BaseBall america

2001 PROSPECT *Handbook*

BaseBall america®
2001 PROSPECT Handbook

PUBLISHED BY
Baseball America Inc.

EDITORS
Jim Callis, Will Lingo, Allan Simpson

CONTRIBUTING WRITERS
James Bailey, Bill Ballew, Mike Berardino, Josh Boyd, Pat Caputo,
Gerry Fraley, Mark Gonzales, Chris Haft, Tom Haudricourt, Jim Ingraham,
Michael Levesque, Lacy Lusk, John Manuel, John Perrotto,
Tracy Ringolsby, Phil Rogers, Casey Tefertiller

EDITORIAL ASSISTANT
Matt Potter

PRODUCTION
Phillip Daquila, Matthew Eddy, Linwood Webb

STATISTICAL CONSULTANT
SportsTicker
Boston

COVER PHOTOS
Corey Patterson by Larry Goren; Ryan Anderson by Frank Ragsdale

BaseBall america
Publisher: Lee Folger
Editor: Allan Simpson
Managing Editor: Will Lingo
Executive Editor: Jim Callis
Design & Production Director: Phillip Daquila

baseballamerica.com

Contents

Foreword

None of us can explain why the future so fascinates us, why we want to know if Josh Hamilton really could be Dave Winfield or Jose Ortiz is the next middle infield 30-30 man. We just do. And since before the Devil Rays' phenom Hamilton was born, Allan Simpson and Baseball America have been the site to see if one cares about every floor of this high-rise complex of baseball.

What has made Baseball America so successful all these years is that it allows you to trace a player from his American Legion roots all the way to the major leagues. Scouting directors, crosscheckers and executives on all levels of the baseball business have long acknowledged that the publication's coverage of the amateur draft—taken to a new level by Baseball America's remarkable Website (baseballamerica.com)—is revered as an integral part of the draft itself. Executives, news services and fans have long waited with expectation for the late summer's league prospect lists, followed by the winter's organization Top 10 Prospects projections.

After creating the Super Register—far and away the most comprehensive register of professional talent ever compiled—Baseball America this year has produced its first Prospect Handbook. It becomes a bible of its kind, for fans of a particular team who want to home in on what players to follow through the season, but also for those interested in those players who are mentioned in or actually traded in pennant race deals. You can survey organizational overviews, and look back on each team's top prospects of the last decade and wonder what would have happened had Frank Rodriguez played shortstop.

Others have tried forms of minor league scouting publications. Baseball America is the only one that can—and now does—get it right.

Peter Gammons
ESPN

Introduction

If you already know about Baseball America, chances are it's because of our annual Top 10 Prospects lists. Even those who aren't regular readers (shame on you) pick up the prospect issues every year to see who's going to turn the fortunes of their favorite team around, or to find a sleeper for their fantasy league draft. The Top 10 Prospects aren't all we do by a far sight, but they are a culmination of everything we do. Baseball America prides itself on covering baseball whenever and wherever it's played, but what we really love—and what people turn to us for—is finding good, young baseball players and telling people their stories.

Allan Simpson, the editor and founder of Baseball America, started the magazine in 1981 because he couldn't readily find the kind of baseball information he wanted. He did something about it, and the result is a company that has become the definitive source for baseball information. There's the magazine, which comes out every two weeks; a Website (baseballamerica.com) that provides comprehensive baseball news around the clock; and a growing library of books. Our annual publications include the Almanac, a review of the year in baseball with statistics and commentary; the Directory, the most comprehensive collection of names, numbers and addresses for anyone who works in the industry; and the Super Register, a one-of-a-kind book that lists career statistics for every active player in the majors and minors.

And you're holding the newest addition to the library, and one we're excited about: the Prospect Handbook. We knew readers loved our prospect information, so we decided to give you more, much more. You'll find 30 prospects for each organization—yes, 900 players—profiled as only Baseball America can do it. We define a prospect as anyone who is still rookie-eligible under Major League Baseball's guidelines (no more than 50 innings pitched or 130 at-bats), without regard to service time. Read the profiles carefully because you'll be hearing them and seeing them in other media throughout the year. Just remember that we're the ones who talk to the general managers, scouting directors, farm directors, scouts, managers, coaches and agents.

On that note, we have to thank the people who made this book so good. First, to all the players, for making us excited about your futures. Also to all the people who work in the game and allow us to take a glimpse into their organizations. Our information wouldn't be so good unless it came straight from the source. Most important, we thank the writers who assembled all of this information. Some are members of the Baseball America staff, while others are trusted correspondents who cover baseball full-time for someone else. A project this massive can't be done by one person or a few people; it takes a large group of people who not only are willing to work hard but also understand who we are and what we were trying to accomplish. We think the contributions of all of these people show in the final product.

So dive into the most complete book on prospects ever assembled, and get ready to enjoy another great season of baseball.

Will Lingo
Managing Editor

Talent Ranking

Rankings, rankings and more rankings. In the pages that follow, we rank the top 30 prospects in each of the 30 major league organizations. But first, we try to put perspective on the whole exercise by ranking the organizations themselves. These rankings represent a blend of quality and quantity of talent in each system. We've favored organizations that have more than their share of high-level prospects and/or a deep farm system.

UPPER ECHELON

1. Chicago White Sox. The White Sox were criticized at the time, but the infamous White Flag trade of 1997 signaled a turnaround for the organization. They went back to the drawing board and rebuilt the organization from the bottom up. And unlike the NBA's Chicago Bulls, owner Jerry Reinsdorf's other team, the White Sox have made the revamped approach work. In three years, Chicago has stockpiled an amazing amount of pitching talent, largely secured in the 1999 draft. They were recognized as Baseball America's Organization of the Year and righthander Jon Rauch was BA's Minor League Player of the Year in 2000.

2. Chicago Cubs. Things aren't rosy in Wrigley Field, where the Cubs brought up the rear in the National League with a .401 winning percentage last year, but this is an organization on the upswing. Cubs affiliates won championships at two levels last year, and the organization has an impressive and well-rounded array of talent making its way to Chicago. That group is led by outfielder Corey Patterson, who was hailed as the savior of the franchise even before he played his first professional game.

3. Cincinnati. The Reds have been near the bottom of this list since Marge Schott's reign of error, but no team did more to upgrade the talent in its farm system in 2000. A plentiful draft netted three premium prospects and trades brought in several more, in particular a deal that brought four quality minor leaguers from the Yankees for Denny Neagle. A tight bottom line impairs Cincinnati's ability to do business, but the club is rich in prospects, particularly young outfielders who one day will flank Ken Griffey.

4. Seattle. Losing Ken Griffey and Alex Rodriguez in the same calendar year would be devastating for any franchise, but 2000 was still upbeat for the Mariners. They made the playoffs for the third time in their checkered history, posted the best winning percentage in the minors—.577, up .094 from 1999—and added impact talent from all corners of the world despite forfeiting their top three draft picks to sign free agents.

5. Atlanta. Pitching has been the heart of the Braves system for a decade, and never more than now with two-thirds of their top 30 doing their work on the mound. Most of the young arms are concentrated at the lower levels, but the next wave should be ready to hit Atlanta about the time Greg Maddux and Tom Glavine start to fade.

6. Tampa Bay. The Devil Rays have switched directions at the big league level more than once in their brief existence but haven't strayed from a solid development plan. They've built from the bottom up, drafting players like Josh Hamilton in 1999. The emergence of pitchers Bobby Seay and Matt White and a midseason purge of the major league roster that netted prospects Brent Abernathy, Jesus Colome and Jason Tyner has helped the Rays make a quantum leap since being ranked 29th on this list two years ago.

7. New York Yankees. Baseball America ranked the Yankees' talent No. 1 at both the major and minor league levels prior to the 2000 season. They defended that lofty ranking by winning their fourth World Series in five years, but it came with a price as trades for David Justice and Denny Neagle siphoned off several premium prospects. A rash of injuries and subpar performances afflicted most of their remaining top players.

8. San Diego. The Padres have an elite group of prospects that can rival any in the game, and can credit the 1999 draft as a reason. They had a windfall that year with six first-round picks and it coincided with a renewed emphasis on the development of power arms. Mix in hitting talents Sean Burroughs and Xavier Nady, and San Diego may be able to re-establish itself in the highly competitive National League West in another year or two.

9. Florida. The Marlins stockpiled the best young talent in the game when they dismantled their 1997 World Series championship team. The transition to a younger, cheaper club hasn't always gone smoothly, as the team overemphasized tools over performance and not all the prospects panned out. But Florida has an impressive array of power arms and bolstered its system with the game's best draft in 2000.

10. Houston. The Astros have assembled an impressive array of frontline talent in the minor leagues. Because of their frugal ways and emphasis on players with raw tools, they rarely make a splash in the early rounds of the draft. Instead they invest in lower-round picks like righthander Roy Oswalt, who became the rage of the farm system in 2000. They've expertly mined Venezuela and are noted for signing Latin talent at less than market value.

MIDDLE OF THE ROAD

11. Oakland. As a small-market team without the resources to support both a contending major league team and a strong farm system, the Athletics pushed toward contention in 2000. They promoted their two best pitching prospects (Mark Mulder and Barry Zito), traded away prospects for immediate help and forfeited their first-round draft pick for 40 innings of Mike Magnante. Their system took a hit, slipping from third on the list a year ago. Still, there's cohesiveness between the player-development and scouting departments and admiration throughout the industry for the way Oakland maximizes limited resources.

12. Philadelphia. The major league team continues to be in a depressed state, but the Phillies system produced its best cumulative record (.568) in 40 years—a sign that things are finally looking up. Years of mismanagement in player development cost Philadelphia dearly, but scouting director Mike Arbuckle has the team pointed in the right direction.

13. Texas. A wholesale makeover of the farm system by GM Doug Melvin was a major reason why Alex Rodriguez signed with the Rangers. The organization is well balanced with the first of the prospects from Melvin's administration, notably first baseman Carlos Pena, ready to hit Triple-A.

14. Kansas City. Ranked fifth a year ago, the Royals suffered the biggest drop in minor league winning percentage in 2000 (.088) while undergoing a shakeup in their front office. With 19 pitchers among their top 30 prospects, the Royals stocked up on catchers in the draft and obtained shortstop prospect Angel Berroa from Oakland in the Johnny Damon trade. They're hoping Dee Brown, the team's top position prospect, can earn at least a major league platoon job in 2001 after a disappointing year in Triple-A.

15. Minnesota. A depressing situation in the Twin Cities casts a pall over the organization, but the farm system boasts a decent array of talent. Triple-A Salt Lake led the minors with 90 wins while short-season Elizabethton's .719 winning percentage was the best overall in the minors. The Twins' top four prospects entering 2000—third baseman Michael Cuddyer, outfielder Michael Restovich, catcher Matthew LeCroy and outfielder B.J. Garbe—all had disappointing seasons, and the club failed to sign two of its top three draft picks.

16. Colorado. The Rockies would rank a couple of rungs higher had they signed righthander Matt Harrington, the consensus best talent in last year's draft. They have made strides in the draft and on the foreign front since they decided to open the pursestrings for new talent in 1998. Catcher Ben Petrick and outfielder Juan Pierre reached Colorado last year, and the next wave of prospects will be two steps away in Double-A this year.

17. Toronto. Once an industry leader in signing talent, Toronto has been strapped financially the last few years and the flow has slowed. The Blue Jays were the only team to spend less than $1 million on its first-round draft picks in each of the last two years, and they got what they paid for. New ownership should return the Jays to their free-spending ways that ended in the early 1990s.

18. Detroit. The Tigers have had their share of setbacks since Randy Smith came aboard as GM in 1997. Prospects have been dealt and a number of pitchers drafted in the first round have been hurt, slow to develop or washed out altogether. Still, the system has improved from the days when it was one of the worst in the game.

19. Pittsburgh. It's been years since Pirates farm clubs have posted a break-even record in the minors, a byproduct of the club's emphasis on raw athletes over players. The big league club also has underachieved, in large part because of the failures of outfielder Chad Hermansen and other top prospects. But the last two drafts may have turned the club's fortunes. Not afraid to outspend other clubs for talent, the Pirates landed righthander Bobby Bradley and catcher J.R. House, their two best prospects.

20. New York Mets. Trades, injuries and free-agent signings at the expense of draft picks have stripped the organization of prospects, particularly at the upper levels. Alex Escobar and

Brian Cole are two of the minors' best outfielders, but the lack of ready pitching has forced the organization to sign free agents like Kevin Appier and Steve Trachsel this offseason.

LOW ACHIEVERS

21. Montreal. The talent in the Expos system doesn't flow as plentifully as in the early 1990s, a result of the team's financial situation. But Montreal showed a renewed willingness to spend in the 2000 draft, and the development of righthander Donnie Bridges and third baseman Scott Hodges provides renewed hope for the team's 1997 draft, when it had eight first-round picks.

22. San Francisco. The opening of Pacific Bell Park sent a positive jolt through the entire organization in 2000, enabling the Giants to add a much-needed sixth farm club while expanding their presence in Latin America. San Francisco operated on a thin margin of error until then. A cumulative .444 minor league record in 2000 suggests it's going to take time to turn the system around, but in Jerome Williams and Kurt Ainsworth they have two of the best arms in the game. And the Giants continue to win at the major league level.

23. St. Louis. The Cardinals had an invigorating 2000, not just at the major league level. Their Triple-A Memphis affiliate had a dream season, both on and off the field, and a farm system that had largely dried up yielded lefthander Bud Smith and third baseman Albert Pujols as legitimate prospects. Trades that enabled the big league team to win now, poor production from mid-round draft picks and lack of impact on the foreign market had sent this traditionally strong organization spiraling downward.

24. Boston. The Red Sox have become increasingly dependent on foreign talent, particularly from the Far East, to prop up their system. Trades of prospects that led to patchwork solutions in the big leagues and a couple of marginally productive drafts have thinned the organization's domestic talent base.

25. Anaheim. The Angels bottomed out in 2000, ranking dead last in minor league winning percentage. That prompted five of their six farm clubs to seek new parent clubs after the season. New Angels management had to bite the bullet for a year but has gone a long way toward breathing new life into the organization. The team's last two drafts were a good starting position in putting the organization back on solid footing.

26. Cleveland. Outside of lefthander C.C. Sabathia, the talent level in the Indians system has reached a dangerously low level. Most of their top prospects are flawed, and the Indians have no one close to being able to replace Manny Ramirez. Even the wisdom of signing Cuban righthander Danys Baez, which cost the organization $14.5 million, is questionable, as he came in less developed than advertised. After years of turnover in the scouting department, John Mirabelli's appointment as scouting director should stabilize that critical area.

27. Baltimore. The Orioles have suffered from a lack of direction at the major league level and a lack of talent in the minors—a lethal combination for an impatient ownership. A promising draft in 1999 could move the organization in the right direction, but none of the seven first-rounders from that crop is a sure thing. The Orioles also have been stung by the fall from grace of lefthander Matt Riley, who had been their best prospect.

28. Los Angeles. The Dodgers won championships at three levels (including the Rookie-level Dominican Summer League) in 2000 and had the second-greatest improvement in minor league winning percentage, but that masks the lack of talent in the organization. The Dodgers still are trying to recover from back-to-back washout drafts in 1997-98, a low point in a decade of suspect drafting. Fallout from Adrian Beltre's illegal signing cost the club six months of signing players in the Dominican Republic, traditionally its most fertile talent hotbed.

29. Arizona. The bottom has fallen out for the Diamondbacks. Desperate to field a big league winner, they sacrificed minor league talent in trades. The 2000 season also had its dark moments. Righthander John Patterson had Tommy John surgery; standout hitter Jack Cust raised more questions about his ability to play defense; and third baseman Corey Myers, the fourth player drafted overall in 1999, showed little signs of progress.

30. Milwaukee. The Brewers system has been down and out for awhile now, but there was reason to get excited about the 2000 season. Indianapolis won the Triple-A World Series, and righthander Ben Sheets shut out Cuba in the Olympic gold-medal game. But years of injuries, curious draft decisions and bad personnel moves have left the organization with little talent. This may be the last year Milwaukee occupies this position, though, as a new stadium and a capable new administration should give the club a better chance to compete for talent.

Elite Eight

Ryan Anderson lhp, Mariners

Seattle fans have grown impatient waiting for the Space Needle, but his development has been handled patiently. Now he's almost ready to fill the Randy Johnson role.

FRANK RAGSDALE

SPORTS ON FILM

Sean Burroughs 3b, Padres

Known forever for his exploits in the Little League World Series, fans soon will realize that he's the best pure hitting prospect around.

Josh Beckett rhp, Marlins

He has Texas-sized talent and the personality to match, and he's so good that he nearly became the first righthander ever drafted No. 1 overall.

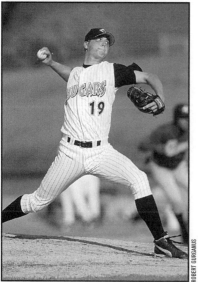

ROBERT GURGANUS

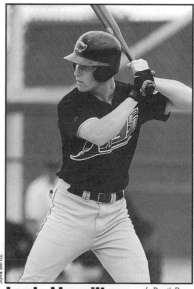

JOHN BATTLE

Josh Hamilton of, Devil Rays

He could have been a first-round pick as a lefthanded pitcher, but his all-around skills as an everyday player should make him a perennial all-star.

L isted in alphabetical order, here are the eight players we consider the best prospects in baseball. Baseball America ranks the Top 100 Prospects in the game in a March issue, so you can see if your pick for No. 1 agrees with ours.

Corey Patterson of, Cubs

Patterson has the best overall package of tools in the game. We just hope fans in Chicago can be patient as he puts the final touches on his development.

WAGNER PHOTOGRAPHY

RICH ABEL

C.C. Sabathia lhp, Indians

With all of the Indians' pitching problems, it won't be long before the stout Sabathia will be called on to stabilize things in Cleveland.

Jon Rauch rhp, White Sox

He came out of nowhere to win BA's Minor League Player of the Year award in 2000, and he soon should become the tallest player in major league history.

BILL SETLIFF

STAN DENNY

Ben Sheets rhp, Brewers

Always considered to be part of the group of the minors' best pitching prospects, he set himself apart with his dominant Olympic performance.

Top50Prospects

At Baseball America, there's nothing we enjoy more than arguing about baseball. And there's no baseball topic we enjoy arguing about more than prospects. After all, it's what we know best. Our Top 100 Prospects list is released every March, and we hope the lists on these two pages—the individual preferences of the three people who put this book together and oversee BA's prospect rankings—will give you a little insight into how the process works.

At least three of us put together individual lists after we've reviewed the prospect reports each year in an effort to put all the rankings in perspective. Each person brings a unique perspective to the process. Some of us prefer polished players who might have lower ceilings to more dynamic athletes who haven't yet proven themselves as baseball players. And it's always hard to gauge the value of recent draft picks who have little professional experience. The overarching philosophy guiding the whole process, though, is that we're looking for the players who will have the greatest long-term value as major league players. We'll always hear comments from those who want to see players with big minor league numbers higher in our rankings, and minor league production is important. But by no means is it everything, or even the most important thing. A player's age in comparison to where he's playing, as well as his overall physical ability—the oft-mentioned tools—are critical factors.

As you'll see, even we have big differences of opinion on how the best players stack up, and sometimes we don't even agree about who they are. From lists like these, we try to compromise and build a consensus list, then we get the opinions of more people who work in the game. The result is what we consider the best of the best up-and-coming players in baseball. Keep in mind that these lists were a snapshot of opinion in January, and those opinions could change by the time the Top 100 Prospects rolls around.

Allan Simpson, Editor

1. Josh Hamilton, of, Devil Rays
2. Ben Sheets, rhp, Brewers
3. Corey Patterson, of, Cubs
4. Josh Beckett, rhp, Marlins
5. Jon Rauch, rhp, White Sox
6. Ryan Anderson, lhp, Mariners
7. C.C. Sabathia, lhp, Indians
8. Nick Johnson, 1b, Yankees
9. Alex Escobar, of, Mets
10. Vernon Wells, of, Blue Jays
11. Sean Burroughs, 3b, Padres
12. Ichiro Suzuki, of, Mariners
13. Roy Oswalt, rhp, Astros
14. Carlos Pena, 1b, Rangers
15. Chris George, lhp, Royals
16. Antonio Perez, ss, Mariners
17. Wilson Betemit, ss, Braves
18. Joe Crede, 3b, White Sox
19. Chin-Hui Tsao, rhp, Rockies
20. Bobby Bradley, rhp, Pirates
21. Hee Seop Choi, 1b, Cubs
22. Drew Henson, 3b, Reds
23. Adam Dunn, of, Reds
24. Alfonso Soriano, ss, Yankees
25. Felipe Lopez, ss, Blue Jays
26. Matt Belisle, rhp, Braves
27. Austin Kearns, of, Reds
28. Donnie Bridges, rhp, Expos
29. Brian Cole, of, Mets
30. Kurt Ainsworth, rhp, Giants
31. Jose Ortiz, 2b, Athletics
32. Joe Borchard, of, White Sox
33. Matt McClendon, rhp, Braves
34. J.R. House, c, Pirates
35. Tim Redding, rhp, Astros
36. Jerome Williams, rhp, Giants
37. Matt Ginter, rhp, White Sox
38. Dee Brown, of, Royals
39. Albert Pujols, 3b, Cardinals
40. Juan Cruz, rhp, Cubs
41. Wes Anderson, rhp, Marlins
42. Joe Torres, lhp, Angels
43. Jimmy Rollins, ss, Phillies
44. Bud Smith, lhp, Cardinals
45. Jovanny Cedeno, rhp, Rangers
46. Wascar Serrano, rhp, Padres
47. Carl Crawford, of, Devil Rays
48. Dan Wright, rhp, White Sox
49. Brad Wilkerson, of, Expos
50. Ben Christensen, rhp, Cubs

Will Lingo, Managing Editor

1. Corey Patterson, of, Cubs
2. Josh Hamilton, of, Devil Rays
3. Jon Rauch, rhp, White Sox
4. Josh Beckett, rhp, Marlins
5. Drew Henson, 3b, Reds
6. Ryan Anderson, lhp, Mariners
7. Sean Burroughs, 3b, Padres
8. Ben Sheets, rhp, Brewers
9. Ichiro Suzuki, of, Mariners
10. Carlos Pena, 1b, Rangers
11. Vernon Wells, of, Blue Jays
12. C.C. Sabathia, lhp, Indians
13. Roy Oswalt, rhp, Astros
14. Juan Cruz, rhp, Cubs
15. Chris George, lhp, Royals
16. J.R. House, c, Pirates
17. Chin-Hui Tsao, rhp, Rockies
18. Nick Johnson, 1b, Yankees
19. Joe Borchard, of, White Sox
20. Jerome Williams, rhp, Giants
21. Austin Kearns, of, Reds
22. Jimmy Rollins, ss, Phillies
23. Bobby Bradley, rhp, Pirates
24. Bud Smith, lhp, Cardinals
25. Brad Wilkerson, of, Expos
26. Antonio Perez, ss, Mariners
27. Donnie Bridges, rhp, Expos
28. Matt Belisle, rhp, Braves
29. Felipe Lopez, ss, Blue Jays
30. Wilson Betemit, ss, Braves
31. Brett Myers, rhp, Phillies
32. Alfonso Soriano, ss, Yankees
33. Wes Anderson, rhp, Marlins
34. Jack Cust, of, Diamondbacks
35. Alex Escobar, of, Mets
36. Jose Ortiz, 2b, Athletics
37. Jacob Peavy, rhp, Padres
38. Hee Seop Choi, 1b, Cubs
39. Jason Standridge, rhp, Devil Rays
40. Pat Strange, rhp, Mets
41. Kurt Ainsworth, rhp, Giants
42. Adam Dunn, of, Reds
43. Adam Johnson, rhp, Twins
44. Albert Pujols, 3b, Cardinals
45. D'Angelo Jimenez, ss, Yankees
46. Joe Crede, 3b, White Sox
47. Brandon Inge, c, Tigers
48. Miguel Cabrera, ss, Marlins
49. Michael Cuddyer, 3b, Twins
50. Ben Christensen, rhp, Cubs

Jim Callis, Executive Editor

1. Corey Patterson, of, Cubs
2. Josh Hamilton, of, Devil Rays
3. Josh Beckett, rhp, Marlins
4. Jon Rauch, rhp, White Sox
5. Sean Burroughs, 3b, Padres
6. Ben Sheets, rhp, Brewers
7. Ryan Anderson, lhp, Mariners
8. C.C. Sabathia, lhp, Indians
9. Antonio Perez, ss, Mariners
10. Juan Cruz, rhp, Cubs
11. Jerome Williams, rhp, Giants
12. Nick Johnson, 1b, Yankees
13. Hee Seop Choi, 1b, Cubs
14. Chin-Hui Tsao, rhp, Rockies
15. Roy Oswalt, rhp, Astros
16. Carlos Pena, 1b, Rangers
17. Ichiro Suzuki, of, Mariners
18. Drew Henson, 3b, Reds
19. Vernon Wells, of, Blue Jays
20. Alex Escobar, of, Mets
21. Donnie Bridges, rhp, Expos
22. Bobby Bradley, rhp, Pirates
23. Joe Borchard, of, White Sox
24. Kurt Ainsworth, rhp, Giants
25. Ben Christensen, rhp, Cubs
26. J.R. House, c, Pirates
27. Alfonso Soriano, ss, Yankees
28. Jack Cust, of, Diamondbacks
29. D'Angelo Jimenez, ss, Yankees
30. Austin Kearns, of, Reds
31. Adam Dunn, of, Reds
32. Jose Ortiz, 2b, Athletics
33. Adam Johnson, rhp, Twins
34. Jacob Peavy, rhp, Padres
35. Matt Belisle, rhp, Braves
36. Jimmy Rollins, ss, Phillies
37. Aubrey Huff, 3b, Devil Rays
38. Marcus Giles, 2b, Braves
39. Albert Pujols, 3b, Cardinals
40. Carlos Zambrano, rhp, Cubs
41. Bud Smith, lhp, Cardinals
42. Chris George, lhp, Royals
43. Mike Bynum, lhp, Padres
44. Brad Wilkerson, of, Expos
45. Felipe Lopez, ss, Blue Jays
46. Wilson Betemit, ss, Braves
47. Joe Crede, 3b, White Sox
48. Kevin Mench, of, Rangers
49. Tony Torcato, 3b, Giants
50. Joe Torres, lhp, Angels

Anaheim
Angels

By Jim Callis

T hese are not your father's Angels, and certainly not Gene Autry's. Last year's surprising 82-80 club was built almost entirely from within. Sixteen players had either 300 at-bats, 10 saves or 10 starts, and 11 of them were signed and developed by Anaheim. Righthander Kent Bottenfield and second baseman Adam Kennedy came in a trade with the Cardinals for homegrown center fielder Jim Edmonds.

The Disney Co.'s one major foray into free agency has been a disappointment. Mo Vaughn has been good, but he's not an elite first baseman outside of Fenway Park. Despite his noted leadership skills, he couldn't keep the clubhouse from imploding in 1999, when almost every high-ranking Angels official lost his job.

The new administration—general manager Bill Stoneman, manager Mike Scioscia, farm director Darrell Miller, scouting director Donny Rowland—turned a 72-90 club into a wild-card contender. More significant for the franchise's future, they breathed new life into a farm system that Baseball America ranked 29th out of 30 at the outset of 2000, though the organization still has a long way to go to boost its talent level.

The Angels touted their homegrown roster for years, conveniently ignoring that its biggest contributors were signed long ago. Even last year's catching surprise, Bengie Molina, came aboard in 1993. The only significant players added in the last half of the 1990s were Darin Erstad and Troy Glaus. Erstad went No. 1 overall in the 1995 draft and Glaus went No. 3 two years later, so neither was a great scouting find.

The Angels shut down their Dominican academy and cut back on their draft budget from 1996-98, and the results showed. Only righthander Seth Etherton (since traded to the Reds) and Scott Schoeneweis surfaced in the majors among Anaheim signees during that period. Righthander Matt Wise is the only member of that group among the organization's top 15 prospects.

In the last two years, the Angels have resumed their Dominican operations while getting more aggressive in Latin America and with the draft. Their prospect list reflects this. The system is still imbalanced, with far more pitchers than position players among the prospects, but things are finally looking up.

OrganizationOverview

General manager: Bill Stoneman. **Farm director:** Darrell Miller. **Scouting director:** Donny Rowland.

2000 PERFORMANCE

Class	Team	League	W	L	Pct.	Finish*	Manager(s)
Majors	Anaheim	American	82	80	.506	8th (14)	Mike Scioscia
Triple-A	#Edmonton Trappers	Pacific Coast	63	78	.447	12th (16)	Garry Templeton
Double-A	†Erie SeaWolves	Eastern	47	94	.333	12th (12)	Don Wakamatsu
High A	^Lake Elsinore Storm	California	70	70	.500	6th (10)	Mario Mendoza
Low A	Cedar Rapids Kernels	Midwest	53	86	.381	13th (14)	M. Seoane/T. Boykin
Short-season	~Boise Hawks	Northwest	41	35	.539	t-1st (8)	Tom Kotchman
Rookie	@Butte Copper Kings	Pioneer	29	47	.382	7th (8)	Joe Urso

OVERALL 2000 MINOR LEAGUE RECORD   303   409   .426   30th (30)

*Finish in overall standings (No. of teams in league). #Affiliate will be in Salt Lake (Pacific Coast) in 2001. †Affiliate will be in Arkansas (Texas) in 2001. ^Affiliate will be in Rancho Cucamonga (California) in 2001. ~Affiliate will be in Rookie-level Arizona League in 2001. @ Franchise is moving to Provo, Utah, in 2001.

ORGANIZATION LEADERS

BATTING
*AVG	Brad Downing, Boise	.337
R	**Gary Johnson**, Erie/Lake Elsinore	100
H	**Gary Johnson**, Erie/Lake Elsinore	164
TB	**Gary Johnson**, Erie/Lake Elsinore	275
2B	Robb Quinlan, Lake Elsinore	35
3B	Elpidio Guzman, Lake Elsinore	16
HR	**Gary Johnson**, Erie/Lake Elsinore	23
RBI	**Gary Johnson**, Erie/Lake Elsinore	118
BB	Bill Mott, Lake Elsinore	76
	Gary Johnson, Erie/Lake Elsinore	76
SO	Darren Blakely, Erie	136
SB	Alfredo Amezaga, Lake Elsinore	73

PITCHING
W	**John Lackey**, Cedar Rapids/LE/Erie	15
L	Dusty Bergman, Cedar Rapids, Lake Els.	16
#ERA	Sean Brummett, Cedar Rapids/Erie	2.74
G	Ben Grezlovski, Lake Els./Cedar Rapids	54
CG	Dusty Bergman, Cedar Rapids, Lake Els.	6
SV	Ben Grezlovski, Lake Els./Cedar Rapids	19
IP	**John Lackey**, Cedar Rapids/LE/Erie	188
BB	Paul Morse, Erie/Edmonton	102
SO	Scot Shields, Edmonton	156

*Minimum 250 at-bats. #Minimum 75 innings.

TOP PROSPECTS OF THE DECADE

TOP DRAFT PICKS OF THE DECADE

Johnson   **Lackey**

BEST TOOLS

Best Hitter for Average	Gary Johnson
Best Power Hitter	Josh Gray
Fastest Baserunner	Ed Welch
Best Fastball	Francisco Rodriguez
Best Breaking Ball	Joe Torres
Best Control	Matt Wise
Best Defensive Catcher	Shawn Wooten
Best Defensive Infielder	Tommy Murphy
Best Infield Arm	Tommy Murphy
Best Defensive Outfielder	Nathan Haynes
Best Outfield Arm	Elpidio Guzman

PROJECTED 2004 LINEUP

Catcher	Bengie Molina
First Base	Mo Vaughn
Second Base	Adam Kennedy
Third Base	Troy Glaus
Shortstop	Brian Specht
Left Field	Darin Erstad
Center Field	Garret Anderson
Right Field	Tim Salmon
Designated Hitter	Gary Johnson
No. 1 Starter	Ramon Ortiz
No. 2 Starter	Joe Torres
No. 3 Starter	Francisco Rodriguez
No. 4 Starter	John Lackey
No. 5 Starter	Jarrod Washburn
Closer	Derrick Turnbow

ALL-TIME LARGEST BONUSES

Troy Glaus, 1997	$2,250,000
Joe Torres, 2000	2,080,000
Chris Bootcheck, 2000	1,800,000
Darin Erstad, 1995	1,575,000
Seth Etherton, 1998	1,075,000

DraftAnalysis

2000 Draft

Best Pro Debut: LHP **Joe Torres** (1) didn't turn 18 until the final week of the short-season Northwest League schedule, but he wasn't overmatched by hitters with college experience. He went 5-1, 2.54 with 52 strikeouts in 46 innings and was the top pitching prospect in the league.

Best Athlete: OF Jason Coulie (9) was an all-conference performer in baseball, football and track at Division III Bates (Maine) College.

Best Hitter: OF Josh Gray (13) didn't get much exposure because of shoulder problems as a senior. He hit .327 with eight homers as a DH at Rookie-level Butte, then had arthroscopic surgery to fix his shoulder.

Best Raw Power: Gray hit 24 homers to spark Rock Creek (Okla.) High to a national record 113 homers last spring. He has well above-average power. C Jared Abruzzo (2) and Coulie also can drive the ball.

Fastest Runner: SS Tommy Murphy (3) was one of the speediest players in the draft. He runs the 60-yard dash in 6.51 seconds.

Best Defensive Player: Murphy was one of the premier defenders available, especially considering the lack of pure college shortstops. Besides his quickness, he also offers a strong arm. His bat is a question, and he did little to dispel that by hitting .225 at Boise.

Best Fastball: Torres will touch 94-95 mph, but RHP Bobby Jenks (5) can reach 96. The Angels also are delighted with RHP Rich Fischer (21), a converted shortstop whom area scout Tim Corcoran found at San Bernardino Valley (Calif.) JC. He can reach 94 mph.

Most Intriguing Background: Jenks left his Idaho high school last spring after failing to qualify academically to play baseball for the third time in four years. He was showcased to scouts in Seattle by his personal trainer. RHP Brett Cimorelli (20) doubles as a backup kicker at Florida State.

Torres

Closest To The Majors: RHP Chris Bootcheck (1) or Charlie Thames (4). Bootcheck was in line to be the first college player drafted, but he slid to 20th and held out all summer before signing for $1.8 million. He already throws 90-92 mph and is projectable. Thames doesn't throw as hard, but his low three-quarters delivery is rough on righthanders. The sleeper is RHP Matt Hensley (10), who throws 89-93 mph with plenty of sink.

Best Late-Round Pick: Gray.

The One Who Got Away: SS Aaron Hill (7), whom the Angels projected as an offensive second baseman. Hill will have a tough time cracking the infield at Louisiana State, which returns Mike Fontenot and Ryan Theriot from a national championship club.

Assessment: Anaheim needs pitching, and took a step in that direction with Torres and Bootcheck in the first round. The Angels signed just three hitters in the first 12 rounds, so arms will determine the success of this draft.

1999 Draft

Even without a first-rounder, the Angels began restocking their organization. SS Brian Specht (9) is the system's top position player, and RHPs John Lackey (2), Philip Wilson (3) and David Wolensky (42, draft-and-follow) are among the best arms.   **Grade: B**

1998 Draft

Anaheim needed to reload in 1999 in part because it did an awful job in 1998. RHP Seth Etherton (1), a safe college senior sign, is the only signee with a future, and he was traded to Cincinnati this offseason.   **Grade: D**

1997 Draft

The Angels hit the jackpot with 3B Troy Glaus (1), the No. 3 overall selection who became the American League home run champ just three years later. RHP Matt Wise (6) could make the big league rotation this year.   **Grade: A–**

1996 Draft

California, as the franchise was known then, didn't have a first-round pick because it signed free agent Randy Velarde and blew its top choice on SS Chuck Abbott (2). LHP Scott Schoeneweis (3) has had his moments, but the club got little else.   **Grade: C–**

Note: Draft analysis prepared by Jim Callis. Numbers in parentheses indicate draft rounds.

. . . Torres is mature and competitive and has the work ethic to get considerably better.

Joe
Torres **lhp**

Born: Sept. 3, 1982.
Ht.: 6-3. **Wt.:** 180.
Bats: L. **Throws:** L.
School: Gateway (Fla.) HS.
Career Transactions: Drafted by Angels in first round (10th overall) of 2000 draft; signed June 17, 2000.

FRANK RAGSDALE

The Angels have plenty of righthanded pitching prospects, but they didn't have a quality lefthander until they selected Torres with the 10th overall pick in the 2000 draft. He signed for $2.08 million, then excelled in the short-season Northwest League against hitters who generally were four years older. He allowed more than two runs just once in 11 outings and limited opponents to a .170 average. He was the top pitching prospect in the league and concluded the season with 13 strikeouts in 6⅓ innings in his final start. Torres has always been precocious. In 1999, Baseball America ranked him as the top 16-year-old player in the United States, after he won the gold-medal game of the World Junior Championship in Taiwan. Though Francisco Rodriguez has slightly better stuff, Torres occupies the top spot on this list because he's lefthanded, projectable and less of a health risk.

Torres reminds the Angels of a young John Candelaria. He already throws a consistent 89-93 mph with the ability to touch 95, and he should add more velocity as he grows and fills out. His arm looks like a whip as he delivers pitches from a low three-quarters arm slot that makes it difficult for batters to pick up the ball. With time, Torres should have at least three solid pitches. His curveball is the best breaking pitch in the organization, and he made progress on his changeup in instructional league as Anaheim didn't allow its pitchers to throw breaking balls. He throws quality strikes, not permitting a single homer in the Northwest League. He's mature and competitive and has the work ethic to get considerably better. Torres needs experience more than any major adjustments. If he improves the consistency of his curveball and changeup, he could have three plus pitches. His body can get stronger and his command can improve.

Torres will be ready for full-season ball at 18, with Class A Cedar Rapids his likely destination. If he performs well, he could move up to high Class A Rancho Cucamonga by the end of 2001. Anaheim won't rush him, but he could be ready for the major leagues in late 2003—before he turns 21.

Year	Club (League)	Class	W	L	ERA	G	GS	CG	SV	IP	H	R	ER	BB	SO
2000	Boise (NWL)	A	4	1	2.54	11	10	0	0	46	27	17	13	23	52
MINOR LEAGUE TOTALS			4	1	2.54	11	10	0	0	46	27	17	13	23	52

2. Francisco Rodriguez, rhp

Born: Jan. 7, 1982. **Ht.:** 6-0. **Wt.:** 165. **Bats:** R. **Throws:** R. **Career Transactions:** Signed out of Venezuela by Angels, Sept. 24, 1998.

The Angels ignored Latin America for three years but returned in a big way by signing Rodriguez to a $900,000 bonus. In his debut a year later, he was the Rookie-level Pioneer League's top prospect. In 121 pro innings, he has allowed just 79 hits and struck out 154. Rodriguez' fastball is just plain filthy, averaging 94-97 mph and reaching as high as 99 mph, with late life to go with the velocity. His quick arm action makes it look even faster. He throws a slurvy slider from a three-quarters arm angle, and the pitch eats up righthanders. His changeup will be a good third pitch. Though Rodriguez has a deceptive motion, it's far from pretty and may have contributed to his arm problems. Shoulder and elbow tendinitis prevented him from making his first start until May 27, and he was shut down for six weeks after three outings because he had a tender forearm. His mechanics have been smoothed out since. Because Rodriguez is so young, there's no reason to promote him from the high Class A California League to begin 2001. If Joe Torres joins him, they'll form one of the best lefty-righty combos in the minors.

Year	Club (League)	Class	W	L	ERA	G	GS	CG	SV	IP	H	R	ER	BB	SO
1999	Butte (Pio)	R	1	1	3.31	12	9	1	0	52	33	21	19	21	69
	Boise (NWL)	A	1	0	5.40	1	1	0	0	5	3	4	3	1	6
2000	Lake Elsinore (Cal)	A	4	4	2.81	13	12	0	0	64	43	29	20	32	79
MINOR LEAGUE TOTALS			6	5	3.12	26	22	1	0	121	79	54	42	54	154

3. Brian Specht, ss

Born: Oct. 19, 1980. **Ht.:** 5-11. **Wt.:** 170. **Bats:** B. **Throws:** R. **School:** Doherty HS, Colorado Springs. **Career Transactions:** Selected by Angels in ninth round of 1999 draft; signed July 14, 1999.

Specht seemed determined to attend Baylor, so he lasted until the ninth round in 1999. The Angels successfully gambled a pick on him, signing him for $600,000, the highest bonus they paid in that draft. They challenged him by letting him make his pro debut in the Cal League last season and he responded, hitting safely in his first 12 games and performing well before fading in August. Specht will have at least average tools across the board. He already has shown the ability to hit, and his speed, arm and shortstop actions are solid. As he develops, he could have average power from both sides of the plate. He's also instinctive and mature. Specht made 34 errors in 2000, several because he rushed plays when he didn't have to. While he has good patience at the plate, he'll have to make more contact. He needs to get stronger in order to hold up over a full season. Spring training will determine whether Specht returns to Class A or moves up to Double-A to start 2001. He's not as flashy defensively as fellow shortstop prospects Wilmy Caceres or Tommy Murphy, but Specht is more likely to produce at the plate.

Year	Club (League)	Class	AVG	G	AB	R	H	2B	3B	HR	RBI	BB	SO	SB
2000	Lake Elsinore (Cal)	A	.269	89	334	70	90	22	5	2	35	52	80	25
MINOR LEAGUE TOTALS			.269	89	334	70	90	22	5	2	35	52	80	25

4. John Lackey, rhp

Born: Oct. 23, 1978. **Ht.:** 6-6. **Wt.:** 205. **Bats:** R. **Throws:** R. **School:** Grayson County (Texas) CC. **Career Transactions:** Selected by Angels in second round of 1999 draft; signed June 9, 1999.

The Angels forfeited their 1999 first-round pick to sign Mo Vaughn, so Lackey was their top pick. He began his college career at Texas-Arlington, then transferred to Grayson County Community College, where he batted .440 with 16 homers as a two-way player in 1999. Though he had more success as a hitter as an amateur, he reached Double-A and pitched well there in his first full season. Lackey has a big, strong body that gives him good leverage and allows him to pitch on a downward plane. Both his low- to mid-90s fastball and his curveball are plus pitches, and his changeup should be at least average. Lackey's control left a lot to be desired after he signed, but he threw a lot more strikes last season. He just needs to fine-tune his command and trust his secondary pitches. The Angels envision Lackey as a workhorse who will pile up lots of innings and wins. He might get more time in Double-A in 2001, but should reach Triple-A by the end of the season.

Year	Club (League)	Class	W	L	ERA	G	GS	CG	SV	IP	H	R	ER	BB	SO
1999	Boise (NWL)	A	6	2	4.98	15	15	1	0	81	81	59	45	50	77
2000	Cedar Rapids (Mid)	A	3	2	2.08	5	5	0	0	30	20	7	7	5	21
	Lake Elsinore (Cal)	A	6	6	3.40	15	15	2	0	101	94	56	38	42	74
	Erie (EL)	AA	6	1	3.30	8	8	2	0	57	58	23	21	9	43
MINOR LEAGUE TOTALS			21	11	3.70	43	43	5	0	270	253	145	111	106	215

5. Chris Bootcheck, rhp

Born: Oct. 24, 1978. **Ht.:** 6-5. **Wt.:** 205. **Bats:** R. **Throws:** R. **School:** Auburn University. **Career Transactions:** Selected by Angels in first round (20th overall) of 2000 draft; signed Sept. 13, 2000.

Bootcheck was considered a potential top-five pick last June, but like all of agent Scott Boras' clients he declined to agree to a predraft deal. The Angels considered him with the 10th pick and got him 10 picks later with a choice from the Athletics for the loss of free agent Mike Magnante. He held out all summer before signing for $1.8 million. Bootcheck has the stuff and command. He is long, lean and projectable, and his fastball already tops out at 94 mph. His most devastating pitch at this point is an 86-90 mph cut fastball with slider action, and it works against both lefthanders and righthanders. He used a curveball in college, and he showed a solid average changeup in instructional league. He has smooth mechanics and throws strikes. He'll need to get stronger. If there's a knock on him, it's that he did not dominate college hitters as much as he should have. The Angels expect Bootcheck to advance rapidly. They'll wait until spring training before determining where he makes his pro debut, but the Cal League is a decent bet.

Year	Club (League)	Class	W	L	ERA	G	GS	CG	SV	IP	H	R	ER	BB	SO
2000					Did Not Play—Signed 2001 Contract										

6. Philip Wilson, rhp

Born: April 1, 1981. **Ht.:** 6-9. **Wt.:** 200. **Bats:** R. **Throws:** R. **School:** Poway (Calif.) HS. **Career Transactions:** Selected by Angels in third round of 1999 draft; signed Aug. 8, 1999.

Shortly after the Angels drafted Wilson, he mentioned he had a lingering arm injury from his final high school game. It turned out to be just a muscle strain, but Anaheim didn't have him pitch after signing him for $525,000. Wilson is the fourth tall, projectable pitcher on this list, and there's another behind him. He can reach 92-93 mph with his fastball, which also has plus life. He's reminiscent of former Angel Mike Witt, with a better changeup and a lesser curveball. Wilson keeps the ball down in the zone and has a strong mound presence. His biggest need is to improve his curve. He has the potential to add another 2-3 mph to his fastball, and he can refine his command. As with John Lackey, the Angels should be more careful with Wilson, who threw 170 innings as a 19-year-old. Wilson could use a few more starts in the Cal League, where he could be part of an impressive Rancho Cucamonga rotation. He's a few years away from being ready for Anaheim.

Year	Club (League)	Class	W	L	ERA	G	GS	CG	SV	IP	H	R	ER	BB	SO
2000	Cedar Rapids (MWL)	A	8	5	3.41	21	21	1	0	129	114	61	49	49	82
	Lake Elsinore (Cal)	A	3	0	1.96	6	6	0	0	41	32	9	9	10	32
MINOR LEAGUE TOTALS			11	5	3.07	27	27	1	0	170	146	70	58	59	114

7. Derrick Turnbow, rhp

Born: Jan. 25, 1978. **Ht.:** 6-3. **Wt.:** 195. **Bats:** R. **Throws:** R. **School:** Franklin (Tenn.) HS. **Career Transactions:** Selected by Phillies in fifth round of 1997 draft; signed July 4, 1997 . . . Selected by Angels from Phillies in major league Rule 5 draft, Dec. 13, 1999.

Turnbow was one of the Phillies' better pitching prospects in 1999. They gambled no one would take him in the major league Rule 5 draft because it required jumping him from low Class A. But the Angels did and were able to keep him in the big leagues for all of 2000. Turnbow's best pitch is a 91-94 mph fastball with late life. Both his curveball and changeup have the potential to be above-average pitches. Anaheim hasn't tagged a closer of the future, but Turnbow might be the guy. They had to relegate him to mop-up duty to keep him in the majors and retain his rights, and it cost him a crucial year of development. Though he wasn't fazed by the experience, it didn't help him. He has a long way to go in terms of his command and his secondary pitches. Turnbow needs to accumulate innings in 2001 so he can make the necessary improvements. He'll likely spend the season at Double-A Arkansas. He'll work as a starter, his role before the Angels drafted him.

Year	Club (League)	Class	W	L	ERA	G	GS	CG	SV	IP	H	R	ER	BB	SO
1997	Martinsville (Appy)	R	1	3	7.40	7	7	0	0	24	34	29	20	16	7
1998	Martinsville (Appy)	R	2	6	5.01	13	13	1	0	70	66	44	39	26	45
1999	Piedmont (SAL)	A	12	8	3.35	26	26	4	0	161	130	67	60	53	149
2000	Anaheim (AL)	MAJ	0	0	4.74	24	1	0	0	38	36	21	20	36	25
MAJOR LEAGUE TOTALS			0	0	4.74	24	1	0	0	38	36	21	20	36	25
MINOR LEAGUE TOTALS			15	17	4.19	46	46	5	0	255	230	140	119	95	201

8. Nathan Haynes, of

RICH ABEL

Born: Sept. 7, 1979. **Ht.:** 5-9. **Wt.:** 170. **Bats:** L. **Throws:** L. **School:** Pinole Valley HS, Pinole, Calif. **Career Transactions:** Selected by Athletics in first round (32nd overall) of 1997 draft; signed June 14, 1997 . . . Traded by Athletics with OF Jeff DaVanon and RHP Elvin Nina to Angels for RHP Omar Olivares and 2B Randy Velarde, July 29, 1999.

When the Angels collapsed in 1999, one of their few highlights was the trade that brought in Haynes, Elvin Nina and Jeff DaVanon. Haynes has been banged up for most of the last two seasons, suffering a hernia in 1999 and battling through wrist, shoulder and knee injuries in 2000. He is the fastest legitimate prospect in the organization. He's also the best center fielder, getting great jumps on balls with the closing speed to steal extra-base hits out of the gaps. His arm is average. The Angels see Haynes as a leadoff hitter, and he occasionally can drive the ball for power. He would be best served by concentrating on making contact and getting on base. The Athletics are sticklers for plate discipline, and Haynes has regressed since he switched organizations. He needs to improve his durability and basestealing skills. After running into an outfield wall, Haynes had minor postseason surgery to clean out his knee. He'll be ready to go in spring training. If Tim Salmon leaves as a free agent after 2001, Garret Anderson could move to right field and Haynes could get a look in center.

Year	Club (League)	Class	AVG	G	AB	R	H	2B	3B	HR	RBI	BB	SO	SB
1997	Athletics (AZL)	R	.278	17	54	8	15	1	0	0	6	7	9	5
	S. Oregon (NWL)	A	.280	24	82	18	23	1	1	0	9	26	21	19
1998	Modesto (Cal)	A	.252	125	507	89	128	13	7	1	41	54	139	42
1999	Visalia (Cal)	A	.310	35	145	28	45	7	1	1	14	17	27	12
	Lake Elsinore (Cal)	A	.327	26	110	19	36	5	5	1	15	12	19	10
	Erie (EL)	AA	.158	5	19	3	3	1	0	0	0	5	5	0
2000	Erie (EL)	AA	.254	118	457	56	116	16	4	6	43	33	107	37
MINOR LEAGUE TOTALS			.266	350	1374	221	366	44	18	9	128	154	327	125

9. Elpidio Guzman, of

JOHN SPEAR

Born: Feb. 24, 1979. **Ht.:** 6-2. **Wt.:** 165. **Bats:** L. **Throws:** L. **Career Transactions:** Signed out of Dominican Republic by Angels, Oct. 15, 1995.

Guzman was one of the last players signed by the Angels before they shut down their Dominican operation. He had a breakout season in the Rookie-level Pioneer League in 1998 and has made steady progress the last two years. He led the minor leagues in triples last season. Guzman has the best all-around package of tools in the system. He's not quite as fast or as good a center fielder as Nathan Haynes, but he's a better basestealer and has a stronger arm. Guzman has plenty of raw power that he's still learning to use, and his strike-zone knowledge keeps getting better. He holds his own against lefthanders but could improve offensively if he adjusts his approach. He tends to get too pull-conscious, and he would make more contact if he shortened his stroke. He also should learn to bunt in order to take more advantage of his speed. Guzman is ready for Double-A, which could make things interesting if the Angels send Haynes back there. Guzman likely would move to right field while still getting some time in center.

Year	Club (League)	Class	AVG	G	AB	R	H	2B	3B	HR	RBI	BB	SO	SB
1996	Rays/Angels (DSL)	R	.233	42	116	11	27	6	0	0	13	19	17	11
1997	Butte (Pio)	R	.302	17	43	12	13	2	1	3	13	5	5	3
1998	Butte (Pio)	R	.331	69	299	70	99	16	5	9	61	24	44	40
1999	Cedar Rapids (Mid)	A	.274	130	526	74	144	26	13	4	48	41	84	52
2000	Lake Elsinore (Cal)	A	.282	135	532	96	150	20	16	9	72	61	116	53
MINOR LEAGUE TOTALS			.286	393	1516	263	433	70	35	25	207	150	266	159

10. Jared Abruzzo, c

Born: Nov. 15, 1981. **Ht.:** 6-3. **Wt.:** 225. **Bats:** B. **Throws:** R. **School:** El Capitan HS, Lakeside, Calif. **Career Transactions:** Selected by Angels in second round of 2000 draft; signed June 8, 2000.

In 40 seasons the Angels have had just three all-star catchers; none since Lance Parrish in 1990. The system had no real chance to end that drought until Abruzzo signed. He has the tools to be a complete catcher. He's a switch-hitter who offers power from both sides of the plate. His 61 walks in 62 games indicate an advanced knowledge of the strike zone. Behind the plate, he's a fine receiver with a solid arm. Abruzzo began his high school career as a third baseman and is still developing as a catcher. He impressed the Angels with his desire to improve all aspects of his defense, including his game-calling and blocking skills. He also needs to improve his arm after throwing out just 23 percent of base-stealers in his debut. At the plate, he'll have to make more contact. Bengie Molina had a surprising rookie season for the Angels in 2000, but he doesn't come close to Abruzzo's offensive ceiling. Abruzzo will move up to Cedar Rapids in 2001.

Year	Club (League)	Class	AVG	G	AB	R	H	2B	3B	HR	RBI	BB	SO	SB
2000	Butte (Pio)	R	.255	62	208	46	53	11	0	8	45	61	58	1
MINOR LEAGUE TOTALS			.255	62	208	46	53	11	0	8	45	61	58	1

11. Matt Wise, rhp

Born: Nov. 18, 1975. **Ht.:** 6-4. **Wt.:** 190. **Bats:** R. **Throws:** R. **School:** Cal State Fullerton. **Career Transactions:** Selected by Angels in sixth round of 1997 draft; signed June 8, 1997.

Wise has recovered from adversity in his short time in the Angels organization. He led the Northwest League in wins in his 1997 pro debut, then jumped all the way to Double-A the following year, when he got rocked pitching in Midland's bandbox. In 1999, Anaheim shifted its Double-A affiliate to more pitcher-friendly Erie, where Wise thrived—until needing surgery to remove bone chips from his elbow. Fully healthy last season, he made it through Triple-A and pitched well in his first six big league outings before getting hammered in his final two starts. His best pitch is a changeup that makes a below-average fastball seem quicker. Because Wise is tall and skinny, there's hope he might get stronger and add velocity, and he did add late running action to his fastball in 2000. He also throws his slider for strikes. Wise works from multiple arm angles, making it difficult for batters to get comfortable. Oddly, lefthanders have hit .231 against him while righthanders have batted .292. Providing that he can make adjustments to counter the ones big league hitters made against him, Wise has a solid chance to make Anaheim's Opening Day rotation.

Year	Club (League)	Class	W	L	ERA	G	GS	CG	SV	IP	H	R	ER	BB	SO
1997	Boise (NWL)	A	9	1	3.25	15	15	0	0	83	62	37	30	34	86
1998	Midland (TL)	AA	9	10	5.42	27	27	3	0	168	195	111	101	46	131
1999	Erie (EL)	AA	8	5	3.77	16	16	3	0	98	102	48	41	24	72
2000	Edmonton (PCL)	AAA	9	6	3.69	19	19	2	0	124	122	54	51	26	82
	Anaheim (AL)	MAJ	3	3	5.54	8	6	0	0	37	40	23	23	13	20
MAJOR LEAGUE TOTALS			3	3	5.54	8	6	0	0	37	40	23	23	13	20
MINOR LEAGUE TOTALS			35	22	4.24	77	77	8	0	473	481	250	223	130	371

12. Elvin Nina, rhp

Born: Nov. 25, 1975. **Ht.:** 6-0. **Wt.:** 185. **Bats:** R. **Throws:** R. **School:** Oklahoma State University. **Career Transactions:** Selected by Athletics in 17th round of 1997 draft; signed June 6, 1997 . . . Traded by Athletics with OF Nathan Haynes and OF Jeff DaVanon to Angels for RHP Omar Olivares and 2B Randy Velarde, July 29, 1999.

When the Angels traded Omar Olivares and Randy Velarde in July 1999, they wanted hard-throwing righthander Jesus Colome from Oakland. Instead they had to settle for Nina, who has been impressive when healthy. He came down with elbow tendinitis at the end of the 1999 season, then began 2000 by pulling an oblique muscle while running in spring training. He missed most of April before taking a no-hitter into the eighth inning in his first start of the season, then missed another month when his mother suddenly died of a stroke. Nina has two plus pitches: a 90-94 mph fastball that tails, and a hard curveball. His third pitch, a changeup, is solid average. Nina's command has been spotty since he left Class A, which is why he hasn't posted dominant numbers at the upper levels. He did do so in the Arizona Fall League, however, where he set a record with a 0.41 ERA. He could use a full, healthy year in Triple-A, and he could be pushing for a callup by the end of 2001.

Year	Club (League)	Class	W	L	ERA	G	GS	CG	SV	IP	H	R	ER	BB	SO
1997	S. Oregon (NWL)	A	1	3	5.23	18	2	0	1	31	36	24	18	18	26
1998	Visalia (Cal)	A	8	8	4.49	30	21	1	0	130	135	77	65	62	131
	Edmonton (PCL)	AAA	0	0	0.00	1	0	0	0	0	1	0	0	2	0
1999	Modesto (Cal)	A	5	2	2.09	17	12	0	0	73	59	31	17	41	74
	Midland (TL)	AA	3	2	4.80	7	4	0	0	30	36	21	16	18	18
	Erie (EL)	AA	3	0	4.07	4	4	0	0	24	20	12	11	15	19
2000	Erie (EL)	AA	2	4	4.24	12	10	2	0	57	51	31	27	24	30
	Edmonton (PCL)	AAA	0	0	2.89	3	2	0	0	9	11	6	3	6	3
MINOR LEAGUE TOTALS			22	19	3.97	92	55	3	1	356	349	202	157	186	301

13. Gary Johnson, of

Born: Oct. 29, 1975. **Ht.:** 6-3. **Wt.:** 210. **Bats:** L. **Throws:** L. **School:** Brigham Young University. **Career Transactions:** Selected by Angels in 19th round of 1999 draft; signed June 2, 1999.

It's hard to get an accurate read on Johnson because he spent two years on a Mormon mission while in college. While his 2000 season was impressive, as he contended for the California League triple crown before he was promoted, he was old for high Class A ball at 24. Cal League managers rated him the best batting prospect in the circuit, and he's definitely the best hitter in the system. He has power to all fields and reasonable discipline at the plate. He's an average baserunner, albeit not much of a stolen-base threat. Johnson is shaky in left field, especially on balls hit over his head, and must work hard to make his defense adequate. He handled Double-A, so he may be ready for Triple-A to start his second full pro season. When Tim Salmon's contract expires after the 2001 season, Johnson should be in the group that will get a shot at starting in the outfield or at DH for Anaheim in 2002.

Year	Club (League)	Class	AVG	G	AB	R	H	2B	3B	HR	RBI	BB	SO	SB
1999	Boise (NWL)	A	.314	71	264	56	83	17	1	2	48	34	44	6
2000	Lake Elsinore (Cal)	A	.338	70	266	56	90	20	2	13	62	41	59	13
	Erie (EL)	AA	.287	71	258	44	74	10	4	10	56	35	63	4
MINOR LEAGUE TOTALS			.313	212	788	156	247	47	7	25	166	110	166	23

14. David Wolensky, rhp

Born: Jan. 15, 1980. **Ht.:** 6-0. **Wt.:** 190. **Bats:** R. **Throws:** R. **School:** Chipola (Fla.) JC. **Career Transactions:** Selected by Angels in 42nd round of 1999 draft; signed May 3, 2000.

Wolensky is one of baseball's top draft-and-follows from 1999, when he was taken in the 42nd round out of Chipola (Fla.) Junior College. He returned for his sophomore season, then signed with Anaheim and laid waste to the Northwest League. He allowed more than two earned runs in only one of his 15 starts and permitted just one homer all summer. Wolensky reminds the Angels of Jason Dickson with better arm strength. He throws a 92-96 mph fastball, complemented by a splitter that gives him a second plus pitch. Both his curveball and changeup should be average pitches. At this point, Wolensky just needs experience so he can learn how to pitch and improve his stuff and ability to throw strikes. He'll spend 2001 in Class A.

Year	Club (League)	Class	W	L	ERA	G	GS	CG	SV	IP	H	R	ER	BB	SO
2000	Boise (NWL)	A	8	3	3.07	15	15	0	0	76	60	29	26	35	88
MINOR LEAGUE TOTALS			8	3	3.07	15	15	0	0	76	60	29	26	35	88

15. Tommy Murphy, ss

Born: Aug. 27, 1979. **Ht.:** 6-0. **Wt.:** 180. **Bats:** R. **Throws:** R. **School:** Florida Atlantic University. **Career Transactions:** Selected by Angels in third round of 2000 draft; signed July 5, 2000.

Murphy opened 2000 as the top-rated shortstop prospect in college baseball, but he struggled offensively and cost himself a chance to go in the first round. After signing with Anaheim as a third-rounder, he continued to have trouble with the bat. The Angels are convinced he'll hit because he has good hand-eye coordination and good balance at the plate. Working against him are his inability to read pitches, particularly sliders, and his poor concept of the strike zone. If he does hit, he'll be a good major league shortstop. He's a tremendous athlete, with 6.5-second speed in the 60-yard dash and an arm that rates a 7 on the 2-to-8 scouting scale. He can cover a lot of ground at shortstop and his hands are solid. It will be interesting to see how he performs offensively in 2001, when he's ticketed for one of Anaheim's Class A clubs.

Year	Club (League)	Class	AVG	G	AB	R	H	2B	3B	HR	RBI	BB	SO	SB
2000	Boise (NWL)	A	.225	55	213	38	48	18	1	2	25	15	52	14
MINOR LEAGUE TOTALS			.225	55	213	38	48	18	1	2	25	15	52	14

16. Wilmy Caceres, ss

Born: Oct. 2, 1978. **Ht.:** 6-0. **Wt.:** 165. **Bats:** B. **Throws:** R. **Career Transactions:** Signed out of Dominican Republic by Reds, Dec. 5, 1996 . . . Traded by Reds to Angels for RHP Seth Etherton, Dec. 10, 2000.

The Angels have struggled to come up with a shortstop as Gary DiSarcina has missed most of the last two seasons with injuries. While they're high on Brian Specht and Tommy Murphy, they felt they needed an insurance policy who could be ready this year or next. So in the first trade of the 2000 Winter Meetings, Anaheim sent 1998 first-round pick Seth Etherton to Cincinnati for Caceres. It was a curious deal, to say the least, because Etherton figured to be in the 2001 rotation while Caceres is a career .266 hitter who has shown no power or on-base ability. He's still young, switch-hits and makes contact, so there's hope for him yet. He needs to be more patient and keep the ball on the ground more frequently. For now, Caceres' forte is baserunning and defense. His considerable speed makes him a threat to steal and gives him plenty of range. This season he'll head to Triple-A, where he'll be on call should DiSarcina get hurt again.

Year	Club (League)	Class	AVG	G	AB	R	H	2B	3B	HR	RBI	BB	SO	SB
1997	Billings (Pio)	R	.263	15	38	10	10	2	0	0	9	2	3	1
1998	Charleston, WV (SAL)	A	.259	103	394	48	102	12	7	0	27	18	62	24
	Burlington (Mid)	A	.293	35	150	23	44	8	0	1	14	4	24	7
1999	Clinton (Mid)	A	.261	117	476	77	124	18	5	1	30	30	65	52
	Reds (GCL)	R	.333	2	9	2	3	0	0	0	0	0	1	0
2000	Chattanooga (SL)	AA	.268	130	534	69	143	23	4	2	33	37	71	36
MINOR LEAGUE TOTALS			.266	402	1601	229	426	63	16	4	113	91	226	120

17. Alfredo Amezaga, 2b

Born: Jan. 16, 1978. **Ht.:** 5-10. **Wt.:** 165. **Bats:** B. **Throws:** R. **School:** St. Petersburg (Fla.) JC. **Career Transactions:** Selected by Angels in 13th round of 1999 draft; signed June 4, 1999.

Amezaga was primarily a shortstop before 2000, but the additions of Brian Specht, Tommy Murphy and Wilmy Caceres have all but cemented his future as a second baseman. He's small and probably never will drive the ball, but Amezaga makes the most of what he has offensively. He makes contact, draws walks and doesn't try to hit the ball in the air, all so he can get on base and use his plus speed. He ranked fifth in the minors in stolen bases last season. Amezaga showed a great feel for second base after switching positions. His hands and range are both plus tools, and his average arm is better suited for second. He already has good footwork and instincts, and he has had little difficulty turning the double play. Adam Kennedy is clearly the franchise's second baseman of the present and future, so Amezaga may have to settle for a utility role in the majors when he's ready in a couple of years.

Year	Club (League)	Class	AVG	G	AB	R	H	2B	3B	HR	RBI	BB	SO	SB
1999	Butte (Pio)	R	.294	8	34	11	10	2	0	0	5	5	5	6
	Boise (NWL)	A	.322	48	205	52	66	6	4	2	29	23	29	14
2000	Lake Elsinore (Cal)	A	.279	108	420	90	117	13	4	4	44	63	70	73
MINOR LEAGUE TOTALS			.293	164	659	153	193	21	8	6	78	91	104	93

18. Charlie Thames, rhp

Born: May 23, 1979. **Ht.:** 6-2. **Wt.:** 190. **Bats:** R. **Throws:** R. **School:** University of Texas. **Career Transactions:** Selected by Angels in 4th round of 2000 draft; signed June 20, 2000.

Though it's possible that a starting pitcher such as Derrick Turnbow could be converted into a closer in the future, Thames is the organization's top relief prospect at the moment. He followed up an All-America season at Texas by earning Northwest League all-star honors, not allowing an earned run in his first 12 pro outings. He throws anywhere from low three-quarters to sidearm, and has better stuff than most pitchers who work at those angles. Thames has an 88-92 mph sinker that dives at the last minute and a solid slider. When he needs it, he also has a changeup he can throw for strikes. Thames, whose brother Damon was an All-America shortstop at Rice and plays in the Cardinals organization, gets lots of ground balls and strikeouts, a reliever's two best friends. He'll probably begin 2001 by returning to the California League, where he pitched well last August with the exception of a seven-run outing.

Year	Club (League)	Class	W	L	ERA	G	GS	CG	SV	IP	H	R	ER	BB	SO
2000	Boise (NWL)	A	1	1	0.35	17	0	0	11	26	18	2	1	5	30
	Lake Elsinore (Cal)	A	0	0	8.68	6	0	0	2	9	15	11	9	1	6
MINOR LEAGUE TOTALS			1	1	2.57	23	0	0	13	35	33	13	10	6	36

19. Josh Gray, of

Born: Feb. 22, 1981. **Ht.:** 6-3. **Wt.:** 210. **Bats:** R. **Throws:** R. **School:** Rock Creek HS, Durant, Okla. **Career Transactions:** Selected by Angels in 13th round of 2000 draft; signed June 16, 2000.

As a high school senior last spring, Gray didn't get a lot of exposure because he had an injured shoulder. The Angels were happy to pluck him in the 13th round. The operative phrase with Gray is light-tower power, and farm director Darrell Miller rates his power as 75 on the 20-to-80 scouting scale. He has fast hands that can drive any pitch in the strike zone for a home run. He struck out a lot in his pro debut, though Anaheim will gladly trade whiffs for longballs. He got into only one game in the field before being shut down in early August, but he runs fine and projects as an average left fielder. Gray had arthroscopic surgery to repair a labrum tear, so his arm remains uncertain. First baseman Casey Kelley led Cedar Rapids last year with 14 homers, a total Gray should dwarf with the Kernels in 2001.

Year	Club (League)	Class	AVG	G	AB	R	H	2B	3B	HR	RBI	BB	SO	SB
2000	Butte (Pio)	R	.327	40	147	31	48	11	3	8	36	19	41	1
MINOR LEAGUE TOTALS			.327	40	147	31	48	11	3	8	36	19	41	1

20. Johan Santana, rhp

Born: Nov. 28, 1973. **Ht.:** 6-2. **Wt.:** 155. **Bats:** R. **Throws:** R. **Career Transactions:** Signed out of Dominican Republic by Angels, Sept. 15, 2000.

Anaheim's most significant international signing in recent years was Venzuelan Francisco Rodriguez. Santana is No. 2 with a bullet after agreeing to an undisclosed six-figure bonus last September. At 6-foot-2 with extremely long arms and fingers, Santana oozes the projectablility the Angels covet. If his fastball gets any quicker he'll be truly overpowering, because he already throws 90-93 mph with a peak of 95. His breaking ball and changeup are still works in progress. He flies open with his delivery and drags his arm when he throws his slider, but both it and his change should become at least average pitches. He's more advanced than fellow Dominican Ramon Ortiz was when he joined the organization, and Ortiz was 19 to Santana's 16. In 2001, Santana could pitch in the Rookie-level Dominican Summer League or make his U.S. debut in the Pioneer League.

Year	Club (League)	Class	AVG	G	AB	R	H	2B	3B	HR	RBI	BB	SO	SB
2000					Did Not Play—Signed 2001 Contract									

21. Scot Shields, rhp

Born: July 22, 1975. **Ht.:** 6-1. **Wt.:** 175. **Bats:** R. **Throws:** R. **School:** Lincoln Memorial (Tenn.) University. **Career Transactions:** Selected by Angels in 38th round of 1997 draft; signed June 9, 1997.

As a late-round pick, Shields was consigned to bullpen duty for his first two seasons as a pro. He earned a promotion to a starting job in 1999 and won 14 games and finished third in the minors in strikeouts. He found the going rockier in Triple-A last season, leading the Pacific Coast League in losses. But he also led the league in strikeouts and finished second to Mariners prospect Ryan Anderson with 8.61 whiffs per nine innings, an indication that Shields has quality stuff. His slider is his best pitch, his fastball fluctuates from 88-93 mph and his changeup has the potential to be average. Shields got into trouble last season by nibbling too much with his pitches, then falling behind in the count and becoming vulnerable. He pitched better toward the end of 2000, and he'll get a shot in Anaheim if he continues to make progress.

Year	Club (League)	Class	W	L	ERA	G	GS	CG	SV	IP	H	R	ER	BB	SO
1997	Boise (NWL)	A	7	2	2.94	30	0	0	2	52	45	20	17	24	61
1998	Cedar Rapids (Mid)	A	6	5	3.65	58	0	0	7	74	62	33	30	29	81
1999	Lake Elsinore (Cal)	A	10	3	2.52	24	9	2	1	107	91	37	30	39	113
	Erie (EL)	AA	4	4	2.89	10	10	1	0	75	57	26	24	26	81
2000	Edmonton (PCL)	AAA	7	13	5.41	27	27	4	0	163	158	114	98	82	156
MINOR LEAGUE TOTALS			34	27	3.80	149	46	7	10	471	413	230	199	200	492

22. Steve Green, rhp

Born: Jan. 26, 1978. **Ht.:** 6-2. **Wt.:** 180. **Bats:** R. **Throws:** R. **School:** Fort Scott (Kan.) CC. **Career Transactions:** Selected by Angels in 10th round of 1997 draft; signed July 15, 1997.

Green was Canada's best pitcher at the 1999 Pan American Games, working a total of 10 scoreless innings in two outings against Cuba as his nation won a bronze medal and narrowly missed qualifying for the Olympics. He has quickly risen through the Angels system, succeeding everywhere but at Triple-A, which he reached in just his third season. Green's repertoire isn't overwhelming. His fastball ranges from 90-95 mph, while his changeup is average and his curveball isn't quite that good. He has succeeded by throwing strikes, though his walk rate has increased as he has moved up and crossed into dangerous territory in Edmonton. Green generally pitches low in the strike zone and keeps the ball in the park. He'll get another chance to prove himself in Triple-A this season with Anaheim's new Salt Lake affiliate.

Year	Club (League)	Class	W	L	ERA	G	GS	CG	SV	IP	H	R	ER	BB	SO
1998	Cedar Rapids (Mid)	A	2	6	4.54	18	10	1	0	83	86	49	42	25	61
1999	Lake Elsinore (Cal)	A	7	6	3.95	19	19	4	0	121	130	70	53	37	91
	Erie (EL)	AA	3	1	3.32	6	6	1	0	41	34	25	15	19	32
2000	Erie (EL)	AA	7	4	3.40	13	13	0	0	79	71	34	30	34	66
	Edmonton (PCL)	AAA	0	4	7.29	8	8	0	0	42	55	35	34	27	24
MINOR LEAGUE TOTALS			19	21	4.28	64	56	6	0	366	376	213	174	142	274

23. Bart Miadich, rhp

Born: Feb. 3, 1976. **Ht.:** 6-4. **Wt.:** 205. **Bats:** R. **Throws:** R. **School:** University of San Diego. **Career Transactions:** Signed as nondrafted free agent by Red Sox, Aug. 31, 1997 . . . Traded by Red Sox to Diamondbacks, Dec. 15, 1998, completing trade in which Diamondbacks sent RHP Bob Wolcott to Red Sox for a player to be named (Nov. 11, 1998) . . . Released by Diamondbacks, March 31, 2000 . . . Signed by Angels, May 23, 2000.

The hiring of Don Wakamatsu to manage Erie last season produced an unexpected benefit for the Angels. Wakamatsu had managed at Double-A El Paso in the Diamondbacks chain the year before, where Miadich posted an 8.10 ERA in 12 appearances. When Arizona released him in spring training, Anaheim signed him on Wakamatsu's recommendation. By the end of the season, Miadich had pitched his way onto the 40-man roster and into contention for a major league bullpen job in 2001. He has two plus pitches: a 90-95 mph fastball and a slider with a late, sharp break. After getting rocked for most of his first two pro seasons, Miadich blossomed after the Angels refined his mechanics and taught him a changeup. His command still needs work, but his future looks much more promising than it did a year ago.

Year	Club (League)	Class	W	L	ERA	G	GS	CG	SV	IP	H	R	ER	BB	SO
1998	Sarasota (FSL)	A	3	2	3.14	22	0	0	7	49	40	20	17	15	64
	Trenton (EL)	AA	1	6	5.96	22	8	0	1	54	66	39	36	26	33
1999	El Paso (TL)	AA	0	2	8.10	12	0	0	1	20	37	22	18	7	16
	High Desert (Cal)	A	3	8	5.42	21	16	0	0	98	125	71	59	40	85
2000	Erie (EL)	AA	3	1	3.35	28	0	0	2	40	27	16	15	21	38
	Edmonton (PCL)	AAA	2	1	4.57	10	0	0	1	22	25	14	11	9	20
MINOR LEAGUE TOTALS			12	20	4.96	115	24	0	12	283	320	182	156	118	256

24. Jaime Escalante, rhp

Born: April 5, 1977. **Ht.:** 6-2. **Wt.:** 210. **Bats:** B. **Throws:** R. **School:** Hagerstown (Md.) JC. **Career Transactions:** Selected by Orioles in 36th round of 1996 draft; signed May 21, 1997 . . . Selected by Angels from Orioles in Rule 5 minor league draft, Dec. 13, 1999.

The Double-A Rule 5 draft isn't a hotbed for prospects by any means. Players are eligible for selection only if they aren't protected among their organization's top 100 or so players, and the cost for taking one is a mere $4,000. Escalante was a strong-armed catcher who had a career .238 average in three seasons in the Orioles organization when the Angels picked him in December 1999. They immediately converted him to a pitcher and were pleased with the results. He reached Double-A in his first season on the mound (not counting one inning in 1997), flashing an 88-93 mph fastball and nice feel for a curveball. As expected, he's pretty raw as a pitcher. His curve, changeup and command all could use improvement. He'll work on those areas of his game in Double-A this year.

Year	Club (League)	Class	AVG	G	AB	R	H	2B	3B	HR	RBI	BB	SO	SB
1997	Orioles (GCL)	R	.273	50	143	12	39	9	1	0	17	18	34	0
1998	Bluefield (Appy)	R	.247	53	166	24	41	9	0	3	12	17	46	3
1999	Frederick (Car)	A	.333	5	3	0	1	1	0	0	1	0	1	0
	Delmarva (SAL)	A	.191	45	141	15	27	4	0	2	14	20	45	0
MINOR LEAGUE TOTALS			.238	153	453	51	108	23	1	5	44	55	126	3

Year	Club (League)	Class	W	L	ERA	G	GS	CG	SV	IP	H	R	ER	BB	SO
2000	Cedar Rapids (Mid)	A	0	1	2.43	25	0	0	7	41	24	14	11	23	41
	Erie (EL)	AA	0	1	15.00	3	1	0	0	3	4	6	5	6	2
	Lake Elsinore (Cal)	A	1	1	2.08	6	0	0	1	9	6	2	2	4	18
MINOR LEAGUE TOTALS*			1	3	3.04	35	1	0	8	53	34	22	18	34	62

*Includes one pitching appearance while a position player.

25. Bobby Jenks, rhp

Born: March 14, 1981. **Ht.:** 6-3. **Wt.:** 225. **Bats:** R. **Throws:** R. **Career Transactions:** Selected by Angels in fifth round of 2000 draft; signed June 13, 2000.

If Hollywood makes a sequel to "Bull Durham," Jenks would be perfect for the part of Nuke LaLoosh. He has a power arm, but everything else about him is questionable. He played only one season of high school ball, as a sophomore, and when he was declared academically ineligible for the third time in four years last spring, he moved from tiny Spirit Lake, Idaho, to Seattle, where he worked out with a personal trainer and showcased himself for scouts. By the fifth round of the June draft, Jenks' 93-96 mph fastball and hard curveball were too much for the Angels to resist. He had absolutely no success after signing because he couldn't throw strikes and had no semblance of an offspeed pitch. He likely won't be ready for full-season ball in 2001, at least not at the start of the season. Jenks could become something special, and he could just as easily go down quickly in flames.

Year	Club (League)	Class	W	L	ERA	G	GS	CG	SV	IP	H	R	ER	BB	SO
2000	Butte (Pio)	R	1	7	7.86	14	12	0	0	53	61	57	46	44	42
MINOR LEAGUE TOTALS			1	7	7.86	14	12	0	0	53	61	57	46	44	42

26. Sergio Contreras, 1b/of

Born: April 30, 1980. **Ht.:** 5-10. **Wt.:** 180. **Bats:** L. **Throws:** L. **School:** Amphitheater HS, Tucson. **Career Transactions:** Signed as nondrafted free agent by Angels, June 5, 1999.

Former Expos righthander Tavo Alvarez and current Diamondbacks first baseman Erubiel Durazo were native Mexicans who played at Tucson's Amphitheater High en route to the major leagues. Contreras hopes to follow the path. His twin brother Albino signed with the Angels on the same day and has played with Sergio in high school, the Dominican Summer League and Butte. Contreras has a less-than-inspiring physique and didn't show much in his pro debut, but he exploded last year. He would have led the Pioneer League in batting if minor injuries hadn't cost him the at-bats to qualify. Contreras will have to hit at every level to move up, because his bat is his only above-average tool. He's more of a gap hitter than a slugger, and his speed and arm are decent. He played first base in 2000, though the Angels say that was out of necessity and project him as a corner outfielder. One Angels official projected Contreras as a Mike Aldrete type who could be useful off a big league bench. This much is certain: When a guy hits .399, you promote him and see if he can continue to rake.

Year	Club (League)	Class	AVG	G	AB	R	H	2B	3B	HR	RBI	BB	SO	SB
1999	Angels (DSL)	R	.252	63	246	33	62	17	0	2	33	37	42	9
2000	Butte (Pio)	R	.399	45	173	44	69	10	8	3	28	19	25	8
MINOR LEAGUE TOTALS			.313	108	419	77	131	27	8	5	61	56	67	17

27. Brandon O'Neal, rhp

Born: Oct. 17, 1978. **Ht.:** 6-1. **Wt.:** 195. **Bats:** B. **Throws:** R. **School:** University of Kansas. **Career Transactions:** Selected by Angels in sixth round of 2000 draft; signed June 30, 2000.

O'Neal didn't take the mound at all as a Kansas freshman and only sparingly as a sophomore, so 2000 was the first year he focused on pitching. He went just 1-6 for the Jayhawks, but the Angels were more interested in the numbers on the radar gun: 91-96 mph with a fastball that has nasty sink. He didn't show that much velocity after signing, quietly trying to pitch through elbow problems with only sporadic success. He had bone spurs removed from his elbow once the season ended and should be healthy again this spring. O'Neal's changeup also dives at the plate, giving him two sinkers with a wide disparity in speeds. His slider needs the most work of his three pitches because he tips it off by slowing down his arm speed. Anaheim officials believe he can move quickly once he gets back to 100 percent. Because of his inexperience and injury, he'd be best served by starting 2001 at Cedar Rapids.

Year	Club (League)	Class	W	L	ERA	G	GS	CG	SV	IP	H	R	ER	BB	SO
2000	Boise (NWL)	A	1	5	5.60	13	10	0	1	53	66	45	33	22	45
MINOR LEAGUE TOTALS			1	5	5.60	13	10	0	1	53	66	45	33	22	45

28. Sean Brummett, lhp

Born: Jan. 10, 1978. **Ht.:** 6-0. **Wt.:** 200. **Bats:** L. **Throws:** L. **School:** Indiana State University. **Career Transactions:** Selected by Angels in 15th round of 1999 draft; signed June 17, 1999.

Though Indiana State went just 21-34 in 1999, the Sycamores had a fine pair of lefthanded pitching prospects in Alex Graman (now with the Yankees) and Brummett. He checks in as one of two lefties (compared to 17 righthanders) on this list, 27 spots lower than the first, Joe Torres. Brummett was more successful as a hitter than as a pitcher in college, batting .303

and compiling a 6.38 ERA. He got shelled in his pro debut, then was untouchable in the Midwest League at the outset of 2000. He skipped high Class A and struggled in Double-A, then rebounded again by ranking among the Arizona Fall League leaders with a 1.97 ERA. Brummett throws three average pitches: a fastball, changeup and curveball. His lack of a plus pitch makes him vulnerable against righthanders. His long-term role may be as a lefty set-up man, though he started last year to get more innings. He'll continue starting in 2001, and could take a step back to the California League to begin the season.

Year	Club (League)	Class	W	L	ERA	G	GS	CG	SV	IP	H	R	ER	BB	SO
1999	Boise (NWL)	A	1	2	6.68	17	3	0	0	32	41	25	24	12	26
2000	Cedar Rapids (Mid)	A	7	4	1.00	32	5	1	5	72	58	16	8	23	53
	Erie (EL)	AA	0	7	5.33	9	9	1	0	49	63	33	29	25	30
MINOR LEAGUE TOTALS			8	13	3.57	58	17	2	5	153	162	74	61	60	109

29. Matt Hensley, rhp

Born: Aug. 18, 1978. **Ht.:** 6-2. **Wt.:** 215. **Bats:** R. **Throws:** R. **School:** Grossmont (Calif.) JC. **Career Transactions:** Selected by Angels in 10th round of 2000 draft; signed June 15, 2000.

The Angels had what looks like a very successful draft in 2000, and Hensley could be one of their real sleepers. After leading the junior college Pacific Coast Conference in ERA (2.24) and strikeouts (101 in 88 innings) during the spring, Hensley reached high Class A at the end of his first pro summer. If not for a disastrous start in which he surrendered 11 earned runs, his ERA would have been 1.76. Hensley's top pitch is his changeup, and his 89-93 mph fastball has nice sink. His breaking ball should become at least average. Hensley has size, command and a bulldog mentality. He'll head back to the California League to continue his climb through the system at the start of 2001.

Year	Club (League)	Class	W	L	ERA	G	GS	CG	SV	IP	H	R	ER	BB	SO
2000	Butte (Pio)	R	1	2	2.57	8	5	0	0	28	29	21	8	10	22
	Cedar Rapids (Mid)	A	2	2	4.15	5	5	1	0	30	33	16	14	10	26
	Lake Elsinore (Cal)	A	0	0	0.00	1	0	0	0	1	1	0	0	0	2
MINOR LEAGUE TOTALS			3	4	3.34	14	10	1	0	59	63	37	22	20	50

30. Shawn Wooten, c

Born: July 24, 1972. **Ht.:** 5-10. **Wt.:** 205. **Bats:** R. **Throws:** R. **School:** Mount San Antonio (Calif.) JC. **Career Transactions:** Selected by Tigers in 18th round of 1993 draft; signed June 7, 1993 . . . Released by Tigers, June 19, 1995 . . . Signed by independent Moose Jaw (Prairie), 1995 . . . Signed by Angels, Feb. 28, 1997.

Wooten doesn't have a prospect pedigree. He's 28 and did two years of time in the independent (and now defunct) Prairie League after the Tigers released him in 1995. He hooked up with the Angels in 1997 and put together three decent seasons while learning to catch. He moved behind the plate full-time in 2000, with surprising results. He hit a career-high 20 homers, and his .327 average was his best since he was the Rookie-level Appalachian League's all-star DH seven years earlier. Wooten also showed an above-average release and arm while throwing out 42 percent of basestealers. He worked hard to get into shape, and his efforts paid off. Wooten had minor surgery on his right ankle after the season but should be healthy at the start of spring training. Wooten might never get a chance to become Anaheim's regular catcher. But at worst, the Angels think he can be a backup catcher/first baseman/third baseman. His offensive upside has to be at least as good as that of Jorge Fabregas, whom Anaheim signed as a free agent during the offseason.

Year	Club (League)	Class	AVG	G	AB	R	H	2B	3B	HR	RBI	BB	SO	SB
1993	Bristol (Appy)	R	.350	52	177	26	62	12	2	8	39	24	20	1
	Fayetteville (SAL)	A	.250	5	16	2	4	0	0	1	5	3	3	0
1994	Fayetteville (SAL)	A	.269	121	439	45	118	25	1	3	61	27	84	1
1995	Jacksonville (SL)	AA	.129	20	70	4	9	1	0	2	7	1	17	0
	Lakeland (FSL)	A	.230	38	135	11	31	10	1	2	11	10	28	0
	Moose Jaw (Prairie)	IND	.373	52	201	38	75	12	2	11	55	18	26	3
1996	Moose Jaw (Prairie)	IND	.305	77	292	44	89	17	0	12	57	18	46	2
1997	Cedar Rapids (Mid)	A	.289	108	353	43	102	23	1	15	75	49	71	0
1998	Lake Elsinore (Cal)	A	.294	105	395	56	116	31	0	16	74	38	82	0
	Midland (TL)	AA	.321	8	28	3	9	4	0	1	6	3	4	0
1999	Erie (EL)	AA	.292	137	518	70	151	27	1	19	88	50	102	3
2000	Erie (EL)	AA	.293	51	191	32	56	12	2	9	35	17	30	4
	Edmonton (PCL)	AAA	.353	66	252	43	89	21	3	11	42	18	38	0
	Anaheim (AL)	MAJ	.556	7	9	2	5	1	0	0	1	0	0	0
MAJOR LEAGUE TOTALS			.556	7	9	2	5	1	0	0	1	0	0	0
MINOR LEAGUE TOTALS			.292	840	3067	417	911	195	13	110	555	276	551	14

Arizona
Diamondbacks

By Mark Gonzales

Despite a disappointing 2000 season, the Diamondbacks' four-year plan remains in place as the franchise enters its third year. The same can't be said, however, for their player-development efforts.

The farm system has been sapped by trades to acquire high-profile major leaguers over the past two seasons, and beset by slow-developing or one-dimensional high school draftees. So with scouting director Mike Rizzo running his first draft last June, Arizona steered in a different direction.

Arizona selected nine college players among its first 10 choices in the draft. This was a clear sign the organization needed to fast-track players to bridge a gap caused by the lack of upper-level minor league talent and the need to have players ready when the contracts of several big leaguers expire after the 2002 season.

The system absorbed several major injury setbacks, most noticeably elbow injuries to two key righthanders: prized prospect John Patterson and reliever Jeremy Ward. They missed nearly all of the 2000 season, though the Diamondbacks hope they'll return healthy with a shot to make the major league roster by 2002, if not sooner.

Despite the well-deserved criticism of the Diamondbacks' past drafts, their ventures into the international market have been largely successful. Latin American coordinator Junior Noboa has injected enough talent from the Caribbean into the system to compensate for draft picks who haven't panned out.

Korean native Byung-Hyun Kim nearly became a National League all-star reliever, though he'll have to gain more confidence and maturity. Former Dominican carpenter Geraldo Guzman pitched his way to the majors after spending 1993-98 out of the game. And Nicaraguan import Vicente Padilla pitched so well in his second full season that the Phillies wanted him in July's Curt Schilling trade.

The Schilling trade also marked the end of the Travis Lee era, four years filled with hope in the form of a $10 million bonus, being ranked as the organization's top prospect and a promising major league debut. Lee hit a brick wall midway through the 1999 season and culminated in his departure after he moved from first base to right field without significant success.

The focus remains the same: win now. But the Diamondbacks are more aware of the need to develop from within, given the high cost of free agents and their own financial concerns. The franchise is in the midst of cutting about $15 million from everywhere but player development.

OrganizationOverview

General manager: Joe Garagiola Jr. **Farm director:** Tommy Jones. **Scouting director:** Mike Rizzo.

2000 PERFORMANCE

Class	Team	League	W	L	Pct.	Finish*	Manager
Majors	Arizona	National	85	77	.525	t-6th (16)	Buck Showalter
Triple-A	Tucson Sidewinders	Pacific Coast	68	73	.482	9th (16)	Tom Spencer
Double-A	El Paso Diablos	Texas	74	66	.529	3rd (8)	Bobby Dickerson
High A	#High Desert Mavericks	California	48	92	.343	10th (10)	Scott Coolbaugh
Low A	So. Bend Silver Hawks	Midwest	60	78	.435	12th (14)	Dave Jorn
Rookie	Missoula Osprey	Pioneer	44	32	.579	2nd (8)	Chip Hale
Rookie	†AZL Diamondbacks	Arizona	27	25	.519	5th (9)	Joe Almaraz
OVERALL 2000 MINOR LEAGUE RECORD			321	368	.466	26th (30)	

* Finish in overall standings (No. of teams in league). #Affiliate will be in Lancaster (California) in 2001. †Affiliate will be in Yakima (Northwest/short-season level) in 2001.

ORGANIZATION LEADERS

BATTING
*AVG	Alex Cabrera, El Paso/Tucscon	.353
R	Jack Cust, El Paso	100
H	**Lyle Overbay**, El Paso/South Bend	172
TB	**Lyle Overbay**, El Paso/South Bend	259
2B	**Lyle Overbay**, El Paso/South Bend	35
3B	Victor Hall, Missoula/South Bend	14
HR	Alex Cabrera, El Paso/Tucscon	39
RBI	**Lyle Overbay**, El Paso/South Bend	96
BB	Jack Cust, El Paso	117
SO	Jack Cust, El Paso	150
SB	Victor Hall, Missoula/South Bend	59

PITCHING
W	Chris Cervantes, South Bend/El Paso	12
L	Todd Thorn, High Desert/El Paso	13
#ERA	**Chris Capuano**, South Bend	2.21
G	Clint Davis, El Paso/Tucson	60
CG	Duaner Sanchez, South Bend	4
SV	Bret Prinz, South Bend/El Paso	27
IP	Duaner Sanchez, South Bend	165
BB	Hatuey Mendoza, High Desert	98
SO	Chris Cervantes, South Bend/El Paso	126

*Minimum 250 at-bats. #Minimum 75 innings.

TOP PROSPECTS OF THE DECADE
1997	Travis Lee, 1b
1998	Travis Lee, 1b
1999	Brad Penny, rhp
2000	John Patterson, rhp

TOP DRAFT PICKS OF THE DECADE
1996	Nick Bierbrodt, lhp
1997	Jack Cust, 1b
1998	Darryl Conyer, of (3)
1999	Corey Myers, ss
2000	Mike Schultz, rhp (2)

BEST TOOLS
Best Hitter for Average	Alex Cintron
Best Power Hitter	Jack Cust
Fastest Baserunner	Victor Hall
Best Fastball	Bret Prinz

Overbay   **Capuano**

Best Breaking Ball	Chris Capuano
Best Control	Mike Koplove
Best Defensive Catcher	Rod Barajas
Best Defensive Infielder	Alex Cintron
Best Infield Arm	Jerry Gil
Best Defensive Outfielder	Luis Terrero
Best Outfield Arm	Luis Terrero

PROJECTED 2004 LINEUP
Catcher	Brad Cresse
First Base	Jack Cust
Second Base	Alex Cintron
Third Base	Tim Olson
Shortstop	Jerry Gil
Left Field	Luis Gonzalez
Center Field	Steve Finley
Right Field	Luis Terrero
No. 1 Starter	Curt Schilling
No. 2 Starter	John Patterson
No. 3 Starter	Brian Anderson
No. 4 Starter	Chris Capuano
No. 5 Starter	Mike Schultz
Closer	Matt Mantei

ALL-TIME LARGEST BONUSES
Travis Lee, 1996	$10,000,000
John Patterson, 1996	6,075,000
Byung-Hyun Kim, 1999	2,000,000
Corey Myers, 1999	2,000,000
Vladimir Nunez, 1996	1,750,000

DraftAnalysis

2000 Draft

Best Pro Debut: C Brad Cresse (5) never stopped hitting. He led NCAA Division I in homers and RBIs, drove in the College World Series-winning run for Louisiana State, then went to high Class A High Desert and put up 17 homers and 56 RBIs in 48 games.

Best Athlete: Tim Olson (7), who played shortstop and center field at Florida, stood out at third base, center field and right field in instructional league. He runs well and has a well above-average arm. The Diamondbacks clocked him at 92-93 mph when he pitched in junior college. Cedrick Harris (10) has similar tools and reminds Arizona of Marquis Grissom with his center-field defense.

Best Hitter: Cresse. Also keep an eye on OF Josh Kroeger (4), who hit .297 in the Rookie-level Arizona League at 17.

Best Raw Power: Cresse, easily.

Fastest Runner: OF Julius Foreman's (15) game is his speed, which rates as a 65 or 70 on the 20-to-80 scouting scale. He hit .288 at Class A South Bend and showed a leadoff man's eye at the plate.

Best Defensive Player: Olson makes great reads as an outfielder and has first-step quickness and plenty of range at the hot corner. At both positions, his arm is an asset.

Best Fastball: RHP Brian Bruney (12) tops out at 98 mph. RHP **Mike Schultz** (2) throws harder on a more consistent basis, regularly throwing 94-96 mph with plenty of life.

Most Intriguing Background: OF Andrew Wishy (47) is an accomplished pianist who opted to study at Arkansas rather than sign. Cresse's father Mark was Tommy Lasorda's bullpen coach with the Dodgers.

Closest To The Majors: Cresse ended 2000 in Double-A and should start there this season. The Diamondbacks have been pleasantly surprised by his catch-and-throw skills, and catching has been their weakest position at the major league level.

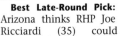
Schultz

Best Late-Round Pick: Arizona thinks RHP Joe Ricciardi (35) could become another Bob Wickman. Ricciardi throws a heavy, 90-94 mph sinker and a good slider. We limit this category to the 10th round and below, but RHP Tanner Eriksen (9) deserves mention. He pitched just six innings at Southern California last spring because he showed no command. But the Diamondbacks signed him after he had one strong outing in the Cape Cod League. Eriksen throws 92-95 mph with a power curve.

The One Who Got Away: C Creighton Kahoalii (48), who's now at California.

Assessment: The Diamondbacks addressed a void in the upper levels of their system by focusing on advanced college players over high schoolers. Schultz, LHP Bill White (3) and RHPs Scott Barber (6) and Brandon Webb (8) all will open 2001 in high Class A or Double-A.

1999 Draft

The Diamondbacks were initially excited about RHP Jeremy Ward (2) and 3B Ryan Owens (7), but both took a step back in 2000. If Ward can't bounce back from reconstructive elbow surgery, 1B Lyle Overbay (18) may be the cream of this crop.   **Grade: C–**

1998 Draft

Arizona forfeited its first two picks and struck out on its top choice, OF Daryl Conyer (3). Sidearming RHP Bret Prinz (18) is the lone highlight from this group, though RHP Andrew Good (8), who missed 2000 with an injury, still holds promise.   **Grade: D**

1997 Draft

In the ultimate hit-or-miss draft, the Diamondbacks found the system's two best prospects in SS Alex Cintron (36) and OF/1B Jack Cust (1). And little else.   **Grade: B**

1996 Draft

Arizona uncovered RHP Brad Penny (5), then traded him to get closer Matt Mantei for the 1999 pennant race. The club's first-ever pick, LHP Nick Bierbrodt (1) has stalled while battling injuries. The Diamondbacks found some role players late, such as OFs Rob Ryan (26) and Jason Conti (32).   **Grade: B**

Note: Draft analysis prepared by Jim Callis. Numbers in parentheses indicate draft rounds.

. . . Cintron is a capable switch-hitter who is tall for a shortstop, yet possesses exceptional range at a demanding position.

Cintron **Alex**
ss

Born: Dec. 17, 1978.
Ht.: 6-2. **Wt.:** 180.
Bats: B. **Throws:** R.
School: Mech Tech HS, Caguas, P.R.
Career Transactions: Selected by Diamondbacks in 36th round of 1997 draft; signed June 15, 1997.

Cintron gives the Diamondbacks system hope amid the criticism it has received for all of the top draft picks who haven't panned out. He has steadily improved in each of his past three seasons, earning league all-star honors in the last two. He has become a more determined player since batting .200 in Rookie ball in 1997 after coming out of a Puerto Rico high school.

There's nothing to dislike about Cintron's physical talents. He's a capable switch-hitter who has batted better than .300 in each of the past two seasons and was among the batting leaders in the Puerto Rican League this winter. He's tall for a shortstop, yet possesses exceptional range at a demanding position. Durability isn't a question, as he has played 253 games over the past two seasons. He also has a tremendous desire to learn and improve. Cintron could be Arizona's shortstop of the future, yet he had no qualms about playing third base in Puerto Rico because big leaguers Alex Cora and Luis Lopez were at shortstop and second base. But there's no masking Cintron's 32 errors last summer. He simply needs to become more consistent. He'll offset a dazzling defensive play with a throwing error on a routine play. Despite his range, he's not a blazing baserunner. Any comparisons to Nomar Garciaparra and Derek Jeter are premature because Cintron has hit just 10 homers in four years. Despite his high batting averages, his on-base percentages have been mediocre because he rarely walks.

If Cintron had a year of Triple-A experience under his belt, the Diamondbacks might have traded Tony Womack this winter in an effort to strengthen their team in other areas. It's a tribute to Cintron's potential that Arizona hasn't made him yet another of its prospects included in a deal for an established veteran. If he continues to improve, he'll be in line for a September callup. Cintron was added to the 40-man roster this winter, so he'll get an opportunity to impress new manager Bob Brenly this spring. Should he establish himself as a big league regular, it would be a shot in the arm for a 1997 Diamondbacks draft that has been largely unsuccessful.

Year	Club (League)	Class	AVG	G	AB	R	H	2B	3B	HR	RBI	BB	SO	SB
1997	Diamondbacks (AZL)	R	.197	43	152	23	30	6	1	0	20	21	32	1
	Lethbridge (Pio)	R	.333	1	3	0	1	0	0	0	0	0	1	0
1998	Lethbridge (Pio)	R	.264	67	258	41	68	11	4	3	34	20	32	8
1999	High Desert (Cal)	A	.307	128	499	78	153	25	4	3	64	19	65	15
2000	El Paso (TL)	AA	.301	125	522	83	157	30	6	4	59	29	56	9
MINOR LEAGUE TOTALS			.285	364	1434	225	409	72	15	10	177	89	186	33

2. Jack Cust, of/1b

Born: Jan. 16, 1979. **Ht.:** 6-1. **Wt.:** 205. **Bats:** L. **Throws:** R. **School:** Immaculata HS, Somerville, N.J. **Career Transactions:** Selected by Diamondbacks in first round (30th overall) of 1997 draft; signed July 14, 1997.

Cust has mashed the ball in four years as a pro. The Diamondbacks wisely let him play the entire 2000 season at Double-A El Paso, where he ranked fourth in the Texas League in runs and on-base percentage (.440). He has the most power of any prospect in the organization. His left-handed uppercut swings have drawn comparisons to Geoff Jenkins and Jeromy Burnitz. Cust enhances his offensive ability with his willingness to take a walk, which means he doesn't help pitchers by getting himself out. Unfortunately for the Diamondbacks, Cust may be better suited for the American League. A former first baseman, he has moved to the outfield and shown little aptitude or hustle there. His big swing makes him susceptible to strikeouts. Cust irked the Diamondbacks by leaving his Dominican League team after playing just three weeks. He could have used the time to work on his planned switch from left to right field. The team was encouraged that Cust was getting better reads on fly balls in right this winter. Should he improve in right, he could reach Arizona by the end of the 2001 season.

Year	Club (League)	Class	AVG	G	AB	R	H	2B	3B	HR	RBI	BB	SO	SB
1997	Diamondbacks (AZL)	R	.306	35	121	26	37	11	1	3	33	31	39	2
1998	South Bend (Mid)	A	.242	16	62	5	15	3	0	0	4	5	20	0
	Lethbridge (Pio)	R	.345	73	223	75	77	20	2	11	56	86	71	15
1999	High Desert (Cal)	A	.334	125	455	107	152	42	3	32	112	96	145	1
2000	El Paso (TL)	AA	.293	129	447	100	131	32	6	20	75	117	150	12
MINOR LEAGUE TOTALS			.315	378	1308	313	412	108	12	66	280	335	425	30

3. Luis Terrero, of

Born: May 18, 1980. **Ht.:** 6-2. **Wt.:** 183. **Bats:** R. **Throws:** R. **Career Transactions:** Signed out of Dominican Republic by Diamondbacks, Sept. 27, 1997.

The Diamondbacks were upset when they lost Abraham Nunez to the Marlins in December 1999 to complete the Matt Mantei trade. They would have been more upset if they didn't have Terrero, a legitimate five-tool player and one of Latin American coordinator Junior Noboa's top finds. Terrero made the most of a brief opportunity by making two exceptional defensive plays in the Hall of Fame game last July. His Coopers-town performance reinforced his ability to play exceptional defense in either center or right field because he has quality range and arm strength. He has stolen 55 bases over the past two seasons, and team officials believe he might hit for power as he gets stronger. Terrero does have a long swing and has averaged more than a strikeout a game as a pro, unacceptable for someone who hasn't produced many home runs. Arizona believes he'll become a more disciplined hitter and less susceptible to outside breaking pitches. A solid full year at Class A in 2001 would put Terrrero back on track after he spent most of the last two seasons at Rookie-level Missoula.

Year	Club (League)	Class	AVG	G	AB	R	H	2B	3B	HR	RBI	BB	SO	SB
1998	Diamondbacks (DSL)	R	.231	56	169	19	39	7	1	2	15	13	44	9
1999	Missoula (Pio)	R	.287	71	272	74	78	13	7	8	40	32	91	27
2000	Missoula (Pio)	R	.261	68	276	48	72	10	0	8	44	10	75	23
	High Desert (Cal)	A	.190	19	79	10	15	3	1	0	1	3	16	5
MINOR LEAGUE TOTALS			.256	214	796	151	204	33	9	18	100	58	226	64

4. John Patterson, rhp

Born: Jan. 30, 1978. **Ht.:** 6-6. **Wt.:** 200. **Bats:** R. **Throws:** R. **School:** West Orange-Stark HS, Orange, Texas. **Career Transactions:** Selected by Expos in first round (fifth overall) of 1996 draft . . . Granted free agency . . . Signed by Diamondbacks, Nov. 7, 1996.

Virtually everyone in the organization noticed something was wrong last spring when Patterson's fastball was clocked at just 90 mph. It took another month before doctors found a torn ligament in his right elbow. A month after that, the Diamondbacks decided he needed Tommy John surgery after seeking several medical opinions. They have a lot invested in Patterson, who received a $6.075 million bonus as a loophole free agent out of high school. Before his elbow injury, everyone held high hopes for Patterson because his 96 mph fastball was only his second-best pitch. When healthy, he throws a knee-buckling curve that he disguises well thanks to his smooth mechanics. He also has excellent command of his fastball and curve. The rehabilitation period has given Patterson time to assess why he has gone 18-29 as a pro. He needs to trust his stuff and not give in to hitters. He hasn't hit a batter since 1998, a sign that he's letting opponents get too comfortable. His changeup and command could use some tweaking. This could have been the season Patterson broke into Arizona's rotation for good. If all goes well, he could return to Triple-A by mid-May. The Diamondbacks expect to bring back their entire 2000 rotation, so there's no need to rush him.

Year	Club (League)	Class	W	L	ERA	G	GS	CG	SV	IP	H	R	ER	BB	SO
1997	South Bend (Mid)	A	1	9	3.23	18	18	0	0	78	63	32	28	34	95
1998	High Desert (Cal)	A	8	7	2.83	25	25	0	0	127	102	54	40	42	148
1999	El Paso (TL)	AA	8	6	4.77	18	18	2	0	100	98	61	53	42	117
	Tucson (PCL)	AAA	1	5	7.04	7	6	0	0	31	43	26	24	18	29
2000	Tucson (PCL)	AAA	0	2	7.80	3	2	0	0	15	21	14	13	9	10
MINOR LEAGUE TOTALS			18	29	4.06	71	69	2	0	351	327	187	158	145	399

5. Jerry Gil, ss

Born: Oct. 14, 1982. **Ht.:** 6-3. **Wt.:** 183. **Bats:** R. **Throws:** R. **Career Transactions:** Signed out of Dominican Republic by Diamondbacks, Nov. 5, 1999.

Everyone in the organization raves about Gil. They don't care that he batted .225 in Rookie ball in his pro debut. They merely want him to get acclimated to playing in the United States and get experience, with the results coming later. Gil has the range and arm strength to play shortstop, and he needs little polish because of his smooth footwork. He's so good defensively that he could push Alex Cintron to second base should both reach the majors. His size gives him good offensive potential, and the Diamondbacks adore his dedication to the game. Gil was a bit overmatched debuting in the United States at 17. He committed 35 errors and had just 12 extra-base hits and 11 walks, though the Diamondbacks insist they weren't disappointed. He just needs experience to work on all facets of his game. He'll continue to get plenty of instruction without being suffocated and will get plenty of time to develop into the big-time player Arizona envisions. With the more established Cintron well ahead of him on the organizational ladder, there's no reason to hurry Gil.

Year	Club (League)	Class	AVG	G	AB	R	H	2B	3B	HR	RBI	BB	SO	SB
2000	Missoula (Pio)	R	.225	58	227	24	51	10	2	0	20	11	63	7
MINOR LEAGUE TOTALS			.225	58	227	24	51	10	2	0	20	11	63	7

6. Brad Cresse, c

Born: July 31, 1978. **Ht.:** 6-4. **Wt.:** 215. **Bats:** R. **Throws:** R. **School:** Louisiana State University. **Career Transactions:** Selected by Diamondbacks in fifth round of 2000 draft; signed June 19, 2000.

If the last name sounds familiar, it's because Cresse is the son of former Dodgers bullpen catcher Mark. Brad made a name for himself by driving in the winning run in the 2000 College World Series title game, capping a senior season in which he led NCAA Division I with 30 homers and 106 RBIs. Cresse loves to play and made an impressive transition from the college game to the high Class A California League. He even held his own after a late promotion to Double-A. Power is his best tool, and it's obvious that he's been around the game for most of his life. His work behind the plate was better than advertised. Though Cresse wouldn't admit it, he showed the effects of a long 2000 season during his rough stint in the Arizona Fall League, where he batted .169. He was vulnerable to breaking pitches in the final weeks. Roving catching instructor Ron Hassey will continue to work with Cresse's defense, which is still the weakest part of his game. Cresse is on the fast track, as evidenced by his start in the Cal League, his jump to Double-A and his placement in the AFL in his first pro summer. He probably needs a full season at Double-A unless he improves dramatically, but his future appears bright.

Year	Club (League)	Class	AVG	G	AB	R	H	2B	3B	HR	RBI	BB	SO	SB
2000	High Desert (Cal)	A	.324	48	173	35	56	7	0	17	·56	17	50	0
	El Paso (TL)	AA	.262	15	42	9	11	1	0	1	10	6	12	0
MINOR LEAGUE TOTALS			.312	63	215	44	67	8	0	18	66	23	62	0

7. Jeremy Ward, rhp

Born: Feb. 24, 1978. **Ht.:** 6-3. **Wt.:** 220. **Bats:** R. **Throws:** R. **School:** Long Beach State University. **Career Transactions:** Selected by Diamondbacks in second round of 1999 draft; signed June 17, 1999.

The Diamondbacks kept their eye on Ward though his stock dropped during his junior year at Long Beach State. He didn't disappoint them, vaulting all the way to Triple-A in his first half-season. Former Diamondbacks manager Buck Showalter raved about Ward last spring, and it was easy to see why. Ward possessed the fearlessness of a veteran reliever instead of someone in his first major league camp. But reconstructive right elbow surgery shelved him for nearly all of 2000. Before his injury, Ward threw 94 mph and had a sharp slider. He probably won't return until midseason because of his rehabilitation, and his maximum-effort delivery is a cause of concern. He hasn't thrown an offspeed pitch since moving to the bullpen. He struggled with his control before the severity of his elbow injury was diagnosed. He also gained extra weight on a thick body during the layoff. The Diamondbacks can afford to be patient with Ward. He already has received a taste of major league camp and a severe injury, so nothing should faze him. He loves to compete, and Arizona's biggest task may be to keep Ward from rushing back too quickly.

Year	Club (League)	Class	W	L	ERA	G	GS	CG	SV	IP	H	R	ER	BB	SO
1999	High Desert (Cal)	A	0	0	2.08	4	4	0	0	9	5	2	2	3	12
	El Paso (TL)	AA	1	1	2.45	19	0	0	7	26	18	7	7	9	26
	Tucson (PCL)	AAA	0	0	0.00	1	0	0	0	2	2	0	0	2	1
2000	Tucson (PCL)	AAA	0	1	5.40	5	0	0	0	3	3	2	2	5	1
MINOR LEAGUE TOTALS			1	2	2.54	29	4	0	7	39	28	11	11	19	40

8. Chris Capuano, lhp

Born: Aug. 19, 1978. **Ht.:** 6-3. **Wt.:** 215. **Bats:** L. **Throws:** L. **School:** Duke University. **Career Transactions:** Selected by Diamondbacks in eighth round of 1999 draft; signed Aug. 24, 1999.

The Diamondbacks respected Capuano's commitment to academics by letting him complete his degree at Duke after he signed as a junior in 1999. They assigned him to extended spring training after he graduated last year, then sent him to Class A South Bend, where he was dazzling. He shared the organization's pitcher-of-the-month award for July, then won it outright in August. The Diamondbacks believe they might have found a late bloomer in Capuano, who now can devote all his time to baseball. He went 10-4 on a 60-78 South Bend team thanks to his great mound presence. His best pitch is his curveball, and he has a 90 mph fastball, good velocity for a lefthander. His delivery is reminiscent of former big leaguer Danny Jackson's. Capuano can refine his control, but his biggest need is experience. He spent time in instructional league and the Arizona Fall League after the season. He's 22 and doesn't have overpowering stuff, so he might be as good as he's going to get. Still, the Diamondbacks are anxious to see what he can do in a full professional season. With lefthanded starters at a premium, the Diamondbacks might have found themselves a jewel if Capuano can improve his command by devoting more time to baseball.

Year	Club (League)	Class	W	L	ERA	G	GS	CG	SV	IP	H	R	ER	BB	SO
2000	South Bend (Mid)	A	10	4	2.21	18	18	0	0	101	68	35	25	45	105
MINOR LEAGUE TOTALS			10	4	2.21	18	18	0	0	101	68	35	25	45	105

9. Bret Prinz, rhp

Born: June 15, 1977. **Ht.:** 6-3. **Wt.:** 200. **Bats:** R. **Throws:** R. **School:** Phoenix JC. **Career Transactions:** Selected by Diamondbacks in 18th round of 1998 draft; signed June 3, 1998.

Prinz is a local kid made good. He attended Centennial High in Peoria, Ariz., and was drafted out of Phoenix College. He made the transition from starter to sidearm reliever prior to the 2000 season, boosting him to prospect status. With the help of former minor league pitching coordinator Gil Patterson and sidearm specialist Brad Clontz, Prinz made a significant improvement to become a closer candidate. He throws a 94 mph fastball that's murder on righthanders. He quickly developed the mentality to want the ball in a save situation, and his arm proved resilient enough to close. He needs to polish his slider as a second pitch. While he throws plenty of strikes, he needs to improve his location because he was hittable last year. That was especially true against lefthanders, who batted .344 off him in Double-A. Prinz still has plenty of room for improvement, which is encouraging considering how far he's come. He probably will be the closer at Triple-A Tucson and could reach the majors in late 2001. He would add youth to a veteran Arizona bullpen.

Year	Club (League)	Class	W	L	ERA	G	GS	CG	SV	IP	H	R	ER	BB	SO
1998	Diamondbacks (AZL)	R	0	0	3.38	4	0	0	0	5	7	3	2	0	3
	Lethbridge (Pio)	R	4	2	3.09	11	10	0	0	47	49	26	16	13	30
1999	South Bend (Mid)	A	6	10	4.48	30	23	0	0	139	129	82	69	52	98
2000	South Bend (Mid)	A	1	0	0.00	6	0	0	1	7	2	2	0	1	10
	El Paso (TL)	AA	9	1	3.56	53	0	0	26	61	71	24	24	16	69
MINOR LEAGUE TOTALS			20	13	3.86	104	33	0	27	259	258	137	111	82	210

10. Jose Valverde, rhp

Born: July 24, 1979. **Ht.:** 6-4. **Wt.:** 220. **Bats:** R. **Throws:** R. **Career Transactions:** Signed out of Dominican Republic by Diamondbacks, Jan. 31, 1997.

Valverde may have closer potential. He struggled at the beginning of 2000 at Class A South Bend, but dominated the competition at Missoula, where he didn't allow a run in 12 appearances. Valverde has an intimidating body and intimidating stuff. He regularly throws in the mid-90s and has touched 98 mph. His slider and splitter can be overpowering as well. He throws with a loose arm action that makes him less susceptible to injury. His biggest problem at South Bend was his inability to harness his fastball, which he did a better job of following his demotion. The Diamondbacks would like to see him throw his splitter more often. Valverde probably will start 2001 at high Class A Lancaster with the hope he can jump to Double-A by the end of the summer. Once he develops into more of a pitcher than a thrower and becomes more acclimated to the United States, the Diamondbacks believe he could make a quick jump through the system.

Year	Club (League)	Class	W	L	ERA	G	GS	CG	SV	IP	H	R	ER	BB	SO
1997	Diamondbacks (DSL)	R	0	0	5.30	14	0	0	0	19	20	12	11	13	19
1998	Diamondbacks (DSL)	R	1	3	1.75	23	4	0	7	51	31	14	10	22	56
1999	Diamondbacks (AZL)	R	1	2	4.08	20	0	0	8	29	34	21	13	10	47
	South Bend (Mid)	A	0	0	0.00	2	0	0	0	3	2	0	0	2	3
2000	Missoula (Pio)	R	1	0	0.00	12	0	0	4	12	3	0	0	4	24
	South Bend (Mid)	A	0	5	5.40	31	0	0	14	32	31	20	19	25	39
MINOR LEAGUE TOTALS			3	10	3.29	102	4	0	33	145	121	67	53	76	188

11. Lyle Overbay, 1b

Born: Jan. 28, 1977. **Ht.:** 6-2. **Wt.:** 215. **Bats:** L. **Throws:** L. **School:** University of Nevada. **Career Transactions:** Selected by Diamondbacks in 18th round of 1999 draft; signed June 8, 1999.

Overbay was a find by former area scout Brian Guinn, who is no longer with the organization. He is a run-producing machine despite not having overwhelming power. He gained recognition by becoming the first player ever to drive in at least 100 runs for a short-season team, then drove in 96 more last year while reaching Double-A. Overbay has solid mechanics at the plate with the ability to drive the ball to all fields and make necessary adjustments. He hit just 14 home runs last season, but team officials believe his swing and maturity might translate into more power as he advances. Though Overbay didn't tear up the Arizona Fall League, he held his own. He still needs work around the first-base bag, but he has made strides defensively. He has shown enough with the bat to start 2001 at Triple-A.

Year	Club (League)	Class	AVG	G	AB	R	H	2B	3B	HR	RBI	BB	SO	SB
1999	Missoula (Pio)	R	.343	75	306	66	105	25	7	12	101	40	53	10
2000	South Bend (Mid)	A	.332	71	259	47	86	19	3	6	47	27	36	9
	El Paso (TL)	AA	.352	62	244	43	86	16	2	8	49	28	39	3
MINOR LEAGUE TOTALS			.342	208	809	156	277	60	12	26	197	95	128	22

12. Oscar Villarreal, rhp

Born: Nov. 22, 1981. **Ht.:** 6-0. **Wt.:** 177. **Bats:** L. **Throws:** R. **Career Transactions:** Signed out of Mexico by Diamondbacks, Nov. 6, 1998.

For all the praise given to Junior Noboa's work in the Dominican, the Diamondbacks also have done a fine job in Mexico. At the major league level, they've gotten a lot of mileage out of veteran Armando Reynoso and struck gold in 1999 with Hermosillo star Erubiel Durazo. Villareal could be another future standout. The team raves about his maturity as a pitcher, specifically his refusal to give in to batters and his cleverness in mixing his array of pitches. Villarreal throws around 90 mph, which is good enough to make his slider and changeup more effective. The Diamondbacks were encouraged by reports from the Mexican Pacific League, where he was Mexicali's best starter. Because of his youth and Arizona's influx of college signees last summer, Villarreal probably will spend his second consecutive season at Class A. The Diamondbacks have plenty of time to decide whether he'll be a full-time starter or reliever. He has split his time between the two roles thus far.

Year	Club (League)	Class	W	L	ERA	G	GS	CG	SV	IP	H	R	ER	BB	SO
1999	Diamondbacks (AZL)	R	1	5	3.78	14	11	0	0	64	64	39	27	25	51
2000	Diamondbacks (AZL)	R	0	0	9.00	1	0	0	0	1	2	1	1	0	1
	South Bend (Mid)	A	1	3	4.41	13	5	0	0	33	37	19	16	17	30
	High Desert (Cal)	A	0	2	3.65	9	4	0	0	25	24	20	10	14	18
MINOR LEAGUE TOTALS			2	10	3.95	37	20	0	0	123	127	79	54	56	100

13. Scott Barber, rhp

Born: Dec. 12, 1978. **Ht.:** 6-3. **Wt.:** 205. **Bats:** R. **Throws:** R. **School:** University of South Carolina. **Career Transactions:** Selected by Diamondbacks in sixth round of 2000 draft; signed July 6, 2000.

Barber might have been the third-best pitcher on a powerful South Carolina team last spring, but he quickly made an impression with the Diamondbacks. He may have been the most mature of the five pitchers the Diamondbacks took with their first eight selections, and he made a quick jump to high Class A High Desert. There was some concern, however, about Barber's workload in college. He split his time between starting and relieving and eventually wore down during his first pro season. Yet Arizona saw enough of him to believe he can become a dependable reliever quickly. He possesses two quality pitches, a sharp slider and a 92 mph fastball. There's an outside chance Barber could begin the season in Double-A is he performs well and has a fresh arm in the spring.

Year	Club (League)	Class	W	L	ERA	G	GS	CG	SV	IP	H	R	ER	BB	SO
2000	Diamondbacks (AZL)	R	0	0	3.00	2	1	0	0	3	0	1	1	2	4
	High Desert (Cal)	A	0	2	6.89	4	4	0	0	15	18	15	12	5	12
MINOR LEAGUE TOTALS			0	2	6.27	6	5	0	0	18	18	16	13	7	16

14. Junior Spivey, 2b

Born: Jan. 28, 1975. **Ht.:** 6-0. **Wt.:** 185. **Bats:** R. **Throws:** R. **School:** Cowley County (Kan.) CC. **Career Transactions:** Selected by Diamondbacks in 36th round of 1996 draft; signed June 14, 1996 . . . Loaned by Diamondbacks to Rangers, July 17-Sept. 14, 1998.

This could finally be the breakout year for Spivey, who has played in just 78 games over the past two years because of left hand and right hamstring injuries. The Diamondbacks still think enough of him that they kept him on the 40-man roster. He's one of the top five athletes in the organization, and the team was encouraged with his play in the Mexican Pacific League. A healthy Spivey could give the team options down the road because he can play second or shortstop adequately. He probably will play second in Triple-A this year while Alex Cintron polishes his skills at shortstop. The organization would love to see Spivey regain the consistency he possessed in 1998, his last injury-free season. He doesn't have much power, but he has plenty of leadoff skills. At one time, the Diamondbacks touted Spivey and Danny Klassen as their keystone combination of the future. Klassen has reached the majors and Spivey definitely has the skills to join him, provided he stays healthy.

Year	Club (League)	Class	AVG	G	AB	R	H	2B	3B	HR	RBI	BB	SO	SB
1996	Diamondbacks (AZL)	R	.333	20	69	13	23	0	0	0	3	12	16	11
	Lethbridge (Pio)	R	.336	31	107	30	36	3	4	2	25	23	24	8
1997	High Desert (Cal)	A	.273	136	491	88	134	24	6	6	53	69	115	14
1998	High Desert (Cal)	A	.281	79	285	64	80	14	5	5	35	64	61	34
	Tulsa (TL)	AA	.311	34	119	26	37	10	1	3	16	28	25	8
1999	El Paso (TL)	AA	.293	44	164	40	48	10	4	3	19	36	27	14
2000	Tucson (PCL)	AAA	.282	28	117	21	33	8	4	3	16	11	17	3
	El Paso (TL)	AA	.421	6	19	5	8	5	0	1	2	0	5	0
MINOR LEAGUE TOTALS			.291	378	1371	287	399	74	24	23	169	243	290	92

15. Mike Schultz, rhp

Born: Nov. 28, 1979. **Ht.:** 6-7. **Wt.:** 205. **Bats:** R. **Throws:** R. **School:** Loyola Marymount University. **Career Transactions:** Selected by Diamondbacks in second round of 2000 draft; signed June 26, 2000.

The Diamondbacks' first choice in the 2000 draft didn't come until the 69th overall selection because they gave up their first-rounder to sign Russ Springer away from the Braves. Arizona wanted a college pitcher with a huge upside and believes it might have found one in Schultz. Though he didn't have a banner junior season at Loyola Marymount, the Diamondbacks were impressed with Schultz' size and ability to throw a 95 mph fastball with consistency. They were careful about giving him rest and limited him to 25 innings in his pro debut. He probably will start 2001 at Lancaster. The club has big plans for him once he gains full command of his fastball and develops a decent breaking pitch and changeup.

Year	Club (League)	Class	W	L	ERA	G	GS	CG	SV	IP	H	R	ER	BB	SO
2000	Diamondbacks (AZL)	R	0	1	6.75	2	0	0	0	3	7	7	2	1	2
	High Desert (Cal)	A	1	2	3.63	7	7	0	0	22	15	9	9	11	16
MINOR LEAGUE TOTALS			1	3	3.96	9	7	0	0	25	22	16	11	12	18

16. Jason Conti, of

Born: Jan. 27, 1975. **Ht.:** 5-11. **Wt.:** 180. **Bats:** L. **Throws:** R. **School:** University of Pittsburgh. **Career Transactions:** Selected by Diamondbacks in 32nd round of 1996 draft; signed June 6, 1996 . . . Loaned by Diamondbacks to Rangers, March 24-Sept. 14, 1998.

Conti was an unheralded part of Arizona's first draft in 1996. He has made the most of his opportunities, hitting .290 or better at each level before receiving a promotion to the big leagues last June. He's one of the most fearless players in the organization, and it showed when he reached base safely in his first three plate appearances, including a pinch-hit RBI single in his first major league at-bat. He is one of the fastest players in the system, which shows in his defense in center and right field, and has one of the strongest arms despite his lean build. He threw out Atlanta's Brian Jordan at third base in consecutive games. Conti struggled in his big league debut, striking out in nearly one-third of his at-bats, and played sparingly in September. He admitted he needed to get stronger and spent the winter on a weight program rather than playing winter ball in the Dominican. Conti will back up Steve Finley in center field and probably will receive some time in right field this year. He's a fourth outfielder whose speed and arm are welcome assets on a team that's aging rapidly.

Year	Club (League)	Class	AVG	G	AB	R	H	2B	3B	HR	RBI	BB	SO	SB
1996	Lethbridge (Pio)	R	.367	63	226	63	83	15	1	4	49	30	29	30
1997	South Bend (Mid)	A	.310	117	458	78	142	22	10	3	43	45	99	30
	High Desert (Cal)	A	.356	14	59	15	21	5	1	2	8	10	12	1
1998	Tulsa (TL)	AA	.315	130	530	125	167	31	12	15	67	63	96	19
1999	Tucson (PCL)	AAA	.290	133	520	100	151	23	8	9	57	55	89	22
2000	Tucson (PCL)	AAA	.305	93	383	75	117	20	5	11	57	23	57	11
	Arizona (NL)	MAJ	.231	47	91	11	21	4	3	1	15	7	30	3
MAJOR LEAGUE TOTALS			.231	47	91	11	21	4	3	1	15	7	30	3
MINOR LEAGUE TOTALS			.313	550	2176	456	681	116	37	44	281	226	382	113

17. Nick Bierbrodt, lhp

Born: May 16, 1978. **Ht.:** 6-5. **Wt.:** 190. **Bats:** L. **Throws:** L. **School:** Millikan HS, Long Beach. **Career Transactions:** Selected by Diamondbacks in first round (30th overall) of 1996 draft; signed June 9, 1996.

Bierbrodt received plenty of notoriety as the team's first-ever draft pick in 1996, then received a bonus that nearly doubled from $525,000 to $1.046 million because of a since-banned clause that was tied to the signings of other first-rounders. Bierbrodt has gotten bigger and stronger without getting too bulky, and he throws in the low 90s. He has a major league curve that impressed scouts last spring. But injuries continue to stunt his development and have hindered his chances of making an impact in the big leagues. He has been called up for brief stints the past two seasons but has yet to throw a big league pitch. Bierbrodt was shut down after two games in the Dominican League this winter with elbow stiffness. That disappointed the Diamondbacks, who hoped he would log enough innings to compete for a bullpen job this spring. He pitched just 15 games in 2000 because of a rib injury. It now looks like a longshot for Bierbrodt to make the Opening Day roster.

Year	Club (League)	Class	W	L	ERA	G	GS	CG	SV	IP	H	R	ER	BB	SO
1996	Diamondbacks (AZL)	R	1	1	1.66	8	8	0	0	38	25	9	7	13	46
	Lethbridge (Pio)	R	2	0	0.50	3	3	0	0	18	12	4	1	5	23
1997	South Bend (Mid)	A	2	4	4.04	15	15	0	0	75	77	43	34	37	64
1998	High Desert (Cal)	A	8	7	3.40	24	23	1	0	129	122	66	49	64	88
1999	El Paso (TL)	AA	5	6	4.62	14	14	2	0	76	78	45	39	37	55
	Tucson (PCL)	AAA	1	4	7.27	11	11	0	0	43	57	42	35	30	43
2000	Tucson (PCL)	AAA	2	1	4.82	4	3	0	0	18	13	10	10	14	11
	Diamondbacks (AZL)	R	0	0	4.50	4	3	0	0	8	4	4	4	5	10
	El Paso (TL)	AA	1	3	7.13	7	7	0	0	35	37	30	28	24	36
MINOR LEAGUE TOTALS			22	26	4.21	90	87	3	0	442	425	253	207	229	376

18. Andrew Good, rhp

Born: Sept. 19, 1979. **Ht.:** 6-2. **Wt.:** 166. **Bats:** R. **Throws:** R. **School:** Rochester (Mich.) HS. **Career Transactions:** Selected by Diamondbacks in eighth round of 1998 draft; signed June 29, 1998.

Much of the hype surrounding Good was deflated when he missed last season because of surgery to repair a torn medial collateral ligament in his right elbow. He was the system's pitcher of the year in 1999 after finishing third in the Midwest League in strikeouts and demonstrating fine control. The Diamondbacks are impressed with Good's maturity. He has an average 89-91 mph fastball and a plus curveball, and his strongest suit is his ability to throw four pitches for strikes. The Diamondbacks won't rush Good back because they drafted a slew of more experienced college pitchers last June. He probably won't be ready to pitch in a game until May, when he'll be sent to Lancaster.

Year	Club (League)	Class	W	L	ERA	G	GS	CG	SV	IP	H	R	ER	BB	SO
1998	Diamondbacks (AZL)	R	1	3	4.28	9	8	0	0	34	46	25	16	7	25
	South Bend (Mid)	A	0	1	3.00	2	0	0	0	6	7	4	2	1	6
1999	South Bend (Mid)	A	11	10	4.10	27	27	0	0	154	160	80	70	42	146
2000							Did Not Play—Injured								
MINOR LEAGUE TOTALS			12	14	4.10	38	35	0	0	193	213	109	88	50	177

19. Casey Daigle, rhp

Born: April 4, 1981. **Ht.:** 6-7. **Wt.:** 215. **Bats:** R. **Throws:** R. **School:** Sulphur (La.) HS. **Career Transactions:** Selected by Diamondbacks in first round (31st overall) of 1999 draft; signed Sept. 14, 1999.

Daigle's draft stock jumped in 1999 when he ended the 47-game winning streak of Barbe High in Lake Charles, La. One of several high draft picks the Diamondbacks have brought along slowly, Daigle might need all the time the organization is giving him. He signed late and didn't begin his career until last summer. He spent time in extended spring training because of a tender right arm. Daigle has the physical presence to dominate but needs plenty of work. He throws his fastball at 90-91 mph. His command and secondary pitches are lacking at this point. Arizona officials believe Daigle will get accustomed to stiffer competition. He likely will start 2001 at South Bend but could jump to Lancaster at midseason.

Year	Club (League)	Class	W	L	ERA	G	GS	CG	SV	IP	H	R	ER	BB	SO
2000	Missoula (Pio)	R	3	5	4.90	15	15	0	0	83	88	57	45	54	56
MINOR LEAGUE TOTALS			3	5	4.90	15	15	0	0	83	88	57	45	54	56

20. Duaner Sanchez, rhp

Born: Oct. 14, 1979. **Ht.:** 6-0. **Wt.:** 160. **Bats:** R. **Throws:** R. **Career Transactions:** Signed out of Dominican Republic by Diamondbacks, Aug. 30, 1996.

Sanchez pitched well enough last year to earn a spot on the 40-man roster. He has been likened to Dodgers lefthander Carlos Perez because of his animated, aggressive demeanor on the mound, but Sanchez throws much harder than Perez. Despite his small frame, Sanchez works in the low 90s. He still needs to improve his breaking pitch and develop a solid third pitch. His competitive nature will help him to advance further. He'll get strong consideration to start the season at El Paso, though Lancaster is a possibility. The Diamondbacks have a few righthanded starters who are more talented, but they have yet to show the durability of Sanchez, who ranked fourth in the Midwest League in innings in 2000.

Year	Club (League)	Class	W	L	ERA	G	GS	CG	SV	IP	H	R	ER	BB	SO
1997	Diamondbacks (DSL)	R	4	4	5.13	21	6	0	1	60	57	50	34	48	44
1998	Diamondbacks (DSL)	R	2	3	1.79	14	8	1	1	50	36	19	10	24	44
1999	High Desert (Cal)	A	0	0	7.53	3	3	0	0	14	15	13	12	9	9
	Missoula (Pio)	R	5	3	3.13	13	11	0	0	63	54	34	22	23	51
2000	South Bend (Mid)	A	8	9	3.65	28	28	4	0	165	152	80	67	54	121
MINOR LEAGUE TOTALS			19	19	3.70	79	56	5	2	353	314	196	145	158	269

21. Tim Olson, 3b/of

Born: Sept. 1, 1978. **Ht.:** 6-2. **Wt.:** 200. **Bats:** R. **Throws:** R. **School:** University of Florida. **Career Transactions:** Selected by Diamondbacks in seventh round of 2000 draft; signed June 14, 2000.

One of the Diamondbacks' weaknesses at the major league level is a lack of athleticism. They took steps to correct that last June, when they drafted the versatile Olson. He threw 92-93 mph when he pitched in junior college and played both shortstop and center field at the University of Florida. Arizona liked his arm and the way he got quick, accurate breaks in the outfield, and figured he had the tools to play third base. He worked out at the hot corner in instructional league and may open 2001 there. Offensively, he has some to work to do after struggling to make contact or hit for power in his pro debut. He did manage to steal 15 bases in 18 attempts. Olson will move up to Lancaster in his first full pro season.

Year	Club (League)	Class	AVG	G	AB	R	H	2B	3B	HR	RBI	BB	SO	SB
2000	South Bend (Mid)	A	.218	68	261	37	57	14	2	2	26	15	49	15
MINOR LEAGUE TOTALS			.218	68	261	37	57	14	2	2	26	15	49	15

22. Jason Martines, rhp

Born: Jan. 21, 1976. **Ht.:** 6-2. **Wt.:** 190. **Bats:** L. **Throws:** R. **School:** Siena Heights (Mich.) College.
Career Transactions: Selected by Diamondbacks in 24th round of 1997 draft; signed June 5, 1997.

Martines established himself as a legitimate prospect in 2000. His 2.26 ERA at High Desert in 1999 and 2.81 mark last season at El Paso are impressive because of the hitter-friendly settings. Martines didn't appear to have much of a future until he followed the same path as Bret Prinz, learning to throw sidearm with the help of former minor league pitching coordinator Gil Patterson and sidearm specialist Brad Clontz. Martines took to his new delivery quickly. He throws around 90 mph with nice command and has become more resilient. He'll need to develop a breaking pitch if he's able to take the final step toward reaching the majors. But he has a chance, based on how quickly he sparked a once-nondescript career.

Year	Club (League)	Class	W	L	ERA	G	GS	CG	SV	IP	H	R	ER	BB	SO
1997	Lethbridge (Pio)	R	3	3	3.14	22	0	0	0	43	45	15	15	11	34
1998	Tucson (PCL)	AAA	0	0	0.00	1	0	0	0	1	0	0	0	2	2
	High Desert (Cal)	A	0	1	7.59	5	0	0	0	11	16	10	9	3	7
	South Bend (Mid)	A	0	2	3.51	21	0	0	0	33	33	16	13	15	31
1999	High Desert (Cal)	A	9	7	2.26	43	0	0	9	72	68	33	18	28	73
2000	El Paso (TL)	AA	9	1	2.81	55	0	0	2	86	72	32	27	27	77
MINOR LEAGUE TOTALS			21	14	3.00	147	0	0	11	246	234	106	82	86	224

23. Josh Kroeger, of

Born: Aug. 31, 1982. **Ht.:** 6-2. **Wt.:** 190. **Bats:** L. **Throws:** L. **School:** Scripps Ranch HS, San Diego.
Career Transactions: Selected by Diamondbacks in fourth round of 2000 draft; signed June 6, 2000.

Kroeger made an impresssive debut coming out of high school. The Diamondbacks marveled over his maturity as a person and as a player, which was exceptional for a 17-year-old. Kroeger led his Rookie-level Arizona League squad in homers and RBIs. His mental approach as a hitter was impressive, as were his swing and bat speed. Kroeger will play in either right or left field, and he'll be at least an adequate defender. He could develop into a David Justice-type hitter with the ability to drive the ball to left field in the future. Kroeger probably will start 2001 at South Bend. Despite his early success, the Diamondbacks want him to move slowly to enhance his chances for success.

Year	Club (League)	Class	AVG	G	AB	R	H	2B	3B	HR	RBI	BB	SO	SB
2000	Diamondbacks (AZL)	R	.297	54	222	40	66	9	3	4	28	21	41	5
MINOR LEAGUE TOTALS			.297	54	222	40	66	9	3	4	28	21	41	5

24. Victor Hall, of

Born: Sept. 16, 1980. **Ht.:** 6-0. **Wt.:** 170. **Bats:** L. **Throws:** L. **School:** Monroe HS, Sepulveda, Calif.
Career Transactions: Selected by Diamondbacks in 12th round of 1998 draft; signed June 3, 1998.

Many players buy a car when they get their signing bonus after turning pro. Not Hall, a former track star in high school. He showed his dedication, using his bonus to purchase a batting cage for his backyard. He has put the cage to good use, showing solid hitting ability as a pro. Better yet, he has the speed and patience to bat leadoff. He led the Pioneer League in walks and stolen bases last season. Hall is as fast as Diamondbacks shortstop Tony Womack and usually makes a mockery of the competition during the farm system's 60-yard dash during spring training. He uses his quickness to get to balls in center but could do a better job reading balls off the bat. Hall has spent most of his three pro years in Rookie ball and must prove he can hit in a full-season league after slumping at South Bend to start 2000. He projects as a Lance Johnson type with a better throwing arm.

Year	Club (League)	Class	AVG	G	AB	R	H	2B	3B	HR	RBI	BB	SO	SB
1998	Diamondbacks (AZL)	R	.188	28	101	10	19	1	1	0	10	10	29	14
1999	Diamondbacks (AZL)	R	.365	27	104	19	38	2	1	0	14	13	25	10
	Missoula (Pio)	R	.279	34	147	27	41	4	0	0	11	15	30	18
2000	South Bend (Mid)	A	.232	41	164	19	38	4	5	2	16	13	41	12
	Missoula (Pio)	R	.307	70	241	70	74	7	9	3	26	77	38	47
MINOR LEAGUE TOTALS			.277	200	757	145	210	18	16	5	77	128	163	101

25. Ryan Owens, 3b

Born: March 18, 1978. **Ht.:** 6-2. **Wt.:** 200. **Bats:** R. **Throws:** R. **School:** Cal State Fullerton. **Career Transactions:** Selected by Diamondbacks in seventh round of 1999 draft; signed July 5, 1999.

The Diamondbacks thought they got a steal in Owens, and he didn't disappoint by reaching Double-A in his first pro summer. But the hype turned to mystery as Owens struggled in his return to El Paso last season and continued to struggle after a demotion to South Bend. Owens' offensive problems carried over to his defense as well. The Diamondbacks are concerned that Owens has lost confidence after not tasting success for the first time. They're hoping he'll get back on track and perhaps hit for more power. The one improvement he did make at the plate in 2000 was increasing his ability to draw walks, though that was somewhat negated by his inability to make consistent contact. He'll start this year at Lancaster with the hope he can revisit El Paso and recapture his 1999 form.

Year	Club (League)	Class	AVG	G	AB	R	H	2B	3B	HR	RBI	BB	SO	SB
1999	High Desert (Cal)	A	.398	26	103	19	41	7	3	4	28	9	30	1
	El Paso (TL)	AA	.319	31	113	11	36	5	1	1	18	8	36	1
2000	El Paso (TL)	AA	.216	60	208	30	45	7	4	5	24	21	60	5
	South Bend (Mid)	A	.248	71	270	52	67	20	0	9	43	47	76	15
MINOR LEAGUE TOTALS			.272	188	694	112	189	39	8	19	113	85	202	22

26. Rod Barajas, c

Born: Sept. 5, 1975. **Ht.:** 6-2. **Wt.:** 220. **Bats:** R. **Throws:** R. **School:** Cerritos (Calif.) JC. **Career Transactions:** Signed as nondrafted free agent by Diamondbacks, Jan. 23, 1996 . . . Loaned by Diamondbacks to co-op Visalia, April 5-June 16, 1996.

The Diamondbacks' expectations for Barajas have become more realistic after a disappointing Triple-A season in 2000. His .226 batting average and .253 on-base percentage were simply dismal. There was plenty of excitement after Barajas, who was signed out of a tryout camp, reached the majors late in his fourth season. But he proved susceptible to outside breaking pitches at Tucson and during a brief stint with the Diamondbacks in September. His stagnation caused concern whether the Diamondbacks could survive with him as the No. 2 catcher, but with Kelly Stinnett gone he's the natural choice to back up Damian Miller. For all of Barajas' offensive shortcomings, though, he received strong praise from former Arizona manager Buck Showalter and several major league pitchers who have thrown to him on minor league rehabilitation assignments. There's no doubt he will be pushed at some point by Brad Cresse and recent signee Melvin Rosario, so it would behoove him to start hitting.

Year	Club (League)	Class	AVG	G	AB	R	H	2B	3B	HR	RBI	BB	SO	SB
1996	Visalia (Cal)	A	.162	27	74	6	12	3	0	0	8	7	21	0
	Lethbridge (Pio)	R	.337	51	175	47	59	9	3	10	50	12	24	2
1997	High Desert (Cal)	A	.266	57	199	24	53	11	0	7	30	8	41	0
1998	High Desert (Cal)	A	.303	113	442	67	134	26	0	23	81	25	81	1
1999	El Paso (TL)	AA	.318	127	510	77	162	41	2	14	95	24	73	2
	Arizona (NL)	MAJ	.250	5	16	3	4	1	0	1	3	1	1	0
2000	Tucson (PCL)	AAA	.226	110	416	43	94	25	0	13	75	14	65	4
	Arizona (NL)	MAJ	.231	5	13	1	3	0	0	1	3	0	4	0
MAJOR LEAGUE TOTALS			.241	10	29	4	7	1	0	2	6	1	5	0
MINOR LEAGUE TOTALS			.283	485	1816	264	514	115	5	67	339	90	305	9

27. Brandon Webb, rhp

Born: May 9, 1979. **Ht.:** 6-4. **Wt.:** 190. **Bats:** R. **Throws:** R. **School:** University of Kentucky. **Career Transactions:** Selected by Diamondbacks in eighth round of 2000 draft; signed June 6, 2000.

The Diamondbacks aren't going to get carried away and rave about their college pitchers in the 2001 draft in the same manner they boasted of their high school troika of Nick Bierbrodt, John Patterson and Brad Penny in 1996. But they do think they acquired more depth this time around, thanks to the quick development of pitchers like Webb. More than one Southeastern Conference coach said last spring that Webb had the best stuff in the conference, and his 123 strikeouts set a Kentucky season record. He has a long, lean pitcher's body. His best pitch is his curveball, and he consistently throws his fastball in the low 90s. He throws both a two-seam and four-seam fastball. Webb projects as a late-inning reliever. After a successful debut at South Bend last summer, he'll move up to Lancaster in 2001.

Year	Club (League)	Class	W	L	ERA	G	GS	CG	SV	IP	H	R	ER	BB	SO
2000	Diamondbacks (AZL)	R	0	0	9.00	1	1	0	0	1	2	1	1	0	3
	South Bend (Mid)	A	0	0	3.24	12	0	0	2	17	10	7	6	9	18
MINOR LEAGUE TOTALS			0	0	3.50	13	1	0	2	18	12	8	7	9	21

28. Doug Slaten, lhp

Born: Feb. 4, 1980. **Ht.:** 6-5. **Wt.:** 190. **Bats:** L. **Throws:** L. **School:** Los Angeles Pierce JC. **Career Transactions:** Selected by Diamondbacks in 17th round of 2000 draft; signed July 5, 2000.

When the Diamondbacks took Slaten last June, they quickly learned how serious he was about pitching at UCLA. He already had spurned a significant offer from the Orioles as a draft-and-follow, and Bruins coach Gary Adams does an exceptional job of recruiting, so the Diamondbacks decided to do so as well. They flew Slaten and his family to Phoenix to attend a game at Bank One Ballpark, let him throw a bullpen session under the watchful eye of then-pitching coach Mark Connor and introduced him to some of the Arizona players. The capper came when Slaten walked into the Diamondbacks clubhouse and found a jersey with his name on the back hanging in one of the empty lockers. He signed soon after his visit. He has the frame to get stronger and add velocity to his 90 mph sinker. He also throws a nifty curveball and added a circle changeup as a sophomore at Pierce. Slaten stands a reasonable chance to start the season at Lancaster, about an hour's drive from where he grew up in Southern California.

Year	Club (League)	Class	W	L	ERA	G	GS	CG	SV	IP	H	R	ER	BB	SO
2000	Diamondbacks (AZL)	R	0	0	0.96	9	4	0	0	9	7	1	1	3	7
MINOR LEAGUE TOTALS			0	0	0.96	9	4	0	0	9	7	1	1	3	7

29. Beltran Perez, rhp

Born: Oct. 24, 1981. **Ht.:** 6-2. **Wt.:** 160. **Bats:** R. **Throws:** R. **Career Transactions:** Signed out of Dominican Republic by Diamondbacks, Feb. 2, 1999.

The Diamondbacks believe they have a potential gem in Perez, who signed as a 17-year-old and was assigned to the Dominican Summer League, where he was undefeated. Working out at the team's academy in the Dominican helped Perez prepare for playing in the United States. He arrived last year, leading the Arizona League club in wins while averaging nearly a strikeout per inning. He even survived a couple of emergency starts in high Class A. At this point, Perez' fastball and curveball are adequate but nothing more. He has a knack for making the right pitch at the right time, and he doesn't try to blow hitters away. Perez stands a strong chance to begin this season at South Bend and could move up to Lancaster if his stuff improves.

Year	Club (League)	Class	W	L	ERA	G	GS	CG	SV	IP	H	R	ER	BB	SO
1999	Diamondbacks (DSL)	R	6	0	2.45	18	0	0	0	29	24	12	8	9	31
2000	Diamondbacks (AZL)	R	5	1	5.81	11	4	0	0	48	61	37	31	25	47
	High Desert (Cal)	A	0	1	3.60	2	2	0	0	10	8	4	4	5	11
MINOR LEAGUE TOTALS			11	2	4.43	31	6	0	0	87	93	53	43	39	89

30. Corey Myers, 3b

Born: June 5, 1980. **Ht.:** 6-2. **Wt.:** 220. **Bats:** R. **Throws:** R. **School:** Desert Vista HS, Phoenix. **Career Transactions:** Selected by Diamondbacks in first round (fourth overall) of 1999 draft; signed June 2, 1999.

Most projections had the Diamondbacks taking Ben Sheets with the fourth overall pick in the 1999 draft, but instead they went for Myers, a local high school product. Myers had an exceptional high school career but wasn't considered a first-round talent by most teams and signed for a below-market $2 million, though Arizona insists he wasn't a signability pick. Perhaps the club should use that excuse, because Sheets has become an Olympic star and a top rookie candidate for 2001, while Myers has struggled as a pro. He has yet to fulfill any of the promise of a top pick, though most scouts will say that expectations were unfair because he was no more than a one-tool player to begin with. Some thought Myers, younger brother of Arizona State All-America catcher Casey Myers, could make it on his hitting alone, but his bat hasn't shown in two seasons. He started his pro career at shortstop before moving to third base because of a lack of range. That hasn't worked so far, as he made 36 errors in 2000. Some believe he might need another position change to first base. The Diamondbacks remain optimistic because Myers' willingness to learn hasn't wavered. He'll be under scrutiny with an expected return to South Bend, where he hit .125 last year.

Year	Club (League)	Class	AVG	G	AB	R	H	2B	3B	HR	RBI	BB	SO	SB
1999	Missoula (Pio)	R	.276	66	272	43	75	13	2	5	44	22	65	6
2000	South Bend (Mid)	A	.125	19	64	5	8	2	0	0	4	7	23	1
	Missoula (Pio)	R	.217	75	272	40	59	16	2	6	49	30	62	5
MINOR LEAGUE TOTALS			.234	160	608	88	142	31	4	11	97	59	150	12

Atlanta
Braves

It may not be obvious to the rest of the baseball world, but the Braves went through a rebuilding effort in 2000. While the major league club won its ninth straight National League East title, several significant changes were made, all with the intent of maintaining one of the most successful runs in the game's history.

The Braves were able to win the division due in part to the midseason additions of righthander Andy Ashby and outfielder B.J. Surhoff. Minor leaguers were moved to acquire both veterans. Two members of last year's top 10 list (righthander Luis Rivera and lefthander Jimmy Osting) were dealt, as were lefthander Bruce Chen and catcher Fernando Lunar. The minors also helped by sending middle infielder Rafael Furcal, Baseball America's Rookie of the Year, and righthander Jason Marquis to Turner Field.

But a lull in talent at the Triple-A and Double-A levels and John Smoltz' season-ending injury in March emphasized that the rotation isn't getting any younger, so the Braves invested more bonus money in the 2000 draft than any team. With five selections among the first 51, first-year scouting director Roy Clark restocked the

lower levels with high-ceiling pitchers, the franchise's calling card over the past 15 years.

The organization also showed steady signs of improving its position prospects, both in quantity and quality. The Braves are particularly strong at the middle-infield positions, with second basemen Marcus Giles and Alejandro Machado and shortstops Wilson Betemit and Kelly Johnson.

Another upgrade came in November when the Braves made a major commitment in Latin America by signing a three-year lease agreement on a state-of-the-art facility in San Francisco de Macoris, Dominican Republic. The complex will allow the Braves to combine their previous camps in the Dominican and Venezuela while reducing the number of 16- and 17-year-olds forced to compete in the Rookie-level Gulf Coast League.

More changes are on the horizon, including the possible shift of third baseman Chipper Jones to the outfield. While GM John Schuerholz will remain active in both the free-agent and trade markets, the Braves are continuing to pump as much energy and money into player development as any organization in baseball.

TOP 30 PROSPECTS

1. Wilson Betemit, ss
2. Matt McClendon, rhp
3. Marcus Giles, 2b
4. Matt Belisle, rhp
5. Jason Marquis, rhp
6. Billy Sylvester, rhp
7. Adam Wainwright, rhp
8. Wes Helms, 3b
9. Christian Parra, rhp
10. Scott Sobkowiak, rhp
11. Horacio Ramirez, lhp
12. Matt Butler, rhp
13. Matt Wright, rhp
14. Bubba Nelson, rhp
15. Tim Spooneybarger, rhp
16. Derrick Lewis, rhp
17. George Lombard, of
18. Damian Moss, lhp
19. Zach Miner, rhp
20. Brett Evert, rhp
21. Scott Thorman, 3b
22. Miguel Bernard, c
23. Cory Aldridge, of
24. John Ennis, rhp
25. Kelly Johnson, ss
26. Alejandro Machado, 2b
27. Brad Voyles, rhp
28. Jung Bong, lhp
29. Chris Waters, rhp
30. Damien Jones, of

By Bill Ballew

OrganizationOverview

General manager: John Schuerholz. **Farm director:** Dick Balderson. **Scouting director:** Roy Clark.

2000 PERFORMANCE

Class	Team	League	W	L	Pct.	Finish*	Manager
Majors	Atlanta	National	95	67	.586	t-2nd (16)	Bobby Cox
Triple-A	Richmond Braves	International	51	92	.357	14th (14)	Randy Ingle
Double-A	Greenville Braves	Southern	68	71	.489	6th (10)	Paul Runge
High A	Myrtle Beach Pelicans	Carolina	88	52	.629	1st (8)	Brian Snitker
Low A	Macon Braves	South Atlantic	69	70	.496	7th (14)	Jeff Treadway
Short-season	Jamestown Jammers	New York-Penn	37	38	.493	8th (14)	Jim Saul
Rookie	Danville Braves	Appalachian	37	29	.561	3rd (10)	J.J. Cannon
Rookie	GCL Braves	Gulf Coast	26	34	.433	10th (13)	Rick Albert
OVERALL 2000 MINOR LEAGUE RECORD			375	386	.493	18th (30)	

*Finish in overall standings (No. of teams in league).

ORGANIZATION LEADERS

BATTING
*AVG	Wilson Betemit, Jamestown	.331
R	Damien Jones, Macon	82
H	Wes Helms, Richmond	155
TB	Wes Helms, Richmond	256
2B	Demond Smith, Greenville	33
	Travis Wilson, Myrtle Beach	33
3B	Charles Thomas, Jamestown	8
HR	Tim Unroe, Richmond	24
RBI	Wes Helms, Richmond	88
BB	Marcus Giles, Greenville	72
SO	Mike Hessman, Greenville	178
SB	Damien Jones, Macon	44

PITCHING
W	Christian Parra, Myrtle Beach	17
L	Steve Avery, Macon/Myr. Beach/Green./Rich.	12
#ERA	Garrett Lee, Myrtle Beach/Richmond	2.08
G	Dan Smith, Greenville/Richmond	55
CG	Horacio Ramirez, Myrtle Beach	3
	Dan Curtis, Macon/Myrtle Beach	3
SV	Brad Voyles, Myrtle Beach	19
IP	Matt Belisle, Macon/Myrtle Beach	181
BB	**Damian Moss**, Richmond	106
SO	Matt Belisle, Macon/Myrtle Beach	168

*Minimum 250 at-bats. #Minimum 75 innings.

TOP PROSPECTS OF THE DECADE

1991	Ryan Klesko, 1b
1992	Chipper Jones, ss
1993	Chipper Jones, ss
1994	Chipper Jones, ss
1995	Chipper Jones, ss/3b
1996	Andruw Jones, of
1997	Andruw Jones, of
1998	Bruce Chen, lhp
1999	Bruce Chen, lhp
2000	Rafael Furcal, ss

TOP DRAFT PICKS OF THE DECADE

1991	Mike Kelly, of
1992	Jamie Arnold, rhp
1993	Andre King, of (2)
1994	Jacob Shumate, rhp
1995	*Chad Hutchinson, rhp
1996	A.J. Zapp, 1b
1997	Troy Cameron, ss
1998	Matt Belisle, rhp (2)
1999	Matt Butler, rhp (2)
2000	Adam Wainwright, rhp

*Did not sign

Wilson   **Moss**

BEST TOOLS

Best Hitter for Average	Wilson Betemit
Best Power Hitter	Wes Helms
Fastest Baserunner	George Lombard
Best Fastball	Bryan Digby
Best Breaking Ball	Billy Sylvester
Best Control	Matt Wright
Best Defensive Catcher	Miguel Bernard
Best Defensive Infielder	Keoni DeRenne
Best Infield Arm	Scott Thorman
Best Defensive Outfielder	Junior Brignac
Best Outfield Arm	Ryan Langerhans

PROJECTED 2004 LINEUP

Catcher	Javy Lopez
First Base	Wes Helms
Second Base	Marcus Giles
Third Base	Wilson Betemit
Shortstop	Rafael Furcal
Left Field	Chipper Jones
Center Field	Andruw Jones
Right Field	Scott Thorman
No. 1 Starter	Greg Maddux
No. 2 Starter	Tom Glavine
No. 3 Starter	Kevin Millwood
No. 4 Starter	Odalis Perez
No. 5 Starter	Matt McClendon
Closer	John Rocker

ALL-TIME LARGEST BONUSES

Matt Belisle, 1998	$1,750,000
Jung Bong, 1997	1,700,000
Adam Wainwright, 2000	1,250,000
Scott Thorman, 2000	1,225,000
Jose Salas, 1998	1,200,000

DraftAnalysis

2000 Draft

Best Pro Debut: RHP Adam Wainwright (1) was Baseball America's Rookie-level Player of the Year, the No. 1 prospect in the Appalachian League and No. 2 in the Gulf Coast League. His 81-12 strikeout-walk ratio was exceptional for a high school pitcher.

Best Athlete: RHP Kenny Nelson (2) made USA Today's all-America high school team as a third baseman. (He made BA's team as a utility player). RHP Zach Miner (4) also was a top two-way player in high school.

Best Hitter: SS Kelly Johnson (1) is a line-drive machine with power to the gaps. The Braves believe he'll develop more pop as he matures.

Best Raw Power: 3B Scott Thorman (1) can hit bombs, which is why Atlanta will keep him in the lineup rather than try to make use of his 94-95 mph fastball.

Fastest Runner: OF Alph Coleman (26) could be a 40-steal guy if he hits enough.

Best Defensive Player: **Keoni DeRenne** (12) played second base because he was on a team with shortstop prospect Wilson Betemit, but he can play short as well. DeRenne played four positions and didn't make an error at short-season Jamestown.

Best Fastball: RHP Blaine Boyer (3), who touches 95. Atlanta concentrated on high school pitching, and Wainwright, Nelson and RHPs Bryan Digby (2), Rodric Douglas (10) and Matt Wright (21) are all a tick behind Boyer.

Most Intriguing Background: The Braves signed the MVPs of the College World Series in Louisiana State RHP Trey Hodges (17) and

the Junior College World Series in Seminole State (Okla.) CC 1B/LHP Adam LaRoche (29). LaRoche, whose father Dave pitched in the majors, is one of five Braves draftees with baseball family connections. The others: SS Aaron Herr (1), son of former Cardinals all-star Tommy; OF Kevin Cust (11), brother of Diamondbacks prospect Jack; RHP Tim McClendon (25), brother of Braves prospect Matt; and OF Anthony Gwynn (33), son of eight-time batting champion Tony. McClendon and Gwynn opted for **DeRenne** college. RHP Brian Montalbo (4), whose father Mel played in the NFL, was the highest-drafted player ever out of Alaska.

DAVID SCHOFIELD

Closest To The Majors: DeRenne, the first of just six players the Braves signed out of Division I colleges. He projects as a utility-man.

Best Late-Round Pick: Wright was unhittable as a reliever in the GCL and will move back into the rotation this year.

The One Who Got Away: Montalbo, who took his 92-94 mph fastball to California.

Assessment: With six picks in the first two rounds, Roy Clark had a luxury in his first year as scouting director. The Braves were last in the draft order but still spent more money on bonuses than any other franchise. As usual, they preferred high school players more than anyone else.

1999 Draft

The Braves didn't have a first-round pick but found a couple of promising righthanders in Matt Butler (2), their top choice, and Matt McClendon (5). RHP Brett Evert (7) still has hope. Otherwise, they came up empty. **Grade: C–**

1998 Draft

Without a first-round choice, Atlanta still found quality arms in RHPs Matt Belisle (2), Scott Sobkowiak (7), Tim Spooneybarger (29, draft-and-follow) and Brad Voyles (45). They failed to sign RHP Josh Karp (8), who's at UCLA and will be a first-rounder in 2001. **Grade: C+**

1997 Draft

SS Troy Cameron (1) has been nothing but a strikeout machine. LHP Joey Nation (2) was traded to the Cubs, but OF Cory Aldridge (4), LHP Horacio Ramirez (5) and RHP Derrick Lewis (20) have emerged as legitimate prospects. **Grade: C**

1996 Draft

RHP Jason Marquis (1) is a big part of the team's future, while 2B Brian Giles (53, draft-and-follow) is one of the best prospects at his position. The Braves failed to sign C Eric Munson (2), who was the No. 3 overall pick three years later. **Grade: B**

Note: Draft analysis prepared by Jim Callis. Numbers in parentheses indicate draft rounds.

. . . Betemit is a 20-year-old switch-hitter who plays a premier position and has produced every time he has taken the field.

Wilson
Betemit ss

Born: Nov. 2, 1981.
Ht.: 6-2. **Wt.:** 155.
Bats: B. **Throws:** R.
Career Transactions: Signed out of Dominican Republic by Braves, July 28, 1996.

Early last spring it appeared Betemit might not live up to his potential in the Atlanta organization. In the offseason, Major League Baseball determined the Braves had signed Betemit before he was 16, in violation of baseball rules. While Atlanta was fined and prohibited from signing Dominican players for six months, Betemit staged a walkout at his agent's direction during spring training. An agreement wasn't reached for several weeks, costing Betemit a shot at playing in a full-season league. After blossoming in 1999 as an all-star in the Rookie-level Appalachian League and ranking as the circuit's No. 2 prospect, Betemit dominated the short-season New York-Penn League by placing second in hits and runs and fourth in average. He also was the loop's best prospect.

What's not to like? Betemit is a 20-year-old switch-hitter who plays a premier position, has outstanding size and has produced every time he has taken the field. He has incredible range and soft, quick hands that make him an ideal candidate for shortstop or third base. His arm also rates above-average, capable of strong, accurate throws in the hole. His defense has improved considerably and attracted rave reviews from NY-P managers. Betemit has plus power that is expected to increase significantly as his body continues to mature. He's reasonably disciplined at the plate and improved his ability to make contact in 2000. Not unlike other young players, Betemit makes careless mistakes, particularly in the field. He tries to make every play a spectacular one instead of recording the out, which has inflated his error total. Experience is a great teacher, and nowhere is that more evident with Betemit than in keeping up with the speed of the game at higher levels. He tends to rush throws and attack pitchers early in the count, so he needs to get more patient on defense and at the plate.

Had he not missed most of spring training, Betemit would have spent 2000 at Class A Macon. But he lost little from an overall development standpoint. That will be proven when Betemit bypasses Macon and opens 2001 at high Class A Myrtle Beach. It would surprise no one if he blazed a trial to Atlanta in less than two more years.

Year	Club (League)	Class	AVG	G	AB	R	H	2B	3B	HR	RBI	BB	SO	SB
1997	Braves (GCL)	R	.212	32	113	12	24	6	1	0	15	9	32	0
1998	Braves (GCL)	R	.220	51	173	23	38	8	4	5	16	20	49	6
1999	Danville (Appy)	R	.320	67	259	39	83	18	2	5	53	27	63	6
2000	Jamestown (NY-P)	A	.331	69	269	54	89	15	2	5	37	30	37	3
MINOR LEAGUE TOTALS			.287	219	814	128	234	47	9	15	121	86	181	15

2. Matt McClendon, rhp

Born: Oct. 13, 1977. **Ht.:** 6-6. **Wt.:** 220. **Bats:** R. **Throws:** R. **School:** University of Florida. **Career Transactions:** Selected by Braves in fifth round of 1999 draft; signed June 18, 1999.

A supplemental first-round pick by the Reds out of high school in 1996, McClendon was expected to go higher in 1999 before a minor shoulder injury robbed him of his velocity. After signing for a $950,000 bonus, McClendon pitched just 23 innings at short-season Jamestown before returning to a normal schedule in 2000. He emerged as hoped and reached Double-A Greenville in May. McClendon has all the ingredients to be a quality starter. His best pitches are his low-90s fastball with good movement and a sharp curveball he added during instructional league in 1999. He has good command and a solid idea of what it takes to get hitters out. An improved changeup would make McClendon much tougher to hit. He could also stand to fine-tune a breaking ball that tends to flatten out at times. Because of his size, refined mechanics are also a must. McClendon could have handled Triple-A at the end of last season. He'll get that opportunity this year at Richmond, with a promotion to Atlanta just around the corner.

Year	Club (League)	Class	W	L	ERA	G	GS	CG	SV	IP	H	R	ER	BB	SO
1999	Jamestown (NY-P)	A	1	1	3.91	7	7	0	0	23	18	11	10	11	24
2000	Myrtle Beach (Car)	A	3	1	1.59	6	6	0	0	40	24	7	7	8	43
	Greenville (SL)	AA	7	6	3.78	22	21	1	0	131	124	59	55	54	90
MINOR LEAGUE TOTALS			11	8	3.34	35	34	1	0	194	166	77	72	73	157

3. Marcus Giles, 2b

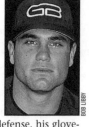

Born: May 18, 1978. **Ht.:** 5-8. **Wt.:** 180. **Bats:** R. **Throws:** R. **School:** Grossmont (Calif.) JC. **Career Transactions:** Selected by Braves in 53rd round of 1996 draft; signed May 26, 1997.

The MVP in the Class A South Atlantic and Carolina leagues in 1998-99, Giles struggled early last season in Double-A before making adjustments to higher quality pitching. He found his groove in June and wound up with another productive season while playing in the Southern League all-star game, Double-A all-star game and the Futures Game. Giles is a pure offensive player. He has a short, compact stroke that packs a line-drive punch to all fields. While he continues to hear criticism about his defense, his glove-work is consistent and better than advertised. Giles' range is only average, though he makes plays on every ball he reaches. His speed is also average, but his knowledge of the basepaths enabled him to steal a career-high 25 bases last season. Once he makes adjustments at the plate, Giles tends to get bored with a league, a trait that should end in the near future. Those who hit play in the major leagues. As long as Giles continues to produce and improve his defense, he'll join his brother Brian, an all-star outfielder with Pittsburgh, at the game's top level. Marcus' trek continues this spring in Triple-A.

Year	Club (League)	Class	AVG	G	AB	R	H	2B	3B	HR	RBI	BB	SO	SB
1997	Danville (Appy)	R	.348	55	207	53	72	13	3	8	45	32	47	5
1998	Macon (SAL)	A	.329	135	505	111	166	38	3	37	108	85	103	12
1999	Myrtle Beach (Car)	A	.326	126	497	80	162	40	7	13	73	54	89	9
2000	Greenville (SL)	AA	.290	132	458	73	133	28	2	17	62	72	71	25
MINOR LEAGUE TOTALS			.320	448	1667	317	533	119	15	75	288	243	310	51

4. Matt Belisle, rhp

Born: June 6, 1980. **Ht.:** 6-3. **Wt.:** 195. **Bats:** R. **Throws:** R. **School:** McCallum HS, Austin. **Career Transactions:** Selected by Braves in second round of 1998 draft; signed Aug. 23, 1998.

The Braves' first pick in 1998, Belisle signed for $1.75 million, still a club record and the largest bonus given a high school pitcher that year. After limited success in the Appalachian League in 1999, he was tabbed as the best pitching prospect in the South Atlantic League last summer. He received a midseason promotion to the Carolina League and pitched well in August. Belisle has outstanding arm strength and the ability to be a top starter. After a rough start, he proved he can make adjustments against better hitters. He has impeccable makeup and a strong inner drive with a desire to learn everything possible about pitching. Belisle needs to improve the command of his curveball and changeup. His curve is on the verge of becoming a solid pitch, but his changeup needs work. He also must be a little more patient, setting hitters up instead of trying to strike out everyone. Belisle could follow in McClendon's footsteps by starting 2001 at Myrtle Beach before moving up to Double-A. If he picks up where he left off in instructional league, he'll open in Greenville.

Year	Club (League)	Class	W	L	ERA	G	GS	CG	SV	IP	H	R	ER	BB	SO
1999	Danville (Appy)	R	2	5	4.67	14	14	0	0	71	86	50	37	23	60
2000	Macon (SAL)	A	9	5	2.37	15	15	1	0	102	79	37	27	18	97
	Myrtle Beach (Car)	A	3	4	3.43	12	12	0	0	78	72	32	30	11	71
MINOR LEAGUE TOTALS			14	14	3.35	41	41	1	0	252	237	119	94	52	228

5. Jason Marquis, rhp

Born: Aug. 21, 1978. **Ht.:** 6-1. **Wt.:** 185. **Bats:** L. **Throws:** R. **School:** Tottenville HS, Staten Island, N.Y. **Career Transactions:** Selected by Braves in first round (35th overall) of 1996 draft; signed July 18, 1996.

Injuries to the Atlanta pitching staff accelerated Marquis' progress to the major leagues last year. He threw well as a starter in Double-A and as a reliever with Atlanta, but showed the effects of bouncing around with six inconsistent starts at Triple-A. Marquis always has been an intense competitor. He showed more maturity last season by making the climb from Double-A to the big leagues. The jump made him more of a pitcher than a thrower, and may serve as the final ingredient for long-term success. Marquis maintains his outstanding arm strength with a mid-90s fastball, a plus curveball and a good changeup. Marquis' greatest need is better overall command. He also discovered in Triple-A and the majors that he can't overpower hitters if he fails to keep his pitches low in the strike zone. The Braves need help in the bullpen. With a successful test run, Marquis is a viable candidate to serve in a set-up role. He could join the rotation as a fifth starter should an opening occur.

Year	Club (League)	Class	W	L	ERA	G	GS	CG	SV	IP	H	R	ER	BB	SO
1996	Danville (Appy)	R	1	1	4.63	7	4	0	0	23	30	18	12	7	24
1997	Macon (SAL)	A	14	10	4.38	28	28	0	0	142	156	78	69	55	121
1998	Danville (Car)	A	2	12	4.87	22	22	1	0	115	120	65	62	41	135
1999	Myrtle Beach (Car)	A	3	0	0.28	6	6	0	0	32	22	2	1	17	41
	Greenville (SL)	AA	3	4	4.58	12	12	1	0	55	52	33	28	29	35
2000	Greenville (SL)	AA	4	2	3.57	11	11	0	0	68	68	35	27	23	49
	Atlanta (NL)	MAJ	1	0	5.01	15	0	0	0	23	23	16	13	12	17
	Richmond (IL)	AAA	0	3	9.00	6	6	0	0	20	26	21	20	13	18
MAJOR LEAGUE TOTALS			1	0	5.01	15	0	0	0	23	23	16	13	12	17
MINOR LEAGUE TOTALS			27	32	4.34	92	89	2	0	455	474	252	219	185	423

6. Billy Sylvester, rhp

Born: Oct. 1, 1976. **Ht.:** 6-5. **Wt.:** 218. **Bats:** R. **Throws:** R. **School:** Spartanburg Methodist (S.C.) JC. **Career Transactions:** Signed as nondrafted free agent by Braves, June 18, 1997.

Signed as a nondrafted free agent out of junior college in 1997, Sylvester blossomed in his fourth professional season. After ending the 1999 campaign with minor arm problems, he didn't allow an earned run until June and was the top relief prospect in the Carolina League. Sylvester is a strong-armed pitcher who came into his own last season thanks to increased confidence. A former starter, he thrived in the closer's role by using his mid-90s fastball and a nasty, sharp-breaking curveball. He also has an average split-finger fastball. Confidence continues to be the key for Sylvester. He must realize that his stuff is good enough to succeed. He also needs to continue throwing strikes consistently by challenging hitters. Improving his splitter and throwing it more often should make his jump to higher levels smoother. The Braves knew they were pushing Sylvester in the Arizona Fall League, where he got rocked after missing the last two months of the season with a broken left hand and a minor ribcage injury. He did show the ability to make adjustments against better hitters, and will have to do that in Double-A in 2001.

Year	Club (League)	Class	W	L	ERA	G	GS	CG	SV	IP	H	R	ER	BB	SO
1997	Braves (GCL)	R	3	4	3.91	12	9	0	0	53	45	25	23	28	58
1998	Eugene (NWL)	A	0	11	6.51	16	16	0	0	55	73	61	40	24	42
1999	Macon (SAL)	A	5	4	3.12	44	1	0	2	84	78	37	29	37	75
2000	Myrtle Beach (Car)	A	3	0	0.79	32	0	0	16	46	16	8	4	15	48
MINOR LEAGUE TOTALS			11	19	3.63	104	26	0	18	238	212	131	96	104	223

7. Adam Wainwright, rhp

Born: Aug. 30, 1981. **Ht.:** 6-7. **Wt.:** 195. **Bats:** R. **Throws:** R. **School:** St. Simons (Ga.) HS. **Career Transactions:** Selected by Braves in 1st round (29th overall) of 2000 draft; signed June 9, 2000.

Wainwright breezed through the Rookie-level Gulf Coast League before receiving a promotion to the Appalachian League after seven starts. He was the Appy League's top prospect and second-best in the GCL. For a teenager, Wainwright's overall command and ability to throw strikes with his changeup are uncanny. He's mature and competitive. In addition to a plus changeup, Wainwright features a low-90s fastball and an average curveball. His maturity can overshadow his inexperience against professional hitters. He wore down in August and must improve his strength to pitch at a high level for a full season. Added strength should add velocity to his four-seam fastball. The progress Wainwright made last season will enable him to open 2001 at Macon. The Braves say finding the right place to challenge Wainwright at this point in his career could be the most difficult decision.

Year	Club (League)	Class	W	L	ERA	G	GS	CG	SV	IP	H	R	ER	BB	SO
2000	Orlando (GCL)	R	4	0	1.13	7	5	0	0	32	15	5	4	10	42
	Danville (Appy)	R	2	2	3.68	6	6	0	0	29	28	13	12	2	39
MINOR LEAGUE TOTALS			6	2	2.36	13	11	0	0	61	43	18	16	12	81

8. Wes Helms, 3b

Born: May 12, 1976. **Ht.:** 6-4. **Wt.:** 230. **Bats:** R. **Throws:** R. **School:** Ashbrook HS, Gastonia, N.C. **Career Transactions:** Selected by Braves in 10th round of 1994 draft; signed June 15, 1994.

Two different shoulder injuries limited Helms to 39 games in 1999, but he bounced back in 2000 and made improvements while posting career-highs in home runs and RBIs at Triple-A. For the first time, Helms displayed his above-average power without hurting his average. He loves the challenge of hitting with the game on the line and has a knack for producing the big hit. His defense at third base also showed a little improvement, though the Braves had the athletic Helms playing first base and the two corner outfield positions in Venezuela during winter ball. On the downside, his big swing continues to show holes. His hands are not soft on defense, and he tends to rush his throws despite possessing a plus arm. Perseverance appears to have paid off for Helms. The Braves could move Chipper Jones to the outfield and giving Helms a shot at the hot corner. This spring is shaping up to be Helms' first real chance at making the 25-man roster.

Year	Club (League)	Class	AVG	G	AB	R	H	2B	3B	HR	RBI	BB	SO	SB
1994	Braves (GCL)	R	.266	56	184	22	49	15	1	4	29	22	36	6
1995	Macon (SAL)	A	.276	136	539	89	149	32	1	11	85	50	107	2
1996	Durham (Car)	A	.322	67	258	40	83	19	2	13	54	12	51	1
	Greenville (SL)	AA	.255	64	231	24	59	13	2	4	22	13	48	2
1997	Richmond (IL)	AAA	.191	32	110	11	21	4	0	3	15	10	34	1
	Greenville (SL)	AA	.296	86	314	50	93	14	1	11	44	33	50	3
1998	Richmond (IL)	AAA	.275	125	451	56	124	27	1	13	75	35	103	6
	Atlanta (NL)	MAJ	.308	7	13	2	4	1	0	1	2	0	4	0
1999	Braves (GCL)	R	.455	9	33	1	15	2	0	0	10	5	4	0
	Greenville (SL)	AA	.301	30	113	15	34	6	0	8	26	7	34	1
2000	Richmond (IL)	AAA	.288	136	539	74	155	27	7	20	88	27	92	0
	Atlanta (NL)	MAJ	.200	6	5	0	1	0	0	0	0	0	2	0
MAJOR LEAGUE TOTALS			.278	13	18	2	5	1	0	1	2	0	6	0
MINOR LEAGUE TOTALS			.282	741	2772	382	782	159	15	87	448	214	559	22

9. Christian Parra, rhp

Born: Feb. 28, 1978. **Ht.:** 6-1. **Wt.:** 255. **Bats:** R. **Throws:** R. **School:** Arizona Western JC. **Career Transactions:** Signed as nondrafted free agent by Braves, Feb. 26, 1999.

Getting the opportunity to pitch on a regular basis allowed Parra to blossom last season. Unknown before the 2000 campaign, he was the Carolina League's top pitcher after leading the circuit in wins and placing second in ERA. Parra is a fearless, barrel-chested pitcher who may be the most competitive in the organization. He believes in his ability to get hitters out and wants the ball with the game on the line. Parra challenges hitters even though his stuff is only slightly above-average. He throws four pitches for strikes and works off an average fastball with good movement. He has a clear understanding of what he wants to accomplish. Parra tends to rush through his delivery, which can affect his mechanics and cause his pitches to rise in the zone, where they become more hittable. He must continue to throw strikes consistently and mix his pitches. Parra is at a place in his career where he needs to improve upon what he's done against better competition. A move one step higher to Double-A is in Parra's immediate future. Proving himself in Greenville will place him firmly in Atlanta's long-term plans.

Year	Club (League)	Class	W	L	ERA	G	GS	CG	SV	IP	H	R	ER	BB	SO
1999	Jamestown (NY-P)	A	1	2	3.10	9	9	0	0	49	46	21	17	19	62
	Macon (SAL)	A	1	1	3.31	6	6	0	0	33	33	15	12	12	37
2000	Myrtle Beach (Car)	A	17	4	2.28	26	25	2	0	158	98	46	40	56	163
MINOR LEAGUE TOTALS			19	7	2.59	41	40	2	0	240	177	82	69	87	262

10. Scott Sobkowiak, rhp

Born: Oct. 26, 1977. **Ht.:** 6-5. **Wt.:** 230. **Bats:** R. **Throws:** R. **School:** University of Northern Iowa. **Career Transactions:** Selected by Braves in seventh round of 1998 draft; signed June 6, 1998.

After ranking as the Braves' No. 4 prospect last year, Sobkowiak made four Double-A starts before going on the disabled list on April 26. He had reconstructive surgery on his right elbow shortly thereafter, costing him the rest of the season. Based on Sobkowiak's rehabilitation efforts in Florida so far, the Braves believe he'll have better stuff than before his injury. He's a power pitcher with good size and the ability to be a workhorse. He challenges hitters with virtually every pitch. Both his fastball, which tops out at 95 mph, and his curveball are plus pitches. He showed an improved changeup prior to getting hurt. The Braves had always been concerned that Sobkowiak's large frame and labored delivery could lead to injury. He needs to fine-tune his mechanics when he's healthy again. Continued improvement with his changeup can do nothing but help. Several scouts thought Sobkowiak would have pitched in the major leagues last year had he not been injured. He's expected to be at full strength in spring training and should open the season at Greenville.

Year	Club (League)	Class	W	L	ERA	G	GS	CG	SV	IP	H	R	ER	BB	SO
1998	Eugene (NWL)	A	3	2	1.55	8	8	0	0	41	25	12	7	13	55
1999	Myrtle Beach (Car)	A	9	4	2.84	27	26	0	0	139	100	50	44	63	161
2000	Greenville (SL)	AA	2	1	4.63	4	4	0	0	23	26	16	12	15	27
MINOR LEAGUE TOTALS			14	7	2.79	39	38	0	0	203	151	78	63	81	243

11. Horacio Ramirez, lhp

Born: Nov. 24, 1979. **Ht.:** 6-1. **Wt.:** 170. **Bats:** L. **Throws:** L. **School:** Inglewood HS, Los Angeles. **Career Transactions:** Selected by Braves in fifth round of 1997 draft; signed June 6, 1997.

Ramirez combined with Christian Parra to give Myrtle Beach the minors' best one-two punch in 2000. The lefthander had battled minor arm injuries throughout his first three seasons before making every start last year and ranking second in the Carolina League in wins and fifth in ERA. Ramirez is a four-pitch pitcher who works off his 92-93 mph fastball and an effective curveball. He also has a natural cut fastball with outstanding movement that produces little strain on his arm. He has made significant improvement with his changeup, which also served as a key to his success last season. Because of Ramirez's health history, the Braves held their breath as he inched toward 150 innings, which is the point he would have been shut down. Though he came within two innings of reaching that level, Ramirez still needs to add strength to help him stay healthy. He also must stay consistent in the strike zone and throw his changeup more often in order to keep hitters off balance. An improved two-seam fastball also will enable him to climb the final rungs of the organization. A promotion to Double-A awaits Ramirez in 2001.

Year	Club (League)	Class	W	L	ERA	G	GS	CG	SV	IP	H	R	ER	BB	SO
1997	Braves (GCL)	R	3	3	2.25	11	8	0	0	44	30	13	11	18	61
1998	Macon (SAL)	A	1	7	5.86	12	12	0	0	55	70	50	36	16	38
	Eugene (NWL)	A	2	7	6.31	16	8	0	0	56	84	51	39	17	39
1999	Macon (SAL)	A	6	3	2.67	17	14	1	0	78	70	30	23	25	43
2000	Myrtle Beach (Car)	A	15	8	3.22	27	26	3	0	148	136	57	53	42	125
MINOR LEAGUE TOTALS			27	28	3.83	83	68	4	0	381	390	201	162	118	306

12. Matt Butler, rhp

Born: Sept. 24, 1979. **Ht.:** 6-3. **Wt.:** 190. **Bats:** R. **Throws:** R. **School:** Hattiesburg (Miss.) HS. **Career Transactions:** Selected by Braves in second round of 1999 draft; signed June 9, 1999.

Butler showed the Braves exactly what they hoped to see during the second half last year. After Matt Belisle was promoted to Myrtle Beach at midseason, Butler took over as Macon's No. 1 starter and dominated, ranking fifth in ERA in the South Atlantic League. His best performance came on Aug. 20, when Butler retired 20 of the first 21 batters he faced to record his second shutout of the season. He began his professional career by allowing one run or less in seven of his 11 outings in the Gulf Coast League. Butler is a power pitcher who throws his four-seam fastball in the low 90s. He showed improvement with his changeup as the season progressed last year. His primary needs center on keeping his pitches low in the strike zone and upgrading his command. Butler also would be more effective if he tightened the spin on his breaking ball. Plans call for him to open the 2001 season at Myrtle Beach, with a midseason promotion to Double-A a possibility.

Year	Club (League)	Class	W	L	ERA	G	GS	CG	SV	IP	H	R	ER	BB	SO
1999	Braves (GCL)	R	2	4	4.03	11	10	0	0	38	36	20	17	22	38
2000	Macon (SAL)	A	13	7	2.94	26	26	2	0	156	132	75	51	66	122
MINOR LEAGUE TOTALS			15	11	3.15	37	36	2	0	194	168	95	68	88	160

13. Matt Wright, rhp

Born: March 13, 1982. **Ht.:** 6-4. **Wt.:** 230. **Bats:** R. **Throws:** R. **School:** Robinson HS, Lorena, Texas. **Career Transactions:** Selected by Braves in 21st round of 2000 draft; signed June 18, 2000.

Members of the Braves front office were unanimous in their belief that Wright made as much progress as any newcomer in 2000. He made minor adjustments to his delivery suggested by the Atlanta coaching staff and emerged as one of the top pitching prospects in the organization. He combines a 92-93 mph fastball with a hard, sharp-breaking curveball that made him almost unhittable late in the Gulf Coast League season and during instructional league. The Braves were most impressed with the command he has of his plus curveball as well as his knowledge of when to use it to his greatest advantage. He'll have to improve his third pitch, an average changeup, to keep hitters from sitting on his fastball. As a late-round pick, Wright was used in relief last year to allow top draft picks to work as starters, limiting his innings. That scenario won't be repeated in 2001 when Wright joins the Macon rotation.

Year	Club (League)	Class	W	L	ERA	G	GS	CG	SV	IP	H	R	ER	BB	SO
2000	Orlando (GCL)	R	0	2	0.86	12	0	0	4	21	8	5	2	11	30
MINOR LEAGUE TOTALS			0	2	0.86	12	0	0	4	21	8	5	2	11	30

14. Bubba Nelson, rhp

Born: Aug. 26, 1981. **Ht.:** 6-2. **Wt.:** 200. **Bats:** R. **Throws:** R. **School:** Riverdale Baptist HS, Upper Marlboro, Md. **Career Transactions:** Selected by Braves in second round of 2000 draft; signed June 23, 2000.

One of Atlanta's crosscheckers liked Nelson better than Adam Wainwright on draft day. Nelson touches 94 mph on the radar gun with a heavy, sinking fastball. It has natural plus movement due to a release point that is slightly above sidearm. Considered a potential third baseman, Nelson has added velocity since he signed because he focused on pitching. The Atlanta scouting department rated Nelson's curveball as the best breaking ball it saw among the 2000 draft class, while his changeup ranked near the top. He also has above-average command, particularly for a pitcher fresh out of high school. Nelson got off to a rocky start before putting the pieces together late in the Gulf Coast League and during instructional league, including one game in which he struck out seven straight batters while using all three pitches. He needs to continue to challenge hitters, use both sides of the plate and get ahead early in the count. Nelson has proven to be advanced for his age, and he could move quickly through the system. His next stop is Class A Macon's rotation.

Year	Club (League)	Class	W	L	ERA	G	GS	CG	SV	IP	H	R	ER	BB	SO
2000	Braves (GCL)	R	3	2	4.23	12	6	1	0	45	40	24	21	13	54
MINOR LEAGUE TOTALS			3	2	4.23	12	6	1	0	45	40	24	21	13	54

15. Tim Spooneybarger, rhp

Born: Oct. 21, 1979. **Ht.:** 6-3. **Wt.:** 190. **Bats:** R. **Throws:** R. **School:** Okaloosa-Walton (Fla.) JC. **Career Transactions:** Selected by Braves in 29th round of 1998 draft; signed May 19, 1999.

Spooneybarger was a 1998 draft-and-follow who blossomed last season. Hitters rarely get good swings against him because of the movement on his pitches and his deceptive delivery. He limited opponents to a .110 average last year after allowing them to bat .179 in 1999.

Spooneybarger has good command of his two fastballs. His four-seamer averages 90-91 mph and has great movement with a natural cutting action. His two-seam fastball looks similar to his four-seamer before diving just prior to reaching the plate. He complements both fastballs with a good, hard curveball. He has spent the past two instructional leagues focusing on improving his changeup. Spooneybarger also needs innings after working just 50 last year because of a minor shoulder ailment. The Braves are uncertain what role fits Spooneybarger best. He prefers to relieve, but Atlanta officials believe he has the arm as well as the athleticism to be a dominating starter. Either way, he's scheduled to open 2001 in Double-A.

Year	Club (League)	Class	W	L	ERA	G	GS	CG	SV	IP	H	R	ER	BB	SO
1999	Danville (Appy)	R	3	0	2.22	12	0	0	0	24	15	11	6	14	36
	Macon (SAL)	A	0	1	3.60	7	0	0	0	10	7	4	4	10	17
2000	Myrtle Beach (Car)	A	3	0	0.91	19	6	0	0	50	18	7	5	19	57
MINOR LEAGUE TOTALS			6	1	1.61	38	6	0	0	84	40	22	15	43	110

16. Derrick Lewis, rhp

Born: May 7, 1976. **Ht.:** 6-5. **Wt.:** 215. **Bats:** R. **Throws:** R. **School:** Florida A&M University. **Career Transactions:** Selected by Braves in 20th round of 1997 draft; signed June 4, 1997.

Atlanta drafted Lewis knowing he was a raw prospect. While he continues to lack polish in some phases of the game, he's on the verge of meriting major league consideration. He started to emerge in 1999 by ranking second in the Carolina League with a 2.40 ERA and followed up with a solid encore in Double-A. Lewis' fastball registers in the low 90s and is hard to hit because of its heavy, sinking action. He also throws a decent slider, though his changeup needs to become more consistent. The albatross throughout Lewis' career has been his lack of control and command. In order to succeed at higher levels, he must reduce his walks and minimize the number of pitches he throws so that he may go deeper in games. Lewis remains a work in progress, which will continue this season at Triple-A Richmond.

Year	Club (League)	Class	W	L	ERA	G	GS	CG	SV	IP	H	R	ER	BB	SO
1997	Danville (Appy)	R	2	4	6.34	16	9	0	0	50	59	48	35	31	46
1998	Macon (SAL)	A	5	6	3.81	23	23	0	0	113	108	64	48	55	100
1999	Myrtle Beach (Car)	A	8	4	2.40	24	23	0	0	131	100	44	35	81	102
2000	Greenville (SL)	AA	7	9	3.30	27	27	1	0	164	146	70	60	83	143
MINOR LEAGUE TOTALS			22	23	3.50	90	82	1	0	458	413	226	178	250	391

17. George Lombard, of

Born: Sept. 14, 1975. **Ht.:** 6-0. **Wt.:** 212. **Bats:** L. **Throws:** R. **School:** The Lovett School, Atlanta. **Career Transactions:** Selected by Braves in second round of 1994 draft; signed June 10, 1994.

Lombard is at a crossroads. Since bypassing a career as a running back at the University of Georgia in 1994, the athletic Lombard has made a slow yet steady climb through the system. Now out of options, he's the leading contender to earn a job as the Braves' fourth outfielder after a late charge last season in Triple-A and a spot on Atlanta's playoff roster. Lombard has world-class speed and an unmatched work ethic. His defense in left field has improved immensely, though his arm remains below average. He also has developed into an outstanding, high-percentage basestealer. Lombard has become more patient at the plate and has shown an increase in power throughout his career. Some scouts wonder, however, if he'll hit well enough to remain in the big leagues, especially because offspeed pitches continue to give him significant difficulty. Some observers believe Lombard will follow in the footsteps of Chris Weinke and play college football if he fails to make Atlanta's 25-man roster this spring. The Braves are confident Lombard won't be faced with that decision.

Year	Club (League)	Class	AVG	G	AB	R	H	2B	3B	HR	RBI	BB	SO	SB
1994	Braves (GCL)	R	.140	40	129	10	18	2	0	0	5	18	47	10
1995	Macon (SAL)	A	.206	49	180	32	37	6	1	3	16	27	44	16
	Eugene (NWL)	A	.252	68	262	38	66	5	3	5	19	23	91	35
1996	Macon (SAL)	A	.245	116	444	76	109	16	8	15	51	36	122	24
1997	Durham (Car)	A	.264	131	462	65	122	25	7	14	72	66	145	35
1998	Greenville (SL)	AA	.308	122	422	84	130	25	4	22	65	71	140	35
	Atlanta (NL)	MAJ	.333	6	6	2	2	0	0	1	1	0	1	1
1999	Richmond (IL)	AAA	.206	74	233	25	48	11	3	7	29	35	98	21
	Atlanta (NL)	MAJ	.333	6	6	1	2	0	0	0	0	1	2	2
2000	Richmond (IL)	AAA	.276	112	424	72	117	25	7	10	48	55	130	32
	Atlanta (NL)	MAJ	.103	27	39	8	4	0	0	0	2	1	14	4
MAJOR LEAGUE TOTALS			.157	39	51	11	8	0	0	1	3	2	17	7
MINOR LEAGUE TOTALS			.253	712	2556	402	647	115	33	76	305	331	817	208

18. Damian Moss, lhp

Born: Nov. 24, 1976. **Ht.:** 6-0. **Wt.:** 187. **Bats:** R. **Throws:** L. **Career Transactions:** Signed out of Australia by Braves, July 30, 1993 . . . On disabled list, March 27-Oct. 29, 1998.

For the first time in several years, the Braves were pleased with the progress Moss made. His arm strength finally returned to where it was prior to his Tommy John surgery during the 1998 season. While his fastball is no better than average, he owns a sharp curveball and an above-average changeup that he mixes well. Batters have difficulty timing Moss, but his control has worsened since his surgery. He tends to nibble instead of challenging batters and appears to lose his concentration at times. While there are major league pitchers who don't have as strong a repertoire as Moss does, his opportunities in Atlanta will be limited until he can discover consistency and command.

Year	Club (League)	Class	W	L	ERA	G	GS	CG	SV	IP	H	R	ER	BB	SO
1994	Danville (Appy)	R	2	5	3.58	12	12	1	0	60	30	28	24	55	77
1995	Macon (SAL)	A	9	10	3.56	27	27	0	0	149	134	73	59	70	177
1996	Durham (Car)	A	9	1	2.25	14	14	0	0	84	52	25	21	40	89
	Greenville (SL)	AA	2	5	4.97	11	10	0	0	58	57	41	32	35	48
1997	Greenville (SL)	AA	6	8	5.35	21	19	1	0	113	111	73	67	58	116
1998							Did Not Play—Injured								
1999	Macon (SAL)	A	0	3	4.32	12	12	0	0	42	33	20	20	15	49
	Greenville (SL)	AA	1	3	8.54	7	7	0	0	33	50	33	31	21	22
2000	Richmond (IL)	AAA	9	6	3.14	29	28	0	0	161	130	67	56	106	123
MINOR LEAGUE TOTALS			38	41	3.99	133	129	2	0	699	597	360	310	400	701

19. Zach Miner, rhp

Born: March 12, 1982. **Ht.:** 6-3. **Wt.:** 190. **Bats:** R. **Throws:** R. **School:** Palm Beach Gardens (Fla.) HS. **Career Transactions:** Selected by Braves in fourth round of 2000 draft; signed Sept. 1, 2000.

Had Adam Wainwright not been available, the Braves would have taken Miner in the first round. They showed how much they wanted Miner by signing him for $1.2 million on the day he was to begin classes at the University of Miami. Miner displayed an impressive knowledge of how to pitch in instructional league. He has an 88-90 mph fastball with good movement, and should add velocity as his body fills out. His curveball and changeup are advanced for a high school pitcher. He impressed the organization with his command of all three pitches, especially after missing the summer. Miner tries to do too much with his pitches at times and needs to use his fastball more often at the expense of his changeup. The greatest challenge awaiting him is the mental and physical drain he'll experience during his first full season at Class A Macon. If he handles it, his ceiling could be considered unlimited.

Year	Club (League)	Class	W	L	ERA	G	GS	CG	SV	IP	H	R	ER	BB	SO
2000						Did Not Play—Signed 2001 Contract									

20. Brett Evert, rhp

Born: Oct. 23, 1980. **Ht.:** 6-6. **Wt.:** 200. **Bats:** L. **Throws:** R. **School:** North Salem HS, Salem, Ore. **Career Transactions:** Selected by Braves in seventh round of 1999 draft; signed June 9, 1999.

Evert opened 2000 in extended spring training before moving to Macon, which proved to be a bigger jump than he could handle. He was demoted to Jamestown when the New York-Penn League season started and regained his rhythm. Evert's body is continuing to develop, with the Braves believing he will become a workhorse once he fully matures. In the meantime, he's making adjustments to his game as his body finds a comfort zone. Evert has an excellent feel for pitching. He works off his plus fastball and is adept at setting hitters up with his average changeup. He's trying to tighten the spin on his curveball and improve his overall command. Braves coaches were impressed with how much Evert learned from his mistakes last year and believe those lessons will accelerate his progress in the Macon rotation.

Year	Club (League)	Class	W	L	ERA	G	GS	CG	SV	IP	H	R	ER	BB	SO
1999	Braves (GCL)	R	5	3	2.03	13	13	0	0	49	37	17	11	9	39
2000	Macon (SAL)	A	1	4	4.64	7	7	0	0	43	53	27	22	9	29
	Jamestown (NY-P)	A	8	3	3.38	15	15	0	0	77	92	52	29	19	64
MINOR LEAGUE TOTALS			14	10	3.31	35	32	0	0	169	182	96	62	37	132

21. Scott Thorman, 3b

Born: Jan. 6, 1982. **Ht.:** 6-3. **Wt.:** 210. **Bats:** R. **Throws:** R. **School:** Preston HS, Cambridge, Ontario. **Career Transactions:** Selected by Braves in 1st round (30th overall) of 2000 draft; signed June 16, 2000.

Thorman possessed as much strength and power potential as any available high school player. The Canadian hit just one home run in the Gulf Coast League after visa problems delayed his professional debut by a month, but he put on a power display during instructional league. Thorman impressed the Braves with his outstanding makeup, impeccable character and strong desire to play the game. He comes to the ballpark ready to play and never gets cheated at the plate. A pitcher in high school who has been clocked as high as 95 mph off the mound, Thorman has a plus arm for third base. His defense needs considerable work, and his range must be increased. Improvements also are needed with his pitch recognition and overall patience. If third base doesn't work out, Thorman has the arm to move to right field. He'll remain at third in 2001, with Macon his most likely destination.

Year	Club (League)	Class	AVG	G	AB	R	H	2B	3B	HR	RBI	BB	SO	SB
2000	Orlando (GCL)	R	.227	29	97	15	22	7	1	1	19	12	23	0
MINOR LEAGUE TOTALS			.227	29	97	15	22	7	1	1	19	12	23	0

22. Miguel Bernard, c

Born: Jan. 1, 1981. **Ht.:** 5-11. **Wt.:** 170. **Bats:** R. **Throws:** R. **Career Transactions:** Signed out of Dominican Republic by Braves, Sept. 15, 1997.

Bernard is the top catching prospect in the organization after his first season in the United States. He's an excellent catch-and-throw receiver. His arm is above-average and his footwork behind the plate has improved considerably. The Braves rave about his enthusiasm, with several coaches saying Bernard reminds them of shortstop Rafael Furcal with his love for playing the game. Bernard does an excellent job of communicating with his pitching staff and has a strong idea of how to call a game. His bat shows considerable promise and budding power, but his big swing has several holes. He sits on fastballs to the point where he becomes overanxious when he gets one. Breaking balls and offspeed pitches eat him alive, so he'll have to make adjustments at higher levels. His next stop is Macon.

Year	Club (League)	Class	AVG	G	AB	R	H	2B	3B	HR	RBI	BB	SO	SB
1998	Braves (DSL)	R	.227	8	22	2	5	0	0	0	2	0	2	0
1999	Braves (DSL)	R	.255	29	98	12	25	4	0	2	20	6	10	3
2000	Braves (GCL)	R	.241	42	137	20	33	5	0	1	10	9	18	0
MINOR LEAGUE TOTALS			.245	79	257	34	63	9	0	3	32	15	30	3

23. Cory Aldridge, of

Born: June 13, 1979. **Ht.:** 6-0. **Wt.:** 210. **Bats:** L. **Throws:** R. **School:** Cooper HS, Abilene, Texas. **Career Transactions:** Selected by Braves in fourth round of 1997 draft; signed June 8, 1997.

Aldridge beat out better-known players such as first baseman A.J. Zapp and second baseman Travis Wilson to earn a spot on the Braves' 40-man roster. He has made impressive strides over the past two years, a byproduct of playing the game daily after focusing on football in high school. Despite having natural athleticism, his tools were rough. He has developed to the point where several scouts compare Aldridge to David Justice. Aldridge has outstanding speed and increasing power that should enable him to hit more than 20 homers a year. His defense has improved considerably, and his arm is average and getting better. Aldridge needs to work on his plate coverage, strike-zone knowledge and basestealing ability. The game isn't second nature to him, which means staying healthy and getting as many repetitions as possible are essential. A strong spring would land Aldridge in Double-A.

Year	Club (League)	Class	AVG	G	AB	R	H	2B	3B	HR	RBI	BB	SO	SB
1997	Braves (GCL)	R	.278	46	169	26	47	8	1	3	37	14	37	1
1998	Danville (Appy)	R	.294	60	214	37	63	16	1	3	33	29	48	16
1999	Macon (SAL)	A	.251	124	443	48	111	19	4	12	65	33	123	9
2000	Myrtle Beach (Car)	A	.249	109	401	51	100	18	5	15	64	33	118	10
MINOR LEAGUE TOTALS			.262	339	1227	162	321	61	11	33	199	109	326	36

24. John Ennis, rhp

Born: Oct. 17, 1979. **Ht.:** 6-5. **Wt.:** 220. **Bats:** R. **Throws:** R. **School:** Monroe HS, Panorama City, Calif. **Career Transactions:** Selected by Braves in 14th round of 1998 draft; signed June 18, 1998.

A light came on for Ennis late in 1999, and his progress carried over to 2000. Ennis has developed into a composed pitcher with an understanding of what he wants to accomplish with all of his pitches. One coach said Ennis pitched like a 10-year veteran during instructional league. His low-90s fastball is his best pitch, followed closely by his hard curveball and effective changeup. Ennis also mixes in a slider, though the Braves would prefer he focus on the curveball to reduce the strain on his arm. As with any young hurler, Ennis needs to improve his consistency, particularly with his curveball, which goes flat when his arm tires. If Ennis continues to develop at the same rate at Myrtle Beach, much bigger things await.

Year	Club (League)	Class	W	L	ERA	G	GS	CG	SV	IP	H	R	ER	BB	SO
1998	Braves (GCL)	R	0	3	4.62	8	2	0	0	25	30	16	13	6	18
1999	Danville (Appy)	R	4	3	5.07	13	13	0	0	66	71	46	37	21	60
2000	Macon (SAL)	A	7	4	2.55	18	16	0	0	99	77	37	28	25	105
MINOR LEAGUE TOTALS			11	10	3.70	39	31	0	0	190	178	99	78	52	183

25. Kelly Johnson, ss

Born: Feb. 22, 1982. **Ht.:** 6-1. **Wt.:** 180. **Bats:** L. **Throws:** R. **School:** Westwood HS, Austin. **Career Transactions:** Selected by Braves in first round (38th overall) of 2000 draft; signed June 12, 2000.

More than a few people looked at one another and said "Who?" when the Braves called Johnson's name last June. Unlike most high-profile draft choices, Johnson hadn't played in national showcases, causing him to slip under the radar screen. The Braves, however, had eight different scouts evaluate him and every report said Johnson is a player. After his solid debut in the Gulf Coast League, Johnson has drawn comparisons to Robin Ventura. A shortstop throughout his career, he has soft hands and a strong arm, but his body is on the verge of necessitating a move to third base. His natural sweet swing attracts the most praise because of his outstanding plate coverage. He also has better-than-average speed and is consistent defensively. Johnson produces a lot of line-drive hits in the gaps, and the Braves believe he'll hit for more power as his body matures naturally. Johnson is in need of more experience, which he'll get in his first full season at Macon.

Year	Club (League)	Class	AVG	G	AB	R	H	2B	3B	HR	RBI	BB	SO	SB
2000	Braves (GCL)	R	.269	53	193	27	52	12	3	4	29	24	45	6
MINOR LEAGUE TOTALS			.269	53	193	27	52	12	3	4	29	24	45	6

26. Alejandro Machado, 2b

Born: April 26, 1982. **Ht.:** 6-0. **Wt.:** 160. **Bats:** R. **Throws:** R. **Career Transactions:** Signed out of Venezuela by Braves, July 2, 1998.

Machado was a solid shortstop prior to making the move to second base. His hands are softer and his arm is stronger than most second basemen. He also has impressive instincts and a knack for positioning himself at the right spot to make plays. Machado has the speed to hit leadoff and to steal bases. A slasher with the bat, he makes good contact and doesn't try to do more than his physical limitations allow. One scout said Machado has all the makings of developing into a complete player should he continue to make the same type of improvements he's made in the past year. He needs to get stronger in order to handle the physical stress of playing every day for a full season. Improved bunting ability would allow him to get on base more often, though he does have a fine eye for drawing walks. Machado also needs to learn the nuances of stealing bases, especially making the proper reads and getting the necessary leads. He'll continue to work on those skills this year at Macon.

Year	Club (League)	Class	AVG	G	AB	R	H	2B	3B	HR	RBI	BB	SO	SB
1999	Braves (GCL)	R	.278	56	223	45	62	11	0	0	14	20	22	19
2000	Danville (Appy)	R	.341	61	217	45	74	6	2	0	16	53	29	30
MINOR LEAGUE TOTALS			.309	117	440	90	136	17	2	0	30	73	51	49

27. Brad Voyles, rhp

Born: Dec. 30, 1976. **Ht.:** 6-1. **Wt.:** 195. **Bats:** R. **Throws:** R. **School:** Lincoln Memorial (Tenn.) University. **Career Transactions:** Selected by Braves in 45th round of 1998 draft; signed June 7, 1998.

Voyles isn't the prettiest pitcher in the game, but he gets the job done. He carried Myrtle Beach to the Carolina League title by handling most of the closing duties after Billy Sylvester was lost for the season in July. He turned the corner last year by working off his fastball instead of his curveball at the behest of Myrtle Beach pitching coach Bruce Dal Canton. Once Voyles used his fastball more often, its velocity and movement increased, making it at least an average pitch, and made his hard curveball more effective. Voyles threw his changeup for strikes last season, giving him three solid pitches. While he was consistent in 2000, he needs to maintain that success against better competition. He also needs to continue working on his changeup. While Voyles is slated to pitch at Double-A this season, the Braves believe Triple-A and even the major leagues aren't out of the question.

Year	Club (League)	Class	W	L	ERA	G	GS	CG	SV	IP	H	R	ER	BB	SO
1998	Eugene (NWL)	A	0	0	3.09	7	0	0	0	12	9	5	4	10	22
1999	Macon (SAL)	A	3	3	2.98	38	0	0	14	51	27	21	17	39	65
	Myrtle Beach (Car)	A	1	1	2.25	5	0	0	0	12	7	3	3	9	13
2000	Myrtle Beach (Car)	A	5	2	1.11	39	0	0	19	57	21	8	7	25	70
MINOR LEAGUE TOTALS			9	6	2.52	89	0	0	33	132	64	37	31	83	170

28. Jung Bong, lhp

Born: July 15, 1980. **Ht.:** 6-3. **Wt.:** 175. **Bats:** L. **Throws:** L. **Career Transactions:** Signed out of Korea by Braves, Nov. 6, 1997.

Bong is an excellent all-around athlete who was considered as promising a prospect as a hitter in Korea as he was on the mound. He hasn't been shy about his continued desire to swing the bat, a longing that may have affected his pitching efforts during the 1999 season. After looking anything but impressive last year during spring training, Bong rededicated himself and started to live up to his tremendous promise. The velocity of his fastball increased to 90-91 mph early last year, and his changeup showed marked improvement. Bong's primary weakness has been his inability to throw a consistent curveball. He has worked on a variety of grips but has yet to find one he can use to throw strikes on a regular basis. The Braves still believe Bong is just scratching the surface regarding his long-term potential. He's slated to return to Myrtle Beach this year to continue his work on his curve and his overall approach with pitching coach Bruce Dal Canton.

Year	Club (League)	Class	W	L	ERA	G	GS	CG	SV	IP	H	R	ER	BB	SO
1998	Braves (GCL)	R	1	1	1.49	11	10	0	0	48	31	9	8	14	56
1999	Macon (SAL)	A	6	5	3.98	26	20	0	1	108	111	61	48	50	100
2000	Macon (SAL)	A	7	7	4.23	20	19	0	0	112	119	65	53	45	90
	Myrtle Beach (Car)	A	3	1	2.18	7	6	0	0	41	33	14	10	7	37
MINOR LEAGUE TOTALS			17	14	3.44	64	55	0	1	311	294	149	119	116	283

29. Chris Waters, rhp

Born: August 17, 1980. **Ht.:** 6-0. **Wt.:** 175. **Bats:** L. **Throws:** L. **School:** South Florida CC. **Career Transactions:** Selected by Braves in fifth round of 2000 draft; signed June 6, 2000.

Waters is yet another pitcher from last year's draft class who attracted rave reviews from the entire organization. He pitched well throughout the Appalachian League season and displayed an easy, fluid motion. Waters then touched 91 mph with his average fastball during the last two weeks of instructional league. He has two other pitches—a changeup and an improving curveball—that are no worse than average. After working intensely with minor league pitching coordinator Rick Adair in Florida, Waters turned his pickoff move into an asset. He must improve his overall strength, which will allow him to go longer in games and reduce his chances for injury. Waters may be one of the more unheralded members of the Macon rotation this spring, but the Braves feel his long-term potential is nearly as promising as that of the pitchers they drafted ahead of him.

Year	Club (League)	Class	W	L	ERA	G	GS	CG	SV	IP	H	R	ER	BB	SO
2000	Danville (Appy)	R	5	3	3.91	13	13	1	0	69	64	33	30	29	73
MINOR LEAGUE TOTALS			5	3	3.91	13	13	1	0	69	64	33	30	29	73

30. Damien Jones, of

Born: July 10, 1979. **Ht.:** 6-2. **Wt.:** 200. **Bats:** L. **Throws:** L. **School:** Vigor HS, Prichard, Ala. **Career Transactions:** Selected by Braves in fifth round of 1998 draft; signed June 5, 1998.

No one in the Atlanta farm system was rawer than Jones two years ago. He was an exceptional all-around athlete whose greatest accomplishments to that point had come on the gridiron, so much so that he had a full scholarship to play wide receiver and cornerback at the University of Alabama awaiting him. Now Jones could be on the verge of a breakout season. He combined a natural aggressiveness with plus speed to emerge as one of the more exciting players in the South Atlantic League last year. His power has been minimal during his first three seasons, but several scouts believe he could hit more than 20 homers a season once he learns how to employ his natural strength into his swing. Placed in center field last season at Macon, his defense improved markedly. His knowledge of the strike zone needs to continue to get better, as does his ability to read the ball off the bat and take the right routes on defense. It wouldn't be surprising if Jones becomes a bigger name after he spends 2001 at Myrtle Beach.

Year	Club (League)	Class	AVG	G	AB	R	H	2B	3B	HR	RBI	BB	SO	SB
1998	Braves (GCL)	R	.271	50	192	25	52	4	1	1	7	10	48	15
1999	Danville (Appy)	R	.296	68	284	56	84	6	5	1	29	37	58	27
2000	Macon (SAL)	A	.268	126	503	82	135	18	4	1	33	63	98	44
MINOR LEAGUE TOTALS			.277	244	979	163	271	28	10	3	69	110	204	86

Baltimore
Orioles

TOP 30 PROSPECTS

1. Keith Reed, of
2. Richard Stahl, lhp
3. Ed Rogers, ss
4. Ntema Ndungidi, of
5. Luis Rivera, rhp
6. Beau Hale, rhp
7. Matt Riley, lhp
8. Ryan Kohlmeier, rhp
9. Octavio Martinez, c
10. Brian Roberts, ss
11. Jay Gibbons, 1b/of
12. Tim Raines Jr., of
13. Tripper Johnson, 3b
14. Larry Bigbie, of
15. Sean Douglass, rhp
16. Darnell McDonald, of
17. Ivanon Coffie, ss/3b
18. John Parrish, lhp
19. Erik Bedard, lhp
20. Josh Towers, rhp
21. Juan Guzman, rhp
22. Juan Figueroa, rhp
23. Lesli Brea, rhp
24. Mike Paradis, rhp
25. Willie Harris, 2b/of
26. Steve Bechler, rhp
27. John Stephens, rhp
28. Fernando Lunar, c
29. Jorge Julio, rhp
30. Doug Gredvig, 1b

By Will Lingo

Knocking the Orioles is a popular sport these days, and Lord knows they've provided critics plenty of opportunities, at least at the big league level.

But the organization actually is doing a good job of adding talent to its once-barren farm system. The system still lacks impact players who are ready to contribute in the major leagues right away, but Orioles fans at least can see players in the pipeline who could turn things around.

In the short term, though, the major league team is a mess. Most of the under-achieving veterans are gone now, traded at midseason when the front office saw another high-priced amalgamation going nowhere. It was the first time the franchise had three straight losing seasons since 1986-88.

The players the Orioles got in all those trades are of questionable value. Of those still in the minor leagues, only righthander Luis Rivera figures into the team's top 20 prospects. The rest of the new players project to play complementary roles in the big leagues, at best.

The most important aspect of the trades, though, may have been the club's recognition it had to scrap the blueprint it was using and try a new plan that includes younger players.

While the organization's prospect list includes just one or two players who might be ready to contribute in Baltimore on Opening Day 2001, prospects can expect to find more opportunities in the big leagues when they're ready. In recent years, the Orioles have been notorious for finding old, expensive veterans to fill holes, blocking youngsters who were ready for major league trials.

Opportunity should be abundant in the coming years. When Opening Day 2001 rolls around, longtime ace Mike Mussina will be pitching in New York. Brady Anderson will be 37, Albert Belle 34 and Cal Ripken 40. Beyond that, the major league team is a largely anonymous bunch.

For the Orioles to contend again, they'll need significant contributions from prospects in the coming years. The team undoubtedly will call on free agents to fill the gaps and prevent a total rebuilding project. For Baltimore to get out of its toxic tailspin, though, owner Peter Angelos and his braintrust will have to show patience, continue to develop young players and give them a chance to succeed.

Organization Overview

General manager: Syd Thrift. **Farm director:** Don Buford. **Scouting director:** Tony DeMacio.

2000 PERFORMANCE

Class	Team	League	W	L	Pct.	Finish*	Manager
Majors	Baltimore	American	74	88	.457	11th (14)	Mike Hargrove
Triple-A	Rochester Red Wings	International	65	79	.451	11th (14)	Marv Foley
Double-A	Bowie Baysox	Eastern	65	77	.458	10th (12)	Andy Etchebarren
High A	Frederick Keys	Carolina	66	71	.482	5th (8)	Dave Machemer
Low A	Delmarva Shorebirds	South Atlantic	74	62	.544	3rd (14)	Joe Ferguson
Rookie	Bluefield Orioles	Appalachian	31	32	.492	7th (10)	Duffy Dyer
Rookie	Sarasota Orioles	Gulf Coast	25	31	.446	9th (13)	Jesus Alfaro
OVERALL 2000 MINOR LEAGUE RECORD			326	352	.481	22nd (30)	

*Finish in overall standings (No. of teams in league).

ORGANIZATION LEADERS

BATTING

*AVG	Rick Short, Bowie/Rochester	.324
R	Willie Harris, Delmarva	106
H	Jose Herrera, Rochester	163
TB	**Rick Short**, Bowie/Rochester	229
2B	**Rick Short**, Bowie/Rochester	40
3B	Wayne Kirby, Rochester	11
HR	David Gibraltar, Bowie	19
	Keith Reed, Delmarva/Frederick	19
RBI	Keith Reed, Delmarva/Frederick	90
BB	Rich Paz, Frederick/Bowie	98
SO	Ntema Ndunigidi, Frederick/Bowie	116
SB	Tim Raines Jr., Frederick	81

PITCHING

W	Jay Spurgeon, Frederick/Bowie	13
L	Steve Bechler, Frederick	12
#ERA	Billy Whitecotton, Blue./Del./Frederick	3.02
G	Two tied at	53
CG	Josh Towers, Rochester	5
SV	Aaron Rakers, Frederick/Bowie	16
IP	Steve Bechler, Frederick	162
BB	**Mike Paradis**, Delmarva/Frederick	73
SO	Matt Achilles, Frederick	137
	Steve Bechler, Frederick	137

*Minimum 250 at-bats. #Minimum 75 innings.

TOP PROSPECTS OF THE DECADE

1991	Arthur Rhodes, lhp
1992	Arthur Rhodes, lhp
1993	Brad Pennington, lhp
1994	Jeffrey Hammonds, of
1995	Armando Benitez, rhp
1996	Rocky Coppinger, rhp
1997	Nerio Rodriguez, rhp
1998	Ryan Minor, 3b
1999	Matt Riley, lhp
2000	Matt Riley, lhp

TOP DRAFT PICKS OF THE DECADE

1991	Mark Smith, of
1992	Jeffrey Hammonds, of
1993	Jay Powell, rhp
1994	Tommy Davis, 1b (2)
1995	Alvie Shepherd, rhp
1996	Brian Falkenborg, rhp (2)
1997	Jayson Werth, c
1998	Rick Elder, 1b-of
1999	Mike Paradis, rhp
2000	Beau Hale, rhp

Short   **Paradis**

BEST TOOLS

Best Hitter for Average	Octavio Martinez
Best Power Hitter	Doug Gredvig
Fastest Baserunner	Tim Raines Jr.
Best Fastball	Richard Stahl
Best Breaking Ball	Sean Douglass
Best Control	Josh Towers
Best Defensive Catcher	Fernando Lunar
Best Defensive Infielder	Ed Rogers
Best Infield Arm	Ed Rogers
Best Defensive Outfielder	Tim Raines Jr.
Best Outfield Arm	Keith Reed

PROJECTED 2004 LINEUP

Catcher	Octavio Martinez
First Base	Chris Richard
Second Base	Brian Roberts
Third Base	Ivanon Coffie
Shortstop	Ed Rogers
Left Field	Ntema Ndungidi
Center Field	Luis Matos
Right Field	Keith Reed
Designated Hitter	Tripper Johnson
No. 1 Starter	Richard Stahl
No. 2 Starter	Beau Hale
No. 3 Starter	Sidney Ponson
No. 4 Starter	Luis Rivera
No. 5 Starter	Sean Douglass
Closer	Ryan Kohlmeier

ALL-TIME LARGEST BONUSES

Beau Hale, 2000	$2,250,000
Darnell McDonald, 1997	1,900,000
Richard Stahl, 1999	1,795,000
Mike Paradis, 1999	1,700,000
Larry Bigbie, 1999	1,200,000

DraftAnalysis

2000 Draft

Best Pro Debut: 3B Tripper Johnson (1) led Baltimore's Rookie-level Gulf Coast League club with a .306 average and 33 RBIs.

Best Athlete: B.J. Littleton (7) is a center fielder built along the lines of Kenny Lofton. He's a switch-hitter with speed.

Best Hitter: Johnson. He has been compared to Chipper Jones, who, by the way, batted just .229 in his professional debut in the GCL. That doesn't mean Johnson will eclipse Jones, but he's off to a nice start.

Best Raw Power: Johnson was one of the top high school sluggers available in the draft. For now, 1B Doug Gredvig (5) is stronger, but Johnson will catch up to him in time.

Fastest Runner: Littleton, who swiped 12 bases in 14 attempts at Rookie-level Bluefield.

Best Defensive Player: C Tommy Arko (3) has a strong arm and solid receiving skills. Baltimore also likes the defensive potential of another catcher, Mike Russell (9).

Best Fastball: RHP **Beau Hale** (1) spent all summer negotiating a $2.25 million bonus, so he has yet to throw a pitch in a game for the Orioles. At Texas, he consistently threw 92-95 mph.

Most Intriguing Background: 1B Andy Hargrove (31) is the son of Orioles manager Mike. Baltimore drafted two other sons of former major leaguers in RHP Jayme Sperring (8, son of Rob) and 3B Brandon Fahey (32, son of Bill). Sperring was the only one of the three to sign. 3B Shayne Ridley's

(19) twin brother Jeremy was taken 15 rounds later by the Blue Jays, who employ their father Jim as assistant director of Canadian scouting.

Closest To The Majors: Hale's showing in instructional league and spring training will determine where he makes his debut, but he's on the fast track, especially since Mike Mussina signed with the Yankees.

JIM VASALOUA

Hale

Best Late-Round Pick: The Orioles are high on two of their lower choices. Kris Wilken (12) has the versatility to play catcher, first or third base, and they like the way he swings the bat. RHP Ryan Keefer (13) didn't get a lot of attention as a Pennsylvania high schooler, but his fastball has jumped from 87-88 to 91 mph.

The One Who Got Away: Though he was drafted 17 rounds after RHP Jon Skaggs (4), who returned for his senior season at Rice, Baltimore feels worse about not landing high school LHP Fraser Dizard (21). Dizard, who's raw but has a 92-94 mph fastball, is at Southern California.

Assessment: Baltimore signed just 19 players out of the draft and didn't get to see its top pick take the field. There's not a whole lot about this crop to get excited about yet.

1999 Draft

The Orioles had seven first-round picks, and while they're optimistic, they don't have a can't-miss player in the bunch. OF Keith Reed (1) and LHP Richard Stahl (1) are the system's two best prospects, and C Octavio Marinez (10) had a breakout 2000 season.   **Grade: C**

1998 Draft

Baltimore may have blown both of its first-rounders, as OF Rick Elder can't stay healthy and OF Mamon Tucker can't hit, and both its second-rounders. OF Tim Raines Jr. (6) has name value and speed, but he needs to round out his game.   **Grade: C–**

1997 Draft

With three first-rounders, the Orioles took C Jayson Werth, since traded to the Blue Jays, and OFs Darnell McDonald and Ntema Ndungidi. They fared better with LHP Matt Riley (3, draft-and-follow) and 2B Jerry Hairston (11).   **Grade: B**

1996 Draft

Baltimore's top pick, RHP Brian Falkenborg (2), has had arm problems, and the club failed to sign three future first-rounders: RHPs Mike MacDougal (22), Jay Gehrke (24) and Ben Christensen (40). OF Luis Matos (10), RHP Ryan Kohlmeier (14) and LHP John Parrish (25) have promise.   **Grade: C**

Note: Draft analysis prepared by Jim Callis. Numbers in parentheses indicate draft rounds.

. . . The organization thinks Reed can become a run producer in the mold of Joe Carter.

Keith Reed of

Born: Oct. 8, 1978.
Ht.: 6-4. **Wt.:** 215.
Bats: R. **Throws:** R.
School: Providence College.
Career Transactions: Selected by Orioles in first round (23rd overall) of 1999 draft; signed June 19, 1999.

Reed's career path has been as improbable as it has been steep. Growing up in Massachusetts he spent most of his athletic energy on basketball, but Providence College recruited him for baseball. He made steady improvement there but remained a virtual unknown heading into his junior season. Even after he hit .398-17-79, winning Big East Conference player-of-the-year honors and leading the Friars to an NCAA regional bid in the program's last season, people took notice of his all-around skills. The Orioles made him the 23rd overall pick in the 1999 draft, but even they have been pleased with his adjustment to pro ball, considering his relative inexperience.

Reed elicits a common response in the organization: "There's nothing he can't do." He has true five-tool potential, and his arm may be his best tool. The most intriguing part of his package, though, is his power, which generates more line drives now but should increase as he matures. Even still, he had 19 home runs in 2000. Given how raw he was supposed to be, he shows a good approach at the plate and should cut down on his strikeouts as he moves up. And let's not forget his speed, which was rated among the best in his draft class. He uses his quickness well, getting caught only four times in 33 basestealing attempts last season. The organization thinks he can be a run producer in the mold of Joe Carter, with a better arm and better speed. The main thing Reed needs is experience. Because he grew up in a cold-weather region, he hasn't played as much baseball as many players his age. Some in the organization think he needs to improve his concentration, to be in the game mentally on every pitch. Others say Reed's concentration is fine, and that he's just one of those players who makes everything look easy.

As surprising as Reed's early success has been, the organization still plans a patient approach. As he did by going back to Class A Delmarva to start the 2000 season, he'll probably go back to high Class A Frederick to start 2001. He's on track for a big league callup in 2002 and a chance for a full-time job in 2003.

Year	Club (League)	Class	AVG	G	AB	R	H	2B	3B	HR	RBI	BB	SO	SB
1999	Bluefield (Appy)	R	.188	4	16	2	3	0	0	0	0	1	3	0
	Delmarva (SAL)	A	.258	61	240	36	62	14	3	4	25	22	53	3
2000	Delmarva (SAL)	A	.290	70	269	43	78	16	1	11	59	25	56	20
	Frederick (Car)	A	.235	65	243	33	57	10	1	8	31	21	58	9
MINOR LEAGUE TOTALS			.260	200	768	114	200	40	5	23	115	69	170	32

WAGNER PHOTOGRAPHY

2. Richard Stahl, lhp

Born: April 11, 1981. **Ht.:** 6-7. **Wt.:** 185. **Bats:** R. **Throws:** L. **School:** Newton HS, Covington, Ga. **Career Transactions:** Selected by Orioles in first round (18th overall) of 1999 draft; signed Aug. 31, 1999.

Stahl's $1.795 million bonus was the largest of any player from the Orioles' big 1999 draft haul. He signed on the day he was to begin classes at Georgia Tech and didn't make his professional debut until last season. He was limited by back trouble, but that's a function of his continuing growth and isn't considered a long-term problem. Stahl has the best arm in the organization and the package of a true No. 1 starter, with a loose, quick delivery and a fastball that gets up to 96 mph. He's big and rangy, and his delivery makes batters feel as though he's right on top of them. He's a good athlete who moves well for a guy his size and could approach Randy Johnson stature by the time he reaches the big leagues. It's a simple question of gaining maturity, with his body, his approach to pitching and his adjustment to the grind of professional baseball. He has the makings of a great curveball but needs to become consistent with it. Stahl has the arm and the athletic ability to advance quickly once everything clicks. That process will continue in 2001 at Frederick.

Year	Club (League)	Class	W	L	ERA	G	GS	CG	SV	IP	H	R	ER	BB	SO
2000	Delmarva (SAL)	A	5	6	3.34	20	20	0	0	89	97	47	33	51	83
MINOR LEAGUE TOTALS			5	6	3.34	20	20	0	0	89	97	47	33	51	83

3. Ed Rogers, ss

Born: Aug. 10, 1981. **Ht.:** 6-1. **Wt.:** 165. **Bats:** R. **Throws:** R. **Career Transactions:** Signed out of Dominican Republic by Orioles, Nov. 7, 1997.

Even the Orioles were stunned by Rogers' emergence as a prospect. He drew a bit of attention in instructional league after the 1998 and '99 seasons, but now he looks like the shortstop of the future. Rogers has the potential to have the offense/defense package of the best modern shortstops. He has pure shortstop tools, with a great arm, plus range and silky actions. Unlike many young shortstops with good tools, he's steady rather than flashy, with little wasted motion. With his slender frame, Rogers needs to add strength to become a bigger offensive threat and hold up to the rigors of a long season. He missed time with a broken finger in 2000. He has the potential to hit .300 with alley power if he refines his approach and adds strength. While the Orioles' comparisons to Derek Jeter and Nomar Garciaparra are premature, Rogers does present an exciting package. He's likely to continue on the fast track by opening the season at Double-A Bowie.

Year	Club (League)	Class	AVG	G	AB	R	H	2B	3B	HR	RBI	BB	SO	SB
1998	Orioles (DSL)	R	.289	58	194	33	56	9	2	2	27	26	29	8
1999	Orioles (GCL)	R	.288	53	177	34	51	5	1	1	19	23	22	20
2000	Delmarva (SAL)	A	.274	80	332	46	91	14	5	5	42	22	63	27
	Bowie (EL)	AA	.286	13	49	4	14	3	0	1	8	3	15	1
MINOR LEAGUE TOTALS			.282	204	752	117	212	31	8	9	96	74	129	56

4. Ntema Ndungidi, of

Born: March 15, 1979. **Ht.:** 6-2. **Wt.:** 199. **Bats:** L. **Throws:** R. **School:** Edouard Montpetit HS, Montreal. **Career Transactions:** Selected by Orioles in first round (36th overall) of 1997 draft; signed June 30, 1997 . . . Placed on disqualified list, Nov. 20, 2000.

Ndungidi was born in Zaire (now known as Congo) and moved with his family to Montreal when he was 3. While his high school in Montreal didn't have a baseball team, he played for the Academy of Baseball select team, made up of Canada's best amateurs. A classic projection draft pick, Ndungidi's package is starting to come together as he gets repetitions and gets stronger. He should grow to have 25-home run power, and he has exciting speed under way with a long, loping stride. He's a 60-65 runner (on the 20-to-80 scouting scale) from home to first, and a 70 runner from first to third. Ndungidi looked overmatched in Double-A and still needs a lot of at-bats against quality pitching. He's still raw in many ways, and his arm will limit him to left field. Ndungidi was scheduled to return to Bowie to start 2001, but his bizarre behavior in the Arizona Fall League landed him on the restricted list in the offseason. He left the Mesa Solar Sox with less than two weeks left in the season after attempting to take infield in street clothes, talking to his locker and yelling at his teammates. He also was arrested twice in two days, charged with possession of marijuana and criminal trespass (both misdemeanors) and spent time in an Arizona psychiatric facility.

Year	Club (League)	Class	AVG	G	AB	R	H	2B	3B	HR	RBI	BB	SO	SB
1997	Orioles (GCL)	R	.185	18	54	10	10	2	1	2	7	12	15	4
1998	Bluefield (Appy)	R	.295	59	210	26	62	10	5	7	35	35	52	6
	Frederick (Car)	A	.000	1	2	0	0	0	0	0	0	0	1	0
1999	Delmarva (SAL)	A	.194	64	217	33	42	8	2	0	24	49	54	18
	Frederick (Car)	A	.266	60	192	40	51	10	3	0	18	39	43	4
2000	Frederick (Car)	A	.284	90	313	53	89	16	4	10	59	60	83	16
	Bowie (EL)	AA	.235	41	136	17	32	6	0	3	14	25	33	2
MINOR LEAGUE TOTALS			.254	333	1124	179	286	52	15	22	157	220	281	50

5. Luis Rivera, rhp

Born: June 21, 1978. **Ht.:** 6-3. **Wt.:** 163. **Bats:** R. **Throws:** R. **Career Transactions:** Signed out of Mexico by Braves, Feb. 18, 1995 . . . Loaned by Braves to Mexico City Tigers (Mexican), May 4-Oct. 18, 1995 . . . Traded by Braves with OF Trenidad Hubbard and C Fernando Lunar to Orioles for OF B.J. Surhoff and RHP Gabe Molina, July 31, 2000.

Rivera was the best prospect the Orioles brought in during their mid-season housecleaning. He was the top prospect in the Rookie-level Appalachian League in 1997 but has battled injury problems ever since. He has dominant stuff and one of the hardest fastballs in the minors, getting it up to 98 mph with good movement. He has a loose, mechanically sound delivery and an aggressive approach. He also has the makings of a good breaking ball, alternately described as a curve or a slider. The Orioles don't know what to think about Rivera because they haven't seen him pitch much. He worked just eight innings after the trade before getting shut down with a tired arm. Persistent blisters on his pitching hand have also been a problem, though he will be ready for spring training. The club is taking a cautious approach, with good reason. Though Rivera has been bothered by injuries, none has been serious yet. If he's really sound, he could contribute in Baltimore in 2001.

Year	Club (League)	Class	W	L	ERA	G	GS	CG	SV	IP	H	R	ER	BB	SO
1996	Braves (GCL)	R	1	1	2.59	8	6	0	0	24	18	9	7	7	26
1997	Danville (Appy)	R	3	1	2.41	9	9	0	0	41	28	15	11	17	57
	Macon (SAL)	A	2	0	1.29	4	4	0	0	21	13	4	3	7	27
1998	Macon (SAL)	A	5	5	3.98	20	20	0	0	93	78	53	41	41	118
1999	Myrtle Beach (Car)	A	0	2	3.11	25	13	0	0	67	45	25	23	23	81
2000	Atlanta (NL)	MAJ	1	0	1.35	5	0	0	0	7	4	1	1	5	5
	Richmond (IL)	AAA	0	2	8.06	8	7	0	0	22	29	20	20	18	12
	Braves (GCL)	R	0	0	0.00	3	3	0	0	4	2	0	0	1	2
	Rochester (IL)	AAA	0	1	3.38	3	3	0	0	8	11	5	3	5	4
	Baltimore (AL)	MAJ	0	0	0.00	1	0	0	0	1	1	0	0	1	0
MAJOR LEAGUE TOTALS			1	0	1.23	6	0	0	0	7	5	1	1	6	5
MINOR LEAGUE TOTALS			11	12	3.47	80	65	0	0	280	224	131	108	119	327

6. Beau Hale, rhp

Born: Dec. 1, 1978. **Ht.:** 6-1. **Wt.:** 185. **Bats:** R. **Throws:** R. **School:** University of Texas. **Career Transactions:** Selected by Orioles in first round (14th overall) of 2000 draft; signed Aug. 18, 2000.

In spite of mediocre numbers in his first two years at Texas, Hale was in scouts' sights after ranking as the No. 9 prospect in the Cape Cod League and pitching well in the NBC World Series in the summer of 1999. He built on that with a 12-6, 3.10 season as the Longhorns' Friday starter, throwing a no-hitter and leading them back to the College World Series for the first time since 1993. Hale is a bulldog with great makeup and a great arm. His fastball tops out at 97 mph, and he pitches comfortably at 92-94. He has a hard slider that could be a plus pitch. He has a durable arm and always has his game face on. The Orioles have to hope Hale's durability in college doesn't translate into arm problems as a professional. He piled up some high pitch counts in his junior season and ranked second in NCAA Division I with 145 innings. He's essentially a two-pitch pitcher now, which could foretell a conversion to closer. Assuming Hale's track record in college carries over to pro ball, he projects as a No. 2 or 3 starter who will be an innings-eater. He'll probably start his career at Frederick after holding out last summer for a $2.25 million bonus, largest in club history.

Year	Club (League)	Class	W	L	ERA	G	GS	CG	SV	IP	H	R	ER	BB	SO
2000			Did Not Play—Signed 2001 Contract												

7. Matt Riley, lhp

Born: Aug. 2, 1979. **Ht.:** 6-1. **Wt.:** 205. **Bats:** L. **Throws:** L. **School:** Sacramento (Calif.) CC. **Career Transactions:** Selected by Orioles in third round of 1997 draft; signed May 28, 1998.

You'd be hard-pressed to find anyone who had a worse year in 2000 than Riley. Invited to big league spring training, he showed his immaturity by arriving late for workouts and drawing the ire of manager Mike Hargrove. Sent back to the minors, he pitched ineffectively before arm trouble ended his season. He had Tommy John surgery in September. When healthy, Riley has three above-average pitches and is the organization's only true premium prospect. His fastball tops out in the mid-90s, and he has a big-breaking curveball and deceptive changeup. He also has an aggressive approach. While Tommy John surgery doesn't carry the stigma it used to, it's still a significant bump in a pitcher's career. The Orioles hope he can return to action by midseason, though that may be optimistic. If he can, he'll get another big league shot in 2002.

Year	Club (League)	Class	W	L	ERA	G	GS	CG	SV	IP	H	R	ER	BB	SO
1998	Delmarva (SAL)	A	5	4	1.19	16	14	0	0	83	42	19	11	44	136
1999	Frederick (Car)	A	3	2	2.61	8	8	0	0	52	34	19	15	14	58
	Bowie (EL)	AA	10	6	3.22	20	20	3	0	126	113	53	45	42	131
	Baltimore (AL)	MAJ	0	0	7.36	3	3	0	0	11	17	9	9	13	6
2000	Rochester (IL)	AAA	0	2	14.14	2	2	0	0	7	15	12	11	4	8
	Bowie (EL)	AA	5	7	6.08	19	14	2	1	74	74	56	50	49	66
MAJOR LEAGUE TOTALS			0	0	7.36	3	3	0	0	11	17	9	9	13	6
MINOR LEAGUE TOTALS			23	21	3.48	65	58	5	1	341	278	159	132	153	399

8. Ryan Kohlmeier, rhp

Born: June 25, 1977. **Ht.:** 6-2. **Wt.:** 195. **Bats:** R. **Throws:** R. **School:** Butler County (Kan.) CC. **Career Transactions:** Selected by Orioles in 14th round of 1996 draft; signed Aug. 16, 1996.

Kohlmeier was slated to be a set-up guy in the Triple-A Rochester bullpen in 2000, but he became the closer and pitched well enough to get an audition in Baltimore, where he shocked everyone by saving 13 games. He has a low-90s fastball and a slider that improved significantly after he learned a new grip from Rochester teammate Mike Grace. His fastball has great natural sink. What puts him over the top is his make-up. He wants the ball in any situation and isn't afraid to challenge hitters, pitching aggressively in the strike zone. Kohlmeier gets the most of his ability and is probably at his ceiling. He has to be fine with his pitches because he isn't overpowering. He might be better suited to a set-up role but will go into the 2001 season as the Orioles' closer. Given the strides he made in 2000, it might be a mistake to underestimate him.

Year	Club (League)	Class	W	L	ERA	G	GS	CG	SV	IP	H	R	ER	BB	SO
1997	Delmarva (SAL)	A	2	2	2.65	50	0	0	24	75	48	22	22	17	99
	Bowie (EL)	AA	0	0	0.00	2	0	0	1	3	0	0	0	2	5
1998	Bowie (EL)	AA	4	4	6.12	42	0	0	7	50	52	37	34	16	56
	Frederick (Car)	A	1	2	7.45	9	0	0	5	10	10	9	8	3	15
1999	Bowie (EL)	AA	3	7	3.16	55	0	0	23	63	44	23	22	29	78
2000	Rochester (IL)	AAA	1	4	2.51	37	0	0	10	47	33	14	13	16	49
	Baltimore (AL)	MAJ	0	1	2.39	25	0	0	13	26	30	9	7	15	17
MAJOR LEAGUE TOTALS			0	1	2.39	25	0	0	13	26	30	9	7	15	17
MINOR LEAGUE TOTALS			11	19	3.62	195	0	0	70	246	187	105	99	83	302

9. Octavio Martinez, c

Born: July 30, 1979. **Ht.:** 6-0. **Wt.:** 195. **Bats:** R. **Throws:** R. **School:** Bakersfield (Calif.) JC. **Career Transactions:** Selected by Orioles in 10th round of 1999 draft; signed June 4, 1999.

Though he was a junior college all-American, Martinez was an unknown when he was drafted but should get attention after his Appalachian League MVP season. Defense was Martinez' calling card coming into the season, but his offense got the attention. He's a strong, heady, hard-working player who's considered a throwback by the organization. He has good, quick feet behind the plate and a strong, accurate arm. While he won't always hit as he did in 2000, he does have good command of the strike zone and a chance to be a .300 hitter with decent power. Martinez' catching skills should carry him to the big leagues, but his ability to hit quality pitching as he moves up will determine what kind of impact he has. The Orioles are concerned about lingering shoulder soreness that could require further treatment. Martinez should return to Frederick in 2001.

Year	Club (League)	Class	AVG	G	AB	R	H	2B	3B	HR	RBI	BB	SO	SB
1999	Orioles (GCL)	R	.237	36	114	11	27	8	1	0	15	4	11	8
2000	Bluefield (Appy)	R	.387	49	181	45	70	14	1	7	46	19	21	0
	Frederick (Car)	A	.375	2	8	0	3	0	0	0	1	0	0	0
MINOR LEAGUE TOTALS			.330	87	303	56	100	22	2	7	62	23	32	8

10. Brian Roberts, ss

RODGER WOOD

Born: Oct. 9, 1977. **Ht.:** 5-9. **Wt.:** 170. **Bats:** B. **Throws:** R. **School:** University of South Carolina. **Career Transactions:** Selected by Orioles in first round (50th overall) of 1999 draft; signed July 14, 1999.

Roberts missed the first half of the 2000 season after having bone chips removed from his elbow, then felt a twinge in the elbow while playing in the Arizona Fall League, so the Orioles shut him down for the year. The son of former North Carolina coach Mike Roberts, he epitomizes the term "baseball player." He has great instincts for the game and a strong desire to reach the big leagues. His tools aren't overwhelming, but the package is greater than the sum of its parts. He's smooth in the field and has a good approach to hitting. The elbow injury raises questions about Roberts' arm, which might have been his best tool. He likely was destined to move to second base anyway. The Orioles compare Roberts to Mike Bordick, but he needs to stay healthy and get more at-bats to see if that comparison is apt. Assuming his elbow is sound, he'll get the chance to move up to Double-A in the spring.

Year	Club (League)	Class	AVG	G	AB	R	H	2B	3B	HR	RBI	BB	SO	SB
1999	Delmarva (SAL)	A	.240	47	167	22	40	12	1	0	21	27	42	17
2000	Frederick (Car)	A	.301	48	163	27	49	6	3	0	16	27	24	13
	Orioles (GCL)	R	.310	9	29	8	9	1	2	1	3	7	4	7
MINOR LEAGUE TOTALS			.273	104	359	57	98	19	6	1	40	61	70	37

11. Jay Gibbons, 1b/of

Born: March 2, 1977. **Ht.:** 6-0. **Wt.:** 200. **Bats:** L. **Throws:** L. **School:** Cal State Los Angeles. **Career Transactions:** Selected by Blue Jays in 14th round of 1998 draft; signed June 4, 1998 . . . Selected by Orioles from Blue Jays in Rule 5 major league draft, Dec. 11, 2000.

A major league Rule 5 draft pick from the Blue Jays, Gibbons must stick with the Orioles throughout 2001 or be offered back. Stocky and strong, he looks like a beer-league hitter, but he drinks no alcohol and was a vegetarian until 2000, when he incorporated lean chicken breasts into his diet to help keep his strength up over the course of the season. Gibbons' short, level, quick swing keeps him out of long slumps and helps him hold his own against lefthanders, whom he hit .329 against last year. He has good power and plate discipline, and showed a surprisingly strong arm in the outfield. He keeps long hours in the gym as well. Gibbons lacks the agility to play anything but first base, left field or DH, which were strong positions in Toronto. He was going to have to display 30-homer power to make the move to SkyDome, but his chances are better in Baltimore. As long as Gibbons continues to hit, he'll be given a chance to play. Whether the Orioles can hold onto him is uncertain.

Year	Club (League)	Class	AVG	G	AB	R	H	2B	3B	HR	RBI	BB	SO	SB
1998	Medicine Hat (Pio)	R	.397	73	290	66	115	29	1	19	98	37	25	2
1999	Hagerstown (SAL)	A	.305	71	292	53	89	20	2	16	69	32	56	3
	Dunedin (FSL)	A	.311	60	212	34	66	14	0	9	39	25	38	2
2000	Tennessee (SL)	AA	.321	132	474	85	152	38	1	19	75	61	67	3
MINOR LEAGUE TOTALS			.333	336	1268	238	422	101	4	63	281	155	186	10

12. Tim Raines Jr., of

Born: Aug. 31, 1979. **Ht.:** 5-10. **Wt.:** 183. **Bats:** B. **Throws:** R. **School:** Seminole HS, Sanford, Fla. **Career Transactions:** Selected by Orioles in sixth round of 1998 draft; signed June 15, 1998.

You'd be hard-pressed to find better bloodlines than those of Raines, whose father had a career that may take him to the Hall of Fame. Tim Jr. actually didn't have a lot of polish coming out of high school, though, so he'll take a level-to-level progression through the organization. He set an organizational record with 81 stolen bases at Frederick in 2000, and that number could rise if he makes more consistent contact. He's strong, fast and athletic, and he can go get the ball in center field. He has an average and potentially plus arm. Raines actually shows a decent eye at the plate, but he doesn't put the bat on the ball enough. He's been switch-hitting for just a few years, and his lefthanded stroke needs a lot of work. Like so many players with outstanding tools, Raines only will make good use of them if he can hit consistently. Facing Double-A pitchers in 2001 will be a true challenge.

Year	Club (League)	Class	AVG	G	AB	R	H	2B	3B	HR	RBI	BB	SO	SB
1998	Orioles (GCL)	R	.244	56	197	40	48	7	4	1	13	30	53	37
1999	Delmarva (SAL)	A	.248	117	415	80	103	24	8	2	49	71	130	49
2000	Frederick (Car)	A	.236	127	457	89	108	21	3	2	36	67	106	81
MINOR LEAGUE TOTALS			.242	300	1069	209	259	52	15	5	98	168	289	167

13. Tripper Johnson, 3b

Born: April 28, 1982. **Ht.:** 6-1. **Wt.:** 195. **Bats:** R. **Throws:** R. **School:** Newport HS, Bellevue, Wash. **Career Transactions:** Selected by Orioles in first round (32nd overall) of 2000 draft; signed June 26, 2000.

Regarded as the top draft prospect in Washington in 2000, Johnson was one of the few legitimate high school power hitters available. He showed good athleticism in his professional debut—he also excelled in football and basketball in high school—and the Orioles see him as a prototypical third baseman. He's built like Ken Caminiti and is a gamer, a quiet grinder who comes to the park and goes about his business every day. On offense he covers the plate well and has a good idea of the strike zone, and he'll hit for power. He should develop into an average defensive player, but that will require work. It was the focus of his time in instructional league, where he worked on getting his glove in better fielding position and improving the accuracy of his throws. He'll make the jump to full-season ball at Delmarva.

Year	Club (League)	Class	AVG	G	AB	R	H	2B	3B	HR	RBI	BB	SO	SB
2000	Orioles (GCL)	R	.306	48	180	22	55	5	3	2	33	13	38	7
MINOR LEAGUE TOTALS			.306	48	180	22	55	5	3	2	33	13	38	7

14. Larry Bigbie, of

Born: Nov. 4, 1977. **Ht.:** 6-4. **Wt.:** 190. **Bats:** L. **Throws:** L. **School:** Ball State University. **Career Transactions:** Selected by Orioles in first round (21st overall) of 1999 draft; signed June 17, 1999.

If you want to know how excited the Orioles are about Bigbie's potential, just check out a few of the names they throw out when discussing him: Will Clark (his swing), B.J. Surhoff (power potential), Andy Van Slyke (body). For those predictions to come true, Bigbie will have to add muscle to his athletic frame. He has great makeup and is a gifted natural hitter with a knack for getting the fat part of the bat on the ball. He should add power as he gets stronger. His tools are best suited for left field, though he has good pursuit speed for chasing fly balls. A hand injury ended his 2000 season early and kept him out of the Arizona Fall League, and the organization thinks he'll also hold up better with added bulk. He'll probably return to Double-A to start the season.

Year	Club (League)	Class	AVG	G	AB	R	H	2B	3B	HR	RBI	BB	SO	SB
1999	Bluefield (Appy)	R	.267	8	30	3	8	0	0	0	4	3	8	1
	Delmarva (SAL)	A	.279	43	165	18	46	7	3	2	27	29	42	3
2000	Frederick (Car)	A	.294	55	201	33	59	11	0	2	28	23	34	7
	Bowie (EL)	AA	.241	31	112	11	27	6	0	0	5	11	28	3
MINOR LEAGUE TOTALS			.276	137	508	65	140	24	3	4	64	66	112	14

15. Sean Douglass, rhp

Born: April 28, 1979. **Ht.:** 6-6. **Wt.:** 200. **Bats:** R. **Throws:** R. **School:** Antelope Valley HS, Lancaster, Calif. **Career Transactions:** Selected by Orioles in second round of 1997 draft; signed July 9, 1997.

Douglass is part of the corps of pitchers from which the Orioles hope to draw their future pitching staffs. He has proceeded quietly through the organization, and that's the kind of pitcher he projects as: a dependable, middle-of-the-rotation starter who won't get a lot of attention but can eat innings. He has the potential to have three solid major league pitches, including a 90 mph fastball with good sink. His breaking ball, an inconsistent slurve, needs refinement. He also has to establish consistency from inning to inning and start to start. Douglass will move up to Triple-A and could contribute in Baltimore sometime in 2001.

Year	Club (League)	Class	W	L	ERA	G	GS	CG	SV	IP	H	R	ER	BB	SO
1997	Orioles (GCL)	R	1	3	6.11	9	1	0	0	18	20	14	12	9	10
1998	Bluefield (Appy)	R	2	2	3.23	10	10	0	0	53	45	20	19	14	62
1999	Frederick (Car)	A	5	6	3.32	16	16	1	0	98	101	48	36	35	89
2000	Bowie (EL)	AA	9	8	4.03	27	27	1	0	161	155	79	72	55	118
MINOR LEAGUE TOTALS			17	19	3.80	62	54	2	0	329	321	161	139	113	279

16. Darnell McDonald, of

Born: Nov. 17, 1978. **Ht.:** 5-11. **Wt.:** 201. **Bats:** R. **Throws:** R. **School:** Cherry Creek HS, Englewood, Colo. **Career Transactions:** Selected by Orioles in first round (26th overall) of 1997 draft; signed Aug. 8, 1997.

McDonald was one of the premium athletes in the 1997 draft, but his reported bonus demands caused him to drop to the 26th pick. He was more of a football prospect in high school and was about to start his career as a running back at the University of Texas when the Orioles signed him for $1.9 million. They're still waiting for the investment to pay off. McDonald, whose brother Donzell is a Yankees prospect, has the same body type and athleticism as Jeffrey Hammonds, who also was an Orioles first-round pick. His potential power-speed combination remains intriguing, but he must control the strike zone better. All things considered, his 2000 performance was better than it looked. His mother died just before spring training and it took him a while to recover. He seems to have worked the football out of his body but is still bothered by nagging injuries. As people have said since McDonald was drafted, if he starts doing the little things he could have a breakout season.

Year	Club (League)	Class	AVG	G	AB	R	H	2B	3B	HR	RBI	BB	SO	SB
1998	Delmarva (SAL)	A	.261	134	528	87	138	24	5	6	44	33	117	35
	Frederick (Car)	A	.222	4	18	3	4	2	0	1	2	3	6	2
1999	Frederick (Car)	A	.266	130	507	81	135	23	5	6	73	61	92	26
2000	Bowie (EL)	AA	.242	116	459	59	111	13	5	6	43	29	87	11
MINOR LEAGUE TOTALS			.257	384	1512	230	388	62	15	19	162	126	302	74

17. Ivanon Coffie, ss/3b

Born: May 16, 1977. **Ht.:** 6-1. **Wt.:** 192. **Bats:** L. **Throws:** R. **Career Transactions:** Signed out of Netherlands Antilles by Orioles, July 28, 1995.

Coffie made it to the big leagues in 2000 after taking a step back to Bowie. The Orioles still are searching for the right position for him, as he has moved back and forth between short and third. He returned to short in 2000 but still played occasionally at the hot corner. His arm and power potential would seem to make him a good fit at third, but he hasn't hit enough to fit the profile there. He also seems more comfortable defensively at short. In the Arizona Fall League, coaches and managers ranked him the best third baseman in the league after he hit .282-2-26. As his AFL performance showed, Coffie has intriguing tools, but he needs to show more than flashes of putting them together.

Year	Club (League)	Class	AVG	G	AB	R	H	2B	3B	HR	RBI	BB	SO	SB
1996	Orioles (GCL)	R	.218	56	193	29	42	8	4	0	20	23	26	6
1997	Delmarva (SAL)	A	.275	90	305	41	84	14	5	3	48	23	45	19
1998	Frederick (Car)	A	.256	130	473	62	121	19	2	16	75	48	109	17
1999	Bowie (EL)	AA	.185	57	195	21	36	9	3	3	23	20	46	2
	Frederick (Car)	A	.283	73	276	35	78	18	4	11	53	28	62	7
2000	Bowie (EL)	AA	.267	87	341	49	91	21	3	9	44	36	53	1
	Baltimore (AL)	MAJ	.217	23	60	6	13	4	1	0	6	5	11	1
	Rochester (IL)	AAA	.218	21	78	4	17	2	1	0	10	2	21	0
MAJOR LEAGUE TOTALS			.217	23	60	6	13	4	1	0	6	5	11	1
MINOR LEAGUE TOTALS			.252	514	1861	241	469	91	22	42	273	180	362	52

18. John Parrish, lhp

Born: Nov. 26, 1977. **Ht.:** 5-11. **Wt.:** 181. **Bats:** L. **Throws:** L. **School:** McCaskey HS, Lancaster, Pa. **Career Transactions:** Selected by Orioles in 25th round of 1996 draft; signed June 7, 1996.

Parrish was a late-round find after an outstanding all-around athletic career in high school. He made it all the way to the big leagues in 2000, striking out the side against the Yankees in his first major league start, when he took a loss against Roger Clemens. Parrish has a strong arm for a lefthander, throwing in the low 90s, and has become a potential big leaguer because he has a full repertoire with three solid major league pitches, including a hard breaking ball. He has a quick, snappy arm with a delivery that's hard for batters to pick up, and he needs it to be effective. His command comes and goes, however, and he needs it to be effective. Parrish could make the big league bullpen if he doesn't go back to Triple-A.

Year	Club (League)	Class	W	L	ERA	G	GS	CG	SV	IP	H	R	ER	BB	SO
1996	Orioles (GCL)	R	2	0	1.86	11	0	0	2	19	13	5	4	11	33
	Bluefield (Appy)	R	2	1	2.70	8	0	0	1	13	11	6	4	9	18
1997	Delmarva (SAL)	A	3	3	3.84	23	10	0	1	73	69	39	31	32	76
	Bowie (EL)	AA	1	0	1.80	1	1	0	0	5	3	1	1	2	3
	Frederick (Car)	A	1	3	6.04	5	5	0	0	22	23	18	15	16	17
1998	Frederick (Car)	A	4	4	3.27	16	16	1	0	83	77	39	30	27	81

1999	Delmarva (SAL)	A	0	1	7.20	4	0	0	0	10	9	8	8	6	10
	Frederick (Car)	A	2	2	4.17	6	6	0	0	37	34	17	17	12	44
	Bowie (EL)	AA	0	2	4.04	12	10	0	0	56	49	28	25	43	42
2000	Bowie (EL)	AA	2	0	1.69	3	3	0	0	16	12	3	3	7	16
	Rochester (IL)	AAA	6	7	4.24	18	18	0	0	104	85	54	49	56	87
	Baltimore (AL)	MAJ	2	4	7.18	8	8	0	0	36	40	32	29	35	28
MAJOR LEAGUE TOTALS			2	4	7.18	8	8	0	0	36	40	32	29	35	28
MINOR LEAGUE TOTALS			23	23	3.85	107	69	1	4	438	385	218	187	221	427

19. Erik Bedard, lhp

Born: March 6, 1979. **Ht.:** 6-1. **Wt.:** 180. **Bats:** L. **Throws:** L. **School:** Norwalk (Conn.) CC. **Career Transactions:** Selected by Orioles in sixth round of 1999 draft; signed June 8, 1999.

An Ontario native, Bedard started the 2000 season in the Delmarva bullpen but blossomed when he was put into the rotation in May. He was one of the big reasons the Shorebirds won the South Atlantic League title, keeping their playoff hopes alive in a late-season start and going 1-0, 2.70 in two postseason starts. He was nearly unhittable in the second half of the season. Bedard runs his fastball to 91 mph and complements it with a hard breaking ball and a developing changeup. He succeeds with an advanced idea of how to pitch and good command. He could jump to Bowie to start the season.

Year	Club (League)	Class	W	L	ERA	G	GS	CG	SV	IP	H	R	ER	BB	SO
1999	Orioles (GCL)	R	2	1	1.86	8	6	0	0	29	20	7	6	13	41
2000	Delmarva (SAL)	A	9	4	3.57	29	22	1	2	111	98	48	44	35	131
MINOR LEAGUE TOTALS			11	5	3.21	37	28	1	2	140	118	55	50	48	172

20. Josh Towers, rhp

Born: Feb. 26, 1977. **Ht.:** 6-1. **Wt.:** 165. **Bats:** R. **Throws:** R. **School:** Oxnard (Calif.) JC. **Career Transactions:** Selected by Orioles in 15th round of 1996 draft; signed June 20, 1996.

Towers would have made his major league debut in 2000 if not for a couple of nagging injuries, including a fall down stairs that hurt his shoulder. He's healthy and will be in the casting call for the big league rotation in the spring. His velocity is nothing special, though he has moved it from the high 80s to the low 90s to establish himself as a legitimate prospect. Towers knows how to go after hitters. He's aggressive in the strike zone, spots his fastball and changes speeds effectively. His command has been great, and it has to be. If he sharpens his breaking ball, he won't have to be perfect with every pitch. Because he's in the strike zone so much, he gives up a lot of hits and home runs, which could spell trouble in the big leagues.

Year	Club (League)	Class	W	L	ERA	G	GS	CG	SV	IP	H	R	ER	BB	SO
1996	Bluefield (Appy)	R	4	1	5.24	14	9	0	0	55	63	35	32	5	61
1997	Delmarva (SAL)	A	0	0	3.44	9	1	0	1	18	18	8	7	2	16
	Frederick (Car)	A	6	2	4.86	25	3	0	1	54	74	36	29	18	64
1998	Frederick (Car)	A	8	7	3.34	25	20	3	1	145	137	58	54	9	122
	Bowie (EL)	AA	2	1	3.50	5	2	0	0	18	20	9	7	4	7
1999	Bowie (EL)	AA	12	7	3.76	29	28	5	0	189	204	86	79	26	106
2000	Rochester (IL)	AAA	8	6	3.47	24	24	5	0	148	157	63	57	21	102
MINOR LEAGUE TOTALS			40	24	3.80	131	87	13	3	627	673	295	265	85	478

21. Juan Guzman, rhp

Born: March 4, 1978. **Ht.:** 6-2. **Wt.:** 184. **Bats:** R. **Throws:** R. **Career Transactions:** Signed out of Dominican Republic by Orioles, Dec. 16, 1994.

Guzman, who isn't related to the major league pitcher of the same name, would have a much brighter outlook if elbow trouble hadn't interrupted his season. Before that, he was on a meteoric rise after converting from catcher in 1998. When healthy, Guzman can throw up to 97 mph with an improving slider and good changeup. He also has surprisingly good command for his level of experience. He was dominant at Frederick, earning a quick promotion before he was shut down with an elbow strain that required minor surgery. The Orioles say his arm strength is almost back and he looked good in instructional league. Guzman remains a work in progress, and the bullpen might be in his future. He'll return to Bowie and could move fast if he stays healthy.

Year	Club (League)	Class	AVG	G	AB	R	H	2B	3B	HR	RBI	BB	SO	SB
1995	Orioles/WS (DSL)	R	.200	37	120	12	24	6	0	0	12	6	20	2
1996	Orioles (DSL)	R	.225	61	200	24	45	8	3	2	19	14	31	5
1997	Orioles (GCL)	R	.149	15	47	1	7	1	0	0	4	1	18	0
1998	Bluefield (Appy)	R	.100	23	20	2	2	1	0	0	0	0	3	0
MINOR LEAGUE TOTALS			.202	136	387	39	78	16	3	2	35	21	72	7

Year	Club (League)	Class	W	L	ERA	G	GS	CG	SV	IP	H	R	ER	BB	SO
1998	Bluefield (Appy)	R	1	2	1.42	15	0	0	1	25	22	12	4	7	26
1999	Delmarva (SAL)	A	9	5	3.55	29	18	0	3	124	124	51	49	44	134
2000	Frederick (Car)	A	3	0	1.53	3	3	0	0	18	11	3	3	4	20
	Bowie (EL)	AA	5	9	4.64	18	18	1	0	97	114	59	50	46	57
MINOR LEAGUE TOTALS			18	16	3.61	65	39	1	4	264	271	125	106	101	237

22. Juan Figueroa, rhp

Born: June 24, 1979. **Ht.:** 6-3. **Wt.:** 150. **Bats:** R. **Throws:** R. **Career Transactions:** Signed out of Dominican Republic by White Sox, Dec. 21, 1995 . . . Traded by White Sox with C Brook Fordyce, RHP Miguel Felix and RHP Jason Lakman to Orioles for C Charles Johnson and DH Harold Baines, July 30, 2000.

With the White Sox Figueroa was another talented arm with potential, but he hadn't set himself apart from the pack. When Baltimore traded for him, it hailed him as if it were one of the best prospects in the minors. Chicago's assessment is more accurate. Figueroa has lots of potential, with a loose, lanky build and a live arm. His fastball has been clocked up to 95 mph, though he pitches more consistently in the low 90s. He has the makings of an excellent slider and average changeup, and he isn't afraid to challenge hitters. But he has yet to show consistency with his stuff and threw only 91 innings last year. He does have the potential to be the best player the Orioles got in their wave of trades.

Year	Club (League)	Class	W	L	ERA	G	GS	CG	SV	IP	H	R	ER	BB	SO
1996	Brewers/WS (DSL)	R	2	6	4.75	15	13	0	0	61	54	43	32	56	60
1997	White Sox (GCL)	R	1	4	3.36	11	10	0	0	64	66	31	24	14	43
1998	Bristol (Appy)	R	5	5	5.06	13	13	2	0	80	87	58	45	22	102
1999	Burlington (Mid)	A	8	4	3.12	17	16	2	0	115	100	51	40	44	139
	Winston-Salem (Car)	A	2	5	5.27	10	10	1	0	56	67	47	33	19	50
2000	Winston-Salem (Car)	A	4	4	4.67	9	7	1	0	52	58	30	27	8	65
	Birmingham (SL)	AA	2	3	3.40	10	9	0	0	56	57	25	21	24	42
	Bowie (EL)	AA	2	2	5.54	7	7	0	0	39	46	24	24	21	42
MINOR LEAGUE TOTALS			26	33	4.23	92	85	6	0	523	535	309	246	208	543

23. Lesli Brea, rhp

Born: Oct. 12, 1978. **Ht.:** 5-11. **Wt.:** 170. **Bats:** R. **Throws:** R. **Career Transactions:** Signed out of Dominican Republic by Mariners, Jan. 20, 1996 . . . Traded by Mariners to Mets for OF Butch Huskey, Dec. 14, 1998 . . . Traded by Mets with RHP Pat Gorman, SS Melvin Mora and 3B Mike Kinkade to Orioles for SS Mike Bordick, July 28, 2000.

Brea's relative value depends on how old you think he is. According to his listed birthdate he's 22, but other reports say he's as old as 27. He's intriguing because he has two power pitches, highlighted by a mid-90s fastball, though it lacks movement. He also throws a hard slider in the mid-80s. But he has struggled with command and has no third pitch, which means he probably needs another year or two of development. The Orioles were happy with his showing in the Arizona Fall League, though he went 1-1, 6.43 in seven innings. He's best suited to a bullpen role. Because the Orioles believe he's really 27, they'll challenge him to make the big league bullpen this spring. It will be a surprise if he proves ready.

Year	Club (League)	Class	W	L	ERA	G	GS	CG	SV	IP	H	R	ER	BB	SO
1996	Mariners (AZL)	R	1	0	5.06	7	0	0	0	10	7	10	6	6	12
1997	Lancaster (Cal)	A	0	0	13.50	1	0	0	0	2	5	5	3	1	1
	Everett (NWL)	A	2	4	7.99	23	0	0	3	32	34	29	29	29	49
1998	Wisconsin (Mid)	A	3	4	2.76	49	0	0	12	58	47	26	18	40	86
1999	St. Lucie (FSL)	A	1	7	3.73	32	18	0	3	120	95	64	50	68	136
2000	Binghamton (EL)	AA	5	8	4.24	19	18	0	0	93	85	53	44	61	86
	Norfolk (IL)	AAA	0	0	0.00	1	1	0	0	5	4	2	0	4	4
	Bowie (EL)	AA	1	1	4.26	2	2	0	0	12	12	6	6	9	3
	Baltimore (AL)	MAJ	0	1	11.00	6	1	0	0	9	12	11	11	10	5
	Rochester (IL)	AAA	1	2	6.05	4	4	0	0	19	27	18	13	8	13
MAJOR LEAGUE TOTALS			0	1	11.00	6	1	0	0	9	12	11	11	10	5
MINOR LEAGUE TOTALS			14	26	4.28	138	43	0	18	355	316	213	169	226	390

24. Mike Paradis, rhp

Born: May 3, 1978. **Ht.:** 6-3. **Wt.:** 190. **Bats:** R. **Throws:** R. **School:** Clemson University. **Career Transactions:** Selected by Orioles in first round (13th overall) of 1999 draft; signed June 22, 1999.

After declining to sign as a seventh-round pick of the Athletics in 1996, Paradis went to Clemson and broke out as a junior after two disappointing years. His first pro year was lost because of a hyperextended elbow, but that appears to be behind him now. His fastball isn't overpowering, peaking in the low 90s, but it's an above-average pitch because of its good sinking life. He has the makings of an excellent slider, with a hard, late break, but he's far from consistent with it. Paradis showed progress by earning a promotion to Frederick last year, but he's still behind in his advancement through the organization. The Orioles would love for him to blow away hitters in spring training and earn a spot in Double-A.

Year	Club (League)	Class	W	L	ERA	G	GS	CG	SV	IP	H	R	ER	BB	SO
1999	Delmarva (SAL)	A	0	1	15.00	2	2	0	0	3	3	5	5	4	6
2000	Delmarva (SAL)	A	6	5	3.99	18	18	0	0	97	95	53	43	49	81
	Frederick (Car)	A	2	5	4.17	8	8	1	0	45	55	24	21	24	32
MINOR LEAGUE TOTALS			8	11	4.27	28	28	1	0	145	153	82	69	77	119

25. Steve Bechler, rhp

Born: Nov. 18, 1979. **Ht.:** 6-2. **Wt.:** 207. **Bats:** R. **Throws:** R. **School:** South Medford HS, Medford, Ore.
Career Transactions: Selected by Orioles in third round of 1998 draft; signed June 5, 1998.

Bechler nearly carried his Medford, Ore., team to the 1997 American Legion World Series title. Medford had to beat Sanford, Fla., twice to win the title, and Bechler went the distance (seven innings) for the win in the first game. He started the second game later that day, but Sanford—led by Tim Raines Jr.'s two home runs—rallied to win after he came out. His minor league career has been a mix of dominant stretches and struggles. He has three above-average pitches but too often has below-average results. He throws comfortably in the low 90s and can reach 95 mph with his fastball, and he throws a knuckle-curve as his breaking pitch. His changeup is a plus pitch when it's on. Bechler fights his mechanics and his command, and he sometimes loses his composure. He'll take the next step to Bowie this year.

Year	Club (League)	Class	W	L	ERA	G	GS	CG	SV	IP	H	R	ER	BB	SO
1998	Orioles (GCL)	R	2	4	2.72	9	9	0	0	49	51	22	15	8	39
1999	Delmarva (SAL)	A	8	12	3.54	26	26	1	0	152	137	69	60	58	139
2000	Frederick (Car)	A	8	12	4.83	27	27	2	0	162	179	98	87	57	137
MINOR LEAGUE TOTALS			18	28	4.01	62	62	3	0	364	367	189	162	123	315

26. Willie Harris, 2b/of

Born: June 22, 1978. **Ht.:** 5-9. **Wt.:** 175. **Bats:** L. **Throws:** R. **School:** Kennesaw State (Ga.) University.
Career Transactions: Selected by Orioles in 24th round of 1999 draft; signed June 7, 1999.

A year ago, Harris was a late-round pick who looked like he could be a solid organizational player. Now Harris, the nephew of former big leaguer Ernest Riles, is viewed as the second coming of Tony Phillips. He's an ornery, gutsy performer who's good but not great in most aspects of the game. He came up as a second baseman but acquitted himself well in center field as well. He has good hands for the infield and a good arm for the outfield. He's a line-drive hitter who shows occasional pop, is willing to take a walk and has good speed on the basepaths. Harris will start the season at Bowie to prove he can be more than a utilityman.

Year	Club (League)	Class	AVG	G	AB	R	H	2B	3B	HR	RBI	BB	SO	SB
1999	Bluefield (Appy)	R	.273	5	22	3	6	1	0	0	3	4	2	1
	Delmarva (SAL)	A	.265	66	272	42	72	13	3	2	32	20	41	17
2000	Delmarva (SAL)	A	.274	133	474	106	130	27	10	6	60	89	89	38
MINOR LEAGUE TOTALS			.271	204	768	151	208	41	13	8	95	113	132	56

27. John Stephens, rhp

Born: Nov. 15, 1979. **Ht.:** 6-1. **Wt.:** 200. **Bats:** R. **Throws:** R. **Career Transactions:** Signed out of Australia by Orioles, July 3, 1996.

Rarely will you find a righthander who throws in the low 80s get any consideration as a prospect. But rarely will you find someone who posts numbers like Stephens. He sustained an injury similar to whiplash in 1998 at Delmarva when he tried to field a bunt. The injury damaged nerves in his arm and when he returned, his velocity had dropped from 89 mph and still hasn't returned. What he has is pinpoint control of the fastball, a plus curveball and plus changeup. He throws all three with the same motion and arm action but different velocity and movement. He has to prove himself almost with every start, and he has to be perfect with his location. He also must stay healthy. He missed time in 2000 with a strained hip flexor, and an impinged nerve in his right hand late in the year cost him a spot on Australia's Olympic team. But he's still young and it's possible his velocity could come back. If that happens, watch out.

Year	Club (League)	Class	W	L	ERA	G	GS	CG	SV	IP	H	R	ER	BB	SO
1997	Orioles (GCL)	R	3	0	0.82	9	3	0	1	33	15	3	3	9	43
	Bluefield (Appy)	R	2	0	2.25	4	4	0	0	24	17	6	6	5	34
1998	Delmarva (SAL)	A	1	2	2.60	6	6	1	0	35	25	11	10	13	40

Yr	Club (League)	Class			ERA					IP						
1999	Delmarva (SAL)	A	10	8	3.22	28	27	4	0	170	148	75	61	36	217	
2000	Frederick (Car)	A	7	6	3.05	20	20	0	0	118	119	45	40	22	121	
MINOR LEAGUE TOTALS			23	16	2.84	67	60	5	1	380	324	140	120	85	455	

28. Fernando Lunar, c

Born: May 25, 1977. **Ht.:** 6-1. **Wt.:** 190. **Bats:** R. **Throws:** R. **Career Transactions:** Signed out of Venezuela by Braves, March 15, 1994 . . . Traded by Braves with RHP Luis Rivera and OF Trenidad Hubbard to Orioles for OF B.J. Surhoff and RHP Gabe Molina, July 31, 2000.

Lunar is a classic defense-first catcher. He looked like nothing better than a major league backup in the Braves organization, though the Orioles hope his offense can improve enough to make him a full-time player. He did show flashes, hitting safely in his first 12 games with Bowie and earning a taste of big league life in Baltimore. He remains a career .222 minor league hitter, however. His catch-and-throw skills are outstanding, and he has good durability and a feel for handling pitchers and calling games. Lunar will get an opportunity to win a big league job this spring, but he'll probably go back to Triple-A to work on his stroke.

Yr	Club (League)	Class	AVG	G	AB	R	H	2B	3B	HR	RBI	BB	SO	SB
1994	Braves (GCL)	R	.240	33	100	9	24	5	0	2	12	1	13	0
1995	Macon (SAL)	A	.179	39	134	13	24	2	0	0	9	10	38	1
	Eugene (NWL)	A	.244	38	131	13	32	6	0	2	16	9	28	0
1996	Macon (SAL)	A	.184	104	343	33	63	9	0	7	33	20	65	3
1997	Macon (SAL)	A	.261	105	380	41	99	26	2	7	37	18	42	0
1998	Danville (Car)	A	.220	91	286	19	63	9	0	3	28	6	52	1
1999	Greenville (SL)	AA	.224	105	343	33	77	15	1	3	35	12	64	0
2000	Greenville (SL)	AA	.167	31	102	6	17	3	0	0	4	8	15	0
	Atlanta (NL)	MAJ	.185	22	54	5	10	1	0	0	5	3	15	0
	Bowie (EL)	AA	.288	22	80	12	23	7	1	0	8	6	8	0
	Baltimore (AL)	MAJ	.125	9	16	0	2	0	0	0	1	0	4	0
MAJOR LEAGUE TOTALS			.171	31	70	5	12	1	0	0	6	3	19	0
MINOR LEAGUE TOTALS			.222	568	1899	179	422	82	4	24	182	90	325	5

29. Jorge Julio, rhp

Born: March 3, 1979. **Ht.:** 6-1. **Wt.:** 190. **Bats:** R. **Throws:** R. **Career Transactions:** Signed out of Venezuela by Expos, Feb. 14, 1996 . . . Traded by Expos to Orioles for 3B Ryan Minor, Dec. 22, 2000.

Julio came over from the Expos as Ryan Minor officially became a footnote in Orioles history. Julio started the year in the Class A Jupiter rotation, but injuries and poor performance sent him to the bullpen. He continued his conversion in the Venezuelan League, and it better suits his ability. He has a big body and had the best velocity in the Expos organization, consistently in the 97-98 mph range. He also throws a power slider and a changeup. Julio has the stuff to be a big league closer but hasn't made the adjustments to get there. His fastball lacks movement, and when he gets hit, he overthrows and has command problems.

Year	Club (League)	Class	W	L	ERA	G	GS	CG	SV	IP	H	R	ER	BB	SO
1996	Expos (DSL)	R	1	1	6.06	10	0	0	0	16	13	12	11	11	21
1997	Expos (GCL)	R	5	6	3.58	15	8	0	1	55	57	25	22	21	42
	W. Palm Beach (FSL)	A	0	0	0.00	1	0	0	0	2	2	1	1	0	0
1998	Vermont (NY-P)	A	3	1	2.57	7	7	0	0	42	30	12	12	15	52
	Cape Fear (SAL)	A	2	2	5.68	6	6	0	0	32	33	20	20	12	20
1999	Jupiter (FSL)	A	4	8	3.92	23	22	0	0	115	116	62	50	34	80
2000	Jupiter (FSL)	A	2	10	5.90	21	15	0	1	79	93	60	52	35	67
MINOR LEAGUE TOTALS			17	28	4.46	83	58	0	2	339	344	192	168	128	282

30. Doug Gredvig, 1b

Born: Aug. 25, 1979. **Ht.:** 6-2. **Wt.:** 195. **Bats:** R. **Throws:** R. **School:** Sacramento CC. **Career Transactions:** Selected by Orioles in fifth round of 2000 draft; signed June 9, 2000.

Gredvig is a pure power prospect, the kind of player who creates a different sound when the ball comes off his bat. He has the approach to be more than an all-or-nothing hitter, but he doesn't show that approach often enough. If he can get consistent in his control of the strike zone, the Orioles think he has Jeff Bagwell offensive potential. He's nothing special on defense, though he did make significant improvements in that area in instructional league. Gredvig will advance to Frederick in 2001 and move as fast as his bat can take him.

Yr	Club (League)	Class	AVG	G	AB	R	H	2B	3B	HR	RBI	BB	SO	SB
2000	Orioles (GCL)	R	.444	2	9	0	4	0	0	0	1	0	1	0
	Delmarva (SAL)	A	.220	56	186	28	41	12	0	6	24	35	48	3
MINOR LEAGUE TOTALS			.231	58	195	28	45	12	0	6	25	35	49	3

Boston
Red Sox

By Jim Callis

Without question, the Red Sox are in much better shape than when Dan Duquette took over as general manager prior to the 1994 season. Boston drafted Nomar Garcia-parra in the first round that June and has advanced to the playoffs three times in seven seasons under Duquette.

Duquette oversaw a commitment to the farm system, as the Red Sox put more money into scouting and signing amateurs. He hired Bob Schaefer as farm director, and Schaefer overhauled the organization's development practices, which ranked somewhere between outmoded and nonexistent.

The system flourished, collecting athletes and quality arms, in contrast to its reputation for producing one-dimensional hitters. Duquette's master stroke came in the 1997 offseason, when he traded pitching prospects Tony Armas Jr. and Carl Pavano to the Expos for Pedro Martinez.

Since acquiring Martinez, the Red Sox have won two wild cards and narrowly missed a third. Despite the on-field success, though, cracks are starting to show in the club's foundation.

Schaefer was fired during the 1998 season after clashing with Duquette and other members of his front office, and the farm system has slipped since his departure. Mark Teixeira, a ninth-round pick that June, and his family didn't like the way the Red Sox treated them, costing the club the consensus top prospect for the 2001 draft. Later in the year, Mo Vaughn departed as a free agent, much as Roger Clemens had two seasons before.

As the system has dried up and Duquette has become more embattled, he has tried to bolster Boston's roster with trades and free-agent signings. The most notable deal he made this winter was signing outfielder Manny Ramirez, which got Red Sox Nation dreaming of the World Series again. But while Duquette has made good deals, others have been short-sighted and bloated the big league payroll.

Among Duquette's regular season moves in 2000, he gave up righthander Dennis Tankersley, who blossomed with the Padres after being included in a package for Ed Sprague, and righthander Chris Reitsma, one of the Red Sox' most advanced mound prospects, who went to the Reds for the overpriced Dante Bichette. This winter he sent Michael Coleman and Donnie Sadler, the two best athletes remaining in Boston's upper minors, to the Reds for Chris Stynes, whom Cincinnati couldn't afford to take to arbitration.

OrganizationOverview

General manager: Dan Duquette. **Farm director:** Kent Qualls. **Scouting director:** Wayne Britton.

2000 PERFORMANCE

Class	Team	League	W	L	Pct.	Finish*	Manager
Majors	Boston	American	85	77	.525	6th (14)	Jimy Williams
Triple-A	Pawtucket Red Sox	International	82	61	.573	3rd (14)	Gary Jones
Double-A	Trenton Thunder	Eastern	67	75	.472	9th (12)	Billy Gardner Jr.
High A	Sarasota Red Sox	Florida State	60	79	.432	12th (14)	Ron Johnson
Low A	Augusta GreenJackets	South Atlantic	83	58	.589	2nd (14)	Mike Boulanger
Short-season	Lowell Spinners	New York-Penn	41	34	.547	5th (14)	Arnie Beyeler
Rookie	GCL Red Sox	Gulf Coast	29	26	.527	7th (13)	John Sanders
OVERALL 2000 MINOR LEAGUE RECORD			**362**	**333**	**.521**	**9th (30)**	

*Finish in overall standings (No. of teams in league).

ORGANIZATION LEADERS

BATTING
*AVG	**Shea Hillenbrand**, Trenton	.323
R	Lew Ford, Augusta	122
H	Shea Hillenbrand, Trenton	171
TB	Lew Ford, Augusta	246
2B	**Shea Hillenbrand**, Trenton	35
	Lew Ford, Augusta	35
3B	Lew Ford, Augusta	11
HR	Israel Alcantara, Pawtucket	29
RBI	Carlos Rodriguez, Augusta	94
BB	Morgan Burkhart, Pawtucket	69
SO	Chris Warren, Augusta	152
SB	Lew Ford, Augusta	52

PITCHING
W	Brad Baker, Augusta	12
L	Three tied at	10
#ERA	Mauricio Lara, Augusta/Lowell	1.92
G	**B.J. Leach**, Augusta	60
CG	Tomokazu Ohka, Pawtucket	3
	Casey Fossum, Sarasota	3
SV	**B.J. Leach**, Augusta	40
IP	Chris Reitsma, Trenton/Sarasota	155
BB	John Curtice, Sarasota	68
SO	Casey Fossum, Sarasota	143

*Minimum 250 at-bats. #Minimum 75 innings.

TOP PROSPECTS OF THE DECADE

TOP DRAFT PICKS OF THE DECADE

RODGER WOOD

RODGER WOOD

Hillenbrand   **Leach**

BEST TOOLS

Best Hitter for Average	Dernell Stenson
Best Power Hitter	Juan Diaz
Fastest Baserunner	Antron Seiber
Best Fastball	Jerome Gamble
Best Breaking Ball	Casey Fossum
Best Control	Paxton Crawford
Best Defensive Catcher	Steve Lomasney
Best Defensive Infielder	Freddy Sanchez
Best Infield Arm	Tony Blanco
Best Defensive Outfielder	Rick Asadoorian
Best Outfield Arm	Rick Asadoorian

PROJECTED 2004 LINEUP

Catcher	Jason Varitek
First Base	Juan Diaz
Second Base	Freddy Sanchez
Third Base	Tony Blanco
Shortstop	Nomar Garciaparra
Left Field	Manny Ramirez
Center Field	Carl Everett
Right Field	Trot Nixon
Designated Hitter	Dernell Stenson
No. 1 Starter	Pedro Martinez
No. 2 Starter	Brad Baker
No. 3 Starter	Tomokazu Ohka
No. 4 Starter	Sun-Woo Kim
No. 5 Starter	Casey Fossum
Closer	Derek Lowe

ALL-TIME LARGEST BONUSES

Rick Asadoorian, 1999	$1,725,500
Adam Everett, 1998	1,725,000
Phil Dumatrait, 2000	1,275,000
Sang-Hoon Lee, 1999	1,050,000
Sun-Woo Kim, 1998	1,000,000

DraftAnalysis

2000 Draft

Best Pro Debut: The Red Sox had a pair of late-rounders post sub-2.00 ERAs in the short-season New York-Penn League: LHP **Chris Elmore** (17), who went 3-3, 1.89, and RHP Brian Bentley (20), who went 4-1, 1.88 with 48 strikeouts in 38 innings. RHP Tony Fontana (7) had the best debut among top prospects, going 5-4, 2.49 on the same club. He throws 89-94 mph with a hard slider.

Best Athlete: LHP Brandon Mims (4) was a solid two-way player in high school. RHP Josh Thigpen (16) was all-state in three sports (baseball, basketball and football) in Alabama. None of the position players stands out as a top-drawer athlete.

Best Hitter: 1B/3B Matt Cooper (3), whom scouts had a difficult time getting a read on because he faced the lowest-level high school competition in Oklahoma. He hit .270 in the Rookie-level Gulf Coast League, where he moved to first to accommodate top prospect Tony Blanco.

Best Raw Power: Cooper.

Fastest Runner: Boston never has championed speed. OF Freddie Money (24) is an above-average runner, but he's not a blazer.

Best Defensive Player: Kenny Perez (6) shows a good arm, actions and hands at shortstop. He may outgrow the position, but the Sox will keep him there for now.

Best Fastball: LHP Phil Dumatrait (1) threw in the low 80s as a high school senior, then shot up to a consistent 92-93 mph at Bakersfield (Calif.) JC last spring after growing and getting on a throwing program. RHP Manny Delcarmen (2) is a year younger

and can touch 93.

Most Intriguing Background: Delcarmen is a Dominican raised in inner-city Boston. The Red Sox have mined New England for prospects in recent years, and he ranks with Rick Asadoorian and Brad Baker, the top two picks from 1999.

Closest To The Majors: The Red Sox went young, signing just six players out of Division I colleges. They won't get any immediate help, with Fontana and Elmore projected to arrive the earliest.

Best Late-Round Pick: SS Freddy Sanchez (11) became the best middle-infield prospect in the system. Thigpen has a loose, free arm to go with a sound delivery. He can throw his fastball up to 92 mph and his curveball has potential. He reminds Boston of a bigger version of 1995 draftee Matt Kinney, who has since been traded to the Twins.

RICH ABEL

Elmore

The One Who Got Away: Mississippi State RHP Ryan Carroll (21), who looked impressive in fall practice.

Assessment: The Red Sox could have scored big had they opted to meet the bonus demands of Texas high school slugger Jason Stokes. Instead they chose Dumatrait, which saved them $750,000. Boston might be better off putting more money into the draft than into the Asian market, where it has spent extravagantly with little to show for it.

1999 Draft

The Red Sox had three first-rounders and spent them on OF Rick Asadoorian, RHP Brad Baker and LHP Casey Fossum. Each is the system's top prospect at his position. **Grade: B**

1998 Draft

Boston will rue losing 3B Mark Teixeira (9), who went to Georgia Tech and could be the No. 1 overall pick in 2001. The best players signed by the club, SS Adam Everett (1), LHP Mike Maroth (3) and RHP Dennis Tankersley (38), were traded. **Grade: C**

1997 Draft

Both Sox first-rounders, LHP John Curtice and OF Mark Fischer, are washouts. Curtice has been traded, as have LHP Greg Miller (5) and RHP Jeff Taglienti (7), while 2B David Eckstein (19) was waived. And after signing RHP Travis Harper (3), the team voided his contract and lost him to the Devil Rays. **Grade: C–**

1996 Draft

Boston traded away most of the talent it found: RHP Chris Reitsma (1), OF John Barnes (7), LHP Rob Ramsay (7). It has kept 1B/OF Dernell Stenson (3), the organization's top prospect. The top pick, RHP Josh Garrett (1), isn't going to make it. **Grade: B**

Note: Draft analysis prepared by Jim Callis. Numbers in parentheses indicate draft rounds.

. . . Stenson has the tools to be an impact hitter who can produce for average and power.

Dernell Stenson 1b/of

Born: June 17, 1978.
Ht.: 6-1. **Wt.:** 230.
Bats: L. **Throws:** L.
School: La Grange (Ga.) HS.
Career Transactions: Selected by Red Sox in third round of 1996 draft; signed July 10, 1996.

At the time, Baseball America rated the Red Sox' 1996 draft the best in the game. Now it appears Stenson may be all they get out of that crop. The other most promising prospects from that draft are all with other teams: righthander Chris Reitsma (first round, now with the Reds), outfielder John Barnes (fourth, Twins) and lefthander Rob Ramsay (seventh, Mariners). And Stenson's star has dimmed. He was named the best batting prospect and No. 2 prospect in the Double-A Eastern League in 1998 and in the Triple-A International League in 1999, but tailed off in a return trip to the IL in 2000. USA Baseball inquired about adding Stenson to the Olympic team, but the Red Sox didn't give their consent—and then didn't promote him in September. He missed time early last year with wrist and hamstring injuries.

Stenson has the tools to be the impact hitter the Red Sox desperately needed before the free-agent signing of Manny Ramirez in December. He has the balance, bat speed, short stroke and pitch recognition to produce for both average and power. Nobody in Boston's lineup outside of Ramirez can match Stenson's power potential. He didn't turn 22 until midseason last year, so he's still ahead of the normal development cycle, and he has never been overmatched despite consistently being one of the youngest players in his league. He made decent progress against lefthanders in 2000 after struggling against them the year before.

For all his offensive gifts, though, Stenson has batted .257, .268 and .268 the last three seasons. And if he doesn't mash in the major leagues, he won't play because he contributes nothing beyond his bat. Originally an outfielder, he put on weight and slowed down, prompting a move to first base in 1999. Stenson led all minor league first basemen with 34 errors and was even worse defensively than that would suggest. He played at first and in left field last year, and he probably will never be more than adequate at either position. Boston is overloaded with first base/left field/DH types, so Stenson could be in for a third trip to Triple-A to begin 2001. In a perfect world, he wouldn't be an organization's No. 1 prospect. But the Red Sox system is far from perfect.

Year	Club (League)	Class	AVG	G	AB	R	H	2B	3B	HR	RBI	BB	SO	SB
1996	Red Sox (GCL)	R	.216	32	97	16	21	3	1	2	15	16	26	4
1997	Michigan (Mid)	A	.291	131	471	79	137	35	2	15	80	72	105	6
1998	Trenton (EL)	AA	.257	138	505	90	130	21	1	24	71	84	135	5
1999	Pawtucket (IL)	AAA	.270	121	440	64	119	28	2	18	82	55	119	2
	Red Sox (GCL)	R	.217	6	23	2	5	0	0	2	7	3	5	0
2000	Pawtucket (IL)	AAA	.268	98	380	59	102	14	0	23	71	45	99	0
MINOR LEAGUE TOTALS			.268	526	1916	310	514	101	6	84	326	275	489	17

2. Brad Baker, rhp

Born: Nov. 6, 1980. **Ht.:** 6-2. **Wt.:** 180. **Bats:** R. **Throws:** R. **School:** Pioneer Valley HS, Northfield, Mass. **Career Transactions:** Selected by Red Sox in first round (40th overall) of 1999 draft; signed July 26, 1999.

RODGER WOOD

Losing Mo Vaughn as a free agent didn't endear the Red Sox to their fans, but the club salvaged something by taking outfielder Rick Asadoorian and Baker with the compensation first-round picks. In his first full pro season, Baker established himself as the organization's top pitching prospect. He can reach 95 mph, though he more comfortably pitches in the low 90s and is more of a pitcher than an overpowering thrower. He has a quick arm that makes his fastball seem harder than it is. His curveball is also a plus pitch, and he brings poise to the mound. He works down in the strike zone, getting groundouts and keeping the ball in the park, allowing just three homers last year. Lefties batted just .204 against him. Baker can improve the consistency of his secondary pitches, which also include a changeup. He also needs to get stronger, which could result in increased velocity. The Red Sox resisted the temptation to promote Baker to high Class A in 2000, when he was just 19. He'll make the move this year and could begin to progress quickly through the system.

Year	Club (League)	Class	W	L	ERA	G	GS	CG	SV	IP	H	R	ER	BB	SO
1999	Red Sox (GCL)	R	1	0	0.79	4	3	0	0	11	10	3	1	2	10
2000	Augusta (SAL)	A	12	7	3.07	27	27	0	0	138	125	58	47	55	126
MINOR LEAGUE TOTALS			13	7	2.90	31	30	0	0	149	135	61	48	57	136

3. Tony Blanco, 3b

Born: Nov. 10, 1981. **Ht.:** 6-1. **Wt.:** 176. **Bats:** R. **Throws:** R. **Career Transactions:** Signed out of Dominican Republic by Red Sox, July 2, 1998.

The Red Sox named Blanco their 1999 player of the year on their Rookie-level Dominican Summer League affiliate, but they weren't prepared for his performance in his stateside debut. He was the No. 1 prospect in the Rookie-level Gulf Coast League, where he and teammate Bryan Barnowski tied the league record with 13 homers each. Blanco has several notable tools. His throwing arm rates the maximum 8 on the 2-to-8 scouting scale. He has exceptional bat speed, which generates light-tower power and allows him to hit for average as well. Blanco also exhibits decent patience at the plate. He did strike out in nearly one-fourth of his at-bats in 2000, though no one can argue with his production. If he can get lighter on his feet and improve his lateral movement, he can be a standout defender at the hot corner. Though Blanco was a bit overmatched in the short-season New York-Penn League, he'll probably go to Class A Augusta in 2001. He's at least three years away from Boston.

Year	Club (League)	Class	AVG	G	AB	R	H	2B	3B	HR	RBI	BB	SO	SB
1999	Red Sox (DSL)	R	.277	67	249	36	69	12	5	8	41	29	65	12
2000	Red Sox (GCL)	R	.384	52	190	32	73	13	1	13	50	18	38	6
	Lowell (NY-P)	A	.143	9	28	1	4	1	0	0	0	2	12	1
MINOR LEAGUE TOTALS				128	467	69	146	26	6	21	91	49	115	19

4. Sun-Woo Kim, rhp

Born: Sept. 4, 1977. **Ht.:** 6-2. **Wt.:** 180. **Bats:** R. **Throws:** R. **Career Transactions:** Signed out of Korea by Red Sox, Jan. 15, 1998.

Kim pitched Korea to the 1994 World Junior Championship title and in 1996 became his nation's youngest baseball Olympian ever. He signed with the Red Sox for $1 million a year later. Kim was the winning pitcher in the Futures Game and was part of an Arizona Fall League championship club in 1999, but his 2000 season at Pawtucket was most notable for a fight with Tomokazu Ohka over who was the better prospect. Kim has the highest ceiling of any of the Asian pitchers in the upper levels of Boston's system. He has excellent movement on his fastball, which touches 95 mph, and he has no problem throwing it for strikes. Kim also has the potential to have an above-average breaking pitch and possibly a plus changeup. He pitches to both sides of the plate. Kim needs to further develop his offspeed stuff and refine his location within the strike zone. He throws too many strikes and is vulnerable when he doesn't get his pitches down. His release point tends to wander, though that may be by design. Kim needs to have success in Triple-A before he's ready for Boston. He has better stuff than Ohka but lacks his feel for pitching.

Year	Club (League)	Class	W	L	ERA	G	GS	CG	SV	IP	H	R	ER	BB	SO
1998	Sarasota (FSL)	A	12	8	4.82	26	24	5	0	153	159	88	82	40	132
1999	Trenton (EL)	AA	9	8	4.89	26	26	1	0	149	160	86	81	44	130
2000	Pawtucket (IL)	AAA	11	7	6.03	26	25	0	0	134	170	98	90	42	116
MINOR LEAGUE TOTALS			32	23	5.22	78	75	6	0	436	489	272	253	126	378

5. Casey Fossum, lhp

Born: Jan. 9, 1978. **Ht.:** 6-1. **Wt.:** 160. **Bats:** B. **Throws:** L. **School:** Texas A&M University. **Career Transactions:** Selected by Red Sox in first round (48th overall) of 1999 draft; signed July 19, 1999.

Boston regrettably gave up righthander Matt Kinney and outfielder John Barnes in a 1998 trade with the Twins for veterans Greg Swindell and Orlando Merced, but got Fossum with a compensation pick after Swindell signed with Arizona. Fossum set season and career strikeout records at Texas A&M. He went 7-2, 2.33 in the second half of 2000, highlighted by a no-hitter with 16 whiffs in August. Fossum reminds scouts of Jimmy Key. He can reach 91-92 mph with his fastball, and his best pitch is a hard slider. He has good command, lots of confidence and a sound delivery. He destroyed lefties in 2000, limiting them to a .105 average with no homers in 95 at-bats. Fossum's changeup is improving, but it still needs more work before he'll be able to keep righties in check. He also could add more strength. Fossum is the only true prospect among lefthanders who pitched in full-season ball for the Red Sox in 2000. He'll start 2001 in Double-A and has an outside chance to reach Boston by the end of the year. At worst, he'll make a good situational reliever.

Year	Club (League)	Class	W	L	ERA	G	GS	CG	SV	IP	H	R	ER	BB	SO
1999	Lowell (NY-P)	A	0	1	1.26	5	5	0	0	14	6	2	2	5	16
2000	Sarasota (FSL)	A	9	10	3.44	27	27	3	0	149	147	71	57	36	143
MINOR LEAGUE TOTALS			9	11	3.26	32	32	3	0	163	153	73	59	41	159

6. Steve Lomasney, c

Born: Aug. 29, 1977. **Ht.:** 6-0. **Wt.:** 195. **Bats:** R. **Throws:** R. **School:** Peabody (Mass.) HS. **Career Transactions:** Selected by Red Sox in fifth round of 1995 draft; signed June 29, 1995.

Ranked as Boston's top prospect after the 1999 season, Lomasney endured a trying year in 2000. The former Boston College football recruit went 0-for-19 in his first five games and couldn't get his average above .200 until late May. He made just six rehab appearances after injuring his hamstring in mid-July. Lomasney shows strong tools behind the plate. He's athletic and has good receiving and throwing skills. As a hitter, he has power potential and a willingness to draw walks. His mental toughness helped him get out of his early-season slump and bat .291 the rest of the way. But Lomasney remains a career .236 hitter. The Red Sox wanted him to focus on hitting breaking pitches in 2000, and he took it to an extreme, letting too many hittable fastballs go by. His release gets sluggish at times, which is why he threw out just 19 percent of basestealers in Double-A Trenton. He has yet to hit much in two Double-A stints, so Lomasney could get a third trip to Trenton before moving up to Triple-A. His ceiling is as a solid backstop who could hit 15-20 homers a year.

Year	Club (League)	Class	AVG	G	AB	R	H	2B	3B	HR	RBI	BB	SO	SB
1995	Red Sox (GCL)	R	.163	29	92	10	15	6	0	0	7	8	16	2
1996	Lowell (NY-P)	A	.139	59	173	26	24	10	0	4	21	42	63	2
1997	Michigan (Mid)	A	.275	102	324	50	89	27	3	12	51	32	98	3
1998	Sarasota (FSL)	A	.239	122	443	74	106	22	1	22	63	59	145	13
1999	Sarasota (FSL)	A	.270	55	189	35	51	10	0	8	28	26	57	5
	Trenton (EL)	AA	.245	47	151	24	37	6	0	12	31	31	44	7
	Boston (AL)	MAJ	.000	1	2	0	0	0	0	0	0	0	2	0
2000	Trenton (EL)	AA	.245	66	233	30	57	16	1	8	27	24	81	4
	Red Sox (GCL)	R	.267	6	15	2	4	2	0	0	1	4	6	0
MAJOR LEAGUE TOTALS			.000	1	2	0	0	0	0	0	0	0	2	0
MINOR LEAGUE TOTALS			.236	486	1620	251	383	99	5	66	229	226	510	36

7. Seung Song, rhp

Born: June 29, 1980. **Ht.:** 6-1. **Wt.:** 192. **Bats:** R. **Throws:** R. **Career Transactions:** Signed out of Korea by Red Sox, Feb. 2, 1999.

Song pitched his high school team to a national championship and was considered the top amateur in Korea when the Red Sox signed him to an $800,000 bonus. After a fine debut in the GCL in 1999, he led the New York-Penn League in strikeouts last season. Song is a power pitcher with exquisite command. He already touches 94 mph and has a 154-40 strikeout-walk ratio as a pro. He has taught himself a curveball that should give him a second above-average pitch. He has allowed just three homers in two years. His body is strong, especially his legs, and he has mastered English quickly, which should accelerate his development. Song tends to rely on his fastball and will need to throw his curve more often at higher levels. Currently his weakest pitch, his change-up will need more work as well. Song easily could go to Augusta this year and dominate to the extent that Brad Baker did. The Red Sox were patient and left Baker there for all of 2000, and may do the same with Song. He's advanced for a young pitcher and could force a more aggressive timetable.

Year	Club (League)	Class	W	L	ERA	G	GS	CG	SV	IP	H	R	ER	BB	SO
1999	Red Sox (GCL)	R	5	5	2.30	13	9	0	0	55	47	29	14	20	61
2000	Lowell (NY-P)	R	5	2	2.60	13	13	0	0	73	63	26	21	20	93
MINOR LEAGUE TOTALS			10	7	2.62	26	22	0	0	120	110	55	35	40	154

8. Mauricio Lara, lhp

Born: April 2, 1979. **Ht.:** 5-11. **Wt.:** 185. **Bats:** B. **Throws:** L. **Career Transactions:** Signed out of Mexico by Red Sox, Sept. 14, 1998.

Lara may be the best prospect signed by Mexico-based scout Lee Sigman since he helped the Brewers obtain Ted Higuera in the mid-1980s. Though Lara hadn't pitched in the United States before 2000, the Red Sox sent him to Augusta after a month in extended spring training. Lara pitched well in relief before getting more innings as a starter in the New York-Penn League, where he was ranked the No. 5 prospect. Though he's not quite 6 feet tall, Lara has excellent velocity for a lefthander. He throws consistently in the low 90s and can touch 94 mph. His curveball also is above-average. Lara has good mound presence and a nice feel for pitching. He didn't permit a homer in 85 NY-P innings. Like many young pitchers, Lara possesses only a rudimentary change-up. If he develops it into an average third pitch, he could rise quickly through the minors. Lara and Song formed a potent lefty-righty one-two punch at Lowell and should do the same at Augusta in 2001. Lara's ceiling is higher than that of any Red Sox lefty, including Casey Fossum.

Year	Club (League)	Class	W	L	ERA	G	GS	CG	SV	IP	H	R	ER	BB	SO
1999	Cagua (VSL)	R	7	0	1.71	10	9	2	0	58	44	15	11	17	63
2000	Augusta (SAL)	A	1	0	1.41	16	0	0	0	32	25	11	5	13	33
	Lowell (NY-P)	A	4	3	2.12	15	14	0	0	85	70	22	20	21	83
MINOR LEAGUE TOTAL			12	3	1.85	41	23	0	0	175	139	48	36	51	179

9. Paxton Crawford, rhp

Born: Aug. 4, 1977. **Ht.:** 6-3. **Wt.:** 205. **Bats:** R. **Throws:** R. **School:** Carlsbad (N.M.) HS. **Career Transactions:** Selected by Red Sox in ninth round of 1995 draft; signed June 6, 1995.

Crawford had trouble regaining his stuff after straining his forearm and breaking his wrist in 1998, but it finally came back in 2000. He earned his first major league win in July, then threw a Triple-A no-hitter in a temporary demotion. The night after his gem, he fell out of bed and onto a glass, requiring eight stitches in his back and delaying his return to Boston until September. Crawford has solid average stuff with a two-seam fastball, slider and changeup. He succeeds with his fastball because it has good sink and his delivery makes it tough to pick up. He works quickly, is durable and throws strikes. Crawford sometimes falls into a power-pitcher mentality, which causes his slider to flatten out. The only pitch he has that has a chance to be above-average is his changeup. Crawford is about as good as he's going to be. He projects as a No. 4 or 5 starter, and the Red Sox will give him the chance to fill that role in spring training.

Year	Club (League)	Class	W	L	ERA	G	GS	CG	SV	IP	H	R	ER	BB	SO
1995	Red Sox (GCL)	R	2	4	2.74	12	7	1	2	46	38	17	14	12	44
1996	Michigan (Mid)	A	6	11	3.58	22	22	1	0	128	120	62	51	42	105
1997	Sarasota (FSL)	A	4	8	4.55	12	11	2	0	65	69	42	33	27	56
1998	Trenton (EL)	AA	6	5	4.17	22	20	1	0	108	104	53	50	39	82
1999	Trenton (EL)	AA	7	8	4.08	28	28	1	0	163	151	81	74	59	111
2000	Trenton (EL)	AA	2	3	3.10	9	9	0	0	52	50	20	18	18	54
	Pawtucket (IL)	AAA	7	4	4.55	12	11	1	0	61	47	32	31	22	47
	Boston (AL)	MAJ	2	1	3.41	7	4	0	0	29	25	15	11	13	17
MAJOR LEAGUE TOTALS			2	1	3.41	7	4	0	0	29	25	15	11	13	17
MINOR LEAGUE TOTALS			36	43	3.91	117	108	7	2	624	579	307	271	219	499

10. Sang-Hoon Lee, lhp

Born: March 11, 1971. **Ht.:** 6-1. **Wt.:** 190. **Bats:** L. **Throws:** L. **Career Transactions:** Signed out of Korea by Red Sox, Dec. 23, 1999.

Lee led the Korea Baseball Organization in wins in 1994 and '95, then moved to the bullpen following a back injury. He led the league in saves in 1997 before being sold to Japan's Chunichi Dragons, whom he helped to a Central League pennant in 1999. He signed a two-year major league contract with a $1.05 million bonus that December. Lee throws 89-93 mph, and his deceptive arm angle and quick arm make his fastball that much tougher. His changeup is his No. 2 pitch, and he shows a curveball and slider. Lee has a closer's mentality and probably has the stuff to be a starter, though he prefers to relieve. He needs to throw his changeup more often. He sometimes drops his arm angle too low, which makes his breaking pitches less effective. In his first year in the United States, it took time for him to understand why he didn't receive the star treatment he got in Asia. More than just a situational lefty, Lee should be a key cog in Boston's 2001 bullpen. He could be an option at closer if the Red Sox decide to move Derek Lowe into their rotation.

Year	Club (League)	Class	W	L	ERA	G	GS	CG	SV	IP	H	R	ER	BB	SO
1993	LG Twins (KBO)	KOR	9	9	3.76	28	—	7	0	151	129	—	63	78	131
1994	LG Twins (KBO)	KOR	18	8	2.47	27	—	8	0	190	140	—	52	64	148
1995	LG Twins (KBO)	KOR	20	5	2.01	30	—	12	0	228	150	—	51	51	142
1996	LG Twins (KBO)	KOR	3	3	2.54	41	—	0	10	99	70	—	28	42	95
1997	LG Twins (KBO)	KOR	10	6	2.11	57	—	0	37	85	56	—	20	27	103
1998	Chunichi (CL)	JPN	1	0	4.68	11	—	0	0	33	32	—	17	12	33
1999	Chunichi (CL)	JPN	6	5	2.83	36	—	0	3	95	75	—	30	30	65
2000	Pawtucket (IL)	AAA	5	2	2.03	45	1	0	2	71	51	23	16	24	73
	Boston (AL)	MAJ	0	0	3.09	9	0	0	0	12	11	4	4	5	6
MAJOR LEAGUE TOTALS			0	0	3.09	9	0	0	0	12	11	4	4	5	6
MINOR LEAGUE TOTALS			5	2	2.03	45	1	0	2	71	51	23	16	24	73

11. Juan Diaz, 1b

Born: Feb. 19, 1976. **Ht.:** 6-2. **Wt.:** 228. **Bats:** R. **Throws:** R. **Career Transactions:** Signed out of Cuba by Dodgers, May 19, 1996 . . . Contract voided, June 25, 1999 . . . Signed by Red Sox, March 4, 2000.

Diaz hit 65 homers in a little more than two seasons in the Dodgers organization when his contract was voided in June 1999. The commissioner's office ruled that Los Angeles had illegally scouted and signed Diaz and outfielder Josue Perez out of Cuba. While Perez signed quickly with the Phillies, Diaz held out for big money that didn't materialize and missed the rest of the year. After signing with Boston, Diaz' 2000 season was delayed by visa trouble and ended prematurely when he fractured and dislocated his right ankle on a bad slide. While he was on the field, Diaz showed the best raw power in Boston's system. He has a short stroke and impressive bat speed. He was suspended for three games after getting caught using a grooved bat in Double-A, though that shouldn't have had anything to do with his power. Diaz is a purely offensive player who is challenged even by the defensive responsibilities of first base. He lacks agility and will never offer much with the glove. Diaz was on the verge of being promoted to Boston when he was injured. The Red Sox have several first baseman/DH types, but they might consider at least platooning Diaz after he batted .385 against lefthanders in 2000.

Year	Club (League)	Class	AVG	G	AB	R	H	2B	3B	HR	RBI	BB	SO	SB
1996	Dodgers (DSL)	R	.362	13	47	15	17	7	0	4	16	11	13	1

Year	Club (League)	Class	AVG	G	AB	R	H	2B	3B	HR	RBI	BB	SO	SB
1997	Savannah (SAL)	A	.230	127	460	63	106	24	2	25	83	48	155	2
	Vero Beach (FSL)	A	.429	2	7	2	3	0	0	1	3	0	4	0
1998	Vero Beach (FSL)	A	.292	67	250	33	73	12	1	17	51	21	52	1
	San Antonio (TL)	AA	.266	56	188	26	50	13	0	13	30	15	45	0
1999	San Antonio (TL)	AA	.303	66	254	42	77	21	1	9	52	26	77	0
2000	Sarasota (FSL)	A	.275	14	51	7	14	2	1	4	12	4	15	0
	Trenton (EL)	AA	.313	50	198	36	129	14	1	17	53	10	56	0
	Pawtucket (IL)	AAA	.279	13	43	11	12	0	0	7	17	6	9	1
MINOR LEAGUE TOTALS			.321	408	1498	235	481	93	6	97	317	141	426	5

12. Jerome Gamble, rhp

Born: April 5, 1980. **Ht.:** 6-2. **Wt.:** 202. **Bats:** R. **Throws:** R. **School:** Benjamin Russell HS, Alexander City, Ala. **Career Transactions:** Selected by Red Sox in fourth round of 1998 draft; signed June 9, 1998.

Gamble may have the best raw arm in the organization, even better than that of his 2000 Augusta teammate, Brad Baker. The Red Sox have nursed him through elbow problems, which is why he has made just 31 appearances in three pro seasons. He was shut down at the end of each of the last two years. Gamble throws a consistent 93-94 mph, and his fastball rides at times and sinks at others. When he fills out his 6-foot-2 frame, scouts think he'll be able to work in the upper 90s on a regular basis. Gamble is a good athlete who played four years of defensive end for his high school football team. He didn't give up a homer in 2000 until his final start. He's still working on the other aspects of pitching, such as developing a curveball (which has its moments) and changeup and improving his command. When he gets that down, he'll be much better at combating lefthanders, who hit 90 points better off him last season than did righties. Gamble should start 2001 at high Class A Sarasota, where he's likely to spend the entire year polishing his craft.

Year	Club (League)	Class	W	L	ERA	G	GS	CG	SV	IP	H	R	ER	BB	SO
1998	Red Sox (GCL)	R	2	3	4.43	11	6	0	1	43	33	24	21	19	49
1999	Lowell (NY-P)	A	1	0	1.75	5	5	0	0	26	18	7	5	9	37
2000	Augusta (SAL)	A	5	3	2.52	15	15	0	0	79	69	26	22	32	71
MINOR LEAGUE TOTALS			8	5	2.94	31	26	0	1	147	120	77	48	60	157

13. Rick Asadoorian, of

Born: July 23, 1980. **Ht.:** 6-2. **Wt.:** 185. **Bats:** R. **Throws:** R. **School:** Northbridge HS, Whitinsville, Mass. **Career Transactions:** Selected by Red Sox in first round (17th overall) of 1999 draft; signed Aug. 16, 1999.

The Red Sox target New England players in the draft, and in 1999 they spent their first pick (17th overall) on Asadoorian, who grew up just 30 miles outside Boston. He held out that summer negotiating a club-record $1.7255 million bonus, and ranked as the No. 12 prospect in the Gulf Coast League in his pro debut last year. His most impressive tool is a throwing arm that has been compared to Dwight Evans', and Asadoorian showed in 2000 that he has center-field range to go with it. While he may be ready to play defensively in Boston now, his bat will take time. He'll need to reduce his strikeouts to hit at higher levels. To his credit, Asadoorian already is making adjustments at the plate. The Red Sox envision him developing at least gap power, and he was caught stealing just twice in 24 attempts. Asadoorian is ticketed for a full season at Augusta in 2001.

Year	Club (League)	Class	AVG	G	AB	R	H	2B	3B	HR	RBI	BB	SO	SB
2000	Red Sox (GCL)	R	.264	54	197	43	52	9	3	5	31	26	56	22
MINOR LEAGUE TOTALS			.264	54	197	43	52	9	3	5	31	26	56	22

14. Phil Dumatrait, lhp

Born: July 12, 1981. **Ht.:** 6-2. **Wt.:** 170. **Bats:** R. **Throws:** L. **School:** Bakersfield (Calif.) JC. **Career Transactions:** Selected by Red Sox in first round (22nd overall) of 2000 draft; signed July 10, 2000.

Of all the 2000 first-round draft picks, Dumatrait was perhaps the unlikeliest a year earlier. He wasn't drafted out of high school, which wasn't at all surprising because he had a low-80s fastball. But a season at Bakersfield (Calif.) Junior College did wonders. He got on a throwing program and suddenly was touching 94 mph. When the Red Sox decided Texas high school slugger Jason Stokes' $2.5 million asking price was too rich, they took Dumatrait 22nd overall and signed him for $1.275 million. John Sanders, his manager in the Gulf Coast League, rated his curveball as a better pitch than his fastball. Dumatrait also showed an easy arm action and formidable mound presence. Though he spent a year in junior college, he's still quite young at 19. It isn't out of the question that he'll spend 2001 at short-season Lowell, though he could make the Augusta staff if he impresses in spring training.

Year	Club (League)	Class	W	L	ERA	G	GS	CG	SV	IP	H	R	ER	BB	SO
2000	Red Sox (GCL)	R	0	1	1.65	6	6	0	0	16	10	6	3	12	12
MINOR LEAGUE TOTALS			0	1	1.65	6	6	0	0	16	10	6	3	12	12

15. Manny Delcarmen, rhp

Born: Feb. 16, 1982. **Ht.:** 6-2. **Wt.:** 190. **Bats:** R. **Throws:** R. **School:** West Roxbury (Mass.) HS. **Career Transactions:** Selected by Red Sox in second round of 2000 draft; signed Aug. 22, 2000.

Boston coveted Rhode Island high school outfielder Rocco Baldelli with its 2000 first-round pick, but the Devil Rays took him sixth overall. The Red Sox got their annual New England fix in the second round, when they drafted Delcarmen, a Dominican from inner-city Boston. He has impressive command of a low-90s fastball and a hard slider, and he should add more velocity as his skinny 6-foot-3 frame fills out. Though he can throw strikes with his two best pitches, Delcarmen is extremely raw and isn't anywhere close to being a finished product. He'll need to develop a changeup and a feel for pitching. Signed to a 2001 contract, he would be best served by making his pro debut in short-season ball.

Year	Club (League)	Class	W	L	ERA	G	GS	CG	SV	IP	H	R	ER	BB	SO
2000					Did Not Play—Signed 2001 Contract										

16. Morgan Burkhart, 1b

Born: Jan. 29, 1972. **Ht.:** 5-11. **Wt.:** 225. **Bats:** B. **Throws:** L. **School:** Central Missouri State University. **Career Transactions:** Signed by independent Richmond (Frontier), June 1995 . . . Signed by Red Sox, Oct. 21, 1998.

A lesser man would have given up far earlier, but Morgan Burkhart saw his perseverance pay off in 2000. After helping Central Missouri State win the 1994 Division II World Series, he was undrafted and spent the next spring coaching at his alma mater before signing with the independent Frontier League. Burkhart tore up the league for four straight seasons, winning MVP awards from 1996-98 and the triple crown in 1998, before a major league club could be bothered to sign him. Burkhart repaid the Red Sox by slamming 35 homers combined in high Class A and Double-A in 1999, his first year in Organized Ball, then was named MVP in the Mexican Pacific League during the winter. He showed he was no fluke last year, punishing Triple-A pitchers for 23 homers in 105 games and making his big league debut. Described by one scout as a poor man's John Kruk or Matt Stairs, Burkhart isn't athletic or pretty. He is an aggressive hitter from both sides of the plate, and he knows how to work counts to get a pitch he can drive. He doesn't run well—though he runs better than Stairs—and isn't much of an outfielder, but he's a passable first baseman. The Red Sox have a glut of first basemen/DHs, so Burkhart may find it difficult to even get a shot at a starting job. But he's a useful offensive player who at the worst could bolster their bench.

Year	Club (League)	Class	AVG	G	AB	R	H	2B	3B	HR	RBI	BB	SO	SB
1995	Richmond (Fron)	IND	.330	70	282	58	93	28	1	9	70	41	24	16
1996	Richmond (Fron)	IND	.357	74	266	60	95	27	1	17	64	49	24	22
1997	Richmond (Fron)	IND	.323	80	285	76	92	22	0	24	74	73	47	8
1998	Richmond (Fron)	IND	.404	80	280	97	113	18	1	36	98	85	38	13
1999	Sarasota (FSL)	A	.363	68	245	56	89	18	0	23	67	37	33	5
	Trenton (EL)	AA	.230	66	239	40	55	14	1	12	41	31	43	3
2000	Pawtucket (IL)	AAA	.255	105	353	59	90	17	1	23	77	69	89	0
	Boston (AL)	MAJ	.288	25	73	16	21	3	0	4	18	17	25	0
MAJOR LEAGUE TOTALS			.288	25	73	16	21	3	0	4	18	17	25	0
MINOR LEAGUE TOTALS			.286	239	817	155	234	49	2	58	185	139	165	8

17. Juan Pena, rhp

Born: June 27, 1977. **Ht.:** 6-5. **Wt.:** 215. **Bats:** R. **Throws:** R. **School:** Miami-Dade CC Wolfson. **Career Transactions:** Selected by Red Sox in 27th round of 1995 draft; signed June 3, 1995.

Little has gone right for Pena since he allowed just one earned run in 13 innings and won his first two major league starts in mid-May 1999. He soon went on the disabled list with shoulder tendinitis, then returned to pitch in the minors only to have his shoulder act up again. A strong candidate to earn a spot in Boston's rotation last spring, he tore the medial collateral ligament in his elbow and had season-ending surgery. Before he got hurt, Pena's best trait was his ability to pitch. He succeeded by precisely locating his pitches, the best of which was his curveball. The sink on his fastball was more impressive than its 89-91 mph velocity. He also throws a slider and changeup. Pena was back on the mound in instructional league and believes he'll be ready for spring training. If he contributes in Boston in 2001, it probably won't be until the second half of the season.

Year	Club (League)	Class	W	L	ERA	G	GS	CG	SV	IP	H	R	ER	BB	SO
1995	Red Sox (GCL)	R	3	2	1.95	13	4	2	1	55	41	17	12	6	47
	Sarasota (FSL)	A	1	1	4.91	2	2	0	0	7	8	4	4	3	5
1996	Michigan (Mid)	A	12	10	2.97	26	26	4	0	188	149	70	62	34	156
1997	Sarasota (FSL)	A	4	6	2.96	13	13	3	0	91	67	39	30	23	88
	Trenton (East)	AA	5	6	4.73	16	14	0	0	97	98	56	51	31	79
1998	Pawtucket (IL)	AAA	8	10	4.38	24	23	1	0	140	141	73	68	51	146
1999	Red Sox (GCL)	R	0	0	0.00	1	1	0	0	2	0	0	0	0	4
	Sarasota (FSL)	A	0	1	7.11	2	2	0	0	6	12	6	5	0	5
	Pawtucket (IL)	AAA	4	2	4.13	10	10	0	0	48	44	28	22	13	61
	Boston	MAJ	2	0	0.69	2	2	0	0	13	9	1	1	3	15
2000							Did Not Play—Injured									
MAJOR LEAGUE TOTALS			2	0	0.69	2	2	0	0	13	9	1	1	3	15
MINOR LEAGUE TOTALS			37	38	3.60	107	95	10	1	635	560	293	254	161	591

18. Luis Garcia, 1b

Born: Nov. 5, 1978. **Ht.:** 6-4. **Wt.:** 184. **Bats:** R. **Throws:** R. **Career Transactions:** Signed out of Mexico by Red Sox, March 14, 1996 . . . Loaned by Red Sox to Monterrey (Mexican), April 30-Sept. 20, 1999.

Garcia signed as a pitcher and threw 91-92 mph before an arm injury finished him on the mound. The Red Sox thought so little of him that they loaned him to Mexico's Monterrey Sultans, who assigned him to a co-op team in the Rookie-level Arizona League, which he promptly led with 13 homers and a .649 slugging percentage. Teams that inquired about signing Garcia then found out he was Red Sox property. Jumped to Class A in 2000, Garcia continued to hit for power. He gets a lot of leverage in his swing, giving him the chance to have above-average power. He has athleticism and arm strength, and might be able to move from first base to the outfield if he hones his defense. Garcia figures to move to high Class A Sarasota this year and see time at both first and in the outfield.

Year	Club (League)	Class	AVG	G	AB	R	H	2B	3B	HR	RBI	BB	SO	SB
1998	Red Sox (DSL)	R	.212	54	189	31	40	6	2	8	32	27	33	3
1999	Mexico (AZL)	R	.330	50	188	35	62	9	6	13	40	22	31	1
2000	Augusta (SAL)	A	.260	128	493	72	128	27	5	20	77	51	112	8
MINOR LEAGUE TOTALS			.279	232	870	138	230	42	13	41	149	100	176	12

19. Luis Peres, lhp

Born: Feb. 10, 1981. **Ht.:** 6-0. **Wt.:** 150. **Bats:** R. **Throws:** L. **Career Transactions:** Signed out of Dominican Republic by Red Sox, Sep. 14, 1998.

Peres has pitched at the lowest rungs on the development ladder, but it's hard not to get at least a little excited about his raw statistics. He resembles a teenage version of fellow Dominican Pedro Martinez. And like Martinez, he throws harder than his build makes it seem possible. Peres consistently throws in the low 90s, and his fastball explodes on hitters, so much so that he can survive up in the strike zone. He also has a late-breaking curveball and shows no fear in challenging batters. Peres still needs to improve his command and his changeup, and he must get stronger after wearing down and missing the final month of the GCL season. Boston may play it safe and assign him to short-season Lowell in 2001.

Year	Club (League)	Class	W	L	ERA	G	GS	CG	SV	IP	H	R	ER	BB	SO
1999	Red Sox (DSL)	R	6	6	1.94	13	13	0	0	70	38	29	15	30	107
2000	Red Sox (GCL)	R	3	1	2.36	9	5	0	1	34	24	12	9	13	43
MINOR LEAGUE TOTALS			9	7	2.07	22	18	0	1	104	62	41	24	43	150

20. Tai-In Che, lhp

Born: Oct. 11, 1982. **Ht.:** 6-2. **Wt.:** 183. **Bats:** L. **Throws:** L. **Career Transactions:** Signed out of Korea by Red Sox, June 4, 2000.

The Red Sox have more depth among lefthanded pitchers than any other position in their system. Most of that talent is in the lower minors, and Che has yet to make his U.S. debut after signing during the summer for $750,000. Che averages 90-91 mph and touches 93, very good velocity for a southpaw, and he projects to add more because he packs little bulk on his 6-foot-2 frame right now. He has a quick breaking ball and should have average or better command. His changeup needs work and he'll have to get acclimated to a new culture, but his upside is intriguing. He'll join Boston in spring training after finishing high school in February.

Year	Club (League)	Class	W	L	ERA	G	GS	CG	SV	IP	H	R	ER	BB	SO
2000							Did Not Play—Signed 2001 Contract									

21. Antron Seiber, of

Born: May 19, 1980. **Ht.:** 6-1. **Wt.:** 185. **Bats:** R. **Throws:** R. **School:** Independence (La.) HS. **Career Transactions:** Selected by Red Sox in third round of 1999 draft; signed July 15, 1999.

Seiber was headed to Louisiana State to play wide receiver before the Red Sox signed him. He's the fastest player in the system and stole 22 bases in 27 attempts last year. He understands what he needs to do to be successful at the plate. He doesn't swing for the fences, instead using a compact swing to hit line drives and enhance his chances of getting on base. He'll need to tighten his strike zone to fit at the top of a batting order. Defensively, he offers outstanding range and a strong, accurate arm, and he takes good routes on fly balls. He has center-field skills, though he played left in 2000 in deference to teammate Rick Asadoorian. Seiber will stay on an outfield corner as he teams with Asadoorian at Augusta this year.

Year	Club (League)	Class	AVG	G	AB	R	H	2B	3B	HR	RBI	BB	SO	SB
1999	Red Sox (GCL)	R	.261	13	46	6	12	0	2	0	10	4	11	2
2000	Red Sox (GCL)	R	.306	49	196	36	60	7	1	4	21	16	31	21
	Lowell (NY-P)	A	.190	6	21	2	4	0	1	0	2	0	5	1
MINOR LEAGUE TOTALS			.289	68	263	44	76	0	4	4	33	20	47	24

22. Mat Thompson, rhp

Born: Aug. 28, 1981. **Ht.:** 6-2. **Wt.:** 205. **Bats:** R. **Throws:** R. **School:** Timberline HS, Boise, Idaho. **Career Transactions:** Selected by Red Sox in second round of 1999 draft; signed July 3, 1999.

After a high school career in which he never lost a game, Thompson became the highest draft pick out of Idaho since the Red Sox took righthander Mike Garman with the third overall pick in 1967. He's still raw and signed at 17, so he'll need time to develop. His best pitch is a 91-92 mph sinker that induces plenty of ground balls. His curveball has potential but lacks consistency, and his changeup is in the rudimentary stages. Thompson throws strikes but almost to a fault, as Gulf Coast League hitters batted .280 against him in 2000. He'll need to improve his command within the strike zone as he moves up the system. The Red Sox have been cautious with Thompson, so he could spend 2001 at short-season Lowell.

Year	Club (League)	Class	W	L	ERA	G	GS	CG	SV	IP	H	R	ER	BB	SO
1999	Red Sox (GCL)	R	0	0	1.20	5	2	0	0	15	7	3	2	4	12
2000	Red Sox (GCL)	R	4	2	3.65	12	11	0	0	57	65	33	23	18	54
MINOR LEAGUE TOTALS			4	2	3.12	17	13	0	0	72	72	36	25	22	66

23. Carlos Rodriguez, of

Born: June 12, 1977. **Ht.:** 6-2. **Wt.:** 210. **Bats:** R. **Throws:** R. **School:** University of Louisville. **Career Transactions:** Selected by Red Sox in 11th round of 1998 draft; signed June 7, 1998.

Born in Cuba, Rodriguez moved to Louisville when his family won an immigration lottery. After bombing at Augusta in 1999 before he was demoted to Lowell, he returned last year and hit for average and power. Rodriguez is a big, strong right fielder with strength and defensive skills. He'll need to make offensive adjustments as he rises through the minors, because his swing is long and his plate discipline is lacking. Don't be misled by his 24 steals in 2000. He does have average speed but was caught stealing 12 times, making for a break-even ratio. At 23, Rodriguez was old for the South Atlantic League, so he could be pushed to Double-A in 2001 if he has a strong first half at Sarasota.

Year	Club (League)	Class	AVG	G	AB	R	H	2B	3B	HR	RBI	BB	SO	SB
1998	Red Sox (GCL)	R	.325	54	197	35	64	14	2	8	37	11	37	14
1999	Augusta (SAL)	A	.193	33	119	14	23	6	1	3	8	8	41	1
	Lowell (NY-P)	A	.250	60	228	37	57	13	5	12	46	13	66	17
2000	Augusta (SAL)	A	.306	116	471	62	144	28	5	18	94	17	108	24
MINOR LEAGUE TOTALS			.284	263	1015	148	288	61	13	41	185	49	252	56

24. Israel Alcantara, 1b

Born: May 6, 1973. **Ht.:** 6-2. **Wt.:** 180. **Bats:** R. **Throws:** R. **Career Transactions:** Signed out of Dominican Republic by Expos, July 2, 1990 . . . Granted free agency, Oct. 17, 1997 . . . Signed by Devil Rays, Dec. 16, 1997 . . . Loaned by Devil Rays to Phillies, June 22-Aug. 18, 1998 . . . Loaned by Devil Rays to Mariners, Aug. 18-Sept. 21, 1998 . . . Granted free agency, Oct. 16, 1998 . . . Signed by Red Sox, Nov. 4, 1998 . . . Granted free agency, Oct. 15, 1999; re-signed by Red Sox, Jan 4, 2000 . . . Granted free agency, Dec. 20, 2000; re-signed by Red Sox, Dec. 21, 2000.

One anecdote sums up the best and worst about Alcantara. On the night he was to be honored as Pawtucket's MVP, he showed up three hours late and was benched. He produced after Boston called him up in late June last year, but made a greater impression by displaying an utter lack of hustle that stood out even more on an overachieving team battling for a wild-card berth. He offers plenty of righthanded power and may hit for a decent average, but that's it. He doesn't walk and strikes out a ton because he's aggressive at the plate, and can't play anywhere but first base or DH. Red Sox manager Jimy Williams didn't care for Alcantara, so he may have a hard time making the team ahead of Juan Diaz and Morgan Burkhart.

Year	Club (League)	Class	AVG	G	AB	R	H	2B	3B	HR	RBI	BB	SO	SB
1991	Expos (DSL)	R	.285	68	239	42	68	9	2	13	51	32	41	8
1992	Expos (GCL)	R	.277	59	224	29	62	14	2	3	37	17	35	6
1993	Burlington (Mid)	A	.245	126	470	65	115	26	3	18	73	20	125	6
1994	W. Palm Beach (FSL)	A	.285	125	471	65	134	26	4	15	69	26	130	9
1995	Harrisburg (EL)	AA	.211	71	237	25	50	12	2	10	29	21	81	1
	W. Palm Beach (FSL)	A	.276	39	134	16	37	7	2	3	22	9	35	3
1996	Harrisburg (EL)	AA	.211	62	218	26	46	5	0	8	19	14	62	1
	Expos (GCL)	R	.300	7	30	4	9	2	0	2	10	3	6	0
	W. Palm Beach (FSL)	A	.311	15	61	11	19	2	0	4	14	3	13	0
1997	Harrisburg (EL)	AA	.282	89	301	48	85	9	2	27	68	29	84	4
1998	St. Petersburg (FSL)	A	.333	38	141	21	47	5	0	10	26	21	29	1
	Reading (EL)	AA	.310	53	203	36	63	12	2	15	44	17	37	0
	Orlando (SL)	AA	.236	15	55	8	13	4	0	3	18	7	15	0
1999	Trenton (EL)	AA	.294	77	293	48	86	26	0	20	60	27	78	4
	Pawtucket (IL)	AAA	.272	24	81	13	22	3	0	9	23	9	29	0
2000	Pawtucket (IL)	AAA	.308	78	299	60	92	17	1	29	76	25	84	2
	Boston (AL)	MAJ	.289	21	45	9	13	1	0	4	7	3	7	0
MAJOR LEAGUE TOTALS			.289	21	45	9	13	1	0	4	7	3	7	0
MINOR LEAGUE TOTALS			.274	946	3457	517	948	179	20	189	639	280	884	45

25. Shea Hillenbrand, 1b/3b

Born: July 27, 1975. **Ht.:** 6-1. **Wt.:** 200. **Bats:** R. **Throws:** R. **School:** Mesa (Ariz.) CC. **Career Transactions:** Selected by Red Sox in 10th round of 1996 draft; signed June 6, 1996.

Hillenbrand would rank considerably higher had he been able to stay behind the plate. He played shortstop in junior college, moved to first base for his first two seasons as a pro, then broke out by hitting .349 in 1998, his first year as a catcher. He caught in Double-A in 1999 but played strictly first and third base last year. Hillenbrand improved his average 64 points in his second shot at Double-A and led the Eastern League in hits and plate appearances per strikeout (14.31). His ability to make contact and penchant for swinging at everything cut into his walks and on-base percentage. And because he lunges at pitches, his strength translates more into gap power than home runs. Some think he feasts on mediocre pitchers and won't hit better ones. Hillenbrand doesn't run or move well enough to offer anything defensively. He best fits as a DH or a bat off the bench. He'll move to Triple-A in 2001.

Year	Club (League)	Class	AVG	G	AB	R	H	2B	3B	HR	RBI	BB	SO	SB
1996	Lowell (NY-P)	A	.315	72	279	33	88	18	2	2	38	18	32	4
1997	Michigan (Mid)	A	.290	64	224	28	65	13	3	3	39	9	20	1
	Sarasota (FSL)	A	.295	57	220	25	65	12	0	2	28	7	29	9
1998	Michigan (Mid)	A	.349	129	498	80	174	33	4	19	93	19	49	13
1999	Trenton (EL)	AA	.259	69	282	41	73	15	0	7	36	14	27	6
2000	Trenton (EL)	AA	.323	135	529	77	171	35	3	11	79	19	39	3
MINOR LEAGUE TOTALS			.313	526	2032	284	636	126	12	44	241	86	196	36

26. Justin Duchscherer, rhp

Born: Nov. 19, 1977. **Ht.:** 6-3. **Wt.:** 165. **Bats:** R. **Throws:** R. **School:** Coronado HS, Lubbock, Texas. **Career Transactions:** Selected by Red Sox in eighth round of 1996 draft; signed June 14, 1996.

Duchscherer didn't reach Double-A until his fifth season, but he responded as Trenton's pitcher of the year. He hasn't been able to add weight to his wiry frame, so his fastball hasn't developed into even an average pitch. He has to have above-average command to succeed. He has so far because he repeats his delivery well. He does throw his breaking pitch, alternately described as a curve and a slider, from a good downward plane and has an effective changeup. He held lefthanders to .213 and .192 averages the last two seasons. Duchscherer is the type who must prove himself each year, and he'll be tested at Triple-A in 2001.

Year	Club (League)	Class	W	L	ERA	G	GS	CG	SV	IP	H	R	ER	BB	SO
1996	Red Sox (GCL)	R	0	2	3.13	13	8	0	1	55	52	26	19	14	45
1997	Red Sox (GCL)	R	2	3	1.81	10	8	0	0	45	34	18	9	17	59
	Michigan (Mid)	A	1	1	5.63	4	4	0	0	24	26	17	15	10	19
1998	Michigan (Mid)	A	7	12	4.79	30	26	0	0	143	166	87	76	47	106
1999	Augusta (SAL)	A	4	0	0.22	6	6	0	0	41	21	1	1	8	39
	Sarasota (FSL)	A	7	7	4.49	20	18	0	0	112	101	62	56	30	105

2000	Trenton (EL)	AA	7	9	3.39	24	24	2	0	143	134	59	54	35	126
MINOR LEAGUE TOTALS			28	34	3.68	107	94	2	1	562	534	270	230	161	499

27. Greg Montalbano, lhp

Born: Aug. 24, 1977. **Ht.:** 6-2. **Wt.:** 185. **Bats:** L. **Throws:** L. **School:** Northeastern University. **Career Transactions:** Selected by Red Sox in fifth round of 1999 draft; signed June 2, 2000.

The Red Sox signed Montalbano nearly a year after he was drafted, having controlled his rights because he was a fifth-year senior. He has just an average fastball but does have a lot going for him. He has a good curveball and cutter. He knows how to pitch, throws strikes, changes speeds and battles his way out of jams. Montalbano overcame adversity before his standout career at Northeastern, recovering from testicular cancer that cost him all of 1996. He'll pitch in Class A in 2001 and projects as an end-of-rotation starter or middle reliever.

Year	Club (League)	Class	W	L	ERA	G	GS	CG	SV	IP	H	R	ER	BB	SO
2000	Red Sox (GCL)	R	0	2	3.75	4	4	0	0	12	13	6	5	3	14
	Lowell (NY-P)	A	0	1	1.74	2	2	0	0	10	4	3	2	4	15
MINOR LEAGUE TOTALS			0	3	2.86	6	6	0	0	22	17	9	7	7	29

28. Bryan Barnowski, c

Born: Sept. 3, 1980. **Ht.:** 6-2. **Wt.:** 205. **Bats:** R. **Throws:** R. **School:** St. Petersburg (Fla.) JC. **Career Transactions:** Selected by Red Sox in 42nd round of June 1998 draft; signed May 25, 1999.

While Tony Blanco received a lot of attention after setting a Gulf Coast League record with 13 homers in 2000, his teammate Barnowski got almost none for doing the same. The grandson of former big leaguer and longtime scout Dick Teed, Barnowski improved after getting into better shape. He has a short stroke, excellent raw power and good balance at the plate. He lacks speed and his future as a catcher is in doubt. He does have arm strength, but he doesn't move well behind the plate and threw out just 19 percent of basestealers last year. Barnowski, who could see time at Class A Augusta in 2001, will probably move to first base.

Year	Club (League)	Class	AVG	G	AB	R	H	2B	3B	HR	RBI	BB	SO	SB
1999	Red Sox (GCL)	R	.227	32	88	13	20	5	1	0	4	10	23	3
2000	Red Sox (GCL)	R	.301	50	166	40	50	9	0	13	33	23	46	1
	Lowell (NY-P)	A	.188	5	16	1	3	1	0	0	1	1	4	0
MINOR LEAGUE TOTALS			.270	87	270	54	73	15	1	13	38	34	73	4

29. Chul Oh, of

Born: May 17, 1981. **Ht.:** 6-3. **Wt.:** 196. **Bats:** L. **Throws:** R. **Career Transactions:** Signed out of Korea by Red Sox, Sept. 9, 1999.

Most of the Red Sox' Asian signings have been pitchers, but in September 1999 they spent $700,000 on Oh, the top Korean high school hitter at the time. He's raw and knew no English before arriving in the United States, so he played sparingly in the Gulf Coast League. He's really closer to 215 pounds than his listed weight and is still just a teenager. Oh shows flashes of being an above-average hitter, as he has a smooth stroke and plenty of raw power. He will need to refine his approach at the plate. He's a solid average runner who should become a decent corner outfielder. Boston is bringing Oh slowly, so he could return to the GCL.

Year	Club (League)	Class	AVG	G	AB	R	H	2B	3B	HR	RBI	BB	SO	SB
2000	Red Sox (GCL)	R	.286	24	70	8	20	6	0	2	9	4	16	0
MINOR LEAGUE TOTALS			.286	24	70	8	20	6	0	2	9	4	16	0

30. Freddy Sanchez, ss

Born: Dec. 21, 1977. **Ht.:** 5-11. **Wt.:** 185. **Bats:** R. **Throws:** R. **School:** Oklahoma City University. **Career Transactions:** Selected by Red Sox in 11th round of 2000 draft; signed June 9, 2000.

Sanchez is the best of a thin middle-infield crop in the Red Sox system. He played at three different colleges, reaching the 1999 NAIA World Series with Dallas Baptist and earning first-team NAIA all-America honors in 2000. Sanchez was Lowell's MVP before moving up to Class A. He doesn't have much power and has average speed, so he'll need to enhance his on-base ability. Defensively, his sure hands are his strongest suit. He should have enough arm to play shortstop, though he has played second base to enhance his versatility. Given his age and his success in his pro debut, he could start 2001 in high Class A.

Year	Club (League)	Class	AVG	G	AB	R	H	2B	3B	HR	RBI	BB	SO	SB
2000	Lowell (NY-P)	A	.288	34	132	24	38	13	2	1	14	9	16	2
	Augusta (SAL)	A	.303	30	109	17	33	7	0	0	15	11	19	4
MINOR LEAGUE TOTALS			.295	64	241	41	71	20	2	1	29	20	35	6

Chicago
Cubs

By Jim Callis

Though they're a franchise associated with losing, the Cubs have been doing more of it than even they are accustomed to over the last two seasons. Their 97 losses last season were the most since 1980, and their two-year total of 192 losses is their worst since 1965-66. Meanwhile, the crosstown White Sox are the American League Central champs, having rebuilt with a farm system so well stocked that they should contend indefinitely.

Hard as it is to believe, the Cubs could be on the verge of doing the same. At the major league level, the Andy MacPhail regime has but one wild-card appearance to show for its six years in Chicago. But down below in the minors, Jim Hendry and Co. have amassed plenty of talent.

Before Hendry was named farm director in November 1994, the system was embarrassingly barren. The top prospects were outfielder Brooks Kieschnick and righthander Amaury Telemaco, and there was little depth behind them. That began to change, especially once Hendry was named scouting director in 1995 and began hitting on each of his first-round picks: Todd Noel (1996), Jon Garland (1997), Corey Patterson (1998), Ben Christensen (1999) and Luis Montanez (2000). All five have star potential, though Noel and Garland were inexplicably jettisoned for veterans during the 1998 wild-card drive.

Under Hendry, the Cubs also mined the international market like never before. Director of Latin American operations Oneri Fleita oversaw the signings of power pitchers Juan Cruz (Dominican Republic) and Carlos Zambrano (Venezuela). Forays into Korea netted slugging first baseman Hee Seop Choi and catcher Yoon-Min Kweon.

Cubs fans got a sneak preview of Patterson last September, though the wave of prospects is still a year away from making an impact at Wrigley Field. That wasn't soon enough to save the job of former general manager Ed Lynch, who resigned last July. MacPhail added GM duties to his titles as team president and quickly rewarded the men who have reshaped the system. Hendry was promoted to assistant GM, while Fleita was named farm director and scouting coordinator/national crosschecker John Stockstill became scouting director.

MacPhail plans to relinquish the GM job at the end of the 2001 season, and it's widely expected that he'll name Hendry as his successor. Soon thereafter, the Cubs should be a young team stocked with athletes and quality arms, giving Hendry the opportunity to reap what he has sown.

OrganizationOverview

General manager: Andy MacPhail. Farm director: Oneri Fleita. Scouting director: John Stockstill.

2000 PERFORMANCE

Class	Team	League	W	L	Pct.	Finish*	Manager
Majors	Chicago	National	65	97	.401	t-15th (16)	Don Baylor
Triple-A	Iowa Cubs	Pacific Coast	57	87	.396	16th (16)	Dave Trembley
Double-A	West Tenn Diamond Jaxx	Southern	80	58	.580	1st (10)	Dave Bialas
High A	Daytona Cubs	Florida State	76	63	.547	5th (14)	Richie Zisk
Low A	Lansing Lugnuts	Midwest	70	68	.507	8th (14)	Steve McFarland
Short-season	#Eugene Emeralds	Northwest	40	36	.526	3rd (8)	Danny Sheaffer
Rookie	Mesa Cubs	Arizona	32	24	.571	3rd (9)	Carmelo Martinez
OVERALL 2000 MINOR LEAGUE RECORD			354	336	.513	12th (30)	

*Finish in overall standings (No. of teams in league). #Affiliate will be in Boise (Northwest) in 2001.

ORGANIZATION LEADERS

BATTING
*AVG	**Ryan Gripp**, Lansing	.333
R	**Ryan Gripp**, Lansing	87
H	**Ryan Gripp**, Lansing	166
TB	**Ryan Gripp**, Lansing	262
2B	**Ryan Gripp**, Lansing	36
3B	Eric Hinske, West Tenn	9
	Jandin Thornton-Murray, Cubs (AZL)	9
HR	Julio Zuleta, Iowa	26
RBI	Hee Seop Choi, Daytona/West Tenn	95
BB	Eric Hinske, West Tenn	78
SO	Eric Hinske, West Tenn	133
SB	Ben Johnstone, Lansing	54

PITCHING
W	Lindsay Gulin, Daytona/West Tenn	16
L	Phil Norton, Iowa	13
	Micah Bowie, Iowa/West Tenn	13
#ERA	Wilton Chavez, Eugene	1.69
G	Courtney Duncan, West Tenn	61
CG	Three tied at	3
SV	**Courtney Duncan**, West Tenn	25
IP	Mike Wuertz, Daytona	171
BB	Phil Norton, Iowa	104
SO	Joey Nation, West Tenn	165

*Minimum 250 at-bats. #Minimum 75 innings.

TOP PROSPECTS OF THE DECADE

1991	Lance Dickson, lhp
1992	Lance Dickson, lhp
1993	Jessie Hollins, rhp
1994	Brooks Kieschnick, of
1995	Brooks Kieschnick, of
1996	Brooks Kieschnick, of
1997	Kerry Wood, rhp
1998	Kerry Wood, rhp
1999	Corey Patterson, of
2000	Corey Patterson, of

TOP DRAFT PICKS OF THE DECADE

1991	Doug Glanville, of
1992	Derek Wallace, rhp
1993	Brooks Kieschnick, of
1994	Jayson Peterson, rhp
1995	Kerry Wood, rhp
1996	Todd Noel, rhp
1997	Jon Garland, rhp
1998	Corey Patterson, of
1999	Ben Christensen, rhp
2000	Luis Montanez, ss

JOHN SPEAR

Gripp   **Duncan**

BEST TOOLS

Best Hitter for Average	Corey Patterson
Best Power Hitter	Hee Seop Choi
Fastest Baserunner	Corey Patterson
Best Fastball	Carlos Zambrano
Best Breaking Ball	Juan Cruz
Best Control	Ben Christensen
Best Defensive Catcher	Ryan Jorgensen
Best Defensive Infielder	Nate Frese
Best Infield Arm	Luis Montanez
Best Defensive Outfielder	Corey Patterson
Best Outfield Arm	Mike Mallory

PROJECTED 2004 LINEUP

Catcher	Todd Hundley
First Base	Hee Seop Choi
Second Base	Bobby Hill
Third Base	David Kelton
Shortstop	Luis Montanez
Left Field	Rondell White
Center Field	Corey Patterson
Right Field	Sammy Sosa
No. 1 Starter	Kerry Wood
No. 2 Starter	Juan Cruz
No. 3 Starter	Jon Lieber
No. 4 Starter	Ben Christensen
No. 5 Starter	John Webb
Closer	Carlos Zambrano

ALL-TIME LARGEST BONUSES

Corey Patterson, 1998	$3,700,000
Luis Montanez, 2000	2,750,000
Bobby Hill, 2000	1,425,000
Jon Garland, 1997	1,325,000
Kerry Wood, 1995	1,265,000

DraftAnalysis

2000 Draft

Best Pro Debut: SS Luis Montanez (1) was MVP and the top prospect in the Rookie-level Arizona League after batting .344-2-37 with 11 steals in 50 games. LHP Mark Freed (9) led the short-season Northwest League with nine victories, while OF Antoine Cameron (12) topped the AZL with 48 RBIs.

Best Athlete: OF Gary Banks (5), who moved from shortstop because he was on the same team as Montanez, won two Alabama state football championships as a high school quarterback. OF Nic Jackson (3) has solid average tools across the board.

Best Hitter: Montanez or 3B J.J. Johnson (6), who batted .316 in the AZL.

Best Raw Power: Johnson.

Fastest Runner: Banks runs a 6.6-second 60-yard dash.

Best Defensive Player: Ryan Jorgensen (7) was the best defensive catcher in the Southeastern Conference, but he also was a backup to Division I home run and RBI leader Brad Cresse at Louisiana State. He's an advanced catcher with good receiving and throwing skills. As a bonus, he hit .300 in the NWL. If he can continue to hit, he might be the catching prospect the Cubs have been seeking for years.

Best Fastball: RHP Todd Wellemeyer (4) throws 93-94 mph. He also has above-average pitches with his splitter and curveball.

Most Intriguing Background: RHP Jason Szuminski (27) may be the first player ever drafted out of the Massachusetts Institute of Technology. He throws 90-93 mph and posted a 3.38 ERA at Class A Lansing. SS Enrique Cruz (49), who didn't sign, is the son of former Astros all-star Jose and the brother of Blue Jays center fielder Jose Jr.

Closest To The Majors: SS **Bobby Hill** (2) has leadoff skills and is expected to start his Cubs career at Double-A. LHP Aaron Krawiec (3) went 6-4, 2.54 at Eugene and could move fast with a 90-93 mph sinker to go with a nice curveball and changeup.

ROBERT GURGANUS

Hill

Best Late-Round Pick: Cameron is a lefthanded hitter who can bat for average and power. LHP Carmen Pignatiello (20), who pitched well for the Team USA junior team in 1999, has command of three pitches and reminds the Cubs of Kirk Rueter.

The One Who Got Away: Hill spent the summer in the independent Atlantic League despite being drafted in the second round by the White Sox in 1999 and the Cubs in 2000, but he finally signed in November. So the best player the Cubs lost was 3B Chad Corona (16), who turned down $150,000 to go to San Diego State.

Assessment: The Cubs got the guy they wanted with the No. 3 overall pick (Montanez) for the price they wanted (a prearranged $2.75 million), then got Hill for $1.425 million. By bringing in two quality middle infielders, they addressed one of the organization's biggest weaknesses.

1999 Draft

RHP Ben Christensen (1) will arrive in Wrigley Field in a hurry. 3B Ryan Gripp (3) won the Midwest League batting title last year, and RHP John Webb (19) is a sleeper. **Grade: B**

1998 Draft

By himself, OF Corey Patterson (1) could make a draft. The Cubs didn't stop there, also grabbing 3B David Kelton (2), C Jeff Golbach (3), LHP Will Ohman (8), SS Nate Frese (10) and 3B Eric Hinske (17). **Grade: A**

1997 Draft

Good move: taking RHP Jon Garland (1) with your top pick. Bad move: trading him for Matt Karchner, to your crosstown rivals, no less. Chicago's consolation prizes are RHPs Mike Wuertz (11) and Matt Bruback (47, draft-and-follow), but neither is a Garland. **Grade: B**

1996 Draft

Two days after dealing Garland in 1998, the Cubs traded RHP Todd Noel (1), who has an electric arm when he's healthy. OF Quincy Carter (2) bolted for football two years after signing, but may return. Chicago did get several players who have or will reach the majors, including 2B/OF Chad Meyers (5) and LHP Philip Norton (10). **Grade: C+**

Note: Draft analysis prepared by Jim Callis. Numbers in parentheses indicate draft rounds.

... Patterson has the best combination of athleticism and baseball skills of any prospect in the game.

Corey Patterson of

Born: Aug. 13, 1979.
Ht.: 5-10. **Wt.:** 180.
Bats: L. **Throws:** R.
School: Harrison HS, Kennesaw, Ga.
Career Transactions: Selected by Cubs in first round (third overall) of 1998 draft; signed Sept. 18, 1998.

When the Cubs signed Patterson to a club-record $3.7 million bonus in 1998, then-scouting director Jim Hendry told club president Andy MacPhail that Patterson would reach the majors within three years. He beat that timetable, arriving last September and hitting his first two big league homers off Juan Acevedo and Alan Benes. Patterson wouldn't have been at Wrigley Field had he made the U.S. Olympic team, but he was chosen only as an alternate and declined. That was the only disappointment in 2000 as he jumped from low Class A to Double-A West Tenn. One of the youngest players in the Southern League, he was batting just .243-6-28 at the end of May before finishing with a .274-16-54 surge over the final three months. He finished second in the league in homers and fourth in RBIs, and managers rated him the circuit's top prospect.

Patterson offers the best combination of athleticism and baseball skills of any prospect in the game. He's the best hitter, the fastest runner and the top outfield defender in the organization. His other two tools, power and arm strength, are both above-average. His top-of-the-line speed is probably his most impressive physical asset, and he has a chiseled physique with biceps that seem a couple of sizes too large for his 5-foot-10 frame. Patterson has more than held his own while being rushed through the minors, and the Cubs love his makeup. He still has to work on the nuances of the game. He has batted just .195 against lefthanders as a pro. He needs to tighten his plate discipline, and his ability to drive pitches that are out of the strike zone actually hampers his ability to draw walks. Despite his blazing speed, he wasn't a particularly effective basestealer in 2000, getting caught 14 times in 41 attempts. Scouts believe Patterson can correct all of those flaws with more experience. They're understandable, considering his age and how much he has been pushed.

If the Cubs trade Sammy Sosa, they'll market Patterson as the cornerstone of the franchise. That would be premature, as his struggles against southpaws show he's not ready for the majors quite yet. While he could make Chicago's Opening Day roster if he performs well in spring training, Patterson would be better served by at least half a season in Triple-A to catch his breath. When he puts it all together, he should be one of the game's superstars.

LARRY GOREN

Year	Club (League)	Class	AVG	G	AB	R	H	2B	3B	HR	RBI	BB	SO	SB
1999	Lansing (Mid)	A	.320	112	475	94	152	35	17	20	79	25	85	33
2000	West Tenn (SL)	AA	.261	118	444	73	116	26	5	22	82	45	115	27
	Chicago (NL)	MAJ	.167	11	42	9	7	1	0	2	2	3	14	1
MAJOR LEAGUE TOTALS			.167	11	42	9	7	1	0	2	2	3	14	1
MINOR LEAGUE TOTALS			.292	230	919	167	268	61	22	42	161	70	200	60

2. Juan Cruz, rhp

Born: Oct. 15, 1980. **Ht.:** 6-2. **Wt.:** 155. **Bats:** R. **Throws:** R. **Career Transactions:** Signed out of Dominican Republic by Cubs, July 4, 1997.

Cruz made the biggest breakthrough in baseball last season. He entered 2000 with a 7-10, 5.99 career record and went 0-5, 9.99 in his first six starts. Then everything clicked, and he went 8-0, 1.86 with 134 strikeouts in 116 innings the rest of the way. Cruz ranked as the No. 2 prospect in both the Midwest and Florida State leagues. He has the best stuff in the organization. He throws a lively 94-97 mph fastball, and wasn't clocked under 94 mph when he threw a 14-strikeout gem in the FSL playoffs. He also has a power slider and a changeup that serves as a good third pitch. He relishes pitching inside, making it difficult to dig in against him. Cruz improved his command as his career took off last year, and it still could get better. Other than that, he just needs a little more experience. It's trendy to compare wispy, hard-throwing Dominicans to Pedro Martinez these days, but Cruz makes a better case than most. He'll prove whether he's for real when he moves up to Double-A in 2001, and the Cubs certainly believe he is. If he progresses like he did a year ago, he could reach Chicago by the end of the season.

Year	Club (League)	Class	W	L	ERA	G	GS	CG	SV	IP	H	R	ER	BB	SO
1998	Cubs (AZL)	R	2	4	6.10	12	5	0	0	41	61	48	28	14	36
1999	Eugene (NWL)	A	5	6	5.94	15	15	0	0	80	97	59	53	33	65
2000	Lansing (Mid)	A	5	5	3.28	17	17	2	0	96	75	50	35	60	106
	Daytona (FSL)	A	3	0	3.25	8	7	1	0	44	30	22	16	18	54
MINOR LEAGUE TOTALS			15	15	4.53	52	44	3	0	262	263	179	132	125	261

3. Hee Seop Choi, 1b

Born: March 16, 1979. **Ht.:** 6-5. **Wt.:** 235. **Bats:** L. **Throws:** L. **Career Transactions:** Signed out of Korea by Cubs, March 4, 1999.

As a 19-year-old, Choi homered in the quarterfinals and semifinals of the 1998 World Championships in Italy. The following March, he became the first Korean position-player prospect to sign with a major league club when he accepted a $1.2 million bonus from the Cubs. He has done nothing but hit ever since, and he led the Arizona Fall League in homers (six) and slugging percentage (.577) after the 2000 season. Choi is a more advanced hitter than Corey Patterson at this point, thanks to his short stroke and understanding of the strike zone. Choi has tremendous power to all fields and he's a better athlete than Chicago thought he would be. He was the high Class A Florida State League's best defensive first baseman and runs well for his size and position. He turned down the team's offer to pay for an interpreter for the 2000 season because he wanted to learn English more quickly. Choi has fanned 184 times in 211 pro games, though he also draws plenty of walks and his extra-base production more than offsets his strikeouts. A big man, he'll have to watch his weight in the future. The Cubs have let Mark Grace go, but scouts who saw Choi in the AFL believe he needs Triple-A time. He could take over the first-base job toward the end of the season, and he won't let it go for a while.

Year	Club (League)	Class	AVG	G	AB	R	H	2B	3B	HR	RBI	BB	SO	SB
1999	Lansing (Mid)	A	.321	79	290	71	93	18	6	18	70	50	68	2
2000	Daytona (FSL)	A	.296	96	345	60	102	25	6	15	70	37	78	4
	West Tenn (SL)	AA	.303	36	122	25	37	9	0	10	25	25	38	3
MINOR LEAGUE TOTALS			.306	211	757	156	232	52	12	43	165	112	184	9

4. Ben Christensen, rhp

Born: Feb. 7, 1978. **Ht.:** 6-4. **Wt.:** 205. **Bats:** R. **Throws:** R. **School:** Wichita State University. **Career Transactions:** Selected by Cubs in first round (26th overall) of 1999 draft; signed June 25, 1999.

Christensen always will be associated with beaning Evansville batter Anthony Molina while they were warming up before a Wichita State game in 1999. But he's making a name for himself as a pitcher, permitting more than three earned runs in just two of his starts last season before he was shut down in early July with shoulder tendinitis. Christensen has two well above-average pitches in his 90-94 mph sinker and his slider. As a bonus, he has good command of both of those offerings, as well as his curveball and an improving changeup. He had nearly as many strikeouts as baserunners allowed last year. Christensen's shoulder problems aren't considered serious. He just needs a few more pro innings and more consistency with his curve and change. He hasn't shown that the Molina incident will affect him. If the Cubs decide to be cautious, they'll give Christensen a month to get going in Double-A before promoting him to Triple-A Iowa this year. Odds are he'll surface in Wrigley Field before the season is over, and he should stick in Chicago's rotation by 2002.

Year	Club (League)	Class	W	L	ERA	G	GS	CG	SV	IP	H	R	ER	BB	SO
1999	Cubs (AZL)	R	0	1	3.00	3	3	0	0	9	8	3	3	5	10
	Eugene (NWL)	A	0	2	5.91	5	5	0	0	21	21	14	14	14	21
	Daytona (FSL)	A	1	3	6.35	4	4	0	0	22	25	16	16	11	18
2000	Daytona (FSL)	A	4	2	2.10	10	10	1	0	64	43	18	15	15	63
	West Tenn (SL)	AA	3	1	2.76	7	7	0	0	42	36	18	13	15	42
MINOR LEAGUE TOTALS			8	9	3.44	29	29	1	0	159	133	69	61	60	154

5. Carlos Zambrano, rhp

Born: June 1, 1981. **Ht.:** 6-4. **Wt.:** 220. **Bats:** L. **Throws:** R. **Career Transactions:** Signed out of Venezuela by Cubs, July 12, 1997.

STEVE MOORE

The Cubs have been aggressively moving their best prospects through the minors, most obviously with Zambrano. After modest success in low Class A in 1999, he opened 2000 in Double-A and was promoted to Triple-A before he turned 19. Upon reaching Iowa, he was converted from a starter to a reliever. Zambrano has a strong pitcher's body and a live, loose arm. He owns the best fastball in the system, a nasty mid-90s sinker that has reached 99 mph. He throws it from two different arm slots, making it tougher. At times, his slider is a good second pitch. Pacific Coast League managers acknowledged Zambrano's quality arm, but they couldn't understand why he was rushed to Triple-A and forced to change roles. His slider is inconsistent, his changeup is nothing special yet and his curveball is more of the get-me-over variety. He needs time to work on his control and his secondary pitches. Zambrano was switched to relief at a time when the major league bullpen was killing the Cubs. With Tom Gordon now on board as the closer, Zambrano's future may be as a starter again. He'll pitch in a rotation this year, likely in Triple-A, to get him as many innings as possible.

Year	Club (League)	Class	W	L	ERA	G	GS	CG	SV	IP	H	R	ER	BB	SO
1998	Cubs (AZL)	R	0	1	3.15	14	2	0	1	40	39	17	14	25	36
1999	Lansing (Mid)	A	13	7	4.17	27	24	2	0	153	150	87	71	62	98
2000	West Tenn (SL)	AA	3	1	1.34	9	9	0	0	60	39	14	9	21	43
	Iowa (PCL)	AAA	2	5	3.97	34	0	0	6	57	54	30	25	40	46
MINOR LEAGUE TOTALS			18	14	3.45	84	35	2	7	310	282	148	119	148	223

6. Luis Montanez, ss

Born: Dec. 15, 1981. **Ht.:** 6-0. **Wt.:** 170. **Bats:** R. **Throws:** R. **School:** Coral Park HS, Miami. **Career Transactions:** Selected by Cubs in first round (third overall) of 2000 draft; signed June 6, 2000.

JOHN SPEAR

The Cubs selected Montanez third overall last June, then announced his signing on the draft conference call in the middle of the third round. They agreed to a predraft deal worth $2.75 million but insisted they would have taken him regardless. His debut Rookie-level Arizona League was spectacular, as he was named MVP and managers rated him as the circuit's top prospect. Montanez has been compared athletically to Alex Gonzalez, and he's a better hitter than the Toronto shortstop. He uses the entire field and the ball jumps off his bat, so he should develop above-average power for a middle infielder. He's a smooth defender with a strong arm. He isn't a blazer and won't be a big-time base-stealer, though he has enough quickness to remain at shortstop. Despite exhibiting good plate discipline in his debut, he'll need to make better contact as he moves up the ladder. The Cubs have had just one all-star shortstop in the last 25 years (Shawon Dunston in 1988 and 1990), but Montanez should end that drought in the near future. He'll likely begin 2001 at Lansing and has a big league ETA of late 2003. Chicago also likes shortstop prospects Nate Frese and Jason Smith, but they won't stand in Montanez' way when he's ready.

Year	Club (League)	Class	AVG	G	AB	R	H	2B	3B	HR	RBI	BB	SO	SB
2000	Cubs (AZL)	R	.344	50	192	50	66	16	7	2	37	25	42	11
	Lansing (Mid)	A	.138	8	29	2	4	1	0	0	0	3	6	0
MINOR LEAGUE TOTALS			.317	58	221	52	70	17	7	2	37	28	48	11

7. David Kelton, 3b

Born: Dec. 17, 1979. **Ht.:** 6-2. **Wt.:** 190. **Bats:** R. **Throws:** R. **School:** Troup County HS, La Grange, Ga. **Career Transactions:** Selected by Cubs in second round of 1998 draft; signed June 3, 1998.

Which will happen first: Ron Santo makes the Hall of Fame or the Cubs find their first long-term replacement for him since he left following the 1973 season? The veterans committee is running out of time to win the race because Chicago has a deep crop of third-base prospects. The most promising is Kelton, who rebounded from a slow start to lead Class A Daytona to a second-half division title and playoff championship in the Florida State League last year. Kelton has legitimate 30-homer power and ranked sixth in the FSL in longballs in 2000. His swing is so pure that the Cubs forbade their minor league instructors from messing with it. He has average speed, good hands and an arm strong enough for third base. Kelton had periodic problems with his right shoulder, which required surgery before his senior year of high school. His shoulder acted up at the start of last season, limiting him to DH duty for a month. He has a 299-100 strikeout-walk ratio as a pro, something that more advanced pitchers may exploit. Kelton is ready for Double-A and is 18-24 months away from Wrigley Field. He'll have to keep producing to hold off players such as Eric Hinske, Ryan Gripp, Brandon Sing and J.J. Johnson, and the Cubs are confident he will.

Year	Club (League)	Class	AVG	G	AB	R	H	2B	3B	HR	RBI	BB	SO	SB
1998	Cubs (AZL)	R	.265	50	181	39	48	7	5	6	29	23	58	16
1999	Lansing (Mid)	A	.269	124	509	75	137	17	4	13	68	39	121	22
2000	Daytona (FSL)	A	.268	132	523	75	140	30	7	18	84	38	120	7
MINOR LEAGUE TOTALS			.268	306	1213	189	325	54	16	37	181	100	299	45

8. Bobby Hill, ss/2b

Born: April 3, 1978. **Ht.:** 5-10. **Wt.:** 180. **Bats:** B. **Throws:** R. **School:** University of Miami. **Career Transactions:** Signed by independent Newark (Atlantic), April 2000 . . . Selected by Cubs in second round of 2000 draft; signed Nov. 17, 2000.

Hill would have gotten a chance to win the White Sox' starting shortstop job in 2000 had he signed as a 1999 second-round pick after leading Miami to the College World Series title. But the two sides never came to terms, so he turned pro with Newark in the independent Atlantic League before the Cubs took him in the second round last June. Hill led the league in hits and on-base percentage (.442) and was named the shortstop on the postseason all-star team. He finally signed with Chicago in November for $1.425 million. Hill is the quintessential leadoff man and has been compared to a young Chuck Knoblauch in that regard. Hill hits for average, makes contact and draws walks, and he's a basestealing threat once he gets on. He has solid range and hands for a middle infielder. While the Cubs believe Hill can play shortstop, they might be in the minority. Most scouts think he doesn't have enough arm to stick at short, prompting an eventual move to second base. Hill will break into the organization at Double-A, where the presence of shortstop Nate Frese may push him to second base. Big league second baseman Eric Young's contract expires after 2001, and in a perfect world Hill would be ready to take over then.

Year	Club (League)	Class	AVG	G	AB	R	H	2B	3B	HR	RBI	BB	SO	SB
2000	Newark (Atl)	IND	.326	132	481	109	157	22	9	13	82	101	57	81

9. John Webb, rhp

Born: May 23, 1979. **Ht.:** 6-3. **Wt.:** 190. **Bats:** R. **Throws:** R. **School:** Manatee (Fla.) CC. **Career Transactions:** Selected by Cubs in 19th round of 1999 draft; signed June 16, 1999.

Webb was primarily a shortstop in his amateur career, but he attracted the Cubs with his work as a late-inning reliever. He stayed in the bullpen for his pro debut, then made a smooth transition to starting last season. Webb has what assistant GM Jim Hendry calls Wrigley Field stuff. He keeps his 90-92 mph sinker and plus slider down in the strike zone, permitting just five homers in 152 innings in 2000 (and only one in 210 at-bats against lefthanders). His changeup is a solid third pitch, and he can throw his entire repertoire for strikes. He's athletic and very projectable, so he could add a touch more velocity. Webb has no glaring need except for added experience. He has three pitches, fine command and durability, and he gets lefthanders out. He will begin 2001 by returning to

Daytona, and he likely will get promoted to Double-A by the end of the year. He hasn't attracted the hype of the higher-ceiling pitchers ahead of him, but he's a legitimate prospect in his own right. He projects as a No. 3 starter, and if the big league rotation gets too crowded, Webb might turn into a closer.

Year	Club (League)	Class	W	L	ERA	G	GS	CG	SV	IP	H	R	ER	BB	SO
1999	Cubs (AZL)	R	0	0	3.58	18	0	0	3	33	33	20	13	8	39
	Eugene (NWL)	A	1	0	0.00	2	0	0	1	4	1	0	0	1	3
2000	Lansing (Mid)	A	7	6	2.47	21	21	1	0	135	125	53	37	40	108
	Daytona (FSL)	A	1	1	4.76	4	2	0	1	17	17	11	9	3	18
MINOR LEAGUE TOTALS			9	7	2.81	45	23	1	5	189	176	84	59	52	168

10. Nate Frese, ss

Born: July 10, 1977. **Ht.:** 6-3. **Wt.:** 200. **Bats:** R. **Throws:** R. **School:** University of Iowa. **Career Transactions:** Selected by Cubs in 10th round of 1998 draft; signed June 6, 1998.

Frese is the great-great-nephew of former Indians slugger Hal Trosky and the cousin of former White Sox righthander Hal Trosky Jr. A first baseman/righthander in his first two seasons at Iowa, Frese didn't become a full-time shortstop until 1998. He was bothered by a hernia in his pro debut that summer, batting just .218. He has made significant offensive improvements in the two seasons since. He may not be the flashiest shortstop, but Frese is effective. He has the most accurate infield arm in the system and made just 13 errors in 113 games at short last year. He has fine on-base ability and possesses unusual size and strength for a shortstop. Frese lacks the speed associated with a shortstop and isn't an effective basestealer. He still has to work to do to translate his strength into home run power. Ricky Gutierrez will be a free agent after 2001, so the Cubs will need a shortstop for next season. Frese might not be quite ready by then, though he'll probably be the system's best candidate to fill the opening. He'll start this year in Double-A.

Year	Club (League)	Class	AVG	G	AB	R	H	2B	3B	HR	RBI	BB	SO	SB
1998	Williamsport (NY-P)	A	.218	54	174	28	38	8	0	2	18	16	38	5
1999	Lansing (Mid)	A	.265	107	373	68	99	27	4	4	49	58	67	10
2000	Daytona (FSL)	A	.296	117	425	70	126	24	5	7	52	64	84	10
MINOR LEAGUE TOTALS			.271	278	972	166	263	59	9	13	119	138	189	25

11. Eric Hinske, 3b

Born: Aug. 5, 1977. **Ht.:** 6-2. **Wt.:** 225. **Bats:** L. **Throws:** R. **School:** University of Arkansas. **Career Transactions:** Selected by Cubs in 17th round of 1998 draft; signed June 17, 1998.

The Cubs have looked for a competent third baseman for almost three decades, and Hinske is the most advanced of a bevy of candidates currently in the system. He may not be destined for the hot corner at Wrigley Field, however. The Cubs signed Bill Mueller to a two-year contract, by which time David Kelton will probably be ready to take over. Hinske projects to have enough bat to play left field or first base, two positions he got a taste of in 2000. He's merely adequate as a third baseman. He has hit 20 homers in each of his two full pro seasons, and he had to hit 17 longballs in the last two months to make it to 20 last year. Though his .255 average was 46 points below his previous career mark, Hinske's patience at the plate bodes well for his ability to hit at higher levels. He'll move up to Triple-A in 2001, and he'll probably get some more time at first base and in left field.

Year	Club (League)	Class	AVG	G	AB	R	H	2B	3B	HR	RBI	BB	SO	SB
1998	Williamsport (NY-P)	A	.298	68	248	46	74	20	0	9	57	35	61	19
	Rockford (Mid)	A	.450	6	20	8	9	4	0	1	4	5	6	1
1999	Daytona (FSL)	A	.297	130	445	76	132	28	6	19	79	62	90	16
	Iowa (PCL)	AAA	.267	4	15	3	4	0	1	1	2	1	4	0
2000	West Tenn (SL)	AA	.259	131	436	76	113	21	9	20	73	78	133	14
MINOR LEAGUE TOTALS			.285	339	1164	209	332	73	16	50	215	181	294	50

12. Julio Zuleta, 1b/of

Born: March 28, 1975. **Ht.:** 6-6. **Wt.:** 230. **Bats:** R. **Throws:** R. **Career Transactions:** Signed out of Panama by Cubs, Sept. 15, 1992.

Signed as a catcher, Zuleta floundered behind the plate and didn't hit much. Three years into his pro career, he was on the verge of getting released before the Cubs decided to give him a shot as a first baseman. With his defensive responsibilities reduced, he began to hit. Zuleta made an impression by launching two bombs off the scoreboard in a spring-training game against the White Sox, and he showed his power to all fields in his first big league trial last year. He has tightened his swing, but he still has holes in it and will chase breaking balls, especially against righthanders. He has no speed and thus no range at either first base or left field, though he does have arm strength. He should make Chicago's Opening Day roster and could share time with free-agent signee Ron Coomer at first base, though they're only keeping the position warm until Hee Seop Choi is ready, which should be in 2002.

Year	Club (League)	Class	AVG	G	AB	R	H	2B	3B	HR	RBI	BB	SO	SB
1993	Cubs (GCL)	R	.245	17	53	3	13	0	1	0	6	3	12	0
1994	Huntington (Appy)	R	.067	6	15	0	1	0	0	0	2	4	4	0
	Cubs (GCL)	R	.310	30	100	11	31	1	0	0	8	8	18	5
1995	Williamsport (NY-P)	A	.173	30	75	9	13	3	1	0	6	11	12	0
1996	Williamsport (NY-P)	A	.258	62	221	35	57	12	2	1	29	19	36	7
1997	Rockford (Mid)	A	.288	119	430	59	124	30	5	6	77	35	88	5
1998	Daytona (FSL)	A	.344	94	366	69	126	25	1	16	86	35	59	6
	West Tenn (SL)	AA	.295	40	139	18	41	9	0	2	20	10	30	0
1999	West Tenn (SL)	AA	.295	133	482	75	142	37	4	21	97	35	122	4
2000	Iowa (PCL)	AAA	.311	107	392	76	122	25	1	26	94	31	77	5
	Chicago (NL)	MAJ	.294	30	68	13	20	8	0	3	12	2	19	0
MAJOR LEAGUE TOTALS			.294	30	68	13	20	8	0	3	12	2	19	0
MINOR LEAGUE TOTALS			.295	638	2273	355	670	142	15	72	425	191	458	32

13. Aaron Krawiec, lhp

Born: March 17, 1979. **Ht.:** 6-6. **Wt.:** 215. **Bats:** L. **Throws:** L. **School:** Villanova University. **Career Transactions:** Selected by Cubs in third round of 2000 draft; signed June 19, 2000.

The Cubs nearly took Krawiec in the second round of the 2000 draft, but opted for Bobby Hill instead. They were delighted when Krawiec lasted until they came around again in the third round, and they're even more enthusiastic after his debut at short-season Eugene. Krawiec led Northwest League starters with 11.4 strikeouts per nine innings and pitched so well that he'll skip a level and open 2001 in high Class A. Krawiec has two above-average pitches: an 89-92 mph sinker and a curveball. His changeup has a chance to be average with more work. At 6-foot-6, he throws on a good downward plane. Krawiec didn't have a lot of success in college at Villanova, mainly because his inconsistent mechanics hurt his command, but that wasn't a problem in his first pro summer.

Year	Club (League)	Class	W	L	ERA	G	GS	CG	SV	IP	H	R	ER	BB	SO
2000	Eugene (NWL)	A	6	4	2.54	14	14	0	0	78	59	28	22	26	99
MINOR LEAGUE TOTALS			6	4	2.54	14	14	0	0	78	59	28	22	26	99

14. Wilton Chavez, rhp

Born: April 30, 1981. **Ht.:** 6-2. **Wt.:** 155. **Bats:** R. **Throws:** R. **Career Transactions:** Signed out of Dominican Republic by Cubs, Feb. 3, 1998.

Aaron Krawiec wasn't the only Eugene pitcher who blew away Northwest League hitters in 2000. Chavez led the league in strikeouts and innings, earning recognition as the righthanded starter on the postseason all-star team. He was signed out of the Dominican by Jose Serra, the same scout who discovered Juan Cruz for the Cubs. Chavez has good command of a nasty slider, though he may use it a little too often at the expense of his other pitches. His fastball is also a plus pitch, as he throws it 90-92 mph, and his changeup is developing. He does a terrific job of pitching down in the strike zone and didn't allow a homer in 90 innings last year. After three seasons in short-season leagues, Chavez will get his first shot at full-season ball with either Lansing or Daytona in 2001.

Year	Club (League)	Class	W	L	ERA	G	GS	CG	SV	IP	H	R	ER	BB	SO
1998	Cubs (DSL)	R	7	5	2.48	20	5	2	1	83	58	33	23	20	84
1999	Cubs (AZL)	R	5	5	5.88	14	13	1	0	67	89	57	44	31	68
2000	Eugene (NWL)	A	7	1	1.69	15	15	0	0	90	69	28	17	25	103
MINOR LEAGUE TOTALS			19	11	3.14	49	33	3	1	241	216	118	84	76	255

15. Ryan Gripp, 3b

Born: April 20, 1978. **Ht.:** 6-1. **Wt.:** 205. **Bats:** R. **Throws:** R. **School:** Creighton University. **Career Transactions:** Selected by Cubs in third round of 1999 draft; signed June 9, 1999.

After taking righthander Ben Christensen and raw high school outfielder Mike Mallory with their first two draft choices in 1999, the Cubs wanted the best college hitter available when they picked in the third round. They went with Gripp, who has justified their evaluation. He batted .333 last year, leading all minor league third basemen and all Midwest

League hitters. Gripp is polished at the plate. He has a compact swing and a selective eye, which allows him to drill doubles and homers to all fields. He has had no problems with wood bats or breaking pitches. He has good hands and makes accurate throws from third base, but his range, mobility and arm strength are all below-average for the position. He may have to move to first base, not something that any prospect who shares an organization with Hee Seop Choi wants to do. At 22, Gripp was a bit old for the Midwest League, though he probably won't skip a level with Eric Hinske and David Kelton ahead of him.

Year	Club (League)	Class	AVG	G	AB	R	H	2B	3B	HR	RBI	BB	SO	SB
1999	Eugene (NWL)	A	.308	73	266	40	82	18	1	12	48	27	65	2
2000	Lansing (Mid)	A	.333	135	498	87	166	36	0	20	92	68	86	4
MINOR LEAGUE TOTALS			.325	208	764	127	248	54	1	32	140	95	151	6

16. Mike Wuertz, rhp

Born: Dec. 15, 1978. **Ht.:** 6-3. **Wt.:** 180. **Bats:** R. **Throws:** R. **School:** Austin (Minn.) HS. **Career Transactions:** Selected by Cubs in 11th round of 1997 draft; signed Aug. 18, 1997.

Despite Weurtz' lackluster performance at Lansing in 1999, his first full pro season, the Cubs still believed he was a sleeper. He proved that correct last year, when he ranked second in the Florida State League in victories. He won seven of his last eight regular season decisions, then earned a 10-strikeout victory in the opener of the playoff finals, spurring Daytona to the championship. Wuertz has two promising pitches, a 90-93 mph fastball and a slider. He also throws a changeup. He's a tough competitor and generally throws strikes. He projects as a No. 3 or 4 starter in the majors, and will pitch in Double-A in 2001.

Year	Club (League)	Class	W	L	ERA	G	GS	CG	SV	IP	H	R	ER	BB	SO
1998	Williamsport (NY-P)	A	7	5	3.44	14	14	1	0	86	79	36	33	19	59
1999	Lansing (Mid)	A	11	12	4.80	28	28	1	0	161	191	104	86	44	127
2000	Daytona (FSL)	A	12	7	3.78	28	28	3	0	171	166	79	72	64	142
MINOR LEAGUE TOTALS			30	24	4.10	70	70	5	0	419	436	219	191	127	328

17. Joey Nation, lhp

Born: Sept. 28, 1978. **Ht.:** 6-2. **Wt.:** 205. **Bats:** L. **Throws:** L. **School:** Putnam City HS, Oklahoma City. **Career Transactions:** Selected by Braves in second round of 1997 draft; signed June 30, 1997 . . . Traded by Braves to Cubs, Aug. 24, 1999, completing trade in which Cubs sent LHP Terry Mulholland and SS Jose Hernandez to Braves for LHP Micah Bowie, RHP Ruben Quevedo and a player to be named (July 31, 1999).

Nation was the player to be named in the deal that sent big leaguers Jose Hernandez and Terry Mulholland to the Braves in July 1999, and he might be the only significant contributor for the Cubs. Lefthander Micah Bowie was released, and righthander Ruben Quevedo had a disappointing big league debut in 2000. Nation got two big league starts after a solid Double-A season in which he ranked second in the Southern League in strikeouts. He's a finesse lefty whose best pitch is a changeup. He also throws an average fastball with nice life, as well as a solid curveball. He'll need to improve his fastball command after leading the Southern League in homers allowed and surrendering longballs to Placido Polanco and Kevin Jordan in the majors. Nation is a back-of-the-rotation starter who could help the Cubs by the second half of 2001. Don't be surprised if he gets passed by several other Cubs pitching prospects, which would put Nation's big league future probably in the bullpen.

Year	Club (League)	Class	W	L	ERA	G	GS	CG	SV	IP	H	R	ER	BB	SO
1997	Danville (Appy)	R	1	2	2.73	8	8	0	0	26	24	11	8	5	41
1998	Macon (SAL)	A	6	12	5.03	29	28	1	0	143	179	102	80	39	141
1999	Macon (SAL)	A	1	1	2.96	6	6	0	0	27	27	10	9	9	31
	Myrtle Beach (Car)	A	5	4	4.39	19	17	0	0	96	88	51	47	37	87
	Daytona (FSL)	A	2	0	1.38	2	2	0	0	13	8	2	2	2	11
2000	West Tenn (SL)	AA	11	10	3.31	27	27	1	0	166	137	72	61	65	165
	Chicago (NL)	MAJ	0	2	6.94	2	2	0	0	12	12	9	9	8	8
MAJOR LEAGUE TOTALS			0	2	6.94	2	2	0	0	12	12	9	9	8	8
MINOR LEAGUE TOTALS			26	29	3.95	91	88	2	0	472	463	248	207	157	476

18. Scott Chiasson, rhp

Born: Aug. 14, 1977. **Ht.:** 6-3. **Wt.:** 200. **Bats:** R. **Throws:** R. **School:** Eastern Connecticut State College. **Career Transactions:** Selected by Royals in fifth round of 1998 draft; signed June 2, 1998 . . . Traded by Royals to Athletics, June 10, 1999, completing trade in which Athletics sent RHP Jay Witasick to Royals for a player to be named and cash (March 30, 1999) . . . Selected by Cubs in major league Rule 5 draft, December 11, 2000.

The Cubs had the first pick in the major league Rule 5 draft at the 2000 Winter Meetings and used it to pluck Chiasson from the Athletics system. He's with his third organization in three years. Chiasson went 9-2, 2.16 in the final three months of 2000 and was part of a combined no-hitter in the high Class A California League playoffs. The key was that he slowed down a maximum-effort delivery, giving him more command of his low-90s fastball and hard slider. His changeup is still developing. Chicago has to keep Chiasson in the majors all season or offer him back to the A's, so he'll get a shot to stick in the bullpen. Considering what a disaster the Cubs' relief corps was last year, he has a good chance of claiming a job.

Year	Club (League)	Class	W	L	ERA	G	GS	CG	SV	IP	H	R	ER	BB	SO
1998	Royals (GCL)	R	2	0	4.81	13	0	0	1	24	24	17	13	11	26
1999	S. Oregon (NWL)	A	2	2	5.22	15	13	0	0	69	80	52	40	39	51
2000	Visalia (Cal)	A	11	4	3.06	31	23	0	2	156	146	66	53	57	150
MINOR LEAGUE TOTALS			15	6	3.83	59	36	0	3	249	250	135	106	107	227

19. Jeff Goldbach, c

Born: Dec. 20, 1979. **Ht.:** 6-0. **Wt.:** 190. **Bats:** R. **Throws:** R. **School:** Princeton (Ind.) Community HS.
Career Transactions: Selected by Cubs in second round of 1998 draft; signed June 14, 1998.

The Cubs have confidence in three of their catching prospects. Goldbach projects as the best hitter, while Ryan Jorgensen is the best defender and Korean signee Yoon-Min Kweon may offer the best all-around package. If Goldbach is going to remain ahead of the other two, he'll have to kick his bat into a higher gear after slumping through 2000. He got worse as the year went on and hit .164 in the Arizona Fall League. Chicago still likes Goldbach's quick bat and power potential. His defense is average at times, though he let his offense affect his play behind the plate. He didn't have much success throwing out baserunners, gunning down just 21 percent. The Cubs would like to move Goldbach to Double-A in 2001, but that wouldn't be the best way to get him back on track offensively.

Year	Club (League)	Class	AVG	G	AB	R	H	2B	3B	HR	RBI	BB	SO	SB
1998	Cubs (AZL)	R	.265	38	136	22	36	11	2	4	25	11	41	5
1999	Lansing (Mid)	A	.271	112	399	82	108	27	3	18	72	64	66	1
2000	Daytona (FSL)	A	.200	119	420	49	84	15	1	10	60	31	76	6
MINOR LEAGUE TOTALS			.239	269	955	153	228	53	6	32	157	106	183	12

20. Mike Mallory, of

Born: Dec. 8, 1980. **Ht.:** 6-4. **Wt.:** 220. **Bats:** R. **Throws:** R. **School:** Dinwiddie (Va.) HS. **Career Transactions:** Selected by Cubs in second round of 1999 draft; signed June 21, 1999.

When the Cubs took Mallory in 1999, they knew he'd be a long-term project. He's living up to that billing, but they still have faith that he'll develop into a big leaguer. His athletic frame reminded Northwest League managers of a young George Foster or Dave Winfield last summer. Mallory already stands out on defense, showing above-average range and arm strength in center field. He has lots of raw power and speed, though he won't be able to take advantage of either until he improves as a hitter. The first step will be tightening his strike zone, and his discipline actually regressed from 1999 to 2000. Mallory probably will take on the challenge of full-season ball for the first time this year.

Year	Club (League)	Class	AVG	G	AB	R	H	2B	3B	HR	RBI	BB	SO	SB
1999	Cubs (AZL)	R	.242	42	149	20	36	6	0	4	15	12	48	2
2000	Eugene (NWL)	A	.210	70	262	39	55	12	3	6	30	16	98	9
MINOR LEAGUE TOTALS			.221	112	411	59	91	18	3	10	45	28	146	11

21. Carlos Urrutia, rhp

Born: Nov. 10, 1981. **Ht.:** 6-3. **Wt.:** 220. **Bats:** R. **Throws:** R. **Career Transactions:** Signed out of Venezuela by Cubs, Sept. 30, 1998.

Urrutia could be another Carlos Zambrano in the making, though he's only five months younger than his fellow Venezuelan and not nearly as advanced. Urrutia has been brought along very slowly, pitching just 61 innings in two years of Rookie ball and walking more batters than he struck out each season. Yet his size and live arm are clearly evident. He throws 94-95 mph and has a promising slider. He still needs plenty of work on developing a changeup, throwing strikes and setting up hitters, though he did start to make strides in instructional league. Urrutia isn't anywhere close to the majors and probably isn't ready for full-season ball, but he definitely bears watching.

Year	Club (League)	Class	W	L	ERA	G	GS	CG	SV	IP	H	R	ER	BB	SO
1999	Cubs (DSL)	R	1	3	7.77	10	6	0	0	22	28	26	19	12	10
2000	Cubs (AZL)	R	2	2	4.94	7	5	0	0	31	32	20	17	12	10
MINOR LEAGUE TOTALS			3	5	6.11	17	11	0	0	53	60	46	36	24	20

22. Ryan Jorgensen, c

Born: May 4, 1979. **Ht.:** 6-2. **Wt.:** 200. **Bats:** R. **Throws:** R. **School:** Louisiana State University. **Career Transactions:** Selected by Cubs in seventh round of 2000 draft; signed June 22, 2000.

The Cubs say Jorgensen was the best defensive catcher in college last season, even better than highly touted Dane Sardinha of Pepperdine, a second-round pick of the Reds. Yet Jorgensen was only the No. 2 backstop on national champion Louisiana State, which started slugger Brad Cresse behind the plate. Jorgensen has advanced catch-and-throw skills, and his arm rates a 65 on the 20-to-80 scouting scale. He has soft hands and is agile behind the plate. He didn't show much with the bat in college but surprised the Cubs with his offense in his pro debut. He hit .300 with gap power and drew a good amount of walks. He'll never hit many home runs and will have to prove his hitting ability at higher levels. After sharing time with Cresse in college and promising Korean Yoon-Min Kweon at Eugene, Jorgensen may finally get a chance to catch every day in 2001. That probably will come at Daytona.

Year	Club (League)	Class	AVG	G	AB	R	H	2B	3B	HR	RBI	BB	SO	SB
2000	Eugene (NWL)	A	.300	41	130	17	39	10	2	1	23	17	27	2
MINOR LEAGUE TOTALS			.300	41	130	17	39	10	2	1	23	17	27	2

23. Steve Smyth, lhp

Born: June 3, 1978. **Ht.:** 6-0. **Wt.:** 195. **Bats:** B. **Throws:** L. **School:** University of Southern California. **Career Transactions:** Selected by Cubs in fourth round of 1999 draft; signed June 8, 1999.

Smyth was part of an all-prospect Daytona rotation—the others were Juan Cruz, John Webb, Mike Wuertz and Matt Bruback—that swept through the Florida State League playoffs with a perfect 5-0 record. Smyth did his part, twirling six shutout innings to win the second game of the finals. The Cubs projected him as a reliever when they drafted him a year earlier, and he did nothing to dispel that notion by posting a 6.09 ERA in 15 starts in his debut. Though he saved the FSL all-star game last year, he made a case for remaining a starter. Smyth throws four pitches for strikes. He features a consistently low-90s fastball and a slider, and he also throws a changeup and cut fastball. He limited lefthanders to a .198 batting average in 2000, so he always can fall back on a role as a lefty specialist. For now, he'll remain in the rotation and move up to Double-A.

Year	Club (League)	Class	W	L	ERA	G	GS	CG	SV	IP	H	R	ER	BB	SO
1999	Eugene (NWL)	A	1	1	4.38	5	5	0	0	25	29	17	12	7	14
	Lansing (Mid)	A	5	3	6.93	10	10	0	0	51	68	40	39	30	46
2000	Daytona (FSL)	A	8	8	3.25	24	23	1	0	138	134	62	50	57	100
MINOR LEAGUE TOTALS			14	12	4.25	39	38	1	0	214	231	119	101	94	160

24. Ross Gload, of/1b

Born: April 5, 1976. **Ht.:** 6-2. **Wt.:** 210. **Bats:** L. **Throws:** L. **School:** University of South Florida. **Career Transactions:** Selected by Marlins in 13th round of 1997 draft; signed June 12, 1997 . . . Traded by Marlins with RHP David Noyce to Cubs for OF Henry Rodriguez, July 31, 2000.

The Cubs were doing little more than dumping salary when they shipped left fielder Henry Rodriguez to the Marlins for two minor leaguers last July. Little did they realize Gload was about to discover his power stroke. He had 41 homers and a .425 slugging percentage in 433 pro games before the trade. The Cubs promoted him to Triple-A only because they had a surplus of lefthanded hitters in Double-A, but Gload moved up and mashed. He had a .942 slugging percentage in 28 games, earning a callup to Chicago. Gload doesn't rank higher in the organization because he has to prove his Triple-A performance wasn't a fluke. His stance reminds several people of former Cubs third baseman Richie Hebner's, and Gload takes a pronounced uppercut. He makes contact but doesn't walk much. He's only adequate at first base and left field, and he lacks arm strength. Other than homering off Brian Rose, Gload didn't show much in the majors and earned himself a ticket back to Triple-A to begin 2001.

Year	Club (League)	Class	AVG	G	AB	R	H	2B	3B	HR	RBI	BB	SO	SB
1997	Utica (NY-P)	A	.261	68	245	28	64	15	2	3	43	28	57	1
1998	Kane County (Mid)	A	.313	132	501	77	157	41	3	12	92	58	84	7
1999	Brevard County (FSL)	A	.298	133	490	80	146	26	3	10	74	53	76	3
2000	Portland (EL)	AA	.284	100	401	60	114	28	4	16	65	29	53	4
	Iowa (PCL)	AAA	.404	28	104	24	42	10	2	14	39	9	13	1
	Chicago (NL)	MAJ	.194	18	31	4	6	0	1	1	3	3	10	0
MAJOR LEAGUE TOTALS			.194	18	31	4	6	0	1	1	3	3	10	0
MINOR LEAGUE TOTALS			.300	461	1741	269	523	120	14	55	313	177	283	16

25. Will Ohman, lhp

Born: Aug. 13, 1977. **Ht.:** 6-2. **Wt.:** 195. **Bats:** L. **Throws:** L. **School:** Pepperdine University. **Career Transactions:** Selected by Cubs in eighth round of 1998 draft; signed June 23, 1998.

Ohman is the best prospect among three relievers who helped West Tenn win the Southern League championship and could shore up the Chicago bullpen in 2001. An all-state kicker as a Colorado high schooler, Ohman focused on baseball at Pepperdine. He has lowered his ERA every year. He throws a 91-92 mph sinker and a plus curveball from a three-quarters angle that makes him tough on lefthanders. His command can get spotty at times, though he helps himself by pitching low in the strike zone. Ohman has a fan in Cubs manager Don Baylor, who was impressed by his fearlessness. Ohman didn't allow a run in his first five big league appearances, highlighted by a called strikeout of Phillies star Bob Abreu on a 3-2 curve. Ohman got rocked to the tune of a 10.20 ERA in the Arizona Fall League, but Chicago attributes that to him being worn out after a long season.

Year	Club (League)	Class	W	L	ERA	G	GS	CG	SV	IP	H	R	ER	BB	SO
1998	Williamsport (NY-P)	A	4	4	6.46	10	7	0	0	39	39	32	28	13	35
	Rockford (Mid)	A	1	1	4.44	4	4	0	0	24	25	13	12	7	21
1999	Daytona (FSL)	A	4	7	3.46	31	15	2	5	107	102	59	41	41	97
2000	West Tenn (SL)	AA	6	4	1.89	59	0	0	3	71	53	20	15	36	85
	Chicago (NL)	MAJ	1	0	8.10	6	0	0	0	3	4	3	3	4	2
MAJOR LEAGUE TOTALS			1	0	8.10	6	0	0	0	3	4	3	3	4	2
MINOR LEAGUE TOTALS			15	16	3.58	104	26	2	8	241	219	124	96	97	238

26. Chris Gissell, rhp

Born: Jan. 4, 1978. **Ht.:** 6-5. **Wt.:** 200. **Bats:** R. **Throws:** R. **School:** Hudson's Bay HS, Vancouver, Wash. **Career Transactions:** Selected by Cubs in fourth round of 1996 draft; signed June 6, 1996.

Ranked with Adam Eaton as the top two prospects in Washington for the 1996 draft, Gissell hasn't developed as quickly as the budding Padres star. He struggled with his confidence and his velocity early in his pro career. After regaining both, he has been shut down in July in each of the last two seasons. In 1999, he had a shoulder strain that required surgery. Last year, he had elbow tendinitis. When he was healthy in 2000, he used a 91-92 mph fastball and plus curveball to limit opponents to a .233 average. His changeup and command still need improvement, however. The Cubs have been patient with Gissell and will remain so. After spending the last two years in Double-A, he'll move up to Triple-A in 2001.

Year	Club (League)	Class	W	L	ERA	G	GS	CG	SV	IP	H	R	ER	BB	SO
1996	Cubs (GCL)	R	4	2	2.35	11	10	0	0	61	54	23	16	8	64
1997	Rockford (Mid)	A	6	11	4.45	26	24	3	0	144	155	89	71	62	105
1998	Rockford (Mid)	A	3	0	0.80	5	5	0	0	34	27	8	3	15	23
	Daytona (FSL)	A	7	6	4.17	22	21	1	0	136	149	80	63	38	123
	West Tenn (SL)	AA	0	1	13.50	1	1	0	0	4	5	7	6	4	4
1999	West Tenn (SL)	AA	3	8	5.99	20	18	0	0	98	121	76	65	62	57
2000	West Tenn (SL)	AA	7	5	3.10	16	16	0	0	93	80	39	32	41	65
MINOR LEAGUE TOTALS			30	33	4.05	101	95	4	0	569	591	322	256	230	441

27. Matt Bruback, rhp

Born: Jan. 12, 1979. **Ht.:** 6-7. **Wt.:** 210. **Bats:** R. **Throws:** R. **School:** Manatee (Fla.) JC. **Career Transactions:** Selected by Cubs in 47th round of 1997 draft; signed May 16, 1998.

Bruback was a projectable 6-foot-6 righthander when the Cubs drafted him in 1997, and it didn't take long for projection to start becoming reality. His fastball jumped to the low 90s and touched 95 the next spring, and he might have been a first-round pick if he hadn't signed as a draft-and-follow. He has moved slowly as a pro, returning to Lansing to start 2000 and struggling initially at Daytona. He did finish strong, with four quality starts in his last five regular season outings and six shutout innings to win the clincher in the Florida State League playoffs. Bruback still has good velocity and life on his fastball, though he has yet to come up with a second plus pitch. His command needs work, and he often has trouble bouncing back if he gets hit early in a game. Chicago has several candidates for its Double-A rotation, so Bruback might get a few more high Class A starts at the outset of 2001.

Year	Club (League)	Class	W	L	ERA	G	GS	CG	SV	IP	H	R	ER	BB	SO
1998	Williamsport (NY-P)	A	2	7	3.93	14	14	0	0	66	62	46	29	45	43
1999	Lansing (Mid)	A	9	8	5.40	25	25	0	0	135	151	92	81	87	118
2000	Lansing (Mid)	A	4	2	2.93	9	9	2	0	55	49	23	18	19	36
	Daytona (FSL)	A	5	5	4.85	18	18	0	0	89	101	57	48	50	69
MINOR LEAGUE TOTALS			20	22	4.58	66	66	2	0	345	363	218	176	201	266

28. Jaisen Randolph, of

Born: Jan. 19, 1979. **Ht.:** 6-0. **Wt.:** 180. **Bats:** B. **Throws:** R. **School:** Hillsborough HS, Tampa. **Career Transactions:** Selected by Cubs in fifth round of 1997 draft; signed June 10, 1997.

Randolph is a product of Tampa's Hillsborough High, which also produced Carl Everett, Dwight Gooden and Gary Sheffield. Randolph's strong points were summed up in the final inning of the Southern League playoffs in 2000. He drew a walk, stole second base and used his speed to score on an infield error, giving West Tenn the championship. In terms of speed and center-field defense, he ranks right with Corey Patterson in the system. But Randolph comes up short in most other areas. He doesn't hit for much average or any power, makes infrequent contact and gets caught stealing more than he should with his wheels. Randolph has tons of athleticism and works hard, so the Cubs remain high on him. However, there's no way he'll be a big league corner infielder, and he's certainly not going to wrest center field away from Patterson.

Year	Club (League)	Class	AVG	G	AB	R	H	2B	3B	HR	RBI	BB	SO	SB
1997	Cubs (AZL)	R	.266	53	218	42	58	1	4	0	26	26	45	24
1998	Rockford (Mid)	A	.289	128	491	78	142	18	9	1	33	40	113	32
1999	Daytona (FSL)	A	.272	130	511	70	139	16	5	2	37	43	86	25
2000	West Tenn (SL)	AA	.243	126	490	76	119	15	5	1	31	56	96	46
MINOR LEAGUE TOTALS			.268	437	1710	266	458	50	23	4	127	165	340	127

29. Jason Smith, ss

Born: July 24, 1977. **Ht.:** 6-3. **Wt.:** 190. **Bats:** L. **Throws:** R. **School:** Meridian (Miss.) CC. **Career Transactions:** Selected by Cubs in 23rd round of 1996 draft; signed May 25, 1997.

Before the Cubs took Luis Montanez with their 2000 first-round pick, Smith had the best tools among the system's shortstops. After missing most of 1999 with hamstring problems, he looked like he was finally translating his athleticism into baseball aptitude last season. But after hitting .322-8-29 through May, he batted just .186-4-32 over the final three months. He has solid pop for a middle infielder, but Smith has woeful plate discipline. His baserunning instincts aren't as impressive as his speed, and he's inconsistent at shortstop. With Bobby Hill and Nate Frese set to form Chicago's Double-A double-play combination in 2001, Smith will have to move up to Triple-A. If he doesn't improve, they'll both pass him by.

Year	Club (League)	Class	AVG	G	AB	R	H	2B	3B	HR	RBI	BB	SO	SB
1997	Williamsport (NY-P)	A	.288	51	205	25	59	5	2	0	11	10	44	9
	Rockford (Mid)	A	.182	9	33	4	6	0	1	0	3	2	11	1
1998	Rockford (Mid)	A	.239	126	464	67	111	15	9	7	60	31	122	23
1999	Daytona (FSL)	A	.261	39	142	22	37	5	2	5	26	12	29	9
2000	West Tenn (SL)	AA	.237	119	481	55	114	22	7	12	61	22	130	16
MINOR LEAGUE TOTALS			.247	344	1325	173	327	47	21	24	161	77	336	58

30. Nic Jackson, of

Born: Sept. 25, 1979. **Ht.:** 6-4. **Wt.:** 205. **Bats:** R. **Throws:** R. **School:** University of Richmond. **Career Transactions:** Selected by Cubs in third round of 2000 draft; signed June 20, 2000.

If Jackson realizes his potential, he could emerge as a right fielder in the mold of fellow University of Richmond product Brian Jordan. The Cubs took Jackson with a draft pick they received as compensation from the Devil Rays for free agent Steve Trachsel, and he might not have been available that late had he been healthy in the spring. Jackson injured the middle finger on his right hand while playing in the Cape Cod League in 1999. It was repeatedly misdiagnosed as a sprain before doctors discovered that a ligament had pulled away from the bone. Jackson had surgery last February and missed 29 of the Spiders' 54 games. In his pro debut, he showed his athleticism by leading the Northwest League in triples and stealing 25 bases in 28 attempts. He'll need to tighten his strike zone, but he does have a quick bat and should develop some home run power. He's a 55 runner on the 20-to-80 scouting scale, and he has a solid average arm. Chicago is considering skipping Jackson a level and sending him to high Class A this year.

Year	Club (League)	Class	AVG	G	AB	R	H	2B	3B	HR	RBI	BB	SO	SB
2000	Eugene (NWL)	A	.255	74	294	39	75	12	7	6	47	22	64	25
MINOR LEAGUE TOTALS			.255	74	294	39	75	12	7	6	47	22	64	25

Chicago
White Sox

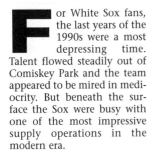

By Phil Rogers

For White Sox fans, the last years of the 1990s were a most depressing time. Talent flowed steadily out of Comiskey Park and the team appeared to be mired in mediocrity. But beneath the surface the Sox were busy with one of the most impressive supply operations in the modern era.

Ron Schueler, who served as GM for a decade before stepping down after the 2000 season, and his lieutenants stocked the organization with the deepest stable of pitching prospects in the game. They began arriving in 2000, when eight White Sox pitchers picked up their first big league victories. And plenty of good arms are coming behind them.

The supersonic rise of Mark Buehrle from a junior college outside St. Louis to Comiskey Park, along with Jon Rauch's jump from third-round pick to Minor League Player of the Year, illustrate the roll the Sox are on.

While Schueler emphasized pitching, he rounded up good position players, too. The Sox already have seen big league success from young players like Paul Konerko, Carlos Lee, Magglio Ordonez and Chris Singleton. Third baseman Joe Crede should make his mark in 2001.

The influx of young talent has posi-tioned the White Sox for a long run at the top. It was among the primary reasons Alex Rodriguez put the Sox on the short list of teams he wanted agent Scott Boras to seriously consider.

White Sox owner Jerry Reinsdorf deserves credit for his commitment to scouting and player development. The Sox have long had an edge on many organizations in staff size and experience on the baseball side. But Reinsdorf went the extra mile by increasing his signing budget even as attendance was shrinking. He spent more than $6 million for draft sign-ings in 1999, then authorized a record $5.3 million deal for top pick Joe Borchard out of Stanford in 2000.

Schueler was vigilant in guarding the talent he amass-ed. He declined to trade pitch-ing prospects like Jon Garland and Kip Wells for a veteran pitcher last July. Righthander Juan Figueroa was the only prospect sent to the Orioles in the Charles Johnson deal.

New GM Kenny Williams, who was Schueler's farm director, is expected to value young talent just as highly. He did have to give the Blue Jays lefthander Mike Sirotka to get David Wells, who provides veteran lead-ership for the rotation. But none of the other three players the Sox gave up figured prominently in their plans.

OrganizationOverview

General manager: Ken Williams. **Farm director:** Bob Fontaine Jr. **Scouting director:** Doug Laumann.

2000 PERFORMANCE

Class	Team	League	W	L	Pct.	Finish*	Manager
Majors	Chicago	American	95	67	.586	1st (14)	Jerry Manuel
Triple-A	Charlotte Knights	International	78	65	.545	6th (14)	Nick Leyva
Double-A	Birmingham Barons	Southern	77	63	.550	2nd (10)	Nick Capra
High A	Winston-Salem Warthogs	Carolina	68	71	.489	4th (8)	Bryan Dayett
Low A	#Burlington Bees	Midwest	51	88	.367	14th (14)	Jerry Terrell
Rookie	Bristol Sox	Appalachian	34	33	.507	5th (10)	R.J. Reynolds
Rookie	AZL White Sox	Arizona	22	32	.407	t-6th (9)	Jerry Hairston

OVERALL 2000 MINOR LEAGUE RECORD   367 317 .537   21st (30)

* Finish in overall standings (No. of teams in league). #Affiliate will be in Kannapolis (South Atlantic) in 2001.

ORGANIZATION LEADERS

BATTING
*AVG	Joe Crede, Birmingham	.306
R	Mario Valenzuela, Winston-Salem	87
H	Joe Crede, Birmingham	163
TB	Joe Crede, Birmingham	261
2B	Joe Crede, Birmingham	35
3B	Terrell Merriman, Winston-Salem	9
HR	**Jeff Liefer**, Charlotte	32
RBI	Aaron Rowand, Birmingham	98
BB	Terrell Merriman, Winston-Salem	94
SO	Jason Dellaero, Birmingham	142
SB	Chad Durham, Burlington	58

PITCHING
W	Jon Rauch, Winston-Salem/Birmingham	16
L	Dennis Ulacia, Burlington	14
#ERA	**Jon Garland**, Charlotte	2.13
G	Joe Davenport, Charlotte	59
CG	Geronimo Mendoza, Winston-Salem	4
SV	Matt Guerrier, Winston-Salem/Birmingham	26
IP	Josh Fogg, Birmingham	192
BB	Rob Purvis, Winston-Salem/Birmingham	90
SO	Jon Rauch, Winston-Salem/Birmingham	187

*Minimum 250 at-bats. #Minimum 75 innings.

TOP PROSPECTS OF THE DECADE

1991	Johnny Ruffin, rhp
1992	Roberto Hernandez, rhp
1993	Jason Bere, rhp
1994	James Baldwin, rhp
1995	Scott Ruffcorn, rhp
1996	Chris Snopek, 3b/ss
1997	Mike Cameron, of
1998	Mike Caruso, ss
1999	Carlos Lee, 3b
2000	Kip Wells, rhp

TOP DRAFT PICKS OF THE DECADE

1991	Scott Ruffcorn, rhp
1992	Eddie Pearson, 1b
1993	Scott Christman, lhp
1994	Mark Johnson, c
1995	Jeff Liefer, 3b
1996	*Bobby Seay, lhp
1997	Jason Dellaero, ss
1998	Kip Wells, rhp
1999	Jason Stumm, rhp
2000	Joe Borchard, of

*Did not sign.

Liefer   **Garland**

BEST TOOLS

Best Hitter for Average	Joe Crede
Best Power Hitter	Joe Borchard
Fastest Baserunner	Bo Ivy
Best Fastball	Dan Wright
Best Breaking Ball	Dan Wright
Best Control	Josh Fogg
Best Defensive Catcher	Miguel Olivo
Best Defensive Infielder	Jason Dellaero
Best Infield Arm	Jason Dellaero
Best Defensive Outfielder	McKay Christensen
Best Outfield Arm	Joe Borchard

PROJECTED 2004 LINEUP

Catcher	Miguel Olivo
First Base	Paul Konerko
Second Base	Ray Durham
Third Base	Joe Crede
Shortstop	Jose Valentin
Left Field	Carlos Lee
Center Field	Joe Borchard
Right Field	Magglio Ordonez
Designated Hitter	Frank Thomas
No. 1 Starter	Jon Rauch
No. 2 Starter	Jon Garland
No. 3 Starter	Mark Buehrle
No. 4 Starter	Dan Wright
No. 5 Starter	James Baldwin
Closer	Matt Ginter

ALL-TIME LARGEST BONUSES

Joe Borchard, 2000	$5,300,000
Jason Stumm, 1999	1,750,000
Kip Wells, 1998	1,495,000
Matt Ginter, 1999	1,275,000
Jason Dellaero, 1997	1,056,000

DraftAnalysis

2000 Draft

Best Pro Debut: SS **Tim Hummel** (2) batted .326-2-30 with 16 doubles while playing for two Class A teams.

Best Athlete: OF Joe Borchard (1) would have started at quarterback for Stanford last fall had he not turned pro for $5.3 million, a record bonus for a draftee signing with the team that selected him. Power and arm strength are his two most exciting tools.

Best Hitter: Hummel, who had more walks than strikeouts. He had a six-hit game at Class A Frederick and finished his first pro summer with a 19-for-39 (.487) streak.

Best Raw Power: Duane Shaffer, who presided over his last draft as scouting director before getting promoted to a more senior position, says Borchard has as much power as anyone he ever scouted, including Mark McGwire at the same stage.

Fastest Runner: The White Sox may have signed more quality speed than anyone. 2B Chris Amador (8) and OF Bo Ivy (6) finished 1-2 in the Rookie-level Arizona League in stolen bases, and OF Eddie Young (7) would have run wild if he hadn't missed his first pro summer with a broken wrist. All three are plus-plus runners, with Ivy the quickest.

Best Defensive Player: Amador has taken to second base after moving from shortstop. His speed gives him plenty of range, and his arm is better suited for second.

Best Fastball: RHP Rylan Reed (23) reaches 96 mph and could add velocity as his body loosens up after he's stopped weight training for football. Shaffer says Reed, at 6-foot-7 and 260 pounds, is the biggest 18-year-old

he has ever seen. Arkansas recruited Reed to play tight end.

Most Intriguing Background: Borchard and Reed aren't the only picks with football connections. OF Freddie Mitchell (50), a backup center fielder at UCLA, is better known as a wide receiver with serious NFL potential. He didn't sign.

ROBERT GURGANUS

Hummel

Closest To The Majors: Borchard reached Double-A then headed to the Arizona Fall League. Chicago has a nice pair of corner outfielders in Carlos Lee and Magglio Ordonez, so Borchard will speed his rise if he can stay in center.

Best Late-Round Pick: Reed, who interestingly didn't get any baseball scholarship offers. He would have gone about 20 rounds earlier had teams been more certain he would give up football.

The One Who Got Away: One of the draft's best high school catching prospects, Tony Richie (5), was disappointed he didn't go in the first round as projected. He's at Florida State.

Assessment: The White Sox took heat for Borchard's bonus, but he was the No. 1 player on their board and they say his deal makes more sense than the major league contracts draftees have gotten in recent years. After loading up on pitching in the last two drafts, Chicago filled the organization with intriguing position players.

1999 Draft

RHP Jon Rauch (3) was a steal. And it's not like the White Sox needed help, considering they also got RHPs Jason Stumm (1), Matt Ginter (1), Brian West (1), Rob Purvis (1), Dan Wright (2), Matt Guerrier (10) and Jeff Bajenaru (36, draft-and-follow). **Grade: A**

1998 Draft

Chicago found arms early in RHPs Kip Wells (1), Gary Majewski (2) and Josh Fogg (3), and late in LHP Mark Buehrle (38, draft-and-follow). OF Aaron Rowand (1) is one of the system's best position players. **Grade: B+**

1997 Draft

The first three first-rounders don't look good: SS Jason Dellaero, RHP Kyle Kane, OF Brett Caradonna. The next three do: RHP Aaron Myette (since traded to Texas), LHP Jim Parque, RHP Rocky Biddle. Imagine the organization if RHP Jeff Weaver (2) had signed. **Grade: C+**

1996 Draft

Chicago lost LHP Bobby Seay (1) to loophole free agency. Like Hill and Weaver, Seay was a Scott Boras client. The Sox did get C Josh Paul (2) and 3B Joe Crede (5), both of whom could be big league regulars by the end of 2001. **Grade: C+**

Note: Draft analysis prepared by Jim Callis. Numbers in parentheses indicate draft rounds.

. . . Rauch sustains his velocity deep into games—he didn't have a fastball clocked below 91 mph in a 14-strikeout, two-hit shutout.

Jon
Rauch rhp

Born: Sept. 27, 1978.
Ht.: 6-10. **Wt.:** 230.
Bats: R. **Throws:** R.
School: Morehead State University.
Career Transactions: Selected by White Sox in third round of 1999 draft; signed June 9, 1999.

While his big frame attracts attention, Rauch wasn't drafted out of high school and received only one Division I scholarship offer, a combination athletic/academic ride at Morehead State. He showed his potential as MVP of the wood-bat Shenandoah Valley League after his sophomore season, going 8-1, 1.69 with 126 strikeouts in 85 innings. Rauch slid in the 1999 draft after an unimpressive junior season, during which he dropped 50 pounds because of a bout with viral meningitis. The White Sox gambled $310,000 he would regain his form of the previous summer, and they hit the jackpot. Rauch, who at 6-foot-11 will become the tallest pitcher in big league history, was Baseball America's Minor League Player of the Year in his first full season. He capped his season with 21 strikeouts and no walks in 11 innings for the gold medal-winning U.S. Olympic team.

Rauch is a polished pitcher with the advantage of the unusual angles that result from his height. He only recently regained the 93-95 mph fastball he had before the meningitis. He sustains his velocity deep into games—he didn't have a fastball clocked below 91 mph in a 14-strikeout, two-hit shutout in his final minor league start in August. Hitters can't sit on the fastball because he has an above-average slider and curveball, both of which he throws for strikes. While many tall pitchers struggle with their mechanics, Rauch is fundamentally sound. He also has excellent control. Rauch didn't have a reliable changeup when he signed but has made progress developing one. Perhaps because he challenges every hitter, he's prone to giving up home runs. His durability is unproven, as his 177 innings (including the Olympics) were a career high.

Rauch has the stuff to be a front-of-the-rotation starter. With youngsters Kip Wells and Jon Garland expected to open the season in the White Sox rotation, there's no reason to rush Rauch. He has pitched just 230 innings as a pro. He's likely to return to Double-A Birmingham, but it would be no big surprise if he spent most of the year at Triple-A Charlotte. He'll be promoted only if the Sox are positive he can help out down the stretch of a playoff race.

Year	Club (League)	Class	W	L	ERA	G	GS	CG	SV	IP	H	R	ER	BB	SO
1999	Bristol (Appy)	R	4	4	4.45	14	9	0	2	57	65	44	28	16	66
	Winston-Salem (Car)	A	0	0	3.00	1	1	0	0	6	4	3	2	3	7
2000	Winston-Salem (Car)	A	11	3	2.86	18	18	1	0	110	102	49	35	33	124
	Birmingham (SL)	AA	5	1	2.25	8	8	2	0	56	36	18	14	16	63
MINOR LEAGUE TOTALS			20	8	3.10	41	36	3	2	229	209	114	79	68	260

2. Joe Borchard, of

Born: Nov. 25, 1978. **Ht.:** 6-5. **Wt.:** 220. **Bats:** B. **Throws:** R. **School:** Stanford University. **Career Transactions:** Selected by White Sox in first round (12th overall) of 2000 draft; signed Aug. 8, 2000.

The White Sox committed a record $5.3 million to keep Borchard from continuing his two-sport career at Stanford, where he had been expected to be the starting quarterback. Some scouts believe he's the best college power prospect since Mark McGwire. He can drive the ball to all fields from both sides of the plate. Borchard's father, an outfielder drafted by the Royals in 1969, had him switch-hitting by age 11. Borchard is a good outfielder with an excellent arm. Stanford coach Mark Marquess says he's the most competitive player he's ever had. Borchard left the Arizona Fall League because of back pain. The Sox blame the injury on football and say their conditioning program will prevent long-term problems. The Sox may be asking too much for Borchard to develop into a center fielder. He'll begin 2001 in Double-A and could be promoted at the end of the year. His situation is complicated by the White Sox' young corner outfielders, Carlos Lee and Magglio Ordonez.

Year	Club (League)	Class	AVG	G	AB	R	H	2B	3B	HR	RBI	BB	SO	SB
2000	White Sox (AZL)	R	.414	7	29	3	12	4	0	0	8	4	4	0
	Winston-Salem (Car)	A	.288	14	52	7	15	3	0	2	7	6	9	0
	Birmingham (SL)	AA	.227	6	22	3	5	0	1	0	3	3	8	0
MINOR LEAGUE TOTALS			.311	27	103	13	32	7	1	2	18	13	21	0

3. Joe Crede, 3b

Born: April 26, 1978. **Ht.:** 6-3. **Wt.:** 195. **Bats:** R. **Throws:** R. **School:** Fatima HS, Westphalia, Mo. **Career Transactions:** Selected by White Sox in fifth round of 1996 draft; signed June 5, 1996.

Crede picked up MVP awards in the Southern League and Carolina League in the last three seasons. The year he wasn't an MVP he was limited by a foot injury. He may have completed his minor league education with a tour of the Arizona Fall League. A pure hitter with a solid approach, Crede has been compared to Scott Rolen. His bat speed generates power without requiring him to pull the ball or swing for the fences. He has shown the mental toughness to recover from slow starts. He's a solid fielder and cut his error total dramatically in 2000. Crede never had a lot of speed and has slowed down after twice having surgery on a toe in 1999. His strikeout total rose above 100 for the first time last season. The only real question is whether Crede will open 2001 as Chicago's third baseman or will displace veteran Herbert Perry along the way.

Year	Club (League)	Class	AVG	G	AB	R	H	2B	3B	HR	RBI	BB	SO	SB
1996	White Sox (GCL)	R	.299	56	221	30	66	17	1	4	32	9	41	1
1997	Hickory (SAL)	A	.271	113	402	45	109	25	0	5	62	24	83	3
1998	Winston-Salem (Car)	A	.315	137	492	92	155	32	3	20	88	53	98	9
1999	Birmingham (SL)	AA	.251	74	291	37	73	14	1	4	42	22	47	2
2000	Birmingham (SL)	AA	.306	138	533	84	163	35	0	21	94	56	111	3
	Chicago (AL)	MAJ	.357	7	14	2	5	1	0	0	3	0	3	0
MAJOR LEAGUE TOTALS			.357	7	14	2	5	1	0	0	3	0	3	0
MINOR LEAGUE TOTALS			.292	518	1939	288	566	123	5	54	318	164	380	18

4. Matt Ginter, rhp

Born: Dec. 24, 1977. **Ht.:** 6-1. **Wt.:** 215. **Bats:** R. **Throws:** R. **School:** Mississippi State University. **Career Transactions:** Selected by White Sox in first round (22nd overall) of 1999 draft; signed June 24, 1999.

In his first full season, Ginter ranked second in the Southern League in ERA and was selected for the U.S. Olympic team. He withdrew when the White Sox considered him for the postseason roster, which he didn't make. Ginter has a plus fastball that he can throw in the mid-90s, but his best pitch is a tight slider that can overmatch righthanders. He's a versatile pitcher who could project as a starter or a reliever. He's willing to knock hitters off the plate, which helped him hold Double-A hitters to a .233 average. Ginter seemed in awe when he was promoted to the big leagues. He respected big league hitters too much, falling behind in counts while nibbling in the strike zone. He gave up five homers in nine innings. The White Sox probably will slow down a bit and give him a full season at Triple-A. He projects as a reliever but could fool the Sox and wind up in the rotation in 2002.

Year	Club (League)	Class	W	L	ERA	G	GS	CG	SV	IP	H	R	ER	BB	SO
1999	White Sox (AZL)	R	1	0	3.24	3	0	0	1	8	5	4	3	3	10
	Burlington (Mid)	A	4	2	4.05	9	9	0	0	40	38	20	18	19	29
2000	Birmingham (SL)	AA	11	8	2.25	27	26	0	0	180	153	72	45	60	126
	Chicago (AL)	MAJ	1	0	13.50	7	0	0	0	9	18	14	14	7	6
MINOR LEAGUE TOTALS			16	10	2.61	39	35	0	1	228	196	96	66	82	165
MAJOR LEAGUE TOTALS			1	0	13.50	7	0	0	0	9	18	14	14	7	6

5. Dan Wright, rhp

Born: Dec. 14, 1977. **Ht.:** 6-5. **Wt.:** 225. **Bats:** R. **Throws:** R. **School:** University of Arkansas. **Career Transactions:** Selected by White Sox in second round of 1999 draft; signed July 10, 1999.

Wright overcame the inconsistency that dogged him throughout his college career and is harnessing the promise that made him a second-round draft choice despite a 2-15 record in his last two years at Arkansas. He held Double-A hitters to a .187 average and performed well in the Southern League playoffs. Wright may be the hardest thrower in the system, which is saying something. His fastball consistently hits 95 mph and has been as high as 98. He has a nasty knuckle-curve with a sharp, downward break. He can be dominating when he's on his game. Control can be a problem for Wright, but the Sox say that also should improve. The key is to build on the confidence he developed in 2000. Outside of perhaps Jon Rauch and the unsung Corwin Malone, Wright has as much upside as any Chicago pitching prospect. The Sox have enough pitching to take their time with Wright, which they will, so he might not be in the big league picture until 2003.

Year	Club (League)	Class	W	L	ERA	G	GS	CG	SV	IP	H	R	ER	BB	SO
1999	Bristol (Appy)	R	2	0	1.00	10	0	0	1	18	14	8	2	9	18
	Burlington (Mid)	A	0	0	6.00	2	0	0	0	6	5	4	4	3	3
2000	Winston-Salem (Car)	A	9	8	3.74	21	21	1	0	132	135	64	55	50	106
	Birmingham (SL)	AA	2	4	2.49	7	7	0	0	43	28	15	12	24	31
MINOR LEAGUE TOTALS			13	12	3.30	40	28	1	1	199	182	91	73	86	158

6. Lorenzo Barcelo, rhp

Born: Aug. 10, 1977. **Ht.:** 6-4. **Wt.:** 220. **Bats:** R. **Throws:** R. **Career Transactions:** Signed out of Dominican Republic by Giants, May 23, 1994 . . . Traded by Giants with SS Mike Caruso, RHP Keith Foulke, RHP Bobby Howry, LHP Ken Vining and OF Brian Manning to White Sox for LHP Wilson Alvarez, RHP Roberto Hernandez and RHP Danny Darwin, July 31, 1997.

Considered the prize prospect from the 1997 White Flag trade, Barcelo was on a fast track to the big leagues before Tommy John surgery. He came back strong in 2000, making his big league debut and serving as a middle reliever in the playoffs. Barcelo is a skilled pitcher with unusual command for such a big man. His fastball, which was approaching 100 mph before surgery, has returned to the mid-90s and is expected to continue upward. His best pitch in 2000 was a sweeping slider that he learned while recovering from surgery. His changeup is another solid secondary pitch. Strength and stamina are still an issue. Barcelo holds back when he's used as a starter, limiting his velocity and effectiveness. Most organizations would love to have a guy like Barcelo in the rotation. The Sox are convinced he's best suited for relief. He'll begin 2001 as a set-up and long reliever, but eventually could emerge as a closer.

Year	Club (League)	Class	W	L	ERA	G	GS	CG	SV	IP	H	R	ER	BB	SO
1994	Giants/Orioles (DSL)	R	0	1	4.32	22	0	0	0	41	45	37	20	28	25
1995	Bellingham (NWL)	A	3	2	3.45	12	11	0	0	47	43	23	18	19	34
1996	Burlington (Mid)	A	12	10	3.54	26	26	1	0	152	138	70	60	46	139
1997	San Jose (Cal)	A	5	4	3.94	16	16	1	0	89	91	45	39	30	89
	Shreveport (TL)	AA	2	0	4.02	5	5	0	0	31	30	19	14	8	20
	Birmingham (SL)	AA	2	1	4.86	6	6	0	0	33	36	20	18	9	29
1998	White Sox (AZL)	R	0	1	1.50	3	3	0	0	6	6	1	1	0	9
1999	White Sox (AZL)	R	2	1	1.69	9	9	0	0	42	36	14	8	6	57
	Burlington (Mid)	A	1	0	3.60	1	1	0	0	5	3	2	2	0	6
	Birmingham (SL)	AA	0	1	3.60	4	4	0	0	20	14	8	8	6	14
2000	Charlotte (IL)	AAA	5	6	4.26	17	17	0	0	99	114	53	47	17	62
	Chicago (AL)	MAJ	4	2	3.69	22	1	0	0	39	34	17	16	9	26
MAJOR LEAGUE TOTALS			4	2	3.69	22	1	0	0	39	34	17	16	9	26
MINOR LEAGUE TOTALS			32	27	3.72	121	98	2	0	568	556	292	235	169	484

7. Brian West, rhp

Born: Aug. 4, 1980. **Ht.:** 6-4. **Wt.:** 230. **Bats:** R. **Throws:** R. **School:** West Monroe (La.) HS. **Career Transactions:** Selected by White Sox in first round (35th overall) of 1999 draft; signed July 1, 1999.

A highly regarded linebacker, West turned down a football scholarship at Texas A&M to sign with the White Sox. His potential as a power pitcher translated to a $1 million bonus. West was just 19 when he pitched in the Class A Midwest League all-star game, an impressive achievement for his first full season. He earned a promotion to the Carolina League but looked tired in two outings there. West is a terrific athlete with an intimidating build. He has a fastball that reaches the mid-90s and a decent curveball. He pitches down in the strike zone unusually well for a raw power pitcher. West still is developing an offspeed pitch. His control is sometimes shaky, which is why his strikeout-walk ratio belied his stuff in 2000. He needs to learn how to put away hitters. The White Sox will take it one step at a time with West, who is likely to open the 2001 season with high Class A Winston-Salem. He's a few years away from getting serious consideration for a big league spot, but he's the kind of kid who could stick around for a long time once he gets there.

Year	Club (League)	Class	W	L	ERA	G	GS	CG	SV	IP	H	R	ER	BB	SO
1999	White Sox (AZL)	R	0	1	13.50	2	0	0	0	5	10	7	7	2	3
	Bristol (Appy)	R	1	2	10.50	8	1	0	2	18	26	25	21	14	17
2000	Burlington (Mid)	A	8	9	3.78	24	24	0	0	148	146	81	62	73	90
	Winston-Salem (Car)	A	0	1	11.37	2	2	0	0	6	10	12	8	6	3
MINOR LEAGUE TOTALS			9	13	4.98	36	27	0	2	177	188	125	98	95	113

8. Aaron Rowand, of

Born: Aug. 29, 1977. **Ht.:** 6-1. **Wt.:** 200. **Bats:** R. **Throws:** R. **School:** Cal State Fullerton. **Career Transactions:** Selected by White Sox in first round (35th overall) of 1998 draft; signed June 12, 1998.

In another organization, Rowand might be well known by now. But his steady development has been obscured by the faster rise of Carlos Lee and Magglio Ordonez. Rowand nevertheless has made an impressive climb, posting all-star seasons in the Carolina and Southern leagues. By leading the Southern League in RBIs in 2000, Rowand added to his reputation as a run producer. He generates power from a short, quick swing and tremendous upper-body strength. He has decent speed and has used his instincts to develop into an above-average baserunner, though he doesn't project as a basestealer. He's a good right fielder with an arm that managers rated the best in the SL. Rowand may feel that he must hit home runs to get attention. His strikeout-walk ratio has gotten worse for two straight years, with his on-base percentage declining to .321 in 2000. Roward could challenge for a job on the bench but needs a trade to get a shot at regular playing time. The Sox can have him spend the 2001 season in Triple-A, but something has to give.

Year	Club (League)	Class	AVG	G	AB	R	H	2B	3B	HR	RBI	BB	SO	SB
1998	Hickory (SAL)	A	.342	61	222	42	76	13	3	5	32	21	36	7
1999	Winston-Salem (Car)	A	.279	133	512	96	143	37	3	24	88	33	94	15
2000	Birmingham (SL)	AA	.258	139	532	80	137	26	5	20	98	38	117	22
MINOR LEAGUE TOTALS			.281	333	1266	218	356	76	11	49	218	92	247	44

9. Josh Fogg, rhp

Born: Dec. 13, 1976. **Ht.:** 6-2. **Wt.:** 205. **Bats:** R. **Throws:** R. **School:** University of Florida. **Career Transactions:** Selected by White Sox in third round of 1998 draft; signed July 3, 1998.

A closer at Florida, Fogg has been used almost exclusively as a starter with the White Sox. They put him in that role to get him more work but have become intrigued by his potential as an innings-eating, end-of-the-rotation starter. He has had three solid seasons as a pro, leading the Southern League with 192 innings in 2000. Fogg has outstanding command, averaging just 2.5 walks per nine innings in the minors. He has an outstanding slider and a decent changeup, and he isn't afraid to throw his offspeed pitches when behind in the count. He's an intelligent pitcher who works to hitters' weaknesses. In a system loaded with hard throwers, Fogg has finesse stuff. His fastball touches the low 90s but often is in the high 80s. He doesn't operate with much margin for error. After pitcher-friendly Birmingham, Fogg may face a tough adjustment at Charlotte, which plays in a bandbox. His chances to advance are more difficult in this system than they would be in others.

Year	Club (League)	Class	W	L	ERA	G	GS	CG	SV	IP	H	R	ER	BB	SO
1998	White Sox (AZL)	R	1	0	0.00	2	0	0	0	4	0	0	0	1	5
	Hickory (SAL)	A	1	3	2.18	8	8	0	0	41	36	17	10	13	29
	Winston-Salem (Car)	A	0	1	0.00	1	0	0	0	2	2	2	0	0	2
1999	Winston-Salem (Car)	A	10	5	2.96	17	17	1	0	103	93	44	34	33	109
	Birmingham (SL)	AA	3	2	5.89	10	10	0	0	55	66	37	36	18	40
2000	Birmingham (SL)	AA	11	7	2.57	27	27	2	0	192	190	68	55	44	136
MINOR LEAGUE TOTALS			26	18	3.06	65	62	3	0	397	387	168	135	109	321

10. Jason Stumm, rhp

Born: April 13, 1981. **Ht.:** 6-2. **Wt.:** 210. **Bats:** R. **Throws:** R. **School:** Centralia (Wash.) HS. **Career Transactions:** Selected by White Sox in first round (15th overall) of 1999 draft; signed June 19, 1999.

Adversity arrived for the former all-everything out of Washington. A league MVP as a quarterback and small forward in high school, Stumm set a since-broken club record when he received a $1.75 million bonus in 1999. He tore an elbow ligament and needed Tommy John surgery last year. When healthy, he throws 96-97 mph consistently and maintains it late into games. Scouts and coaches rave about his character. He's a leader and a competitor. Stumm was able to get by with his fastball in high school but needs a lot of work on his slider and changeup. The White Sox aren't too worried about Stumm. He's still young and they've had plenty of Tommy John survivors in the organization, including Lorenzo Barcelo and Rocky Biddle. Because Stumm didn't have surgery until late in the 2000 season, he'll miss most of 2001. The Sox hope he can be back in time for instructional league.

Year	Club (League)	Class	W	L	ERA	G	GS	CG	SV	IP	H	R	ER	BB	SO
1999	White Sox (AZL)	R	0	0	3.27	3	2	0	0	11	13	8	4	3	9
	Burlington (Mid)	A	3	3	5.32	10	10	0	0	44	47	31	26	27	33
2000	Burlington (Mid)	A	2	7	4.61	13	13	2	0	66	66	46	34	30	62
MINOR LEAGUE TOTALS			5	10	4.76	26	25	2	0	121	126	85	64	60	104

11. Gary Majewski, rhp

Born: Feb. 26, 1980. **Ht.:** 6-2. **Wt.:** 200. **Bats:** R. **Throws:** R. **School:** St. Pius X HS, Houston. **Career Transactions:** Selected by White Sox in second round of 1998 draft; signed Sept. 2, 1998.

The private-school kid from Houston has a real mean streak. He pitches inside with a fearlessness not often seen in young pitchers. How else do you explain a 29-5 hit batter-wild pitch ratio during his first two pro seasons? The White Sox started Majewski slowly after he signed late in 1998. He has a low-90s fastball with natural sinking action, and he complements it with an above-average slider and changeup. He's considered an outstanding competitor and led his high school team to a private-school title in Texas. Majewski figures to be advanced slowly because of the pitching depth in the White Sox system. He's unlikely to reach Comiskey Park before 2003.

Year	Club (League)	Class	W	L	ERA	G	GS	CG	SV	IP	H	R	ER	BB	SO
1999	Bristol (Appy)	R	7	1	3.05	13	13	1	0	77	67	34	26	37	91
	Burlington (Mid)	A	0	0	37.80	2	0	0	0	3	11	14	14	4	1
2000	Burlington (Mid)	A	6	7	3.07	22	22	3	0	135	83	53	46	68	137
	Winston-Salem (Car)	A	2	4	5.11	6	6	0	0	37	32	21	21	17	24
MINOR LEAGUE TOTALS			15	12	3.83	43	41	4	0	252	193	122	107	126	253

12. Jeff Liefer, 1b/of

Born: Aug. 17, 1974. **Ht.:** 6-3. **Wt.:** 195. **Bats:** L. **Throws:** R. **School:** Long Beach State University. **Career Transactions:** Selected by White Sox in first round (25th overall) of 1995 draft; signed Aug. 18, 1995.

It may be now or never for Liefer, who has spent most of the last four seasons at Triple-A or Double-A without establishing himself as a big leaguer. Liefer long has been the best left-handed hitter in a system heavy on righthanders, but he hasn't used that to his advantage. He has impressive potential as a power hitter but has failed to homer in 124 at-bats with the White Sox. He hasn't received regular playing time, however, getting most of his at-bats when he was wasting the first half of the 1999 season on the Sox bench. Liefer was drafted as a third baseman but since elbow surgery has been limited to first base and occasional starts in the outfield. Liefer's stats argue for him to get a look as at least a platoon player for the Sox, but that won't happen unless something happens to Paul Konerko or Frank Thomas.

Year	Club (League)	Class	AVG	G	AB	R	H	2B	3B	HR	RBI	BB	SO	SB
1996	South Bend (Mid)	A	.325	74	277	60	90	14	0	15	58	30	62	6
	Prince William (Car)	A	.224	37	147	17	33	6	0	1	13	11	27	0
1997	Birmingham (SL)	AA	.238	119	474	67	113	24	9	15	71	38	115	2
1998	Birmingham (SL)	AA	.291	127	471	84	137	33	6	21	89	60	125	1
	Calgary (PCL)	AAA	.258	8	31	3	8	3	0	1	10	2	12	0
1999	Chicago (AL)	MAJ	.248	45	113	8	28	7	1	0	14	8	28	2
	Charlotte (IL)	AAA	.339	46	171	36	58	17	1	9	34	21	26	2
2000	Charlotte (IL)	AAA	.281	120	445	75	125	29	1	32	91	53	107	2
	Chicago (AL)	MAJ	.182	5	11	0	2	0	0	0	0	0	4	0
MAJOR LEAGUE TOTALS			.242	50	124	8	30	7	1	0	14	8	32	2
MINOR LEAGUE TOTALS			.280	531	2016	342	564	126	17	94	366	215	474	13

13. Rocky Biddle, rhp

Born: May 21, 1976. **Ht.:** 6-3. **Wt.:** 230. **Bats:** R. **Throws:** R. **School:** Long Beach State University.
Career Transactions: Selected by White Sox in first round (51st overall) of 1997 draft; signed June 12, 1997.

No one could have guessed how quickly Biddle would move after returning from Tommy John surgery. He won a job on the Double-A staff in spring training and wound up getting an audition in the Sox rotation. Former general manager Ron Schueler fell in love with Biddle's work ethic in 1999, when he was rehabbing at the Sox complex in Arizona. He not only regained his low-90s velocity after the surgery but also showed a hard curveball. His fastball has natural movement when it's thrown down. He credited the time "shadow-boxing" for improving his mechanics. Biddle doesn't have as high a ceiling as other pitchers in the system, but he has a competitive spirit that won't be denied. He could wind up as a reliever.

Year	Club (League)	Class	W	L	ERA	G	GS	CG	SV	IP	H	R	ER	BB	SO
1997	Hickory (SAL)	A	0	1	4.64	13	0	0	1	21	22	18	11	10	25
1998	Winston-Salem (Car)	A	4	5	4.57	16	16	0	0	82	92	55	42	45	72
	White Sox (AZL)	R	1	0	3.94	5	2	0	0	16	15	9	7	8	18
1999					Did Not Play—Injured										
2000	Birmingham (SL)	AA	11	6	3.08	23	23	2	0	146	138	63	50	54	118
	Chicago (AL)	MAJ	1	2	8.34	4	4	0	0	22	31	25	21	8	7
MAJOR LEAGUE TOTALS			1	2	8.34	4	4	0	0	22	31	25	21	8	7
MINOR LEAGUE TOTALS			16	12	3.72	57	41	2	1	266	267	145	110	117	233

14. Corwin Malone, lhp

Born: July 3, 1980. **Ht.:** 6-3. **Wt.:** 200. **Bats:** R. **Throws:** L. **School:** Thomasville (Ala.) HS. **Career Transactions:** Selected by White Sox in ninth round of 1999 draft; signed June 7, 1999.

Malone was among the 14 pitchers the Sox took with their first 15 picks in the 1999 draft. He had a standout high school career in Alabama, throwing one no-hitter and four one-hitters as a senior. He held opponents to a .180 average in the Rookie-level Arizona League in 1999. He's 6-foot-3 and can intimidate lefthanders. He has tremendous tools, including a fastball in the 92-93 range, but is raw. Malone struggles to throw strikes, especially with breaking pitches. He has averaged almost a walk an inning in his career, frequently winging the ball to the screen. The White Sox can move slowly with him because he's so young. He'll spend at least one more year in Class A before being considered for bigger challenges.

Year	Club (League)	Class	W	L	ERA	G	GS	CG	SV	IP	H	R	ER	BB	SO
1999	White Sox (AZL)	R	0	2	8.00	10	0	0	0	18	16	19	16	16	24
2000	Burlington (Mid)	A	2	3	4.90	38	1	0	0	72	67	52	39	60	82
MINOR LEAGUE TOTALS			2	5	5.52	48	1	0	0	90	83	71	55	76	106

15. Jeff Bajenaru, rhp

Born: March 21, 1978. **Ht.:** 6-1. **Wt.:** 190. **Bats:** R. **Throws:** R. **School:** University of Oklahoma. **Career Transactions:** Selected by White Sox in 36th round of 1999 draft; signed May 29, 2000.

How do the White Sox keep finding guys like Bajenaru? They took a flier on the right fielder/reliever in 1999 but couldn't sign him. Because he was a fifth-year senior at Oklahoma, the Sox retained his rights until a week before the 2000 draft. They signed him after he hit .342 with 11 homers and saved 20 games to earn third-team All-America honors. Bajenaru had smooth sailing as a pro, using his 93-95 mph fastball to overpower hitters. The Sox believe they'll really have something after he finds a breaking ball he can consistently throw for strikes. Because he's 23, he'll probably be pushed to Double-A as soon as possible.

Year	Club (League)	Class	W	L	ERA	G	GS	CG	SV	IP	H	R	ER	BB	SO
2000	Bristol (Appy)	R	1	1	3.77	12	0	0	5	14	10	6	6	5	31
	Winston-Salem (Car)	A	2	0	4.38	10	0	0	2	12	7	6	6	5	15
MINOR LEAGUE TOTALS			3	1	4.05	22	0	0	7	26	17	12	12	10	46

16. Matt Guerrier, rhp

Born: Aug. 2, 1978. **Ht.:** 6-3. **Wt.:** 190. **Bats:** R. **Throws:** R. **School:** Kent University. **Career Transactions:** Selected by White Sox in 10th round of 1999 draft; signed June 17, 1999.

A move to the bullpen has allowed Guerrier to climb quickly, with a strong showing down the stretch in Double-A last year. He's a sinker/slider pitcher who keeps the ball down, allowing only one homer in 58 innings in 2000. He has averaged more than a strikeout an inning as a pro but will see that ratio drop as he faces better competition. Guerrier has a closer's mindset, but the real test comes when he starts getting hit. If Guerrier continues to progress, they might consider Keith Foulke's wish to move into the rotation.

Year	Club (League)	Class	W	L	ERA	G	GS	CG	SV	IP	H	R	ER	BB	SO
1999	Bristol (Appy)	R	5	0	1.05	21	0	0	10	26	18	9	3	14	37
	Winston-Salem (Car)	A	0	0	5.40	4	0	0	2	3	3	2	2	0	5
2000	Winston-Salem (Car)	A	0	3	1.30	30	0	0	19	35	25	13	5	12	35
	Birmingham (SL)	AA	3	1	2.70	23	0	0	7	23	17	9	7	12	19
MINOR LEAGUE TOTALS			8	4	1.76	78	0	0	38	87	63	33	17	38	96

17. Rob Purvis, rhp

Born: Aug. 11, 1977. **Ht.:** 6-2. **Wt.:** 200. **Bats:** R. **Throws:** R. **School:** Bradley University. **Career Transactions:** Selected by White Sox in first round (45th overall) of 1999 draft; signed July 7, 1999.

Like a jet trying to land at O'Hare, Purvis is stacked behind a ton of outstanding pitching in the organization. He might not stand out like a 747, but his stuff is a long way from making him look like a prop plane. Purvis has a fastball that can reach 94 mph on his best days and complements it with a hard curveball. The Sox have done extensive work with his mechanics and allowed him to spend all of last season in the Carolina League, where he held hitters to a .222 average. He's prone to bouts of wildness but should get more consistent as he settles into his improved delivery. Purvis will open 2001 in Double-A.

Year	Club (League)	Class	W	L	ERA	G	GS	CG	SV	IP	H	R	ER	BB	SO
1999	White Sox (AZL)	R	0	1	4.00	4	0	0	2	9	12	10	4	6	7
	Burlington (Mid)	A	0	0	2.38	6	0	0	1	11	10	5	3	4	8
2000	Winston-Salem (Car)	A	11	10	3.38	27	27	2	0	168	139	81	63	87	114
	Birmingham (SL)	AA	0	1	4.50	1	1	0	0	4	6	8	2	3	3
MINOR LEAGUE TOTALS			11	12	3.38	38	28	2	3	192	167	104	72	100	132

18. Miguel Olivo, c

Born: July 15, 1978. **Ht.:** 6-1. **Wt.:** 215. **Bats:** R. **Throws:** R. **Career Transactions:** Signed out of Dominican Republic by Athletics, Sept. 30, 1996 . . . Traded by Athletics to White Sox, Dec. 12, 2000, completing trade in which White Sox sent RHP Chad Bradford to Athletics for a player to be named (Dec. 7, 2000).

Olivo's calling card is an arm that may rank with Ivan Rodriguez' as the strongest in the game, but the Athletics soured on him after a disappointing 2000 season. Olivo is a solid receiver who moves well behind the plate, but his arm strength caused him problems last season because he threw wildly. His offense showed little development last year. He didn't show the ability to make adjustments at the plate. He also battled minor injuries much of the season, which retarded his progress. Olivo has trouble working with pitchers partly because of his difficulty in learning the English language. He bolsters the catching depth in a system that was lacking in that area. If all goes according to plan, Olivo will be ready for Chicago when Sandy Alomar's contract expires after the 2002 season.

Year	Club (League)	Class	AVG	G	AB	R	H	2B	3B	HR	RBI	BB	SO	SB
1997	Athletics (DSL)	R	.271	63	221	37	60	11	4	6	57	34	36	6
1998	Athletics (AZL)	R	.311	46	164	30	51	11	3	2	23	8	43	2
1999	Modesto (Cal)	A	.305	73	243	46	74	13	6	9	42	21	60	4
2000	Modesto (Cal)	A	.282	58	227	40	64	11	5	5	35	16	53	5
	Midland (TL)	AA	.237	19	59	8	14	2	0	1	9	5	15	0
MINOR LEAGUE TOTALS			.288	259	914	161	263	48	18	23	166	84	207	17

19. Tim Hummel, ss

Born: Nov. 18, 1978. **Ht.:** 6-1. **Wt.:** 185. **Bats:** R. **Throws:** R. **School:** Old Dominion University. **Career Transactions:** Selected by White Sox in second round of 2000 draft; signed June 21, 2000.

The Padres drafted Hummel in the fifth round in 1997, but he went to Old Dominion, where he was the 2000 Colonial Athletic Association player of the year. The White Sox quickly got a look at him at his two possible positions: shortstop in the Midwest League and third base in the Carolina League. Hummel is a solid fundamental player who never wastes a step. He's smooth at shortstop but has problems getting to some grounders. His arm is average for the position. He has good bat speed and knowledge of the strike zone, which resulted in more walks than strikeouts last year. It will be a bonus if he develops into a double-digit homer hitter, but he should drive the ball to the gaps. His speed is average. The Sox will give him a chance to win their Double-A shortstop job and could move him fast if he keeps hitting.

Year	Club (League)	Class	AVG	G	AB	R	H	2B	3B	HR	RBI	BB	SO	SB
2000	Burlington (Mid)	A	.326	39	144	22	47	9	1	1	21	21	20	8
	Winston-Salem (Car)	A	.327	27	98	15	32	7	0	1	9	13	12	1
MINOR LEAGUE TOTALS			.326	66	242	37	79	16	1	2	30	34	32	9

20. Josh Paul, c

Born: May 19, 1975. **Ht.:** 6-1. **Wt.:** 185. **Bats:** R. **Throws:** R. **School:** Vanderbilt University. **Career Transactions:** Selected by White Sox in second round of 1996 draft; signed June 25, 1996.

The White Sox are looking to Paul to share catching duties with Sandy Alomar in 2001. They thought enough of him to place him on their 2000 playoff roster over Mark Johnson, but Paul is still an unknown commodity. An outfielder and third baseman at Vanderbilt, he is a terrific athlete and has worked hard to become a good receiver. He threw out 42 percent of basestealers in his big league stint last year. Paul hasn't hit with authority since breaking the hamate bone in his right wrist in 1997. While he hit for a decent average last year, he could be in trouble when teams compile a scouting report on him. The Sox value his leadership skills and versatility. He runs well enough to serve as a pinch-runner. But his bat will determine if he can stick around, and he hasn't shown much improvement in recent years.

Year	Club (League)	Class	AVG	G	AB	R	H	2B	3B	HR	RBI	BB	SO	SB
1996	White Sox (GCL)	R	.000	1	0	0	0	0	0	0	0	1	0	0
	Hickory (SAL)	A	.327	59	226	41	74	16	0	8	37	21	53	13
1997	Birmingham (SL)	AA	.296	34	115	18	34	5	0	1	16	12	25	6
	White Sox (GCL)	R	.429	5	14	3	6	0	1	0	0	1	3	1
1998	Winston-Salem (Car)	A	.255	123	444	66	113	20	7	11	63	38	91	20
1999	Birmingham (SL)	AA	.279	93	319	47	89	19	3	4	42	29	68	6
	Chicago (AL)	MAJ	.222	6	18	2	4	1	0	0	1	0	4	0
2000	Chicago (AL)	MAJ	.282	36	71	15	20	3	2	1	8	5	17	1
	Charlotte (IL)	AAA	.238	51	168	28	40	5	1	4	19	13	38	6
MAJOR LEAGUE TOTALS			.270	42	89	17	24	4	2	1	9	5	21	1
MINOR LEAGUE TOTALS			.277	366	1286	203	356	65	12	28	177	115	278	52

21. Julio Ramirez, of

Born: Aug. 10, 1977. **Ht.:** 5-11. **Wt.:** 170. **Bats:** R. **Throws:** R. **Career Transactions:** Signed out of Dominican Republic by Marlins, Dec. 6, 1993 . . . Traded by Marlins to White Sox for OF Jeff Abbott, Dec. 10, 2000.

Once the Marlins' top position-player prospect, Ramirez' stock has dropped. Though blessed with five-tool talent, Ramirez has struggled to master the game's subtleties. A nagging quadriceps injury and sore shoulder bothered him in 2000, and he missed close to two months. His frustration at the plate carried over to his defense, where his effort sometimes lagged on balls he used to run down with ease. He still projects as a No. 3 hitter with speed and power to all fields, but the clock is ticking. One positive out of his difficult season was an increased willingness to take instruction. Ramirez realized his free-swinging ways leave him open to lengthy slumps, and he shortened his stroke late in the year. The Sox have been trying to upgrade in center field, though Ramirez likely will begin 2001 in Triple-A.

Year	Club (League)	Class	AVG	G	AB	R	H	2B	3B	HR	RBI	BB	SO	SB
1994	Marlins (DSL)	R	.274	67	274	54	75	18	0	7	32	28	41	29
1995	Marlins (GCL)	R	.284	48	204	35	58	9	4	2	13	13	42	17
1996	Marlins (GCL)	R	.287	43	174	35	50	5	4	0	16	15	34	26
	Brevard County (FSL)	A	.246	17	61	11	15	0	1	0	2	4	18	2
1997	Kane County (Mid)	A	.255	99	376	70	96	18	7	14	53	37	122	41
1998	Brevard County (FSL)	A	.279	135	559	90	156	20	12	13	58	45	147	71
1999	Portland (EL)	AA	.261	138	568	87	148	30	10	13	64	39	150	64
	Florida (NL)	MAJ	.143	15	21	3	3	1	0	0	2	1	6	0
2000	Calgary (PCL)	AAA	.266	94	350	45	93	18	3	7	52	21	86	20
MAJOR LEAGUE TOTALS			.143	15	21	3	3	1	0	0	2	1	6	0
MINOR LEAGUE TOTALS			.269	641	2566	427	691	118	41	56	290	202	640	270

22. Gary Glover, rhp

Born: Dec. 3, 1976. **Ht.:** 6-5. **Wt.:** 205. **Bats:** R. **Throws:** R. **School:** De Land (Fla.) HS. **Career Transactions:** Selected by Blue Jays in 15th round of 1994 draft; signed June 27, 1994 . . . Traded by Blue Jays to White Sox for LHP Scott Eyre, Nov. 7, 2000.

Glover ranked as the Blue Jays' No. 6 prospect a year ago, and would have remained their top starter prospect if he hadn't been traded. His fastball ranks near the top of any organization when he has good mechanics and good command. He can get slow with his front side and inconsistent with the placement of his lead leg, which slowed his arm and dropped his velocity from 92-95 mph to 85-88 at times last season. Glover throws a true slider, which some organizations call a cut fastball because of its good velocity (85-88 mph) and late movement. He also can mix in a solid 70-72 mph curve. If he keeps his mechanics together, he still projects as a No. 3 starter in a big league rotation.

Year	Club (League)	Class	W	L	ERA	G	GS	CG	SV	IP	H	R	ER	BB	SO
1994	Blue Jays (GCL)	R	0	0	47.25	2	0	0	0	1	4	8	7	4	2
1995	Blue Jays (GCL)	R	3	7	4.91	12	10	2	0	62	62	48	34	26	46
1996	Medicine Hat (Pio)	R	3	12	7.75	15	15	2	0	84	119	94	72	29	54
1997	Hagerstown (SAL)	A	6	17	3.73	28	28	3	0	174	165	94	72	58	155
1998	Knoxville (SL)	AA	0	5	6.75	8	8	0	0	37	41	36	28	28	14
	Dunedin (FSL)	A	7	6	4.28	19	18	0	0	109	117	66	52	36	88
1999	Knoxville (SL)	AA	8	2	3.56	13	13	1	0	86	70	39	34	27	77
	Syracuse (IL)	AAA	4	6	5.19	14	14	0	0	76	93	50	44	35	57
	Toronto (AL)	MAJ	0	0	0.00	1	0	0	0	1	0	0	0	1	0
2000	Syracuse (IL)	AAA	9	9	5.02	27	27	1	0	167	181	104	93	62	119
MAJOR LEAGUE TOTALS			0	0	0.00	1	0	0	0	1	0	0	0	1	0
MINOR LEAGUE TOTALS			40	64	4.93	138	133	9	0	797	852	539	436	305	612

23. Ken Vining, lhp

Born: Dec. 5, 1974. **Ht.:** 6-0. **Wt.:** 180. **Bats:** L. **Throws:** L. **School:** Clemson University. **Career Transactions:** Selected by Giants in fourth round of 1996 draft; signed June 28, 1996 . . . Traded by Giants with RHP Lorenzo Barcelo, RHP Keith Foulke, RHP Bobby Howry, SS Mike Caruso and OF Brian Manning to White Sox for LHP Wilson Alvarez, RHP Roberto Hernandez and RHP Danny Darwin, July 31, 1997.

The third starter on the 1996 Clemson staff that featured Kris Benson and Billy Koch, Vining has been slowed by injury. He came over in the 1997 White Flag trade and made only three starts in 1999 before Tommy John surgery. Vining emerged as a reliable reliever on a team good enough to go to the Southern League championship series. His best pitch is a big-breaking curveball, and he has a 90 mph fastball. He uses a changeup effectively to keep hitters from sitting on his fastball. He locates his pitches well and does a good job keeping the ball down. Vining went to the Arizona Fall League as the Sox evaluated whether to give him a spot on the 40-man roster, which they did. Given the way teams covet lefties, there was no hiding Vining in the minors. He'll get a chance in the majors before long.

Year	Club (League)	Class	W	L	ERA	G	GS	CG	SV	IP	H	R	ER	BB	SO
1996	Bellingham (NWL)	A	4	2	2.09	12	11	0	0	60	45	16	14	23	69
1997	San Jose (Cal)	A	9	6	4.21	23	23	1	0	137	140	77	64	60	142
	Winston-Salem (Car)	A	2	2	2.86	5	5	0	0	35	36	17	11	11	38
1998	Birmingham (SL)	AA	10	12	4.07	29	28	1	0	173	187	103	78	91	133
1999	Birmingham (SL)	AA	0	2	9.26	3	3	0	0	12	20	16	12	9	8
2000	Birmingham (SL)	AA	1	5	4.08	43	0	0	1	46	36	26	21	18	41
MINOR LEAGUE TOTALS			26	29	3.89	115	70	2	1	462	464	255	200	212	431

24. Geronimo Mendoza, rhp

Born: Jan. 23, 1978. **Ht.:** 6-4. **Wt.:** 180. **Bats:** L. **Throws:** R. **Career Transactions:** Signed out of Dominican Republic by White Sox, April 22, 1995.

Mendoza had been in the shadow of fellow Dominican Juan Figueroa. But after his best friend was traded to the Orioles, Mendoza bloomed as a talent worthy of a reputation of his own. He had a breakthrough in the Carolina League, showing improved velocity and a new-found ability to battle hitters. He led the league with four complete games and three shutouts while finishing ninth in ERA. That's especially impressive considering he opened in the bullpen, becoming a starter after Figueroa and Jon Rauch moved on. Mendoza had been an afterthought but earned a longer look. He should be in Birmingham's rotation this season.

Year	Club (League)	Class	W	L	ERA	G	GS	CG	SV	IP	H	R	ER	BB	SO
1995	White Sox (GCL)	R	0	1	4.30	10	0	0	0	15	8	9	7	7	11
1996	White Sox (GCL)	R	1	8	9.78	12	7	0	0	39	55	49	42	26	29
1997	White Sox (GCL)	R	2	7	3.67	12	8	0	0	54	51	32	22	28	41
1998	Bristol (Appy)	R	5	2	3.83	13	13	0	0	80	78	40	34	30	70
1999	Burlington (Mid)	A	9	8	4.63	28	28	0	0	157	186	96	81	60	119
2000	Winston-Salem (Car)	A	11	6	3.41	31	19	4	0	145	146	65	55	65	117
MINOR LEAGUE TOTALS			28	32	4.43	106	75	4	0	490	524	291	241	216	387

25. McKay Christensen, of

Born: Aug. 14, 1975. **Ht.:** 5-11. **Wt.:** 180. **Bats:** L. **Throws:** L. **School:** Clovis (Calif.) West HS. **Career Transactions:** Selected by Angels in first round (sixth overall) of 1994 draft; signed July 28, 1994 . . . Traded by Angels with RHP John Snyder, LHP Andrew Lorraine and RHP Bill Simas to White Sox for LHP Jim Abbott and LHP Tim Fortugno, July 27, 1995.

Christensen is an excellent defensive center fielder and has the speed to be an outstanding leadoff man, but he must improve as a hitter. For years that has been the book on the former blue-chip tailback, and it remains true. The start of his career was delayed while he was on a Morman mission. He teases the White Sox with his potential but hasn't mounted a strong campaign for playing time in the big leagues. This could be the year he does. Power pitchers can knock the bat out of his hands. All pitchers go right at him, making it tough to work walks. He's a skilled bunter but loses lots of hits because outfielders play shallow on him. Christensen has tremendous range in center but only an average arm. He has learned to use his speed well on the bases, but has had too much trouble getting on in the first place.

Year	Club (League)	Class	AVG	G	AB	R	H	2B	3B	HR	RBI	BB	SO	SB
1995			Did Not Play—Mormon Mission											
1996	White Sox (GCL)	R	.263	35	133	17	35	7	5	1	16	10	23	10
	Hickory (SAL)	A	.000	6	11	0	0	0	0	0	0	1	4	0
1997	Hickory (SAL)	A	.280	127	503	95	141	12	12	5	47	52	61	28
1998	Winston-Salem (Car)	A	.285	95	361	69	103	17	6	4	32	53	54	20
1999	Chicago (AL)	MAJ	.226	28	53	10	12	1	0	1	6	4	7	2
	Birmingham (SL)	AA	.290	75	293	53	85	8	6	3	28	31	46	18
	Charlotte (IL)	AAA	.250	1	4	0	1	0	0	0	0	0	0	1
2000	Chicago (AL)	MAJ	.105	32	19	4	2	0	0	0	1	2	6	1
	Charlotte (IL)	AAA	.264	90	337	49	89	13	2	6	29	32	51	28
MAJOR LEAGUE TOTALS			.194	60	72	14	14	1	0	1	7	6	13	3
MINOR LEAGUE TOTALS			.276	429	1642	283	454	57	31	19	152	179	239	105

26. Chris Amador, 2b

Born: Dec. 14, 1982. **Ht.:** 5-10. **Wt.:** 160. **Bats:** R. **Throws:** R. **School:** Luis Felipe Crespo HS, Camuy, P.R. **Career Transactions:** Selected by White Sox in eighth round of 2000 draft; signed June 15, 2000.

Drafted as a 17-year-old, Amador made a smooth transition to second base. He has excellent range and good hands for the position. He immediately took to the pivot from the other side of the bag, doing a nice job turning double plays. He has the potential to develop into an outstanding leadoff or No. 2 hitter and is an outstanding baserunner, tying an Arizona League record with 40 stolen bases last year. He works pitchers deep into the count and bunts well. His power potential is limited, but that's the only real drawback to his game.

Year	Club (League)	Class	AVG	G	AB	R	H	2B	3B	HR	RBI	BB	SO	SB
2000	White Sox (AZL)	R	.302	53	212	48	64	10	3	0	31	30	46	40
MINOR LEAGUE TOTALS			.302	53	212	48	64	10	3	0	31	30	46	40

27. Bo Ivy, of

Born: Sept. 20, 1981. **Ht.:** 5-10. **Wt.:** 175. **Bats:** R. **Throws:** R. **School:** Shannon (Miss.) HS. **Career Transactions:** Selected by White Sox in sixth round of 2000 draft; signed June 9, 2000.

Ivy can flat-out fly. Chris Amador and Ivy ranked 1-2 in the Arizona League in stolen bases, though Ivy was caught 11 times, which included more than his share of pickoffs. His instincts can only improve. Baseball wasn't his game growing up, so his skills are raw. The White Sox were thrilled by his approach at the plate, and he used his speed to get lots of infield hits. He hit .341 despite playing most of the year with jammed wrists. He should get stronger and develop some power as he matures, but for now he's a dangerous leadoff man. He's solid in center field but needs to work on his throwing.

Year	Club (League)	Class	AVG	G	AB	R	H	2B	3B	HR	RBI	BB	SO	SB
2000	White Sox (AZL)	R	.341	36	129	35	44	4	2	0	13	34	24	34
MINOR LEAGUE TOTALS			.341	36	129	35	44	4	2	0	13	34	24	34

28. Amaury Garcia, 2b

Born: May 20, 1975. **Ht.:** 5-10. **Wt.:** 160. **Bats:** R. **Throws:** R. **Career Transactions:** Signed out of Dominican Republic by Marlins, Dec. 14, 1992 . . . Traded by Marlins to White Sox for RHP Mark Roberts, Nov. 27, 2000.

Ken Williams made several minor deals in his first few months as Chicago's general manager, including acquiring Garcia. His ceiling isn't terribly high, but he could be a useful utilityman if Tony Graffanino fades. Garcia doesn't draw enough walks to bat at the top of the order, but he does hit for average with gap power. He also runs well enough to be a stolen-base threat. Garcia has played second base and the outfield in the minors. He's adequate at best at second, where he's stiff and has shown little range and concentration. He hasn't worked hard at becoming a quality outfielder either. His performance tailed off when he was asked to repeat Triple-A in 2000, and Florida was more than happy to trade him.

Year	Club (League)	Class	AVG	G	AB	R	H	2B	3B	HR	RBI	BB	SO	SB
1993	Marlins (DSL)	R	.283	64	237	35	67	5	3	4	29	31	41	9
1994	Marlins (GCL)	R	.313	58	208	46	65	9	3	0	25	33	49	10
1995	Kane County (Mid)	A	.241	26	58	19	14	4	1	1	5	18	12	5
	Elmira (NY-P)	A	.273	62	231	40	63	7	3	0	17	34	50	41
1996	Kane County (Mid)	A	.263	106	395	65	104	19	7	6	36	62	84	37
1997	Brevard County (FSL)	A	.288	124	479	77	138	30	2	7	44	49	97	45
1998	Portland (EL)	AA	.270	137	544	79	147	19	6	13	62	45	126	23
1999	Calgary (PCL)	AAA	.317	119	479	94	152	37	9	17	53	44	79	17
	Florida (NL)	MAJ	.250	10	24	6	6	0	1	2	2	3	11	0
2000	Calgary (PCL)	AAA	.292	120	479	83	140	26	3	13	47	41	79	35
MAJOR LEAGUE TOTALS			.250	10	24	6	6	0	1	2	2	3	11	0
MINOR LEAGUE TOTALS			.286	816	3110	538	890	156	37	61	318	357	617	222

29. Danny Sandoval, ss/2b

Born: April 7, 1979. **Ht.:** 5-11. **Wt.:** 160. **Bats:** R. **Throws:** R. **Career Transactions:** Signed out of Venezuela by White Sox, Dec. 8, 1996.

The Sox aren't sure what they have on their hands in Sandoval, but they're intrigued. He hit his way to a Triple-A cameo last year, then continued his rise with a strong winter at Zulia in the Venezuelan League. While Sandoval is a promising contact hitter, he has little power and there's no sign the Sox are looking to him as a long-term option anywhere. He was an all-star shortstop in the Midwest League, but is error-prone and lacks both range and arm strength. He played second and third base at Winston-Salem, but was back as a full-time shortstop in winter ball. His future is probably as a utilityman, but he needs another season like his last one to get the White Sox' full attention.

Year	Club (League)	Class	AVG	G	AB	R	H	2B	3B	HR	RBI	BB	SO	SB
1997	Guacara 1 (VSL)	R	.341	31	82	16	28	0	1	0	9	11	7	8
1998	Hickory (SAL)	A	.230	126	430	43	99	12	2	0	30	29	88	13
1999	Burlington (Mid)	A	.227	76	255	34	58	5	1	3	37	17	39	8
2000	Burlington (Mid)	A	.323	75	269	34	87	9	3	0	34	18	22	37
	Winston-Salem (Car)	A	.266	52	199	29	53	11	2	2	17	18	21	11
	Charlotte (IL)	AAA	.125	2	8	0	1	0	0	0	1	1	1	0
MINOR LEAGUE TOTALS			.262	362	1243	156	326	37	9	5	128	94	178	77

30. Jason Dellaero, ss

Born: Dec. 17, 1976. **Ht.:** 6-2. **Wt.:** 195. **Bats:** R. **Throws:** R. **School:** University of South Florida. **Career Transactions:** Selected by White Sox in first round (15th overall) of 1997 draft; signed June 24, 1997.

Look out below. Dellaero received the organization's first seven-figure signing bonus and was among the top 15 prospects in each of the last three years. But he has lost it at the plate. He abandoned switch-hitting last season, hoping he would get on base more often if he hit exclusively from the right side. He was overmatched in his second year of Double-A, had major problems making contact with his long swing and remained nearly impossible to walk. But the success of Birmingham, which went to the Southern League championship series with him in the lineup, enforces his value. He's a first-rate fielder. He has worked to improve his defensive skills and his arm is one of the best in the minors. There's speculation he may be tried as a pitcher, but that's only a rumor for now. Dellaero still could get to the big leagues as a shortstop, but only if he figures out how to crawl above the Mendoza line.

Year	Club (League)	Class	AVG	G	AB	R	H	2B	3B	HR	RBI	BB	SO	SB
1997	White Sox (GCL)	R	.200	5	15	1	3	2	0	0	1	1	2	0
	Hickory (SAL)	A	.277	55	191	37	53	10	3	6	29	17	49	3
1998	Winston-Salem (Car)	A	.208	121	428	45	89	23	3	10	49	25	147	12
1999	Winston-Salem (Car)	A	.223	54	184	22	41	13	0	2	19	18	59	9
	Birmingham (SL)	AA	.268	81	272	40	73	13	3	10	44	14	76	6
	Chicago (AL)	MAJ	.091	11	33	1	3	0	0	0	2	1	13	0
2000	Birmingham (SL)	AA	.185	122	438	36	81	18	1	7	42	20	142	9
MAJOR LEAGUE TOTALS			.091	11	33	1	3	0	0	0	2	1	13	0
MINOR LEAGUE TOTALS			.223	438	1528	181	340	79	10	35	184	95	475	39

Cincinnati
Reds

By Chris Haft

Though the Reds fell short of expectations in the big leagues in 2000, their minor league system exceeded them. The organization has chipped away at the years of neglect that characterized the Marge Schott regime, when the farm and scouting departments were an afterthought. Cincinnati is drafting, acquiring and developing players more efficiently, establishing a consistency that should continue.

Reds officials believe their river of talent is fed by three essential streams. First, highly touted prospects whose names are already familiar to Cincinnati fans, such as outfielders Austin Kearns and Adam Dunn, progressed last year.

Then several players emerged as pleasant surprises and established themselves as potential major leaguers, such as shortstop Rainer Olmedo and lefthander Lance Davis.

And finally, the Reds probably brought more significant talent into their system in 2000 than any other organization. Of the players on Cincinnati's list of 30 prospects, 10 came in trades. Three players in the top 10—catcher Dane Sardinha, second baseman David Espinosa and righthander Dustin Moseley—came out of the first two rounds of the draft.

"When you look at us now, the way every-thing turned out," said Bill Doran, special assistant to Reds general manager Jim Bowden, "we're deeper than I thought we were going to be at the beginning of the year."

The Reds wouldn't have been nearly as deep if they hadn't come up with creative ways to sign their premium draft choices. The cash-poor front office persuaded Espinosa and Sardinha to accept major league contracts without bonuses, and delayed a deal with Moseley until November, after the 2001 fiscal year began.

"To win championships, you must put money in player development and scouting," Bowden said. "You have to sign your draft choices. We want to keep up the process."

Part of the process has spread to Latin America, where the Reds have accelerated their efforts. For example, outfielders Juan Acevedo and Elvin Andujar were signed out of the Dominican Republic. Olmedo was discovered in Venezuela.

The Reds have new men in charge of their minor league and scouting operations. Scouting director DeJon Watson was promoted to major league scout in July and replaced by national crosschecker Kasey McKeon, the son of deposed manager Jack McKeon. Two months later, then-farm director Doran switched roles with Tim Naehring.

OrganizationOverview

General manager: Jim Bowden. **Farm director:** Tim Naehring. **Scouting director:** Kasey McKeon.

2000 PERFORMANCE

Class	Team	League	W	L	Pct.	Finish*	Manager
Majors	Cincinnati	National	85	77	.525	t-6th (16)	Jack McKeon
Triple-A	Louisville RiverBats	International	71	73	.493	10th (14)	Dave Miley
Double-A	Chattanooga Lookouts	Southern	70	68	.507	t-3rd (10)	Mike Rojas
Low A	Dayton Dragons	Midwest	70	67	.511	7th (14)	Freddie Benavides
Low A	#Clinton Lumber Kings	Midwest	71	69	.507	t-8th (14)	Jay Sorg
Rookie	Billings Mustangs	Pioneer	39	36	.520	5th (8)	Russ Nixon
Rookie	GCL Reds	Gulf Coast	14	41	.255	13th (13)	Luis Quinones
OVERALL 2000 MINOR LEAGUE RECORD			335	354	.486	19th (30)	

*Finish in overall standings (No. of teams in league). #Affiliate will be in Mudville (California/high A) in 2001.

ORGANIZATION LEADERS

BATTING
*AVG	Chris Sexton, Louisville	.324
R	Austin Kearns, Dayton	110
H	**Brady Clark**, Louisville	148
	Austin Kearns, Dayton	148
TB	Austin Kearns, Dayton	270
2B	Randy Stegall, Dayton	43
3B	Three tied at	8
HR	Austin Kearns, Dayton	27
RBI	Austin Kearns, Dayton	104
BB	Adam Dunn, Dayton	100
SO	Samone Peters, Clinton	198
SB	Wilmy Caceres, Chattanooga	36

PITCHING
W	Travis Thompson, Dayton/Chattanooga	17
L	**Ty Howington**, Dayton	15
#ERA	Lance Davis, Chattanooga/Louisville	2.44
G	Michael Neu, Clinton	58
CG	Jim Manias, Dayton/Chattanooga	7
SV	Bo Donaldson, Chattanooga	24
	Michael Neu, Clinton	24
IP	Travis Thompson, Dayton/Chattanooga	189
BB	Scott Dunn, Clinton	89
SO	Paul Darnell, Clinton	164

*Minimum 250 at-bats. #Minimum 75 innings.

TOP PROSPECTS OF THE DECADE

1991	Reggie Sanders, of
1992	Reggie Sanders, of
1993	Willie Greene, 3b
1994	Pokey Reese, ss
1995	Pokey Reese, ss
1996	Pokey Reese, ss
1997	Aaron Boone, 3b
1998	Damian Jackson, ss/2b
1999	Rob Bell, rhp
2000	Gookie Dawkins, ss

TOP DRAFT PICKS OF THE DECADE

1991	Pokey Reese, ss
1992	Chad Mottola, of
1993	Pat Watkins, of
1994	C.J. Nitkowski, lhp
1995	Brett Tomko, rhp (2)
1996	John Oliver, of
1997	Brandon Larson, ss/3b
1998	Austin Kearns, of
1999	Ty Howington, lhp
2000	David Espinosa, ss

Clark **Howington**

BEST TOOLS

Best Hitter for Average	Austin Kearns
Best Power Hitter	Adam Dunn
Fastest Baserunner	Gookie Dawkins
Best Fastball	Ty Howington
Best Breaking Ball	John Riedling
Best Control	Dustin Moseley
Best Defensive Catcher	Dane Sardinha
Best Defensive Infielder	Rainer Olmedo
Best Infield Arm	Drew Henson
Best Defensive Outfielder	Alejandro Diaz
Best Outfield Arm	Jackson Melian

PROJECTED 2004 LINEUP

Catcher	Dane Sardinha
First Base	Sean Casey
Second Base	David Espinosa
Third Base	Drew Henson
Shortstop	Pokey Reese
Left Field	Adam Dunn
Center Field	Ken Griffey Jr.
Right Field	Austin Kearns
No. 1 Starter	Rob Bell
No. 2 Starter	Ty Howington
No. 3 Starter	Dustin Moseley
No. 4 Starter	Scott Williamson
No. 5 Starter	Chris Reitsma
Closer	Danny Graves

ALL-TIME LARGEST BONUSES

Austin Kearns, 1998	$1,950,000
Ty Howington, 1999	1,750,000
Brandon Larson, 1997	1,330,000
Alejandro Diaz, 1999	1,175,000
Dustin Moseley, 2000	930,000

DraftAnalysis

2000 Draft

Best Pro Debut: OF Steve Smitherman (23) batted .316-15-65 with 14 stolen bases at Rookie-level Billings. RHP David Gil (3) was one of three drafted pitchers to reach Double-A.

Best Athlete: SS David Espinosa (1) is a switch-hitter who can run, hit and sting the ball, and he has a plus arm and range. C **Dane Sardinha** (2) is athletic for his position. Cash flow jeopardized the chances of signing either player until Espinosa (eight years, up to $5 million) and Sardinha (four years, up to $2.4 million) accepted big league contracts without bonuses.

Best Hitter: Espinosa not only has the physical tools to hit, but he also has the knowledge, plate discipline and makeup. He should be an effective leadoff hitter, and in a best-case scenario Cincinnati can see him growing into a Chipper Jones.

Best Raw Power: OF/1B Chris Williamson (11), who hit eight homers between Billings and Class A Dayton, and Smitherman. They need to control their swings better but can punish mistakes.

Fastest Runner: Espinosa is an above-average runner who can run a 6.6-second 60-yard dash.

Best Defensive Player: Sardinha is so talented behind the plate that he probably could play defensively in the majors now.

Best Fastball: RHP Dan Fletcher (7) touched 95 mph last spring but didn't throw as hard after signing. RHP Bryan Edwards (9) also threw 95 but with an ugly delivery. Cincinnati retooled his mechanics

in instructional league, and Edwards was more effective throwing 88-92 mph.

Most Intriguing Background: Edwards dropped out of Texas and pitched in the independent Atlantic League. 3B Rod Allen (34), who didn't sign, is the son of the former big leaguer of the same name.

Closest To The Majors: Sardinha, whose timetable will be based on how much he hits. RHP Dustin Moseley (1) is very advanced for a high school pitcher, but he signed late and that could slow down his timetable.

Sardinha

Best Late-Round Pick: Williamson and Smitherman. RHP Bradley George (12) was clocked as fast as 93 mph while striking out 55 in 48 innings at Billings.

The One Who Got Away: Once the Reds announced the signing of Moseley when their new fiscal year began in November, the only significant players they lost were RHP Marc Kaiser (4), the highest-drafted high school player who definitely won't sign, and OF Roydell Williams (5). Kaiser is at Arizona and Williams is a wide receiver at Tulane.

Assessment: In spite of a budget crunch, the Reds found a way to sign arguably the draft's best shortstop (Espinosa), most polished high school pitcher (Moseley) and best catcher (Sardinha).

1999 Draft

The Reds remain high on LHP Ty Howington (1), but he struggled in his 2000 pro debut. 1B/OF Ben Broussard (2) crushed the ball until hurting his wrist last summer. **Grade: C–**

1998 Draft

Cincinnati found its corner outfielders of the future in Austin Kearns (1) and Adam Dunn (2), the system's best prospects. LHP B.J. Ryan (17) rocketed to the majors and was traded to Baltimore. **Grade: B+**

1997 Draft

2B/SS Gookie Dawkins (2) won an Olympic gold medal with Team USA and RHP Scott Williamson (9) was the 1999 National League rookie of the year, though both had rocky seasons in 2000. 3B Brandon Larson (1) shows power when healthy. OF Dewayne Wise (5) was lost to Toronto, while RHP Robert Averett (21) was traded to Colorado. **Grade: B**

1996 Draft

The two first-rounders were OF John Oliver, a flop, and RHP Matt McClendon, who didn't sign and is now a top prospect with the Braves. RHP Buddy Carlyle (2), the best player in the crop, was traded for Marc Kroon and will play in Japan in 2001. **Grade: D–**

Note: Draft analysis prepared by Jim Callis. Numbers in parentheses indicate draft rounds.

. . . Kearns' power is in full bloom, and he distributes it to all fields.

Austin Kearns of

Born: May 20, 1980.
Ht.: 6-3. **Wt.:** 220.
Bats: R. **Throws:** R.
School: Lafayette HS, Lexington, Ky.
Career Transactions: Selected by Reds in first round (seventh overall) of 1998 draft; signed July 30, 1998.

Kearns was a highly regarded high school pitching prospect until his senior year, when his velocity plunged from the low 90s to the low 80s. Undaunted, the Reds made him the seventh overall pick in the 1998 draft as a position player and refused to panic when he homered just once in 108 Rookie-level at-bats. He made steady progress in the low Class A Midwest League in 1999, then dominated when the organization's lack of a high Class A club (which finally was addressed with the addition of the California League's Mudville franchise for 2001) sent him back there last season. He ranked among the league leaders in nearly every offensive category and topped the circuit in runs, homers, RBIs and extra-base hits (66). He shared the league's official prospect-of-the-year award with Cardinals third baseman Albert Pujols.

Kearns' power is now in full bloom. He homered in eight consecutive games from July 17-24, establishing a Midwest League record and falling two games short of the all-time minor league mark. Reds officials like Kearns' ability to distribute that power to all fields. Another of his assets is the ability to make adjustments at the plate. He made impressive strides with his strike-zone judgment in 2000, and the dividends were obvious. Kearns has decent speed, a strong arm and is proficient enough in right field to keep Cincinnati from considering switching him to first base. Though his attitude has earned praise, the Reds want to see him continue to push himself. Some say he's so good that he occasionally eases up a little bit. Developing a gameday routine—extra hitting, mental preparation and even a short work-out, similar to the regimen most top major leaguers maintain—would benefit him. That also could help him fine-tune his swing, which gets a little long from time to time.

The blueprints for Great American Ball Park, which is scheduled to open on Cincinnati's riverfront in 2003, might as well have Kearns' name etched in right field. He tops the group of prospects whom the Reds hope will provide an influx of young, economical talent as they move into their new stadium. The organization braintrust loves the idea of Kearns and Adam Dunn, the system's gems, flanking Ken Griffey, the franchise's crown jewel. For 2001, the Reds will be happy to watch Kearns continue to improve at Double-A Chattanooga.

Year	Club (League)	Class	AVG	G	AB	R	H	2B	3B	HR	RBI	BB	SO	SB
1998	Billings (Pio)	R	.315	30	108	17	34	9	0	1	14	23	22	1
1999	Rockford (Mid)	A	.258	124	426	72	110	36	5	13	48	50	120	21
2000	Dayton (Mid)	A	.306	136	484	110	148	37	2	27	104	90	93	18
MINOR LEAGUE TOTALS			.287	290	1018	199	292	82	7	41	166	163	235	40

2. Adam Dunn, of

Born: Nov. 9, 1979. **Ht.:** 6-6. **Wt.:** 235. **Bats:** L. **Throws:** R. **School:** New Caney (Texas) HS. **Career Transactions:** Selected by Reds in second round of 1998 draft; signed June 11, 1998.

Dunn continued his conversion to becoming exclusively a baseball player with a solid all-around performance. The former University of Texas quarterback announced his commitment to baseball in spring training 1999, thrilling Reds management. It's easy to understand when you look at Dunn's dimensions and then watch him move. Not only has he displayed power potential, but he also stole 24 bases in 29 tries at Dayton in 2000. He enhances his skill with a keen eye and patience, leading the Midwest League with a .428 on-base percentage last year. Dunn still shows the effects of spending all that time on the gridiron, though. Reading balls off the bat and taking the proper routes when tracking balls sometimes challenges him. His arm isn't what you would expect from a former quarterback, which is why he has been playing left field. Dunn's size-speed-power combination gives him the potential to be a more spectacular player than Kearns. He'll play with Kearns for the fourth straight season, this time in Double-A.

Year	Club (League)	Class	AVG	G	AB	R	H	2B	3B	HR	RBI	BB	SO	SB
1998	Billings (Pio)	R	.288	34	125	26	36	3	1	4	13	22	23	4
1999	Rockford (Mid)	A	.307	93	313	62	96	16	2	11	44	46	64	21
2000	Dayton (Mid)	A	.281	122	420	101	118	29	1	16	79	100	101	24
MINOR LEAGUE TOTALS			.291	249	858	189	250	48	4	31	136	168	188	49

3. Drew Henson, 3b

Born: Feb. 13, 1980. **Ht.:** 6-5. **Wt.:** 222. **Bats:** R. **Throws:** R. **School:** Brighton (Mich.) HS. **Career Transactions:** Selected by Yankees in third round of 1998 draft; signed July 24, 1998 . . . Traded by Yankees with OF Jackson Melian, LHP Ed Yarnall and RHP Brian Reith to Reds for LHP Denny Neagle and OF Mike Frank, July 12, 2000.

The Yankees drafted Henson and signed him for a $2 million bonus, aware that the pull of football might prevent the University of Michigan quarterback from ever reaching the Bronx. Henson's future became the Reds' headache when they acquired him in the Denny Neagle deal. Obviously, his all-around athleticism is enviable. He displays nimble feet at third base, outstanding hands and a cannon arm. He runs well for his size and hits proficiently to all fields. His power is his best tool. It almost goes without saying that he has poise, as he thrives in front of 110,000 fans at Michigan on home Saturdays. A baseball chauvinist might say that Henson's only weakness is football. He needs at-bats—which may never come—to polish his plate technique. Though he passed on the 2001 NFL draft, football remains a big lure, and rumors persist that he won't play baseball unless it's with the Yankees. The NFL also offers him a shot at playing at the highest level right away, while baseball will require a couple of additional years in the minors. Idealists who think Henson will choose baseball over football should repeat these two words: John Elway.

Year	Club (League)	Class	AVG	G	AB	R	H	2B	3B	HR	RBI	BB	SO	SB
1998	Yankees (GCL)	R	.316	10	38	5	12	3	0	1	2	3	9	0
1999	Tampa (FSL)	A	.280	69	254	37	71	12	0	13	37	26	71	3
2000	Tampa (FSL)	A	.333	5	21	4	7	2	0	1	1	1	7	0
	Norwich (EL)	AA	.287	59	223	39	64	9	2	7	39	20	75	0
	Chattanooga (SL)	AA	.172	16	64	7	11	8	0	1	9	4	25	2
MINOR LEAGUE TOTALS			.275	159	600	92	165	34	2	23	88	54	187	5

4. Dane Sardinha, c

Born: April 8, 1979. **Ht.:** 6-0. **Wt.:** 200. **Bats:** R. **Throws:** R. **School:** Pepperdine University. **Career Transactions:** Selected by Reds in second round of 2000 draft; signed Sept. 1, 2000.

The knowledge that agent Scott Boras was "advising" Sardinha scared most teams off, though his skills prompted some to project him as an early first-round choice. But little intimidates Reds general manager Jim Bowden, who ordered his staff to take Sardinha in the second round. Signing Sardinha did prove to be a chore, but the Reds got it done with a six-year big league contract worth $1.75 million guaranteed that didn't include a signing bonus. The consensus in the organization is that Sardinha could catch and throw in the big leagues right now. His hands, release and arm strength are all considered assets. For a player with no professional experience, he exudes leadership that should help him work with pitchers. His speed and opposite-field power were encouraging in instructional league. Yet his next professional game will be his first, so he needs plenty of at-bats and innings behind the plate. As with many young catchers, Sardinha must continue to refine his footwork before he truly can be considered big league material. Some scouts have questioned his ability to hit since he struggled in the wood-bat Cape Cod League in the summer of 1999. Because catching has been the weakest position in the Reds organization for about a decade, and no holdover prospects are around to complement Jason LaRue, Sardinha could ascend rapidly to Cincinnati. He has been stamped as part of the 2003 group, though he could arrive sooner. Sardinha may debut at high Class A Mudville and reach Double-A by the end of the season.

Year	Club (League)	Class	AVG	G	AB	R	H	2B	3B	HR	RBI	BB	SO	SB
2000				Did Not Play—Signed 2001 Contract										

5. David Espinosa, 2b

Born: Dec. 16, 1981. **Ht.:** 6-2. **Wt.:** 175. **Bats:** B. **Throws:** R. **School:** Gulliver Prep, Miami. **Career Transactions:** Selected by Reds in first round (23rd overall) of 2000 draft; signed Sept. 1, 2000.

Like Dane Sardinha—a fellow Scott Boras client—Espinosa didn't sign until September, when he got a major league, bonus-free deal. Espinosa's was for eight years and $2.75 million guaranteed, and it kept intact Cincinnati's streak of always signing its top pick. The Reds like Espinosa's aggressive approach from both sides of the plate. It's not mindless aggression, either. Coaches noticed in instructional league that he has a good idea at the plate, seldom looking overmatched or fooled. He also has above-average speed and arm strength. As with most young players, Espinosa needs to refine his defensive footwork. This could be especially challenging, given his move from shortstop to second base. The plethora of experienced shortstop prospects in the organization and the need to accelerate his progress because he's on the major league roster prompted the decision. The Reds also want Espinosa to gain flexibility, which they think he'll develop over time. He shouldn't regard his position switch as a negative. The Reds are fond of major league second baseman Pokey Reese, but he's likely to move to shortstop once all-star Barry Larkin retires. Espinosa will have to stick in the majors by 2004, when he'll run out of options, but that isn't expected to be a problem. The club's leadoff man of the future, he'll break in at low Class A Dayton.

Year	Club (League)	Class	AVG	G	AB	R	H	2B	3B	HR	RBI	BB	SO	SB
2000				Did Not Play—Signed 2001 Contract										

6. Ty Howington, lhp

Born: Nov. 4, 1980. **Ht.:** 6-5. **Wt.:** 220. **Bats:** B. **Throws:** L. **School:** Hudson's Bay HS, Vancouver, Wash. **Career Transactions:** Selected by Reds in first round (14th overall) of 1999 draft; signed Nov. 1, 1999.

Howington was considered the best high school lefthander available in the 1999 draft. The Reds chose him in the first round but didn't sign him until late August, preventing him from making his pro debut until 2000. He showed promise despite his ugly stats. Howington's lively fastball regularly reaches 95 mph. He complements it with an above-average curveball and a changeup. The Reds were thrilled that he managed to make every start in his first professional season, reflecting his physical and mental durability. With continued work on his mechanics, he should manage to improve the late life on his fastball and the break on his curve. He must develop consistency in his mechanics, which hindered his command and effectiveness last year. His delivery was considered unorthodox before the Reds tried to streamline it. As this ranking indicates, the Reds remain enthusiastic about Howington. He'll move up to Mudville in 2001 and probably won't be ready for the majors until sometime in 2003, at the earliest.

Year	Club (League)	Class	W	L	ERA	G	GS	CG	SV	IP	H	R	ER	BB	SO
2000	Dayton (Mid)	A	5	15	5.27	27	26	0	0	142	150	91	83	86	119
MINOR LEAGUE TOTALS			5	15	5.27	27	26	0	0	142	150	91	83	86	119

7. Dustin Moseley, rhp

Born: Dec. 26, 1981. **Ht.:** 6-3. **Wt.:** 190. **Bats:** R. **Throws:** R. **School:** Arkansas HS, Texarkana, Ark. **Career Transactions:** Selected by Reds in first round (34th overall) of 2000 draft; signed Nov. 21, 2000.

Among high school prospects in the 2000 draft, Baseball America regarded Moseley as closest to the majors. His precociousness attracted the attention of the pitching-poor Reds, who couldn't sign him until mid-November after a new fiscal year started. They landed him with a $930,000 bonus and a $100,000 scholarship plan. Moseley already shows a seasoned professional's polish and control. Scouts who have met him say he's confident and knows what he must do to get to the majors. He spots his fastball well, complementing it with a wicked curveball and an adequate changeup. His intelligence allows him to survive on the mound even on days when his stuff falls a little short. Moseley's velocity is good but not great. The Reds hope he can push it to 90-92 mph with maturity and added strength. He needs experience to test his impressive self-assurance. Moseley is expected to start 2001 at Dayton. Though his maturity suggests that he might not stay there for long, the Reds might want to keep him in low Class A for most of the season.

Year	Club (League)	Class	W	L	ERA	G	GS	CG	SV	IP	H	R	ER	BB	SO
2000	Did Not Play—Signed 2001 Contract														

8. Gookie Dawkins, 2b/ss

Born: May 12, 1979. **Ht.:** 6-1. **Wt.:** 180. **Bats:** R. **Throws:** R. **School:** Newberry (S.C.) HS. **Career Transactions:** Selected by Reds in second round of 1997 draft; signed June 8, 1997.

Dawkins is collecting more medals than an Armed Forces veteran. He hit .273 in the 1999 Pan American Games as Team USA captured the silver medal and qualified for the 2000 Sydney Olympics. In Australia he appeared in seven games, starting twice, for the gold medal-winning Americans. The Reds' plethora of shortstops in the majors and in the system led them to try Dawkins at second base last year. If he were to play a full season alongside two-time Gold Glove second baseman Pokey Reese, the Reds might be able to count the number of ground-ball base hits up the middle on one hand. Like Reese, Dawkins has excellent range and a sure, strong arm. Though Dawkins could stand to polish his footwork, he proved he could hold his own defensively in the majors already. But he regressed offensively last year. He made less contact, hit for less average and power and wasn't as much of a factor on the bases. The Reds say he'll thrive if he can develop a consistent approach at the plate. With Barry Larkin signed through 2003, Dawkins may encounter the proverbial glass ceiling if he stays with the Reds. He can use another minor league season to improve offensively but may be ready in 2002—with no clear job awaiting him.

Year	Club (League)	Class	AVG	G	AB	R	H	2B	3B	HR	RBI	BB	SO	SB
1997	Billings (Pio)	R	.241	70	253	47	61	5	0	4	37	30	38	16
1998	Burlington (Mid)	A	.264	102	367	52	97	7	6	1	30	37	60	37
1999	Rockford (Mid)	A	.272	76	305	56	83	10	6	8	32	35	38	38
	Chattanooga (SL)	AA	.364	32	129	24	47	7	0	2	13	14	17	15
	Cincinnati (NL)	MAJ	.143	7	7	1	1	0	0	0	0	0	4	0
2000	Chattanooga (SL)	AA	.231	95	368	54	85	20	6	6	31	40	71	22
	Cincinnati (NL)	MAJ	.220	14	41	5	9	2	0	0	3	2	7	0
MAJOR LEAGUE TOTALS			**.208**	21	48	6	10	2	0	0	3	2	11	0
MINOR LEAGUE TOTALS			.262	375	1422	233	373	49	18	21	143	156	224	128

9. John Riedling, rhp

Born: Aug. 29, 1975. **Ht.:** 5-11. **Wt.:** 190. **Bats:** R. **Throws:** R. **School:** Ely HS, Pompano Beach, Fla. **Career Transactions:** Selected by Reds in 22nd round of 1994 draft; signed June 15, 1994 . . . Released by Reds, Dec. 14, 1998; re-signed by Reds, Dec. 22, 1998.

After he was put on the 40-man roster, released and re-signed by the Reds after the 1998 season, Riedling's career was revived by a move from the rotation to the bullpen in 1999. In 2000, the only question was why he wasn't called up earlier. He was called to Cincinnati on Aug. 28 when Scott Williamson went on the disabled list, and Riedling breezed through his first big league stint. When he joined the Reds, catcher Jason LaRue compared his stuff to that of closer Danny Graves. Skeptics scoffed, then agreed once they saw Riedling pitch.

He has a quick, darting fastball that indeed rivals Graves', and a sharp breaking ball. Riedling's makeup also thrills Cincinnati. He needs no help with his pitches but could benefit from more consistent command in the strike zone. He'll need to cut down on his walks to maintain his effectiveness. Riedling will open the season in Cincinnati's bullpen. His late-season effectiveness seeded trade rumors involving Scott Sullivan, the workhorse set-up artist whose arbitration-eligible status might make him too expensive for the Reds.

Year	Club (League)	Class	W	L	ERA	G	GS	CG	SV	IP	H	R	ER	BB	SO
1994	Billings (Pio)	R	4	1	5.48	15	5	0	0	44	62	36	27	28	27
1995	Billings (Pio)	R	2	2	7.04	13	7	0	1	38	51	38	30	21	28
1996	Charleston, WV (SAL)	A	6	10	3.99	26	26	0	0	140	135	85	62	66	90
1997	Burlington (Mid)	A	7	6	5.26	35	16	0	0	103	101	70	60	47	104
1998	Chattanooga (SL)	AA	3	10	5.00	24	20	0	0	103	112	70	57	60	86
1999	Chattanooga (SL)	AA	9	5	3.43	40	0	0	5	42	41	23	16	20	38
	Indianapolis (IL)	AAA	1	0	1.54	24	0	0	1	35	19	9	6	18	26
2000	Louisville (IL)	AAA	6	3	2.52	53	0	0	5	75	63	24	21	30	75
	Cincinnati (NL)	MAJ	3	1	2.35	13	0	0	1	15	11	7	4	8	18
MAJOR LEAGUE TOTALS			3	1	2.35	13	0	0	1	15	11	7	4	8	18
MINOR LEAGUE TOTALS			38	37	4.33	230	74	0	12	580	584	355	279	290	474

10. Chris Reitsma, rhp

Born: Dec. 31, 1977. **Ht.:** 6-5. **Wt.:** 214. **Bats:** R. **Throws:** R. **School:** Calgary Christian HS. **Career Transactions:** Selected by Red Sox in first round (34th overall) of 1996 draft; signed June 30, 1996 . . . Selected by Devil Rays from Red Sox in Rule 5 major league draft, Dec. 13, 1999 . . . Returned to Red Sox, March 28, 2000 . . . Traded by Red Sox with LHP John Curtice to Reds for OF Dante Bichette, Aug. 31, 2000.

JOHN SPEAR

Acquired from the Red Sox, Reitsma has overcome a broken elbow he suffered while pitching in 1997 and a stress fracture in his elbow the following year that set him back. Finally healthy in 2000, he pitched nearly as many innings as he had in his first four years as a pro combined. Able to touch 95-97 mph before his injuries, Reitsma has pushed his fastball back into the low 90s, hard enough to be assertive. Like some hard throwers who lose their blazing stuff, Reitsma has survived by improving his offspeed deliveries, including a pitch described as a power changeup. The Reds like his ability to set up batters and work both sides of the plate. Having been robbed of close to two seasons of development, Reitsma needs innings to complete his big league entrance exam. The Reds wouldn't mind if a little more of his velocity would return, too. Some optimists think Reitsma can pitch in the majors this year. Since he hasn't pitched above Double-A, that might be a little unrealistic. Nevertheless, he's clearly the organization's top pitching prospect in the upper levels of the minors.

Year	Club (League)	Class	W	L	ERA	G	GS	CG	SV	IP	H	R	ER	BB	SO
1996	Red Sox (GCL)	R	3	1	1.35	7	6	0	0	27	24	7	4	1	32
1997	Michigan (Mid)	A	4	1	2.90	9	9	0	0	50	57	23	16	13	41
1998	Sarasota (FSL)	A	0	0	2.84	8	8	0	0	13	12	6	4	5	9
1999	Sarasota (FSL)	A	4	10	5.61	19	19	0	0	96	116	71	60	31	79
2000	Sarasota (FSL)	A	3	4	3.66	11	11	0	0	64	57	29	26	17	47
	Trenton (EL)	AA	7	2	2.58	14	14	1	0	91	78	28	26	21	58
MINOR LEAGUE TOTALS			21	18	3.60	68	67	1	0	340	344	164	136	88	266

11. Jackson Melian, of

Born: Jan. 7, 1980. **Ht.:** 6-2. **Wt.:** 190. **Bats:** R. **Throws:** R. **Career Transactions:** Signed out of Venezuela by Yankees, July 2, 1996 . . . Traded by Yankees with 3B Drew Henson, LHP Ed Yarnall and RHP Brian Reith to Reds for LHP Denny Neagle and OF Mike Frank, July 12, 2000.

The Reds made sure to trumpet Melian's skills loudly after they acquired him in the Denny Neagle trade with the Yankees. That trade initially was unpopular with fans, so the organization had to put as good a spin on it as possible. If Melian develops, he might be able to make the fans forget about Neagle. Though hamstring problems bothered the center fielder throughout the 2000 season, the Reds know what he can do. He has excellent instincts that enhance his tools, which include power and excellent throwing ability. Though he's strong, he needs to work on his conditioning, particularly to ward off further problems with his hamstrings. He'll also need to tighten his strike zone if he's to maximize his offensive potential. Melian likely will return to Double-A Chattanooga to start 2001. He could be blocked in the future, as he won't ever displace Ken Griffey in Cincinnati and is unlikely to take a corner spot away from Austin Kearns or Adam Dunn.

Year	Club (League)	Class	AVG	G	AB	R	H	2B	3B	HR	RBI	BB	SO	SB
1997	Yankees (GCL)	R	.263	57	213	32	56	11	2	3	36	20	52	9
1998	Greensboro (SAL)	A	.255	135	467	66	119	18	2	8	45	41	120	15
1999	Tampa (FSL)	A	.283	128	467	65	132	17	13	6	61	49	98	11
2000	Norwich (EL)	AA	.252	81	290	34	73	8	4	9	38	18	69	17
	Chattanooga (SL)	AA	.167	2	6	0	1	0	0	0	0	0	0	0
MINOR LEAGUE TOTALS			.264	403	1443	197	381	54	21	26	180	128	339	52

12. Brian Reith, rhp

Born: Feb. 28, 1978. **Ht.:** 6-5. **Wt.:** 190. **Bats:** R. **Throws:** R. **School:** Concordia Lutheran HS, Fort Wayne, Ind. **Career Transactions:** Selected by Yankees in sixth round of 1996 draft; signed June 22, 1996 . . . Traded by Yankees with 3B Drew Henson, OF Jackson Melian and LHP Ed Yarnall to Reds for LHP Denny Neagle and OF Mike Frank, July 12, 2000.

Reith established himself as a prospect in 1998, when his 2.28 ERA at Class A Greensboro ranked fifth among all minor leaguers. The Reds believe he can be a major league starter with continued experience. He's durable, with good life on a low-90s fastball and a nifty slider. Reith complements his harder stuff with a deceptive changeup. He has maintained favorable strikeout-walk ratios throughout his climb. Reith probably will begin the season at Chattanooga. Given Cincinnati's eternal hunger for pitching, he might not stay there long.

Year	Club (League)	Class	W	L	ERA	G	GS	CG	SV	IP	H	R	ER	BB	SO
1996	Yankees (GCL)	R	2	3	4.13	10	4	0	0	33	31	16	15	16	21
1997	Yankees (GCL)	R	4	2	2.86	12	11	1	0	63	70	28	20	14	40
1998	Greensboro (SAL)	A	6	7	2.28	20	20	3	0	118	86	42	30	32	116
1999	Tampa (FSL)	A	9	9	4.70	26	23	0	0	140	174	87	73	35	101
2000	Tampa (FSL)	A	9	4	2.18	18	18	1	0	120	101	39	29	33	100
	Dayton (Mid)	A	2	1	2.88	5	5	0	0	34	33	12	11	8	30
	Chattanooga (SL)	AA	1	3	3.90	5	5	0	0	30	31	14	13	11	29
MINOR LEAGUE TOTALS			33	29	3.20	96	86	5	0	538	526	238	191	149	437

13. Ben Broussard, 1b/of

Born: Sept. 24, 1976. **Ht.:** 6-2. **Wt.:** 220. **Bats:** L. **Throws:** L. **School:** McNeese State University. **Career Transactions:** Selected by Reds in second round of 1999 draft; signed June 2, 1999.

Broussard was the talk of the organization in 1999 after getting drafted. He soared from Rookie ball to Double-A, batting .332 overall. He followed that by hitting .387-9-34 in the California Fall League. A wrist injury bothered Broussard throughout 2000, and he hit .353 before he got hurt and just .094 afterward. A good low-ball hitter, he can drive the ball out of the park to all fields. He's selective at the plate, though he can improve his contact. The Reds expect him to play mostly first base, after shifting him between first and the outfield the last two years. Broussard will return to Double-A, though he could be promoted quickly.

Year	Club (League)	Class	AVG	G	AB	R	H	2B	3B	HR	RBI	BB	SO	SB
1999	Billings (Pio)	R	.407	38	145	39	59	11	2	14	48	34	30	1
	Clinton (Mid)	A	.550	5	20	8	11	4	1	2	6	3	4	0
	Chattanooga (SL)	AA	.213	35	127	26	27	5	0	8	21	11	41	1
2000	Chattanooga (SL)	AA	.255	87	286	64	73	8	4	14	51	72	78	15
MINOR LEAGUE TOTALS			.294	165	578	137	170	28	7	38	126	120	153	17

14. Ed Yarnall, lhp

Born: Dec. 4, 1975. **Ht.:** 6-3. **Wt.:** 234. **Bats:** L. **Throws:** L. **School:** Louisiana State University. **Career Transactions:** Selected by Mets in third round of 1996 draft; signed Aug. 12, 1996 . . . Traded by Mets with OF Preston Wilson and a player to be named to Marlins for C Mike Piazza, May 22, 1998; Marlins acquired LHP Geoff Goetz to complete trade (July 3, 1998) . . . Traded by Marlins with RHP Todd Noel and RHP Mark Johnson to Yankees for 3B Mike Lowell, Feb. 1, 1999.

Yarnall was handed the Yankees' No. 5 starter's job last year but gave it back with a series of poor spring performances. That didn't deter the Reds, who are intrigued by his arsenal. He throws a sneaky fastball that reaches the low 90s, a slider that he commands well and a curveball that he uses to put batters away. He has a pitcher's physique, marked by strong thighs and hips, as well as a competitive attitude. They want him to gain consistency and believe he can reach his potential more quickly out of the New York spotlight. He pitched better after the trade, though his control never was as sharp as in 1999. Yarnall will compete for a rotation spot this spring and will open in Triple-A Louisville if he doesn't win it.

Year	Club (League)	Class	W	L	ERA	G	GS	CG	SV	IP	H	R	ER	BB	SO
1997	St. Lucie (FSL)	A	5	8	2.48	18	18	2	0	105	93	33	29	30	114
	Norfolk (IL)	AAA	0	1	14.40	1	1	0	0	5	11	8	8	7	2

	Club	Class	W	L	ERA	G	GS	CG	SV	IP	H	R	ER	BB	SO
1998	Binghamton (EL)	AA	3	2	3.06	5	5	0	0	32	20	11	11	11	32
	Binghamton (EL)	AA	7	0	0.39	7	7	0	0	47	20	5	2	17	52
	Portland (EL)	AA	2	0	2.93	2	2	0	0	15	9	5	5	4	15
	Charlotte (IL)	AAA	4	5	6.20	15	13	2	0	70	79	60	48	39	47
1999	Columbus (IL)	AAA	13	4	3.47	23	23	1	0	145	136	61	56	57	146
	New York (AL)	MAJ	1	0	3.71	5	2	0	0	17	17	8	7	10	13
2000	Columbus (IL)	AAA	2	1	4.56	10	10	1	0	49	43	27	25	26	34
	New York (AL)	MAJ	0	0	15.00	2	1	0	0	3	5	5	5	3	1
	Louisville (IL)	AAA	3	4	3.86	11	11	0	0	68	72	32	29	34	59
MAJOR LEAGUE TOTALS			1	0	5.40	7	3	0	0	20	22	13	12	13	14
MINOR LEAGUE TOTALS			39	25	3.57	92	90	6	0	537	427	242	213	225	501

15. Leo Estrella, rhp

Born: Feb. 20, 1975. **Ht.:** 6-1. **Wt.:** 185. **Bats:** R. **Throws:** R. **Career Transactions:** Signed out of Dominican Republic by Mets, Sept. 28, 1993 . . . Traded by Mets to Blue Jays for OF Tony Phillips, July 31, 1998 . . . Traded by Blue Jays with LHP Clayton Andrews to Reds for RHP Steve Parris, Nov. 22, 2000.

Estrella came over when the Reds decided to trade Steve Parris rather than offer him arbitration. He threw two no-hitters in 2000: a six-inning job in Double-A that required just 64 pitches, and a seven-inning perfect game in his first Triple-A start. He has a lively fastball that has good movement low in the zone. When his mechanics are sound, he combines his fastball with a solid splitter and changeup to keep hitters off balance. His breaking ball, which is a slurvy slider, can be his out pitch when he stays on top of it and gets the proper break. Estrella tends to lose his mechanics by flying open with his left side. The Reds believe he can excel as a starter, though his resilience makes him a candidate for bullpen duty.

Year	Club (League)	Class	W	L	ERA	G	GS	CG	SV	IP	H	R	ER	BB	SO
1994	Mets (DSL)	R	5	0	3.47	30	0	0	3	36	33	28	14	32	20
1995	Mets (DSL)	R	2	4	5.44	12	8	0	0	43	61	37	26	13	32
1996	Kingsport (Appy)	R	6	3	3.88	15	7	1	0	58	54	32	25	24	52
1997	Pittsfield (NY-P)	A	7	6	3.03	15	15	0	0	92	91	48	31	27	55
1998	Capital City (SAL)	A	10	8	3.93	20	20	3	0	119	120	66	52	23	97
	Hagerstown (SAL)	A	1	3	4.50	5	5	0	0	30	34	19	15	13	27
1999	Dunedin (FSL)	A	14	7	3.21	27	24	2	0	168	166	74	60	47	116
2000	Tennessee (SL)	AA	5	5	3.67	13	13	3	0	76	68	36	31	30	63
	Syracuse (IL)	AAA	5	4	4.01	15	15	3	0	90	68	42	40	40	48
	Toronto (AL)	MAJ	0	0	5.79	2	0	0	0	5	9	3	3	0	3
MAJOR LEAGUE TOTALS			0	0	5.79	2	0	0	0	5	9	3	3	0	3
MINOR LEAGUE TOTALS			55	40	3.72	152	107	12	3	712	695	382	294	249	510

16. Michael Coleman, of

Born: Aug. 16, 1975. **Ht.:** 5-11. **Wt.:** 215. **Bats:** R. **Throws:** R. **School:** Stratford HS, Nashville. **Career Transactions:** Selected by Red Sox in 18th round of 1994 draft; signed June 8, 1994 . . . Traded by Red Sox with 2B Donnie Sadler to Reds for 3B Chris Stynes, Nov. 16, 2000.

After obtaining Coleman for Chris Stynes, another arbitration-eligible player they couldn't afford, the Reds released Kimera Bartee and Brian Hunter. That was an indication of their faith in Coleman, a five-tool prospect who could have attended the University of Alabama on a football scholarship. Coleman was leading the International League in homers in April when he broke his left wrist diving for a fly ball, ending his season. His tools still overshadow his skills, as he lacks polish at the plate and on the bases. He does have plus range and arm strength in center field. He had attitude problems in the Red Sox system, which led to counseling in the summer of 1998. Cincinnati believes he can thrive with a fresh opportunity. He could be the Reds' fifth outfielder, though Triple-A is also a possibility.

Year	Club (League)	Class	AVG	G	AB	R	H	2B	3B	HR	RBI	BB	SO	SB
1994	Red Sox (GCL)	R	.274	25	95	15	26	6	1	3	15	10	20	5
	Utica (NY-P)	A	.169	23	65	16	11	2	0	1	3	14	21	11
1995	Michigan (Mid)	A	.268	112	422	70	113	16	2	11	61	40	93	29
1996	Sarasota (FSL)	A	.246	110	407	54	100	20	5	1	36	38	86	24
1997	Trenton (EL)	AA	.301	102	385	56	116	17	8	14	58	41	89	20
	Pawtucket (IL)	AAA	.319	28	113	27	36	9	2	7	19	12	27	4
	Boston (AL)	MAJ	.167	8	24	2	4	1	0	0	2	0	11	1
1998	Pawtucket (IL)	AAA	.253	93	340	47	86	13	0	14	37	27	92	12
1999	Pawtucket (IL)	AAA	.268	115	467	95	125	29	2	30	74	51	128	14
	Boston (AL)	MAJ	.200	2	5	1	1	0	0	0	0	1	0	0
2000	Pawtucket (IL)	AAA	.258	18	66	11	17	5	1	6	15	3	23	3
MAJOR LEAGUE TOTALS			.172	10	29	3	5	1	0	0	2	1	11	1
MINOR LEAGUE TOTALS			.267	626	2360	391	630	117	21	87	318	236	579	122

17. Brandon Larson, 3b

Born: May 24, 1976. **Ht.:** 6-0. **Wt.:** 210. **Bats:** R. **Throws:** R. **School:** Louisiana State University. **Career Transactions:** Selected by Reds in first round (14th overall) of 1997 draft; signed July 22, 1997.

Staying healthy has been Larson's biggest challenge since he was drafted in 1997. He was the College World Series MVP that year, leading Louisiana State to the championship and setting a college record for shortstops with 40 homers. After enduring ankle and knee injuries in his first two pro years, Larson has stayed in the lineup and shown his power the last two seasons. Of course, the Reds always knew Larson could hit. He also has continued to develop defensively. He still needs more patience at the plate. Larson will begin the season at Triple-A and could arrive in Cincinnati if Aaron Boone's knee gives him any trouble.

Year	Club (League)	Class	AVG	G	AB	R	H	2B	3B	HR	RBI	BB	SO	SB
1997	Chattanooga (SL)	AA	.268	11	41	4	11	5	1	0	6	1	10	0
1998	Burlington (Mid)	A	.221	18	68	5	15	3	0	2	9	4	16	2
1999	Rockford (Mid)	A	.300	69	250	38	75	18	1	13	52	25	67	12
	Chattanooga (SL)	AA	.285	43	172	28	49	10	0	12	42	10	51	4
2000	Chattanooga (SL)	AA	.272	111	427	61	116	26	0	20	64	31	122	15
	Louisville (IL)	AAA	.286	17	63	11	18	7	1	2	4	4	16	0
MINOR LEAGUE TOTALS			.278	269	1021	147	284	69	3	49	177	75	282	33

18. Brandon Love, rhp

Born: April 5, 1980. **Ht.:** 6-2. **Wt.:** 190. **Bats:** R. **Throws:** R. **School:** Viola (Ark.) HS. **Career Transactions:** Selected by Reds in third round of 1999 draft; signed June 28, 1999.

The Reds beat out the University of Arkansas to sign Love. As a high school senior, he allowed just nine hits and four walks while striking out 120 in 54 innings. He has had intermittent success as a pro, and shoulder problems limited him to nine appearances last season. When he's right, he had a hard fastball with late life to go with a bulldog attitude. Love won't advance much, however, unless he develops a second pitch. He hasn't been able to throw a breaking ball or changeup for strikes, enabling hitters to sit on his fastball. Love probably will return to Dayton until he proves he's healthy and shows improvement.

Year	Club (League)	Class	W	L	ERA	G	GS	CG	SV	IP	H	R	ER	BB	SO
1999	Reds (GCL)	R	0	4	7.66	7	6	0	0	25	30	21	21	9	17
2000	Dayton (Mid)	A	2	1	3.63	7	7	0	0	35	33	18	14	19	32
	Reds (GCL)	R	0	1	0.00	2	2	0	0	7	4	4	0	6	8
MINOR LEAGUE TOTALS			2	6	4.77	16	15	0	0	66	67	43	35	34	57

19. Ranier Olmedo, ss

Born: May 31, 1981. **Ht.:** 5-11. **Wt.:** 155. **Bats:** R. **Throws:** R. **Career Transactions:** Signed out of Venezuela by Reds, Jan. 21, 1999.

Olmedo is as raw as he is gifted. Cincinnati officials, some of whom rate Olmedo above the since-traded Wilmy Caceres, say his defensive skills are reminiscent of perennial Gold Glover Omar Vizquel's. Olmedo has incredible hands, though he must remind himself to stay down on ground balls. A natural righthanded batter, he's working on hitting from the left side, which would enhance his value. He's a quick learner with excellent instincts who's willing to bunt and move runners along. Olmedo stole 17 bases at Dayton but still needs to refine his technique. He'll probably begin 2001 in Double-A.

Year	Club (League)	Class	AVG	G	AB	R	H	2B	3B	HR	RBI	BB	SO	SB
1999	Reds (GCL)	R	.236	54	195	30	46	12	1	1	19	12	28	13
2000	Dayton (Mid)	A	.255	111	369	50	94	19	1	4	41	30	70	17
MINOR LEAGUE TOTALS			.248	165	564	80	140	31	2	5	60	42	98	30

20. Clayton Andrews, lhp

Born: May 15, 1978. **Ht.:** 6-0. **Wt.:** 175. **Bats:** R. **Throws:** L. **School:** Seminole (Fla.) HS. **Career Transactions:** Selected by Blue Jays in third round of 1996 draft; signed June 5, 1996 . . . Traded by Blue Jays with RHP Leo Estrella to Reds for RHP Steve Parris, Nov. 22, 2000.

Andrews was regarded as one of the Blue Jays' top prospects after he led the Class A South Atlantic League in ERA in 1998. He wasn't burdened by similar expectations when he came to the Reds in November, but he was compared to various lefties who aren't overpowering but pitch intelligently. The comparisons are apt. Andrews' repertoire includes a fastball with a slight tail and a changeup with a nice sink that's thrown with good arm speed. His fastball has aroused concern. Jays scouts say it used to hit 93 mph but rarely exceeds the 88-90 range now. The pitch now cuts more than it runs, which could be indicative of a mechanical problem. Still, Andrews can move the ball around both sides of the plate, essential for a finesse pitcher. The Reds believe Andrews will help anchor the back of a rotation someday.

Year	Club (League)	Class	W	L	ERA	G	GS	CG	SV	IP	H	R	ER	BB	SO
1996	Medicine Hat (Pio)	R	2	4	7.36	8	4	0	0	26	37	23	21	10	14
1997	Hagerstown (SAL)	A	7	7	4.55	28	15	0	0	115	120	70	58	47	112
1998	Hagerstown (SAL)	A	10	7	2.28	27	26	2	0	162	112	59	41	46	193
1999	Knoxville (SL)	AA	10	8	3.93	25	25	0	0	133	143	85	58	69	93
	Syracuse (IL)	AAA	0	1	7.80	3	3	0	0	15	10	14	13	13	9
2000	Syracuse (IL)	AAA	8	7	4.82	19	18	0	0	103	114	56	55	42	59
	Toronto (AL)	MAJ	1	2	10.02	8	2	0	0	21	34	23	23	9	12
MAJOR LEAGUE TOTALS			1	2	10.02	8	2	0	0	21	34	23	23	9	12
MINOR LEAGUE TOTALS			37	34	4.01	110	91	2	0	553	536	307	246	227	480

21. Lance Davis, lhp

Born: Sept. 1, 1976. **Ht.:** 6-0. **Wt.:** 160. **Bats:** R. **Throws:** L. **School:** Lake Gibson HS, Lakeland, Fla. **Career Transactions:** Selected by Reds in 16th round of 1995 draft; signed June 1, 1995.

Davis has been in the organization since 1995, a long gestation period for a prospect. But being lefthanded has bought him time. Shoulder tendinitis bothered Davis late in the year, and he later was diagnosed with a small rotator-cuff tear that won't require surgery. That came after he led all Reds farmhands with a 2.44 ERA last season. Though his fastball hovers in the 87-89 mph range, he has good command of it and supplements it with a sharp curveball. He needs a better changeup to succeed at the game's highest levels. The Reds aren't sure where they'll start Davis in 2001. They'd like him to prove he's healthy first.

Year	Club (League)	Class	W	L	ERA	G	GS	CG	SV	IP	H	R	ER	BB	SO
1995	Princeton (Appy)	R	3	7	3.88	15	9	0	0	58	77	39	25	25	43
1996	Charleston, WV (SAL)	A	1	0	2.45	4	0	0	0	4	4	1	1	2	5
	Billings (Pio)	R	2	3	6.70	16	5	0	0	46	59	41	34	33	43
	Princeton (Appy)	R	2	0	1.20	2	2	1	0	15	6	4	2	3	19
1997	Burlington (Mid)	A	4	6	6.59	30	13	0	0	97	121	78	71	55	51
1998	Burlington (Mid)	A	4	2	1.99	25	4	0	0	54	35	17	12	29	38
1999	Rockford (Mid)	A	7	5	3.82	22	20	1	0	127	135	62	54	49	95
2000	Chattanooga (SL)	AA	7	5	2.18	25	16	1	0	116	96	41	28	52	98
	Louisville (IL)	AAA	1	0	3.38	5	5	0	0	32	32	19	12	8	14
MINOR LEAGUE TOTALS			31	28	3.92	144	74	3	0	549	565	302	239	256	406

22. Robert Pugmire, rhp

Born: Sept. 5, 1978. **Ht.:** 6-3. **Wt.:** 205. **Bats:** R. **Throws:** R. **School:** Cascade HS, Everett, Wash. **Career Transactions:** Selected by Indians in third round of 1997 draft; signed June 9, 1997 . . . Traded by Indians with RHP Jim Brower to Reds for C Eddie Taubensee, Nov. 16, 2000.

Pugmire perpetuates the jinx of the Bob Feller award. Only one of the previous nine winners of the award, which is given to Cleveland's top minor league pitcher, remains with the Tribe. Pugmire's exit was hastened by a partially torn labrum that required surgery in May, a disappointment after a breakthrough 1999 season, which came after he missed all of 1998 with a stress fracture in his back. Cincinnati, which has supreme faith in its medical staff, is gambling that Pugmire can stay healthy. The Reds are impressed by his ability to keep his deliveries low in the strike zone, particularly his fastball and curveball, which has a nice, tight rotation. Pugmire's changeup lacks deception and must improve. Of course, keeping his arm sound would help. He'll probably be assigned to Double-A when he's ready to pitch.

Year	Club (League)	Class	W	L	ERA	G	GS	CG	SV	IP	H	R	ER	BB	SO
1997	Burlington (Appy)	R	1	2	3.92	14	14	0	0	67	72	42	29	29	62
1998	Did Not Play—Injured														
1999	Columbus (SAL)	A	6	1	2.65	10	10	0	0	58	43	20	17	14	71
	Kinston (Car)	A	7	1	3.66	16	16	0	0	96	85	44	39	25	89
2000	Akron (EL)	AA	1	1	5.51	4	4	0	0	16	22	11	10	6	14
	Mahoning Valley (NY-P)	A	0	1	4.26	5	5	0	0	13	16	10	6	8	10
MINOR LEAGUE TOTALS			15	6	3.65	49	49	0	0	249	238	127	101	82	246

23. Scott Dunn, rhp

Born: May 23, 1978. **Ht.:** 6-3. **Wt.:** 185. **Bats:** R. **Throws:** R. **School:** University of Texas. **Career Transactions:** Selected by Reds in 10th round of 1999 draft; signed June 5, 1999.

Dunn had one of the best seasons of any pitcher in the organization and fired a perfect game Aug. 3 against Lansing, striking out 12 as part of a nine-game winning streak. He has several qualities that suggest he has potential for advancement: smooth mechanics, an above-average fastball with plenty of life and a curveball that can be downright nasty. He's quick to the plate and holds runners on base proficiently. Dunn still needs to work on his command, especially with his curveball, and must work on developing his changeup. He's yet another candidate for what seems certain to be a prospect-laden team at Chattanooga.

Year	Club (League)	Class	W	L	ERA	G	GS	CG	SV	IP	H	R	ER	BB	SO
1999	Billings (Pio)	R	1	3	4.31	9	8	0	0	40	36	24	19	24	36
2000	Clinton (Mid)	A	11	3	3.96	26	26	2	0	148	123	78	65	89	159
MINOR LEAGUE TOTALS			12	6	4.04	35	34	2	0	187	159	102	84	113	195

24. Brady Clark, of

Born: April 18, 1973. **Ht.:** 6-2. **Wt.:** 195. **Bats:** R. **Throws:** R. **School:** University of San Diego. **Career Transactions:** Signed as nondrafted free agent by Reds, Jan. 13, 1996 . . . Released by Reds, April 10, 1996; re-signed by Reds, Feb. 15, 1997.

Clark is the organization's poster child for desire. He hasn't given up despite not being drafted, then spraining his left wrist and breaking the hamate bone in his left hand after the Reds signed him. They released him but re-signed him when he returned to health. He won the Southern League batting title and MVP award in 1999. His late-season promotion to Cincinnati in 2000 was deserved, and he followed up by hitting .303 in the Arizona Fall League and being named to the circuit's all-prospect team. Clark has gap power and above-average speed, totaling 121 extra-base hits and 37 steals over the last two seasons. He draws walks and makes good contact. Defensively, he reads balls off the bat well, compensating for his mediocre throwing arm. With nothing left to prove in the minors, Clark has a shot at a reserve spot in Cincinnati, though a numbers crunch easily could force him back to Triple-A.

Year	Club (League)	Class	AVG	G	AB	R	H	2B	3B	HR	RBI	BB	SO	SB
1997	Burlington (Mid)	A	.325	126	459	108	149	29	7	11	63	76	71	31
1998	Chattanooga (SL)	AA	.270	64	222	41	60	13	1	2	16	31	34	12
1999	Chattanooga (SL)	AA	.326	138	506	103	165	37	4	17	75	89	58	25
2000	Louisville (IL)	AAA	.304	132	487	90	148	41	6	16	79	72	51	12
	Cincinnati (NL)	MAJ	.273	11	11	1	3	1	0	0	2	0	2	0
MAJOR LEAGUE TOTALS			.273	11	11	1	3	1	0	0	2	0	2	0
MINOR LEAGUE TOTALS			.312	460	1674	342	522	120	18	46	233	268	214	80

25. David Gil, rhp

Born: Oct. 1, 1978. **Ht.:** 6-4. **Wt.:** 215. **Bats:** R. **Throws:** R. **School:** University of Miami. **Career Transactions:** Selected by Reds in third round of 2000 draft; signed June 29, 2000.

The only one of Cincinnati's top five draft choices in 2000 who has actually played professionally, Gil showed plenty of polish and was one of just three pitchers selected in June to reach Double-A. That reflected his background at the University of Miami, where he went 12-0 for the Hurricanes' 1999 College World Series champions and 31-5 overall in four seasons. Gil showed late life on an 88-92 mph fastball and a decent assortment of breaking pitches. The Reds like his poise and makeup. They're looking forward to seeing him again once he has a chance to refresh himself after throwing a combined 162 innings in 2000. He's a strong possibility to return to Chattanooga to start the season and could ascend quickly.

Year	Club (League)	Class	W	L	ERA	G	GS	CG	SV	IP	H	R	ER	BB	SO
2000	Dayton (Mid)	A	1	1	2.70	4	4	0	0	27	20	13	8	11	15
	Chattanooga (SL)	AA	2	0	2.16	6	3	0	1	25	15	7	6	13	25
MINOR LEAGUE TOTALS			3	1	2.44	10	7	0	1	52	35	20	14	24	40

26. John Curtice, lhp

Born: Nov. 1, 1979. **Ht.:** 6-2. **Wt.:** 228. **Bats:** L. **Throws:** L. **School:** Great Bridge HS, Chesapeake, Va. **Career Transactions:** Selected by Red Sox in first round (17th overall) of 1997 draft; signed July 23, 1997 . . . Traded by Red Sox with RHP Chris Reitsma to Reds for OF Dante Bichette, Aug. 31, 2000.

Curtice's migration to the Reds system wasn't a complete surprise. Former manager Jack McKeon scouted him as an amateur and encouraged the Reds to draft him in the first round instead of Brandon Larson in 1997. McKeon compared Curtice to David Wells, down to the free-spirit demeanor and girth. Curtice might never match Wells' effectiveness, however. He has had problems with his arm, weight and command. The Reds hope Curtice can exceed expectations if he regains consistency with his fastball, which travels between 88-92 mph. Curtice still is regaining strength after shoulder surgery in 1999. After a disastrous season in high Class A last year, he'll probably need to repeat that level.

Year	Club (League)	Class	W	L	ERA	G	GS	CG	SV	IP	H	R	ER	BB	SO
1997	Red Sox (GCL)	R	2	0	0.79	4	3	0	0	11	6	2	1	5	11
1998	Michigan (Mid)	A	6	6	3.37	25	25	1	0	133	96	61	50	79	146

1999	Red Sox (GCL)	R	0	5	7.36	8	6	0	0	14	16	22	12	12	19
2000	Sarasota (FSL)	A	4	10	6.49	25	23	0	0	112	114	87	81	68	83
MINOR LEAGUE TOTALS			12	21	4.76	62	57	1	0	272	232	172	144	164	259

27. Elvin Andujar, of

Born: Jan. 19, 1981. **Ht.:** 6-3. **Wt.:** 205. **Bats:** R. **Throws:** R. **Career Transactions:** Signed out of Dominican Republic by Reds, June 22, 1999.

Andujar spent his second year in a row in the Rookie-level Dominican Summer League, leading his team in homers and RBIs. The Reds are impressed by Andujar's physical tools, which become evident with just a glance at his 6-foot-3, 205-pound physique. He has above-average power, decent speed for his size and a hunger to play. Defensively, Andujar gets good jumps but his arm strength is a little short, which may limit him to left field. He'll make his U.S. debut this year, probably in the Rookie-level Gulf Coast League.

Year	Club (League)	Class	AVG	G	AB	R	H	2B	3B	HR	RBI	BB	SO	SB
1999	Reds (DSL)	R	.284	67	218	47	62	7	5	4	39	25	51	25
2000	Reds (DSL)	R	.288	66	233	37	67	15	4	8	52	33	49	11
MINOR LEAGUE TOTALS			.286	133	451	84	129	22	9	12	91	58	100	36

28. Brad Salmon, rhp

Born: Jan. 3, 1980. **Ht.:** 6-4. **Wt.:** 210. **Bats:** R. **Throws:** R. **School:** Jefferson Davis (Ala.) CC. **Career Transactions:** Selected by Reds in 21st round of 1999 draft; signed June 3, 1999.

Salmon began his pro career in uninspiring fashion in 1999. He blossomed in 2000, however, and the Reds may have a sleeper on their hands. He picked up velocity and now throws in the low 90s. He also improved his curveball and his delivery, and developed a tricky fosh changeup, a forkball/split/change hybrid that few pitchers master. He also showed a strong work ethic. Salmon needs to continue refining his mechanics and gaining experience. The Reds have plenty of starter candidates for Double-A, so he may wind up at Class A Mudville.

Year	Club (League)	Class	W	L	ERA	G	GS	CG	SV	IP	H	R	ER	BB	SO
1999	Billings (Pio)	R	2	2	7.48	16	6	0	1	49	67	46	41	19	43
2000	Clinton (Mid)	A	7	5	4.29	22	22	1	0	124	134	71	59	46	119
MINOR LEAGUE TOTALS			9	7	5.20	38	28	1	1	173	201	117	100	65	162

29. Alejandro Diaz, of

Born: July 9, 1978. **Ht.:** 5-9. **Wt.:** 190. **Bats:** R. **Throws:** R. **Career Transactions:** Signed by Hiroshima (Japan), 1998 . . . Signed by Reds, March 2, 1999.

A Japanese League veteran who received a $1.175 million bonus to sign with the Reds, Diaz has gained more skeptics than fans. Nobody denies his obvious tools. He has a quick bat which can generate power to all fields, and his speed makes him a threat on the bases. He has excellent range in center field and one of the best arms in the organization. But he needs to discipline himself at the plate, where he swings at bad pitches, and on the base-paths, where he makes poor decisions. The additions of Ken Griffey and Jackson Melian to the organization last year don't bode well for Diaz' future.

Year	Club (League)	Class	AVG	G	AB	R	H	2B	3B	HR	RBI	BB	SO	SB
1998	Hiroshima (CL)	JAP	.311	—	61	8	19	1	0	3	9	—	—	0
1999	Clinton (Mid)	A	.285	55	221	39	63	14	3	6	41	12	35	28
	Chattanooga (SL)	AA	.264	55	220	27	58	9	8	7	35	8	31	6
2000	Chattanooga (SL)	AA	.267	122	491	69	131	19	8	13	66	14	77	18
MINOR LEAGUE TOTALS			.270	232	932	135	252	42	19	26	142	34	143	52

30. Juan Acevedo, of

Born: Aug. 4, 1981. **Ht.:** 6-2. **Wt.:** 180. **Bats:** B. **Throws:** R. **Career Transactions:** Signed out of Dominican Republic by Reds, Oct. 4, 1999.

Acevedo put up woeful statistics in his debut, but the Reds insist his shortcomings mask a wealth of talent. Where others might see an undisciplined hacker, the Reds see a switch-hitter with power to all fields from both sides of the plate. They like his aggressive approach, which is helped by good bat speed. Acevedo takes his gung-ho attitude to the outfield, where he has displayed a decent arm. As the numbers indicate, he has plenty of work to do. He tends to pull off the ball from the right side of the plate. He also must hone his baserunning. The Reds believe Acevedo could make significant improvement at Dayton this year.

Year	Club (League)	Class	AVG	G	AB	R	H	2B	3B	HR	RBI	BB	SO	SB
2000	Reds (GCL)	R	.180	49	172	23	31	5	2	2	13	20	71	8
MINOR LEAGUE TOTALS			.180	49	172	23	31	5	2	2	13	20	71	8

Cleveland
Indians

TOP 30 PROSPECTS

1. C.C. Sabathia, lhp
2. Danys Baez, rhp
3. Corey Smith, 3b
4. Willy Taveras, of
5. Sean DePaula, rhp
6. Zach Day, rhp
7. Jake Westbrook, rhp
8. Tim Drew, rhp
9. Maicer Izturis, ss
10. Alex Requena, of
11. Danny Peoples, 1b
12. Martin Vargas, rhp
13. John McDonald, ss
14. Brian Tallet, lhp
15. David Riske, rhp
16. Roy Padilla, lhp
17. Jamie Brown, rhp
18. Jorge Moreno, of
19. Jhonny Peralta, ss
20. Hector Luna, ss
21. Zach Sorensen, ss
22. Derek Thompson, lhp
23. Eric Johnson, of
24. Kyle Evans, rhp
25. Sean Swedlow, 1b
26. Mark Folsom, of
27. Osmany Santana, of
28. Scott Pratt, 2b
29. Ryan Church, of
30. Jason Fitzgerald, of

By Jim Ingraham

The loss of Manny Ramirez to free agency this offseason was an ironic twist for the Indians. Ramirez is arguably the best player ever drafted and developed by the organization, and his exit came amid growing concerns about the depth of talent in the system.

The farm system appears to be in a down cycle at the upper levels as the front office attempts to recycle and reload. Lefthander C.C. Sabathia is one of just a handful of players who appear ready to challenge for big league jobs.

The organization's lack of big-time prospects was evident in Baseball America's Top 100 Prospects list before the 2000 season, and the top 10 lists from each minor league after the season. Only righthander Danys Baez made the overall top 50, though Sabathia certainly will in 2001. And Sabathia was the only Indian to make a top 10 in a full-season league.

The bulk of the Indians' talent is at the lower levels, where there's a nice mix of pitchers and position players who in many cases have higher ceilings than the higher-profile names closer to the majors. Still, 2000 first-round pick Corey Smith, a third baseman, was the only Indian on a short-season top 10 list.

Where has all of the talent gone? Mostly to other teams. In their quest to return to the World Series—and win it for the first time since 1948—the Indians have been willing to package prospects in go-for-broke trades to bolster the roster for the postseason.

In recent years the club has traded such players as David Bell, Sean Casey, Alan Embree, Brian Giles, Danny Graves, Damian Jackson, Steve Kline, Jason Rakers, Alex Ramirez, Paul Rigdon, Richie Sexson, Julian Tavarez and Enrique Wilson.

Most of those players were originally drafted, signed and developed by the Indians. Many of them are alumni of Indians Top 10 Prospects lists from years past. Few organizations would be able to withstand such a steady drain of talent without an impact somewhere down the road. The Tribe is somewhere down that very road.

The Indians have tried to compensate by expanding their international presence. Nearly half of the players on the top 10 hail from foreign countries. They signed Baez after he defected from Cuba, found outfielder Willy Taveras in the Dominican Republic, and shortstop Maicer Izturis and outfielder Alex Requena in Venezuela.

OrganizationOverview

General manager: John Hart. **Farm director:** Neal Huntington. **Scouting director:** John Mirabelli.

2000 PERFORMANCE

Class	Team	League	W	L	Pct.	Finish*	Manager
Majors	Cleveland	American	90	72	.566	4th (14)	Charlie Manuel
Triple-A	Buffalo Bisons	International	86	59	.593	1st (14)	Joel Skinner
Double-A	Akron Aeros	Eastern	75	68	.524	6th (12)	Eric Wedge
High A	Kinston Indians	Carolina	68	69	.496	3rd (8)	Brad Komminsk
Low A	Columbus RedStixx	South Atlantic	67	70	.489	t-8th (14)	Rick Gutierrez
Short-season	Mahoning Valley Scrappers	New York-Penn	48	28	.632	1st (14)	Ted Kubiak
Rookie	Burlington Indians	Appalachian	21	46	.313	10th (10)	Dave Turgeon
OVERALL 2000 MINOR LEAGUE RECORD			365	340	.517	10th (30)	

*Finish in overall standings (No. of teams in league).

ORGANIZATION LEADERS

BATTING

*AVG	Nate Janowicz, Mahoning Valley	.340
R	**Dave Roberts**, Buffalo	93
H	Victor Rodriguez, Kinston/Akron	157
TB	Billy Munoz, Kinston/Akron	257
2B	Victor Rodriguez, Kinston/Akron	38
3B	Dennis Malave, Mahoning Valley/Akron	10
HR	Billy Munoz, Kinston/Akron	25
	Corey Erickson, Kinston/Akron	25
RBI	Nate Grindell, Columbus	98
BB	Mike Edwards, Akron	68
SO	Alex Requena, Columbus	137
SB	Alex Requena, Columbus	87

PITCHING

W	Wilson Sido, Kinston/Akron/Buffalo	12
	Jason Stanford, Columbus/Kinston/Akron	12
L	Danys Baez, Kinston/Akron	11
#ERA	Roy Smith, Kinston/Akron	2.34
G	**Martin Vargas**, Akron	53
CG	Three tied at	2
SV	Chris Nichting, Buffalo	26
IP	Mike Bacsik, Kinston/Akron/Buffalo	165
BB	Alberto Garza, Kinston	81
SO	C.C. Sabathia, Kinston/Akron	159

*Minimum 250 at-bats. #Minimum 75 innings.

TOP PROSPECTS OF THE DECADE

1991	Mark Lewis, ss
1992	Kenny Lofton, of
1993	Manny Ramirez, of
1994	Manny Ramirez, of
1995	Jaret Wright, rhp
1996	Bartolo Colon, rhp
1997	Bartolo Colon, rhp
1998	Sean Casey, 1b
1999	Russell Branyan, 3b
2000	C.C. Sabathia, lhp

TOP DRAFT PICKS OF THE DECADE

1991	Manny Ramirez, of
1992	Paul Shuey, rhp
1993	Daron Kirkreit, rhp
1994	Jaret Wright, rhp
1995	David Miller, 1b/of
1996	Danny Peoples, 1b/of
1997	Tim Drew, rhp
1998	C.C. Sabathia, lhp
1999	Will Hartley, c (2)
2000	Corey Smith, 3b

RICH ABEL

RICH ABEL

Roberts   **Vargas**

BEST TOOLS

Best Hitter for Average	Maicer Izturis
Best Power Hitter	Mark Folsom
Fastest Baserunner	Alex Requena
Best Fastball	C.C. Sabathia
Best Breaking Ball	J.D. Brammer
Best Control	Jake Westbrook
Best Defensive Catcher	Victor Martinez
Best Defensive Infielder	John McDonald
Best Infield Arm	Corey Smith
Best Defensive Outfielder	Osmany Santana
Best Outfield Arm	Ryan Church

PROJECTED 2004 LINEUP

Catcher	Einar Diaz
First Base	Jim Thome
Second Base	Roberto Alomar
Third Base	Corey Smith
Shortstop	Maicer Izturis
Left Field	Russell Branyan
Center Field	Willy Taveras
Right Field	Alex Requena
Designated Hitter	Juan Gonzalez
No. 1 Starter	C.C. Sabathia
No. 2 Starter	Bartolo Colon
No. 3 Starter	Jaret Wright
No. 4 Starter	Danys Baez
No. 5 Starter	Zach Day
Closer	Sean DePaula

ALL-TIME LARGEST BONUSES

Danys Baez, 1999	$4,500,000
Tim Drew, 1997	1,600,000
Corey Smith, 2000	1,375,000
C.C. Sabathia, 1998	1,300,000
Jaret Wright, 1994	1,150,000

DraftAnalysis

2000 Draft

Best Pro Debut: OF Ryan Church (14) was named MVP of the short-season New York-Penn League after hitting .288 with 10 homers and a league-high 63 RBIs. Fellow Mahoning Valley OF Nate Janowicz (15) also hammered NY-P pitching, batting .340-3-43.

Best Athlete: SS Rodney Choy Foo (26) was a running back recruited by Pacific-10 Conference schools until he failed to qualify academically. He packs a lot of athleticism into his 6-foot, 180-pound frame, though he's very raw. OF Rashad Eldridge (5) is a switch-hitter with power who runs well when a knee he hurt in 1999 isn't bothering him.

Best Hitter: 3B Corey Smith (1) batted .557 as a high school senior and should hit for both power and average as he matures. He hit .256-4-39 at Rookie-level Burlington last summer but showed flashes of his potential.

Best Raw Power: OF Mark Folsom (2). Smith and 1Bs Sean Swedlow (3) and Jeff Haase (13) all have above-average power potential.

Fastest Runner: Choy Foo has above-average speed but isn't a blazer.

Best Defensive Player: Church (14) is a solid right fielder. 2B Joe Inglett (8), Church's college teammate at Nevada, made a nice transition to the infield after playing center field in college.

Best Fastball: RHP Chad Cislak (19), who didn't pitch much in 2000 at UCLA because of severe control problems, has a 92-94 mph fastball.

Most Intriguing Background: 3B Conor Jackson's (31) father John plays an admiral on the CBS television series "JAG." Jackson is succeeding Xavier Nady at third base for California.

Closest To The Majors: LHP Brian Tallet (2) and RHP **Kyle Evans** (6) may start their first full seasons at high Class A Kinston. Tallet started the College World Series championship game for Louisiana State in June but didn't get the decision. RHP Jason Davis, who signed as a 25th-round draft-and-follow out of Cleveland State

RICH ABEL

Evans

(Tenn.) CC, where he also played basketball, is also on a fast track after showing a 93-mph fastball last summer.

Best Late-Round Pick: Church.

The One Who Got Away: RHP Scott Tolbert (9) threw 90-93 mph in high school when he wasn't bothered by a sore arm. The Indians never were convinced he was healthy enough to make a run at him before he went to Georgia Southern.

Assessment: First-year scouting director John Mirabelli didn't think the pitching ran deep in the draft, so he focused on power bats instead. Most of Cleveland's early pitching picks were used on lefthanders with plus arms, such as Derek Thompson (1), Tallet and Victor Kleine (7).

1999 Draft

One year later, the lone player of even mild promise appears to be OF Eric Johnson (1). C Will Hartley (2), the top pick, hasn't shown much. **Grade: F**

1998 Draft

One of the two best lefthanders in the minors, C.C. Sabathia (1) may be ready to contribute in 2001. SS Zach Sorensen (2) and 2B Scott Pratt (3) have a shot. **Grade: B+**

1997 Draft

The Indians didn't help RHP Tim Drew (1) by rushing him to the majors last year. His future appears brighter than that of the club's other first-rounder, OF Jason Fitzgerald. The only other notable pick was RHP Rob Pugmire (3), who was traded to Cincinnati in the off-season. **Grade: C–**

1996 Draft

None looks like a superstar, but 1B Danny Peoples (1), SS John McDonald (12) and RHPs Sean DePaula (9), Jamie Brown (21, draft-and-follow) and David Riske (56, draft-and-follow) all rank among Cleveland's better prospects. RHP Paul Rigdon (6) surfaced in the majors and was dealt to the Brewers last summer. **Grade: C**

Note: Draft analysis prepared by Jim Callis. Numbers in parentheses indicate draft rounds.

. . . Sabathia is intelligent and coachable, a ferocious competitor and an intimidating presence on the mound.

Sabathia **C.C.**
lhp

Born: July 21, 1980.
Ht.: 6-7. **Wt.:** 260.
Bats: L. **Throws:** L.
School: Vallejo (Calif.) HS.
Career Transactions: Selected by Indians in first round (20th overall) of 1998 draft; signed June 29, 1998.

It would be difficult for any player to have a wider range of experience than did Sabathia during the 2000 season. In addition to pitching in high Class A and Double-A, Sabathia also was selected to the Eastern League all-star team; participated in the Futures Game; pitched in the Hall of Fame game at Cooperstown; and finished the season with the big league club in September, though he never was formally activated. Sabathia also was among the finalists for the U.S. Olympic team, but the Indians balked at letting him be used as a reliever, so he didn't make the final cut. Through it all, the mature beyond his years Sabathia handled the spotlight gracefully, as he continued his freight-train ascent through the minors. His biggest accomplishment was pitching a career-high 146 innings without incident, putting to rest any doubts raised by missing the first 2½ months of 1999 with a bone bruise in his elbow.

Sabathia is the whole package—and a gigantic one at that. He has a tremendous fastball that consistently sits at 97-98 mph, a good changeup, terrific feel for pitching and off-the-charts makeup. He's intelligent and coachable, a ferocious competitor, and at 6-foot-7 and upward of 260 pounds he can be an intimidating presence on the mound. He's strong with durable mechanics. That he's a lefthander and only 20 is icing on the cake. He has a chance to be a dominant No. 1 starter at the big league level, the most overpowering lefty the organization has produced since Sam McDowell. Sabathia has no glaring flaws. He needs to continue to refine his breaking ball and changeup, and his body is always going to be a concern. He will have to work hard throughout his career to keep himself in top shape in order to avoid injuries. Beyond that, he could use a little more experience.

Though he has yet to pitch above Double-A, Sabathia will get a chance to win a spot in the major league rotation in the spring, as the Indians could have multiple openings. Sabathia would benefit from at least a half-season at Triple-A Buffalo, but team officials are going to let his talent dictate where he starts 2001.

Year	Club (League)	Class	W	L	ERA	G	GS	CG	SV	IP	H	R	ER	BB	SO
1998	Burlington (Appy)	R	1	0	4.50	5	5	0	0	18	20	14	9	8	35
1999	Mahoning Valley (NY-P)	A	0	0	1.83	6	6	0	0	20	9	5	4	12	27
	Columbus (SAL)	A	2	0	1.08	3	3	0	0	17	8	2	2	5	20
	Kinston (Car)	A	3	3	5.34	7	7	0	0	32	30	22	19	19	29
2000	Kinston (Car)	A	3	2	3.54	10	10	2	0	56	48	23	22	24	69
	Akron (EL)	AA	3	7	3.59	17	17	0	0	90	75	41	36	48	90
MINOR LEAGUE TOTALS			12	12	3.57	48	48	2	0	232	190	107	92	116	270

2. Danys Baez, rhp

Born: Sept. 10, 1977. **Ht.:** 6-4. **Wt.:** 225. **Bats:** R. **Throws:** R. **Career Transactions:** Signed out of Cuba by Indians, Nov. 6, 1999.

Baez, who defected from the Cuban national team during the 1999 Pan American Games in Winnipeg, was the Tribe's first big-money gamble on the international market. The Tribe signed him to a four-year, $14.5 million contract last winter, expecting him to be in their rotation in 2000. But one look in spring training told club officials he was going to be a project. His mechanics needed a major overhaul, and it took him time to adjust culturally. Baez' fastball just keeps getting better. He threw 94-95 mph early in the 2000 season, and in the Arizona Fall League he was at 97 mph with life. He gets great leverage on his fastball, which helps him keep it down in the zone. He has an above-average curve, mental toughness and desire. Baez lacks a third pitch and needs more consistent mechanics. He struggles working out of the stretch and controlling his emotions. He needs more innings to allow him to refine everything. Following his AFL performance, Baez will get a chance to win a spot on the big league staff in spring training. A better bet is that he starts the season in the Triple-A Buffalo rotation.

Year	Club (League)	Class	W	L	ERA	G	GS	CG	SV	IP	H	R	ER	BB	SO
2000	Kinston (Car)	A	2	2	4.71	9	9	0	0	49	45	29	26	20	56
	Akron (EL)	AA	4	9	3.68	18	18	0	0	102	98	46	42	32	77
MINOR LEAGUE TOTALS			6	11	4.02	27	27	0	0	152	143	75	68	52	133

3. Corey Smith, 3b

Born: April 15, 1982. **Ht.:** 6-0. **Wt.:** 210 **Bats:** R. **Throws:** R. **School:** Piscataway (N.J.) HS. **Career Transactions:** Selected by Indians in first round (26th overall) of 2000 draft; signed June 13, 2000.

The first high school infielder selected by the Indians in the first round since Mark Lewis in 1988, Smith signed for $1.375 million. A shortstop in high school, he immediately converted to third base, where the reviews were better than his numbers. Smith made 32 errors in 57 games, but club officials maintain his transition is going fine. He projects as a four-tool third baseman. He's athletic, has good power and should hit for average as well. Though he was shaky defensively in his professional debut, he shows a plus arm and has great first-step reactions. He has a tremendous work ethic, listens and applies what he's taught. Smith is a below-average runner. Though he has a strong arm, it's not especially accurate right now. His swing tends to get long on pitches up in the strike zone. But there's nothing that can't be fixed by more experience. His high error total is attributed to youthful aggressiveness. Smith will start his first full pro season at Class A Columbus. If his bat develops as expected, he could be ready for the majors in three years.

Year	Club (League)	Class	AVG	G	AB	R	H	2B	3B	HR	RBI	BB	SO	SB
2000	Burlington (Appy)	R	.256	57	207	21	53	8	2	4	39	27	50	8
MINOR LEAGUE TOTALS			.256	57	207	21	53	8	2	4	39	27	50	8

4. Willy Taveras, of

Born: Dec. 25, 1981. **Ht.:** 6-0. **Wt.:** 160. **Bats:** R. **Throws:** R. **Career Transactions:** Signed out of Dominican Republic by Indians, May 27, 1999.

A product of the Indians' Dominican program, Taveras emerged in 2000, though his .354 average in the Rookie-level Dominican Summer League in 1999 should have been a tipoff that the potential was there. He was on nobody's radar screen at the start of last season, but that has changed dramatically. Taveras is a center fielder with speed, so the comparisons with Kenny Lofton already have started. He is a 6 or 7 runner on the 2-to-8 scouting scale, which makes him a dangerous basestealer and gives him fine range in center field, where his arm is also a plus tool. He has a good idea of how to hit, and the Indians envision him as a contact hitter who drives the ball to all fields. Taveras is still raw as a hitter, however, especially in the power department. He needs to work on going back on balls in the outfield. He's still learning how to read pitchers in order to maximize his threat as a basestealer. Like Corey Smith, Taveras will jump from Rookie-level Burlington to Columbus in 2001. He too could be ready for Cleveland by the end of 2003.

Year	Club (League)	Class	AVG	G	AB	R	H	2B	3B	HR	RBI	BB	SO	SB
1999	Indians (DSL)	R	.354	68	277	57	98	19	6	3	44	32	32	26
2000	Burlington (Appy)	R	.263	50	190	46	50	4	3	1	16	23	44	36
	MINOR LEAGUE TOTALS		.263	118	467	103	148	23	9	4	60	55	76	62

5. Sean DePaula, rhp

TYLER BOLDEN

Born: Nov. 7, 1973. **Ht.:** 6-4. **Wt.:** 215. **Bats:** R. **Throws:** R. **School:** Wake Forest University. **Career Transactions:** Selected by Indians in ninth round of 1996 draft; signed June 7, 1996.

A strong September earned DePaula a spot on the Tribe's 1999 postseason roster, and he was the club's only reliable reliever in the American League Division Series flameout against the Red Sox. He came to camp in 2000 favored to win a bullpen spot, but an inflamed elbow limited his effectiveness and cost him almost half the season. DePaula has three quality pitches—fastball, slider, splitter—and throws all of them with confidence. He has shown the mental toughness necessary to pitch in the back end of the bullpen. At times, he has trouble throwing strikes consistently. DePaula's biggest drawback right now is the uncertainty about his elbow. It didn't require surgery after extended rest. Indians officials hope that's all he needs to return to 1999 form. If healthy, DePaula will make a serious run at winning a job in the Cleveland bullpen during spring training. If he doesn't pitch well in camp, he could start the season in Triple-A. In a couple of years, he could emerge as the Tribe's closer.

Year	Club (League)	Class	W	L	ERA	G	GS	CG	SV	IP	H	R	ER	BB	SO
1996	Burlington (Appy)	R	4	2	3.82	23	0	0	1	35	31	16	15	13	42
	Watertown (NY-P)	A	0	0	0.00	1	0	0	0	2	0	0	0	0	5
1997	Columbus (SAL)	A	4	5	5.20	29	1	0	0	71	71	56	41	43	75
	Watertown (NY-P)	A	1	1	2.84	9	0	0	0	19	21	6	6	8	17
1998	Kinston (Car)	A	3	2	2.36	28	1	0	1	50	50	20	13	18	59
	Akron (EL)	AA	1	1	4.76	8	1	0	0	17	16	10	9	15	17
1999	Kinston (Car)	A	4	2	2.28	23	0	0	7	51	36	17	13	17	75
	Akron (EL)	AA	1	0	3.54	14	0	0	1	28	20	11	11	17	31
	Buffalo (IL)	AAA	0	0	0.00	5	0	0	2	5	0	0	0	3	7
	Cleveland (AL)	MAJ	0	0	4.63	11	0	0	0	12	8	6	6	3	18
2000	Buffalo (IL)	AAA	1	0	5.54	9	0	0	1	13	16	10	8	7	11
	Cleveland (AL)	MAJ	0	0	5.94	13	0	0	0	17	20	11	11	14	16
	Akron (EL)	AA	0	0	1.80	4	0	0	0	5	1	1	1	2	4
	MAJOR LEAGUE TOTALS		0	0	5.40	24	0	0	0	28	28	17	17	17	34
	MINOR LEAGUE TOTALS		19	13	3.55	153	3	0	13	296	262	147	117	143	343

6. Zach Day, rhp

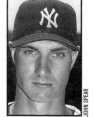

JOHN SPEAR

Born: June 15, 1978. **Ht.:** 6-4. **Wt.:** 185. **Bats:** R. **Throws:** R. **School:** LaSalle HS, Cincinnati. **Career Transactions:** Selected by Yankees in fifth round of 1996 draft; signed July 14, 1996 . . . Traded by Yankees with RHP Jake Westbrook to Indians, July 24, 2000, completing trade in which Indians sent OF David Justice to Yankees for OF Ricky Ledee and two players to be named (June 29, 2000).

Day was one of three players obtained from the Yankees in last June's David Justice trade. The others were righthander Jake Westbrook and outfielder Ricky Ledee, since traded to the Rangers for David Segui. Day bounced back from rotator-cuff surgery in 1999 to rank among the minor league strikeout leaders in 2000. He and Westbrook gave the Indians a couple of much-needed upper-level pitching prospects. Day has a big, strong body and relies mainly on a fastball and changeup. His fastball shows good sink and has improved from 90 to 93 mph since his surgery. He has a good feel for pitching and an ability to make big pitches when needed. Day could use a more consistent curveball and more experience. His performance in 2000 erased concerns about his health. Day started eight games at Double-A Akron following the trade, and that's probably where he'll begin 2001. He easily could pitch his way to Triple-A or the majors by the end of the season.

Year	Club (League)	Class	W	L	ERA	G	GS	CG	SV	IP	H	R	ER	BB	SO
1996	Yankees (GCL)	R	5	2	5.61	7	5	0	0	34	41	26	21	3	23
1997	Oneonta (NY-P)	A	7	2	2.15	14	14	0	0	92	82	26	22	23	92
1998	Tampa (FSL)	A	5	8	5.49	18	17	0	0	100	142	89	61	32	69
	Greensboro (SAL)	A	1	2	2.75	7	6	1	0	36	35	22	11	6	37
1999	Yankees (GCL)	R	1	1	3.78	5	4	0	0	17	20	10	7	4	17

Year	Club (League)	Class	W	L	ERA	G	GS	CG	SV	IP	H	R	ER	BB	SO
	Greensboro (SAL)	A	0	1	2.25	2	2	0	0	8	14	11	2	1	4
2000	Greensboro (SAL)	A	9	3	1.90	13	13	1	0	85	72	29	18	31	101
	Tampa (FSL)	A	2	4	4.19	7	7	0	0	34	33	22	16	15	36
	Akron (EL)	AA	4	2	3.52	8	8	0	0	46	38	20	18	21	43
MINOR LEAGUE TOTALS			34	25	3.50	81	76	2	0	452	477	255	176	136	422

7. Jake Westbrook, rhp

Born: Sept. 29, 1977. **Ht.:** 6-3. **Wt.:** 190. **Bats:** R. **Throws:** R. **School:** Madison County HS, Danielsville, Ga. **Career Transactions:** Selected by Rockies in first round (21st overall) of 1996 draft; signed June 13, 1996 . . . Traded by Rockies with RHP John Nicholson and OF Mark Hamlin to Expos for 2B Mike Lansing, Dec. 16, 1997 . . . Traded by Expos with two players to be named to Yankees for RHP Hideki Irabu, Dec. 22, 1999 . . . Traded by Yankees with RHP Zach Day to Indians, July 24, 2000, completing trade in which Indians sent OF David Justice to Yankees for OF Ricky Ledee and two players to be named (June 29, 2000).

Cleveland is Westbrook's fourth team in five years. The Rockies drafted him in the first round in 1996, then traded him to the Expos as part of a Mike Lansing deal a year later. In 2000, he was used in packages to acquire Hideki Irabu from the Yankees and David Justice from the Indians. Westbrook has yet to pitch for the Tribe, as a fractured rib had sidelined him before the trade. He has a big, strong body and an average fastball with hard sink. He complements it with an occasionally plus slider and average changeup. He's intelligent and has a feel for mixing his pitches. Some see him as a Chad Ogea with better stuff. Lacking an overwhelming pitch, Westbrook hasn't shown any signs of dominating hitters since pitching in short-season ball in 1996. The top concern at the moment is getting him healthy again after he averaged 172 innings in the three previous seasons. His breaking ball could be more consistent. Westbrook joins the roll of candidates for Cleveland's Opening Day rotation. More likely, he'll begin the season in Triple-A.

Year	Club (League)	Class	W	L	ERA	G	GS	CG	SV	IP	H	R	ER	BB	SO
1996	Rockies (AZL)	R	4	2	2.87	11	11	0	0	63	66	33	20	14	57
	Portland (NWL)	A	1	1	2.55	4	4	0	0	25	22	8	7	5	19
1997	Asheville (SAL)	A	14	11	4.29	28	27	3	0	170	176	93	81	55	92
1998	Jupiter (FSL)	A	11	6	3.26	27	27	2	0	171	169	70	62	60	79
1999	Harrisburg (EL)	AA	11	5	3.92	27	27	2	0	175	180	88	76	63	90
2000	Columbus (IL)	AAA	5	7	4.65	16	15	2	0	89	94	53	46	38	61
MINOR LEAGUE TOTALS			46	32	3.79	113	111	9	0	693	707	345	292	235	398

8. Tim Drew, rhp

Born: Aug. 31, 1978. **Ht.:** 6-1. **Wt.:** 195. **Bats:** R. **Throws:** R. **School:** Lowndes HS, Valdosta, Ga. **Career Transactions:** Selected by Indians in first round (28th overall) of 1997 draft; signed July 27, 1997.

Drew and his older brother J.D. (Cardinals) became the first siblings chosen in the first round of the same draft. Against their better judgment, the Indians rushed Drew to the big leagues in 2000. He wasn't ready, but a glut of injuries stripped the pitching staff and they took a chance. Drew had a 10.00 ERA in three starts and got crushed in Triple-A after being sent back down. Despite his bumpy debut with the Indians, Drew remains a solid prospect. His out pitch is a changeup, and his slider is becoming a weapon as well. He's intelligent, mentally tough and intense, and possesses a good feel for pitching. Because he doesn't have overpowering velocity, Drew must mix all his pitches to get batters out. He needs to locate his fastball precisely, because it arrives at 90 mph and hitters don't have any trouble picking it up. Drew still needs to prove he can pitch at the Triple-A level. Once he does, he'll get a second chance in Cleveland.

Year	Club (League)	Class	W	L	ERA	G	GS	CG	SV	IP	H	R	ER	BB	SO
1997	Burlington (Appy)	R	0	1	6.17	4	4	0	0	12	16	15	8	4	14
	Watertown (NY-P)	A	0	0	1.93	1	1	0	0	5	4	1	1	3	9
1998	Columbus (SAL)	A	4	3	3.79	13	13	0	0	71	68	43	30	26	64
	Kinston (Car)	A	3	8	5.20	15	15	0	0	90	105	58	52	31	67
1999	Kinston (Car)	A	13	5	3.73	28	28	2	0	169	154	79	70	60	125
2000	Akron (EL)	AA	3	2	2.42	9	9	0	0	52	41	19	14	15	22
	Cleveland (AL)	MAJ	1	0	10.00	3	3	0	0	9	17	12	10	8	5
	Buffalo (IL)	AAA	7	8	5.87	16	16	2	0	95	122	69	62	31	53
MAJOR LEAGUE TOTALS			1	0	10.00	3	3	0	0	9	17	12	10	8	5
MINOR LEAGUE TOTALS			30	27	4.32	86	86	4	0	494	510	284	237	170	354

9. Maicer Izturis, ss

Born: Sept. 12, 1980. **Ht.:** 5-8. **Wt.:** 155. **Bats:** B. **Throws:** R. **Career Transactions:** Signed out of Venezuela by Indians, April 1, 1998.

The Izturis family churns out shortstops, as Maicer's older brother Cesar is the Blue Jays' No. 3 prospect. Maicer might have as high a ceiling as any player in the organization, but he missed a large chunk of the 1999 season following shoulder surgery and barely played in 2000 because of elbow problems. When healthy, Izturis has drawn comparisons to fellow Venezuelan Omar Vizquel. He is a solid all-around player who can run, throw and hit. He has great hands, reads balls well off the bat and moves to the ball well. His arm is both strong and accurate. Offensively, he makes consistent contact and is a basestealing threat. Izturis' lack of durability has been a problem, costing him most of the last two years. He needs to get stronger in order to hold up for an entire season, and he could also stand to develop a dose of pop at the plate. Having played a total of just 67 games at Columbus over the last two seasons, Izturis may head back to low Class A at the start of 2001. Vizquel's contract expires after the 2002 season, but Izturis might not be quite ready at that point.

Year	Club (League)	Class	AVG	G	AB	R	H	2B	3B	HR	RBI	BB	SO	SB
1998	Burlington (Appy)	R	.290	55	217	33	63	8	2	2	33	17	32	16
1999	Columbus (SAL)	A	.300	57	220	46	66	5	3	4	23	20	28	14
2000	Columbus (SAL)	A	.276	10	29	4	8	1	0	0	1	3	3	0
MINOR LEAGUE TOTALS			.294	122	466	83	137	14	5	6	57	40	63	30

10. Alex Requena, of

Born: Aug. 13, 1980. **Ht.:** 5-11. **Wt.:** 155. **Bats:** B. **Throws:** R. **Career Transactions:** Signed out of Venezuela by Indians, July 25, 1998.

Requena has established himself as the most prolific basestealer in the organization and one of the fastest runners in the minor leagues. He led the short-season New York-Penn League with 44 steals in 1999 and the Class A South Atlantic League with 87 in 2000, when he swiped a league-record six in one game. His strengths are speed, speed and more speed. Requena is aggressive and fearless on the bases. While his bat leaves a lot to be desired, he has shown a willingness to take a walk. He also displays an above-average arm and range in center field. Requena's bat is a major question mark. He has hit a soft .251 since coming to the United States, with just 22 extra-base hits and 201 strikeouts in 696 at-bats. He began switch-hitting three years ago and is still learning. Making contact remains a challenge, and he hits too many balls in the air. He needs to put the ball on the ground to take full advantage of his speed. Requena will open 2001 at high Class A Kinston, where he'll face more advanced pitching than he has seen before. His development as a hitter will dictate how quickly he moves through the organization.

Year	Club (League)	Class	AVG	G	AB	R	H	2B	3B	HR	RBI	BB	SO	SB
1999	Mahoning Valley (NY-P)	A	.234	61	214	44	50	6	3	0	18	36	64	44
2000	Columbus (SAL)	A	.259	126	482	90	125	6	6	1	24	66	137	87
MINOR LEAGUE TOTALS			.251	187	696	134	175	12	9	1	42	102	201	131

11. Danny Peoples, 1b

Born: Jan. 20, 1975. **Ht.:** 6-1. **Wt.:** 207. **Bats:** R. **Throws:** R. **School:** University of Texas. **Career Transactions:** Selected by Indians in first round (28th overall) of 1996 draft; signed June 5, 1996.

The clock continues to tick for the Indians' top draft pick from 1996. Peoples has flirted with breakthrough seasons—34 homers in 1997 at Kinston, and 21 homers in each of the last two years—but never has been able to put it all together. Drafted as a first baseman, he was later moved to third base and the outfield, and now he's back at first base. Peoples has very good raw power and bat speed. He's considered a solid hitter, though he never has batted higher than .279 in the minors. Defensively, he's a good enough athlete to be tried at three different positions but not proficient enough to excel at any one of them. He's adequate at best with the glove. But his biggest problem is making consistent contact. He has struck out a combined 264 times the last two years, and has averaged one whiff per 3.3 at-bats as a pro. His age also is becoming a factor. Peoples likely will begin 2001 at Buffalo, especially after the Indians signed Juan Gonzalez to be the DH, but he could be one of the first hitters called up when injuries strike the big league club.

Year	Club (League)	Class	AVG	G	AB	R	H	2B	3B	HR	RBI	BB	SO	SB
1996	Watertown (NY-P)	A	.239	35	117	20	28	7	0	3	26	28	36	3
1997	Kinston (Car)	A	.249	121	409	82	102	21	1	34	84	84	145	8
1998	Akron (EL)	AA	.279	60	222	30	62	19	0	8	32	29	61	1
1999	Akron (EL)	AA	.251	127	494	75	124	23	3	21	78	55	142	2
2000	Buffalo (IL)	AAA	.260	124	420	68	109	19	2	21	74	63	122	2
MINOR LEAGUE TOTALS			.256	467	1662	275	425	89	6	87	294	259	506	16

12. Martin Vargas, rhp

Born: Feb. 22, 1978. **Ht.:** 6-0. **Wt.:** 155. **Bats:** R. **Throws:** R. **Career Transactions:** Signed out of Dominican Republic by Indians, July 5, 1995.

Vargas was oringally signed as a catcher and used to go by the name Martin Bautista. By either name, he has shown one of the liveliest arms in the organization since coverting to pitcher. Originally a starter, he moved to the bullpen in the middle of the 1999 season. He has tremendous athleticism, an easy delivery and a well above-average fastball with good sink, the best sinker in the organization. He's also making progress in throwing a quality splitter. Vargas is still developing a feel for pitching, and at times he's inconsistent. His secondary stuff needs to be further refined, but the arm is definitely there. He projects as a reliever at the big league level, with a chance at developing into a closer.

Year	Club (League)	Class	AVG	G	AB	R	H	2B	3B	HR	RBI	BB	SO	SB
1996	Indians (DSL)	R	.223	39	103	7	23	6	1	0	12	12	25	1
MINOR LEAGUE TOTALS			.223	39	103	7	23	6	1	0	12	12	25	1

Year	Club (League)	Class	W	L	ERA	G	GS	CG	SV	IP	H	R	ER	BB	SO
1997	Indians (DSL)	R	3	5	2.45	14	14	0	0	70	52	33	19	39	43
1998	Columbus (SAL)	A	1	4	10.01	7	7	0	0	30	42	36	33	24	25
	Burlington (Appy)	R	3	7	4.76	13	13	1	0	74	78	49	39	35	64
1999	Columbus (SAL)	A	6	3	4.95	15	12	0	0	67	80	46	37	20	51
	Kinston (Car)	A	6	1	2.76	20	0	0	2	42	31	16	13	20	44
2000	Akron (EL)	AA	10	8	5.42	53	0	0	7	81	96	52	49	30	58
MINOR LEAGUE TOTALS			29	28	4.70	122	46	1	9	364	379	232	190	167	255

13. John McDonald, ss

Born: Sept. 24, 1974. **Ht.:** 5-11. **Wt.:** 175. **Bats:** R. **Throws:** R. **School:** Providence College. **Career Transactions:** Selected by Indians in 12th round of 1996 draft; signed June 5, 1996.

The trade of Enrique Wilson to the Pirates last season was a break for McDonald, now the heir apparent as the Indians' utility infielder. Unfortunately for him, when the injury bug was sweeping Cleveland in 2000, he was limited to 75 games at Buffalo by a pulled quad. McDonald is above-average at shortstop, and his defensive skills are superior to many major league starters. He has soft hands, is good on the transfer, shows excellent quickness around the bag and has a quick release. He has terrific makeup and loves to play the game. There are questions about whether he will hit enough to be an everyday player in the majors. Right now he's a No. 8 or 9 hitter who would have to play on a big offensive team that could carry him offensively. McDonald also needs to improve his bunting and his ability to play the little game. He'll go to camp with a good chance at opening the season as the Indians' utilityman. Defensively, there isn't much of a dropoff from Omar Vizquel to McDonald.

Year	Club (League)	Class	AVG	G	AB	R	H	2B	3B	HR	RBI	BB	SO	SB
1996	Watertown (NY-P)	A	.270	75	278	48	75	11	0	2	26	32	49	11
1997	Kinston (Car)	A	.259	130	541	77	140	27	3	5	53	51	75	6
1998	Akron (EL)	AA	.230	132	514	68	118	18	2	2	43	43	61	17
1999	Akron (EL)	AA	.296	55	226	31	67	12	0	1	26	19	26	7
	Buffalo (IL)	AAA	.316	66	237	30	75	12	1	0	25	11	23	6
	Cleveland (AL)	MAJ	.333	18	21	2	7	0	0	0	0	0	3	0
2000	Buffalo (IL)	AAA	.269	75	286	37	77	17	2	1	36	21	29	4
	Cleveland (AL)	MAJ	.444	9	9	0	4	0	0	0	0	0	1	0
MAJOR LEAGUE TOTALS			.367	27	30	2	11	0	0	0	0	0	4	0
MINOR LEAGUE TOTALS			.265	533	2082	291	552	97	8	11	209	177	263	51

14. Brian Tallet, lhp

Born: Nov. 28, 1977. **Ht.:** 6-7. **Wt.:** 193. **Bats:** L. **Throws:** L. **School:** Louisiana State University. **Career Transactions:** Selected by Indians in second round of 2000 draft; signed August 1, 2000.

Tallet comes out of a big-time program at Louisiana State and has experience pitching big games. He was the starter in the 2000 College World Series championship, getting no decision as the Tigers rallied to beat Stanford. Tallet has three solid average pitches: a low-90s fastball, slider and changeup. He has good size and that most precious commodity of all: being lefthanded. Tallet tends to throw across his body, but that's correctable. He has good mound presence. With his advanced college background, Tallet could move quickly. He was effective in his stint at Mahoning Valley, helping the Scrappers to the New York-Penn League championship. He'll likely begin his first full pro season in the high Class A Kinston rotation.

Year	Club (League)	Class	W	L	ERA	G	GS	CG	SV	IP	H	R	ER	BB	SO
2000	Mahoning Valley (NY-P)	A	0	0	1.15	6	6	0	0	16	10	2	2	3	20
MINOR LEAGUE TOTALS			0	0	1.15	6	6	0	0	16	10	2	2	3	20

15. David Riske, rhp

Born: Oct. 23, 1976. **Ht.:** 6-2. **Wt.:** 175. **Bats:** R. **Throws:** R. **School:** Green River (Wash.) CC. **Career Transactions:** Selected by Indians in 56th round of 1996 draft; signed Oct. 21, 1996.

Riske first made it to Cleveland in 1999 and didn't pitch like a 56th-round draft pick. He showed poise and wasn't awed at all by big league hitters. He was a candidate for the bullpen in 2000, but a bulging disc hampered him early and led to surgery in May to remove the disc. When he attempted to pitch again in September, he was halted by a labrum tear in his shoulder. When healthy, Riske gets by on guts and guile. He doesn't have overpowering stuff but is utterly fearless on the mound and uses good deception to make the most of an average fastball. He has good command of the fastball but lacks a quality second pitch, which sometimes gets him into trouble. He'll go to camp with a chance to win a job in the bullpen.

Year	Club (League)	Class	W	L	ERA	G	GS	CG	SV	IP	H	R	ER	BB	SO
1997	Kinston (Car)	A	4	4	2.25	39	0	0	2	72	58	22	18	33	90
1998	Kinston (Car)	A	1	1	2.33	53	0	0	33	54	48	15	14	15	67
	Akron (EL)	AA	0	0	0.00	2	0	0	1	3	1	0	0	1	5
1999	Akron (EL)	AA	0	0	1.90	23	0	0	12	24	5	6	5	13	33
	Buffalo (IL)	AAA	3	0	0.65	23	0	0	6	28	14	3	2	7	22
	Cleveland (AL)	MAJ	1	1	8.36	12	0	0	0	14	20	15	13	6	16
2000	Akron (EL)	AA	0	0	0.00	3	1	0	1	4	2	0	0	0	4
	Buffalo (IL)	AAA	0	0	3.00	2	0	0	0	3	2	1	1	2	2
MAJOR LEAGUE TOTALS			1	1	8.36	12	0	0	0	14	20	15	13	6	16
MINOR LEAGUE TOTALS			8	5	1.93	145	1	0	55	187	130	47	40	71	223

16. Roy Padilla, lhp

Born: Aug. 4, 1975. **Ht.:** 6-5. **Wt.:** 227. **Bats:** L. **Throws:** L. **Career Transactions:** Signed out of Panama by Red Sox, Sept. 30, 1992 . . . Loaned by Red Sox to co-op Butte, June 12-Sept. 5, 1995 . . . Selected by Indians from Red Sox in minor league Rule 5 draft, Dec. 14, 1998.

A minor league Rule 5 draftee out of the Boston organization, Padilla has had a strange career. Drafted as a pitcher, he converted to the outfield and was the starting left fielder in the 1996 Midwest League all-star game. He stalled the next two years in high Class A, then was drafted by the Indians and moved back to the mound. He has tremendous arm strength, unleashing a fastball that can at times be overpowering, clocking in at a C.C. Sabathia-like 99 mph. Because he spent about half of his minor league time as a position player, Padilla still is learning to develop his secondary pitches. His feel for pitching is also lacking. But he is a stunning physical specimen on the mound with the potential to make an impact at the big league level, once he improves his repertoire and the consistency of his mechanics. He's expected to start this season in the Double-A bullpen.

Year	Club (League)	Class	W	L	ERA	G	GS	CG	SV	IP	H	R	ER	BB	SO
1993	Red Sox (GCL)	R	0	1	2.35	13	1	0	0	31	25	10	8	17	18
1994	Red Sox (GCL)	R	6	1	2.99	15	12	0	1	72	68	39	24	34	52
1995	Michigan (Mid)	A	0	1	6.48	4	1	0	0	8	10	9	6	7	7
	Butte (Pio)	R	2	7	5.91	15	14	0	0	70	80	60	46	54	49
1999	Columbus (SAL)	A	2	2	3.02	30	0	0	3	60	53	27	20	27	56
	Kinston (Car)	A	0	0	4.15	8	0	0	1	13	9	6	6	10	7
2000	Kinston (Car)	A	1	1	4.94	14	0	0	0	24	14	21	13	21	32
	Akron (EL)	AA	0	1	4.24	16	0	0	0	23	20	16	11	25	18
MINOR LEAGUE TOTALS			11	14	4.01	115	28	0	5	301	279	188	134	195	239

Year	Club (League)	Class	AVG	G	AB	R	H	2B	3B	HR	RBI	BB	SO	SB
1995	Butte (Pio)	R	.000	16	1	0	0	0	0	0	0	0	0	0
1996	Michigan (Mid)	A	.280	103	386	58	108	20	6	2	40	34	56	21
	Sarasota (FSL)	A	.296	8	27	2	8	2	0	0	2	2	3	4
1997	Sarasota (FSL)	A	.246	130	463	66	114	16	4	2	38	41	80	24
1998	Sarasota (FSL)	A	.255	109	365	46	93	17	3	3	53	28	66	12
MINOR LEAGUE TOTALS			.260	366	1242	172	323	55	13	7	133	105	205	61

17. Jamie Brown, rhp

Born: March 31, 1977. **Ht.:** 6-2. **Wt.:** 205. **Bats:** R. **Throws:** R. **School:** Meridian (Miss.) CC. **Career Transactions:** Selected by Indians in 21st round of 1996 draft; signed May 15, 1997.

Brown has been on the verge of a breakthrough for the last couple of years. His best season remains his first, though. Brown's 2000 performance at Akron was unremarkable. But the stuff is there. He has a good feel for pitching and has two above-average pitches in his fastball and change. His third pitch is a slider, which could use a little work. He had back problems in 2000, which may have contributed to an inconsistent delivery. Inconsistency in the strike zone has also been a problem at times. The back trouble last season and a sore shoulder in 1999 have raised questions about his durability. Brown remains one of the organization's more intriguing arms and could start 2001 in the Triple-A rotation.

Year	Club (League)	Class	W	L	ERA	G	GS	CG	SV	IP	H	R	ER	BB	SO
1997	Watertown (NY-P)	A	10	2	3.08	13	13	1	0	73	66	35	25	15	57
1998	Kinston (Car)	A	11	9	3.81	27	27	2	0	172	162	91	73	44	148
	Akron (EL)	AA	1	0	2.57	1	1	0	0	7	5	2	2	1	5
1999	Akron (EL)	AA	5	9	4.57	23	23	1	0	138	140	72	70	39	98
	Buffalo (IL)	AAA	1	0	5.40	1	0	0	0	5	8	4	3	1	2
2000	Akron (EL)	AA	7	6	4.38	17	17	1	0	96	95	49	47	26	57
MINOR LEAGUE TOTALS			35	26	4.02	82	81	5	0	492	476	253	220	126	367

18. Jorge Moreno, of

Born: Oct. 26, 1980. **Ht.:** 6-0. **Wt.:** 175. **Bats:** R. **Throws:** R. **Career Transactions:** Signed out of Venezuela by Indians, May 10, 1998.

Moreno hit .303 in full-season Class A ball at 19. He came on even stronger in instructional league, where he really opened eyes. Defensively, he's a good left fielder with a decent arm. Some compare him to Magglio Ordonez. Moreno has good power and is a warrior. With his tools and tremendous makeup, there's no telling how good he could be. The knock on him is there isn't one part of his game that stands out. He's solid in all areas but not exceptional in any. If he continues to develop at his current pace, he projects as a potential starter at the big league level. The Indians won't rush him. He'll start the 2001 season with one of the Tribe's Class A affiliates.

Year	Club (League)	Class	AVG	G	AB	R	H	2B	3B	HR	RBI	BB	SO	SB
1998	Guacara 2 (VSL)	R	.259	44	147	18	38	14	1	1	18	10	34	3
1999	Mahoning Valley (NY-P)	A	.257	69	230	38	59	10	2	9	38	31	61	15
2000	Columbus (SAL)	A	.303	55	211	37	64	15	2	7	32	19	57	10
MINOR LEAGUE TOTALS			.274	168	588	93	161	39	5	17	88	60	152	28

19. Jhonny Peralta, ss

Born: May 28, 1982. **Ht.:** 6-1. **Wt.:** 185. **Bats:** R. **Throws:** R. **Career Transactions:** Signed out of Dominican Republic by Indians, April 14, 1999.

The Indians surprised some by assigning Peralta to a full-season Class A team at age 17, but he held his own. He is mechanically sound defensively, with soft hands and good range to his left, but he needs more work going into the hole. He has a strong arm and is already a quality defensive shortstop. Offensively there are adjustments he needs to make. He draws walks and has potential gap power but must make more consistent contact. He's only an average runner and not an accomplished basestealer. Peralta already is halfway up the ladder, though the Indians will be patient with him. He likely will start 2001 in high Class A, and if his development continues, it's not out of the question that he could reach Triple-A as a teenager. He might be the most advanced young player in the system.

Year	Club (League)	Class	AVG	G	AB	R	H	2B	3B	HR	RBI	BB	SO	SB
1999	Indians (DSL)	R	.303	62	208	48	63	14	6	6	43	33	49	14
2000	Columbus (SAL)	A	.241	106	349	52	84	13	1	3	34	59	102	7
MINOR LEAGUE TOTALS			.264	168	557	100	147	27	7	9	77	92	151	21

20. Hector Luna, ss

Born: Feb. 1, 1982. **Ht.:** 6-1. **Wt.:** 170. **Bats:** R. **Throws:** R. **Career Transactions:** Signed out of Dominican Republic by Indians, Feb. 2, 1999. •

A product of the Indians' growing Dominican program, Luna is another in the organization's growing inventory of middle infielders. His defense is ahead of his offense, mostly because he's already an accomplished shortstop. He's a solid athlete with quick, soft hands. His glove is his No. 1 tool, but his speed is a close second. He has 48 stolen bases in 121 games in his two years in the system. Luna's bat is still a question mark, and his ability to hit will determine how far he'll rise. He'll have to get stronger to give himself a chance. The Indians will have legitimate prospects playing shortstop at every level of their system in 2001. That includes Luna, who's expected to be the starting shortstop at Columbus.

Year	Club (League)	Class	AVG	G	AB	R	H	2B	3B	HR	RBI	BB	SO	SB
1999	Indians (DSL)	R	.256	61	234	44	60	13	2	1	24	27	36	29
2000	Burlington (Appy)	R	.204	55	201	25	41	5	0	1	15	27	35	19
	Mahoning Valley (NY-P)	A	.316	5	19	2	6	2	0	0	4	1	3	0
MINOR LEAGUE TOTALS			.236	121	454	71	107	20	2	2	43	55	74	48

21. Zach Sorensen, ss

Born: Jan. 3, 1977. **Ht.:** 6-0. **Wt.:** 190. **Bats:** B. **Throws:** R. **School:** Wichita State University. **Career Transactions:** Selected by Indians in second round of 1998 draft; signed July 1, 1998.

Sorensen is an intelligent player with a tremendous work ethic and makeup. After not showing much with the bat the last two years, he made progress in the Arizona Fall League that could indicate he's turned the corner. He could become a Jay Bell type of infielder because he lacks a true No. 1 tool. Defensively, he's solid if unspectacular. His arm is fringe for a shortstop and he hasn't exhibited a lot of range. He'll have to make up for his short-age of defensive tools by precise positioning. But it's his temperament and personality that everyone talks about. Sheer effort and will make up for shortages in other areas, and Sorensen has all the intangibles. He has risen through the system with his double-play part-ner, second baseman Scott Pratt, and the duo will start the 2001 season in Double-A or Triple-A. Sorensen, however, might be better suited for second base at the major league level.

Year	Club (League)	Class	AVG	G	AB	R	H	2B	3B	HR	RBI	BB	SO	SB
1998	Watertown (NY-P)	A	.300	53	200	38	60	7	8	4	26	35	35	14
1999	Kinston (Car)	A	.238	130	508	79	121	16	7	7	59	62	126	24
2000	Akron (EL)	AA	.259	96	382	62	99	17	4	6	38	42	62	16
	Buffalo (IL)	AAA	.263	12	38	5	10	1	1	0	2	3	9	1
MINOR LEAGUE TOTALS			.257	291	1128	184	290	41	20	17	125	142	232	55

22. Derek Thompson, lhp

Born: Jan. 8, 1981. **Ht.:** 6-3. **Wt.:** 180. **Bats:** L. **Throws:** L. **School:** Land O'Lakes (Fla.) HS. **Career Transactions:** Selected by Indians in first round (37th overall) of 2000 draft; signed June 13, 2000.

The Indians believed the 2000 draft was strong in high school hitters and pitchers, par-ticularly lefthanders. The Indians wasted little time in picking a high school lefty, choosing Thompson with the No. 37 overall pick, compensation for losing free agent Mike Jackson to the Phillies. Thompson signed for an $850,000 bonus. He has a good feel for pitching and throws strikes with three pitches—a low 90s fastball, a slider and changeup—a rarity for a high school pitcher. Thompson was undefeated as a high school senior, averaging 16.7 strikeouts per nine innings. The Indians think he's very projectable. Though his numbers at Rookie-level Burlington were unimpressive, he may bypass Mahoning Valley and begin 2001 in the Columbus rotation.

Year	Club (League)	Class	W	L	ERA	G	GS	CG	SV	IP	H	R	ER	BB	SO
2000	Burlington (Appy)	R	0	4	5.82	12	12	0	0	43	50	38	28	14	40
MINOR LEAGUE TOTALS			0	4	5.82	12	12	0	0	43	50	38	28	14	40

23. Eric Johnson, of

Born: Aug. 14, 1977. **Ht.:** 6-1. **Wt.:** 210. **Bats:** R. **Throws:** R. **School:** Western Carolina University. **Career Transactions:** Selected by Indians in third round of 1999 draft; signed June 6, 1999.

Johnson is a converted football player who actually logged more time on the gridiron than on the diamond at Western Carolina. He still is wrestling with the transition from foot-ball, but he's a tremendous athlete with superior baseball abilities. His instincts in the out-field are good and he has all the tools necessary to be an above-average defender. He has a plus arm and plus speed, though he's still working on tracking fly balls. Offensively, Johnson will be more of a project. He struggled after being promoted to Kinston and has been slow to make adjustments offensively. His mechanics are inconsistent and he needs a better approach. He does just fine on the bases, where he stole a combined 56 bases in 68 attempts last year. Johnson likely will start the 2001 season back at Kinston.

Year	Club (League)	Class	AVG	G	AB	R	H	2B	3B	HR	RBI	BB	SO	SB
1999	Burlington (Appy)	R	.231	39	147	26	34	9	1	3	22	25	29	13
	Mahoning Valley (NY-P)	A	.257	28	105	23	27	4	1	1	10	18	17	12

Year	Club (League)	Class	AVG	G	AB	R	H	2B	3B	HR	RBI	BB	SO	SB
2000	Columbus (SAL)	A	.309	67	262	63	81	11	2	4	45	37	49	41
	Kinston (Car)	A	.207	55	213	23	44	4	2	2	21	27	47	15
MINOR LEAGUE TOTALS			.256	189	727	135	186	28	6	10	98	107	142	81

24. Kyle Evans, rhp

Born: Oct. 10, 1978. **Ht.:** 6-3. **Wt.:** 190. **Bats:** R. **Throws:** R. **School:** Baylor University. **Career Transactions:** Selected by Indians in sixth round of 2000 draft; signed June 15, 2000.

Evans, another product of new scouting director John Mirabelli's first draft, is a very athletic pitcher. He has a quality sinker, great makeup and good pitchability. He showed a lot of promise in his first year, reminding some of a young Charles Nagy. Evans moves his fastball around the strike zone, and mixes in a slider and changeup. He throws strikes down in the zone and is more of a pitcher than a thrower. That's somewhat surprising, because he's a converted infielder who's still learning the nuances of pitching. His inexperience on the mound is at times noticeable and costly, but that can be fixed. Evans' biggest need right now is for innings. He showed so much in his debut that he might skip Columbus and begin this season in the Kinston rotation.

Year	Club (League)	Class	W	L	ERA	G	GS	CG	SV	IP	H	R	ER	BB	SO
2000	Mahoning Valley (NY-P)	A	5	2	3.14	12	11	0	0	63	56	29	22	22	53
MINOR LEAGUE TOTALS			5	2	3.14	12	11	0	0	63	56	29	22	22	53

25. Sean Swedlow, 1b

Born: May 25, 1982. **Ht.:** 6-3. **Wt.:** 225. **Bats:** L. **Throws:** R. **School:** San Dimas (Calif.) HS. **Career Transactions:** Selected by Indians in third round of 2000 draft; signed June 12, 2000.

A catcher in high school, Swedlow was converted to a first baseman after signing. His best tool is his raw power, though he's still looking for his first professional home run. A big left-handed hitter, Swedlow has a nice swing and a chance to be an impact power source. The consensus is that he's further along than Richie Sexson was at the same age. Defensively, Swedlow is barely adequate at first base. He needs a lot of work around the bag, though he did show some improvement in instructional league. Swedlow needs to go out and play, learn his new position and settle in at the plate. He's expected to spend 2001 at Columbus.

Year	Club (League)	Class	AVG	G	AB	R	H	2B	3B	HR	RBI	BB	SO	SB
2000	Burlington (Appy)	R	.226	36	115	13	26	5	0	0	7	23	41	1
MINOR LEAGUE TOTALS			.226	36	115	13	26	5	0	0	7	23	41	1

26. Mark Folsom, of

Born: June 7, 1981. **Ht.:** 6-5. **Wt.:** 215. **Bats:** R. **Throws:** R. **School:** West Orange HS, Winter Garden, Fla. **Career Transactions:** Selected by Indians in second round of 2000 draft; signed June 20, 2000.

Folsom signed for $700,000 and immediately opened eyes with his jaw-dropping power. He has off-the-charts raw power that rivals that of any hitter in the minors. He's a big, muscular slugger who at times has a tendency to overswing. He averaged a Russell Branyanesque one strikeout per 2.8 at-bats in his debut, so obviously making consistent contact is a problem. His strike zone discipline needs a lot of work, as does his defense. He played center field in high school but mostly left field at Burlington, and was only adequate at best. Folsom has a lot of upside, though he needs to work on his swing and acknowledge that a 350-foot homer counts the same as a 500-foot blast. Columbus is his likely destination this season.

Year	Club (League)	Class	AVG	G	AB	R	H	2B	3B	HR	RBI	BB	SO	SB
2000	Burlington (Appy)	R	.227	51	176	11	40	8	0	4	16	10	62	3
MINOR LEAGUE TOTALS			.227	51	176	11	40	8	0	4	16	10	62	3

27. Osmany Santana, of

Born: Aug. 9, 1976. **Ht.:** 5-11. **Wt.:** 185. **Bats:** L. **Throws:** L. **Career Transactions:** Signed out of Cuba by Indians, March 11, 1998.

A Cuban defector, Santana didn't generate nearly as much hoopla when he signed as Danys Baez did a year later. But Santana has positioned himself to make a run at a big league job in the next year or two. As a center fielder, Santana is as good at running down balls as anyone in the system. He gets a tremendous jump on flies and covers a lot of ground. At the plate, he's a contact hitter who must use the bunt to greater advantage. He doesn't have Kenny Lofton's speed or power, but the best may be yet to come. Though he has above-average speed, Santana doesn't steal as many bases as he should. He also doesn't necessarily project as a leadoff hitter because he doesn't draw enough walks. He posted a .325 on-base percentage after his promotion to Akron, and may head back there to start 2001.

Year	Club (League)	Class	AVG	G	AB	R	H	2B	3B	HR	RBI	BB	SO	SB
1998	Watertown (NY-P)	A	.282	19	78	17	22	4	3	2	13	11	8	3
1999	Columbus (SAL)	A	.323	38	133	23	43	6	0	0	17	10	21	15
	Kinston (Car)	A	.241	43	145	16	35	8	0	3	20	8	26	7
2000	Kinston (Car)	A	.326	44	190	27	62	12	2	0	14	15	27	13
	Akron (EL)	AA	.283	51	191	16	54	6	0	1	23	11	23	14
MINOR LEAGUE TOTALS			.293	195	737	99	216	36	5	6	87	55	105	52

28. Scott Pratt, 2b

Born: Feb. 4, 1977. **Ht.:** 5-10. **Wt.:** 185. **Bats:** L. **Throws:** R. **School:** Auburn University. **Career Transactions:** Selected by Indians in third round of 1998 draft; signed July 13, 1998.

Pratt led the New York-Penn League in hitting in his pro debut in 1998, and a year later he led the Carolina League with 47 stolen bases. Last season his big statistical accomplishment was ranking among the Eastern League leaders with 500 at-bats—which wasn't a positive. The main reason he had so many at-bats is that he's reluctant to take a walk, and his lack of patience has contributed to his .239 average the last two years. His main offensive strength is his solid pop for a middle infielder, and he has good instincts on the bases. However, he has to learn to use his speed to greater effect by making better use of the bunt. Defensively he's adequate and should improve with more experience. A lack of consistency in all phases of the game is holding him back right now. As he has in his first three seasons, Pratt probably will team with shortstop Zach Sorensen in 2001, at either Buffalo or Akron.

Year	Club (League)	Class	AVG	G	AB	R	H	2B	3B	HR	RBI	BB	SO	SB
1998	Watertown (NY-P)	A	.351	47	174	37	61	12	3	2	14	34	26	15
1999	Kinston (Car)	A	.247	133	486	86	120	27	6	9	54	77	95	47
2000	Akron (EL)	AA	.236	129	500	67	118	18	6	7	51	39	98	22
	Buffalo (IL)	AAA	.083	4	12	0	1	0	0	0	1	0	4	0
MINOR LEAGUE TOTALS			.256	313	1172	190	300	57	15	18	120	150	223	84

29. Ryan Church, of

Born: Oct. 14, 1978. **Ht.:** 6-1. **Wt.:** 190. **Bats:** L. **Throws:** L. **School:** University of Nevada. **Career Transactions:** Selected by Indians in 14th round of 2000 draft; signed June 7, 2000.

Church had the best debut of any of Cleveland's 2000 draft picks, leading the New York-Penn League in RBIs and earning MVP honors. He has a lot of upside but may take some time to develop because up until three years ago he was a pitcher. A shoulder injury in college moved him back to the outfield, his main position in high school. Though Church lacks an exceptional tool, he's solid in all phases of the game. He runs fairly well and will take a walk, as evidenced by his .396 on base percentage. The jury is still out on what kind of power Church may eventually show. He's a corner outfielder, so the power better arrive eventually. He'll get the chance to develop it in Class A this season.

Year	Club (League)	Class	AVG	G	AB	R	H	2B	3B	HR	RBI	BB	SO	SB
2000	Mahoning Valley (NY-P)	A	.298	73	272	51	81	16	5	10	65	38	49	11
MINOR LEAGUE TOTALS			.298	73	272	51	81	16	5	10	65	38	49	11

30. Jason Fitzgerald, of

Born: Sept. 16, 1975. **Ht.:** 6-1. **Wt.:** 190. **Bats:** L. **Throws:** L. **School:** Tulane University. **Career Transactions:** Selected by Indians in first round (41st overall) of 1997 draft; signed July 28, 1997.

There's nothing glamorous about Fitzgerald, a blue-collar player with great makeup. Taken with a compensation pick for the loss of free agent Albert Belle, he hasn't shown the power Indians officials had hoped to see. He also hasn't produce much in terms of average or walks, though he has been effective running the bases. His biggest drawback has been a lack of health. In 1998 he had surgery to remove the hamate bone from his right wrist, and a year later he had reconstructive surgery on his left elbow. Healthy again in 2000, he reached Double-A. He has yet to light up the minor leagues, but does enough things to project as a role player, a solid fourth or fifth outfielder at the major league level.

Year	Club (League)	Class	AVG	G	AB	R	H	2B	3B	HR	RBI	BB	SO	SB
1997	Watertown (NY-P)	A	.196	34	112	11	22	8	0	1	13	17	31	2
1998	Columbus (SAL)	A	.273	132	490	60	134	28	3	16	80	38	117	21
1999	Kinston (Car)	A	.239	82	310	26	74	17	3	4	39	22	77	15
2000	Kinston (Car)	A	.252	82	318	42	80	16	3	4	44	29	55	21
	Akron (EL)	AA	.279	56	208	27	58	8	4	4	30	23	38	7
MINOR LEAGUE TOTALS			.256	386	1438	166	368	77	13	29	206	129	318	66

Colorado
Rockies

TOP 30 PROSPECTS

1. Chin-Hui Tsao, rhp
2. Juan Uribe, ss
3. Choo Freeman, of
4. Aaron Cook, rhp
5. Jason Young, rhp
6. Jason Jennings, rhp
7. Craig House, rhp
8. Shawn Chacon, rhp
9. Josh Kalinowski, lhp
10. Matt Holliday, 3b/of
11. Luke Hudson, rhp
12. Jose Vasquez, of
13. Randy Dorame, lhp
14. Elvis Pena, 2b/ss
15. Cory Vance, lhp
16. Robert Averette, rhp
17. Garrett Atkins, 1b/of
18. Brad Hawpe, of
19. Justin Lincoln, 3b
20. Esteban Montero, ss
21. Chuck Crowder, lhp
22. Jeff Winchester, c
23. Josh Bard, c
24. Cam Esslinger, rhp
25. Tim Christman, lhp
26. Brent Butler, 2b
27. Ryan Kibler, rhp
28. Enemencio Pacheco, rhp
29. Julio DePaula, rhp
30. Jody Gerut, of

By Tracy Ringolsby

The Rockies believe they're still two quality drafts away from having the top-to-bottom depth they desire. But they are starting to feel the benefits from the last three drafts—the final two of former scouting director Pat Daugherty, when he was freed from the signability edicts of former general manager Bob Gebhard, and the initial draft of his successor, Bill Schmidt.

They ran into a setback with their struggles to sign 2000 first-round pick Matt Harrington despite a $4 million bonus offer to the California prep righthander, who was considered the best prospect available. Colorado eased some of the sting by getting Stanford righthander Jason Young in the second round.

The club's commitment to player development is apparent. If the Rockies eventually come to terms with Harrington—and there were positive signs in January—only the Braves will have spent more on signing amateurs in 2000.

Talent is finally reaching the upper levels of the system. Infielder Brent Butler is the only prospect among the top 30 who played most of the season with Triple-A Colorado Springs in 2000. At least seven members of the list figure to make the Sky Sox' Opening Day 2001 roster, though.

Double-A Carolina will benefit even more from the Rockies' recent efforts. The Mudcats project a rotation of Chin-Hui Tsao, Jason Jennings, Josh Kalinowski, Luke Hudson and Chuck Crowder. Other prospects should include relievers Cam Esslinger and Tim Christman, catcher Josh Bard, shortstop Juan Uribe and third baseman-turned-outfielder Matt Holliday.

Besides putting more money into the draft, the Rockies also are undertaking a major effort on the international market. They're focusing initially on Latin America. Rolando Fernandez, who had been a roving instructor, has assumed the duties of the director of Latin operations. He signed nine Dominicans in a one-week span in December and is attempting to open doors in Venezuela, Mexico and Panama as well.

Fernandez was just one of several scouting changes. Pacific Rim director Tim Ireland resigned and was replaced by Kent Blasingame, son of former big league infielder and Japanese League veteran Don. The big league scouting staff was restructured in the wake of Mark Wiley's departure to become Orioles pitching coach. Among the hirings were Bill Geivett, who has extensive international experience from his days with the Expos, Devil Rays and Dodgers; and Terry Wetzel, former Royals scouting director.

OrganizationOverview

General manager: Dan O'Dowd. **Farm director:** Mike Hill. **Scouting director:** Bill Schmidt.

2000 PERFORMANCE

Class	Team	League	W	L	Pct.	Finish*	Manager
Majors	Colorado	National	82	80	.506	8th (16)	Buddy Bell
Triple-A	Colo. Springs Sky Sox	Pacific Coast	74	68	.521	7th (16)	Chris Cron
Double-A	Carolina Mudcats	Southern	64	75	.460	t-9th (10)	Ron Gideon
High A	Salem Avalanche	Carolina	73	67	.521	2nd (8)	Alan Cockrell
Low A	Asheville Tourists	South Atlantic	66	69	.489	t-8th (14)	Joe Mikulik
Short-season	#Portland Rockies	Northwest	32	44	.421	8th (8)	Bill White
Rookie	†AZL Rockies	Arizona	35	19	.648	2nd (9)	P.J. Carey
OVERALL 2000 MINOR LEAGUE RECORD			344	341	.502	14th (30)	

*Finish in overall standings (No. of teams in league). #Franchise will move in Tri-Cities, Wash., in 2001. †Affiliate will be in Butte (Pioneer) in 2001.

ORGANIZATION LEADERS

BATTING

*AVG	Carlos Mendoza, Colorado Springs	.354
R	Phil Hiatt, Colorado Springs	106
H	Phil Hiatt, Colorado Springs	157
TB	Phil Hiatt, Colorado Springs	303
2B	Kevin Burford, Salem	40
3B	Chone Figgins, Salem	14
	Carlos Mendoza, Colorado Springs	14
HR	Phil Hiatt, Colorado Springs	36
RBI	Phil Hiatt, Colorado Springs	109
BB	Jody Gerut, Carolina	76
SO	Justin Lincoln, Asheville	161
SB	**Elvis Pena**, Carolina	48

PITCHING

W	**Chuck Crowder**, Salem	14
L	Ryan Kibler, Asheville	14
#ERA	Matt Roney, Portland	3.14
G	Pete Walker, Colorado Springs	58
CG	Doug Linton, Colorado Springs	6
SV	Cam Esslinger, Asheville	24
IP	Jason Jennings, Salem/Carolina	187
BB	**Chuck Crowder**, Salem	86
SO	Julio DePaula, Asheville	187
	Chin-hui Tsao, Asheville	187

*Minimum 250 at-bats. #Minimum 75 innings.

TOP PROSPECTS OF THE DECADE

1993	David Nied, rhp
1994	John Burke, rhp
1995	Doug Million, lhp
1996	Derrick Gibson, of
1997	Todd Helton, 1b
1998	Todd Helton, 1b
1999	Choo Freeman, of
2000	Choo Freeman, of

TOP DRAFT PICKS OF THE DECADE

1992	John Burke, rhp
1993	Jamey Wright, rhp
1994	Doug Million, lhp
1995	Todd Helton, 1b
1996	Jake Westbrook, rhp
1997	Mark Mangum, rhp
1998	Choo Freeman, of
1999	Jason Jennings, rhp
2000	*Matt Harrington, rhp

*Had not signed.

Pena

Crowder

BEST TOOLS

Best Hitter for Average	Garrett Atkins
Best Power Hitter	Matt Holliday
Fastest Baserunner	Elvis Pena
Best Fastball	Chin-Hui Tsao
Best Breaking Ball	Jason Jennings
Best Control	Chin-Hui Tsao
Best Defensive Catcher	Josh Bard
Best Defensive Infielder	Juan Uribe
Best Infield Arm	Juan Uribe
Best Defensive Outfielder	Jody Gerut
Best Outfield Arm	Dan Phillips

PROJECTED 2004 LINEUP

Catcher	Ben Petrick
First Base	Todd Helton
Second Base	Juan Uribe
Third Base	Jeff Cirillo
Shortstop	Neifi Perez
Left Field	Matt Holliday
Center Field	Choo Freeman
Right Field	Larry Walker
No. 1 Starter	Mike Hampton
No. 2 Starter	Chin-Hui Tsao
No. 3 Starter	Pedro Astacio
No. 4 Starter	Aaron Cook
No. 5 Starter	Denny Neagle
Closer	Craig House

ALL-TIME LARGEST BONUSES

Jason Young, 2000	$2,750,000
Chin-Hui Tsao, 1999	2,200,000
Jason Jennings, 1999	1,675,000
Choo Freeman, 1998	1,400,000
Doug Million, 1994	905,000

DraftAnalysis

2000 Draft

Best Pro Debut: 1B/OF **Garrett Atkins** (5) shared MVP honors in the short-season Northwest League after hitting .303-7-47. 3B Eric Storey (24) won the home-run crown in the Rookie-level Arizona League and batted .328-9-40, though at 22 he was much older than most of his competition.

Best Athlete: SS Clint Barmes (10) has no outstanding tool, but he's steady across the board. He's also versatile, having played center field in junior college before moving to short at Indiana State.

Best Hitter: Atkins will hit for average, and the Rockies hope his propensity for hitting doubles develops into a propensity for hitting home runs.

Best Raw Power: OF Jose Vasquez (16), who hit .311-5-38 in the AZL. He was headed for Louisiana State before calling a Rockies area scout before the draft to say he wanted to sign. OF Brad Hawpe (11), who tied an NCAA Division I record with 36 doubles last year for LSU, just needs to add loft to his swing to become a homer threat.

Fastest Runner: Colorado didn't sign any speed. Its quickest player is Barmes, an average runner.

Best Defensive Player: C Dan Conway's (8) catch-and-throw skills played as well in the pros as they did in college. But he has work to do adjusting to wood bats.

Best Fastball: RHP Matt Harrington's (1) 98 mph heat was as hot as any in the draft, but the Rockies' ability to get him signed remains in doubt. RHP Jason Young (2), whom Colorado would have taken in the first round if Harrington hadn't been available, hits 94 mph at his best.

Most Intriguing Background: OF Michael Vick (30) hasn't played baseball since he was 14 and is better known for his football exploits, formerly at Virginia Tech and soon to be in the NFL. He was tempted by the idea of signing but had to attend summer school.

ROBERT GURGANUS

Atkins

Closest To The Majors: Young held out all summer before signing for $2.75 million, and his shoulder bothered him at times during the spring at Stanford. The Rockies will be patient with him at first. As a result, LHP Cory Vance (4) is the favorite to reach Colorado first. He has an average fastball and a plus curveball.

Best Late-Round Pick: Hawpe and Vasquez.

The One Who Got Away: The Rockies, who offered $4 million, and Harrington, who wanted $4.95 million, were at a stalemate entering 2001. But the first face-to-face meeting between the club and the family may have set the stage for a signing. The best player that Colorado definitely lost is raw 6-foot-5 RHP Bob Zimmerman (14), who's at Southwest Missouri State.

Assessment: First-year scouting director Bill Schmidt wasn't necessarily looking for pitching, but he took five arms in the first six rounds. The Rockies will have two of the best if Harrington joins Young.

1999 Draft

RHPs Jason Jennings (1) and Craig House (12) look like they'll come through for a club always in need of arms. Signing RHP Bobby Brownlie (26) would have helped. Now at Rutgers, he projects as one of the first picks in 2002.   **Grade: C**

1998 Draft

One day, Choo Freeman (1), Matt Holliday (7) and Juan Pierre (13) could form the starting outfield in Colorado. C Jeff Winchester (1) and RHP Luke Hudson (4) also could contribute. A third first-rounder, RHP Matt Roney, has moved slowly.   **Grade: B**

1997 Draft

RHP Mark Mangum (1) was a pure signability pick, and he pales in comparison to RHP Aaron Cook (2). RHP Justin Miller (5) was traded to Oakland, so Cook might be all the Rockies get out of this crop.   **Grade: C–**

1996 Draft

RHP Jake Westbrook (1) was traded to Montreal for Mike Lansing and was passed on to two other clubs last year. RHPs Shawn Chacon (3), Tim Christman (11) and Josh Kalinowski (33, draft-and-follow) are the best of what remains in the system.   **Grade: C–**

Note: Draft analysis prepared by Jim Callis. Numbers in parentheses indicate draft rounds.

. . . Tsao is a legitimate power pitcher with the ability to be a quality No. 1 starter in the big leagues.

Chin-Hui
Tsao rhp

Born: June 2, 1981.
Ht.: 6-1. **Wt.:** 180.
Bats: R. **Throws:** R.
Career Transactions: Signed out of Taiwan by Rockies, Oct. 7, 1999.

Tsao was the Rockies' first impact move on the international market. He signed for a then-franchise-record $2.2 million bonus as the franchise's first Asian signee after he went 3-0 with 23 shutout innings for Taiwan in the 1999 World Junior Championship. The only amateur to participate in the Asia Cup (a qualifying tournament for the 2000 Olympics), he pitched a 15-strikeout one-hitter against China in his lone start. Tsao continued to dominate in his pro debut. He got the attention of big league scouts when he pitched a perfect inning in an exhibition game against the Mariners, which was televised live back to Taiwan. Among the honors he earned were selection to the Futures Game, Class A Asheville team MVP honors, South Atlantic League midseason and postseason all-star recognition, and selection as the league's pitcher of the year. He was slowed briefly by a midseason blister problem and a late-season tender elbow, but neither injury was considered serious and he finished strong. He tied for second in the SAL in strikeouts and finished fourth in ERA.

Tsao is a legitimate power pitcher. He has a fastball that is consistently in the 93-94 mph range, a hard slider, curveball and a changeup. His fastball, slider and curve already are quality big league pitches. The fastball has good sinking action and he'll pitch inside. And he does throw strikes. He walked only 40 batters, although hitting five, in 145 innings. Tsao needs to maintain his focus. His changeup has the makings of a top-quality pitch but he hasn't had to use it enough to gain total command of it yet. He also is working to adjust to American culture, including taking advanced English courses. The Rockies kept him at Asheville all of last season so they wouldn't disrupt his routine off the field and have that interfere with his development on the field.

Tsao has the ability to be a quality No. 1 starter in the big leagues. He could be pushed to Double-A Carolina in 2001 but likely will go to high Class A Salem. Don't look for him to be moved once the season starts, as the Rockies again want to give him time to adjust.

Year	Club (League)	Class	W	L	ERA	G	GS	CG	SV	IP	H	R	ER	BB	SO
2000	Asheville (SAL)	A	11	8	2.73	24	24	0	0	145	119	54	44	40	187
MINOR LEAGUE TOTALS			11	8	2.73	24	24	0	0	145	119	54	44	40	187

2. Juan Uribe, ss

Born: July 22, 1979. **Ht.:** 5-11. **Wt.:** 173. **Bats:** R. **Throws:** R. **Career Transactions:** Signed out of Dominican Republic by Rockies, Jan. 15, 1997.

Signed as a 16-year-old out of a tryout camp in his native Dominican Republic, Uribe has put together three quality seasons since coming to the United States. He even has shown power in two years at full-season Class A, hitting a total of 22 home runs. Uribe is capable of playing in the big leagues right now defensively. He has a rifle arm that's accurate, soft hands and quick feet. Neifi Perez, the National League's Gold Glove shortstop in 2000, says he expects Uribe to push him to second base before long. Uribe has basestealing speed and showed a better feel for the art last year, getting caught just five times. He has plus power potential for a middle infielder. But he is still young and learning. He needs to have a more consistent approach at the plate, working deeper counts and making more frequent contact. With the Rockies finally showing depth with middle infielders, there's no reason to rush Uribe. He'll make the natural progression to Double-A this year, and could be in the big leagues by the end of the 2002 season.

Year	Club (League)	Class	AVG	G	AB	R	H	2B	3B	HR	RBI	BB	SO	SB
1997	Rockies (DSL)	R	.269	65	234	32	63	12	0	0	29	31	22	7
1998	Rockies (AZL)	R	.277	40	148	25	41	5	3	0	17	12	25	8
1999	Asheville (SAL)	A	.267	125	430	57	115	28	3	9	46	20	79	11
2000	Salem (Car)	A	.256	134	485	64	124	22	7	13	65	38	100	22
MINOR LEAGUE TOTALS			.264	364	1297	178	343	67	13	22	157	101	226	48

3. Choo Freeman, of

Born: Oct. 20, 1979. **Ht.:** 6-2. **Wt.:** 200. **Bats:** R. **Throws:** R. **School:** Dallas Christian HS, Mesquite, Texas. **Career Transactions:** Selected by Rockies in first round (36th overall) of 1998 draft; signed July 13, 1998.

Freeman was the first player who showed that the Rockies were going to start taking chances with the draft. After living by signability in previous years, they didn't hesitate to take Freeman and give him the $1.4 million to keep him from accepting a football scholarship from Texas A&M. A three-sport start at Dallas Christian High, he was a Connie Mack teammate of Blue Jays outfield prospect Vernon Wells. He is a pure athlete with the physical abilities to be an impact center fielder, as well as the power potential to play left field. He's mentally tough and willing to put in the time it takes to be successful. He was the organization's top prospect for the previous two years but has been passed by players who are coming along a little more quickly. Freeman just needs to play so he can turn his tools into skills. He has started to develop his timing at the plate but needs to be more selective. He has the speed to steal 50 bases once he gets a better feel for that part of the game. Freeman could start at Salem for the second year in a row, with the possibility of moving to Carolina during the season. He has been pushed each of the last two years and would benefit from being allowed to dominate a league.

Year	Club (League)	Class	AVG	G	AB	R	H	2B	3B	HR	RBI	BB	SO	SB
1998	Rockies (AZL)	R	.320	40	147	35	47	3	6	1	24	15	25	14
1999	Asheville (SAL)	A	.274	131	485	82	133	22	4	14	66	39	132	16
2000	Salem (Car)	A	.266	127	429	73	114	18	7	5	54	37	104	16
MINOR LEAGUE TOTALS			.277	298	1061	190	294	43	17	20	144	91	261	46

4. Aaron Cook, rhp

Born: Feb. 8, 1979. **Ht.:** 6-3. **Wt.:** 175. **Bats:** R. **Throws:** R. **School:** Hamilton (Ohio) HS. **Career Transactions:** Selected by Rockies in second round of 1997 draft; signed July 13, 1997.

Cook was considered the top talent of the Rockies' 1997 draft, in which first-round pick Mark Mangum was a pure budget decision. Cook blossomed last year when he returned to Asheville, finishing eighth in the Sally League with a 2.96 ERA. His combined 11 wins were one more than the total from his three previous pro seasons. Cook has good pitchability. He has three quality pitches, and builds off a mid-90s fastball. He's durable and competes well, responding to the challenge of being in the same rotation as Chin-Hui Tsao last year. Like so many young pitchers who always have been able to dominate with their fastball, Cook still is gaining confidence in his changeup. He has the makings of a quality offspeed pitch but doesn't use it enough. As he moves up in pro ball, he'll realize how useful changing speeds can be. Cook got a taste of Salem at the end of last season and struggled. He'll return there to start 2001.

Year	Club (League)	Class	W	L	ERA	G	GS	CG	SV	IP	H	R	ER	BB	SO
1997	Rockies (AZL)	R	1	3	3.13	9	8	0	0	46	48	27	16	17	35
1998	Portland (NWL)	A	5	8	4.88	15	15	1	0	79	87	50	43	39	38
1999	Asheville (SAL)	A	4	12	6.44	25	25	2	0	121	157	99	87	42	73
2000	Asheville (SAL)	A	10	7	2.96	21	21	4	0	142	130	54	47	23	118
	Salem (Car)	A	1	6	5.44	7	7	1	0	43	52	33	26	12	37
MINOR LEAGUE TOTALS			21	36	4.56	77	76	8	0	432	474	263	219	133	301

5. Jason Young, rhp

Born: Sep. 28, 1979. **Ht.:** 6-5. **Wt.:** 210. **Bats:** B. **Throws:** R. **School:** Stanford University. **Career Transactions:** Selected by Rockies in second round of 2000 draft; signed Sept. 26, 2000.

Considered a possible No. 1 pick in the 2000 draft before the college season began, Young was slowed by tightness in his right shoulder. After leading NCAA Division I with 178 strikeouts as a sophomore, he had only 120 as a junior while going 9-1, 3.73. The Rockies, who had planned to take him in the first round until Matt Harrington slipped, were able to get Young in the second round. He didn't come cheap. He received a franchise-record $2.75 million bonus, fourth-highest for any player in the 2000 draft. Young has size and strength. His fastball topped out at 94 mph when he was healthy. He has command of a hard slider that dominates hitters. Young needs to use his changeup better. Once he masters that pitch, he has the potential of being a legitimate No. 1 starter. His command was inconsistent during the college season, which might have been the result of his shoulder troubles. Because of prolonged negotiations, Young won't make his pro debut until this spring, most likely at Salem. With his background and arm he could move quickly, and he figures to get to Double-A by midseason. He could arrive in Colorado sometime in 2002.

Year	Club (League)	Class	W	L	ERA	G	GS	CG	SV	IP	H	R	ER	BB	SO
2000						Did Not Play—Signed 2001 Contract									

6. Jason Jennings, rhp

Born: July 17, 1978. **Ht.:** 6-2. **Wt.:** 230. **Bats:** L. **Throws:** R. **School:** Baylor University. **Career Transactions:** Selected by Rockies in first round (16th overall) of 1999 draft; signed June 9, 1999.

One of just three college players the Rockies have taken with their top pick in nine years of drafting, Jennings was Baseball America's 1999 College Player of the Year as a two-way standout at Baylor. He went 13-2, 2.58 with 172 strikeouts in 147 innings for the Bears that season, and hit .386-17-68 as a DH. His father Jim played baseball at Texas and in the Rangers farm system, and his grandfater was a longtime public-address announcer for the Dallas Cowboys. Jennings has three pitches he can command in the strike zone. What makes him so attractive for Coors Field is a solid, low-90s sinker. He complements it with a hard slider. He draws physical comparisons to Rick Reuschel, who like Jennings was a deceptively good athlete despite his bulk. He'll be an interesting hitting pitcher if he gets to Coors Field. Jennings can be a bit stubborn at times, but he's competitive enough that he eventually will make the adjustments necessary to succeed at the upper levels. He's still getting the confidence necessary to throw his changeup in key situations. He got a taste of Double-A at the end of last season and will open 2001 back with Carolina. He could be promoted quickly and figures to be in the big leagues in 2002 with a future as a No. 3 starter.

Year	Club (League)	Class	W	L	ERA	G	GS	CG	SV	IP	H	R	ER	BB	SO
1999	Portland (NWL)	A	1	0	1.00	2	2	0	0	9	5	1	1	2	11
	Asheville (SAL)	A	2	2	3.70	12	12	0	0	58	55	27	24	8	69
2000	Salem (Car)	A	7	10	3.47	22	22	3	0	150	136	66	58	42	133
	Carolina (SL)	AA	1	3	3.44	6	6	0	0	37	32	19	14	11	33
MINOR LEAGUE TOTALS			11	15	3.43	42	42	3	0	254	228	113	97	63	246

7. Craig House, rhp

Born: July 8, 1977. **Ht.:** 6-2. **Wt.:** 210. **Bats:** R. **Throws:** R. **School:** University of Memphis. **Career Transactions:** Selected by Rockies in 12th round of 1999 draft; signed June 18, 1999.

House made a rapid rise in his first full year of pro ball, opening 2000 in Class A and making stops at Double-A and Triple-A before finishing the season in the big leagues. A starter in college, he has worked exclusively out of the bullpen in 81 professional appearances. Combine a funky delivery that has his body going in different directions with an upper-90s fastball that could be headed just about anywhere, and House is very intimidating. He also has a mid-80s slider and a changeup that understandably freezes hitters when he throws it for strikes. House must find a more consistent release point in order to have better command. He got hitters to chase pitches in the lower minors, but more advanced hitters forced him to throw strikes. When he had trouble doing so in the majors, he got hammered. House has closer potential, but there's work to be done before he's ready to return to Colorado. He'll start 2001 at Triple-A Colorado Springs.

Year	Club (League)	Class	W	L	ERA	G	GS	CG	SV	IP	H	R	ER	BB	SO
1999	Portland (NWL)	A	2	1	2.08	26	0	0	11	35	28	14	8	14	58
2000	Salem (Car)	A	2	0	2.25	13	0	0	8	16	7	4	4	10	24
	Carolina (SL)	AA	0	2	3.80	18	0	0	9	21	14	11	9	15	28
	Colo. Spr. (PCL)	AAA	0	0	3.24	8	0	0	4	8	6	4	3	2	8
	Colorado (NL)	MAJ	1	1	7.24	16	0	0	0	14	13	11	11	17	8
MAJOR LEAGUE TOTALS			1	1	7.24	16	0	0	0	14	13	11	11	17	8
MINOR LEAGUE TOTALS			4	3	2.69	65	0	0	32	80	55	33	24	41	118

8 Shawn Chacon, rhp

Born: Dec. 23, 1977. **Ht.:** 6-3. **Wt.:** 212. **Bats:** R. **Throws:** R. **School:** Greeley (Colo.) Central HS. **Career Transactions:** Selected by Rockies in third round of 1996 draft; signed June 18, 1996.

After two years wasted by injuries and off-field problems, Chacon reaffirmed his potential in 2000. He led the Double-A Southern League in strikeouts and shutouts (three), while finishing second in complete games and third in innings. He turned down a scholarship to Arizona State to sign with the Rockies. Chacon has power-pitcher potential. He has a solid 94 mph fastball and hard slider, which have allowed him to consistently rack up strikeouts. He's a tough competitor. Whether he winds up a starter or reliever will depend on how well he develops a changeup. Right now it's a raw pitch, though he does throw it with decent action. He needs to get on the mound and get experience after pitching just 128 innings combined in 1998-99. Chacon will make the jump to Triple-A in 2001. He's on pace to get his first taste of the big leagues in September.

Year	Club (League)	Class	W	L	ERA	G	GS	CG	SV	IP	H	R	ER	BB	SO
1996	Rockies (AZL)	R	1	2	1.60	11	11	1	0	56	46	17	10	15	64
	Portland (NWL)	A	0	2	6.86	4	4	0	0	19	24	18	15	9	17
1997	Asheville (SAL)	A	11	7	3.89	28	27	1	0	162	155	80	70	63	149
1998	Salem (Car)	A	0	4	5.30	12	12	0	0	56	53	35	33	31	54
1999	Salem (Car)	A	5	5	4.13	12	12	0	0	72	69	44	33	34	66
2000	Carolina (SL)	AA	10	10	3.16	27	27	4	0	173	151	71	61	85	172
MINOR LEAGUE TOTALS			27	30	3.70	94	93	6	0	539	498	265	222	237	522

9 Josh Kalinowski, lhp

Born: Dec. 12, 1976. **Ht.:** 6-2. **Wt.:** 190. **Bats:** L. **Throws:** L. **School:** Indian Hills (Iowa) CC. **Career Transactions:** Selected by Rockies in 33rd round of 1996 draft; signed May 28, 1997.

Kalinowski is a product of Natrona County High in Casper, Wyo., which also churned out big leaguers Tom Browning, Mike Devereaux and Mike Lansing. Signed as a draft-and-follow, Kalinowski led his league in strikeouts in each of his first two full years and was named the high Class A Carolina League pitcher of the year in 1999. But a nagging elbow problem sidelined him for the bulk of 2000 and resulted in arthroscopic surgery. Kalinowski has three-pitch potential. His strikeout pitch is a curveball, and there are no concerns about how the mile-high altitude of Coors Field will affect its break because he learned to throw the pitch at altitude in Wyoming. Kalinowski also has a quality fastball that touches 90 mph on a consistent basis. An all-state selection as a high school football and basketball player, he's an excellent athlete who fields his position well. He must learn to work off his fastball instead of the curveball. He also has to refine a changeup, an important pitch for him to claim a rotation spot. His command will need to improve as he rises up the ladder. Kalinowski has been given a clean bill of health after his surgery. He figures to open 2001 back at Carolina with the possibility of a quick promotion to Colorado Springs.

Year	Club (League)	Class	W	L	ERA	G	GS	CG	SV	IP	H	R	ER	BB	SO
1997	Portland (NWL)	A	0	1	2.41	6	6	0	0	19	15	6	5	10	27
1998	Asheville (SAL)	A	12	10	3.92	28	28	3	0	172	159	93	75	65	215
1999	Salem (Car)	A	11	6	2.11	27	27	1	0	162	119	47	38	71	176
2000	Carolina (SL)	AA	1	3	6.23	6	6	0	0	26	30	22	18	12	27
MINOR LEAGUE TOTALS			24	20	3.23	67	67	4	0	379	323	168	136	158	445

10 Matt Holliday, 3b/of

Born: Jan. 10, 1980. **Ht.:** 6-4. **Wt.:** 215. **Bats:** R. **Throws:** R. **School:** Stillwater (Okla.) HS. **Career Transactions:** Selected by Rockies in seventh round of 1998 draft; signed July 24, 1998.

Holliday comes from a baseball family. His father Tom is the head coach at Oklahoma State, his uncle Dave scouts for the Rockies and his brother Josh is a first baseman in the Blue Jays system. Matt was one of the nation's top prep quarterbacks when he came out of Stillwater (Okla.) High, but the Rockies gambled a pick on him and signed him for $865,000, the most ever for a seventh-round draft choice. Holliday's bat is the key to his future. His size, bat speed and swing equate to big league power, and he has a good understanding of hitting. He has struggled at third base, committing 32 errors last year, and his future likely will be in left field, where he has the power to be an impact player. He's not a burner, but he does have a feel for the game and it shouldn't take long for him to get comfortable in the outfield. He'll improve at the plate if he develops a little more discipline. It's uncertain where Holliday will begin his transition to the outfield. He's in line for a move to Double-A, though he might be sent back to Salem to have the benefit of a comfortable environment while changing positions. He's at least two years away from Colorado.

Year	Club (League)	Class	AVG	G	AB	R	H	2B	3B	HR	RBI	BB	SO	SB
1998	Rockies (AZL)	R	.342	32	117	20	40	4	1	5	23	15	21	2
1999	Asheville (SAL)	A	.264	121	444	76	117	28	0	16	64	53	116	10
2000	Salem (Car)	A	.274	123	460	64	126	28	2	7	72	43	74	11
MINOR LEAGUE TOTALS			.277	276	1021	160	283	60	3	28	159	111	211	23

11. Luke Hudson, rhp

Born: May 2, 1977. **Ht.:** 6-3. **Wt.:** 195. **Bats:** R. **Throws:** R. **School:** University of Tennessee. **Career Transactions:** Selected by Rockies in fourth round of 1998 draft; signed June 5, 1998.

As an amateur, Hudson won two California state high school titles and national championships in Pony League (13-14) and Colt League (15-16) competition. He has had elbow soreness as a pro, but shook it off to finish strong in 2000. With his size, Hudson projects to add velocity to a fastball that already reaches the low 90s with regularity. He also has command of a slider and changeup, but has to be more aggressive throwing strikes. His biggest need is staying healthy. He was hit in the face by a line drive during instructional league in 1998 and has faced nagging, unrelated injuries ever since. His 110 innings last year were the most he has worked in three pro seasons. He'll pitch in Double-A to start this season.

Year	Club (League)	Class	W	L	ERA	G	GS	CG	SV	IP	H	R	ER	BB	SO
1998	Portland (NWL)	A	3	6	4.74	15	15	0	0	80	68	46	42	51	82
1999	Asheville (SAL)	A	6	5	4.30	21	20	1	0	88	89	47	42	24	96
2000	Salem (Car)	A	5	8	3.27	19	19	2	0	110	101	47	40	34	80
MINOR LEAGUE TOTALS			14	19	4.02	55	54	3	0	278	258	140	124	109	258

12. Jose Vasquez, of

Born: Dec. 28, 1982. **Ht.:** 6-3 **Wt.:** 220 **Bats:** L. **Throws:** L. **School:** Sarasota (Fla.) HS. **Career Transactions:** Selected by Rockies in 16th round of 2000 draft; signed June 7, 2000.

Vazquez is the type of low-round pick who can make a draft a success. He showed his offensive tools in the Rookie-level Arizona League but played his first pro season at 17 and will have to be brought along slowly. He has legitimate power potential and decent speed (10-for-12 in stolen bases). He is still quite raw, as evidenced by his 73 strikeouts and 11 errors in just 29 games in the field. But he did show the potential to develop a good eye at the plate. He split the first season between first base and the outfield, but figures to wind up in the outfield for the long term. He'll play for the Rockies' new short-season Casper affiliate in 2001.

Year	Club (League)	Class	AVG	G	AB	R	H	2B	3B	HR	RBI	BB	SO	SB
2000	AZL Rockies	R	.311	46	177	37	55	12	5	5	38	27	73	10
MINOR LEAGUE TOTALS			.311	46	177	37	55	12	5	5	38	27	73	10

13. Randy Dorame, lhp

Born: Jan. 23, 1979. **Ht.:** 6-2. **Wt.:** 205. **Bats:** L. **Throws:** L. **Career Transactions:** Signed out of Mexico by Dodgers, May 16, 1997 . . . Loaned by Dodgers to Reynosa (Mexican), March 18-Oct. 28, 1998 . . . Traded by Dodgers with OF Todd Hollandsworth and OF Kevin Gibbs to Rockies for OF Tom Goodwin, July 31, 2000.

Dorame was the 1999 California League pitcher of the year after leading the high Class A circuit in wins and ERA. He was the key to the July trade that netted three players from Los Angeles for speedster Tom Goodwin. It was a curious decision by the Dodgers to trade Dorame, because he was one of their better prospects and Goodwin is a limited big leaguer. Dorame was slowed by elbow problems late last year but was able to pitch during the winter in the Mexican Pacific League. He has a build that can get stronger, which should add to the velocity on his average fastball. He throws an excellent curveball and a changeup. He has good arm action and throws strikes. Dorame probably will go back to Double-A to start 2001 and move up to Triple-A during the season.

Year	Club (League)	Class	W	L	ERA	G	GS	CG	SV	IP	H	R	ER	BB	SO
1997	Dodgers (DSL)	R	8	0	0.97	12	9	0	0	65	33	9	7	11	69
1998	Reynosa (Mex)	AAA	6	13	4.03	24	23	2	0	132	143	73	59	73	71
1999	Vero Beach (FSL)	A	0	2	5.73	3	2	0	0	11	15	9	7	1	5
	San Bernardino (Cal)	A	14	3	2.51	24	24	1	0	154	130	52	43	37	159
2000	Vero Beach (FSL)	A	7	1	2.21	9	9	2	0	57	50	15	14	13	49
	San Antonio (TL)	AA	3	4	3.86	9	9	0	0	58	53	29	25	18	28
	Carolina (SL)	AA	0	2	5.06	2	2	0	0	11	7	6	6	4	9
MINOR LEAGUE TOTALS			38	25	2.97	83	78	5	0	488	431	193	161	157	390

14. Elvis Pena, 2b/ss

Born: Sept. 15, 1976. **Ht.:** 5-11. **Wt.:** 155. **Bats:** B. **Throws:** R. **Career Transactions:** Signed out of Dominican Republic by Rockies, June 22, 1993.

Pena has made a dramatic move into prospect status, ranking among the batting leaders in the Carolina and Southern leagues over the last two years. He also led the Southern League with 48 stolen bases, giving him 231 in his pro career. Pena is adept at either second base or shortstop, though his arm is probably best suited for second base. He has soft hands and quick feet. A close friend of Rockies shortstop Neifi Perez, Pena isn't a power guy and understands his job is to get on base, which he does with regularity. He could be forced into a utility role in 2001 but most likely will get to play every day at shortstop in Triple-A.

Year	Club (League)	Class	AVG	G	AB	R	H	2B	3B	HR	RBI	BB	SO	SB
1994	Rockies (AZL)	R	.228	49	171	31	39	5	2	0	9	35	47	20
1995	Asheville (SAL)	A	.228	48	145	27	33	2	0	0	4	28	32	23
	Portland (NWL)	A	.251	58	215	29	54	6	3	0	18	26	45	28
1996	Salem (Car)	A	.223	102	341	48	76	9	4	0	28	61	70	30
1997	Salem (Car)	A	.222	93	279	41	62	9	2	1	30	37	53	16
1998	Asheville (SAL)	A	.287	115	428	93	123	24	4	6	48	70	85	41
1999	Carolina (SL)	AA	.301	110	356	57	107	24	6	2	31	48	64	21
	Colo. Spr. (PCL)	AAA	.163	13	43	5	7	1	0	0	1	3	7	4
2000	Carolina (SL)	AA	.300	126	477	92	143	16	7	3	37	69	76	48
	Colorado (NL)	MAJ	.333	10	9	1	3	1	0	0	1	1	1	1
MAJOR LEAGUE TOTALS			.333	10	9	1	3	1	0	0	1	1	1	1
MINOR LEAGUE TOTALS			.262	714	2455	423	644	96	28	12	206	377	479	231

15. Cory Vance, lhp

Born: June 20, 1979. **Ht.:** 6-1. **Wt.:** 195. **Bats:** L. **Throws:** L. **School:** Georgia Tech. **Career Transactions:** Selected by Rockies in 4th round of 2000 draft; signed July 17, 2000.

Vance was the second Georgia Tech lefty drafted in the fourth round by the Rockies in as many years, following Chuck Crowder in 1999. Vance led the Atlantic Coast Conference with 13 victories last year before turning pro. He has command of three pitches, and his best is a big-breaking curveball. His fastball comes in at 87-90 mph, enough velocity for a left-hander. After a lengthy negotiation he was impressive in his brief debut at short-season Portland. His durability is a key asset and he projects as a third or fourth starter in the majors. He figures to open his first full season at Class A Salem.

Year	Club (League)	Class	W	L	ERA	G	GS	CG	SV	IP	H	R	ER	BB	SO
2000	Portland (NWL)	A	0	2	1.11	7	3	0	0	24	11	5	3	8	26
MINOR LEAGUE TOTALS			0	2	1.11	7	3	0	0	24	11	5	3	8	26

16. Robert Averette, rhp

Born: Sept. 30, 1976. **Ht.:** 6-2. **Wt.:** 195. **Bats:** R. **Throws:** R. **School:** Florida A&M University. **Career Transactions:** Selected by Reds in 21st round of 1997 draft; signed June 6, 1997 . . . Traded by Reds to Rockies for OF Brian L. Hunter, Aug. 6, 2000.

Averette led the Southern League in wins and complete games while ranking seventh in ERA last year. As with the deal that brought Randy Dorame from Los Angeles, this was another example of Colorado general manager Dan O'Dowd doing a masterful job of turning a one-dimensional big leaguer into a pitching prospect. Averette has won in double figures in each of his three full minor league seasons. He has an impressive curveball and an average fastball, and he throws strikes. He'll have to improve his changeup if he's going to pitch in a big league rotation. He does throw strikes. He'll open the 2001 season at Colorado Springs, which always provides a stern test for finesse pitchers.

Year	Club (League)	Class	W	L	ERA	G	GS	CG	SV	IP	H	R	ER	BB	SO
1997	Billings (Pio)	R	0	0	0.00	2	1	0	0	3	3	0	0	1	3
	Charleston, WV (SAL)	A	2	2	7.86	11	3	0	1	26	42	28	23	12	20
1998	Charleston, WV (SAL)	A	5	4	2.79	14	14	3	0	84	84	38	26	26	68
	Chattanooga (SL)	AA	5	8	5.11	14	14	0	0	81	97	51	46	36	32
1999	Rockford (Mid)	A	9	5	2.58	19	19	2	0	126	117	54	36	40	98
	Chattanooga (SL)	AA	2	1	5.20	6	6	1	0	36	42	22	21	19	15
2000	Chattanooga (SL)	AA	12	6	2.44	19	19	5	0	136	126	51	37	28	87
	Louisville (IL)	AAA	0	1	8.38	2	2	0	0	10	9	10	9	10	4
	Carolina (SL)	AA	1	3	3.19	5	5	0	0	31	25	12	11	10	29
MINOR LEAGUE TOTALS			36	30	3.53	92	83	11	1	533	545	266	209	182	356

17. Garrett Atkins, 1b/of

Born: Dec. 12, 1979. **Ht.:** 6-3. **Wt.:** 210. **Bats:** R. **Throws:** R. **School:** UCLA. **Career Transactions:** Selected by Rockies in fifth round of 2000 draft; signed June 22, 2000.

Atkins collected several awards in 2000. He was a third-team All-American and an all-Pacific-10 Conference pick at UCLA during the spring, then shared MVP honors in the short-season Northwest League in his pro debut. Atkins has power potential with a compact approach at the plate and an ability to hit the ball to all fields. Now that he's in a pro program and will be put through a year-round conditioning routine, his body should firm up and he should become more of a home run threat. Atkins handles himself well around the bag, and he's a good enough athlete that he could see time in the outfield to create versatility in light of Todd Helton's presence in Colorado. Atkins figures to skip Asheville and open 2001 at Salem.

Year	Club (League)	Class	AVG	G	AB	R	H	2B	3B	HR	RBI	BB	SO	SB
2000	Portland (NWL)	A	.303	69	251	34	76	12	0	7	47	45	48	2
MINOR LEAGUE TOTALS			.303	69	251	34	76	12	0	7	47	45	48	2

18. Brad Hawpe, of

Born: June 22, 1979. **Ht.:** 6-2. **Wt.:** 200. **Bats:** L. **Throws:** L. **School:** Louisiana State University. **Career Transactions:** Selected by Rockies in 11th round of 2000 draft; signed June 21, 2000.

Hawpe batted .362 with an NCAA Division I record-tying 36 doubles for Louisiana State's College World Series championship team last spring. He was a second-team All-America first baseman, relegating Garrett Atkins to the third team. Hawpe made such a good impression in his pro debut that Portland manager Billy White actually mentioned him in the same breath as Todd Helton among hitters White has seen come through the organization. Hawpe has a beautiful lefthanded swing with line-drive power, and he concentrates on hitting the ball to left field. As he gets stronger and develops a better understanding of how pitchers work him, there's every reason to expect he'll lift the ball more and turn some of his doubles into homers. He also showed that he's capable of playing the outfield as a pro. Like Atkins, he'll probably bypass Asheville and head straight to Salem this year.

Year	Club (League)	Class	AVG	G	AB	R	H	2B	3B	HR	RBI	BB	SO	SB
2000	Portland (NWL)	A	.288	62	205	38	59	19	2	7	29	40	51	2
MINOR LEAGUE TOTALS			.288	62	205	38	59	19	2	7	29	40	51	2

19. Justin Lincoln, 3b

Born: April 4, 1979. **Ht.:** 6-2. **Wt.:** 200. **Bats:** R. **Throws:** R. **School:** Manatee (Fla.) JC. **Career Transactions:** Selected by Rockies in eighth round of 1998 draft; signed May 31, 1999.

The Rockies had hoped to sign Lincoln immediately, but a lengthy negotiation turned him into a draft-and-follow and he didn't make his pro debut until 1999. A member of a Florida state championship team at Sarasota High, he's expected to make the conversion from shortstop to third baseman this spring after leading the organization with 39 errors in 2000. He definitely has the arm strength to play on the hot corner, and he has shown glimpses of the power he'll need to stick there. Lincoln will have to develop better plate discipline and make more contact to become a true threat, however. He'll probably move up to Salem in 2001.

Year	Club (League)	Class	AVG	G	AB	R	H	2B	3B	HR	RBI	BB	SO	SB
1999	Portland (NWL)	A	.241	68	253	36	61	14	2	6	44	28	102	6
2000	Asheville (SAL)	A	.235	126	451	58	106	22	0	17	60	35	161	18
MINOR LEAGUE TOTALS			.237	194	704	94	167	36	2	23	104	63	263	24

20. Esteban Montero, ss

Born: April 16, 1983. **Ht.:** 5-11. **Wt.:** 170. **Bats:** R. **Throws:** R. **Career Transactions:** Signed out of Dominican Republic by Rockies, March 10, 2000.

Montero caught the organization's attention in a hurry. He's an exciting middle infielder with a strong arm, soft hands, quick feet and an aggressive approach to the game. He does need to play under control more after making 26 errors in 47 games at shortstop, but that should come with maturity. He has a natural tendency to try and make the impossible play, which led to several of his miscues. He hit for average with gap power in his pro debut, and contributed more than his share of stolen bases and walks. Montero will need to make more contact, however, if he's going to hit at the top of a lineup. As he benefits from the conditioning and diet programs in the Rockies organization, he should get stronger and drive the ball more. Portland is his likely destination this season.

Year	Club (League)	Class	AVG	G	AB	R	H	2B	3B	HR	RBI	BB	SO	SB
2000	Rockies (AZL)	R	.314	49	175	41	55	12	4	0	28	29	49	9
MINOR LEAGUE TOTALS			.314	49	175	41	55	12	4	0	28	29	49	9

21. Chuck Crowder, lhp

Born: Sept. 30, 1976. **Ht.:** 6-2. **Wt.:** 200. **Bats:** L. **Throws:** L. **School:** Georgia Tech. **Career Transactions:** Selected by Rockies in fourth round of 1999 draft; signed July 29, 1999.

Crowder was drafted in the third round out of high school by the Orioles in 1995, and again in the eighth round as a Georgia Tech junior by the Pirates in 1998, before finally signing as a fourth-rounder in 1999. He might have been drafted higher if not for arm problems while in college. He's healthy now and came on strong in 2000, his first full pro season. He led the Carolina League in innings while ranking third in victories and strikeouts. He set a Salem franchise record with 16 strikeouts in one game. Crowder has three quality pitches: a low-90s fastball, a curveball and a changeup. He has fairly good command of his fastball, though he sometimes fights himself to keep his pitches down in the strike zone. Crowder should be part of an all-prospect rotation in Carolina this year. Because he ranks down the list of Colorado's pitching prospects, he could wind up in the bullpen when he reaches the majors.

Year	Club (League)	Class	W	L	ERA	G	GS	CG	SV	IP	H	R	ER	BB	SO
1999	Portland (NWL)	A	2	1	4.33	6	6	0	0	27	24	14	13	16	39
2000	Salem (Car)	A	14	9	3.52	28	28	0	0	168	124	78	66	86	154
MINOR LEAGUE TOTALS			16	10	3.63	34	34	0	0	195	148	92	79	102	193

22. Jeff Winchester, c

Born: Jan. 21, 1980. **Ht.:** 6-0. **Wt.:** 205. **Bats:** R. **Throws:** R. **School:** Archbishop Rummel HS, Metairie, La. **Career Transactions:** Selected by Rockies in first round (40th overall) of 1998 draft; signed June 5, 1998.

After the Rockies lost Walt Weiss as a free agent, they selected Winchester with the supplemental first-round pick they received as compensation. Though he played in the South Atlantic League all-star game in 1999, Winchester was questioning his decision to play pro ball after his first full pro season. He repeated at Asheville last year, was an all-star again, and enjoyed the type of success that has him looking forward to now continuing a baseball career. He's the best catching prospect in the system. He has a legitimate power bat and a strong arm, but he still has work to do. He needs better plate discipline and faces the challenge of refining his skills as a receiver. After two years in the Sally League, he's ready for high Class A.

Year	Club (League)	Class	AVG	G	AB	R	H	2B	3B	HR	RBI	BB	SO	SB
1998	Rockies (AZL)	R	.208	43	125	22	26	8	0	3	16	22	46	2
1999	Asheville (SAL)	A	.232	86	310	45	72	18	1	18	48	27	92	0
2000	Asheville (SAL)	A	.262	110	397	62	104	29	0	17	73	31	109	9
MINOR LEAGUE TOTALS			.243	239	832	129	202	55	1	38	137	80	247	11

23. Josh Bard, c

Born: March 30, 1978. **Ht.:** 6-3. **Wt.:** 205. **Bats:** B. **Throws:** R. **School:** Texas Tech. **Career Transactions:** Selected by Rockies in third round of 1999 draft; signed Aug. 12, 1999.

Bard was a local Denver star at Cherry Creek High, leading his team to consecutive Colorado state titles and a 45-1 overall record in games he started. He teamed with Jason Jennings on the U.S. team that won a bronze medal at the 1996 World Junior Championship, where Bard hit a team-high .462. His brother Mike is an assistant coach at the University of Kansas. Josh has strong leadership qualities and is a polished defensive catcher who could handle the chores behind the plate in the big leagues now. The question will be how much he hits, though he fared well in his pro debut in high Class A last year. He makes contact, but he has a bit of a loop in his stroke and didn't produce much power or many walks. He has the size that leads to expectations of pop, which will be the key for him to get a chance to play every day in the big leagues. This year, Bard will be the regular catcher on a Carolina team loaded with pitching prospects.

Year	Club (League)	Class	AVG	G	AB	R	H	2B	3B	HR	RBI	BB	SO	SB
2000	Salem (Car)	A	.285	93	309	40	88	17	0	2	25	32	33	3
	Colo. Spr. (PCL)	AAA	.235	4	17	0	4	0	0	0	1	0	2	0
MINOR LEAGUE TOTALS			.282	97	326	40	92	17	0	2	26	32	35	3

24. Cam Esslinger, rhp

Born: Dec. 28, 1976. **Ht.:** 6-0. **Wt.:** 180. **Bats:** R. **Throws:** R. **School:** Seton Hall University. **Career Transactions:** Selected by Rockies in 16th round of 1999 draft; signed June 9, 1999.

Esslinger was a starter in college and in his pro debut at Portland in 1999. Last year, however, he was converted into a reliever, and two months into the season emerged as a legitimate closer candidate. He led the system with 24 saves despite earning just three in the first two months of the season. Esslinger was more aggressive coming out of the bullpen, going after hitters and throwing strikes. He has a power fastball that's consistently in the mid-90s, plus a back-door slider. He struggled with offspeed stuff, which is why the the Rockies decided to work him in relief. Now it's a matter of just letting him pitch more and get acclimated to the closer's role.

Year	Club (League)	Class	W	L	ERA	G	GS	CG	SV	IP	H	R	ER	BB	SO
1999	Portland (NWL)	A	6	3	3.83	14	14	0	0	80	76	37	34	35	68
2000	Asheville (SAL)	A	4	2	3.06	47	2	0	24	65	55	23	22	23	84
MINOR LEAGUE TOTALS			10	5	3.48	61	16	0	24	145	131	60	56	58	152

25. Tim Christman, lhp

Born: March 31, 1975. **Ht.:** 6-0. **Wt.:** 195. **Bats:** L. **Throws:** L. **School:** Siena College. **Career Transactions:** Selected by Rockies in 11th round of 1996 draft; signed June 13, 1996.

Christman was on the verge of making the jump from Class A to the big leagues last spring. But after eight Double-A appearances he had surgery for a torn labrum in his shoulder, his second major operation in three years. He missed the 1998 season following reconstructive elbow surgery. Now it's a question of Christman bouncing back and proving he's healthy. He's not overpowering, but he has mastered the command of his fastball. His out pitch is a big-breaking curveball. Toss in a funky delivery that gives him deception and he can be particularly tough on lefthanders. Christman has averaged more than a strikeout an inning as a pro and hasn't allowed a homer since 1998. If he's 100 percent in 2001, he could surface in Colorado at some point.

Year	Club (League)	Class	W	L	ERA	G	GS	CG	SV	IP	H	R	ER	BB	SO
1996	Portland (NWL)	A	1	2	4.28	21	0	0	2	40	30	23	19	23	56
1997	Asheville (SAL)	A	7	3	3.41	29	0	0	3	63	55	32	24	18	87
1998						Did Not Play—Injured									
1999	Salem (Car)	A	1	2	2.42	38	0	0	2	48	38	18	13	12	64
2000	Carolina (SL)	AA	0	0	2.53	8	0	0	0	10	6	3	3	7	13
MINOR LEAGUE TOTALS			9	7	3.27	96	0	0	7	162	129	76	59	60	220

26. Brent Butler, 2b

Born: Feb. 11, 1978. **Ht.:** 6-0. **Wt.:** 180. **Bats:** R. **Throws:** R. **School:** Scotland County HS, Laurinburg, N.C. **Career Transactions:** Selected by Cardinals in third round of 1996 draft; signed June 9, 1996 . . . Traded by Cardinals with RHP Manny Aybar, RHP Jose Jimenez and RHP Rick Croushore to Rockies for RHP Darryl Kile, RHP Dave Veres and RHP Luther Hackman, Nov. 16, 1999.

Butler came to the Rockies after the 1999 season as part of a seven-player trade that also brought closer Jose Jimenez to Colorado. Butler originally was signed as a shortstop and has been tried at all the infield positions except first base. He settled in at second base at Colorado Springs in 2000, though he also made 25 starts at shortstop. There's nothing about Butler that stands out physically, but he has a good feel for the game and doesn't make mistakes. He makes contact, hits for average and can provide an occasional double or walk. He likely will wind up as a utility player in the big leagues, but if he develops more upper-body strength he could win a full-time job at second base. He figures to return to Colorado Springs to open 2001 and share the middle-infield chores with Elvis Pena.

Year	Club (League)	Class	AVG	G	AB	R	H	2B	3B	HR	RBI	BB	SO	SB
1996	Johnson City (Appy)	R	.343	62	248	45	85	21	1	8	50	25	29	8
1997	Peoria (Mid)	A	.306	129	480	81	147	37	2	15	71	63	69	6
1998	Prince William (Car)	A	.286	126	475	63	136	27	2	11	76	39	74	3
1999	Arkansas (TL)	AA	.269	139	528	68	142	21	1	13	54	26	47	0
2000	Colo. Spr. (PCL)	AAA	.292	122	438	73	128	35	1	8	54	44	46	1
MINOR LEAGUE TOTALS			.294	578	2169	330	638	141	7	55	305	197	265	18

27. Ryan Kibler, rhp

Born: Sept. 17, 1980. **Ht.:** 6-2. **Wt.:** 185. **Bats:** R. **Throws:** R. **School:** King HS, Tampa. **Career Transactions:** Selected by Rockies in second round of 1999 draft; signed June 17, 1999.

Kibler was part of an impressive rotation at Asheville last year in which all five starters threw 90 mph or harder. He has a lively fastball with sinking action that's considered vital for success at Coors Field. An excellent competitor, he has confidence in a changeup that's a solid No. 2 pitch. More than anything, Kibler needs to physically mature and get stronger so he can handle the demands of starting every fifth day. He also needs to develop an effective breaking pitch. Kibler was jumped from Rookie ball to full-season Class A in 2000, and because of a growing pitching depth in the system he could return to Asheville so he can maintain steady work.

Year	Club (League)	Class	W	L	ERA	G	GS	CG	SV	IP	H	R	ER	BB	SO
1999	Rockies (AZL)	R	6	2	2.55	14	14	2	0	81	77	35	23	14	55
	Portland (NWL)	A	0	0	21.60	1	1	0	0	3	8	8	8	4	4
2000	Asheville (SAL)	A	10	14	4.41	26	26	0	0	155	173	107	76	67	110
MINOR LEAGUE TOTALS			16	16	4.02	41	41	2	0	240	258	150	107	85	169

28. Enemencio Pacheco, rhp

Born: March 30, 1979. **Ht.:** 6-0. **Wt.:** 160. **Bats:** R. **Throws:** R. **Career Transactions:** Signed out of Dominican Republic by Rockies, Jan. 15, 1997.

A lanky righthander with whiplike arm action and a lively fastball, Pacheco draws comparisons to a young Pedro Martinez. Then again, every short Dominican righty with good stuff is compared to Martinez these days. Pacheco struggled at Asheville in 1999 and was sent back to the Northwest League, where he finished eighth in ERA. He was ready for the Asheville challenge in 2000, however, and will make the move to Salem for 2001. Along with his fastball, Pacheco has a hard slider that ties up lefthanders. He needs to build upper-body strength, and if he wants to remain a starter he'll have to come up with a changeup.

With the resiliency his arm has shown, there's a growing sentiment that the bullpen could be his future, regardless.

Year	Club (League)	Class	W	L	ERA	G	GS	CG	SV	IP	H	R	ER	BB	SO
1997	Rockies (DSL)	R	1	6	5.26	11	10	1	0	51	70	49	30	22	39
1998	Rockies (AZL)	R	5	0	3.99	12	11	0	0	59	51	31	26	17	59
	Asheville (SAL)	A	0	0	6.75	2	0	0	0	4	5	5	3	1	2
1999	Asheville (SAL)	A	3	9	5.29	15	15	1	0	85	98	60	50	29	59
	Portland (NWL)	A	4	3	3.95	12	12	1	0	73	73	43	32	21	44
2000	Asheville (SAL)	A	8	10	3.69	21	21	0	0	117	129	67	48	35	79
MINOR LEAGUE TOTALS			21	28	4.37	73	69	3	0	389	426	255	189	125	282

29. Julio DePaula, rhp

Born: July 27, 1979. **Ht.:** 6-1. **Wt.:** 160. **Bats:** R. **Throws:** R. **Career Transactions:** Signed out of Dominican Republic by Rockies, Jan. 13, 1997.

DePaula has the makings of a dominating pitcher, but whether it will be as a starter or reliever remains to be seen. After finishing fourth in the Northwest League in strikeouts in 1999, he finished second in the South Atlantic League in the same category last season. Despite his lackluster record, there were glimpses of his ability to overpower in 2000, including a no-hitter in which he hit the first batter and retired the next 27. He can reach the mid-90s with his fastball and maintain his velocity into the late innings. He's an innings eater with strain-free mechanics and an exceptional work ethic. If DePaula is going to remain a starter as he moves up the ladder, he'll need to improve his breaking ball and changeup.

Year	Club (League)	Class	W	L	ERA	G	GS	CG	SV	IP	H	R	ER	BB	SO
1997	Rockies (DSL)	R	3	6	4.75	15	11	1	0	66	77	46	35	28	59
1998	Rockies (AZL)	R	5	5	3.81	17	9	0	2	54	54	30	23	18	62
1999	Portland (NWL)	A	6	6	6.01	16	16	0	0	85	97	67	57	43	77
2000	Asheville (SAL)	A	8	13	4.70	28	27	1	0	155	151	90	81	62	187
MINOR LEAGUE TOTALS			22	30	4.89	76	63	2	2	361	379	233	196	151	385

30. Jody Gerut, of

Born: Sept. 18, 1977. **Ht.:** 6-0. **Wt.:** 190. **Bats:** L. **Throws:** L. **School:** Stanford University. **Career Transactions:** Selected by Rockies in second round of 1998 draft; signed Aug. 8, 1998.

In addition to getting Jeff Winchester with a 1998 sandwich pick after they lost free agent Walt Weiss, the Rockies also got a second-rounder from the Braves, which they spent on Gerut. He spent that summer holding out but since has moved up quickly. He can play all three outfield positions and projects as a fourth outfielder in the big leagues. Gerut doesn't have the speed needed for a center fielder at Coors Field, and so far hasn't shown the power expected from a corner outfielder. He is, however, a fundamentally sound player with a short, quick stroke. As he gets stronger he could surprise with power, learning to lift the line drives in the gaps. He'll spend 2001 in Triple-A.

Year	Club (League)	Class	AVG	G	AB	R	H	2B	3B	HR	RBI	BB	SO	SB
1999	Salem (Car)	A	.289	133	499	80	144	33	11	11	63	61	65	25
2000	Carolina (SL)	AA	.285	109	362	48	103	32	3	3	57	76	54	18
MINOR LEAGUE TOTALS			.287	242	861	128	247	65	14	14	120	137	119	43

Detroit
Tigers

TOP 30 PROSPECTS

1. Brandon Inge, c
2. Ramon Santiago, ss
3. Eric Munson, 1b
4. Matt Wheatland, rhp
5. Nate Cornejo, rhp
6. Shane Loux, rhp
7. Andres Torres, of
8. Omar Infante, ss
9. Andy VanHekken, lhp
10. Exavier Logan, of/ss
11. Shane Heams, rhp
12. Kris Keller, rhp
13. Tommy Marx, lhp
14. Cody Ross, of
15. Mike Maroth, lhp
16. Adam Bernero, rhp
17. Neil Jenkins, 3b
18. Matt Miller, lhp
19. Fernando Rodney, rhp
20. Adam Pettyjohn, lhp
21. Miles Durham, of
22. Chad Petty, lhp
23. Calvin Chipperfield, rhp
24. Jermaine Clark, 2b
25. Chris Wakeland, of
26. Brant Ust, 3b
27. Javier Cardona, c
28. Luis Pineda, rhp
29. Mark Woodyard, rhp
30. Richard Gomez, of

By Pat Caputo

With a new philosophy in the big leagues under manager Phil Garner and a push to contend instead of rebuild, the changes are being felt throughout the organization.

The Tigers have concentrated their top minor league prospects at two levels in the past. They put their younger prospects at low Class A West Michigan and their more advanced prospects at Double-A Jacksonville. The better prospects often skipped high Class A Lakeland and Triple-A Toledo on their way to the major leagues.

The records of the clubs reflected this, especially in 2000. Jacksonville and West Michigan went a combined 157-123, while Toledo and Lakeland were 107-174.

That should change in 2001. For the first time in eons, the organization will have a solid nucleus of young prospects in Triple-A, particularly on the pitching staff. Catcher Brandon Inge and pitchers Shane Heams, Kris Keller, Shane Loux, Mike Maroth, Matt Miller and Adam Pettyjohn all figure to start the season at Toledo. Bruce Fields, who had managed West Michigan since 1997, will jump to Triple-A to oversee the talent.

The new approach results partly from Garner, who is not as likely to use young prospects as previous managers Larry Parrish and Buddy Bell. Garner hardly used catcher Javier Cardona and first baseman Eric Munson during their stints in the major leagues in 2000.

From a development standpoint, the upside is that it gives Detroit's prospects more time in the minor leagues. They won't be rushed as often as before.

Catching is the position of greatest strength in the organization. Inge, Cardona and Michael Rivera provide a surplus behind newly acquired Mitch Meluskey.

There's also pitching depth, shown by the number of prospects who will be at Triple-A. What Detroit continues to lack is a potential breakout star. Most of the pitching prospects project as No. 3 or No. 4 starters or situational relievers. Likewise, no position players can be categorized as potential superstars.

Detroit hasn't signed and developed an everyday middle infielder since Alan Trammell and Lou Whitaker came up together during the late 1970s. That could change. Shortstops Ramon Santiago and Omar Infante have good tools and are coming off solid seasons, especially defensively, at the Class A level.

OrganizationOverview

General manager: Randy Smith. **Farm director:** Steve Lubratich. **Scouting director:** Greg Smith.

2000 PERFORMANCE

Class	Team	League	W	L	Pct.	Finish*	Manager(s)
Majors	Detroit	American	79	83	.488	9th (14)	Phil Garner
Triple-A	Toledo Mud Hens	International	55	86	.390	12th (14)	D. Anderson/G. Ezell
Double-A	#Jacksonville Suns	Southern	69	71	.493	5th (10)	Gene Roof
High A	Lakeland Tigers	Florida State	52	88	.371	14th (14)	Skeeter Barnes
Low A	West Mich. Whitecaps	Midwest	88	52	.629	1st (14)	Bruce Fields
Short-season	Oneonta Tigers	New York-Penn	35	41	.461	10th (14)	Gary Green
Rookie	GCL Tigers	Gulf Coast	34	26	.567	t-5th (13)	Kevin Bradshaw
OVERALL 2000 MINOR LEAGUE RECORD			333	364	.478	23rd (30)	

*Finish in overall standings (No. of teams in league). #Affiliate will be in Erie (Eastern) in 2001.

ORGANIZATION LEADERS

BATTING
*AVG	Billy McMillon, Toledo	.345
R	Andres Torres, Lakeland/Jacksonville	85
H	**Chris Wakeland**, Toledo	133
TB	**Chris Wakeland**, Toledo	246
2B	Stoney Briggs, Jacksonville	39
3B	Andres Torres, Lakeland/Jacksonville	11
HR	**Chris Wakeland**, Toledo	28
RBI	Alejandro Freire, Jacksonville	77
BB	Corey Richardson, West Michigan	94
SO	Neil Jenkins, West Michigan	151
SB	Andres Torres, Lakeland/Jacksonville	67

PITCHING
W	Andy Van Hekken, West Michigan	16
L	Mike Oquist, Toledo	15
#ERA	**Calvin Chipperfield**, West Michigan	2.13
G	Kris Keller, Jacksonville	62
	Greg Watson, West Michigan	62
CG	Three tied at	3
SV	Greg Watson, West Michigan	30
IP	Nate Cornejo, Lakeland/Jacksonville	169
BB	Doug Walls, Toledo/Jacksonville	76
SO	**Calvin Chipperfield**, West Michigan	151

*Minimum 250 at-bats. #Minimum 75 innings.

Wakeland   **Chipperfield**

TOP PROSPECTS OF THE DECADE
1991	Rico Brogna, 1b
1992	Greg Gohr, rhp
1993	Greg Gohr, rhp
1994	Justin Thompson, lhp
1995	Tony Clark, 1b
1996	Mike Drumright, rhp
1997	Mike Drumright, rhp
1998	Juan Encarnacion, of
1999	Gabe Kapler, of
2000	Eric Munson, 1b/c

TOP DRAFT PICKS OF THE DECADE
1991	Jason Thompson, lhp
1992	Rick Greene, rhp
1993	Matt Brunson, ss
1994	Cade Gaspar, rhp
1995	Mike Drumright, rhp
1996	Seth Greisinger, rhp
1997	Matt Anderson, rhp
1998	Jeff Weaver, rhp
1999	Eric Munson, c/1b
2000	Matt Wheatland, rhp

BEST TOOLS
Best Hitter for Average	Andres Torres
Best Power Hitter	Eric Munson
Fastest Baserunner	Exavier Logan
Best Fastball	Shane Heams
Best Breaking Ball	Calvin Chipperfield
Best Control	Matt Wheatland
Best Defensive Catcher	Brandon Inge
Best Defensive Infielder	Ramon Santiago
Best Infield Arm	Ramon Santiago
Best Defensive Outfielder	Andres Torres
Best Outfield Arm	Cody Ross

PROJECTED 2004 LINEUP
Catcher	Brandon Inge
First Base	Eric Munson
Second Base	Omar Infante
Third Base	Deivi Cruz
Shortstop	Ramon Santiago
Left Field	Bobby Higginson
Center Field	Andres Torres
Right Field	Juan Encarnacion
Designated Hitter	Dean Palmer
No. 1 Starter	Jeff Weaver
No. 2 Starter	Matt Wheatland
No. 3 Starter	Brian Moehler
No. 4 Starter	Nate Cornejo
No. 5 Starter	Shane Loux
Closer	Matt Anderson

ALL-TIME LARGEST BONUSES
Eric Munson, 1999	$3,500,000
Matt Anderson, 1997	2,505,000
Matt Wheatland, 2000	2,150,000
Jeff Weaver, 1998	1,750,000
Seth Greisinger, 1996	1,415,000

DraftAnalysis

2000 Draft

Best Pro Debut: RHP Mike Steele (29) struck out 41 in 27 innings at short-season Oneonta while going 2-1, 2.70.

Best Athlete: OF/SS Exavier Logan (3) is a raw athlete with blazing speed, which is why he's being moved to center field. His hitting ability and his arm strength at short aren't nearly as good.

Best Hitter: OF Miles Durham (5), a pomising hitter who got through just three games in the Rookie-level Gulf Coast League before hamstring problems ended his pro debut last summer. He had similar trouble at Texas Tech.

Best Raw Power: C Forrest Johnson (13), though he didn't get the opportunity to show it last summer. A broken hamate bone in his left wrist has delayed his debut until 2001.

Fastest Runner: Logan can fly through the 60-yard dash in 6.35 seconds. Durham, when he's healthy, wouldn't be far behind him.

Best Defensive Player: 3B Hugh Quattlebaum (25) is a solid if not spectacular defender. He also batted .301 at Oneonta.

Best Fastball: RHP **Matt Wheatland** (1) has a 90-94 mph sinker that draws comparisons to that of Kevin Brown. On the right day, RHP Mark Woodyard (4) has an electric fastball, but his mechanics are far from consistent.

Most Intriguing Background: Wheatland and Rangers catcher Scott Heard, coming out of the powerful Rancho Bernardo High program in San Diego, were the third pair of high school teammates to go in the first round of the same draft.

Closest To The Majors: Wheatland shows a lot of polish for a high school pitcher, but the Tigers have no plans to rush him. They signed few players from major college programs, and those they did sign are not expected to provide any immediate help in the big leagues.

Best Late-Round Pick: Johnson. Detroit has faith in his hitting ability but isn't sure if he'll be a catcher, outfielder or first baseman. OF Ryan Neill (22), an unheralded player out of Oral Roberts who hit .274-5-39 with 16 steals at Oneonta, has more offensive promise than most of the players in this crop.

LARRY GOREN
Wheatland

The One Who Got Away: RHP Ryan Schroyer (16), who throws 92-93 mph and has a tight curveball, became part of college baseball's best recruiting class at Arizona State.

Assessment: The Tigers focused on the middle of the field with this draft, stocking up on catchers, pitchers, shortstops and center fielders. Wheatland and LHP Chad Petty (2) were a nice start, but Detroit didn't pick up much in the way of offense. As noted above, there also isn't much from this draft class that will provide immediate help.

1999 Draft

1B Eric Munson (3) was supposed to make a quick impact after getting a $6.75 million major league contract, but back problems slowed him considerably last year. The Tigers didn't look for many pitchers and didn't find any.   **Grade: C**

1998 Draft

RHP Jeff Weaver (1) reached Detroit in less than a year. RHP Nate Cornejo (1), C Brandon Inge (2), LHP Tommy Marx (3) and OF Andres Torres (4) rank among the system's best prospects.   **Grade: B+**

1997 Draft

RHP Matt Anderson (1) has been a mild disappointment as the No. 1 overall pick, and the Tigers could have stopped drafting after taking RHP Shane Loux (2). Failing to sign LHP Bud Smith (9) and OF Brian Cole (36) as draft-and-follows really hurt.   **Grade: C**

1996 Draft

RHP Seth Greisinger (1) made it to the majors in two years before arm troubles ruined his career. Now RHP Kris Keller (4) and 1B/C Robert Fick (5) may be all Detroit gets out of this draft.   **Grade: C**

Note: Draft analysis prepared by Jim Callis. Numbers in parentheses indicate draft rounds.

. . . Inge is fluid, quick and instinctive behind the plate. He's exceptionally strong for his size and has power.

Brandon Inge c

Born: May 19, 1977.
Ht.: 5-11. **Wt.:** 185.
Bats: B. **Throws:** R.
School: Virginia Commonwealth University.
Career Transactions: Selected by Tigers in second round of 1998 draft; signed June 27, 1998.

Inge was pleased in 1998 when he found out the Tigers had drafted him in the second round. His reaction was mixed moments later when he received another call from the organization, to tell him he was going to catch as a pro. Inge had been a shortstop and closer at Virginia Commonwealth, and he hadn't caught since Little League. He had little problem making the move, however. He played well defensively from the time he put on the catcher's gear. He did struggle at the plate in his first two professional seasons, hitting just .230 and .244 with little power. His breakthrough came in the now-defunct California Fall League in 1999 after he changed his stroke and hit a resounding .407, best in the league. He got off to a fast start in 2000 for Jacksonville, but didn't finish the first half strong and batted .221 at Triple-A Toledo.

Inge is fluid, quick and instinctive behind the plate. Not only does he have a strong and accurate arm, but his feet are also quick and he gets into position to throw swiftly. He has a quick release. He gets into a low crouch and presents the pitcher with an excellent target. Inge's hands are soft and he frames pitches well. He's exceptionally strong for his size and has power. A classic aluminum-bat pull hitter coming out of college, Inge changed his stroke to stay behind the ball and drive it to right field. Many of his 49 extra-base hits last year went up the right-center field gap. He still is capable of pulling offspeed pitches with power. He runs well for the position. Inge needs to make more consistent contact and grasp the strike zone better. The more experienced pitchers he faced in Triple-A just toyed with him. As a former pitcher, Inge is hesitant to get on pitchers much, saying he remembers what it was like on the mound when things aren't going well. His coaches and team officials would like him to be more aggressive in that area, however.

Inge will start the 2001 season at Toledo. Ideally the Tigers would like to keep him there the entire season. That might have been easier to do if the team had not traded Brad Ausmus to the Astros for Mitch Meluskey in December. Meluskey isn't nearly as accomplished defensively as Ausmus and might be better suited as a DH.

Year	Club (League)	Class	AVG	G	AB	R	H	2B	3B	HR	RBI	BB	SO	SB
1998	Jamestown (NY-P)	A	.230	51	191	24	44	10	1	8	29	17	53	8
1999	West Michigan (Mid)	A	.244	100	352	54	86	25	2	9	46	39	87	15
2000	Jacksonville (SL)	AA	.258	78	298	39	77	25	1	6	53	26	73	10
	Toledo (IL)	AAA	.221	55	190	24	42	9	3	5	20	15	51	2
MINOR LEAGUE TOTALS			.242	284	1031	141	249	69	7	28	148	97	264	35

2. Ramon Santiago, ss

Born: Aug. 31, 1981. **Ht.:** 5-11. **Wt.:** 150. **Bats:** B. **Throws:** R. **Career Transactions:** Signed out of Dominican Republic by Tigers, July 29, 1998.

Santiago's 2000 season was cut short late by a torn labrum in his right shoulder. That's the only thing that has slowed him in his career so far. He played for Class A West Michigan at just 18 years old. In his pro debut, he batted a combined .326 for the Rookie-level Gulf Coast League Tigers and short-season Oneonta. Santiago is already a major league-caliber shortstop on defense. He rarely boots a routine play, has plus range and had a plus arm before he got hurt. He's expected to fully recover from the injury. He has above-average speed, though he's more quick than flat-out fast, and he's a smart baserunner. He makes consistent contact at the plate and is extraordinarily poised for his age. Santiago is a little guy who takes a big man's stance at the plate—and then takes a little guy's swing. His swing isn't grooved or refined. He often just flips the bat onto the ball, and he had just 17 extra-base hits in 2000. He has a long way to go as a hitter, and there are questions about his arm because of the injury. Santiago will start 2001 at high Class A Lakeland. He may have to DH to start the season until he regains strength in his shoulder.

Year	Club (League)	Class	AVG	G	AB	R	H	2B	3B	HR	RBI	BB	SO	SB
1999	Tigers (GCL)	R	.321	35	134	25	43	9	2	0	11	9	17	20
	Oneonta (NY-P)	A	.340	12	50	9	17	1	2	1	8	2	12	5
2000	West Michigan (Mid)	A	.272	98	379	69	103	15	1	1	42	34	60	39
	MINOR LEAGUE TOTALS		.290	145	563	103	163	25	5	2	61	45	89	64

3. Eric Munson, 1b

Born: Oct. 3, 1977. **Ht.:** 6-3. **Wt.:** 220. **Bats:** L. **Throws:** R. **School:** University of Southern California. **Career Transactions:** Selected by Tigers in first round (third overall) of 1999 draft; signed June 24, 1999.

An All-America catcher as a sophomore whose junior season was interrupted by injuries, Munson still managed to hit .346-15-41 at Southern California. The Tigers signed him to a major league contract worth $6.75 million, including a $3.5 million bonus, and moved him to first base. He has yet to put up overwhelming stats but has been pitched around as a pro. He was limited during the second half of 2000 because of a back injury sustained when he caught a couple of times in the bullpen. Munson has an exceptionally quick, fluid lefthanded stroke that produces a lot of power. He can pull any fastball and is capable of hitting offspeed pitches if he stays on the ball. He can drive the ball to left-center field with power. Munson is awkward defensively both fielding grounders and receiving throws. He's not a patient hitter and sometimes gets pull-happy. He ended 2000 in a back brace but is expected to be ready for spring training. He missed the Arizona Fall League and will start 2001 at Double-A Erie. The Tigers would like him to develop quickly because they need lefthanded hitters and a first baseman.

Year	Club (League)	Class	AVG	G	AB	R	H	2B	3B	HR	RBI	BB	SO	SB
1999	Lakeland (FSL)	A	.333	2	6	0	2	0	0	0	1	1	1	0
	West Michigan (Mid)	A	.266	67	252	42	67	16	1	14	44	37	47	3
2000	Jacksonville (SL)	AA	.252	98	365	52	92	21	4	15	68	39	96	5
	Detroit (AL)	MAJ	.000	3	5	0	0	0	0	0	1	0	1	0
	MAJOR LEAGUE TOTALS		.000	3	5	0	0	0	0	0	1	0	1	0
	MINOR LEAGUE TOTALS		.258	167	623	94	161	37	5	29	113	77	144	8

4. Matt Wheatland, rhp

Born: Oct. 18, 1981. **Ht.:** 6-5. **Wt.:** 215. **Bats:** R. **Throws:** R. **School:** Rancho Bernardo HS, San Diego. **Career Transactions:** Selected by Tigers in first round (8th overall) of 2000 draft; signed June 5, 2000.

Wheatland started slowly last spring for national power Rancho Bernardo High but closed strong with several good outings in front of Detroit officials, including general manager Randy Smith. He and catcher Scott Heard, who went to the Rangers, became just the third pair of high school teammates to go in the first round of the same draft. Wheatland consistently tops 90 mph with a sinking fastball that has been compared to Kevin Brown's. He has excellent command for a pitcher so young, walking just five batters in 46 pro innings. His breaking ball is an effective pitch and he has the makings of a good changeup. He wasn't as effective in Oneonta as he was in the Gulf Coast League, in part because he developed a mysterious pain in his middle and index fingers while throwing his breaking pitch. The problem cleared up in instructional league but is still a concern. His changeup needs improvement. Wheatland will start 2001 at West Michigan. With his poise and polish, he could advance quickly if the finger problem does not return.

Year	Club (League)	Class	W	L	ERA	G	GS	CG	SV	IP	H	R	ER	BB	SO
2000	Lakeland (GCL)	R	2	1	1.25	5	4	0	0	22	14	4	3	1	21
	Oneonta (NY-P)	A	1	2	5.55	5	5	0	0	24	30	18	15	4	25
MINOR LEAGUE TOTALS			3	3	3.52	10	9	0	0	46	44	22	18	5	26

5. Nate Cornejo, rhp

Born: Sept. 24, 1979. **Ht.:** 6-5. **Wt.:** 200. **Bats:** R. **Throws:** R. **School:** Wellington (Kan.) HS. **Career Transactions:** Selected by Tigers in second round of 1998 draft; signed Aug. 6, 1998.

After having surgery on both knees in high school, Cornejo slid from a projected first-rounder to the second round of the 1998 draft. He has been durable in his two full professional seasons, starting a total of 56 games. Sixteen of those came in 2000 in Double-A at age 20. His father Mardie is a former big league reliever. Cornejo consistently sits between 90-92 mph with sinking action on his fastball. He throws a heavy ball. His slider has late break when it's working. It could be an effective pitch in the major leagues if he develops more consistency with it. He's an excellent athlete who moves exceptionally well for someone his size. Cornejo's changeup needs a lot of work before he reaches the majors. He throws too many pitches about the same speed. His breaking ball often lacks crispness. When he gets his fastball up, it flattens out and he gets hit hard. Cornejo will start 2001 back in Double-A and likely will remain there for the entire season. There's no need to rush him.

Year	Club (League)	Class	W	L	ERA	G	GS	CG	SV	IP	H	R	ER	BB	SO
1998	Tigers (GCL)	R	1	0	1.26	5	0	0	1	14	12	2	2	2	9
1999	West Michigan (Mid)	A	9	11	3.71	28	28	4	0	174	173	87	72	67	125
2000	Lakeland (FSL)	A	5	5	3.04	12	12	1	0	77	67	37	26	31	60
	Jacksonville (SL)	AA	5	7	4.61	16	16	0	0	91	91	52	47	43	60
MINOR LEAGUE TOTALS			20	23	3.70	61	56	5	1	357	343	178	147	143	254

6. Shane Loux, rhp

Born: Aug. 13, 1979. **Ht.:** 6-2. **Wt.:** 205. **Bats:** R. **Throws:** R. **School:** Highland HS, Gilbert, Ariz. **Career Transactions:** Selected by Tigers in second round of 1997 draft; signed June 14, 1997.

Loux turned down a scholarship to Arizona State to sign with the Tigers out of high school and promptly dominated the Gulf Coast League in 1997. During the next two seasons, he struggled with his conditioning and his poise. He started putting it all together in Double-A in 2000. Loux throws hard, usually in the low 90s and sometimes going a bit higher. But it's the movement on his fastball that makes him effective. He also has a good curveball and an excellent feel for pitching. He's a competitive kid who makes a good pitch when he really needs one. He has been durable as a pro and is advanced for a 21-year-old. Loux needs to improve his changeup if he's going to be an effective pitcher in the major leagues. He'd be wise to continue harnessing his emotions on the mound as well. He will start 2001 in Triple-A. It's possible he will reach the major leagues later in the season if he performs well.

Year	Club (League)	Class	W	L	ERA	G	GS	CG	SV	IP	H	R	ER	BB	SO
1997	Tigers (GCL)	R	4	1	0.84	10	9	1	0	43	19	7	4	10	33
1998	West Michigan (Mid)	A	7	13	4.64	28	28	2	0	157	184	96	81	52	88
1999	West Michigan (Mid)	A	1	3	6.27	8	8	0	0	47	55	39	33	16	43
	Lakeland (FSL)	A	6	5	4.05	17	17	0	0	91	92	48	41	47	52
2000	Lakeland (FSL)	A	0	1	1.80	1	1	0	0	5	2	1	1	3	6
	Jacksonville (SL)	AA	12	9	3.82	26	26	2	0	158	150	78	67	55	130
MINOR LEAGUE TOTALS			30	32	4.08	90	89	5	0	501	502	269	227	183	352

7. Andres Torres, of

Born: Jan. 26, 1978. **Ht.:** 5-10. **Wt.:** 175. **Bats:** B. **Throws:** R. **School:** Miami-Dade CC North. **Career Transactions:** Selected by Tigers in fourth round of 1998 draft; signed June 23, 1998.

Raised in Puerto Rico, Torres was still raw when drafted by the Tigers. He didn't hit well his first two seasons but broke through in 2000. Torres has better than average speed, getting from home to first in 4.0 seconds from the right side of the plate. He starts quickly and has developed a good feel for stealing bases. He didn't start switch-hitting until he was in junior college and has made progress from the left side. He has good range as a center fielder and throws adequately. Torres needs to get stronger and drive the ball with more authority. He can be overpowered by a good fastball and isn't selective enough, given the threat he presents on the bases. He runs himself into outs sometimes on batted balls. On defense, he has a tendency to turn the wrong way on fly balls. Juan Encarnacion isn't anything special as a center fielder, so Detroit is looking forward to putting Torres in center and Encarnacion in right in a couple of years.

Year	Club (League)	Class	AVG	G	AB	R	H	2B	3B	HR	RBI	BB	SO	SB
1998	Jamestown (NY-P)	A	.234	48	192	28	45	2	6	1	21	25	50	13
1999	West Michigan (Mid)	A	.236	117	407	72	96	20	5	2	34	92	116	39
2000	Lakeland (FSL)	A	.296	108	398	82	118	11	11	3	33	63	82	65
	Jacksonville (SL)	AA	.148	14	54	3	8	0	0	0	0	5	14	2
MINOR LEAGUE TOTALS			.254	287	1051	185	267	33	22	6	88	185	262	119

8. Omar Infante, ss

Born: Dec. 26, 1981. **Ht.:** 6-0. **Wt.:** 150. **Bats:** R. **Throws:** R. **Career Transactions:** Signed out of Venezuela by Tigers, April 28, 1999.

Because Ramon Santiago was ticketed for West Michigan in 2000, Infante was pushed to Lakeland out of necessity. He held his own despite having just 75 pro at-bats entering the year. Eric Munson's back problems opened a spot for Infante in the Arizona Fall League, where he batted .218 as the youngest player in league history. An adroit fielder, Infante has better range than his speed would dictate. He shows a good, accurate arm and makes the backhanded play in the hole particularly well. He doesn't mess up routine plays and has good instincts for the game. The best thing about his offensive game is that he puts the ball in play, but he is much more advanced defensively than he is offensively. He needs to get stronger because he doesn't drive the ball much. He swings at too many bad pitches. For a shortstop, he has average speed. Infante may return to Lakeland or start 2001 in Double-A, again depending on where Santiago goes. When both of them are ready for Detroit, Infante probably faces a move to second base.

Year	Club (League)	Class	AVG	G	AB	R	H	2B	3B	HR	RBI	BB	SO	SB
1999	Tigers (GCL)	R	.268	25	97	11	26	4	0	0	7	4	11	4
2000	Lakeland (FSL)	A	.274	79	259	35	71	11	0	2	24	20	29	11
	West Michigan (Mid)	A	.229	12	48	7	11	0	0	0	5	5	7	1
MINOR LEAGUE TOTALS			.267	116	404	53	108	15	0	2	36	29	47	16

9. Andy VanHekken, lhp

Born: July 31, 1979. **Ht.:** 6-3. **Wt.:** 175. **Bats:** R. **Throws:** L. **School:** Holland (Mich.) HS. **Career Transactions:** Selected by Mariners in third round of 1998 draft; signed June 26, 1998 . . . Traded by Mariners to Tigers, June 26, 1999, completing trade in which Tigers sent OF Brian Hunter to Mariners for two players to be named (April 21, 1999); Tigers acquired OF Jerry Amador to complete trade (Aug. 26, 1999).

The Mariners surely regret the trade that sent VanHekken to Detroit for speedster Brian Hunter in 1999. VanHekken, a Michigan high school product, led the Midwest League in wins and ranked second in ERA in 2000. He is a good athlete with an exceptional feel for pitching. He sets up his fastball with his other pitches, which include a curveball with nice bite and a change-up. He's poised on the mound and always seems to be in control. He works the outer half of the plate well, often expanding the strike zone on the hitter. He allowed just three homers in 2000. VanHekken's fastball doesn't register well on the radar gun, usually around 87 mph without exceptional movement, and he may not have enough velocity to pitch in the strike zone at the major league level. He needs to develop more consistency with his offspeed pitches and must pitch inside more, especially against righthanders. VanHekken is a proto-type crafty lefthander. He'll start 2001 at Lakeland and could reach Erie by season's end.

Year	Club (League)	Class	W	L	ERA	G	GS	CG	SV	IP	H	R	ER	BB	SO
1998	Mariners (AZL)	R	6	3	4.43	11	8	0	0	41	34	23	20	18	55
1999	Oneonta (NY-P)	A	4	2	2.15	11	10	0	0	50	44	17	12	16	50
2000	West Michigan (Mid)	A	16	6	2.45	26	25	3	1	158	139	48	43	37	126
MINOR LEAGUE TOTALS			26	11	2.71	48	43	3	1	249	217	88	75	71	231

10. Exavier Logan, of/ss

RICK BATTLE

Born: Nov. 28, 1979. **Ht.:** 6-2. **Wt.:** 180. **Bats:** R. **Throws:** R. **School:** Copiah-Lincoln (Miss.) CC. **Career Transactions:** Selected by Tigers in third round of 2000 draft; signed July 8, 2000.

Logan was drafted as a shortstop and played there in the Gulf Coast League, where he used his exceptional speed to steal 20 bases in 23 attempts. But he was selected with the idea of converting him to center field, where he excelled in instructional league. The athletic Logan has been clocked in less than 6.4 seconds in the 60-yard dash. Team officials drool when they see Logan shagging fly balls because he covers ground so effortlessly. He also offers arm strength. He is about as raw as they come, however, and miles away from being refined enough to be a major leaguer. He has no previous outfield experience. Offensively, he's all about speed. He has little power, though he has a body that could allow him to develop some in time. If Logan continues to progress during spring training, he'll open the 2001 season at West Michigan. If not, he'll head to extended spring until the short-season New York-Penn League schedule starts in June.

Year	Club (League)	Class	AVG	G	AB	R	H	2B	3B	HR	RBI	BB	SO	SB
2000	Tigers (GCL)	R	.279	43	136	29	38	2	2	0	14	31	36	20
	Lakeland (FSL)	A	.333	11	42	4	14	1	0	0	3	2	13	2
MINOR LEAGUE TOTALS			.292	54	178	33	52	3	2	0	17	33	49	22

11. Shane Heams, rhp

Born: Sept. 29, 1975. **Ht.:** 6-1. **Wt.:** 175. **Bats:** R. **Throws:** R. **School:** Parkland (Ill.) JC. **Career Transactions:** Selected by Mariners in 41st round of 1994 draft; signed May 23, 1995 . . . Voluntarily retired, March 24, 1998 . . . Released by Mariners, April 9, 1998 . . . Signed by Tigers, April 23, 1998.

After little success as a draft-and-follow sign of the Mariners, Heams switched from being an outfielder to pitching, then decided to leave the game near the end of spring training in 1998. Tigers scout Clyde Weir remembered him from Lambertville High in western Michigan and signed him. After solid years in Jamestown and West Michigan, Heams finally got attention at Jacksonville before joining the U.S. Olympic team last year. He has been used strictly in relief and primarily as a set-up man. He hits 97 mph at times, and his fastball has good sink. His slider is either excellent or awful, and it often dictates his effectiveness on a given night. Heams sometimes lets his emotions overwhelm him on the mound, though there's hope his Olympic experience will help him. He'll start this season in Triple-A.

Year	Club (League)	Class	AVG	G	AB	R	H	2B	3B	HR	RBI	BB	SO	SB
1995	Everett (NWL)	A	.197	27	61	5	12	4	0	1	4	3	28	2
MINOR LEAGUE TOTALS			.197	27	61	5	12	4	0	1	4	3	28	2

Year	Club (League)	Class	W	L	ERA	G	GS	CG	SV	IP	H	R	ER	BB	SO
1996	Mariners (AZL)	R	1	1	2.93	9	0	0	2	15	10	7	5	6	12
1997	Mariners (AZL)	R	6	2	1.70	21	0	0	2	37	30	20	7	22	42
1998	Jamestown (NY-P)	A	2	2	3.99	24	0	0	6	47	43	27	21	16	73
1999	West Michigan (Mid)	A	5	4	2.35	51	0	0	10	69	41	26	18	39	101
2000	Jacksonville (SL)	AA	6	2	2.59	39	0	0	5	56	35	17	16	34	67
	Toledo (IL)	AAA	0	0	11.17	6	0	0	0	10	13	12	12	12	7
MINOR LEAGUE TOTALS			20	11	3.04	150	0	0	25	234	172	109	79	129	302

12. Kris Keller, rhp

Born: March 1, 1978. **Ht.:** 6-2. **Wt.:** 225. **Bats:** R. **Throws:** R. **School:** Fletcher HS, Neptune Beach, Fla. **Career Transactions:** Selected by Tigers in fourth round of 1996 draft; signed June 29, 1996.

Until last season, Keller was an enigma. He can reach as high as 98 mph on the radar gun and is consistently in the mid-90s, but his coaches and club officials often complained about his lack of maturity. After three years in short-season leagues, he started to emerge at

West Michigan in 1999 and broke through last season at Jacksonville. Keller's breaking ball has improved but needs to get better before he reaches the major leagues. He also needs to develop more consistent command. Keller is the type of pitcher who will strike out the side two innings in a row and get shelled in the third. He's at his best when he keeps the ball down in the zone. He'll be at Toledo to begin the 2001 season.

Year	Club (League)	Class	W	L	ERA	G	GS	CG	SV	IP	H	R	ER	BB	SO
1996	Tigers (GCL)	R	1	1	2.38	8	6	0	0	34	23	12	9	21	23
1997	Jamestown (NY-P)	A	0	2	8.67	16	0	0	0	27	37	33	26	20	18
1998	Jamestown (NY-P)	A	1	3	3.27	27	0	0	8	33	29	12	12	16	41
1999	West Michigan (Mid)	A	5	3	2.92	49	0	0	8	77	63	28	25	36	87
2000	Jacksonville (SL)	AA	2	3	2.91	62	0	0	26	68	58	24	22	44	60
MINOR LEAGUE TOTALS			9	12	3.54	162	6	0	42	239	210	109	94	137	229

13. Tommy Marx, lhp

Born: Sept. 5, 1979. **Ht.:** 6-7. **Wt.:** 220. **Bats:** R. **Throws:** L. **School:** Brother Rice HS, Bloomfield Hills, Mich. **Career Transactions:** Selected by Tigers in third round of 1998 draft; signed June 9, 1998.

Marx was on the verge of dominating the Midwest League last season when he was shut down because of a shoulder ailment. It's not expected to be a long-term problem. At 6-foot-7, Marx cuts an imposing figure on the mound. His fastball consistently tops 90 mph and he has good rotation on his breaking ball. Marx was raw when Detroit drafted him in the second round in 1998, signing him away from the University of Miami. There are times when the rough edges still show, but he has come a long way in a short period of time. His mechanics are solid for a pitcher his size. Marx is a hard worker who's just starting to learn how to compete. He may return to West Michigan to start 2001.

Year	Club (League)	Class	W	L	ERA	G	GS	CG	SV	IP	H	R	ER	BB	SO
1998	Tigers (GCL)	R	1	3	4.29	12	12	0	0	42	33	27	20	39	38
1999	Tigers (GCL)	R	3	2	3.43	8	8	0	0	42	35	24	16	32	39
	Oneonta (NY-P)	A	2	1	3.22	6	4	0	0	22	20	14	8	13	19
2000	West Michigan (Mid)	A	7	6	2.74	18	18	1	0	99	74	35	30	51	83
MINOR LEAGUE TOTALS			13	12	3.25	44	42	1	0	205	162	100	74	135	179

14. Cody Ross, of

Born: Dec. 23, 1980. **Ht.:** 5-11. **Wt.:** 180. **Bats:** R. **Throws:** L. **School:** Carlsbad (N.M.) HS. **Career Transactions:** Selected by Tigers in fourth round of 1999 draft; signed June 12, 1999.

Ross isn't particularly big or fast, but he's a scrappy player with a strong arm and power potential. Playing right field last season, Ross was consistent with his effort and production. He hit seven home runs playing in one of the bigger home parks in the Midwest League, and had nine triples. He's a rare player who bats righthanded and throws lefthanded. He has a good, compact stroke and a clue about the strike zone. Ross pitched with great effectiveness in high school and some Tigers scouts still believe his future would be brighter on the mound. Ross has thrown on the side for minor league pitching coaches but hasn't shown the same potential as a pitcher he did before he was drafted. He's ticketed for Lakeland in 2001.

Year	Club (League)	Class	AVG	G	AB	R	H	2B	3B	HR	RBI	BB	SO	SB
1999	Tigers (GCL)	R	.218	42	142	19	31	8	3	4	18	16	28	3
2000	West Michigan (Mid)	A	.267	122	434	71	116	17	9	7	68	55	83	11
MINOR LEAGUE TOTALS			.255	164	576	90	147	25	12	11	86	71	111	14

15. Mike Maroth, lhp

Born: Aug. 17, 1977. **Ht.:** 6-0. **Wt.:** 180. **Bats:** L. **Throws:** L. **School:** University of Central Florida. **Career Transactions:** Selected by Red Sox in third round of 1998 draft; signed July 5, 1998 . . . Traded by Red Sox to Tigers for RHP Bryce Florie, July 31, 1999.

On the verge of being demoted to Lakeland after going 0-9, 6.35 to start the 2000 season, Maroth recovered to have a remarkably good performance at Jacksonville. He accented his strong finish by pitching well in the Arizona Fall League. Maroth has a good fastball, the best among Detroit's advanced lefthanded pitching prospects, often hitting 90 mph. He likes to work the outer half of the plate, so he hasn't pitched inside effectively to righthanders. As a result, he worked on a cut fastball in Arizona. Maroth had minor arm problems early last year, but mostly it just seemed he was in some sort of malaise. As his attitude improved, so did his results. He'll work out of Toledo's rotation to begin this season.

Year	Club (League)	Class	W	L	ERA	G	GS	CG	SV	IP	H	R	ER	BB	SO
1998	Red Sox (GCL)	R	1	1	0.00	4	2	0	0	13	9	3	0	2	14
	Lowell (NY-P)	A	2	3	2.90	6	6	0	0	31	22	13	10	13	34
1999	Sarasota (FSL)	A	11	6	4.04	20	19	0	0	111	124	65	50	35	64
	Lakeland (FSL)	A	2	1	3.24	3	3	0	0	17	18	7	6	7	11
	Jacksonville (SL)	AA	1	2	4.79	4	4	0	0	21	27	15	11	7	10
2000	Jacksonville (SL)	AA	9	14	3.94	27	26	2	0	164	176	79	72	58	85
MINOR LEAGUE TOTALS			26	27	3.76	64	60	2	0	357	376	182	149	122	218

16. Adam Bernero, rhp

Born: Nov. 28, 1976. **Ht.:** 6-4. **Wt.:** 205. **Bats:** R. **Throws:** R. **School:** Armstrong Atlantic State (Ga.) College. **Career Transactions:** Signed as nondrafted free agent by Tigers, May 21, 1999.

Bernero signed for an $8,000 bonus, using a napkin at a Denny's restaurant as a contract. As a fifth-year college senior, he was eligible to sign with any club before the draft. A year later he reached Detroit, becoming the first Armstrong Atlantic alumnus to make it to the majors. Bernero doesn't throw particularly hard, topping out in the low 90s and usually pitching in the high 80s. But his fastball has good sinking action that makes it effective. His slider and splitter are adequate, but he could use a straight changeup because he throws too many pitches at the same speed. While his stuff isn't overwhelming, Bernero helps himself by being stingy with walks and home runs, and it's hard to argue with his success as a pro. He'll get a shot at making Detroit's rotation this spring, but might fit better in long relief because of the makeup of the major league staff.

Year	Club (League)	Class	W	L	ERA	G	GS	CG	SV	IP	H	R	ER	BB	SO
1999	West Michigan (Mid)	A	8	4	2.54	15	15	2	0	96	75	36	27	23	80
2000	Jacksonville (SL)	AA	2	5	2.79	10	10	0	0	61	54	26	19	24	46
	Toledo (IL)	AAA	3	1	2.47	7	7	1	0	47	34	16	13	10	37
	Detroit (AL)	MAJ	0	1	4.19	12	4	0	0	34	33	18	16	13	20
MAJOR LEAGUE TOTALS			0	1	4.19	12	4	0	0	34	33	18	16	13	20
MINOR LEAGUE TOTALS			13	10	2.60	32	32	3	0	204	163	78	59	57	163

17. Neil Jenkins, 3b

Born: July 17, 1980. **Ht.:** 6-5. **Wt.:** 205. **Bats:** R. **Throws:** R. **School:** Dwyer HS, West Palm Beach, Fla. **Career Transactions:** Selected by Tigers in third round of 1999 draft; signed July 7, 1999.

This much is certain about Jenkins, even at this early stage of his professional career: He'll go only as far as his bat takes him. He made 46 errors in 99 games at third base in 2000 while displaying next to no range. His future probably lies at first base. Hitting is a different story, though. Jenkins is strong and has an exceptionally live bat. When he lays the bat on the ball, it carries. He was the only player at West Michigan, which has a spacious home ballpark, to reach double figures in home runs last season. But he doesn't put the bat on the ball consistently enough, as his 151-38 strikeout-walk ratio indicates. Jenkins was considered the best power-hitting high school prospect in the 1999 draft but needs to work on the other aspects of his game. Depending on how he performs this spring, he'll either return to West Michigan or move up to Lakeland.

Year	Club (League)	Class	AVG	G	AB	R	H	2B	3B	HR	RBI	BB	SO	SB
1999	Tigers (GCL)	R	.297	33	111	18	33	13	3	2	15	16	37	2
2000	West Michigan (Mid)	A	.253	112	411	56	104	16	5	13	65	38	151	0
MINOR LEAGUE TOTALS			.262	145	522	74	137	29	8	15	80	54	188	2

18. Matt Miller, lhp

Born: Aug. 2, 1974. **Ht.:** 6-3. **Wt.:** 175. **Bats:** L. **Throws:** L. **School:** Texas Tech. **Career Transactions:** Selected by Tigers in second round of 1996 draft; signed Aug. 7, 1996.

Long considered a disappointment, Miller pulled his career together in 2000. He displayed the command that was envisioned when he was picked in the second round of the 1996 draft. Elbow problems, severe enough to require major surgery, sidelined Miller for all of 1997. He didn't regain his form until the second half of 1999, when he was pushed to Jacksonville. He pitched in relief in the Arizona Fall League after being used exclusively as a starter, and he pitched well. He doesn't throw hard, usually working in the 88 mph range, and has a good breaking ball but a below-average changeup. If Miller is going to be a starter in the major leagues, conventional wisdom says he'll have to develop that third pitch. If he doesn't, his best chance may be as a middle reliever. Miller will be part of the Toledo rotation in 2001.

Year	Club (League)	Class	W	L	ERA	G	GS	CG	SV	IP	H	R	ER	BB	SO
1996	Jamestown (NY-P)	A	1	3	4.62	6	6	0	0	25	33	16	13	13	21
1997	Did Not Play—Injured														
1998	West Michigan (Mid)	A	7	4	1.52	14	14	3	0	95	59	20	16	26	102
	Jacksonville (SL)	AA	3	7	7.04	13	13	0	0	61	70	49	48	50	49
1999	Lakeland (FSL)	A	4	9	4.15	19	19	1	0	108	108	58	50	45	82
	Jacksonville (SL)	AA	4	1	4.43	7	7	0	0	41	43	23	20	12	25
2000	Jacksonville (SL)	AA	8	5	3.18	20	20	1	0	122	126	50	43	32	99
MINOR LEAGUE TOTALS			27	29	3.78	79	79	5	0	452	439	216	190	178	378

19. Fernando Rodney, rhp

Born: March 17, 1981. **Ht.:** 5-11. **Wt.:** 170. **Bats:** R. **Throws:** R. **Career Transactions:** Signed out of Dominican Republic by Tigers, Nov. 1, 1997.

The good news about Rodney is that he's the hardest thrower in Detroit's system. The bad news is that his fastball is straight as an arrow. Even so, 98 mph is 98 mph. Rodney is difficult to hit, limiting opponents to a .238 average last season. He started 10 games, but that was so he could get innings and develop more pitches, and his long-term future will be in the bullpen. The fear also was that his fastball is so good that he would use it to overpower Class A hitters and wouldn't throw his breaking ball and changeup if he was used only an inning at a time. He's viewed as a potential closer because of his fastball, and his presence made it easier for the Tigers to include Francisco Cordero in the ill-fated Juan Gonzalez trade with the Rangers in November 1999. Rodney probably will move up a level to Lakeland in 2001.

Year	Club (League)	Class	W	L	ERA	G	GS	CG	SV	IP	H	R	ER	BB	SO
1998	Tigers (DSL)	R	1	3	3.38	11	5	0	1	32	25	16	12	19	37
1999	Tigers (GCL)	R	3	3	2.40	22	0	0	9	30	20	8	8	21	39
	Lakeland (FSL)	A	1	0	1.42	4	0	0	2	6	7	1	1	5	
2000	West Michigan (Mid)	A	6	4	2.94	22	10	0	0	83	74	34	27	35	56
MINOR LEAGUE TOTALS			11	10	2.86	59	15	0	12	151	126	59	48	76	137

20. Adam Pettyjohn, lhp

Born: June 11, 1977. **Ht.:** 6-3. **Wt.:** 190. **Bats:** R. **Throws:** L. **School:** Fresno State University. **Career Transactions:** Selected by Tigers in second round of 1998 draft; signed June 22, 1998.

The 2000 season was close to being a washout for Pettyjohn because of a shoulder injury. After being on the fast track to the major leagues, he made just 15 starts and got shelled in Triple-A as his usually sharp control deserted him. And control is paramount for Pettyjohn. He doesn't throw hard, usually in the neighborhood of 86 mph. He must be precise with the location of his fastball or he gets hit hard. His release point is three-quarters, so he cuts across the ball, producing a fastball that tails away from righthanders. His out pitch is a curveball that he often induces hitters to chase out of the strike zone. Pettyjohn was a teammate of Detroit righthander Jeff Weaver at Fresno State and was taken one round behind him in the Tigers' 1998 draft. If all goes well in the spring, Pettyjohn will be back at Toledo to open 2001.

Year	Club (League)	Class	W	L	ERA	G	GS	CG	SV	IP	H	R	ER	BB	SO
1998	Jamestown (NY-P)	A	2	2	2.86	4	4	0	0	22	21	10	7	4	24
	West Michigan (Mid)	A	4	2	1.97	8	8	1	0	50	46	15	11	9	64
1999	Lakeland (FSL)	A	3	4	3.77	9	9	2	0	60	62	35	25	11	51
	Jacksonville (SL)	AA	9	5	4.69	20	20	0	0	127	134	75	66	35	92
2000	Jacksonville (SL)	AA	2	2	3.40	8	8	0	0	50	43	20	19	12	45
	Toledo (IL)	AAA	0	4	6.69	7	7	0	0	39	45	34	29	22	23
MINOR LEAGUE TOTALS			20	19	4.06	56	56	3	0	348	351	189	157	93	299

21. Miles Durham, of

Born: Aug. 19, 1978. **Ht.:** 6-3. **Wt.:** 195. **Bats:** L. **Throws:** R. **School:** Texas Tech. **Career Transactions:** Selected by Tigers in fifth round of 2000 draft; signed July 3, 2000.

Despite missing most of his college season at Texas Tech because of chronic hamstring pulls, Durham was selected in the fifth round. The reason: speed. Durham consistently runs from the left side of the plate to first base in 3.9 seconds. He missed almost all of his first professional season, playing just the final three games of the Gulf Coast League schedule. The idea was to get his legs 100 percent healthy. Durham played nearly every day during instructional league last fall. He has a sleek frame and a relatively short hitting stroke that produces line drives. He played center field in college and during instructional league, but could see time on an outfield corner depending on what the organization does with Exavier Logan, who is moving to center field. Durham likely will start the 2001 season at West Michigan.

Year	Club (League)	Class	AVG	G	AB	R	H	2B	3B	HR	RBI	BB	SO	SB
2000	Tigers (GCL)	R	.286	3	14	1	4	2	0	0	0	0	4	1
MINOR LEAGUE TOTALS			.286	3	14	1	4	2	0	0	0	0	4	1

22. Chad Petty, lhp

Born: Feb. 17, 1982. **Ht.:** 6-3. **Wt.:** 185. **Bats:** L. **Throws:** L. **School:** Chalker (Ohio) HS. **Career Transactions:** Selected by Tigers in second round of 2000 draft; signed June 6, 2000.

Though he isn't nearly as refined as first-rounder Matt Wheatland, second-rounder Petty has plenty of upside. He already tops out at 94 mph, though most of the time he pitches in the 88-90 mph range. Petty has the making of a good curveball and is a good athlete who moves well for his size. At times his command is good and he doesn't seem quite as raw. At other times his command is poor and his inexperience is obvious. He lacks a changeup and needs one. Petty will start the 2001 season at West Michigan.

Year	Club (League)	Class	W	L	ERA	G	GS	CG	SV	IP	H	R	ER	BB	SO
2000	Lakeland (GCL)	R	2	3	3.00	9	7	1	0	39	31	18	13	20	38
MINOR LEAGUE TOTALS			2	3	3.00	9	7	1	0	39	31	18	13	20	38

23. Calvin Chipperfield, rhp

Born: March 7, 1978. **Ht.:** 6-1. **Wt.:** 170. **Bats:** R. **Throws:** R. **School:** Mount San Antonio (Calif.) JC. **Career Transactions:** Selected by Tigers in 14th round of 1998 draft; signed June 9, 1998.

Because Chipperfield isn't tall and doesn't throw very hard, he's the type of righthander scouts often take one look at before they pack up their radar guns and head home. But his 2000 performance was too good to be ignored. He led the Midwest League in ERA and shutouts (three) while fanning more than a batter an inning and limiting opponents to a .186 average. His fastball usually is in the 87 mph range, so he has little margin for error. But he has excellent command and a curveball that he uses effectively as a strikeout pitch. A native of Australia, Chipperfield will be 23 this season, so he likely will be pushed to Double-A. That would be a huge step from low Class A, and a level where hitters aren't nearly as prone to chase curveballs out of the strike zone. The 2001 season figures to go a long way in determining whether Chipperfield has enough savvy to compensate for his physical shortcomings.

Year	Club (League)	Class	W	L	ERA	G	GS	CG	SV	IP	H	R	ER	BB	SO
1998	Tigers (GCL)	R	3	2	3.10	12	12	0	0	52	44	23	18	24	69
1999	Oneonta (NY-P)	A	4	4	3.28	15	15	0	0	79	55	32	29	33	83
2000	West Michigan (Mid)	A	12	3	2.13	24	22	3	0	143	95	45	34	65	151
MINOR LEAGUE TOTALS			19	9	2.64	51	49	3	0	275	194	100	81	122	303

24. Jermaine Clark, 2b

Born: Sept. 29, 1976. **Ht.:** 5-10. **Wt.:** 175. **Bats:** L. **Throws:** R. **School:** University of San Francisco. **Career Transactions:** Selected by Mariners in fifth round of 1997 draft; signed June 10, 1997 . . . Selected by Tigers in major league Rule 5 draft, December 11, 2000.

Clark hit well over .300 in each of his first three professional seasons in the Mariners system, moving steadily up the ladder despite a perceived lack of tools. He was off to a tremendous start last year at Double-A New Haven, hitting .400 through mid-May before tailing off late. Clark has a quick swing, but he typically uppercuts and pulls off the ball. He has made the swing work for him at every stop, despite predictions that better pitching would overmatch him. Somehow he keeps getting on base, and he's a threat to run when he gets there. Defensively, Clark has held his own, though he's not the rangiest infielder around. Detroit selected him in the major league Rule 5 draft, so he has to be kept in the majors or offered back to Seattle for half the $50,000 draft price. Damion Easley has declined in each of the last two seasons, but Clark doesn't project to take his starting job at this point.

Year	Club (League)	Class	AVG	G	AB	R	H	2B	3B	HR	RBI	BB	SO	SB
1997	Everett (NWL)	A	.337	59	199	42	67	13	2	3	29	34	31	22
1998	Wisconsin (Mid)	A	.324	123	448	81	145	24	13	6	55	57	64	40
1999	Lancaster (Cal)	A	.315	126	502	112	158	27	8	6	61	58	80	33
2000	New Haven (EL)	AA	.293	133	447	80	131	23	9	2	44	87	69	38
MINOR LEAGUE TOTALS			.314	441	1596	315	501	87	32	17	189	236	244	133

25. Chris Wakeland, of

Born: June 15, 1974. **Ht.:** 6-0. **Wt.:** 185. **Bats:** L. **Throws:** L. **School:** Oregon State University. **Career Transactions:** Selected by Tigers in 15th round of 1996 draft; signed June 11, 1996.

Being a lefthanded hitter in an organization that needs help from the left side of the plate gives Wakeland a chance to make it to the major leagues, perhaps as soon as this year. He has a smooth stroke with power. He drives the ball up the gaps with authority, particularly to left-center field, where there's lots of room at Comerica Park. But he is an older prospect who hasn't been as consistently productive as Tigers officials have desired. He's also suspect defensively, not so much because he doesn't have adequate ability but because his mind tends to wander. The lack of concentration sometimes hinders him on the bases as well. Wakeland will get a look in big league camp but figures to begin the season back in Triple-A. He must hit to contribute.

Year	Club (League)	Class	AVG	G	AB	R	H	2B	3B	HR	RBI	BB	SO	SB
1996	Jamestown (NY-P)	A	.309	70	220	38	68	14	5	10	49	43	83	8
1997	West Michigan (Mid)	A	.285	111	414	64	118	38	2	7	75	43	120	20
1998	Lakeland (FSL)	A	.302	131	487	82	147	26	5	18	89	66	111	19
1999	Jacksonville (SL)	AA	.321	55	212	42	68	16	3	13	36	35	53	6
	Tigers (GCL)	R	.071	4	14	2	1	0	0	0	1	0	4	0
	Lakeland (FSL)	A	.412	4	17	3	7	1	0	0	7	0	0	1
2000	Toledo (IL)	AAA	.270	141	492	65	133	25	2	28	76	60	148	4
MINOR LEAGUE TOTALS			.292	516	1856	296	542	120	17	76	333	247	519	58

26. Brant Ust, 3b

Born: July 17, 1978. **Ht.:** 6-2. **Wt.:** 200. **Bats:** R. **Throws:** R. **School:** University of Notre Dame. **Career Transactions:** Selected by Tigers in sixth round of 1999 draft; signed June 10, 1999.

That Ust struggled offensively for Jacksonville last season wasn't a shock. It was a reach to jump him from short-season ball to Double-A, at least in terms of offense. Defense is another story. Ust played shortstop at Notre Dame and was moved to third base by the Tigers. He has excellent hands and plus range to go with a strong, accurate arm. He also has strong makeup, which is why there was little hesitation about pushing him up the ladder so quickly. He's mature enough to understand what was happening. Ust needs to refine his swing, be more patient at the plate and make more consistent contact before he progresses as a hitter.

Year	Club (League)	Class	AVG	G	AB	R	H	2B	3B	HR	RBI	BB	SO	SB
1999	Oneonta (NY-P)	A	.261	58	226	23	59	12	3	5	34	16	54	3
2000	Jacksonville (SL)	AA	.217	111	383	37	83	15	4	4	28	33	95	2
MINOR LEAGUE TOTALS			.233	169	609	60	142	27	7	9	62	49	149	5

27. Javier Cardona, c

Born: Sept. 15, 1975. **Ht.:** 6-1. **Wt.:** 185. **Bats:** R. **Throws:** R. **School:** Lake Land (Ill.) JC. **Career Transactions:** Selected by Tigers in 23rd round of 1994 draft; signed June 4, 1994.

After having a breakout season in Double-A in 1999, Cardona dropped off in 2000. He may have been trying too hard, and Jacksonville is a hitter's ballpark. Making matters worse, he hardly played when he was summoned to the major leagues. And on the few occasions when he saw action, he didn't do much. Cardona does have power and makes consistent contact. He isn't going to win a Gold Glove, but he's adequate across the board defensively. Brandon Inge, the organization's top prospect, will be at Toledo this season, making Cardona the leading candidate to back up Mitch Meluskey in Detroit. He has to make more of that opportunity than he did last year.

Year	Club (League)	Class	AVG	G	AB	R	H	2B	3B	HR	RBI	BB	SO	SB
1994	Jamestown (NY-P)	A	.261	19	46	6	12	2	0	0	5	7	9	0
1995	Fayetteville (SAL)	A	.206	51	165	18	34	8	0	3	19	13	30	1
1996	Fayetteville (SAL)	A	.282	97	348	42	98	21	0	4	28	28	53	1
1997	Lakeland (FSL)	A	.289	85	284	28	82	15	0	7	38	25	51	1
1998	Jacksonville (SL)	AA	.331	46	163	31	54	16	1	4	40	15	29	0
	Toledo (IL)	AAA	.191	47	162	12	31	4	0	5	16	9	32	0
1999	Jacksonville (SL)	AA	.309	108	418	84	129	31	0	26	92	46	69	4
2000	Toledo (IL)	AAA	.275	56	218	29	60	10	0	11	43	15	33	0
	Detroit (AL)	MAJ	.175	26	40	1	7	1	0	1	2	0	9	0
MAJOR LEAGUE TOTALS			.175	26	40	1	7	1	0	1	2	0	9	0
MINOR LEAGUE TOTALS			.277	509	1804	250	500	107	1	60	281	158	306	7

28. Luis Pineda, rhp

Born: June 10, 1978. **Ht.:** 6-1. **Wt.:** 160. **Bats:** R. **Throws:** R. **Career Transactions:** Signed out of Dominican Republic by Rangers, June 14, 1995 . . . Released by Rangers, May 22, 1997 . . . Signed by Diamondbacks, June 25, 1998 . . . Released by Diamondbacks, July 4, 1998 . . . Signed by Tigers, July 30, 1998 . . . Granted free agency, Oct. 16, 1998; re-signed by Tigers, Dec. 29, 1998.

Pineda has been in pro baseball since 1995 without pitching above Class A. He was released by both the Rangers and Diamondbacks before hooking on with the Tigers. So what gives him a chance? His fastball. He throws 98 mph consistently and has nice life to go with his velocity. He also throws a slider and a curveball, and both are effective pitches. Though hindered by arm problems, Pineda averaged 14.2 strikeouts per nine innings last season. He carries a reputation for having a lot of personality—a little too much at times for his managers, teammates and club officials. He also needs better command of his fastball. The Tigers are leaning toward putting Pineda at Double-A to start the 2001 season.

Year	Club (League)	Class	W	L	ERA	G	GS	CG	SV	IP	H	R	ER	BB	SO
1995	Rangers (DSL)	R	6	1	3.00	12	5	0	0	39	36	17	13	31	19
1996	Rangers (GCL)	R	6	3	3.52	11	11	1	0	72	67	31	28	25	66
1997						Did Not Play—Injured									
1998	Tigers (DSL)	R	2	0	0.89	12	0	0	5	20	7	3	2	14	43
1999	West Michigan (Mid)	A	0	2	3.57	24	3	0	7	40	30	18	16	26	55
	Lakeland (FSL)	A	0	1	1.04	8	0	0	0	9	6	2	1	7	8
2000	Lakeland (FSL)	A	1	3	3.38	18	0	0	4	27	23	13	10	19	42
MINOR LEAGUE TOTALS			15	10	3.04	85	19	1	16	207	169	84	70	122	233

29. Mark Woodyard, rhp

Born: Dec. 19, 1978. **Ht.:** 6-2. **Wt.:** 195. **Bats:** R. **Throws:** R. **School:** Bethune-Cookman College. **Career Transactions:** Selected by Tigers in fourth round of 2000 draft; signed June 24, 2000.

The Tigers went off the beaten path to find Woodyard. He was mostly a position player at Florida's tiny Bethune-Cookman until last spring, when he began pitching and impressed Detroit's scouts enough to get drafted in the fourth round. He obviously is raw, but not as much as might be expected. His mechanics come and go, and as they do so do his radar-gun readings, which fluctuate from the high 80s to as much as 94 mph. His breaking ball isn't bad given his lack of experience, and he's a good athlete with solid work habits. Woodyard didn't get totally overwhelmed during his first pro season, showing the ability to battle through innings, but he was fairly wild and still needs a lot of work on his changeup. He has a good chance of starting this season at West Michigan.

Year	Club (League)	Class	W	L	ERA	G	GS	CG	SV	IP	H	R	ER	BB	SO
2000	Oneonta (NY-P)	A	1	5	4.59	11	9	0	0	51	48	32	26	39	38
MINOR LEAGUE TOTALS			1	5	4.59	11	9	0	0	51	48	32	36	39	38

30. Richard Gomez, of

Born: Aug. 19, 1977. **Ht.:** 5-11. **Wt.:** 190. **Bats:** R. **Throws:** R. **Career Transactions:** Signed out of Dominican Republic by Tigers, Sept. 5, 1996.

If this were track instead of baseball, Gomez might be the Tigers' top prospect. He's a big, strong outfielder who runs the 60-yard dash in 6.4 seconds. He got a late start, not signing out of the Dominican Republic until he was 19, and is still raw in many areas. While he has learned to use his speed effectively, his power has been slower to develop. He has a long swing and doesn't turn on pitches well. His bat is slow, so good fastballs give him problems. Defensively, Gomez is awkward and doesn't throw well. Given his speed, he doesn't cover a lot of ground. He will be at Double-A this season, which should provide a stern test.

Year	Club (League)	Class	AVG	G	AB	R	H	2B	3B	HR	RBI	BB	SO	SB
1997	Tigers (DSL)	R	.351	63	222	48	78	14	6	1	42	28	39	19
1998	Tigers (GCL)	R	.333	47	162	42	54	11	4	6	40	21	37	20
1999	West Michigan (Mid)	A	.303	130	479	89	145	26	12	8	81	54	122	66
2000	Lakeland (FSL)	A	.277	128	455	78	126	20	10	8	57	50	102	48
MINOR LEAGUE TOTALS			.306	368	1318	257	403	71	32	23	220	153	300	153

Florida
Marlins

TOP 30 PROSPECTS

1. Josh Beckett, rhp
2. Wes Anderson, rhp
3. Miguel Cabrera, ss
4. Adrian Gonzalez, 1b
5. Abraham Nunez, of
6. Claudio Vargas, rhp
7. Blaine Neal, rhp
8. Jason Stokes, of/1b
9. Pablo Ozuna, 2b
10. Nate Rolison, 1b
11. Chip Ambres, of
12. Gary Knotts, rhp
13. Rob Henkel, lhp
14. Denny Bautista, rhp
15. Geoff Goetz, lhp
16. Luis Ugueto, ss
17. Josh Wilson, ss
18. Chris Aguila, of
19. Cesar Crespo, of
20. Jason Grilli, rhp
21. Terry Byron, rhp
22. Jose Soto, of
23. Hector Almonte, rhp
24. Will Smith, of
25. Derek Wathan, ss
26. Jesus Medrano, 2b
27. Manuel Esquivia, rhp
28. Mark Roberts, rhp
29. Brandon Harper, c
30. Nate Bump, rhp

By Mike Berardino

The long climb back to respectability accelerated for the Marlins in 2000. They closed with a flourish to go 79-82, a 15-win improvement over the previous year, and became just the second National League team in the past half-century to post double-digit improvements in the win column in consecutive seasons.

Even better, the Marlins escaped last place for the first time since the Great Purge. They finished comfortably in third place in the NL East and did it with a payroll just under $20 million, lowest in the majors except for the Twins. That figure should rise into the low 30s in 2001, as the organization navigates its way through deals with nine arbitration-eligible players. The team even reached a tentative deal for a ballpark in downtown Miami that would open in 2004 and result in a franchise name change to the Miami Marlins.

Alex Fernandez saw his comeback derailed by a recurrence of shoulder problems and made just eight starts in 2000. But there were plenty of positives. Ryan Dempster, the 23-year-old righthander, won 14 games and made the all-star team in his breakthrough season. Closer Antonio Alfonseca led the majors with 45 saves.

Second baseman Luis Castillo led the majors with 62 stolen bases. Center fielder Preston Wilson blossomed into the game's only 30-30 player and drove in a franchise-record 121 runs.

Three of the Marlins' six affiliates posted winning records, led by Class A Kane County and the Rookie-level Gulf Coast League Marlins. Overall, the organization posted a .496 minor league winning percentage, a 19-point improvement over 1999.

Having retooled around young starting pitching, the Marlins continued to add quality position prospects in 2000. Five of their top six draft picks were spent on position players. The re-emergence of first baseman Nate Rolison, and the drafting of Jason Stokes and Jim Kavourias added power. Speed is in abundance in Quincy Foster, Pablo Ozuna and Anthony Brewer.

The system remains rich in righthanded starting pitching, first basemen, middle infielders and multitooled outfielders. A lack of depth is apparent at catcher and third base, though they addressed the former position by signing Charles Johnson, the franchise's first-ever draft pick in 1992. Prized Venezuelan shortstop Miguel Cabrera may move to the hot corner and fill the other hole.

Organization Overview

General manager: Dave Dombrowski. **Farm director:** Rick Williams. **Scouting director:** Al Avila.

2000 PERFORMANCE

Class	Team	League	W	L	Pct.	Finish*	Manager
Majors	Florida	National	79	82	.491	9th (16)	John Boles
Triple-A	Calgary Cannons	Pacific Coast	60	82	.423	14th (16)	Lynn Jones
Double-A	Portland Sea Dogs	Eastern	71	70	.504	8th (12)	Rick Renteria
High A	Brevard Cty. Manatees	Florida State	66	74	.471	10th (14)	Dave Huppert
Low A	Kane County Cougars	Midwest	74	65	.532	4th (14)	Russ Morman
Short-season	Utica Blue Sox	New York-Penn	35	40	.467	9th (14)	Jon Deeble
Rookie	GCL Marlins	Gulf Coast	40	20	.667	2nd (13)	Kevin Boles
OVERALL 2000 MINOR LEAGUE RECORD			345	351	.496	15th (30)	

*Finish in overall standings (No. of teams in league).

ORGANIZATION LEADERS

BATTING

*AVG	Josh Wilson, Utica/Kane County	.331
R	**Cesar Crespo**, Portland	96
H	Nate Rolison, Calgary	146
TB	Nate Rolison, Calgary	258
2B	Mike Gulan, Calgary	40
3B	Derek Wathan, Brevard/Portland	8
HR	Luis Raven, Calgary	24
RBI	Nate Rolison, Calgary	88
BB	**Cesar Crespo**, Portland	77
	Brett Roneberg, Brevard	77
SO	Matt Padgett, Kane County	139
SB	**Cesar Crespo**, Portland	41

PITCHING

W	**Brandon Leese**, Portland	12
L	Ryan Moskau, Portland/Brevard	13
#ERA	Joe Sergent, Kane County	2.67
G	Brandon Bowe, Kane County	61
CG	**Brandon Leese**, Portland	6
SV	Bryan Moore, Kane County	27
IP	**Brandon Leese**, Portland	174
BB	Mike Drumright, Calgary	101
SO	Claudio Vargas, Brevard/Portland	156

*Minimum 250 at-bats. #Minimum 75 innings.

TOP PROSPECTS OF THE DECADE

1993	Nigel Wilson, of
1994	Charles Johnson, c
1995	Charles Johnson, c
1996	Edgar Renteria, ss
1997	Felix Heredia, lhp
1998	Mark Kotsay, of
1999	A.J. Burnett, rhp
2000	A.J. Burnett, rhp

TOP DRAFT PICKS OF THE DECADE

1992	Charles Johnson, c
1993	Marc Valdes, rhp
1994	Josh Booty, ss
1995	Jaime Jones, of
1996	Mark Kotsay, of
1997	Aaron Akin, rhp
1998	Chip Ambres, of
1999	Josh Beckett, rhp
2000	Adrian Gonzalez, 1b

Crespo   **Leese**

BEST TOOLS

Best Hitter for Average	Adrian Gonzalez
Best Power Hitter	Jason Stokes
Fastest Baserunner	Quincy Foster
Best Fastball	Josh Beckett
Best Breaking Ball	Josh Beckett
Best Control	Todd Moser
Best Defensive Catcher	Brandon Harper
Best Defensive Infielder	Luis Ugueto
Best Infield Arm	Luis Ugueto
Best Defensive Outfielder	Chris Aguila
Best Outfield Arm	Abraham Nunez

PROJECTED 2004 LINEUP

Catcher	Charles Johnson
First Base	Derrek Lee
Second Base	Luis Castillo
Third Base	Miguel Cabrera
Shortstop	Alex Gonzalez
Left Field	Jason Stokes
Center Field	Abraham Nunez
Right Field	Preston Wilson
No. 1 Starter	Ryan Dempster
No. 2 Starter	Josh Beckett
No. 3 Starter	A.J. Burnett
No. 4 Starter	Wes Anderson
No. 5 Starter	Brad Penny
Closer	Blaine Neal

ALL-TIME LARGEST BONUSES

Josh Beckett, 1999	$3,625,000
Adrian Gonzalez, 2000	3,000,000
Livan Hernandez, 1996	2,500,000
Jason Stokes, 2000	2,027,000
Miguel Cabrera, 1999	1,900,000

DraftAnalysis

2000 Draft

Best Pro Debut: OF Will Smith (6) batted .368 and tied for the Rookie-level Gulf Coast League lead with 21 doubles. Finesse LHP Chris Key (18) had a 1.75 ERA while reaching Class A.

Best Athlete: OF Anthony Brewer (4) has raw physical skills, including speed, arm strength and surprising power.

Best Hitter: 1B **Adrian Gonzalez** (1) was the top high school hitter in the draft. That and his willingness to accept a $3 million bonus endeared him to the Marlins as the No. 1 overall pick. After going 4-for-28 to start his pro career, Gonzalez hit .320 the rest of the summer.

Best Raw Power: 1B Jason Stokes (2) was the top high school power hitter in the draft, and he would have gone early in the first round had teams not been concentrating on signability. OF Jim Kavourias (5), who led NCAA Division II with 23 homers last spring, also has a lot of pop. His season was abbreviated by back problems. Smith set the Arizona high school record for career homers, but he's not in the class of Stokes or Kavourias.

Fastest Runner: Brewer is exceptionally quick. He gets from the right side of the plate to first base in 4.08 seconds, the equivalent of a 6.4-second 60-yard dash.

Best Defensive Player: The Marlins didn't sign any outstanding glove men at a premium position. The best defender is Gonzalez, who's slick at first base. As a result, Stokes is moving to left field.

Best Fastball: In his first season back at UCLA after Tommy John surgery, LHP Rob Henkel (3) peaked at 94-95 mph before tiring later in the spring. His knuckle-curve may have been the best breaking pitch in the draft. RHP Phillip Akens (13), a 6-foot-5 high school kid, saw his velocity jump from 88-89 mph to an occasional 94 after signing.

Most Intriguing Background: RHP Jared Brite (41) is punting and playing baseball at Kansas State. Gonzalez' older brother Edgar signed as a 30th-round pick of the Rangers.

Closest To The Majors: Henkel, though he held out all summer before signing for $650,000. He'll probably make his pro debut at Class A Kane County in April.

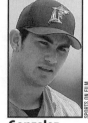

Gonzalez

Best Late-Round Pick: Akens. RHP Steve Sawyer (11) threw 93 mph in relief.

The One Who Got Away: LHP Daniel Moore (23), who's projectable because he's 6-foot-5 and already throws 90 mph. He would have gone in the top three or four rounds had a North Carolina scholarship offer not been more tempting.

Assessment: No team had a better draft. The Gonzalez signing made it seem the Marlins were most concerned about costs, but they spent to add the equivalent of two more first-round picks in Stokes and Henkel. They continued to make astute picks in later rounds, and most of their players enjoyed successful debuts.

1999 Draft

There isn't a pitching prospect in the game who can match RHP Josh Beckett's (1) potential. The Marlins like what they've seen from their next two picks, too: RHP Terry Byron (2) and SS Josh Wilson (3). **Grade: B+**

1998 Draft

OF Chip Ambres (1) is a premium athlete, but he's also very raw. After Florida picked SS Derek Wathan (2), the talent thinned out. **Grade: C–**

1997 Draft

RHP Wes Anderson (14) slid in the draft because he was committed to the University of Arkansas, and his ceiling is within shouting distance of Beckett's. He makes up for RHP Aaron Akin (1) not panning out. **Grade: C**

1996 Draft

The Marlins lost second- and third-round picks for free-agent signings and signed just nine players from the first 15 rounds. OF Mark Kotsay (1) has been a three-year starter in Florida, while RHP Blaine Neal (4) is the closer of the future. LHP Brent Billingsley (5) got a cup of coffee. **Grade: C**

Note: Draft analysis prepared by Jim Callis. Numbers in parentheses indicate draft rounds.

. . . Beckett has a prototypical power pitcher's build, a fastball that reaches 97 mph and a devastating 12-to-6 curveball.

Josh
Beckett rhp

Born: May 15, 1980.
Ht.: 6-4. **Wt.:** 190.
Bats: R. **Throws:** R.
School: Spring (Texas) HS.
Career Transactions: Selected by Marlins in first round (second overall) of 1999 draft; signed Sept. 1, 1999.

Beckett was taken No. 2 overall in 1999, the first high school righthander taken that high since Bill Gullickson 20 years earlier. After a summer-long holdout he received a four-year, $7 million big league contract just days before he was to begin classes at Blinn (Texas) Junior College, wisecracking his way through a press conference at the Astrodome. Beckett made two appearances at his first big league spring training, blowing away the Royals before getting rocked by the more experienced Braves. He returned to minor league camp to begin his professional climb at Class A Kane County, where he was named the Midwest League's No. 1 prospect.

Beckett has a prototypical power pitcher's build and has been clocked as high as 97 mph, though he generally pitches at 93-94 mph. He has a devastating 12-to-6 curveball that breaks hard and late. The combination has drawn comparisons to a young Bert Blyleven. Though confident and bordering on cocky, Beckett is generally coachable and willing to learn. His changeup is developing, but the arm speed and command are there already. Two starts into his pro career, Beckett was shut down for seven weeks with shoulder tendinitis. The condition flared again in August, and the Marlins again proved cautious with their huge investment. Beckett attended instructional league but wasn't allowed to throw. He still needs to mature physically and improve his upper-body conditioning. Suddenly, there are doubts about his durability and deep-seated fears about the long-term health of his prized shoulder. He needs to work on finishing his pitches, and a little more emotional maturity wouldn't hurt either.

Beckett had hoped to make it to Double-A by the end of last season. Now there's a good chance he won't get there until 2002. He'll get another crack at big league spring training, but this time the emphasis should be on staying healthy and fine-tuning his repertoire rather than trying to impress the brass. His contract calls for him to be in the big leagues for good by 2004, so there's time for development. Some believe the first health scare of his young career could work to his advantage. If he ever took his gift for granted before, he probably won't now.

ROBERT GURGANUS

Year	Club (League)	Class	W	L	ERA	G	GS	CG	SV	IP	H	R	ER	BB	SO
2000	Kane County (Mid)	A	2	3	2.12	13	12	0	0	59	45	18	14	15	61
MINOR LEAGUE TOTALS			2	3	2.12	13	12	0	0	59	45	18	14	15	61

2. Wes Anderson, rhp

Born: Sept. 10, 1979. **Ht.:** 6-4. **Wt.:** 175. **Bats:** R. **Throws:** R. **School:** Pine Bluff (Ark.) HS. **Career Transactions:** Selected by Marlins in 14th round of 1997 draft; signed Aug. 18, 1997.

Anderson was stolen in the 14th round in 1997 as teams thought he was headed to the University of Arkansas. Even with Josh Beckett in hand, some still believe Anderson has the best fastball in the system. He pitches at 92-93 mph but has topped out at 97. He has a plus slider and an average changeup, though the slider came and went last year. His lanky frame and fluid delivery have drawn comparisons to John Smoltz. When he's on, Anderson can absolutely dominate opposing hitters and make it look easy. He's considered a future No. 1 or 2 starter. For the second straight season Anderson's shoulder wore down late, causing him to miss starts. Some felt he kept quiet and tried to pitch through pain to prove he's not soft, but he was told that's the wrong approach. Anderson is a classic worrier and honestly doesn't seem to grasp his talent. He could use a little of Beckett's swagger. Anderson should start the year at Double-A Portland, where he must prove he can stay healthy and pitch with more bravado. The stuff is there. It's the rest of the package that needs work.

Year	Club (League)	Class	W	L	ERA	G	GS	CG	SV	IP	H	R	ER	BB	SO
1998	Marlins (GCL)	R	5	2	1.39	11	11	1	0	65	44	25	10	18	66
1999	Kane County (Mid)	A	9	5	3.21	23	23	2	0	137	111	55	49	51	134
2000	Brevard County (FSL)	A	6	9	3.42	22	21	0	0	116	108	55	44	66	91
MINOR LEAGUE TOTALS			20	16	2.92	56	55	3	0	318	263	135	103	135	291

3. Miguel Cabrera, ss

Born: April 18, 1983. **Ht.:** 6-2. **Wt.:** 185. **Bats:** R. **Throws:** R. **Career Transactions:** Signed out of Venezuela by Marlins, July 2, 1999.

Cabrera signed for a Venezuelan-record $1.9 million. A false rumor that he contracted elephantiasis was spread in Venezuela by a jilted scout, though the truth is slowly making its way through the country. Making his pro debut at 17, Cabrera stood out as the best position prospect on a stacked Rookie-level Gulf Coast League club. For his age, Cabrera has an advanced approach at the plate. He has a great eye and a compact swing to go with plus power. He could contend for batting crowns and home run titles. In the field he has a solid, accurate arm and a quick release. His hands are soft and more than sufficient to play shortstop. Cabrera's speed is below-average, he has a stocky build and his legs tend to be a bit heavy. Those attributes, plus his long frame, have prompted speculation about a move to third base. He still had baby fat after signing but has worked hard to turn it into muscle. After getting a taste of short-season Utica late in the 2000 season, Cabrera could start out as high as the Midwest League. If all goes well he should challenge for a big league job by 2003.

Year	Club (League)	Class	AVG	G	AB	R	H	2B	3B	HR	RBI	BB	SO	SB
2000	Marlins (GCL)	R	.260	57	219	38	57	10	2	2	22	23	46	1
	Utica (NY-P)	A	.250	8	32	3	8	2	0	0	6	2	6	0
MINOR LEAGUE TOTALS			.259	65	251	41	65	12	2	2	28	25	52	1

4. Adrian Gonzalez, 1b

Born: May 8, 1982. **Ht.:** 6-2. **Wt.:** 190. **Bats:** L. **Throws:** L. **School:** Eastlake HS, Chula Vista, Calif. **Career Transactions:** Selected by Marlins in first round (first overall) of 2000 draft; signed June 6, 2000.

A late bloomer on the San Diego scene, Gonzalez rocketed to the top of the 2000 draft. His older brother Edgar was a 30th-round pick and signed with the Devil Rays. Their father David was a top first baseman in Mexican semipro leagues into his early 40s. Gonzalez has a smooth stroke and easy actions around the bag. His hitting has drawn comparisons to Rafael Palmeiro, while his glove evokes Mark Grace. He has tremendous makeup and a willingness to take instruction. His hand-eye coordination makes him tough to strike out and a treat to watch in the field. Gonzalez has gap power but some wonder if his wiry frame will ever produce 20-plus homers in the majors. He gets jammed with inside pitches and has a tendency to get too closed with his stride. He has an elaborate leg kick, but so far Marlins instructors have been reluctant to quiet down his lower half. In an organization full of first basemen, Gonzalez has the most polished all-around game. He already has moved Jason Stokes to left field and should start 2001 in the Midwest League.

Year	Club (League)	Class	AVG	G	AB	R	H	2B	3B	HR	RBI	BB	SO	SB
2000	Marlins (GCL)	R	.295	53	193	24	57	10	1	0	30	32	35	0
	Utica (NY-P)	A	.310	8	29	7	9	3	0	0	3	7	6	0
MINOR LEAGUE TOTALS			.297	61	222	31	66	13	1	0	33	39	41	0

5. Abraham Nunez, of

RICH ABEL

Born: Feb. 5, 1980. **Ht.:** 6-2. **Wt.:** 186. **Bats:** B. **Throws:** R. **Career Transactions:** Signed out of Dominican Republic by Diamondbacks, Aug. 22, 1996 . . . Traded by Diamondbacks to Marlins, Dec. 14, 1999, completing trade in which Diamondbacks sent RHP Vladimir Nunez, RHP Brad Penny and a player to be named to Marlins for RHP Matt Mantei (July 9, 1999).

Nunez moved to Florida as the player to be named in the Matt Mantei trade. The Diamondbacks contested his inclusion, but after a three-month controversy the commissioner's office let it stand. You'll find all five tools in this package. Nunez has plus power from both sides of the plate. He has the arm to play either center or right field. He showed admirable patience and work ethic after an injury to the back of his throwing shoulder kept him out of the field most of the year. Nunez sustained a tear when he failed to warm up properly before playing catch with friends at home. He also had to deal with a brain aneurysm that struck his father at midseason. His father survived, and Nunez came back and finished the season strong. His speed is the weakest of his tools, average at best, but Nunez uses it well. He tends to jump at pitches, forcing him to spend time seeing thousands of curveballs from a pitching machine. Nunez figures to return for a second go-round at Double-A. His shoulder was healthy for instructional league, though he missed six weeks in winter ball when he broke his left hand sliding.

Year	Club (League)	Class	AVG	G	AB	R	H	2B	3B	HR	RBI	BB	SO	SB
1997	Diamondbacks (AZL)	R	.305	54	213	52	65	17	4	0	21	26	40	3
	Lethbridge (Pio)	R	.167	2	6	2	1	0	0	0	1	1	0	0
1998	South Bend (Mid)	A	.255	110	364	44	93	14	2	9	47	67	81	12
1999	High Desert (Cal)	A	.273	130	488	106	133	29	6	22	93	86	122	40
2000	Portland (EL)	AA	.276	74	221	39	61	17	3	6	42	44	64	8
	Brevard County (FSL)	A	.194	31	103	17	20	4	0	1	9	28	34	11
MINOR LEAGUE TOTALS			.267	401	1395	260	373	81	15	38	213	252	341	74

6. Claudio Vargas, rhp

Born: May 19, 1979. **Ht.:** 6-3. **Wt.:** 210. **Bats:** R. **Throws:** R. **Career Transactions:** Signed out of Dominican Republic by Marlins, Aug. 25, 1995.

Signed at 16, Vargas has made slow but steady progress. His star took off in late 1999, when he came back from shoulder tendinitis to throw 96 mph in a playoff game for Kane County. That earned him an invitation to big league camp last spring, and he has been climbing ever since. Vargas pitches at 92-93 mph and has touched 97 with his lively fastball. He has a smooth delivery and a live, loose arm to go with a solid pitcher's frame. He has a good feel for both his curveball and changeup. He has a bulldog mentality on the mound and isn't afraid to pitch inside. His curve tends to get slurvy as he struggles with his arm slot. Vargas probably will have to make it a full-fledged slider at some point, but the Marlins discourage younger pitchers from throwing sliders or splitters. His fastball command escapes him now and again, and he'll leave pitches up and over the middle of the plate. Vargas should be in the next wave of young Marlins starters to reach the majors. He should get his first taste of Triple-A in 2001, and a big league callup is possible in September.

Year	Club (League)	Class	W	L	ERA	G	GS	CG	SV	IP	H	R	ER	BB	SO
1996	Marlins (DSL)	R	2	3	3.09	15	4	0	0	47	41	25	16	26	37
1997	Marlins (DSL)	R	6	2	2.50	13	10	3	0	72	62	32	20	31	81
1998	Brevard County (FSL)	A	0	1	4.66	2	2	0	0	10	15	5	5	4	9
	Marlins (GCL)	R	0	4	4.08	5	4	0	0	29	24	15	13	7	27
1999	Kane County (Mid)	A	5	5	3.88	19	19	1	0	100	97	47	43	41	88
2000	Brevard County (FSL)	A	10	5	3.28	24	23	0	0	145	126	64	53	44	143
	Portland (EL)	AA	1	1	3.60	3	2	0	0	15	16	9	6	6	13
MINOR LEAGUE TOTALS			24	21	3.37	81	64	4	0	417	381	197	156	159	398

7. Blaine Neal, rhp

Born: April 6, 1978. **Ht.:** 6-5. **Wt.:** 205. **Bats:** L. **Throws:** R. **School:** Bishop Eustace HS, Pennsauken, N.J. **Career Transactions:** Selected by Marlins in fourth round of 1996 draft; signed July 13, 1996.

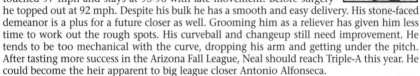

Neal languished with elbow problems through his first two pro seasons before the Marlins opted to give him a last chance as a first baseman. He flopped at the plate as well. Surgery to remove bone spurs and other debris in his throwing elbow at the end of the 1998 season led to his re-emergence as a pitching prospect. Neal comes at hitters with a fastball that has touched 97 mph and stays at 95-96 with late movement. Before surgery he topped out at 92 mph. Despite his bulk he has a smooth and easy delivery. His stone-faced demeanor is a plus for a future closer as well. Grooming him as a reliever has given him less time to work out the rough spots. His curveball and changeup still need improvement. He tends to be too mechanical with the curve, dropping his arm and getting under the pitch. After tasting more success in the Arizona Fall League, Neal should reach Triple-A this year. He could become the heir apparent to big league closer Antonio Alfonseca.

Year	Club (League)	Class	AVG	G	AB	R	H	2B	3B	HR	RBI	BB	SO	SB
1998	Utica (NY-P)	A	.190	53	121	13	23	4	0	0	13	23	32	2
MINOR LEAGUE TOTALS			.190	53	121	13	23	4	0	0	13	23	32	2

Year	Club (League)	Class	W	L	ERA	G	GS	CG	SV	IP	H	R	ER	BB	SO
1996	Marlins (GCL)	R	1	1	4.60	7	5	0	1	29	32	18	15	6	15
1997	Marlins (GCL)	R	4	1	3.63	10	0	0	1	22	24	11	9	11	19
1999	Kane County (Mid)	A	4	2	2.32	26	0	0	6	31	21	8	8	10	31
2000	Brevard County (FSL)	A	2	2	2.15	41	0	0	11	54	40	27	13	24	65
MINOR LEAGUE TOTALS			11	6	2.96	84	5	0	19	137	117	64	45	51	130

8. Jason Stokes, of/1b

Born: Jan. 23, 1982. **Ht.:** 6-5. **Wt.:** 233. **Bats:** R. **Throws:** R. **School:** Coppell (Texas) HS. **Career Transactions:** Selected by Marlins in second round of 2000 draft; signed August 27, 2000.

Stokes set a Texas high school record with 23 homers last spring and was considered the top high school power hitter in the draft. He dropped only because of signability concerns and was ready to attend Texas until the Marlins forked over $2.027 million in late August. He signed too late to make his pro debut. Stokes has raw, brute strength and generates upper-deck clout with a relatively compact swing. He put on a batting-practice show on the eve of his signing. He showed no scare during instructional league, where a pulled hamstring slowed him down but he whetted the organization's appetite. Stokes has poise and confidence, especially at the plate, where his strike-zone recognition is advanced. His defense at first base was below-average, and with Adrian Gonzalez at first, Stokes has moved to left field. His feet are quick enough and he's a good enough athlete to at least make that transition stick for a few years, but he'll never be a plus outfielder. A late bloomer in high school, Stokes has a first-rate makeup and work ethic. The Marlins fully expect him to develop into one of their premier position players, starting in the Gulf Coast League.

Year	Club (League)	Class	AVG	G	AB	R	H	2B	3B	HR	RBI	BB	SO	SB
2000			Did Not Play—Signed 2001 Contract											

9. Pablo Ozuna, 2b

Born: Aug. 25, 1978. **Ht.:** 6-0. **Wt.:** 160. **Bats:** R. **Throws:** R. **Career Transactions:** Signed out of Dominican Republic by Cardinals, April 8, 1996 . . . Traded by Cardinals with RHP Braden Looper and LHP Armando Almanza to Marlins for SS Edgar Renteria, Dec. 14, 1998.

Ozuna was the key player in the trade that sent Edgar Renteria to the Cardinals. His star has dimmed somewhat in the two seasons since, but not by much. Speed is his primary tool. Close behind is tremendous hand-eye coordination that enables him to make contact on pitches anywhere near the plate. Though slight, he's wiry strong and has some gap power. He has a solid makeup and takes instruction well. An erratic arm prompted a move from shortstop to second. Ozuna's defense has been shaky as he makes the transition. He's learning to harness his speed. Lapses in concentration and overaggressiveness cause him to run into outs. Doubts are beginning to build about Ozuna. He looked overmatched in a big league audition. Now that Luis Castillo has put his vast tools to use, Florida may look to move Ozuna yet again, perhaps to center field. He should get his first crack at Triple-A in 2001.

Year	Club (League)	Class	AVG	G	AB	R	H	2B	3B	HR	RBI	BB	SO	SB
1996	Cardinals (DSL)	R	.363	74	295	57	107	12	4	6	60	23	19	18
1997	Johnson City (Appy)	R	.323	56	232	40	75	13	1	5	24	10	24	23
1998	Peoria (Mid)	A	.357	133	538	122	192	27	10	9	62	29	56	62
1999	Portland (EL)	AA	.281	117	502	62	141	25	7	7	46	13	50	31
2000	Portland (EL)	AA	.308	118	464	74	143	25	6	7	59	40	55	35
	Florida (NL)	MAJ	.333	14	24	2	8	1	0	0	0	0	2	1
MAJOR LEAGUE TOTALS			.333	14	24	2	8	1	0	0	0	0	2	1
MINOR LEAGUE TOTALS			.324	498	2031	355	658	102	28	34	251	115	204	169

10. Nate Rolison, 1b

Born: March 27, 1977. **Ht.:** 6-6. **Wt.:** 240. **Bats:** L. **Throws:** R. **School:** Petal (Miss.) HS. **Career Transactions:** Selected by Marlins in second round of 1995 draft; signed June 30, 1995.

Rolison has developed slowly, failing to hit .300 or more than 17 home runs in any of his first five professional seasons. He finally graduated to Triple-A Calgary in 2000 and enjoyed a breakout season as Marlins minor league player of the year. A hulking figure, Rolison has possessed some of the best power in the organization for years. He finally figured out how to turn on pitches on the inner half and drive them. He's one of the few Marlins prospects willing to take a walk. At times he can be too passive with pitches on the outer half, but Rolison did a much better job of driving those balls to left and left-center last season. He's a below-average runner and defender, though he has improved his footwork around the bag. A freak injury during batting practice wiped out Rolison's planned tour of duty in the Puerto Rican League and likely wrecked whatever chance he had to make the Marlins this spring. He had surgery to repair the hamate bone in his right hand.

Year	Club (League)	Class	AVG	G	AB	R	H	2B	3B	HR	RBI	BB	SO	SB
1995	Marlins (GCL)	R	.276	37	134	22	37	10	2	1	19	15	34	0
1996	Kane County (Mid)	A	.243	131	474	63	115	28	1	14	75	66	170	3
1997	Brevard County (FSL)	A	.256	122	473	59	121	22	0	16	65	38	143	3
1998	Portland (EL)	AA	.277	131	484	80	134	35	2	16	83	64	150	5
1999	Portland (EL)	AA	.299	124	438	71	131	20	1	17	69	68	112	0
2000	Calgary (PCL)	AAA	.330	123	443	88	146	37	3	23	88	70	117	3
	Florida (NL)	MAJ	.077	8	13	0	1	0	0	0	2	1	4	0
MAJOR LEAGUE TOTALS			.077	8	13	0	1	0	0	0	2	1	4	0
MINOR LEAGUE TOTALS			.280	668	2446	383	684	152	9	87	399	321	726	14

11. Chip Ambres, of

Born: Dec. 19, 1979. **Ht.:** 6-1. **Wt.:** 190. **Bats:** R. **Throws:** R. **School:** West Brook HS, Beaumont, Texas. **Career Transactions:** Selected by Marlins in first round (27th overall) of 1998 draft; signed Aug. 3, 1998.

The Marlins thought Ambres had put his right hamstring problems behind him with a strong 1999 season, but those woes returned in 2000. It was lingering concerns over knee and hamstring injuries, as well as a football scholarship to play quarterback for Texas A&M, that caused Ambres to slip in the 1998 draft. The Marlins got him with a $1.5 million bonus. When healthy he has outstanding speed and has worked hard to improve his basestealing instincts. He draws high marks for his makeup, intelligence and leadership skills. He has shown he can handle the best of fastballs, but regressed in his approach against good breaking balls. He has gap power but projects as more of a .300 hitter with 15-18 homers. He could lead off or bat third, depending on his progress with strike-zone judgment. His arm is accurate but just average, relegating him to left field.

Year	Club (League)	Class	AVG	G	AB	R	H	2B	3B	HR	RBI	BB	SO	SB
1999	Marlins (GCL)	R	.353	37	139	29	49	13	3	1	15	25	19	22
	Utica (NY-P)	A	.267	28	105	24	28	3	6	5	15	21	25	11
2000	Kane County (Mid)	A	.231	84	320	46	74	16	3	7	28	52	72	26
MINOR LEAGUE TOTALS			.268	149	564	99	151	32	12	13	58	98	116	59

12. Gary Knotts, rhp

Born: Feb. 12, 1977. **Ht.:** 6-4. **Wt.:** 200. **Bats:** R. **Throws:** R. **School:** Northwest Alabama CC. **Career Transactions:** Selected by Marlins in 11th round of 1995 draft; signed May 11, 1996 . . . Granted free agency, Dec. 21, 1999; re-signed by Marlins, Dec. 21, 1999.

Knotts signed in 1996 for $35,000 as a draft-and-follow. He has filled out considerably, adding at least 35 pounds to a once-lanky frame. He was the only Marlins starter to make it through the full Arizona Fall League schedule, and he may have done enough to earn a promotion to Triple-A. His strong pitcher's body and durability make him a future workhorse. His fastball tops out at 94 mph, and his two-seamer has heavy sink that produces ground balls when he's on. He's a good athlete for his size. Knotts projects as a No. 3 or 4 starter who will gobble up innings. He has a power curve but tends to overthrow it. Some scouts wonder if he'll develop his secondary pitches enough to be more than a middle reliever in the majors.

Year	Club (League)	Class	W	L	ERA	G	GS	CG	SV	IP	H	R	ER	BB	SO
1996	Marlins (GCL)	R	4	2	2.04	12	9	1	0	57	35	16	13	17	46
1997	Kane County (Mid)	A	1	5	13.05	7	7	0	0	20	33	34	29	17	19
	Utica (NY-P)	A	3	5	3.62	12	12	1	0	70	70	34	28	27	65
1998	Kane County (Mid)	A	8	8	3.87	27	27	3	0	158	144	84	68	66	148
1999	Brevard County (FSL)	A	9	6	4.60	16	16	3	0	94	101	52	48	29	65
	Portland (EL)	AA	6	3	3.75	12	12	1	0	82	79	39	34	33	63
2000	Portland (EL)	AA	9	8	4.66	27	27	2	0	156	161	102	81	63	113
MINOR LEAGUE TOTALS			40	37	4.25	113	110	11	0	637	623	361	301	252	519

13. Rob Henkel, lhp

Born: Aug. 3, 1978. **Ht.:** 6-2. **Wt.:** 210. **Bats:** R. **Throws:** L. **School:** UCLA. **Career Transactions:** Selected by Marlins in third round of 2000 draft; signed Sept. 19, 2000.

Some consider Henkel the most intriguing lefthander in the organization. He signed too late to pitch in 2000 after accepting a $650,000 bonus in September. He attended instructional league but had shoulder fatigue related to an arm-strengthening program. He was limited to fastballs when he got on the mound. Henkel came back from Tommy John surgery in March 1998 to shine in the Cape Cod League the following summer. He turned down $700,000 from the Mets, who took him in the 20th round of the 1999 draft, then went out and piled up 121 strikeouts in his first 79 innings at UCLA in 2000. A late-season fade cost him a spot in the top half of the first round. Henkel's fastball is 90-93 mph when he's on, but his strikeout pitch is a vicious knuckle-curve. The Marlins like to imagine Henkel and A.J. Burnett in the same rotation in a few years, each trying to outdo the other's knuckle-curve.

Year	Club (League)	Class	W	L	ERA	G	GS	CG	SV	IP	H	R	ER	BB	SO
2000					Did Not Play—Signed 2001 Contract										

14. Denny Bautista, rhp

Born: Oct. 23, 1982. **Ht.:** 6-5. **Wt.:** 170. **Bats:** R. **Throws:** R. **Career Transactions:** Signed out of Dominican Republic by Marlins, April 11, 2000.

Bautista's family is friends with the Martinez family, which means Pedro and Ramon Martinez have guided him to this point. Largely on Pedro's advice, Bautista signed with Florida for about $350,000 after the commissioner's office forced the Braves to release their rights to Bautista in the aftermath of the Wilson Betemit flap. Scrawny when he signed, Bautista added weight and velocity. His fastball was up to 91 mph by instructional league. Tall with long, loose limbs, Bautista is open to instruction and has made mechanical adjustments that gave him better tilt and break on his curveball. He has good natural movement and his changeup is advanced for his age. He controls his emotions well for a teenager but tends to be hard on himself. His upside is tremendous.

Year	Club (League)	Class	W	L	ERA	G	GS	CG	SV	IP	H	R	ER	BB	SO
2000	Marlins (GCL)	R	6	2	2.43	11	11	2	0	63	49	24	17	17	58
	Utica (NY-P)	A	0	0	3.60	1	1	0	0	5	4	3	2	2	5
MINOR LEAGUE TOTALS			6	2	2.51	12	12	2	0	68	53	27	19	19	63

15. Geoff Goetz, lhp

Born: April 3, 1979. **Ht.:** 5-11. **Wt.:** 163. **Bats:** L. **Throws:** L. **School:** Jesuit HS, Tampa. **Career Transactions:** Selected by Mets in first round (sixth overall) of 1997 draft; signed July 1, 1997 . . . Traded by Mets to Marlins, July 3, 1998, completing trade in which Marlins sent C Mike Piazza to Mets for OF Preston Wilson, LHP Ed Yarnall and a player to be named (May 22, 1998).

Nagging injuries slowed Goetz in 1999, but a move to the bullpen restored momentum to his career. Working on a program that had him pitching two or three innings every third day, Goetz dominated at Class A Brevard County. He took to the unusual plan with enthusiasm and mixed a 91 mph fastball with a plus knuckle-curve to great effect. He also smoothed out a delivery that used to be violent and led to bouts of shoulder tendinitis as well as a strained lat muscle. Promoted to Double-A for the first time, Goetz struggled as he eased back into a less structured work schedule. A finalist for the U.S. Olympic team, Goetz reported instead to the Arizona Fall League, where the advanced hitters knocked him around and likely sent him back to Double-A for more seasoning. His stuff is good but not overwhelming, and there's some concern about both his durability and his eventual role.

Year	Club (League)	Class	W	L	ERA	G	GS	CG	SV	IP	H	R	ER	BB	SO
1997	Mets (GCL)	R	0	2	2.73	8	6	0	1	26	23	11	8	18	28
1998	Capital City (SAL)	A	5	4	3.96	15	15	0	0	77	68	45	34	37	68
	Kane County (Mid)	A	1	4	4.64	9	9	0	0	43	44	22	22	24	36
1999	Kane County (Mid)	A	5	3	4.26	16	12	0	0	51	52	28	24	24	43
2000	Brevard County (FSL)	A	6	2	1.75	27	0	0	5	67	43	19	13	36	61
	Portland (EL)	AA	1	2	5.96	17	0	0	1	23	27	15	15	11	21
MINOR LEAGUE TOTALS			18	17	3.64	92	42	0	7	287	257	140	116	150	257

16. Luis Ugueto, ss

Born: Feb. 15, 1979. **Ht.:** 5-11. **Wt.:** 185. **Bats:** B. **Throws:** R. **Career Transactions:** Signed out of Venezuela by Marlins, April 28, 1996.

Ugueto has shown little pop at the plate but remains intriguing because of his defensive talents. He has the best infield arm in the organization and is hands-down the best defensive infielder. He can make all the plays and has tremendous range. The switch-hitter has shown progress at the plate, where he was too stiff in his first four seasons. Ugueto is getting more relaxed and generating better bat speed. His makeup is solid. He needs to improve his strike-zone judgment if he's going to keep climbing the ladder. Ugueto missed the first few weeks of the 2000 season with a broken knuckle on his right ring finger. The injury came when he was jumped by several assailants while leaving his girlfriend's house in Venezuela. He's still a work in progress, but should his bat approach his glove in a couple of years, he could be something special.

Year	Club (League)	Class	AVG	G	AB	R	H	2B	3B	HR	RBI	BB	SO	SB
1996	Marlins (DSL)	R	.254	70	240	37	61	4	2	0	12	41	33	14
1997	Maracay 1 (VSL)	R	.180	50	111	17	20	3	2	0	17	18	16	7
1998	Brevard County (FSL)	A	.182	3	11	0	2	0	0	0	0	0	5	0
	Marlins (GCL)	R	.229	50	166	20	38	8	2	0	15	8	37	7
1999	Brevard County (FSL)	A	.133	12	30	1	4	0	0	0	3	7	5	1
	Marlins (GCL)	R	.000	1	3	0	0	0	0	0	2	1	0	0
	Utica (NY-P)	A	.276	56	217	33	60	11	2	1	26	18	46	9
2000	Kane County (Mid)	A	.234	114	393	43	92	13	2	1	32	28	83	12
MINOR LEAGUE TOTALS			.237	356	1171	151	277	39	10	2	107	121	225	50

17. Josh Wilson, ss

Born: March 26, 1981. **Ht.:** 6-1. **Wt.:** 165. **Bats:** R. **Throws:** R. **School:** Mount Lebanon (Pa.) HS. **Career Transactions:** Selected by Marlins in third round of 1999 draft; signed June 5, 1999.

Son of the head baseball coach at Duquesne University, Wilson gathered significant experience as a member of the U.S. junior national team. He wraps his bat and his swing tends to get a little long, but so far he's been able to get away with it. He ranked among the batting leaders in the New York-Penn League, though pitchers may learn to pound him inside as he climbs the ladder. Wilson's speed is just average and his defense, while steady, probably ranks behind the organization's other pure shortstops. Wilson has a strong arm and average range. He got a taste of the Midwest League after Luis Ugueto's late-season injury, and that's probably where he will open 2001.

Year	Club (League)	Class	AVG	G	AB	R	H	2B	3B	HR	RBI	BB	SO	SB
1999	Marlins (GCL)	R	.266	53	203	29	54	9	4	0	27	24	36	14
2000	Utica (NY-P)	A	.344	66	259	43	89	13	6	3	43	29	47	9
	Kane County (Mid)	A	.269	13	52	2	14	3	1	1	6	3	14	0
MINOR LEAGUE TOTALS			.305	53	514	74	157	25	11	4	76	56	97	23

18. Chris Aguila, of

Born: Feb. 23, 1979. **Ht.:** 5-11. **Wt.:** 180. **Bats:** R. **Throws:** R. **School:** McQueen HS, Reno, Nev. **Career Transactions:** Selected by Marlins in third round of 1997 draft; signed June 18, 1997.

Aguila, who tied the national high school record with 29 home runs in 1997, has made improvement across the board, and club officials consider him a potential sleeper if it continues. He played center field last year, showing smooth actions and good judgment. His arm is strong enough for a move to right field. At the plate he tends to be streaky. When he's on he makes consistently hard contact and has power to all fields. Aguila's speed is just average, but he has solid instincts on the bases and knows how to steal a meaningful base. His makeup and instincts make him a candidate to climb higher on this list in the coming years.

Year	Club (League)	Class	AVG	G	AB	R	H	2B	3B	HR	RBI	BB	SO	SB
1997	Marlins (GCL)	R	.217	46	157	12	34	7	0	1	17	21	49	2
1998	Marlins (GCL)	R	.269	51	171	29	46	12	3	4	29	19	49	6
1999	Kane County (Mid)	A	.244	122	430	74	105	21	7	15	78	40	127	14
2000	Brevard County (FSL)	A	.241	136	518	68	125	27	3	9	56	37	105	8
MINOR LEAGUE TOTALS			.243	355	1276	183	310	67	13	29	180	117	330	30

19. Cesar Crespo, of

Born: May 23, 1979. **Ht.:** 5-11. **Wt.:** 170. **Bats:** B. **Throws:** R. **School:** Notre Dame HS, Caguas, P.R.
Career Transactions: Selected by Mets in third round of 1997 draft; signed Sept. 2, 1997 . . . Traded by Mets to Marlins, Sept. 12, 1998, completing trade in which Marlins sent OF Robert Stratton to Mets for a player to be named (March 20, 1998).

The younger brother of Giants infielder Felipe, Cesar was advised by agent Scott Boras during a lengthy holdout and got first-round money from the Mets. When the Marlins got outfielder Robert Stratton in a February 1998 trade, then discovered that Stratton was injured, they sent him back to New York for Crespo. Crespo has established his value as a switch-hitting utilityman. He lit up the Eastern League for the first month of 2000, then cooled off when he changed his approach and started trying to hit for more power. A classic tinkerer, he changed his stance and hand position repeatedly, and his average plummeted. He has a good enough arm to play center or left field. He just needs to gain maturity and experience to carve out a spot in the majors. Crespo is solid enough defensively not to hurt his team wherever he spots into the lineup.

Year	Club (League)	Class	AVG	G	AB	R	H	2B	3B	HR	RBI	BB	SO	SB
1998	Capital City (SAL)	A	.252	116	428	61	108	18	4	6	48	44	114	47
1999	Brevard County (FSL)	A	.286	115	427	63	122	17	2	6	40	62	86	22
2000	Portland (EL)	AA	.257	134	482	96	124	21	6	9	60	77	118	41
MINOR LEAGUE TOTALS			.265	365	1337	220	354	56	12	21	148	183	318	110

20. Jason Grilli, rhp

Born: Nov. 11, 1976. **Ht.:** 6-4. **Wt.:** 185. **Bats:** R. **Throws:** R. **School:** Seton Hall University. **Career Transactions:** Selected by Giants in first round (fourth overall) of 1997 draft; signed July 24, 1997 . . . Traded by Giants with RHP Nate Bump to Marlins for RHP Livan Hernandez, July 24, 1999.

Grilli won his big league debut last May 11, beating the Braves. He showed flashes of the ability that earned him a $1.875 million bonus from the Giants in 1997 and made him the key to the Livan Hernandez trade. But it was the aberration in a season of misery. Invited to spring training to audition for the fifth starter's spot, Grilli pitched poorly and didn't get the part. Next came another round of Triple-A bashings, interrupted only by his night in the majors, then his first trip to the disabled list. A bout of elbow tendinitis led to arthroscopic surgery in August. His stock has plummeted to the point where you wonder if he shouldn't just go by Grilli.com. Overthrowing has been a persistent problem for the son of former big league pitcher Steve Grilli, now a Cardinals scout. He still has great sink on his two-seam fastball, which he throws in the low 90s. But his curve has flattened out and his changeup needs work. Maybe his first health scare will convince him harder isn't always better.

Year	Club (League)	Class	W	L	ERA	G	GS	CG	SV	IP	H	R	ER	BB	SO
1998	Shreveport (TL)	AA	7	10	3.79	21	21	3	0	123	113	60	52	37	100
	Fresno (PCL)	AAA	2	3	5.14	8	8	0	0	42	49	30	24	18	37
1999	Fresno (PCL)	AAA	7	5	5.54	19	19	1	0	101	124	69	62	39	76
	Calgary (PCL)	AAA	1	5	7.68	8	8	0	0	41	56	48	35	23	27
2000	Calgary (PCL)	AAA	1	4	7.19	8	8	0	0	41	58	37	33	23	21
	Florida (NL)	MAJ	1	0	5.40	1	1	0	0	7	11	4	4	2	3
MAJOR LEAGUE TOTALS			1	0	5.40	1	1	0	0	7	11	4	4	2	3
MINOR LEAGUE TOTALS			18	27	5.32	64	64	4	0	348	400	244	206	140	261

21. Terry Byron, rhp

Born: March 28, 1979. **Ht.:** 6-0. **Wt.:** 200. **Bats:** R. **Throws:** R. **School:** Indian River (Fla.) CC. **Career Transactions:** Selected by Marlins in second round of 1999 draft; signed July 18, 1999.

Byron made the top 10 after a standout debut but took a few steps back in his sophomore campaign. A Virgin Islands native, Byron has a hammer-like changeup and a fastball that has hit 94 mph. But he couldn't stay healthy. He missed time early in the season with a stress fracture in his shin, then missed a few turns late with shoulder tendinitis. Byron claims his circle change is self-taught, the grip stolen from a Baseball America photo of Pedro Martinez. His curveball needs work. He's listed at 6 feet but is really closer to 5-foot-9. He has a short, stocky build and puts weight on easily. In fact, the Marlins lectured Byron about his weight at instructional league, where his shoulder woes kept him from throwing. Byron turned down a scholarship from Louisiana State to sign for $350,000, the lowest among 1999's second-rounders. If he continues to struggle with his curve, a move to the bullpen is possible, particularly with the starting depth throughout the system.

Year	Club (League)	Class	W	L	ERA	G	GS	CG	SV	IP	H	R	ER	BB	SO
1999	Utica (NY-P)	A	3	0	1.24	6	6	1	0	29	17	7	4	7	31
2000	Kane County (Mid)	A	1	2	4.18	6	4	0	0	23	18	16	11	15	13
MINOR LEAGUE TOTALS			4	2	2.56	12	10	1	0	52	35	23	15	22	44

22. Jose Soto, of

Born: June 20, 1980. **Ht.:** 6-0. **Wt.:** 160. **Bats:** B. **Throws:** R. **Career Transactions:** Signed out of Dominican Republic by Marlins, Nov. 5, 1996.

When it comes to raw tools, only Abraham Nunez can come close to Soto among Marlins outfield prospects. An injury to his throwing shoulder limited him to mostly pinch-hitting and DH duty in 2000. A switch-hitter with power from both sides of the plate, Soto remains a free swinger. He might have the highest ceiling of any Marlins position player, but so far he has struggled to convert those skills into production. He has tremendously quick hands, but tends to jump at pitches and get himself out that way. He can drive the ball out of the park to all fields. He has the same swing from both sides, which makes his stroke relatively low-maintenance. He has played both left and right field but could take a crack at center down the road. He may get his first taste of full-season ball in 2001.

Year	Club (League)	Class	AVG	G	AB	R	H	2B	3B	HR	RBI	BB	SO	SB
1997	Marlins (DSL)	R	.247	40	77	13	19	2	0	2	5	14	33	5
1998	Marlins (DSL)	R	.250	66	232	46	58	10	1	6	36	33	64	17
1999	Marlins (GCL)	R	.229	49	175	17	40	8	0	4	20	14	56	10
2000	Marlins (GCL)	R	.218	42	165	24	36	9	2	3	19	12	62	8
MINOR LEAGUE TOTALS			.236	197	649	100	153	29	3	15	80	73	215	40

23. Hector Almonte, rhp

Born: Oct. 17, 1975. **Ht.:** 6-2. **Wt.:** 190. **Bats:** R. **Throws:** R. **Career Transactions:** Signed out of Dominican Republic by Marlins, Feb. 9, 1993 . . . Granted free agency, Dec. 18, 1998; re-signed by Marlins, Dec. 19, 1998.

Armed with a fastball that has reached 98 mph, Almonte has been groomed as a closer for years. He got his first taste of the big leagues late in the 1999 season but suffered through a miserable 2000. Sent back to Triple-A, he sulked and got hammered. Shoulder instability plagued him in the first half, though his velocity never dropped. He needs to strengthen his shoulder but there's no major structural damage. Because his fastball tends to be straight, Almonte needs to develop a second pitch. The Marlins have been telling him to throw more sliders, but he's stubborn and lacks confidence with the pitch. Some have suggested he try a splitter. He has lost luster in the organization, but there's still time to turn things around.

Year	Club (League)	Class	W	L	ERA	G	GS	CG	SV	IP	H	R	ER	BB	SO
1993	Marlins (DSL)	R	1	6	4.79	13	7	1	1	56	59	39	30	29	20
1994	Marlins (DSL)	R	3	5	4.34	20	4	0	5	58	68	40	28	26	26
1995	Marlins (DSL)	R	1	2	4.26	20	1	0	9	32	28	17	15	11	27
1996	Marlins (DSL)	R	0	0	0.00	2	0	0	0	2	0	0	0	1	2
1997	Marlins (GCL)	R	2	0	0.76	8	0	0	3	24	12	3	2	6	25
	Kane County (Mid)	A	0	1	3.86	8	1	0	1	14	11	6	6	6	10
1998	Kane County (Mid)	A	1	5	3.95	43	0	0	21	43	51	22	19	19	51
1999	Portland (EL)	AA	1	4	2.84	47	0	0	23	44	42	14	14	26	42
	Florida (NL)	MAJ	0	2	4.20	15	0	0	0	15	20	7	7	6	8
2000	Calgary (PCL)	AAA	0	4	11.17	18	0	0	3	19	36	24	24	9	16
	Marlins (GCL)	R	0	0	4.50	1	1	0	0	2	3	1	1	1	2
	Brevard County (FSL)	A	1	1	2.35	8	2	0	0	15	11	6	4	5	16
	Portland (EL)	AA	0	1	3.60	4	0	0	3	5	5	2	2	4	6
MAJOR LEAGUE TOTALS			0	2	4.20	15	0	0	0	15	20	7	7	6	8
MINOR LEAGUE TOTALS			10	29	4.15	192	16	1	69	315	326	174	145	143	243

24. Will Smith, of/1b

Born: Oct. 23, 1981. **Ht.:** 6-1. **Wt.:** 185. **Bats:** L. **Throws:** R. **School:** Palo Verde (Ariz.) HS. **Career Transactions:** Selected by Marlins in sixth round of 2000 draft; signed June 8, 2000.

Smith set the Arizona high school record for career home runs. He showed a surprisingly complete offensive game in the Gulf Coast League, smashing line drives all over the yard with a smooth lefthanded stroke. Club officials were surprised by his ability to make consistently hard contact. In the outfield he has a good enough arm to play right but probably projects as more of a left fielder because his routes need a lot of work. Smith has average speed and played first base as well in his debut season. Some aren't convinced he has a position at all and wonder about the value of a one-way player in a National League organization.

Year	Club (League)	Class	AVG	G	AB	R	H	2B	3B	HR	RBI	BB	SO	SB
2000	Marlins (GCL)	R	.368	54	204	37	75	21	2	2	34	26	24	7
MINOR LEAGUE TOTALS			.368	54	204	37	75	21	2	2	34	26	24	7

25. Derek Wathan, ss

Born: Dec. 13, 1976. **Ht.:** 6-3. **Wt.:** 190. **Bats:** B. **Throws:** R. **School:** University of Oklahoma. **Career Transactions:** Selected by Marlins in second round of 1998 draft; signed June 8, 1998.

Like his father, former Royals catcher and manager John, and older brother, Mariners catching prospect Dusty, Derek is a take-charge type who commands respect. He doesn't have the strongest arm, but he compensates with a quick release and always seems to make the play. His instincts are among the best in the organization and at least one club official considers him the fiercest competitor in the system. A switch-hitter, he has greatly improved his stroke from the left side. He has learned to use his legs better, relax his hands and generate more bat speed. For the first time in three pro seasons he began to show gap power in 2000. If he hits, he'll play. Wathan was the only position prospect the Marlins sent to the Arizona Fall League. He'll start 2001 in Double-A after struggling there last season.

Year	Club (League)	Class	AVG	G	AB	R	H	2B	3B	HR	RBI	BB	SO	SB
1998	Utica (NY-P)	A	.268	60	224	32	60	8	2	0	23	21	35	10
1999	Kane County (Mid)	A	.254	125	469	71	119	18	4	1	49	53	54	33
2000	Brevard County (FSL)	A	.258	91	364	53	94	18	6	6	49	45	54	19
	Portland (EL)	AA	.220	41	141	13	31	3	2	0	17	13	20	3
MINOR LEAGUE TOTALS			.254	317	1198	169	304	47	14	7	138	132	163	65

26. Jesus Medrano, 2b

Born: Sept. 11, 1978. **Ht.:** 6-0. **Wt.:** 185. **Bats:** R. **Throws:** R. **School:** Bishop Amat HS, La Puente, Calif. **Career Transactions:** Selected by Marlins in 11th round of 1997 draft; signed June 19, 1997.

Medrano has opened eyes with his steady improvement. He projects as an everyday second baseman in the majors. He doesn't have much power, but he knows how to get on base and he has proven to be an aggressive basestealer. He takes great pride in his ability to wreak havoc on the bases, at times to the detriment of the rest of his game. Some in the organization would like to see him show similar devotion to improving his bat. Medrano has worked on shortening his swing with two strikes and has cut down on his unproductive outs. He has the ability to play all the infield spots and is athletic enough to stick in the outfield in a pinch. Medrano will be teamed with Derek Wathan again this year in Double-A.

Year	Club (League)	Class	AVG	G	AB	R	H	2B	3B	HR	RBI	BB	SO	SB
1997	Marlins (GCL)	R	.279	40	111	20	31	4	0	0	16	19	18	16
1998	Marlins (GCL)	R	.286	48	175	42	50	11	1	2	15	21	30	26
1999	Kane County (Mid)	A	.274	118	445	64	122	26	5	5	46	36	92	42
2000	Brevard County (FSL)	A	.219	117	466	56	102	18	3	3	46	48	98	32
MINOR LEAGUE TOTALS			.255	323	1197	182	305	59	9	10	123	124	238	116

27. Manuel Esquivia, rhp

Born: May 30, 1980. **Ht.:** 6-0. **Wt.:** 165. **Bats:** R. **Throws:** R. **Career Transactions:** Signed out of Colombia by Marlins, Jan. 19, 1997.

Esquivia spent three seasons in the Marlins' Venezuelan program before coming to the United States and remains raw. His four-seam fastball reaches 88-92 mph and he has yet to add a two-seamer to his repertoire. Esquivia also throws a curveball and changeup, and he can throw all three of his pitches for strikes. He has a short-arm delivery that recalls Ken Hill. Esquivia made some mechanical adjustments at instructional league that produced quick results. He's intelligent with a willingness to learn, as shown by his rapidly improving English. He has a competitive streak that club officials like.

Year	Club (League)	Class	W	L	ERA	G	GS	CG	SV	IP	H	R	ER	BB	SO
1997	Maracay 1 (VSL)	R	4	4	4.27	19	0	0	0	59	70	42	28	24	33
1998	Guacara 1 (VSL)	R	0	2	5.46	7	6	0	0	31	30	20	19	16	34
1999	Ciudad Alianza (VSL)	R	5	4	3.00	13	11	1	0	69	47	31	23	37	94
2000	Marlins (GCL)	R	6	1	2.78	12	11	0	0	65	42	20	20	24	77
	Utica (NY-P)	A	1	0	2.45	2	2	0	0	11	9	3	3	4	14
MINOR LEAGUE TOTALS			16	11	3.56	53	30	1	0	235	198	116	93	105	252

28. Mark Roberts, rhp

Born: Sept. 29, 1975. **Ht.:** 6-2. **Wt.:** 205. **Bats:** R. **Throws:** R. **School:** University of South Florida. **Career Transactions:** Selected by White Sox in fourth round of 1996 draft; signed June 13, 1996 . . . Traded by White Sox to Marlins, Dec. 12, 2000, completing trade in which Marlins sent 2B Amaury Garcia to White Sox for a player to be named (Nov. 27, 2000).

When the Marlins tired of Amaury Garcia and decided he wasn't suited for a big league utility role, they traded him for Roberts. He started the 2000 season as a reliever with Double-A Birmingham but wound up as a big winner in the Triple-A rotation. Roberts still was stuck behind several prospects in baseball's most pitching-rich organization. He had a tendency to nibble but went right after hitters last season, when his fastball jumped from the high 80s to 92-94 mph. He also threw his slider harder than in recent years. With the added velocity, both pitches had more bite. Roberts might have a future as a starter, though his shortest road would be as a swingman. He could force his way into the Florida picture this year.

Year	Club (League)	Class	W	L	ERA	G	GS	CG	SV	IP	H	R	ER	BB	SO
1996	Hickory (SAL)	A	4	6	4.88	13	13	0	0	72	70	42	39	19	62
1997	Hickory (SAL)	A	0	2	3.68	4	4	0	0	22	23	12	9	9	14
	Winston-Salem (Car)	A	5	9	4.04	14	14	3	0	91	78	48	41	45	64
1998	Winston-Salem (Car)	A	9	9	3.92	27	25	2	0	165	165	88	72	50	142
1999	Birmingham (SL)	AA	5	8	3.40	33	17	0	2	124	108	64	47	41	84
2000	Birmingham (SL)	AA	6	3	3.75	17	8	0	3	60	65	27	25	17	46
	Charlotte (IL)	AAA	7	2	2.10	14	10	1	0	64	58	16	15	20	38
MINOR LEAGUE TOTALS			36	39	3.72	122	91	6	5	599	567	297	248	201	450

29. Brandon Harper, c

Born: April 29, 1976. **Ht.:** 6-4. **Wt.:** 200. **Bats:** R. **Throws:** R. **School:** Dallas Baptist University. **Career Transactions:** Selected by Marlins in fourth round of 1997 draft; signed June 24, 1997.

Harper has inherited the mantle as the Marlins' top catching prospect. He has yet to distinguish himself with the bat, but injuries have slowed his progress. The latest was a strained oblique muscle that kept him out of instructional league. He missed the first half of 2000 after he tore a ligament in his right thumb blocking home plate. A classic catch-and-throw guy, he's solid behind the plate. Harper shows leadership and calls a good game. He is learning to use his hands more rather than rely on his thick upper body. When he does make contact, he can hit balls hard to all fields. Florida's signing of Charles Johnson to a five-year contract likely cuts off any chance Harper will have of starting for the Marlins.

Year	Club (League)	Class	AVG	G	AB	R	H	2B	3B	HR	RBI	BB	SO	SB
1997	Marlins (GCL)	R	.000	2	6	0	0	0	0	0	1	0	1	0
	Utica (NY-P)	A	.257	47	152	27	39	7	2	2	22	19	32	1
1998	Kane County (Mid)	A	.231	113	412	34	95	22	2	4	50	42	64	1
1999	Brevard County (FSL)	A	.268	81	280	35	75	9	0	4	40	30	31	1
2000	Portland (EL)	AA	.208	37	125	15	26	3	0	5	17	12	23	0
	Marlins (GCL)	R	.296	8	27	8	8	1	0	0	2	7	4	0
MINOR LEAGUE TOTALS			.243	288	1002	119	243	42	4	15	132	110	155	3

30. Nate Bump, rhp

Born: July 24, 1976. **Ht.:** 6-2. **Wt.:** 185. **Bats:** R. **Throws:** R. **School:** Penn State University. **Career Transactions:** Selected by Giants in first round (25th overall) of 1998 draft; signed June 17, 1998 . . . Traded by Giants with RHP Jason Grilli to Marlins for RHP Livan Hernandez, July 24, 1999.

Bump hoped to use the 2000 Arizona Fall League the way Brad Penny did the year before, to create momentum after a disappointing year at Double-A. Instead, a recurrence of tendinitis in the back of his shoulder ended Bump's AFL experience after just 2⅔ innings. He missed his final three turns at Portland with the same ailment, but an MRI revealed no damage. His upper-80s fastball won't blow hitters away, and Bump admits he threw too many "get-me-over" curves to thrive at Double-A. But he made good progress with his changeup in the second half and learned to relax on the mound. His two-seamer has good life, but Bump has a tendency not to trust it. Assuming he's healthy, he'll move to Triple-A in 2001.

Year	Club (League)	Class	W	L	ERA	G	GS	CG	SV	IP	H	R	ER	BB	SO
1998	Salem-Keizer (NWL)	A	0	0	0.00	2	2	0	0	8	5	0	0	3	8
	San Jose (Cal)	A	6	1	1.75	11	11	0	0	61	37	13	12	24	61
1999	Shreveport (TL)	AA	4	10	3.31	17	17	1	0	92	85	40	34	32	59
	Portland (EL)	AA	2	6	6.07	8	8	0	0	43	57	38	29	12	33
2000	Portland (EL)	AA	8	9	4.57	26	26	3	0	149	169	85	76	49	98
MINOR LEAGUE TOTALS			20	26	3.83	64	64	4	0	354	353	176	151	120	259

Houston
Astros

I n one sense, the Astros' 2000 performance was shocking. Their 30-57 record before the all-star break was the worst in baseball, and their overall 72-90 finish ended streaks of eight straight seasons at .500 or better and three consecutive National League Central titles—all accomplished with a less-than-Texas-sized budget.

While last season was tremendously disappointing, it wasn't a portent of Houston's future. The club will return to contender status soon, perhaps even in 2001.

Houston had the majors' worst record in one-run games last year at 15-31. Repeated analysis has shown that performance in one-run contests is more a function of fortune than the quality of a team. When the Astros weren't dropping tight games, they were 57-59, playing nearly .500 ball in a season in which most of their breaks were bad. Craig Biggio, Shane Reynolds and Billy Wagner suffered the first significant injuries of their major league careers. Ken Caminiti's return to Houston was a failure. And Jose Lima turned back into a pumpkin. After regrouping, the Astros went 42-33 after the all-star break.

General manager Gerry Hunsicker took heat for two salary-dictated trades after the 1999 season, but in retrospect he didn't do

By Jim Callis

too badly. Mike Hampton pitched well for the Mets, but both he and the overrated Derek Bell fled New York as free agents, while the Astros will hang on to flamethrowing righthander Octavio Dotel. Carl Everett had a monster year for the Red Sox, but his replacement in center, Richard Hidalgo, did the same and was less volatile. Shortstop Adam Everett and lefthander Greg Miller, the two prospects Hunsicker got from Boston, now rank among the organization's best.

Everett and Miller joined a thriving farm system that should be able to plug the holes on the big league roster. Each of the Astros' six affiliates has won a championship in the last three seasons: Triple-A New Orleans and short-season Auburn in 1998, high Class A Kissimmee and Rookie-level Martinsville in 1999, and Double-A Round Rock and Class A Michigan in 2000.

Round Rock was Baseball America's Minor League Team of the Year, setting a Double-A attendance record and featuring several prospects who should establish themselves in Houston in the next couple of years: righthanders Roy Oswalt, Tim Redding, Tony McKnight and Scott Linebrink; lefthanders Wilfredo Rodriguez and Miller; second baseman Keith Ginter; and third baseman Morgan Ensberg.

OrganizationOverview

General manager: Gerry Hunsicker. Farm director: Tim Purpura. Scouting director: David Lakey.

2000 PERFORMANCE

Class	Team	League	W	L	Pct.	Finish*	Manager
Majors	Houston	National	72	90	.444	12th (16)	Larry Dierker
Triple-A	New Orleans Zephyrs	Pacific Coast	68	74	.479	11th (16)	Tony Pena
Double-A	Round Rock Express	Texas	83	57	.593	1st (8)	Jackie Moore
High A	#Kissimmee Cobras	Florida State	73	66	.525	6th (14)	Manny Acta
Low A	Michigan Battle Cats	Midwest	82	56	.594	2nd (14)	Al Pedrique
Short-season	†Auburn Doubledays	New York-Penn	32	42	.432	11th (14)	John Massarelli
Rookie	Martinsville Astros	Appalachian	30	36	.455	8th (10)	Brad Wellman
OVERALL 2000 MINOR LEAGUE RECORD			367	331	.526	8th (30)	

*Finish in overall standings (No. of teams in league). #Affiliate will be in Lexington (South Atlantic/low A) in 2001. †Affiliate will be in Pittsfield (New York-Penn) in 2001.

ORGANIZATION LEADERS

BATTING
*AVG	Keith Ginter, Round Rock	.333
R	Keith Ginter, Round Rock	108
H	**Eric Cole**, Round Rock	158
TB	**Eric Cole**, Round Rock	270
2B	**Eric Cole**, Round Rock	46
3B	Jon Topolski, Michigan	12
HR	Morgan Ensberg, Round Rock	28
RBI	Jason Lane, Michigan	104
BB	Jon Topolski, Michigan	105
SO	Mike Rosamond, Kissimmee	151
SB	Donaldo Mendez, Michigan	39

PITCHING
W	Roy Oswalt, Kissimmee/Round Rock	15
L	Esteban Maldonado, Kissimmee	12
#ERA	Ryan Jamison, Michigan	2.10
G	**Travis Wade**, Kissimmee/Round Rock	61
CG	Mike Nannini, Michigan/Kissimmee	5
SV	Chris George, Michigan	24
	Travis Wade, Kissimmee/Round Rock	24
IP	Tim Redding, Kissimmee/Round Rock	181
BB	Derek Stanford, Michigan	92
SO	Tim Redding, Kissimmee/Round Rock	192

*Minimum 250 at-bats. #Minimum 75 innings.

TOP PROSPECTS OF THE DECADE

1991	Andujar Cedeno, ss
1992	Brian Williams, rhp
1993	Todd Jones, rhp
1994	Phil Nevin, 3b
1995	Brian Hunter, of
1996	Billy Wagner, lhp
1997	Richard Hidalgo, of
1998	Richard Hidalgo, of
1999	Lance Berkman, of
2000	Wilfredo Rodriguez, lhp

TOP DRAFT PICKS OF THE DECADE

1991	*John Burke, rhp
1992	Phil Nevin, 3b
1993	Billy Wagner, lhp
1994	Ramon Castro, c
1995	Tony McKnight, rhp
1996	Mark Johnson, rhp
1997	Lance Berkman, 1b
1998	Brad Lidge, rhp
1999	Mike Rosamond, of
2000	Robert Stiehl, rhp

*Did not sign.

Cole   **Wade**

BEST TOOLS

Best Hitter for Average	Keith Ginter
Best Power Hitter	Morgan Ensberg
Fastest Baserunner	Modesto de Aza
Best Fastball	Tim Redding
Best Breaking Ball	Brad Lidge
Best Control	Roy Oswalt
Best Defensive Catcher	John Buck
Best Defensive Infielder	Adam Everett
Best Infield Arm	Adam Everett
Best Defensive Outfielder	Gavin Wright
Best Outfield Arm	Mike Rosamond

PROJECTED 2004 LINEUP

Catcher	John Buck
First Base	Jeff Bagwell
Second Base	Keith Ginter
Third Base	Morgan Ensberg
Shortstop	Adam Everett
Left Field	Lance Berkman
Center Field	Gavin Wright
Right Field	Richard Hidalgo
No. 1 Starter	Scott Elarton
No. 2 Starter	Roy Oswalt
No. 3 Starter	Octavio Dotel
No. 4 Starter	Wilfredo Rodriguez
No. 5 Starter	Tim Redding
Closer	Billy Wagner

ALL-TIME LARGEST BONUSES

Robert Stiehl, 2000	$1,250,000
Brad Lidge, 1998	1,070,000
Lance Berkman, 1997	1,000,000
Mark Johnson, 1996	775,000
Scott Elarton, 1994	750,000

DraftAnalysis

2000 Draft

Best Pro Debut: RHP Robert Stiehl (1) pitched just 11 innings in short-season and Class A, but they were 11 overpowering innings. He had a 1.69 ERA and a 20-5 strikeout-walk ratio, and opponents batted .135 against him.

Best Athlete: Described by assistant scouting director Pat Murphy as "5-foot-11 and 190 pounds of muscle," OF Jake Whitesides (5) reminds the Astros of Lenny Dykstra.

Best Hitter: Whitesides, though he batted just .178-1-6 at Rookie-level Martinsville with 49 strikeouts in 129 at-bats in his pro debut.

Best Raw Power: Though he didn't show it in Martinsville, Whitesides' best tool is power, and he hit 11 home runs in 20 swings at Kauffman Stadium in a predraft workout for the Royals. Houston also likes the pop in the bats of 3B Nate Nelson (10) and OF Anthony Acevedo (13).

Fastest Runner: The Astros didn't sign any speedsters. Whitesides is the only above-average runner, and he's only slightly better than average.

Best Defensive Player: Tommy Whiteman (6) is a slick 6-foot-3 shortstop with a strong arm.

Best Fastball: Stiehl threw 97 mph during the summer, a velocity surpassed by RHP Anthony Pluta (3) in instructional league. They both average 93-95 mph. RHP **Chad Qualls** (2) tops out at 95 mph, but his fastball might be even nastier. It has a lot of sink, and righthanders have trouble

picking it up from his low three-quarters angle.

Most Intriguing Background: Stiehl was primarily a catcher at El Camino (Calif.) JC but began closing games last season. He would often catch the first eight innings of a game and pitch the ninth. The Astros envision him following the same career path that Troy Percival did successfully with the Angels.

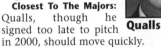
Qualls

Closest To The Majors: Qualls, though he signed too late to pitch in 2000, should move quickly.

Best Late-Round Pick: Acevedo generates plenty of leverage with a 6-foot-5 frame and he runs well enough to have moved from first base, his position at Fresno State, to left field.

The One Who Got Away: Power-hitting 3B Eric Keefner (4) would have been the best athlete signed by Houston, but he decided to play baseball and football at Arizona State instead.

Assessment: This was a typical Astros draft in that they went after raw arms and inexpensive college seniors, such as Qualls, Nelson and Acevedo. Just 12 of their 43 selections were used on high school players. Stiehl (inexperience) and Pluta (4-3, 4.76 as a high school senior) were gambles, though Houston likes the early returns.

1999 Draft

Disappointing OF Mike Rosamond (1) is one more bad season away from being written off. The Astros think RHP Ryan Jamison (17) is a sleeper, while RHP Jimmy Barrett (3) and OF/1B Jason Lane (6) have a chance. **Grade: C–**

1998 Draft

Houston forfeited two top picks and didn't sign its third- or fourth-rounders. It still did a fine job, hauling in RHPs Brad Lidge (1) and Mike Nannini (1), C John Buck (7), 3B Morgan Ensberg (9), 2B Keith Ginter (10) and OF Gavin Wright (33, draft-and-follow). **Grade: B**

1997 Draft

The Astros didn't sign their third- through fifth-round picks. But they did get OF Lance Berkman (1), who looks like he'll be a big league star this year, and RHP Tim Redding (20, draft-and-follow), who could be one in a couple of seasons. **Grade: A–**

1996 Draft

RHP Mark Johnson is pedestrian as far as first-round picks go. But RHPs Roy Oswalt (23) and Wade Miller (20) are frontline starters who came late in the draft. Houston could have saved itself some money if it had signed Rosamond (71) out of high school. **Grade: B+**

Note: Draft analysis prepared by Jim Callis. Numbers in parentheses indicate draft rounds.

. . . Righthanders have no chance when Oswalt throws his heat knee-high on the outside corner.

Roy
Oswalt rhp

Born: Aug. 29, 1977.
Ht.: 6-0. **Wt.:** 170.
Bats: R. **Throws:** R.
School: Holmes (Miss.) JC.
Career Transactions: Selected by Astros in 23rd round of 1996 draft; signed May 18, 1997.

One way the Astros try to keep player-development costs down is by using the draft-and-follow process. They identify raw players and try to sign them after they refine their skills in junior college. Their best work may have been done with Oswalt, though he didn't come cheap. He would have been a first-round pick had Houston not handed him a $500,000 bonus shortly before the 1997 draft.

Oswalt has a plus fastball, but he seemed more concerned with his velocity than in becoming a refined pitcher in his first three pro seasons. That changed in 2000. He was promoted to Double-A Round Rock for what was supposed to be an emergency start. When he responded with a 15-strikeout shutout, he never looked back. He went on to lead Texas League starters in strikeouts (9.8) and fewest hits (7.4) per nine innings, and his 1.94 ERA was the circuit's lowest in a decade. Then he went to Sydney with the U.S. Olympic team. He contributed to the gold-medal effort with two strong starts against Korea, allowing two runs in 13 innings. Oswalt pitched more under control in 2000, which is why his career took off. He still pitches up in the strike zone with his fastball at times, but for the most part he worried about painting the black at 92-94 mph rather than trying to reach back and throw 96. Righthanders have no chance when he throws his heat knee-high on the outside corner. He hides the ball well, and when he doesn't try to max out his velocity, his fastball explodes out of his hand with late life. His curveball jumps straight down, and his changeup at times serves as a third above-average pitch. He's an absolute warrior who always gives his best effort.

Oswalt must remember that less is more when it comes to his fastball. He needs to get more consistent with his curveball and changeup, as he doesn't always finish off the latter pitch. If Oswalt continues to progress like he did last year, he'll be ready for Houston after spending a half-season in Triple-A. He has the stuff to be the club's No. 1 starter down the road.

Year	Club (League)	Class	W	L	ERA	G	GS	CG	SV	IP	H	R	ER	BB	SO
1997	Astros (GCL)	R	1	1	0.64	5	5	0	0	28	25	7	2	7	28
	Auburn (NY-P)	A	2	4	4.53	9	9	1	0	52	50	29	26	15	44
1998	Astros (GCL)	R	1	1	2.25	4	4	0	0	16	10	6	4	1	27
	Auburn (NY-P)	A	4	5	2.18	11	11	0	0	70	49	24	17	31	67
1999	Michigan (Mid)	A	13	4	4.46	22	22	2	0	151	144	78	75	54	143
2000	Kissimmee (FSL)	A	4	3	2.98	8	8	0	0	45	52	15	15	11	47
	Round Rock (TL)	AA	11	4	1.94	19	18	2	0	130	106	37	28	22	141
MINOR LEAGUE TOTALS			36	22	3.05	78	77	5	0	493	436	196	167	141	497

2. Wilfredo Rodriguez, lhp

Born: March 20, 1979. **Ht.:** 6-3. **Wt.:** 180. **Bats:** L. **Throws:** L. **Career Transactions:** Signed out of Venezuela by Astros, July 20, 1995.

The Astros have mined Venezuela better than any organization, signing 12 major leaguers. None has earned a victory for Houston, though Rodriguez should change that soon. After leading the high Class A Florida State League in wins and strikeouts in 1999, he was stymied by shoulder tendinitis and a hamstring pull last year. Rodriguez was at this best in the postseason, winning the opener and clincher in the Texas League finals. He is a rare power lefthander. He throws a 93-95 mph fastball with plenty of life, as well as a hard curveball. At 6-foot-3 and with long arms, he throws his pitches on a nasty downward plane. Rodriguez needs to polish his mechanics. He has an inconsistent release point that costs him command. He'll need to throw his changeup more often and for more strikes as he moves up through the organization. After pitching well in the playoffs and in the Venezuelan League, Rodriguez appears to be back. He'll begin 2001 in Double-A and needs another year and a half in the minors. The Astros haven't had a lefty in their rotation since trading Mike Hampton, and they're looking to Rodriguez to fill that void.

Year	Club (League)	Class	W	L	ERA	G	GS	CG	SV	IP	H	R	ER	BB	SO
1996	Astros/Red Sox (DSL)	R	1	2	2.97	18	0	0	0	33	28	17	11	21	29
1997	Astros (GCL)	R	8	2	3.04	12	12	1	0	68	54	30	23	32	71
1998	Quad City (Mid)	A	11	5	3.05	28	27	1	0	165	122	70	56	62	170
1999	Kissimmee (FSL)	A	15	7	2.88	25	24	0	0	153	108	55	49	62	148
2000	Kissimmee (FSL)	A	3	5	4.75	9	9	1	0	53	43	29	28	30	52
	Round Rock (TL)	AA	2	4	5.77	11	11	0	0	58	54	42	37	52	55
MINOR LEAGUE TOTALS			40	25	3.46	103	83	3	0	530	409	243	204	259	525

3. Tim Redding, rhp

Born: Feb. 12, 1978. **Ht.:** 6-0. **Wt.:** 180. **Bats:** R. **Throws:** R. **School:** Monroe (N.Y.) CC. **Career Transactions:** Selected by Astros in 20th round of 1997 draft; signed May 21, 1998.

Redding was a center fielder as well as a pitcher at Monroe Community College before signing as a draft-and-follow in 1998. He stalled as a pro starter in 1999 before moving to the bullpen and blowing away Class A Midwest League hitters. Returned to the rotation in 2000, Redding was the most valuable pitcher in the Florida State League and didn't permit an earned run in 16⅔ innings in the Texas League playoffs. Managers rated Redding's fastball the best in the FSL. He repeatedly hits the mid-90s, and he's capable of touching 98 mph with a four-seamer that rides or getting filthy sink with a two-seamer. His power curveball can be unhittable, and at times his changeup is above-average. Redding sometimes tries to guide his pitches, which leads to lapses in control. He needs to improve the consistency of his curveball and changeup, as well as a slider he added last year. He's competitive but sometimes gets too emotional. Once he tweaks his command and his secondary pitches, Redding will be ready for the majors. He should reach Triple-A in 2001. Because Houston has pitching depth, he could become a big league closer one day.

Year	Club (League)	Class	W	L	ERA	G	GS	CG	SV	IP	H	R	ER	BB	SO
1998	Auburn (NY-P)	A	7	3	4.52	16	15	0	1	74	49	44	37	50	98
1999	Michigan (Mid)	A	8	6	4.97	43	11	0	14	105	84	69	58	76	141
2000	Kissimmee (FSL)	A	12	5	2.68	24	24	0	0	155	125	62	46	57	170
	Round Rock (TL)	AA	2	0	3.46	5	5	0	0	26	14	12	10	22	22
MINOR LEAGUE TOTALS			29	14	3.78	88	55	0	15	359	272	187	151	205	431

4. Tony McKnight, rhp

Born: June 29, 1977. **Ht.:** 6-5. **Wt.:** 205. **Bats:** R. **Throws:** R. **School:** Arkansas HS, Texarkana, Ark. **Career Transactions:** Selected by Astros in first round (22nd overall) of 1995 draft; signed June 2, 1995.

McKnight was a signability pick who accepted $500,000, the lowest bonus among first-rounders in 1995. He was overworked in high school, throwing more than 250 pitches one day, and resulting elbow and shoulder problems hindered him in his first two years as a pro. He had a breakthrough season in Double-A in 1999 and made four quality starts in six tries in his big league debut last year. He reminds scouts of Ron Darling because he'll show three plus pitches at times. He works with a 92-94 mph fastball, a curveball and a changeup. He throws strikes and has a deceptive delivery. When he was less than 100 percent, he was tagged with a reputation for being soft, but he has shed that and is recognized as a competitor. McKnight must understand he's not a power pitcher. His fastball isn't lively, and moves less when he gets it up in the zone. He'll sometimes overthrow and hang his pitches. He didn't overmatch hitters in the minors last year before his September callup. McKnight pitched well in Houston but would benefit from more Triple-A experience. He'll probably get it, though he could make the big league rotation with a strong spring.

Year	Club (League)	Class	W	L	ERA	G	GS	CG	SV	IP	H	R	ER	BB	SO
1995	Astros (GCL)	R	1	1	3.86	3	3	0	0	12	14	5	5	2	8
1996	Astros (GCL)	R	2	2	6.66	9	6	0	0	24	34	26	18	7	17
1997	Quad City (Mid)	A	4	9	4.68	20	20	0	0	115	116	71	60	55	92
1998	Kissimmee (FSL)	A	11	13	4.67	28	28	0	0	154	191	101	80	50	104
1999	Jackson (TL)	AA	9	9	2.75	24	24	0	0	160	134	60	49	44	118
2000	Round Rock (TL)	AA	0	2	4.78	6	6	0	0	32	39	19	17	10	24
	New Orleans (PCL)	AAA	4	8	4.56	19	19	0	0	118	129	66	60	36	63
	Houston (NL)	MAJ	4	1	3.86	6	6	1	0	35	35	19	15	9	23
MAJOR LEAGUE TOTALS			4	1	3.86	6	6	1	0	35	35	19	15	9	23
MINOR LEAGUE TOTALS			31	44	4.22	109	106	0	0	616	657	348	289	204	426

5. Robert Stiehl, rhp

Born: Dec. 9, 1980. **Ht.:** 6-3. **Wt.:** 205. **Bats:** R. **Throws:** R. **School:** El Camino (Calif.) JC. **Career Transactions:** Selected by Astros in first round (27th overall) of 2000 draft; signed July 21, 2000.

RICH ABEL

The Astros hope Stiehl can make the same catcher-to-closer transition that Ricky Bottalico and Troy Percival did. Stiehl barely pitched until last spring, when he threw 97 mph in front of 80 scouts in his first start. Most of the time, he caught for eight innings and then took the mound in the ninth. Stiehl has a fresh, loose arm that can throw 93-94 mph fastballs with regularity. He also has a power curveball that breaks straight down. Pro hitters went 5-for-37 (.135) with 20 strikeouts against him in his pro debut. He's strong and athletic but developed a sore shoulder toward the end of the season and was shut down with tendinitis. It's not a long-term concern. He's obviously raw as a pitcher and in need of experience. Houston will make him a starter next year to get him innings. In that role, he'll have to pick up a changeup and learn to keep his pitch counts down. The Astros realize Stiehl will need plenty of time to develop and will remain patient. To that end, he'll start this season in the low Class A Michigan rotation. His future remains in the bullpen.

Year	Club (League)	Class	W	L	ERA	G	GS	CG	SV	IP	H	R	ER	BB	SO
2000	Auburn (NY-P)	A	1	0	0.93	5	0	0	1	10	4	1	1	4	19
	Michigan (Mid)	A	0	0	9.00	1	0	0	0	1	1	1	1	1	1
MINOR LEAGUE TOTALS			1	0	1.69	6	0	0	1	11	5	2	2	5	20

6. Adam Everett, ss

Born: Feb. 6, 1977. **Ht.:** 6-1. **Wt.:** 167. **Bats:** R. **Throws:** R. **School:** University of South Carolina. **Career Transactions:** Selected by Red Sox in first round (12th overall) of 1998 draft; signed Aug. 4, 1998 . . . Traded by Red Sox with LHP Greg Miller to Astros for OF Carl Everett, Dec. 15, 1999.

JOHN SPEAR

Everett was the key player Houston received from Boston after it decided it couldn't afford Carl Everett (no relation). Just before making the trade, the Red Sox paid Everett $725,000 and put him on the major league roster, apparently as part of a side deal to defer part of his original $1.725 million signing bonus. Despite a lackluster Triple-A performance last year, Everett started for gold medal-winning Team USA at the Olympics, where he went 1-for-23. Rated the Triple-A Pacific Coast League's best defensive shortstop in 2000, Everett has Gold Glove tools. His range and arm are outstanding, and he has sure hands and keen instincts. Those who believe in him offensively envision him as a No. 2 hitter in a couple of years, based on his bat control, ability to draw walks and speed. He did bat .292 in his final two months in the PCL after a .215 start. Everett will have to get a lot stronger to become a No. 2 hitter, though, and several PCL managers think that projection is too optimistic. He can't handle inside fastballs, and he chases sliders off the plate. He has a little power, which can be a detriment because he hits too many fly balls. Everett's defense could be so overwhelming that he'll beat out Julio Lugo for Houston's shortstop job in spring training. He would be much better off working on his hitting in Triple-A.

Year	Club (League)	Class	AVG	G	AB	R	H	2B	3B	HR	RBI	BB	SO	SB
1998	Lowell (NY-P)	A	.296	21	71	11	21	6	2	0	9	11	13	2
1999	Trenton (EL)	AA	.263	98	338	56	89	11	0	10	44	41	64	21
2000	New Orleans (PCL)	AAA	.245	126	453	82	111	25	2	5	37	75	100	13
MINOR LEAGUE TOTALS			.256	245	862	149	221	42	4	15	90	127	177	36

7. Greg Miller, lhp

Born: Sept. 30, 1979. **Ht.:** 6-5. **Wt.:** 215. **Bats:** L. **Throws:** L. **School:** Aurora (Ill.) West HS. **Career Transactions:** Selected by Red Sox in fifth round of 1997 draft; signed July 2, 1997 . . . Traded by Red Sox with SS Adam Everett to Astros for OF Carl Everett, Dec. 15, 1999.

Adam Everett was the bigger name in the Carl Everett trade, but the Astros did their homework and got Miller as well. An all-state basketball player at his Illinois high school, he made four appearances in the Texas League playoffs last year without allowing an earned run. Miller has a tremendous pitcher's body and is creative on the mound. He mixes four pitches, all of which are at least average, and throws them for strikes. He has an 89-93 mph fastball, a vastly improved curveball, a changeup and a slider. Unlike a lot of lefties with not-quite-dominating stuff, he doesn't have any problems getting righthanders out. Because he lacks a consistently plus pitch, Miller might have trouble with more advanced hitters. His arm action is a little long, so he's not as deceptive as he could be, though he counters by hiding the ball with his delivery. Miller will return to Double-A to start 2001.

Year	Club (League)	Class	W	L	ERA	G	GS	CG	SV	IP	H	R	ER	BB	SO
1997	Red Sox (GCL)	R	0	2	3.72	4	4	0	0	10	8	6	4	6	6
1998	Red Sox (GCL)	R	6	0	2.49	11	7	0	0	43	33	18	12	18	47
1999	Augusta (SAL)	A	10	6	3.10	25	25	1	0	137	109	54	47	56	146
2000	Kissimmee (FSL)	A	10	8	3.70	24	24	1	0	146	131	63	60	46	109
	Round Rock (TL)	AA	0	0	0.00	2	0	0	0	2	0	0	0	1	2
MINOR LEAGUE TOTALS			26	16	3.28	66	60	2	0	338	281	141	123	127	310

8. John Buck, c

Born: July 7, 1980. **Ht.:** 6-3. **Wt.:** 200. **Bats:** R. **Throws:** R. **School:** Taylorsville (Utah) HS. **Career Transactions:** Selected by Astros in seventh round of 1998 draft; signed June 11, 1998.

Buck really put his game together last season, when Midwest League managers thought he was a better prospect than Seattle's Ryan Christianson, the top catcher taken in the 1999 draft. Buck has solid all-around skills. Offensively, he has a quick bat and fine patience. One day, some of his doubles will turn into home runs. Behind the plate, he took charge of Michigan's pitching staff and ranked third in the league by throwing out 39 percent of basestealers. Buck doesn't extend his arms enough on his swing, leaving him vulnerable inside and making it difficult for him to pull the ball. He'll cut down on his strikeouts once he learns to read breaking pitches. He doesn't run well and could become a baseclogger down the road. His release sometimes gets long, robbing him of accuracy on his throws. It's uncertain where Buck will play this year because the Astros have no high Class A club, but they hope he'll be ready to take over when Brad Ausmus slows down.

Year	Club (League)	Class	AVG	G	AB	R	H	2B	3B	HR	RBI	BB	SO	SB
1998	Astros (GCL)	R	.286	36	126	24	36	9	0	3	15	13	22	2
1999	Auburn (NY-P)	A	.245	63	233	36	57	17	0	3	29	25	48	7
	Michigan (Mid)	A	.100	4	10	1	1	1	0	0	0	2	3	0
2000	Michigan (Mid)	A	.282	109	390	57	110	33	0	10	71	55	81	2
MINOR LEAGUE TOTALS			.269	212	759	118	204	60	0	16	115	95	154	11

9. Mike Nannini, rhp

Born: Aug. 9, 1980. **Ht.:** 5-11. **Wt.:** 170. **Bats:** R. **Throws:** R. **School:** Green Valley HS, Henderson, Nev. **Career Transactions:** Selected by Astros in first round (37th overall) of 1998 draft; signed July 1, 1998.

At Green Valley High, Nannini threw back-to-back no-hitters as a senior and was part of four straight Nevada state championships. He broke into pro ball with 16 consecutive scoreless innings in the Rookie-level Gulf Coast League in 1998. He has moved quickly, reaching high Class A at age 19 last season. Though he lacks size, Nannini doesn't lack stuff. He can touch the mid-90s with his fastball, and he has a plus slider and a decent changeup. He didn't allow a home run in 256 at-bats against lefthanders in 2000. His competitive makeup has spurred the Astros to challenge him with promotions more than they usually do. Like Roy Oswalt and Tony McKnight, Nannini gets into trouble when he thinks he's a power pitcher. At times he'll overthrow, and he'll lose command and movement on his fastball. His heater usually arrives in the low 90s, but occasionally it will dip into the high 80s. His secondary pitches could use more consistency. After the progress he showed in the Florida State League in 2000, Nannini could move up to Double-A to begin this season. At this rate, he'll be pushing to arrive in Houston by late 2002.

Year	Club (League)	Class	W	L	ERA	G	GS	CG	SV	IP	H	R	ER	BB	SO
1998	Astros (GCL)	R	1	1	1.49	8	6	1	0	36	23	6	6	13	39
1999	Michigan (Mid)	A	4	10	4.43	15	15	0	0	87	107	56	43	31	68
	Auburn (NY-P)	A	5	3	1.90	11	11	2	0	76	55	19	16	17	86
2000	Michigan (Mid)	A	7	4	3.55	15	15	3	0	101	85	45	40	33	86
	Kissimmee (FSL)	A	7	3	3.33	12	12	2	0	78	83	34	29	14	56
MINOR LEAGUE TOTALS			24	21	3.18	61	59	8	0	379	353	160	134	108	335

10 Keith Ginter, 2b

Born: May 5, 1976. **Ht.:** 5-10. **Wt.:** 190. **Bats:** R. **Throws:** R. **School:** Texas Tech. **Career Transactions:** Selected by Astros in 10th round of 1998 draft; signed June 7, 1998.

Ginter exploded in 2000. He was Texas League MVP after leading the minors in on-base percentage (.457) and his league in average and hit by pitches (24). In September, he led Round Rock to a playoff championship, then hit his first big league homer off Jimmy Haynes. Ginter is a student of hitting who has a short, quick stroke reminiscent of Paul Molitor's. He has strong hands and arms, and he excels at reading pitches, so he doesn't struggle with breaking balls. He showed more power and speed in 2000 than he had in his first two years as a pro. Defensively, his biggest asset is his quick release when turning double plays. Though he can go the other way, Ginter likes to pull everything he sees. That aside, most of the work he needs to do concerns his defense. He's average at best as a second baseman. He's a bit stiff in the field, and his arm is just adequate. If he can continue to mash, the Astros will be likely to forgive his defense. It's also possible he could be moved to third base. Assuming Craig Biggio is healthy this year, Ginter will spend 2001 in Triple-A.

Year	Club (League)	Class	AVG	G	AB	R	H	2B	3B	HR	RBI	BB	SO	SB
1998	Auburn (NY-P)	A	.315	71	241	55	76	22	1	8	41	60	68	10
1999	Kissimmee (FSL)	A	.263	103	376	66	99	15	4	13	46	61	90	9
	Jackson (TL)	AA	.382	9	34	9	13	1	0	1	6	4	6	0
2000	Round Rock (TL)	AA	.333	125	462	108	154	30	3	26	92	82	127	24
	Houston (NL)	MAJ	.250	5	8	3	2	0	0	1	3	1	3	0
MAJOR LEAGUE TOTALS			.250	5	8	3	2	0	0	1	3	1	3	0
MINOR LEAGUE TOTALS			.307	308	1113	238	342	68	8	48	185	207	291	43

11. Brad Lidge, rhp

Born: Dec. 23, 1976. **Ht.:** 6-5. **Wt.:** 200. **Bats:** R. **Throws:** R. **School:** University of Notre Dame. **Career Transactions:** Selected by Astros in first round (17th overall) of 1998 draft; signed July 2, 1998.

The Astros absolutely love Lidge's arm—when it's healthy. And it has rarely been healthy since they made him the 17th overall pick in the 1998 draft. After three years as a pro, Lidge has racked up more elbow operations (three) than victories (two), and his eight starts last year were a career high. His latest surgery came in November, when he had bone chips removed after they prompted his early exit from the Arizona Fall League. Houston has changed his mechanics and had him scrap his curveball in favor of a slider in order to reduce the stress on his elbow. When he's 100 percent, Lidge has touched 98 mph and throws a consistent 94-95. His slider can be unhittable at times and has draw comparisons to those of J.R. Richard and Todd Worrell. Because Lidge has yet to pick up a changeup or show any durability, his future may lie in the bullpen. He's expected to pitch in Double-A in 2001.

Year	Club (League)	Class	W	L	ERA	G	GS	CG	SV	IP	H	R	ER	BB	SO
1998	Quad City (Mid)	A	0	1	3.27	4	4	0	0	11	10	5	4	5	6
1999	Kissimmee (FSL)	A	0	2	3.38	6	6	0	0	21	13	8	8	11	19
2000	Kissimmee (FSL)	A	2	1	2.81	8	8	0	0	42	28	14	13	15	46
MINOR LEAGUE TOTALS			2	4	3.04	18	18	0	0	74	51	27	25	31	71

12. Gavin Wright, of

Born: May 6, 1979. **Ht.:** 6-2. **Wt.:** 175. **Bats:** R. **Throws:** R. **School:** Blinn (Texas) JC. **Career Transactions:** Selected by Astros in 33rd round of June 1998 draft; signed May 21, 1999.

The Astros don't have much in the way of minor league outfield depth, which isn't a major problem because the big club is stacked with Moises Alou, Lance Berkman, Richard Hidalgo and Daryle Ward. The exception in the system is Wright, who strained his right wrist and hurt his right shoulder in center-field mishaps last year, injuries that limited him to 43 games. He's a line-drive hitter with stolen base speed and home run potential. If all goes well, he could be a 20-homer, 40-steal guy. Wright projects as a .275-.280 hitter who could bat leadoff if he tightens his strike zone. He's also the best defensive outfielder in the system, getting good jumps and using his wheels to make up for an adequate arm. Because he missed much of 2000, he'll spend 2001 with one of Houston's low Class A teams.

Year	Club (League)	Class	AVG	G	AB	R	H	2B	3B	HR	RBI	BB	SO	SB
1999	Martinsville (Appy)	R	.309	61	236	37	73	17	3	2	29	25	46	31
2000	Michigan (Mid)	A	.288	43	163	22	47	10	5	2	19	18	37	10
MINOR LEAGUE TOTALS			.301	104	399	59	120	27	8	4	48	43	83	41

13. Ryan Jamison, rhp

Born: Jan. 5, 1978. **Ht.:** 6-3. **Wt.:** 185. **Bats:** R. **Throws:** R. **School:** University of Missouri. **Career Transactions:** Selected by Astros in 17th round of 1999 draft; signed June 4, 1999.

Jamison is the sleeper of the organization, and the Astros believe he'll have a break-through season in Double-A. They rated him as a second- to fifth-rounder at the beginning of 1999, but he went 5-1, 6.24 as a junior at Missouri and slid to the 17th round. In his first full season, he limited opponents to a .190 average and would have led the Midwest League in ERA had he had enough innings to qualify. He came up just short because he spent the first five months in the bullpen. Once he moved to the rotation and had his pitch count raised, he responded with five quality starts in six tries, including a playoff victory. Jamison throws 89-94 mph, and the late movement on his fastball and quality slider induces a lot of swinging strikes and ground balls. His changeup is good for a third pitch. He has issued a few more walks than desired as a pro, though they haven't gotten him into much trouble.

Year	Club (League)	Class	W	L	ERA	G	GS	CG	SV	IP	H	R	ER	BB	SO
1999	Auburn (NY-P)	A	5	3	4.11	15	15	0	0	88	83	45	40	36	83
2000	Michigan (Mid)	A	8	3	2.10	41	7	0	7	99	66	32	23	38	95
MINOR LEAGUE TOTALS			13	6	3.04	56	22	0	7	186	149	77	63	74	178

14. Carlos Hernandez, lhp

Born: April 22, 1980. **Ht.:** 5-10. **Wt.:** 145. **Bats:** L. **Throws:** L. **Career Transactions:** Signed out of Venezuela by Astros, April 15, 1997.

When Hernandez is on, he's really on. He clinched an Appalachian League division title with an 18-strikeout gem in 1999, and threw a Midwest League no-hitter last May after missing all of April with a lower-back strain. The key for him is his curveball. When he has it working, it's devastating, but there are plenty of occasions when he can't throw it for strikes. Hernandez needs to learn to pitch off his fastball, which has average velocity and can touch 93 mph, rather than fall in love with his curve. His changeup is developing, though he alternately abandons and overuses it. His stuff is better than his feel for pitching, but he's still young enough to figure it out. Hernandez will start out at Class A Lexington in 2001.

Year	Club (League)	Class	W	L	ERA	G	GS	CG	SV	IP	H	R	ER	BB	SO
1997	San Joaquin 1 (VSL)	R	5	1	2.54	22	0	0	3	46	47	20	13	21	53
1998	Astros (DSL)	R	2	0	1.33	17	0	0	9	27	16	4	4	12	33
1999	Martinsville (Appy)	R	5	1	1.79	13	9	0	0	55	36	21	11	23	82
2000	Michigan (Mid)	A	6	6	3.82	22	22	2	0	111	92	57	47	63	115
MINOR LEAGUE TOTALS			18	8	2.82	74	31	2	12	239	191	102	75	119	283

15. Morgan Ensberg, 3b

Born: Aug. 26, 1975. **Ht.:** 6-2. **Wt.:** 210. **Bats:** R. **Throws:** R. **School:** University of Southern California. **Career Transactions:** Selected by Astros in ninth round of 1998 draft; signed June 18, 1998.

Ensberg played on Southern California's 1998 College World Series-winning club, stealing home on the front end of a triple steal in the championship game against Arizona State. He ranks fourth all-time in homers in the Trojans' storied history, trailing only Mark McGwire, Geoff Jenkins and Eric Munson. Ensberg joined those three in the majors at the end of 2000, his breakthrough season. After batting .236 with a total of 20 homers in his first two years as a pro, he surged while helping Round Rock win the Texas League title. He improved his plate discipline and his ability to read pitches. He can get pull-conscious, leaving him vulnerable to breaking balls or pitches on the outer half. Though he was rated the Texas League's best defensive third baseman, Ensberg still has work to do on the hot corner. He needs to be more consistent with his footwork and throwing. Ticketed for Triple-A to begin 2001, he has more upside than Houston's big league third basemen, Chris Truby and Charlie Hayes. He may have to fight off Keith Ginter, who could move from second, in the future.

Year	Club (League)	Class	AVG	G	AB	R	H	2B	3B	HR	RBI	BB	SO	SB
1998	Auburn (NY-P)	A	.230	59	196	39	45	10	1	5	31	46	51	15
1999	Kissimmee (FSL)	A	.239	123	427	72	102	25	2	15	69	68	90	17
2000	Round Rock (TL)	AA	.300	137	483	95	145	34	0	28	90	92	107	9
	Houston (NL)	MAJ	.286	4	7	0	2	0	0	0	0	0	1	0
MAJOR LEAGUE TOTALS			.286	4	7	0	2	0	0	0	0	0	1	0
MINOR LEAGUE TOTALS			.264	319	1106	206	292	69	3	48	190	206	248	41

16. Scott Linebrink, rhp

Born: Aug. 4, 1976. **Ht.:** 6-3. **Wt.:** 185. **Bats:** R. **Throws:** R. **School:** Southwest Texas State University. **Career Transactions:** Selected by Giants in second round of 1997 draft; signed July 3, 1997 . . . Traded by Giants to Astros for RHP Doug Henry, July 30, 2000.

Linebrink was San Francisco's No. 2 prospect entering 1999, but was slow to bounce back from arthroscopic shoulder surgery that offseason. He struggled for a year and half until the Giants traded him for Doug Henry last July, then started to regain his past form. The Astros made mechanical adjustments so Linebrink would stop throwing across his body, which had made it difficult for him to pitch inside against lefthanders. He throws three pitches, none of them soft: a 92-94 mph fastball, a slider and a splitter. His splitter can be effective when he stays on top of it. A former starter, he has taken to relieving because he doesn't need an offspeed pitch and it takes less of a toll on his arm. After a strong Arizona Fall League showing, he'll compete for a major league bullpen job this spring.

Year	Club (League)	Class	W	L	ERA	G	GS	CG	SV	IP	H	R	ER	BB	SO
1997	Salem-Keizer (NWL)	A	0	0	4.50	3	3	0	0	10	7	5	5	6	6
	San Jose (Cal)	A	2	1	3.18	6	6	0	0	28	29	11	10	10	40
1998	Shreveport (TL)	AA	10	8	5.02	21	21	0	0	113	101	66	63	58	128
1999	Shreveport (TL)	AA	1	8	6.44	10	10	0	0	43	48	31	31	14	33
2000	Fresno (PCL)	AAA	1	4	5.23	28	7	0	4	62	54	42	36	12	49
	San Francisco (NL)	MAJ	0	0	11.57	3	0	0	0	2	7	3	3	2	0
	Houston (NL)	MAJ	0	0	4.66	8	0	0	0	10	11	5	5	6	6
	New Orleans (PCL)	AAA	2	0	1.80	11	0	0	1	15	15	4	3	7	22
MAJOR LEAGUE TOTALS			0	0	6.00	11	0	0	0	12	18	8	8	8	6
MINOR LEAGUE TOTALS			16	21	4.90	79	47	0	5	272	254	159	148	107	278

17. Aaron McNeal, 1b

Born: April 28, 1978. **Ht.:** 6-3. **Wt.:** 230. **Bats:** R. **Throws:** R. **School:** Chabot (Calif.) JC. **Career Transactions:** Selected by Astros in 27th round of 1995 draft; signed May 14, 1996.

McNeal was the Midwest League MVP in 1999, when he led the circuit with 38 homers and 131 RBIs. Those numbers plunged to 11 and 69 last year, when he skipped a level and went to Double-A. Part of the problem was an injured tendon in his right wrist, which required surgery after ending his season in mid-August. But another part of the problem is that he doesn't pull the ball, lacks the instincts to make adjustments and stubbornly resists instruction. He's more of a cripple hitter than a true power hitter who can turn around a quality fastball. He doesn't have good balance and is too aggressive at the plate. For a player with a Cecil Fielder physique, McNeal is actually pretty agile. He was named the best defensive first baseman in the Texas League last year and has surprisingly quick feet and hands. His spring-training performance will determine whether McNeal returns to Double-A or moves to Triple-A this year.

Year	Club (League)	Class	AVG	G	AB	R	H	2B	3B	HR	RBI	BB	SO	SB
1996	Astros (GCL)	R	.250	55	200	22	50	10	2	2	31	13	52	0
1997	Auburn (NY-P)	A	.250	12	40	5	10	3	0	0	3	4	10	1
	Astros (GCL)	R	.293	46	164	22	48	12	0	3	26	11	28	0
1998	Quad City (Mid)	A	.284	112	370	54	105	15	1	14	61	31	112	3
1999	Michigan (Mid)	A	.310	133	536	95	166	29	3	38	131	40	121	7
2000	Round Rock (TL)	AA	.310	97	361	40	112	20	2	11	69	24	91	0
MINOR LEAGUE TOTALS			.294	455	1671	238	491	89	8	68	321	123	414	11

18. Anthony Pluta, rhp

Born: Oct. 28, 1982. **Ht.:** 6-2. **Wt.:** 190. **Bats:** R. **Throws:** R. **School:** Las Vegas HS. **Career Transactions:** Selected by Astros in third round of 2000 draft; signed Aug. 22, 2000.

Pluta was a power-hitting outfielder until he threw 90 mph at a workout as a freshman in high school. He has pitched full-time for just three years, and it showed during his senior year at Las Vegas High. Despite a mid-90s fastball, he went just 4-3, 4.76 (though he continued to hit, batting .478-8-43). Pluta signed late and has yet to make his pro debut. He was impressive in instructional league, touching 98-99 mph on occasion. He'll need to learn there's more to pitching that velocity, however. Pluta tends to fly open with his delivery and overthrow, which makes him wild up in the strike zone and less deceptive. The life on his fastball is also inconsistent. His hard curveball and changeup have potential but need work. His upside could be higher than that of 2000 first-rounder Robert Stiehl. But Pluta also could continue to struggle if he can't make the transition from thrower to pitcher.

Year	Club (League)	Class	W	L	ERA	G	GS	CG	SV	IP	H	R	ER	BB	SO
2000	Did Not Play—Signed 2001 Contract														

19. Chad Qualls, rhp

Born: Aug. 17, 1978. **Ht.:** 6-5. **Wt.:** 205. **Bats:** R. **Throws:** R. **School:** University of Nevada. **Career Transactions:** Selected by Astros in second round of 2000 draft; signed Aug. 16, 2000.

Undrafted following his 1999 junior year at Nevada, Qualls added 15 pounds of muscle in the offseason. His stuff got stronger, too, as he started throwing 91-95 mph with a plus slider. His fastball has nasty sinking action, and righthanders have little chance against him when he throws it from a low three-quarters arm angle. Like Anthony Pluta, he signed late and won't debut until 2001. Qualls is much more polished than Pluta and should be the first draftee from the Astros' 2000 class to reach the majors. His mechanics are a bit of a concern, however. He's a maximum-effort guy who has trouble maintaining his arm slot. That might mean his best long-term role will be as a reliever, though he'll remain a starter for now.

Year	Club (League)	Class	W	L	ERA	G	GS	CG	SV	IP	H	R	ER	BB	SO
2000	Did Not Play—Signed 2001 Contract														

20. Jimmy Barrett, rhp

Born: June 7, 1981. **Ht.:** 6-2. **Wt.:** 190. **Bats:** R. **Throws:** R. **School:** Fort Hill HS, Cumberland, Md. **Career Transactions:** Selected by Astros in third round of 1999 draft; signed June 25, 1999.

Barrett didn't win a game at Martinsville in 1999, then returned there last year and was the Appalachian League's second-best pitching prospect, trailing only Braves first-rounder Adam Wainwright. Barrett has a live arm, capable of reaching 95 mph and most often pitching at 88-93. His curveball has fine rotation and deception, and he has a good changeup for a teenager. He has a feel for pitching and is working on a slider as a fourth pitch. Barrett will need to improve his mechanics, as he throws mostly with his upper body and doesn't use his legs to generate leverage. Making changes also might help him throw more strikes. Barrett will get his first taste of full-season ball in 2001 in Michigan's rotation.

Year	Club (League)	Class	W	L	ERA	G	GS	CG	SV	IP	H	R	ER	BB	SO
1999	Martinsville (Appy)	R	0	1	4.42	6	3	0	0	18	15	9	9	10	12
2000	Martinsville (Appy)	R	6	2	4.73	13	13	0	0	66	60	37	35	32	72
MINOR LEAGUE TOTALS			6	3	4.66	19	16	0	0	85	75	46	44	42	84

21. Mike Hill, of

Born: Sept. 30, 1976. **Ht.:** 6-4. **Wt.:** 210. **Bats:** R. **Throws:** R. **School:** Oral Roberts University. **Career Transactions:** Selected by Astros in 18th round of 1999 draft; signed June 6, 1999.

The Astros like to save money by taking college seniors in the draft, though they've also found a number of prospects that way. Hill is one of six such players on this list, joining Keith Ginter, Morgan Ensberg, Chad Qualls, Ryan Lane and Royce Huffman. Hill capped his college career by ranking among the NCAA Division I leaders and topping the Mid-Continent Conference with 23 homers and 88 RBIs in 1999, then showed power and speed in his pro debut that summer. He continued to do the same in 2000, though he missed most of the year with a ribcage pull and a knee strain. He has a quick bat that enables him to catch up to quality fastballs, and the ball jumps off his bat. He has instincts to match his quickness on the bases, and he'd make a good right fielder if he could improve his throwing. He'll also need to work on his plate discipline. Because he's already 24, Hill figures to reach Double-A at some point in 2001 despite his inexperience as a pro.

Year	Club (League)	Class	AVG	G	AB	R	H	2B	3B	HR	RBI	BB	SO	SB
1999	Auburn (NY-P)	A	.297	69	269	44	80	11	2	6	39	29	65	22
2000	Michigan (Mid)	A	.313	56	198	38	62	18	4	6	35	11	43	6
MINOR LEAGUE TOTALS			.304	125	467	82	142	29	6	12	74	40	108	28

22. Jason Lane, of/1b

Born: Dec. 22, 1976. **Ht.:** 6-2. **Wt.:** 220. **Bats:** R. **Throws:** L. **School:** University of Southern California. **Career Transactions:** Selected by Astros in sixth round of 1999 draft; signed June 7, 1999.

Lane played with Morgan Ensberg on Southern California's 1998 championship team, hitting a grand slam and earning the victory in the College World Series finale against Arizona State. He tied a CWS record with four homers in the tournament, and his overall .517 average matched Mark Kotsay's career mark. He has led his league in RBIs in each of his two pro seasons, though he also has been older than most of his competition each time. His biggest assets are his bat, which produces line-drive power to all fields, and his makeup. He sometimes looks for breaking balls too much, allowing pitchers to sneak a fastball by him, and he's just adequate as a baserunner and defender. As an outfielder, he has a decent arm but his range limits him to left field. Lane probably should have been promoted out of low Class A in 2000, though he never complained. He'll probably head straight to Double-A to begin this season because the Astros don't have a high Class A club.

Year	Club (League)	Class	AVG	G	AB	R	H	2B	3B	HR	RBI	BB	SO	SB
1999	Auburn (NY-P)	A	.279	74	283	46	79	18	5	13	59	38	46	6
2000	Michigan (Mid)	A	.299	133	511	98	153	38	0	23	104	62	91	20
MINOR LEAGUE TOTALS			.292	207	794	144	232	56	5	36	163	100	137	26

23. Wayne Franklin, lhp

Born: March 9, 1974. **Ht.:** 6-2. **Wt.:** 195. **Bats:** L. **Throws:** L. **School:** University of Maryland-Baltimore County. **Career Transactions:** Selected by Dodgers in 36th round of 1996 draft; signed June 8, 1996 . . . Selected by Astros from Dodgers in minor league Rule 5 draft, Dec. 14, 1998.

The Dodgers have one of the weakest farm systems in baseball, but didn't protect Franklin before the 1998 Winter Meetings, allowing the Astros to grab him in the Triple-A portion of the Rule 5 draft. Franklin reached Double-A in his first year in the Houston organization, and spent the final two months of 2000 in the majors. His repertoire—an 88 mph fastball, a slider and a changeup—is unremarkable, but he gets outs, especially against lefthanders. Franklin limited lefties to a .257 average, no homers and a 26-4 strikeout-walk ratio in 105 at-bats last year. His numbers weren't as pretty against righties. Franklin might be nothing more than a lefty specialist, but he can be a good one. Closer Billy Wagner is Houston's only other southpaw reliever, so Franklin should make the Astros to open 2001.

Year	Club (League)	Class	W	L	ERA	G	GS	CG	SV	IP	H	R	ER	BB	SO
1996	Yakima (NWL)	A	1	0	2.52	20	0	0	1	25	32	10	7	12	22
1997	Savannah (SAL)	A	5	3	3.18	28	7	1	2	82	79	41	29	35	58
	San Bernardino (Cal)	A	0	0	0.00	1	0	0	0	2	2	0	0	0	1
1998	Vero Beach (FSL)	A	9	3	3.53	48	0	0	10	87	81	43	34	26	78
1999	Kissimmee (FSL)	A	3	0	1.53	12	0	0	1	18	11	4	3	6	22
	Jackson (TL)	AA	3	1	1.61	46	0	0	20	50	31	11	9	16	40
2000	New Orleans (PCL)	AAA	3	3	3.63	48	0	0	4	45	51	29	18	19	37
	Houston (NL)	MAJ	0	0	5.48	25	0	0	0	21	24	14	13	12	21
MAJOR LEAGUE TOTALS			0	0	5.48	25	0	0	0	21	24	14	13	12	21
MINOR LEAGUE TOTALS			24	10	2.92	203	7	1	38	308	287	138	100	114	258

24. Kyle Kessel, lhp

Born: June 2, 1976. **Ht.:** 6-0. **Wt.:** 187. **Bats:** R. **Throws:** L. **School:** Mundelein (Ill.) HS. **Career Transactions:** Signed as nondrafted free agent by Mets, July 24, 1994 . . . Traded by Mets with OF Roger Cedeno and RHP Octavio Dotel to Astros for OF Derek Bell and LHP Mike Hampton, Dec. 23, 1999.

Kessel was the lone minor leaguer in the trade that sent Mike Hampton and Derek Bell to the Mets. He hadn't progressed past Class A in five years in the Mets system. Shoulder surgery in 1998 was partly to blame, and spending two years playing point guard for Texas A&M's basketball team also retarded his development. He still owns Aggies records for assists by a freshman and sophomore. Kessel showed the Astros enough to make the 40-man roster this winter. His best pitch may be a curveball he added in 2000, though he throws his slider more often. His fastball is more notable for its movement than its velocity, and he uses his changeup effectively. Kessel will have to be more precise with his command to succeed at higher levels. His velocity tends to fade quickly, so he projects as a middle reliever/spot starter. He needs at least another year in the minors before he'll be ready for Houston.

Year	Club (League)	Class	W	L	ERA	G	GS	CG	SV	IP	H	R	ER	BB	SO
1995	Mets (GCL)	R	3	0	1.80	7	7	0	0	40	29	12	8	11	47
	Kingsport (Appy)	R	4	0	1.80	5	5	0	0	30	33	11	6	10	23
1996	Pittsfield (NY-P)	A	2	6	4.74	13	13	0	0	80	80	44	42	19	67
1997	Capital City (SAL)	A	11	11	2.72	27	27	5	0	169	131	63	51	53	151
1998	St. Lucie (FSL)	A	2	7	5.14	16	16	0	0	89	101	58	51	27	61
	Mets (GCL)	R	1	1	0.64	4	4	0	0	14	5	4	1	5	19
1999	Mets (GCL)	R	0	1	3.38	3	3	0	0	8	5	4	3	2	11
	St. Lucie (FSL)	A	1	2	4.63	8	8	0	0	35	35	22	18	16	24
2000	Kissimmee (FSL)	A	4	5	3.36	12	12	0	0	75	74	37	28	24	56
	Round Rock (TL)	AA	6	5	4.88	14	13	0	0	72	68	45	39	48	43
MINOR LEAGUE TOTALS			34	38	3.63	109	108	5	0	612	561	300	247	215	502

25. Royce Huffman, 3b/2b

Born: Jan. 11, 1977. **Ht.:** 6-0. **Wt.:** 195. **Bats:** R. **Throws:** R. **School:** Texas Christian University. **Career Transactions:** Selected by Astros in 12th round of 1999 draft; signed June 4, 1999.

A punter/wide receiver/defensive back/punt returner at Texas Christian, Huffman was named one of college football's 10 best special-teamers by Sports Illustrated in 1999. His versatility extends to the diamond, where he was the Florida State League's all-star utilityman in 2000. Huffman won't hit for power, but he can do almost everything else offensively. He makes contact, hits the ball where it's pitched, enhances his on-base ability by drawing walks and is an effective basestealer, succeeding in 32 of 37 attempts last season. While he's a tremendous athlete, he doesn't have a home defensively. He can't play shortstop, and he's nothing special at second or third base because he needs to improve his hands, throwing and footwork. If he does that, he could be a useful big league utilityman in a couple of years, especially because there's no reason he can't play the outfield as well.

Year	Club (League)	Class	AVG	G	AB	R	H	2B	3B	HR	RBI	BB	SO	SB
1999	Martinsville (Appy)	R	.296	53	196	39	58	16	7	2	36	31	29	18
2000	Kissimmee (FSL)	A	.298	129	450	82	134	32	4	5	55	84	49	31
	Round Rock (TL)	AA	.353	4	17	2	6	1	0	0	2	0	2	1
MINOR LEAGUE TOTALS			.299	186	663	123	198	49	11	7	93	115	80	50

26. Cory Doyne, rhp

Born: Aug. 13, 1981. **Ht.:** 6-2. **Wt.:** 185. **Bats:** R. **Throws:** R. **School:** Land O' Lakes (Fla.) HS. **Career Transactions:** Selected by Astros in eighth round of 2000 draft; signed June 26, 2000.

Doyne's makeup was questioned after he attended four high schools in four years, surfacing last spring at Land O'Lakes (Fla.) High, where he was the ace of an all-prospect rotation that also included lefthander Derek Thompson (second round, Indians) and righthander Kurt Shafer (eighth round, Pirates). Doyne was academically ineligible at Tampa's Catholic High as a junior, in part because of a learning disability. The Astros say his reputation is unfounded, and that he's a good kid with a solid makeup. No one doubts his fastball, which consistently reaches 94-95 mph and maxes out at 98 mph. At least one manager thought Doyne had the best raw arm in the Appalachian League. But at this point, velocity is all he has going for him. He pitches up in the strike zone and rarely throws strikes. His maximum-effort, over-the-top delivery causes scouts to cringe because he looks like an injury waiting to happen. His curveball should be at least average in time, but he's just learning to throw a changeup. Doyne has plenty of potential but needs plenty of polish.

Year	Club (League)	Class	W	L	ERA	G	GS	CG	SV	IP	H	R	ER	BB	SO
2000	Martinsville (Appy)	R	3	6	5.45	12	8	0	0	40	25	27	24	35	54
MINOR LEAGUE TOTALS			3	6	5.45	12	8	0	0	40	25	27	24	35	54

27. Ramon German, 1b

Born: Jan. 15, 1980. **Ht.:** 5-11. **Wt.:** 160. **Bats:** B. **Throws:** R. **Career Transactions:** Signed out of Dominican Republic by Astros, Jan. 19, 1997.

German spent three seasons in the Rookie-level Dominican Summer League before making his U.S. debut in 2000. He earned all-star recognition in the Appalachian League after hitting .320 with a league-high 24 doubles. He has a quick bat and plenty of raw power that should produce more homers in time. He's too aggressive at the plate, trying to pull everything and not taking walks. His bat will have to carry him. He played some third base last year and has the arm and hands for the position, but he lacks range and doesn't read balls well off the bat. Those also are handicaps at first base, where he's merely adequate. German also has below-average speed. He likely will play at Michigan in 2001.

Year	Club (League)	Class	AVG	G	AB	R	H	2B	3B	HR	RBI	BB	SO	SB
1997	Astros (DSL)	R					Statistics Unavailable							
1998	Astros (DSL)	R	.276	51	181	28	50	16	1	3	27	21	25	3
1999	Astros (DSL)	R	.289	69	249	48	72	23	1	9	47	41	44	19
2000	Martinsville (Appy)	R	.320	59	225	42	72	24	1	7	44	23	64	16
MINOR LEAGUE TOTALS			.295	179	655	118	194	63	3	19	118	85	133	38

28. Jake Whitesides, of

Born: June 23, 1981. **Ht.:** 5-11. **Wt.:** 190. **Bats:** L. **Throws:** R. **School:** Hickman HS, Columbia, Mo. **Career Transactions:** Selected by Astros in fifth round of 2000 draft; signed July 15, 2000.

Missouri's career high school home run leader, Whitesides hit 11 longballs in 20 swings during a predraft workout at Kauffman Stadium for the Royals. Compact and muscular, he reminds the Astros of Lenny Dykstra. Whitesides didn't show much power or anything else in his pro debut, primarily because he has a classic aluminum-bat swing and will need time to adjust to wood. He also must learn the strike zone and the art of reading pitches. He has a lot of pure speed, but he's still in the process of realizing how to use it on the bases. Though Whitesides played center field last year, he doesn't get good reads on fly balls. He also doesn't have the arm for right field, so he may wind up in left. Houston may want to take it slow with Whitesides and keep him in short-season ball at Auburn this year.

Year	Club (League)	Class	AVG	G	AB	R	H	2B	3B	HR	RBI	BB	SO	SB
2000	Martinsville (Appy)	R	.178	37	129	14	23	2	1	1	6	15	49	7
MINOR LEAGUE TOTALS			.178	37	129	14	23	2	1	1	6	15	49	7

29. Jon Helquist, 3b/ss

Born: Aug. 17, 1980. **Ht.:** 6-0. **Wt.:** 175. **Bats:** R. **Throws:** R. **School:** University Christian HS, Jacksonville. **Career Transactions:** Selected by Astros in ninth round of 1999 draft; signed June 3, 1999.

Helquist had a lackluster first full year in pro ball. After hitting .365 in his first 23 Midwest League games, he batted just .191 the rest of the way and missed much of the last two months with nagging muscle pulls in his legs. He has no outstanding tool, but he's average across the board and has above-average instincts. Helquist has some bat speed and raw power. He has worked on shortening his swing so he can make better contact, and he needs better balance at the plate. Righthanders can trouble him with breaking balls, holding him to a .206 average in 2000. Drafted as a shortstop, he played mostly third base last year because Donaldo Mendez handled shortstop for Michigan. With Mendez lost at least temporarily in the major league Rule 5 draft to the Padres, Helquist may get a chance to play short this year. That's certainly an idea worth exploring, as is letting Helquist return to low Class A to work on his hitting.

Year	Club (League)	Class	AVG	G	AB	R	H	2B	3B	HR	RBI	BB	SO	SB
1999	Martinsville (Appy)	R	.301	49	173	33	52	15	3	4	17	18	50	5
2000	Michigan (Mid)	A	.238	96	320	59	76	19	2	5	42	48	101	4
MINOR LEAGUE TOTALS			.260	145	493	92	128	34	5	9	59	66	151	9

30. Mike Rosamond, of

Born: April 18, 1978. **Ht.:** 6-5. **Wt.:** 225. **Bats:** R. **Throws:** R. **School:** University of Mississippi. **Career Transactions:** Selected by Astros in first round (42nd overall) of 1999 draft; signed June 27, 1999.

Rosamond has four impressive tools, but lacks the most important one. That didn't stop the Astros from making him their top pick in the 1999 draft, a supplemental pick received as compensation for losing Randy Johnson as a free agent. Three years earlier, they took him in the 71st round out of Madison (Miss.) Central High, where he was coached by his father Mike. Built like Dale Murphy, Rosamond has center-field range and a right-field arm. He has plenty of speed and power. He hasn't shown the aptitude to hit, however. He batted just .292 in college at Mississippi and has dropped to .224 since turning pro. Rosamond doesn't show much instinct at the plate, struggling to read pitches or make adjustments. He chases balls out of the strike zone and has whiffed 217 times in 194 pro games. Rosamond is tough on himself, which doesn't make hitting any easier. He skipped a level last year, so perhaps Houston will return him to the Florida State League in 2001. The Astros aren't giving up on him yet, but they sound like they might if he doesn't hit this year.

Year	Club (League)	Class	AVG	G	AB	R	H	2B	3B	HR	RBI	BB	SO	SB
1999	Auburn (NY-P)	A	.265	61	230	34	61	9	4	6	24	23	63	22
	Michigan (Mid)	A	.100	4	10	0	1	0	0	0	2	2	3	0
2000	Kissimmee (FSL)	A	.206	129	446	60	92	14	7	16	60	60	151	17
MINOR LEAGUE TOTALS			.224	194	686	94	154	23	11	22	86	85	217	39

Kansas City
Royals

TOP 30 PROSPECTS

1. Chris George, lhp
2. Dee Brown, of
3. Mike MacDougal, rhp
4. Jimmy Gobble, lhp
5. Jeff Austin, rhp
6. Angel Berroa, ss
7. Ken Harvey, 1b
8. Mike Stodolka, lhp
9. Alexis Gomez, of
10. Kyle Snyder, rhp
11. Shawn Sonnier, rhp
12. Ryan Bukvich, rhp
13. Brian Sanches, rhp
14. Mike Tonis, c
15. Corey Thurman, rhp
16. Jeremy Affeldt, lhp
17. Orber Moreno, rhp
18. Junior Guerrero, rhp
19. Scott Mullen, lhp
20. Mike Curry, of
21. Robbie Morrison, rhp
22. Jeremy Dodson, of
23. Paul Phillips, c
24. Tony Cogan, lhp
25. Jason Kaanoi, rhp
26. Scott Walter, c
27. Wes Obermueller, rhp
28. Ryan Baerlocher, rhp
29. Byron Gettis, of
30. Jonathan Guzman, of

By Jim Callis

The Royals have been singing the small-revenue blues ever since the 1994 strike. They haven't been above .500 or finished closer than 16 games to first place in the American League Central since. Before that, their longest streak of consecutive losing seasons was two, 1969-70, the first two years of the franchise.

Between the strike and the beginning of the 2000 season, the only major change in the organization came when the Royals fired manager Bob Boone in July 1997 and hired Tony Muser. Herk Robinson remained the general manager and Bob Hegman served as farm director. Before the 1997 season, longtime scouting director Art Stewart was promoted to special assistant and replaced by crosschecker Terry Wetzel.

In the midst of their sixth straight losing season, the Royals shook up their front office. David Glass' purchase of the club was finalized in April. Seven weeks later he booted Robinson upstairs and removed the first word from assistant GM Allard Baird's title. Baird asked for and received Wetzel's resignation and replaced him with Braves major league scout Deric Ladnier. Wetzel said he and Baird had philosophical differences.

Baird couldn't have had any legitimate quarrel with Wetzel's job performance. The Royals may have a narrow window within which they actually can contend, and players selected in the four drafts Wetzel ran for the franchise will determine how successful Kansas City will be.

The Royals have a young, potent lineup built primarily via the draft and trades. Kansas City finished fifth in the American League in scoring last year and probably can weather the departure of outfielder Johnny Damon, if 1999 AL rookie of the year Mark Quinn and prospect Dee Brown pick up the slack. But getting closer Roberto Hernandez, much-needed shortstop prospect Angel Berroa and catcher A.J. Hinch wasn't a good return in a three-team January trade that cost the Royals Damon, sparkplug infielder Mark Ellis and a player to be named. At least Baird followed up by signing a two-year contract extension with slugger Mike Sweeney.

To take advantage of their window of hope, the Royals need to revamp a pitching staff that was the second-worst in the AL in 2000. Their rotation of the very near future could consist entirely of first-round picks piled up in the last few years.

OrganizationOverview

General manager: Allard Baird. **Farm director:** Bob Hegman. **Scouting director:** Deric Ladnier.

2000 PERFORMANCE

Class	Team	League	W	L	Pct.	Finish*	Manager(s)
Majors	Kansas City	American	77	85	.475	12th (16)	Tony Muser
Triple-A	Omaha Golden Spikes	Pacific Coast	64	79	.448	11th (16)	John Mizerock
Double-A	Wichita Wranglers	Texas	76	61	.555	2nd (8)	Keith Bodie
High A	Wilmington Blue Rocks	Carolina	63	76	.453	7th (8)	Jeff Garber
Low A	#Charleston Alley Cats	South Atlantic	53	80	.398	14th (14)	Joe Szekely
Short-season	Spokane Indians	Northwest	38	38	.500	5th (8)	Tom Poquette
Rookie	GCL Royals	Gulf Coast	20	40	.333	11th (13)	R. Karkovice/A. David
OVERALL 2000 MINOR LEAGUE RECORD			314	373	.457	27th (30)	

*Finish in overall standings (No. of teams in league). #Affiliate will be in Burlington (Midwest) in 2001.

ORGANIZATION LEADERS

BATTING
*AVG	**Pat Hallmark**, Wichita	.326
R	Mike Curry, Wichita	104
H	**Pat Hallmark**, Wichita	156
TB	Dee Brown, Omaha	235
2B	Mark Ellis, Wilmington/Wichita	28
3B	Three tied at	6
HR	Dee Brown, Omaha	23
RBI	**Pat Hallmark**, Wichita	79
	Brandon Berger, Wilmington/Wichita	79
BB	Mike Curry, Wichita	94
SO	Chad Santos, Spokane/Charleston	165
SB	Mike Curry, Wichita	52

PITCHING
W	**Shawn Sedlacek**, Wichita	15
L	Jeremy Affeldt, Wilmington	15
#ERA	Ryan Baerlocher, Charleston/Wilmington	2.40
G	Scott Mullen, Wichita/Omaha	49
CG	Jimmy Gobble, Charleston	3
SV	Shawn Sonnier, Wichita	21
IP	Jeff Austin, Wichita/Omaha	170
BB	Mike MacDougal, Wilmington/Wichita	83
SO	Ryan Baerlocher, Charleston/Wilmington	193

*Minimum 250 at-bats. #Minimum 75 innings.

TOP PROSPECTS OF THE DECADE

1991	Jeff Conine, 1b
1992	Joel Johnston, rhp
1993	Johnny Damon, of
1994	Jeff Granger, lhp
1995	Johnny Damon, of
1996	Jim Pittsley, rhp
1997	Glendon Rusch, lhp
1998	Dee Brown, of
1999	Carlos Beltran, of
2000	Dee Brown, of

TOP DRAFT PICKS OF THE DECADE

1991	Joe Vitiello, of/1b
1992	Michael Tucker, ss
1993	Jeff Granger, lhp
1994	Matt Smith, lhp/1b
1995	Juan LeBron, of
1996	Dee Brown, of
1997	Dan Reichert, of
1998	Jeff Austin, rhp
1999	Kyle Snyder, rhp
2000	Mike Stodolka, lhp

Hallmark   **Sedlacek**

BEST TOOLS

Best Hitter for Average	Ken Harvey
Best Power Hitter	Dee Brown
Fastest Baserunner	Mike Curry
Best Fastball	Mike MacDougal
Best Breaking Ball	Robbie Morrison
Best Control	Chris George
Best Defensive Catcher	Paul Phillips
Best Defensive Infielder	Angel Berroa
Best Infield Arm	Angel Berroa
Best Defensive Outfielder	Jeremy Dodson
Best Outfield Arm	Jeremy Dodson

PROJECTED 2004 LINEUP

Catcher	Mike Tonis
First Base	Mike Sweeney
Second Base	Carlos Febles
Third Base	Joe Randa
Shortstop	Angel Berroa
Left Field	Dee Brown
Center Field	Carlos Beltran
Right Field	Jermaine Dye
Designated Hitter	Ken Harvey
No. 1 Starter	Chris George
No. 2 Starter	Dan Reichert
No. 3 Starter	Mike MacDougal
No. 4 Starter	Jimmy Gobble
No. 5 Starter	Chad Durbin
Closer	Shawn Sonnier

ALL-TIME LARGEST BONUSES

Jeff Austin, 1998	$2,700,000
Mike Stodolka, 2000	2,500,000
Kyle Snyder, 1999	2,100,000
Dan Reichert, 1997	1,450,000
Chris George, 1998	1,162,500

DraftAnalysis

2000 Draft

Best Pro Debut: RHP Ryan Bukvich (11) posted a 2.37 ERA, six saves and 35 strikeouts in 30 innings with three teams, peaking at high Class A Wilmington. RHP Mike Natale (22) put up similar numbers at short-season Spokane with a 1.32 ERA, eight saves and 43 strikeouts in 41 innings.

Best Athlete: LHP Mike Stodolka (1) had a chance to make it to the majors as a first baseman. But the Royals drafted him fourth overall and handed him $2.5 million so they could take advantage of his 90-93 mph fastball on the mound. He's polished for a teenaged lefty.

Best Hitter: Though he went just 4-for-34 (.114) at Spokane, C Scott Walter (3) has offensive upside for his position. He has good receiving skills and arm strength.

Best Raw Power: C **Mike Tonis** (2) gets the nod over Walter.

Fastest Runner: OF David DeJesus (4), who has yet to make his pro debut because of a shoulder injury in NCAA regional play that kept him out of action all summer.

Best Defensive Player: Tonis is more advanced as a catcher than Walter. He has an above-average arm, better footwork and moves well behind the plate.

Best Fastball: RHP Jason Kaanoi (7) and Bukvich both can hit 96 mph with their fastballs. Bukvich's fastball is probably more effective, because at 6-foot-3 he throws on more of a downward plane than the 5-foot-11 Kaanoi does. Kaanoi is also recovering from offseason rotator-cuff surgery.

Most Intriguing Background: RHP Jason

Fingers (10) is the son of Hall of Fame reliever Rollie. LHP Hector Rosado (50) is the cousin of Royals starter Jose.

Closest To The Majors: Tonis was the only 2000 draftee to play in Triple-A, going 4-for-8 at Omaha. Once he makes a couple of adjustments to his swing, he'll be able to fill the black hole that was Royals catching last season. Stodolka should be one of the first high school players from the draft to reach the majors.

Best Late-Round Pick: Bukvich. Kansas City kept **Tonis** track of him after he dropped out of Mississippi.

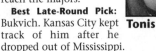

The One Who Got Away: RHP Adam Peterson (15) was the only Royals draft pick in the first 22 rounds who didn't sign. Owner of a consistent 92-93 mph fastball and a solid breaking ball, he returned to Wichita State for his junior season and could be a 2001 first-rounder if he continues to develop.

Assessment: Terry Wetzel departed as scouting director shortly after the draft, though there was nothing wrong with this effort. Stodolka wasn't the fourth-best player available, but he was a solid choice for a franchise determined to have a predraft deal in place. With Tonis and Walter, the Royals got two of the three best college players at the big league club's weakest position.

1999 Draft

With four first-rounders, the Royals may have found 60 percent of a future rotation in RHPs Kyle Snyder and Mike MacDougal and LHP Jimmy Gobble. RHP Jay Gehrke (1) has been disappointing, but RHP Brian Sanches (2) and 1B Ken Harvey (5) were solid picks. Since traded to Oakland, SS Mark Ellis was a potential bargain as a ninth-round pick. **Grade: B+**

1998 Draft

Kansas City had three first-round choices this time, scoring with RHP Jeff Austin and LHP Chris George and missing with RHP Matt Burch. The club also got several players who reached Double-A quickly, including RHP Robbie Morrison (2). **Grade: B**

1997 Draft

The Royals chose RHP Dan Reichert (1) seventh overall because of his signability, but he has plenty of ability as well. C Dane Sardinha (2) would have filled a void in the system had he not gone to Pepperdine and become a 2000 second-round pick of the Reds. **Grade: C**

1996 Draft

Kansas City may have landed three big league regulars in OFs Dee Brown (1) and Jeremy Giambi (6), plus RHP Chad Durbin (3). The downside is that they traded Giambi to Oakland for Brett Laxton. **Grade: B+**

Note: Draft analysis prepared by Jim Callis. Numbers in parentheses indicate draft rounds.

. . . Kansas City hasn't had a left-hander win more than 10 games in a season since 1988. George should end that drought soon.

Chris
George lhp

Born: Sept. 16, 1979.
Ht.: 6-1. **Wt.:** 165.
Bats: L. **Throws:** L.
School: Klein (Texas) HS.
Career Transactions: Selected by Royals in first round (31st overall) of 1998 draft; signed July 9, 1998.

It has become a cliché to compare lefthanded pitching prospects without overwhelming velocity to Tom Glavine, but George just might be the real deal. He has been following the same career path as the two-time Cy Young Award winner: debut in Rookie ball, solid first full season in Class A, second season split between succeeding in Double-A and struggling for the first time after reaching Triple-A. Glavine went back to Triple-A the next year before surfacing in the majors, and George probably will do the same. He might already have gotten a look in Kansas City had he not spent September with the gold medal-winning U.S. Olympic team as the second-youngest pitcher on the staff. George was the third of three pitchers selected by the Royals in the first 31 picks of the 1998 draft, and his ceiling appears significantly higher than college righthanders Jeff Austin and Matt Burch, who were taken before him.

George throws in the low 90s and hit 96 mph in about a third of his starts in 2000. His changeup is his best pitch, and he already has an advanced feel for changing speeds. George has been equally successful against left-handers and righthanders. He has a sound pitcher's frame (a near carbon copy of Glavine's), a smooth delivery and generally throws strikes. He's tough to run on, as just 42 percent of basestealers succeeded against him in 2000. Before 2000, George's fastball had maxed out at 94 mph. When he picked up a little more velocity, he at times fell into a power pitcher's mentality, which wreaked havoc with his command. He was more effective when he didn't try to blow the ball by hitters. If he has learned that lesson, his only need is an improved breaking ball. He throws both a slider and a curveball, with the slider the more effective pitch.

Kansas City hasn't had a lefthander win more than 10 games in a season since 1988. That drought should end soon, with George and youngsters Jimmy Gobble and Mike Stodolka on the way. The Royals need starters and don't have another lefty candidate besides George. Making the club out of spring training isn't a certainty, though he shouldn't need more than another half-season in Triple-A.

Year	Club (League)	Class	W	L	ERA	G	GS	CG	SV	IP	H	R	ER	BB	SO
1998	Royals (GCL)	R	0	1	2.87	5	4	0	0	16	14	9	5	4	10
1999	Wilmington (Car)	A	9	7	3.60	27	27	0	0	145	142	65	58	53	142
2000	Wichita (TL)	AA	8	5	3.14	18	18	0	0	97	92	41	34	51	80
	Omaha (PCL)	AAA	3	2	4.84	8	8	0	0	45	47	29	24	20	27
MINOR LEAGUE TOTALS			20	15	3.60	58	57	0	0	303	295	144	121	128	259

2. Dee Brown, of

Born: March 27, 1978. **Ht.:** 6-0. **Wt.:** 215. **Bats:** L. **Throws:** R. **School:** Marlboro (N.Y.) Central HS. **Career Transactions:** Selected by Royals in first round (14th overall) of 1996 draft; signed Aug. 7, 1996.

The Royals have a good track record of spending first-round picks on University of Maryland-bound tailbacks. In 1974, they signed Willie Wilson. Twenty-two years later, they got Brown. After a breakthrough 1999, Brown regressed a bit in 2000 and was suspended for five games after an altercation with Triple-A Omaha manager John Mizerock. Brown hasn't met a fastball he can't crush. His bat is extremely quick and can drive the ball out of any part of any ballpark. In 1999, he hit for average and showed fine plate discipline. He also runs well enough to be a 30-30 threat. Brown was too aggressive at the plate in 2000, and his slugging and on-base percentages plummeted. He was raw defensively when he signed, and he must work if he's to become an average left fielder with an average arm. Multiple Pacific Coast League managers didn't like Brown's attitude. With the trade of Johnny Damon, Brown has a realistic shot at a big league job in 2001, and the Royals would like him to show he's ready to replace Damon in left field.

Year	Club (League)	Class	AVG	G	AB	R	H	2B	3B	HR	RBI	BB	SO	SB
1996	Royals (GCL)	R	.050	7	20	1	1	1	0	0	1	0	6	0
1997	Spokane (NWL)	A	.326	73	298	67	97	20	6	13	73	38	65	17
1998	Wilmington (Car)	A	.258	128	442	64	114	30	2	10	58	53	115	26
	Kansas City (AL)	MAJ	.000	5	3	2	0	0	0	0	0	0	1	0
1999	Wilmington (Car)	A	.308	61	221	49	68	10	2	13	46	44	56	20
	Wichita (TL)	AA	.353	65	235	58	83	14	3	12	56	35	41	10
	Kansas City (AL)	MAJ	.080	12	25	1	2	0	0	0	0	2	7	0
2000	Omaha (PCL)	AAA	.269	125	479	76	129	25	6	23	70	37	112	20
	Kansas City (AL)	MAJ	.160	15	25	4	4	1	0	0	4	3	9	0
MAJOR LEAGUE TOTALS			.113	32	53	7	6	1	0	0	4	5	17	0
MINOR LEAGUE TOTALS			.290	459	1695	315	492	100	19	71	304	207	395	93

3. Mike MacDougal, rhp

Born: March 5, 1977. **Ht.:** 6-4. **Wt.:** 195. **Bats:** R. **Throws:** R. **School:** Wake Forest University. **Career Transactions:** Selected by Royals in first round (25th overall) of 1999 draft; signed July 1, 1999.

Eligible for the 1998 draft as a college sophomore, MacDougal projected as a first-round pick but came down with mononucleosis and slid to the 17th round. He returned for his junior year, then went in the first round with a compensation pick the Red Sox surrendered to sign free agent Jose Offerman. MacDougal has the best stuff in the organization, including the major leagues. He can touch 99 mph and throw 96 with ease, and he's best at 93-94 mph because then his fastball just dives at the plate. His slider and changeup also are above-average pitches when he throws them for strikes. MacDougal has so much life on his pitches that it's difficult to control them. He needs to more consistently throw his fastball on the corners and his secondary pitches for strikes. After a brief taste of Double-A at the end of 2000, MacDougal will return there to begin 2001. As soon as he learns to harness his pitches, he'll get the call to Kansas City.

Year	Club (League)	Class	W	L	ERA	G	GS	CG	SV	IP	H	R	ER	BB	SO
1999	Spokane (NWL)	A	2	2	4.47	11	11	0	0	46	43	25	23	17	57
2000	Wilmington (Car)	A	9	7	3.92	26	25	0	1	145	115	79	63	76	129
	Wichita (TL)	AA	0	1	7.71	2	2	0	0	12	16	10	10	7	9
MINOR LEAGUE TOTALS			11	10	4.26	39	38	0	1	203	174	114	96	100	195

4. Jimmy Gobble, lhp

Born: July 19, 1981. **Ht.:** 6-3. **Wt.:** 175. **Bats:** L. **Throws:** L. **School:** John S. Battle HS, Bristol, Va. **Career Transactions:** Selected by Royals in first round (43rd overall) of 1999 draft; signed June 21, 1999.

Gobble was the fourth of four pitchers selected by Kansas City before the second round of the 1999 draft. He too was a free-agent compensation choice, the result of the Tigers signing Dean Palmer away. After barely pitching in the Rookie-level Gulf Coast League in 1999, Gobble held his own in the Class A South Atlantic League as a teenager. He finished strong, going 7-2, 2.58 in his final 11 starts. Gobble has the same build and better stuff than Chris George. Like George, he can throw in the low 90s and isn't afraid to use his plus changeup when he's behind in the count. The difference is that Gobble's curveball is an upgrade over either of George's breaking pitches. What he doesn't have is George's advanced feel for pitching. Gobble's curveball breaks so much he struggles to keep it in the strike zone. More advanced hitters may not chase his curve as much, so he may need to refine it. Gobble still needs polish, so the Royals will be patient with his progress. He'll move up to high Class A Wilmington in 2001 and probably will spend the entire season there.

Year	Club (League)	Class	W	L	ERA	G	GS	CG	SV	IP	H	R	ER	BB	SO
1999	Royals (GCL)	R	0	0	2.70	4	1	0	0	7	6	3	2	5	8
2000	Charleston, WV (SAL)	A	12	10	3.66	25	25	3	0	145	144	75	59	34	115
MINOR LEAGUE TOTALS			12	10	3.62	29	26	3	0	152	150	78	61	39	123

5. Jeff Austin, rhp

Born: Oct. 19, 1976. **Ht.:** 6-0. **Wt.:** 185. **Bats:** R. **Throws:** R. **School:** Stanford University. **Career Transactions:** Selected by Royals in first round (fourth overall) of 1998 draft; signed Feb. 20, 1999.

Austin was Baseball America's College Player of the Year at Stanford and the No. 4 overall draft pick in 1998. He didn't sign until the following February, when he agreed to a club-record $2.7 million bonus. If not for his holdout, the Royals believe he already would have been a member of the big league rotation. His command is a strong suit. He needed just 30 pro starts to reach Triple-A. Austin's best pitch always has been a hard-breaking curveball. He has made strides with his changeup, a key because his fastball is nothing more than average. He pitches at 89-90 mph and can reach 92. Not only does Austin's fastball lack overpowering velocity, but it also lacks movement. It's fairly straight, and he got hit in Triple-A when he threw it over the plate. He'll have to learn to work the corners better. Austin could win a big league rotation job in spring training but might be better off with a few more starts in Triple-A. He projects as a solid starter, albeit not as a No. 1 guy.

Year	Club (League)	Class	W	L	ERA	G	GS	CG	SV	IP	H	R	ER	BB	SO
1999	Wilmington (Car)	A	7	2	3.77	18	18	0	0	112	108	52	47	39	97
	Wichita (TL)	AA	3	1	4.46	6	6	0	0	34	40	19	17	11	21
2000	Wichita (TL)	AA	2	2	2.93	6	6	1	0	43	33	16	14	4	31
	Omaha (PCL)	AAA	7	9	4.48	23	19	1	0	127	150	85	63	35	57
MINOR LEAGUE TOTALS			19	14	4.01	53	49	2	0	316	331	172	141	89	206

6. Angel Berroa, ss

Born: Jan. 27, 1980. **Ht.:** 6-0. **Wt.:** 175. **Bats:** R. **Throws:** R. **Career Transactions:** Signed out of Dominican Republic by Athletics, Aug. 14, 1997 . . . Traded by Athletics with C A.J. Hinch and cash to Royals, as part of three-way trade in which Athletics acquired OF Johnny Damon, SS Mark Ellis and a player to be named from Royals and RHP Cory Lidle from Devil Rays; Royals acquired RHP Roberto Hernandez from Devil Rays; and Devil Rays acquired OF Ben Grieve and a player to be named or cash from Athletics, Jan. 8, 2001.

Berroa was a key player in the Johnny Damon deal because he filled the Royals' need for a pure shortstop prospect. He got attention first for his defense but showed he could hit, too, batting .290 in his U.S. debut in the Arizona League and reaching double figures in homers in 2000. Berroa's potential as a shortstop is still his calling card. He has tremendous range, an outstanding arm and an innate sense of how to catch the ball. He also has good pop for a middle infielder, can hit for average and runs well. Berroa does have much to learn. He ranked third in the minors with 54 errors last season, most the result of aggressiveness. He could use patience at the plate as well. He needs to prepare better mentally and concentrate on every pitch. With Miguel Tejada settled at shortstop for the immediate future and an abundance of infielders in the farm system, Oakland could afford to trade Berroa, who will probably start his Royals career in Double-A.

Year	Club (League)	Class	AVG	G	AB	R	H	2B	3B	HR	RBI	BB	SO	SB
1998	Athletics (DSL)	R	.245	58	196	51	48	7	4	8	37	25	37	4
1999	Athletics (AZL)	R	.290	46	169	42	49	11	4	2	24	16	26	11
	Midland (TL)	AA	.059	4	17	3	1	1	0	0	0	0	2	0
2000	Visalia (Cal)	A	.277	129	429	61	119	25	6	10	63	30	70	11
MINOR LEAGUE TOTALS			.268	237	811	157	217	44	14	20	124	71	135	26

7. Ken Harvey, 1b

Born: March 1, 1978. **Ht.:** 6-2. **Wt.:** 240. **Bats:** R. **Throws:** R. **School:** University of Nebraska. **Career Transactions:** Selected by Royals in fifth round of 1999 draft; signed June 4, 1999.

Harvey is the highest-ranking draft-eligible player on this list who was not a first-round draft pick. He was part of the Royals' big haul in the 1999 draft, though he was the ninth player the team picked. He won the NCAA Division I (.478) and short-season Northwest League (.397) batting titles in 1999, and might have done the same in the high Class A Carolina League in 2000 had a toe injury not sidelined him. Harvey doesn't have a classic baseball physique, but he can hit for average and gap power. He excels at hitting to the opposite field and has the size to develop over-the-fence power if he starts pulling more pitches. For his size, he runs surprisingly well. Despite having surgery on his right foot after the 1999 season, Harvey never fully recovered and played just 46 games in 2000. Though he's listed at 240 pounds, he was up to 255 last season and must watch his weight. He has stiff hands that limit his effectiveness at first base. Harvey showed that high Class A pitchers were no match for him. He's probably ready for Double-A despite just 102 games of pro experience. He could put up huge numbers at Double-A Wichita and Omaha, which have hitter's parks in hitter's leagues.

Year	Club (League)	Class	AVG	G	AB	R	H	2B	3B	HR	RBI	BB	SO	SB
1999	Spokane (NWL)	A	.397	56	204	49	81	17	0	8	41	23	30	7
2000	Wilmington (Car)	A	.335	46	164	20	55	10	0	4	25	14	29	0
MINOR LEAGUE TOTALS			.370	102	368	69	136	27	0	12	66	37	59	7

8. Mike Stodolka, lhp

Born: Sept. 9, 1981. **Ht.:** 6-2. **Wt.:** 210. **Bats:** L. **Throws:** L. **School:** Corona (Calif.) HS. **Career Transactions:** Selected by Royals in first round (fourth overall) of 2000 draft; signed June 7, 2000.

Stodolka's willingness to accept a $2.5 million predraft deal made him attractive to the Royals. While he wouldn't have gone quite as high as fourth overall on pure ability, he's still loaded with talent. A year earlier, some teams weren't sure if he was better as a hitter or a pitcher. Stodolka's future was determined when his fastball jumped from 88 mph in 1999 to 90-93 mph last spring. He also throws a hard curveball and has been working on adding a changeup. The Royals love both his stuff and his ability to throw strikes with it. Like many pitchers fresh out of high school, Stodolka needs to improve the command of his curveball and refine his changeup. There's nothing that can't be cured with experience. Stodolka will spend his first full pro season at Kansas City's new low Class A Burlington affiliate. He should be one of the first high school pitchers from the 2000 draft to reach the majors. Late 2003 is a realistic ETA.

Year	Club (League)	Class	W	L	ERA	G	GS	CG	SV	IP	H	R	ER	BB	SO
2000	Royals (GCL)	R	0	3	2.68	9	6	0	0	37	31	18	11	16	32
	Charleston (SAL)	A	0	0	7.71	1	1	0	0	5	3	4	4	4	0
MINOR LEAGUE TOTALS			0	3	3.21	10	7	0	0	42	34	22	15	20	32

9. Alexis Gomez, of

Born: Aug. 6, 1980. **Ht.:** 6-2. **Wt.:** 160. **Bats:** L. **Throws:** L. **Career Transactions:** Signed out of Dominican Republic by Royals, Feb. 21, 1997.

The Royals have never had a Dominican all-star. Big league second baseman Carlos Febles has a chance to be their first, and Gomez is their next best hope. He ranked as the No. 4 prospect in the Rookie-level Gulf Coast League and No. 7 in the Carolina League the last two years. Gomez is the best all-around athlete in the system. He's a center fielder who can run (6.5-6.6 seconds in the 60-yard dash) and throw, and he can put on a power display in batting practice. He also exhibits a strong work ethic. Gomez has tools but not skills, however. He lacks strength or plate discipline, which makes him a weak hitter. Especially troubling is the way he still buckles against breaking pitches from lefthanders after four years as a pro. He batted .237 and slugged .255 against southpaws in 2000. He lacks basestealing instincts and doesn't make good reads in the outfield. The Royals hustled Gomez to high Class A at age 19 because of his tools. They need to send him back there in 2001 so he can develop his baseball aptitude.

Year	Club (League)	Class	AVG	G	AB	R	H	2B	3B	HR	RBI	BB	SO	SB
1997	Royals (DSL)	R	.351	64	248	51	87	12	9	0	42	33	52	9
1998	Royals (DSL)	R	.283	67	233	51	66	11	3	1	34	50	46	17
1999	Royals (GCL)	R	.276	56	214	44	59	12	1	5	31	32	48	13
2000	Wilmington (Car)	A	.254	121	461	63	117	13	4	1	33	45	121	21
MINOR LEAGUE TOTALS			.285	308	1156	209	329	48	17	7	140	160	267	60

10. Kyle Snyder, rhp

Born: Sept. 9, 1977. **Ht.:** 6-8. **Wt.:** 215. **Bats:** B. **Throws:** R. **School:** University of North Carolina. **Career Transactions:** Selected by Royals in first round (seventh overall) of 1999 draft; signed June 8, 1999.

Paul Faulk lived an area scout's dream in 1999, when he bagged three first-round picks in Mike MacDougal, Jimmy Gobble and Snyder. Snyder was the No. 1 prospect in the Northwest League that year. In 2000, he did not pitch until August because of a stress fracture in his elbow and an impinged nerve in his hand. When he returned, he worked two innings before blowing out his elbow, requiring Tommy John surgery. When healthy, Snyder has it all. Start with a classic pitcher's body and uncommon athleticism for his size. He has three quality pitches: a 95-96 mph fastball, a hard curveball and a devastating changeup. Some thought Snyder's curve was at the root of his elbow problems, which included tendinitis in college. He may rework his breaking ball when he returns. Despite the successful track record for Tommy John patients, he faces a long road back. Snyder could start throwing off a mound in August. He may not see any real action until instructional league. The Royals were cautious with him before, and they'll take extra care now.

Year	Club (League)	Class	W	L	ERA	G	GS	CG	SV	IP	H	R	ER	BB	SO
1999	Spokane (NWL)	A	1	0	4.13	7	7	0	0	24	20	13	11	7	25
2000	Royals (GCL)	R	0	0	0.00	1	1	0	0	2	1	0	0	0	4
	Wilmington (Car)	A	0	0	0.00	1	1	0	0	0	0	1	0	1	0
MINOR LEAGUE TOTALS			1	0	3.81	9	9	0	0	26	21	14	11	8	29

11. Shawn Sonnier, rhp

Born: July 5, 1976. **Ht.:** 6-5. **Wt.:** 210. **Bats:** R. **Throws:** R. **School:** Louisiana Tech. **Career Transactions:** Signed as nondrafted free agent by Royals, Aug. 18, 1998.

The Royals have endured bullpen trouble in recent years, and Sonnier may be the closer they've been looking for. If he is, scouts Craig Struss and Bill Price deserve credit for uncovering him after he spent time at two junior colleges and Louisiana Tech. Sonnier offers intimidating size and stuff. He has a mid-90s fastball and a hard slider, and he uses a splitter as a strikeout pitch. He ranked third among minor league relievers last year with 12.7 per nine innings, and he led Double-A Texas League relievers with 5.8 hits allowed per nine innings. He comes straight over the top, which costs him a little life and deception on his pitches, and he could tweak his command, but it's hard to argue with his results. Sonnier could factor into the Kansas City bullpen sometime in 2001.

Year	Club (League)	Class	W	L	ERA	G	GS	CG	SV	IP	H	R	ER	BB	SO
1998	Spokane (NWL)	A	0	0	1.35	7	0	0	1	7	7	1	1	1	10
1999	Wilmington (Car)	A	1	2	2.88	44	0	0	13	59	46	20	19	19	73
2000	Wichita (TL)	AA	0	3	2.25	48	0	0	21	64	41	22	16	26	90
MINOR LEAGUE TOTALS			1	5	2.49	99	0	0	35	130	94	43	36	46	173

12. Ryan Bukvich, rhp

Born: May 13, 1978. **Ht.:** 6-3. **Wt.:** 237. **Bats:** R. **Throws:** R. **Career Transactions:** Selected by Royals in 11th round of 2000 draft; signed June 9, 2000.

Like Shawn Sonnier, Bukvich is a tribute to fine scouting. He spent a year at NCAA Division II Delta State (Miss.), then two at Mississippi, where he had an 8.44 ERA and more walks than strikeouts before being declared academically ineligible for his senior year. But area scout Mark Willoughby stayed on Bukvich, and persuaded the Royals to draft him in the 11th round. Upon signing, Bukvich showed a 96 mph fastball and reached high Class A without allowing a home run. He also displayed a closer's mentality. He still needs to throw more strikes and refine his second pitch, a hard slurve that the Royals would like to become a true slider. If he doesn't open 2001 at Double-A Wichita, he certainly could get there by the end of the season.

Year	Club (League)	Class	W	L	ERA	G	GS	CG	SV	IP	H	R	ER	BB	SO
2000	Spokane (NWL)	A	2	0	0.64	10	0	0	2	14	5	1	1	9	15

Charleston, WV (SAL)	A	0	0	1.88	11	0	0	4	14	6	3	3	7	17
Wilmington (Car)	A	0	1	18.00	2	0	0	0	2	3	4	4	5	3
MINOR LEAGUE TOTALS		2	1	2.37	23	0	0	6	30	14	8	8	21	35

13. Brian Sanches, rhp

Born: Aug. 8, 1978. **Ht.:** 6-1. **Wt.:** 175. **Bats:** R. **Throws:** R. **School:** Lamar University. **Career Transactions:** Selected by Royals in second round of 1999 draft; signed July 6, 1999.

Sanches led all short-season pitchers with 13.5 strikeouts per nine innings in his pro debut in 1999, and began 2000 by overmatching the Carolina League. He opened May by throwing a no-hitter and one-hitter in consecutive starts, improving his record to 2-1, 1.77 with 35 strikeouts in 36 innings. At that point the Royals believe the game was coming too easily to Sanches, who lost focus and slumped the rest of the way. He doesn't have the stuff that allows him a great margin for error. His best pitch is his curveball, and his fastball can touch 90 mph with average movement. He has a feel for a changeup, though it still is developing. Sanches must improve his command, both throwing more strikes and locating his pitches in the strike zone. If he doesn't, he could be in for a rude awakening at hitter-friendly Wichita this year.

Year	Club (League)	Class	W	L	ERA	G	GS	CG	SV	IP	H	R	ER	BB	SO
1999	Spokane (NWL)	A	1	1	4.76	9	9	0	0	34	32	19	18	12	51
2000	Wilmington (Car)	A	6	12	3.53	28	27	2	0	158	132	77	62	69	122
MINOR LEAGUE TOTALS			7	13	3.75	37	36	0	0	192	164	96	80	81	173

14. Mike Tonis, c

Born: Feb. 9, 1979. **Ht.:** 6-3. **Wt.:** 215. **Bats:** R. **Throws:** R. **School:** University of California. **Career Transactions:** Selected by Royals in second round of 2000 draft; signed July 10, 2000.

The Royals have been looking for a catcher since moving Mike Sweeney from behind the plate. Last year, they used a four-headed monster of Gregg Zaun, Jorge Fabregas, Brian Johnson and Hector Ortiz, and got the expected mediocre production. As a result, they spent their second- and third-round picks in June on catchers, choosing Tonis and Scott Walter out of California colleges. Tonis is better defensively than Walter and could catch up to him with the bat. Tonis is athletic for a catcher, to the point where he played all nine positions in a game for Cal last spring, during which his fastball was clocked at 90 mph. His strong arm enabled him to throw out 33 percent of basestealers after turning pro, and he's durable behind the plate. Offensively, his swing needs a couple of adjustments and he probably won't hit for a high average, but Kansas City sees him as a run producer capable of 15-25 homers a season. Tonis, the only 2000 draftee to play in Triple-A, is ticketed for Double-A this season.

Year	Club (League)	Class	AVG	G	AB	R	H	2B	3B	HR	RBI	BB	SO	SB
2000	Charleston (SAL)	A	.200	28	100	10	20	8	0	0	17	9	22	1
	Omaha (PCL)	AAA	.500	2	8	1	4	0	0	0	3	0	3	0
MINOR LEAGUE TOTALS			.222	30	108	11	24	8	0	0	20	9	25	1

15. Corey Thurman, rhp

Born: Nov. 5, 1978. **Ht.:** 6-1. **Wt.:** 215. **Bats:** R. **Throws:** R. **School:** Texas HS, Texarkana, Texas. **Career Transactions:** Selected by Royals in fourth round of 1996 draft; signed June 7, 1996.

Thurman had four undistinguished seasons in the Royals system before 2000, when he finally made a breakthrough by leading the Carolina League in ERA. He was 17 when he was drafted, so Kansas City knew he would take time. His best pitch is his changeup, though he falls in love with it on occasion and costs himself velocity on his fastball. When his delivery is sound, Thurman can touch 93 mph, though he more often pitches in the 88-90 range. He didn't have a breaking ball before he turned pro, and since has made progress with a curveball. If he can throw his curveball for strikes and mix in some more fastballs, he could move quickly. He has a big league body that reminds the Royals of a stronger Dave Stewart. Thurman is ready to move up to Double-A in 2001.

Year	Club (League)	Class	W	L	ERA	G	GS	CG	SV	IP	H	R	ER	BB	SO
1996	Royals (GCL)	R	1	6	6.08	11	11	0	0	47	53	32	32	28	52
1997	Royals (GCL)	R	2	1	2.38	8	8	1	0	34	28	12	9	22	42
	Spokane (NWL)	A	1	2	5.16	5	5	0	0	23	23	19	13	13	24
1998	Lansing (Mid)	A	5	6	3.61	14	11	0	0	62	47	31	25	30	61
	Spokane (NWL)	A	3	3	4.05	12	12	0	0	60	72	35	27	31	49
1999	Wilmington (Car)	A	8	11	4.88	27	27	0	0	149	160	89	81	64	131

2000	Wilmington (Car)	A	10	5	2.26	19	19	1	0	116	97	33	29	46	96
	Wichita (TL)	AA	4	5	4.83	9	9	0	0	50	46	34	27	24	47
MINOR LEAGUE TOTALS			34	39	4.04	105	102	2	0	542	526	285	243	258	502

16. Jeremy Affeldt, lhp

Born: June 6, 1979. **Ht.:** 6-5. **Wt.:** 185. **Bats:** L. **Throws:** L. **School:** Northwest Christian HS, Spokane, Wash. **Career Transactions:** Selected by Royals in third round of 1997 draft; signed June 21, 1997.

Affeldt has 18 wins in four seasons as a pro, and he led the Carolina League in losses in 2000. His reward? A spot on the 40-man roster, because he's a projectable 6-foot-5 left-hander. For now he has only average velocity, though the Royals believe he'll throw in the low 90s if he can get stronger. His fastball is more effective than its radar-gun readings because it has good life and he pitches inside as well as anyone in the system. Affeldt uses a curveball as his second pitch and is developing a changeup. This season is an important one for him. He needs to get stronger and improve his stuff after being more hittable than ever last year. Making the jump to Double-A in a hitter's park in a hitter's league will be difficult if he doesn't.

Year	Club (League)	Class	W	L	ERA	G	GS	CG	SV	IP	H	R	ER	BB	SO
1997	Royals (GCL)	R	2	0	4.50	10	9	0	0	40	34	24	20	21	36
1998	Lansing (Mid)	A	0	3	9.53	6	3	0	0	17	27	21	18	12	8
	Royals (GCL)	R	4	3	2.89	12	9	0	0	56	50	24	18	24	67
1999	Charleston, WV (SAL)	A	7	7	3.83	27	24	2	0	143	140	78	61	80	111
2000	Wilmington (Car)	A	5	15	4.09	27	26	0	0	147	158	87	67	59	92
MINOR LEAGUE TOTALS			18	28	4.10	82	71	2	0	404	409	234	184	196	314

17. Orber Moreno, rhp

Born: April 27, 1977. **Ht.:** 6-2. **Wt.:** 190. **Bats:** R. **Throws:** R. **Career Transactions:** Signed out of Venezuela by Royals, Nov. 10, 1993.

The Royals might not have had to turn to Ricky Bottalico and Jerry Spradlin as closers if Moreno hadn't been hurt. Converted to relief in 1998, he immediately began dominating in Double-A and earned a big league promotion in May 1999. Once in Kansas City, Moreno tried to overthrow, and he went on the disabled list with biceps tendinitis. He also injured his elbow, tearing a tendon in spring training last year and requiring Tommy John surgery. There was no need for Moreno to overthrow, because he already possessed a mid-90s fastball that peaked at 98 mph. He also throws a slider and changeup. The success rate of pitchers coming back from Tommy John surgery keeps increasing, though Moreno will have to show he's healthy before being projected as the club's closer of the future again.

Year	Club (League)	Class	W	L	ERA	G	GS	CG	SV	IP	H	R	ER	BB	SO
1994	Royals/Rock (DSL)	R	3	3	3.19	16	11	0	1	68	51	33	24	27	44
1995	Royals (GCL)	R	1	1	2.45	8	3	0	0	22	15	9	6	7	21
1996	Royals (GCL)	R	5	1	1.36	12	7	0	1	46	37	15	7	10	50
1997	Lansing (Mid)	A	4	8	4.81	27	25	0	0	138	150	83	74	45	128
1998	Wilmington (Car)	A	3	2	0.82	23	0	0	7	33	8	3	3	10	50
	Wichita (TL)	AA	0	1	2.88	24	0	0	7	34	28	13	11	12	40
1999	Omaha (PCL)	AAA	3	1	2.10	16	0	0	4	26	17	6	6	4	30
	Kansas City (AL)	MAJ	0	0	5.63	7	0	0	0	8	4	5	5	6	7
	Royals (GCL)	R	0	0	0.00	1	1	0	0	1	0	0	0	0	1
2000							Did Not Play—Injured								
MAJOR LEAGUE TOTALS			0	0	5.63	7	0	0	0	8	4	5	5	6	7
MINOR LEAGUE TOTALS			19	17	3.20	127	47	0	20	368	306	162	131	115	364

18. Junior Guerrero, rhp

Born: Aug. 21, 1979. **Ht.:** 6-2. **Wt.:** 175. **Bats:** R. **Throws:** R. **Career Transactions:** Signed out of Dominican Republic by Royals, Dec. 5, 1996.

The nephew of famed Latin American scout Epy Guerrero, Junior looked like a great find in 1999, when he dominated the Carolina League and ranked among the minor league leaders in ERA and strikeouts per nine innings (10.46). But last year he was probably the most disappointing player in the system. Double-A hitters feasted on Guerrero, showing that a pitcher can't live on velocity alone. He throws in the mid-90s and can reach 98 mph, but his fastball is straight and up in the strike zone, and advanced hitters can pound it. Compounding his troubles, he has no secondary pitches he can trust. His mid-80s slider has potential, though he can't throw it for strikes and Double-A batters refused to chase it. He's also working on a splitter and a changeup, and neither is close to average yet. Guerrero will get a second chance in Wichita in 2001.

Year	Club (League)	Class	W	L	ERA	G	GS	CG	SV	IP	H	R	ER	BB	SO
1997	Royals (DSL)	R	4	4	5.30	16	15	0	0	71	70	61	42	45	67
1998	Royals (GCL)	R	4	4	3.23	13	6	0	0	61	57	24	22	19	58
1999	Charleston, WV (SAL)	A	7	3	2.76	19	19	0	0	104	90	39	32	45	113
	Wilmington (Car)	A	4	2	1.40	9	9	0	0	51	30	10	8	26	68
2000	Wichita (TL)	AA	4	10	5.70	28	24	0	0	131	153	93	83	69	79
MINOR LEAGUE TOTALS			23	23	4.01	85	73	0	0	419	400	227	187	204	385

19. Scott Mullen, lhp

Born: Jan. 17, 1975. **Ht.:** 6-2. **Wt.:** 190. **Bats:** R. **Throws:** L. **School:** Dallas Baptist University. **Career Transactions:** Selected by Royals in seventh round of 1996 draft; signed June 5, 1996.

Mullen got a wakeup call after the 1999 season. He had been placed on the 40-man roster after winning 16 games in 1998, then was removed following a rocky Triple-A debut the following year. He also found out that he'd be moving from the rotation to the bullpen. Mullen definitely responded. Told to air it out while working shorter stints, he saw his previously nondescript fastball jump to a consistent 88-92 mph and touch 93-94. His slider and changeup gave him two other trustworthy pitches. He pitched well in 11 outings with the Royals, especially against lefthanders, whom he limited to a .143 average. He'll need to fare better against righthanders, who hit .350 with a .550 slugging percentage, but Kansas City thinks he can be more than a situational lefty. Mullen had shoulder irritation for most of the season and had minor surgery to correct it during the offseason. He should be ready to go by spring training.

Year	Club (League)	Class	W	L	ERA	G	GS	CG	SV	IP	H	R	ER	BB	SO
1996	Spokane (NWL)	A	5	6	3.92	15	15	0	0	80	78	45	35	29	78
1997	Lansing (Mid)	A	5	2	3.70	16	16	0	0	92	90	46	38	31	78
	Wilmington (Car)	A	4	4	4.55	11	11	0	0	59	64	35	30	26	43
1998	Wilmington (Car)	A	8	4	2.21	14	14	1	0	86	68	28	21	25	56
	Wichita (TL)	AA	8	2	4.11	12	12	0	0	70	66	34	32	26	42
1999	Wichita (TL)	AA	4	3	4.01	9	9	0	0	49	47	28	22	18	30
	Omaha (PCL)	AAA	6	7	6.26	20	20	0	0	119	150	91	83	53	87
2000	Wichita (TL)	AA	3	2	3.19	33	1	0	7	73	65	27	26	26	61
	Omaha (PCL)	AAA	2	1	3.05	16	0	0	0	21	15	10	7	8	21
	Kansas City (AL)	MAJ	0	0	4.35	11	0	0	0	10	10	5	5	3	7
MAJOR LEAGUE TOTALS			0	0	4.35	11	0	0	0	10	10	5	5	3	7
MINOR LEAGUE TOTALS			45	31	4.07	146	98	1	7	650	643	344	294	242	496

20. Mike Curry, of

Born: Feb. 15, 1977. **Ht.:** 5-10. **Wt.:** 190. **Bats:** L. **Throws:** R. **School:** University of South Carolina. **Career Transactions:** Selected by Royals in sixth round of 1998 draft; signed June 10, 1998.

Curry is all about speed, which isn't surprising considering that his mother Irene was a U.S. Olympic track athlete. Curry set the single-season Southeastern Conference record for stolen bases as a junior in 1998, and he led all Double-A players with 52 swipes last year, when Texas League managers rated him the circuit's best baserunner. He also understands that he needs to reach base to maximize his value, and he has done just that, posting a career .394 on-base percentage. Curry wasn't protected on the 40-man roster after last season, in part because he doesn't do much else well. He's merely average in center field and has a below-average arm, though it has improved from a 3 to a 4 on the 2-to-8 scouting scale. He needs to add strength, not that he'll ever be much of a slugger. Curry will start in center this year in Triple-A but may have difficulty cracking a deep Kansas City outfield after that.

Year	Club (League)	Class	AVG	G	AB	R	H	2B	3B	HR	RBI	BB	SO	SB
1998	Spokane (NWL)	A	.251	67	227	53	57	8	2	1	25	46	41	30
1999	Charleston, WV (SAL)	A	.311	85	318	70	99	13	3	0	25	48	58	61
	Wilmington (Car)	A	.230	54	200	31	46	4	2	1	16	34	39	24
2000	Wichita (TL)	AA	.289	123	461	104	133	18	6	4	52	94	99	52
MINOR LEAGUE TOTALS			.278	329	1206	258	335	43	13	6	118	222	237	167

21. Robbie Morrison, rhp

Born: Dec. 7, 1976. **Ht.:** 6-0. **Wt.:** 215. **Bats:** R. **Throws:** R. **School:** University of Miami. **Career Transactions:** Selected by Royals in second round of 1998 draft; signed June 25, 1998.

Morrison gave up the most famous home run in college baseball history—Louisiana State's Warren Morris' two-out, two-run shot to win the 1996 College World Series—but has done a nice job putting it behind him. He finished second on Miami's career saves list and reached Double-A before the end of his first full pro season. He returned to Wichita in 2000, serving as a set-up man to Shawn Sonnier, but was shut down in early August with a partial rotator-cuff tear that required surgery. The shoulder problem explained why he wasn't quite as effective as he had been the previous two years. Morrison primarily works with a 90-92 mph fastball and a sharp curveball. His changeup is average, though he doesn't go to his third pitch very often. Aside from regaining his health, Morrison's biggest need is to improve his control. The Royals expect he'll be 100 percent in spring training. He doesn't project as a big league closer, but he can help the Kansas City bullpen in the near future.

Year	Club (League)	Class	W	L	ERA	G	GS	CG	SV	IP	H	R	ER	BB	SO
1998	Spokane (NWL)	A	3	0	2.13	26	0	0	13	25	15	8	6	18	33
1999	Wilmington (Car)	A	2	5	2.27	28	0	0	6	44	31	13	11	13	47
	Wichita (TL)	AA	2	0	2.01	15	0	0	5	22	26	7	5	7	21
2000	Wichita (TL)	AA	3	3	3.38	34	1	0	5	61	58	30	23	29	49
MINOR LEAGUE TOTALS			10	8	2.65	103	1	0	29	153	130	58	45	67	150

22. Jeremy Dodson, of

Born: May 3, 1977. **Ht.:** 6-2. **Wt.:** 200. **Bats:** L. **Throws:** R. **School:** Baylor University. **Career Transactions:** Selected by Royals in seventh round of 1998 draft; signed June 5, 1998.

The Royals haven't done Dodson any favors. After he tore up the Northwest League in his 1998 pro debut, they skipped him past two affiliates and sent him to Double-A, where he was a bit overmatched but still managed to hold his own. As a reward, they handed him an invitation to big league camp in 2000. Dodson so impressed manager Tony Muser with his hustle that he stuck around until the next-to-last cut, albeit while getting just 17 at-bats. When he returned to Double-A, his spring inactivity contributed to a two-month slump that didn't see him cross the Mendoza Line for good until June 21. And once he started hitting for average, his home run power disappeared. Dodson has intriguing tools—above-average bat speed and power, average foot speed and an outfield arm that has been rated the Texas League's best for two years running—but his confidence and possibly his career have been damaged by the way he has been handled. He probably needs to head back to Wichita for a third try in 2001.

Year	Club (League)	Class	AVG	G	AB	R	H	2B	3B	HR	RBI	BB	SO	SB
1998	Spokane (NWL)	A	.336	69	268	56	90	19	5	9	59	25	59	8
1999	Wichita (TL)	AA	.257	133	452	63	116	20	1	21	58	51	95	9
2000	Wichita (TL)	AA	.238	128	450	69	107	16	4	18	57	52	111	17
MINOR LEAGUE TOTALS			.268	330	1170	188	313	55	10	48	174	128	265	34

23. Paul Phillips, c

Born: April 15, 1977. **Ht.:** 5-11. **Wt.:** 180. **Bats:** R. **Throws:** R. **School:** University of Alabama. **Career Transactions:** Selected by Royals in ninth round of 1998 draft; signed June 6, 1998.

Before the Royals took Mike Tonis and Scott Walter in the first three rounds of the 2000 draft, Phillips was their only real catching prospect. Interestingly, he was more of a center fielder at Alabama. Kansas City made him a full-time catcher after signing him, and he responded by being named the Northwest League's No. 1 propsect in his pro debut in 1998. Like Jeremy Dodson, Phillips was jumped two levels to Double-A, where he has been mediocre with the bat for two seasons. He hasn't had as much trouble hitting for average as Dodson, but Phillips has shown little power or on-base ability. He needs to get stronger and more patient to contribute offensively. He's athletic for a catcher and excels in all phases of the game defensively. Phillips has a strong, accurate arm, and his 54 percent success rate at gunning down basestealers would have led the Texas League last year had a hip-flexor injury not cost him the necessary attempts to qualify. He also moves well behind the plate, and receives and blocks well. Kansas City needs a catcher, and Phillips could get a look if he produces in Triple-A.

Year	Club (League)	Class	AVG	G	AB	R	H	2B	3B	HR	RBI	BB	SO	SB
1998	Spokane (NWL)	A	.308	59	234	55	72	12	2	4	25	18	19	12
	Wilmington (Car)	A	.400	2	5	0	2	0	0	0	2	0	1	0
1999	Wichita (TL)	AA	.267	108	393	58	105	20	2	3	56	26	38	8
2000	Wichita (TL)	AA	.292	82	291	49	85	11	5	4	30	21	22	4
MINOR LEAGUE TOTALS			.286	251	923	162	264	43	9	11	113	65	80	24

24. Tony Cogan, lhp

Born: Dec. 21, 1976. **Ht.:** 6-2. **Wt.:** 195. **Bats:** L. **Throws:** L. **School:** Stanford University. **Career Transactions:** Selected by Royals in 12th round of 1999 draft; signed June 21, 1999.

Stanford has lost heartbreakers to end each of the last two College World Series, and Cogan took the defeat in a wild 14-11, 13-inning semifinal against Florida State in 1999.

Cogan made the Northwest League all-star team as a reliever in his pro debut, but when he struggled at Wilmington at the outset of 2000, he was demoted to low Class A Charleston and put in the rotation. Counting two outings at Wilmington, Cogan didn't allow a run until his fourth pro start. His fastball, curveball and changeup are all average, and he seems to do better when he has more time to mix his pitches and set hitters up. Cogan helps himself by throwing strikes and keeping the ball in the park, having permitted just four homers in 160 pro innings. His ceiling isn't as high as the average Stanford pro product, but the Royals just may have something in Cogan.

Year	Club (League)	Class	W	L	ERA	G	GS	CG	SV	IP	H	R	ER	BB	SO
1999	Spokane (NWL)	A	1	3	1.36	27	0	0	4	39	26	10	6	14	37
2000	Wilmington (Car)	A	2	4	4.35	16	3	0	1	39	39	22	19	18	31
	Charleston, WV (SAL)	A	6	2	1.83	13	13	0	0	78	65	19	16	14	51
	Wichita (TL)	AA	1	1	11.57	2	0	0	0	2	6	4	3	2	1
MINOR LEAGUE TOTALS			10	10	2.48	58	16	0	5	160	136	55	44	48	120

25. Jason Kaanoi, rhp

Born: Aug. 19, 1982. **Ht.:** 5-11. **Wt.:** 175. **Bats:** L. **Throws:** R. **School:** Kamehameha HS, Honolulu. **Career Transactions:** Selected by Royals in seventh round of 2000 draft; signed June 12, 2000.

High school righthanders who can touch 96 mph don't usually last until the seventh round, but Kaanoi had two strikes against him: He's just 5-foot-11, and most clubs thought he was headed to Arizona State. Area scout Dave Herrera determined he was signable and was proven correct. Kaanoi is built similar to former Royals phenom Tom Gordon, so the club isn't concerned about his size. The only worry is how he'll bounce back from arthroscopic surgery to repair a partial tear of his rotator cuff. Kaanoi has a free and easy arm action, so the cause of his injury is somewhat of a mystery. When he returns, he'll need to add secondary pitches. He has good arm speed, so Kansas City is confident he'll be able to develop a nice curveball. Because he's coming off surgery, he'll be handled carefully and may not pitch in 2001 until the Northwest League season begins in June.

Year	Club (League)	Class	W	L	ERA	G	GS	CG	SV	IP	H	R	ER	BB	SO
2000	Royals (GCL)	R	2	1	0.56	4	4	0	0	16	13	2	1	2	20
	Charleston, WV (SAL)	A	0	1	4.29	4	4	0	0	21	23	13	10	11	9
MINOR LEAGUE TOTALS			2	2	2.68	8	8	0	0	37	36	15	11	13	29

26. Scott Walter, c

Born: Dec. 28, 1978. **Ht.:** 6-2. **Wt.:** 200. **Bats:** R. **Throws:** R. **School:** Loyola Marymount University. **Career Transactions:** Selected by Royals in third round of 2000 draft; signed June 22, 2000.

In Walter and second-round pick Mike Tonis, the Royals snagged two of the three best college catching prospects in the 2000 draft. Walter may have the most offensive upside of the three (Dane Sardinha of the Reds is the other), though Northwest League managers thought he had an aluminum-bat swing that would need a lot of refinement. He didn't get a chance to make any adjustments, as a broken hand ended his pro debut after 13 games. Based on the brief time he played, he'll definitely need to make more contact and show more patience at the plate. Though he's still considered a bit raw behind the plate and will have to improve his footwork, he did throw out five of the nine basestealers who tested him. Tonis is slated for Double-A in 2001, so Walter likely will be catching every day in high Class A.

Year	Club (League)	Class	AVG	G	AB	R	H	2B	3B	HR	RBI	BB	SO	SB
2000	Spokane (NWL)	A	.114	13	35	2	4	1	0	0	2	1	10	1
MINOR LEAGUE TOTALS			.114	13	35	2	4	1	0	0	2	1	10	1

27. Wes Obermueller, rhp

Born: Dec. 22, 1976. **Ht.:** 6-2. **Wt.:** 195. **Bats:** R. **Throws:** R. **School:** University of Iowa. **Career Transactions:** Selected by Royals in second round of 1999 draft; signed June 22, 1999.

One of the most appealing things about Obermueller when the Royals drafted him was that he had been primarily an outfielder in college, meaning he had limited mileage on his arm and was less of an injury risk. But he spent most of 2000, his first full season as a pitcher, on the sidelines. Obermueller's mechanics got out of whack in spring training, leading to shoulder tendinitis. He didn't appear in a game until May 27, and after just seven outings he had to be shut down for a month. He made one final start at the end of July, then was diagnosed with a partially torn labrum in his shoulder, which necessitated surgery. When healthy, Obermueller throws in the low 90s and can reach 96 mph. He also has a curveball and changeup that project as major league average, and he hasn't had any difficulty throwing strikes. Once he returns in 2001, his biggest concerns will be getting a sounder delivery and more experience.

Year	Club (League)	Class	W	L	ERA	G	GS	CG	SV	IP	H	R	ER	BB	SO
1999	Royals (GCL)	R	2	1	2.58	11	7	0	0	38	33	16	11	12	39
2000	Charleston, WV (SAL)	A	3	0	1.14	8	7	0	0	32	19	6	4	5	29
MINOR LEAGUE TOTALS			5	1	1.93	19	14	0	0	70	52	22	15	17	68

28. Ryan Baerlocher, rhp

Born: Aug. 6, 1977. **Ht.:** 6-5. **Wt.:** 220. **Bats:** R. **Throws:** R. **School:** Lewis-Clark State (Idaho) College. **Career Transactions:** Selected by Royals in sixth round of 1999 draft; signed June 3, 1999.

One look at Baerlocher's size and dominant 2000 season—he led the South Atlantic League in ERA and ranked second in the minors in strikeouts—might lead to the conclusion that he has overpowering stuff. In fact, it's far from it. Baerlocher's best pitch is an outstanding changeup that Class A hitters couldn't touch even when they knew it was coming. However, he falls in love with it at the expense of his fastball, which averages 88-89 mph. He might improve the velocity slightly, though his body is fairly well filled out. He'll also need a consistent breaking ball to succeed at higher levels. Wichita is one of the toughest Double-A proving grounds for finesse pitchers, and Baerlocher will face that challenge this year.

Year	Club (League)	Class	W	L	ERA	G	GS	CG	SV	IP	H	R	ER	BB	SO
1999	Spokane (NWL)	A	7	2	4.70	15	15	0	0	74	78	43	39	32	68
2000	Charleston, WV (SAL)	A	5	6	2.14	19	19	0	0	113	88	43	27	33	139
	Wilmington (Car)	A	5	1	2.98	8	8	0	0	51	35	18	17	17	54
MINOR LEAGUE TOTALS			17	9	3.12	42	42	0	0	239	201	104	83	82	261

29. Byron Gettis, of

Born: March 13, 1980. **Ht.:** 6-2. **Wt.:** 220. **Bats:** R. **Throws:** R. **School:** Cahokia (Ill.) HS. **Career Transactions:** Signed as nondrafted free agent by Royals, June 29, 1998.

The cousin of former NFL linebacker Dana Howard, Gettis planned on pursuing football himself. He was a quarterback who signed with the University of Minnesota, then changed his mind and joined the Royals as a nondrafted free agent. His power potential and arm strength are intriguing, though he has yet to prove he can hit advanced pitching. He got blown away in the Carolina League last year, and wasn't much better after getting demoted to the South Atlantic League. Gettis needs to find a batting stance and stick to it, and he has to do a much better job of making contact. His raw strength has translated into just 12 career homers. While Gettis can throw, he has played almost solely in left field because he's been too heavy (up to 245 pounds) and still is learning the nuances of outfield play. He's a classic boom-or-bust player who can become special or struggle to make it out of Class A.

Year	Club (League)	Class	AVG	G	AB	R	H	2B	3B	HR	RBI	BB	SO	SB
1998	Royals (GCL)	R	.216	27	88	11	19	2	0	0	4	4	20	0
1999	Royals (GCL)	R	.316	28	95	20	30	6	2	5	21	17	21	3
	Charleston, WV (SAL)	A	.295	43	149	19	44	7	2	2	13	10	36	10
2000	Wilmington (Car)	A	.155	30	97	13	15	2	0	0	10	13	33	2
	Charleston, WV (SAL)	A	.215	94	344	43	74	18	3	5	50	31	95	11
MINOR LEAGUE TOTALS			.235	222	773	106	182	35	7	12	98	75	205	26

30. Jonathan Guzman, of

Born: Aug. 8, 1980. **Ht.:** 6-1. **Wt.:** 170. **Bats:** R. **Throws:** R. **Career Transactions:** Signed out of Dominican Republic by Mets, June 5, 1998 . . . Traded by Mets to Royals for 2B Shane Halter, March 22, 1999.

Like Byron Gettis, Guzman is a hit-or-miss prospect. He spent 1999 in the United States after being acquired from the Mets, then returned home for a second stint in the Dominican Summer League last season. Guzman is a potential five-tool player. A right fielder capable of playing center, he has an arm that rivals any outfielder's in the organization and he can run the 60-yard dash in 6.5 seconds. He has considerable power potential as well, though he has yet to do much at the plate because he hasn't made consistent contact. The Royals obviously are being patient with Guzman, who probably isn't quite ready for full-season ball.

Year	Club (League)	Class	AVG	G	AB	R	H	2B	3B	HR	RBI	BB	SO	SB
1998	Mets 2 (DSL)	R	.251	67	227	50	57	0	5	7	38	33	73	32
1999	Royals (GCL)	R	.241	43	141	23	34	4	1	2	14	21	46	11
MINOR LEAGUE TOTALS			.247	110	368	73	91	4	6	9	52	54	119	43

Los Angeles
Dodgers

By Bill Ballew

It appears the tide may be turning in Los Angeles. Distractions have become commonplace throughout the Dodgers organization over the past few years. Yet with the hiring of manager Jim Tracy to replace Davey Johnson, combined with a talented major league roster and some positive signs from the farm system, the Dodgers may be on the verge of returning to their place as one of the game's marquee franchises.

The franchise may have reached its ebb in 2000, when the major league team and its $98 million payroll finished eight games out of the playoffs. The farm system provided little help to the big league team and little ammunition for deadline deals. And the organization changed four minor league affiliates after years of stability.

The Dodgers will continue to build on a long legacy of premier pitching. General manager Kevin Malone signed free agent Andy Ashby and retained Darren Dreifort to team with Kevin Brown, Chan Ho Park and young righthander Eric Gagne in one of the deeper rotations in the game. Several other promising pitchers are in the minors as well.

The Dodgers are coming off their most successful minor league effort in several seasons on the field. Dodgers minor league affiliates were a combined 67 games over .500 last year (counting the Rookie-level Dominican Summer League club), representing a 101-game improvement over the previous campaign and ending a streak of four consecutive losing years.

Class A San Bernardino won the California League title for the second straight season, joining short-season Yakima (Northwest) and Santo Domingo (DSL) as league champions. Triple-A Albuquerque (Pacific Coast) and Rookie-level Great Falls (Pioneer) also made the playoffs.

And the revamped organizational ladder could prove to be beneficial. While Los Angeles won't have a Cal League club for the first time in 60 seasons after dropping San Bernardino, the system added a much-needed low Class A affiliate in the South Atlantic League. The Dodgers also have new homes at Triple-A (Las Vegas) and Double-A (Jacksonville).

More important, the Dodgers are on the way to upgrading the depth of talent in the organization. After getting four players in the 1999 draft who are ranked among the team's best 17 prospects, they had another productive draft last year. Those selections and a renewed aggressive approach to signing foreign players have the Dodgers on the verge of producing strong teams in the lower minors in 2001.

OrganizationOverview

General manager: Kevin Malone. **Farm director:** Jerry Weinstein. **Scouting director:** Matt Slater.

2000 PERFORMANCE

Class	Team	League	W	L	Pct.	Finish*	Manager
Majors	Los Angeles	National	86	76	.531	5th (16)	Davey Johnson
Triple-A	#Albuquerque Dukes	Pacific Coast	86	58	.597	3rd (16)	Tom Gamboa
Double-A	†San Antonio Missions	Texas	64	76	.457	t-6th (8)	Rick Burleson
High A	^San Bern. Stampede	California	77	63	.550	4th (10)	Dino Ebel
High A	Vero Beach Dodgers	Florida State	66	71	.482	8th (14)	John Shoemaker
Short-season	~Yakima Bears	Northwest	41	35	.539	t-1st (8)	Butch Hughes
Rookie	Great Falls Dodgers	Pioneer	42	34	.553	3rd (8)	Juan Bustabad
OVERALL 2000 MINOR LEAGUE RECORD			375	337	.527	7th (30)	

*Finish in overall standings (No. of teams in league). #Affiliate will be in Las Vegas (Pacific Coast) in 2001. †Affiliate will be in Jacksonville (Southern) in 2001. ^Affiliate will be in Wilmington (South Atlantic/low A) in 2001. ~Affiliate will be in Gulf Coast League (Rookie level) in 2001.

ORGANIZATION LEADERS

BATTING
*AVG	Paul LoDuca, Albuquerque	.351
R	Hiram Bocachica, Albuquerque	99
H	Joe Thurston, San Bernardino	167
TB	Hiram Bocachica, Albuquerque	270
2B	Hiram Bocachica, Albuquerque	38
3B	**Lamont Matthews**, San Bernardino	9
HR	Chris Donnels, Albuquerque	27
RBI	**Lamont Matthews**, San Bernardino	90
BB	**Lamont Matthews**, San Bernardino	88
SO	**Lamont Matthews**, San Bernardino	170
SB	Jorge Nunez, Vero Beach/Albuquerque	54

PITCHING
W	**Carlos Garcia**, San Bernardino	14
L	Adam Williams, Vero Beach	12
#ERA	Steve Langone, Yakima	3.08
G	Maximo Regalado, Vero Beach/San Antonio	56
CG	Allen Davis, San Antonio	3
	Heath Murray, Albuquerque	3
SV	Maximo Regalado, Vero Beach/San Antonio	30
IP	**Carlos Garcia**, San Bernardino	182
BB	Three tied at	68
SO	Ricardo Rodriguez, Great Falls	129

*Minimum 250 at-bats. #Minimum 75 innings.

TOP PROSPECTS OF THE DECADE

1991	Jose Offerman, ss
1992	Pedro Martinez, rhp
1993	Mike Piazza, c
1994	Darren Dreifort, rhp
1995	Todd Hollandsworth, of
1996	Karim Garcia, of
1997	Paul Konerko, 3b
1998	Paul Konerko, 1b
1999	Angel Pena, c
2000	Chin-Feng Chen, of

TOP DRAFT PICKS OF THE DECADE

1991	Todd Hollandsworth, of (3)
1992	Ryan Luzinski, c
1993	Darren Dreifort, rhp
1994	Paul Konerko, c
1995	David Yocum, lhp
1996	Damian Rolls, 3b
1997	Glenn Davis, 1b
1998	Bubba Crosby, of
1999	Jason Repko, ss/of
2000	Ben Diggins, rhp

JOHN SPEAR

Matthews   **Garcia**

BEST TOOLS

Best Hitter for Average	Chin-Feng Chen
Best Power Hitter	Chin-Feng Chen
Fastest Baserunner	Travis Ezi
Best Fastball	Kris Foster
Best Breaking Ball	Luke Prokopec
Best Control	Luke Prokopec
Best Defensive Catcher	Geronimo Gil
Best Defensive Infielder	Jason Repko
Best Infield Arm	Jorge Nunez
Best Defensive Outfielder	Ramon Moreta
Best Outfield Arm	Tony Mota

PROJECTED 2004 LINEUP

Catcher	Angel Pena
First Base	Eric Karros
Second Base	Jason Repko
Third Base	Adrian Beltre
Shortstop	Alex Cora
Left Field	Chin-Feng Chen
Center Field	Shawn Green
Right Field	Gary Sheffield
No. 1 Starter	Kevin Brown
No. 2 Starter	Chan Ho Park
No. 3 Starter	Darren Dreifort
No. 4 Starter	Ben Diggins
No. 5 Starter	Hong-Chih Kuo
Closer	Mike Judd

ALL-TIME LARGEST BONUSES

Ben Diggins, 2000	$2,200,000
Hideo Nomo, 1995	2,000,000
Willie Aybar, 2000	1,400,000
Darren Dreifort, 1993	1,300,000
Hong-Chih Kuo, 1999	1,250,000

DraftAnalysis

2000 Draft

Best Pro Debut: RHP Heath Totten (5) was the best pitcher on a short-season Yakima club that won the Northwest League title. Armed with a 90-91 mph fastball and a good slider, Totten went 8-2, 2.30 with 67 strikeouts in 74 innings.

Best Athlete: RHP **Ben Diggins** (1) is an agile, 6-foot-7 athlete reminiscent of Dave Winfield. Diggins was a supplemental first-round pick of the Cardinals out of high school in 1998—as a hitter. He complements one of the draft's best fastballs with a slider that will be a plus pitch.

Best Hitter: C/3B Koyie Hill (4) should hit for average with gap power. An outstanding defensive third baseman at Wichita Sate, Hill will move behind the plate for the Dodgers.

Best Raw Power: Diggins, though he won't pick up a bat until he reaches Double-A and faces a National League affiliate. Of the hitters, 1B Derek Michaelis (15), who played baseball and basketball at Rice, uses his 6-foot-7 frame to get tremendous loft on the ball—when he makes contact.

Fastest Runner: OF Travis Ezi (12) can fly, with a 6.3-second time in the 60-yard dash. He'll be a terror if he can learn to hit. He already has taken up switch-hitting.

Best Defensive Player: C Jared Price (7) has a strong body and a slightly above-average arm.

Best Fastball: Diggins pitches at 96 mph and was clocked up to 98 mph at Arizona.

Most Intriguing Background: 3B Brooks Bollinger (50) is the quarterback at Wisconsin, which doesn't have a baseball team. He had interest in signing while continuing to play football before Badgers coaches discouraged the idea. The Dodgers petitioned the commissioner's office to allow Bollinger to be treated as a draft-and-follow, but were turned down.

Diggins

Closest To The Majors: After holding out for a $2.2 million bonus, Diggins will make his pro debut at low Class A Wilmington in 2001. Totten and LHP Greg Withelder (6) also could move quickly.

Best Late-Round Pick: RHP Jonathan Lorenzen (14) topped out at 88 mph in high school but was up to 92-93 mph in instructional league.

The One Who Got Away: RHP Humberto Sanchez (9) reminds the Dodgers of Roberto Hernandez, and they'll try to sign him as a draft-and-follow after a season at Rockland (N.Y.) CC. They no longer control the rights to RHP Ryan Sadowski (29), who has a low-90s fastball. He's at Florida.

Assessment: After targeting high school athletes in 1999, the Dodgers earmarked pitchers in 2000. RHPs Joel Hanrahan (2) and Jeff Tibbs (3) have live arms to go with Diggins'. They signed just two hitters from the first 11 rounds, and only one position player (1B Nicholas Alvarez, 26) who batted better than .259 in his pro debut.

1999 Draft

Desperately seeking athletes in a barren system, the Dodgers found SS Jason Repko (1), 3B Brennan King (2), SS Joe Thurston (4), 2B/OF Shane Victorino (6) and OF Reggie Abercrombie (23, draft-and-follow). They haven't shown impact potential, however.   **Grade: C–**

1998 Draft

The hands-down worst draft of 1996-99. OF Bubba Crosby (1) didn't even make the 40-man roster this offseason, and he's the best of this crop. Los Angeles didn't even take a promising player among the ones it couldn't sign.   **Grade: F**

1997 Draft

This draft is only slightly better than 1998. LHP Steve Colyer (2, draft-and-follow) has a slightly better chance of amounting to something than Crosby does, though 1B Glenn Davis (1) is just about done. At least the Dodgers identified some talent in the form of several players who went on to become premium picks in 2000, led by 2B Chase Utley (2).   **Grade: F**

1996 Draft

Los Angeles' two best picks, OF Peter Bergeron (4) and LHP Ted Lilly (23), were traded to Montreal. SS Alex Cora (1) could be a big league starter, though. 3B Damian Rolls (1) was lost in the 1999 major league Rule 5 draft.   **Grade: C+**

Note: Draft analysis prepared by Jim Callis. Numbers in parentheses indicate draft rounds.

. . . Diggins has a 96 mph fastball, but his athleticism is most impressive, especially for a 6-foot-7 pitcher.

Ben
Diggins rhp

Born: June 13, 1979.
Ht.: 6-7. **Wt.:** 230.
Bats: R. **Throws:** R.
School: University of Arizona.
Career Transactions: Selected by Dodgers in first round
(17th overall) of 2000 draft; signed Aug. 23, 2000.

Teams entered last year's draft with mixed feelings about
Diggins. Some clubs liked his bat, others preferred his arm and
several teams were interested in both. That was the case in
1998, when the Cardinals used a supplemental first-round pick
to draft him in hopes of developing both aspects of his game.
He instead attended the University of Arizona and went 10-4,
3.83 as a draft-eligible sophomore last spring. Diggins wound
up as the 17th overall pick, but didn't come to terms until the
day before classes were to resume for Arizona's fall semester,
netting a club-record $2.2 million signing bonus. He reported
to instructional league and proved to be even better than advertised.

Diggins has a 96 mph fastball that was clocked as high as 98 at
Arizona and rated by Baseball America as the best in the draft. He
also throws a good changeup and is continuing to work on the
consistency of a slider that already is average and has all the makings of a plus pitch. While those will get any pitcher noticed, the
Dodgers are most impressed with Diggins' athleticism, especially for
a 6-foot-7 pitcher. Comparisons to Dave Kingman and Dave Winfield
have been common. Considering that Chin-Feng Chen hit just six homers while Willie
Aybar drilled four in 2000, a case could be made that Diggins has the organization's best
power potential. But he's definitely sticking to the mound. Inexperience is the biggest hur-
dle for Diggins to clear. He's still learning how to pitch and has yet to face professional hitters. Some scouts are concerned about his tendency to throw his fastball across his body. His
delivery and mechanics need fine-tuning to enable him to control his arm action and
improve his overall command. Diggins also showed fatigue late in the college season, meaning an improvement in his overall conditioning is being addressed in order for him to handle the longer pro season. Of course, focusing strictly on pitching instead of playing a position in between starts will keep him fresher.

Diggins is coming off an outstanding showing during instructional league that included
several overpowering performances and will be expected to open the 2001 season at Class A
Wilmington. A midseason promotion to high Class A Vero Beach would excite all parties,
but isn't considered mandatory. The Dodgers believe that once Diggins gets his feet wet in
the pro ranks, he could move quickly.

Year	Club (League)	Class	W	L	ERA	G	GS	CG	SV	IP	H	R	ER	BB	SO
2000					Did Not Play—Signed 2001 Contract										

2. Chin-Feng Chen, of

Born: Oct. 28, 1977. **Ht.:** 6-1. **Wt.:** 189. **Bats:** R. **Throws:** R. **Career Transactions:** Signed out of Taiwan by Dodgers, Jan. 4, 1999.

Chen had a difficult first season in Double-A. The organization's top prospect last year after becoming the first 30-30 performer in high Class A California League history, Chen hit .344 last April but just .262 with four homers after that. Chen is the most natural baseball player and has the best power in the system. He has good instincts on the basepaths and in the field. He also possesses above-average strength and the hitting ability to be a middle-of-the-lineup run producer in the majors. While his throws are accurate, his arm strength is below-average. His speed is no better than average, which led to his being caught 15 times in 38 steal attempts last year. When slumping, Chen has difficulty catching up to plus fastballs. Chen had surgery to remove scar tissue in his right shoulder after a strong start in the Arizona Fall League. He's still on pace to become the first Taiwanese native to reach the majors. His performance this spring will determine whether he returns to Double-A or moves up to Triple-A.

Year	Club (League)	Class	AVG	G	AB	R	H	2B	3B	HR	RBI	BB	SO	SB
1999	San Bernardino (Cal)	A	:316	131	510	98	161	22	10	31	123	75	129	31
2000	San Antonio (TL)	AA	.277	133	516	66	143	27	3	6	67	61	131	23
MINOR LEAGUE TOTALS			.296	264	1026	164	304	49	13	37	190	136	260	54

3. Hong-Chih Kuo, lhp

Born: July 23, 1981. **Ht.:** 6-0. **Wt.:** 200. **Bats:** L. **Throws:** L. **Career Transactions:** Signed out of Taiwan by Dodgers, June 19, 1999.

After receiving a reported $1.25 million signing bonus, Kuo made one dominating appearance in 2000 by striking out seven batters in three innings before feeling a minor twinge in his left elbow. To everyone's surprise, he required Tommy John surgery, costing him the remainder of the season. The Dodgers believe Kuo is one of the most talented pitchers in professional baseball. His forte is a 95-97 mph fastball from the left side. With a flexible upper body and a thick, strong lower body, he has all the makings of a power pitcher. The Dodgers also like his high-energy personality and aggressiveness on the mound. Kuo relied strictly on his fastball as an amateur in Taiwan, and surgery slowed the necessary improvement with his curveball and changeup. While he's expected to make a full recovery, that can take two full years. Kuo has given every indication that he's ahead of schedule with his rehab. The Dodgers believe he'll be at full strength by the end of spring training and able to open the season at Vero Beach.

Year	Club (League)	Class	W	L	ERA	G	GS	CG	SV	IP	H	R	ER	BB	SO
2000	San Bernardino (Cal)	A	0	0	0.00	1	1	0	0	3	0	0	0	0	7
MINOR LEAGUE TOTALS			0	0	0.00	1	1	0	0	3	0	0	0	0	7

4. Jason Repko, ss

Born: Dec. 27, 1980. **Ht.:** 5-11. **Wt.:** 175. **Bats:** R. **Throws:** R. **School:** Hanford HS, Richland, Wash. **Career Transactions:** Selected by Dodgers in first round (37th overall) of 1999 draft; signed June 3, 1999.

The 2000 season was a wasted one for Repko, who battled a hamstring problem followed by a strained back. Though he got just 17 at-bats at short-season Yakima, the Dodgers aren't worried about his progress based on his showings in spring training and instructional league. Repko is a top-of-the-lineup hitter who has attracted comparisons to Paul Molitor. His offensive potential is as good as anyone in the organization. He brings considerable energy and athleticism to the lineup with his outstanding speed. He also continues to display more power than most scouts expected when he signed out of high school. His arm strength is also above-average. He needs experience more than anything else. A natural athlete with five tools, Repko tries to do too much at times, especially on defense. The Dodgers believe his errors will decrease as he learns the nuances of pro ball. He'll experience his first taste of a full-season league by opening the year at Wilmington.

Year	Club (League)	Class	AVG	G	AB	R	H	2B	3B	HR	RBI	BB	SO	SB
1999	Great Falls (Pio)	R	.304	49	207	51	63	9	9	8	32	21	43	12
2000	Yakima (NWL)	A	.294	8	17	3	5	2	0	0	1	1	7	0
MINOR LEAGUE TOTALS			.304	57	224	54	68	11	9	8	33	22	50	12

5. Luke Prokopec, rhp

Born: Feb. 23, 1978. **Ht.:** 5-11. **Wt.:** 166. **Bats:** L. **Throws:** R. **Career Transactions:** Signed out of Australia by Dodgers, Aug. 28, 1994.

Prokopec made major strides in his second season in the Double-A Texas League after he was removed from the 40-man roster prior to the season. He ranked second in the circuit with a 2.45 ERA, then received a September promotion to Los Angeles and won his second start. He reaches the low 90s with a fastball that looks better than it may be, thanks to a hard slider that was rated the best breaking ball in the TL last year. His control is the best in the system. He's a warrior with outstanding aggressiveness. After signing as an outfielder, Prokopec didn't begin pitching as a professional until 1997, and his inexperience shows at times. Though not afraid to pitch inside, he needs to continue to work both sides of the plate while improving his changeup. The Dodgers were criticized for promoting Prokopec instead of allowing him to pitch for Australia in the Olympics last fall. That cup of coffee, however, could mean the difference this spring between whether Prokopec earns a job in the Los Angeles rotation or returns to Triple-A.

Year	Club (League)	Class	AVG	G	AB	R	H	2B	3B	HR	RBI	BB	SO	SB
1995	Great Falls (Pio)	R	.244	43	119	16	29	6	2	2	24	8	37	5
1996	Savannah (SAL)	A	.216	82	245	34	53	12	1	4	29	27	78	0
1997	Savannah (SAL)	A	.232	61	164	11	38	7	3	2	20	12	49	3
MINOR LEAGUE TOTALS*			.229	241	593	69	136	31	7	10	78	51	182	9

*Includes plate appearances as a pitcher since 1997.

Year	Club (League)	Class	W	L	ERA	G	GS	CG	SV	IP	H	R	ER	BB	SO
1997	Savannah (SAL)	A	3	1	4.07	13	6	0	0	42	37	21	19	12	45
1998	San Bernardino (Cal)	A	8	5	2.69	20	20	0	0	110	98	43	33	33	148
	San Antonio (TL)	AA	3	0	1.38	5	5	0	0	26	16	5	4	13	25
1999	San Antonio (TL)	AA	8	12	5.42	27	27	0	0	158	172	113	95	46	128
2000	San Antonio (TL)	AA	7	3	2.45	22	22	1	0	129	118	40	35	23	124
	Los Angeles (NL)	MAJ	1	1	3.00	5	3	0	0	21	19	10	7	9	12
MAJOR LEAGUE TOTALS			1	1	3.00	5	3	0	0	21	19	10	7	9	12
MINOR LEAGUE TOTALS			29	21	3.60	87	80	1	0	465	441	222	186	127	470

6. Mike Judd, rhp

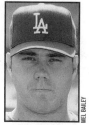

Born: June 30, 1975. **Ht.:** 6-1. **Wt.:** 217. **Bats:** R. **Throws:** R. **School:** Grossmont (Calif.) JC. **Career Transactions:** Selected by Yankees in ninth round of 1995 draft; signed June 4, 1995 . . . Traded by Yankees to Dodgers for LHP Billy Brewer, June 22, 1996.

Judd has accumulated 46 innings with the Dodgers over the last four years while spending most of the past three seasons as a Triple-A starter. He's coming off his best year in Triple-A and finally looking more like a pitcher than a thrower. Judd's entire repertoire consists of hard stuff. He works off his 93-96 mph fastball, which has excellent movement and moves up and in against righthanders. Judd also throws a good, sharp slider as well as an average changeup and curveball. He needs to be more consistent with his delivery. Smoother mechanics also will improve his command. He continues to throw too many breaking balls early in the count instead of going right after hitters with his heat. Judd has yet to live up to expectations in the big leagues, but most members of the front office say this will be the year he puts everything together by earning a job in the major league bullpen.

Year	Club (League)	Class	W	L	ERA	G	GS	CG	SV	IP	H	R	ER	BB	SO
1995	Yankees (GCL)	R	1	1	1.11	21	0	0	8	32	18	5	4	6	30
	Greensboro (SAL)	A	0	0	0.00	1	0	0	0	3	2	0	0	0	1
1996	Greensboro (SAL)	A	2	2	3.81	29	0	0	10	28	22	14	12	8	36
	Savannah (SAL)	A	4	2	2.44	15	8	1	3	55	40	21	15	15	62
1997	Vero Beach (FSL)	A	6	5	3.53	14	14	1	0	87	67	37	34	39	104
	San Antonio (TL)	AA	4	2	2.73	12	12	0	0	79	69	27	24	33	65
	Los Angeles (NL)	MAJ	0	0	0.00	1	0	0	0	3	4	0	0	0	4
1998	Albuquerque (PCL)	AAA	5	7	4.56	17	17	3	0	95	98	62	48	44	77
	Los Angeles (NL)	MAJ	0	0	15.09	7	0	0	0	11	19	19	19	9	14
1999	Albuquerque (PCL)	AAA	8	7	6.67	21	21	1	0	111	132	90	82	47	122
	Los Angeles (NL)	MAJ	3	1	5.46	7	4	0	0	28	30	17	17	12	22
2000	Albuquerque (PCL)	AAA	7	6	4.51	24	23	1	0	142	153	86	71	62	92
	Los Angeles (NL)	MAJ	0	1	15.75	1	1	0	0	4	4	7	7	3	5
MAJOR LEAGUE TOTALS			3	2	8.41	16	5	0	0	46	57	43	43	24	45
MINOR LEAGUE TOTALS			37	32	4.13	154	95	7	21	631	601	342	290	254	589

7. Willy Aybar, 3b

Born: March 9, 1983. **Ht.:** 6-0. **Wt.:** 175. **Bats:** B. **Throws:** R. **Career Transactions:** Signed out of Dominican Republic by Dodgers, Jan. 31, 2000.

The Dodgers signed Aybar for a $1.4 million bonus, which established a new high for a Dominican amateur. He showed the ability to make adjustments against more experienced players in the Rookie-level Pioneer League. Scouts rave about the different sound the ball makes off Aybar's bat. Though aggressive at the plate, he remains under control most of the time. The switch-hitter has power from both sides that should enable him to hit 30-plus homers annually. Aybar also made the move to third after playing shortstop as an amateur. He has good hands, a consistent glove and a strong arm. Not unlike most players his age, Aybar needs to add strength, which should occur naturally as his body continues to mature. He handled an advanced Rookie league last year with no problem. The Dodgers will be patient because of his youth and may have him return to Great Falls in 2001, though a promotion to Wilmington is a definite possibility.

Year	Club (League)	Class	AVG	G	AB	R	H	2B	3B	HR	RBI	BB	SO	SB
2000	Great Falls (Pio)	R	.263	70	266	39	70	15	1	4	49	36	45	5
MINOR LEAGUE TOTALS			.263	70	266	39	70	15	1	4	49	36	45	5

8. Hiram Bocachica, 2b

Born: March 4, 1976. **Ht.:** 5-11. **Wt.:** 165. **Bats:** R. **Throws:** R. **School:** Rexville HS, Bayamon, P.R. **Career Transactions:** Selected by Expos in first round (21st overall) of 1994 draft; signed June 6, 1994 . . . Traded by Expos with SS Mark Grudzielanek to Dodgers for 2B Wilton Guerrero, OF Peter Bergeron, 1B Jonathan Tucker and LHP Ted Lilly, July 31, 1998.

Bocachica had one of the best seasons in the organization last year and was the second baseman on Baseball America's Triple-A all-star team. He also performed well during his first stint in the majors. He could turn out to be the best thing to come out of a regrettable July 1998 trade with the Expos and gave every indication last year that he has put the finishing touches on all aspects of his game and is close to being a polished product. An exciting offensive performer with his excellent speed, he combines good strength and bat speed to drive the ball into the gaps. He also has an above-average arm and is a steady fielder. The Dodgers envision him as a utilityman. He tried playing the outfield during winter ball, but the results weren't overwhelming. Dogged by a reputation for a lack of dedication to the game, he has proven his critics wrong. The Dodgers plan to give Bocachica a shot this spring at earning a job as a reserve infielder in the big leagues.

Year	Club (League)	Class	AVG	G	AB	R	H	2B	3B	HR	RBI	BB	SO	SB
1994	Expos (GCL)	R	.280	43	168	31	47	9	0	5	16	15	42	11
1995	Albany (SAL)	A	.284	96	380	65	108	20	10	2	30	52	78	47
1996	W. Palm Beach (FSL)	A	.337	71	267	50	90	17	5	2	26	34	47	21
	Expos (GCL)	R	.250	9	32	11	8	3	0	0	2	5	3	2
1997	Harrisburg (EL)	AA	.278	119	443	82	123	19	3	11	35	41	98	29
1998	Harrisburg (EL)	AA	.264	80	296	39	78	18	4	4	27	21	61	20
	Ottawa (IL)	AAA	.195	12	41	5	8	3	1	0	5	6	14	2
	Albuquerque (PCL)	AAA	.238	26	101	16	24	7	1	4	16	13	24	5
1999	San Antonio (TL)	AA	.291	123	477	84	139	22	10	11	60	60	71	30
2000	Albuquerque (PCL)	AAA	.322	124	482	99	155	38	4	23	84	40	100	10
	Los Angeles (NL)	MAJ	.300	8	10	2	3	0	0	0	0	0	2	0
MAJOR LEAGUE TOTALS			.300	8	10	2	3	0	0	0	0	0	2	0
MINOR LEAGUE TOTALS			.290	703	2687	482	780	156	38	62	301	287	538	177

9. Joe Thurston, ss

Born: Sept. 29, 1979. **Ht.:** 5-11. **Wt.:** 175. **Bats:** L. **Throws:** R. **School:** Sacramento CC. **Career Transactions:** Selected by Dodgers in fourth round of 1999 draft; signed June 6, 1999.

Thurston was the Dodgers' minor league player of the year in 2000, his first full professional season. He impressed California League managers enough last year to earn recognition as an all-star and the league's most exciting player. His game is built around his outstanding speed and quickness. He makes solid contact and uses his legs to get on base, enabling him to lead the Cal League in hits. He possesses excellent range and has a lightning-quick first step out of the box and in the field. He's a good baserunner who placed second in the organization in stolen bases last year. While some scouts like Thurston as a shortstop, his high error totals could land him at second base. His defense remains raw, though he has improved with his routes to grounders. He took his game to a higher level last year by learning how to hit to the opposite field. With impeccable character, he could move up the list with a strong season at Double-A Jacksonville.

Year	Club (League)	Class	AVG	G	AB	R	H	2B	3B	HR	RBI	BB	SO	SB
1999	Yakima (NWL)	A	.285	71	277	48	79	10	3	0	32	27	34	27
	San Bernardino (Cal)	A	.000	2	3	0	0	0	0	0	0	0	1	0
2000	San Bernardino (Cal)	A	.303	138	551	97	167	31	8	4	70	56	61	43
MINOR LEAGUE TOTALS			.296	211	831	145	246	41	11	4	102	83	96	70

10. Chad Ricketts, rhp

Born: Feb. 12, 1975. **Ht.:** 6-5. **Wt.:** 225. **Bats:** R. **Throws:** R. **School:** Polk (Fla.) CC. **Career Transactions:** Selected by Cubs in ninth round of 1995 draft; signed June 2, 1995 . . . Traded by Cubs with RHP Willie Adams and a player to be named to Dodgers for RHP Ismael Valdes and 2B Eric Young, Dec. 12, 1999; Dodgers acquired RHP Brian Stephenson to complete trade (Dec. 16, 1999).

Acquired last winter from the Cubs, Ricketts was the Dodgers' most effective Triple-A reliever in 2000. He led Albuquerque in appearances while placing second in ERA and third in saves. Ricketts has an intimidating presence, combining above-average height and stuff to dominate out of the bullpen. His fastball is clocked consistently in the low 90s with good side-to-side movement. He also throws an above-average changeup and an improving slider. Ricketts tends to lose confidence in his second and third pitches and winds up going with his fastball when he needs to throw strikes. His delivery needs regular fine-tuning in order to maintain his control. Ricketts has an outside shot of earning a job in the Los Angeles bullpen this spring but is likely to return to Triple-A to gain more consistency with his secondary pitches.

Year	Club (League)	Class	W	L	ERA	G	GS	CG	SV	IP	H	R	ER	BB	SO
1995	Cubs (GCL)	R	1	0	0.00	2	2	0	0	9	1	1	0	1	5
	Williamsport (NY-P)	A	4	5	4.19	12	12	0	0	69	89	46	32	16	37
1996	Rockford (Mid)	A	3	8	5.03	37	9	0	4	88	89	60	49	29	70
1997	Rockford (Mid)	A	4	0	2.48	16	0	0	3	29	19	9	8	11	32
	Daytona (FSL)	A	3	1	0.44	20	0	0	8	20	13	4	1	6	18
	Orlando (SL)	AA	0	0	18.00	2	0	0	0	2	7	4	4	2	3
1998	Daytona (FSL)	A	2	1	1.84	47	0	0	19	49	41	15	10	11	59
	West Tenn (SL)	AA	0	2	3.52	13	0	0	6	15	19	7	6	4	13
1999	West Tenn (SL)	AA	6	4	3.09	57	0	0	8	67	55	25	23	21	80
2000	Albuquerque (PCL)	AAA	6	2	3.46	54	0	0	7	68	59	35	26	36	75
MINOR LEAGUE TOTALS			29	23	3.44	260	23	0	55	416	392	206	159	137	392

11. Brennan King, 3b

Born: Jan. 20, 1981. **Ht.:** 6-3. **Wt.:** 190. **Bats:** R. **Throws:** R. **School:** Oakland HS, Murfreesboro, Tenn. **Career Transactions:** Selected by Dodgers in second round of 1999 draft; signed June 11, 1999.

King has made a successful move from shortstop in high school to third base as a professional. He has attracted comparisons to Travis Fryman with outstanding athletic ability, impressive size, a strong arm and good mobility at the hot corner. While he has just three professional homers, he projects to have above-average power if he gets stronger. The greatest concerns regarding his game center on his ability to add strength and hit consistently enough to play third base in the major leagues. The Dodgers love his makeup, but his confidence tends to wane, which is to be expected for such a young player. With a solid season under his belt, King will move up the organizational ladder to Wilmington this spring.

Year	Club (League)	Class	AVG	G	AB	R	H	2B	3B	HR	RBI	BB	SO	SB
1999	Great Falls (Pio)	R	.291	61	247	37	72	13	1	2	30	24	45	9
2000	Yakima (NWL)	A	.239	61	238	27	57	10	1	1	30	29	49	14
MINOR LEAGUE TOTALS			.266	122	485	64	129	23	2	3	60	53	94	23

12. Carlos Garcia, rhp

Born: Sept. 23, 1978. **Ht.:** 6-3. **Wt.:** 232. **Bats:** R. **Throws:** R. **Career Transactions:** Signed out of Mexico by Dodgers, July 14, 1996 . . . Loaned by Dodgers to Mexico City Red Devils (Mexican), March 18-Oct. 28, 1998 . . . Loaned to Mexico City, June 18-Sept. 20, 1999.

Garcia made a strong impression in his first season pitching in the United States. He was named the Dodgers' top minor league pitcher as well as the California League's pitcher of the year after leading the league in wins and ERA. He got stronger as the season progressed, going 3-0, 1.82 in the playoffs. Garcia is a workhorse who worked at least six innings in 25 of his 27 starts in 2000. He has an above-average fastball in the 92-93 mph range that has good sinking action. He also mixes a plus changeup well to keep hitters off balance. In addition to his excellent command, the Dodgers love Garcia's makeup, work ethic and desire to be his best. He tends to be too fine with his pitches on occasion, and the Dodgers would like to see him go after hitters more often by pitching inside. A veteran of two seasons with the Mexico City Reds, Garcia will continue his development this season at Jacksonville.

Year	Club (League)	Class	W	L	ERA	G	GS	CG	SV	IP	H	R	ER	BB	SO
1997	Dodgers (DSL)	R	8	1	1.70	12	12	0	0	69	57	17	13	19	58
1998	M.C. Reds (Mex)	AAA	2	1	5.74	17	0	0	0	31	37	21	20	15	11
1999	M.C. Reds (Mex)	AAA	12	4	4.05	25	25	2	0	153	170	78	69	78	58
2000	San Bernardino (Cal)	A	14	7	2.57	27	27	2	0	182	162	61	52	49	106
MINOR LEAGUE TOTALS			36	13	3.18	81	64	4	0	436	426	177	154	161	233

13. Luke Allen, 3b

Born: Aug. 4, 1978. **Ht.:** 6-2. **Wt.:** 208. **Bats:** L. **Throws:** R. **School:** Newton County HS, Covington, Ga. **Career Transactions:** Signed as nondrafted free agent by Dodgers, Aug. 4, 1996.

Though injuries, including a fractured left eye socket sustained on a bad-hop grounder, hampered Allen during 2000, he wound up having a productive season in his second year at Double-A. He finished second on San Antonio in RBIs despite having his season conclude at the end of July, and he cut his errors in half after making a minor league-high 53 in 1999. Managers ranked Allen's arm as the best among Texas League infielders last year. The problem is, he still hasn't found a home in the field. His hands aren't soft and he hasn't shown the necessary consistency to handle the hot corner at higher levels. Those limitations could land Allen in right field. With his quick wrists, improving power and good speed for a player of his size, he's a budding offensive player who could develop into a middle-of-the-lineup run producer. After a solid showing in the Arizona Fall League, Allen was placed on the Dodgers' 40-man roster. His next stop is scheduled to be Triple-A Las Vegas.

Year	Club (League)	Class	AVG	G	AB	R	H	2B	3B	HR	RBI	BB	SO	SB
1997	Great Falls (Pio)	R	.345	67	258	50	89	12	6	7	40	19	53	12
1998	San Bernardino (Cal)	A	.298	105	399	51	119	25	6	4	46	30	93	18
	San Antonio (TL)	AA	.333	23	78	9	26	3	1	3	10	6	16	1
1999	San Antonio (TL)	AA	.281	137	533	90	150	16	12	14	82	44	102	14
2000	San Antonio (TL)	AA	.265	90	339	55	90	15	5	7	60	40	71	14
MINOR LEAGUE TOTALS			.295	422	1607	255	474	71	30	35	238	139	335	59

14. Joel Hanrahan, rhp

Born: Oct. 6, 1981. **Ht.:** 6-3. **Wt.:** 215. **Bats:** R. **Throws:** R. **School:** Norwalk (Iowa) Community HS. **Career Transactions:** Selected by Dodgers in second round of 2000 draft; signed June 22, 2000.

The Dodgers rarely tout players from recent drafts. A college player such as Ben Diggins is an exception because of his experience and obvious high ceiling. A pitcher such as Hanrahan is a different story in more ways than one. Because the state of Iowa doesn't play a spring high school schedule, many scouts and crosscheckers have trouble getting an accurate read on potential picks heading into the draft. Hanrahan, however, was so impressive with his low-90s fastball and projectable body during the previous summer and fall that several teams considered him a potential first-round pick. He made a successful debut in the Pioneer League. In addition to his above-average fastball, he showed a promising changeup and slider, which should give him three average offerings. Experience, particularly against a higher level of competition, is his greatest need, along with a better overall knowledge of how to work hitters and both sides of the plate. He'll work on that at Wilmington in 2001.

Year	Club (League)	Class	W	L	ERA	G	GS	CG	SV	IP	H	R	ER	BB	SO
2000	Great Falls (Pio)	R	3	1	4.75	12	11	0	0	55	49	32	29	23	40
MINOR LEAGUE TOTALS			3	1	4.75	12	11	0	0	55	49	32	29	23	40

15. Adrian Burnside, lhp

Born: March 15, 1977. **Ht.:** 6-4. **Wt.:** 190. **Bats:** R. **Throws:** L. **Career Transactions:** Signed out of Australia by Dodgers, July 12, 1995 . . . Selected by Reds from Dodgers in major league Rule 5 draft, Dec. 13, 1999 . . . Returned to Dodgers, March 14, 2000.

Before tendinitis and other elbow problems shelved him for the season, Burnside joined fellow Australian Luke Prokopec as two of Los Angeles' few bright spots at the Double-A level last year. The Dodgers were concerned late in the season when Burnside's elbow didn't improve after he was sent to minor league rehab and feared he had contracted Lyme disease when he had discomfort in his knee and ankle joints, but that didn't prove to be the case. He was slated to pitch for Australia in the Olympics before he got hurt. Burnside has outstanding arm strength for a lefthander. His fastball has been clocked as high as 94 mph, and he throws an average changeup that has improved over the past two years. Burnside's albatross has been both his command and control, or lack thereof. He tends to become too fine and goes deeper into counts than he should. He's a candidate to pitch at Las Vegas this season.

Year	Club (League)	Class	W	L	ERA	G	GS	CG	SV	IP	H	R	ER	BB	SO
1996	Great Falls (Pio)	R	1	3	6.80	14	5	0	0	41	44	35	31	38	33
1997	Yakima (NWL)	A	6	3	4.93	15	13	0	0	65	67	53	36	49	66
1998	San Bernardino (Cal)	A	1	10	7.81	21	12	0	0	78	97	79	68	48	65
	Yakima (NWL)	A	1	4	4.05	8	6	0	0	33	27	21	15	30	34
1999	San Bernardino (Cal)	A	10	9	4.17	26	22	0	0	131	124	69	61	55	129
2000	San Antonio (TL)	AA	6	5	2.90	17	17	0	0	93	73	40	30	55	82
MINOR LEAGUE TOTALS			25	34	4.90	101	75	0	0	443	432	297	241	275	409

16. Kris Foster, rhp

Born: Aug. 30, 1974. **Ht.:** 6-1. **Wt.:** 200. **Bats:** R. **Throws:** R. **School:** Edison (Fla.) CC. **Career Transactions:** Selected by Expos in 39th round of 1992 draft; signed May 26, 1993 . . . Traded by Expos to Dodgers for SS Rafael Bournigal, June 10, 1995 . . . Granted free agency, Oct. 15, 1999; re-signed by Dodgers, Oct. 22, 1999.

Shoulder surgery to remove scar tissue cost Foster all but the final few weeks of the 2000 season. He then pitched in the Arizona Fall League. Foster is a power pitcher who was clocked as high as 99 mph and consistently at 96 prior to surgery. He was back to 95 last summer and reported no pain in his shoulder after battling tenderness in both his shoulder and elbow in 1997 and '98. The operation doesn't appear to have affected the control of his fastball, which hindered his progress during his early days in the organization. Foster's slider showed impressive improvement prior to his surgery. The development of a changeup would help him immensely. At age 26, Foster is no longer a pup. If he hadn't needed surgery, the Dodgers believe he might have pitched in the major leagues last year. How he pitches this spring will determine his destination, with Triple-A the most likely choice.

Year	Club (League)	Class	W	L	ERA	G	GS	CG	SV	IP	H	R	ER	BB	SO
1993	Expos (GCL)	R	1	6	3.43	17	3	0	1	45	44	26	17	16	30
1994	Expos (GCL)	R	4	2	1.55	18	5	0	4	52	34	21	9	32	65
1995	Yakima (NWL)	A	2	3	2.89	15	10	0	3	56	38	27	18	38	55
1996	San Bernardino (Cal)	A	3	5	3.86	30	8	0	2	82	66	46	35	54	78
1997	Vero Beach (FSL)	A	6	3	5.32	17	17	2	0	90	97	69	53	44	77
1998	Vero Beach (FSL)	A	3	5	6.79	24	6	0	1	53	59	45	40	27	52
1999	Vero Beach (FSL)	A	1	1	1.76	8	0	0	0	15	10	5	3	2	15
	San Antonio (TL)	AA	0	2	3.59	33	0	0	4	53	43	24	21	26	53
2000	San Bernardino (Cal)	A	0	0	0.77	10	1	0	2	12	7	2	1	1	19
MINOR LEAGUE TOTALS			20	27	3.88	172	50	2	17	457	398	265	197	240	444

17. Shane Victorino, 2b/of

Born: Nov. 30, 1980. **Ht.:** 5-9. **Wt.:** 160. **Bats:** R. **Throws:** R. **School:** St. Anthony HS, Wailuku, Hawaii. **Career Transactions:** Selected by Dodgers in sixth round of 1999 draft; signed June 8, 1999.

Having led Great Falls with 53 runs and 20 stolen bases in his first pro season, Victorino continued to use his legs to create havoc at Yakima in 2000. Reviews were mixed regarding the speedster's performance last year. Those who like him compare Victorino to Lenny Dykstra. He's a gritty leadoff hitter who plays hard from start to finish. Those who aren't impressed labeled Victorino as a one-tool talent who has a long way to go in order to develop another average tool. He tends to swing for power when he should focus on slapping the ball on the ground and going the other way with pitches. He also whiffs too often for a player at the top of the lineup, and he needs to improve his knowledge of the strike zone in order to draw more walks. After watching Victorino play a modest second base last year in the Northwest League, the Dodgers will take a look at him in the outfield as well in order to maximize his speed. The good news is that age is on Victorino's side. He's scheduled to play both second base and the outfield this season at Wilmington.

Year	Club (League)	Class	AVG	G	AB	R	H	2B	3B	HR	RBI	BB	SO	SB
1999	Great Falls (Pio)	R	.280	55	225	53	63	7	6	2	25	20	31	20
2000	Yakima (NWL)	A	.246	61	236	32	58	7	2	2	20	20	44	21
MINOR LEAGUE TOTALS			.262	116	461	85	121	14	8	4	45	40	75	41

18. Ricardo Rodriguez, rhp

Born: May 21, 1979. **Ht.:** 6-3. **Wt.:** 195. **Bats:** R. **Throws:** R. **Career Transactions:** Signed out of Dominican Republic by Dodgers, Sept. 2, 1996.

Rodriguez got stronger as the 2000 season progressed. He went 3-1, 1.02 in August, capping a year in which he was Pioneer League pitcher of the week five times. He led the league in wins, ERA and strikeouts to earn a berth on Baseball America's short-season all-star team. Rodriguez has above-average arm strength and good command. He throws a hard slider and a fastball that clocks consistently in the 93-94 mph range. Though he was old for the Pioneer League, he showed the ability to pitch along with a strong competitive streak. After three years in the Rookie-level Dominican Summer League, Rodriguez isn't as far up the organizational ladder as he should be. He can't afford an injury or extended difficulties. The Dodgers would like to start pushing him faster now. He'll open the season Wilmington.

Year	Club (League)	Class	W	L	ERA	G	GS	CG	SV	IP	H	R	ER	BB	SO
1997	Dodgers (DSL)	R	1	2	6.40	12	10	0	0	32	42	39	23	26	20
1998	Dodgers (DSL)	R	1	1	3.55	13	9	1	0	33	28	19	13	34	36
1999	Dodgers (DSL)	R	3	2	3.43	9	9	0	0	42	34	22	16	18	51
2000	Great Falls (Pio)	R	10	3	1.88	15	15	2	0	96	66	32	20	23	129
MINOR LEAGUE TOTALS			15	8	3.19	49	43	3	0	203	170	112	72	101	236

19. Jorge Nunez, ss

Born: March 3, 1978. **Ht.:** 5-10. **Wt.:** 158. **Bats:** R. **Throws:** R. **Career Transactions:** Signed out of Dominican Republic by Blue Jays, April 17, 1995 . . . Traded by Blue Jays with OF Shawn Green to Dodgers for OF Raul Mondesi and LHP Pedro Borbon, Nov. 8, 1999 . . . Granted free agency, Dec. 20, 2000; re-signed by Dodgers, Dec. 21, 2000.

Nunez spent his first season in the organization last year after leading all Class A players with 116 runs in 1999. He led Vero Beach in runs, hits and triples while topping the entire system in stolen bases. He has a wiry, athletic body that projects to be even more productive as he continues to mature. His arm was rated as the best among Florida State League infielders last year. He also has outstanding speed that he parlays into impressive baserunning skills. His athleticism, however, can cause Nunez to play out of control on occasion. He also isn't as disciplined as he needs to be at the plate. He has some power and produces a decent number of extra-base hits, but Nunez would be better served spraying the ball to all fields in order to get on base more often. The Dodgers believe he's just beginning to reveal his vast potential and are looking for more progress this year at Jacksonville.

Year	Club (League)	Class	AVG	G	AB	R	H	2B	3B	HR	RBI	BB	SO	SB
1995	Blue Jays (DSL)	R	.133	13	15	1	2	0	0	1	4	1	5	0
1996	Blue Jays (DSL)	R	.295	69	258	51	76	10	2	7	40	19	36	19
1997	Blue Jays (DSL)	R	.252	71	262	46	66	5	5	4	33	29	48	44
1998	Hagerstown (SAL)	A	.250	4	16	0	4	0	0	0	1	0	1	1
	Medicine Hat (Pio)	R	.319	74	317	74	101	9	11	6	52	28	45	31
1999	Hagerstown (SAL)	A	.268	133	564	116	151	28	11	14	61	40	103	51
2000	Vero Beach (FSL)	A	.288	128	534	86	154	17	8	4	39	38	104	54
	Albuquerque (PCL)	AAA	.000	1	3	0	0	0	0	0	0	0	0	0
MINOR LEAGUE TOTALS			.281	493	1969	374	554	69	37	36	230	155	342	200

20. Steve Colyer, lhp

Born: Feb. 22, 1979. **Ht.:** 6-4. **Wt.:** 205. **Bats:** L. **Throws:** L. **School:** Meramec (Mo.) JC. **Career Transactions:** Selected by Dodgers in second round of 1997 draft; signed May 23, 1998.

After two solid years that had him ranked ninth in the organization entering 2000, Colyer struggled. He had difficulty once again with his control, relegating him to bullpen duty at midseason. While Colyer would have benefited from being able to report to a low Class A league, he did show two plus pitches in a mid-90s fastball and an overhand curveball. He's continuing to work on his changeup, but it has yet to develop into an average offering. Colyer is his own worst enemy with his inconsistent approach and overall lack of maturity. There continues to be a strong movement within the organization to move the strong-armed Colyer to the bullpen permanently. The hope remains for him to discover some consistency this year in Double-A.

Year	Club (League)	Class	W	L	ERA	G	GS	CG	SV	IP	H	R	ER	BB	SO
1998	Yakima (NWL)	A	2	2	4.96	15	12	0	0	65	72	46	36	36	75
1999	San Bernardino (Cal)	A	7	9	4.70	27	25	1	0	145	145	82	76	86	131
2000	Vero Beach (FSL)	A	5	7	5.76	26	18	1	0	95	97	74	61	68	80
MINOR LEAGUE TOTALS			14	18	5.08	68	55	2	0	306	314	202	173	190	286

21. Heath Totten, rhp

Born: Sep. 30, 1978. **Ht.:** 6-3. **Wt.:** 210. **Bats:** R. **Throws:** R. **School:** Lamar University. **Career Transactions:** Selected by Dodgers in fifth round of 2000 draft; signed June 21, 2000.

Totten was selected to Baseball America's short-season all-star team after heading a Yakima rotation that won the Northwest League title. He had the best professional debut among the Dodgers' 2000 draft class by topping the league in ERA. Totten throws strikes, keeps the ball down in the strike zone and isn't afraid to challenge hitters. While not overpowering, he moves his average fastball around in the strike zone. His best pitch is a plus slider that he'll throw when behind in the count. He still needs to upgrade his changeup in order to keep hitters honest. He'll open the 2001 season at Wilmington, with a midseason promotion to Vero Beach within reach.

Year	Club (League)	Class	W	L	ERA	G	GS	CG	SV	IP	H	R	ER	BB	SO
2000	Yakima (NWL)	A	8	2	2.30	13	13	0	0	74	55	24	19	15	67
MINOR LEAGUE TOTALS			8	2	2.30	13	13	0	0	74	55	24	19	15	67

22. Jeff Williams, lhp

Born: June 6, 1972. **Ht.:** 6-0. **Wt.:** 185. **Bats:** R. **Throws:** L. **School:** Southeastern Louisiana University. **Career Transactions:** Signed as nondrafted free agent by Dodgers, July 3, 1996.

Williams became the ninth Australian to play in the major leagues when he made his major league debut late in 1999. He experienced numbness in his left hand and wrist during an early-season callup last year, then returned to Triple-A and tried to pitch through the discomfort before a pinched nerve was discovered. He had surgery, forcing him to miss the Arizona Fall League. Williams also has experienced a dead arm in the past. In 1996, he logged a lot of innings with Southeastern Louisiana and the Australian Olympic team. The result was a fastball that had difficulty breaking 80 mph for more than a year. He now throws in the low 90s with good movement, along with an average curveball and changeup. While he has had success during his stints in the majors, Williams remains an unproven 28-year-old pitcher who's coming off an injury, so his clock is ticking.

Year	Club (League)	Class	W	L	ERA	G	GS	CG	SV	IP	H	R	ER	BB	SO
1997	San Bernardino (Cal)	A	10	4	3.10	18	18	0	0	116	101	52	40	34	72
	San Antonio (TL)	AA	2	1	5.40	5	5	0	0	28	30	17	17	7	14
1998	San Antonio (TL)	AA	3	0	2.59	7	7	0	0	42	43	19	12	13	35
	Albuquerque (PCL)	AAA	8	8	4.98	21	21	0	0	121	160	87	67	49	93
1999	Albuquerque (PCL)	AAA	9	7	5.01	42	14	1	4	126	151	77	70	47	86
	Los Angeles (NL)	MAJ	2	0	4.08	5	3	0	0	18	12	10	8	9	7
2000	Albuquerque (PCL)	AAA	4	3	4.26	12	12	0	0	63	64	33	30	28	38
	Los Angeles (NL)	MAJ	0	0	15.88	7	0	0	0	6	12	11	10	8	3
MAJOR LEAGUE TOTALS			2	0	6.75	12	3	0	0	24	24	21	18	17	10
MINOR LEAGUE TOTALS			36	23	4.28	105	77	1	4	496	549	285	236	178	338

23. Tony Mota, of

Born: Oct. 31, 1977. **Ht.:** 6-1. **Wt.:** 170. **Bats:** B. **Throws:** R. **School:** Miami Springs (Fla.) HS. **Career Transactions:** Selected by Dodgers in 17th round of 1995 draft; signed Aug. 22, 1995 . . . Released by Dodgers, Dec. 11, 2000; re-signed by Dodgers, Dec. 18, 2000.

The son of longtime Dodgers player and coach Manny made the jump to Triple-A last year but had difficulty adjusting. He also battled injury problems again after a season-ending thumb ailment in 1999 and right shoulder surgery that cost him playing time in both 1996 and '97. When healthy, Mota is a solid contact hitter with good plate coverage. He showed a considerable increase in power in 1999 but had a mere 21 extra-base hits last year. Mota is an above-average defender with an arm strong enough to play right field in the major leagues. He also covers a large amount of ground with his plus speed. Mota's progress has been hampered by injuries and a lack of overall consistency in all phases of the game. While he remained on the 40-man roster in November, Mota needs to upgrade his performance this year in Triple-A in order to remain in the Dodgers' plans.

Year	Club (League)	Class	AVG	G	AB	R	H	2B	3B	HR	RBI	BB	SO	SB
1996	Yakima (NWL)	A	.276	60	225	29	62	11	3	3	29	13	37	13
1997	San Bernardino (Cal)	A	.240	111	420	53	101	14	13	4	49	30	97	11
1998	Vero Beach (FSL)	A	.319	61	254	45	81	18	5	7	35	18	27	13
	San Antonio (TL)	AA	.243	59	222	20	54	10	6	2	22	12	36	16
1999	San Antonio (TL)	AA	.325	98	345	65	112	31	2	15	75	41	56	13
2000	Albuquerque (PCL)	AAA	.269	102	372	57	100	11	4	6	47	28	61	8
MINOR LEAGUE TOTALS			.277	491	1838	269	510	95	33	37	257	142	314	74

24. Reggie Abercrombie, of

Born: July 15, 1981. **Ht.:** 6-3. **Wt.:** 210. **Bats:** R. **Throws:** R. **School:** Lake City (Fla.) CC. **Career Transactions:** Selected by Dodgers in 23rd round of 1999 draft; signed May 24, 2000.

The Dodgers signed the unheralded Abercrombie as a draft-and-follow and watched him blossom. A potential five-tool talent, Abercrombie succeeds with his plus speed. He has excellent range in center field, takes the proper route to most fly balls and possesses an above-average arm for his position. His ability to run is also evident on the basepaths, as he ranked second in the Pioneer League in stolen bases while succeeding on 32 of 40 attempts. The Dodgers were a little surprised about how well Abercrombie made adjustments at the plate. The one area his game is lacking is in power, particularly for a player his size, but that could come as he continues to mature. He'll likely head to Wilmington in 2001.

Year	Club (League)	Class	AVG	G	AB	R	H	2B	3B	HR	RBI	BB	SO	SB
2000	Great Falls (Pio)	R	.273	54	220	40	60	7	1	2	29	22	66	32
MINOR LEAGUE TOTALS			.273	54	220	40	60	7	1	2	29	22	66	32

25. Bubba Crosby, of

Born: Aug. 11, 1976. **Ht.:** 5-11. **Wt.:** 185. **Bats:** L. **Throws:** L. **School:** Rice University. **Career Transactions:** Selected by Dodgers in first round (23rd overall) of 1998 draft; signed June 19, 1998.

Few players have caused more organizational head-scratching than Crosby. He was a consensus first-rounder after hitting 25 home runs in his final season at Rice. But his power has been virtually nonexistent since he started swinging wood bats. His all-around hitting has not been spectacular, either. He did provide a ray of hope in the Arizona Fall League, where he hit .346-3-13 in 104 at-bats. He has above-average speed, resulting in a career-high 27 steals last year. He is an adequate defender with a decent arm, but has shown nothing to merit his $995,000 bonus. The Dodgers have been patient with Crosby, but he's going to be pushed to see how he reacts against better competition, beginning this year at Double-A.

Year	Club (League)	Class	AVG	G	AB	R	H	2B	3B	HR	RBI	BB	SO	SB
1998	San Bernardino (Cal)	A	.216	56	199	25	43	9	2	0	14	17	38	3
1999	San Bernardino (Cal)	A	.296	96	371	53	110	21	3	1	37	42	71	19
2000	Vero Beach (FSL)	A	.266	73	274	50	73	13	8	8	51	31	41	27
	San Bernardino (Cal)	A	.250	3	12	2	3	0	0	0	2	0	4	1
MINOR LEAGUE TOTALS			.268	228	856	130	229	43	13	9	104	90	154	50

26. Jose Diaz, c

Born: April 13, 1980. **Ht.:** 6-0. **Wt.:** 205. **Bats:** R. **Throws:** R. **Career Transactions:** Signed out of Dominican Republic by Dodgers, Aug. 24, 1996.

Diaz held his own last year in the Pioneer League and made the league's postseason all-star team. He got high marks for his blocking skills, glovework and arm strength. What hurts Diaz is his hitting. His .219 average established a new career best. He does have average power, but his inability to make consistent contact, especially against breaking balls, is affecting his development. Also working against Diaz is the fact that he missed all of the 1999 season due to an injury and has played just one year in the United States. Given his age, he'll be provided every opportunity to earn a job at Wilmington during spring training.

Year	Club (League)	Class	AVG	G	AB	R	H	2B	3B	HR	RBI	BB	SO	SB
1997	Dodgers (DSL)	R	.147	30	95	12	14	1	0	1	5	6	30	3
1998	Dodgers (DSL)	R	.209	51	163	24	34	6	0	1	27	15	34	4
1999						Did Not Play—Injured								
2000	Great Falls (Pio)	R	.219	57	210	29	46	9	1	7	31	18	52	2
MINOR LEAGUE TOTALS			.201	138	468	65	94	16	1	9	63	39	116	9

27. Marcos Castillo, rhp

Born: Feb. 15, 1979. **Ht.:** 6-2. **Wt.:** 172. **Bats:** R. **Throws:** R. **Career Transactions:** Signed out of Venezuela by Dodgers, Aug. 26, 1995.

Inconsistency continues to be the defining term in Castillo's career. After a breakthrough in 1999 that included the fourth perfect game in California League history, he floundered in his third season at the high Class A level. Castillo is a finesse pitcher who tends to nibble instead of going right at hitters. He works off an 88-90 mph fastball with excellent sinking action. He complements it with an above-average changeup that he can become infatuated with, and an average curveball. He also possesses sterling control. If he's to succeed at higher levels, he must not give up the inside half of the plate and must challenge hitters more often. The Dodgers hope to see him make those strides this season in Double-A.

Year	Club (League)	Class	W	L	ERA	G	GS	CG	SV	IP	H	R	ER	BB	SO
1996	Dodgers (DSL)	R	1	2	3.27	5	2	0	0	11	7	4	4	6	9
1997	San Joaquin 2 (VSL)	R	6	2	2.41	18	0	0	0	74	67	22	20	15	67
1998	Vero Beach (FSL)	A	5	15	4.99	25	25	2	0	139	141	95	77	47	77
1999	San Bernardino (Cal)	A	14	9	4.10	27	27	1	0	167	182	90	76	48	130
2000	Vero Beach (FSL)	A	7	9	3.89	25	22	2	0	141	150	77	61	34	91
MINOR LEAGUE TOTALS			33	37	4.02	100	76	5	0	532	547	288	238	150	374

28. Maximo Regalado, rhp

Born: Nov. 18, 1976. **Ht.:** 6-1. **Wt.:** 198. **Bats:** R. **Throws:** R. **Career Transactions:** Signed out of Dominican Republic by Dodgers, April 7, 1994.

Regalado made Baseball America's minor league all-star team last year after moving to the bullpen during instructional league 1999 at the suggestion of roving pitching instructor Jim Benedict. The combination of natural maturation and learning from adversity enabled Regalado to blossom in his new role. Regalado succeeds with a 95 mph fastball. While his lack of a consistent changeup or breaking pitch always hurt him as a starter, it's not as big a problem as a reliever. He still needs to develop at least one more average offering to succeed at higher levels. Regalado needs another strong season to become part of the Dodgers' plans.

Year	Club (League)	Class	W	L	ERA	G	GS	CG	SV	IP	H	R	ER	BB	SO
1994	Dodgers (DSL)	R	2	1	3.33	6	6	0	0	24	22	16	9	12	14
1995	Dodgers (DSL)	R	0	2	7.85	11	3	0	0	18	21	20	16	14	13
1996	Dodgers (DSL)	R	3	5	4.70	14	13	0	1	54	44	32	28	48	19
1997	Great Falls (Pio)	R	2	1	1.96	9	6	0	0	37	27	12	8	21	24
1998	Vero Beach (FSL)	A	0	2	6.75	4	4	0	0	16	17	15	12	13	14
	Great Falls (Pio)	R	0	0	0.00	3	0	0	0	6	2	0	0	3	7
	San Bernardino (Cal)	A	3	3	4.18	14	3	0	0	47	45	30	22	24	42
1999	Vero Beach (FSL)	A	2	12	5.80	20	19	1	0	90	110	65	58	49	58
2000	Vero Beach (FSL)	A	0	0	0.88	30	0	0	21	31	15	4	3	8	45
	San Antonio (TL)	AA	1	2	3.09	26	0	0	9	23	22	8	8	15	27
MINOR LEAGUE TOTALS			13	28	4.27	137	54	1	31	346	325	202	164	207	263

29. Jose Nunez, lhp

Born: March 14, 1979. **Ht.:** 6-2. **Wt.:** 175. **Bats:** L. **Throws:** L. **Career Transactions:** Signed out of Dominican Republic by Mets, Feb. 21, 1996 . . . Selected by Dodgers from Mets in major league Rule 5 draft, Dec. 11, 2000.

The Dodgers rolled the dice by taking Nunez from the Mets in the major league Rule 5 draft. A starter in 1998 and '99, he spent most of last season (his first in a full-season league) in the bullpen. Nunez has excellent command of all his pitches, including an above-average fastball that reaches the low 90s with outstanding movement. He also throws a good changeup and an average curveball. Nunez may be a longshot to stay on the major league roster, but the Dodgers have just one lefty (Onan Masaoka) in their major league bullpen. His all-around stuff and ability to dominate hitters make him intriguing.

Year	Club (League)	Class	W	L	ERA	G	GS	CG	SV	IP	H	R	ER	BB	SO
1996	Mets (DSL)	R	0	1	6.46	11	3	0	0	24	33	19	17	9	25
1997	Mets (DSL)	R	2	2	2.91	18	6	0	0	46	43	21	15	15	37
1998	Mets (GCL)	R	3	7	2.38	13	11	1	0	68	60	26	18	12	69
1999	Kingsport (Appy)	R	3	4	3.75	13	13	0	0	70	75	36	29	15	63
2000	Capital City (SAL)	A	3	4	3.02	34	5	0	8	95	82	36	32	23	112
MINOR LEAGUE TOTALS			11	18	3.30	89	38	1	8	303	293	138	111	74	306

30. Koyie Hill, c/3b

Born: March 9, 1979. **Ht.:** 6-0. **Wt.:** 190. **Bats:** B. **Throws:** R. **School:** Wichita State University. **Career Transactions:** Selected by Dodgers in fourth round of 2000 draft; signed June 22, 2000.

Hill made a strong pro debut, impressing with his ability to swing the bat. A solid defensive third baseman at Wichita State with good hands and an above-average arm, Hill saw activity at catcher in Yakima. His inexperience was obvious, resulting in several catcher-interference calls. The Dodgers like his footwork and overall athleticism and plan to give him more catching experience. As a hitter, Hill uses the entire field and can drive the ball to all fields. He needs better plate coverage and must get ahead in the count more often. While he's a work in progress, Hill has the versatility to develop into a productive utilityman.

Year	Club (League)	Class	AVG	G	AB	R	H	2B	3B	HR	RBI	BB	SO	SB
2000	Yakima (NWL)	A	.259	64	251	26	65	13	1	2	29	25	47	0
MINOR LEAGUE TOTALS			.259	64	251	26	65	13	1	2	29	25	47	0

Milwaukee
Brewers

In the fall of 1999, the new Brewers regime led by general manager Dean Taylor encountered a crisis, with a farm system desperately thin in position-player prospects.

A look back at the organization's top prospects from last year shows the situation hasn't improved. Four of the five hitters among the organization's Top 10 Prospects entering 2000 are out of the picture. First baseman Kevin Barker flopped so badly that he was removed from the 40-man roster. Disappointing outfielder Chad Green and shortstop Santiago Perez were traded after the season. Third baseman-turned-outfielder Scott Kirby couldn't handle the jump from Class A to Double-A. Only outfielder Cristian Guerrero emerged unscathed.

"It's no secret that the farm system is thin in regards to position players," Taylor said. "That's why we are making such a big commitment to scouting and player development."

The Brewers have good reason to be excited about righthander Ben Sheets, a first-round draft pick in 1999 who became the hero for Team USA in the Sydney Olympics. Nick Neugebauer, Allen Levrault and Jose Mieses are also promising righthanders.

But faced with budget limitations and the lack of hitting prospects at the top levels, the Brewers will have to look elsewhere for lineup regulars for now. Their major move in the offseason was signing free agent Jeffrey Hammonds to a three-year contract, and they hope he can hold up in center field and hit away from Coors Field.

At least things appear to be moving in the right direction after eight consecutive losing seasons. The Brewers were a much more competitive team after acquiring slugger Richie Sexson from Cleveland in late July, going 30-27 with him in their lineup. And 2001 brings the long-awaited move to Miller Park, the retractable-roof facility that will generate more money for the team. The climate-controlled conditions also should help the Brewers attract players, a noticeable problem in the past.

Milwaukee did shore up its pitching last year, and stopped the daily track meet on the bases by acquiring catcher Henry Blanco. The Brewers also hired former Tigers GM Bill Lajoie to advise Taylor and former Pirates GM Larry Doughty to serve as a national crosschecker.

They couldn't turn around the franchise in a year's time, but Taylor and feisty manager Dave Lopes have given long-suffering Brewers fans reason for hope. More about how much progress they're making will be known after 2001.

TOP 30 PROSPECTS

1. Ben Sheets, rhp
2. Nick Neugebauer, rhp
3. David Krynzel, of
4. Cristian Guerrero, of
5. Allen Levrault, rhp
6. Jose Mieses, rhp
7. Kade Johnson, c
8. Mike Penney, rhp
9. Horacio Estrada, lhp
10. Brandon Kolb, rhp
11. Jason Belcher, c
12. Carlos Chantres, rhp
13. Mark Ernster, ss
14. Dane Artman, lhp
15. Roberto Miniel, rhp
16. Matt Childers, rhp
17. Gene Altman, rhp
18. J.M. Gold, rhp
19. Daryl Clark, 3b/1b
20. Scott Kirby, of
21. Will Hall, ss
22. Jason Fox, of
23. Chris Rowan, ss
24. Jose Garcia, rhp
25. Ryan Poe, rhp
26. Kane Davis, rhp
27. Brian Moon, c
28. Justin Gordon, lhp
29. Ruddy Lugo, rhp
30. Bucky Jacobsen, 1b/of

By Tom Haudricourt

Organization Overview

General manager: Dean Taylor. Farm director: Greg Riddoch. Scouting director: Jack Zduriencik.

2000 PERFORMANCE

Class	Team	League	W	L	Pct.	Finish*	Manager(s)
Majors	Milwaukee	National	73	89	.451	11th (16)	Davey Lopes
Triple-A	Indianapolis Indians	International	81	63	.563	5th (14)	Steve Smith
Double-A	Huntsville Stars	Southern	64	75	.460	t-9th (10)	Carlos Lezcano
High A	#Mudville Nine	California	68	72	.486	7th (10)	Moss/Keeter/Kremblas
Low A	Beloit Snappers	Midwest	71	64	.526	t-5th (14)	Don Money
Rookie	†Helena Brewers	Pioneer	26	50	.342	8th (8)	Dan Norman
Rookie	Ogden Raptors	Pioneer	41	34	.520	4th (8)	Ed Sedar
OVERALL 2000 MINOR LEAGUE RECORD			351	358	.495	16th (30)	

*Finish in overall standings (No. of teams in league). #Affiliate will be High Desert (California) in 2001. †Affiliate will be in Arizona League in 2001.

ORGANIZATION LEADERS

BATTING
*AVG	**Bobby Darula**, Beloit/Huntsville	.336
R	Mickey Lopez, Indianapolis/Huntsville	80
H	Jeff Pickler, Huntsville/Indianapolis	135
TB	Mark Cridland, Mudville	231
2B	Jose Fernandez, Indianapolis	37
3B	Santiago Perez, Indianapolis	7
	Jeff Deardorff, Mudville	7
HR	Lance Burkhart, Beloit/Huntsville	23
RBI	Lance Burkhart, Beloit/Huntsville	83
BB	Jon Macalutas, Mudville	104
SO	Will Hall, Beloit	127
SB	Jason Fox, Mudville	53

PITCHING
W	**Jose Mieses**, Beloit/Mudville	17
L	Paul Stewart, Huntsville/Mudville	11
	Matt Childers, Mudville/Beloit	11
#ERA	Jack Krawczyk, Mudville/Huntsville	1.60
G	Scott Huntsman, Huntsville	59
CG	Horacio Estrada, Indianapolis	3
SV	Bob Scanlan, Indianapolis	35
IP	**Jose Mieses**, Beloit/Mudville	169
BB	Nick Neugebauer, Mudville/Huntsville	134
SO	Jason Childers, Mudville	177

*Minimum 250 at-bats. #Minimum 75 innings.

TOP PROSPECTS OF THE DECADE

1991	Chris George, rhp
1992	Tyrone Hill, lhp
1993	Tyrone Hill, lhp
1994	Jeff D'Amico, rhp
1995	Antone Williamson, 3b
1996	Jeff D'Amico, rhp
1997	Todd Dunn, of
1998	Valerio de los Santos, lhp
1999	Ron Belliard, 2b
2000	Nick Neugebauer, rhp

TOP DRAFT PICKS OF THE DECADE

1991	*Kenny Henderson, rhp
1992	Ken Felder, of
1993	Jeff D'Amico, rhp
1994	Antone Williamson, 3b
1995	Geoff Jenkins, of
1996	Chad Green, of
1997	Kyle Peterson, rhp
1998	J.M. Gold, rhp
1999	Ben Sheets, rhp
2000	David Krynzel, of

*Did not sign.

Darula

Mieses

BEST TOOLS

Best Hitter for Average	David Krynzel
Best Power Hitter	Kade Johnson
Fastest Baserunner	David Krynzel
Best Fastball	Nick Neugebauer
Best Breaking Ball	Ben Sheets
Best Control	Ben Sheets
Best Defensive Catcher	Brian Moon
Best Defensive Infielder	Steve Scarborough
Best Infield Arm	Will Hall
Best Defensive Outfielder	David Krynzel
Best Outfield Arm	Cristian Guerrero

PROJECTED 2004 LINEUP

Catcher	Kade Johnson
First Base	Richie Sexson
Second Base	Ron Belliard
Third Base	Daryl Clark
Shortstop	Mark Loretta
Left Field	Geoff Jenkins
Center Field	David Krynzel
Right Field	Cristian Guerrero
No. 1 Starter	Ben Sheets
No. 2 Starter	Jeff D'Amico
No. 3 Starter	Nick Neugebauer
No. 4 Starter	Jose Mieses
No. 5 Starter	Horacio Estrada
Closer	Allen Levrault

ALL-TIME LARGEST BONUSES

Ben Sheets, 1999	$2,450,000
David Krynzel, 2000	1,950,000
J.M. Gold, 1998	1,675,000
Kyle Peterson, 1997	1,400,000
Chad Green, 1996	1,060,000

DraftAnalysis

2000 Draft

Best Pro Debut: 3B Daryl Clark (17) hit .339-15-64 in the Rookie-level Pioneer League. A pair of high school players, OF **David Krynzel** (1) and C Jason Belcher (5), also fared well in the same circuit, batting .359 and .333, respectively.

Best Athlete: Krynzel was the fastest true prospect in the draft, and he has tremendous range in center field to go with a solid arm.

Best Hitter: OF Bill Scott (8) led the Pacific-10 Conference with a .421 average last spring at UCLA despite playing much of the spring with a broken bone in his right hand. The Brewers are excited about both Krynzel and Belcher.

Best Raw Power: Clark. Belcher could give him a run as his body matures, and so could Scott once he makes his pro debut in 2001.

Fastest Runner: Krynzel has been clocked as fast as 6.3 seconds in the 60-yard dash. OF Bryan Hicks (6), who was recruited as a quarterback by Louisiana-Monroe, also runs well.

Best Defensive Player: Krynzel.

Best Fastball: RHP Matt Yeatman (13), who signed late, was throwing 93 mph in instructional league. RHPs Gerry Oakes (7) and Heath McMurray (12) are also in that class.

Most Intriguing Background: Canadian RHP Michael Reiss' (26) twin brother Stephen was drafted one round later by the Twins. Neither signed and they are attending college at Houston. C Casey Myers (30), who returned to Arizona State, is the brother of Corey, the No. 4 overall pick in the 1999 draft who is playing in the Diamondbacks organization.

Closest To The Majors: Scott didn't sign until late September while the Brewers waited for his hand to heal. As advanced a hitter as he is, that shouldn't hold him back.

Best Late-Round Pick: The Brewers look at 1B Jon Hart (11) and see a Richie Sexson body, and this is an organization that obviously appreciates Sexson. They also have hopes for McMurray, Yeatman and Clark.

Krynzel

The One Who Got Away: Milwaukee says it signed everyone it targeted. The highest-drafted player who didn't come to terms was RHP Scott Roehl (16), the best prospect in a weak Wisconsin draft crop. He's at Arkansas.

Assessment: Many players who get drafted in the first round based almost solely on their speed don't work out—just ask the Brewers about Chad Green—but Krynzel may have the all-around skills to be an exception. An organization with one of the weakest systems in the game didn't need to give away its second-round pick to sign Jose Hernandez as a free agent, however.

1999 Draft

RHP Ben Sheets (1) was a welcomed change from the Brewers' dismal track record with its top choices in previous drafts. As a bonus, they also got Kade Johnson (2), the best catcher in the system. **Grade: B+**

1998 Draft

RHP Nick Neugebauer (2) might really be something if he ever harnesses his tremendous stuff well enough to throw strikes. Milwaukee thought getting RHP J.M. Gold (1) was a coup, but he blew out his elbow last year. RHP Mike Penney (8) has promise. **Grade: C**

1997 Draft

RHP Kyle Peterson (1) is another injury casualty, missing most of 2000 after shoulder surgery. If he doesn't bounce back, the Brewers could wind up with nothing from this draft, though there is hope for RHP Matt Childers (9). **Grade: C–**

1996 Draft

Milwaukee blew its top pick on speedy OF Chad Green (1), a signability guy who was exiled to the Padres this winter. 1B Kevin Barker (3) once ranked as Milwaukee's top prospect but fizzled in 2000. The lone bright spot is RHP Allen Levrault (13), who could blossom into the closer of the future. **Grade: D+**

Note: Draft analysis prepared by Jim Callis. Numbers in parentheses indicate draft rounds.

... Sheets answered questions with his eye-popping showing in the pressurized atmosphere of the Olympics.

Ben
Sheets rhp

Born: July 18, 1978.
Ht.: 6-1. **Wt.:** 195.
Bats: R. **Throws:** R.
School: Northeast Louisiana University.
Career Transactions: Selected by Brewers in first round (10th overall) of 1999 draft; signed July 30, 1999.

Sheets was projected to go well before Milwaukee grabbed him with the 10th overall pick in the 1999 draft, but he fell into the Brewers' lap. As soon as they selected him, the plan was to fast-track him to the big leagues. And by all appearances, that's exactly what will happen. Sheets gave a remarkable performance for Team USA in the Sydney Olympics. Immediately tabbed as the team ace, Sheets lived up to that billing and then some with a stunning shutout of favored Cuba in the gold-medal game. Manager Tommy Lasorda became so enamored of Sheets that he even traveled to Louisiana after the Olympics to attend his wedding. The Brewers' decision to allow Sheets to play in the Olympics rather than come to the major leagues in September for a few meaningless starts was an astute one. "He has a burning desire to be a major league player," Brewers farm director Greg Riddoch said. "He rose to the occasion in the biggest game of his life. That tells you all you need to know."

Sheets has an above-average fastball that he throws regularly in the 92-95 mph range, but his bread-and-butter pitch is an old-fashioned, 12-to-6 curveball that buckles the knees of hitters. Because he has a good, sinking fastball and a decent changeup, you can't sit on his curve. Beyond his repertoire, Sheets is an intense competitor who doesn't lose his cool on the mound. Everyone involved with Team USA raved about the way he handled himself on the mound. "He's a throwback player," Brewers minor league pitching coach Mike Caldwell said. "He does all the things right. And he's as competitive as it gets." Lack of professional experience is about all that can be counted against Sheets, and he answered that shortcoming (and most other questions) with his eye-popping showing in the pressurized atmosphere of the Olympics. He still needs to work on his changeup, and he could stand to add a bit of muscle to his frame. When his curveball takes the day off, he has to keep his fastball down to avoid an early exit.

Never say never in baseball, but nothing short of an injury will keep Sheets from opening the 2001 season in the Brewers rotation. Management will put him toward the back of the starting five to avoid putting any undue pressure on him, but Sheets will have the best stuff of anyone in the rotation from the first day of camp. He's a legitimate top-of-the-rotation pitcher who could go a long way toward returning the Brewers to respectability.

Year	Club (League)	Class	W	L	ERA	G	GS	CG	SV	IP	H	R	ER	BB	SO
1999	Ogden (Pio)	R	0	1	5.63	2	2	0	0	8	8	5	5	2	12
	Stockton (Cal)	A	1	0	3.58	5	5	0	0	28	23	11	11	14	28
2000	Huntsville (SL)	AA	5	3	1.88	13	13	0	0	72	55	17	15	25	60
	Indianapolis (IL)	AAA	3	5	2.87	14	13	1	0	82	77	31	26	31	59
MINOR LEAGUE TOTALS			9	9	2.71	34	33	1	0	189	163	64	57	72	159

2. Nick Neugebauer, rhp

Born: July 15, 1980. **Ht.:** 6-3. **Wt.:** 225. **Bats:** R. **Throws:** R. **School:** Arlington HS, Riverside, Calif. **Career Transactions:** Selected by Brewers in second round of 1998 draft; signed Aug. 27, 1998.

In an effort to protect the strongest arm in the organization, the Brewers kept Neugebauer on a strict pitch count at the outset of the 2000 season. Because he continued to battle control problems, he rarely qualified for a win. But he wasn't intimidated and continued to show progress, so he was elevated to Double-A Huntsville in the second half of the season. The Brewers pushed his development even further by sending him to the Arizona Fall League, where he finished with eight hitless innings in his last two outings. Simply put, Neugebauer has a blazing fastball. When he really rears back, he can approach 100 mph, though instructors have tried to show him the value of backing off a bit to achieve better control. He has a nasty slider that makes him nearly unhittable when he gets it over the plate. He continues to work on a changeup that could be a devastating pitch. But Neugebauer has averaged a little more than a walk an inning. He has overcome that wildness so far by allowing few hits and striking out hitters when he has to. He has worked hard on his mechanics and release point and must continue to do so. Improving his control is all that's holding him back. As with a young Nolan Ryan and Randy Johnson, Neugebauer must harness his pitches to pave the way to a successful major league career. If the Brewers are able to advance him to Triple-A for at least half a season in 2001, Neugebauer could be a very young, very promising pitcher by the time he makes it to Milwaukee.

Year	Club (League)	Class	W	L	ERA	G	GS	CG	SV	IP	H	R	ER	BB	SO
1999	Beloit (Mid)	A	7	5	3.90	18	18	0	0	81	50	41	35	80	125
2000	Mudville (Cal)	A	4	4	4.19	18	18	0	0	77	43	40	36	87	117
	Huntsville (SL)	AA	1	3	3.73	10	10	0	0	51	35	28	21	47	57
MINOR LEAGUE TOTALS			12	12	3.97	46	46	0	0	209	128	109	92	214	299

3. David Krynzel, of

Born: Nov. 7, 1981. **Ht.:** 6-1. **Wt.:** 180. **Bats:** L. **Throws:** L. **School:** Green Valley HS, Henderson, Nev. **Career Transactions:** Selected by Brewers in first round (11th overall) of 2000 draft; signed June 12, 2000.

Krynzel is the player the Brewers targeted from the get-go in the 2000 draft, and they were thrilled he was on the board when they made the 11th pick. He was considered the fastest player in the high school ranks and a prototype leadoff hitter/center fielder, exactly what Milwaukee sought. His $1.95 million bonus was the second-highest in club history. Speed is Krynzel's calling card, and he is a good defensive player who has all of the tools except power. As he fills out, the Brewers believe he'll develop more pop at the plate. He's a hard worker with a desire to succeed. Other than the lack of power, Krynzel has a lot going for him. As with most high school players, he needs to develop more strength but has the frame to do so. He'll need to make more consistent contact to be an effective leadoff man. Though Krynzel missed the second half of the Rookie-level Pioneer League season with a thumb injury, managers named him the circuit's No. 1 prospect. The Brewers will give him the chance to show he can handle Class A Beloit in 2001.

Year	Club (League)	Class	AVG	G	AB	R	H	2B	3B	HR	RBI	BB	SO	SB
2000	Ogden (Pio)	R	.359	34	131	25	47	8	3	1	29	16	23	8
MINOR LEAGUE TOTALS			.359	34	131	25	47	8	3	1	29	16	23	8

4. Cristian Guerrero, of

Born: April 12, 1981. **Ht.:** 6-5. **Wt.:** 200. **Bats:** R. **Throws:** R. **Career Transactions:** Signed out of Dominican Republic by Brewers, Aug. 28, 1997.

Because Guerrero was so young, the Brewers weren't discouraged when he struggled at Beloit and had to be sent back to Rookie-level Ogden. By the end of the year, he was playing so well that he rejoined Beloit in the playoffs and more than held his own. Guerrero not only has power but also runs well. In fact, he has five-tool potential along the lines of cousin Vladimir Guerrero. With a lanky frame that should fill out as he gets older, Cristian's ceiling is very high. His failure at Beloit, where he was bothered by the cold weather, showed he has work to do mentally. Projected as a right fielder because of his power potential and arm, he must continue to work on his defense to be a complete player. At this stage, comparisons to his cousin are premature and counterproductive. Guerrero could be something special, though. He's still a teenager, so the Brewers have no reason to rush him. This time around, he should be ready for Beloit.

Year	Club (League)	Class	AVG	G	AB	R	H	2B	3B	HR	RBI	BB	SO	SB
1998	Brewers (DSL)	R	.268	64	213	45	57	9	3	5	37	43	54	5
1999	Ogden (Pio)	R	.310	65	226	51	70	7	3	5	28	23	59	26
2000	Beloit (Mid)	A	.164	15	55	5	9	4	0	2	8	1	18	1
	Ogden (Pio)	R	.341	66	255	56	87	14	4	12	54	37	42	24
MINOR LEAGUE TOTALS			.298	210	749	157	223	34	10	24	127	104	173	56

5. Allen Levrault, rhp

Born: Aug. 15, 1977. **Ht.:** 6-3. **Wt.:** 230. **Bats:** R. **Throws:** R. **School:** CC of Rhode Island. **Career Transactions:** Selected by Brewers in 13th round of 1996 draft; signed June 10, 1996.

Levrault had an up-and-down season in his first full year at the Triple-A level but got his feet wet in a stint with the Brewers. Used sporadically out of the bullpen, the confident Levrault showed no fear of big league hitters. But his inexperience did show at times. An aggressive pitcher who goes right at hitters, Levrault has a low-90s fastball and effective change-up. He seems to pitch better in small spurts, which is why there's a movement afoot to convert him from a starter to a set-up man. He has the bulldog mentality to pitch at the end of games. He has had trouble stringing together wins as a starter because he too often is a two-pitch pitcher who struggles with his breaking ball. He can be stubborn at times, throwing too many fastballs, and his confidence sometimes crosses the line to cockiness. Levrault may get the chance to win a spot in the Milwaukee bullpen during the spring. He has been primarily a starter in the minors, but his future in the big leagues probably is at the end of games, possibly as a closer.

Year	Club (League)	Class	W	L	ERA	G	GS	CG	SV	IP	H	R	ER	BB	SO
1996	Helena (Pio)	R	4	3	5.32	18	11	0	1	71	70	43	42	22	68
1997	Beloit (Mid)	A	3	10	5.28	24	24	1	0	131	141	89	77	40	112
1998	Stockton (Cal)	A	9	3	2.87	16	15	4	0	97	76	33	31	27	86
	El Paso (TL)	AA	1	5	5.89	11	11	0	0	63	77	51	41	17	46
1999	Huntsville (SL)	AA	9	2	3.43	16	16	2	0	100	77	44	38	33	82
	Louisville (IL)	AAA	1	3	8.65	9	5	0	0	34	48	37	33	16	33
2000	Indianapolis (IL)	AAA	6	8	4.24	21	18	1	0	108	98	55	51	46	78
	Milwaukee (NL)	MAJ	0	1	4.50	5	1	0	0	12	10	7	6	7	9
MAJOR LEAGUE TOTALS			0	1	4.50	5	1	0	0	12	10	7	6	7	9
MINOR LEAGUE TOTALS			33	34	4.66	115	100	8	1	605	587	352	313	201	505

6. Jose Mieses, rhp

Born: Oct. 14, 1979. **Ht.:** 6-1. **Wt.:** 180. **Bats:** R. **Throws:** R. **Career Transactions:** Signed out of Dominican Republic by Brewers, Dec. 11, 1996.

Mieses has been the biggest winner in the Brewers system the past two years, going 27-9, 2.61. He pitched two seasons in the Rookie-level Dominican Summer League before he was brought to the states for Rookie ball but could prove to be a real find. With a palmball that throws hitters off balance, plus an average fastball and curveball, Mieses mixes his pitches with maximum effectiveness. He has shown good poise on the mound and appears mature for his age. His solid strikeout-walk ratios are indicative of his plus command. He shelved his palmball in instructional league to concentrate on his fastball and curveball. He's not an overpowering pitcher, topping out around 89 mph, so he has to hit his spots. Most Midwest League managers felt more advanced hitters would lay off his palmball and take advantage of his other pitches. After pitching well at both Class A levels last season, Mieses probably will begin the 2001 season in Double-A. He could make it to the big leagues before the end of 2002.

Year	Club (League)	Class	W	L	ERA	G	GS	CG	SV	IP	H	R	ER	BB	SO
1997	Brewers (DSL)	R	3	2	2.40	20	5	0	1	56	34	22	15	36	49
1998	Brewers (DSL)	R	4	5	3.00	14	13	3	0	84	70	39	28	38	77
1999	Helena (Pio)	R	10	2	2.67	15	15	3	0	108	79	36	32	28	87
2000	Beloit (Mid)	A	13	6	2.53	21	21	2	0	135	107	43	38	37	132
	Mudville (Cal)	A	4	1	2.65	6	6	0	0	34	25	11	10	18	40
MINOR LEAGUE TOTALS			34	16	2.65	76	60	8	1	417	315	151	123	157	385

7. Kade Johnson, c

Born: Sept. 28, 1978. **Ht.:** 6-1. **Wt.:** 205. **Bats:** R. **Throws:** R. **School:** Seminole State (Okla.) JC. **Career Transactions:** Selected by Brewers in second round of 1999 draft; signed Sept. 3, 1999.

Johnson was an unknown quantity until the end of the 2000 season. He set a junior college record with 38 homers in 1999 after transferring from the University of Texas. He signed too late to make his pro debut, then showed up last spring with a shoulder injury that required surgery. He turned heads with six homers in three playoff games for Ogden. Even before his playoff explosion, Johnson displayed his chief tool by socking 10 homers in just 98 at-bats. It was a welcome sight for an organization hurting for a legitimate power-hitting prospect. Prior to his shoulder surgery, he showed good arm strength, and he's a take-charge guy behind the plate. Johnson must show he can stay healthy, and he needs to play after barely seeing action since turning pro. He was throwing fine in instructional league, so the Brewers hope the shoulder surgery won't make him a liability with the running game. Though Johnson has played little as a pro, the Brewers believe he can handle a Class A assignment to begin the 2001 season. Catching depth is a real problem in the organization, so he could move up fast if he gets the job done.

Year	Club (League)	Class	AVG	G	AB	R	H	2B	3B	HR	RBI	BB	SO	SB
2000	Ogden (Pio)	R	.316	28	98	16	31	7	0	10	35	14	20	2
MINOR LEAGUE TOTALS			.316	28	98	16	31	7	0	10	35	14	20	2

8. Mike Penney, rhp

Born: March 29, 1977. **Ht.:** 6-1. **Wt.:** 190. **Bats:** R. **Throws:** R. **School:** University of Southern California. **Career Transactions:** Selected by Brewers in eighth round of 1998 draft; signed July 3, 1998.

Penney was strictly a starter for 2½ professional seasons before finding a niche as short reliever in the second half of 2000. After proving he could close games at Huntsville, he was promoted to Triple-A Indianapolis and served as a capable set-up man. Penney's Arizona Fall League debut was halted after three outings when he cut his finger in an off-field accident. Penny has a low- to mid-90s fastball and an above-average curveball. He has the poise and makeup to be a short reliever, and he has the ability to reach back and get a strikeout when he gets into trouble. As a starter, he habitually lost velocity as the game wore on, which led to his conversion to a short reliever. He's really a two-pitch pitcher with no reliable slider or changeup. Thanks to his new role, Penney realizes the big leagues are within his grasp. He'll probably start 2001 as the closer at Indy. Getting hurt in Arizona was unfortunate during what otherwise was a breakthrough year.

Year	Club (League)	Class	W	L	ERA	G	GS	CG	SV	IP	H	R	ER	BB	SO
1998	Helena (Pio)	R	1	5	7.38	10	10	0	0	46	63	47	38	20	36
1999	Beloit (Mid)	A	9	12	4.24	27	27	4	0	170	171	94	80	70	109
2000	Mudville (Cal)	A	2	4	3.24	13	13	0	0	67	63	31	24	28	45
	Huntsville (SL)	AA	0	1	2.66	20	0	0	7	20	19	7	6	6	22
	Indianapolis (IL)	AAA	1	1	3.44	17	0	0	1	18	16	9	7	10	13
MINOR LEAGUE TOTALS			13	23	4.34	87	50	4	8	322	332	188	155	134	225

9. Horacio Estrada, lhp

Born: Oct. 19, 1975. **Ht.:** 6-0. **Wt.:** 160. **Bats:** L. **Throws:** L. **Career Transactions:** Signed out of Venezuela by Brewers, July 3, 1992.

Until last season, Estrada had muddled through his minor league career with the Brewers. But 2000 was a breakthrough year as he pitched Indianapolis to the Triple-A World Series crown and emerged as a possible starter in Milwaukee this season. Estrada throws a fastball, curveball and changeup. He's at his best when he's moving the ball around, inside and out, up and down. With a good move to first, he's difficult to run on, and he fields his position well. Estrada is a painter, which means he has to hit his spots to be effective. His mid- to high-80s fastball isn't quite average, so he can't make mistakes up in the strike zone without consequences. To be successful, he has to get his curveball over when behind in the count. Estrada could give the Milwaukee rotation the lefthander it lacked in 2000. He'll get every chance to make the club in spring training.

Year	Club (League)	Class	W	L	ERA	G	GS	CG	SV	IP	H	R	ER	BB	SO
1993	Brewers (DSL)	R	1	2	4.41	22	3	0	0	51	39	33	25	37	60
1994	Astros/Brewers (DSL)	R	3	4	2.67	26	2	0	7	61	41	27	18	46	52
1995	Brewers (AZL)	R	0	1	3.71	8	1	0	2	17	13	9	7	8	21
	Helena (Pio)	R	1	2	5.40	13	0	0	0	30	27	21	18	24	30
1996	Beloit (Mid)	A	2	1	1.23	17	0	0	1	29	21	8	4	11	34
	Stockton (Cal)	A	1	3	4.59	29	0	0	3	51	43	29	26	21	62
1997	El Paso (TL)	AA	8	10	4.74	29	23	1	1	154	174	93	81	70	127
1998	El Paso (TL)	AA	5	0	4.53	8	8	0	0	50	50	27	25	21	37
	Louisville (IL)	AAA	0	0	3.00	2	2	0	0	12	10	4	4	5	4
1999	Louisville (IL)	AAA	6	6	5.67	25	24	1	0	132	128	87	83	65	112
	Milwaukee (NL)	MAJ	0	0	7.36	4	0	0	0	7	10	6	6	4	5
2000	Indianapolis (IL)	AAA	14	4	3.33	25	25	3	0	159	149	63	59	45	103
	Milwaukee (NL)	MAJ	3	0	6.29	7	4	0	0	24	30	18	17	20	13
MAJOR LEAGUE TOTALS			3	0	6.54	11	4	0	0	32	40	24	23	24	18
MINOR LEAGUE TOTALS			41	33	4.23	204	88	5	14	745	695	401	350	353	642

10. Brandon Kolb, rhp

Born: Nov. 20, 1973. **Ht.:** 6-1. **Wt.:** 190. **Bats:** R. **Throws:** R. **School:** Texas Tech. **Career Transactions:** Selected by Padres in fourth round of 1995 draft; signed June 2, 1995 . . . Traded by Padres to Brewers for SS Santiago Perez and a player to be named or cash, Dec. 1, 2000.

After a solid showing as the closer at Triple-A Las Vegas, Kolb got his feet wet in the big leagues with 11 relief outings with the Padres. Kolb is a power pitcher who gets his fastball up to 96 mph at times. He also has a hard, sharp-breaking slider and can mix in a curveball. Lefthanders didn't homer against him in the minors or majors in 2000. A starting pitcher at the outset of his pro career, Kolb was moved to short relief because he's primarily a two-pitch pitcher. His control has been erratic in the minors and was even worse in San Diego last season. Kolb is the oldest player in the Brewers' top 10, but sometimes power pitchers take a little longer to develop. He'll be given the opportunity to win a spot in the big league bullpen this spring but has minor league options remaining if needed.

Year	Club (League)	Class	W	L	ERA	G	GS	CG	SV	IP	H	R	ER	BB	SO
1995	Idaho Falls (Pio)	R	2	3	7.04	9	8	0	0	38	42	33	30	29	21
	Padres (AZL)	R	1	1	1.17	4	4	1	0	23	13	10	3	13	21
1996	Clinton (Mid)	A	16	9	3.42	27	27	3	0	181	170	84	69	76	138
1997	Rancho Cuca. (Cal)	A	3	2	3.00	10	10	0	0	63	60	29	21	22	49
1998	Rancho Cuca. (Cal)	A	0	2	3.05	4	4	0	0	21	14	8	7	18	16
	Mobile (SL)	AA	4	3	4.50	21	6	0	1	62	46	33	31	40	58
1999	Mobile (SL)	AA	0	2	0.79	7	0	0	2	11	8	4	1	4	14
	Las Vegas (PCL)	AAA	2	1	3.94	42	0	0	4	62	72	36	27	29	63
2000	Las Vegas (PCL)	AAA	3	3	4.47	47	0	0	16	56	53	35	28	21	59
	San Diego (NL)	MAJ	0	1	4.50	11	0	0	0	14	16	8	7	11	12
MAJOR LEAGUE TOTALS			0	1	4.50	11	0	0	0	14	16	8	7	11	12
MINOR LEAGUE TOTALS			31	26	3.77	171	59	4	23	518	478	272	217	252	439

11. Jason Belcher, c

Born: Jan. 13, 1982. **Ht.:** 6-1. **Wt.:** 190. **Bats:** L. **Throws:** R. **School:** Walnut Ridge (Ark.) HS. **Career Transactions:** Selected by Brewers in fifth round of 2000 draft; signed June 30, 2000.

Belcher impressed scouts and Pioneer League managers with his debut at Rookie-level Helena. He hit for both average and power, a continuation from high school, where he earned All-America honors with a .676 average and 15 homers. That he bats from the left side is just an added perk. His defense is lagging at this stage, and some wondered before the draft if he might have to be moved to another position, but the Brewers want to keep him at catcher for now to see if he improves. Belcher is strong and has a solid catcher's body. He's a tough competitor who shows up to play every day and appears mature for his age. If he improves behind the plate enough to establish himself as a legitimate catcher, he could move quickly through the system because of his advanced offense. The Brewers like his work ethic, so they aren't about to make any rash decisions about whether he can handle the work defensively. He'll get a chance to catch at Beloit this season.

Year	Club (League)	Class	AVG	G	AB	R	H	2B	3B	HR	RBI	BB	SO	SB
2000	Helena (Pio)	R	.333	46	162	30	54	18	2	4	36	20	25	3
MINOR LEAGUE TOTALS			.333	46	162	30	54	18	2	4	36	20	25	3

12. Carlos Chantres, rhp

Born: April 1, 1976. **Ht.:** 6-3. **Wt.:** 175. **Bats:** R. **Throws:** R. **School:** Columbus HS, Miami. **Career Transactions:** Selected by White Sox in 12th round of 1994 draft; signed June 6, 1994 . . . Granted free agency, Oct. 15, 2000 . . . Signed by Brewers, Nov. 20, 2000.

It's not often that a six-year free agent is among an organization's top prospects, but Chantres left the pitching-rich White Sox organization in hopes of getting a better shot with the Brewers. He went from baseball's deepest system to the leanest. Milwaukee thought so much of Chantres that it placed him on the 40-man roster. He's a finesse pitcher who knows how to work both sides of the plate. His fastball tops out at 90 mph or so, and he has a good curveball. He also throws a changeup and has dabbled with a splitter. Chantres could break through and make an impact in the big leagues because he has a feel for pitching and recognizes hitters' tendencies. At the very least, he gives the Brewers a reliable pitcher in Triple-A.

Year	Club (League)	Class	W	L	ERA	G	GS	CG	SV	IP	H	R	ER	BB	SO
1994	White Sox (GCL)	R	0	1	3.60	16	2	0	1	35	28	21	14	13	29
1995	White Sox (GCL)	R	2	3	3.21	11	11	2	0	61	65	32	22	14	47
1996	Hickory (SAL)	A	6	7	3.76	18	18	0	0	119	108	63	50	38	93
	South Bend (Mid)	A	4	5	3.60	10	10	1	0	65	61	31	26	19	41
1997	Winston-Salem (Car)	A	9	11	4.70	26	26	2	0	164	152	94	86	71	158
1998	Birmingham (SL)	AA	2	4	5.81	20	5	0	1	52	58	35	34	42	49
	Winston-Salem (Car)	A	5	5	3.77	13	13	1	0	88	71	43	37	41	86
1999	Birmingham (SL)	AA	6	8	3.50	28	21	1	2	141	122	64	55	61	105
2000	Charlotte (IL)	AAA	10	4	3.53	29	22	0	0	142	136	59	56	54	85
MINOR LEAGUE TOTALS			44	48	3.93	171	128	7	4	871	801	442	380	353	693

13. Mark Ernster, ss

Born: Dec. 10, 1977. **Ht.:** 6-0. **Wt.:** 190. **Bats:** R. **Throws:** R. **School:** Arizona State University. **Career Transactions:** Selected by Brewers in sixth round of 1999 draft; signed June 11, 1999.

Ernster made it to Double-A in 2000, no small feat considering he broke his wrist after five games the previous year and missed the rest of his rookie season. Drafted after playing second base at Arizona State, he's getting the chance to play shortstop as a pro. The Brewers know he can play second and are trying to increase his value as a possible utilityman. Ernster held his own in the Arizona Fall League, batting .295 in 26 games. He has extra-base pop in his bat, and at this stage he's more of an offensive than defensive player. The game plan for Ernster in 2001 is to start him at Double-A with the hope he can move up to Triple-A by the end of the season.

Year	Club (League)	Class	AVG	G	AB	R	H	2B	3B	HR	RBI	BB	SO	SB
1999	Ogden (Pio)	R	.227	5	22	3	5	1	1	0	2	1	1	1
2000	Mudville (Cal)	A	.230	61	204	30	47	9	1	3	22	13	40	4
	Huntsville (SL)	AA	.244	57	205	27	50	9	0	5	26	35	46	10
MINOR LEAGUE TOTALS			.237	123	431	60	102	19	2	8	50	49	87	15

14. Dane Artman, lhp

Born: June 3, 1982. **Ht.:** 6-3. **Wt.:** 215. **Bats:** L. **Throws:** L. **School:** Westminster Academy, Fort Lauderdale. **Career Transactions:** Selected by Brewers in third round of 2000 draft; signed July 3, 2000.

Artman didn't take long to make an impression with the Brewers. His numbers weren't overwhelming in Rookie ball, but he was fresh out of high school and displayed the ability to make adjustments. He has a fluid delivery and good poise on the mound, and the Brewers expect he'll pick up 4-5 mph on his fastball as he gets older and stronger. Artman has a solid frame and should get stronger. He's not a power pitcher at this point with a high-80s fastball. He mixes in a sharp-breaking curveball and a decent changeup. The Brewers have a dearth of bona fide lefthanded pitching prospects in the organization and had no lefties in their rotation in 2000, which is why they targeted Artman as an early draft pick.

Year	Club (League)	Class	W	L	ERA	G	GS	CG	SV	IP	H	R	ER	BB	SO
2000	Ogden (Pio)	R	1	0	5.33	7	7	0	0	25	35	18	15	11	19
MINOR LEAGUE TOTALS			1	0	5.33	7	7	0	0	25	35	18	15	11	19

15. Roberto Miniel, rhp

Born: May 12, 1980. **Ht.:** 6-4. **Wt.:** 160. **Bats:** R. **Throws:** R. **Career Transactions:** Signed out of Dominican Republic by Brewers, Oct. 12, 1996.

Miniel was signed as a skinny, raw 17-year-old pitcher in 1997 by famed scout Epy Guerrero. Used as a starter and a reliever the past two years, Miniel came into his own as the best pitcher in Ogden's rotation in 2000. Getting stronger as he fills out his wiry 6-foot-4 frame, he has a fastball that tops out in the 91-92 mph neighborhood. He also throws a curveball and changeup and has been dabbling with a splitter. A year makes a big difference with some players, especially those signed in their teens, and scouts were amazed at the step forward Miniel took last season. He showed improved control and seemed more confident on the mound. Depending on how things shape up in spring camp, Miniel will begin 2001 at Beloit or high Class A High Desert.

Year	Club (League)	Class	W	L	ERA	G	GS	CG	SV	IP	H	R	ER	BB	SO
1997	Brewers (DSL)	R	3	2	3.69	13	12	0	0	54	58	32	22	30	38
1998	Ogden (Pio)	R	3	2	4.39	16	0	0	2	41	39	24	20	24	39
1999	Beloit (Mid)	A	0	0	9.37	10	0	0	0	16	23	19	17	16	11
	Ogden (Pio)	R	5	4	4.41	15	14	1	0	86	98	58	42	34	77
2000	Ogden (Pio)	R	9	3	2.70	16	14	0	0	83	84	41	25	22	80
MINOR LEAGUE TOTALS			20	11	4.05	70	40	1	2	280	302	174	126	126	245

16. Matt Childers, rhp

Born: Dec. 3, 1978. **Ht.:** 6-5. **Wt.:** 195. **Bats:** R. **Throws:** R. **School:** Westside HS, Augusta, Ga. **Career Transactions:** Selected by Brewers in ninth round of 1997 draft; signed June 6, 1997.

If raw ability and a strong arm were all it took to make it to the big leagues, Childers would be in the express lane. But after a successful first half at Beloit in 2000—his third stint in the Midwest League—he struggled in high Class A. In fact, Childers pitched much worse than his older brother Jason, a Mudville teammate who's not considered a prospect. Matt throws his fastball consistently in the low 90s and reaches 95 mph on occasion, but he gets the ball up too often and gives up the longball (10 in 85 innings at Mudville). He doesn't lose his cool often and bounces back from tough outings, but he must get his curveball over when behind in the count to keep hitters off his fastball. Childers probably will start 2001 back in the California League. At 23, it's time for him to get to Double-A and stop spinning his wheels.

Year	Club (League)	Class	W	L	ERA	G	GS	CG	SV	IP	H	R	ER	BB	SO
1997	Helena (Pio)	R	1	4	6.20	14	10	0	1	61	81	49	42	24	19
1998	Helena (Pio)	R	1	0	0.64	2	2	1	0	14	9	1	1	4	4
	Beloit (Mid)	A	3	7	5.10	14	12	3	0	67	89	55	38	20	49
1999	Beloit (Mid)	A	3	10	5.94	20	19	0	0	100	129	72	66	30	52
2000	Beloit (Mid)	A	8	2	2.71	12	12	1	0	73	64	33	22	17	47
	Mudville (Cal)	A	3	9	4.75	15	15	0	0	85	103	59	45	32	43
MINOR LEAGUE TOTALS			19	32	4.81	77	70	5	1	400	475	269	214	127	214

17. Gene Altman, rhp

Born: Sept. 1, 1978. **Ht.:** 6-7. **Wt.:** 235. **Bats:** R. **Throws:** R. **School:** Hudgens Academy, Lynchburg, S.C. **Career Transactions:** Selected by Reds in 20th round of 1996 draft; signed June 8, 1996 . . . Traded by Reds to Brewers, May 15, 2000, completing trade in which Brewers sent OF Alex Ochoa to Reds for OF Mark Sweeney and a player to be named (Jan. 14, 2000).

The major league portion of the trade that sent Alex Ochoa to the Reds for Mark Sweeney didn't work out very well for the Brewers. Hampered by knee and shoulder problems, Sweeney batted just .219. The Brewers were much more pleased with what they saw from Altman, a big righthander who also arrived in the deal. Formerly a starting pitcher, he made the adjustment to closer without missing a beat, and Milwaukee now projects him to stay in that role. He throws his fastball in the mid-90s, and he has a decent slider as well as a curveball that he shows on occasion. As a power pitcher, Altman has the stuff to protect leads in the ninth inning and get strikeouts when the game is on the line. He'll probably go to High Desert at the outset of the 2001 season.

Year	Club (League)	Class	W	L	ERA	G	GS	CG	SV	IP	H	R	ER	BB	SO
1996	Princeton (Appy)	R	2	0	4.10	18	1	0	3	42	34	24	19	15	36
1997	Charleston, WV (SAL)	A	1	4	7.79	17	1	0	0	32	45	31	28	10	35
	Billings (Pio)	R	3	2	7.83	20	5	0	3	33	48	36	29	19	34
1998	Burlington (Mid)	A	6	9	4.49	25	24	1	0	130	129	73	65	48	108
1999	Rockford (Mid)	A	2	6	6.08	11	11	0	0	53	63	41	36	34	51
	Reds (GCL)	R	1	0	1.80	3	3	0	0	10	6	2	2	4	10
	Clinton (Mid)	A	0	2	3.86	3	3	0	0	14	7	9	6	7	19
2000	Dayton (Mid)	A	2	0	3.78	9	0	0	0	17	17	10	7	13	16
	Beloit (Mid)	A	4	0	2.15	33	0	0	17	38	32	11	9	18	42
MINOR LEAGUE TOTALS			21	23	4.90	139	48	1	23	369	381	237	201	168	351

18. J.M. Gold, rhp

Born: April 18, 1980. **Ht.:** 6-5. **Wt.:** 220. **Bats:** R. **Throws:** R. **School:** Toms River North HS, Toms River, N.J. **Career Transactions:** Selected by Brewers in first round (13th overall) of 1998 draft; signed June 24, 1998.

The organization's No. 5 prospect a year ago, Gold blew out his elbow after seven starts at Beloit and required Tommy John surgery. Because he struggled with his mechanics from the time he was drafted, his injury didn't surprise many scouts who have seen him pitch. Concerns about the flaws in his delivery as well as past arm problems prompted some clubs to pass on him out of high school. The good news is that Gold is only 20 and has plenty of time to bounce back. Whether he can regain the 95 mph fastball and sharp-breaking curve that made him a first-rounder remains to be seen, though it seems most pitchers these days are returning from Tommy John surgery better than ever. Once he's deemed ready to pitch, Gold probably will go back to Beloit, but not until the weather warms up.

Year	Club (League)	Class	W	L	ERA	G	GS	CG	SV	IP	H	R	ER	BB	SO
1998	Ogden (Pio)	R	1	0	2.61	5	5	0	0	21	21	13	6	7	15
1999	Beloit (Mid)	A	6	10	5.40	21	21	2	0	112	120	82	67	54	93
2000	Beloit (Mid)	A	3	1	2.91	7	7	0	0	34	27	13	11	16	33
MINOR LEAGUE TOTALS			10	11	4.55	33	33	2	0	166	168	108	84	77	141

19. Daryl Clark, 3b/1b

Born: Sept. 25, 1979. **Ht.:** 6-2. **Wt.:** 205. **Bats:** L. **Throws:** R. **School:** UNC Charlotte. **Career Transactions:** Selected by Brewers in 17th round of 2000 draft; signed June 15, 2000.

Clark was the biggest surprise among the Brewers' 2000 draftees. He not only compiled an impressive average but also ranked second in the Pioneer League in homers. Questions about his position hurt Clark in the draft, and the Brewers still aren't sure where he'll play in the field in 2001. He saw extensive action at first base in instructional league but still may be used at the hot corner this year. Clark's bat will be his ticket through the farm system, though. A lefthanded power hitter is valued by an organization that has very few. Equally impressive in his professional debut, Clark walked more times than he struck out, showing he has a good eye and discipline to go with his power. He'll spend 2001 in Class A.

Year	Club (League)	Class	AVG	G	AB	R	H	2B	3B	HR	RBI	BB	SO	SB
2000	Ogden (Pio)	R	.339	64	218	54	74	12	4	15	64	67	53	5
MINOR LEAGUE TOTALS			.339	64	218	54	74	12	4	15	64	67	53	5

20. Scott Kirby, of

Born: July 18, 1977. **Ht.:** 6-2. **Wt.:** 190. **Bats:** R. **Throws:** R. **School:** Polk (Fla.) CC. **Career Transactions:** Selected by Brewers in 30th round of 1995 draft; signed May 12, 1996.

Kirby's history has been to struggle after first moving up the ladder, then to make adjustments and do significantly better upon repeating the level. The Brewers hope the pattern holds true again in 2001 because the former third baseman had a bad year at Huntsville. He righted himself somewhat in the pitching-rich Arizona Fall League by batting .265-3-18. One of the few positives form last season is that he has handled the move to the outfield well and appears set there for the future. Thanks to his third baseman's arm, Kirby is a natural in right field. Ranked No. 9 in the organization after the 1999 season, he now must re-establish himself as a player to watch. He'll try to do so at Huntsville.

Year	Club (League)	Class	AVG	G	AB	R	H	2B	3B	HR	RBI	BB	SO	SB
1996	Helena (Pio)	R	.200	47	145	26	29	4	0	4	21	19	42	0
1997	Helena (Pio)	R	.262	68	248	65	65	10	1	11	47	53	65	8
1998	Beloit (Mid)	A	.203	107	359	51	73	19	2	8	40	47	109	5
1999	Beloit (Mid)	A	.304	68	247	54	75	14	1	17	47	47	59	3
	Stockton (Cal)	A	.287	60	202	35	58	15	3	10	36	25	59	3
2000	Huntsville (SL)	AA	.218	118	344	54	75	11	1	12	45	66	112	7
MINOR LEAGUE TOTALS			.243	468	1545	285	375	73	8	62	236	257	446	26

21. Will Hall, ss

Born: Dec. 28, 1979. **Ht.:** 6-0. **Wt.:** 175. **Bats:** R. **Throws:** R. **School:** Nettleton (Miss.) HS. **Career Transactions:** Selected by Brewers in sixth round of 1998 draft; signed June 7, 1998.

After spending two seasons in Rookie ball, Hall moved up to low Class A last season and made the Midwest League all-star team at midseason. He wore down as the season progressed, however, and he must work on his strength. Pitchers found holes in his swing often enough to strike him out more than seven times as much as he walked. Hall made 40 errors, but many came on a tough infield surface at Beloit. He came a long way defensively, showing a good arm and decent range. He appeared more comfortable going up the middle for balls than in the hole. Hall has time to work on his offense and concentrate on putting the ball in play. He's ticketed for High Desert but could make it to Double-A before the year is out.

Year	Club (League)	Class	AVG	G	AB	R	H	2B	3B	HR	RBI	BB	SO	SB
1998	Helena (Pio)	R	.176	29	85	11	15	3	0	0	5	9	27	5
1999	Ogden (Pio)	R	.289	69	280	41	81	15	2	6	31	15	61	19
2000	Beloit (Mid)	A	.262	130	470	57	123	30	6	3	41	18	127	10
MINOR LEAGUE TOTALS			.262	228	835	109	219	48	8	9	77	42	215	34

22. Jason Fox, of

Born: March 30, 1977. **Ht.:** 6-2. **Wt.:** 185. **Bats:** B. **Throws:** R. **School:** Florida Southern College. **Career Transactions:** Selected by Brewers in seventh round of 1998 draft; signed June 6, 1998.

Fox has one tool that is in short supply in the organization: speed. He put it to good use at Mudville last year, swiping 53 bases in 70 chances, pretty amazing considering he batted just .249 and struggled to make contact. Because he has virtually no power, Fox must bunt more and keep the ball on the ground to take advantage of his speed. Otherwise, his value as a leadoff hitter decreases. He showed an ability to get bunts down last season by leading his club with 10 sacrifices. In center field, Fox can go get the ball with the best of them. After spending two seasons in Class A, Fox will get the chance to open 2001 in Double-A.

Year	Club (League)	Class	AVG	G	AB	R	H	2B	3B	HR	RBI	BB	SO	SB
1998	Helena (Pio)	R	.302	43	179	40	54	13	1	5	23	15	36	21
1999	Stockton (Cal)	A	.234	70	248	34	58	8	3	1	18	14	63	15
	Beloit (Mid)	A	.221	41	163	18	36	3	1	1	6	11	34	8
2000	Mudville (Cal)	A	.249	130	493	58	123	17	2	2	43	52	92	53
MINOR LEAGUE TOTALS			.250	284	1083	150	271	41	7	9	90	92	225	97

23. Chris Rowan, ss

Born: March 18, 1979. **Ht.:** 6-1. **Wt.:** 195. **Bats:** R. **Throws:** R. **School:** Mount Vernon (N.Y.) HS. **Career Transactions:** Selected by Brewers in 14th round of 1997 draft; signed June 26, 1997.

When people in the organization talk about tools, Rowan's name often comes up. There's a lot to like: strong arm, some pop in his bat, good head on his shoulders. Yet Rowan hasn't been able to put it together. He shows flashes of breaking through but has been unable to maintain consistency at the plate. He's a free swinger who hasn't learned the value of a walk. Rowan hasn't always shown good instincts at shortstop, which is why the Brewers are thinking about moving him to third base. On top of that, he missed all but 39 games at Mudville last season with a shoulder injury. How his arm bounces back remains to be seen.

Year	Club (League)	Class	AVG	G	AB	R	H	2B	3B	HR	RBI	BB	SO	SB
1997	Ogden (Pio)	R	.251	55	211	46	53	10	3	9	34	27	65	2
1998	Ogden (Pio)	R	.221	56	195	38	43	8	5	11	45	24	75	4
1999	Stockton (Cal)	A	.237	121	431	53	102	25	4	11	55	30	142	9
2000	Ogden (Pio)	R	.267	4	15	0	4	0	0	0	1	1	5	1
	Mudville (Cal)	A	.175	39	143	13	25	5	1	2	4	3	55	0
MINOR LEAGUE TOTALS			.228	275	995	150	227	48	13	33	139	85	342	16

24. Jose Garcia, rhp

Born: April 29, 1978. **Ht.:** 6-3. **Wt.:** 195. **Bats:** R. **Throws:** R. **School:** Baldwin Park (Calif.) HS. **Career Transactions:** Selected by Brewers in second round of 1996 draft; signed June 25, 1996.

Once considered among the top pitching prospects in the organization, Garcia still is trying to catch up after missing the entire 1999 season with a somewhat mysterious elbow problem. At times last year he showed his old low-90s fastball and sharp curveball, but Garcia's command still came and went as usual. The Brewers then sent him to the Arizona Fall League, where he was solid if not sensational. Conditioning has been a problem at times for Garcia, who has a good pitcher's body as long as he doesn't let it go soft. After two consecutive years of making the organization's top 10, his stock has dropped considerably. He'll get a shot to win a spot in the Triple-A rotation and re-establish himself as a prospect.

Year	Club (League)	Class	W	L	ERA	G	GS	CG	SV	IP	H	R	ER	BB	SO
1996	Helena (Pio)	R	0	0	16.20	2	0	0	0	2	1	3	3	3	2
1997	Beloit (Mid)	A	6	11	4.00	27	26	2	0	155	145	89	69	70	126
1998	Stockton (Cal)	A	11	12	3.67	28	28	1	0	169	147	89	69	91	167
1999						Did Not Play—Injured									
2000	Huntsville (SL)	AA	4	8	3.76	19	18	0	0	103	107	52	43	54	78
MINOR LEAGUE TOTALS			21	31	3.86	76	72	3	0	429	400	233	184	218	373

25. Ryan Poe, rhp

Born: Sept. 3, 1977. **Ht.:** 6-2. **Wt.:** 220. **Bats:** R. **Throws:** R. **School:** Saddleback (Calif.) CC. **Career Transactions:** Selected by Brewers in 21st round of 1998 draft; signed June 13, 1998.

Not much was expected of Poe, but he began to gain some notice at Beloit in 1999 when he posted a 6-1 strikeout-walk ratio, mostly in relief. Poe has a low-90s fastball and knows how to move the ball around. Given a chance to close games as well as make a handful of starts at Mudville last year, he continued to excel. His versatility eventually earned him a promotion to Double-A, where he handled himself very well. Now the Brewers must figure out where Poe can help them most, as a starter, middle reliever or set-up man.

Year	Club (League)	Class	W	L	ERA	G	GS	CG	SV	IP	H	R	ER	BB	SO
1998	Helena (Pio)	R	3	3	4.66	14	5	0	1	46	52	30	24	15	43
1999	Beloit (Mid)	A	6	10	3.56	49	5	0	9	96	94	46	38	16	108
2000	Mudville (Cal)	A	7	5	1.96	33	7	0	9	83	56	19	18	21	98
	Huntsville (SL)	AA	1	3	3.38	9	0	0	3	21	18	8	8	9	20
MINOR LEAGUE TOTALS			17	21	3.22	105	17	0	22	246	220	103	88	61	269

26. Kane Davis, rhp

Born: June 25, 1975. **Ht.:** 6-3. **Wt.:** 194. **Bats:** R. **Throws:** R. **School:** Spencer HS, Reedy, W.Va. **Career Transactions:** Selected by Pirates in 13th round of 1993 draft; signed June 6, 1993 . . . Granted free agency, Oct. 15, 1999 . . . Signed by Indians, Dec. 10, 1999 . . . Traded to Indians with OF Richie Sexson, RHP Paul Rigdon and a player to be named to Brewers for RHP Bob Wickman, RHP Steve Woodard and RHP Jason Bere, July 28, 2000; Brewers acquired 2B Marcos Scutaro to complete trade (Aug. 30, 2000).

Davis rode the shuttle from Triple-A Buffalo to Cleveland and back again last season until he was included in the trade that brought Richie Sexson to the Brewers. Davis has a good arm, particularly considering he had reconstructive elbow surgery while in the Pirates organization in 1997. A power pitcher who relies too much on his fastball at times, Davis has been erratic yet shows enough potential to tease. He has been a starter throughout his minor league career but may have to pitch out of the bullpen to find a niche in the majors. He's out of options, so spring training will be important for Davis. He could prove to be one of those Quadruple-A pitchers who never quite makes it in the big leagues.

Year	Club (League)	Class	W	L	ERA	G	GS	CG	SV	IP	H	R	ER	BB	SO
1993	Pirates (GCL)	R	0	4	7.07	11	4	0	0	28	34	30	22	19	24
1994	Welland (NY-P)	A	5	5	2.65	15	15	2	0	98	90	36	29	32	74
1995	Augusta (SAL)	A	12	6	3.75	26	25	1	0	139	136	73	58	43	78
1996	Lynchburg (Car)	A	11	9	4.29	26	26	3	0	157	160	84	75	56	116
1997	Carolina (SL)	AA	0	3	3.77	6	6	0	0	29	22	17	12	16	23
1998	Augusta (SAL)	A	0	0	6.00	2	2	0	0	9	8	6	6	3	6
	Carolina (SL)	AA	1	11	9.24	18	16	0	0	74	102	84	76	38	39
1999	Altoona (EL)	AA	4	6	3.78	16	16	0	0	95	97	51	40	41	53
	Nashville (PCL)	AAA	3	2	6.75	12	9	0	0	49	65	38	37	17	31
2000	Akron (EL)	AA	0	1	2.70	5	5	0	0	20	17	7	6	5	13
	Buffalo (IL)	AAA	2	0	4.20	6	4	0	0	30	30	16	14	12	19
	Cleveland (AL)	MAJ	0	3	14.73	5	2	0	0	11	20	21	18	8	2
	Milwaukee (NL)	MAJ	0	0	6.75	3	0	0	0	4	7	3	3	5	2
	Indianapolis (IL)	AAA	1	1	3.54	4	4	0	0	20	19	8	8	7	12
MAJOR LEAGUE TOTALS			0	3	12.60	8	2	0	0	15	27	24	21	13	4
MINOR LEAGUE TOTALS			39	48	4.60	147	132	6	0	750	780	450	383	289	488

27. Brian Moon, c

Born: July 15, 1977. **Ht.:** 6-0. **Wt.:** 190. **Bats:** B. **Throws:** R. **School:** Southern Union State (Ala.) JC. **Career Transactions:** Selected by Brewers in 48th round of 1996 draft; signed May 22, 1997.

One of the best defensive catchers in the organization, Moon took a significant downward turn at the plate in 2000. The Brewers thought he would hold his own in Double-A after two years in Class A, but he struggled. Moon performed much better in the Arizona Fall League, where he hit .266. He has little hope of being more than a backup catcher in the big leagues if he doesn't produce more at the plate. Moon is an adept catcher who shows a good arm and handles pitchers well. He needs to get stronger and develop more pop. After last year's poor showing, he'll have to repeat Double-A in 2001 and show he can make adjustments.

Year	Club (League)	Class	AVG	G	AB	R	H	2B	3B	HR	RBI	BB	SO	SB
1997	Helena (Pio)	R	.282	49	170	15	48	5	0	0	22	8	23	2
1998	Beloit (Mid)	A	.256	118	438	62	112	20	1	1	54	46	62	0
1999	Stockton (Cal)	A	.265	116	385	52	102	14	2	2	30	37	40	6

2000	Huntsville (SL)	AA	.183	106	312	34	57	13	1	1	33	45	49	2
MINOR LEAGUE TOTALS			.244	389	1305	163	319	52	4	4	139	136	174	10

28. Justin Gordon, lhp

Born: May 26, 1979. **Ht.:** 6-5. **Wt.:** 215. **Bats:** L. **Throws:** L. **School:** Massasoit (Mass.) CC. **Career Transactions:** Selected by Brewers in 32nd round of 1999 draft; signed June 14, 1999.

Gordon was converted from an outfielder to a pitcher and was understandably erratic with his command in Rookie ball in his pro debut. He looked much more comfortable when he returned to the Pioneer League last season and even caught the eye of some scouts and opposing managers. He's a fastball/curveball pitcher with a strong arm, and he simply needs to log more innings on the mound. His control was much better the second time around, though he still uncorked 10 wild pitches in 76 innings. The Brewers plan to give him a shot at the Beloit rotation in 2001. He's raw, but as a lefty who's still young at 21, Gordon is an interesting project to monitor.

Year	Club (League)	Class	W	L	ERA	G	GS	CG	SV	IP	H	R	ER	BB	SO
1999	Helena (Pio)	R	1	2	6.03	15	4	0	0	31	31	31	21	29	36
2000	Ogden (Pio)	R	5	5	4.26	16	15	0	0	76	69	45	36	42	53
MINOR LEAGUE TOTALS			6	7	4.78	31	19	0	0	107	100	76	57	71	89

29. Ruddy Lugo, rhp

Born: May 22, 1980. **Ht.:** 5-11. **Wt.:** 180. **Bats:** R. **Throws:** R. **School:** Xaverian HS, Brooklyn. **Career Transactions:** Selected by Brewers in third round of 1999 draft; signed June 21, 1999.

Like his brother Julio, an Astros infielder, Ruddy was born in the Dominican Republic but grew up in Brooklyn. He was also a good shortstop in high school, but more teams liked him as a pitcher because of his arm strength. With all the similarities in their backgrounds, Lugo has drawn comparisons to former Mariners righthander Frank Rodriguez. Lugo has heard more than once that he's too short to pitch in the big leagues, and the odds are longer for small righthanders. But most of those pitchers don't have Lugo's velocity. He gets his fastball to the plate in the mid-90s and has shown a good changeup and curveball. Control was a problem for him last year, when he hit 12 batters and had seven wild pitches. He also logged 88 strikeouts and showed an ability to work out of jams. Because he didn't play against much top-flight competition in high school, Lugo will need time to develop. But he has great determination and the desire to prove critics wrong.

Year	Club (League)	Class	W	L	ERA	G	GS	CG	SV	IP	H	R	ER	BB	SO
1999	Ogden (Pio)	R	1	2	7.88	6	6	0	0	24	35	23	21	12	26
2000	Ogden (Pio)	R	5	5	3.44	16	16	1	0	92	82	48	35	52	88
MINOR LEAGUE TOTALS			6	7	4.36	22	22	1	0	116	117	71	56	64	114

30. Bucky Jacobsen, 1b/of

Born: Aug. 30, 1975. **Ht.:** 6-4. **Wt.:** 220. **Bats:** R. **Throws:** R. **School:** Lewis-Clark State (Idaho) College. **Career Transactions:** Selected by Brewers in seventh round of 1997 draft; signed June 4, 1997.

Whatever else you might say about Jacobsen, how many minor leaguers have such a loyal following? The Bucky Backers were formed in 1998, when Jacobsen was playing for Beloit and a group of Kane County Cougars fans adopted him because they liked his name. They've been following his career ever since and have their own Website (buckybackers.8m.com). On the downside, Jacobsen's stock has dropped in recent years because of inconsistent play and his lack of a position. He originally was an outfielder but moved to first base because he's slow afoot. He didn't shine there, either. He has good power and draws plenty of walks, though he also strikes out a lot. Jacobsen was off to a good start at Double-A last year, among the Southern League leaders in home runs and slugging percentage, before an injury ended his season in July. He broke two bones in his left wrist in a collision while playing first base. He showed he was healthy in Venezuela, batting .304-8-28 in 138 at-bats. But Jacobsen needs to prove himself because his window of opportunity is closing rapidly.

Year	Club (League)	Class	AVG	G	AB	R	H	2B	3B	HR	RBI	BB	SO	SB
1997	Ogden (Pio)	R	.328	67	238	57	78	17	2	8	52	41	44	6
1998	Beloit (Mid)	A	.293	135	499	96	146	31	1	27	100	83	133	5
1999	Huntsville (SL)	AA	.193	47	150	20	29	6	1	3	19	20	32	4
	Stockton (Cal)	A	.250	46	156	22	39	8	0	5	22	21	40	3
2000	Huntsville (SL)	AA	.276	81	268	44	74	14	0	18	50	51	69	4
MINOR LEAGUE TOTALS			.279	376	1311	239	366	76	4	61	243	216	318	22

Minnesota
Twins

The World Series title of 1991 seems like ages ago. For the most part, the Twins have the same people in charge and the same problems that have persisted since then. Maybe a cash infusion and a wave of twentysomething players will change things.

Owner Carl Pohlad made his only significant hire in recent years in May, when he brought in former Northwest Airlines executive Chris Clouser to take over daily operation of the franchise. General manager Terry Ryan and manager Tom Kelly went all season without knowing their futures.

After another year at the bottom of the American League Central, both Ryan and Kelly were retained, at Pohlad's behest. Clouser, who had pushed for changes, resigned as CEO in December in frustration, as did general counsel Ben Hirst, who had been hired to lead the Twins' efforts to get a new ballpark.

It's difficult to blame Ryan for not gathering a wealth of big league talent. The club's payroll has decreased each year since the 1994 strike, but that could change. Ryan has been cleared to raise the ante from a major league-low $16.5 million to as much as $30 million.

The money would be best spent on power, which has been seriously lacking. No Twin

TOP 30 PROSPECTS

1. Adam Johnson, rhp
2. Michael Cuddyer, 3b
3. Michael Restovich, of
4. Luis Rivas, 2b
5. Justin Morneau, 1b/c
6. Matt Kinney, rhp
7. Rob Bowen, c
8. Bobby Kielty, of
9. Brad Thomas, lhp
10. B.J. Garbe, of
11. Jeff Randazzo, lhp
12. John Barnes, of
13. Juan Rincon, rhp
14. Colby Miller, rhp
15. Grant Balfour, rhp
16. Kyle Lohse, rhp
17. Ryan Mills, lhp
18. A.J. Pierzynski, c
19. Todd Sears, 1b
20. J.D. Durbin, rhp
21. Jason Miller, lhp
22. Rafael Boitel, of
23. Chad Moeller, c
24. Lew Ford, of
25. Brian Buchanan, of
26. Brandon Knight, rhp
27. Saul Rivera, rhp
28. Jon Pridie, rhp
29. Danny Mota, rhp
30. Ruben Salazar, 3b

By Lacy Lusk

has hit 20 homers since Matt Lawton racked up 21 in 1998. Just four reached double figures last season, led by Jacque Jones with 19.

Having the worst record in the AL in 2000 affords Minnesota a shot at a pure power hitter—perhaps local high school catcher/first baseman Joe Mauer or Georgia Tech third baseman Mark Teixeira—with the No. 1 pick in the 2001 draft. Money will almost certainly play a part in the decision, though, as it did when the Twins took Adam Johnson last June.

With the club's top five prospects averaging 20.8 years old on Opening Day 2001, help could be on the way in the middle infield, the pitching staff and perhaps even the middle of the lineup. After signing Brad Radke through 2003 and seeing lefthander Mark Redman have a breakout rookie season, Minnesota has a decent core of pitchers with eight more on the way. Eric Milton will continue to anchor the rotation, and the Twins are optimistic Joe Mays can return to his 1999 form.

The small bump up in payroll represents a positive sign, but a new ballpark—whether it's at the latest proposed site near Target Center, elsewhere in the Twin Cities or in another city—might be what it takes for this club to become competitive again.

OrganizationOverview

General manager: Terry Ryan. **Farm director:** Jim Rantz. **Scouting director:** Mike Radcliff.

2000 PERFORMANCE

Class	Team	League	W	L	Pct.	Finish*	Manager(s)
Majors	Minnesota	American	69	93	.426	14th (14)	Tom Kelly
Triple-A	#Salt Lake Buzz	Pacific Coast	90	53	.629	1st (16)	Phil Roof
Double-A	New Britain Rock Cats	Eastern	51	91	.359	11th (12)	John Russell
High A	Fort Myers Miracle	Florida State	83	57	.593	2nd (14)	Jose Marzan
Low A	Quad City River Bandits	Midwest	64	75	.460	t-10th (14)	Stan Cliburn
Rookie	Elizabethton Twins	Appalachian	46	18	.719	1st (10)	Jeff Carter
Rookie	GCL Twins	Gulf Coast	33	23	.589	4th (13)	Al Newman
OVERALL 2000 MINOR LEAGUE RECORD			367	317	.537	4th (30)	

* Finish in overall standings (No. of teams in league). #Affiliate will be in Edmonton (Pacific Coast) in 2001.

ORGANIZATION LEADERS

BATTING

*AVG	John Barnes, Salt Lake	.365
R	John Barnes, Salt Lake	107
H	Doug Mientkiewicz, Salt Lake	162
TB	Doug Mientkiewicz, Salt Lake	254
2B	John Barnes, Salt Lake	37
	Luis Rivas, Salt Lake/New Britain	37
3B	Michael Restovich, Fort Myers	9
HR	**Brian Buchanan**, Salt Lake	27
RBI	**Brian Buchanan**, Salt Lake	103
BB	Bobby Kielty, New Britain/Salt Lake	105
SO	Bobby Kielty, New Britain/Salt Lake	119
SB	Michael Restovich, Fort Myers	19
	Brett Tamburrino, Quad City/GCL Twins	19

PITCHING

W	Brad Thomas, Fort Myers/New Britain	12
L	Kyle Lohse, New Britain	18
#ERA	Tony Cento, Quad City	1.97
G	Brent Stentz, Salt Lake/New Britain	66
CG	Joe Foote, Quad City/New Britain	4
SV	Brent Stentz, Salt Lake/New Britain	20
IP	Kyle Lohse, New Britain	167
BB	**Ryan Mills**, Quad City/New Britain	98
SO	Matt Kinney, New Britain/Salt Lake	152

*Minimum 250 at-bats. #Minimum 75 innings.

TOP PROSPECTS OF THE DECADE

1991	Rich Garces, rhp
1992	David McCarty, of
1993	David McCarty, of
1994	Rich Becker, of
1995	LaTroy Hawkins, rhp
1996	Todd Walker, 3b
1997	Todd Walker, 3b
1998	Luis Rivas, ss
1999	Michael Cuddyer, 3b
2000	Michael Cuddyer, 3b

TOP DRAFT PICKS OF THE DECADE

1991	David McCarty, of
1992	Dan Serafini, lhp
1993	Torii Hunter, of
1994	Todd Walker, 2b
1995	Mark Redman, lhp
1996	*Travis Lee, 1b
1997	Michael Cuddyer, ss
1998	Ryan Mills, lhp
1999	B.J. Garbe, of
2000	Adam Johnson, rhp

*Did not sign.

Buchanan

Mills

BEST TOOLS

Best Hitter for Average	Justin Morneau
Best Power Hitter	Michael Restovich
Fastest Baserunner	Luis Rivas
Best Fastball	Adam Johnson
Best Breaking Ball	Matt Kinney
Best Control	Adam Johnson
Best Defensive Catcher	Rob Bowen
Best Defensive Infielder	Luis Rivas
Best Infield Arm	Michael Cuddyer
Best Defensive Outfielder	Bobby Kielty
Best Outfield Arm	B.J. Garbe

PROJECTED 2004 LINEUP

Catcher	Rob Bowen
First Base	Corey Koskie
Second Base	Luis Rivas
Third Base	Michael Cuddyer
Shortstop	Cristian Guzman
Left Field	Michael Restovich
Center Field	Torii Hunter
Right Field	Jacque Jones
Designated Hitter	Matthew LeCroy
No. 1 Starter	Eric Milton
No. 2 Starter	Brad Radke
No. 3 Starter	Mark Redman
No. 4 Starter	Matt Kinney
No. 5 Starter	Brad Thomas
Closer	Adam Johnson

ALL-TIME LARGEST BONUSES

B.J. Garbe, 1999	$2,750,000
Adam Johnson, 2000	2,500,000
Ryan Mills, 1998	2,000,000
Michael Cuddyer, 1997	1,850,000
Mark Redman, 1995	830,000

DraftAnalysis

2000 Draft

Best Pro Debut: RHP **Adam Johnson** (1) dominated the high Class A Florida State League, going 5-3, 2.47 while striking out 92 in 69 innings and limiting opponents to a .186 average.

Best Athlete: RHP J.D. Durbin (2) was an all-state wide receiver for his Arizona high school. Shortstop Edgardo LeBron (5) has above-average speed and arm strength to go with his power potential.

Best Hitter: OF James Tomlin (7), who hit .338 in the Rookie-level Gulf Coast League, gets the nod over OF Jason Kubel (12).

Best Raw Power: OF Josh Rabe (11) or C Cory Agar (14). Neither is in the class of 1B Taggert Bozied (2), whom the Twins failed to sign.

Fastest Runner: Tomlin would edge LeBron, though neither is a true blazer.

Best Defensive Player: The Twins believe LeBron can be a solid shortstop or center fielder. He played mostly third base in the GCL and could end up there if he grows too big for the other two positions.

Best Fastball: Johnson's heavy fastball tops out at 94-95 mph and would be there more often if Minnesota turns him into a closer. For now, he will remain a starter. Durbin has the same peak velocity, though he didn't show it before he was shut down with elbow tendinitis. RHP Andy Persby (18), a former Minnesota backup quarterback, also can touch 95.

Most Intriguing Background: Persby wasn't the only passer drafted by the Twins. RHPs Shane Boyd (13) and T.J. Prunty (20) are backups at Kentucky and Miami, respectively. C Kelley Gulledge (10) is the son of Rangers public-address announcer Chuck Morgan. RHP Stephen Reiss' (27) twin brother Michael was taken one round earlier the Brewers. Neither Reiss signed, nor did Boyd or Prunty.

Closest To The Majors: Johnson. His Cal State Fullerton teammate, RHP Ron Corona (6), was one of three pitchers drafted in June who reached Double-A. His fastball touches 94 mph and he throws strikes.

Johnson

Best Late-Round Pick: Persby, who didn't pitch for the Golden Gophers until last spring. Besides his fastball, the Twins love his size (6-foot-5, 240 pounds) and makeup.

The One Who Got Away: Missing on Bozied was a major loss, as was RHP Aaron Heilman (1). Minnesota was much closer to signing Heilman, whose best pitch is a 92-93 mph sinker. He returned to Notre Dame and Bozied went back to San Francisco for their senior seasons. If Prunty sticks with baseball, he could be a high pick in three years.

Assessment: The Twins were doomed by their penurious budget yet again. They failed to sign two premium picks and settled for signability with the No. 2 overall choice, though it's hard to argue with Johnson's initial success.

1999 Draft

OF B.J. Garbe's (1) career took a downturn last season. C Rob Bowen (2), 1B/C Justin Morneau (3) and LHP Jeff Randazzo (4) show a lot of promise, but the Twins' draft petered out after that. It didn't help that they didn't sign eight of their top 15 picks.   **Grade: C**

1998 Draft

LHP Ryan Mills (1) has either been hurt of ineffective. The only player from this crop who makes Minnesota's top 30 is RHP Saul Rivera (9), and he checks in at No. 27.   **Grade: F**

1997 Draft

The Twins got the heart of their future batting order in 3B Michael Cuddyer (1), C Matthew LeCroy (1) and OF Michael Restovich (2). They drafted but didn't sign RHP Adam Johnson (25), whom they chose No. 2 overall in 2000, and 3B Marques Tuiasosopo (34), who quarterbacked Washington to an 11-1 record and Rose Bowl victory this winter.   **Grade: B+**

1996 Draft

Minnesota lost 1B Travis Lee (1) as a loophole free agent after granting his wish not to negotiate until after the Olympics. OF Jacque Jones (2) is part of the club's future, and OF Chad Allen (4), C Chad Moeller (7) and RHP Mike Lincoln (13) have gotten looks. **Grade: C**

Note: Draft analysis prepared by Jim Callis. Numbers in parentheses indicate draft rounds.

. . . . With Johnson's power repertoire, he could become a closer in the Billy Koch mold.

Adam Johnson rhp

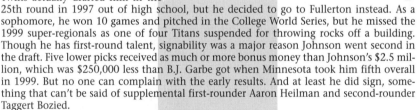

Born: July 12, 1979.
Ht.: 6-2. **Wt.:** 210.
Bats: R. **Throws:** R.
School: Cal State Fullerton.
Career Transactions: Selected by Twins in first round (second overall) of 2000 draft; signed June 19, 2000.

Johnson was the No. 2 overall pick in the 2000 draft after an outstanding junior year at Cal State Fullerton. He went 7-4, 2.72 with 166 strikeouts and 28 walks in 119 innings, setting school strikeout records for a season and a career (365). He also holds the San Diego County high school career strikeout mark. The Twins actually drafted him in the 25th round in 1997 out of high school, but he decided to go to Fullerton instead. As a sophomore, he won 10 games and pitched in the College World Series, but he missed the 1999 super-regionals as one of four Titans suspended for throwing rocks off a building. Though he has first-round talent, signability was a major reason Johnson went second in the draft. Five lower picks received as much or more bonus money than Johnson's $2.5 million, which was $250,000 less than B.J. Garbe got when Minnesota took him fifth overall in 1999. But no one can complain with the early results. And at least he did sign, something that can't be said of supplemental first-rounder Aaron Heilman and second-rounder Taggert Bozied.

Among Twins prospects who haven't already appeared in Minnesota, Johnson may be the closest to the majors. He locates his fastball well and has excellent mound presence. With his power repertoire—a consistent 91 mph fastball that touches 94-95 and a hard, late-breaking 85-86 mph slider—he could become a closer in the Billy Koch mold. He has a good approach and would benefit from a full summer in the minor leagues. Johnson is an emotional pitcher who sometimes comes off as arrogant. He needs to behave more professionally, but club officials like his focus on each game and on pitching in general. He could use more consistency with his curveball and slider. After frequently going deep in counts in his first professional start, he showed more command the rest of the season.

For now, Johnson remains a starter. Koch, another early first-round pick, was a starter in the minor leagues before Toronto called him up in 1999. Expect Johnson to begin 2001 at Double-A New Britain with the possibility of ending it in Minnesota's rotation or bullpen. He already would have gotten his first look at Double-A in 2000, but New Britain finished in a tailspin and Fort Myers was in a pennant race.

Year	Club (League)	Class	W	L	ERA	G	GS	CG	SV	IP	H	R	ER	BB	SO
2000	Fort Myers (FSL)	A	5	4	2.47	13	12	1	0	69	45	21	19	20	92
MINOR LEAGUE TOTALS			5	4	2.47	13	12	1	0	69	45	21	19	20	92

2. Michael Cuddyer, 3b

Born: March 27, 1979. **Ht.:** 6-2. **Wt.:** 202. **Bats:** R. **Throws:** R. **School:** Great Bridge HS, Chesapeake, Va. **Career Transactions:** Selected by Twins in first round (ninth overall) of 1997 draft; signed Aug. 19, 1997.

Cuddyer was Minnesota's No. 1 prospect after each of his first two pro seasons but drops a notch following a shaky 2000 season. He hit just six homers in Double-A, which prompted the Twins to send him to instructional league so he could work on driving the ball for more power. Off the field, he's an amateur magician. Twins officials like Cuddyer's attitude and leadership qualities. With experience, he's expected to become a 20-25 home run threat. He flashes power to the opposite field and can hit offspeed pitches well. For a player frequently compared to Angels third baseman Troy Glaus, six homers don't quite measure up. In addition to concerns about Cuddyer's power, he has below-average speed, and his error total went from 28 to 34 in his second full year at third base. He has trouble fielding balls cleanly and throwing accurately. Cuddyer likely will return to Double-A in 2001, which isn't a terrible setback considering he'll be just 22. He's at least a year or two away from forcing Minnesota to decide where to move incumbent third baseman Corey Koskie.

Yr	Club (League)	Class	AVG	G	AB	R	H	2B	3B	HR	RBI	BB	SO	SB
1998	Fort Wayne (Mid)	A	.276	129	497	82	137	37	7	12	81	61	107	16
1999	Fort Myers (FSL)	A	.298	130	466	87	139	24	4	16	82	76	91	14
2000	New Britain (EL)	AA	.263	138	490	72	129	30	8	6	61	55	93	5
MINOR LEAGUE TOTALS			.279	397	1453	241	405	91	19	34	224	192	291	35

3. Michael Restovich, of

Born: Jan. 3, 1979. **Ht.:** 6-4. **Wt.:** 233. **Bats:** R. **Throws:** R. **School:** Mayo HS, Rochester, Minn. **Career Transactions:** Selected by Twins in second round of 1997 draft; signed Aug. 15, 1997.

A home state product, Restovich rejected a Notre Dame baseball scholarship to sign with the Twins. He broke his high school's record for career points in basketball. The No. 2 prospect behind Braves infielder Rafael Furcal in the Rookie-level Appalachian League in 1998, he stumbled in 2000. Restovich has the best raw power among Twins farmhands, and the big league club needs sluggers like him. He also runs well for a player his size and led Minnesota minor leaguers with 19 stolen bases. He has improved his two-strike approach in each of the last two seasons. After a slow start in 2000, Restovich was able to get around better on inside fastballs. He also demonstrated improvement with his baserunning instincts, but will need to keep progressing. His outfield jumps and throwing accuracy are also developing. Managers ranked Resto the 17th-best prospect in the Florida State League, and he may return there to begin 2001. He hit 19 homers in the Class A Midwest League in 1999, and the Twins hope he becomes a threat to hit 25-30 a season.

Year	Club (League)	Class	AVG	G	AB	R	H	2B	3B	HR	RBI	BB	SO	SB
1998	Elizabethton (Appy)	R	.355	65	242	68	86	20	1	13	64	54	58	5
	Fort Wayne (Mid)	A	.444	11	45	9	20	5	2	0	6	4	12	0
1999	Quad City (Mid)	A	.312	131	493	91	154	30	6	19	107	74	100	7
2000	Fort Myers (FSL)	A	.263	135	475	73	125	27	9	8	64	61	100	19
MINOR LEAGUE TOTALS			.307	342	1255	241	385	82	18	40	241	193	270	31

4. Luis Rivas, 2b

Born: Aug. 30, 1979. **Ht.:** 5-10. **Wt.:** 175. **Bats:** R. **Throws:** R. **Career Transactions:** Signed out of Venezuela by Twins, Dec. 13, 1995.

Rivas has been playing in the United States since he was 16, and was the top prospect in the Rookie-level Gulf Coast League in his debut. He made a smooth transition to second base in 2000. Rivas' speed has dropped a notch to above-average as he has filled out, but he's still the quickest player in the system. He has good range and a shortstop's arm at second base. He hit only .262 as he was pushed through the system, but he seemed to blossom in 2000 when he reached the hitter-friendly Pacific Coast League and Minnesota. After the position change, Rivas can still improve on making the pivot and turning the double play. He improved his plate discipline in 2000 but still needs to draw more walks. If all goes well for Rivas in the Venezuelan League and spring training, he could win Minnesota's starting second-base job over Jay Canizaro and Denny Hocking. Rivas and

Cristian Guzman could form the Twins' double-play combination for years.

Year	Club (League)	Class	AVG	G	AB	R	H	2B	3B	HR	RBI	BB	SO	SB
1996	Twins (GCL)	R	.259	53	201	29	52	12	1	1	13	18	37	35
1997	Fort Wayne (Mid)	A	.239	121	419	61	100	20	6	1	30	33	90	28
1998	Fort Myers (FSL)	A	.281	126	463	58	130	21	5	4	51	14	75	34
1999	New Britain (EL)	AA	.254	132	527	78	134	30	7	7	49	41	92	31
2000	New Britain (EL)	AA	.250	82	328	56	82	23	6	3	40	36	41	11
	Salt Lake (PCL)	AAA	.318	41	157	33	50	14	1	3	25	13	21	7
	Minnesota (AL)	MAJ	.310	16	58	8	18	4	1	0	6	2	4	2
MAJOR LEAGUE TOTALS			.310	16	58	8	18	4	1	0	6	2	4	2
MINOR LEAGUE TOTALS			.262	555	2095	315	548	120	26	19	208	155	356	146

5. Justin Morneau, 1b/c

RICK BATTLE

Born: May 15, 1981. **Ht.:** 6-4. **Wt.:** 205. **Bats:** L. **Throws:** R. **School:** New Westminster (British Columbia) Secondary School. **Career Transactions:** Selected by Twins in third round of 1999 draft; signed June 17, 1999.

After wrenching his knee while sliding, Morneau didn't even play in extended spring training in 2000 until just before the Gulf Coast League season started in June. A gamer, he came back faster than expected and set GCL records for average and RBIs. The Twins believe Morneau could be their No. 3 hitter of the future. Shortly after he was drafted in 1999, he drilled several balls into the Metrodome's upper deck. He's already mature offensively and still has room to grow. Prior to 2000, Morneau's throwing mechanics were subpar. Though he showed improvement behind the plate and caught during the Rookie-level Appalachian League playoffs, he is best suited for first base—where he won't be blocked in the system. He has below-average speed but isn't considered a base clogger. Morneau left instructional league with a sore elbow, which could tie him to first base for awhile. He and Rob Bowen could form an impressive tandem at Class A Quad City in 2001. Morneau's bat is his ticket to the majors, and catching would be a bonus.

Year	Club (League)	Class	AVG	G	AB	R	H	2B	3B	HR	RBI	BB	SO	SB
1999	Twins (GCL)	R	.302	17	53	3	16	5	0	0	9	2	6	0
2000	Twins (GCL)	R	.402	52	194	47	78	21	0	10	58	30	18	3
	Elizabethton (Appy)	R	.217	6	23	4	5	0	0	1	3	1	6	0
MINOR LEAGUE TOTALS			.367	75	270	54	99	26	0	11	70	33	30	3

6. Matt Kinney, rhp

RICH ABEL

Born: Dec. 16, 1976. **Ht.:** 6-5. **Wt.:** 220. **Bats:** R. **Throws:** R. **School:** Bangor (Maine) HS. **Career Transactions:** Selected by Red Sox in sixth round of 1995 draft; signed June 30, 1995 . . . Traded by Red Sox with LHP Joe Thomas and OF John Barnes to Twins for LHP Greg Swindell and 1B Orlando Merced, July 31, 1998.

Kinney is another New Englander who got away from the Red Sox. He is on par with Adam Johnson as the hardest thrower in the system. He can touch 95-96 mph but is usually around 91. Kinney had bone chips removed from his elbow in 1999 but generally is durable like Johnson. Kinney often reaches his pitch limits too soon, as he lacks the concentration to put hitters away early in the count. His curve's not as big and loopy as it once was, but he must continue to tighten it, and his changeup is just ordinary. He has shown more consistency since ditching his glasses in favor of contact lenses. Kinney has an excellent shot at leaving spring training as one of Minnesota's starters. He even has drawn praise from Twins manager Tom Kelly, who habitually finds fault with young players.

Year	Club (League)	Class	W	L	ERA	G	GS	CG	SV	IP	H	R	ER	BB	SO
1995	Red Sox (GCL)	R	1	3	2.93	8	2	0	2	28	29	13	9	10	11
1996	Lowell (NY-P)	A	3	9	2.68	15	15	0	0	87	68	51	26	44	72
1997	Michigan (Mid)	A	8	5	3.53	22	22	2	0	117	93	59	46	78	123
1998	Sarasota (FSL)	A	9	6	4.01	22	20	2	1	121	109	70	54	75	96
	Fort Myers (FSL)	A	3	2	3.13	7	7	0	0	37	31	18	13	18	39
1999	New Britain (EL)	AA	4	7	7.12	14	13	0	0	61	69	54	48	36	50
	Twins (GCL)	R	0	1	4.76	3	3	0	0	6	6	4	3	3	8
2000	New Britain (EL)	AA	6	1	2.71	15	15	0	0	86	74	31	26	35	93
	Salt Lake (PCL)	AAA	5	2	4.25	9	9	0	0	55	42	26	26	26	59
	Minnesota (AL)	MAJ	2	2	5.10	8	8	0	0	42	41	26	24	25	24
MAJOR LEAGUE TOTALS			2	2	5.10	8	8	0	0	42	41	26	24	25	24
MINOR LEAGUE TOTALS			39	36	3.77	115	106	4	3	599	521	326	251	325	551

7. Rob Bowen, c

Born: Feb. 24, 1981. **Ht.:** 6-2. **Wt.:** 195. **Bats:** B. **Throws:** R. **School:** Homestead HS, Fort Wayne, Ind. **Career Transactions:** Selected by Twins in second round of 1999 draft; signed July 10, 1999.

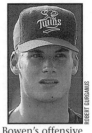

Bowen was Indiana's high school player of the year in 1999. He did not hit a home run in 77 at-bats in the big ballparks of the Gulf Coast League that summer, but showed increased power numbers in 2000. Managers rated him the No. 7 prospect in the Appalachian League. A switch-hitter, Bowen gets most of his power from the right side. He made progress with the bat while staying as dominant as ever on defense. He's mobile behind the plate and has a strong arm. Less than a month into the 2000 season, Bowen's offensive breakout was put on hold as a foul tip gave him a hairline fracture of his collarbone. Like so many of the youngsters on the Twins list, he'll need all the repetitions he can get at this stage of his development. Bowen and Justin Morneau were drafted in back-to-back rounds in 1999 and have been teammates for two seasons. The next probable step is Quad City, where Bowen will do most of the catching. He doesn't have Morneau's bat, but Bowen's defensive skills put him on an identical track right now.

Year	Club (League)	Class	AVG	G	AB	R	H	2B	3B	HR	RBI	BB	SO	SB
1999	Twins (GCL)	R	.260	29	77	10	20	4	0	0	11	20	15	2
2000	Elizabethton (Appy)	R	.288	21	73	17	21	3	0	4	19	11	18	0
MINOR LEAGUE TOTALS			.273	50	150	27	41	7	0	4	30	31	33	2

8. Bobby Kielty, of

Born: Aug. 5, 1976. **Ht.:** 6-1. **Wt.:** 215. **Bats:** B. **Throws:** R. **School:** University of Mississippi. **Career Transactions:** Signed as nondrafted free agent by Twins, Feb. 16, 1999.

Kielty commanded a $500,000 bonus as a nondrafted free agent after bursting into prominence after the 1998 draft as the Cape Cod League player of the year. He missed six weeks in 1999 because of allergies that affected his vision. Laser eye surgery corrected the problem. Kielty is a solid hitter who has good gap power from both sides of the plate. He also has a good eye at the plate, leading the Eastern League in walks before finishing the year in Triple-A. Defensively, he gets the best jumps of any outfielder in the organization and has a playable arm. Kielty doesn't hit with consistent over-the-fence power, so the longer he can stay in center field the better. He struck out more than usual in the Arizona Fall League. At times, he gets too tough on himself. If Jacque Jones and Torii Hunter lay long-term claim to their outfield jobs in Minnesota, Kielty could run into a wall. But he has blossomed when least expected before, and he'll start 2001 a step away at new Triple-A affiliate Edmonton.

Year	Club (League)	Class	AVG	G	AB	R	H	2B	3B	HR	RBI	BB	SO	SB
1999	Quad City (Mid)	A	.294	69	245	52	72	13	1	13	43	43	56	12
2000	New Britain (EL)	AA	.262	129	451	79	118	30	3	14	65	98	109	6
	Salt Lake (PCL)	AAA	.242	9	33	8	8	4	0	0	2	7	10	0
MINOR LEAGUE TOTALS			.272	207	729	139	198	47	4	27	110	148	175	18

9. Brad Thomas, lhp

Born: Oct. 22, 1977. **Ht.:** 6-3. **Wt.:** 204. **Bats:** L. **Throws:** L. **Career Transactions:** Signed out of Australia by Dodgers, July 2, 1995 . . . Released by Dodgers, May 9, 1997 . . . Signed by Twins, May 12, 1997.

Thomas signed with the Dodgers but was released because of a visa snafu in May 1997. The Twins grabbed him three days later. He had a busy 2000, pitching in the Futures Game and for the home team in the Olympics. Minnesota has been aggressive in Australia, where scout Howard Norsetter also uncovered prospect Grant Balfour. Thomas has good stuff for a lefthander. He has an above-average fastball, consistently throwing 91 mph and higher, to go with a solid changeup and curve. He doesn't get rattled and concerns himself more with outs than strikeouts. He's heavier than his listed weight, yet the Twins like his athleticism. As his one hot and one cold start in Sydney demonstrated, Thomas needs to do a better job locating his fastball. He can get velocity-happy, which is when he usually gets into trouble. Thomas remained effective even while New Britain lost its final 17 games of the 2000 season. If he has a good spring, he'll begin 2001 in Triple-A.

Year	Club (League)	Class	W	L	ERA	G	GS	CG	SV	IP	H	R	ER	BB	SO
1996	Great Falls (Pio)	R	3	2	6.31	11	5	0	0	36	48	27	25	11	28
1997	Elizabethton (Appy)	R	3	4	4.48	14	13	0	0	70	78	43	35	21	53
1998	Fort Wayne (Mid)	A	11	8	2.95	27	26	1	0	152	146	68	50	45	126
1999	Fort Myers (FSL)	A	8	11	4.78	27	27	1	0	153	182	99	81	46	108
2000	Fort Myers (FSL)	A	6	2	1.66	12	12	0	0	65	62	33	12	16	57
	New Britain (EL)	AA	6	6	4.06	14	13	1	0	75	80	47	34	46	66
MINOR LEAGUE TOTALS			37	33	3.87	105	96	3	0	551	596	317	237	185	438

10. B.J. Garbe, of

Born: Feb. 3, 1981. **Ht.:** 6-2. **Wt.:** 195. **Bats:** R. **Throws:** R. **School:** Moses Lake (Wash.) HS. **Career Transactions:** Selected by Twins in first round (fifth overall) of 1999 draft; signed July 7, 1999.

Garbe's 1999 high school team also featured outfielder Jason Cooper (now playing college ball at Stanford) and catcher Ryan Doumit (now with the Pirates), both of whom were drafted in the second round. He signed for a club-record $2.75 million bonus. He's a strong-bodied kid with the chance to develop power and the speed to leg out hits. He played well against older pitchers in instructional league in the fall and has the best outfield arm in the system and the range to play center field. Tools aside, Garbe didn't impress much of anybody in the Midwest League. He chased too many sliders and seldom got into hitter's counts. He never found a swing he liked. Reviews of his overall defense were mixed as well. Garbe likely will repeat the Midwest League, at least to start the season. A star quarterback in high school, he remains the best all-around athlete in the organization, even if it hasn't translated on the baseball diamond yet.

Year	Club (League)	Class	AVG	G	AB	R	H	2B	3B	HR	RBI	BB	SO	SB
1999	Elizabethton (Appy)	R	.316	41	171	33	54	8	0	3	32	20	34	4
2000	Quad City (Mid)	A	.233	133	476	62	111	12	3	5	51	63	91	14
MINOR LEAGUE TOTALS			.255	174	647	95	165	20	3	8	83	83	125	18

11. Jeff Randazzo, lhp

Born: Aug. 12, 1981. **Ht.:** 6-7. **Wt.:** 200. **Bats:** R. **Throws:** L. **School:** Cardinal O'Hara HS, Springfield, Pa. **Career Transactions:** Selected by Twins in fourth round of 1999 draft; signed Aug. 18, 1999.

Rated as the No. 19 prospect in the Gulf Coast League, the lanky lefthander succeeded in a two-start taste of Class A. Though he's 6-foot-7, Twins officials don't believe Randazzo will get too bulky because he's an avid runner who stays in excellent shape. Randazzo's fastball is a consistent 87 mph and could get to 90-91 as he becomes a finished product. He has good spin to his curveball and a nice feel for his changeup, which he already can throw for strikes. In instructional league, he was aggressive and effective against more experienced hitters. Randazzo is one of four members of Minnesota's 1999 draft class among the organization's top 11 prospects. The Twins also like righthanders Brent Schoening (fifth round) and Brian Wolfe (sixth).

Year	Club (League)	Class	W	L	ERA	G	GS	CG	SV	IP	H	R	ER	BB	SO
2000	Fort Myers (GCL)	R	7	2	3.15	13	12	3	0	69	70	35	24	19	58
	Quad City (Mid)	A	1	1	3.97	2	2	0	0	11	10	5	5	8	12
MINOR LEAGUE TOTALS			8	3	3.26	15	14	3	0	80	80	40	29	27	70

12. John Barnes, of

Born: April 24, 1976. **Ht.:** 6-2. **Wt.:** 205. **Bats:** R. **Throws:** R. **School:** Grossmont (Calif.) JC. **Career Transactions:** Selected by Red Sox in fourth round of 1996 draft; signed July 22, 1996 . . . Traded by Red Sox with RHP Matt Kinney and LHP Joe Thomas to Twins for LHP Greg Swindell and 1B Orlando Merced, July 31, 1998.

The leading hitter in the minor leagues in 2000, Barnes wasn't even supposed to start at Triple-A Salt Lake. He was sent to the Buzz as a fourth outfielder but hit his way into the lineup. Barnes began last year with a lifetime .280 minor league average in 1,494 at-bats and had topped .300 just once. With an accurate, major league average arm and good defensive instincts, he has the ability to play all three outfield positions. Barnes could use more aggressiveness on the bases, but he should get plenty of practice. He sprays line drives everywhere, has gap power and walks as much as he strikes out. He joined the organization in the same trade that brought Matt Kinney from the Red Sox. Barnes will have a shot at making the big league club as a fourth or fifth outfielder—a scenario that worked for him last year.

Year	Club (League)	Class	AVG	G	AB	R	H	2B	3B	HR	RBI	BB	SO	SB
1996	Red Sox (GCL)	R	.277	30	101	9	28	4	0	1	17	5	17	4
1997	Michigan (Mid)	A	.304	130	490	80	149	19	5	6	73	65	42	19
1998	Trenton (EL)	AA	.274	100	380	53	104	18	0	14	36	40	47	3
	New Britain (EL)	AA	.268	20	71	9	19	4	1	0	8	9	9	1
1999	New Britain (EL)	AA	.263	129	452	62	119	21	1	13	58	49	40	10
2000	Salt Lake (PCL)	AAA	.365	119	441	107	161	37	6	13	87	57	48	7
	Minnesota (AL)	MAJ	.351	11	37	5	13	4	0	0	2	2	6	0
MAJOR LEAGUE TOTALS			.351	11	37	5	13	4	0	0	2	2	6	0
MINOR LEAGUE TOTALS			.300	528	1935	320	580	103	13	47	279	225	203	44

13. Juan Rincon, rhp

Born: Jan. 23, 1979. **Ht.:** 5-11. **Wt.:** 187. **Bats:** R. **Throws:** R. **Career Transactions:** Signed out of Venezuela by Twins, Nov. 4, 1996.

Stuck in the haze of a horrible New Britain season, Rincon took a step back after leading the Midwest League in strikeouts and ranking second in wins and third in ERA a year earlier. He had no such success after his promotion to the Eastern League last June. He had been his usual self at Fort Myers, holding opponents to a .238 average. He'll have the same catching up to do this year in Double-A. His offspeed stuff has yet to complement his 92-95 mph fastball and sharp slider. He also must improve his command, though his ceiling remains high.

Year	Club (League)	Class	W	L	ERA	G	GS	CG	SV	IP	H	R	ER	BB	SO
1997	Twins (GCL)	R	3	3	2.95	11	10	1	0	58	55	21	19	24	46
	Elizabethton (Appy)	R	0	1	3.86	2	1	0	0	9	11	4	4	3	7
1998	Fort Wayne (Mid)	A	6	4	3.83	37	13	0	6	96	84	51	41	54	74
1999	Quad City (Mid)	A	14	8	2.92	28	28	0	0	163	146	67	53	66	153
2000	Fort Myers (FSL)	A	5	3	2.12	13	13	0	0	76	67	26	18	23	55
	New Britain (EL)	AA	3	9	4.65	15	15	2	0	89	96	55	46	39	79
MINOR LEAGUE TOTALS			31	28	3.31	96	70	3	6	492	459	224	181	209	414

14. Colby Miller, rhp

Born: March 19, 1982. **Ht.:** 6-2. **Wt.:** 185. **Bats:** R. **Throws:** R. **School:** Weatherford (Olka.) HS. **Career Transactions:** Selected by Twins in third round of 2000 draft; signed June 19, 2000.

Miller has been called a baby Brad Radke. He's mature and a good competitor who has Radke-like focus as a pitcher. He was a winner as a high school quarterback and has carried that intensity to the mound. Miller turned down a baseball scholarship to Oklahoma to join the Twins. Rated the best talent in Oklahoma entering the 2000 draft, he went 11-0, 0.83 with 141 strikeouts in 68 innings as a senior and played a solid shortstop in high school. His fastball is in the 92-93 mph range, and his other pitches show promise. While Miller couldn't quite match the success of Jeff Randazzo at Quad City, the pair should anchor the River Bandits rotation in 2001.

Year	Club (League)	Class	W	L	ERA	G	GS	CG	SV	IP	H	R	ER	BB	SO
2000	Twins (GCL)	R	3	2	3.09	14	10	0	0	55	44	26	19	21	55
	Quad City (Mid)	A	0	1	6.75	2	2	0	0	7	10	6	5	7	6
MINOR LEAGUE TOTALS			3	3	3.48	16	12	0	0	62	54	32	24	28	61

15. Grant Balfour, rhp

Born: Dec. 30, 1977. **Ht.:** 6-2. **Wt.:** 170. **Bats:** R. **Throws:** R. **Career Transactions:** Signed out of Australia by Twins, Jan. 19, 1997.

A stringbean catcher on a youth team in Australia that featured Twins prospect Brad Thomas and Braves signees Damian Moss and Glenn Williams, Balfour has bloomed into a bullpen prospect. He pitched in the Olympics after flashing brilliant stuff in relief for Fort Myers. He had been throwing 89-91 mph as a starter, but now operates at 92-94 mph. He also has an 83-87 mph slider with late downward tilt and a changeup that has a chance to be major league average. Balfour is a fitness fanatic who has the lowest percentage of body fat in the system, and he actually has a tendency to overtrain. He has a closer mentality and closer stuff, but he needs to come up with a better way to attack lefthanded hitters. He has a spot on Minnesota's 40-man roster and likely will start 2001 in Double-A.

Year	Club (League)	Class	W	L	ERA	G	GS	CG	SV	IP	H	R	ER	BB	SO
1997	Twins (GCL)	R	2	4	3.76	13	12	0	0	67	73	31	28	20	43
1998	Elizabethton (Appy)	R	7	2	3.36	13	13	0	0	77	70	36	29	27	75
1999	Quad City (Mid)	A	8	5	3.53	19	14	0	1	91	66	39	36	37	95
2000	Fort Myers (FSL)	A	8	5	4.25	35	10	0	6	89	91	46	42	34	90
MINOR LEAGUE TOTALS			25	16	3.73	80	49	0	7	325	300	152	135	118	303

16. Kyle Lohse, rhp

Born: Oct. 4, 1978. **Ht.:** 6-2. **Wt.:** 190. **Bats:** R. **Throws:** R. **School:** Butte (Calif.) CC. **Career Transactions:** Selected by Cubs in 29th round of 1996 draft; signed May 20, 1997 . . . Traded by Cubs with RHP Jason Ryan to Twins for RHP Rick Aguilera and LHP Scott Downs, May 21, 1999.

No one in the organization is giving up on Lohse, even after he put up ghastly numbers for New Britain. A year earlier, he was the Twins' No. 7 prospect because of a hard slider, 90 mph fastball and solid changeup. He won 10 games in 1999 but showed a sign of things to come when he got rocked at New Britain. His troubles in his first full Eastern League season were attributed to his inability to locate his pitches. He threw the ball down the middle too much, especially for a righthander without a blazing fastball. His breaking stuff held up a little better, but he and the Rock Cats (who finished the season with 17 straight losses) would like to forget 2000. He did finish on a strong note, however, posting a 1.80 ERA with 35 strikeouts in as many innings in the Arizona Fall League.

Year	Club (League)	Class	W	L	ERA	G	GS	CG	SV	IP	H	R	ER	BB	SO
1997	Cubs (AZL)	R	2	2	3.02	12	11	0	0	48	46	22	16	22	49
1998	Rockford (Mid)	A	13	8	3.22	28	26	3	0	171	158	76	61	45	121
1999	Daytona (FSL)	A	5	3	2.89	9	9	1	0	53	48	21	17	16	41
	Fort Myers (FSL)	A	2	3	5.18	7	7	0	0	42	47	28	24	9	33
	New Britain (EL)	AA	3	4	5.89	11	11	1	0	70	87	49	46	23	41
2000	New Britain (EL)	AA	3	18	6.04	28	28	0	0	167	196	123	112	55	124
MINOR LEAGUE TOTALS			28	38	4.51	95	92	5	0	550	582	319	276	170	409

17. Ryan Mills, lhp

Born: July 21, 1977. **Ht.:** 6-5. **Wt.:** 205. **Bats:** R. **Throws:** L. **School:** Arizona State University. **Career Transactions:** Selected by Twins in first round (sixth overall) of 1998 draft; signed June 30, 1998.

Mills, regarded as one of the most polished arms available in the 1998 draft, has yet to pan out as a pro. The Twins hoped he would take a quick path to the big leagues, but he was immediately beset by elbow problems, then endured a dreadful 1999. He rebounded briefly last season but pitched poorly after a promotion to Double-A and looked uninspiring in the Arizona Fall League. The Twins hold out hope that Mills will do an about-face similar to 1995 first-round pick Mark Redman's. Mills' stuff is better than Redman's at this stage, as he has more velocity and a better curveball, though an inferior changeup. Mills averages 89-91 mph and can touch 93 with his fastball, but he still has a long way to go if he's going to follow his father Dick to the major leagues.

Year	Club (League)	Class	W	L	ERA	G	GS	CG	SV	IP	H	R	ER	BB	SO
1998	Fort Myers (FSL)	A	0	0	1.80	2	2	0	0	5	2	3	1	1	3
1999	Fort Myers (FSL)	A	3	10	8.87	27	21	0	0	95	121	107	94	87	70
2000	Quad City (Mid)	A	3	6	3.53	20	20	0	0	120	101	54	47	64	110
	New Britain (EL)	AA	0	7	9.28	8	8	0	0	32	47	49	33	34	21
MINOR LEAGUE TOTALS			6	23	6.25	57	51	0	0	252	271	213	175	186	204

18. A.J. Pierzynski, c

Born: Dec. 30, 1976. **Ht.:** 6-3. **Wt.:** 220. **Bats:** L. **Throws:** R. **School:** Dr. Phillips HS, Orlando, Fla. **Career Transactions:** Selected by Twins in third round of 1994 draft; signed June 9, 1994.

Pierzynski received a 33-game opportunity to see what he could do as a major league catcher, and he made the most of it. Some in the organization think he has the inside track to be Minnesota's Opening Day starter, thanks to his reliable lefthanded bat and decent defensive skills. Danny Ardoin, a 2000 acquisition from the Athletics system, plays the best defense among the top four catchers in the organization, but his offense lags behind Pierzynski's. Matthew LeCroy has the best bat, but his below-average arm and release could force a move to first base. Chad Moeller has the best balance of tools, but a knee injury last year helped pave the way for Pierzynski's chance. Pierzynski makes good contact but still could use more patience at the plate. Though he won't hit many homers, his gap power is good for a fair share of doubles. Considering the multiple catching options presented by the system, Pierzynski's surge came just in time for him.

Year	Club (League)	Class	AVG	G	AB	R	H	2B	3B	HR	RBI	BB	SO	SB
1994	Twins (GCL)	R	.289	43	152	21	44	8	1	1	19	12	19	0
1995	Fort Wayne (Mid)	A	.310	22	84	10	26	5	1	2	14	2	10	0
	Elizabethton (Appy)	R	.332	56	205	29	68	13	1	7	45	14	23	0
1996	Fort Wayne (Mid)	A	.274	114	431	48	118	30	3	7	70	22	53	0
1997	Fort Myers (FSL)	A	.279	118	412	49	115	23	1	9	64	16	59	2
1998	New Britain (EL)	AA	.297	59	212	30	63	11	0	3	17	10	25	0

Year	Club (League)	Class	AVG	G	AB	R	H	2B	3B	HR	RBI	BB	SO	SB
	Salt Lake (PCL)	AAA	.255	59	208	29	53	7	2	7	30	9	24	3
	Minnesota (AL)	MAJ	.300	7	10	1	3	0	0	0	1	1	2	0
1999	Salt Lake (PCL)	AAA	.259	67	228	29	59	10	0	1	25	16	29	0
	Minnesota (AL)	MAJ	.273	9	22	3	6	2	0	0	3	1	4	0
2000	New Britain (EL)	AA	.298	62	228	36	68	17	2	4	34	8	22	0
	Salt Lake (PCL)	AAA	.335	41	155	22	52	14	1	4	25	5	22	1
	Minnesota (AL)	MAJ	.307	33	88	12	27	5	1	2	11	5	14	1
MAJOR LEAGUE TOTALS			.300	49	120	16	36	7	1	2	15	7	20	1
MINOR LEAGUE TOTALS			.288	641	2315	303	666	138	12	45	343	114	286	6

19. Todd Sears, 1b

Born: Oct. 23, 1975. **Ht.:** 6-6. **Wt.:** 205. **Bats:** L. **Throws:** R. **School:** University of Nebraska. **Career Transactions:** Selected by Rockies in third round of 1997 draft; signed July 3, 1997 . . . Traded by Rockies with a player to be named to Twins for OF Butch Huskey and 2B Todd Walker, July 16, 2000.

Starved for power, the Twins dealt for the hulking Sears last summer. Though his 16 homers in 2000 represented a career high, he has the build and potential for more. In his first year in Double-A, he led Carolina in home runs and RBIs despite playing the last month in the Twins organization. Sears is a decent athlete who offers some mobility around the first-base bag. Colorado tried him at third base for part of 1999. He could start 2001 in the middle of Minnesota's Triple-A lineup. The Twins have several alternatives at the infield corners, so Sears will have to blast his way to a major league role.

Year	Club (League)	Class	AVG	G	AB	R	H	2B	3B	HR	RBI	BB	SO	SB
1997	Portland (NWL)	A	.270	55	200	37	54	13	1	2	29	41	49	2
1998	Asheville (SAL)	A	.290	130	459	71	133	26	2	11	82	72	89	10
1999	Salem (Car)	A	.281	109	385	58	108	21	0	14	59	58	99	11
2000	Carolina (SL)	AA	.301	86	299	54	90	21	0	12	72	72	76	12
	New Britain (EL)	AA	.314	40	140	15	44	8	1	3	15	18	40	1
	Salt Lake (PCL)	AAA	.364	3	11	2	4	1	0	1	4	1	2	0
MINOR LEAGUE TOTALS			.290	423	1494	237	433	90	4	43	261	262	375	36

20. J.D. Durbin, rhp

Born: Feb. 24, 1982. **Ht.:** 6-1. **Wt.:** 185. **Bats:** R. **Throws:** R. **School:** Coronado HS, Scottsdale, Ariz. **Career Transactions:** Selected by Twins in second round of 2000 draft; signed July 18, 2000.

With four pitchers from the 2000 draft class in the top 30 (and former University of Minnesota quarterback Andy Persby just missing), the Twins are optimistic about their pitching future. Durbin missed most of his first summer because of elbow tendinitis, but he didn't need surgery. He's a little undersized but makes up for it with tenacity. He throws plus stuff from a three-quarters release point. His fastball touches 94 mph and he has a hard, late-breaking slider. Minnesota can't wait to see more of Durbin when he's healthy in 2001.

Year	Club (League)	Class	W	L	ERA	G	GS	CG	SV	IP	H	R	ER	BB	SO
2000	Twins (GCL)	R	0	0	0.00	2	0	0	0	2	2	0	0	0	4
MINOR LEAGUE TOTALS			0	0	0.00	2	0	0	0	2	2	0	0	0	4

21. Jason Miller, lhp

Born: July 20, 1982. **Ht.:** 6-1. **Wt.:** 195. **Bats:** R. **Throws:** L. **School:** Sarasota (Fla.) HS. **Career Transactions:** Selected by Twins in fourth round of 2000 draft; signed July 4, 2000.

Miller reminds one Twins official of the Cubs' Joey Nation, who may not be a frontline starter but did reach the big leagues three years after he was drafted out of high school. A product of national power Sarasota (Fla.) High, Miller is a finesse lefthander who touches 89-90 mph, hits his spots and has a mature approach to pitching. He enjoys studying and talking about the game. He has an excellent curveball and works both sides of the plate. He wasn't quite as in demand as the three Sarasota hurlers (Matt Drews, Doug Million and Bobby Seay) who went in the first round in a four-year period during the 1990s, but he has a promising future.

Year	Club (League)	Class	W	L	ERA	G	GS	CG	SV	IP	H	R	ER	BB	SO
2000	Twins (GCL)	R	0	0	0.00	2	1	0	0	4	2	1	0	0	3
	Elizabethton (Appy)	R	2	1	4.50	9	5	0	0	26	23	16	13	5	22
MINOR LEAGUE TOTALS			2	1	3.90	11	6	0	0	30	25	17	13	5	25

22. Rafael Boitel, of

Born: Jan. 21, 1981. **Ht.:** 6-3. **Wt.:** 165. **Bats:** B. **Throws:** L. **Career Transactions:** Signed out of Dominican Republic by Twins, Jan. 24, 1998.

Boitel could be the Twins' best leadoff prospect. He has a nice swing from both sides of the plate, a quick bat and a knack for hitting balls to the opposite field. As he matures, Boitel could hit for a little pop, but that never will be his forte. He improved his basestealing ability in 2000, and needs to do the same with his patience. He's solid defensively in center field at running down balls and throwing. In addition to his switch-hitting skills, Boitel can throw with either arm, though Minnesota has him throwing lefthanded. After rating as the Appalachian League's No. 8 prospect, he'll get his first taste of full-season ball in 2001.

Year	Club (League)	Class	AVG	G	AB	R	H	2B	3B	HR	RBI	BB	SO	SB
1998	Twins (DSL)	R	.280	63	218	33	61	3	3	2	28	32	35	22
1999	Twins (GCL)	R	.286	45	161	23	46	6	2	0	14	18	39	6
2000	Elizabethton (Appy)	R	.263	55	224	43	59	7	2	2	27	25	47	16
MINOR LEAGUE TOTALS			.275	163	603	99	166	16	7	4	69	75	121	44

23. Chad Moeller, c

Born: Feb. 18, 1975. **Ht.:** 6-3. **Wt.:** 210. **Bats:** R. **Throws:** R. **School:** University of Southern California.
Career Transactions: Selected by Twins in seventh round of 1996 draft; signed June 8, 1996.

If he hadn't torn cartilage in his right knee and missed much of 2000, Moeller might have been the frontrunner to start at catcher for the Twins this year. Instead, A.J. Pierzynski played well in Minnesota down the stretch and moved to the front of the line. Moeller is by no means out of the competition for a major league job this year, however. His offense and defense both fit into the middle of the pack in the catching corps that includes Pierzynski, Matthew LeCroy and Danny Ardoin. Moeller led the 1999 Arizona Fall League in hitting, a springboard to a successful season offensively in 2000—when he was in the lineup. He will need to improve his plate discipline if he's going to continue to produce. His defense may have slipped a bit, as he gunned down just 10 percent of basestealers.

Year	Club (League)	Class	AVG	G	AB	R	H	2B	3B	HR	RBI	BB	SO	SB
1996	Elizabethton (Appy)	R	.356	17	59	17	21	4	0	4	13	18	9	1
1997	Fort Wayne (Mid)	A	.289	108	384	58	111	18	3	9	39	48	76	11
1998	Fort Myers (FSL)	A	.327	66	254	37	83	24	1	6	39	31	37	2
	New Britain (EL)	AA	.235	58	187	21	44	10	0	6	23	24	41	2
1999	New Britain (EL)	AA	.248	89	250	29	62	11	3	4	24	21	44	0
2000	Salt Lake (PCL)	AAA	.287	47	167	30	48	13	1	5	20	9	45	0
	Minnesota (AL)	MAJ	.211	48	128	13	27	3	1	1	9	9	33	1
MAJOR LEAGUE TOTALS			.211	48	128	13	27	3	1	1	9	9	33	1
MINOR LEAGUE TOTALS			.284	385	1301	192	369	80	8	34	158	151	252	16

24. Lew Ford, of

Born: Aug. 12, 1976. **Ht.:** 6-0. **Wt.:** 190. **Bats:** R. **Throws:** R. **School:** Dallas Baptist University. **Career Transactions:** Selected by Red Sox in 12th round of 1999 draft; signed June 7, 1999 . . . Traded by Red Sox to Twins for RHP Hector Carrasco, Sept. 10, 2000.

Ford, who was caught just four times in 56 stolen-base attempts in 2000, immediately became one of the fastest players in the system after joining the Twins last fall. He led the minors with 122 runs and dominated the South Atlantic League in his first full pro season, though he should have done so as one of the circuit's older players. He needs to be pushed to Double-A in 2001 to get a true reading on his abilities, though he's a center fielder who appears fairly solid across the board, with the exception of power. Ford is a late bloomer who didn't even plan on playing college baseball, instead choosing to attend Texas A&M to study computer engineering. He stayed there two years before trying out for the team, where he got stuck behind eventual major leaguers Chad Allen and Jason Tyner. Ford wound up playing four different colleges over the next three years before joining the Red Sox.

Year	Club (League)	Class	AVG	G	AB	R	H	2B	3B	HR	RBI	BB	SO	SB
1999	Lowell (NY-P)	A	.280	62	250	48	70	17	4	7	34	19	35	15
2000	Augusta (SAL)	A	.315	126	514	122	162	35	11	9	74	52	83	52
MINOR LEAGUE TOTALS			.304	188	764	170	232	52	15	16	108	71	118	67

25. Brian Buchanan, of

Born: July 21, 1973. **Ht.:** 6-4. **Wt.:** 230. **Bats:** R. **Throws:** R. **School:** University of Virginia. **Career Transactions:** Selected by Yankees in first round (24th overall) of 1994 draft; signed July 11, 1994 . . . Traded by Yankees with SS Cristian Guzman, RHP Danny Mota, LHP Eric Milton and cash to Twins for 2B Chuck Knoblauch, Feb. 6, 1998.

The 24th pick in the 1994 draft, Buchanan's career was thrown off track a year later by a gruesome compound fracture of his left ankle when he hit the first-base bag running out a ground ball. He was off to a .302-3-12 start at Class A Greensboro in what would have been his first full season. Buchanan's long climb finally reached the majors after he tore up the Pacific Coast League in his third try last season. Buchanan hit 22 home runs in his last year in college and was projected to be a power threat, but he didn't hit more than 17 in a minor league season until 2000. Buchanan is only adequate defensively and struggled to make contact in the majors, but he still has a shot at a reserve outfield job in Minnesota this year.

Year	Club (League)	Class	AVG	G	AB	R	H	2B	3B	HR	RBI	BB	SO	SB
1994	Oneonta (NY-P)	A	.226	50	177	28	40	9	2	4	26	24	53	5
1995	Greensboro (SAL)	A	.302	23	96	19	29	3	0	3	12	9	17	7
1996	Tampa (FSL)	A	.260	131	526	65	137	22	4	10	58	37	108	23
1997	Norwich (EL)	AA	.309	116	470	75	145	25	2	10	69	32	85	11
	Columbus (IL)	AAA	.279	18	61	8	17	1	0	4	7	4	11	2
1998	Salt Lake (PCL)	AAA	.278	133	500	74	139	29	3	17	82	36	90	14
1999	Salt Lake (PCL)	AAA	.297	107	391	67	116	24	1	10	60	28	85	11
2000	Salt Lake (PCL)	AAA	.297	95	364	82	108	20	1	27	103	41	75	5
	Minnesota (AL)	MAJ	.232	30	82	10	19	3	0	1	8	8	22	0
MAJOR LEAGUE TOTALS			.232	30	82	10	19	3	0	1	8	8	22	0
MINOR LEAGUE TOTALS			.283	673	2585	418	731	133	13	85	417	211	524	78

26. Brandon Knight, rhp

Born: Oct. 1, 1975. **Ht.:** 6-0. **Wt.:** 170. **Bats:** L. **Throws:** R. **School:** Ventura (Calif.) JC. **Career Transactions:** Selected by Rangers in 14th round of 1995 draft; signed June 3, 1995 . . . Traded by Rangers with RHP Sam Marsonek to Yankees for OF Chad Curtis, Dec. 14, 1999 . . . Selected by Twins from Yankees in major league Rule 5 draft, Dec. 11, 2000.

The second pick in the 2000 Rule 5 draft, Knight could become the Twins' No. 5 starter or take a spot in the bullpen. He's with his third organization in little more than a year, having been traded by the Rangers to the Yankees for Chad Curtis in December 1999. He throws strikes with all four of his pitches: a low-90s fastball, as well as a curveball, slider and changeup. Knight was more accomplished as a hitter in junior college, and it has taken him a while to learn the difference between throwing strikes and quality strikes. If he continues to make progress, Minnesota's Rule 5 gamble may pay off.

Year	Club (League)	Class	W	L	ERA	G	GS	CG	SV	IP	H	R	ER	BB	SO
1995	Rangers (GCL)	R	2	1	5.25	3	2	0	0	12	12	7	7	6	11
	Charleston, SC (SAL)	A	4	2	3.13	9	9	0	0	55	37	22	19	21	52
1996	Charlotte (FSL)	A	4	10	5.12	19	17	2	0	102	118	65	58	45	74
	Hudson Valley (NY-P)	A	2	2	4.42	9	9	0	0	53	59	29	26	21	52
1997	Charlotte (FSL)	A	7	4	2.23	14	12	3	0	93	82	33	23	22	91
	Tulsa (TL)	AA	6	4	4.50	14	14	2	0	90	83	52	45	35	84
1998	Tulsa (TL)	AA	6	6	5.11	14	14	0	0	86	94	54	49	37	87
	Oklahoma (PCL)	AAA	0	7	9.74	16	12	0	0	65	100	75	70	29	52
1999	Oklahoma (PCL)	AAA	9	8	4.91	27	26	5	0	163	173	96	89	47	97
2000	Columbus (IL)	AAA	10	12	4.44	28	28	8	0	185	172	105	91	61	138
MINOR LEAGUE TOTALS			50	56	4.75	153	143	20	0	903	930	538	477	324	738

27. Saul Rivera, rhp

Born: Dec. 7, 1977. **Ht.:** 5-11. **Wt.:** 165. **Bats:** R. **Throws:** R. **School:** University of Mobile (Ala.). **Career Transactions:** Selected by Twins in ninth round of 1998 draft; signed June 11, 1998.

Rivera, who also played in the outfield in college, showed enough command of his 92-94 mph fastball to earn a spot on the Twins' 40-man roster. Most of his 134 minor league appearances have been out of the bullpen, and he's one of several prospects (starting with No. 1 Adam Johnson) who eventually could help Minnesota in relief. Rivera is a little undersized, but he may throw hard enough to make up for it. In 1998, he led Appy League relievers with 16.3 strikeouts per nine innings. That figure has remained impressive, at 13.2 in 1999 and 11.1 last year. However, his control has regressed a bit as he has moved up the ladder. After picking up 23 saves in 1999, Rivera was used more as a set-up man in 2000. With all the up-and-coming relievers in this system, he may have to grow accustomed to that role.

Year	Club (League)	Class	W	L	ERA	G	GS	CG	SV	IP	H	R	ER	BB	SO
1998	Elizabethton (Appy)	R	3	3	2.25	23	0	0	7	36	19	10	9	19	65
1999	Quad City (Mid)	A	4	1	1.42	60	0	0	23	70	42	12	11	36	102
2000	Fort Myers (FSL)	A	8	1	3.58	29	0	0	5	38	34	15	15	19	45
	New Britain (EL)	AA	4	5	6.24	17	9	0	0	62	94	53	43	18	28
MINOR LEAGUE TOTALS			19	10	3.45	100	9	0	35	206	189	99	79	92	240

28. Jon Pridie, rhp

Born: Dec. 7, 1979. **Ht.:** 6-4. **Wt.:** 205. **Bats:** R. **Throws:** R. **School:** Prescott (Ariz.) HS. **Career Transactions:** Selected by Twins in 11th round of 1998 draft; signed July 13, 1998.

In his first professional season, Pridie pitched one inning and played 14 games at third base and five at first. He has found more success as an intimidating presence on the mound. His fastball touches 94-95 mph and he has the makings of a well above-average slider. Pridie is still raw and working to develop offspeed pitches. Curiously, the Twins used him primarily in relief last season, a role in which he could rely almost solely on his hard stuff. He may return to the rotation in 2001, when he'll make the jump to high Class A.

Year	Club (League)	Class	AVG	G	AB	R	H	2B	3B	HR	RBI	BB	SO	SB
1998	Twins (GCL)	R	.217	31	106	10	23	6	0	1	15	6	24	0
MINOR LEAGUE TOTALS			.217	31	106	10	23	6	0	1	15	6	24	0

Year	Club (League)	Class	W	L	ERA	G	GS	CG	SV	IP	H	R	ER	BB	SO
1998	Twins (GCL)	R	0	0	6.75	1	0	0	0	1	2	1	1	2	1
1999	Elizabethton (Appy)	R	5	6	4.48	14	14	0	0	76	93	44	38	33	64
2000	Quad City (Mid)	A	7	7	3.43	45	8	0	2	97	89	47	37	42	91
MINOR LEAGUE TOTALS			12	13	3.92	60	22	0	2	175	184	92	76	77	156

29. Danny Mota, rhp

Born: Oct. 9, 1975. **Ht.:** 6-0. **Wt.:** 180. **Bats:** R. **Throws:** R. **Career Transactions:** Signed out of Dominican Republic by Yankees, April 15, 1994 . . . Traded by Yankees with SS Cristian Guzman, LHP Eric Milton, OF Brian Buchanan and cash to Twins for 2B Chuck Knoblauch, Feb. 6, 1998.

With Mota's inclusion on the 40-man roster, all four players acquired from the Yankees for Chuck Knoblauch still have a chance to contribute to the Twins. Mota's improved command allowed him to join the others in the big leagues in 2000, a far cry from the year before, when he missed most of the season with a sprained elbow. Healthy again, Mota showed a 94 mph fastball and a good slider. He had no trouble with lefthanders in the minors, though they batted .417 against him during his brief stint with the Twins. After going from Class A to the majors in one season, he'll probably settle in at Triple-A to start 2001.

Year	Club (League)	Class	W	L	ERA	G	GS	CG	SV	IP	H	R	ER	BB	SO
1994	Yankees (DSL)	R	2	3	4.53	13	12	0	0	58	50	39	29	24	51
1995	Yankees (GCL)	R	2	3	2.20	14	0	0	0	33	27	9	8	4	35
1996	Oneonta (NY-P)	A	0	1	4.50	10	0	0	7	10	10	5	5	2	11
1997	Greensboro (SAL)	A	2	0	1.82	20	0	0	1	30	17	6	6	11	30
	Oneonta (NY-P)	A	1	0	2.22	27	0	0	17	28	21	8	7	16	40
1998	Fort Wayne (Mid)	A	4	3	2.25	25	0	0	7	32	24	14	8	8	39
	Fort Myers (FSL)	A	3	5	2.85	19	4	0	0	47	45	21	15	22	49
1999	Fort Myers (FSL)	A	1	1	2.41	11	0	0	0	19	19	5	5	5	22
	New Britain (EL)	AA	0	1	3.55	6	0	0	0	13	11	5	5	5	12
2000	Fort Myers (FSL)	A	2	2	2.05	29	1	0	4	48	38	20	11	23	52
	New Britain (EL)	AA	3	1	2.86	24	0	0	4	28	19	13	9	8	40
	Salt Lake (PCL)	AAA	0	0	1.59	6	0	0	0	6	5	1	1	1	5
	Minnesota (AL)	MAJ	0	0	8.44	4	0	0	0	5	10	5	5	1	3
MAJOR LEAGUE TOTALS			0	0	8.44	4	0	0	0	5	10	5	5	1	3
MINOR LEAGUE TOTALS			20	20	2.79	202	17	0	40	351	286	146	109	129	386

30. Ruben Salazar, 3b

Born: Jan. 16, 1978. **Ht.:** 5-9. **Wt.:** 162. **Bats:** R. **Throws:** R. **Career Transactions:** Signed out of Venezuela by Twins, June 3, 1997.

Salazar was the Appalachian League MVP in 1999 and joined Tony Oliva as the only Twins to hit .400 in a minor league (Justin Morneau joined the club in 2000). He earned a spot in the Futures Game and continued to hit after jumping to high Class A in 2000, which was crucial because his bat must carry him. Salazar doesn't have a position; his lack of range hampered him at second base last year. He likely will move to third base in 2001, though his arm may not be strong enough to stay there. His power may be lacking, too, as he's more of a gap hitter. His plate discipline deteriorated last year, another discouraging sign.

Year	Club (League)	Class	AVG	G	AB	R	H	2B	3B	HR	RBI	BB	SO	SB
1997	Maracay 1 (VSL)	R	.247	45	81	13	20	4	1	2	9	11	13	2
1998	Twins (GCL)	R	.248	50	161	16	40	5	1	3	25	9	29	10
1999	Elizabethton (Appy)	R	.401	64	262	66	105	24	2	14	65	48	43	11
2000	Fort Myers (FSL)	A	.311	124	499	80	155	25	0	11	64	37	81	3
MINOR LEAGUE TOTALS			.319	283	1003	175	320	58	4	30	163	105	166	26

Montreal
Expos

By Michael Levesque

It wasn't entirely business as usual for the Expos in 2000. Though the team did endure its third straight season with 90-plus losses, the tide of talented players leaving town for financial reasons has stopped for the time being. New owner Jeffery Loria has given the team a much-needed infusion of cash on the major league level, as well as in the scouting and player-development departments.

The biggest and most productive result of the new ownership's willingness to spend will be felt in the stability it will bring to the major league roster and the organization in general. The revolving door of players and front-office staff that has departed over the last several years had created an organization with no direction.

Vladimir Guerrero leads a core of young Montreal talent that also includes Tony Armas, Michael Barrett, Peter Bergeron, Milton Bradley, Carl Pavano, Ugueth Urbina, Javier Vazquez and Jose Vidro. That group compares favorably to any in the game. The key for the Expos will be getting these players, particularly Guerrero, signed to long-term deals while surrounding them with quality veterans.

The Expos have more youngsters on the way in the near future, with righthander Donnie Bridges and outfielder Brad Wilkerson the most likely candidates to make an impact in 2001. Jim Fleming, in his fourth year as scouting director, and Fred Ferreira, director of international operations, continue to bring in prospects. Last summer, Montreal spent more aggressively than ever, handing draft picks Justin Wayne ($2.95 million) and Grady Sizemore ($2 million) club-record bonuses.

General manager Jim Beattie continued to upgrade the talented scouting and development staff as well. Braves crosschecker Tony LaCava was hired in September as farm director, with Don Reynolds moving into an assistant GM role. In October, Mets minor league manager Doug Davis came aboard as minor league field coordinator, a position that was vacant in 2000. A month later, Devil Rays crosschecker Stan Meek assumed the same duties with Montreal, filling a void left when Len Strelitz left the organization to become an agent. The Expos also added a five-man pro scouting staff and restored the Midwest crosschecker position that had been eliminated under the previous regime.

OrganizationOverview

General manager: Jim Beattie. **Farm director:** Tony LaCava. **Scouting director:** Jim Fleming.

2000 PERFORMANCE

Class	Team	League	W	L	Pct.	Finish*	Manager(s)
Majors	Montreal	National	67	95	.414	14th (16)	Felipe Alou
Triple-A	Ottawa Lynx	International	53	88	.376	13th (14)	Jeff Cox/Rick Sweet
Double-A	Harrisburg Senators	Eastern	76	67	.531	5th (12)	Doug Sisson
High A	Jupiter Hammerheads	Florida State	61	79	.436	11th (14)	Luis Dorante
Low A	#Cape Fear Crocs	South Atlantic	64	74	.464	10th (14)	Bill Masse
Short-season	Vermont Expos	New York-Penn	45	30	.600	4th (14)	Tim Leiper
Rookie	GCL Expos	Gulf Coast	17	43	.283	12th (13)	Steve Phillips

OVERALL 2000 MINOR LEAGUE RECORD 315 381 .453 28th (30)

*Finish in overall standings (No. of teams in league). #Affiliate will be in Clinton (Midwest) in 2001.

ORGANIZATION LEADERS

BATTING
*AVG	Rich Lane, Cape Fear	.310
R	Wilken Ruan, Cape Fear	95
H	Wilken Ruan, Cape Fear	165
TB	Brad Wilkerson, Harrisburg/Ottawa	237
2B	Brad Wilkerson, Harrisburg/Ottawa	47
3B	Dan McKinley, Harrisburg	14
HR	Brad Wilkerson, Harrisburg/Ottawa	18
RBI	**Matt Cepicky**, Jupiter	88
	Scott Hodges, Jupiter/Harrisburg	88
BB	Noah Hall, Jupiter/Harrisburg	92
SO	Valentino Pascucci, Cape Fear/Jupiter	113
SB	Wilken Ruan, Cape Fear	64

PITCHING
W	Donnie Bridges, Jupiter/Harrisburg	16
L	Bryan Hebson, Harrisburg	15
#ERA	Donnie Bridges, Jupiter/Harrisburg	2.68
G	Gabe Gonzalez, Harrisburg/Ottawa	58
CG	Donnie Bridges, Jupiter/Harrisburg	6
SV	**Jim Serrano**, Harrisburg	16
IP	Donnie Bridges, Jupiter/Harrisburg	201
BB	Pat Collins, Cape Fear/Jupiter	81
SO	Donnie Bridges, Jupiter/Harrisburg	150

*Minimum 250 at-bats. #Minimum 75 innings.

TOP PROSPECTS OF THE DECADE
1991	Wil Cordero, ss
1992	Wil Cordero, ss
1993	Cliff Floyd, 1b/of
1994	Cliff Floyd, 1b/of
1995	Ugueth Urbina, rhp
1996	Vladimir Guerrero, of
1997	Vladimir Guerrero, of
1998	Brad Fullmer, 1b
1999	Michael Barrett, 3b/c
2000	Tony Armas, rhp

TOP DRAFT PICKS OF THE DECADE
1991	Cliff Floyd, 1b
1992	B.J. Wallace, lhp
1993	Chris Schwab, of
1994	Hiram Bocachica, ss
1995	Michael Barrett, ss
1996	*John Patterson, rhp
1997	Donnie Bridges, rhp
1998	Josh McKinley, ss
1999	Josh Girdley, lhp
2000	Justin Wayne, rhp

*Did not sign.

Cepicky

Serrano

RICH ABEL

BEST TOOLS
Best Hitter for Average	Brad Wilkerson
Best Power Hitter	Felix Lugo
Fastest Baserunner	Wilken Ruan
Best Fastball	Kris Tetz
Best Breaking Ball	Donnie Bridges
Best Control	Donnie Bridges
Best Defensive Catcher	Brian Schneider
Best Defensive Infielder	Wilson Valdez
Best Infield Arm	Felix Lugo
Best Defensive Outfielder	Wilken Ruan
Best Outfield Arm	Wilken Ruan

PROJECTED 2004 LINEUP
Catcher	Michael Barrett
First Base	Brad Wilkerson
Second Base	Jose Vidro
Third Base	Fernando Tatis
Shortstop	Brandon Phillips
Left Field	Grady Sizemore
Center Field	Milton Bradley
Right Field	Vladimir Guerrero
No. 1 Starter	Donnie Bridges
No. 2 Starter	Javier Vazquez
No. 3 Starter	Tony Armas
No. 4 Starter	Carl Pavano
No. 5 Starter	Josh Girdley
Closer	Ugueth Urbina

ALL-TIME LARGEST BONUSES
Justin Wayne, 2000	$2,950,000
Grady Sizemore, 2000	2,000,000
Josh Girdley, 1999	1,700,000
Josh McKinley, 1998	1,250,000
Brad Wilkerson, 1998	1,000,000

DraftAnalysis

2000 Draft

Best Pro Debut: RHP **Derrick DePriest** (17) befuddled hitters with his submarine delivery. He had a combined 11 saves and 1.54 ERA for two Class A teams before becoming one of three pitchers drafted last year to reach Double-A.

Best Athlete: OF Grady Sizemore (3) was one of the most complete athletes in the draft, which is why it cost Montreal $2 million to buy him away from a Washington football scholarship. Besides his impressive physical tools, he also earns praise for his instincts, work ethic and aptitude. The only reason he was available in the third round was due to concerns about his signability.

Best Hitter: Sizemore and another Washington high school product, 3B Seth Johnson (11). Johnson outhit Sizemore .299 to .293 in the Rookie-level Gulf Coast League.

Best Raw Power: Sizemore, though he had just one home run in 205 at-bats in the GCL.

Fastest Runner: 3B Darryl Jenkins (10) is a long strider who can run a 6.6-second 60-yard dash. Sizemore runs a 6.7 and stole 16 bases in 18 attempts in the GCL.

Best Defensive Player: Sizemore again. He gets after balls well in center field.

Best Fastball: LHP Cliff Lee (4) and RHP Thomas Mitchell (5) both can reach 94 mph, with Lee doing so more consistently.

Most Intriguing Background: RHP Justin Wayne (1), the No. 5 overall selection, was the highest-drafted Hawaiian ever. His brother Hawkeye pitches in the Mariners system. DePriest punted for North Carolina's football team.

Closest To The Majors: Wayne, who has an 88-91 mph fastball and a plus slider, is so advanced that he's compared to fellow Stanford product Mike Mussina. He's an innings-eater with excellent makeup. DePriest will continue to rise quickly if batters don't figure out his submarine style.

DePriest

Best Late-Round Pick: Johnson, who figured to go in the first five rounds. DePriest may be a real find as well, and the Expos also like RHP Ben Washburn (14), a fastball-slider guy who had a 1.30 ERA at Class A Cape Fear.

The One Who Got Away: RHP Wes Littleton (7) headlines a banner Cal State Fullerton recruiting class.

Assessment: Are these the Expos? First they lost a second-round pick by signing a free agent, though the wisdom of giving up a pick for Graeme Lloyd is debatable. Then they spent $2.95 million, the draft's third-largest bonus, on Wayne, before breaking the bank again for Sizemore, much to the consternation of the commissioner's office. Wayne's bonus equaled the combined amount Montreal gave its top picks from 1998 and '99.

1999 Draft

LHP Josh Girdley (1) was a signability choice, and he may have been a good one. SS Brandon Phillips (2) is the organization's best position-player prospect, and the Expos are high on OFs Matt Cepicky (4) and Valentino Pascucci (15), and LHP Luke Lockwood (8). **Grade: C+**

1998 Draft

Montreal went cheap with SS Josh McKinley (1) and got what it paid for. The other first-rounder, OF Brad Wilkerson, is a keeper, but this draft petered out quickly after LHP Eric Good (2). **Grade: C**

1997 Draft

The Expos didn't make enough of their eight first-round choices. RHP Donnie Bridges is their top prospect, and 3B Scott Hodges and RHP T.J. Tucker are two other first-rounders on their top 10 list. The other five have faded into obscurity. **Grade: B**

1996 Draft

After losing RHP John Patterson (1) as a loophole free agent, Montreal bounced back with OF Milton Bradley (2). RHP Christian Parker (4) blossomed in 2000—following his trade to the Yankees. **Grade: C**

Note: Draft analysis prepared by Jim Callis. Numbers in parentheses indicate draft rounds.

. . . Bridges has the stuff to blow hitters away, but his ability to throw with command and purpose may be more impressive.

Donnie Bridges
rhp

Born: Dec. 10, 1978.
Ht.: 6-4. **Wt.:** 220.
Bats: R. **Throws:** R.
School: Oak Grove HS, Hattiesburg, Miss.
Career Transactions: Selected by Expos in first round (23rd overall) of 1997 draft; signed July 21, 1997.

Bridges was the first of eight selections the Expos had before the start of the second round in the 1997 draft as compensation for the loss of Moises Alou and Mel Rojas to free agency, and the failure to sign 1996 first-rounder John Patterson. After two undistinguished years, Bridges began to assert himself as a prospect in 1999 and continued his rise last season. After starting 2000 at high Class A Jupiter, he was promoted to Double-A Harrisburg, where Eastern League managers selected him as the circuit's No. 3 prospect. He started 30 games between the two levels and showed the makings of a workhorse, ranking second overall in the minors with 201 total innings. His 16 wins were one off the minor league lead. Bridges pitched briefly in the Arizona Fall League but the Expos wisely sent him home after two outings.

Bridges is a big, strong power pitcher with a full assortment of above-average pitches. Though he has the stuff to blow hitters away, his ability to throw with command and purpose to both sides of the plate may be more impressive. He has an easy delivery and throws a consistent 94-95 mph fastball with late movement. He complements it with a devastating 80-82 mph power curve that gets good spin and bite, and an improving 75-78 mph changeup. Expos officials praise Bridges for his pitching acumen, bulldog makeup and intelligence. He also can wield the bat quite well for a pitcher, as his five pinch-hit at-bats attest. Bridges made huge strides in the control department last year, but still needs to continue to improve the command of his changeup, which he has a habit of overthrowing at times. Like most young pitchers, he needs to be more consistent from start to start. Pitching more than 200 innings at 21 isn't the best way to prepare for a long career, though Bridges wasn't responsible for how he was used.

The Expos are hoping their pitching staff at the major league level returns to health so Bridges can receive a full season at Triple-A Ottawa before he vies for a spot in Montreal. He projects to be an innings eater at the front of a rotation.

Year	Club (League)	Class	W	L	ERA	G	GS	CG	SV	IP	H	R	ER	BB	SO
1997	Expos (GCL)	R	0	2	6.30	5	2	0	0	10	14	9	7	5	6
1998	Vermont (NY-P)	A	5	6	4.90	13	13	0	0	68	71	42	37	37	43
1999	Cape Fear (SAL)	A	6	1	2.28	8	8	1	0	47	37	12	12	17	44
	Jupiter (FSL)	A	4	6	4.09	18	18	1	0	99	116	53	45	36	63
2000	Jupiter (FSL)	A	5	5	3.19	11	11	0	0	73	58	29	26	20	66
	Harrisburg (EL)	AA	11	7	2.39	19	19	6	0	128	104	39	34	49	84
MINOR LEAGUE TOTALS			31	27	3.40	74	71	8	0	425	400	184	161	164	306

2. Brandon Phillips, ss

Born: June 28, 1981. **Ht.:** 5-10. **Wt.:** 170. **Bats:** R. **Throws:** R. **School:** Redan HS,
Stone Mountain, Ga. **Career Transactions:** Selected by Expos in second round of
1999 draft; signed June 21, 1999.

Phillips comes from a family of athletes. His mother was a basketball
star at Shaw University in North Carolina, where she met his father, a
running back on the football team. Brandon's older brother Jamil played
in the Rangers system and his sister Porsha is a nationally ranked junior
sprinter. Brandon has been compared to a young Barry Larkin. He is a
high-ceiling middle infielder with a live, athletic body; an above-average
shortstop with soft hands, solid range, plus arm strength and superior lateral movement.
He's a line-drive hitter with plenty of bat speed and projects above-average power for his
position. Phillips is an average runner with good baserunning skills. The Expos speak highly of his intelligence. For all his tools, Phillips still needs to refine his skills. His youth sometimes shows up in the field and he loses concentration. He's prone to not squaring up on
his throws, causing throwing errors. The Expos have an abundance of slick-fielding shortstops, but he's their long-term answer. He'll begin the 2001 season at high Class A Jupiter.

Year	Club (League)	Class	AVG	G	AB	R	H	2B	3B	HR	RBI	BB	SO	SB
1999	Expos (GCL)	R	.290	47	169	23	49	11	3	1	21	15	35	12
2000	Cape Fear (SAL)	A	.242	126	484	74	117	17	8	11	72	38	97	23
MINOR LEAGUE TOTALS			.254	173	653	97	166	28	11	12	93	53	132	35

3. Brad Wilkerson, of

Born: June 1, 1977. **Ht.:** 6-0. **Wt.:** 190. **Bats:** L. **Throws:** L. **School:** University of
Florida. **Career Transactions:** Selected by Expos in first round (33rd overall) of 1998
draft; signed Aug. 29, 1998.

One of the top two-way players in NCAA history, Wilkerson struggled
when he made his pro debut in 1999. He returned to Double-A and flourished in 2000, earning a promotion to Triple-A and ranking second in the
minors with a combined 47 doubles. He finished the season in Sydney as
the center fielder on the U.S. Olympic team. Bad news came after that,
though, as Wilkerson tried to play in the Arizona Fall League but suc-
cumbed to shoulder pain. He had surgery to repair the labrum and rotator cuff in his left
shoulder in December and was expected to miss spring training. Assuming a full recovery, he
has the classic tools of a right fielder. He has a smooth, compact swing from the left side, with
outstanding bat speed and extension that should enable him to hit with above-average
power. He's disciplined at the plate. He's a solid corner outfielder with a strong arm and average speed. Wilkerson's troubles two years ago were a blessing in disguise. He realized he needed to improve and entered 2000 in much better condition. He lacks the speed to play center,
and with right field blocked by Vladimir Guerrero, Wilkerson could be bound for left or first
base in Montreal. He'll head to Triple-A when he's ready to play again, probably in May.

Year	Club (League)	Class	AVG	G	AB	R	H	2B	3B	HR	RBI	BB	SO	SB
1999	Harrisburg (EL)	AA	.235	138	422	66	99	21	3	8	49	88	100	3
2000	Harrisburg (EL)	AA	.336	66	229	53	77	36	2	6	44	42	38	8
	Ottawa (IL)	AAA	.250	63	212	40	53	11	1	12	35	45	60	5
MINOR LEAGUE TOTALS			.265	267	863	159	229	68	6	26	128	175	198	16

4. Josh Girdley, lhp

Born: Aug. 29, 1980. **Ht.:** 6-3. **Wt.:** 185. **Bats:** L. **Throws:** L. **School:** Jasper
(Texas) HS. **Career Transactions:** Selected by Expos in first round (sixth overall) of
1999 draft; signed June 2, 1999.

Girdley gained national notoriety when he stuck out 29 batters in a 10-
inning game in high school in 1999. He dominated the New York-Penn
League last year and was named the circuit's No. 3 prospect. Girdley has a
projectable body with long arms and legs. He comes at batters with three
above-average pitches: a 92-93 mph fastball with late life, a curveball that
has a tight downward rotation, and a changeup that he throws with excellent arm speed. His mechanics are smooth and effortless, which gives him the potential for
plus command, and he does an outstanding job of repeating his delivery. Girdley is physically immature and needs to add weight and strength. Expos officials rave about the way he
competes but would like to see him pitch inside more. He missed instructional league with a

double hernia but should be fine by spring training. Girdley projects as a frontline starter. He'll get his first taste of full-season ball in 2001 at low Class A Clinton.

Year	Club (League)	Class	W	L	ERA	G	GS	CG	SV	IP	H	R	ER	BB	SO
1999	Expos (GCL)	R	0	2	3.32	12	11	0	1	43	41	19	16	16	49
2000	Vermont (NY-P)	A	5	0	2.95	14	14	0	0	79	60	32	26	28	70
MINOR LEAGUE TOTALS			5	2	3.08	26	25	0	1	123	101	51	42	44	119

5. Justin Wayne, rhp

Born: April 16, 1979. **Ht.:** 6-3. **Wt.:** 200. **Bats:** R. **Throws:** R. **School:** Stanford University. **Career Transactions:** Selected by Expos in first round (fifth overall) of 2000 draft; signed July 20, 2000.

Wayne became the first native Hawaiian selected in the first round of the draft when the Expos grabbed him fifth overall. An All-American at Stanford, where he set school records for single-season victories and career strikeouts, he lost the College World Series championship game in relief against Louisiana State. Wayne, whose brother Hawkeye pitches in the Mariners system, signed for a team-record $2.95 million bonus. Wayne is a polished pitcher with a smooth delivery and four solid pitches. His fastball is more notable for its movement than its 88-91 mph velocity, and his slider is his best pitch. He has a plus changeup and solid curveball, and he can command all of his pitches. The Expos can't say enough about his intelligence and makeup. Wayne has a deep repertoire but doesn't have a go-to pitch that strikes fear in the heart of batters. Though the Expos gave Wayne some time off after his long college season, he's definitely on the fast track. He should get to Double-A this season and could be in Montreal by early 2002.

Year	Club (League)	Class	W	L	ERA	G	GS	CG	SV	IP	H	R	ER	BB	SO
2000	Jupiter (FSL)	A	0	3	5.81	5	5	0	0	26	26	22	17	11	24
MINOR LEAGUE TOTALS			0	3	5.81	5	5	0	0	26	26	22	17	11	24

6. Grady Sizemore, of

Born: Aug. 2, 1982. **Ht.:** 6-2. **Wt.:** 195. **Bats:** L. **Throws:** L. **School:** Cascade (Wash) HS. **Career Transactions:** Selected by Expos in third round of 2000 draft; signed June 8, 2000.

Sizemore was a standout football player—he rushed for 1,199 yards and eight touchdowns as a senior quarterback/running back—who planned to play both baseball and football at Washington before Montreal lured him away with a $2 million bonus. The Expos view Sizemore as a special player. They rave about his athleticism and ability to pick up instruction. He has impressive bat speed, uses the whole field, and has an advanced understanding of the strike zone. He keeps the bat head in the hitting zone a long time and projects to hit with above-average power. He runs a 6.6 60-yard dash and gets good jumps in center field. Sizemore has average arm strength and still displays some stiffness in his throwing stroke because of his football background. Montreal officials believe it will smooth out with time. He has trouble catching up to anything up in the strike zone. Sizemore has the ability and makeup to move quickly. The Expos expect him to start 2001 with short-season Vermont but think Clinton is a realistic possibility.

Year	Club (League)	Class	AVG	G	AB	R	H	2B	3B	HR	RBI	BB	SO	SB
2000	Expos (GCL)	R	.293	55	205	31	60	8	3	1	14	23	24	16
MINOR LEAGUE TOTALS			.293	55	205	31	60	8	3	1	14	23	24	16

7. Scott Hodges, 3b

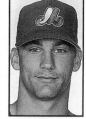

Born: Dec. 26, 1978. **Ht.:** 6-0. **Wt.:** 190. **Bats:** L. **Throws:** R. **School:** Henry Clay HS, Lexington, Ky. **Career Transactions:** Selected by Expos in first round (38th overall) of 1997 draft; signed June 5, 1997.

Hodges is yet another member of Montreal's vaunted 1997 draft bonanza who asserted himself as a bona fide prospect last year. He set career highs across the board while earning a spot on Baseball America's postseason high Class A all-star team. Hodges' best tool is his bat, which is one of the best in the system. He has above-average bat speed with quiet hands to the ball when he strides. He has a smooth, level swing with good top-hand extension and follow-though. Hodges is an aggressive hitter with plus power potential. He's a solid third baseman with an average arm and speed. Hodges shortened his stroke in 2000 and abandoned the high leg kick that had triggered his swing. The changes kept his head still and increased his ability to make contact. He still needs to develop physically and work on the mental aspects of his game. Hodges appeared to be the third baseman of the future until the Expos traded for Fernando Tatis. He should begin the 2000 season at Double-A, with a chance for a promotion to Triple-A.

Year	Club (League)	Class	AVG	G	AB	R	H	2B	3B	HR	RBI	BB	SO	SB
1997	Expos (GCL)	R	.235	57	196	26	46	13	2	2	23	23	47	2
1998	Vermont (NY-P)	A	.278	67	266	35	74	13	3	3	35	11	59	8
1999	Cape Fear (SAL)	A	.258	127	449	62	116	31	2	8	59	45	105	8
2000	Jupiter (FSL)	A	.306	111	422	75	129	32	1	14	83	49	66	8
	Harrisburg (EL)	AA	.176	6	17	2	3	0	0	1	5	2	4	1
MINOR LEAGUE TOTALS			.273	368	1350	200	368	89	8	28	205	130	281	27

8. T.J. Tucker, rhp

Born: Aug. 20, 1978. **Ht.:** 6-3. **Wt.:** 245. **Bats:** R. **Throws:** R. **School:** River Ridge HS, New Port Richey, Fla. **Career Transactions:** Selected by Expos in first round (47th overall) of 1997 draft; signed June 9, 1997.

Tucker began 2000 at Double-A and pitched well in seven starts before a promotion to Montreal. In his second start with the Expos, he left with a strained right forearm. He made one rehab start with Harrisburg before getting shut down for the season and undergoing arthroscopic elbow surgery. Tucker is a big body who's praised for his competitiveness, acumen and feel for pitching. He has outstanding command of a 90-93 mph fastball that has a bit of tail. He supplements his fastball with a nasty 75-78 mph curveball with a 12-to-6 downward break, and a straight changeup. It's imperative that Tucker improve both his strength and conditioning. He lacks command with his curveball at times, but it's a dominant pitch when he throws it for strikes. After pitching well in instructional league, Tucker is expected to be healthy and ready for spring training. If he's able to get in a full Triple-A season, he should challenge for a spot in the Montreal rotation in 2002.

Year	Club (League)	Class	W	L	ERA	G	GS	CG	SV	IP	H	R	ER	BB	SO
1997	Expos (GCL)	R	1	0	1.93	3	2	0	0	5	5	1	1	1	11
1998	Expos (GCL)	R	1	0	0.75	7	7	0	0	36	23	5	3	5	40
	Vermont (NY-P)	A	3	1	2.18	6	6	0	0	33	24	9	8	15	34
	Jupiter (FSL)	A	1	1	1.00	2	1	0	0	9	5	1	1	0	10
1999	Jupiter (FSL)	A	5	1	1.23	7	7	0	0	44	24	7	6	16	35
	Harrisburg (EL)	AA	8	5	4.10	19	19	1	0	116	110	55	53	38	85
2000	Harrisburg (EL)	AA	2	1	3.60	8	8	0	0	45	33	19	18	17	24
	Montreal (NL)	MAJ	0	1	11.57	2	2	0	0	7	11	9	9	3	2
MAJOR LEAGUE TOTALS			0	1	11.57	2	2	0	0	7	11	9	9	3	2
MINOR LEAGUE TOTALS			21	9	2.81	52	50	1	0	288	224	97	90	92	239

9. Wilken Ruan, of

Born: Nov. 18, 1979. **Ht.:** 6-0. **Wt.:** 170. **Bats:** R. **Throws:** R. **Career Transactions:** Signed out of Dominican Republic by Expos, Nov. 15, 1996.

Ruan emerged in 2000, finishing second in the Class A South Atlantic League in hits and stolen bases. Ruan has a wiry athletic body with well-defined muscles and loose flexible actions. He's an outstanding center fielder with well above-average flychasing skills and a cannon for an arm. In addition, he's a top-of-the-scale runner with good first-step quickness and keen baserunning ability. At the plate, Ruan has impressive bat speed and sprays line drives from line to line. He's aggressive at the plate to a fault. He's never going to have much power—he has just six career homers—and needs to concentrate on getting on base. His strike-zone judgment and pitch selection leave a lot to be desired. After two seasons in the Sally League, Ruan is ready for high Class A in 2002. The Expos already have a pair of young center fielders in the big leagues in Peter Bergeron and Milton Bradley, so competition awaits Ruan in the future.

Year	Club (League)	Class	AVG	G	AB	R	H	2B	3B	HR	RBI	BB	SO	SB
1997	Expos (DSL)	R	.348	69	293	53	102	16	5	4	46	31	34	33
1998	Jupiter (FSL)	A	.167	5	18	2	3	0	0	0	0	1	3	2
	Expos (GCL)	R	.239	54	201	22	48	9	3	1	19	5	43	13
1999	Cape Fear (SAL)	A	.224	112	397	43	89	16	4	1	47	18	79	29
2000	Cape Fear (SAL)	A	.287	134	574	95	165	29	10	0	51	24	75	64
MINOR LEAGUE TOTALS			.274	374	1483	215	407	70	22	6	163	79	234	141

10. Luke Lockwood, of

Born: July 21, 1981. **Ht.:** 6-2. **Wt.:** 165. **Bats:** L. **Throws:** L. **School:** Silverado HS, Victorville, Calif. **Career Transactions:** Selected by Expos in eighth round of 1999 draft; signed June 3, 1999.

Lockwood was a standout baseball and football player in high school. He was a two-way star on the diamond, leading his league in homers while dominating on the mound. On the gridiron, he was an all-area quarterback who topped his league in touchdown passes. Lockwood has a lanky athletic frame that projects to get bigger and stronger. His balanced delivery and quick, easy arm action provide the foundation for above-average command. His fastball has good movement and consistently hits 87-90 mph, and he can top out at 91-92 when he needs a little extra. Lockwood also has a nasty curveball with plenty of tilt. His circle changeup is still in the early stages of development because he never had to use it much in high school. With work, it can be a plus pitch. He needs to improve his strength. When Expos officials talk about Lockwood, the first word is always "moxie" or "mature." Those traits are the reason they'll challenge him with a full season in the Florida State League at 19.

Year	Club (League)	Class	W	L	ERA	G	GS	CG	SV	IP	H	R	ER	BB	SO
1999	Expos (GCL)	R	1	2	4.57	11	7	0	0	41	46	21	21	13	32
2000	Jupiter (FSL)	A	0	1	10.93	3	3	0	0	14	24	17	17	5	2
	Vermont (NY-P)	A	1	0	2.25	2	2	0	0	12	12	3	3	1	8
	Cape Fear (SAL)	A	2	4	4.50	9	9	0	0	48	49	32	24	20	33
MINOR LEAGUE TOTALS			4	7	5.07	25	21	0	0	115	131	73	65	39	75

11. Matt Cepicky, of

Born: Nov. 10, 1977. **Ht.:** 6-2. **Wt.:** 215. **Bats:** L. **Throws:** R. **School:** Southwest Missouri State University. **Career Transactions:** Selected by Expos in fourth round of 1999 draft; signed June 12, 1999.

Cepicky made scouts take notice when he ranked among the leaders in all three triple-crown categories in the prestigious Cape Cod League in the summer of 1998, then did the same in NCAA Division I while earning All-America honors the following spring. He's a heavy-hitting outfielder who frequently draws comparisons to Ryan Klesko because of his bat and tools. Power potential and work ethic are Cepicky's strong suits, with his lefthanded power grading out as a 70 on the 20-to-80 scouting scale. His power didn't translate into home runs last season, in part because he doesn't always wait for pitches he can drive. He has good bat speed and makes consistent contact, however. Cepicky runs well for a man his size, and his prowess on the basepaths enabled him to swipe 32 bags last season. Defensively, his range and arm are average for a left fielder. He'll probably open 2001 in Double-A.

Year	Club (League)	Class	AVG	G	AB	R	H	2B	3B	HR	RBI	BB	SO	SB
1999	Vermont (NY-P)	A	.307	74	323	50	99	15	5	12	53	20	49	10
2000	Jupiter (FSL)	A	.299	131	536	61	160	32	7	5	88	24	64	32
MINOR LEAGUE TOTALS			.302	205	859	111	259	47	12	17	141	44	113	42

12. Vince Rooi, 3b

Born: Dec. 13, 1981. **Ht.:** 6-0. **Wt.:** 185. **Bats:** R. **Throws:** R. **Career Transactions:** Signed out of Netherlands by Expos, Aug. 4, 1998.

Rooi signed with the Expos in 1998 after helping the Dutch national team win the European youth championships. He won the Ron Fraser Award as the Netherlands' most talented youth player that year. He's a big kid with an athletic body, and he hasn't stopped growing. Rooi is a polished hitter for his age, though he has been overmatched in his first two seasons in the United States. His stance is similar to Carlos Delgado's, and Rooi has a smooth righthanded stroke with first-rate bat speed, which enables him to drive the ball to all fields when he makes contact. He projects to hit with plus power down the road. At third base, he offers good range, soft hands and a solid arm. Rooi isn't a burner but he doesn't clog up the bases either. Considering he's 19 and has struggled, he might be best off with a third stint in short-season ball this year.

Year	Club (League)	Class	AVG	G	AB	R	H	2B	3B	HR	RBI	BB	SO	SB
1999	Expos (GCL)	R	.189	36	111	17	21	4	0	0	10	22	24	3
2000	Vermont (NY-P)	A	.231	65	234	36	54	9	1	6	43	40	60	9
MINOR LEAGUE TOTALS			.217	101	345	53	75	13	1	6	53	62	84	12

13. Brian Schneider, c

Born: Nov. 26, 1976. **Ht.:** 6-1. **Wt.:** 180. **Bats:** L. **Throws:** R. **School:** Northampton (Pa.) HS. **Career Transactions:** Selected by Expos in fifth round of 1995 draft; signed June 3, 1995.

Schneider made his big league debut in 2000, when he had three separate stints with Montreal. He didn't hit as well in Triple-A or the majors as he had in Double-A the year before, but he still projects as an offensive catcher with power potential. He has a compact swing, and as he continues to add strength and plate discipline, he should increase his power numbers. He has catlike agility behind the plate, with quick feet and outstanding receiving skills. Schneider has only average arm strength but compensates with accuracy and a quick release. He threw out 32 percent of the basestealers who tested him last season. Montreal's offseason trade for Fernando Tatis cemented Michael Barrett's future behind the plate and essentially cut off Schneider's chances of starting for the Expos. But he could make the big league club as his backup in 2001.

Year	Club (League)	Class	AVG	G	AB	R	H	2B	3B	HR	RBI	BB	SO	SB
1995	Expos (GCL)	R	.227	30	97	7	22	3	0	0	4	14	23	2
1996	Expos (GCL)	R	.268	52	164	26	44	5	2	0	23	24	15	2
	Delmarva (SAL)	A	.333	5	9	0	3	0	0	0	1	1	1	0
1997	Cape Fear (SAL)	A	.252	113	381	46	96	20	1	4	49	53	45	3
1998	Cape Fear (SAL)	A	.299	38	134	33	40	7	2	7	30	16	9	6
	Jupiter (FSL)	A	.272	82	302	32	82	12	1	3	30	22	38	4
1999	Harrisburg (EL)	AA	.264	121	421	48	111	19	1	17	66	32	56	2
2000	Ottawa (IL)	AAA	.248	67	238	22	59	22	3	4	31	16	42	1
	Montreal (NL)	MAJ	.235	45	115	6	27	6	0	0	11	7	24	0
MAJOR LEAGUE TOTALS			.235	45	115	6	27	6	0	0	11	7	24	0
MINOR LEAGUE TOTALS			.262	508	1746	214	457	88	10	35	234	178	229	20

14. Henry Mateo, 2b

Born: Oct. 14, 1976. **Ht.:** 5-11. **Wt.:** 180. **Bats:** B. **Throws:** R. **School:** Centro Estudios Libres, Santurce, P.R. **Career Transactions:** Selected by Expos in second round of 1995 draft; signed June 11, 1995.

It has been a slow, steady climb for Mateo. Drafted as shortstop in 1995, he switched to second base to accommodate first-rounder Michael Barrett. Barrett since has become a catcher/third baseman, while Mateo has remained at second. He's a switch-hitting, athletic middle infielder with solid tools across the board. His speed registers a 65 on the 20-to-80 scouting scale, and he enhances it with good first-step quickness. He swings the bat well from both sides of the plate with gap power. Defensively he has smooth actions, plus range and plenty of arm strength. Mateo projects as a No. 2 hitter, but still needs to improve his ability to make contact and draw walks. He made strides in doing so last season. Mateo is ready for Triple-A, though his future is clouded by the emergence of Jose Vidro as a star in Montreal.

Year	Club (League)	Class	AVG	G	AB	R	H	2B	3B	HR	RBI	BB	SO	SB
1995	Expos (GCL)	R	.148	38	122	11	18	0	0	0	6	14	47	2
1996	Expos (GCL)	R	.250	14	44	8	11	3	0	0	3	5	11	5
1997	Vermont (NY-P)	A	.246	67	228	32	56	9	3	1	31	30	44	21
1998	Cape Fear (SAL)	A	.276	114	416	72	115	20	5	4	41	40	111	22
	Jupiter (FSL)	A	.279	12	43	11	12	3	1	0	6	2	6	3
1999	Jupiter (FSL)	A	.260	118	447	69	116	27	7	4	58	44	112	32
2000	Harrisburg (EL)	AA	.287	140	530	91	152	25	11	5	63	58	97	48
MINOR LEAGUE TOTALS			.262	503	1830	294	480	87	27	14	208	193	428	133

15. Britt Reames, rhp

Born: Aug. 19, 1973. **Ht.:** 5-11. **Wt.:** 175. **Bats:** R. **Throws:** R. **School:** The Citadel. **Career Transactions:** Selected by Cardinals in 17th round of 1995 draft; signed June 4, 1995 . . . Traded by Cardinals with 3B Fernando Tatis to Expos for RHP Dustin Hermanson and LHP Steve Kline, Dec. 14, 2000.

Many people think the Expos fleeced the Cardinals when they got Fernando Tatis for Dustin Hermanson and Reames could prove to be a nice throw-in. He was the Cardinals' minor league pitcher of the year in 1996, when he fell one win short of the Class A Midwest League's pitching triple crown. Then he tore a ligament in his elbow, had Tommy John surgery and missed all of 1997 and 1998. Like many recent pitchers, Reames has come back stronger than ever. His fastball now works at 90-93 mph with good sink and run. He complements it with a solid average curveball, a plus changeup and a bulldog mentality on the mound. Reames was effective after joining the Cardinals last year, including allowing just one run in 10 postseason innings. Montreal will give him every opportunity to replace Hermanson in the rotation this spring.

Year	Club (League)	Class	W	L	ERA	G	GS	CG	SV	IP	H	R	ER	BB	SO
1995	New Jersey (NY-P)	A	2	1	1.52	5	5	0	0	30	19	7	5	12	42
	Savannah (SAL)	A	3	5	3.46	10	10	1	0	55	41	23	21	15	63
1996	Peoria (Mid)	A	15	7	1.90	25	25	2	0	161	97	43	34	41	167
1997	Did Not Play—Injured														
1998	Did Not Play—Injured														
1999	Potomac (Car)	A	3	2	3.19					37	34	21	13	21	22
2000	Arkansas (TL)	AA	2	3	6.13	8	8	0	0	40	46	28	27	18	39
	Memphis (PCL)	AAA	6	2	2.28	13	13	2	0	75	55	20	19	20	77
	St. Louis (NL)	MAJ	2	1	2.88	8	7	0	0	41	30	17	13	23	31
MAJOR LEAGUE TOTALS			2	1	2.88	8	7	0	0	41	30	17	13	23	31
MINOR LEAGUE TOTALS			31	20	2.70	71	69	5	0	397	292	142	119	127	410

16. Felix Lugo, 3b

Born: Aug. 1, 1980. **Ht.:** 6-2. **Wt.:** 175. **Bats:** B. **Throws:** R. **Career Transactions:** Signed out of Dominican Republic by Expos, Oct. 20, 1996.

Lugo is a young, raw, work in progress with a great upside. He has spent almost all of his four years in pro ball in short-season leagues and has yet to demonstrate that he's ready for full-season Class A in 2001. But he has an athletic body with loose, flexible actions and a pretty swing from both sides of the plate. Lugo displays good bat speed and has tremendous raw power potential. He also has solid average foot speed with good first-step quickness and baserunning instincts. He's a standout at third base with plus range, soft hands and a strong, accurate arm that has good carry. Lugo still has a lot of work to do. He needs to make much better contact and be far more selective at the plate. He must learn to make adjustments and keep his swing under control. He struggles against both hard stuff in on his hands and breaking pitches in general, and he tends to get pull-conscious. Montreal has been exceedingly patient with Lugo and will continue to be.

Year	Club (League)	Class	AVG	G	AB	R	H	2B	3B	HR	RBI	BB	SO	SB
1997	Expos (DSL)	R	.244	66	250	47	61	14	5	5	36	30	76	24
1998	Expos (GCL)	R	.232	57	194	22	45	9	6	1	26	14	69	9
1999	Expos (GCL)	R	.368	6	19	6	7	2	1	1	4	3	4	2
	Vermont (NY-P)	A	.206	46	170	19	35	6	3	5	25	12	67	3
2000	Jupiter (FSL)	A	.143	2	7	2	1	0	0	0	0	0	3	0
	Vermont (NY-P)	A	.250	39	140	22	35	13	0	3	19	7	47	11
	Cape Fear (SAL)	A	.186	16	59	7	11	2	0	2	7	2	20	3
MINOR LEAGUE TOTALS			.232	232	839	125	195	46	15	17	117	68	286	52

17. Thomas Mitchell, rhp

Born: Nov. 20, 1980. **Ht.:** 6-2. **Wt.:** 190. **Bats:** R. **Throws:** R. **School:** Bladenboro (N.C.) HS. **Career Transactions:** Selected by Expos in fifth round of 2000 draft; signed June 6, 2000.

Mitchell had an impressive resume as an amateur. In the summer of 1999, he was named the top prospect at the East Coast Professional Baseball Showcase and pitched in the Dixie Majors World Series. Last spring, he pitched Bladenboro High to the North Carolina 1-A state championship while going 10-1, 0.39 with 157 strikeouts and 18 walks in 71 innings. Mitchell has a medium-sized pitcher's build with a loose, tension-free arm. His delivery is solid and compact. He throws a 90-94 mph with explosive sink and complements it with a promising 76-78 mph curveball with good spin. The most impressive thing about him is the late break he gets on both his fastball and curve. He also throws a slider and changeup, which are less advanced. After holding his own in the Gulf Coast League, Mitchell probably will step up to Clinton in 2001.

Year	Club (League)	Class	W	L	ERA	G	GS	CG	SV	IP	H	R	ER	BB	SO
2000	Expos (GCL)	R	2	3	3.72	10	9	0	0	46	43	29	19	18	26
MINOR LEAGUE TOTALS			2	3	3.72	10	9	0	0	46	43	29	19	18	26

18. Eric Good, lhp

Born: April 10, 1980. **Ht.:** 6-3. **Wt.:** 180. **Bats:** R. **Throws:** L. **School:** Mishawaka (Ind.) HS. **Career Transactions:** Selected by Expos in second round of 1998 draft; signed June 15, 1998.

Outside of Brad Wilkerson, the Expos don't have a lot to show for their 1998 draft. That crop took a hit in spring training when Good, its second-most promising player, sprained a nerve in his elbow. He didn't pitch in a game until June, then lasted just eight starts before getting shut down. His rehab has gone according to plan, so Good should start 2001 with a clean bill of health. He has a lean, athletic body with an effortless delivery. His two-seam fastball sits in the 88-91 mph range with good life, and should reach 92-94 mph once he fills out. He supplements his fastball with a plus curveball that has a tight rotation and a sharp downward break. Good's approach to pitching is solid, but he needs to get stronger and learn how to compete and not make excuses. If all goes well, he'll start 2001 at Clinton.

Year	Club (League)	Class	W	L	ERA	G	GS	CG	SV	IP	H	R	ER	BB	SO
1998	Expos (GCL)	R	1	2	2.08	6	3	0	0	17	11	4	4	8	20
1999	Vermont (NY-P)	A	5	5	5.79	15	15	0	0	70	77	49	45	30	59
2000	Cape Fear (SAL)	A	1	2	2.75	8	8	0	0	36	31	15	11	12	32
MINOR LEAGUE TOTALS			7	9	4.38	29	26	0	0	123	119	68	60	50	111

19. Luis Torres, rhp

Born: March 12, 1981. **Ht.:** 6-5. **Wt.:** 180. **Bats:** R. **Throws:** R. **Career Transactions:** Signed out of Venezuela by Expos, Nov. 26, 1998.

The Expos outbid the Braves, Indians and Yankees for Torres in 1998, giving him a $300,000 bonus—a club record for an international player since broken by Venezuelan righthander Williams Figueroa, who signed for $400,000 last July. Torres has a major league body with big shoulders, a loose arm action and an easy delivery; all the things scouts like to see in a young pitcher. His fastball has been clocked as high as 92-93 mph with late tailing action, and he complements it with a slider and a straight changeup. An intelligent young man, Torres needs to stay on top of the ball when he throws his slider and learn to pitch inside with command. His first two years as a pro have gone smoothly, and Montreal hopes that trend continues as he makes the jump to full-season Clinton.

Year	Club (League)	Class	W	L	ERA	G	GS	CG	SV	IP	H	R	ER	BB	SO
1999	Expos (GCL)	R	5	3	2.85	12	9	1	0	60	55	28	19	28	36
2000	Vermont (NY-P)	A	7	5	3.43	15	15	0	0	87	82	45	33	34	56
MINOR LEAGUE TOTALS			12	8	3.18	27	24	1	0	147	137	73	52	62	92

20. Valentino Pascucci, of

Born: Nov. 17, 1978. **Ht.:** 6-6. **Wt.:** 225. **Bats:** R. **Throws:** R. **School:** University of Oklahoma. **Career Transactions:** Selected by Expos in 15th round of 1999 draft; signed June 2, 1999.

Pascucci starred in baseball, basketball and water polo in high school, and turned down the Brewers as an 11th-round pick in 1996 to attend Oklahoma. Primarily a pitcher for the Sooners, he caught the eye of Expos area scout Joe Jordan while playing the outfield as a freshman. Pascucci has had no problems hitting as a pro, showing the ability to drive the ball out of any part of the park. He also has exceptional discipline at the plate and average speed on the bases. He has a short swing for a player of his size, reminiscent of Brewers first baseman Richie Sexson. Pascucci has adequate range and a plus arm that makes him a right fielder. He'll have to keep proving himself, and he has earned the chance to do so in Double-A this season.

Year	Club (League)	Class	AVG	G	AB	R	H	2B	3B	HR	RBI	BB	SO	SB
1999	Vermont (NY-P)	A	.351	72	259	62	91	26	1	7	48	53	46	17
2000	Cape Fear (SAL)	A	.319	20	69	17	22	4	0	3	10	16	15	5
	Jupiter (FSL)	A	.284	113	405	70	115	30	2	14	66	66	98	14
MINOR LEAGUE TOTALS			.311	205	733	149	228	60	3	24	124	135	159	36

21. Cliff Lee, lhp

Born: Aug. 30, 1978. **Ht.:** 6-3. **Wt.:** 190. **Bats:** L. **Throws:** L. **School:** University of Arkansas. **Career Transactions:** Selected by Expos in fourth round of 2000 draft; signed July 6, 2000.

Based on pure stuff, the Expos thought Lee was one of the top three college lefthanders available in the 2000 draft. He was selected out of high school by the Marlins (eighth round, 1997) and out of Meridian (Miss.) Community College by the Orioles (20th round, 1998). He has a prototype pitcher's body with long arms and legs. Lee has two plus pitches, an 88-94 mph fastball and a curveball. He also throws a slider and a straight changeup. Lee didn't have much success in 2000 at Arkansas or Cape Fear, primarily because he has an inconsistent delivery that hampers his ability to throw strikes. He has a tendency to lose his stuff quickly after dominating for a couple of innings, and responded when the Razorbacks moved him to the bullpen. Montreal used him as a starter in his pro debut, and will do so again this year in Class A.

Year	Club (League)	Class	W	L	ERA	G	GS	CG	SV	IP	H	R	ER	BB	SO
2000	Cape Fear (SAL)	A	1	4	5.24	11	11	0	0	45	50	39	26	36	63
MINOR LEAGUE TOTALS			1	4	5.24	11	11	0	0	45	50	39	26	36	63

22. Troy Mattes, rhp

Born: Aug. 26, 1975. **Ht.:** 6-7. **Wt.:** 230. **Bats:** R. **Throws:** R. **School:** Miami-Dade CC South. **Career Transactions:** Selected by Expos in 16th round of 1993 draft; signed May 17, 1994.

Mattes spent one season at junior college before signing as a draft-and-follow. He made good progress and made Montreal's top 15 list after the 1996 season. Arm trouble over the next couple of seasons stunted his development until he rebounded in 2000 at Double-A and in the Arizona Fall League, where he ranked fourth with a 1.50 ERA. Mattes has regained his velocity and can maintain it, reaching as high as 97 mph but more regularly pitching in the low 90s. His size allows him to pitch on a nice downhill plane, and he supplements his heat with an 82-83 mph slurve. While he has made enormous progress, some parts of his game still need work. He needs to improve his command of his slurve and changeup, and he needs to learn to set a tempo that will allow him to pitch deeper into games. Mattes will move up to Triple-A this season and could get a look in Montreal at some point.

Year	Club (League)	Class	W	L	ERA	G	GS	CG	SV	IP	H	R	ER	BB	SO
1994	Expos (GCL)	R	3	2	3.40	12	11	1	0	56	35	25	21	21	51
1995	Albany (SAL)	A	0	2	5.03	4	4	0	0	20	21	12	11	12	15
	Vermont (NY-P)	A	3	4	3.72	10	10	0	0	46	51	34	19	25	23
	Expos (GCL)	R	2	0	0.00	2	2	0	0	12	7	0	0	3	8
1996	Delmarva (SAL)	A	10	9	2.86	27	27	5	0	173	142	77	55	50	151
1997	W. Palm Beach (FSL)	A	6	9	4.94	20	16	2	1	102	123	61	56	20	61
1998	Jupiter (FSL)	A	7	6	3.07	17	10	0	0	73	73	33	25	19	42
1999	Jupiter (FSL)	A	3	0	3.70	5	5	0	0	24	27	11	10	7	12
	Harrisburg (EL)	AA	5	8	5.36	20	19	0	0	97	114	67	58	38	58
2000	Harrisburg (EL)	AA	11	9	4.18	28	28	4	0	174	170	91	81	56	109
MINOR LEAGUE TOTALS			50	49	3.89	145	132	12	1	778	763	411	336	251	530

23. Josh Reding, ss

Born: March 7, 1977. **Ht.:** 6-2. **Wt.:** 175. **Bats:** R. **Throws:** R. **School:** Rancho Santiago (Calif.) JC. **Career Transactions:** Selected by Expos in third round of 1997 draft; signed June 8, 1997.

As a freshman pitcher in junior college, Reding caught the eye of former Expos area scout Mark Baca, who became even more impressed by Reding's overall athleticism when he moved to shortstop. He was named the South Atlantic League's best defensive shortstop in 1998, but the highlights have dwindled since then. He's still outstanding with the glove, as he has soft hands to go with above-average arm strength and range. He also has plus speed and the instincts to steal bases. But Reding's career .311 on-base percentage and .300 slugging percentage beg the question about whether he'll ever hit enough to play in the major leagues. He has good balance and bat speed, but he lacks the strength to drive the ball and the selectivity to make consistent contact and get on base. At times he'll let a bad at-bat affect his play in the field. After a disastrous 2000 performance in Double-A, Reding should return there and try again this season.

Year	Club (League)	Class	AVG	G	AB	R	H	2B	3B	HR	RBI	BB	SO	SB
1997	Expos (GCL)	R	.255	56	196	34	50	11	1	2	19	22	31	14
	Vermont (NY-P)	A	.167	8	24	2	4	2	1	0	0	3	11	0
1998	Cape Fear (SAL)	A	.233	73	253	32	59	6	0	1	21	22	71	13
	Expos (GCL)	R	.375	2	8	2	3	1	0	0	0	0	3	1
	Jupiter (FSL)	A	.250	4	12	2	3	1	0	0	2	0	3	0
1999	Jupiter (FSL)	A	.263	121	415	54	109	10	2	2	31	22	73	30
2000	Harrisburg (EL)	AA	.219	137	457	58	100	11	5	2	48	58	110	25
MINOR LEAGUE TOTALS			.240	401	1365	184	328	42	9	7	121	127	302	83

24. Josh McKinley, 2b

Born: Sept. 14, 1979. **Ht.:** 6-2. **Wt.:** 200. **Bats:** B. **Throws:** R. **School:** Malvern (Pa.) Prep School. **Career Transactions:** Selected by Expos in first round (11th overall) of 1998 draft; signed June 3, 1998.

McKinley was the 11th overall selection in the 1998 draft, in large part because he agreed to a predraft deal for a below-market $1.25 million. He was named to the Gulf Coast League all-star team in his pro debut but has stalled in low Class A since then. Drafted as a shortstop, McKinley now finds himself at second base. The Expos are pleased with the adjustments that he has made defensively. Now he needs to the same at the plate. He has a short swing from both sides of the plate and he's willing to draw a walk. But his occasional gap power isn't an acceptable tradeoff for inconsistent contact. He has average speed and can steal bases with his terrific instincts. The Florida State League will provide a strong test for McKinley this season.

Year	Club (League)	Class	AVG	G	AB	R	H	2B	3B	HR	RBI	BB	SO	SB
1998	Expos (GCL)	R	.269	57	208	36	56	11	5	1	19	24	40	14
	Vermont (NY-P)	A	.136	6	22	2	3	0	0	0	4	1	9	0
1999	Cape Fear (SAL)	A	.262	48	168	18	44	12	0	0	17	16	38	9
	Vermont (NY-P)	A	.251	69	283	47	71	12	3	4	32	33	52	9
2000	Cape Fear (SAL)	A	.256	129	480	73	123	34	3	5	64	54	100	46
MINOR LEAGUE TOTALS			.256	309	1161	176	297	69	11	10	136	128	239	78

25. Wilson Valdez, ss

Born: May 20, 1980. **Ht.:** 5-11. **Wt.:** 150. **Bats:** R. **Throws:** R. **Career Transactions:** Signed out of Dominican Republic by Expos, Feb. 4, 1997.

Valdez was signed out of Nizao Bani, the same hometown as Vladimir Guerrero. An outstanding defensive shortstop with instincts beyond his years, he possesses soft hands and excellent range. His arm strength is above-average and he has quick, smooth actions to the ball. His body has matured and started to fill out since he came to the United States in 1999. He projects as a line-drive hitter with potential gap power, but he has a long swing and is too impatient at the plate. Valdez makes the most of his average speed by getting solid jumps and reads on the basepaths. As with Josh Reding and Josh McKinley, Valdez will have to hit in order to show off his defensive prowess in Montreal. He's finally ready for his first extended stint in full-season ball.

Year	Club (League)	Class	AVG	G	AB	R	H	2B	3B	HR	RBI	BB	SO	SB
1997	Expos (DSL)	R	.303	62	244	39	74	13	1	2	29	25	19	19
1998	Expos (DSL)	R	.300	64	247	42	74	9	0	3	30	19	12	15
1999	Expos (GCL)	R	.293	22	82	12	24	2	0	0	7	5	7	10
	Vermont (NY-P)	A	.246	36	130	19	32	7	0	1	10	7	21	4
2000	Vermont (NY-P)	A	.266	65	248	32	66	8	1	1	30	17	32	16
	Cape Fear (SAL)	A	.245	15	49	6	12	2	0	0	3	2	9	3
MINOR LEAGUE TOTALS			.282	264	1000	150	282	41	2	7	109	75	100	51

26. Danny Rombley, of

Born: Nov. 26, 1979. **Ht.:** 6-1. **Wt.:** 185. **Bats:** R. **Throws:** R.. **Career Transactions:** Signed out of Netherlands by Expos, Dec. 14, 1998.

Rombley caught the eye of Expos officials with his athleticism while playing for the Netherlands at the 1997 World Junior Championship. The native Aruban immediately was converted to the outfield and adjusted quickly. Though he played mainly left field in 2000, Rombley is a quality defender with a strong, accurate arm. He did play some center and right and should be able to handle a more challenging position. He moves instinctively at the crack of the bat and has outstanding fly-chasing skills. Rombley roams the basepaths with plus speed and heady baserunning skills. He's an aggressive gap hitter with quick hands and wrists, good strength and some power. But like many of the position players on the second half of this list, Rombley has done little with the bat since turning pro. Both his pitch recognition and strike-zone judgment are raw. He was overmatched in his first taste of full-season ball, and may not be ready to try that level again at the beginning of 2001.

Year	Club (League)	Class	AVG	G	AB	R	H	2B	3B	HR	RBI	BB	SO	SB
1999	Expos (GCL)	R	.246	45	134	20	33	4	1	0	15	12	29	8
2000	Cape Fear (SAL)	A	.258	24	89	8	23	1	2	0	10	2	30	2
	Vermont (NY-P)	A	.234	49	192	32	45	3	2	0	28	16	51	14
MINOR LEAGUE TOTALS			.243	118	415	60	101	8	5	0	53	30	110	24

27. Jose Docen, ss/2b

Born: Jan. 10, 1980. **Ht.:** 5-9. **Wt.:** 160. **Bats:** B. **Throws:** R. **Career Transactions:** Signed out of Dominican Republic by Expos, May 11, 1998.

Docen made his pro debut by batting .227 with 34 steals in the Dominican Summer League. Expos director of international operations Fred Ferreira told Docen he would give him a visa to play in the United States if he batted .300 and stole 50 bases in 1999. He had a .361 average that year while stealing 49 bases, which Ferreira deemed close enough. Docen began last year in extended spring training, spent six weeks at Class A Cape Fear and headed to Vermont when short-season leagues opened in June. He's not very big, but he's a gamer with shortstop tools. He has smooth, quick feet with good range and excellent body control. His arm strength is a bit above-average and his hands are adequate for the position. Docen is a switch-hitter with bat speed but little power. He's short to the ball and makes consistent contact, and more important, he has a solid understanding of the strike zone for a young player. He has above-average speed and his overall baserunning grades out at 65 on the 20-to-80 scouting scale. Docen is likely to play at Clinton in 2001.

Year	Club (League)	Class	AVG	G	AB	R	H	2B	3B	HR	RBI	BB	SO	SB
1998	Expos (DSL)	R	.227	60	203	47	46	3	2	3	20	57	41	34
1999	Expos (DSL)	R	.361	68	244	63	88	9	1	2	23	71	31	49
2000	Cape Fear (SAL)	A	.276	34	116	19	32	3	0	0	15	14	18	6
	Vermont (NY-P)	A	.293	59	229	44	67	16	2	0	30	34	33	27
MINOR LEAGUE TOTALS			.294	221	792	173	233	31	5	5	88	176	123	116

28. Kris Tetz, rhp

Born: Sept. 3, 1978. **Ht.:** 6-5. **Wt.:** 230. **Bats:** R. **Throws:** R. **School:** Lodi (Calif.) HS. **Career Transactions:** Selected by Expos in second round of 1997 draft; signed June 12, 1997.

After righthander Jorge Julio was traded to the Orioles in December for third baseman Ryan Minor, Tetz inherited Julio's title as having the best fastball in the system. Tetz has a mature body made for power pitching. His fastball tops out in the 94-96 mph range and features good boring action and life. The reason he doesn't rank higher is that he doesn't have much else going for him at this point. He scrapped his curveball last season at the suggestion of Montreal officials, and while his slider has plus potential, it still needs considerable work. He throws a changeup that isn't terribly effective. The Expos have cleaned up Tetz' delivery, but he can be erratic with his release point, causing problems with his command. He got hit after his promotion to high Class A, where he'll probably return in 2001. Tetz moved to the bullpen last year, and the Expos believe he has a chance to be a closer.

Year	Club (League)	Class	W	L	ERA	G	GS	CG	SV	IP	H	R	ER	BB	SO
1997	Expos (GCL)	R	0	0	4.15	3	0	0	0	4	2	2	2	3	5
1998	Vermont (NY-P)	A	5	5	3.79	17	11	0	1	76	76	41	32	19	51
1999	Expos (GCL)	R	0	0	2.25	1	0	0	0	4	1	1	1	1	4
	Cape Fear (SAL)	A	3	3	4.35	10	9	0	0	50	54	25	24	12	36
2000	Cape Fear (SAL)	A	1	0	5.64	19	0	0	6	22	15	19	14	18	19
	Jupiter (FSL)	A	1	3	3.91	25	0	0	9	25	30	13	11	18	19
MINOR LEAGUE TOTALS			10	11	4.16	75	20	0	16	182	178	101	84	71	134

29. Lorvin Leandro Louisa, of

Born: Feb. 7, 1983. **Ht.:** 6-4. **Wt.:** 190. **Bats:** R. **Throws:** R. **Career Transactions:** Signed out of Curacao (Netherlands Antilles) by Expos, July 15, 1999.

Louisa is from Willemstad, Curacao, the hometown of Braves all-star Andruw Jones. He made his debut last season, and Montreal was more pleased with his performance than the numbers would indicate. He's loaded with raw talent. He's a towering athlete with long arms and legs, and he projects to get bigger and stronger. The Expos envision him reaching 220 pounds by the time he fills out. Though he's too aggressive at the plate, he looks like he'll hit for plus power down the road. He has a quick bat but needs a trigger to get his swing started. He also offers speed and first-step quickness. As a corner outfielder, Louisa has good range and above-average arm strength. His throwing mechanics will need adjustments. Because he's so raw, he might not be ready for full-season ball for a couple of years.

Year	Club (League)	Class	AVG	G	AB	R	H	2B	3B	HR	RBI	BB	SO	SB
2000	Expos (GCL)	R	.136	38	118	7	16	4	1	0	6	11	49	1
MINOR LEAGUE TOTALS			.136	38	118	7	16	4	1	0	6	11	49	1

30. Jason Norderum, lhp

Born: Nov. 21, 1981. **Ht.:** 6-1. **Wt.:** 185. **Bats:** L. **Throws:** L. **School:** Sacramento CC. **Career Transactions:** Selected by Expos in 31st round of 1999 draft; signed May 16, 2000.

Norderum became one of 2000's top draft-and-follow prospects after an outstanding season at Sacramento City College. He pitched well at one of the nation's best junior college programs, going 9-1, 2.10 with 91 strikeouts in 65 innings. He decided to sign with Montreal for a $500,000 bonus rather than going back into the draft. Norderum has a mature pitcher's body with strong legs and thighs. He has a solid, balanced delivery that should translate into plus command, though he struggled with his control in his pro debut. Norderum throws an 87-92 mph fastball with above-average movement and a curveball with nice downward break. His third pitch is a changeup that's still in development. The Expos expect bigger things out of him this year, when he'll open at Clinton.

Year	Club (League)	Class	W	L	ERA	G	GS	CG	SV	IP	H	R	ER	BB	SO
2000	Vermont (NY-P)	A	5	3	3.77	15	15	0	0	76	66	44	32	47	40
MINOR LEAGUE TOTALS			5	3	3.77	15	15	0	0	76	66	44	32	47	40

New York
Mets

By Lacy Lusk

General manager Steve Phillips and his staff have built a pennant winner, a team with enough stars that he could tell Alex Rodriguez to look elsewhere over the winter. They may not be the toast of New York, but the Mets have a core of veterans and up-and-comers capable of making another run at the World Series. The question is how long their window of opportunity will remain open.

Eight members of the projected 2001 pitching staff—which won't include departed free agent Mike Hampton—are older than 30. So is the heart of the batting order: catcher Mike Piazza, third baseman Robin Ventura and first baseman Todd Zeile. Conventional wisdom is that Piazza should move to first base, perhaps after Zeile's contract expires following the 2002 season, but the Mets might have to go find catching help. They're low on catching prospects, and in fact they're pretty slim in all areas except pitching and outfielders.

Phillips hasn't been reluctant to trade young players for veterans. Many of those deals have worked out, but to get guys like Hampton, Al Leiter and Piazza he has parted with A.J. Burnett, Octavio Dotel and Preston Wilson. Two 1999 trades with the Athletics netted disappointing Kenny Rogers and Billy Taylor and cost Jason Isringhausen and Terrence Long. Alex Escobar likely would have been sent to Cincinnati for Barry Larkin last summer had Larkin not vetoed the trade.

And the Mets' recent draft history is spotty. They haven't really hit on a first-round pick since 1994, when they took Long and Jay Payton. There's just one first-rounder in the top 10, and lefthander Billy Traber joined the organization in 2000. Of the five draft picks in the top 10, three were taken in the 11th round or later. That means that the club has made some astute late picks—but hasn't done much earlier.

This year, the organization will hope playoff wonder Timoniel Perez proves he's not a flash in the pan in right field. If he continues to develop, that should give the Mets an easy transition to an outfield that will include Escobar and/or Brian Cole in the next season or two. Combined with Payton, the outfielders could make life easier on a rotation that had to plug a few holes. Free agents Kevin Appier and Steve Trachsel were signed because the system didn't have replacements ready.

OrganizationOverview

General manager: Steve Phillips. **Farm director:** Jim Duquette. **Scouting director:** Gary LaRocque.

2000 PERFORMANCE

Class	Team	League	W	L	Pct.	Finish*	Manager
Majors	New York	National	94	68	.580	4th (16)	Bobby Valentine
Triple-A	Norfolk Tides	International	65	79	.452	10th (14)	John Gibbons
Double-A	Binghamton Mets	Eastern	82	58	.586	2nd (12)	Doug Davis
High A	St. Lucie Mets	Florida State	81	58	.583	3rd (14)	Dave Engle
Low A	Capital City Bombers	South Atlantic	56	81	.409	t-12th (14)	John Stephenson
Short-season	#Pittsfield Mets	New York-Penn	38	37	.507	7th (14)	Tony Tijerina
Rookie	Kingsport Mets	Appalachian	35	32	.522	4th (10)	Edgar Alfonzo
OVERALL 2000 MINOR LEAGUE RECORD			357	344	.509	13th (30)	

*Finish in overall standings (No. of teams in league). #Affiliate will be in Brooklyn (New York-Penn) in 2001.

ORGANIZATION LEADERS

BATTING

*AVG	Mike Kinkade, Binghamton	.366
R	Brian Cole, St. Lucie/Binghamton	104
H	Brian Cole, St. Lucie/Binghamton	166
TB	Brian Cole, St. Lucie/Binghamton	272
2B	Earl Snyder, St. Lucie	36
3B	Alex Escobar, Binghamton	7
	Brian Cole, St. Lucie/Binghamton	7
HR	**Robert Stratton**, St. Lucie	29
RBI	Earl Snyder, St. Lucie	93
BB	Ryan McGuire, Norfolk	87
SO	**Robert Stratton**, St. Lucie	180
SB	Brian Cole, St. Lucie/Binghamton	69

PITCHING

W	Pat Strange, St. Lucie/Binghamton	14
L	Three tied at	12
#ERA	Jason Roach, Binghamton/St. Lucie	2.58
G	Corey Brittan, Binghamton	55
CG	Grant Roberts, Norfolk	5
SV	Jerrod Riggan, Binghamton	28
IP	Grant Roberts, Norfolk	157
BB	Jason Saenz, St. Lucie	83
SO	Dicky Gonzalez, Binghamton	138
	Jeremy Griffiths, Capital City	138

*Minimum 250 at-bats. #Minimum 75 innings.

TOP PROSPECTS OF THE DECADE

1991	Anthony Young, rhp
1992	Todd Hundley, c
1993	Bobby Jones, rhp
1994	Bill Pulsipher, lhp
1995	Bill Pulsipher, lhp
1996	Paul Wilson, rhp
1997	Jay Payton, of
1998	Grant Roberts, rhp
1999	Alex Escobar, of
2000	Alex Escobar, of

TOP DRAFT PICKS OF THE DECADE

1991	Al Shirley, of
1992	Preston Wilson, ss
1993	Kirk Presley, rhp
1994	Paul Wilson, rhp
1995	Ryan Jaroncyk, ss
1996	Robert Stratton, of
1997	Geoff Goetz, lhp
1998	Jason Tyner, of
1999	Neal Musser, lhp (2)
2000	Billy Traber, lhp

Stratton

Griffiths

BEST TOOLS

Best Hitter for Average	Chris Basak
Best Power Hitter	Robert Stratton
Fastest Baserunner	Brian Cole
Best Fastball	Nick Maness
Best Breaking Ball	Grant Roberts
Best Control	Pat Strange
Best Defensive Catcher	Jason Phillips
Best Defensive Infielder	Jose Reyes
Best Infield Arm	Enrique Cruz
Best Defensive Outfielder	Timoniel Perez
Best Outfield Arm	Alex Escobar

PROJECTED 2004 LINEUP

Catcher	Mike Piazza
First Base	Robin Ventura
Second Base	Edgardo Alfonzo
Third Base	Enrique Cruz
Shortstop	Rey Ordonez
Left Field	Brian Cole
Center Field	Jay Payton
Right Field	Alex Escobar
No. 1 Starter	Pat Strange
No. 2 Starter	Al Leiter
No. 3 Starter	Kevin Appier
No. 4 Starter	Grant Roberts
No. 5 Starter	Glendon Rusch
Closer	Armando Benitez

ALL-TIME LARGEST BONUSES

Geoff Goetz, 1997	$1,700,000
Paul Wilson, 1994	1,550,000
Jason Tyner, 1998	1,070,000
Robert Stratton, 1996	975,000
Kirk Presley, 1993	900,000

DraftAnalysis

2000 Draft

Best Pro Debut: SS Chris Basak (6) hit .349 to win the short-season New York-Penn League batting title and stole 32 bases. RHP Chad Bowen (9) was co-pitcher of the year in the Rookie-level Appalachian League after going 7-2, 3.00.

Best Athlete: Basak or OF Jeff Duncan (7). OF Skyler Fulton (25) was one of the better athletes in the draft but chose not to sign.

Best Hitter: Basak.

Best Raw Power: C John Wilson (11) didn't homer in the NY-P, but his 16 doubles are indicative of his power potential. In the last two years in college at Kentucky, Wilson hit 41 homers.

Fastest Runner: Duncan has above-average speed, though it doesn't compare to that of SS Angel Pagan, a draft-and-follow from 1999 who signed in May. Basak also has good speed.

Best Defensive Player: Basak has solid range and hands at shortstop. Duncan is a standout center fielder.

Best Fastball: In the first five rounds, the Mets got five pitchers who can throw in the low 90s. The guy who throws the hardest most often is RHP Quenten Patterson (5).

Most Intriguing Background: Wilson was nearly killed in September 1996 when his father, who was stalking his mother, fired two shotgun blasts through a door, striking Wilson in the chest. 3B Brett Harper (45), who didn't sign and is attending Scottsdale (Ariz.) CC, is the son of former big leaguer Brian.

Closest To The Majors: It's still LHP **Billy**

Traber (1), though his $1.7 million bonus was slashed to $400,000 when a routine physical revealed elbow damage that he did not know about and had apparently pitched with. He throws an 88-91 mph fastball and a plus splitter, and he gets ahead of hitters. He threw well in instructional league and will make his pro debut in the spring.

Traber

Best Late-Round Pick: Wilson. In addition to his power, the Mets like his arm and the way he takes charge behind the plate.

The One Who Got Away: Fulton couldn't be swayed from playing running back and outfield for Arizona State. 1B Todd Faulkner was a first-team All-American after batting .423-22-103 as a junior at Auburn, setting a handful of school records in the process. As a fifth-year senior, Faulkner will still remain eligible to sign with the Mets until a week before the 2001 draft.

Assessment: As compensation for losing John Olerud to free agency, the Mets received a pair of first-round picks that they turned into Traber and RHP Bob Keppel. Ten of the 14 players they signed out of the first 20 rounds were pitchers, and they have some promising arms, especially if Traber proves his elbow will not be a long-term problem.

1999 Draft

The Mets didn't pick in the first round and didn't distinguish themselves afterward. LHP Neal Musser (2) and RHPs Jake Joseph (2) and Jeremy Griffiths (3) are the best of a lean crop. OF Angel Pagan (4, draft-and-follow) has some speed.   **Grade: C–**

1998 Draft

New York's Nos. 2 and 3 prospects are RHP Pat Strange (2) and OF Eric Cole (18). RHP Ken Chenard (46, draft-and-follow) could be another Jason Isringhausen, and OF Jason Tyner (1) reached the majors last year before being traded to Tampa Bay.   **Grade: B**

1997 Draft

LHP Geoff Goetz (1) and OF Cesar Crespo (3) were shipped to Florida in deals for Mike Piazza and Al Leiter, respectively. Of the players who remain, RHPs Tyler Walker (2), Nick Maness (12) and Eric Cammack (13) have the best shot.   **Grade: C**

1996 Draft

LHP Ed Yarnall (3) and LHP Scott Comer (10) went to the Marlins in trades for Piazza and Dennis Cook, respectively. OF Robert Stratton (1) could be the next Rob Deer or the next Earl Cunningham.   **Grade: C–**

Note: Draft analysis prepared by Jim Callis. Numbers in parentheses indicate draft rounds.

. . . Escobar could be the most exciting player in a young, talented Mets outfield in the near future.

Alex Escobar of

Born: Sept. 6, 1978.
Ht.: 6-1. **Wt.:** 185.
Bats: R. **Throws:** R.
Career Transactions: Signed out of Venezuela by Mets, July 1, 1995.

When Escobar has been healthy, he has been awesome. He's capable of playing any of the three outfield positions, is projected as a 20-30 stolen base threat in the big leagues, can hit for average and power and has an above-average arm. The only problem is that before 2000, those tools often were on the disabled list. In his first four years in the system, Escobar averaged just 153 at-bats a season. He was restricted to three games in 1999 because of two injuries: a lower-back problem and then a separated left shoulder that required surgery. Despite the lost season, he remained the organization's No. 1 prospect because no one could forget his scintillating 1998 season at Class A Capital City, when he hit .310-27-91 while stealing 49 bases. He was as good a power/speed combination as anyone in the minor leagues.

At Double-A Binghamton in 2000, Escobar did all the things he needed to do and stayed healthy while doing them. His work with a personal trainer paid off as he hit well after a slow start. Almost halfway through the year, he had just four stolen bases. That was by design, though, so his sore hamstrings could heal. Afterward, he was back to his Sally League dominance on the bases, finishing with 24 steals. All of his other tools looked as impressive as they had two seasons earlier. By all accounts, Escobar just needs the benefit of time. In the outfield, he could use improvement on picking up hard-hit ground balls and on the accuracy of his throws. He'll still have to answer questions about his durability and scouts would like to see him cut down on his strikeouts, but Escobar could be the most exciting player in a young, talented Mets outfield in the near future.

Escobar is seen as a pure center fielder, but incumbent Jay Payton has a slight defensive edge on him at that spot and probably will push Escobar to right. As long as the Mets' top prospect keeps his health, he'll get a chance to show off his skills as an everyday player at Triple-A Norfolk in 2001. If all goes well, he may get a chance to continue New York's recent tradition of finding key late-season outfield additions from the farm system.

Year	Club (League)	Class	AVG	G	AB	R	H	2B	3B	HR	RBI	BB	SO	SB
1996	Mets (GCL)	R	.360	24	75	15	27	4	0	0	10	4	9	7
1997	Kingsport (Appy)	R	.194	10	36	6	7	3	0	0	3	3	8	1
	Mets (GCL)	R	.247	26	73	12	18	4	1	1	11	10	17	0
1998	Capital City (SAL)	A	.310	112	416	90	129	23	5	27	91	54	133	49
1999	Mets (GCL)	R	.375	2	8	1	3	2	0	0	1	1	2	0
	St. Lucie (FSL)	A	.667	1	3	1	2	0	0	1	3	1	1	1
2000	Binghamton (EL)	AA	.288	122	437	79	126	25	7	16	67	57	114	24
MINOR LEAGUE TOTALS			.298	297	1048	204	312	61	13	45	186	130	284	82

2. Pat Strange, rhp

JOANNE COLENZO

Born: Aug. 23, 1980. **Ht.:** 6-5. **Wt.:** 240. **Bats:** R. **Throws:** R. **School:** Central HS, Springfield, Mass. **Career Transactions:** Selected by Mets in second round of 1998 draft; signed July 29, 1998.

The organization's minor league pitcher of the year, Strange has advanced faster than expected for a New Englander who didn't get a full year of baseball until 1999. He is durable and shows no signs of the loss in velocity that dropped him out of the first round of the 1998 draft. Strange has a nice feel for his offspeed stuff. His best pitch might be a changeup that he cuts a little, giving it the appearance of a slider when it feeds off his fastball. When he stays on top of his pitches, he has heavy sink on his 91-94 mph fastball and excellent control. He loves to have the ball late in the game. Compared to Bill Pulsipher because of how quickly he tackled Double-A, Strange already was considered a righthanded Pulsipher because of concerns about his mechanics. The Mets think Strange will overcome his inconsistent delivery, but his motion is something he'll always battle. An exception in the organization's philosophy, he doesn't throw a curveball. His slider needs improvement. Look for Strange to start 2001 back in Double-A, with an excellent chance at a taste of Triple-A by the halfway mark.

Year	Club (League)	Class	W	L	ERA	G	GS	CG	SV	IP	H	R	ER	BB	SO
1998	Mets (GCL)	R	1	1	1.42	4	4	0	0	19	18	3	3	7	19
1999	Capital City (SAL)	A	12	5	2.63	28	21	2	1	154	138	57	45	29	113
2000	St. Lucie (FSL)	A	10	1	3.58	19	13	2	0	88	78	48	35	32	77
	Binghamton (EL)	AA	4	3	4.55	10	10	0	0	55	62	30	28	30	36
MINOR LEAGUE TOTALS			27	10	3.16	61	48	4	1	316	296	138	111	98	245

3. Brian Cole, of

JOHN SPEAR

Born: Sept. 28, 1978. **Ht.:** 5-9. **Wt.:** 168. **Bats:** R. **Throws:** R. **School:** Navarro (Texas) JC. **Career Transactions:** Selected by Mets in 18th round of 1998 draft; signed June 23, 1998.

If Cole were a couple of inches taller, he would have been a much higher draft pick after he was named Baseball America's Junior College Player of the Year in 1998. He and similarly diminutive Timoniel Perez are two of the most exciting prospects in the system. Cole has a combination similar to Alex Escobar in terms of his power, speed, aggressiveness at the plate and baserunning instincts. He's a plus defensive player and his arm—a notch below Escobar's—is at least average. Likely a future No. 2, 3 or 6 hitter in a major league lineup, Cole projects as more of an RBI threat than a speedster. He has a sweet swing and gets power Perez won't ever have, but Cole can be a little too pull-conscious. He also could stand to draw a few more walks. Cole's only cold spell last year came in his first few weeks in Double-A after a midseason promotion, but he adjusted and thrived, then finished strong in the Arizona Fall League. He's expected to try switch-hitting this spring, and that may carry over to Binghamton for the start of the minor league season.

Year	Club (League)	Class	AVG	G	AB	R	H	2B	3B	HR	RBI	BB	SO	SB
1998	Kingsport (Appy)	R	.300	56	230	36	69	13	8	5	35	7	23	15
	Pittsfield (NY-P)	A	.250	2	8	0	2	1	0	0	1	0	1	1
1999	Capital City (SAL)	A	.316	125	500	97	158	41	4	18	71	37	77	50
2000	St. Lucie (FSL)	A	.312	91	375	73	117	26	5	15	61	29	51	54
	Binghamton (EL)	AA	.278	46	176	31	49	9	2	4	25	13	28	15
MINOR LEAGUE TOTALS			.306	320	1289	237	395	90	19	42	193	86	180	135

4. Timoniel Perez, of

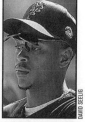

DAVID SEELIG

Born: April 8, 1977. **Ht.:** 5-9. **Wt.:** 167. **Bats:** L. **Throws:** L. **Career Transactions:** Contract purchased by Mets from Hiroshima (Japan), March 27, 2000.

Though Perez' bubble burst in the World Series, he was an important part of the Mets' run in October. He provided an invaluable spark to the team in the National League playoffs but might be most remembered for getting thrown out at home plate by Derek Jeter in the World Series. Before he became Derek Bell's postseason replacement, he was signed by the Mets in 2000 after four years in Japan, mostly in the minor leagues. Hiroshima signed him out of its academy in the Dominican Republic. Perez already has stepped into the big leagues and shown what he can do. He stood out with his offense, defense and excitement on the bases. The Mets see him as a leadoff hitter who has a little punch. He covers ground in the gap and has good accuracy on his throws. Perez' weaknesses are almost identical to Brian Cole's. The Yankees exposed his impatience by getting him to chase breaking stuff out of the zone. His arm strength is only average. Perez should open 2001 as at least the Mets' platoon right fielder. He'll be more of a known commodity to National League pitchers and must make adjustments, and for that reason some scouts wonder if his postseason performance might be a flash in the pan. He'll also have to hold off a bevy of outfielders who will be competing for major league outfield spots.

Year	Club (League)	Class	AVG	G	AB	R	H	2B	3B	HR	RBI	BB	SO	SB
1994	Hiroshima (DSL)	R	.340	51	206	40	70	9	8	0	21	31	7	8
1995					Played in Japanese minor leagues									
1996	Hiroshima (CL)	JAP	.278	31	54	8	15	1	0	1	7	2	7	3
1997	Hiroshima (CL)	JAP	.245	86	139	17	34	4	2	3	15	10	16	2
	Hiroshima (WL)	JAP	.304	19	69	9	21	3	1	2	12	10	3	9
1998	Hiroshima (CL)	JAP	.296	98	230	22	68	8	1	5	35	20	21	4
	Hiroshima (WL)	JAP	.286	2	7	0	2	0	0	0	0	0	0	0
1999	Hiroshima (CL)	JAP	.174	12	23	2	4	0	0	0	2	3	3	0
	Hiroshima (WL)	JAP	.363	60	160	19	58	13	4	1	24	34	13	6
2000	St. Lucie (FSL)	A	.355	8	31	3	11	4	0	1	8	2	1	3
	Norfolk (IL)	AAA	.357	72	291	45	104	17	5	6	37	16	25	13
	New York (NL)	MAJ	.286	24	49	11	14	4	1	1	3	3	5	1
MAJOR LEAGUE TOTALS			.286	24	49	11	14	4	1	1	3	3	5	1
MINOR LEAGUE TOTALS			.350	131	528	88	185	30	13	7	66	49	33	24

5. Grant Roberts, rhp

Born: Sept. 13, 1977. **Ht.:** 6-3. **Wt.:** 205. **Bats:** R. **Throws:** R. **School:** Grossmont HS, La Mesa, Calif. **Career Transactions:** Selected by Mets in 11th round of 1995 draft; signed June 11, 1995.

Once the system's top prospect, Roberts has always needed a little extra push. He may have gotten a wakeup call last year when the Expos rocked him in his first big league start. He has come back from November 1997 elbow surgery to flash excellent stuff again, and now his makeup may come closer to matching his repertoire. The durable Roberts has a good, live arm with a low- to mid-90s fastball, a hard curveball and an average slider. After returning to Norfolk after his first glimpse of the majors, he worked harder than ever. He picked up his running program on his own and ended the season with four complete games. His weakest pitch is a changeup that has made enough progress to border on average. Most of Roberts' difficulty, though, has been his makeup. He hasn't been nearly as dominant after his surgery as he was before it. After ending 2000 on a good note, showing positives in a couple of relief outings against Montreal, Roberts should make a bid as a long man or swing man on New York's Opening Day staff.

Year	Club (League)	Class	W	L	ERA	G	GS	CG	SV	IP	H	R	ER	BB	SO
1995	Mets (GCL)	R	2	1	2.15	11	3	0	0	29	19	13	7	14	24
1996	Kingsport (Appy)	R	9	1	2.10	13	13	2	0	69	43	18	16	37	92
1997	Capital City (SAL)	A	11	3	2.36	22	22	2	0	130	98	37	34	44	122
1998	St. Lucie (FSL)	A	4	5	4.23	17	17	0	0	72	72	37	34	37	70
1999	Binghamton (EL)	AA	7	6	4.87	23	23	0	0	131	135	81	71	49	94
	Norfolk (IL)	AAA	2	1	4.50	5	5	0	0	28	32	15	14	11	30
2000	Norfolk (IL)	AAA	7	8	3.38	25	25	5	0	157	154	67	59	63	115
	New York (NL)	MAJ	0	0	11.57	4	1	0	0	7	11	10	9	4	6
MAJOR LEAGUE TOTALS			0	0	11.57	4	1	0	0	7	11	10	9	4	6
MINOR LEAGUE TOTALS			42	25	3.43	116	108	9	0	617	553	268	235	255	547

6. Enrique Cruz, 3b/ss

Born: Nov. 21, 1981. **Ht.:** 6-1. **Wt.:** 190. **Bats:** R. **Throws:** R. **Career Transactions:** Signed out of Dominican Republic by Mets, Aug. 5, 1998.

Cruz' father played professionally in the Dominican. The climb from the Rookie-level Gulf Coast League proved to be a little much for him, so he was demoted from Capital City to Rookie-level Kingsport. He rebounded to become the No. 2 prospect in the Appalachian League. Cruz received a $400,000 bonus because he has a major league average arm and plus power potential. He's not as strong defensively at shortstop as Jose Reyes—who occupied the position most of the season at

Kingsport—but he has good defensive tools. Cruz draws a healthy amount of walks. Mets officials aren't sure which position best suits Cruz, so he'll continue to play shortstop and third base for now. He has started growing into his body and becoming more coordinated and balanced in the field. He has been slow to make adjustments, but he was more coachable in 2000. He'll need to make more consistent contact. He's ready for Capital City, take two. By the end of the year the Mets will know a lot more about his position and his adaptability.

Year	Club (League)	Class	AVG	G	AB	R	H	2B	3B	HR	RBI	BB	SO	SB
1999	Mets (GCL)	R	.306	54	183	34	56	14	2	4	24	28	41	0
2000	Capital City (SAL)	A	.185	49	157	19	29	12	0	1	12	25	44	1
	Kingsport (Appy)	R	.251	63	223	35	56	14	0	9	39	26	56	19
MINOR LEAGUE TOTALS			.250	166	563	88	141	40	2	14	75	79	141	20

7. Nick Maness, rhp

Born: Oct. 17, 1978. **Ht.:** 6-4. **Wt.:** 210. **Bats:** R. **Throws:** R. **School:** North Moore HS, Robbins, N.C. **Career Transactions:** Selected by Mets in 12th round of 1997 draft; signed June 12, 1997.

Aside from Perez, Maness is the highest-ranking newcomer on the Mets' prospect list. His cousin Dwight is a minor league outfielder who played in the Mets system after an August 1995 trade with the Dodgers for Brett Butler. Dwight spent last year in Double-A with the Mariners. Maness has a power arm that finally showed up in his results in 2000— though he did have a 0.40 ERA as senior in high school. His low-90s fastball is the best in the system. His changeup gives him a second above-average pitch, and he also throws a curveball. When Maness is on, he can be unhittable. He came on last year as he started taking his profession more seriously. Maness' emotions can get the best of him. Command of his pitches remains an issue as well, as he walked the leadoff hitter in his first five Arizona Fall League starts this offseason. Even after he settles in, he sometimes has trouble finding consistency in his delivery. Maness finished 2000 with a so-so performance in the AFL, where he had a 4.36 ERA in 33 innings. He'll start this season in Double-A after making two appearances there last June.

Year	Club (League)	Class	W	L	ERA	G	GS	CG	SV	IP	H	R	ER	BB	SO
1997	Mets (GCL)	R	3	2	3.02	11	6	0	0	45	52	25	15	20	54
1998	Kingsport (Appy)	R	5	3	4.48	13	13	0	0	64	68	41	32	30	76
1999	Capital City (SAL)	A	5	6	4.95	23	22	0	0	107	92	74	59	57	99
2000	St. Lucie (FSL)	A	11	7	3.22	26	25	0	0	145	116	58	52	68	124
	Binghamton (EL)	AA	1	0	1.93	2	1	0	0	9	8	2	2	4	3
MINOR LEAGUE TOTALS			25	18	3.88	75	67	0	0	371	336	200	160	179	356

8. Billy Traber, lhp

Born: Sep. 18, 1979. **Ht.:** 6-3. **Wt.:** 190. **Bats:** L. **Throws:** L. **School:** Loyola Marymount University **Career Transactions:** Selected by Mets in first round (16th overall) of 2000 draft.; signed September 1, 2000.

Traber was the first college lefthander drafted in 2000. After holding out for two months while the market for first-round picks was established, he was set to sign for a club-record-tying $1.7 million bonus. But a physical revealed abnormalities in his pitching elbow that suggested damage to the medial collateral ligament. He wound up signing reluctantly for $400,000 and getting his first taste of pro ball in instructional league. Based on his work in college and instructional league, Traber has impressed the Mets with his four-pitch repertoire. He throws 88-91 mph, giving him good velocity for a lefty, and picks up strikeouts with an above-average splitter. He also throws a curveball and slider. Traber hasn't required surgery yet, but he may have to keep his splitter under wraps because of the uncertainty about his elbow. His curve hasn't been as effective as his slider. Traber's MRI yielded an all-too-familiar result for an organization that has been stung by injuries to its top prospects. If he stays healthy, his fastball and medley of breaking pitches could put him on the fast track. He would have headed to St. Lucie had he pitched in 2000, and he'll likely make his debut there this year.

Year	Club (League)	Class	W	L	ERA	G	GS	CG	SV	IP	H	R	ER	BB	SO
2000						Did Not Play—Signed 2001 Contract									

9. Tsuyoshi Shinjo, of

WAYNE GRACZYK

Born: Jan. 28, 1972. **Ht.:** 6-1. **Wt.:** 185. **Bats:** R. **Throws:** R. **Career Transactions:** Contract purchased by Mets from Hanshin (Japan), Dec. 11, 2000.

Shinjo became the second Japanese position player (after the Mariners' Ichiro Suzuki) to sign a major league contract when the Mets gave the seven-time Central League Gold Glove outfielder a guaranteed one-year, $700,000 deal. In his 10 years in Japan, Shinjo made four all-star teams. He is a good fastball hitter who can run and has the ability to play all three outfield positions. He has a little power, as he showed with his 28 home runs and 85 RBIs for the Hanshin Tigers in 2000. In the annual U.S.-Japan major league exhibition series in November, he hit .409 in 22 at-bats. Shinjo doesn't draw many walks and never has hit for a particularly high average. His on-base percentage last year was just .321, and major league pitchers may be able to exploit his impatience. Considering how U.S. journeymen such as Sherman Obando and Bobby Rose dominated in Japan, Shinjo's statistics aren't inspiring. Shinjo projects as a reserve outfielder for the Mets. He'll likely be used as a defensive replacement, pinch-runner and pinch-hitter.

Year	Club (League)	Class	AVG	G	AB	R	H	2B	3B	HR	RBI	BB	SO	SB
1991	Hanshin (CL)	JAP	.118	13	17	—	2	—	—	0	1	—	—	0
1992	Hanshin (CL)	JAP	.278	95	353	—	98	—	—	11	46	—	—	5
1993	Hanshin (CL)	JAP	.257	102	408	50	105	13	1	23	62	—	—	19
1994	Hanshin (CL)	JAP	.251	122	466	—	117	—	—	17	68	—	—	7
1995	Hanshin (CL)	JAP	.225	87	311	—	70	—	—	7	37	—	—	6
1996	Hanshin (CL)	JAP	.238	113	408	97	97	—	—	19	66	—	—	2
1997	Hanshin (CL)	JAP	.232	136	482	—	112	—	—	20	68	—	—	8
1998	Hanshin (CL)	JAP	.222	132	414	—	92	—	—	6	27	—	—	1
1999	Hanshin (CL)	JAP	.255	123	471	53	120	21	7	14	58	—	—	8
2000	Hanshin (CL)	JAP	.278	131	511	71	142	23	1	28	85	32	93	15

10. Dicky Gonzalez, rhp

STEVE MOORE

Born: Dec. 21, 1978. **Ht.:** 5-11. **Wt.:** 170. **Bats:** R. **Throws:** R. **School:** Adolfina Irizarry HS, Bayamon, P.R. **Career Transactions:** Selected by Mets in 16th round of 1996 draft; signed June 12, 1996.

Growing up in Puerto Rico, Gonzalez played basketball at Puig High, but had to play baseball at nearby Toa Baja because Puig, like most high schools in Puerto Rico, didn't offer the sport. In his first few years in the minors, he was a wiry pitcher who looked more like a middle infielder. He has filled out a little, but no one will confuse him with Roger Clemens. Gonzalez has an idea of how to pitch. He uses both sides of the plate with a fastball that sinks or runs in on a hitter's hands. Gonzalez can throw his curve and slider for strikes, plus he has a deceptive changeup. His command is impeccable. Gonzalez doesn't light radar guns up with his fastball and must locate his pitches with precision in order to succeed. He has bumped his velocity up a tick or two each of the last couple of years, to the point where he can reach 89-91 mph. Maturity has been Gonzalez' greatest feature since he was a 17-year-old pitching against major leaguers and veteran minor leaguers in winter ball. He's ready to try his hand at Triple-A.

Year	Club (League)	Class	W	L	ERA	G	GS	CG	SV	IP	H	R	ER	BB	SO
1996	Mets (GCL)	R	4	2	2.66	11	8	2	0	47	50	19	14	3	51
	Kingsport (Appy)	R	1	0	1.80	1	1	0	0	5	4	2	1	0	7
1997	Capital City (SAL)	A	1	4	4.94	10	7	1	0	47	50	28	26	15	49
	Kingsport (Appy)	R	3	6	4.36	12	12	1	0	66	70	38	32	10	76
1998	Capital City (SAL)	A	10	3	3.31	18	18	1	0	111	104	57	41	14	107
	St. Lucie (FSL)	A	2	1	3.09	8	8	0	0	47	46	22	16	13	23
1999	St. Lucie (FSL)	A	14	9	2.83	25	25	3	0	169	156	66	53	30	143
	Norfolk (IL)	AAA	0	1	2.70	1	1	0	0	7	5	2	2	1	3
2000	Binghamton (EL)	AA	13	5	3.84	26	25	2	0	148	130	75	63	36	138
MINOR LEAGUE TOTALS			48	31	3.45	112	105	10	0	647	615	309	248	122	597

11. Eric Cammack, rhp

Born: Aug. 14, 1975. **Ht.:** 6-1. **Wt.:** 185. **Bats:** R. **Throws:** R. **School:** Lamar University. **Career Transactions:** Selected by Mets in 13th round of 1997 draft; signed June 9, 1997.

Cammack put up another year with astounding hits-to-innings numbers. He made his major league debut in 2000 and could be competing with the vastly improved Jerrod Riggan for the last spot in the Mets' Opening Day bullpen this year. Cammack throws a fastball that tops out at 92 mph and backs it up with a curveball and slider. He has a sneaky delivery and a good feel for pitching. Most relievers don't even worry about a fourth pitch, but Cammack also has a changeup. It needs work but is usable. If his control improves against major league hitters, Cammack could be a keeper. Otherwise, the paucity of hits probably won't last long. Younger and perhaps a little more polished than Riggan, Cammack is the favorite to fill the righthanded relief role in an already deep New York bullpen.

Year	Club (League)	Class	W	L	ERA	G	GS	CG	SV	IP	H	R	ER	BB	SO
1997	Pittsfield (NY-P)	A	0	1	0.86	23	0	0	8	31	9	4	3	14	32
1998	Capital City (SAL)	A	4	0	2.81	25	0	0	8	32	17	13	10	13	49
	St. Lucie (FSL)	A	3	2	2.02	29	0	0	11	35	22	12	8	14	53
1999	Binghamton (EL)	AA	4	2	2.38	45	0	0	15	56	28	17	15	38	83
	Norfolk (IL)	AAA	0	0	3.12	9	0	0	4	8	7	3	3	1	17
2000	Norfolk (IL)	AAA	6	2	1.70	47	0	0	9	63	38	14	12	31	67
	New York (NL)	MAJ	0	0	6.30	8	0	0	0	10	7	7	7	10	9
MAJOR LEAGUE TOTALS			0	0	6.30	8	0	0	0	10	7	7	7	10	9
MINOR LEAGUE TOTALS			17	7	2.01	178	0	0	55	228	121	63	51	111	301

12. Jerrod Riggan, rhp

Born: May 16, 1974. **Ht.:** 6-3. **Wt.:** 197. **Bats:** R. **Throws:** R. **School:** San Diego State University. **Career Transactions:** Selected by Angels in eighth round of 1996 draft; signed June 10, 1996 . . . Released by Angels, April 17, 1998 . . . Signed by Mets, July 9, 1998.

Riggan came into his own last year, making his major league debut in just his third season after getting released by the Angels. When he was still in the Anaheim system following the 1997 season, Riggan was pitching in Hawaii Winter Baseball. Mets scouting director Gary LaRocque and minor league manager John Gibbons took note of him there. The next spring, Anaheim wanted to send Riggan back to low Class A so he requested his release. After sitting out a month, he accepted a low Class A spot—and a new opportunity—with New York. He spent that summer in the South Atlantic League before beginning his rapid ascent to Shea Stadium. Last year, Riggan picked up 4 mph on his fastball and touched 92 on occasion. He also throws a slider and an effective and consistent split-finger fastball. Riggan always has thrown strikes, but he has been less hittable since switching organizations. He'll fight Eric Cammack for a bullpen spot in New York this spring.

Year	Club (League)	Class	W	L	ERA	G	GS	CG	SV	IP	H	R	ER	BB	SO
1996	Boise (NWL)	A	3	5	4.63	15	15	1	0	89	90	62	46	38	80
1997	Cedar Rapids (Mid)	A	9	8	4.89	19	19	3	0	116	132	70	63	36	65
	Lake Elsinore (Cal)	A	2	5	6.07	8	8	0	0	43	60	36	29	16	31
1998	Capital City (SAL)	A	4	1	3.70	14	0	0	1	41	38	21	17	14	40
1999	St. Lucie (FSL)	A	5	5	3.33	44	0	0	12	73	69	33	27	24	66
2000	Binghamton (EL)	AA	2	0	1.11	52	0	0	28	65	43	9	8	18	79
	New York (NL)	MAJ	0	0	0.00	1	0	0	0	2	3	2	0	0	1
MAJOR LEAGUE TOTALS			0	0	0.00	1	0	0	0	2	3	2	0	0	1
MINOR LEAGUE TOTALS			25	24	4.00	152	42	4	41	428	432	231	190	146	361

13. Ken Chenard, rhp

Born: Aug. 30, 1978. **Ht.:** 6-3. **Wt.:** 185. **Bats:** R. **Throws:** R. **School:** Fullerton (Calif.) JC. **Career Transactions:** Selected by Mets in 46th round of 1998 draft; signed May 12, 1999.

Chenard's story is similar to that of Athletics closer Jason Isringhausen. Both were selected 40-plus rounds into the draft, signed as draft-and-follows, then saw their fastballs suddenly shoot from 84 mph to 94 the next season. Along with his fastball, Chenard's curveball and changeup are also above-average pitches. His command was erratic last season, but there were extenuating circumstances. He was shut down twice in 2000 with shoulder soreness. A lesion was attached to his labrum, so he spent much of the season resting and then trying to get cranked up again. If he had enough innings to qualify, Chenard would have ranked fifth in the South Atlantic League in ERA last year after finishing ninth in the Appy League ERA race in his pro debut. Providing he stays healthy in 2001, Chenard very well could jump into the organization's top 10 for the first time.

Year	Club (League)	Class	W	L	ERA	G	GS	CG	SV	IP	H	R	ER	BB	SO
1999	Kingsport (Appy)	R	6	3	3.07	14	13	1	0	76	64	32	26	25	80
2000	Capital City (SAL)	A	4	5	2.86	21	21	0	0	94	75	39	30	48	112
MINOR LEAGUE TOTALS			10	8	2.95	35	34	1	0	170	139	71	56	73	192

14. Robert Stratton, of

Born: Oct. 7, 1977. **Ht.:** 6-2. **Wt.:** 240. **Bats:** R. **Throws:** R. **School:** San Marcos HS, Santa Barbara, Calif.
Career Transactions: Selected by Mets in first round (13th overall) of 1996 draft; signed July 12, 1996 . . . Traded by Mets with LHP Jesus Sanchez and RHP A.J. Burnett to Marlins for LHP Al Leiter and 2B Ralph Milliard, Feb. 6, 1998 . . . Traded by Marlins to Mets for RHP Brandon Villafuerte and a player to be named, March 20, 1998; Marlins acquired 2B Cesar Crespo to complete trade (Sept. 14, 1998).

Stratton was the 13th overall pick in 1996 because of his power potential. His other tools are only average, while he's certainly below-average as a hitter for average. He hit .512 as a senior in high school but strikes out way too much now. Mets officials say Stratton at least had a little bit more of a plan as a hitter in 2000, when he came within four of the Florida State League's single-season home run mark. Stratton has lost some of his stubbornness, yet he still continues to go down looking at too many curveballs. Earlier in his career, Stratton too often followed a pattern of trying to back up a light-tower home run with an even longer one. He drew a career-high 60 walks last year, which is an encouraging sign. If back problems hadn't prevented him from passing a physical in 1998, he'd be with the Marlins as part of the Al Leiter trade. Instead, Florida returned him to New York after discovering the problem. Stratton could get his first taste of Double-A in 2001.

Year	Club (League)	Class	AVG	G	AB	R	H	2B	3B	HR	RBI	BB	SO	SB
1996	Mets (GCL)	R	.254	17	59	5	15	2	0	2	9	2	22	3
1997	Kingsport (Appy)	R	.249	63	245	51	61	11	5	15	50	19	94	11
1998	Mets (GCL)	R	.261	12	46	4	12	1	0	3	13	2	15	1
	Pittsfield (NY-P)	A	.226	34	124	18	28	5	4	6	18	11	55	3
1999	Capital City (SAL)	A	.274	95	318	58	87	17	3	21	60	48	112	7
2000	St. Lucie (FSL)	A	.228	108	381	61	87	18	4	29	87	60	180	3
MINOR LEAGUE TOTALS			.247	329	1173	197	290	54	16	76	237	142	478	28

15. Tyler Walker, rhp

Born: May 15, 1976. **Ht.:** 6-3. **Wt.:** 255. **Bats:** R. **Throws:** R. **School:** University of California. **Career Transactions:** Selected by Mets in second round of 1997 draft; signed July 29, 1997.

Walker followed a 12-win season in 1999 with another outstanding year at the upper levels of the Mets system. Producing another solid encore will be more difficult in 2001. He left the Arizona Fall League early with a torn labrum that required surgery. His goal is to return in the spring, though the Mets would like to take things slowly and have him pitching again some time around May. Walker threw 95-96 mph when he was a closer in college, but a little of that velocity has been sacrificed since he became a starter in 1998. In exchange, he has developed a potentially above-average changeup. Walker is intelligent, and he has shown good control and durability. His curveball needs work, and its development may dictate whether he winds up a third or fourth starter or a reliever as he finishes his climb through the minors.

Year	Club (League)	Class	W	L	ERA	G	GS	CG	SV	IP	H	R	ER	BB	SO
1997	Mets (GCL)	R	0	0	1.00	5	0	0	3	9	8	1	1	2	9
	Pittsfield (NY-P)	A	0	0	13.50	1	0	0	0	1	2	2	1	1	1
1998	Capital City (SAL)	A	5	5	4.12	34	13	0	1	116	122	63	53	38	110
1999	St. Lucie (FSL)	A	6	5	2.94	13	13	2	0	80	64	31	26	29	64
	Binghamton (EL)	AA	6	4	6.22	13	13	0	0	68	78	49	47	32	59
2000	Binghamton (EL)	AA	7	6	2.75	22	22	0	0	121	82	43	37	55	111
	Norfolk (IL)	AAA	1	3	2.39	5	5	0	0	26	29	7	7	9	17
MINOR LEAGUE TOTALS			25	23	3.69	93	66	2	4	420	385	196	172	166	371

16. Jeremy Griffiths, rhp

Born: March 22, 1978. **Ht.:** 6-7. **Wt.:** 230. **Bats:** R. **Throws:** R. **School:** University of Toledo. **Career Transactions:** Selected by Mets in third round of 1999 draft; signed June 9, 1999.

Griffiths starred at Toledo, where he set the season strikeout record and was Mid-American Conference pitcher of the year in 1999. Though he has gone just 10-17 in two pro seasons, he has pitched better than his record indicates. One of the taller pitching prospects in the game, Griffiths throws his low-90s fastball on a nasty downward plane. His change-up is decent already, and his slider has some potential. He also throws a curveball that lags behind his other pitches. Griffiths lacks Ken Chenard's consistency, but he lit up instructional league for the second straight fall and could be ready for a breakout year at St. Lucie in 2001.

Year	Club (League)	Class	W	L	ERA	G	GS	CG	SV	IP	H	R	ER	BB	SO
1999	Kingsport (Appy)	R	3	5	3.30	14	14	1	0	76	68	40	28	36	74
2000	Capital City (SAL)	A	7	12	4.34	26	26	0	0	129	120	78	62	39	138
MINOR LEAGUE TOTALS			10	17	3.95	40	40	1	0	205	188	118	90	75	212

17. Jake Joseph, rhp

Born: Jan. 24, 1978. **Ht.:** 6-1. **Wt.:** 210. **Bats:** R. **Throws:** R. **School:** Cosumnes River (Calif.) JC. **Career Transactions:** Selected by Mets in second round of 1999 draft; signed July 7, 1999.

Joseph's career has been marked by success mixed with disappointment. In his first year, he was the starter in the first no-hitter in Pittsfield's franchise history (a combined effort)—but was saddled with a 2-0 loss. Last year, he would have ranked fifth in the South Atlantic League in ERA if he had enough innings to qualify. He battled ribcage problems after lifting more weight than the Mets would have liked. Once he made it back, Joseph was weakened again by an infection in his lower leg. When he was able to pitch, he was quite impressive. Reliant on his fastball and slider, Joseph could project as a Turk Wendell type out of the bullpen. The front office, though, hopes he can continue to be successful as a starter. His control was better than it was in his pro debut but still needs improvement.

Year	Club (League)	Class	W	L	ERA	G	GS	CG	SV	IP	H	R	ER	BB	SO
1999	Pittsfield (NY-P)	A	3	2	2.91	11	6	0	1	43	35	19	14	27	26
2000	Capital City (SAL)	A	4	3	2.85	15	15	0	0	85	81	45	27	29	59
MINOR LEAGUE TOTALS			7	5	2.87	26	21	0	1	129	116	64	41	56	85

18. Jason Saenz, lhp

Born: Feb. 13, 1977. **Ht.:** 6-2. **Wt.:** 195. **Bats:** L. **Throws:** L. **School:** University of Southern California. **Career Transactions:** Selected by Mets in third round of 1998 draft; signed June 25, 1998.

In his draft year at Southern California, Saenz didn't pitch at all in the postseason as the Trojans won the College World Series. Scouts loved his power arm, but he was so raw that he couldn't be trusted to get hitters out in key situations. His ERA has gone down each year as a pro as he has gained a better feel for pitching. If Barry Larkin hadn't vetoed a trade to the Mets last July, Saenz would have gone to Cincinnati with Alex Escobar and Eric Cammack. He throws 93-94 mph and has improved his slider, but still has bouts of wildness. If he continues to make the strides he did last year, he could follow a similar career path to former Met Mike Remlinger. He'll move up to the Double-A rotation in 2001.

Year	Club (League)	Class	W	L	ERA	G	GS	CG	SV	IP	H	R	ER	BB	SO
1998	Pittsfield (NY-P)	A	2	3	6.75	12	7	0	0	44	56	37	33	23	34
1999	Capital City (SAL)	A	10	8	5.44	27	27	0	0	134	147	89	81	68	125
2000	St. Lucie (FSL)	A	6	9	4.40	28	28	0	0	153	165	98	75	83	107
MINOR LEAGUE TOTALS			18	20	5.14	67	62	0	0	331	368	224	189	174	266

19. Marvin Seale, of

Born: June 16, 1979. **Ht.:** 6-0. **Wt.:** 195. **Bats:** B. **Throws:** R. **School:** Durango (Colo.) HS. **Career Transactions:** Selected by Mets in sixth round of 1998 draft; signed June 3, 1998.

Because of an inability to hit the breaking ball as a strictly righthanded hitter, Seale learned to switch-hit in the offseason before 2000. He still has a ways to go from the left side of the plate after hitting just .258 with four homers in 330 at-bats against righthanders. His explosive speed has been his most obvious tool for a while. If he can develop as a hitter from the left side, he'd become a leadoff candidate. Seale will draw some walks, though his strike-zone discipline needs improvement. He also has the strength to hit 10-15 homers a year. Seale has played all three outfield positions, though he'll probably settle in left as he approaches the big leagues.

Year	Club (League)	Class	AVG	G	AB	R	H	2B	3B	HR	RBI	BB	SO	SB
1998	Mets (GCL)	R	.220	37	132	24	29	4	5	0	7	10	40	11
1999	Kingsport (Appy)	R	.233	63	210	46	49	7	3	2	20	24	75	22
2000	Capital City (SAL)	A	.291	120	453	76	132	23	6	6	37	53	125	52
	St. Lucie (FSL)	A	.353	5	17	5	6	1	0	1	2	2	6	0
MINOR LEAGUE TOTALS			.266	225	812	151	216	35	14	9	66	89	246	85

20. Ty Wigginton, 2b

Born: Oct. 11, 1977. **Ht.:** 6-0. **Wt.:** 195. **Bats:** R. **Throws:** R. **School:** UNC Asheville. **Career Transactions:** Selected by Mets in 17th round of 1998 draft; signed June 3, 1998.

Wigginton isn't the prettiest second baseman in the minors, but those who have seen him over long periods have been impressed. Nothing looks smooth, but he makes the plays and does the little things to help his team win. He has pretty good pop for a middle infielder. His 21 homers in 1999 set a St. Lucie record (broken by Robert Stratton last year), and he followed up with 20 more in Double-A. Wigginton was far less patient in 2000, when his on-base percentage dropped 54 points from the season before. That doesn't bode well for his ability to keep hitting as he moves up the ladder. In the Arizona Fall League, he enhanced his versatility by playing third base, first base and left field. A possible righthanded bat off the bench for the Mets in 2002, he'll probably start this year at Triple-A.

Year	Club (League)	Class	AVG	G	AB	R	H	2B	3B	HR	RBI	BB	SO	SB
1998	Pittsfield (NY-P)	A	.239	70	272	39	65	14	4	8	29	16	72	11
1999	St. Lucie (FSL)	A	.292	123	456	69	133	23	5	21	73	56	82	9
2000	Binghamton (EL)	AA	.285	122	453	64	129	27	3	2	77	24	107	5
MINOR LEAGUE TOTALS			.277	315	1181	172	327	64	12	31	179	96	261	25

21. Neal Musser, lhp

Born: Aug. 25, 1980. **Ht.:** 6-2. **Wt.:** 195. **Bats:** L. **Throws:** L. **School:** Benton Central HS, Oxford, Ind. **Career Transactions:** Selected by Mets in second round of 1999 draft; signed June 23, 1999.

Like Jake Joseph, Musser overdid his weightlifting last offseason. He was just beyond the guidelines the Mets had set for him, which contributed to a pulled ribcage and strained elbow in his second pro season. His development hasn't gone quite as fast as New York hoped when it made him their initial selection (second round) in the 1999 draft, but he still has a live arm and plenty of promise. Musser has an average fastball and the makings of a plus changeup. When he's healthy, his curveball also works well. There's some question about his size and durability. While he's listed at 6-foot-2, he's really closer to 6 feet and has worked just 66 innings in two years. If he's 100 percent in the spring, he could open 2001 in Capital City.

Year	Club (League)	Class	W	L	ERA	G	GS	CG	SV	IP	H	R	ER	BB	SO
1999	Mets (GCL)	R	2	1	2.01	8	7	0	0	31	26	13	7	18	22
2000	Kingsport (Appy)	R	3	2	2.10	7	7	0	0	34	33	10	8	6	21
MINOR LEAGUE TOTALS			5	3	2.06	15	14	0	0	66	59	23	15	24	43

22. Matt Peterson, rhp

Born: Feb. 11, 1982. **Ht.:** 6-5. **Wt.:** 185. **Bats:** R. **Throws:** R. **School:** Rapides HS, Alexandria, La. **Career Transactions:** Selected by Mets in second round of 2000 draft; signed Aug. 9, 2000.

With a refined delivery for a pitcher fresh out of high school, Peterson has the potential to have above-average command of solid stuff. He already possesses an above-average fastball (94-95 mph with an effortless delivery), an effective curveball and a developing changeup. He has a long, loose and lean body. Rated as the best draft prospect in Louisiana in 2000, he went 11-1, 0.63 with 149 strikeouts in 78 innings as a high school senior. He signed for $575,000 at the end of the summer, so he didn't get to show his stuff off until instructional league. Peterson performed well during the fall and made Mets officials even happier that they landed him in the second round.

Year	Club (League)	Class	W	L	ERA	G	GS	CG	SV	IP	H	R	ER	BB	SO
2000										Did Not Sign—Signed 2001 Contract					

23. Chad Bowen, rhp

Born: April 28, 1982. **Ht.:** 6-4. **Wt.:** 205. **Bats:** R. **Throws:** R. **School:** Gallatin (Tenn.) HS. **Career Transactions:** Selected by Mets in eighth round of 2000 draft; signed June 6, 2000.

In the first five rounds of the 2000 draft, New York nabbed four pitchers who bring it in the 90s on a consistent basis. Bowen didn't go until the eighth round, and he has a different kind of upside. His stuff reminds some in the organization of Dicky Gonzalez' at the same age. Neither one lights up radar guns, but both are competitors and consistent winners. Co-pitcher of the year in the Rookie-level Appalachian League, Bowen won his first seven decisions as a pro. His fastball is a notch below-average, but he can throw his curve for strikes on any count, which enables him to keep hitters off balance. His pitching smarts are unusual for a high school draftee. He has good mound presence and the ability to succeed when he doesn't have his best stuff.

Year	Club (League)	Class	W	L	ERA	G	GS	CG	SV	IP	H	R	ER	BB	SO
2000	Kingsport (Appy)	R	7	2	3.00	11	11	0	0	63	59	22	21	23	41
MINOR LEAGUE TOTALS			7	2	3.00	11	11	0	0	63	59	22	21	23	41

24. Chris Basak, ss

Born: Jan. 26, 1978. **Ht.:** 6-2. **Wt.:** 185. **Bats:** R. **Throws:** R. **School:** University of Illinois. **Career Transactions:** Selected by Mets in sixth round of 2000 draft; signed June 20, 2000.

Taking to short-season Pittsfield's leadoff spot with ease, Basak drove opposing defenses crazy with his knack for fouling off pitches until he saw one he liked. He led the New York-Penn League in hitting and was solid defensively. The only tool he lacks is power, as he's still looking for his first professional home run. Basak can drive liners to the gaps and seems to catch everything at shortstop. With above-average speed and baserunning skills, plus his knack for making plays, he reminds the Mets a little of Mike Bordick. Basak has just an average arm, but he's steady, intelligent and hard-nosed enough to avoid a move to second base for the time being. He was promoted to St. Lucie for the Florida State League playoffs and could start 2001 there.

Year	Club (League)	Class	AVG	G	AB	R	H	2B	3B	HR	RBI	BB	SO	SB
2000	Pittsfield (NY-P)	A	.349	63	249	46	87	18	4	0	15	26	36	32
	St. Lucie (FSL)	A	.412	4	17	2	7	1	0	0	3	4	2	3
MINOR LEAGUE TOTALS			.353	67	266	48	94	19	4	0	18	30	38	35

25. Bob Keppel, rhp

Born: June 11, 1982. **Ht.:** 6-5. **Wt.:** 185. **Bats:** R. **Throws:** R. **School:** DeSmet HS, St. Louis. **Career Transactions:** Selected by Mets in first round (36th overall) of 2000 draft; signed July 7, 2000.

Keppel could have been on the roster for Notre Dame's basketball team but chose to play professional baseball instead. He was inconsistent after joining Kingsport midway through the 2000 season, and some of the league's managers weren't impressed by what they saw. But he showed an aptitude for three pitches, throwing a sinking, low-90s fastball, a good slider and an average changeup. The slider was his most effective pitch by the end of the summer, which wasn't bad considering the knock on him before the draft was his breaking stuff. With his frame, the Mets project him to add velocity in time. Keppel lacks strength now but has the potential to be a No. 2 starter in the big leagues.

Year	Club (League)	Class	W	L	ERA	G	GS	CG	SV	IP	H	R	ER	BB	SO
2000	Kingsport (Appy)	R	1	2	6.83	8	6	0	0	29	31	22	22	13	29
MINOR LEAGUE TOTALS			1	2	6.83	8	6	0	0	29	31	22	22	13	29

26. Jorge Toca, 1b

Born: Jan. 7, 1975. **Ht.:** 6-3. **Wt.:** 220. **Bats:** R. **Throws:** R. **Career Transactions:** Signed out of Cuba by Mets, Sept. 7, 1998.

Listed at age 26 but really 29, Toca is running out of time to earn a major league job. Big league first baseman Todd Zeile is signed through 2002 and Toca hasn't done anything to take his job away. He could give New York a righthanded bat off the bench or serve as a temporary replacement for Zeile or a corner outfielder. A Cuban defector, Toca lived at baseball academies with current Met Rey Ordonez as a teenager. He has excellent bat speed and is capable of hitting a few more home runs than he did in 2000. Power is his only impressive tool. He doesn't walk, which hampers his ability to hit for average, and he has below-average speed and arm strength. In 1999, Toca was the Mets' No. 7 prospect after winning the organization's minor league player of the year honor. He also played in the inaugural Futures Game at Fenway Park. But his stock has slipped considerably since then.

Year	Club (League)	Class	AVG	G	AB	R	H	2B	3B	HR	RBI	BB	SO	SB
1999	Binghamton (EL)	AA	.308	75	279	60	86	15	1	20	67	32	43	5
	Norfolk (IL)	AAA	.335	49	176	25	59	12	1	5	29	6	23	0
	New York (NL)	MAJ	.333	4	3	0	1	0	0	0	0	0	2	0
2000	Binghamton (EL)	AA	.091	3	11	1	1	0	0	0	0	0	0	0
	Norfolk (IL)	AAA	.272	120	453	58	123	25	3	11	70	17	72	9
	New York (NL)	MAJ	.429	8	7	1	3	1	0	0	4	0	1	0
MAJOR LEAGUE TOTALS			.400	12	10	1	4	1	0	0	4	0	3	0
MINOR LEAGUE TOTALS			.296	247	915	144	271	53	5	36	166	55	138	14

27. Jae Weong Seo, rhp

Born: May 24, 1977. **Ht.:** 6-1. **Wt.:** 215. **Bats:** R. **Throws:** R. **Career Transactions:** Signed out of Korea by Mets, Jan. 6, 1998.

Seo ranked as the Mets' No. 4 prospect entering 1999. He had bounced back from an elbow injury to pitch St. Lucie to Florida State League championship, winning both of his playoff starts without allowing a run. Then he went to the Asian Games, where he helped

Korea win the title and earned an exemption from compulsory military service. Little has gone right for Seo since then, however. He made just three starts in 1999 before succumbing to Tommy John surgery and didn't pitch at all in 2000. When healthy, Seo has a 90-92 mph fastball, a plus changeup, a promising curveball and solid command. Mets officials have been extra-cautious with his throwing program, especially after he experienced unrelated tightness in his forearm area. Added to the 40-man roster this offseason, he should be ready for spring training. He'll probably start 2001 at St. Lucie, then move to Double-A Binghamton when the weather warms up.

Year	Club (League)	Class	W	L	ERA	G	GS	CG	SV	IP	H	R	ER	BB	SO
1998	St. Lucie (FSL)	A	3	1	2.31	8	7	0	0	35	26	13	9	10	37
	Mets (GCL)	R	0	0	0.00	2	0	0	0	5	4	0	0	0	5
1999	St. Lucie (FSL)	A	2	0	1.84	3	3	0	0	15	8	3	3	2	14
2000					Did Not Play—Injured										
MINOR LEAGUE TOTALS			5	1	1.98	13	10	0	0	55	38	16	12	12	56

28. Prentice Redman, of

Born: Aug. 23, 1979. **Ht.:** 6-3. **Wt.:** 180. **Bats:** R. **Throws:** R. **School:** Bevill State (Ala.) CC. **Career Transactions:** Selected by Mets in 10th round of 1999 draft; signed June 4, 1999.

Redman is a tools player who struggled in his first full minor league season in 2000. He wore down and lost a lot of weight during the year. From July 1 to the end of the season, Redman managed just six extra-base hits and a .243 average in 218 at-bats. That should prove to be a good learning experience for him as he moves to the Florida State League in 2001. One Mets official called Redman a poor man's Preston Wilson, a Mets first-round pick in 1992. Redman already is a stolen-base threat, though his power potential has yet to manifest itself. He has played all three outfield positions, but may not quite have the range for center field and his below-average arm might limit him to left.

Year	Club (League)	Class	AVG	G	AB	R	H	2B	3B	HR	RBI	BB	SO	SB
1999	Kingsport (Appy)	R	.295	58	200	40	59	14	1	6	29	24	42	16
2000	Capital City (SAL)	A	.260	131	497	60	129	19	1	3	46	52	90	26
MINOR LEAGUE TOTALS			.270	189	697	100	188	33	2	9	75	76	132	42

29. Angel Pagan, of

Born: July 2, 1981. **Ht.:** 6-1. **Wt.:** 175. **Bats:** B. **Throws:** R. **School:** Indian River (Fla.) CC. **Career Transactions:** Selected by Mets in fourth round of 1999 draft; signed May 28, 2000.

Pagan was the highest-selected draft-and-follow to sign from the 1999 draft. His performance in junior college was uninspiring, and he played just 19 games before going on the disabled list in mid-July with a wrist injury. Before his season ended, he impressed managers with a well-rounded package of tools. Pagan has projectable power and runs well, though he's raw on the bases. He also showed good range in center field and a strong arm. Pagan will face his first full pro season this year, so he may want to check with Prentice Redman about the rigors of a long campaign.

Year	Club (League)	Class	AVG	G	AB	R	H	2B	3B	HR	RBI	BB	SO	SB
2000	Kingsport (Appy)	R	.361	19	72	13	26	5	1	0	8	6	8	6
MINOR LEAGUE TOTALS			.361	19	72	13	26	5	1	0	8	6	8	6

30. Josh Reynolds, rhp

Born: Sept. 27, 1979. **Ht.:** 6-2. **Wt.:** 195. **Bats:** R. **Throws:** R. **School:** Central Missouri State University. **Career Transactions:** Selected by Mets in third round of 2000 draft; signed July 12, 2000.

Reynolds was dominant last spring in NCAA Division II, supporting his rating (57 on the 20-80 scale) as Missouri's top prospect by the Major League Scouting Bureau. He went 11-1, 2.35, thanks to a 90-93 mph fastball that has excellent run. He also has an above-average slider and an improving changeup. Reynolds had health problems with muscles in his back in 2000, but he looked fine by the end of the year. He has come a long way from his days as a high school shortstop, when he threw only 84-85. Reynolds was one of several members of the Mets' 2000 draft class that gave the system an injection of power arms.

Year	Club (League)	Class	W	L	ERA	G	GS	CG	SV	IP	H	R	ER	BB	SO
2000	Pittsfield (NY-P)	A	1	1	4.39	7	6	0	0	27	35	13	13	11	23
MINOR LEAGUE TOTALS			1	1	4.39	7	6	0	0	27	35	13	13	11	23

New York
Yankees

TOP 30 PROSPECTS

1. Nick Johnson, 1b
2. Alfonso Soriano, ss
3. D'Angelo Jimenez, ss
4. Adrian Hernandez, rhp
5. Alex Graman, lhp
6. Randy Keisler, lhp
7. Erick Almonte, ss
8. Deivi Mendez, ss
9. Wily Mo Pena, of
10. Todd Noel, rhp
11. Juan Rivera, of
12. Brandon Claussen, lhp
13. Chien-Ming Wang, rhp
14. David Martinez, lhp
15. Elvis Corporan, 3b
16. Ricardo Aramboles, rhp
17. Danny Borrell, lhp
18. Ted Lilly, lhp
19. David Walling, rhp
20. Christian Parker, rhp
21. Donzell McDonald, of
22. Craig Dingman, rhp
23. Brett Jodie, rhp
24. Brian Rogers, rhp
25. Andy Brown, of
26. Jeremy Blevins, rhp
27. Mitch Jones, of
28. David Parrish, c
29. Scott Seabol, 3b
30. Marcus Thames, of

By Jim Callis

Though they stumbled at the end of the regular season, the Yankees righted themselves in time to win their third consecutive World Series and fourth in five years. And while they did so with a predominantly veteran team—Derek Jeter (26), Andy Pettitte (28) and Jorge Posada (29) were the only key players under 30—the farm system also made significant contributions.

Providing fresh talent is the most obvious way the minor league department can assist a big league team. And the Yankees did originally sign Jeter, Pettitte, Posada, Orlando Hernandez, Mariano Rivera and Bernie Williams. In recent years, they haven't been as successful integrating home-grown talent into the majors.

As a result the Yankees have used excess minor league talent to acquire proven veterans. When holes arose in 2000, they dealt off some of the farm system's depth. The most significant trade sent Ricky Ledee and minor league righthanders Zach Day and Jake Westbrook to the Indians for David Justice. The most costly shipped third baseman Drew Henson, center fielder Jackson Melian and lefthander Ed Yarnall—three of New York's top six prospects at the start of the year—along with promising righthander Brian Reith to the Reds for Denny Neagle, who flopped with the Yankees before signing as a free agent with the Rockies as a free agent.

The Yankees' deep pockets give them an advantage over other teams, in that they're able to take on the salary of a Justice or Neagle for a playoff drive. But if they didn't have a deep farm system, they wouldn't have the ammunition to acquire them in the first place.

The Yankees also have astutely worked these trades in reverse. When they didn't have a spot for Mike Lowell, they sent him to the Marlins for pitchers Mark Johnson, Todd Noel and Yarnall. Likewise, when they tired of Hideki Irabu, they got three arms (Ted Lilly, Christian Parker and Westbrook) from the Expos.

While New York still ranks among the best systems in the game, it's not at the top any longer, as it was entering 2000. Most of the top prospects from a year ago were injured for most of the season (Nick Johnson, D'Angelo Jimenez, Todd Noel), disappointing (Alfonso Soriano, Wily Mo Pena) or traded (Henson, Melian, Yarnall, Westbrook). The lone player to emerge unscathed was Randy Keisler, who could compete for a rotation job in spring training.

OrganizationOverview

General manager: Brian Cashman. **Farm director:** Mark Newman. **Scouting director:** Lin Garrett.

2000 PERFORMANCE

Class	Team	League	W	L	Pct.	Finish*	Manager(s)
Majors	New York	American	87	74	.540	5th (14)	Joe Torre
Triple-A	Columbus Clippers	International	75	69	.521	8th (14)	Trey Hillman
Double-A	Norwich Navigators	Eastern	76	66	.535	4th (12)	Dan Radison
High A	Tampa Yankees	Florida State	70	70	.500	7th (14)	Tom Nieto
Low A	Greensboro Bats	South Atlantic	56	81	.409	t-12th (14)	Stan Hough
Short-season	Staten Island Yankees	New York-Penn	46	28	.622	2nd (14)	Joe Arnold
Rookie	GCL Yankees	Gulf Coast	38	22	.633	3rd (13)	Derek Shelton
OVERALL 2000 MINOR LEAGUE RECORD			361	336	.518	11th (30)	

*Finish in overall standings (No. of teams in league).

ORGANIZATION LEADERS

BATTING

*AVG	Kerry Robinson, Columbus	.318
R	Alfonso Soriano, Columbus	90
H	**Scott Seabol**, Norwich	146
TB	**Scott Seabol**, Norwich	255
2B	**Scott Seabol**, Norwich	45
3B	Kerry Robinson, Columbus	9
HR	Mike Coolbaugh, Columbus	23
	Ryan Thompson, Columbus	23
RBI	Juan Rivera, Norwich/Tampa	81
BB	Torre Tyson, Greensboro	76
SO	Andy Brown, Greensboro	182
SB	Kerry Robinson, Columbus	37

PITCHING

W	**Christian Parker**, Norwich	14
	Randy Keisler, Norwich/Columbus	14
L	Mike Knowles, Greensboro	14
#ERA	Brian Reith, Tampa	2.18
G	Domingo Jean, Norwich	62
CG	Brandon Knight, Columbus	8
SV	Jay Tessmer, Columbus	34
IP	**Christian Parker**, Norwich	204
BB	Jason Beverlin, Columbus/Norwich	101
SO	Randy Keisler, Norwich/Columbus	156

*Minimum 250 at-bats. #Minimum 75 innings.

Seabol   **Parker**

BEST TOOLS

Best Hitter for Average	Nick Johnson
Best Power Hitter	Wily Mo Pena
Fastest Baserunner	Donzell McDonald
Best Fastball	Todd Noel
Best Breaking Ball	Brian Rogers
Best Control	Brett Jodie
Best Defensive Catcher	Michel Hernandez
Best Defensive Infielder	Deivi Mendez
Best Infield Arm	Elvis Corporan
Best Defensive Outfielder	Wily Mo Pena
Best Outfield Arm	Juan Rivera

TOP PROSPECTS OF THE DECADE

1991	Bernie Williams, of
1992	Brien Taylor, lhp
1993	Brien Taylor, lhp
1994	Derek Jeter, ss
1995	Ruben Rivera, of
1996	Ruben Rivera, of
1997	Ruben Rivera, of
1998	Eric Milton, lhp
1999	Nick Johnson, 1b
2000	Nick Johnson, 1b

TOP DRAFT PICKS OF THE DECADE

1991	Brien Taylor, lhp
1992	Derek Jeter, ss
1993	Matt Drews, rhp
1994	Brian Buchanan, of
1995	Shea Morenz, of
1996	Eric Milton, lhp
1997	*Tyrell Godwin, of
1998	Andy Brown, of
1999	David Walling, rhp
2000	David Parrish, c

*Did not sign.

PROJECTED 2004 LINEUP

Catcher	Jorge Posada
First Base	Nick Johnson
Second Base	D'Angelo Jimenez
Third Base	Alfonso Soriano
Shortstop	Derek Jeter
Left Field	Bernie Williams
Center Field	Wily Mo Pena
Right Field	Juan Rivera
Designated Hitter	David Justice
No. 1 Starter	Andy Pettitte
No. 2 Starter	Mike Mussina
No. 3 Starter	Orlando Hernandez
No. 4 Starter	Adrian Hernandez
No. 5 Starter	Alex Graman
Closer	Mariano Rivera

ALL-TIME LARGEST BONUSES

Hideki Irabu, 1997	$8,500,000
Wily Mo Pena, 1999	2,440,000
Drew Henson, 1998	2,000,000
Jackson Melian, 1996	1,600,000
Brien Taylor, 1991	1,550,000

DraftAnalysis

2000 Draft

Best Pro Debut: After going 2-11 at Vanderbilt in the spring, LHP Andy Beal (5) went 9-3, 2.34 to lead the short-season New York-Penn League in victories and help Staten Island win the league title. OF Mitch Jones (7), who challenged for the NCAA Division I home run title, topped the NY-P with 28 doubles and 11 homers.

Best Athlete: LHP Danny Borrell (2) reminds the Yankees of Twins lefty Eric Milton, a 1996 Yankees first-rounder. Both were two-way standouts in the Atlantic Coast Conference, Borrell at Wake Forest and Milton at Maryland. Milton was more of a pitcher in college, while Borrell was the No. 3 hitter in his lineup.

Best Hitter: New York still is waiting to see OF Jason Grove's (3) sweet swing. A broken hamate bone in his wrist hampered him last spring at Washington State, then he broke a bone in his foot at midseason and never appeared in a pro game. Grove also has an above-average arm and average speed.

Best Raw Power: Jones. The Yankees love the way the ball explodes off his bat and can't believe they got him in the seventh round.

Fastest Runner: New York didn't sign anyone with better than average speed. The quickest player is actually RHP Jason Smith (11), who runs a 6.7-second 60-yard dash. He shows a lot of athleticism as an outfielder, but he's staying on the mound.

Best Defensive Player: The Yankees surprised a lot of teams by taking C **David Parrish** (1) with their top pick. They've

liked him since they drafted him in the 10th round out of high school three years earlier and believe he'll be a standout offensive and defensive catcher. His arm is quite strong.

Best Fastball: RHP Jason Anderson (10) threw 92-94 mph as a starter and moved up to 96 when he pitched in relief.

Most Intriguing Background: Parrish resembles his father Lance, a former all-star catcher. OF Tim Nettles (47) is the son of former Yankees all-star Graig.

RICH ABEL

Closest To The Majors: Parrish
Beal's fastball is less than overpowering, but that's fine because he has pinpoint control. His 87-17 strikeout-walk ratio was the best in the NY-P.

Best Late-Round Pick: The only thing questioned about Smith was his signability. He's 6-foot-5 and 205 pounds, has a live, loose arm and throws a projectable 90-91 mph fastball. His slider is another potential plus pitch.

The One Who Got Away: RHP Darric Merrell (20) has an average fastball and plenty of polish. He turned down New York for Cal State Fullerton.

Assessment: Parrish still needs refinement to prove he wasn't a first-round reach. Even if he fizzles, the Yankees got a trio of promising lefties in Borrell, Matt Smith (4) and Beal.

1999 Draft

RHP David Walling (1) and LHP Alex Graman (3) both reached Double-A in their first full season. Other than that, the Yankees didn't do much. **Grade: C–**

1998 Draft

New York got talented 3B Drew Henson (3) but traded him to the Reds. The club did find keepers in LHP Randy Keisler (2) and two draft-and-follows, 3B Elvis Corporan (31) and LHP Brandon Claussen (34). OF Andy Brown (1) has started slowly, while RHP Mark Prior (1) went to college and could be the No. 1 overall pick this year. **Grade: B+**

1997 Draft

The Yankees identified talent, choosing OF Tyrell Godwin (1), C David Parrish (10) and RHPs Beau Hale (22) and Aaron Heilman (55). But they didn't sign any of the four. RHP Ryan Bradley (1) hasn't emerged, making LHP Randy Choate (5) the top signee. **Grade: C–**

1996 Draft

New York found a budding superstar in 1B Nick Johnson (3), plus three quality arms it used in trades—LHP Eric Milton (1) and RHPs Zach Day (5) and Brian Reith (6). 3B Scott Seabol may be the best 88th-round pick ever. **Grade: A**

Note: Draft analysis prepared by Jim Callis. Numbers in parentheses indicate draft rounds.

. . . There's no reason to assume Johnson won't regain his place among the most feared minor league hitters.

Nick Johnson 1b

Born: Sept. 19, 1978.
Ht.: 6-3. **Wt.:** 224.
Bats: L. **Throws:** L.
School: McClatchy HS, Sacramento.
Career Transactions: Selected by Yankees in third round of 1996 draft; signed June 14, 1996.

Johnson's extraordinary 1999 season in Double-A had the Yankees excited about what he might do in 2000. He led the Eastern League in '99 in hitting (.345) and topped the entire minors in walks (123), hit by pitches (37) and on-base percentage (.525). Johnson was ticketed for Triple-A to start 2000, though he had a chance to make the big league club at some point. And with Tino Martinez' contract set to expire, Johnson was in position to take over the first-base job in 2001. But all that went awry in spring training, when Johnson felt something pop in his right hand when he checked a swing. Doctors struggled to diagnose the injury, which didn't heal until his hand was placed in a cast. As a result, he didn't play in a game all season.

Johnson is a tremendously gifted all-around hitter. He obviously produces for average and his power is coming. He had 14 home runs in 1999, when he played his home games in a park (Norwich's Dodd Memorial Stadium) not conducive to power. Johnson was seen as a Mark Grace type when he signed, but since has put on 44 pounds and should be much more of a masher. The Grace comparisons were a tribute to Johnson's glove, and he was named the EL's best defensive first baseman in 1999. He also made a league-high 20 errors at first base that season, though the Yankees think he only needs to be more aggressive to avoid getting caught in between hops.

The biggest negative surrounding Johnson is his lost year of development. To try to overcome that, he spent much of the offseason in Tampa going through daily hitting drills. He's not going to overwhelm anyone as a runner, but he doesn't need to. Defensively, he just has to charge more grounders. The Yankees picked up Martinez' option for 2001, so he'll return while Johnson gets Triple-A at-bats. Martinez has been slumping since bashing 44 homers in 1997, and New York got the worst production out of its first basemen among all American League clubs in 2000. There's no reason to assume Johnson won't regain his place among the most feared minor league hitters, which will put him in line to replace Martinez in 2002.

Year	Club (League)	Class	AVG	G	AB	R	H	2B	3B	HR	RBI	BB	SO	SB
1996	Yankees (GCL)	R	.287	47	157	31	45	11	1	2	33	30	35	0
1997	Greensboro (SAL)	A	.273	127	433	77	118	23	1	16	75	76	99	16
1998	Tampa (FSL)	A	.317	92	303	69	96	14	1	17	58	68	76	1
1999	Norwich (EL)	AA	.345	132	420	114	145	33	5	14	87	123	88	8
2000						Did Not Play—Injured								
MINOR LEAGUE TOTALS			.308	398	1313	291	404	81	8	49	253	297	298	25

2. Alfonso Soriano, ss

Born: Jan. 7, 1978. **Ht.:** 6-1. **Wt.:** 160. **Bats:** R. **Throws:** R. **Career Transactions:** Signed out of Dominican Republic by Hiroshima (Japan), November 1994 . . . Contract purchased by Yankees from Hiroshima, Sept. 29, 1998.

RICH ABEL

Soriano originally signed with Japan's Hiroshima Toyo Carp, then "retired" in 1998 in order to become a free agent. He got a four-year major league contract worth $3.1 million from the Yankees, then wowed observers in the 1998 Arizona Fall League and at the 1999 Futures Game, leading the World team to victory with two home runs. The furor has died down a bit since then. Soriano's tools are beyond reproach. He has a lightning-quick bat and can hit for average power. He runs well and has the arm and quickness to be an above-average shortstop. Soriano needs to translate those tools into baseball skills, however. He presently lacks the discipline to be the offensive threat he can be, the instincts to be an effective basestealer and the consistency to be a steady defender. Some don't think he'll be able to play shortstop in the big leagues. In three stints with the Yankees in 2000, Soriano didn't impress offensively or defensively, so he'll get more time in Triple-A. He won't take Derek Jeter's job, so a move to second base, third base or the outfield is in Soriano's future.

Year	Club (League)	Class	AVG	G	AB	R	H	2B	3B	HR	RBI	BB	SO	SB
1995	Hiroshima (DSL)	R	.366	63	227	52	83	12	3	4	55	30	19	8
1996	Hiroshima West	JPN	.214	57	131	11	28	—	—	0	13	—	—	—
1997	Hiroshima (CL)	JPN	.118	9	17	2	2	0	0	0	2	0	4	0
1998							Did Not Play							
1999	Norwich (EL)	AA	.305	89	361	57	110	20	3	15	68	32	67	24
	Yankees (GCL)	R	.263	5	19	7	5	2	0	1	5	1	3	0
	Columbus (IL)	AAA	.183	20	82	8	15	5	1	2	11	5	18	1
	New York (AL)	MAJ	.125	9	8	2	1	0	0	1	1	0	3	0
2000	Columbus (IL)	AAA	.290	111	459	90	133	32	6	12	66	25	85	14
	New York (AL)	MAJ	.180	22	50	5	9	3	0	2	3	1	15	2
MAJOR LEAGUE TOTALS			.172	31	58	7	10	3	0	3	4	1	18	2
MINOR LEAGUE TOTALS			.301	288	1148	214	346	71	13	34	205	93	192	47

3. D'Angelo Jimenez, ss

Born: Dec. 21, 1977. **Ht.:** 6-0. **Wt.:** 194. **Bats:** B. **Throws:** R. **Career Transactions:** Signed out of Dominican Republic by Yankees, Aug. 1, 1994.

RICH ABEL

Jimenez led all minor league shortstops with a .327 average in 1999, putting him in line to serve in a big league utility role in 2000. Those plans were dashed in January when he broke his neck when his car hit a bus in the Dominican Republic. He was sidelined until July. All of Jimenez' tools are average or better with the exception of his power, and he can sting the ball well for a shortstop. He draws walks and makes contact. Defensively, he's solid at short and has shown an aptitude for playing second base. Unlike Alfonso Soriano, who's still a work in progress, Jimenez is a refined player. He's not an above-average runner and he's still working on turning the double play at second, but those are minor flaws. Fully healthy again, Jimenez should claim that utility job this spring. If the Yankees decide Chuck Knoblauch can't play second base, Jimenez would be the logical in-house candidate to replace him.

Year	Club (League)	Class	AVG	G	AB	R	H	2B	3B	HR	RBI	BB	SO	SB
1995	Yankees (GCL)	R	.280	57	214	41	60	14	8	2	28	23	31	6
1996	Greensboro (SAL)	A	.244	138	537	68	131	25	5	6	48	56	113	15
1997	Tampa (FSL)	A	.281	94	352	52	99	14	6	6	48	50	50	8
	Columbus (IL)	AAA	.143	2	7	1	1	0	0	0	1	0	1	0
1998	Norwich (EL)	AA	.270	40	152	21	41	6	2	2	21	25	26	5
	Columbus (IL)	AAA	.256	91	344	55	88	19	4	8	51	46	67	6
1999	Columbus (IL)	AAA	.327	126	526	97	172	32	5	15	88	59	75	26
	New York (AL)	MAJ	.400	7	20	3	8	2	0	0	4	3	4	0
2000	GCL Yankees (GCL)	R	.100	4	10	2	1	0	0	0	0	5	1	0
	Tampa (FSL)	A	.195	12	41	8	8	1	1	1	2	8	7	0
	Columbus (IL)	AAA	.233	21	73	11	17	3	1	1	5	7	12	2
MAJOR LEAGUE TOTALS			.400	7	20	3	8	2	0	0	4	3	4	0
MINOR LEAGUE TOTALS			.274	585	2256	356	618	114	32	41	292	279	383	68

4. Adrian Hernandez, rhp

Born: Aug. 30, 1974. **Ht.:** 6-2. **Wt.:** 185. **Bats:** R. **Throws:** R. **Career Transactions:** Signed out of Cuba by Yankees, June 2, 2000.

Though initial reports claimed Hernandez defected from Cuba disguised as a woman, he insists his escape was far less dramatic. What is certain is that he signed a four-year, $4 million major league contract and reached Triple-A before a sprained ligament in his left knee ended his season. Hernandez' delivery resembles that of fellow Cuban Orlando Hernandez (no relation), which is why he earned the nickname El Duquecito. He throws a variety of pitches (sinker, cutter, curveball, slider, changeup) from a variety of arm angles, and his delivery and the life on his pitches make him difficult to hit. He can reach 92-93 mph when needed. Like Orlando Hernandez before him, Adrian needs to refine his changeup to combat lefthanders. They hit .250 against him with a walk for every four at-bats, while righties batted .209 with a walk for every 14 ABs. The Yankees will give Hernandez the opportunity to win the fifth spot in their rotation.

Year	Club (League)	Class	W	L	ERA	G	GS	CG	SV	IP	R	ER	H	BB	SO
2000	Tampa (FSL)	A	1	0	1.35	1	1	0	0	7	1	1	3	1	13
	Norwich (EL)	AA	5	1	4.04	6	6	1	0	36	17	16	34	18	44
	Columbus (IL)	AAA	2	1	4.40	5	5	2	0	31	18	15	24	18	29
MINOR LEAGUE TOTALS			8	2	3.89	12	12	3	0	74	36	32	61	37	86

5. Alex Graman, lhp

Born: Nov. 17, 1977. **Ht.:** 6-4. **Wt.:** 200. **Bats:** L. **Throws:** L. **School:** Indiana State University. **Career Transactions:** Selected by Yankees in third round of 1999 draft; signed June 5, 1999.

The Yankees are deep in lefthanders, and Graman has the highest ceiling. As a result, both the Tigers and Cubs tried to get him when New York explored trades for Juan Gonzalez and Sammy Sosa at midseason. He was the short-season New York-Penn League's top prospect in 1999. Graman is a legitimate four-pitch pitcher, with a great package for a lefthander, starting with a low-90s fastball that can touch 94 mph. With his frame, he's projectable and could add more velocity. He's fearless when it comes to throwing his changeup behind in the count, has good bite on his curveball and puts hitters away with his splitter. Graman needs to improve his command, mostly of his pitches but also of his emotions. That should come with experience. He'll begin 2001 in Double-A and might be ready if the Yankees need him toward the end of the season, though a 2002 ETA is more likely.

Year	Club (League)	Class	W	L	ERA	G	GS	CG	SV	IP	H	R	ER	BB	SO
1999	Staten Island (NY-P)	A	6	3	2.99	14	14	0	0	81	74	30	27	16	85
2000	Tampa (FSL)	A	8	9	3.65	28	28	3	0	143	120	64	58	58	111
	Norwich (EL)	AA	0	1	11.81	1	1	0	0	5	6	7	7	4	3
MINOR LEAGUE TOTALS			14	13	3.62	43	43	3	0	229	200	101	92	78	199

6. Randy Keisler, lhp

Born: Feb. 24, 1976. **Ht.:** 6-3. **Wt.:** 190. **Bats:** L. **Throws:** L. **School:** Louisiana State University. **Career Transactions:** Selected by Yankees in second round of 1998 draft; signed July 21, 1998.

Keisler recovered from Tommy John surgery in college to reach New York barely two years after he was drafted. He beat the Red Sox with five solid innings of work in his major league debut in September. He was made available to the Indians in the David Justice trade, but they chose righthander Zach Day instead. Keisler has three major league pitches. He throws his fastball from 88-92 mph, his curveball is slightly above-average and he has picked up a nice changeup. After defeating the Red Sox, Keisler got rocked by major league hitters, allowing 13 runs in six innings. He must improve the command of his fastball. Though Adrian Hernandez is the frontrunner, Keisler also will contend for the vacancy in New York's rotation. A few more Triple-A starts won't hurt if he gets sent down.

Year	Club (League)	Class	W	L	ERA	G	GS	CG	SV	IP	H	R	ER	BB	SO
1998	Oneonta (NY-P)	A	1	1	7.45	6	2	0	1	10	14	10	8	7	11
1999	Greensboro (SAL)	A	1	1	2.38	4	4	0	0	23	12	6	6	10	42
	Tampa (FSL)	A	10	3	3.30	15	15	1	0	90	67	43	33	40	77
	Norwich (EL)	AA	3	4	4.57	8	8	0	0	43	45	24	22	17	33

Year	Club (League)		Class													
2000	Norwich (EL)		AA	6	2	2.60	11	11	1	0	73	63	29	21	34	70
	Columbus (IL)		AAA	8	3	3.02	17	17	1	0	113	104	44	38	42	86
	New York (AL)		MAJ	1	0	11.81	4	1	0	0	11	16	14	14	8	6
MAJOR LEAGUE TOTALS				1	0	11.81	4	1	0	0	11	16	14	14	8	6
MINOR LEAGUE TOTALS				29	14	3.27	61	57	3	1	352	305	156	128	150	319

7. Erick Almonte, ss

RICH ABEL

Born: Feb. 1, 1978. **Ht.:** 6-2. **Wt.:** 180. **Bats:** R. **Throws:** R. **Career Transactions:** Signed out of Dominican Republic by Yankees, Feb. 12, 1996.

Almonte was the No. 4 prospect in the Rookie-level Gulf Coast League in 1997, but his progress stalled over the next two years. He came on in 2000, batting .297 during the final three months of the season and opening eyes in the Arizona Fall League, where he batted .301-4-21. Built along the lines of Derek Jeter, Almonte is an impressive athlete. He can run, throw and hit for power. The Yankees always had faith in him, and he responded as he matured. Like many young shortstops, Almonte alternates between making spectacular defensive plays and botching routine ones. He's a free swinger who needs to gain better control of the strike zone. Unfortunately for Almonte, he's in an organization loaded with shortstops, starting with Jeter. Almonte is ready for Triple-A, where it might be time for him to try another position, especially if Alfonso Soriano or D'Angelo Jimenez returns there. He spent most of his time in the AFL playing second base.

Year	Club (League)	Class	AVG	G	AB	R	H	2B	3B	HR	RBI	BB	SO	SB
1996	Yankees (DSL)	R	.282	58	216	37	61	7	0	8	36	15	30	3
1997	Yankees (GCL)	R	.283	52	180	32	51	4	4	3	31	21	27	8
1998	Greensboro (SAL)	A	.209	120	450	53	94	13	0	6	33	29	121	6
1999	Tampa (FSL)	A	.257	61	230	36	59	8	2	5	25	18	49	3
	Yankees (GCL)	R	.300	9	30	5	9	2	0	2	9	3	10	1
2000	Norwich (EL)	AA	.271	131	454	56	123	18	4	15	77	35	129	12
MINOR LEAGUE TOTALS			.254	431	1560	219	397	52	10	39	211	121	366	33

8. Deivi Mendez, ss

SPORTS ON FILM

Born: June 24, 1983. **Ht.:** 6-1. **Wt.:** 165. **Bats:** R. **Throws:** R. **Career Transactions:** Signed out of Dominican Republic by Yankees, July 2, 1999.

Mendez is the fourth shortstop among the Yankees' top eight prospects, and he has the best defensive tools of the bunch. He was 16 when he made his pro debut, though he had no trouble in the Gulf Coast League and finished up as the league's No. 3 prospect. Mendez is unbelievably polished for a shortstop so young. His hands, range and arm are all plus tools. Not only that, but he also showed hitting ability, gap power and the willingness to take a walk. As he develops physically, his penchant for doubles may translate into decent over-the-fence power. Mendez will need to tone down his strikeouts, but his youth and knowledge of the strike zone bode well for his ability to do so. He also must improve his defensive consistency, but the main thing he needs is experience. At 17, it's unlikely he'll be sent to a full-season league in 2001. If he advances one level a year, he would reach New York in 2006, when he'll be 22 and Jeter will be 31.

Year	Club (League)	Class	AVG	AB	G	R	H	2B	3B	HR	RBI	BB	SO	SB
2000	Yankees (GCL)	R	.300	210	56	37	63	20	1	2	25	26	39	4
MINOR LEAGUE TOTALS			.300	210	56	37	63	20	1	2	25	26	39	4

9. Wily Mo Pena, of

RODGER WOOD

Born: Jan. 23, 1982. **Ht.:** 6-3. **Wt.:** 215. **Bats:** R. **Throws:** R. **Career Transactions:** Signed out of Dominican Republic by Yankees, July 15, 1998.

Pena previously signed with the Marlins and Mets before both contracts were ruled invalid and he accepted a four-year big league deal worth $3.7 million from the Yankees. After batting .184 in the first two months of 2000, he hit .294 before straining a ligament in his right knee in an outfield collision. Pena is probably the most impressive five-tool prospect the Yankees have had since Ruben Rivera. He's a pure athlete with awesome power, and he can run, throw and play center field. But he's as raw as he is gifted. He has a .234 average and a 168-32 strikeout-walk ratio in 132 professional games. He'll need time to develop into a productive hitter. The Yankees knew sending Pena to a full-season club at age 18 was a stretch, and it may be again at the start of 2001. Because he signed a major league contract, he must stick in New York to open 2003 or be exposed to waivers. That timetable appears too ambitious at this point.

Year	Club (League)	Class	AVG	G	AB	R	H	2B	3B	HR	RBI	BB	SO	SB
1999	Yankees (GCL)	R	.247	45	166	21	41	10	1	7	26	12	54	3
2000	Greensboro (SAL)	A	.205	67	249	41	51	7	1	10	28	18	91	6
	Staten Island (NY-P)	A	.301	20	73	7	22	1	2	0	10	2	23	2
MINOR LEAGUE TOTALS			.234	132	488	69	114	18	4	17	64	32	168	11

10. Todd Noel, rhp

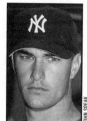

Born: Sept. 28, 1978. **Ht.:** 6-4. **Wt.:** 225. **Bats:** R. **Throws:** R. **School:** North Vermillion HS, Maurice, La. **Career Transactions:** Selected by Cubs in first round (17th overall) of 1996 draft; signed June 30, 1996 . . . Traded by Cubs with 3B Kevin Orie and RHP Justin Speier to Marlins for LHP Felix Heredia and LHP Steve Hoff, July 31, 1998 . . . Traded by Marlins with LHP Ed Yarnall and RHP Mark Johnson to Yankees for 3B Mike Lowell, Feb. 1, 1999.

Noel missed the first six weeks of 2000, then made just four starts before needing arthroscopic surgery to clean up the labrum in his right shoulder. The Yankees say he has the best pure arm in the organization since 1991 No. 1 overall pick Brien Taylor. He pitches at 95-96 mph and can reach 98. He has a smooth delivery, which should lead to good control, and his secondary pitches (curveball, slider, changeup) are fine. Noel has elite stuff. He just needs innings and health. He has pitched just 293 innings and has yet to advance past Class A. The Yankees consider Noel's surgery a minor setback and expect him to be ready for spring training. Pitching a full season in 2001 would be a big step forward. He'll probably begin his third consecutive season in the Florida State League.

Year	Club (League)	Class	W	L	ERA	G	GS	CG	SV	IP	H	R	ER	BB	SO
1996	Cubs (GCL)	R	0	0	6.75	3	0	0	0	4	4	4	3	2	4
1997	Cubs (AZL)	R	5	1	1.98	12	11	0	1	59	39	27	13	30	63
1998	Rockford (Mid)	A	6	6	4.03	16	16	1	0	89	83	45	40	37	70
	Kane County (Mid)	A	2	2	5.30	7	5	0	0	37	45	25	22	17	26
1999	Tampa (FSL)	A	3	7	4.34	17	17	0	0	93	101	56	45	33	80
2000	Tampa (FSL)	A	0	0	10.80	4	4	0	0	10	18	13	12	8	11
MINOR LEAGUE TOTALS			16	16	4.15	59	59	1	1	293	290	170	135	127	254

11. Juan Rivera, of

Born: July 3, 1978. **Ht.:** 6-2. **Wt.:** 170. **Bats:** R. **Throws:** R. **Career Transactions:** Signed out of Venezuela by Yankees, April 12, 1996.

Rivera spent two seasons in the Rookie-level Dominican and Venezuelan summer leagues before making his U.S. debut in 1998, when he led the Gulf Coast League in homers and RBIs and ranked as its No. 1 prospect. He hasn't excelled like that since, repeating the Florida State League last year and struggling after a late-season promotion to Double-A. Rivera makes decent contact and has hit for gap power, but he won't hit for a higher average or tap into his raw power until he develops more patience at the plate. He's an average runner with a plus arm, which makes him a legitimate right fielder. When Jackson Melian was included in the Denny Neagle trade with the Reds, Rivera became the Yankees' top upper-level outfield prospect. But he's still at least two years away from New York.

Year	Club (League)	Class	AVG	G	AB	R	H	2B	3B	HR	RBI	BB	SO	SB
1996	Yankees (DSL)	R	.167	10	18	0	3	0	0	0	2	0	1	0
1997	Maracay 2 (VSL)	R	.282	52	142	25	40	9	0	0	14	12	16	12
1998	Yankees (GCL)	R	.333	57	210	43	70	9	1	12	45	26	27	8
	Oneonta (NY-P)	A	.278	6	18	2	5	0	0	1	3	1	4	1
1999	Tampa (FSL)	A	.263	109	426	50	112	20	2	14	77	26	67	5
	Yankees (GCL)	R	.333	5	18	7	6	0	0	1	4	4	1	0
2000	Norwich (EL)	AA	.226	17	62	9	14	5	0	2	12	6	15	0
	Tampa (FSL)	A	.276	115	409	62	113	26	1	14	69	33	56	11
MINOR LEAGUE TOTALS			.279	371	1303	198	363	69	4	44	226	118	187	37

12. Brandon Claussen, lhp

Born: May 1, 1979. **Ht.:** 6-2. **Wt.:** 175. **Bats:** L. **Throws:** L. **School:** Howard (Texas) JC. **Career Transactions:** Selected by Yankees in 34th round of 1998 draft; signed May 20, 1999.

The Yankees have worked the draft-and-follow process as well as any club, with Exhibit A being Andy Pettitte. Claussen returned for his sophomore year at Howard (Texas) Junior College before joining the Yankees in 1999. He reached high Class A Tampa in his first full pro season and has plenty of upside. He has a fastball that has above-average movement and velocity (90-91 mph). His curveball is his second pitch and his changeup is developing. Claussen's biggest needs are to consistently repeat his delivery and improve his command within the strike zone, two things that go hand in hand. He may start 2001 in Double-A.

Year	Club (League)	Class	W	L	ERA	G	GS	CG	SV	IP	H	R	ER	BB	SO
1999	Yankees (GCL)	R	0	1	3.18	2	2	0	0	11	7	4	4	2	16
	Staten Island (NY-P)	A	6	4	3.38	12	12	1	0	72	70	30	27	12	89
	Greensboro (SAL)	A	0	1	10.50	1	1	1	0	6	8	7	7	2	5
2000	Greensboro (SAL)	A	8	5	4.05	17	17	1	0	98	91	49	44	44	98
	Tampa (FSL)	A	2	5	3.10	9	9	1	0	52	49	24	18	17	44
MINOR LEAGUE TOTALS			16	16	3.77	41	41	4	0	239	225	114	100	77	252

13. Chien-Ming Wang, rhp

Born: March 31, 1980. **Ht.:** 6-2. **Wt.:** 180. **Bats:** R. **Throws:** R. **Career Transactions:** Signed out of Taiwan by Yankees, May 5, 2000.

The Yankees made their first foray into Taiwan when they gave Wang a $1.5 million bonus in May. He had the best arm in an all-prospect rotation that led Staten Island to the New York-Penn League championship. Wang showed a lot of polish for a 20-year-old pitcher making his U.S. debut. Opponents batted just .233 with two homers against him. He throws strikes with quality stuff: a consistent 92-mph fastball that can reach 94, a splitter, a slider and a changeup. He also keeps his pitches down and has a projectable body, a sound delivery and plenty of poise. Nicknamed "Tiger," he'll move up to Class A Greensboro this year.

Year	Club (League)	Class	W	L	ERA	G	GS	CG	SV	IP	H	R	ER	BB	SO
2000	Staten Island (NY-P)	A	4	4	2.48	14	14	2	0	87	77	34	24	21	75
MINOR LEAGUE TOTALS			4	4	2.48	14	14	2	0	87	77	34	24	21	75

14. David Martinez, lhp

Born: June 7, 1980. **Ht.:** 6-1. **Wt.:** 165. **Bats:** L. **Throws:** L. **Career Transactions:** Signed out of Venezuela by Yankees, Dec. 23, 1996.

Martinez threw a no-hitter in the Gulf Coast League in his U.S. debut in 1999, then began 2000 at Staten Island. He earned a quick promotion to Greensboro, and when he returned to Staten Island just before the New York-Penn League playoffs, he paid two dividends. First, he won the championship clincher over Mahoning Valley. And when Martinez joined the rotation it sent Jason Anderson to the bullpen, where his fastball soared to 96 mph. Martinez has exceptional velocity as well, particularly for a lefthander. He consistently works at 91-92 mph with a high of 94. He also has a promising curveball and changeup. All he needs are more experience to refine his secondary pitches and command. New York has handled him carefully, but he's ready for his first full season in 2001, when he'll be assigned to Greensboro.

Year	Club (League)	Class	W	L	ERA	G	GS	CG	SV	IP	H	R	ER	BB	SO
1997	Maracay 2 (VSL)	R	2	1	1.66	6	0	0	0	22	19	7	4	9	15
1998	La Pradera (VSL)	R	2	4	4.27	15	13	0	0	72	75	42	34	25	67
1999	Yankees (GCL)	R	5	3	2.97	12	11	2	0	67	52	29	22	22	67
2000	Staten Island (NY-P)	A	2	2	2.51	6	4	0	0	32	20	12	9	11	33
	Greensboro (SAL)	A	2	5	2.92	8	8	1	0	49	33	24	16	27	44
MINOR LEAGUE TOTALS			13	15	3.17	47	36	3	0	241	199	114	85	94	226

15. Elvis Corporan, 3b

Born: June 9, 1980. **Ht.:** 6-3. **Wt.:** 200. **Bats:** B. **Throws:** R. **School:** Lake City (Fla.) CC. **Career Transactions:** Selected by Yankees in 31st round of 1998 draft; signed May 19, 1999.

Like Brandon Claussen, Corporan is a promising draft-and-follow from the 1998 draft. Corporan did a nice job of recovering last year after being overmatched in the Class A South Atlantic League as a teenager. Demoted to the New York-Penn League, he ranked as the circuit's No. 2 prospect. Switch-hitting third basemen with power abound in the Yankees system—Donny Leon and Juan Camacho are others of note—but Corporan is easily the best. He has good pop from both sides of the plate and should be a terror once he fills out his 6-foot-2 frame. He has the arm and lateral movement to be an exceptional third baseman. Corporan is ready for another shot at the Sally League in 2001.

Year	Club (League)	Class	AVG	G	AB	R	H	2B	3B	HR	RBI	BB	SO	SB
1999	Yankees (GCL)	R	.278	56	212	29	59	13	3	4	30	19	41	3
2000	Staten Island (NY-P)	A	.260	73	281	37	73	14	2	8	36	23	61	7
	Greensboro (SAL)	A	.247	63	255	37	63	10	1	4	31	28	66	10
MINOR LEAGUE TOTALS			.261	192	748	103	195	37	6	16	97	70	168	20

16. Ricardo Aramboles, rhp

Born: Dec. 4, 1981. **Ht.:** 6-2. **Wt.:** 170. **Bats:** R. **Throws:** R. **Career Transactions:** Signed out of Dominican Republic by Marlins, July 2, 1996 . . . Contract voided, Dec. 3, 1997 . . . Signed by Yankees Feb. 26, 1998.

Aramboles signed with the Marlins in 1996, but the commissioner's office struck down the contract because he was underage when he signed. Spirited bidding from several teams ensued, with New York winning out for $1.52 million. After a fine debut, he injured his elbow and required Tommy John surgery that knocked him out for much of 1999. Back at full strength last year, he held his own at Greensboro. His fastball once again was topping out at 95 mph, and he has good secondary pitches. His changeup is outstanding, and his curveball is slightly above-average. In 2000, Aramboles got hit a little more than a pitcher with his stuff should because he relied on his changeup at the expense of his fastball. He has the heat to overpower hitters and needs to do so. Aramboles will move up to Tampa this season.

Year	Club (League)	Class	W	L	ERA	G	GS	CG	SV	IP	H	R	ER	BB	SO
1997	Marlins (DSL)	R	1	1	1.71	8	2	0	0	21	15	7	4	7	14
1998	Yankees (GCL)	R	2	1	2.93	10	9	0	0	40	33	14	13	13	44
	Oneonta (NY-P)	A	1	0	1.50	1	1	0	0	6	4	2	1	1	8
1999	Yankees (GCL)	R	2	3	3.89	9	7	0	0	35	35	18	15	14	42
	Greensboro (SAL)	A	1	2	2.34	6	6	1	0	35	25	9	9	12	34
2000	Greensboro (SAL)	A	5	13	4.31	25	25	2	0	138	150	81	66	47	150
MINOR LEAGUE TOTALS			12	20	3.48	59	50	3	0	274	262	131	106	94	292

17. Danny Borrell, lhp

Born: Jan. 24, 1979. **Ht.:** 6-3. **Wt.:** 195. **Bats:** L. **Throws:** L. **School:** Wake Forest University. **Career Transactions:** Selected by Yankees in second round of 2000 draft; signed June 19, 2000.

Borrell reminds the Yankees of Eric Milton, another lefthander from an Atlantic Coast Conference school (Maryland) whom they took early in the draft (first round, 1996). Both were two-way players in college, though Borrell was more effective as a first baseman/outfielder (.336-37-172) for Wake Forest than he was as a pitcher (10-8, 6.21). Focusing fully on pitching as a pro, he performed much better. Borrell has an average fastball and a plus changeup. Very athletic, he has a fluid delivery and a nice, loose arm. He needs to come up with a breaking pitch and has worked on both a curveball and a slider. Because he's relatively inexperienced as a pitcher, Borrell probably will be assigned to Greensboro in 2001.

Year	Club (League)	Class	W	L	ERA	G	GS	CG	SV	IP	H	R	ER	BB	SO
2000	Yankees (GCL)	R	0	1	0.00	1	1	0	0	3	2	0	0	0	2
	Staten Island (NY-P)	A	4	2	3.20	10	10	0	0	56	39	21	20	19	44
MINOR LEAGUE TOTALS			4	3	3.05	11	11	0	0	59	41	21	20	19	46

18. Ted Lilly, lhp

Born: Jan. 4, 1976. **Ht.:** 6-0. **Wt.:** 185. **Bats:** L. **Throws:** L. **School:** Fresno CC. **Career Transactions:** Selected by Dodgers in 23rd round of 1996 draft; signed June 7, 1996 . . . Traded by Dodgers with 2B Wilton Guerrero, OF Peter Bergeron and 1B Jonathan Tucker to Expos for SS Mark Grudzielanek, LHP Carlos Perez and OF Hiram Bocachica, July 31, 1998 . . . Traded by Expos to Yankees, March 17, 2000, as part of trade in which Yankees sent RHP Hideki Irabu to Expos for RHP Jake Westbrook and two players to be named (Dec. 22, 2000); Yankees acquired RHP Christian Parker to complete trade (March 22, 2000).

Lilly has been involved in two trades as a pro, and both teams that got rid of him regret the deals. After offseason surgery to clean up the labrum in his shoulder, Lilly turned in a decent season in Triple-A. He can reach the low 90s with a four-seam fastball, though it tends to get pounded when he leaves it up in the strike zone. His curveball is his best pitch, and his changeup is solid. Lilly would do well to refine a two-seam fastball that would have more life than his four-seamer. With his curve he should dominate lefthanders, but they have hit .335 off him in Triple-A. Lilly was used as a reliever when he was promoted to New York in 2000, but he could factor into the race for a rotation spot this spring, albeit as a long-shot behind Adrian Hernandez and Randy Keisler.

Year	Club (League)	Class	W	L	ERA	G	GS	CG	SV	IP	H	R	ER	BB	SO
1996	Yakima (NWL)	A	4	0	0.84	13	8	0	0	54	25	9	5	14	75
1997	San Bernardino (Cal)	A	7	8	2.81	23	21	2	0	135	116	52	42	32	158
1998	San Antonio (TL)	AA	8	4	3.30	17	17	0	0	112	114	50	41	37	96
	Albuquerque (PCL)	AAA	1	3	4.94	5	5	0	0	31	39	20	17	9	25
	Ottawa (IL)	AAA	2	2	4.85	7	7	0	0	39	45	28	21	19	49
1999	Ottawa (IL)	AAA	8	5	3.84	16	16	0	0	89	81	40	38	23	78
	Montreal (NL)	MAJ	0	1	7.61	9	3	0	0	24	30	20	20	9	28

Year	Club (League)	Class	W	L	ERA	G	GS	CG	SV	IP	H	R	ER	BB	SO
2000	Columbus (IL)	AAA	8	11	4.19	22	22	3	0	137	157	77	64	48	127
	New York (AL)	MAJ	0	0	5.63	7	0	0	0	8	8	6	5	5	11
MINOR LEAGUE TOTALS			38	33	3.44	103	96	5	0	596	577	276	228	182	608
MAJOR LEAGUE TOTALS			0	1	7.03	16	3	0	0	32	38	26	25	14	39

19. David Walling, rhp

Born: Nov. 12, 1978. **Ht.:** 6-5. **Wt.:** 210. **Bats:** R. **Throws:** R. **School:** University of Arkansas. **Career Transactions:** Selected by Yankees in first round (27th overall) of 1999 draft; signed June 5, 1999.

The Yankees made Walling just the 16th pitcher they have drafted in the first round. The track record of the first 15 is dubious, as only Bill Burbach (1965) reached New York. Scott McGregor (1972) and Eric Milton (1996) enjoyed major league success after being traded. Walling is on track to escape that history, having reached Double-A in his first full season. The Yankees compared him to Orlando Hernandez without a curveball after signing him, and they still think that's what he'll become. He throws an 88-93 mph fastball and a quality changeup, both with command. He got knocked around at Norwich after dominating the lower minors because he lacks a good breaking pitch. He needs to tighten his curveball, and New York may try to get him to experiment with a slider or a cut fastball. Though Walling will return to Norwich to start 2001, he remains on the fast track.

Year	Club (League)	Class	W	L	ERA	G	GS	CG	SV	IP	H	R	ER	BB	SO
1999	Staten Island (NY-P)	A	8	2	3.14	14	14	0	0	80	76	31	28	18	82
2000	Tampa (FSL)	A	7	2	1.99	9	9	2	0	59	48	17	13	12	45
	Norwich (EL)	AA	3	9	5.27	14	14	2	0	85	101	54	50	26	70
MINOR LEAGUE TOTALS			18	13	3.66	37	37	4	0	224	225	102	91	56	197

20. Christian Parker, rhp

Born: July 3, 1975. **Ht.:** 6-1. **Wt.:** 200. **Bats:** R. **Throws:** R. **School:** University of Notre Dame. **Career Transactions:** Selected by Expos in fourth round of 1996 draft; signed June 13, 1996 . . . Traded by Expos to Yankees, March 22, 2000, as part of trade in which Yankees sent RHP Hideki Irabu to Expos for RHP Jake Westbrook and two players to be named (Dec. 22, 2000); Yankees acquired LHP Ted Lilly to complete trade (March 17, 2000).

Parker was a throw-in in the Hideki Irabu deal with Montreal last spring. He wasn't protected on the Expos' 40-man roster the previous winter and wasn't picked in the Rule 5 draft. So the term "breakthrough" doesn't quite do justice to Parker's 2000 season, when he threw 40 consecutive scoreless innings in Double-A and led the minors in innings. His fastball shot up from 86-90 mph to 91-93, and he touched 93-94 mph every game. Parker already knew how to throw strikes, change speeds and mix his pitches, which also include a cut fastball, slider and changeup. After surrendering 11 homers in 89 Double-A innings in 1999, he permitted just eight in 204 innings last year. Parker will get Triple-A experience in 2001 but has a good chance to surface in New York in the second half.

Year	Club (League)	Class	W	L	ERA	G	GS	CG	SV	IP	H	R	ER	BB	SO
1996	Vermont (NY-P)	A	7	1	2.48	14	14	2	0	80	63	26	22	22	61
1997	Cape Fear (SAL)	A	11	10	3.12	25	25	0	0	153	146	72	53	49	106
	W. Palm Beach (FSL)	A	0	1	3.32	3	3	0	0	19	22	7	7	5	10
1998	Harrisburg (EL)	AA	6	6	3.48	36	16	0	5	127	124	66	49	47	73
1999	Ottawa (IL)	AAA	0	1	7.59	7	0	0	0	11	10	9	9	7	5
	Harrisburg (EL)	AA	8	5	3.65	36	6	0	3	89	86	39	36	37	45
2000	Norwich (EL)	AA	14	6	3.13	28	28	4	0	204	196	86	71	58	147
MINOR LEAGUE TOTALS			46	30	3.26	149	92	6	8	682	647	305	247	225	447

21. Donzell McDonald, of

Born: Feb. 20, 1975. **Ht.:** 5-11. **Wt.:** 165. **Bats:** B. **Throws:** R. **School:** Yavapai (Ariz.) JC. **Career Transactions:** Selected by Yankees in 22nd round of 1995 draft; signed July 22, 1995.

McDonald's younger brother Darnell was an Orioles first-round pick in 1997, but Donzell has become the better prospect. After missing half of 2000 recovering from a broken right thumb incurred while sliding in May, Donzell tore up the Arizona Fall League. He batted .354, missing out on the batting title by .001, and led the AFL in runs (29), hits (45), stolen bases (18) and on-base percentage (.435). A chic prospect in 1997 who nevertheless was unprotected in the expansion draft, McDonald endured a disappointing 1998 season before resurrecting his career. He has taken his role to heart: get on base by any means necessary so he can use his disruptive speed. He is drawing more walks and cutting down his swing. He's also a switch-hitter, which enhances his ability to contribute offensively. He's a plus defender in center field. McDonald won't hit for much power, but he won't be expected to as a leadoff hitter. He'll begin 2001 in Triple-A. If Wily Mo Pena and Juan Rivera don't improve their offensive production, then McDonald could wind up in New York's outfield of the future.

Year	Club (League)	Class	AVG	G	AB	R	H	2B	3B	HR	RBI	BB	SO	SB
1995	Yankees (GCL)	R	.236	28	110	23	26	5	1	0	9	16	24	11
1996	Oneonta (NY-P)	A	.277	74	282	57	78	8	10	2	30	43	62	54
1997	Tampa (FSL)	A	.296	77	297	69	88	23	8	3	23	48	75	39
1998	Norwich (EL)	AA	.253	134	495	80	125	20	7	6	36	55	127	35
	Tampa (FSL)	A	.333	5	18	6	6	1	2	0	2	2	7	2
1999	Norwich (EL)	AA	.272	137	533	95	145	19	10	4	33	90	110	54
2000	Norwich (EL)	AA	.241	44	170	23	41	7	2	2	10	35	36	13
	Columbus (IL)	AAA	.247	24	77	17	19	4	4	1	6	23	11	12
MINOR LEAGUE TOTALS			.266	523	1982	370	528	87	44	18	149	312	452	220

22. Craig Dingman, rhp

Born: March 12, 1974. **Ht.:** 6-4. **Wt.:** 215. **Bats:** R. **Throws:** R. **School:** Hutchinson (Kan.) CC. **Career Transactions:** Selected by Yankees in 36th round of 1993 draft; signed May 22, 1994.

Dingman is another draft-and-follow, returning for his sophomore season at Hutchinson (Kan.) Community College after getting drafted in 1992. He showed potential with 51 strikeouts in 32 innings in the Gulf Coast League in 1994, then missed all of 1995 after elbow surgery. Dingman made a full recovery and has posted remarkable minor league numbers. He's a pure power pitcher, throwing a 93-95 mph fastball and a high-80s slider. He's also working on a splitter that would make him tougher on lefthanders. Dingman has a deceptive delivery, which gives batters less time to pick up his pitches. He got knocked around in 10 big league appearances last year, but he's ready for a spot in New York's bullpen.

Year	Club (League)	Class	W	L	ERA	G	GS	CG	SV	IP	H	R	ER	BB	SO
1994	Yankees (GCL)	R	0	5	3.38	17	1	0	1	32	27	17	12	10	51
1995							Did Not Play—Injured								
1996	Oneonta (NY-P)	A	0	2	2.04	20	0	0	9	35	17	11	8	9	52
1997	Greensboro (SAL)	A	2	0	1.91	30	0	0	19	33	19	7	7	12	41
	Tampa (FSL)	A	0	4	5.24	19	0	0	6	22	15	14	13	14	26
1998	Tampa (FSL)	A	5	4	3.18	50	0	0	7	71	48	29	25	39	95
1999	Norwich (EL)	AA	8	6	1.57	55	0	0	9	74	56	16	13	12	90
2000	Columbus (IL)	AAA	6	1	3.05	47	2	0	1	74	60	31	25	20	65
	New York (AL)	MAJ	0	0	6.55	10	0	0	0	11	18	8	8	3	8
MAJOR LEAGUE TOTALS			0	0	6.55	10	0	0	0	11	18	8	8	3	8
MINOR LEAGUE TOTALS			21	22	2.71	238	3	0	52	342	242	125	103	116	420

23. Brett Jodie, rhp

Born: March 25, 1977. **Ht.:** 6-4. **Wt.:** 208. **Bats:** R. **Throws:** R. **School:** University of South Carolina. **Career Transactions:** Selected by Yankees in sixth round of 1998 draft; signed June 8, 1998.

Known as a control specialist, Jodie's career took off in 2000 when his velocity did the same. His fastball, which used to top out at 90 mph, suddenly averaged 90-91 mph and reached 94. He always had a projectable pitcher's body, and his fastball suddenly caught up with it. He can locate his fastball with precision, and he developed his secondary pitches when he lacked velocity. He throws a curveball and isn't afraid to come in with a changeup when he's behind in the count. Jodie doesn't need to do much except keep throwing strikes with all his pitches. He'll return to Double-A, where he did well at the end of 2000.

Year	Club (League)	Class	W	L	ERA	G	GS	CG	SV	IP	H	R	ER	BB	SO
1998	Oneonta (NY-P)	A	7	6	2.59	15	15	1	0	94	87	40	27	21	73
1999	Greensboro (SAL)	A	9	6	3.81	25	20	2	1	120	125	59	51	18	106
2000	Tampa (FSL)	A	11	4	2.57	25	18	3	0	144	134	53	41	29	122
	Norwich (EL)	AA	2	1	3.15	3	3	1	0	20	16	8	7	5	9
MINOR LEAGUE TOTALS			29	17	3.00	68	56	7	1	378	362	160	126	73	310

24. Brian Rogers, rhp

Born: Feb. 13, 1977. **Ht.:** 6-6. **Wt.:** 210. **Bats:** R. **Throws:** R. **School:** The Citadel. **Career Transactions:** Selected by Yankees in fifth round of 1998 draft; signed June 13, 1998.

Rogers led the Cape Cod League in strikeouts in 1997 and finished second in NCAA Division I in whiffs in 1998. In between, he had knee surgery that cost him velocity and messed up his mechanics, knocking him from a sure first-round pick to a fifth-rounder. It worked out for the Yankees, as Rogers has had no knee problems as a pro. His best pitch is a hammer curveball that drops straight down, and he has a fastball capable of reaching 93 mph. Rogers has put up solid numbers in the minors, but he hasn't overmatched hitters. He needs to improve his command, and he's working on a changeup and a cut fastball. It wouldn't be a bad idea to send him back to Double-A for a big first half before going to Triple-A.

Year	Club (League)	Class	W	L	ERA	G	GS	CG	SV	IP	H	R	ER	BB	SO
1998	Oneonta (NY-P)	A	2	2	2.31	6	6	0	0	35	23	9	9	10	34
	Tampa (FSL)	A	0	0	4.20	3	3	0	0	15	12	7	7	14	13
	Greensboro (SAL)	A	2	1	7.88	3	3	0	0	16	18	15	14	6	19
1999	Tampa (FSL)	A	8	10	3.83	25	23	1	0	134	141	62	57	43	129
2000	Norwich (EL)	AA	11	6	3.94	27	27	1	0	164	155	90	72	70	132
MINOR LEAGUE TOTALS			23	19	3.93	64	62	2	0	364	349	183	159	143	327

25. Andy Brown, of

Born: April 14, 1980. **Ht.:** 6-6. **Wt.:** 190. **Bats:** L. **Throws:** L. **School:** Richmond (Ind.) HS. **Career Transactions:** Selected by Yankees in first round (24th overall) of 1998 draft; signed June 14, 1998.

Brown didn't perform like a first-rounder until the final two months of 2000. Entering August, he had a career .219 average and 26 homers. He finished by batting .291 with eight homers in 48 games. Power usually takes a while to develop, and it seems to be happening for Brown. At 6-foot-6 he has a frame for generating leverage. He's more than a one-dimensional slugger, too. He's a decent athlete with average speed and a good arm in right field. Brown led the South Atlantic League in strikeouts and had nearly six whiffs for every walk, so he has to tighten his strike zone. He also needs to add strength. The Yankees like his work ethic and believe he'll do both. He'll make the jump to high Class A this season.

Year	Club (League)	Class	AVG	G	AB	R	H	2B	3B	HR	RBI	BB	SO	SB
1998	Yankees (GCL)	R	.229	36	131	19	30	5	2	3	24	16	38	0
1999	Greensboro (SAL)	A	.176	29	108	14	19	5	1	5	15	10	49	0
	Staten Island (NY-P)	A	.214	67	215	38	46	8	5	7	22	27	97	5
2000	Greensboro (SAL)	A	.257	122	463	56	119	31	1	19	63	35	182	4
MINOR LEAGUE TOTALS			.233	254	917	127	214	49	9	34	124	88	366	9

26. Jeremy Blevins, rhp

Born: Oct. 5, 1977. **Ht.:** 6-3. **Wt.:** 190. **Bats:** R. **Throws:** R. **School:** Sullivan East HS, Bristol, Tenn. **Career Transactions:** Selected by Angels in third round of 1995 draft; signed June 6, 1995 . . . Traded by Angels with 3B Ryan Kane to Yankees for C Jim Leyritz, Dec. 9, 1996.

The Yankees got Blevins and third baseman Ryan Kane the first time they traded Jim Leyritz. Kane was released in 1998, but Blevins blossomed into a relief prospect. He hit the wall as a starter in Class A, then converted saves in his first 13 relief appearances in 2000. His velocity picked up when he was used in shorter stints, as Blevins threw 92-93 mph repeatedly and reached 95. He continued to use the slider and changeup he employed as a starter, but his new role allowed him to rely on his fastball more often. His command is still spotty at best and remains his biggest point of concern. The Yankees will promote him to Double-A in 2001 and see if he can climb the ladder in relief. He threw well in the Arizona Fall League.

Year	Club (League)	Class	W	L	ERA	G	GS	CG	SV	IP	H	R	ER	BB	SO
1995	Angels (AZL)	R	5	1	2.45	11	9	0	0	51	39	20	14	32	48
1996	Boise (NWL)	A	2	3	6.60	14	13	0	0	59	54	49	43	58	39
1997	Yankees (GCL)	R	5	3	2.43	11	9	0	0	56	50	27	15	23	46
1998	Greensboro (SAL)	A	5	8	4.81	24	23	0	0	120	121	80	64	66	110
1999	Tampa (FSL)	A	0	0	0.00	1	0	0	0	2	4	3	0	1	0
	Greensboro (SAL)	A	10	5	4.05	19	19	0	0	107	105	56	48	30	81
2000	Tampa (FSL)	A	3	7	4.44	42	12	0	20	95	96	50	47	49	104
MINOR LEAGUE TOTALS			30	27	4.25	122	85	0	20	489	469	285	231	259	428

27. Mitch Jones, of

Born: Oct. 15, 1977. **Ht.:** 6-2. **Wt.:** 215. **Bats:** R. **Throws:** R. **School:** Arizona State University. **Career Transactions:** Selected by Yankees in seventh round of 2000 draft; signed June 15, 2000.

Jones broke Bob Horner's Arizona State season home run record with 27, and he set a Sun Devils career mark with a .731 slugging percentage. The Yankees are still trying to figure out how they got him with the 218th pick in the draft, especially after he led the short-season New York-Penn League in doubles, homers and extra-base hits. He generates a lot of bat speed, and the ball jumps off his bat. He has a decent eye at the plate, though he'll have to cut down on his strikeouts if he's going to hit for average. He's an average runner with a plus arm, and he can play a solid left or right field. Jones also worked out at third base in a Yankees mini-camp, though he'll stay in the outfield for now. Considering his 2000 success and his age, Jones is a prime candidate to skip Greensboro and go straight to high Class A Tampa.

Year	Club (League)	Class	AVG	G	AB	R	H	2B	3B	HR	RBI	BB	SO	SB
2000	Staten Island (NY-P)	A	.268	74	284	46	76	28	3	11	54	35	66	8
MINOR LEAGUE TOTALS			.268	74	284	46	76	28	3	11	54	35	66	8

28. David Parrish, c

Born: June 13, 1979. **Ht.:** 6-3. **Wt.:** 220. **Bats:** R. **Throws:** R. **School:** University of Michigan. **Career Transactions:** Selected by Yankees in first round (28th overall) of 2000 draft; signed June 22, 2000.

The Yankees also drafted Parrish in the 10th round out of high school in 1997. Though he was Michigan's MVP as a junior in 2000, several teams were surprised when New York took him in the first round. But without any other catching prospects, the Yankees are intrigued by Parrish's upside, which resembles that of his father, former big league all-star Lance. David has raw power and arm strength, which he showed in his pro debut at Staten Island. Though he hit just four homers, he did stroke 20 doubles, and he finished second among New York-Penn League regulars by gunning down 37 percent of basestealers. Parrish still needs to refine all aspects of his game. He needs to improve his plate discipline as well as his blocking and receiving skills. He'll probably begin 2001 at Greensboro.

Year	Club (League)	Class	AVG	G	AB	R	H	2B	3B	HR	RBI	BB	SO	SB
2000	Staten Island (NY-P)	A	.240	63	221	29	53	20	1	4	29	25	54	0
MINOR LEAGUE TOTALS			.240	63	221	29	53	20	1	4	29	25	54	0

29. Scott Seabol, 3b

Born: May 17, 1975. **Ht.:** 6-4. **Wt.:** 200. **Bats:** R. **Throws:** R. **School:** West Virginia University. **Career Transactions:** Selected by Yankees in 88th round of 1996 draft; signed June 25, 1996.

If Seabol reaches the major leagues, he'll be the lowest-drafted player ever to do so. Seabol was the 1,719th of 1,740 players selected in 1996. The Yankees didn't hand him an every-day job in the minors until 1999, his third season in the South Atlantic League. He responded with a 35-game hitting streak and a minor league-best 55 doubles. He jumped to Double-A in 2000 and led the Eastern League in doubles with a career-high 20 homers. Seabol made himself a hitter by working hard and adding strength, though he still could tighten his strike zone. Defensively, he offers solid hands and agility, and his arm is good enough to play third base. He's capable of playing at first base or in left field, or even at second base in 2000. Seabol has passed Donny Leon on the organization's depth chart, which means he'll be the Triple-A starter this season. When they tire of Scott Brosisus, the Yankees are more likely to convert one of their shortstops to third base rather than hand their starting job at the hot corner to Seabol, but he could be a versatile big league reserve.

Year	Club (League)	Class	AVG	G	AB	R	H	2B	3B	HR	RBI	BB	SO	SB
1996	Oneonta (NY-P)	A	.211	43	142	16	30	9	1	3	10	15	30	2
1997	Greensboro (SAL)	A	.265	48	136	11	36	12	2	2	15	9	26	3
1998	Greensboro (SAL)	A	.286	71	210	24	60	11	0	7	33	13	40	2
1999	Greensboro (SAL)	A	.315	138	543	86	171	55	6	15	89	45	91	6
2000	Norwich (EL)	AA	.296	132	493	82	146	45	2	20	78	42	108	2
MINOR LEAGUE TOTALS			.291	432	1524	219	443	132	11	47	225	124	295	15

30. Marcus Thames, of

Born: March 6, 1977. **Ht.:** 6-2. **Wt.:** 205. **Bats:** R. **Throws:** R. **School:** East Central (Miss.) CC. **Career Transactions:** Selected by Yankees in 30th round of 1996 draft; signed May 16, 1997.

Few players in the system can match the array of tools possessed by Thames, yet another draft-and-follow. His power potential, speed and arm all are above-average, though he's still learning how to put them to good use. He's too undisciplined at the plate, which is why he makes inconsistent contact. He also needs to improve his baserunning skills after going 1-for-6 stealing bases in 2000. Regularly used in right field, Thames could play center field if needed. He has been at Norwich since midseason 1999, but he'll have to return there yet again this year to show he can handle Double-A pitching. It will be a pivotal season for Thames, who likely will fall by the wayside if he doesn't show improvement.

Year	Club (League)	Class	AVG	G	AB	R	H	2B	3B	HR	RBI	BB	SO	SB
1997	Yankees (GCL)	R	.344	57	195	51	67	17	4	7	36	16	26	6
	Greensboro (SAL)	A	.313	4	16	2	5	1	0	0	2	0	3	1
1998	Tampa (FSL)	A	.284	122	457	62	130	18	3	11	59	24	78	13
1999	Norwich (EL)	AA	.225	51	182	25	41	6	2	4	26	22	40	0
	Tampa (FSL)	A	.244	69	266	47	65	12	4	11	38	33	58	3
2000	Norwich (EL)	AA	.241	131	474	72	114	30	2	15	79	50	89	1
MINOR LEAGUE TOTALS			.265	434	1590	259	422	84	15	48	240	145	294	24

Oakland
Athletics

By Casey Tefertiller

The Athletics had a master plan last spring. They would send their highly touted prospects back to the minor leagues, let them gain seasoning, then maybe after September callups they would be armed and ready with a kiddie corps for 2001.

So much for well-laid plans.

By late July, Terrence Long, Mark Mulder, Adam Piatt and Barry Zito were in the majors and the young A's were on the way to winning the American League West. The expectation now is that Oakland has developed a young core of talent that can keep it in contention for years to come.

The formula is simple: draft, development, Dominicans. The A's stutter-stepped through most of the 1990s as the organization rebuilt through the draft, selecting carefully and developing expertly. Oakland established a major presence in the Dominican Republic and began attracting some of the best young talent to its inviting complex. The result has been an infusion of young talent with high potential, just beginning to blossom.

General manager Billy Beane has to be creative at the helm of a small-revenue club. After the 2000 season ended, he traded veterans Matt Stairs and Randy Velarde, added three prospects and saved payroll to try to sign American League MVP Jason Giambi to a long-term deal. Then he traded to get Johnny Damon from the Royals in a three-way deal, a sign the A's are going for broke in 2001.

Yet the A's are remarkably homegrown. They're likely to start the 2001 season with a lineup featuring six position players from their farm system. With Tim Hudson, Mulder and Zito, the rotation is built around pitchers drafted and developed by Oakland.

Former first-rounders Eric Chavez (1996), Mulder (1998) and Zito (1999) are locks for the big league club and another, Ariel Prieto (1995), is likely to battle for a rotation or bullpen job. Oakland could start 2001 with just one first-rounder in the minors: righthander Chris Enochs (1997). This is an unusual record of success, and the A's consider it a tribute to scouting director Grady Fuson, farm director Keith Lieppman and their staffs.

In an era when franchises complain that enormous contracts and high expenses isolate success to just an elite few, Beane and his predecessor Sandy Alderson were charged with trying to reverse that trend. The plan has worked better and faster than even the organization had expected.

OrganizationOverview

General manager: Billy Beane. **Farm director:** Keith Lieppman. **Scouting director:** Grady Fuson.

2000 PERFORMANCE

Class	Team	League	W	L	Pct.	Finish*	Manager
Majors	Oakland	American	91	70	.565	2nd (14)	Art Howe
Triple-A	Sacramento RiverCats	Pacific Coast	90	54	.625	2nd (16)	Bob Geren
Double-A	Midland RockHounds	Texas	70	69	.504	4th (8)	Tony DeFrancesco
High A	Modesto A's	California	76	64	.543	5th (10)	Greg Sparks
High A	Visalia Oaks	California	78	62	.557	3rd (10)	Juan Navarrette
Short-season	Vancouver Canadians	Northwest	39	37	.513	4th (8)	Dave Joppie
Rookie	AZL Athletics	Arizona	29	25	.537	4th (9)	John Kuehl
OVERALL 2000 MINOR LEAGUE RECORD			381	311	.551	3rd (30)	

*Finish in overall standings (No. of teams in league).

ORGANIZATION LEADERS

BATTING

*AVG	Jose Ortiz, Sacramento	.351
R	**Mark Bellhorn**, Sacramento	111
H	Jason Hart, Midland/Sacramento	183
TB	Jason Hart, Midland/Sacramento	327
2B	Eric Byrnes, Midland/Sacramento	48
3B	**Mark Bellhorn**, Sacramento	11
HR	Jason Hart, Midland/Sacramento	31
RBI	Jason Hart, Midland/Sacramento	125
BB	**Mark Bellhorn**, Sacramento	94
SO	Caonabo Cosme, Midland	163
SB	Esteban German, Visalia/Midland	83

PITCHING

W	Mario Ramos, Modesto/Midland	14
L	Kevin Gregg, Midland	14
#ERA	Mario Ramos, Modesto/Midland	2.66
G	Bert Snow, Midland/Sacramento	62
CG	Several tied at	1
SV	Bert Snow, Midland/Sacramento	27
IP	**Denny Wagner**, Midland	180
BB	Wayne Nix, Visalia	76
SO	Juan Pena, Modesto	177

*Minimum 250 at-bats. #Minimum 75 innings.

TOP PROSPECTS OF THE DECADE

1991	Todd Van Poppel, rhp
1992	Todd Van Poppel, rhp
1993	Todd Van Poppel, rhp
1994	Steve Karsay, rhp
1995	Ben Grieve, of
1996	Ben Grieve, of
1997	Miguel Tejada, ss
1998	Ben Grieve, of
1999	Eric Chavez, 3b
2000	Mark Mulder, lhp

TOP DRAFT PICKS OF THE DECADE

1991	Brent Gates, ss
1992	Benji Grigsby, rhp
1993	John Wasdin, rhp
1994	Ben Grieve, of
1995	Ariel Prieto, rhp
1996	Eric Chavez, 3b
1997	Chris Enochs, rhp
1998	Mark Mulder, lhp
1999	Barry Zito, lhp
2000	Freddie Bynum, ss (2)

Bellhorn **Wagner**

BEST TOOLS

Best Hitter for Average	Jose Ortiz
Best Power Hitter	Jason Hart
Fastest Baserunner	Esteban German
Best Fastball	Chad Harville
Best Breaking Ball	Bert Snow
Best Control	Mario Ramos
Best Defensive Catcher	Gerald Laird
Best Defensive Infielder	Francis Alfonseca
Best Infield Arm	Freddie Bynum
Best Defensive Outfielder	Ryan Ludwick
Best Outfield Arm	Mario Encarnacion

PROJECTED 2004 LINEUP

Catcher	Ramon Hernandez
First Base	Jason Hart
Second Base	Jose Ortiz
Third Base	Eric Chavez
Shortstop	Miguel Tejada
Left Field	Terrence Long
Center Field	Johnny Damon
Right Field	Ryan Ludwick
Designated Hitter	Jason Giambi
No. 1 Starter	Tim Hudson
No. 2 Starter	Barry Zito
No. 3 Starter	Mark Mulder
No. 4 Starter	Justin Miller
No. 5 Starter	Mario Ramos
Closer	Jason Isringhausen

ALL-TIME LARGEST BONUSES

Mark Mulder, 1998	$3,200,000
Barry Zito, 1999	1,625,000
Chris Enochs, 1997	1,204,000
Ben Grieve, 1994	1,200,000
Ariel Prieto, 1995	1,200,000

DraftAnalysis

2000 Draft

Best Pro Debut: RHPs Mike Ziegler (14) and Richie Rodarmel (40) were outstanding in the short-season Northwest League. Ziegler went 3-0, 1.27. Rodarmel went 1-0, 1.17 with 10 saves. SS Freddie Bynum (2), Oakland's first pick, batted .256 with 22 steals to earn top prospect honors in the NWL.

Best Athlete: Bynum, who had a low profile before he was drafted out of Pitt County (N.C.) CC. His speed and arm are plus tools, and he has the strength in his hands and wrists to develop decent power for a middle infielder.

Best Hitter: OF **Daylan Holt** (3) has a feel for hitting, though his aggressive nature stands out in an organization that preaches the virtues of patience at the plate. Holt will need to learn the strike zone to hit for average at higher levels.

Best Raw Power: Holt led NCAA Division I with 34 homers in 1999 before dipping to 15 as a junior last spring. He's a good athlete, combining his offensive ability with a quality right-field arm and average speed.

Fastest Runner: Bynum goes from the left side to first base in 3.9 to 4.0 seconds.

Best Defensive Player: Bynum has the range and arm to make highlight plays at shortstop, but he must improve his consistency. 2B Marshall McDougall (9) is a more solid defender with a strong arm and good hands.

Best Fastball: The A's emphasize pitching savvy and command more than most organizations, and they didn't sign any power arms. RHPs Kevin McGerry (4), Marcus Gwyn (7), Kyle Crowell (8), Ziegler, Chris Scarcella (16) and Rodarmel all peak in the low 90s. Ziegler probably throws harder more consistently than the others.

Most Intriguing Background: McDougall set an NCAA record in 1999 with a six-homer game and won the College World Series MVP award. C John Suomi (22) was the first player drafted from the University College of the Cariboo in Kamloops, B.C., which has earned him the nickname Bullwinkle.

Closest To The Majors: Gwyn or Ziegler, the most polished of the pitchers. Gwyn also pitched well at Vancouver, going 2-1, 2.86 with a 31-2 strikeout-walk ratio in 28 inings.

Holt

Best Late-Round Pick: Ziegler. OF Chris Tritle (19) is raw but has a lot of upside.

The One Who Got Away: RHP Kenny Baugh (5), a college teammate of Gwyn, returned to Rice for his senior season. RHP Kip Bouknight (21) led Divison I with 17 wins despite marginal stuff. He's back at South Carolina for his senior year.

Assessment: Giving up a first-round pick to sign free-agent middle reliever Mike Magnante made no sense, and the move looked worse when the Angels used that choice to get righthander Chris Bootcheck. The Athletics didn't spend much money on the draft. Bynum got the largest bonus at $495,000, the third-lowest figure among second-rounders.

1999 Draft

LHP Barry Zito (1) tore up the big leagues just a year later. Five of the next seven picks are on the A's top 30 list, led by OF Ryan Ludwick (2) and LHP Mario Ramos (6).   **Grade: B+**

1998 Draft

Oakland found another rotation anchor in LHP Mark Mulder (1). Afterward it landed four of its best 12 prospects in C Gerald Laird (2, draft-and-follow), 1B Jason Hart (5), OF Eric Byrnes (8) and RHP Bert Snow (10).   **Grade: C+**

1997 Draft

The A's get a top grade despite blowing first-round picks on RHPs Chris Enochs and Denny Wagner and LHP Eric DuBose. Later in the draft, Oakland rebounded with 2000 American League Cy Young Award runner-up Tim Hudson (6) and slugging OF Adam Piatt (8). RHP Chad Harville (2) could be a future closer.   **Grade: A**

1996 Draft

3B Eric Chavez (1) looks like an all-star for years to come. C A.J. Hinch (3) and RHP Brett Laxton (24) didn't work out, but brought Johnny Damon and Jeremy Giambi, respectively, in trades with the Royals.   **Grade: B+**

Note: Draft analysis prepared by Jim Callis. Numbers in parentheses indicate draft rounds.

. . . . Ortiz has developed into an offensive force who can hit for unusual average and power for a middle infielder.

Jose
Ortiz 2b

Born: June 13, 1977.
Ht.: 5-9. **Wt.:** 177.
Bats: R. **Throws:** R.
Career Transactions: Signed out of Dominican Republic by Athletics, Nov. 8, 1994.

LARRY GOREN

Almost since the day he joined the Athletics, Ortiz has had a corps of believers who expected him to become something special. He showed remarkable offensive skills at a young age, hitting .330 in the Rookie-level Arizona League in 1996. Then came three years of injuries and moderate production as the A's awaited his maturation. There were lingering questions about whether he could play middle-infield defense or would be forced to third base. His game came together last season. He won the Pacific Coast League MVP and was the best position-player prospect in the Triple-A league.

Ortiz has developed into an offensive force. He can hit for unusual average and power for a middle infielder, and if he can translate the numbers at the big league level, it will make him a factor in the lineup. Ortiz made major strides in defining his strike zone and quit swinging at so many pitcher's pitches. "When he stopped being his own worst enemy, he found out how good he was," Sacramento manager Bob Geren said. "He has good balance, good eye-hand coordination, his bat path to the zone is perfect, his swing is short, he's strong. Once he got a feel for the strike zone and started understanding the game, he made remarkable improvement."

His glove remains the biggest problem. Ortiz made 32 errors last season, but most were at shortstop before moving to second base. He is far better at second, where he has more time to recover from a mistake. Once he got the call to the majors, Ortiz worked with infield instructor Ron Washington and made great progress in fielding balls hit to his right. His range is only average and he needs more experience at second. He also needs to improve his strike zone discipline and patience at the plate.

The A's pulled a surprise in November, trading veteran Randy Velarde to the Rangers and opening a big league job for Ortiz, who otherwise might have been cast in a utility role in 2001. Ortiz will face competition from Frank Menechino and Mark Bellhorn, but if all goes according to plan he will be the A's second baseman of the future, and the future begins now.

Year	Club (League)	Class	AVG	G	AB	R	H	2B	3B	HR	RBI	BB	SO	SB
1995	Oakland (DSL)	R	.300	61	217	45	65	12	2	9	41	32	22	14
1996	Athletics (AZL)	R	.330	52	200	43	66	12	8	4	25	20	34	16
	Modesto (Cal)	A	.250	1	4	0	1	0	0	0	0	0	1	0
1997	Modesto (Cal)	A	.245	128	497	92	122	25	7	16	58	60	107	22
1998	Huntsville (SL)	AA	.277	94	354	70	98	24	2	6	55	48	63	22
1999	Vancouver (PCL)	AAA	.284	107	377	66	107	29	2	9	45	29	50	13
2000	Sacramento (PCL)	AAA	.351	131	518	107	182	34	5	24	108	47	64	22
	Oakland (AL)	MAJ	.182	7	11	4	2	0	0	0	1	2	3	0
MAJOR LEAGUE TOTALS			.182	7	11	4	2	0	0	0	1	2	3	0
MINOR LEAGUE TOTALS			.296	574	2167	423	641	136	26	68	332	236	341	109

2. Jason Hart, 1b

Born: Sept. 5, 1977. **Ht.:** 6-3. **Wt.:** 225. **Bats:** R. **Throws:** R. **School:** Southwest Missouri State University. **Career Transactions:** Selected by Athletics in fifth round of 1998 draft; signed June 5, 1998.

Hart spent his youth in Contra Costa County, just north of Oakland. He finished among the NCAA Division I leaders in home runs and RBIs in 1998, then batted .305-19-123 at Class A Modesto in his first full pro season a year later. He surpassed those numbers in 2000, and fared as well on the road as he did at hitter-friendly Double-A Midland. Hart possesses impressive power and backs it up with big numbers in average. He has developed the ability to use the whole field. What has most impressed the A's is his dramatic improvement on defense, where thousands of ground balls have led to huge advancements in his first-base play. Hart still needs to improve his selectivity at the plate and refine his stroke. More than anything he needs experience against higher-level pitching. He's probably limited to playing first, though he's working at third base to increase his versatility. A year at Triple-A at Sacramento will provide Hart the opportunity to test his skills against more advanced pitching. He has the bat to be an everyday first baseman in the major leagues.

Year	Club (League)	Class	AVG	G	AB	R	H	2B	3B	HR	RBI	BB	SO	SB
1998	S. Oregon (NWL)	A	.258	75	295	58	76	19	1	20	69	36	67	0
1999	Modesto (Cal)	A	.305	135	550	96	168	48	2	19	123	56	105	2
2000	Midland (TL)	AA	.326	135	546	98	178	44	3	30	121	67	112	4
	Sacramento (PCL)	AAA	.278	5	18	4	5	1	0	1	4	3	7	0
MINOR LEAGUE TOTALS			.303	350	1409	256	427	112	6	70	317	162	291	6

3. Ryan Ludwick, of

Born: July 13, 1978. **Ht.:** 6-3. **Wt.:** 200. **Bats:** R. **Throws:** L. **School:** University of Nevada-Las Vegas. **Career Transactions:** Selected by Athletics in second round of 1999 draft; signed July 17, 1999.

After an impressive summer with Team USA in 1998, Ludwick was projected as a first-round pick at the beginning of the 1999 college season. When he failed to show the power most scouts had expected, hitting only 13 homers, Oakland got him in the second round. Once he signed with the A's, his power quickly became apparent. The A's have high expectations for Ludwick. He hit for a high average in college, and they hope he can do the same as a pro without sacrificing power. He has shown outstanding defensive skills, and the A's hope he can become a legitimate center fielder. He has good speed, though not as good as usually exhibited by big league center fielders. He has a strong arm and may be best suited to right field. Ludwick is raw and must refine his swing, use the whole field and define his strike zone. Too often he's fooled by offspeed pitches because he hasn't seen much pro-level pitching. Ludwick is ticketed for Midland. He could use two full seasons in the upper minors before challenging for an outfield job in Oakland in 2003.

Year	Club (League)	Class	AVG	G	AB	R	H	2B	3B	HR	RBI	BB	SO	SB
1999	Modesto (Cal)	A	.275	43	171	28	47	11	3	4	34	19	45	2
2000	Modesto (Cal)	A	.264	129	493	86	130	26	3	29	102	68	128	10
MINOR LEAGUE TOTALS			.267	172	664	114	177	37	6	33	136	87	173	12

4. Mario Encarnacion, of

Born: Sept. 24, 1977. **Ht.:** 6-2. **Wt.:** 205. **Bats:** R. **Throws:** R. **Career Transactions:** Signed out of Dominican Republic by Athletics, July 2, 1994.

Since the day he signed, Encarnacion has excited the A's. He's a complete package but has needed two years at each stop before advancing, and he was hampered by injuries most of 2000. Encarnacion is a five-tool player with an abundance of natural ability. He has proven himself as a legitimate center fielder, though his future is more likely in right because he has a strong arm. He also has shown an excellent attitude and great desire. Encarnacion never has hit for average because he misses hittable pitches and swings at bad ones. He has been slow to make adjustments. His power potential continues to exceed his production, and he continues to make mistakes of youth in the outfield, missing cutoff men and throwing to the wrong base. Encarnacion has an outside shot at winning Oakland's right-field job in spring training. More likely, Jeremy Giambi and Adam Piatt will platoon while Encarnacion returns to Triple-A.

Year	Club (League)	Class	AVG	G	AB	R	H	2B	3B	HR	RBI	BB	SO	SB
1995	Athletics (DSL)	R	.345	64	229	56	79	11	5	8	44	40	36	17
1996	West Michigan (Mid)	A	.229	118	401	55	92	14	3	7	43	49	131	23
1997	Modesto (Cal)	A	.297	111	364	70	108	17	9	18	78	42	121	14
1998	Huntsville (SL)	AA	.272	110	357	70	97	15	2	15	61	60	123	11
1999	Midland (TL)	AA	.309	94	353	69	109	21	4	18	71	47	86	9
	Vancouver (PCL)	AAA	.241	39	145	18	35	5	0	3	17	6	44	5
2000	Sacramento (PCL)	AAA	.269	81	301	51	81	16	3	13	61	36	95	15
	Modesto (Cal)	A	.200	5	15	1	3	0	0	0	1	1	4	0
MINOR LEAGUE TOTALS			.279	622	2165	390	604	99	26	82	376	281	640	94

5. Justin Miller, rhp

Born: Aug. 27, 1977. **Ht.:** 6-2. **Wt.:** 195. **Bats:** R. **Throws:** R. **School:** Los Angeles Harbor JC. **Career Transactions:** Selected by Rockies in fifth round of 1997 draft; signed June 17, 1997 . . . Traded by Rockies with cash to Athletics as part of three-way trade in which Devil Rays sent RHP Rolando Arrojo and SS Aaron Ledesma to Rockies, Rockies sent 3B Vinny Castilla to Devil Rays and RHP Jamey Wright and C Henry Blanco to Brewers, Brewers sent 3B Jeff Cirillo, LHP Scott Karl and cash to Rockies and Athletics sent RHP Jimmy Haynes to Brewers, Dec. 13, 1999.

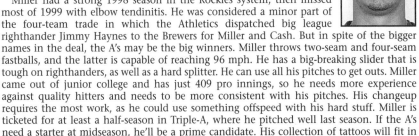

Miller had a strong 1998 season in the Rockies system, then missed most of 1999 with elbow tendinitis. He was considered a minor part of the four-team trade in which the Athletics dispatched big league righthander Jimmy Haynes to the Brewers for Miller and Cash. But in spite of the bigger names in the deal, the A's may be the big winners. Miller throws two-seam and four-seam fastballs, and the latter is capable of reaching 96 mph. He has a big-breaking slider that is tough on righthanders, as well as a hard splitter. He can use all his pitches to get outs. Miller came out of junior college and has just 409 pro innings, so he needs more experience against quality hitters and needs to be more consistent with his pitches. His changeup requires the most work, as he could use something offspeed with his hard stuff. Miller is ticketed for at least a half-season in Triple-A, where he pitched well last season. If the A's need a starter at midseason, he'll be a prime candidate. His collection of tattoos will fit in well in a clubhouse presided over by Jason Giambi.

Year	Club (League)	Class	W	L	ERA	G	GS	CG	SV	IP	H	R	ER	BB	SO
1997	Portland (NWL)	A	4	2	2.14	14	11	0	0	67	68	26	16	20	54
1998	Asheville (SAL)	A	13	8	3.69	27	27	3	0	163	177	89	67	40	142
1999	Salem (Car)	A	1	2	4.14	8	8	0	0	37	35	18	17	11	35
2000	Midland (TL)	AA	5	4	4.55	18	18	0	0	87	74	49	44	41	82
	Sacramento (PCL)	AAA	4	1	2.47	9	9	0	0	55	42	18	15	13	34
MINOR LEAGUE TOTALS			27	17	3.50	76	73	3	0	409	396	200	159	125	347

6. Freddie Bynum, ss

Born: March 15, 1980. **Ht.:** 6-2. **Wt.:** 180. **Bats:** L. **Throws:** R. **School:** Pitt County (N.C.) CC. **Career Transactions:** Selected by Athletics in second round of 2000 draft; signed June 19, 2000.

With no first-round pick in 2000, Oakland came up with a shocker when it selected Bynum. Despite batting .521 and succeeding on all 27 of his steal attempts in junior college, he received little predraft hype. But he showed great tools and was the top prospect in the short-season Northwest League. Bynum's speed and arm are plus tools, and he has excellent hand-eye coordination. He shows a great joy for the game. At instructional league, he played second, short and third, but the A's will keep him at shortstop for now. If he can make consistent contact, he has the ability to bat at the top of a lineup. Bynum has little experience against pro-caliber pitching. He probably won't ever hit for much power, but he can do better than the .256 average he put up in his debut. He is learning how to approach different types of grounders and become consistent in catching the ball cleanly and making the quick transfer to his throwing hand. Bynum will go to one of the A's California League affiliates. As with Angel Berroa, Oakland has no need to rush him.

Year	Club (League)	Class	AVG	G	AB	R	H	2B	3B	HR	RBI	BB	SO	SB
2000	Vancouver (NWL)	A	.256	72	281	52	72	10	1	1	26	31	58	22
MINOR LEAGUE TOTALS			.256	72	281	52	72	10	1	1	26	31	58	22

7. Chad Harville, rhp

Born: Sept. 16, 1976. **Ht.:** 5-9. **Wt.:** 180. **Bats:** R. **Throws:** R. **School:** University of Memphis. **Career Transactions:** Selected by Athletics in second round of 1997 draft; signed June 19, 1997.

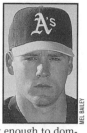

Harville reached Oakland in 1999 but has been unable to stick in the big leagues. He earned all-Conference USA honors as a reliever and a starter but has pitched primarily out of the bullpen since joining the A's. He has excelled in that role, leading Pacific Coast League relievers in strikeouts per nine innings (10.83) last season. Harville can launch his fastball at 98 mph, and he complements it with an above-average slider. He has the makeup and confidence to become a major league closer. Heat alone is not enough to dominate big league hitters, though, as Harville found out in Oakland. He fires too many of his fastballs up in the strike zone and is trying to master a sinking two-seamer to give him another weapon. He was slow to make either adjustment in 2000. His violent delivery concerns scouts, but he has remained healthy. Harville again will go to spring training competing for a job in the Oakland bullpen, though Jason Isringhausen is the unquestioned closer now. If Harville can make the necessary improvements, he will be a quality reliever.

Year	Club (League)	Class	W	L	ERA	G	GS	CG	SV	IP	H	R	ER	BB	SO
1997	S. Oregon (NWL)	A	1	0	0.00	3	0	0	0	5	3	0	0	3	6
	Visalia (Cal)	A	0	0	5.79	14	0	0	0	19	25	14	12	13	24
1998	Visalia (Cal)	A	4	3	3.00	24	7	0	4	69	59	25	23	31	76
	Huntsville (SL)	AA	0	0	2.45	12	0	0	8	15	6	4	4	13	24
1999	Midland (TL)	AA	2	0	2.01	17	0	0	7	22	13	6	5	9	35
	Vancouver (PCL)	AAA	1	0	1.75	22	0	0	11	26	24	5	5	11	36
	Oakland (AL)	MAJ	0	2	6.91	15	0	0	0	14	18	11	11	10	15
2000	Sacramento (PCL)	AAA	5	3	4.50	53	0	0	9	64	53	35	32	35	77
MAJOR LEAGUE TOTALS			0	2	6.91	15	0	0	0	14	18	11	11	10	15
MINOR LEAGUE TOTALS			13	6	3.32	145	7	0	39	219	183	89	81	115	278

8. Mario Ramos, lhp

Born: Oct. 19, 1977. **Ht.:** 5-11. **Wt.:** 165. **Bats:** L. **Throws:** L. **School:** Rice University. **Career Transactions:** Selected by Athletics in sixth round of 1999 draft; signed Aug. 23, 1999.

Ramos may not intimidate folks with his size, but the slender lefty continues to succeed. He led Rice to the 1999 College World Series by going 12-2, 2.51, then signed late and didn't make his pro debut until 2000. He dominated the California League and fared even better when he was bumped up to Double-A. Ramos is intelligent and knows how to pitch. He understands how to evaluate hitters and pitch to their weaknesses. He lives by changing speeds off his 88 mph fastball, and his changeup makes it seem faster. He throws strikes and keeps the ball in the park by pitching down in the strike zone. His changeup is his lone plus pitch. Ramos has yet to develop a legitimate breaking ball, though he has worked hard to add a curveball. He'll need it if he's going to survive his lack of velocity. Midland will provide a stern test for Ramos, who will face Double-A hitters in an unforgiving home ballpark. If all goes well, he might be ready for the major leagues in 2002.

Year	Club (League)	Class	W	L	ERA	G	GS	CG	SV	IP	H	R	ER	BB	SO
2000	Modesto (Cal)	A	12	5	2.90	26	24	1	0	152	131	63	49	50	134
	Midland (TL)	AA	2	0	1.32	4	4	0	0	27	24	6	4	6	19
MINOR LEAGUE TOTALS			14	5	2.66	30	28	1	0	179	155	69	53	56	153

9. Eric Byrnes, of

Born: Feb. 16, 1976. **Ht.:** 6-2. **Wt.:** 205. **Bats:** R. **Throws:** R. **School:** UCLA. **Career Transactions:** Selected by Athletics in eighth round of 1998 draft; signed June 12, 1998.

Despite winning the California League batting title with a .337 average in 1999, Byrnes was regarded as more of a blue-collar player than a prospect. He changed that in 2000 by adding power on his way to a September callup. Byrnes has hit at every stop in the system, and he has solid power potential. He runs well and continues to impress with his makeup. His work ethic has led to continual improvement, and he plays with all-out hustle. Despite his speed, Byrnes still needs work to become a good defensive outfielder, and he'll have to hit more home runs if he's to become more than a fourth outfielder at the big league level. Byrnes may have difficulty finding a spot in Oakland. Johnny Damon will be the left fielder for at least a year, and Jeremy Giambi and Adam Piatt likely will platoon in right. All three have higher ceilings than Byrnes, as do Ryan Ludwick and Mario Encarnacion. Byrnes will begin 2001 in Triple-A while he awaits an opening.

Year	Club (League)	Class	AVG	G	AB	R	H	2B	3B	HR	RBI	BB	SO	SB
1998	S. Oregon (NWL)	A	.314	42	169	36	53	10	2	7	31	16	16	6
	Visalia (Cal)	A	.426	29	108	26	46	9	2	4	21	18	15	11
1999	Modesto (Cal)	A	.337	96	365	86	123	28	1	6	66	58	37	28
	Midland (TL)	AA	.238	43	164	25	39	14	0	1	22	17	32	6
2000	Midland (TL)	AA	.301	67	259	49	78	25	2	5	37	43	38	21
	Sacramento (PCL)	AAA	.333	67	243	55	81	23	1	9	47	31	30	12
	Oakland (AL)	MAJ	.300	10	10	5	3	0	0	0	0	0	1	2
MAJOR LEAGUE TOTALS			.300	10	10	5	3	0	0	0	0	0	1	2
MINOR LEAGUE TOTALS			.321	344	1308	277	420	109	8	32	224	183	168	84

10. Bert Snow, rhp

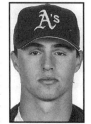

Born: March 23, 1977. **Ht.:** 6-1. **Wt.:** 190. **Bats:** R. **Throws:** R. **School:** Vanderbilt University. **Career Transactions:** Selected by Athletics in 10th round of 1998 draft; signed June 20, 1998.

Snow has been a revelation and led all minor league relievers with an average of 13.05 strikeouts per nine innings last year. He lives by an exceptional slider, which he mixes with a sinking fastball to keep hitters off balance. Snow came to instructional league to develop a split-finger pitch, and if he can get the feel for it the splitter could smooth his way to the majors. He has shown the ability to enter a game and throw strikes quickly, a key requirement for a reliever. The A's expect him to be ready for Oakland in 2001 should the need arise. Some in the organization believe he has the potential to grow into a major league closer, but the current plan is to move him into the hard-to-fill set-up role.

Year	Club (League)	Class	W	L	ERA	G	GS	CG	SV	IP	H	R	ER	BB	SO
1998	S. Oregon (NWL)	A	1	3	5.64	11	8	0	0	45	52	38	28	18	35
	Modesto (Cal)	A	1	1	3.12	2	2	0	0	9	12	8	3	6	12
1999	Visalia (Cal)	A	3	2	5.15	31	3	0	5	65	55	43	37	40	90
	Midland (TL)	AA	1	1	1.71	21	0	0	13	21	14	4	4	9	32
	Vancouver (PCL)	AAA	1	0	3.86	2	0	0	0	2	3	1	1	1	3
2000	Midland (TL)	AA	1	7	3.59	59	0	0	27	68	58	33	27	36	98
	Vancouver (PCL)	AAA	0	0	4.50	3	0	0	0	2	1	1	1	3	3
MINOR LEAGUE TOTALS			8	14	4.31	129	13	0	45	211	195	128	101	113	273

11. Gerald Laird, c

Born: Nov. 13, 1979. **Ht.:** 6-2. **Wt.:** 195. **Bats:** R. **Throws:** R. **School:** Cypress (Calif.) JC. **Career Transactions:** Selected by Athletics in second round of 1998 draft; signed June 1, 1999.

A second-round pick in 1998, Laird didn't sign until the following spring as a draft-and-follow. He's athletic and even played center field in college when he wasn't catching during the 1999 season. Once he joined the A's, he made an immediate impression, earning a position on the Northwest League all-star team. He has matured greatly since signing, developing from a kid who wanted to have fun into a serious worker. Injuries sidetracked his progress during 2000, but he still managed to show distinct improvement, particularly with his defense. He still has much development ahead and needs to refine his swing with a wood bat. The A's consider him a solid defensive catcher with legitimate offensive potential. He has shown signs of the ability to work with pitchers and handle a pitching staff.

Year	Club (League)	Class	AVG	G	AB	R	H	2B	3B	HR	RBI	BB	SO	SB
1999	S. Oregon (NWL)	A	.285	60	228	45	65	7	2	2	39	28	43	10
2000	Visalia (Cal)	A	.243	33	103	14	25	3	0	0	13	14	27	7
	Athletics (AZL)	R	.300	14	50	10	15	2	1	0	9	6	7	2
MINOR LEAGUE TOTALS			.276	107	381	69	105	12	3	2	61	48	77	19

12. Todd Belitz, lhp

Born: Oct. 23, 1975. **Ht.:** 6-3. **Wt.:** 200. **Bats:** L. **Throws:** L. **School:** Washington State University. **Career Transactions:** Selected by Devil Rays in fourth round of 1997 draft; signed June 5, 1997 . . . Traded by Devil Rays with RHP Jim Mecir to Athletics for RHP Jesus Colome and cash, July 28, 2000.

Belitz was brought to the organization to fill a specific role. The A's have been desperate for a second lefty in the bullpen, and he will have the opportunity to win the job this year. His father Stan played linebacker for the NFL's Miami Dolphins before working as a Secret

Service agent. Todd was a high school first baseman who didn't start pitching until college, and he still needs experience. He worked as a starter through his first three seasons in the Devil Rays chain, then was switched to the bullpen in 2000. He was much more effective in his new role after struggling mightily in Double-A the year before. As a reliever, he throws in the low 90s and mixes in a two-seam sinker to get ground balls. He also throws a slider.

Year	Club (League)	Class	W	L	ERA	G	GS	CG	SV	IP	H	R	ER	BB	SO
1997	Hudson Valley (NY-P)	A	4	5	3.53	15	15	0	0	74	65	41	29	18	78
1998	Charleston, SC (SAL)	A	6	4	2.42	21	21	0	0	130	99	44	35	48	123
	St. Petersburg (FSL)	A	2	2	5.04	7	7	0	0	44	39	28	25	14	40
1999	Orlando (SL)	AA	9	9	5.77	28	28	0	0	160	169	114	103	65	118
2000	Durham (IL)	AAA	1	1	3.83	43	0	0	2	47	33	24	20	28	46
	Sacramento (PCL)	AAA	0	1	4.38	12	0	0	1	12	12	6	6	5	10
	Oakland (AL)	MAJ	0	0	2.70	5	0	0	0	3	4	2	1	4	3
MAJOR LEAGUE TOTALS			0	0	2.70	5	0	0	0	3	4	2	1	4	3
MINOR LEAGUE TOTALS			22	22	4.19	126	71	0	3	468	417	257	218	178	415

13. Keith Surkont, rhp

Born: April 4, 1977. **Ht.:** 6-2. **Wt.:** 205. **Bats:** R. **Throws:** R. **School:** Williams (Mass.) College. **Career Transactions:** Selected by Athletics in fourth round of 1999 draft; signed June 12, 1999.

A product of Division III Williams (the alma mater of George Steinbrenner and Fay Vincent), Surkont has steadily improved since being drafted. He throws a heavy, low-90s fastball with good sink. He mixes in a fine breaking ball and an excellent changeup, and his overall command is solid. As with many New England players, he hasn't had the on-field time to match other players and still requires far more experience. He has shown the ability to learn quickly. Surkont needs to develop consistency with the breaking ball and the ability to throw it for strikes when needed. He can at times be dominant, as his 2.72 ERA in the tough Cal League indicates. The A's view him as a potential big league starter. Max Surkont, his grandfather, pitched for five major league teams between 1949-57.

Year	Club (League)	Class	W	L	ERA	G	GS	CG	SV	IP	H	R	ER	BB	SO
1999	S. Oregon (NWL)	A	5	3	4.48	17	13	0	1	74	85	45	37	35	39
2000	Visalia (Cal)	A	8	7	2.72	27	22	0	1	126	104	60	38	54	122
MINOR LEAGUE TOTALS			13	10	3.38	44	35	0	2	200	189	105	75	89	161

14. Luis Vizcaino, rhp

Born: June 10, 1977. **Ht.:** 5-11. **Wt.:** 170. **Bats:** R. **Throws:** R. **Career Transactions:** Signed out of Dominican Republic by Athletics, Dec. 9, 1994.

The hard-throwing Vizcaino has touched down in the big leagues in the last two seasons but has yet to find a way to stick. He has great ability and maddening inconsistency. He'll cruise along, then offer up a series of mistake pitches that get hammered. He often leaves the ball too high in the strike zone, and his mid-90s fastball has a tendency to straighten out. Vizcaino has started and relieved in the minors, though the A's see his future in the bullpen. If he can become more consistent, he could be an imposing force in relief. He's still trying to tighten up his slider, and he has yet to come up with much of an offspeed pitch. Vizcaino is likely to spend 2001 on the bubble, bouncing between Triple-A and the majors.

Year	Club (League)	Class	W	L	ERA	G	GS	CG	SV	IP	H	R	ER	BB	SO
1995	Athletics (DSL)	R	10	2	2.27	16	15	5	0	115	93	41	29	29	89
1996	Athletics (AZL)	R	6	3	4.07	15	10	0	1	60	58	36	27	24	52
1997	Modesto (Cal)	A	0	3	13.19	7	0	0	0	14	24	24	21	13	15
	S. Oregon (NWL)	A	1	6	7.93	22	5	0	0	48	62	51	42	27	42
1998	Modesto (Cal)	A	6	3	2.74	23	16	0	0	102	72	39	31	43	108
	Huntsville (SL)	AA	3	2	4.66	7	7	0	0	39	43	27	20	22	26
1999	Midland (TL)	AA	8	7	5.85	25	19	0	0	105	120	74	68	48	88
	Oakland (AL)	MAJ	0	0	5.40	1	0	0	0	3	3	2	2	3	2
	Vancouver (PCL)	AAA	0	1	1.38	7	0	0	0	13	13	4	2	6	7
2000	Oakland (AL)	MAJ	0	1	7.45	12	0	0	0	19	25	17	16	11	18
	Vancouver (PCL)	AAA	6	2	5.03	33	2	0	5	48	48	27	27	21	41
MAJOR LEAGUE TOTALS			0	1	7.36	13	0	0	0	22	28	19	18	14	20
MINOR LEAGUE TOTALS			40	29	4.43	155	74	5	6	543	533	323	267	233	468

15. Oscar Salazar, 2b/ss

Born: June 27, 1978. **Ht.:** 6-0. **Wt.:** 155. **Bats:** R. **Throws:** R. **Career Transactions:** Signed out of Dominican Republic by Athletics, July 2, 1994.

The happy-go-lucky Salazar is a throwback to many players of the 1960s. He's an undisciplined hitter who swings at many bad pitches, yet still hits for a high average. His approach clashes with the organization's philosophies on pitch selection and walks, but he has succeeded in his own way. Salazar is a loose player, and his personality makes him a favorite of teammates and coaches. He's most competent at second base and can function adequately at shortstop and third. With decent hands and a good arm, he has the tools to become a legitimate middle infielder. After adding him to the 40-man roster, Oakland will keep moving him up the ladder to see if he can produce enough to get to the majors.

Year	Club (League)	Class	AVG	G	AB	R	H	2B	3B	HR	RBI	BB	SO	SB
1995	Athletics (DSL)	R	.271	53	166	29	45	10	1	0	23	22	23	5
1996	Athletics (DSL)	R	.256	69	219	49	56	9	4	3	29	47	37	9
1997	Athletics (DSL)	R	.299	66	268	65	80	20	4	12	48	34	39	3
1998	Athletics (AZL)	R	.324	26	102	29	33	7	5	2	18	12	15	4
	S. Oregon (NWL)	A	.317	28	101	19	32	4	1	5	28	16	22	5
1999	Modesto (Cal)	A	.295	130	525	100	155	26	18	18	105	39	106	14
2000	Midland (TL)	AA	.300	111	427	70	128	27	1	13	57	39	71	4
	Vancouver (PCL)	AAA	.154	4	13	0	2	1	0	0	1	1	1	1
MINOR LEAGUE TOTALS			.292	487	1821	361	531	104	34	53	309	210	314	45

16. Claudio Galva, lhp

Born: Nov. 28, 1979. **Ht.:** 6-2. **Wt.:** 205. **Bats:** L. **Throws:** L. **Career Transactions:** Signed out of Dominican Republic by Athletics, July 19, 1996.

Galva first raised eyebrows when he put together an 11-0, 1.00 season in the Rookie-level Dominican Summer League in 1998, and he backed it up with an all-star season in the Arizona League in 1999. Moved to the bullpen last season, Galva continued to make an impression. He's being groomed as a closer, and he embraced the role with relish. He relies on a fastball/slider combination and can throw strikes with both pitches. He has remarkable resilience and can pitch several days in a row. The A's will bring him to spring training with the hope they can place him in Double-A, but an overload of pitchers at that level could force his return to the Cal League. His command gives him the chance to develop quickly.

Year	Club (League)	Class	W	L	ERA	G	GS	CG	SV	IP	H	R	ER	BB	SO
1997	Athletics (DSL)	R	2	1	1.30	18	0	0	5	28	18	4	4	8	21
1998	Athletics (DSL)	R	11	0	1.00	13	12	4	0	90	39	15	10	14	97
1999	Athletics (AZL)	R	6	2	2.38	14	11	0	0	68	64	23	18	16	59
2000	Visalia (Cal)	A	7	4	3.61	48	7	0	15	97	103	54	39	29	98
MINOR LEAGUE TOTALS			26	7	2.26	93	30	4	20	283	224	96	71	67	275

17. Mark Ellis, ss

Born: June 6, 1977. **Ht.:** 5-11. **Wt.:** 180. **Bats:** R. **Throws:** R. **School:** University of Florida. **Career Transactions:** Selected by Royals in ninth round of 1999 draft; signed June 3, 1999 . . . Traded by Royals with OF Johnny Damon and a player to be named to Athletics, as part of three-way trade in which Royals acquired C A.J. Hinch, SS Angel Berroa and cash from Athletics and RHP Roberto Hernandez from Devil Rays, Devil Rays acquired OF Ben Grieve and a player to be named or cash from Athletics, and Athletics acquired RHP Cory Lidle from Devil Rays, Jan. 8, 2001.

Ellis accepted a $1,000 bonus from the Royals and was a real bargain, earning all-star honors in both of his seasons as a pro and leading the Carolina League in hits and on-base percentage (.404) in 2000. The Royals included him in the Johnny Damon deal in order to get a pure shortstop from the A's in Angel Berroa. Ellis is the quintessential heady ballplayer, an overachiever in terms of his raw ability. He gets on base by making contact and drawing walks, and he can steal an occasional base more on instincts than on speed. He's a steady if unspectacular defender. Ellis' arm strength isn't quite up to par for shortstop, which means he may have to settle for being a second baseman or a utilityman. Ellis will have to keep proving himself, especially in a new, deep system, and in 2001 he'll do so in Double-A.

Year	Club (League)	Class	AVG	G	AB	R	H	2B	3B	HR	RBI	BB	SO	SB
1999	Spokane (NWL)	A	.327	71	281	67	92	14	0	7	47	47	40	21
2000	Wilmington (Car)	A	.302	132	484	83	146	27	4	6	62	78	72	25
	Wichita (TL)	AA	.318	7	22	4	7	1	0	0	4	5	5	1
MINOR LEAGUE TOTALS			.311	210	787	154	245	42	4	13	113	130	117	47

18. Juan Pena, lhp

Born: June 4, 1979. **Ht.:** 6-3. **Wt.:** 195. **Bats:** L. **Throws:** L. **Career Transactions:** Signed out of Dominican Republic by Athletics, Nov. 1, 1995.

Pena is a lefthander of great potential if he can find the strike zone consistently. He spent the last two years in the California League, leading the league in strikeouts in 2000. He'll move to the Midland rotation 2001 amid concerns whether he can command his fastball well enough against better hitters. His fastball has both low-90s velocity and life, and he complements it with an excellent change, which he can throw 25 times a game and keep fooling hitters. Much of his success has come by inducing aggressive young hitters to swing at pitches out of the strike zone, and more advanced opponents may have more success in waiting him out. He's from a pitching family, with his brother Juan having pitched with the Red Sox and another brother expected to be a prized signee in 2001.

Year	Club (League)	Class	W	L	ERA	G	GS	CG	SV	IP	H	R	ER	BB	SO
1996	Athletics (DSL)	R	8	2	3.21	12	12	0	0	70	75	34	25	15	59
1997	Athletics (AZL)	R	6	2	2.91	14	13	0	0	65	54	38	21	33	67
1998	S. Oregon (NWL)	A	1	2	2.15	8	8	0	0	46	46	21	11	10	38
	Modesto (Cal)	A	3	2	5.18	6	6	0	0	33	50	25	19	7	32
1999	Visalia (Cal)	A	9	5	5.76	33	18	0	1	131	168	106	84	61	107
2000	Modesto (Cal)	A	6	9	3.86	29	27	0	0	154	132	85	66	75	177
MINOR LEAGUE TOTALS			33	22	4.08	102	84	0	1	499	525	309	226	201	480

19. Jon Adkins, rhp

Born: Aug. 30, 1977. **Ht.:** 6-0. **Wt.:** 200. **Bats:** L. **Throws:** R. **School:** Oklahoma State University. **Career Transactions:** Selected by Athletics in ninth round of 1998 draft; signed June 27, 1998.

After going 19-5 in his last two seasons at Oklahoma State, Adkins sat out in 1998 to heal a partially torn ligament in his elbow. He came back and made the Cal League midseason all-star team the next year, but was shut down in August with elbow and shoulder soreness. A month later he had Tommy John surgery on his elbow. His comeback has been remarkable. He returned to the mound 10 months later, featuring better stuff than he had before. His low-90s fastball has more sinking action, his slider has improved, and he developed his change while his arm was bouncing back. With three solid pitches, Adkins has a legitimate shot at starting in a big league rotation. The surgery also helped Adkins mature off the mound. He returned from the injury with new dedication and has become a devotee of the weight room, putting extra hours into conditioning. He should move up to Double-A this season.

Year	Club (League)	Class	W	L	ERA	G	GS	CG	SV	IP	H	R	ER	BB	SO
1998					Did Not Play—Injured										
1999	Modesto (Cal)	A	9	5	4.76	26	15	0	1	102	113	65	54	30	93
2000	Athletics (AZL)	R	1	1	3.00	4	2	0	0	15	15	6	5	3	17
	Sacramento (PCL)	AAA	0	1	9.00	1	1	0	0	4	6	4	4	1	2
	Modesto (Cal)	A	5	2	1.81	9	7	1	0	50	41	17	10	17	38
MINOR LEAGUE TOTALS			15	9	3.85	40	25	1	1	171	175	92	73	51	150

20. Eric Ireland, rhp

Born: March 11, 1977. **Ht.:** 6-1. **Wt.:** 170. **Bats:** R. **Throws:** R. **School:** Millikan HS, Long Beach. **Career Transactions:** Selected by Astros in second round of 1995 draft; signed Aug. 15, 1995 . . . Claimed on waivers by Cubs from Astros, Nov. 20, 2000 . . . Traded by Cubs to Athletics for OF Matt Stairs, Nov. 20, 2000.

Ireland was a member of three different teams on Nov. 20. He began the day as a member of the Astros, who cleared space on their 40-man roster by removing him. The Cubs claimed him, then traded him to the A's for arbitration-eligible outfielder Matt Stairs. Ireland is a curveball pitcher whose fastball ranges into the high 80s. Though he doesn't throw hard, he consistently has posted solid numbers in wins, innings and strikeouts. He pitched the first perfect game in Astros organization history at Class A Kissimmee in 1999. Scouts say he has a good feel for pitching. The A's plan to place Ireland in their Triple-A rotation in 2001 and believe he could be an emergency starter at the big league level if necessary.

Year	Club (League)	Class	W	L	ERA	G	GS	CG	SV	IP	H	R	ER	BB	SO
1996	Astros (GCL)	R	3	4	4.70	12	11	0	0	54	54	33	28	23	43
1997	Auburn (NY-P)	A	5	7	3.70	16	16	2	0	107	111	55	44	21	78
1998	Quad City (Mid)	A	14	9	2.88	29	28	6	0	206	172	80	66	71	191
1999	Kissimmee (FSL)	A	10	7	2.06	24	24	5	0	170	145	59	39	30	133
	Jackson (TL)	AA	0	1	4.30	3	3	0	0	15	19	9	7	2	15
2000	Round Rock (TL)	AA	11	9	3.41	29	29	2	0	180	171	84	68	64	123
MINOR LEAGUE TOTALS			43	37	3.10	113	111	15	0	731	672	320	252	211	583

21. Justin Lehr, rhp

Born: Aug. 3, 1977. **Ht.:** 6-1. **Wt.:** 200. **Bats:** R. **Throws:** R. **School:** University of Southern California. **Career Transactions:** Selected by Athletics in eighth round of 1999 draft; signed June 29, 1999.

After growing up as a catcher and spending his first three college seasons mostly behind the plate at UC Santa Barbara, Lehr transferred to Southern California in 1999, where he went 7-3, 4.29 on the mound and hit .297-4-27 as a DH. The 2000 season was the first time he concentrated on pitching, and he responded by winning 13 games. While Lehr can crank his fastball up to the low 90s, he usually works in the high 80s with good movement. He complements it with a superlative change, as well as a slider and a forkball. He has excellent command of the strike zone and knowledge of pitching that may be a result of his years of catching. Lehr knows how to pitch backward, taking a little off his fastball instead of trying to overpower hitters in tense situations. He also has a calm about him, so he doesn't get rattled at difficult times. He's ready to move to Double-A this season.

Year	Club (League)	Class	W	L	ERA	G	GS	CG	SV	IP	H	R	ER	BB	SO
1999	S. Oregon (NWL)	A	2	6	5.95	14	4	0	0	42	62	36	28	17	40
2000	Modesto (Cal)	A	13	6	3.19	29	25	0	0	175	161	71	62	46	138
	Sacramento (PCL)	AAA	0	0	11.25	1	1	0	0	4	7	5	5	3	3
MINOR LEAGUE TOTALS			15	12	3.86	44	30	0	0	221	230	112	95	66	181

22. Chad Bradford, rhp

Born: Sept. 14, 1974. **Ht.:** 6-5. **Wt.:** 205. **Bats:** R. **Throws:** R. **School:** University of Southern Mississippi.
Career Transactions: Selected by White Sox in 13th round of 1996 draft; signed June 6, 1996 . . . Traded to Athletics for player to be named, Dec. 7, 2000. C Miguel Olivo sent to White Sox to complete trade, Dec. 12, 2000.

When the A's became disenchanted with catching prospect Miguel Olivo, they traded him to the White Sox for Bradford, who joined former Sox farmhands Frank Menechino, Olmedo Saenz and Mario Valdez on the 40-man roster. The submarining Bradford spent time in the majors in each of the last three seasons, but the White Sox never trusted him enough to keep him around. They took a leap of faith by putting him on their 2000 playoff roster, and when he came in to protect a 4-3 lead in Game One of the Division Series against Seattle, Mike Cameron delivered a game-tying single. It was one of the few low moments in a terrific year for Bradford, who has proven he's too good for the minor leagues. In 131 Triple-A appearances, he has a 1.81 ERA. He throws in the high 80s, but his funky delivery makes him nasty on righthanders. His fastball has sinking action but straightens out when he leaves it up in the strike zone. He has a good curveball that helps against lefthanders, and he shows hitters an occasional changeup. He's always around the strike zone. Managers have been reluctant to use him in save situations, but he should be effective as a set-up man.

Year	Club (League)	Class	W	L	ERA	G	GS	CG	SV	IP	H	R	ER	BB	SO
1996	Hickory (SAL)	A	0	2	0.90	28	0	0	18	30	21	7	3	7	27
1997	Winston-Salem (Car)	A	3	7	3.95	46	0	0	15	54	51	30	24	25	43
1998	Birmingham (SL)	AA	1	1	2.60	10	0	0	1	17	13	6	5	8	14
	Calgary (PCL)	AAA	4	1	1.94	29	0	0	0	51	50	12	11	11	27
	Chicago (AL)	MAJ	2	1	3.23	29	0	0	1	30	27	16	11	7	11
1999	Charlotte (IL)	AAA	9	3	1.94	47	0	0	5	74	63	19	16	15	56
	Chicago (AL)	MAJ	0	0	19.64	3	0	0	0	3	9	8	8	5	0
2000	Charlotte (IL)	AAA	2	4	1.51	55	0	0	10	53	38	18	9	12	42
	Chicago (AL)	MAJ	1	0	1.98	12	0	0	0	13	13	4	3	1	9
MAJOR LEAGUE TOTALS			3	1	4.13	44	0	0	1	48	49	28	22	13	20
MINOR LEAGUE TOTALS			19	18	2.18	215	0	0	49	281	236	92	68	78	209

23. Mike Lockwood, of

Born: Dec. 27, 1976. **Ht.:** 6-0. **Wt.:** 190. **Bats:** L. **Throws:** L. **School:** Ohio State University. **Career Transactions:** Selected by Athletics in 23rd round of 1999 draft; signed June 13, 1999.

Lockwood has been amazing since coming to the A's, reaching Triple-A in his first full season. He has shown the ability to make adjustments at the plate and has been mostly a singles hitter, though the A's would like to see him spend more time in the weight room to add to his power production. He's above-average defensively at the corner outfield positions, and can move to center in an emergency. His arm strength has improved since signing, and his throwing accuracy is solid. Lockwood is a driven player who's ready to play every day and prepared for each at-bat. Because he lacks the power to play regularly on an outfield corner and the speed to start in center, he'll have to prove himself at every level. He has done that to this point, stalling only in Triple-A, where he'll return this season.

Year	Club (League)	Class	AVG	G	AB	R	H	2B	3B	HR	RBI	BB	SO	SB
1999	S. Oregon (NWL)	A	.361	69	255	48	92	18	5	7	51	39	49	6
2000	Modesto (Cal)	A	.314	47	159	42	50	12	0	6	35	46	25	9
	Sacramento (PCL)	AAA	.254	36	126	14	32	3	0	1	13	17	14	0
	Midland (TL)	AA	.309	56	236	45	73	16	1	4	31	21	33	1
MINOR LEAGUE TOTALS			.318	208	776	149	247	49	6	18	130	123	121	16

24. Francis Alfonseca, ss/2b

Born: Sept. 2, 1981. **Ht.:** 6-1. **Wt.:** 165. **Bats:** R. **Throws:** R. **Career Transactions:** Signed out of Dominican Republic by Athletics, Dec. 5, 1998.

The half-brother of Marlins closer Antonio Alfonseca made his U.S. debut in 2000 under the name Francis Gomez. His Arizona League season was cut short by nagging hamstring injuries, but he still played well enough to be ranked the No. 3 prospect in the league. He has exceptional tools, with excellent hands and range on defense and quick hands with the bat. The A's compare him to Miguel Tejada because of his defensive skills and power potential. In his first game back in the Arizona League after a month on the disabled list, he pinch-hit a game-winning grand slam. Alfonseca can play all three infield positions, and the A's have been moving him around to increase his versatility. He has shown he can hit to all fields. He's aggressive, both in the field and with the bat, and he has shown great desire to play.

Year	Club (League)	Class	AVG	G	AB	R	H	2B	3B	HR	RBI	BB	SO	SB
1999	Athletics (DSL)	R	.233	66	257	50	60	14	2	4	43	50	52	10
2000	Athletics (AZL)	R	.355	17	62	17	22	3	1	3	28	11	10	8
MINOR LEAGUE TOTALS			.257	83	319	67	82	17	3	7	71	61	62	18

25. Daylan Holt, of

Born: Oct. 4, 1978. **Ht.:** 6-1. **Wt.:** 205. **Bats:** R. **Throws:** R. **School:** Texas A&M University. **Career Transactions:** Selected by Athletics in third round of 2000 draft; signed Aug. 2, 2000.

After leading NCAA Division I with 34 homers in 1999, Holt projected as an early first-round pick in 2000. But with a mediocre team surrounding him, Holt slipped to 15 homers as a junior and the third round. He spent most of the summer of 2000 in the amateur Cape Cod League before signing. Holt followed with major strides during instructional league, improving his approach from hard, wild thrusts to consistent line-drive production. He's learning to use his hands and reduce his swing, which should help him keep his power and improve his consistency. Holt needs to improve his right-field defense, but he has a plus arm and unusual speed for his size. He must develop a professional mentality for the long season, rather than carry every failure with him. He's an intense competitor with high expectations for himself. A promotion to the Cal League in 2001 is probably in order.

Year	Club (League)	Class	AVG	G	AB	R	H	2B	3B	HR	RBI	BB	SO	SB
2000	Vancouver (NWL)	A	.271	32	118	17	32	6	0	2	17	10	26	1
MINOR LEAGUE TOTALS			.271	32	118	17	32	6	0	2	17	10	26	1

26. Josh Hochgesang, 3b

Born: April 16, 1977. **Ht.:** 6-3. **Wt.:** 210. **Bats:** R. **Throws:** R. **School:** Stanford University. **Career Transactions:** Selected by Athletics in seventh round of 1999 draft; signed July 22, 1999.

After a distinguished career for college powerhouse Stanford, Hochgesang drew attention with his power and continual improvement. He has shown the ability to understand the game and make adjustments, but his streaks of success have been mixed with serious down periods. He spent 2000 battling elbow problems, which prompted the A's to shut him down for instructional league. His elbow didn't prevent him from drilling 20 homers in his first full season. He also showed a fine eye at the plate, fitting in with the organization's philosophy. Hochgesang also made great strides on defense and plays a solid third base. His attitude and personality make him an organization favorite. He is expected to land at Double-A in 2001.

Year	Club (League)	Class	AVG	G	AB	R	H	2B	3B	HR	RBI	BB	SO	SB
1999	S. Oregon (NWL)	A	.155	21	71	10	11	2	0	1	8	14	23	0
2000	Visalia (Cal)	A	.246	126	443	78	109	23	3	20	80	90	135	20
MINOR LEAGUE TOTALS			.233	147	514	88	120	25	3	21	88	104	158	20

27. Aaron Harang, rhp

Born: May 9, 1978. **Ht.:** 6-7. **Wt.:** 240. **Bats:** R. **Throws:** R. **School:** San Diego State University. **Career Transactions:** Selected by Rangers in sixth round of 1999 draft; signed June 7, 1999 . . . Traded by Rangers with LHP Ryan Cullen to Athletics for 2B Randy Velarde, Nov. 17, 2000.

When the A's decided Jose Ortiz was ready to take over second base in 2001, they traded Randy Velarde for Harang and lefty reliever Ryan Cullen. Harang lit up the Rookie-level Appalachian League in his pro debut, earning pitcher-of-the-year honors after leading the circuit in wins and ranking third in ERA and strikeouts. He had no difficulty jumping to the Florida State League in his first full season. Harang has a fastball that touches 90 mph, and he mixes it with an effective slider. He has poise and a feel for pitching, impressing the A's enough to trade for him. He'll pitch in either the Cal League or the Texas League this season.

Year	Club (League)	Class	W	L	ERA	G	GS	CG	SV	IP	H	R	ER	BB	SO
1999	Pulaski (Appy)	R	9	2	2.30	16	10	1	1	78	64	22	20	17	87
2000	Charlotte (FSL)	A	13	5	3.32	28	27	3	0	157	128	68	58	50	136
MINOR LEAGUE TOTALS			22	7	2.98	44	37	4	1	235	192	90	78	67	223

28. Beau Craig, c

Born: Feb. 12, 1979. **Ht.:** 5-10. **Wt.:** 170. **Bats:** B. **Throws:** R. **School:** University of Southern California. **Career Transactions:** Selected by Athletics in sixth round of 2000 draft; signed July 6, 2000.

Craig made a quick impression before his pro debut ended early. His jaw was broken when a batter hit him with a wild backswing, so he had his jaw wired shut and took his meals through a straw before he finally returned to limited duty in instructional league. Craig was drafted in the third round by the Padres out of high school in 1998, in part because of his arm strength, but elbow injuries at Southern Cal diminished his throwing ability. By adjusting his arm slot during instructional league, he showed improvement. He moves well behind the plate, though he will need work in calling games. At the plate, Craig shows power potential. His next chore will be to refine his strike zone and quit swinging at bad pitches.

Year	Club (League)	Class	AVG	G	AB	R	H	2B	3B	HR	RBI	BB	SO	SB
2000	Vancouver (NWL)	A	.247	24	77	6	19	8	0	0	11	5	19	0
MINOR LEAGUE TOTALS			.247	24	77	6	19	8	0	0	11	5	19	0

29. Chris Enochs, rhp

Born: Oct. 11, 1975. **Ht.:** 6-3. **Wt.:** 225. **Bats:** R. **Throws:** R. **School:** West Virginia University. **Career Transactions:** Selected by Athletics in first round (11th overall) of 1997 draft; signed June 12, 1997.

The sole remaining first-round pick in the farm system, Enochs' advancement has been derailed by a series of injuries. Ironically, his durability was one of the main reasons Oakland drafted him. A 1998 hip injury and recurring bouts of tendinitis have limited Enochs' progress. He still needs to refine his arm angle and learn to pitch at the professional level. When he's right, he throws a lively 93 mph fastball and a plus curve. He shows excellent mound presence and competitiveness, and his size and strength indicate he has the potential to become a workhorse. But he'll have to rebuild his confidence after three years of struggles. He still has time, though. He's ticketed for Double-A in 2001, a critical year in his career.

Year	Club (League)	Class	W	L	ERA	G	GS	CG	SV	IP	H	R	ER	BB	SO
1997	S. Oregon (NWL)	A	0	0	3.48	3	3	0	0	10	12	4	4	2	10
	Modesto (Cal)	A	3	0	2.78	10	9	0	0	45	51	20	14	12	45
1998	Huntsville (SL)	AA	9	10	4.74	26	26	0	0	148	159	101	78	64	100
1999	Midland (TL)	AA	3	5	10.00	13	11	0	0	45	69	57	50	34	33
	Visalia (Cal)	A	0	0	4.91	4	4	0	0	18	24	10	10	10	19
2000	Visalia (Cal)	A	2	5	4.64	18	18	0	0	97	116	61	50	38	75
MINOR LEAGUE TOTALS			17	20	5.09	74	71	0	0	364	431	253	206	160	282

30. Bobby Vaz, of

Born: March 15, 1975. **Ht.:** 5-9. **Wt.:** 195. **Bats:** L. **Throws:** L. **School:** University of Alabama. **Career Transactions:** Selected by Athletics in seventh round of 1997 draft; signed June 14, 1997.

Vaz had a sterling college career, first as MVP of the 1996 Junior College World Series. He helped Alabama to the 1997 College World Series as a center fielder/closer. Strictly a left fielder as a pro, Vaz' bat is his best tool. He sprays line drives from foul pole to foul pole and has decent speed, especially when he keeps his weight down. He hasn't shown enough power for a corner outfield spot, though. He has had injury problems, from a broken foot that kept him out of the 1997 CWS to a shoulder injury in the 2000 Pacific Coast League playoffs that required offseason surgery. He hit two home runs to lead Vancouver to the Triple-A World Series crown in 1999 and maintained the momentum in 2000. Vaz won't throw until April, so he probably won't play until May unless it's as a DH. When he gets healthy, he's a candidate for a reserve outfield job in Oakland. Vaz is a contact hitter and lefty bat off the bench, though Eric Byrnes can play all three outfield positions and provides more speed.

Year	Club (League)	Class	AVG	G	AB	R	H	2B	3B	HR	RBI	BB	SO	SB
1997	S. Oregon (NWL)	A	.321	22	78	11	25	6	0	3	15	7	4	5
	Visalia (Cal)	A	.356	19	73	9	26	5	0	3	13	8	10	2
1998	Huntsville (SL)	AA	.295	131	457	54	135	18	5	8	62	56	63	23
1999	Midland (TL)	AA	.406	10	32	4	13	3	0	1	12	8	5	0
	Vancouver (PCL)	AAA	.264	109	367	54	97	18	4	7	38	51	72	7
2000	Vancouver (PCL)	AAA	.289	114	426	56	123	22	3	10	72	49	72	20
MINOR LEAGUE TOTALS			.292	405	1433	188	419	72	12	32	212	179	226	57

Philadelphia
Phillies

TOP 30 PROSPECTS

1. Jimmy Rollins, ss
2. Brett Myers, rhp
3. Brad Baisley, rhp
4. Ryan Madson, rhp
5. Chase Utley, 2b
6. Anderson Machado, ss
7. Reggie Taylor, of
8. Eric Valent, of
9. Brandon Duckworth, rhp
10. Marlon Byrd, of
11. Carlos Rosario, ss
12. Doug Nickle, rhp
13. Yoel Hernandez, rhp
14. Jorge Padilla, of
15. Russ Jacobson, c
16. Dave Coggin, rhp
17. Evan Thomas, rhp
18. Nate Espy, 1b
19. Johnny Estrada, c
20. Carlos Silva, rhp
21. Josue Perez, of
22. Keith Bucktrot, rhp
23. Jimmy Osting, lhp
24. Jason Michaels, of
25. Jay Sitzman, of
26. Taylor Buchholz, rhp
27. Danny Gonzalez, ss
28. Franklin Nunez, rhp
29. Nick Punto, 2b/ss
30. Alejandro Giron, of

By Josh Boyd

Last year was disastrous for the Phillies at the major league level. They tied the Cubs for the worst record with 97 losses. Excluding their unlikely 1993 trip to the World Series, they haven't finished over .500 since 1986.

It looked like things were headed in the right direction in 1999, but a late-season collapse dashed all of the hopes and carried over into 2000. Manager Terry Francona's tenure ended with an uninspiring .440 winning percentage and two last-place finishes.

He couldn't control the limited payroll or the poor conditions at Veterans Stadium, though, and his players didn't help much either. The Phillies had the worst bullpen ERA and the third-lowest on-base percentage in the majors last year, and hit fewer homers than any National League club. New manager Larry Bowa has his work cut out for him.

After losing young talent during last offseason, including righthander Adam Eaton and righthander Derrick Turnbow, Philadelphia reversed course once its 2000 season fell apart. Andy Ashby was shipped to the Braves for promising lefthanders Bruce Chen and Jimmy Osting, and Curt Schilling went to the Diamondbacks for four players, with first baseman Travis Lee and righthander Vicente Padilla the most significant.

The organization seemed to switch plans again this offseason. GM Ed Wade tried to shore up the bullpen by spending $17 million on free agents Ricky Bottalico, Rheal Cormier and Jose Mesa—which will also cost the club its second- and third-round draft picks in June.

Despite the parent club's recent adversity, Wade and his braintrust have stockpiled a deep stable of prospects. Philadelphia's .567 minor league winning percentage in 2000 was the system's best record in 40 years.

As Jimmy Rollins prepares to take over the shortstop and leadoff roles, the 2001 Phillies could boast the NL's only homegrown infield: Pat Burrell, Marlon Anderson, Scott Rolen and Rollins. And while the system took a hit by losing Eaton and Turnbow, a wealth of young guns led by Brett Myers, Brad Baisley and Ryan Madson makes it easier to stomach. And not only have the drafts been fruitful, but the Phillies also have become prominent in the international market, signing such players as Anderson Machado, who with Rollins heads up a deep crop of middle-infield talent.

OrganizationOverview

General manager: Ed Wade. **Farm director:** Steve Noworyta. **Scouting director:** Mike Arbuckle.

2000 PERFORMANCE

Class	Team	League	W	L	Pct.	Finish*	Manager
Majors	Philadelphia	National	65	97	.401	t-15th (16)	Terry Francona
Triple-A	Scranton/W-B Barons	International	85	60	.586	2nd (14)	Marc Bombard
Double-A	Reading Phillies	Eastern	85	57	.599	1st (12)	Gary Varsho
High A	Clearwater Phillies	Florida State	64	71	.474	9th (14)	Ken Oberkfell
Low A	#Piedmont Boll Weevils	South Atlantic	90	47	.657	1st (14)	Greg Legg
Short-season	Batavia Muckdogs	New York-Penn	39	37	.513	6th (14)	Frank Klebe
Rookie	Clearwater Phillies	Appalachian	31	29	.517	8th (13)	Ramon Aviles
OVERALL 2000 MINOR LEAGUE RECORD			394	300	.568	2nd (30)	

*Finish in overall standings (No. of teams in league). #Affiliate will be in Lakewood, N.J. (South Atlantic) in 2001.

ORGANIZATION LEADERS

BATTING
*AVG	Jay Sitzman, Piedmont	.316
R	Marlon Byrd, Piedmont	104
H	Marlon Byrd, Piedmont	159
TB	Marlon Byrd, Piedmont	265
2B	**Nate Espy**, Piedmont	32
3B	Marlon Byrd, Piedmont	13
HR	Eric Valent, Reading	22
RBI	Marlon Byrd, Piedmont	93
BB	**Nate Espy**, Piedmont	101
SO	Carlos Duncan, Clearwater	113
SB	Jay Sitzman, Piedmont	69

PITCHING
W	Adam Walker, Piedmont/Clearwater	15
L	Carlos Silva, Clearwater	13
#ERA	**Tom Jacquez**, Reading/Scranton	2.30
G	Barry Johnson, Scranton	56
CG	Mark Brownson, Scranton	4
	Carlos Silva, Clearwater	4
SV	Cary Hiles, Clearwater	20
IP	Frank Brooks, Piedmont	178
BB	Jason Brester, Reading	89
SO	Brandon Duckworth, Reading	178

*Minimum 250 at-bats. #Minimum 75 innings.

TOP PROSPECTS OF THE DECADE

1991	Mickey Morandini, 2b
1992	Tyler Green, rhp
1993	Tyler Green, rhp
1994	Tyler Green, rhp
1995	Scott Rolen, 3b
1996	Scott Rolen, 3b
1997	Scott Rolen, 3b
1998	Ryan Brannan, rhp
1999	Pat Burrell, 1b
2000	Pat Burrell, 1b/of

TOP DRAFT PICKS OF THE DECADE

1991	Tyler Green, rhp
1992	Chad McConnell, of
1993	Wayne Gomes, rhp
1994	Carlton Loewer, rhp
1995	Reggie Taylor, of
1996	Adam Eaton, rhp
1997	*J.D. Drew, of
1998	Pat Burrell, 1b
1999	Brett Myers, rhp
2000	Chase Utley, 2b

*Did not sign.

Espy   Jacquez

BEST TOOLS

Best Hitter for Average	Chase Utley
Best Power Hitter	Nate Espy
Fastest Baserunner	Jay Sitzman
Best Fastball	Brett Myers
Best Breaking Ball	Brandon Duckworth
Best Control	Evan Thomas
Best Defensive Catcher	Russ Jacobson
Best Defensive Infielder	Jimmy Rollins
Best Infield Arm	Anderson Machado
Best Defensive Outfielder	Reggie Taylor
Best Outfield Arm	Reggie Taylor

PROJECTED 2004 LINEUP

Catcher	Mike Lieberthal
First Base	Pat Burrell
Second Base	Chase Utley
Third Base	Scott Rolen
Shortstop	Jimmy Rollins
Left Field	Eric Valent
Center Field	Reggie Taylor
Right Field	Bobby Abreu
No. 1 Starter	Brett Myers
No. 2 Starter	Randy Wolf
No. 3 Starter	Bruce Chen
No. 4 Starter	Brad Baisley
No. 5 Starter	Ryan Madson
Closer	Vicente Padilla

ALL-TIME LARGEST BONUSES

Pat Burrell, 1998	$3,150,000
Brett Myers, 1999	2,050,000
Chase Utley, 2000	1,780,000
Adam Eaton, 1996	1,100,000
Reggie Taylor, 1995	850,000
Josue Perez, 1999	850,000

DraftAnalysis

2000 Draft

Best Pro Debut: 1B Reggie Griggs (18) batted .340-6-42 to rank in the top five in all three triple-crown categories in the Rookie-level Gulf Coast League. He was old for the GCL at 22, though he came from a small-college background at Florida A&M. OF Anthony Hensley (20) led the short-season New York-Penn League in stolen bases (43 in 52 attempts), walks (60) and on-base percentage (.430).

Best Athlete: RHP Keith Bucktrot (3) has a live arm; some teams liked him better as a multi-tooled outfielder.

Best Hitter: 2B **Chase Utley** (1), who hit .307-2-22 with 13 doubles for short-season Batavia, was the best pure hitter in the college ranks. Some teams didn't like his hands and range at second base, but the Phillies say he has shown improvement and should be able to stay there.

Best Raw Power: For now, it's Griggs. 1B Tony Cancio (7), who's four years younger, has more power potential and a better chance of reaching the majors.

Fastest Runner: Hensley has good leadoff skills and baserunning instincts to go with his 6.55-second speed in the 60-yard dash.

Best Defensive Player: Danny Gonzalez (4) is a pure shortstop who's so fluid that he has been compared to Roberto Alomar. SS Scott Youngbauer (10) is less flashy but more reliable at this point.

Best Fastball: RHP Andrew Elskamp (36), the lowest-drafted player signed by Philadelphia, has hit 94-95 mph when used in relief. RHP Matt Riethmaier (5) has thrown 93-94 mph in the same role.

Most Intriguing Background: OF Brandon Caraway (12) hit in 40 straight games at Houston in 1998-99, the eighth-longest streak in NCAA Division I history. He batted only .218 at Batavia, however.

Closest To The Majors: If Utley can handle the defensive responsibilities of second base, Marlon Anderson better start looking over his shoulder.

RICH ABEL

Utley

Best Late-Round Pick: Emil Belich, the 2000 scout of the year honoree in the Midwest, uncovered both Elskamp and RHP Chad Sadowski (23) in Wisconsin, which isn't exactly a prospect hotbed. Sadowski throws 92-93 mph.

The One Who Got Away: Philadelphia signed 25 of its top 27 picks and got everyone it really wanted. The best player it didn't get is projectable LHP Chad White (30), who may also play some outfield at Alabama.

Assessment: In time, Utley will fit nicely at the top of a Phillies lineup that already includes standouts Bob Abreu, Pat Burrell, Mike Lieberthal and Scott Rolen. Losing their second-round pick for signing free agent Mike Jackson, who got hurt before pitching in a regular-season game, was a blow.

1999 Draft

RHP Brett Myers (1) instantly became the Phillies' best pitching prospect, while Russ Jacobson (3) is their top catching hopeful. OF Marlon Byrd (10) is a raw athlete with potential. **Grade: C**

1998 Draft

With the No. 1 overall pick, Philadelphia wisely chose 3B Pat Burrell, who could have batting and home run titles in his future. It also did well with its next two choices, OF Eric Valent (1) and RHP Brad Baisley (2). **Grade: A**

1997 Draft

The good news is that the Phillies stole Randy Wolf in the second round. The bad news is that they didn't sign OF J.D. Drew (1), and lost RHP Derrick Turnbow (5) in the 1999 major league Rule 5 draft. **Grade: C+**

1996 Draft

Promising RHP Adam Eaton (1) was dealt to San Diego, but starting this season, Jimmy Rollins (2) should plug Philadelphia's gaping void at shortstop. The club struck out afterward, though, with the possible exception of RHP Evan Thomas (10). **Grade: C+**

Note: Draft analysis prepared by Jim Callis. Numbers in parentheses indicate draft rounds.

. . . Rollins has surprising pop from both sides of the plate and puts pressure on opposing defenses with his quickness.

Rollins **Jimmy**
ss

Born: Nov. 27, 1978.
Ht.: 5-8. **Wt.:** 160.
Bats: B. **Throws:** R.
School: Encinal HS, Alameda, Calif.
Career Transactions: Selected by Phillies in second round of 1996 draft; signed June 24, 1996.

Rollins has been among his league's youngest players at every level since coming out of high school in the East Bay, but that hasn't stopped him from turning heads. Traditionally a slow starter, Rollins hit .134 in April and was below .200 through mid-May last year, before busting out and hitting .327 in the last two months. He was one of the final candidates to join the U.S. Olympic team, and many thought he would have been a better choice at shortstop than Adam Everett or Gookie Dawkins, who went a combined 1-for-29. Rollins continued to exceed expectations by shining in his September callup. He's the cousin of former big league outfielder Tony Tarasco.

Rollins' play belies his stature, as he has improved all facets of his game each year. His batting average, on-base percentage and slugging percentage all have increased steadily in each of the last three seasons. He displays surprising pop from both sides of the plate and puts a lot of pressure on opposing defenses with his quickness. At shortstop, he's a slick fielder with great range in the hole and up the middle, and he possesses the arm strength to make those plays. Rollins has all of the tools to become an exciting leadoff hitter, including bunting skills, basestealing success and bat control. The fact he starts slow and makes in-season adjustments is a tribute to his work ethic and instincts. At times Rollins gets anxious at the plate and chases pitches early in the count. His pitch selection improved during the year and has been solid throughout his career, but he'll be tested against big league hurlers. The Phillies want him to concentrate on doing the little things atop the lineup, and he'll need to draw a few more walks to be effective in the No. 1 slot. He tends to get home run conscious and needs to stay within his limitations.

New manager Larry Bowa got his first look at Rollins in the Arizona Fall League and was inspired. Rollins was named to the AFL's all-prospect team, setting the stage for his arrival atop Bowa's first lineup card. He could set the tone for the offense in the same way Rafael Furcal did for Atlanta last year.

BILL SETLIFF

Year	Club (League)	Class	AVG	G	AB	R	H	2B	3B	HR	RBI	BB	SO	SB
1996	Martinsville (Appy)	R	.238	49	172	22	41	3	1	1	16	28	20	11
1997	Piedmont (SAL)	A	.270	139	560	94	151	22	8	6	59	52	80	46
1998	Clearwater (FSL)	A	.244	119	495	72	121	18	9	6	35	41	62	23
1999	Reading (EL)	AA	.273	133	532	81	145	21	8	11	56	51	47	24
	Scranton/W-B (IL)	AAA	.077	4	13	0	1	1	0	0	0	1	1	1
2000	Scranton/W-B (IL)	AAA	.274	133	470	67	129	28	11	12	69	49	55	24
	Philadelphia (NL)	MAJ	.321	14	53	5	17	1	1	0	5	2	7	3
MAJOR LEAGUE TOTALS			.321	14	53	5	17	1	1	0	5	2	7	3
MINOR LEAGUE TOTALS			.262	577	2242	336	588	93	37	36	235	222	265	129

2. Brett Myers, rhp

Born: Aug. 17, 1980. **Ht.:** 6-4. **Wt.:** 215. **Bats:** R. **Throws:** R. **School:** Englewood HS, Jacksonville. **Career Transactions:** Selected by Phillies in first round (12th overall) of 1999 draft; signed July 9, 1999.

After an All-America high school career, Myers took the first step last year toward backing up his claim to be the next Curt Schilling. He's built along the same lines and displayed similar workhorse capabilities by logging at least six innings in 15 consecutive starts last summer. Myers appeared to get stronger and more polished as the season went on. Armed with the best fastball in the system, Myers comes right after hitters with a pure power arsenal. He fires his lively heater consistently at 92-93 mph and can pump it up as high as 96. His hard-breaking curveball already is becoming a second plus pitch to put hitters away with. A former amateur boxer, Myers brings a fighting mentality to the mound. He is learning to control his emotions and his pitches. His mindset and his maximum-effort delivery have led some to wonder if his future is as a closer, but his performance last year buried those concerns. He's a future No. 1 prospect and potential ace. He'll be handled with care, though it will be hard to hold him back when he starts to overpower Class A hitters.

Year	Club (League)	Class	W	L	ERA	G	GS	CG	SV	IP	H	R	ER	BB	SO
1999	Phillies (GCL)	R	2	1	2.33	7	5	0	0	27	17	8	7	7	30
2000	Piedmont (SAL)	A	13	7	3.18	27	27	2	0	175	165	78	62	69	140
MINOR LEAGUE TOTALS			15	8	3.07	34	32	2	0	202	182	86	69	76	170

3. Brad Baisley, rhp

Born: Aug. 24, 1979. **Ht.:** 6-9. **Wt.:** 205. **Bats:** R. **Throws:** R. **School:** Land O' Lakes (Fla.) HS. **Career Transactions:** Selected by Phillies in second round of 1998 draft; signed July 16, 1998.

On the heels of Baisley's breakout 1999 campaign, expectations were sky-high. A tender elbow forced the lanky righthander to sit out most of the summer as a precautionary measure. He was back on track by instructional league. Baisley uses his size as a weapon, bearing down on hitters with a lively 89-93 mph fastball that could improve, and a sharp curveball. His balanced delivery also gives him an advantage, as his stuff bores on hitters from a tough downward angle. Baisley demonstrates an advanced understanding of what he's doing on the mound and changes speeds well, though his changeup lacks consistency. It shows promise as an effective third option. His body still is growing and there may be some necessary mechanical adjustments to make along the way to avoid further injury. Despite having last season interrupted by tendinitis, Baisley is expected to compete for a spot in Double-A Reading's rotation in 2001. His ceiling ranks right below Brett Myers', as a potential No. 2 or 3 starter who should be ready for the majors in a couple of years.

Year	Club (League)	Class	W	L	ERA	G	GS	CG	SV	IP	H	R	ER	BB	SO
1998	Martinsville (Appy)	R	3	2	3.58	7	7	0	0	27	27	12	11	4	14
1999	Piedmont (SAL)	A	10	7	2.26	23	23	3	0	147	116	56	37	55	110
2000	Clearwater (FSL)	A	3	9	3.74	16	15	2	1	89	95	47	37	34	60
MINOR LEAGUE TOTALS			16	18	2.89	46	45	5	1	264	238	115	85	93	184

4. Ryan Madson, rhp

Born: Aug. 28, 1980. **Ht.:** 6-6. **Wt.:** 180. **Bats:** L. **Throws:** R. **School:** Valley View HS, Moreno Valley, Calif. **Career Transactions:** Selected by Phillies in ninth round of 1998 draft; signed June 10, 1998.

Madson's stock soared in his first exposure to full-season ball. He tied teammate Frank Brooks for the South Atlantic League lead in wins while ranking third in ERA. Madson fits the mold of the young, projectable arms the Phillies are trying to build around. He has imposing size on the mound, and his stuff further sets him apart. Like Baisley, he throws an effortless 91-93 mph fastball that still has room to add velocity, along with a biting, overhand curveball. He's sound mechanically and able to consistently repeat his delivery. Madson already displays good control, but he could use a little refinement of his offspeed offerings. He's working on tightening the spin on his 12-to-6 curve, while his changeup is showing signs of improvement. The Phillies think the towering trio of Brett Myers, Brad Baisley and Madson can be special. Baisley is one step ahead right now, but they could climb the ladder together. Madson will pitch at high Class A Clearwater in 2001.

Year	Club (League)	Class	W	L	ERA	G	GS	CG	SV	IP	H	R	ER	BB	SO
1998	Martinsville (Appy)	R	3	3	4.83	12	10	0	0	54	57	38	29	20	52
1999	Batavia (NY-P)	A	5	5	4.72	15	15	0	0	88	80	51	46	43	75
2000	Piedmont (SAL)	A	14	5	2.59	21	21	2	0	136	113	50	39	45	123
MINOR LEAGUE TOTALS			22	13	3.70	48	46	2	0	277	250	139	114	108	250

5. Chase Utley, 2b

RICK BATTLE

Born: Dec. 17, 1978. **Ht.:** 6-0. **Wt.:** 180. **Bats:** L. **Throws:** R. **School:** UCLA. **Career Transactions:** Selected by Phillies in first round (15th overall) of 2000 draft; signed July 29, 2000.

Drafted as a shortstop in the second round out of high school by the Dodgers, Utley went to UCLA and was an All-American as a junior, batting .382 and leading the Pacific-10 Conference with 82 runs. The Phillies gave him a $1.7 million bonus. Utley was considered the best pure hitter available among college draft prospects, and he has plenty of sock for a middle infielder. He lived up to his reputation in his pro debut. He always has demonstrated a good idea of the strike zone and handles the bat well. Utley has drawn comparisons to Todd Walker (Rockies) and Adam Kennedy (Angels), two former first-round picks, based on both his offensive prowess and defensive shortcomings. At the plate, Utley needs to use the whole field more effectively. He's improving in that regard by staying inside pitches better and driving them to left-center. He's adjusting to the finer points of playing second base and will have to prove he can stick there. The Phillies envision Utley's bat fitting in nicely with their young nucleus in the near future. He's expected to begin a rapid ascent through the system by beginning 2001 in Clearwater.

Year	Club (League)	Class	AVG	G	AB	R	H	2B	3B	HR	RBI	BB	SO	SB
2000	Batavia (NY-P)	A	.307	40	153	21	47	13	1	2	22	18	23	5
MINOR LEAGUE TOTALS			.307	40	153	21	47	13	1	2	22	18	23	5

6. Anderson Machado, ss

Born: Jan. 25, 1981. **Ht.:** 5-11. **Wt.:** 165. **Bats:** B. **Throws:** R. **Career Transactions:** Signed out of Venezuela by Phillies, Jan. 14, 1998.

Machado did little offensively during his first two years that would merit a promotion all the way to the Florida State League last season. But not only did he hold his own as one of the FSL's youngest everyday players, but he also started for Double-A Reading in the Eastern League playoffs. Machado has drawn comparisons to Dave Concepcion for his smooth actions, cannon arm and flashy range. Despite committing 43 errors, managers ranked him the FSL's best defensive shortstop. The Phillies applaud his instincts. But he hasn't shown proficiency from either side of the plate and has struggled to make consistent contact. Power is the one tool he'll never have, but Machado should have more success ripping balls into the gaps as he matures physically. His speed is raw, as he was caught stealing 18 times in 2000. With Jimmy Rollins set to take over in Philadelphia, there's no need to continue rushing Machado. He'll start back at Reading.

Year	Club (League)	Class	AVG	G	AB	R	H	2B	3B	HR	RBI	BB	SO	SB
1998	Phillies (DSL)	R	.201	68	219	26	44	7	0	0	17	30	44	4
1999	Phillies (GCL)	R	.259	43	143	26	37	6	3	2	12	15	38	6
	Clearwater (FSL)	A	.000	1	2	0	0	0	0	0	0	0	1	0
	Piedmont (SAL)	A	.233	20	60	7	14	4	2	0	7	7	20	2
2000	Clearwater (FSL)	A	.245	117	417	55	102	19	7	1	35	54	103	32
	Reading (EL)	AA	.364	3	11	2	4	1	0	1	2	0	4	0
MINOR LEAGUE TOTALS			.236	252	852	116	201	37	12	4	73	106	210	44

7. Reggie Taylor, of

Born: Jan. 12, 1977. **Ht.:** 6-1. **Wt.:** 175. **Bats:** L. **Throws:** R. **School:** Newberry (S.C.) HS. **Career Transactions:** Selected by Phillies in first round (14th overall) of 1995 draft; signed June 13, 1995.

Taylor has made the top 10 six straight years since being drafted in the first round. A separated shoulder in the Venezuelan League nearly derailed his 2000 season, but to his credit he battled back to return by the end of May. He still had time to show off his five-tool potential and tie a career-high in home runs. Some scouts believe Taylor would be among the best defensive center fielders in the majors right now. He can close the gaps with impressive bursts of speed, while his arm cuts down runners with its strength and accuracy. He generates above-average pop with a quick bat and his wiry athletic strength. Considered a raw athlete six years ago, Taylor has yet to shed that label. His lack of concern for working counts is the key factor holding him back. A career .296 on-base percentage is a major concern. Taylor is the most athletic player in the system, but the perennial prospect is entering a pivotal season. He showed steady improvement in Venezuela this winter.

Year	Club (League)	Class	AVG	G	AB	R	H	2B	3B	HR	RBI	BB	SO	SB
1995	Martinsville (Appy)	R	.222	64	239	36	53	4	6	2	32	23	58	18
1996	Piedmont (SAL)	A	.263	128	499	68	131	20	6	0	31	29	136	36
1997	Clearwater (FSL)	A	.244	134	545	73	133	18	6	12	47	30	130	40
1998	Reading (EL)	AA	.273	79	337	49	92	14	6	5	22	12	73	22
1999	Reading (EL)	AA	.266	127	526	75	140	17	10	15	61	18	79	38
2000	Scranton/W-B (IL)	AAA	.275	98	422	60	116	10	8	15	43	21	87	23
	Philadelphia (NL)	MAJ	.091	9	11	1	1	0	0	0	0	0	8	1
MAJOR LEAGUE TOTALS			.091	9	11	1	1	0	0	0	0	0	8	1
MINOR LEAGUE TOTALS			.259	630	2568	361	665	83	42	49	236	133	563	177

8. Eric Valent, of

Born: April 4, 1977. **Ht.:** 6-0. **Wt.:** 191. **Bats:** L. **Throws:** L. **School:** UCLA. **Career Transactions:** Selected by Phillies in first round (42nd overall) of 1998 draft; signed July 1, 1998.

Valent broke Troy Glaus' home run record at UCLA, but won't approach his power exploits in the majors. Valent finished third in the Eastern League in home runs and RBIs en route to earning recognition as the loop's sixth-best prospect. Valent's 30-point decline in average from 1999 to 2000 isn't a major concern because of his excellent plate discipline. Dating back to college, he has shown a knack for driving in runs. His intensity and solid makeup also will work to his advantage in the upper levels. His arm is one of the best in the organization, and he displays good all-around skills in right field. Valent hit just .238 from July on last year. He has been prone to peaks and valleys and can become too pull conscious at times, compounding his slumps. He's no more than an average runner. Entering his third full season, Valent will have to turn up his offensive production a notch and make the adjustments to avoid stagnating in Triple-A. With Bob Abreu in Philadelphia, Valent projects as a left fielder in the majors.

Year	Club (League)	Class	AVG	G	AB	R	H	2B	3B	HR	RBI	BB	SO	SB
1998	Piedmont (SAL)	A	.427	22	89	24	38	12	0	8	28	14	19	0
	Clearwater (FSL)	A	.264	34	125	24	33	8	1	5	25	16	29	1
1999	Clearwater (FSL)	A	.288	134	520	91	150	31	9	20	106	58	110	5
2000	Reading (EL)	AA	.258	128	469	81	121	22	5	22	90	70	89	2
MINOR LEAGUE TOTALS			.284	318	1203	220	342	73	15	55	249	158	247	8

9. Brandon Duckworth, rhp

Born: Jan. 23, 1976. **Ht.:** 6-2. **Wt.:** 185. **Bats:** B. **Throws:** R. **School:** Cal State Fullerton. **Career Transactions:** Signed as nondrafted free agent by Phillies, Aug. 13, 1997.

Duckworth has risen from not getting drafted after his senior college season to the verge of the Phillies rotation. He led the Eastern League in strikeouts and earned recognition as an all-star and the circuit's No. 5 prospect. He doesn't try to blow hitters away, but he can show surprising pop and movement on his fastball. It regularly sits in the 87-92 mph range, topping out at 94. His sharp, 12-to-6 curveball was rated the best breaking pitch in the EL, and he also has a changeup. He'll throw any of his three pitches at any point in the count. There are no glaring weaknesses in Duckworth's arsenal, but at 25, he has to prove his breakthrough was no fluke. He'll need to maintain his increased velocity to enjoy success in the majors. Duckworth placed himself on the fast track by outdueling hitters in Double-A. He'll get a long look in spring training, and has the inside track over Dave Coggin and Evan Thomas for consideration on the big league staff.

Year	Club (League)	Class	W	L	ERA	G	GS	CG	SV	IP	H	R	ER	BB	SO
1998	Piedmont (SAL)	A	9	8	2.80	21	21	5	0	148	116	58	46	24	119
	Clearwater (FSL)	A	6	2	3.74	9	9	1	0	53	64	25	22	22	46
1999	Clearwater (FSL)	A	11	5	4.84	27	17	0	1	132	164	84	71	40	101
2000	Reading (EL)	AA	13	7	3.16	27	27	1	0	165	145	70	58	52	178
MINOR LEAGUE TOTALS			39	22	3.56	84	74	7	1	498	489	237	197	138	444

10. Marlon Byrd, of

Born: Aug. 30, 1977. **Ht.:** 6-0. **Wt.:** 225. **Bats:** R. **Throws:** R. **School:** Georgia Perimeter JC. **Career Transactions:** Selected by Phillies in 10th round of 1999 draft; signed June 4, 1999.

Byrd attended Georgia Tech to play football out of high school, but quickly changed his path by focusing on baseball and transferring to Georgia Perimeter Junior College. He resembles Dee Brown, a high school gridiron standout turned Royals prospect. Byrd's assault on the South Atlantic League earned him the organization's minor league player of the year award. He generates tremendous power with his muscular build and compact stroke. He can mash fastballs into the gaps and his over-the-fence power should increase with experience. He's a gifted baserunner and a potential 30-30 threat in the future. Though he pulverized the Sally League, Byrd needs to prove he can hit pitching at the higher levels by sharpening his command of the strike zone. His arm is his biggest weakness and will relegate him to left field. Given his lack of baseball experience, the Phillies were thrilled with the aptitude Byrd showed in a full-season league in 2000. His work ethic is off the charts, which should give him an edge as he takes on the challenges of the upper levels.

Year	Club (League)	Class	AVG	G	AB	R	H	2B	3B	HR	RBI	BB	SO	SB
1999	Batavia (NY-P)	A	.296	65	243	40	72	7	6	13	50	28	70	8
2000	Piedmont (SAL)	A	.309	133	515	104	159	29	13	17	93	51	110	41
MINOR LEAGUE TOTALS			.305	198	758	144	231	36	19	30	143	79	180	49

11. Carlos Rosario, ss

Born: Feb. 22, 1980. **Ht.:** 5-8. **Wt.:** 160. **Bats:** B. **Throws:** R. **Career Transactions:** Signed out of Dominican Republic by Athletics, Dec. 10, 1996.

Rosario put himself on display at the Area Code Games in Long Beach in August, where he emerged as one of the top prospects at one of the nation's premier amateur showcases. The Phillies signed him for $700,000, the equivalent of a second-round bonus. The switch-hitting shortstop's game revolves around speed. While his quickness, arm strength and fluid actions stand out on the bases and in the field, the Phillies believe he can develop into an exciting offensive player as well once he matures into his projectable frame. Rosario made his first professional appearance in instructional league, flashing his tools for the player-development staff. They were encouraged by his bat from the left side and plan on getting him initiated in extended spring before launching his career in a short-season league in 2001.

Year	Club (League)	Class	AVG	G	AB	R	H	2B	3B	HR	RBI	BB	SO	SB
2000			Did Not Play—Signed 2001 Contract											

12. Doug Nickle, rhp

Born: Oct. 2, 1974. **Ht.:** 6-4. **Wt.:** 210. **Bats:** R. **Throws:** R. **School:** University of California. **Career Transactions:** Selected by Angels in 13th round of 1997 draft; signed June 9, 1997 . . . Traded by Angels to Phillies, Sept. 10, 1998, completing trade in which Phillies sent OF Gregg Jefferies to Angels for a player to be named (Aug. 28, 1998).

When Nickle came over, most people saw a 23-year-old starter toiling in Class A. But the Phillies saw something different. A shift to the bullpen and mechanical tinkering increased Nickle's velocity from the high 80s to the 94 mph range. In his first year in the system, he emerged as a closer prospect on the fast track. He continued to flourish last season, when managers named him the Eastern League's best reliever. He relies on his fastball and a good knuckle-curve, and he will mix in a slider and change. He has the ideal demeanor for a closer, but he needs to hone his command and learn to put hitters away. Nickle overpowered righthanders in Double-A last year, limiting them to a .164 average, a factor that could help his chances of breaking into the Phillies' relief corps. The additions of Ricky Bottalico, Rheal Cormier and Jose Mesa buy him time and will allow him to be eased into a lesser relief role.

Year	Club (League)	Class	W	L	ERA	G	GS	CG	SV	IP	H	R	ER	BB	SO
1997	Boise (NWL)	A	0	1	6.41	17	2	0	0	20	27	17	14	8	22
1998	Cedar Rapids (Mid)	A	8	4	3.78	20	7	1	0	69	66	30	29	20	59
	Lake Elsinore (Cal)	A	3	4	4.48	11	10	1	0	66	68	40	33	25	69
1999	Clearwater (FSL)	A	2	4	2.29	60	0	0	28	71	60	25	18	23	70
2000	Reading (EL)	AA	8	3	2.44	49	0	0	16	77	55	25	21	22	58
	Philadelphia (NL)	MAJ	0	0	13.50	4	0	0	0	3	5	4	4	2	0
MAJOR LEAGUE TOTALS			0	0	13.50	4	0	0	0	3	5	4	4	2	0
MINOR LEAGUE TOTALS			21	16	3.42	157	19	2	44	303	276	137	115	98	278

13. Yoel Hernandez, rhp

Born: April 15, 1982. **Ht.:** 6-2. **Wt.:** 170. **Bats:** R. **Throws:** R. **Career Transactions:** Signed out of Venezuela by Phillies, Nov. 5, 1998.

One of the most pleasant surprises in the organization last year, Hernandez made his U.S. debut an overwhelming success by winning the Rookie-level Gulf Coast League's ERA title and recognition as the circuit's No. 6 prospect. The Phillies would have been happy if the teenager kept his head above water, but they came away raving about his advanced feel for pitching. Hernandez already shows the ability to locate four quality pitches: a projectable 89-92 mph fastball, a good curveball and changeup, and a developing slider. After his encouraging effort in the GCL, he continued to show his poise and pitchability by competing in the Venezuelan Winter League. Hernandez has shown that he's more than capable of handling the challenge of a promotion to the full-season South Atlantic League this year.

Year	Club (League)	Class	W	L	ERA	G	GS	CG	SV	IP	H	R	ER	BB	SO
1999	La Victoria (VSL)	R	2	2	3.32	14	11	0	1	60	48	27	22	29	57
2000	Phillies (GCL)	R	4	1	1.35	10	9	2	0	60	39	10	9	17	46
MINOR LEAGUE TOTALS			6	3	2.33	24	20	2	1	120	87	37	31	46	103

14. Jorge Padilla, of

Born: Aug. 11, 1979. **Ht.:** 6-2. **Wt.:** 200. **Bats:** R. **Throws:** R. **School:** Florida Air Academy, Melbourne, Fla. **Career Transactions:** Selected by Phillies in third round of 1998 draft; signed July 19, 1998.

The Phillies view Padilla as an exciting prospect who only has begun to scratch the surface of his potential. He was the organization's No. 7 prospect two years ago, but he showed up out of shape in 1999 and left a lot to be desired with his overall approach. Padilla responded to the criticism and turned the corner last year by showing up in tremendous shape. He displays an above-average arm and plays a solid right field. He uses the whole field and is beginning to develop some of the power that Philadelphia's scouts projected when they drafted the Puerto Rican native out of a Florida high school. He's still impatient at the plate and needs to lay off of breaking stuff out of the zone. He can put a charge into the ball just based on his raw strength, but he still is learning which pitches to turn on. Padilla should continue to improve and will play in the Florida State League this year.

Year	Club (League)	Class	AVG	G	AB	R	H	2B	3B	HR	RBI	BB	SO	SB
1998	Martinsville (Appy)	R	.356	23	90	10	32	3	0	5	25	4	24	2
1999	Piedmont (SAL)	A	.208	44	168	13	35	10	1	3	17	5	44	0
	Batavia (NY-P)	A	.252	65	238	28	60	10	1	3	30	22	79	2
2000	Piedmont (SAL)	A	.305	108	413	62	126	24	8	11	67	26	89	8
MINOR LEAGUE TOTALS			.278	240	909	113	253	47	10	22	139	57	236	12

15. Russ Jacobson, c

Born: Oct. 14, 1977. **Ht.:** 6-3. **Wt.:** 210. **Bats:** R. **Throws:** R. **School:** University of Miami. **Career Transactions:** Selected by Phillies in third round of 1999 draft; signed July 13, 1999.

A member of Miami's 1999 College World Series champions, Jacobson didn't play in Omaha because of a broken hand. A much-improved commodity in scout's eyes before the injury, the big receiver hit .380 for the Hurricanes and was regarded as one of the draft's best defensive players before the Phillies nabbed him in the third round. When he was healthy enough to make his pro debut in 2000, he lived up to his billing as a catcher. Jacobson sets a good target for pitchers and works well with them. Basestealers will have to run at their own risk, as he owns excellent arm strength that produces good carry on his throws. He has raw power potential that's really evident in batting practice, when he tattoos pitches and the ball jumps off of his bat. In games, pro pitchers were able to exploit his long swing and questionable strike-zone judgment. If he can address those weaknesses in the Florida State League this year, he'll be on his way to developing into a double threat as a catcher.

Year	Club (League)	Class	AVG	G	AB	R	H	2B	3B	HR	RBI	BB	SO	SB
2000	Piedmont (SAL)	A	.247	102	348	43	86	17	0	19	71	29	105	0
MINOR LEAGUE TOTALS			.247	102	348	43	86	17	0	19	71	29	105	0

16. Dave Coggin, rhp

Born: Oct. 30, 1976. **Ht.:** 6-4. **Wt.:** 205. **Bats:** R. **Throws:** R. **School:** Upland (Calif.) HS. **Career Transactions:** Selected by Phillies in first round (30th overall) of 1995 draft; signed June 15, 1995.

Since ranking as the organization's No. 2 prospect entering 1996, Coggin's career has rarely looked like that of a high-profile first-rounder. Drafted as a power pitcher, he had a scholarship to play quarterback at Clemson before the Phillies persuaded him to turn pro.

He never has lived up to expectations and all but disappeared from prospect consideration when shoulder injuries limited him to just 42 innings in 1999. He worked hard to regain his velocity by building lower-body strength, and found himself filling Robert Person's shoes in the Phillies rotation briefly last summer. Coggin's four-pitch arsenal isn't overpowering, but he mixes a solid array of breaking pitches along with a 91-93 mph fastball to keep hitters off balance. Controlling his stuff, specifically his fastball, has been an issue that has plagued Coggin as a pro. Now that he has his confidence and stamina back, and has had a taste of the majors, he'll try to establish himself as a legitimate callup candidate in Triple-A this year.

Year	Club (League)	Class	W	L	ERA	G	GS	CG	SV	IP	H	R	ER	BB	SO
1995	Martinsville (Appy)	R	5	3	3.00	11	11	0	0	48	45	25	16	31	37
1996	Piedmont (SAL)	A	9	12	4.31	28	28	3	0	169	156	87	81	46	129
1997	Clearwater (FSL)	A	11	8	4.70	27	27	3	0	155	160	96	81	86	110
1998	Reading (EL)	AA	4	8	4.14	20	20	0	0	108	106	58	50	62	65
1999	Reading (EL)	AA	2	5	7.50	9	9	0	0	42	55	37	35	20	21
2000	Clearwater (FSL)	A	2	2	2.67	6	5	0	0	33	25	11	10	13	26
	Reading (EL)	AA	2	3	4.93	7	7	0	0	42	49	24	23	13	30
	Philadelphia (NL)	MAJ	2	0	5.33	5	5	0	0	27	35	20	16	12	17
	Scranton/W-B (IL)	AAA	3	2	4.34	9	9	0	0	45	35	27	22	33	27
MAJOR LEAGUE TOTALS			2	0	5.33	5	5	0	0	27	35	20	16	12	17
MINOR LEAGUE TOTALS			38	43	4.44	117	116	6	0	644	631	365	318	304	445

17. Evan Thomas, rhp

Born: June 14, 1974. **Ht.:** 5-10. **Wt.:** 180. **Bats:** R. **Throws:** R. **School:** Florida International University.
Career Transactions: Selected by Phillies in 10th round of 1996 draft; signed June 17, 1996.

Not much has been heard from Thomas since he led NCAA Division I with 220 strikeouts in 1996. The former Florida International All-American resurfaced last year after four non-descript campaigns as a pro. Thomas improved his conditioning and it paid off with a career-high 171 innings, and he finished second in the International League in strikeouts. He hasn't attracted a lot of attention because of his size and radar-gun readings, but he came together as a pitcher in Triple-A and no longer can be ignored. He draws praise for his bull-dog approach on the mound and work ethic. He's a finesse pitcher who relies on spotting an average 89-91 mph fastball to complement his outstanding curveball and solid average changeup. He's not young and will have to continue to be precise with his command to survive against major leaguers. If anything, he has proved to be durable and intelligent enough to fool hitters, which should help him get a look this year as a potential swingman.

Year	Club (League)	Class	W	L	ERA	G	GS	CG	SV	IP	H	R	ER	BB	SO
1996	Batavia (NY-P)	A	10	2	2.78	13	13	0	0	81	60	29	25	23	75
1997	Clearwater (FSL)	A	5	5	2.44	13	12	2	0	85	68	30	23	23	89
	Reading (EL)	AA	3	6	4.12	15	15	0	0	83	98	51	38	32	83
1998	Reading (EL)	AA	8	5	3.35	24	24	3	0	158	180	66	59	44	134
	Scranton/W-B (IL)	AAA	0	1	8.00	2	2	0	0	9	9	8	8	6	5
1999	Reading (EL)	AA	9	5	3.25	36	15	1	3	127	123	53	46	50	127
2000	Scranton/W-B (IL)	AAA	13	10	3.53	29	27	3	0	171	163	70	67	50	127
MINOR LEAGUE TOTALS			48	34	3.35	132	108	9	3	714	701	307	266	228	640

18. Nate Espy, 1b

Born: April 24, 1978. **Ht.:** 6-3. **Wt.:** 215. **Bats:** R. **Throws:** R. **School:** Lurleen B. Wallace State (Ala.) JC.
Career Transactions: Selected by Phillies in 18th round of 1998 draft; signed June 6, 1998.

The Phillies have had some success delving into the junior college ranks, with Marlon Byrd, Espy, Johnny Estrada and Nick Punto showing upside. Espy torched the South Atlantic League last year, finishing in the top five in batting average, home runs, on-base percentage (.439) and slugging percentage (.531). A big masher, he owns the best raw power in the system. He's a baseball junkie with outstanding work habits keeping his muscular physique in shape throughout the season. Espy isn't a feast-or-famine slugger either. He was one of just eight minor leaguers to surpass the 100-walk plateau. In the field, he operates with limited mobility, but has good hands and isn't a liability. Many have been quick to discredit his monster offensive campaign due to his age, so he'll have to continue to prove himself at each level. The pitcher-friendly Florida State League is up next for Espy.

Year	Club (League)	Class	AVG	G	AB	R	H	2B	3B	HR	RBI	BB	SO	SB
1998	Martinsville (Appy)	R	.361	66	227	50	82	20	1	13	56	51	55	2
1999	Piedmont (SAL)	A	.254	83	295	37	75	18	2	11	38	48	56	3
2000	Piedmont (SAL)	A	.312	130	452	88	141	32	2	21	87	101	105	7
MINOR LEAGUE TOTALS			.306	279	974	175	298	70	5	45	181	200	216	12

19. Johnny Estrada, c

Born: June 27, 1976. **Ht.:** 5-11. **Wt.:** 209. **Bats:** B. **Throws:** R. **School:** JC of the Sequoias (Calif.). **Career Transactions:** Selected by Phillies in 17th round of 1997 draft; signed June 5, 1997.

Estrada has shown marked improvement since coming out of junior college. He has added 20 pounds to his stocky frame and made himself into a prospect worth noting through hard work. As a switch-hitting catcher, Estrada already has one thing going for him, and he puts the bat on nearly everything. He rarely strikes out, going down just once in every 16 plate appearance over the course of his career. On the flip side, Estrada has drawn just 44 career walks. He possesses gap power and swings the bat well from both sides of the plate, hitting .338 against southpaws last season. Managers named Estrada the best defensive catcher in the Eastern League last season, and he rates solid average across the board. He has become a good signal caller and his pitchers like to have him as a target. After a stint in the Arizona Fall League, he'll head into 2001 as the starting backstop at Triple-A Scranton/Wilkes-Barre with a chance to backup Mike Lieberthal in the not-too-distant future. It will be interesting to see how his ultra-aggressive approach works against more experienced pitching, though.

Year	Club (League)	Class	AVG	G	AB	R	H	2B	3B	HR	RBI	BB	SO	SB
1997	Batavia (NY-P)	A	.314	58	223	28	70	17	2	6	43	9	15	0
1998	Piedmont (SAL)	A	.310	77	303	33	94	14	2	7	44	6	19	0
	Clearwater (FSL)	A	.222	37	117	8	26	8	0	0	13	5	7	0
1999	Clearwater (FSL)	A	.277	98	346	35	96	15	0	9	52	14	26	1
2000	Reading (EL)	AA	.295	95	356	42	105	18	0	12	42	10	20	1
MINOR LEAGUE TOTALS			.291	365	1345	146	391	72	4	34	194	44	87	2

20. Carlos Silva, rhp

Born: April 23, 1979. **Ht.:** 6-4. **Wt.:** 225. **Bats:** R. **Throws:** R. **Career Transactions:** Signed out of Venezuela by Phillies, March 22, 1996.

Silva's live arm rivals the system's best. But since signing, he hasn't developed the secondary pitches and polish to accompany his blazing fastball. For a guy who consistently blows his fastball in the mid- to upper 90s, Silva has been surprisingly hittable. He also has averaged a mere 4.9 strikeouts per nine innings. Last year, he led the Florida State League in innings pitched, losses and complete games, and it may have been his last experience as a starter. The Phillies liked what they saw from him in shorter relief stints during instructional league and think he could have a future in that capacity. Silva's changeup is showing signs of coming around. He has experimented with a curveball and slider that he's struggled to throw consistently. A shift to the pen could prove to be the turning point in his career.

Year	Club (League)	Class	W	L	ERA	G	GS	CG	SV	IP	H	R	ER	BB	SO
1996	Martinsville (Appy)	R	0	0	4.00	7	1	0	0	18	20	11	8	5	16
1997	Martinsville (Appy)	R	2	2	5.15	11	11	0	0	58	66	46	33	14	31
1998	Martinsville (Appy)	R	1	4	5.05	7	7	1	0	41	48	24	23	4	21
	Batavia (NY-P)	A	2	3	6.35	9	7	0	0	45	61	37	32	9	27
1999	Piedmont (SAL)	A	11	8	3.12	26	26	3	0	164	176	79	57	41	99
2000	Clearwater (FSL)	A	8	13	3.57	26	24	4	0	176	229	99	70	26	82
MINOR LEAGUE TOTALS			24	30	4.00	86	76	8	0	502	600	296	223	99	276

21. Josue Perez, of

Born: Aug. 12, 1977. **Ht.:** 6-0. **Wt.:** 180. **Bats:** B. **Throws:** R. **Career Transactions:** Signed out of Cuba by Dodgers, March 27, 1998 . . . Contract voided, June 25, 1999 . . . Signed by Phillies, Aug. 5, 1999.

After Perez spent a little more than a year in the Dodgers system, the commissioner's office ruled that he was illegally signed out of Cuba in 1998. Perez and fellow Los Angeles prospect Juan Diaz had their contracts voided and were immediately declared free agents. The Phillies spent $850,000 for the speedster's services, while the Red Sox landed Diaz for considerably less. Perez' progress has been stunted by injuries since he signed with Philadelphia. Last season, he fractured a finger on a headfirst slide and also spent much of the season playing with a bronchial infection, unbeknownst to the Phillies. He was weak and lethargic by the end of the season before heading to the disabled list. Perez projects as a potential top-of-the-order threat with his wheels and ability to put the ball in play from both sides of the plate. He's a line-drive hitter with marginal gap power in his wiry body. Perez' speed is put to use in center field, as he has shown the ability to cover alley to alley. While he's blessed with great running speed, he needs to learn the finer points of stealing bases and reading moves. The Phillies anticipate getting their first yearlong look at the multi-tooled outfielder in Double-A.

Year	Club (League)	Class	AVG	G	AB	R	H	2B	3B	HR	RBI	BB	SO	SB
1998	Dodgers (DSL)	R	.335	48	167	56	56	8	7	2	17	39	16	24
1999	Vero Beach (FSL)	A	.279	62	201	24	56	14	1	2	22	21	29	14
	Clearwater (FSL)	A	.247	23	93	15	23	2	0	0	6	7	17	6
2000	Clearwater (FSL)	A	.297	70	279	41	83	9	8	3	32	28	48	18
	Reading (EL)	AA	.240	32	96	10	23	5	1	1	8	9	19	2
MINOR LEAGUE TOTALS			.288	235	836	146	241	38	17	8	85	104	129	64

22. Keith Bucktrot, rhp

Born: Nov. 27, 1980. **Ht.:** 6-3. **Wt.:** 195. **Bats:** L. **Throws:** R. **School:** Claremore (Okla.) HS. **Career Transactions:** Selected by Phillies in third round of 2000 draft; signed June 26, 2000.

Some teams might have drafted and developed the athletic Bucktrot as a slugging left-handed-hitting outfielder, but the Phillies were enamored with his powerful right arm. He fires an above-average fastball into the low 90s and also has a sharp-breaking curveball. He's still learning how to put it all together and showed some dominating potential in the Gulf Coast League. Given his two-way background, Bucktrot still is learning how to set up hitters. Because he was able to rely on two power pitches in high school, he never threw a changeup, but he'll get a chance to develop one as a starter. With his lively arm and projectable 6-foot-3 frame, Bucktrot is a candidate to have a breakthrough season. The Phillies believe he'll be able to handle the South Atlantic League this year.

Year	Club (League)	Class	W	L	ERA	G	GS	CG	SV	IP	H	R	ER	BB	SO
2000	Phillies (GCL)	R	3	2	4.78	11	7	0	0	37	39	21	20	19	40
MINOR LEAGUE TOTALS			3	2	4.78	11	7	0	0	37	39	21	20	19	40

23. Jimmy Osting, lhp

Born: April 7, 1977. **Ht.:** 6-5. **Wt.:** 190. **Bats:** R. **Throws:** L. **School:** Trinity HS, Louisville. **Career Transactions:** Selected by Braves in fourth round of 1995 draft; signed June 30, 1995 . . . On disabled list, April 2-Sept. 23, 1998 . . . Traded by Braves with LHP Bruce Chen to Phillies for RHP Andy Ashby, July 12, 2000.

Rated the Braves' 10th-best prospect before Tommy John surgery in 1997, Osting was acquired last summer in the Andy Ashby deal. After missing the entire 1998 season, Osting dominated the South Atlantic League in 1999 and pitched well in Double-A last year. He always has been a control pitcher, relying on spotting his lively 86-90 mph fastball on both sides of the plate. He changes speed effectively, using his curveball and changeup to keep hitters off balance. The Phillies would like to see him become more aggressive and improve the arc on his big breaking ball to help combat righties. His up-and-down performance in the Venezuelan Winter League factored into Philadelphia's decision to leave Osting off the 40-man roster. He's expected to compete for a job in Triple-A, but because he's not over-powering his ceiling as a starter is just average. He should have a future role in the majors as a middle reliever if he continues to get lefties out, however.

Year	Club (League)	Class	W	L	ERA	G	GS	CG	SV	IP	H	R	ER	BB	SO
1995	Danville (Appy)	R	2	7	7.15	11	10	0	0	39	46	34	31	25	43
1996	Eugene (NWL)	A	2	1	2.59	5	5	0	0	24	14	11	7	13	35
1997	Macon (SAL)	A	2	3	3.28	15	15	0	0	58	54	28	21	29	62
1998						Did Not Play—Injured									
1999	Macon (SAL)	A	14	4	2.88	27	22	0	2	147	130	52	47	30	131
2000	Myrtle Beach (Car)	A	2	2	3.13	4	4	0	0	23	25	8	8	5	17
	Greenville (SL)	AA	2	6	2.65	11	11	0	0	71	67	30	21	29	52
	Richmond (IL)	AAA	0	2	11.57	3	3	0	0	9	15	12	12	11	2
	Reading (EL)	AA	4	2	2.38	10	9	1	0	57	53	17	15	26	31
MINOR LEAGUE TOTALS			28	27	3.40	86	79	1	2	428	404	192	162	168	373

24. Jason Michaels, of

Born: May 4, 1976. **Ht.:** 6-0. **Wt.:** 204. **Bats:** R. **Throws:** R. **School:** University of Miami. **Career Transactions:** Selected by Phillies in fourth round of 1998 draft; signed June 19, 1998.

Michaels was drafted in the 15th round by the Cardinals in 1997, after hitting .411 with 32 doubles and 15 home runs as a junior in the shadows of Pat Burrell at Miami. Unsatisfied with his draft position, Michaels returned for a senior season and batted .378 with 19 home runs to cap off a standout collegiate career. In the process he improved his draft status, as the Phillies scooped him up three rounds after taking Burrell with the first overall choice in 1998. Michaels' tools are solid across the board. He can play all three outfield positions, though he's best suited for a corner. Until last year, he exhibited a professional understanding of pitch selection. Michaels hits the ball hard and can drive pitches the other way into the gaps. He has proven he can hit, though his lack of power may preclude him from earning a regular role in the majors. Seemingly destined to be a fourth outfielder or a platoon player, he'll play everyday in Triple-A this year.

Year	Club (League)	Class	AVG	G	AB	R	H	2B	3B	HR	RBI	BB	SO	SB
1998	Batavia (NY-P)	A	.268	67	235	45	63	14	3	11	49	40	69	4
1999	Clearwater (FSL)	A	.306	122	451	91	138	31	6	14	65	68	103	10
2000	Reading (EL)	AA	.295	113	437	71	129	30	4	10	74	28	87	7
MINOR LEAGUE TOTALS			.294	302	1123	207	330	75	13	35	188	136	259	21

25. Jay Sitzman, of

Born: March 13, 1978. **Ht.:** 6-3. **Wt.:** 195. **Bats:** L. **Throws:** L. **School:** Arizona State University. **Career Transactions:** Selected by Phillies in 32nd round of 1999 draft; signed June 10, 1999.

Sitzman was overshadowed at Arizona State and not highly regarded as a pro prospect. He did flourish as a junior, however, hitting .373 and leading the Pacific-10 Conference with 33 steals in 1999. In his full-season debut, speed was his most evident tool again as he led all Philadelphia farmhands with 53 steals in 65 attempts. Sitzman's 6.38-second 60-yard-dash time is the best in the organization, and the fact that he knows how to use his speed makes him an intriguing player to watch. He was able to eliminate the loop in his swing that scared away scouts during college and finished second in the South Atlantic League batting race. As expected, he covers a lot of ground in center field and his wheels augment his average arm strength a little bit. Sitzman sprays line drives to all fields, but doesn't drive the ball with much authority. He's expected to move up to Clearwater, where he'll need to focus more on getting on base to maximize the value of his speed.

Year	Club (League)	Class	AVG	G	AB	R	H	2B	3B	HR	RBI	BB	SO	SB
1999	Batavia (NY-P)	A	.296	49	169	33	50	5	5	2	22	9	37	15
2000	Piedmont (SAL)	A	.316	107	418	95	132	17	8	6	55	38	88	53
MINOR LEAGUE TOTALS			.310	156	587	128	182	22	13	8	77	47	125	68

26. Taylor Buchholz, rhp

Born: Oct. 13, 1981. **Ht.:** 6-3. **Wt.:** 220. **Bats:** R. **Throws:** R. **School:** Springfield (Pa.) HS. **Career Transactions:** Selected by Phillies in sixth round of 2000 draft; signed June 19, 2000.

Though the Phillies didn't have a second-round pick in 2000, they were able to land a few prizes in the first 10 rounds because of scouting director Mike Arbuckle's willingness to take chances. Keith Bucktrot, Buchholz and Danny Gonzalez all had been projected to go higher than they did. Buchholz was strongly committed to attend North Carolina, but Philadelphia believed it owned a regional advantage and selected the Pennsylvania high school product. It still took third-round money ($365,000) to sign him, but the move could pay off. Buchholz has the size of a future workhorse and he's developing the repertoire to go with it. He consistently can hit 90 mph and has topped out at 92. He has the makings of an above-average curveball and already owns a great feel for his changeup. Buchholz shows an impressive aptitude considering he's not even a year removed from the prep ranks. His command and poise should help him as he's expected to jump to a full-season circuit this year.

Year	Club (League)	Class	W	L	ERA	G	GS	CG	SV	IP	H	R	ER	BB	SO
2000	Phillies (GCL)	R	2	3	2.25	12	7	0	0	44	46	22	11	14	41
MINOR LEAGUE TOTALS			2	3	2.25	12	7	0	0	44	46	22	11	14	41

27. Danny Gonzalez, ss

Born: Nov. 20, 1981. **Ht.:** 6-0. **Wt.:** 175. **Bats:** B. **Throws:** R. **School:** Florida Air Academy, Melbourne, Fla. **Career Transactions:** Selected by Phillies in fourth round of 2000 draft; signed Aug. 25, 2000.

Like Padilla, Gonzalez was drafted in the top five rounds out of the Florida Air Academy via Puerto Rico. The Phillies believe if it weren't for his lack of speed, Gonzalez would have been regarded among the upper echelon of 2000 draft prospects. But as it is, they may have uncovered a gem with promising potential on both sides of the ball. In instructional league, Gonzalez provided a glimpse of his impressive tools. In particular, his bat shows signs of being a plus, with the potential to add some loft power as he bulks up his frame. At shortstop, he displays soft hands and a strong arm, but his range and the presence of Jimmy Rollins, Anderson Machado and Carlos Rosario in the system could force Gonzalez to shift to second base. The next look the Phillies will get at him will be in extended spring training, before deciding which short-season club he should debut with.

Year	Club (League)	Class	AVG	G	AB	R	H	2B	3B	HR	RBI	BB	SO	SB
2000			Did Not Play—Signed 2001 Contract											

28. Franklin Nunez, rhp

Born: Jan. 18, 1977. **Ht.:** 6-0. **Wt.:** 175. **Bats:** R. **Throws:** R. **Career Transactions:** Signed out of Dominican Republic by Dodgers, Sept. 1, 1994 . . . Released by Dodgers, Jan. 12, 1996 . . . Signed by Phillies, June 20, 1998.

Originally signed in 1994 by the Dodgers, Nunez was released after just one season in the Rookie-level Dominican Summer League. After he spent two years out of baseball, the Phillies discovered he had physically matured and signed him in 1998. He finally made his stateside debut that year, following a second and more decisive tour of the DSL. His fastball, which touches 98 mph, was rated the best in the South Atlantic League in 1999. Because he lacks an above-average secondary offering, Nunez will be used in short relief. The Phillies hoped his time in the rotation would help him develop his breaking stuff. He was able to air out his heater and became more effective in his nine relief appearances last year. A late bloomer, he may see his ascent helped by the shift to the bullpen. Improving his rudimentary curve or changeup would raise his profile even more.

Year	Club (League)	Class	W	L	ERA	G	GS	CG	SV	IP	H	R	ER	BB	SO
1995	Dodgers (DSL)	R	1	0	7.36	12	1	0	0	22	27	25	18	20	17
1996							Did Not Play								
1997							Did Not Play								
1998	Phillies (DSL)	R	0	2	2.18	5	5	1	0	33	23	14	8	14	37
	Martinsville (Appy)	R	2	2	2.49	6	4	0	0	25	23	10	7	8	19
1999	Piedmont (SAL)	A	4	8	3.39	13	13	1	0	77	69	39	29	25	88
2000	Clearwater (FSL)	A	10	4	3.62	23	14	1	2	112	112	54	45	57	81
MINOR LEAGUE TOTALS			17	16	3.58	59	37	3	2	269	254	142	107	124	242

29. Nick Punto, 2b/ss

Born: Nov. 8, 1977. **Ht.:** 5-9. **Wt.:** 170. **Bats:** B. **Throws:** R. **School:** Saddleback (Calif.) JC. **Career Transactions:** Selected by Phillies in 21st round of 1998 draft; signed June 7, 1998.

Drafted as a shortstop, Punto has spent all of his first three years in the system at that position. But the Phillies' abundance of shortstop prospects has forced him across the bag to second base. The scrappy Punto made a relatively smooth transition to the keystone in the Arizona Fall League. He has the hands and footwork to handle the move. In an effort to mold him into a utility player, Punto also got some work at the hot corner in Arizona. He plays the game hard and is a solid line-drive hitter from both sides of the plate who battles and works the count. His speed adds another necessary dimension to becoming a quality utility player, though his lack of power should prevent him from earning a full-time job. He's slated to learn the nuances of second base in Triple-A this year.

Year	Club (League)	Class	AVG	G	AB	R	H	2B	3B	HR	RBI	BB	SO	SB
1998	Batavia (NY-P)	A	.247	72	279	51	69	9	4	1	20	42	48	19
1999	Clearwater (FSL)	A	.305	106	400	65	122	18	6	1	48	67	53	16
2000	Reading (EL)	AA	.254	121	456	77	116	15	4	5	47	69	71	33
MINOR LEAGUE TOTALS			.270	299	1135	193	307	42	14	7	115	178	172	68

30. Alejandro Giron, of

Born: April 26, 1979. **Ht.:** 6-2. **Wt.:** 180. **Bats:** R. **Throws:** R. **Career Transactions:** Signed out of Dominican Republic by Phillies, Oct. 3, 1995.

The Phillies' commitment to scouting in Latin America is starting to pay dividends. They have yet to develop a bona-fide major league player from their efforts, but their Top 30 list has more of an international flavor than ever before. Club officials Sal Artiaga, Sal Agostinelli and the Amaros, Ruben Sr. and Ruben Jr., have been integral in building that link. Giron was signed at the age of 16 and quietly has developed into a noteworthy prospect. His tools are average across the board. Giron has to improve his routes in the outfield, and will be limited to a corner position. More attention to the strike zone also could help him tap into some of his power potential. He'll spend most of 2001 in Double-A.

Year	Club (League)	Class	AVG	G	AB	R	H	2B	3B	HR	RBI	BB	SO	SB
1996	Phillies (DSL)	R	.326	66	273	31	89	15	4	1	37	16	26	10
1997	Martinsville (Appy)	R	.302	54	202	26	61	15	1	1	27	11	40	6
1998	Piedmont (SAL)	A	.228	51	180	14	41	5	2	0	19	9	34	8
1999	Piedmont (SAL)	A	.287	99	387	43	111	15	6	8	59	15	75	12
2000	Clearwater (FSL)	A	.291	115	433	59	126	31	7	4	47	33	100	16
MINOR LEAGUE TOTALS			.290	385	1475	173	428	81	20	14	189	84	275	52

Pittsburgh
Pirates

By John Perrotto

The lack of talent in the upper levels of the Pirates farm system last season was obvious just by looking at Baseball America's annual rankings of talent in each minor league.

Pittsburgh had just one player in the Pacific Coast League top 20 list at Triple-A Nashville. That was Chad Hermansen, who sneaked on at No. 20 following a miserable year with the Sounds (.224-11-38) and a failed six-week audition as the Pirates' starting center fielder at the beginning of the season. He hit just .185-2-8 in 78 games with the Pirates.

Double-A Altoona didn't have anyone crack the Eastern League top 20.

The failure of prospects to make adjustments at the major league level, along with not having replacement parts in the high minors when injuries struck, proved fatal to the Pirates last season. They had a miserable 69-93 finish in a year that started with owner Kevin McClatchy hinting at dark horse contention for a playoff spot and ended with manager Gene Lamont being replaced by hitting coach Lloyd McClendon.

Hermansen wasn't the only young player to struggle. Third baseman Aramis Ramirez, a 21-year-old, and rookie lefthander Jimmy Anderson came into the season counted on to perform key roles. Yet they needed to go back

to the minors before finishing the season in Pittsburgh.

Ramirez was shipped to Nashville after hitting just .167 in April. He came back in late June and finished at .256-6-35 in 73 games, reestablishing himself as the starter at the hot corner. Anderson went 5-11, 5.25 despite an outstanding 3-1 ground ball-fly ball ratio. But he needed two side trips to Nashville and Altoona during the season when he got off track.

The good news for the Pirates is that help is coming. They are developing premium prospects in the lower levels of their farm system. In fact, most of their top prospects were at Class A or lower last year. And with the opening of PNC Park, the franchise could have more money at its disposal.

The Pirates have had two strong drafts since Mickey White took over as scouting director. McClatchy, a proponent of player development, has given White the money to gamble on players with signability questions. That has paid off with White consistently landing players who scared off other clubs with their demands, such as Princeton basketball star Chris Young. Furthermore, McClatchy doesn't skimp on the minor league operation, making sure each club is fully staffed with coaches and trainers.

OrganizationOverview

General manager: Cam Bonifay. **Farm director:** Paul Tinnell. **Scouting director:** Mickey White.

2000 PERFORMANCE

Class	Team	League	W	L	Pct.	Finish*	Manager
Majors	Pittsburgh	National	69	93	.426	13th (16)	Gene Lamont
Triple-A	Nashville Sounds	Pacific Coast	63	79	.444	14th (16)	Trent Jewett
Double-A	Altoona Curve	Eastern	74	68	.521	7th (12)	Marty Brown
High A	Lynchburg Hillcats	Carolina	66	72	.478	6th (8)	Tracy Woodson
Low A	Hickory Crawdads	South Atlantic	75	66	.532	t-4th (14)	Jay Loviglio
Short-season	Williamsport Crosscutters	New York-Penn	29	44	.397	13th (14)	Curtis Wilkerson
Rookie	GCL Pirates	Gulf Coast	34	26	.567	t-5th (13)	Woody Huyke
OVERALL 2000 MINOR LEAGUE RECORD			341	354	.491	18th (30)	

*Finish in overall standings (No. of teams in league).

ORGANIZATION LEADERS

BATTING
*AVG	J.R. House, Hickory	.348
R	Adam Hyzdu, Altoona	96
H	Jose Castillo, Hickory	158
TB	Adam Hyzdu, Altoona	285
2B	Adam Hyzdu, Altoona	39
3B	**Tike Redman**, Nashville	11
HR	Craig Wilson, Nashville	33
RBI	Adam Hyzdu, Altoona	106
BB	Adam Hyzdu, Altoona	94
SO	J.J. Davis, Lynchburg	171
SB	Tony Alvarez, Hickory	52

PITCHING
W	Larry Wimberly, Lynchburg/Altoona	16
L	Geraldo Padua, Lynchburg/Altoona	15
#ERA	Landon Jacobsen, Williamsport/Hickory	2.17
G	Cory Bailey, Nashville	55
CG	Justin Reid, Hickory	5
SV	Clint Chrysler, Lynchburg	14
	Tony Pavlovich, Lynchburg	14
IP	Joe Beimel, Lynchburg/Altoona	183
BB	Brian O'Connor, Altoona/Nashville	75
SO	**Dave Williams**, Hickory/Lynchburg	201

*Minimum 250 at-bats. #Minimum 75 innings.

TOP PROSPECTS OF THE DECADE

1991	Kurt Miller, rhp
1992	Steve Cooke, lhp
1993	Kevin Young, 1b
1994	Midre Cummings, of
1995	Trey Beamon, of
1996	Jason Kendall, c
1997	Kris Benson, rhp
1998	Kris Benson, rhp
1999	Chad Hermansen, of
2000	Chad Hermansen, of

TOP DRAFT PICKS OF THE DECADE

1991	Jon Farrell, c/of
1992	Jason Kendall, c
1993	Charles Peterson, of
1994	Mark Farris, ss
1995	Chad Hermansen, ss
1996	Kris Benson, rhp
1997	J.J. Davis, of
1998	Clint Johnston, lhp/of
1999	Bobby Bradley, rhp
2000	Sean Burnett, lhp

Redman   **Williams**

BEST TOOLS

Best Hitter for Average	J.R. House
Best Power Hitter	J.J. Davis
Fastest Baserunner	Manuel Ravelo
Best Fastball	Luis Torres
Best Breaking Ball	Bobby Bradley
Best Control	Jason Reid
Best Defensive Catcher	Ryan Doumit
Best Defensive Infielder	Jack Wilson
Best Infield Arm	Jose Castillo
Best Defensive Outfielder	Tike Redman
Best Outfield Arm	Jeremy Harts

PROJECTED 2004 LINEUP

Catcher	Jason Kendall
First Base	J.R. House
Second Base	Warren Morris
Third Base	Aramis Ramirez
Shortstop	Jack Wilson
Left Field	Brian Giles
Center Field	Aron Weston
Right Field	J.J. Davis
No. 1 Starter	Kris Benson
No. 2 Starter	Bobby Bradley
No. 3 Starter	Chris Young
No. 4 Starter	Sean Burnett
No. 5 Starter	Jimmy Anderson
Closer	Luis Torres

ALL-TIME LARGEST BONUSES

Bobby Bradley, 1999	$2,250,000
Kris Benson, 1996	2,000,000
J.J. Davis, 1997	1,675,000
Sean Burnett, 2000	1,650,000
Chris Young, 2000	1,650,000

DraftAnalysis

2000 Draft

Best Pro Debut: RHP Josh Higgins (23) went 3-1, 1.04 with eight saves and a 40-8 strikeout-walk ratio in 35 innings at short-season Williamsport. His changeup is his best pitch, and because he's 6-foot-5 he has the potential for plus velocity.

Best Athlete: RHP Chris Young (3) was a standout basketball player at Princeton and had legitimate NBA potential. He has smooth mechanics for a 6-foot-11 pitcher and is agile for his size. The Pirates were confident they could sign him and got him for $1.65 million after he spent the summer dominating the Cape Cod League.

Best Hitter: 2B Nate McLouth (25) spent all summer negotiating but looked good in instructional league.

Best Raw Power: 1B Jon Pagan (18) has terrific strength but needs to learn the strike zone.

Fastest Runner: OFs Troy Veleber (13) and Victor Buttler (14) combine well above-average speed and sound baserunning instincts.

Best Defensive Player: SS Brandon Chaves (10) is a smooth glove man with outstanding hands and range. He batted just .154 at Williamsport and must get stronger to have a chance to hit.

Best Fastball: RHP David Beigh (2) is a 6-foot-5, 230-pound horse who throws in the low to mid-90s. Though Young is still learning to pitch and tops out at 92 mph, the ceiling on his fastball is high.

Most Intriguing Background: For the second straight year, the Pirates spent their first pick on a polished pitcher from Wellington (Fla.) High. In 1999 it was righthander Bobby Bradley. In 2000 it was LHP Sean Burnett (1). He throws in the high 80s with an impressive changeup. RHP Chris Gale (30), who didn't sign, is the son of former major league pitcher Rich.

Boyd

Closest To The Majors: Burnett has a tremendous feel for pitching and is the most advanced of the high school pitchers who dominate the top of Pittsburgh's draft list. Young is attending Princeton and won't rejoin the Pirates until May.

Best Late-Round Pick: McLouth. LHP Mike Connolly (19) has a 90 mph fastball and reminds Pittsburgh of Mike Stanton.

The One Who Got Away: OF **Patrick Boyd** (4) has exceptional tools and projected as a high first-round pick before he had a disappointing junior season at Clemson. When they decided not to meet his asking price, the Pirates freed up the money to sign RHP Jason Sharber (5) and McLouth.

Assessment: Getting Young was one of the draft's bigger coups. He's just one of several promising young arms hoarded by Pittsburgh, which departed from its small-revenue ways. Young got the second-highest bonus among third-rounders, while Sharber ($500,000) and RHP Cole Burzynski ($175,000) led the way among fifth- and seventh-rounders, respectively.

1999 Draft

The Pirates got two potential stars in RHP Bobby Bradley (1) and C J.R. House (5), who dominated the South Atlantic League last year. They rank 1-2 on the club's Top 30 list, and OF Aron Weston (3) is right behind at No. 4. **Grade: A**

1998 Draft

LHP/OF Clint Johnston (1) was a curious first-round choice and he hasn't gotten it done on the mound. Two years later, LHP Joe Biemel (18) appears to be the only real prospect from this group. **Grade: D–**

1997 Draft

OF J.J. Davis (1) is the system's most impressive slugger, while LHP John Grabow (3) has had his moments. 3B/2B Rico Washington (10) looked intriguing until his stock plummeted last season. **Grade: C**

1996 Draft

After struggling for two years in the minors, No. 1 overall pick Kris Benson became the ace righthander everyone projected. Beyond OF Tike Redman (5), Pittsburgh didn't land much else. **Grade: C+**

Note: Draft analysis prepared by Jim Callis. Numbers in parentheses indicate draft rounds.

. . . House has been called a young Mike Piazza by some for his ability to hit for both average and power as a catcher.

J.R. House c

Born: Nov. 11, 1979.
Ht.: 6-1. **Wt.:** 202.
Bats: R. **Throws:** R.
School: Seabreeze HS, Daytona Beach, Fla.
Career Transactions: Selected by Pirates in fifth round of 1999 draft; signed June 12, 1999.

House had a most intriguing high school career. Not only was he a two-sport star, but he was a two-state standout as well. In the fall, House was a record-setting quarterback in West Virginia at Nitro High. He would move to Florida in the spring and catch for Seabreeze High in Ormond Beach. House's father maintained residences in both West Virginia and Florida, and both states' high school athletic associations had liberal transfer policies. House passed for more than 14,000 yards in his career at Nitro, a national record. In baseball, House led Seabreeze to the Florida 4-A semifinals as a senior while slugging 15 homers.

Though he had scholarship offers from major college football programs, he opted to sign with the Pirates for a bonus of $250,000. He moved all the way to a full-season Class A league by the end of his first pro summer. House likely would have won the Class A South Atlantic League triple crown in 2000 if he hadn't missed a month with mononucleosis. An outstanding hitter, he has been called a young Mike Piazza by some for his ability to hit for both average and power as a catcher. His catching skills are still raw but he showed improvement in all areas last season. Despite his quarterback pedigree, House's arm is just average, though his accuracy was better in 2000. He also showed more mobility behind the plate and a better idea of calling a game. Like most catchers, he doesn't run real well and it's unlikely he ever will be a Gold Glove catcher. But with Jason Kendall now signed through 2007 and holding a no-trade clause, House's future probably doesn't lie behind the plate with the Pirates anyway. He has played first base, and the Pirates might try him at third base or one the corner outfield spots this year.

Though his path to Pittsburgh at catcher is blocked, House will force his way into the Pirates' plans with his outstanding bat—if he sticks to baseball. He flirted with the idea of resuming his football career in the offseason after Rich Rodriguez, noted for his passing attacks, replaced the retiring Don Nehlen as coach at West Virginia. House also hinted at asking to be traded in the wake of Kendall's contract. The Pirates believe House will stay with baseball and continue on the fast track to the major leagues, arriving sometime in 2002.

Year	Club (League)	Class	AVG	G	AB	R	H	2B	3B	HR	RBI	BB	SO	SB
1999	Pirates (GCL)	R	.327	33	113	13	37	9	3	5	23	11	23	1
	Williamsport (NY-P)	A	.300	26	100	11	30	6	0	1	13	9	21	0
	Hickory (SAL)	A	.273	4	11	1	3	0	0	0	0	0	3	0
2000	Hickory (SAL)	A	.348	110	420	78	146	29	1	23	90	46	91	1
MINOR LEAGUE TOTALS			.335	173	644	103	216	44	4	29	126	66	138	2

2. Bobby Bradley, rhp

Born: Dec. 15, 1980. **Ht.:** 6-1. **Wt.:** 170. **Bats:** R. **Throws:** R. **School:** Wellington (Fla.) Community HS. **Career Transactions:** Selected by Pirates in first round (eighth overall) of 1999 draft; signed July 7, 1999.

The Pirates gave Bradley a club-record $2.25 million bonus as their first-round draft pick in 1999. He got off to a great start at Class A Hickory last year in his first full pro season, but sprained a ligament in his pitching elbow in June and missed two months. Bradley did come back late in the season, then threw well in instructional league. He has extraordinary control, shown by his 149-25 strikeout-walk ratio. He has two nasty curveballs thrown from different arm angles: a big bender that's his out pitch and one with a tighter break and more velocity. Bradley, who gets high marks for competitiveness, doesn't light up radar guns but his fastball has good life. His changeup continues to improve. His elbow problems are cause for at least mild concern. Some believe his reliance on curves might lead to continued arm trouble. The Pirates say they aren't worried about Bradley after seeing him back at 100 percent in instructional league. While he has adapted quickly to pro ball, the Pirates will try to avoid rushing him. Yet it's realistic to think he'll be in the majors at some point in 2002, particularly if his elbow holds up, and have the chance to become a top-of-the-rotation starter.

Year	Club (League)	Class	W	L	ERA	G	GS	CG	SV	IP	H	R	ER	BB	SO
1999	Pirates (GCL)	R	1	1	2.90	6	6	0	0	31	31	13	10	4	31
2000	Hickory (SAL)	A	8	2	2.29	14	14	3	0	82	62	31	21	21	118
MINOR LEAGUE TOTALS			9	3	2.45	20	20	3	0	113	93	44	31	25	149

3. J.J. Davis, of

Born: Oct. 25, 1978. **Ht.:** 6-4. **Wt.:** 250. **Bats:** R. **Throws:** R. **School:** Baldwin Park (Calif.) HS. **Career Transactions:** Selected by Pirates in first round (eighth overall) of 1997 draft; signed June 3, 1997.

Davis was a standout pitcher and first baseman in high school, compared to Dave Winfield for his two-way ability. The Pirates drafted him as a right fielder. Davis generates great power with his 6-foot-6 frame and a body he started building up two years ago through weight training. He also runs well for a big man, especially once he gets his large body in motion. But he strikes out a ton. The strikeouts are a result of his struggles to recognize breaking pitches, which he sees frequently. Davis has an above-average arm in right field. He also made 18 errors last season, many of them careless mistakes on bobbles or ground balls that got through his legs. He is still unpolished but has as much raw ability as anyone in the system. He likely will get his first taste of Double-A this season, and it will be instructive to see how he fares against better pitching. While he may take a while to reach the majors, the Pirates are intrigued by the potential payoff of 40 homers a season.

Year	Club (League)	Class	AVG	G	AB	R	H	2B	3B	HR	RBI	BB	SO	SB
1997	Pirates (GCL)	R	.255	45	165	19	42	10	2	1	18	14	44	0
	Erie (NY-P)	A	.077	4	13	1	1	0	0	0	0	0	4	0
1998	Augusta (SAL)	A	.198	30	106	11	21	6	0	4	11	3	24	1
	Erie (NY-P)	A	.270	52	196	25	53	12	2	8	39	20	54	4
1999	Hickory (SAL)	A	.265	86	317	58	84	26	1	19	65	44	99	2
2000	Lynchburg (Car)	A	.243	130	485	77	118	36	1	20	80	52	171	9
MINOR LEAGUE TOTALS			.249	347	1282	191	319	90	6	52	213	133	396	16

4. Aron Weston, of

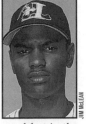

Born: Nov. 5, 1980. **Ht.:** 6-5. **Wt.:** 173. **Bats:** L. **Throws:** L. **School:** Solon (Ohio) HS. **Career Transactions:** Selected by Pirates in third round of 1999 draft; signed June 13, 1999.

The 1999 draft, Mickey White's first as scouting director, yielded two potential superstars for the Pirates in House and Bradley. Weston, a superb high school athlete from suburban Cleveland, hasn't gotten the same hype but also could make it big. He is a potential five-tool player. His lanky body is reminiscent of a young Darryl Strawberry and he should generate good power as his body fills out. He already showed signs of learning to hit for average last year after batting just .218 in his pro debut in the Rookie-level Gulf Coast League. He also has above-average speed, a good grasp of the art of basestealing and fine range in center field. What he lacks are experience and physical maturity. He is learning the finer points of the game, though he draws raves for his intelligence, and needs to get stronger. His arm strength and accuracy also need work, as does his plate discipline. Weston is a high-ceiling player who adapted well in going from extended spring training to a full-season club last May. He's a bit of project and the Pirates will let him develop at his own pace, both physically and mentally.

Year	Club (League)	Class	AVG	G	AB	R	H	2B	3B	HR	RBI	BB	SO	SB
1999	Pirates (GCL)	R	.218	33	119	26	26	2	1	0	5	20	36	14
2000	Hickory (SAL)	A	.267	82	315	52	84	13	2	2	21	36	89	28
MINOR LEAGUE TOTALS			.253	115	434	78	110	15	3	2	26	56	125	142

5. Jose Castillo, ss

Born: March 19, 1981. **Ht.:** 5-11. **Wt.:** 185. **Bats:** R. **Throws:** R. **Career Transactions:** Signed out of Venezuela by Pirates, July 2, 1997.

Castillo burst onto the scene last year in his first taste of full-season ball. He established himself as one of the better prospects in the South Atlantic League by showing plenty of tools. He greatly improved his power last season, as he more than tripled his GCL homer output from the previous year. He has a cannon arm, easily making throws from deep in the hole at shortstop, while also showing good range. He is erratic in the field and tries to force too many plays, and he led the minor leagues with 60 errors last year. However, many slick-fielding shortstops in the major leagues had high error totals in Class A, and Castillo committed just 18 miscues in the second half of the season. His strike-zone judgment isn't good and he needs work on his baserunning. A shortstop with above-average power is intriguing, though Castillo must gain defensive consistency to make it to the major leagues at the position. If he doesn't show enough improvement with the glove, he has the arm and power to shift to third base. He likely will move one step at a time, making 2004 his ETA in Pittsburgh.

Year	Club (League)	Class	AVG	G	AB	R	H	2B	3B	HR	RBI	BB	SO	SB
1998	Montalban (VSL)	R	.291	55	179	31	52	9	1	1	13	20	30	23
1999	Pirates (GCL)	R	.266	47	173	27	46	9	0	4	30	11	23	8
2000	Hickory (SAL)	A	.299	125	529	95	158	32	8	16	72	29	107	16
MINOR LEAGUE TOTALS			.291	227	881	153	256	50	9	21	115	60	160	47

6. Jack Wilson, ss

Born: Dec. 29, 1977. **Ht.:** 6-0. **Wt.:** 170. **Bats:** R. **Throws:** R. **School:** Oxnard (Calif.) JC. **Career Transactions:** Selected by Cardinals in ninth round of 1998 draft; signed June 3, 1998 . . . Traded by Cardinals to Pirates for LHP Jason Christiansen, July 30, 2000.

The Pirates acquired Wilson last July after Pirates manager Lloyd McClendon, then the club's hitting coach, highly recommended him to general manager Cam Bonifay. McClendon knew Wilson from managing him in the California Fall League in 1999. Wilson doesn't have eye-popping tools, but his total package makes him an above-average shortstop. He has solid range, a good arm and soft hands. What makes Wilson stand out are his great instincts and knowledge of the game. He also will take a walk while being a good bat handler and bunter, making him a potential No. 2 hitter. He has no glaring weaknesses. He has only moderate pop in his bat and doesn't look like he'll hit for much power in the major leagues. He is only an average runner, making it doubtful he'll steal many bases. The Pirates are contractually committed to shortstop Pat Meares through 2003, but they would like to upgrade defensively and Wilson could be their answer by 2002 if he continues to improve in Triple-A this year. In that case, Pittsburgh either could find a taker for Meares or eat his contract.

Year	Club (League)	Class	AVG	G	AB	R	H	2B	3B	HR	RBI	BB	SO	SB
1998	Johnson City (Appy)	R	.373	61	241	50	90	18	4	4	29	18	30	22
1999	Peoria (Mid)	A	.343	64	251	47	86	22	4	3	28	15	23	11
	Potomac (Car)	A	.296	64	257	44	76	10	1	2	18	19	31	7
2000	Potomac (Car)	A	.277	13	47	7	13	0	1	2	7	5	10	2
	Arkansas (TL)	AA	.294	88	343	65	101	29	8	6	34	36	59	2
	Altoona (EL)	AA	.252	33	139	17	35	7	2	1	16	14	17	1
MINOR LEAGUE TOTALS			.314	323	1278	230	401	86	20	18	132	107	170	45

7. Chris Young, rhp

Born: May 25, 1979. **Ht.:** 6-11. **Wt.:** 250. **Bats:** R. **Throws:** R. **School:** Princeton University. **Career Transactions:** Selected by Pirates in third round of 2000 draft; signed Aug. 30, 2000.

Young was an all-Ivy League center at Princeton and appeared to have an NBA future before following his heart to baseball. The Pirates persuaded Young to give up basketball with a $1.65 million signing bonus last August after he starred in the Cape Cod League. Young has outstanding mechanics and coordination for such a big man. Scouts are impressed with how he consistently repeats his delivery, a difficult task for tall pitchers. He also is graceful and moves well around the mound. Young's fastball routinely hits 90 mph and has the potential to max out at 95-96 mph because of his large frame. His breaking and offspeed pitches need work, which is understandable because he lacks experience. His progress will be slowed this year because he'll participate in spring training for just a week or so while continuing to take classes at Princeton. He likely will begin his professional career in June with short-season Williamsport.

Year	Club (League)	Class	W	L	ERA	G	GS	CG	SV	IP	H	R	ER	BB	SO
2000					Did Not Play—Signed 2001 Contract										

8. Sean Burnett, lhp

Born: Sept. 17, 1982. **Ht.:** 6-1. **Wt.:** 172. **Bats:** L. **Throws:** L. **School:** Wellington (Fla.) Community HS. **Career Transactions:** Selected by Pirates in first round (19th overall) of 2000 draft; signed July 7, 2000.

Burnett followed in the footsteps of Bobby Bradley, his close friend. Burnett was a first-round pick out of Wellington (Fla.) High last spring, after Bradley was their first-round choice in 1999. Burnett received a $1.65 million signing bonus. He is also like Bradley in that he doesn't possess an overpowering fastball but succeeds with outstanding secondary pitches, good command and a great understanding of pitching. Burnett has an advanced changeup for a young pitcher and consistently spots it on the outside corner of the plate. He also has a fine curveball and plenty of intangibles, with a fierce competitiveness and great poise. His fastball tops out at 87-88 mph, below average in an era when seemingly everyone throws 90-plus. Other than that, he only lacks professional experience. The Pirates envision Bradley and Burnett forming a dynamic righty-lefty duo at the top of their rotation for many years. Burnett likely will start off with Hickory this season, putting him on pace to get to the major leagues in 2005. He has the potential to get there sooner.

Year	Club (League)	Class	W	L	ERA	G	GS	CG	SV	IP	H	R	ER	BB	SO
2000	Pirates (GCL)	R	2	1	4.06	8	6	0	0	31	31	17	14	3	24
MINOR LEAGUE TOTALS			2	1	4.06	8	6	0	0	31	31	17	14	3	24

9. John Grabow, lhp

Born: Nov. 4, 1978. **Ht.:** 6-2. **Wt.:** 189. **Bats:** L. **Throws:** L. **School:** San Gabriel (Calif.) HS. **Career Transactions:** Selected by Pirates in third round of 1997 draft; signed June 12, 1997.

The Pirates love lefthanders and have been infatuated with Grabow since drafting him. He throws harder than the average lefty, as his fastball routinely reaches 91-92 mph and makes him a strikeout pitcher. He also has a curveball, which he sometimes struggles to control, and an above-average changeup that could become an out pitch. He doesn't back down to hitters or rattle easily. Grabow's control regressed last season at Double-A Altoona. Making the jump past high Class A had something to do with it, as he had a harder time getting less experienced hitters to chase pitches out of the strike zone. Grabow has made rapid progress through the system, but arthroscopic surgery on his elbow in September could slow him down. He is expected to be ready for spring training and will go to Triple-A if he's healthy. He could be in the Pittsburgh rotation by 2002 if all goes well.

Year	Club (League)	Class	W	L	ERA	G	GS	CG	SV	IP	H	R	ER	BB	SO
1997	Pirates (GCL)	R	2	7	4.57	11	8	0	0	45	57	32	23	14	28
1998	Augusta (SAL)	A	6	3	5.78	17	16	0	0	72	84	59	46	34	67
1999	Hickory (SAL)	A	9	10	3.80	26	26	0	0	156	152	82	66	32	164
2000	Altoona (EL)	AA	8	7	4.33	24	24	1	0	145	145	81	70	65	109
MINOR LEAGUE TOTALS			25	27	4.41	78	74	1	0	419	438	254	205	145	368

10. Ryan Doumit, c

Born: April 3, 1981. **Ht.:** 6-0. **Wt.:** 180. **Bats:** B. **Throws:** R. **School:** Moses Lake (Wash.) HS. **Career Transactions:** Selected by Pirates in second round of 1999 draft; signed June 16, 1999.

Doumit was the catcher on the powerful Moses Lake team in 1999 that produced a first-round draft pick (B.J. Garbe, Twins) and two second-rounders (Doumit and Jason Cooper, who went to Stanford rather than signing with the Phillies). A rare switch-hitting catcher, Doumit swings the bat well from both sides of the plate. He has shown the ability to hit for average and flashed better gap power last season, and some of his doubles should turn into home runs as he matures. On defense, he can stop a running game with his strong arm, and he's agile behind the plate. Like Jason Kendall, Doumit is small for a catcher but has a strong body. He still is learning how to call a game, something that should come with experience because he's bright. Like every other catcher in the organization, he faces the specter of Kendall. Considering Doumit is still three or four years away from the major leagues, he has no need to concern himself with that yet.

Year	Club (League)	Class	AVG	G	AB	R	H	2B	3B	HR	RBI	BB	SO	SB
1999	Pirates (GCL)	R	.282	29	85	17	24	5	0	1	7	15	14	4
2000	Williamsport (NY-P)	A	.313	66	246	25	77	15	5	2	40	23	33	2
MINOR LEAGUE TOTALS			.305	95	331	42	101	20	5	3	47	38	47	6

11. Luis Torres, rhp

Born: June 6, 1980. **Ht.:** 5-10. **Wt.:** 175. **Bats:** R. **Throws:** R. **Career Transactions:** Signed out of Dominican Republic by Pirates, Feb. 20, 1998.

Torres has established himself as the hardest thrower in the organization but missed a month in the second half of 2000 with a sore shoulder. Torres' fastball reaches as high as 97-98 mph and consistently settles in around 93-95. Despite being only 5-foot-10, he gets exceptional leverage and throws everything on a downhill plane. The ball seems to jump out of his hand. Torres needs better movement on his fastball, a tighter slider and an off-speed pitch to combat advanced hitters. Stamina is also a concern because he isn't big. The Pirates aren't sure whether Torres projects as a starter or closer. He'll stay in the rotation this year, likely beginning the season at high Class A Lynchburg.

Year	Club (League)	Class	W	L	ERA	G	GS	CG	SV	IP	H	R	ER	BB	SO
1998	Pirates (DSL)	R	1	3	2.87	4	2	0	0	16	15	14	5	8	6
1999	Pirates (GCL)	R	1	2	1.69	8	8	0	0	43	24	9	8	7	33
	Hickory (SAL)	A	3	2	3.26	7	7	0	0	39	40	17	14	20	26
2000	Hickory (SAL)	A	5	7	4.49	23	21	0	0	110	121	73	55	60	68
MINOR LEAGUE TOTALS			10	14	3.56	42	38	0	0	207	200	113	82	95	133

12. Tike Redman, of

Born: March 10, 1977. **Ht.:** 5-11. **Wt.:** 166. **Bats:** L. **Throws:** L. **School:** Tuscaloosa (Ala.) Academy. **Career Transactions:** Selected by Pirates in fifth round of 1996 draft; signed June 5, 1996.

Redman made his major league debut last season, holding his own in limited appearances. He had two straight solid Arizona Fall League seasons and was named to the all-prospect team in 2000. Redman has outstanding speed, making him a potential leadoff hitter if he refines his offensive game. He has outstanding range in center field and an accurate arm. While a small guy, Redman has gap power and defenses have to play him honest. He has to become more consistent at playing the little man's game. After making great strides in strike zone judgment, Redman regressed last season and went back to swinging at everything. He needs to learn to read pickoff moves better, which would improve his basestealing success. Though Redman likely will repeat Triple-A, the Pirates believe he can become a big league center fielder if he shows more consistency at the plate.

Year	Club (League)	Class	AVG	G	AB	R	H	2B	3B	HR	RBI	BB	SO	SB
1996	Pirates (GCL)	R	.298	26	104	20	31	4	1	1	16	12	12	15
	Erie (NY-P)	A	.294	43	170	31	50	4	6	2	21	17	30	7
1997	Lynchburg (Car)	A	.251	125	415	55	104	18	5	4	45	45	82	21
1998	Lynchburg (Car)	A	.257	131	525	70	135	26	10	6	46	32	73	36
1999	Altoona (EL)	AA	.269	136	532	84	143	20	12	3	60	52	52	29
2000	Nashville (PCL)	AAA	.261	121	506	62	132	24	11	4	51	32	73	24
	Pittsburgh (NL)	MAJ	.333	9	18	2	6	1	0	1	1	1	7	1
MAJOR LEAGUE TOTALS			.333	9	18	2	6	1	0	1	1	1	7	1
MINOR LEAGUE TOTALS			.264	582	2252	322	595	96	45	20	239	190	322	132

13. Humberto Cota, c

Born: Feb. 7, 1979. **Ht.:** 6-0. **Wt.:** 175. **Bats:** R. **Throws:** R. **Career Transactions:** Signed out of Mexico by Braves, Dec. 22, 1995 . . . Loaned by Braves to Mexico City Tigers (Mexican), June 23-Sept. 23, 1996 . . . Released by Braves, Jan. 27, 1997 . . . Signed by Devil Rays, May 22, 1997 . . . Traded by Devil Rays with C Joe Oliver to Pirates for OF Jose Guillen and RHP Jeff Sparks, July 23, 1999.

Cota has a chance to be an offensive catcher with the ability to hit for average and power. He struggled to make the jump from low Class A to Double-A, but hit better in the second half. He's agile behind the plate. Cota lost his plate discipline last season and was often fooled by the offspeed offerings of more experienced pitchers. His arm strength is OK, but he has a slow release and struggles with the accuracy of his throws. Cota was in over his head at Double-A, and the Pirates may put him back there this year. With Jason Kendall ahead of him and prospects J.R. House and Ryan Doumit behind him, his future is cloudy.

Year	Club (League)	Class	AVG	G	AB	R	H	2B	3B	HR	RBI	BB	SO	SB
1997	Devil Rays (GCL)	R	.241	44	133	14	32	6	1	2	20	17	27	3
	Hudson Valley (NY-P)	A	.222	3	9	0	2	0	0	0	2	0	1	0
1998	Princeton (Appy)	R	.310	67	245	48	76	13	4	15	61	32	59	4
1999	Charleston, SC (SAL)	A	.280	85	336	42	94	21	1	9	61	20	51	1
	Hickory (SAL)	A	.271	37	133	28	36	11	2	2	20	21	20	3
2000	Altoona (EL)	AA	.261	112	429	49	112	20	1	8	44	21	80	6
MINOR LEAGUE TOTALS			.274	348	1285	181	352	71	9	36	208	111	238	17

14. Craig Wilson, c/1b

Born: Nov. 30, 1976. **Ht.:** 6-2. **Wt.:** 220. **Bats:** R. **Throws:** R. **School:** Marina HS, Huntington Beach, Calif. **Career Transactions:** Selected by Blue Jays in second round of 1995 draft; signed June 22, 1995 . . . Traded by Blue Jays to Pirates, Dec. 11, 1996, completing trade in which Pirates sent 2B Carlos Garcia, 1B Orlando Merced and LHP Dan Plesac to Blue Jays for LHP Mike Halperin, SS Abraham Nunez, RHP Jose Pett, RHP Jose Silva, SS Brandon Cromer and a player to be named (Nov. 14, 1996).

Wilson has homered every 17 at-bats during his four years in the system. He broke through last season, slamming an organization-best 33 homers for Triple-A Nashville. He's strong enough to the hit the ball out of the park to all fields and generates his power with an effortless swing. A typical laid-back Southern Californian, he handles the ups and downs of baseball better than most players. Wilson has trouble handling breaking and offspeed pitches, often chasing them out of the strike zone. He's a subpar catcher with a long throwing motion, perhaps an offshoot of reconstructive elbow surgery in 1998. Wilson also isn't mobile behind the plate and his game-calling abilities have been brought into question, making many believe he's better suited for first base. Despite his 2000 performance, Wilson needs more minor league at-bats and time to find a new position, which means another trip to Nashville. He might be best off as a DH in the American League.

Year	Club (League)	Class	AVG	G	AB	R	H	2B	3B	HR	RBI	BB	SO	SB
1995	Medicine Hat (Pio)	R	.283	49	184	33	52	14	1	7	35	24	41	8
1996	Hagerstown (SAL)	A	.261	131	495	66	129	27	5	11	70	32	120	17
1997	Lynchburg (Car)	A	.264	117	401	54	106	26	1	19	69	39	98	6
1998	Lynchburg (Car)	A	.269	61	219	26	59	12	2	12	45	22	53	2
	Carolina (SL)	AA	.331	45	148	20	49	11	0	5	21	14	32	4
1999	Altoona (EL)	AA	.268	111	362	57	97	21	3	20	69	40	104	1
2000	Nashville (PCL)	AAA	.283	124	396	83	112	24	2	33	86	44	121	1
MINOR LEAGUE TOTALS			.274	638	2205	339	604	135	14	107	395	215	569	39

15. Joe Beimel, lhp

Born: April 19, 1977. **Ht.:** 6-2. **Wt.:** 201. **Bats:** L. **Throws:** L. **School:** Duquesne University. **Career Transactions:** Selected by Pirates in 18th round of 1998 draft; signed June 5, 1998.

Beimel grew up a Pirates fan in the mountain town of St. Mary's, Pa., two hours northeast of Pittsburgh. He became a rare Duquesne draft pick when the Pirates selected him in 1998. Beimel has a wide assortment of pitches and a good idea of how to use them. His fastball routinely reaches 90 mph with good movement. He also changes speeds on his curveball, throws a plus changeup and mixes in a slider that can be tough on lefthanders. Beimel is a good fielder and holds runners well. He struggled after moving up to Double-A midway through last season, and there were concerns he may have hit a wall in his career. Once he learned he couldn't fool advanced hitters so easily with his curve, he made adjustments and had success. He still needs to be sharper with all his pitches. Beimel projects as a starter because of his ability to mix pitches, yet his fastball and curveball could make him an effective set-up man. He will start 2001 back at Double-A but could be in Pittsburgh by 2002.

Year	Club (League)	Class	W	L	ERA	G	GS	CG	SV	IP	H	R	ER	BB	SO
1998	Erie (NY-P)	A	1	4	6.32	17	6	0	0	47	56	39	33	22	37
1999	Hickory (SAL)	A	5	11	4.43	29	22	0	0	130	146	81	64	43	102
2000	Lynchburg (Car)	A	10	6	3.36	18	18	2	0	120	111	49	45	44	82
	Altoona (EL)	AA	1	6	4.16	10	10	1	0	62	72	38	29	21	28
MINOR LEAGUE TOTALS			17	27	4.27	74	56	3	0	360	385	207	171	130	249

16. Jeremy Harts, of

Born: June 6, 1980. **Ht.:** 6-1. **Wt.:** 186. **Bats:** B. **Throws:** L. **School:** Columbia HS, Decatur, Ga. **Career Transactions:** Selected by Pirates in third round of 1998 draft; signed June 18, 1998.

Harts was regarded as a lefthanded pitching prospect by many clubs heading into the draft, but the Pirates liked his offensive potential more. As you might expect, Harts has a cannon arm, the best of any outfielder in the organization. His arm makes his long-range position right field, though he has the speed to play center. All of Harts' tools grade out above-average because he has the potential to hit for average and power while being a plus runner with basestealing capabilities. Harts began to develop power last season but strikes out too frequently and doesn't walk enough to take advantage of his speed. He did improve his pitch recognition during instructional league, an encouraging sign. He'll move slowly through the system as he learns the game, but he's an intriguing player who could blossom.

Year	Club (League)	Class	AVG	G	AB	R	H	2B	3B	HR	RBI	BB	SO	SB
1998	Pirates (GCL)	R	.268	34	123	21	33	9	3	1	11	7	37	10
1999	Pirates (GCL)	R	.295	28	122	20	36	3	2	2	15	8	21	8
	Hickory (SAL)	A	.132	22	68	8	9	1	0	0	1	10	24	1
2000	Hickory (SAL)	A	.242	124	459	75	111	14	2	12	62	32	147	25
MINOR LEAGUE TOTALS			.245	208	772	124	189	27	7	15	89	57	229	44

17. Brian O'Connor, lhp

Born: Jan. 4, 1977. **Ht.:** 6-2. **Wt.:** 190. **Bats:** L. **Throws:** L. **School:** Reading HS, Cincinnati. **Career Transactions:** Selected by Pirates in 11th round of 1995 draft; signed June 3, 1995.

O'Connor played for a team called the Pirates in Little League while growing up in suburban Cincinnati and adopted former Pittsburgh catcher Tony Pena as his favorite player. He wound up being drafted by the real Pirates and made his major league debut last season. He's the antithesis of most lefthanders, relying on power rather than finesse. He has a fastball that tops out at 92-93 mph with good movement. His slider has developed into a quality pitch, giving him something to attack lefthanders. Control has been O'Connor's bugaboo as he has reached the higher levels of the organization. The Pirates know he has a live arm, but they're torn between using him as a starter or reliever. If he moves to the bullpen, he could land in Pittsburgh as early as Opening Day 2001. If he keeps starting, he'll get a full year at Triple-A.

Year	Club (League)	Class	W	L	ERA	G	GS	CG	SV	IP	H	R	ER	BB	SO
1995	Pirates (GCL)	R	2	2	1.88	14	5	0	1	43	33	22	9	13	43
1996	Augusta (SAL)	A	0	1	3.06	19	0	0	1	35	33	13	12	8	37
	Erie (NY-P)	A	4	10	5.85	15	15	0	0	68	75	60	44	47	60
1997	Augusta (SAL)	A	2	7	4.41	25	14	0	0	86	90	54	42	39	91
	Lynchburg (Car)	A	2	1	3.46	11	0	0	2	13	11	5	5	6	14
1998	Lynchburg (Car)	A	6	2	2.60	14	14	1	0	87	86	34	25	22	84
	Carolina (SL)	AA	2	4	8.25	14	13	0	0	64	86	65	59	53	41
1999	Altoona (EL)	AA	7	11	4.70	28	27	1	0	153	152	98	80	92	106
2000	Altoona (EL)	AA	12	4	3.76	22	22	4	0	129	120	69	54	61	76
	Nashville (PCL)	AAA	2	2	6.84	5	5	0	0	26	30	23	20	14	19
	Pittsburgh (NL)	MAJ	0	0	5.11	6	1	0	0	12	12	11	7	11	7
MAJOR LEAGUE TOTALS			0	0	5.11	6	·1	0	0	12	12	11	7	11	7
MINOR LEAGUE TOTALS			39	44	4.47	167	115	6	4	705	716	443	350	355	571

18. Tony Alvarez, of

Born: May 10, 1979. **Ht.:** 6-1. **Wt.:** 202. **Bats:** R. **Throws:** R. **Career Transactions:** Signed out of Venezuela by Pirates, Sept. 27, 1995.

Alvarez came from nowhere to become the New York-Penn League's MVP in 1999. He followed that up by stealing an organization-best 52 bases last year. Alvarez is a good all-around offensive player with his power and speed. He has raw power, and some scouts think he can hit 30-35 homers a year if he gets stronger and develops a better knowledge of the strike zone. He has a good grasp of situational hitting for a young player. Alvarez isn't a burner but always looks to run. He swings at too many bad pitches and runs into outs on the bases. Though he can play all three outfield positions and both corner infield spots, he's a below-average defender. Alvarez is intriguing because of his power/speed combination, though he still has many shortcomings. He likely won't surface in the majors until 2004.

Year	Club (League)	Class	AVG	G	AB	R	H	2B	3B	HR	RBI	BB	SO	SB
1996	Pirates (DSL)	R	.138	39	109	12	15	2	0	1	9	8	12	6
1997	Guacara 1 (VSL)	R	.220	38	91	15	20	3	0	0	6	9	10	3
1998	Pirates (GCL)	R	.247	50	190	27	47	13	1	4	29	13	24	19
1999	Williamsport (NY-P)	A	.321	58	196	44	63	14	1	7	45	21	36	38
2000	Hickory (SAL)	A	.285	118	442	75	126	25	4	15	77	39	93	52
MINOR LEAGUE TOTALS			.264	303	1028	173	271	57	6	27	166	90	175	118

19. B.J. Barns, of

Born: July 21, 1977. **Ht.:** 6-4. **Wt.:** 195. **Bats:** L. **Throws:** L. **School:** Duquesne University. **Career Transactions:** Selected by Pirates in sixth round of 1999 draft; signed June 8, 1999.

Jon Mercurio's mission was to find local talent when the Pirates named him coordinator of amateur baseball development and scouting supervisor in 1998. He has delivered by drafting Joe Beimel and B.J. Barns from Duquesne in Pittsburgh. Barns rewrote the Dukes record book and was the Atlantic 10 Conference player of the year in 1999. He uses the whole field better than most hitters and hits the ball where it's pitched. He also can turn on inside pitches and drive them out of the park. He tends to be streaky and needs to gain more consistency. He also must cut down on his strikeouts and improve his strike-zone judgment. Barns is only an average fielder and runner, though his arm is strong enough for right field. He could begin 2001 at Altoona with a strong spring. Double-A is the place where prospects separate from suspects. If Barns passes that test, he could get to the majors quickly.

Year	Club (League)	Class	AVG	G	AB	R	H	2B	3B	HR	RBI	BB	SO	SB
1999	Williamsport (NY-P)	A	.400	14	50	10	20	4	0	1	11	12	11	0
·	Hickory (SAL)	A	.230	52	174	16	40	8	4	6	25	25	47	5
2000	Lynchburg (Car)	A	.244	120	398	46	97	20	1	8	48	44	95	8
MINOR LEAGUE TOTALS			.252	186	622	72	157	32	5	15	84	81	153	13

20. Chris Spurling, rhp

Born: June 28, 1977. **Ht.:** 6-6. **Wt.:** 240. **Bats:** R. **Throws:** R. **School:** Sinclair (Ohio) CC. **Career Transactions:** Selected by Yankees in 41st round of 1997 draft; signed May 14, 1998 . . . Traded by Yankees to Pirates for 2B Luis Sojo, Aug. 7, 2000.

Spurling throws fairly hard, but his success comes from consistently throwing strikes. He's aggressive and challenges hitters with a 91-93 mph fastball, along with a good slider. His fastball appears harder because he has a smooth delivery. Spurling put up decent numbers in the Yankees organization after signing as a draft-and-follow, but he was far from spectacular. So it's hard to tell whether his success with the Pirates is a trend or a one-month aberration. While Spurling has had success by just attacking opponents in the lower levels, it remains to be seen if his stuff is good enough to get more advanced hitters out. Spurling will begin this season in Double-A and has the chance for a promotion to Triple-A.

Year	Club (League)	Class	W	L	ERA	G	GS	CG	SV	IP	H	R	ER	BB	SO
1998	Yankees (GCL)	R	2	1	2.28	13	6	0	1	51	57	21	13	11	44
	Greensboro (SAL)	A	1	0	3.00	1	1	0	0	6	7	2	2	1	5
1999	Greensboro (SAL)	A	4	6	3.66	49	0	0	4	76	78	34	31	23	68
2000	Tampa (FSL)	A	4	6	3.79	34	0	0	1	57	50	27	24	22	55
	Lynchburg (Car)	A	1	0	0.98	9	0	0	5	18	8	2	2	3	17
MINOR LEAGUE TOTALS			12	13	3.10	106	7	0	11	209	200	86	72	60	189

21. Alex Hernandez, of

Born: May 28, 1977. **Ht.:** 6-4. **Wt.:** 186. **Bats:** L. **Throws:** L. **School:** Pedro Alviso Campos HS, Levittown, P.R. **Career Transactions:** Selected by Pirates in fourth round of 1995 draft; signed June 5, 1995.

After three straight years in Double-A, Hernandez finally moved up to Triple-A last June then received a September callup. He seemed destined to become a Pirate after growing up playing baseball at Roberto Clemente Sports City in San Juan. Hernandez does many things well, though nothing spectacularly. He hits for a decent average, has some power and speed, and is solid defensively. His strong arm makes him a good right fielder, and he shows good agility around the first-base bag when he plays there. The Pirates long have believed there's big-time power locked in Hernandez' lanky 6-foot-4 frame, but it has yet to emerge. Hernandez, like seemingly every hitter in the organization, has little understanding of the strike zone and his walk numbers get worse each year. The Pirates have waited a long time for him to blossom and will send him back to Triple-A this season for more seasoning.

Year	Club (League)	Class	AVG	G	AB	R	H	2B	3B	HR	RBI	BB	SO	SB
1995	Pirates (GCL)	R	.269	49	186	24	50	5	3	1	17	17	33	4
1996	Erie (NY-P)	A	.289	61	225	38	65	13	4	4	30	20	47	7
1997	Lynchburg (Car)	A	.290	131	520	75	151	37	4	5	68	27	140	13
1998	Carolina (SL)	AA	.259	115	452	62	117	22	7	8	48	41	81	11
1999	Altoona (EL)	AA	.257	126	475	76	122	26	3	15	63	54	110	11
2000	Altoona (EL)	AA	.337	50	199	28	67	16	1	4	34	13	42	1
	Nashville (PCL)	AAA	.275	76	276	29	76	17	2	8	37	11	60	6
	Pittsburgh (NL)	MAJ	.200	20	60	4	12	3	0	1	5	0	13	1
MAJOR LEAGUE TOTALS			.200	20	60	4	12	3	0	1	5	0	13	1
MINOR LEAGUE TOTALS			.278	608	2333	332	648	136	24	45	297	183	513	53

22. Wilson Guzman, lhp

Born: July 14, 1977. **Ht.:** 5-9. **Wt.:** 200. **Bats:** L. **Throws:** L. **Career Transactions:** Signed out of Dominican Republic by Pirates, July 14, 1994.

Guzman has slowly worked his way up the chain in six seasons. His patience paid off as he was the Pirates' minor league pitcher of the year in 2000. Guzman stands only 5-foot-9 but succeeds with guile. His fastball has average velocity with nice life, and he mixes it with a good changeup and decent slider. His unorthodox delivery and ability to change speeds keep hitters off balance. He's a strong competitor who never backs down. Guzman's stature leaves his long-term future as a starter in doubt because of potential stamina problems. He was primarily a reliever in five previous pro seasons, and his arm isn't used to a lot of innings. He also needs to tighten his slider to better combat lefthanders. Guzman came a long way last season and likely will get a chance in Triple-A this year.

Year	Club (League)	Class	W	L	ERA	G	GS	CG	SV	IP	H	R	ER	BB	SO
1995	Pirates (DSL)	R	5	0	1.47	16	6	1	4	55	52	17	9	17	48
1996	Pirates (DSL)	R	1	6	4.22	14	11	1	1	60	61	33	28	21	56
1997	Pirates (GCL)	R	4	1	2.90	9	8	0	0	40	43	15	13	8	48
	Erie (NY-P)	A	1	2	5.06	5	5	0	0	27	26	20	15	6	25
1998	Augusta (SAL)	A	6	3	2.57	42	0	0	4	70	55	24	20	24	73
	Lynchburg (Car)	A	0	1	13.50	3	0	0	0	3	4	4	4	5	2
1999	Lynchburg (Car)	A	1	2	3.44	35	0	0	2	65	70	35	25	12	78
2000	Lynchburg (Car)	A	4	3	2.88	10	10	0	0	59	65	28	19	19	58
	Altoona (EL)	AA	10	4	3.02	18	18	3	0	119	99	49	40	45	77
MINOR LEAGUE TOTALS			32	22	3.12	152	58	5	11	498	475	225	173	157	465

23. Paul Weichard, of

Born: Nov. 7, 1979. **Ht.:** 5-11. **Wt.:** 195. **Bats:** B. **Throws:** L. **Career Transactions:** Signed out of Australia by Diamondbacks, April 3, 1997 . . . Traded by Diamondbacks with a player to be named to Pirates for 2B Tony Womack, Feb. 26, 1999.

Weichard is the first Australian to play in the Pirates organization. He has plenty of raw skills that have yet to translate into baseball ability. He's strong and has power potential. He has above-average speed, which gives him a chance to become an accomplished defensive center fielder and basestealer. He didn't play much baseball growing up in Australia and is learning the basics of the game. His swing is mechanical and stiff, and combined with his free-swinging tendencies, has held him back as a hitter. Weichard is tightly muscled and prone to injury. He has been bothered by hamstring pulls and back strains throughout his four pro seasons. He has the tools to become a fine player. Whether he ever learns how to put those tools to work remains to be seen. He's at least three years away from the majors.

Year	Club (League)	Class	AVG	G	AB	R	H	2B	3B	HR	RBI	BB	SO	SB
1997	Diamondbacks (AZL)	R	.183	36	115	27	21	3	1	0	7	30	54	4
1998	Lethbridge (Pio)	R	.293	54	188	37	55	10	2	0	28	38	45	19
1999	Hickory (SAL)	A	.225	89	316	44	71	7	3	5	37	28	92	23
2000	Lynchburg (Car)	A	.251	80	263	39	66	10	2	5	26	30	84	20
MINOR LEAGUE TOTALS			.250	223	767	120	192	27	7	10	91	96	221	62

24. David Williams, rhp

Born: March 12, 1979. **Ht.:** 6-2. **Wt.:** 208. **Bats:** L. **Throws:** L. **School:** Delaware Tech CC. **Career Transactions:** Selected by Pirates in 17th round of 1998 draft; signed June 3, 1998.

Williams led the minor leagues with 201 strikeouts last year. He doesn't rack up strikeouts with pure stuff, instead using movement and deception to confuse hitters. His fastball is average in velocity but an effective pitch because of its good running action. He also hides the ball well, making it hard for hitters to pick up his pitches. He does the little things well, including holding runners with a quick pickoff move. Pitchers who post high strikeout totals without a plus fastball in the lower minors tend to struggle as they move up, though. He needs to improve his secondary pitches, a slider and changeup, especially if hitters catch up to his fastball. Williams will open 2001 at Lynchburg or Altoona.

Year	Club (League)	Class	W	L	ERA	G	GS	CG	SV	IP	H	R	ER	BB	SO
1998	Erie (NY-P)	A	2	2	3.23	22	2	0	0	47	45	21	17	14	38
1999	Williamsport (NY-P)	A	4	2	2.56	7	7	1	0	46	33	17	13	11	47
	Hickory (SAL)	A	3	1	3.20	9	9	1	0	59	42	22	21	11	46
2000	Hickory (SAL)	A	11	9	2.96	24	24	1	0	170	145	66	56	39	193
	Lynchburg (Car)	A	1	0	6.55	2	2	0	0	11	18	8	8	3	8
MINOR LEAGUE TOTALS			21	14	3.11	64	44	3	0	333	283	134	115	78	332

25. Steve Sparks, rhp

Born: March 28, 1975. **Ht.:** 6-4. **Wt.:** 210. **Bats:** R. **Throws:** R. **School:** University of South Alabama. **Career Transactions:** Selected by Pirates in 28th round of 1998 draft; signed June 3, 1998.

Two players named Steve Sparks pitched in the major leagues last season. The better-known Steve Sparks is a knuckleballer. This one is the opposite, a hard thrower with little finesse. He's a prototypical power pitcher, a big guy who can throw his fastball as high as 96-97 mph. Sparks has added velocity as a professional by making mechanical adjustments and building arm strength. He also throws a hard slider. Sparks has yet to gain command of his fastball/slider combination. He may have to take a little off his fastball to get it over the plate. He never has been able to master a changeup, which held him back as a starter. The Pirates have decided Sparks is better suited for relief, and he'll work out of the bullpen this season, either in Triple-A or Double-A depending on how he performs in spring training.

Year	Club (League)	Class	W	L	ERA	G	GS	CG	SV	IP	H	R	ER	BB	SO
1998	Erie (NY-P)	A	2	7	4.43	14	10	0	0	63	55	38	31	30	61
	Augusta (SAL)	A	0	1	6.23	2	2	0	0	9	11	9	6	4	12
1999	Hickory (SAL)	A	4	6	4.47	25	12	1	0	89	97	60	44	51	72
	Lynchburg (Car)	A	2	3	6.23	5	5	1	0	26	36	20	18	15	20
2000	Altoona (EL)	AA	6	7	4.77	23	17	3	0	109	103	66	58	54	66
	Pittsburgh (NL)	MAJ	0	0	6.75	3	0	0	0	4	4	3	3	5	2
MAJOR LEAGUE TOTALS			0	0	6.75	3	0	0	0	4	4	3	3	5	2
MINOR LEAGUE TOTALS			14	24	4.78	69	46	5	0	296	302	193	157	154	231

26. Rico Washington, 3b/2b

Born: May 30, 1978. **Ht.:** 5-10. **Wt.:** 179. **Bats:** L. **Throws:** R. **School:** Jones County HS, Gray, Ga. **Career Transactions:** Selected by Pirates in 10th round of 1997 draft; signed June 12, 1997.

Washington is a product of the same high school that produced Willie Greene and Rondell White. Greene, the Pirates' 1989 first-round pick, is his cousin. Washington made the Arizona Fall League's all-prospect team but was dropped off Pittsburgh's 40-man roster a week later. He has a pretty line-drive stroke that led some to believe he can hit .300 in the major leagues. He also has a decent eye and will take a walk. Washington provides versatility with his ability to catch and play first, second and third base. But he struggled in Double-A adjusting to better breaking and offspeed pitches. He doesn't have a true position, and his stock has clearly dropped. The Pirates insist they still believe he's a prospect, though his future seems to be in a utility role. He probably will go back to Double-A this year.

Year	Club (League)	Class	AVG	G	AB	R	H	2B	3B	HR	RBI	BB	SO	SB
1997	Pirates (GCL)	R	.245	28	98	12	24	6	0	1	11	4	13	1
1998	Erie (NY-P)	A	.330	51	197	31	65	14	2	6	31	17	33	1
	Augusta (SAL)	A	.300	12	50	12	15	2	1	2	12	7	9	2
1999	Hickory (SAL)	A	.355	76	287	70	102	15	1	13	50	48	45	5
	Lynchburg (Car)	A	.283	57	205	31	58	7	0	7	32	30	45	4
2000	Altoona (EL)	AA	.258	135	503	74	130	22	7	8	59	55	74	4
MINOR LEAGUE TOTALS			.294	359	1340	230	394	66	11	37	195	161	219	17

27. Edwin Yan, ss

Born: Feb. 18, 1982. **Ht.:** 6-0. **Wt.:** 165. **Bats:** B. **Throws:** R. **Career Transactions:** Signed out of Dominican Republic by Pirates, Jan. 4, 1999.

Yan was limited to 12 games in the Gulf Coast League last year because of hamstring injuries. He has outstanding speed and is capable of taking an extra base or stealing a base at any time. That speed, coupled with his willingness to take a walk, could make him a future leadoff hitter. Yan's solid range at shortstop, along with a strong arm and soft hands, makes him an above-average defender. He also has an infectious personality and great enthusiasm for the game. Yan has little strength and his power is negligible. Like many young middle infielders, Yan is prone to making careless errors but should outgrow that in time. Depending on what happens in spring training, Yan either will start this season with Hickory or stay in extended spring training before joining Williamsport.

Year	Club (League)	Class	AVG	G	AB	R	H	2B	3B	HR	RBI	BB	SO	SB
1999	Pirates (DSL)	R	.300	69	250	61	75	6	1	3	21	49	49	48
2000	Pirates (GCL)	R	.357	12	42	10	15	0	1	0	1	12	8	5
MINOR LEAGUE TOTALS			.308	81	292	71	90	6	2	3	22	61	57	53

28. Humberto Aliendo, of

Born: Oct. 31, 1980. **Ht.:** 6-1. **Wt.:** 170. **Bats:** R. **Throws:** R. **Career Transactions:** Signed out of Venezuela by Pirates, Jan. 19, 1998.

The Pirates haven't had many prospects from Venezuela in recent years, but Aliendo made a good first impression last season with a team-high 38 RBIs in the Gulf Coast League. Aliendo has power, as his quick wrists enable him to hit the ball hard to all fields. He also has a knack for driving in runs. He's a good defensive outfielder with a plus arm and will wind up on a corner because he doesn't have the range for center field. Aliendo swings at too many bad pitches and rarely walks. He isn't a great runner and won't steal many bases. He was the talk of instructional league last fall, hitting a string of long home runs in games and batting practice. He's at least four years away from the majors but has opened the eyes of the Pirates, who don't have many big-time power threats.

Year	Club (League)	Class	AVG	G	AB	R	H	2B	3B	HR	RBI	BB	SO	SB
1998	Montalban (VSL)	R	.211	48	147	19	31	3	1	3	14	12	33	1
1999	Chivacoa (VSL)	R	.328	52	189	37	62	15	2	6	37	12	42	12
2000	Pirates (GCL)	R	.271	54	203	33	55	15	1	6	38	17	41	6
MINOR LEAGUE TOTALS			.275	154	539	89	148	33	4	15	89	41	116	19

29. Lee Evans, c

Born: July 20, 1977. **Ht.:** 6-1. **Wt.:** 185. **Bats:** B. **Throws:** R. **School:** Tuscaloosa County HS, Northport, Ala. **Career Transactions:** Selected by Pirates in fourth round of 1996 draft; signed June 6, 1996.

Evans showed signs of blossoming last year and finally reached Double-A. He has outstanding catch-and-throw skills, moves well behind the plate and sets a good target while possessing an above-average arm. He is learning the nuances of calling a game and is beginning to take charge of a pitching staff. He also is developing decent power and runs well for a catcher. Evans always has been inconsistent offensively. His biggest problems have been pitch recognition and difficulty adjusting to breaking pitches and offspeed stuff. He could be a decent starting catcher in the big leagues if he continues to improve with the bat. But he looks more like an above-average No. 2 backstop.

Year	Club (League)	Class	AVG	G	AB	R	H	2B	3B	HR	RBI	BB	SO	SB
1996	Pirates (GCL)	R	.279	32	111	27	31	5	2	3	20	18	26	3
1997	Augusta (SAL)	A	.194	54	186	19	36	9	2	2	23	14	52	6
	Erie (NY-P)	A	.298	40	141	20	42	6	0	5	16	11	30	1
1998	Augusta (SAL)	A	.223	98	337	43	75	19	1	5	43	28	90	6
1999	Lynchburg (Car)	A	.225	117	413	44	93	18	2	11	58	37	129	3
2000	Lynchburg (Car)	A	.259	90	305	45	79	15	3	9	37	43	88	16
	Altoona (EL)	AA	.237	32	118	18	28	4	1	1	8	14	28	1
MINOR LEAGUE TOTALS			.238	463	1611	216	384	76	11	36	205	165	443	36

30. Josh Bonifay, 2b

Born: July 30, 1978. **Ht.:** 6-0. **Wt.:** 190. **Bats:** R. **Throws:** R. **School:** UNC Wilmington. **Career Transactions:** Selected by Pirates in 24th round of 1999 draft; signed June 5, 1999.

Bonifay is the son of longtime Pirates general manager Cam Bonifay, but he is proving he isn't with the organization because of nepotism. He is considered a heady player, not surprising since he has been around the game his entire life. He's developing decent power for a middle infielder and uses the whole field as a hitter as well as anyone in the system. He also has decent speed and will steal an occasional base. Bonifay sometimes gets too anxious at the plate. Bonifay is a scrapper and a student of the game, so he shouldn't be counted out. He has shown enough to think he could be a major league second baseman, though probably not until at least 2004.

Year	Club (League)	Class	AVG	G	AB	R	H	2B	3B	HR	RBI	BB	SO	SB
1999	Williamsport (NY-P)	A	.260	52	200	42	52	10	2	4	17	25	55	2
2000	Hickory (SAL)	A	.281	106	377	62	106	17	2	14	62	48	104	11
MINOR LEAGUE TOTALS			.274	158	577	104	158	27	4	18	79	73	159	13

St. Louis
Cardinals

By Will Lingo

A glance down the St. Louis prospect list will show a minor league system that isn't loaded with talent. But don't cry for the Cardinals.

The Cardinals have used their young talent effectively to build their major league roster. The results are hard to argue with. The team cruised to the National League Central title and made it to the NL Championship Series before its pitching fell apart.

GM Walt Jocketty, Baseball America's 2000 Executive of the Year, made several key moves to rebuild his rotation, but the best came in spring training when he traded for outfielder Jim Edmonds, who responded with the best season of his career. Jocketty traded more prospects in the middle of the playoff drive. The deals continued the franchise's willingness to part with young, talented players for established major leaguers, and most have worked out. Darryl Kile, Mark McGwire, Edgar Renteria and Fernando Vina have been worth the price. St. Louis may have taken its biggest gamble this offseason, however, shipping third baseman Fernando Tatis and righthander Britt Reames to the Expos for righthander Dustin Hermanson and lefty reliever Steve Kline.

St. Louis has held on to the players it con-siders cornerstones. Elite prospects such as lefthander Rick Ankiel and J.D. Drew have been worked into the big leagues, and the team is counting on them to be long-term Cardinals.

The club's overall philosophy is starting to take a toll on the farm system, though. None of the organization's prospects is considered a sure-fire major league standout—though Bud Smith and Albert Pujols emerged in 2000—and just one of the Cardinals' farm teams had a winning record last year. That team was Triple-A Memphis, which is shaping up as one of the premier franchises in the minor leagues.

The Cardinals have had mostly solid drafts in recent years, but it may be time to let a couple of classes stay in the organization to rebuild depth.

To boost its scouting efforts, the organization did some shuffling in the offseason. Jeff Scott moves from director of player procurement to director of international operations, former scouting director Marty Maier returned as director of amateur scouting and Marteese Robinson was hired as director of professional scouting. Former scouting director John Mozeliak was named director of baseball operations, while former Rockies GM Bob Gebhard was hired as a special assistant to Jocketty.

OrganizationOverview

General manager: Walt Jocketty. **Farm director:** Mike Jorgensen. **Scouting director:** Marty Maier.

2000 PERFORMANCE

Class	Team	League	W	L	Pct.	Finish*	Manager
Majors	St. Louis	National	95	67	.586	t-2nd (16)	Tony La Russa
Triple-A	Memphis Redbirds	Pacific Coast	83	61	.576	4th (16)	Gaylen Pitts
Double-A	#Arkansas Travelers	Texas	68	71	.489	5th (8)	Chris Maloney
High A	Potomac Cannons	Carolina	62	76	.449	8th (8)	Joe Cunningham
Low A	Peoria Chiefs	Midwest	63	74	.460	t-10th (14)	Tom Lawless
Short-season	New Jersey Cardinals	New York-Penn	31	45	.408	12th (14)	Jeff Shireman
Rookie	Johnson City Cardinals	Appalachian	24	44	.353	9th (10)	Luis Melendez
OVERALL 2000 MINOR LEAGUE RECORD			331	370	.472	25th (30)	

*Finish in overall standings (No. of teams in league). #Affiliate will be in New Haven (Eastern) in 2001.

ORGANIZATION LEADERS

BATTING

*AVG	Bill Ortega, Arkansas	.325
R	**Stubby Clapp**, Memphis	89
	Andy Bevins, Arkansas/Memphis	89
H	Albert Pujols, Peoria/Potomac/Memphis	154
TB	Albert Pujols, Peoria/Potomac/Memphis	266
2B	Albert Pujols, Peoria/Potomac/Memphis	41
3B	Jack Wilson, Potomac/Arkansas	11
HR	Ernie Young, Memphis	35
RBI	Troy Farnsworth, Potomac	113
BB	**Stubby Clapp**, Memphis	80
SO	Travis Bailey, Peoria	154
SB	Esix Snead, Potomac	109

PITCHING

W	Bud Smith, Arkansas/Memphis	17
L	Patrick Coogan, Arkansas	13
#ERA	Bud Smith, Arkansas/Memphis	2.26
G	Jim Dougherty, Memphis	60
CG	Bud Smith, Arkansas/Memphis	3
SV	Jason Marr, Potomac	30
IP	**Clint Weibl**, Arkansas/Memphis	178
BB	B.R. Cook, Peoria/Potomac	79
SO	Les Walrond, Potomac	153

*Minimum 250 at-bats. #Minimum 75 innings.

TOP PROSPECTS OF THE DECADE

1991	Ray Lankford, of
1992	Donovan Osborne, lhp
1993	Allen Watson, lhp
1994	Brian Barber, rhp
1995	Alan Benes, rhp
1996	Alan Benes, rhp
1997	Matt Morris, rhp
1998	Rick Ankiel, lhp
1999	J.D. Drew, of
2000	Rick Ankiel, lhp

TOP DRAFT PICKS OF THE DECADE

1991	Dmitri Young, 3b/of
1992	Sean Lowe, rhp
1993	Alan Benes, rhp
1994	Bret Wagner, lhp
1995	Matt Morris, rhp
1996	Braden Looper, rhp
1997	Adam Kennedy, ss
1998	J.D. Drew, of
1999	Chance Caple, rhp
2000	Shaun Boyd, of

Clapp   **Weibl**

BEST TOOLS

Best Hitter for Average	Bill Ortega
Best Power Hitter	Chris Haas
Fastest Baserunner	Esix Snead
Best Fastball	Jim Journell
Best Breaking Ball	Chad Hutchinson
Best Control	Bud Smith
Best Defensive Catcher	Shawn Schumacher
Best Defensive Infielder	Jason Bowers
Best Infield Arm	Albert Pujols
Best Defensive Outfielder	Esix Snead
Best Outfield Arm	Luis Saturria

PROJECTED 2004 LINEUP

Catcher	Eli Marrero
First Base	Bill Ortega
Second Base	Fernando Vina
Third Base	Albert Pujols
Shortstop	Edgar Renteria
Left Field	Luis Saturria
Center Field	Jim Edmonds
Right Field	J.D. Drew
No. 1 Starter	Rick Ankiel
No. 2 Starter	Darryl Kile
No. 3 Starter	Bud Smith
No. 4 Starter	Chad Hutchinson
No. 5 Starter	Dustin Hermanson
Closer	Matt Morris

ALL-TIME LARGEST BONUSES

J.D. Drew, 1998	$3,000,000
Rick Ankiel, 1997	2,500,000
Chad Hutchinson, 1998	2,300,000
Shaun Boyd, 2000	1,750,000
Braden Looper, 1996	1,675,000

DraftAnalysis

2000 Draft

Best Pro Debut: RHP Blake Williams (1) went 3-1, 1.59 for short-season New Jersey. C Ryan Hamill (25), who was mostly a back-up at UCLA, batted .263-12-46 at Rookie-level Johnson City.

Best Athlete: SS Chase Voshell (3) and OF Justin Woodrow (6) have solid tools across the board.

Best Hitter: OF **Shaun Boyd** (1) has a line-drive swing and plus speed. If he can learn to draw walks, he'll make a nifty lead-off man. SS Justin Hileman (16) already uses the entire field and will add power as he matures.

Best Raw Power: OF Dee Haynes, the NCAA Division II player of the year at Delta State (Miss.), has more pop now, but 3B Billy Schmitt (22) will surpass him with more growth and experience.

Fastest Runner: OF Chris Morris (15) led Division I with 84 steals in 94 attempts last spring at The Citadel. He swiped 42 more bases at New Jersey even though he batted just .170. He's a switch-hitter who goes from the right side of the plate to first base in 4.0 seconds.

Best Defensive Player: Woodrow has center-field skills and a right-field arm. He played in right at Johnson City because Boyd was in center.

Best Fastball: RHP John Novinsky (9), who spent the summer in the Cape Cod League, throws 92-93 mph and also has an outstanding curveball.

Most Intriguing Background: Yedeal

Molina (4) hopes to become the third member of his family to catch in the majors, following brothers Bengie (Angels) and Jose (Cubs). 2B Matt Galante (13) is the son of the Astros dugout coach of the same name. SS Kaulana Kuhaulua's (17) father Fred pitched in the majors. Kuhaulua (who headed to Long Beach State) did not sign.

Boyd

Closest To The Majors: Williams should move rapidly because he not only has a low-90s fastball and hard slurve, but he also knows how to pitch.

Best Late-Round Pick: Hileman, who dropped because of signability concerns. Hamill has some potential, though he isn't quite the power hitter he looked like at Johnson City.

The One Who Got Away: RHP Marc LaMacchia needs to develop physically, but he has the potential for three average or better pitches. He took that repertoire to Florida State.

Assessment: The Cardinals had a pair of first-round picks thanks to the loss of Darren Oliver, though some teams believe they squandered that advantage by over-drafting Boyd and Williams. If Boyd hits like he should and Williams continues to build on his strong debut, St. Louis will be vindicated.

1999 Draft

RHPs Chance Caple and Nick Stocks have been OK, while 1B Chris Duncan has been disappointing—not what you hope for from three first-round picks. St. Louis' best choices may be 3B Albert Pujols (13) and OF Ben Johnson (4), who was traded to the Padres. **Grade: C+**

1998 Draft

The Cardinals found possible standouts in OF J.D. Drew (1), who was expected, and LHP Bud Smith (4), who was not. A second first-rounder, RHP Ben Diggins, didn't sign and was a first-round pick of the Dodgers in 2000. RHP Chad Hutchinson (2) has yet to live up to his $3.4 million major league contract. **Grade: B+**

1997 Draft

If LHP Rick Ankiel's (2) control hadn't disintegrated in the playoffs, the Cardinals would have an even higher grade. 2B Adam Kennedy (1) signed a below-market deal, clearing up the money to sign Ankiel, then was traded last year for Jim Edmonds. **Grade: B+**

1996 Draft

The highlights of this draft were RHP Braden Looper (1), 2B Brent Butler (3) and RHP Mark Nussbeck (29), who were used to acquire Edgar Renteria, Darryl Kile and Mike Timlin, respectively. No one else is likely to reach the majors. **Grade: C**

Note: Draft analysis prepared by Jim Callis. Numbers in parentheses indicate draft rounds.

. . . Smith is unflappable on the mound and always thinks a step ahead of batters.

Smith **Bud**
lhp

Born: Oct. 23, 1979.
Ht.: 6-0. **Wt.:** 170.
Bats: L. **Throws:** L.
School: Los Angeles Harbor JC.
Career Transactions: Selected by Cardinals in fourth round of 1998 draft; signed June 3, 1998.

Smith didn't come out of nowhere—he was No. 13 on the Cardinals prospect list last year—but his degree of success in 2000 was a surprise to everyone. He opened the season at Double-A Arkansas and was dominant in the Texas League, earning a promotion to Memphis and serving as the Redbirds' ace at age 20 as the team went to the Triple-A World Series. Smith pitched two seven-inning no-hitters in Arkansas, finished tied for the minor league lead in wins with 17 and was the Texas League pitcher of the year. Double-A batters had just a .213 average against him, and Triple-A batters fared even worse, hitting .206.

Smith was a good outfielder at St. John Bosco High in Bellflower, Calif., where he broke some of Nomar Garciaparra's batting records. He became strictly a pitcher when he went to Los Angeles Harbor Junior College. To say Smith is poised doesn't do him justice. He's unflappable on the mound and always thinks a step ahead of batters. He's like Rick Ankiel with his advanced approach, good curveball and excellent change-up, though his fastball is a few ticks slower. But he might have a better feel for pitching, which earns the inevitable comparison to Tom Glavine. The Cardinals weren't even sure they'd put Smith in the Arkansas rotation last year, but he showed in spring training he was ready to do something special. As his 2000 walk numbers show, he also has developed plus command. He's a good athlete and a good fielder. On pure velocity, Smith's fastball is below average, though he worked out in the offseason in hopes of adding to it. His listed height and weight are generous, and he'll never be at the front of a rotation. But he knows his limitations and pitches to his strengths.

The Cardinals plan to start Smith back in Triple-A to open the season, though they have opened their minds to let him move at whatever pace he dictates. They hope he'll become something of a cross between Ankiel and Jamie Moyer and occupy a spot in the middle of their rotation for years. It would be a surprise if he doesn't contribute in St. Louis at some point in 2001.

Year	Club (League)	Class	W	L	ERA	G	GS	CG	SV	IP	H	R	ER	BB	SO
1998	Johnson City (Appy)	R	3	3	5.18	14	14	0	0	64	85	47	37	34	65
1999	Peoria (Mid)	A	4	1	2.83	9	9	0	0	54	53	20	17	16	59
	Potomac (Car)	A	4	9	2.96	18	18	0	0	103	91	47	34	32	93
2000	Arkansas (TL)	AA	12	1	2.32	18	18	3	0	109	93	32	28	27	102
	Memphis (PCL)	AAA	5	1	2.15	9	8	0	0	54	40	24	13	15	34
MINOR LEAGUE TOTALS			28	15	3.02	68	67	3	0	385	362	170	129	124	353

LARRY GOREN

2. Albert Pujols, 3b

Born: Jan. 16, 1980. **Ht.:** 6-3. **Wt.:** 210. **Bats:** R. **Throws:** R. **School:** Maple Woods (Mo.) CC. **Career Transactions:** Selected by Cardinals in 13th round of 1999 draft; signed Aug. 17, 1999.

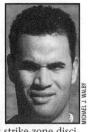

The Cardinals offered Pujols $10,000 to sign in 1999, so he went to the summer amateur Jayhawk League instead and hit .343-5-17, good enough to earn a bonus close to $60,000. Then he proved to be a bargain, with a monster pro debut in which he was MVP of the Class A Midwest League and the Pacific Coast League playoffs. He followed up by hitting .323 in the Arizona Fall League. Pujols started hitting in instructional league just after he signed and hasn't stopped. He uses the whole field and has great strike-zone discipline. He goes the other way well and should add power as he moves up. He's still young, but he has the approach of a veteran. He has a strong arm at third base. Pujols wasn't a more notable amateur prospect because he was heavier and didn't move well. He's in good shape now, but the Cardinals aren't sure about his defense. He's passable at third, but he already has played a few games in the outfield and could wind up there. The Cardinals are trying to temper expectations, but he could be in the big leagues by 2002, especially with the void at third created by the Fernando Tatis trade. He will start 2001 at Double-A New Haven.

Year	Club (League)	Class	AVG	G	AB	R	H	2B	3B	HR	RBI	BB	SO	SB
2000	Peoria (Mid)	A	.324	109	395	62	128	32	6	17	84	38	37	2
	Potomac (Car)	A	.284	21	81	11	23	8	1	2	10	7	8	1
	Memphis (PCL)	AAA	.214	3	14	1	3	1	0	0	2	1	2	1
MINOR LEAGUE TOTALS			.314	133	490	74	154	41	7	19	96	46	47	4

3. Chad Hutchinson, rhp

Born: Feb. 21, 1977. **Ht.:** 6-5. **Wt.:** 230. **Bats:** R. **Throws:** R. **School:** Stanford University. **Career Transactions:** Selected by Cardinals in second round of 1998 draft; signed June 30, 1998.

Before Joe Borchard, Hutchinson was the Stanford quarterback getting the big bucks. He signed a major league deal with a $2.3 million bonus. After a promising spring in 2000, he got shelled in Triple-A before returning to Double-A and righting himself. Then he missed much of the second half with elbow tendinitis. Hutchinson's numbers haven't been impressive in college or pro ball, but scouts remain agog over his stuff. He's a horse with a 94 mph fastball, but his breaking ball is his out pitch. Whether you call it a curve or a slurve, it gives him a second hard offering. His changeup showed progress in the Arizona Fall League, where he led the league in strikeouts. Command of the fastball is everything for Hutchinson. He lost it at Memphis last year and blew up. A little of the problem is mental and a little of it is mechanical. There's also debate about his future role. The Cardinals want him to remain in the rotation because frontline starters are so hard to find. They think he is ready to compete for a big league job, but he would be better served by Triple-A success. Their larger point is that when he's on, he can get hitters out at any level.

Year	Club (League)	Class	W	L	ERA	G	GS	CG	SV	IP	H	R	ER	BB	SO
1998	New Jersey (NY-P)	A	0	1	3.52	3	3	0	0	15	15	7	6	4	20
	Prince William (Car)	A	2	0	2.79	5	5	0	0	29	20	12	9	11	31
1999	Arkansas (TL)	AA	7	11	4.72	25	25	0	0	141	127	79	74	85	150
	Memphis (PCL)	AAA	2	0	2.19	2	2	0	0	12	4	3	3	8	16
2000	Memphis (PCL)	AAA	0	1	25.92	5	4	0	0	8	10	24	24	27	9
	Arkansas (TL)	AA	2	3	3.38	11	11	1	0	48	40	21	18	27	54
MINOR LEAGUE TOTALS			13	16	4.75	51	50	1	0	254	216	146	134	162	280

4. Chance Caple, rhp

Born: Aug. 9, 1978. **Ht.:** 6-6. **Wt.:** 215. **Bats:** R. **Throws:** R. **School:** Texas A&M University. **Career Transactions:** Selected by Cardinals in first round (30th overall) of 1999 draft; signed July 15, 1999.

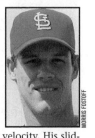

Caple was an eighth-round pick out of high school, but went to Texas A&M instead and became a first-round pick three years later. He struggled in his first pro experience in 1999, then didn't pitch until May in 2000 because of a ribcage injury. His brother Kyle was a minor league catcher for three seasons. Caple has all the tools of a frontline starter. He has a big frame that's still filling out and should make him a workhorse. He has whiplike arm action and throws around 92 mph, and he could add more velocity. His slider is probably his best pitch right now. He's a great competitor and willing to learn. Caple didn't have any problems once he got started last year, but he still has to prove he'll be durable. He needs to learn to keep the ball down, but he may not have a good enough feel for his mechanics to know how yet. He also needs to improve his changeup. Success has eluded Caple so far, but the Cardinals still like his potential. He has the all-around package and just needs to refine it to have success. He'll take the next step to Double-A in 2001.

Year	Club (League)	Class	W	L	ERA	G	GS	CG	SV	IP	H	R	ER	BB	SO
1999	New Jersey (NY-P)	A	0	4	4.38	7	7	0	0	37	35	24	18	18	36
2000	Potomac (Car)	A	7	9	4.39	22	22	0	0	125	128	68	61	34	97
MINOR LEAGUE TOTALS			7	13	4.39	29	29	0	0	162	163	92	79	52	133

5. Nick Stocks, rhp

Born: Aug. 27, 1978. **Ht.:** 6-2. **Wt.:** 185. **Bats:** R. **Throws:** R. **School:** Florida State University. **Career Transactions:** Selected by Cardinals in first round (36th overall) of 1999 draft; signed Aug. 29, 1999.

Another in the growing legion of Tommy John surgery survivors, Stocks missed his freshman year at Florida State after his elbow ligament popped off the bone. Like so many, he came back stronger than ever after the operation, and the Cardinals took him with a supplemental first-round pick they got for losing Brian Jordan. Stocks touched 90-91 mph before his surgery, and now he pitches comfortably at 92-93 and reaches 94-95. He also has a major league curveball and makeup that's off the charts. He has the heart of a lion and refuses to give in to hitters. Stocks probably isn't quite as big as he's listed, which raises questions about his durability. With just one professional season under his belt, he still has work to do on his changeup and on his command. Even with the good Tommy John track record, Stocks' health will always be a concern. The early returns on Stocks are positive, especially the innings he piled up at Class A Peoria with no problems. The next step is high Class A Potomac, but he'll probably finish this season in Double-A.

Year	Club (League)	Class	W	L	ERA	G	GS	CG	SV	IP	H	R	ER	BB	SO
2000	Peoria (Mid)	A	10	10	3.78	25	24	1	0	150	133	88	63	52	118
MINOR LEAGUE TOTALS			10	10	3.78	25	24	1	0	150	133	88	63	52	118

6. Blake Williams, rhp

Born: Feb. 22, 1979. **Ht.:** 6-5. **Wt.:** 210. **Bats:** R. **Throws:** R. **School:** Southwest Texas State University. **Career Transactions:** Selected by Cardinals in first round (24th overall) of 2000 draft; signed July 19, 2000.

Williams wasn't the first player the Cardinals drafted in 2000, but he was the most impressive. He came with the team's second pick in the first round, which they received for losing Darren Oliver to the Rangers. St. Louis has taken a college pitcher in the first round of nine of the last 11 drafts. Williams added 15 pounds of muscle before his junior season and 5-6 mph to his fastball, which now peaks in the mid-90s. His best pitch may be his slurvy curve. He's a big kid who carries himself well and has good mound presence. He has a solid pitcher's body and mechanics, as well as an idea about how to work in the strike zone. The Cardinals haven't seen much they don't like yet. After his strong debut and an impressive instructional league, Williams has the organization excited about seeing him in spring training. He could jump to high Class A with a good performance.

Year	Club (League)	Class	W	L	ERA	G	GS	CG	SV	IP	H	R	ER	BB	SO
2000	New Jersey (NY-P)	A	3	1	1.59	6	6	0	0	28	20	7	5	9	25
MINOR LEAGUE TOTALS			3	1	1.59	6	6	0	0	28	20	7	5	9	25

7. Bill Ortega, of

Born: July 24, 1975. **Ht.:** 6-4. **Wt.:** 205. **Bats:** R. **Throws:** R. **Career Transactions:** Signed out of Cuba by Cardinals, March 11, 1997.

A Cuban defector, Ortega signed with the Cardinals in 1997 but didn't look comfortable until last year, when he became a Texas League all-star. His season ended early, though, when he collided with an umpire and broke his wrist. He's expected to be healthy for spring training. Ortega was projected as a power hitter when he signed, and he showed it last season. He scorched the ball and hit it all over the park, and when he pulled the ball he showed real juice. He has the potential to hit 25-30 home runs a season if he keeps developing. While Ortega's defense in right field has improved, the Cardinals were a little surprised when a survey of Texas League managers named him as the league's best defensive outfielder. They think he'll be an adequate left fielder, and he definitely has a left-field arm. His reluctance to draw walks could be exploited by more experienced pitchers. His bat will take him as far as he's going to go, so the Cardinals will move Ortega up to Memphis and see if he keeps hitting.

Year	Club (League)	Class	AVG	G	AB	R	H	2B	3B	HR	RBI	BB	SO	SB
1997	Prince William (Car)	A	.229	73	249	23	57	14	0	0	15	21	42	1
1998	Peoria (Mid)	A	.276	105	398	57	110	23	2	2	60	39	69	4
1999	Potomac (Car)	A	.306	110	421	66	129	27	4	9	74	38	69	7
	Arkansas (TL)	AA	.377	20	69	10	26	9	0	2	10	10	9	0
2000	Arkansas (TL)	AA	.325	86	332	51	108	18	5	12	62	28	42	1
MINOR LEAGUE TOTALS			.293	394	1469	207	430	91	11	25	221	136	231	13

8. Gene Stechschulte, rhp

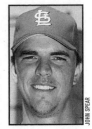

JOHN SPEAR

Born: Aug. 12, 1973. **Ht.:** 6-5. **Wt.:** 210. **Bats:** R. **Throws:** R. **School:** Ashland (Ohio) University. **Career Transactions:** Signed as nondrafted free agent by Cardinals, June 13, 1996.

Stechschulte wasn't drafted out of Ashland University, where he spent most of his career as a first baseman. He hadn't pitched for several years when the Cardinals signed him, and worked in middle relief in his first season. By 1999, he was a Double-A all-star. Biceps tendinitis ended that season early, but he showed no signs of the trouble in 2000. A nondrafted free agent pitcher works his way into an organization's plans by throwing hard and getting people out. Stechschulte has a plus fastball that can reach the mid-90s and a good slider. More important, he has the makeup for late-inning work. Stechschulte is strictly a two-pitch pitcher, but because his role in the organization is so clearly defined, that's not as much of a concern. He pitched too tentatively in the majors in 2000, falling behind in the count and allowing six homers in 26 innings. Against the odds, Stechschulte is ready to compete for a spot in the big league bullpen. He has closer stuff if he can get big league hitters out consistently.

Year	Club (League)	Class	W	L	ERA	G	GS	CG	SV	IP	H	R	ER	BB	SO
1996	New Jersey (NY-P)	A	1	2	3.27	20	1	0	0	33	41	17	12	16	27
1997	New Jersey (NY-P)	A	1	1	3.22	30	0	0	1	36	45	16	13	16	28
1998	Peoria (Mid)	A	4	8	2.59	57	0	0	33	66	58	26	19	21	70
1999	Arkansas (TL)	AA	2	6	3.40	39	0	0	19	42	41	26	16	20	41
	Memphis (PCL)	AAA	0	0	7.71	2	0	0	0	2	2	2	2	5	2
2000	Memphis (PCL)	AAA	4	1	2.45	41	0	0	26	48	38	13	13	18	37
	St. Louis (NL)	MAJ	1	0	6.31	20	0	0	0	26	24	22	18	17	12
	Arkansas (TL)	AA	0	0	0.00	2	0	0	0	2	0	0	0	0	3
MAJOR LEAGUE TOTALS			1	0	6.31	20	0	0	0	26	24	22	18	17	12
MINOR LEAGUE TOTALS			12	18	2.94	191	1	0	79	230	225	100	75	96	208

9. Luis Saturria, of

STEVE MOORE

Born: July 21, 1976. **Ht.:** 6-2. **Wt.:** 165. **Bats:** R. **Throws:** R. **Career Transactions:** Signed out of Dominican Republic by Cardinals, March 5, 1994 . . . Selected by Blue Jays from Cardinals in major league Rule 5 draft, Dec. 15, 1997 . . . Returned to Cardinals, March 20, 1998.

Saturria has teased the Cardinals with his athletic ability since he signed. But every step forward is followed by a step back. He played in the Dominican League this winter to get more experience against good pitching and hit just .194. Scouts love Saturria because the tools are all there. He has power and speed and is an exciting player when he's on his game. He has a good arm and is a solid defensive outfielder. When he plays with confidence, his athleticism shines. "Enigmatic" is the best word for Saturria. He never has established consistency and hasn't been able to make the adjustments necessary to get out of slumps. He remains undisciplined at the plate. Despite all of his experience, St. Louis thinks he needs more at-bats. The Cardinals would like to lock Saturria in a room with Albert Pujols in hopes of making him the same kind of hitter. This will be a big year for him. He needs to start strong and perform well in Triple-A because time and patience are running out.

Year	Club (League)	Class	AVG	G	AB	R	H	2B	3B	HR	RBI	BB	SO	SB
1994	Cardinals/Phillies (DSL)	R	.278	61	227	29	63	2	6	1	23	25	49	16

1995	Phillies/Cardinals (DSL)	R	.318	66	245	48	78	16	7	2	33	34	26	12
1996	Johnson City (Appy)	R	.256	57	227	43	58	7	1	5	40	24	61	12
1997	Peoria (Mid)	A	.274	122	445	81	122	19	5	11	51	44	95	23
1998	Prince William (Car)	A	.294	129	462	70	136	25	9	12	73	28	104	26
1999	Arkansas (TL)	AA	.244	139	484	66	118	30	4	16	61	35	134	16
2000	Arkansas (TL)	AA	.274	129	478	78	131	25	10	20	76	45	124	18
	St. Louis (NL)	MAJ	.000	12	5	1	0	0	0	0	0	1	3	0
MAJOR LEAGUE TOTALS			.000	12	5	1	0	0	0	0	0	1	3	0
MINOR LEAGUE TOTALS			.275	703	2568	415	706	124	42	67	357	235	593	123

10. Josh Pearce, rhp

JOHN SPEAR

Born: Aug. 20, 1977. **Ht.:** 6-3. **Wt.:** 215. **Bats:** R. **Throws:** R. **School:** University of Arizona. **Career Transactions:** Selected by Cardinals in second round of 1999 draft; signed June 18, 1999.

Pearce put together a solid pro debut in 1999, followed by an instructional league performance that was among the best in the organization. Then the Cardinals figured out that between college fall ball in 1998 and instructional league in 1999, Pearce had thrown almost 300 innings. They promptly shut him down for the winter, and he showed no ill effects last year. Pearce is a strong, workmanlike, competitive pitcher whose best pitch is a hard breaking ball that has been called both a curve and a slider. His fastball is on the high side of average and has good sink. As he has shown so far, he's durable. To be effective at higher levels, Pearce needs to improve his changeup. He would get hit a lot less with an effective third pitch and improved command in the strike zone. He's moving at a good rate, jumping to Double-A in his first full season. He may return there to start 2001. If his changeup improves, he'll be an innings-eater in a rotation. If not, he'll take his two good pitches to the bullpen.

Year	Club (League)	Class	W	L	ERA	G	GS	CG	SV	IP	H	R	ER	BB	SO
1999	New Jersey (NY-P)	A	3	7	4.98	14	14	1	0	78	78	45	43	20	78
2000	Potomac (Car)	A	5	3	3.45	10	10	1	0	63	70	25	24	10	42
	Arkansas (TL)	AA	5	6	5.46	17	17	0	0	97	117	68	59	35	63
MINOR LEAGUE TOTALS			13	16	4.77	41	41	2	0	238	265	138	126	65	183

11. Clint Weibl, rhp

Born: March 17, 1975. **Ht.:** 6-3. **Wt.:** 180. **Bats:** R. **Throws:** R. **School:** University of Miami. **Career Transactions:** Selected by Cardinals in 37th round of 1996 draft; signed June 25, 1996.

Weibl pitched in the powerful Miami program in college but was a draft afterthought and looked like nothing more than an organization player until 2000. Called up for an emergency start at Memphis, he took off and pitched himself into the Cardinals' plans. Weibl is a player-development poster boy. He has added velocity and now has a solid average fastball, as well as a good slider and changeup. His command is also above-average, and his newfound success came from a more aggressive approach. He forgot about finesse and started going after hitters. After four uninspiring seasons, though, he'll have to prove the fifth wasn't a fluke. He has made mental and mechanical adjustments to become more successful, though he still pitches with a smaller margin for error than many pitchers. Weibl has made himself a legitimate part of the Cardinals' future plans. He'll go to his first big league camp and try to surprise people again. More than likely, though, he'll head back to Memphis.

Year	Club (League)	Class	W	L	ERA	G	GS	CG	SV	IP	H	R	ER	BB	SO
1996	Johnson City (Appy)	R	4	1	2.05	7	7	0	0	44	27	12	10	12	51
	Peoria (Mid)	A	1	2	4.85	5	5	0	0	30	27	16	16	7	21
1997	Prince William (Car)	A	12	11	4.64	29	29	0	0	163	185	90	84	62	135
1998	Arkansas (TL)	AA	12	10	5.37	25	23	0	0	139	161	86	83	53	85
	Memphis (PCL)	AAA	0	1	6.35	1	1	0	0	6	6	5	4	2	2
1999	Memphis (PCL)	AAA	1	0	5.40	5	0	0	0	8	10	9	5	2	8
	Arkansas (TL)	AA	4	9	4.66	28	17	1	0	110	121	59	57	49	75
2000	Arkansas (TL)	AA	3	3	4.74	10	9	0	0	57	57	35	30	19	51
	Memphis (PCL)	AAA	9	4	2.83	19	18	2	0	121	98	45	38	37	92
MINOR LEAGUE TOTALS			46	41	4.34	129	109	3	0	677	692	357	327	243	520

12. Jim Journell, rhp

Born: Dec. 29, 1977. **Ht.:** 6-4. **Wt.:** 205. **Bats:** R. **Throws:** R. **School:** University of Illinois. **Career Transactions:** Selected by Cardinals in fourth round of 1999 draft; signed Aug. 12, 1999.

Journell is another Tommy John surgery survivor. The Cardinals drafted him knowing he had arm problems but took a chance that his stuff would return. He didn't throw a profes-sional pitch until the 2000 season, and even then he was limited to three innings every four days in the New York-Penn League. The organization was happy with his progress. Journell was the most intimidating closer in college baseball at Illinois in 1999, and when healthy he has explosive velocity. He reaches the mid-90s with his fastball. He threw from a low three-quarters slot in college, which made his fastball almost frightening for righthanders, but the arm angle flattened out his slider and put strain on his arm. The Cardinals moved his arm slot up and saw positive results, especially with the slider. They're excited about see-ing Journell in spring training, and he could move fast if his arm is all the way back.

Year	Club (League)	Class	W	L	ERA	G	GS	CG	SV	IP	H	R	ER	BB	SO
2000	New Jersey (NY-P)	A	1	0	1.97	13	1	0	0	32	12	12	7	24	39
MINOR LEAGUE TOTALS			1	0	1.97	13	1	0	0	32	12	12	7	24	39

13. Esix Snead, of

Born: June 7, 1976. **Ht.:** 5-10. **Wt.:** 175. **Bats:** B. **Throws:** R. **School:** University of Central Florida. **Career Transactions:** Selected by Cardinals in 18th round of 1998 draft; signed June 24, 1998.

Snead set a new high Class A Carolina League standard with 109 stolen bases last year, breaking the record of 105 set by Lenny Dykstra. Almost as amazing, Snead was caught 35 times. So much for the element of surprise. Snead is a true speedster. He's a go-getter and a hard worker who loves to play, and he's a strong defender who can really go get the ball in center field. Unless he improves his hitting and gets on base more, though, he won't make an impact in the big leagues. He's relatively inexperienced and still doesn't have much of a hitting approach. He could add 30 points to his average if he just bunted effectively. His real problem is that he's not strong enough to hit the ball with authority. Opposing teams cheat in on him, making it harder for him to get leg hits. Snead's speed makes him intriguing, though, and the Cardinals will give him every chance. He didn't fare any better in the Arizona Fall League, so hitting against Double-A pitchers could provide a real challenge.

Year	Club (League)	Class	AVG	G	AB	R	H	2B	3B	HR	RBI	BB	SO	SB
1998	New Jersey (NY-P)	A	.233	58	193	38	45	4	4	1	16	33	54	42
1999	Potomac (Car)	A	.181	67	249	37	45	8	5	0	14	32	57	35
	Peoria (Mid)	A	.193	59	181	35	35	7	1	2	18	35	42	29
2000	Potomac (Car)	A	.235	132	493	82	116	14	3	1	34	72	98	109
MINOR LEAGUE TOTALS			.216	316	1116	192	241	33	13	4	82	172	251	215

14. Luther Hackman, rhp

Born: Oct. 6, 1974. **Ht.:** 6-4. **Wt.:** 195. **Bats:** R. **Throws:** R. **School:** Columbus (Miss.) HS. **Career Transactions:** Selected by Rockies in sixth round of 1994 draft; signed June 4, 1994 . . . Traded by Rockies with RHP Darryl Kile and RHP Dave Veres to Cardinals for RHP Manny Aybar, RHP Jose Jimenez, RHP Rick Croushore and 2B Brent Butler, Nov. 16, 1999.

Hackman was the only minor leaguer the Cardinals got in the seven-player deal with the Rockies that brought in Darryl Kile and Dave Veres. He has been on the fringe of the majors for the past couple of seasons and had big league stints in 1999 and 2000. He's a big, strong pitcher who has been compared to Jim Bibby. He can bring his fastball in the mid-90s and has a good slider. His changeup is a decent third pitch. His command has improved signif-icantly over the course of his career. But Hackman is a question mark because he hasn't proven he's ready to make the jump to the big leagues. He has been hit hard in brief audi-tions but could be more effective coming out of the bullpen, allowing him to rely on just his fastball and slider. Hackman will go to spring training with a chance to win a big league job, but he'll probably wind up back in Memphis, where he makes his offseason home.

Year	Club (League)	Class	W	L	ERA	G	GS	CG	SV	IP	H	R	ER	BB	SO
1994	Rockies (AZL)	R	1	3	2.10	12	12	0	0	56	50	21	13	16	63
1995	Asheville (SAL)	A	11	11	4.64	28	28	2	0	165	162	95	85	65	108
1996	Salem (Car)	A	5	7	4.24	21	21	1	0	110	93	60	52	69	83
1997	New Haven (EL)	AA	0	6	7.82	10	10	0	0	51	58	49	44	34	34
	Salem (Car)	A	1	4	5.80	15	15	2	0	81	99	60	52	37	59
1998	New Haven (EL)	AA	3	12	5.44	28	23	1	0	139	169	102	84	54	90
1999	Carolina (SL)	AA	4	3	4.04	11	10	0	0	62	53	33	28	28	50
	Colo. Spr. (PCL)	AAA	7	6	3.74	15	15	1	0	101	106	49	42	44	88
	Colorado (NL)	MAJ	1	2	10.69	5	3	0	0	16	26	19	19	12	10
2000	Memphis (PCL)	AAA	8	9	4.74	21	21	0	0	120	134	71	63	36	66
	St. Louis (NL)	MAJ	0	0	10.13	1	0	0	0	.3	4	3	3	4	0
MAJOR LEAGUE TOTALS			1	2	10.61	6	3	0	0	19	30	22	22	16	10
MINOR LEAGUE TOTALS			40	61	4.71	161	155	7	0	884	924	540	463	383	641

15. Chris Narveson, lhp

Born: Dec. 20, 1981. **Ht.:** 6-3. **Wt.:** 180. **Bats:** L. **Throws:** L. **School:** T.C. Roberson HS, Skyland, N.C. **Career Transactions:** Selected by Cardinals in second round of 2000 draft; signed June 27, 2000.

Narveson reminds the Cardinals of Bud Smith a couple of years ago. His draft status rose dramatically in his senior year of high school, as he added velocity to his fastball and compiled a 10-0, 0.71 record for one of North Carolina's best prep teams. He was an outstanding student but turned down a scholarship to Wake Forest to sign with the Cardinals for $675,000. With his improving fastball, which he consistently throws in the low 90s, he has better raw stuff than Smith. Narveson also has more of a bulldog approach. He throws both a slider and curveball, though the Cardinals will direct him more in the slider direction. His changeup is strictly a third pitch now but shows potential. He has solid mechanics and should have good command with more experience. He'll move up to low Class A for 2001.

Year	Club (League)	Class	W	L	ERA	G	GS	CG	SV	IP	H	R	ER	BB	SO
2000	Johnson City (Appy)	R	2	4	3.27	12	12	0	0	55	57	33	20	25	63
MINOR LEAGUE TOTALS			2	4	3.27	12	12	0	0	55	57	33	20	25	63

16. Cristobal Correa, rhp

Born: Dec. 27, 1979. **Ht.:** 6-1. **Wt.:** 175. **Bats:** R. **Throws:** R. **Career Transactions:** Signed out of Venezuela by Cardinals, May 20, 1998.

The Cardinals' foreign efforts have been hit and miss. Correa was probably the most promising pitcher in their international corps until he had Tommy John surgery last year. St. Louis can only hope he recovers as well as Nick Stocks and Jim Journell have. But Correa is still early in the rehabilitation process and isn't expected to pitch much in 2001, if at all. When healthy, he has two plus pitches, a sinker and a curveball, a combination that leads to a lot of ground balls. His command was the area he needed to work the most on, though his changeup could use improvement as well. The injury makes all those question marks bigger, as he'll have to make up for lost development time when he returns. The Cardinals hope he'll be ready by instructional league in the fall.

Year	Club (League)	Class	W	L	ERA	G	GS	CG	SV	IP	H	R	ER	BB	SO
1998	San Joaquin 2 (VSL)	R	1	1	3.15	23	2	0	5	34	28	14	12	28	27
1999	New Jersey (NY-P)	A	3	3	2.94	9	9	0	0	52	41	20	17	26	59
	Peoria (Mid)	A	0	2	10.35	5	5	0	0	20	26	24	23	14	15
2000	Potomac (Car)	A	6	6	3.24	18	18	0	0	100	82	41	36	49	76
MINOR LEAGUE TOTALS			10	12	3.84	55	34	0	5	206	177	99	88	117	177

17. Shaun Boyd, of/2b

Born: Aug. 15, 1981. **Ht.:** 5-10. **Wt.:** 175. **Bats:** R. **Throws:** R. **School:** Vista HS, Oceanside, Calif. **Career Transactions:** Selected by Cardinals in first round (13th overall) of 2000 draft; signed June 26, 2000.

Boyd was a UCLA recruit, and many people thought he would fall in the draft and head to college after struggling in the field in his senior season of high school. The Cardinals took him in the first round because of his athleticism. He had a solid debut at Rookie-level Johnson City playing in the outfield, where he moved because of defensive struggles at shortstop. He was bothered by nagging hamstring and groin injuries. When he came to instructional league, Boyd told the Cardinals he wanted to move back to shortstop. The organization doesn't think he's suited for the position but said it would try him at second base. He also is going to become a switch-hitter, which may work because he has a nice hitting stroke. He has a quick bat and potential leadoff skills. All in all, it should be a busy spring as Boyd tries to find his niche. The organization still isn't sure where he fits best, but will try to put him where he's comfortable and where he can advance the quickest.

Year	Club (League)	Class	AVG	G	AB	R	H	2B	3B	HR	RBI	BB	SO	SB
2000	Johnson City (Appy)	R	.263	43	152	15	40	9	0	2	15	10	22	6
MINOR LEAGUE TOTALS			.263	43	152	15	40	9	0	2	15	10	22	6

18. Jason Karnuth, rhp

Born: May 15, 1976. **Ht.:** 6-2. **Wt.:** 190. **Bats:** R. **Throws:** R. **School:** Illinois State University. **Career Transactions:** Selected by Cardinals in eighth round of 1997 draft; signed June 7, 1997.

Karnuth has shown potential but little else since a standout season in Class A in 1998. He could find new life in the organization as a reliever. Karnuth is a sinker/slider pitcher, and his sinker is a major league-quality pitch already. His slider has improved to become a good complement. He has plus command of both pitches as well. His changeup never has come along, though, and he tended to tire as a starter. The organization thinks that's why he floundered in Double-A and Triple-A in spite of his stuff. So they put him in the bullpen in the Arizona Fall League, with promising results. His control and sinker should make him effective in the role. The Cardinals plan to keep him in the bullpen and send him back to Memphis, where he could close if Gene Stechschulte makes the big league team.

Year	Club (League)	Class	W	L	ERA	G	GS	CG	SV	IP	H	R	ER	BB	SO
1997	New Jersey (NY-P)	A	4	1	1.86	7	7	0	0	39	33	8	8	9	23
	Peoria (Mid)	A	0	3	6.65	4	4	0	0	23	29	19	17	7	12
1998	Prince William (Car)	A	8	1	1.67	16	15	2	0	108	86	26	20	14	53
1999	Arkansas (TL)	AA	7	11	5.22	26	26	2	0	160	175	105	93	55	71
2000	Arkansas (TL)	AA	2	3	3.75	8	8	1	0	50	59	30	21	14	31
	Memphis (PCL)	AAA	5	4	4.04	16	13	0	0	78	89	47	35	27	28
MINOR LEAGUE TOTALS			26	23	3.81	77	73	5	0	458	471	235	194	126	218

19. Chase Voshell, ss

Born: March 29, 1979. **Ht.:** 6-2. **Wt.:** 185. **Bats:** R. **Throws:** R. **School:** Wake Forest University. **Career Transactions:** Selected by Cardinals in third round of 2000 draft; signed July 17, 2000.

Voshell was a fourth-round pick of the Diamondbacks in 1997 but went to Wake Forest, where he was a three-year starter for a team that won two Atlantic Coast Conference championships. His grandfather Les played four seasons of minor league ball and led the Florida State League with 31 stolen bases in 1941. His brother Key is an assistant coach at Wake Forest who played at Peoria last season. Chase made tremendous improvements in the field and especially at the plate in college. He won't make his professional debut until this spring. He had shoulder problems last summer and was examined by doctors, who found an infection in his leg that was caused by an ingrown hair. He had minor surgery to fix the problem and should be healthy for spring training. He has an athletic body, and the Cardinals expect him to be a productive hitter, albeit without much power. He's the type of player who's solid in all areas of the game but not spectacular in any. He should debut in a full-season league.

Year	Club (League)	Class	AVG	G	AB	R	H	2B	3B	HR	RBI	BB	SO	SB
2000			Did Not Play—Signed 2001 Contract											

20. Chris Haas, 1b

Born: Oct. 15, 1976. **Ht.:** 6-2. **Wt.:** 210. **Bats:** L. **Throws:** R. **School:** St. Mary HS, Paducah, Ky. **Career Transactions:** Selected by Cardinals in first round (29th overall) of 1995 draft; signed June 4, 1995.

The Cardinals are woefully thin at a couple of positions, and first base is one of them. They'll give Haas the opportunity to step in there, as he has proven that he isn't suited to play third. He is a former member of the organization's top 10, but he hasn't been able to hit Triple-A pitching and his stock has dropped. He was hampered in 2000 by bone chips in his right elbow, which required surgery. Albert Pujols passed him among organization third basemen, and his elbow makes him even less likely to remain at third, where he has not refined his defensive skills and lacks the tools to excel. He has light-tower power—and that's his only plus tool. He's willing to take a walk but still strikes out too much. He has great makeup and won't ever stop working to get better. The organization hopes settling him at first will allow his bat to take off again. He'll go back to Memphis for a make-or-break year.

Year	Club (League)	Class	AVG	G	AB	R	H	2B	3B	HR	RBI	BB	SO	SB
1995	Johnson City (Appy)	R	.269	67	242	43	65	15	3	7	50	52	93	1
1996	Peoria (Mid)	A	.240	124	421	56	101	19	1	11	65	64	169	3
1997	Peoria (Mid)	A	.313	36	115	23	36	11	0	5	22	22	38	3
	Prince William (Car)	A	.238	100	361	58	86	10	2	14	54	42	144	1
1998	Arkansas (TL)	AA	.274	132	445	75	122	27	4	20	83	73	129	1
1999	Memphis (PCL)	AAA	.229	114	397	63	91	19	2	18	73	66	155	4
2000	Arkansas (TL)	AA	.271	82	291	52	79	14	2	17	59	40	84	0
	Memphis (PCL)	AAA	.214	23	56	7	12	1	0	1	9	9	11	0
MINOR LEAGUE TOTALS			.254	678	2328	377	592	116	14	93	415	368	823	13

21. Les Walrond, lhp

Born: Nov. 7, 1976. **Ht.:** 6-0. **Wt.:** 195. **Bats:** L. **Throws:** L. **School:** University of Kansas. **Career Transactions:** Selected by Cardinals in 13th round of 1998 draft; signed June 30, 1998.

Walrond was an outfielder in college at Kansas, until a scout told him he had more potential as a pitcher. He turned to the mound and has made himself into a prospect. He ranked among the Carolina League ERA leaders in 2000 and had a stretch of 21 innings without giving up an earned run. He's a workmanlike pitcher who doesn't overwhelm hitters. The Cardinals jokingly say Walrond has the kind of stuff that puts you to sleep, meaning he doesn't have spectacular pitches but finds a way to get people out. His fastball velocity is average at best, but he's effective because he throws his two-seam and four-seam fastballs, curve and change from the same release point and with the same arm speed, giving him great deception. He also has the good movement typical of lefthanders, and he has become adept at working hitters. He has little margin for error, and he still could stand to improve his command. He'll continue his quiet progression at Double-A in 2001.

Year	Club (League)	Class	W	L	ERA	G	GS	CG	SV	IP	H	R	ER	BB	SO
1998	New Jersey (NY-P)	A	2	4	4.01	13	10	0	0	52	52	31	23	24	52
1999	Peoria (Mid)	A	7	10	5.70	21	20	0	0	109	115	77	69	59	78
2000	Potomac (Car)	A	10	5	3.34	27	27	0	0	151	134	66	56	54	153
MINOR LEAGUE TOTALS			19	19	4.27	61	57	0	0	312	301	174	148	137	283

22. B.R. Cook, rhp

Born: March 2, 1978. **Ht.:** 6-4. **Wt.:** 200. **Bats:** R. **Throws:** R. **School:** Oregon State University. **Career Transactions:** Selected by Cardinals in third round of 1999 draft; signed June 18, 1999.

Cook wasn't drafted out of high school after helping his Salem, Ore., team to the American Legion World Series in 1995 as a high school junior. He won his last start against Chino, Calif., the eventual national runner-up, allowing just one run in 8⅓ innings of work. He was considered a potential first-rounder after he pitched a one-hitter against Oklahoma State early in his junior year at Oregon State, but he tailed off after that. The same thing that held back Cook's draft status has held back his prospect status: He has electric stuff at times but is inconsistent with it. He was the organization's pitcher of the month last April, with an ERA of 0.38 in four Peoria starts. His ERA soared after that, and he ended up leading the organization with 79 walks. When he's on, Cook throws his fastball in the mid-90s and has a plus curveball. He's a bulldog on the mound and goes right after hitters. He needs to work on his consistency, and his command obviously is not where it should be. As a college pitcher, Cook needs to graduate from Class A. He'll try to make the Double-A rotation in spring training.

Year	Club (League)	Class	W	L	ERA	G	GS	CG	SV	IP	H	R	ER	BB	SO
1999	New Jersey (NY-P)	A	5	1	2.84	9	8	0	0	44	42	19	14	16	42
2000	Peoria (Mid)	A	5	7	3.69	18	18	0	0	97	90	66	40	52	83
	Potomac (Car)	A	0	4	5.53	8	8	0	0	42	48	31	26	27	23
MINOR LEAGUE TOTALS			10	12	3.91	35	34	0	0	184	180	116	80	95	148

23. Tim Lemon, of

Born: Sept. 23, 1980. **Ht.:** 6-1. **Wt.:** 180. **Bats:** R. **Throws:** R. **School:** La Mirada (Calif.) HS. **Career Transactions:** Selected by Cardinals in second round of 1998 draft; signed June 20, 1998.

As if Esix Snead weren't enough, Lemon is another speedy, athletic outfielder in the organization who has no clue at the plate. The organization is more disappointed in Lemon because more was expected of his bat and it hasn't happened yet. He's the nephew of former big leaguer Chet. He had limited baseball experience in high school and turned down a Washington State football scholarship to sign, and his case illustrates the risk of taking raw athletes. But teams hate to give up on tools like these. Lemon has the potential for good power, and his athleticism, speed and arm make him a good outfielder. But he doesn't bring his full talent to the field every day, and as his statistics show, he hasn't given any sign that he's learning about hitting. The Cardinals hope Lemon sees his friends and teammates passing him in the organization, and that he's ready to do something about it.

Year	Club (League)	Class	AVG	G	AB	R	H	2B	3B	HR	RBI	BB	SO	SB
1998	Johnson City (Appy)	R	.226	50	190	25	43	6	2	4	23	15	50	11
1999	New Jersey (NY-P)	A	.198	72	242	25	48	5	3	4	29	22	62	16
2000	Peoria (Mid)	A	.225	127	466	64	105	25	5	10	52	17	105	25
MINOR LEAGUE TOTALS			.218	249	898	114	196	36	10	18	104	54	217	52

24. Jason Woolf, ss

Born: June 6, 1977. **Ht.:** 6-1. **Wt.:** 170. **Bats:** B. **Throws:** R. **School:** American HS, Hialeah, Fla. **Career Transactions:** Selected by Cardinals in second round of 1995 draft; signed June 7, 1995.

If it weren't for bad luck, Woolf wouldn't have any luck at all. Since the Cardinals drafted him, he has put together just one full, healthy season. Strained groin, dislocated finger, migraine headaches, sprained elbow, strained hamstring, back spasms—Woolf has seen it all. Or almost all. He blew out his knee at the end of the 2000 season and had ACL surgery, and he's not expected back until June. On pure talent, Woolf is a top 10 player. But he's the organization's biggest enigma, not only because of his continual injuries but also because he doesn't always seem to give his best effort. His arm and power are both plus tools, and he's not lacking in any area. He has an athletic body when healthy. He tends to be lackadaisical on defense, and the organization also has tried him at third base and in the outfield. Woolf needs to come back strong from his injury and make an impression at Memphis.

Year	Club (League)	Class	AVG	G	AB	R	H	2B	3B	HR	RBI	BB	SO	SB
1995	Johnson City (Appy)	R	.279	31	111	16	31	7	1	0	14	8	21	6
1996	Peoria (Mid)	A	.257	108	362	68	93	12	8	1	27	57	87	28
1997	Prince William (Car)	A	.247	70	251	59	62	11	3	6	18	55	75	26
1998	Arkansas (TL)	AA	.265	76	294	63	78	22	5	4	16	34	84	28
1999	Arkansas (TL)	AA	.272	86	320	46	87	18	4	8	15	28	86	11
2000	Arkansas (TL)	AA	.236	45	165	22	39	8	2	3	13	16	40	7
	Memphis (PCL)	AAA	.243	32	103	21	25	5	1	0	6	19	23	5
MINOR LEAGUE TOTALS			.258	448	1606	295	415	83	24	22	109	217	416	111

25. Aneuris Diaz, 3b

Born: Jan. 20, 1981. **Ht.:** 6-2. **Wt.:** 165. **Bats:** R. **Throws:** R. **Career Transactions:** Signed out of Dominican Republic by Cardinals, Jan. 2, 1998.

When your Rookie-level club supplies four members of the top 30, it's either a loaded club or you have a picked-over system. We'll leave that question for history to answer, though we'll note Johnson City was 24-44 in 2000. The Cardinals do have several promising Dominican players entering the system, and Diaz leads the way at this point. He has the build of a ballplayer and the potential to have at least average power. On defense he has good hands and good actions, and he should have enough arm to stay at third base. Diaz has a long way to go in his development, though, and needs polish in just about every aspect. He'll be a more effective hitter when he learns to take the ball the other way. The Cardinals look at Diaz as a sleeper. He could go to Peoria but is more likely headed for New Jersey.

Year	Club (League)	Class	AVG	G	AB	R	H	2B	3B	HR	RBI	BB	SO	SB
1998	Cardinals (DSL)	R	.200	67	240	29	48	7	1	8	41	26	68	5
1999	Johnson City (Appy)	R	.229	56	205	30	47	9	2	4	27	10	55	6
2000	Johnson City (Appy)	R	.268	53	179	27	48	11	1	5	25	10	65	4
MINOR LEAGUE TOTALS			.229	176	624	86	143	27	4	17	93	46	188	15

26. Jason Bowers, ss

Born: Jan. 27, 1978. **Ht.:** 5-11. **Wt.:** 170. **Bats:** R. **Throws:** R. **School:** Gulf Coast (Fla.) CC. **Career Transactions:** Selected by Cardinals in 14th round of 1998 draft; signed June 6, 1998.

The Cardinals' numerous trades in the last few years have clearly taken a lot of talent out of the system. But for the players who remain, the trades have created opportunity that might not have existed before. Bowers was clearly behind Jack Wilson in the organization before Wilson was traded to the Pirates. Now Bowers is one of the organization's more advanced infield prospects. He has played mostly shortstop throughout his career but profiles better as a second baseman. He has limited range but should be able to handle second. He'll have to hit to continue his advance, though. He has a good approach and is willing to take a walk. He'll never hit for much power. The Cardinals will let Bowers take the next step to Double-A, hoping he continues his offensive development and holds his own on defense.

Year	Club (League)	Class	AVG	G	AB	R	H	2B	3B	HR	RBI	BB	SO	SB
1998	Johnson City (Appy)	R	.291	60	213	31	62	10	5	3	38	13	43	10
1999	Peoria (Mid)	A	.263	112	414	53	109	14	8	2	49	32	78	10
2000	Potomac (Car)	A	.272	91	342	53	93	16	6	1	35	48	72	10
MINOR LEAGUE TOTALS			.272	263	969	137	264	40	19	6	122	93	193	30

27. Troy Farnsworth, 1b/3b

Born: Feb. 4, 1976. **Ht.:** 6-2. **Wt.:** 200. **Bats:** R. **Throws:** R. **School:** Brigham Young University. **Career Transactions:** Selected by Cardinals in 32nd round of 1998 draft; signed June 5, 1998.

As a late-round college pick, Farnsworth knew he would have to produce on the field to get the organization's attention. What better way than to go out and lead the Carolina League in home runs and RBIs last year—and win the RBI race by 26. He's a professional hitter and has the knack for hitting with men on base (.321 in 2000, compared to .154 with the bases empty). He does strike out a lot, and he was old for his league, so he'll have to prove himself against better pitching. He has holes defensively and made 17 errors between first and third last year. Because he doesn't run well, first is probably his long-term position. Farnsworth is the kind of player organizations draft to fill spots in the minor leagues, and not the kind they project to make it to the majors. But every now and then a player like that breaks through, and Farnsworth hit enough last year to earn a longer look in Double-A.

Year	Club (League)	Class	AVG	G	AB	R	H	2B	3B	HR	RBI	BB	SO	SB
1998	New Jersey (NY-P)	A	.257	65	218	33	56	14	1	6	37	25	64	2
1999	Peoria (Mid)	A	.250	134	500	76	125	33	3	19	78	55	124	3
2000	Potomac (Car)	A	.240	137	512	67	123	24	3	23	113	44	133	7
MINOR LEAGUE TOTALS			.247	336	1230	176	304	71	7	48	228	124	321	12

28. Shawn Schumacher, c

Born: Aug. 18, 1976. **Ht.:** 6-1. **Wt.:** 200. **Bats:** L. **Throws:** R. **School:** Texas A&M University. **Career Transactions:** Selected by Cardinals in eighth round of 1999 draft; signed June 19, 1999.

A college teammate of Chance Caple at Texas A&M, Schumacher is the Cardinals' best prospect at catcher, which may be the organization's thinnest position. Another catcher who has a chance to join the list in future years is Dan Moylan, a 2000 eighth-round pick out of North Carolina who swings a good bat but will have to prove himself on defense. Schumacher attended Panola (Texas) Junior College and went to Texas as a junior in 1998 before transferring to Texas A&M for his senior year. The Pirates picked him in the 18th round of the 1997 draft but couldn't sign him. Schumacher missed all but 13 games last year with a broken leg, but the Cardinals like his all-around package and his lefthanded bat from the catcher's spot. He has solid catch-and-throw skills and is athletic enough to play third base. Schumacher will jump to Potomac in 2001 to accelerate his path toward the big leagues.

Year	Club (League)	Class	AVG	G	AB	R	H	2B	3B	HR	RBI	BB	SO	SB
1999	New Jersey (NY-P)	A	.227	47	154	14	35	6	0	3	23	11	8	2
2000	Peoria (Mid)	A	.283	13	46	5	13	5	0	0	5	2	6	0
MINOR LEAGUE TOTALS			.240	60	200	19	48	11	0	3	28	13	14	2

29. Billy Schmitt, 3b

Born: Aug. 16, 1982. **Ht.:** 6-1. **Wt.:** 200. **Bats:** R. **Throws:** R. **School:** Green Valley HS, Henderson, Nev. **Career Transactions:** Selected by Cardinals in 22nd round of 2000 draft; signed June 15, 2000.

The Cardinals are counting on the 2000 draft to restock the farm system, as shown by the presence of the first four players they drafted—Shaun Boyd, Blake Williams, Chris Narveson, Chase Voshell—high on this list. Schmitt could be the sleeper of the group. Playing for powerful Green Valley High, he was overshadowed by more heralded prospects like outfielder David Krynzel, a first-round pick of the Brewers. After struggling initially, he put together a 10-game hitting streak in August to finish third in the Rookie-level Appalachian League batting race. His tools are solid across the board and he should develop a little pop as he matures. He has a good approach at the plate and can hit the ball to all fields with alley power. He worked out to add muscle over the winter. Schmitt has the physical skills to be a solid third baseman, though he left a lot to be desired there last year. He committed 11 errors in just 29 games and spent most of his time as a DH. He has a bad throwing motion and will need work. With a good spring, Schmitt could jump to full-season ball at Peoria in 2001.

Year	Club (League)	Class	AVG	G	AB	R	H	2B	3B	HR	RBI	BB	SO	SB
2000	Johnson City (Appy)	R	.321	46	165	21	53	5	3	2	21	10	23	3
MINOR LEAGUE TOTALS			.321	46	165	21	53	5	3	2	21	10	23	3

30. T.J. Maier, 2b

Born: Feb. 24, 1975. **Ht.:** 6-0. **Wt.:** 180. **Bats:** R. **Throws:** R. **School:** Cal Poly San Luis Obispo. **Career Transactions:** Selected by Cardinals in 30th round of 1997 draft; signed June 6, 1997.

From the organization that developed utilityman Joe McEwing comes Maier. It's a good bet that he's the only player in the Prospect Handbook who was born in Tehran, Iran, though he grew up in California. His father was in the Army and stationed in Iran when he was born. His mother is from Thailand. Maier played shortstop at Cal Poly San Luis Obispo, the same school that produced Ozzie Smith, but his tools are far more pedestrian. He's the type of player who appeals more to managers than scouts. He moved to second base right away as a pro and has played at third as well. Maier will make it to the big leagues on his bat, though. He walks more than he strikes out and is working on driving the ball and getting full extension with every swing so he can become more than just a contact hitter. He should be able to take the next step to Memphis in 2001.

Year	Club (League)	Class	AVG	G	AB	R	H	2B	3B	HR	RBI	BB	SO	SB
1997	New Jersey (NY-P)	A	.213	50	155	19	33	9	1	2	22	20	30	6
1998	Peoria (Mid)	A	.269	84	271	47	73	14	1	2	28	45	52	6
1999	Potomac (Car)	A	.263	102	353	53	93	15	0	2	38	55	61	12
2000	Arkansas (TL)	AA	.294	110	364	59	107	16	3	6	42	49	42	13
MINOR LEAGUE TOTALS			.268	346	1143	178	306	54	5	12	130	169	185	37

San Diego
Padres

TOP 30 PROSPECTS

1. Sean Burroughs, 3b
2. Jacob Peavy, rhp
3. Wascar Serrano, rhp
4. Mike Bynum, lhp
5. Gerik Baxter, rhp
6. Mark Phillips, lhp
7. Xavier Nady, 3b
8. Ben Johnson, of
9. Dennis Tankersley, rhp
10. Junior Herndon, rhp
11. Brian Lawrence, rhp
12. Nobuaki Yoshida, lhp
13. Vince Faison, of
14. Kevin Eberwein, 1b/3b
15. Kevin Nicholson, ss
16. Nick Trzesniak, c
17. Omar Falcon, c
18. Justin Germano, rhp
19. Kory DeHaan, of
20. Santiago Perez, ss
21. Jeremy Owens, of
22. Steve Watkins, rhp
23. Andres Pagan, c
24. Omar Ortiz, rhp
25. Mike Colangelo, of
26. Christian Berroa, ss
27. Oliver Perez, lhp
28. Mike Thompson, rhp
29. Mewelde Moore, of
30. J.J. Trujillo, rhp

By Jim Callis

As recently as the fall of 1998, it was a great time to be a Padres fan. In October, San Diego made an exhilarating run to the second World Series in franchise history. A month later, local voters approved Proposition C, allowing the sale of bonds to finance half of a $450 million ballpark and redevelopment plan.

Shortly after that initiative passed, Kevin Brown, Ken Caminiti and Steve Finley left the Padres as free agents, and Joey Hamilton was traded. The following spring, Greg Vaughn was dealt off as well. The club said it didn't have the cash to afford those players, but pledged it would be competitive and in solid shape when the new park opened in 2002.

Many voters felt betrayed, and they probably feel worse now. In October, construction on the new park was halted when money ran out. The city has been barred from selling the bonds in the wake of a federal investigation into councilwoman Valerie Stallings' stock dealings in a company controlled by Padres owner John Moores during a period when she voted in favor of the ballpark deal.

As for the team, it has been rebuilding with an eye on 2002. Its farm system ranks among the best in game, and the Padres tied the Cubs for leadership among all organizations with nine players on Baseball America's minor league Top 10 Prospects lists. San Diego has drafted as well as any team over the last three years.

Yet the Padres have stockpiled talent at some positions while remaining thin at others. Their top two hitters in the minors, Sean Burroughs and Xavier Nady, both play third base, the same position as the top player on the big league club, Phil Nevin. Meanwhile, San Diego remains weak up the middle.

Catcher Ben Davis, the No. 2 overall pick in the 1995 draft, has yet to prove he can hit at the major league level. The Padres' three best catching prospects all were teenagers who spent 2000 in Rookie ball, so no help is imminent if Davis and Wiki Gonzalez don't pan out. San Diego also is weak in the middle infield, so it spent this offseason grabbing as many shortstops as possible. If Mike Darr isn't an upgrade over Ruben Rivera in center, the Padres future options are Kory DeHaan, whose development was stunted as a major league Rule 5 pick last year, or Vince Faison and Jeremy Owens, who combined to strike out 342 times in 255 Class A games.

OrganizationOverview

General manager: Kevin Towers. **Farm director:** Tye Waller. **Scouting director:** Bill Gayton.

2000 PERFORMANCE

Class	Team	League	W	L	Pct.	Finish*	Manager(s)
Majors	San Diego	National	76	86	.469	10th (16)	Bruce Bochy
Triple-A	#Las Vegas Stars	Pacific Coast	73	70	.510	7th (16)	D. Espy/T. Franklin
Double-A	Mobile BayBears	Southern	66	73	.475	8th (10)	Mike Basso
High A	†Rancho Cuca. Quakes	California	61	79	.436	8th (10)	Tom LeVasseur
Low A	Fort Wayne Wizards	Midwest	72	65	.526	t-5th (14)	Craig Colbert
Rookie	Idaho Falls Padres	Pioneer	45	29	.608	1st (8)	Don Werner
Rookie	^AZL Padres	Arizona	17	38	.309	9th (9)	Howard Bushong
OVERALL 2000 MINOR LEAGUE RECORD			334	354	.485	20th (30)	

*Finish in overall standings (No. of teams in league). #Affiliate will be in Portland (Pacific Coast) in 2001. †Affiliate will be in Lake Elsinore (California) in 2001. ^Affiliate will be in Eugene (Northwest/short-season) in 2001.

ORGANIZATION LEADERS

BATTING
*AVG	Joe Vitiello, Las Vegas	.350
R	Jeremy Owens, Rancho Cucamonga	99
H	Al Benjamin, Rancho Cucamonga	154
TB	Jeremy Owens, Rancho Cucamonga	243
2B	Greg LaRocca, Las Vegas	42
3B	Jeremy Owens, Rancho Cucamonga	10
HR	J.P. Woodward, Idaho Falls	20
RBI	**Graham Koonce**, Rancho Cucamonga	93
BB	**Graham Koonce**, Rancho Cucamonga	107
SO	Jeremy Owens, Rancho Cucamonga	183
SB	Jeremy Owens, Rancho Cucamonga	54

PITCHING
W	Jacob Peavy, Fort Wayne	13
L	Jason Middlebrook, Mobile/Las Vegas	14
#ERA	Shawn Camp, Rancho Cucamonga/Mobile	2.19
G	Keith Forbes, Rancho Cucamonga	74
CG	Junior Herndon, Las Vegas	3
SV	J.J. Trujillo, Fort Wayne	42
IP	**Brian Lawrence**, Mobile/Las Vegas	173
BB	Ben Howard, Rancho Cucamonga	111
SO	**Brian Lawrence**, Mobile/Las Vegas	165

*Minimum 250 at-bats. #Minimum 75 innings.

TOP PROSPECTS OF THE DECADE
1991	Rafael Valdez, rhp
1992	Joey Hamilton, rhp
1993	Ray McDavid, of
1994	Joey Hamilton, rhp
1995	Dustin Hermanson, rhp
1996	Ben Davis, c
1997	Derrek Lee, 1b
1998	Matt Clement, rhp
1999	Matt Clement, rhp
2000	Sean Burroughs, 3b

TOP DRAFT PICKS OF THE DECADE
1991	Joey Hamilton, rhp
1992	*Todd Helton, of (2)
1993	Derrek Lee, 1b
1994	Dustin Hermanson, rhp
1995	Ben Davis, c
1996	Matt Halloran, ss
1997	Kevin Nicholson, ss
1998	Sean Burroughs, 3b
1999	Vince Faison, of
2000	Mark Phillips, lhp

*Did not sign.

JEFF GOLDEN

RODGER WOOD

Koonce

Lawrence

BEST TOOLS
Best Hitter for Average	Sean Burroughs
Best Power Hitter	Xavier Nady
Fastest Baserunner	Jeremy Owens
Best Fastball	Wascar Serrano
Best Breaking Ball	Mike Bynum
Best Control	Brian Lawrence
Best Defensive Catcher	Andres Pagan
Best Defensive Infielder	Christian Berroa
Best Infield Arm	Cesar Saba
Best Defensive Outfielder	Jeremy Owens
Best Outfield Arm	Jeremy Owens

PROJECTED 2004 LINEUP
Catcher	Ben Davis
First Base	Ryan Klesko
Second Base	Kevin Nicholson
Third Base	Sean Burroughs
Shortstop	Damian Jackson
Left Field	Xavier Nady
Center Field	Mike Darr
Right Field	Ben Johnson
No. 1 Starter	Matt Clement
No. 2 Starter	Adam Eaton
No. 3 Starter	Jacob Peavy
No. 4 Starter	Wascar Serrano
No. 5 Starter	Mike Bynum
Closer	Trevor Hoffman

ALL-TIME LARGEST BONUSES
Mark Phillips, 2000	$2,200,000
Sean Burroughs, 1998	2,100,000
Vince Faison, 1999	1,415,000
Ben Davis, 1995	1,300,000
Gerik Baxter, 1999	1,100,000
Xavier Nady, 2000	1,100,000

DraftAnalysis

2000 Draft

Best Pro Debut: 1B J.P. Woodward (14) batted .317 and led the Rookie-level Pioneer League with 20 homers and 92 RBIs, though he'll need to shorten his swing to succeed at higher levels. SS J.J. Furmaniak (22) hit .343-5-38 and OF Craig Thompson (23) batted .358-10-62 on Woodward's Idaho Falls club, which won the league title.

Best Athlete: OF Mewelde Moore (4) ranked second among NCAA Division I-A freshmen in rushing last fall with an average of 89 yards a game at Tulane. His speed and offensive potential in baseball are exciting if he chooses the diamond over the gridiron. He'll make his pro debut next summer.

Best Hitter: 3B Xavier Nady (2) ranked as college baseball's premier all-around hitter entering the 2000 season, but then had somewhat disappointing performances at California (.329, 19 homers) and with wood bats with the U.S. national team (.238, one homer). The Padres believe those numbers were an aberration.

Best Raw Power: Few players in the draft can match Nady's power.

Fastest Runner: Moore has breakaway speed. He can run the 60-yard dash in 6.39 seconds.

Best Defensive Player: C Omar Falcon (3) has an above-average arm with a short release. He also offers some power at the plate.

Best Fastball: LHP **Mark Phillips** (1) threw as hard as 96 mph after signing, and he has command of three pitches.

Most Intriguing Background: OF Jarrett Roenicke's (17) father Gary and uncle Ron both played outfield in the majors.

Closest To The Majors: Nady already reached the majors under terms of his four-year, $2.85 million big league contract. He singled off the Dodgers' Eric Gagne in his only at-bat and has the tools to return on merit soon. San Diego hoped playing in the Arizona Fall League would prepare Nady for Triple-A in 2001, but he had to leave the AFL with elbow tendinitis.

FRANK RAGSDALE

Phillips

Best Late-Round Pick: RHP Justin Germano (13), who has a 88-92 mph fastball and a nifty curveball. He's a better pitcher than the Padres thought they were getting, and he reminds them of Junior Herndon, another advanced high school pitcher whom they took in the ninth round in 1997.

The One Who Got Away: RHP Chad Cordero (26), who throws 93-95 mph, went to Cal State Fullerton.

Assessment: Brad Sloan's last draft as Padres scouting director could pay huge dividends. San Diego got the best left-hander available (Phillips), one of the best hitters (Nady), a two-way catcher (Falcon) and an elite athlete (Moore) in the first four rounds.

1999 Draft

The Padres had six first-round choices, but their biggest find may have been RHP Jacob Peavy (15). LHP Mike Bynum is the best of the first-rounders, followed by RHP Gerik Baxter, OF Vince Faison and C Nick Trzesniak. The other two, RHPs Omar Ortiz and Casey Burns, have not lived up to expectations so far. **Grade: A–**

1998 Draft

3B Sean Burroughs (1) is one of the most advanced hitters in the minors and may be a big league starter before he turns 21. 1B/3B Kevin Eberwein (5), OF Jeremy Owens (8) and RHP Brian Lawrence (17) are the best of the rest of the crop. **Grade: A–+**

1997 Draft

SS Kevin Nicholson (1) and RHP Junior Herndon (9) have advanced quickly. They're the only standouts from an otherwise forgettable draft. **Grade: C–**

1996 Draft

When the Royals took Dee Brown just ahead of them, the Padres' fallback choice was SS Matt Halloran, one of the worst first-rounders in recent memory. If oft-injured RHP Jason Middlebrook (9) doesn't make it, San Diego will wind up with nothing. **Grade: F**

Note: Draft analysis prepared by Jim Callis. Numbers in parentheses indicate draft rounds.

. . . Burroughs is the best pure hitter in the minor leagues and will be an above-average major league power hitter.

Sean Burroughs 3b

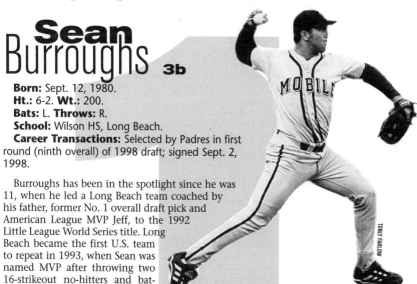

TONY FARLOW

Born: Sept. 12, 1980.
Ht.: 6-2. **Wt.:** 200.
Bats: L. **Throws:** R.
School: Wilson HS, Long Beach.
Career Transactions: Selected by Padres in first round (ninth overall) of 1998 draft; signed Sept. 2, 1998.

Burroughs has been in the spotlight since he was 11, when he led a Long Beach team coached by his father, former No. 1 overall pick and American League MVP Jeff, to the 1992 Little League World Series title. Long Beach became the first U.S. team to repeat in 1993, when Sean was named MVP after throwing two 16-strikeout no-hitters and batting .600. He added another world championship in 2000 as a member of the U.S. Olympic team, hitting .375 in limited action as manager Tommy Lasorda inexplicably played Orioles journeyman Mike Kinkade ahead of him. Earlier in the year, Burroughs was MVP of the Futures Game in Atlanta after going 3-for-4 with a key defensive play.

The Padres have been aggressive with Burroughs, playing him in Double-A last season as a teenager. He has responded to every challenge. Burroughs is the best pure hitter in the minor leagues. Despite being much younger than his opposition, he has batted .329 as a pro. More impressive, he has walked more times (135) than he has struck out (107). He has a tremendous understanding of the strike zone, reaching base in 57 consecutive games in 1999-2000. Much has been made of Burroughs' paltry home run total, but he'll be an above-average power hitter. It's typical for young lefthanded hitters to drive the ball to the middle of the ballpark, with home run power the last thing to develop. Burroughs has the bat speed and the approach to drive the ball out of the park as he gets more experience and learns to turn on pitches. He's not a one-dimensional player, either. He has above-average arm strength and hands at third base. He improved his footwork in 2000, cutting his errors to 16 after making 37 the year before. Power is Burroughs' most obvious shortcoming, but it will come. The only thing he won't do is impress anyone with his speed on the bases. He has been caught stealing in 24 of his 47 pro attempts.

If the Padres trade Phil Nevin, their most marketable major leaguer, some say Burroughs could be their Opening Day starter at third. While he probably wouldn't be scarred by the experience, Burroughs isn't quite ready. He'll be better off spending most of the year at Triple-A Portland. Regardless, he's a future batting champion and an all-star for years to come.

Year	Club (League)	Class	AVG	G	AB	R	H	2B	3B	HR	RBI	BB	SO	SB
1999	Fort Wayne (Mid)	A	.359	122	426	65	153	30	3	5	80	74	59	17
	Rancho Cuca. (Cal)	A	.435	6	23	3	10	3	0	1	5	3	3	0
2000	Mobile (SL)	AA	.291	108	392	46	114	29	4	2	42	58	45	6
MINOR LEAGUE TOTALS			.329	236	841	114	277	62	7	8	127	135	107	23

2. Jacob Peavy, rhp

Born: May 31, 1981. **Ht.:** 6-1. **Wt.:** 180. **Bats:** R. **Throws:** R. **School:** St. Paul's Episcopal HS, Mobile, Ala. **Career Transactions:** Selected by Padres in 15th round of 1999 draft; signed June 9, 1999.

The Padres spent four first-round picks on pitchers in 1999, but 15th-rounder Peavy has been the best from that draft so far. He lasted that long because he was considered frail, wild and committed to an Auburn scholarship. He won the Rookie-level Arizona League's pitching triple crown in his pro debut, and had another strong season in 2000 despite missing two weeks with viral meningitis in April. Peavy used a fastball that reaches the mid-90s, good slider and nice changeup to tie for the Class A Midwest League lead in strikeouts last season. He makes it tougher for hitters by varying his arm angle and pitching down in the strike zone. His control has been better than expected as a pro. He has allowed just 10 homers in 208 innings and hasn't had any trouble with lefthanders. Like all young pitchers, he can refine his command and the consistency of his pitches. Peavy's pure stuff isn't as good as that of Wascar Serrano, Gerik Baxter and Mark Phillips. It's his savvy that elevates him ahead of them on this list, and it will be interesting to see if it can keep him there. Peavy will move up to high Class A Lake Elsinore in 2001 and could reach Double-A late in the season.

Year	Club (League)	Class	W	L	ERA	G	GS	CG	SV	IP	H	R	ER	BB	SO
1999	Padres (AZL)	R	7	1	1.34	13	11	1	0	74	52	16	11	23	90
	Idaho Falls (Pio)	R	2	0	0.00	2	2	0	0	11	5	0	0	1	13
2000	Fort Wayne (Mid)	A	13	8	2.90	26	25	0	0	134	107	61	43	53	164
MINOR LEAGUE TOTALS			22	9	2.23	41	38	1	0	218	164	77	54	77	267

3. Wascar Serrano, rhp

Born: June 2, 1978. **Ht.:** 6-2. **Wt.:** 180. **Bats:** R. **Throws:** R. **Career Transactions:** Signed out of Dominican Republic by Padres, May 31, 1995.

For the first time in his four seasons in the United States, Serrano failed to make his league's Top 10 Prospects list. It still was a successful year, with the exception of a disastrous four-start stint in Triple-A at midseason. Serrano has the best fastball in the system. He can touch the mid-90s with his four-seam fastball, and his low-90s two-seamer is more effective because of its additional movement. He improved his breaking ball in 2000, and it's now more of a slider than a slurve. Serrano has been slow to pick up a changeup. After six pro seasons, it's still not effective or deceptive. He generally has been stingy with walks and homers, but that wasn't the case in Triple-A. Serrano will get a second shot at Triple-A in 2001, when the Padres' new affiliate (Portland) should be more pitcher-friendly than their old one (Las Vegas). The back end of San Diego's rotation is far from stable, so he could get a big league shot if he passes the Triple-A test this time around.

Year	Club (League)	Class	W	L	ERA	G	GS	CG	SV	IP	H	R	ER	BB	SO
1995	Cubs/Padres (DSL)	R	3	3	3.11	12	7	0	0	46	63	24	16	15	23
1996	Cubs/Padres (DSL)	R	3	7	7.88	22	2	0	1	54	77	58	47	24	44
1997	Idaho Falls (Pio)	R	0	1	11.88	2	2	0	0	8	13	12	11	4	13
	Padres (AZL)	R	6	3	3.18	12	11	0	1	71	60	43	25	22	75
	Clinton (Mid)	A	0	1	6.00	1	1	1	0	6	6	5	4	2	2
1998	Clinton (Mid)	A	9	7	3.22	26	26	0	0	157	150	74	56	54	143
1999	Rancho Cuca. (Cal)	A	9	8	3.33	21	21	1	0	132	110	58	49	43	129
	Mobile (SL)	AA	2	3	5.53	7	7	0	0	42	48	27	26	17	29
2000	Mobile (SL)	AA	9	4	2.80	20	20	1	0	112	93	42	35	42	112
	Las Vegas (PCL)	AAA	0	1	14.18	4	4	0	0	13	24	23	21	10	19
MINOR LEAGUE TOTALS			41	38	4.07	127	101	3	2	642	644	366	290	233	589

4. Mike Bynum, lhp

Born: March 20, 1978. **Ht.:** 6-4. **Wt.:** 200. **Bats:** L. **Throws:** L. **School:** University of North Carolina. **Career Transactions:** Selected by Padres in first round (19th overall) of 1999 draft; signed July 1, 1999.

After being overshadowed by Kyle Snyder (the seventh overall pick in 1999) at North Carolina, Bynum burst into the spotlight by pitching 27 scoreless innings to start his pro career. He hasn't slowed down must since, reaching Double-A in his season and a half as a pro. He was rated the best lefty pitching prospect in the high Class A California League and pitched a scoreless inning in the Futures Game last year. Bynum's best pitch is a slider that has been compared to Hall of Famer Steve Carlton's. He changed his grip on it as a college junior, increasing its break. Lefthanders have little chance against him, hitting .170 with no homers in 123 at-bats last year. He's an intelligent, composed pitcher who has the ability to read a batter's swing and make adjustments. Bynum's fastball and changeup aren't nearly as dominating as his slider. He has average velocity at 89-90 mph but admitted he was disappointed with his fastball command in 2000. He doesn't throw his changeup as much as he should. As he moves to higher levels, he'll need a full repertoire. Scott Karl is the only lefthander with a chance to make the big league rotation this year, so the Padres are looking forward to the day when Bynum will be ready to join them. He could go to Triple-A if he has a strong spring, though a return to Double-A is also a possibility.

Year	Club (League)	Class	W	L	ERA	G	GS	CG	SV	IP	H	R	ER	BB	SO
1999	Idaho Falls (Pio)	R	1	0	0.00	5	3	0	0	17	7	0	0	4	21
	Rancho Cuca. (Cal)	A	3	1	3.29	7	7	0	0	38	35	17	14	8	44
2000	Rancho Cuca. (Cal)	A	9	6	3.00	21	21	0	0	126	101	55	42	51	129
	Mobile (SL)	AA	3	1	2.91	6	6	0	0	34	31	12	11	16	27
MINOR LEAGUE TOTALS			16	8	2.80	39	37	0	0	215	174	84	67	79	221

5. Gerik Baxter, rhp

Born: March 11, 1980. **Ht.:** 6-2. **Wt.:** 185. **Bats:** R. **Throws:** R. **School:** Edmonds-Woodway HS, Edmonds, Wash. **Career Transactions:** Selected by Padres in first round (28th overall) of 1999 draft; signed June 5, 1999.

Baxter struggled at the beginning of 2000, his first full season, going 1-3, 6.96 in his first seven starts. Then he hit his stride, posting a 1.71 ERA and limiting opponents to a .190 average the rest of the way. The only downside came in late June, when he was hit in the head by a line drive and missed seven weeks with a concussion. Baxter has a 92-93 mph fastball that can touch 96. At times, his slider gives him a second plus pitch. He has a surprisingly advanced changeup for his age. He keeps the ball in the park, allowing just eight homers in 161 pro innings, and challenges hitters. Baxter was supposed to pitch in Australia over the winter, but he left after one outing with what's considered a minor elbow problem. His biggest need is to develop a consistent delivery. If he does that, he should throw more strikes and improve his secondary pitches. Baxter should be 100 percent by spring training. He'll move up to Lancaster in 2001 and probably will stay there for the entire season. He's at least two years away from being ready for the majors.

Year	Club (League)	Class	W	L	ERA	G	GS	CG	SV	IP	H	R	ER	BB	SO
1999	Padres (AZL)	R	3	0	1.50	8	7	0	0	36	27	7	6	15	45
	Idaho Falls (Pio)	R	2	0	4.81	5	5	0	0	24	21	15	13	17	29
2000	Fort Wayne (Mid)	A	5	6	3.40	20	19	0	0	100	81	46	38	44	103
MINOR LEAGUE TOTALS			10	6	3.19	33	31	0	0	161	129	68	57	76	177

6. Mark Phillips, lhp

Born: Dec. 30, 1981. **Ht.:** 6-3. **Wt.:** 205. **Bats:** L. **Throws:** L. **School:** Hanover (Pa.) HS. **Career Transactions:** Selected by Padres in first round (ninth overall) of 2000 draft; signed July 6, 2000.

Phillips may have the most upside of any pitcher from the 2000 draft. He agreed to a predraft deal with the Padres worth a club-record $2.2 million. He blossomed late, with his velocity shooting up last spring after he didn't attend any of the national showcases the previous summer. Phillips best pro outing came in the Rookie-level Pioneer League playoffs, when he threw 7⅓ shutout innings and struck out 11 to win the clincher. Phillips has the best fastball among 2000 high school draftees who signed, throwing 93-94 mph on a regular basis. That's exceptional velocity for a lefthander. He also has a curveball that he throws so hard it looks like a slider. When he throws strikes with both pitches, he's untouchable. Phillips is more of a thrower than a pitcher. His command needs a lot of improvement and he'll have to add a changeup after not needing one in high school. Fairly skinny, he needs to get stronger, which should boost his fastball even more. Considering his stuff and the fact that he's lefthander, Phillips is a good bet to be the first high schooler from last year's draft to reach the majors. That said, he's going to have to add a lot of polish before he's ready for San Diego. He's ticketed for low Class A Fort Wayne in 2001.

Year	Club (League)	Class	W	L	ERA	G	GS	CG	SV	IP	H	R	ER	BB	SO
2000	Idaho Falls (Pio)	R	1	1	5.35	10	10	0	0	37	35	30	22	24	37
MINOR LEAGUE TOTALS			1	1	5.35	10	10	0	0	37	35	30	22	24	37

7. Xavier Nady, 3b

Born: Nov. 14, 1978. **Ht.:** 6-1. **Wt.:** 185. **Bats:** R. **Throws:** R. **School:** University of California. **Career Transactions:** Selected by Padres in second round of 2000 draft; signed Sept. 17, 2000.

Entering last spring, Nady was the top-rated prospect for the 2000 draft. Because his junior year at California (.329-19-59) wasn't as strong as his previous two seasons and because of his bonus demands, Nady slid to the 49th pick. He spent the summer with Team USA before agreeing to a four-year big league contract that includes a $1.1 million bonus. Nady was the best all-around hitter in the draft. He broke Mark McGwire's Pacific-10 Conference record with a .718 slugging percentage. With his strength and eye at the plate, Nady should hit for both power and average as a pro. He lacks speed and a definite position. He played second base and shortstop as a freshman, then moved to third base as a sophomore. It's uncertain he can play the hot corner as a pro, but it's moot because Sean Burroughs is the franchise's third baseman of the future. Scouts soured on Nady a bit after he slumped as a junior, then batted .238 with one homer using a wood bat for Team USA. He became the first 2000 draftee to reach the majors last September (per the terms of his contract), singling off Eric Gagne in his lone at-bat. The Padres hoped the Arizona Fall League would prepare Nady for Triple-A in 2001, but he had to leave after one game with elbow tendinitis. His likely destination now is Double-A. He'll play third base and may even get a look at second. The guess here is that he'll reach the majors as a left fielder.

Year	Club (League)	Class	AVG	G	AB	R	H	2B	3B	HR	RBI	BB	SO	SB
2000	San Diego (NL)	MAJ	1.000	1	1	1	1	0	0	0	0	0	0	0
MAJOR LEAGUE TOTALS			1.000	1	1	1	1	0	0	0	0	0	0	0

8. Ben Johnson, of

Born: June 18, 1981. **Ht.:** 6-1. **Wt.:** 200. **Bats:** R. **Throws:** R. **School:** Germantown (Tenn.) HS. **Career Transactions:** Selected by Cardinals in fourth round of 1999 draft; signed June 24, 1999 . . . Traded by Cardinals with RHP Heathcliff Slocumb to Padres for C Carlos Hernandez and SS Nate Tebbs, July 31, 2000.

Kevin Towers made some astute deals before the 2000 trading deadline. In one fell swoop, he shed the Padres of the last 14 months of Carlos Hernandez' excessive contract and acquired Johnson, the best prospect drafted by the Cardinals in 1999. The Padres' scouting reports compare Johnson to a young Brian Jordan. Johnson's most obvious gifts are size, strength and speed. For a young hitter, he has a good idea of the strike zone. Defensively, he has a solid arm and range for right field. A gifted athlete, he played both football and baseball at Germantown (Tenn.) High, one of the nation's top high school baseball programs. After wearing down in the second half of 2000, Johnson will have to adjust to the extended pro season. He showed the ability to make adjustments at the plate the year before, so there are no long-term concerns about his hitting. Johnson could move up to high Class A in 2001, though he could return to Fort Wayne if the Padres decide to promote some older outfielders from last year's championship club at Rookie-level Idaho Falls ahead of him. In either case, Johnson is about three years away from San Diego.

Year	Club (League)	Class	AVG	G	AB	R	H	2B	3B	HR	RBI	BB	SO	SB
1999	Johnson City (Appy)	R	.330	57	203	38	67	9	1	10	51	29	57	14
2000	Peoria (Mid)	A	.242	93	330	58	80	22	1	13	46	53	78	17
	Fort Wayne (Mid)	A	.193	29	109	11	21	6	2	3	13	7	25	0
MINOR LEAGUE TOTALS			.262	179	642	107	168	37	4	26	110	89	160	31

9. Dennis Tankersley, rhp

Born: Feb. 24, 1979. **Ht.:** 6-2. **Wt.:** 185. **Bats:** R. **Throws:** R. **School:** Meramec (Mo.) JC. **Career Transactions:** Selected by Red Sox in 38th round of 1998 draft; signed May 18, 1999 . . . Traded by Red Sox with SS Cesar Saba to Padres for 3B Ed Sprague, June 30, 2000.

Few trades work out better than the one in which the Padres sent Ed Sprague to the Red Sox last June. San Diego received two players: shortstop Cesar Saba, who ranked No. 8 on Boston's 2000 Top 10 Prospects list, and the unheralded Tankersley, who developed into a far better prospect. After switching organizations, Tankersley had nearly twice as many double-digit strikeout outings (five) as he did games in which he allowed more than two runs (three). Making the deal look worse for the Red Sox, they released Sprague in August and the Padres re-signed him. Tankersley's out pitch is a two-seam fastball that arrives at 91-92 mph and dives toward the plate. He's also capable of throwing a four-seamer that tops out at 94-95 mph. His slider and curveball are effective, and he throws all three pitches for strikes to both sides of the plate. His deceptive delivery has been compared to Kevin Appier's. Tankersley has yet to run into any roadblocks as a pro. His primary need is experience, though like any pitcher, he'll need to improve his command and consistency to enjoy continued success as he rises through the minors. Tankersley is yet another example of the Red Sox underestimating the worth of their prospects before including them in trades. He likely will start 2001 in the California League. His age and past performance make him a candidate to reach Double-A Mobile by the end of the year.

Year	Club (League)	Class	W	L	ERA	G	GS	CG	SV	IP	H	R	ER	BB	SO
1999	Red Sox (GCL)	R	1	0	0.76	11	6	0	1	36	14	7	3	9	57
2000	Augusta (SAL)	A	5	3	4.06	15	15	1	0	75	73	41	34	32	74
	Fort Wayne (Mid)	A	5	2	2.85	12	12	0	0	66	48	25	21	25	87
MINOR LEAGUE TOTALS			11	5	2.94	38	33	1	1	177	135	73	58	66	218

10. Junior Herndon, rhp

Born: Sept. 11, 1978. **Ht.:** 6-1. **Wt.:** 190. **Bats:** R. **Throws:** R. **School:** Moffat County HS, Craig, Colo. **Career Transactions:** Selected by Padres in ninth round of 1997 draft; signed June 5, 1997.

Herndon is the most precocious pitcher in the system. After being named the Padres' 1998 minor league pitcher of the year, he moved to Double-A at age 20 and Triple-A at 21. He started slowly at Las Vegas in 2000 before seemingly turning the corner by going 2-1, 1.91 in five July starts, but went 3-6, 7.21 in his final 12 outings. Herndon throws in the low 90s with life on is fastball. Pacific Coast League managers liked his slider last season, though the Padres would prefer him to throw a curveball. His changeup is effective. After lefthanders batted .317 off him in 1999, he limited them to a .254 average in 2000. Herndon may have been moved too quickly for his own good. He doesn't have a dominant pitch, so he has to win with location and command. He has been too tentative since leaving Class A, as his strikeout-walk ratio has declined from 198-80 to 162-117 and his ERA has risen from 3.43 to 4.89. Herndon definitely needs another season in Triple-A to catch his breath. He's still just 22, so he has time to make adjustments. He must start doing so in 2001.

Year	Club (League)	Class	W	L	ERA	G	GS	CG	SV	IP	H	R	ER	BB	SO
1997	Padres (AZL)	R	3	2	4.42	14	14	0	0	77	80	51	38	32	65
	Idaho Falls (Pio)	R	0	0	0.00	1	1	0	0	5	5	0	0	1	3
1998	Clinton (Mid)	A	10	8	2.99	21	21	3	0	132	119	59	44	34	101
	Rancho Cuca. (Cal)	A	3	2	3.40	6	6	0	0	40	37	18	15	13	29
1999	Mobile (SL)	AA	10	9	4.69	26	26	2	0	163	172	96	85	52	87
2000	Las Vegas (PCL)	AAA	10	11	5.13	26	26	3	0	135	151	90	77	65	75
MINOR LEAGUE TOTALS			36	32	4.22	94	94	8	0	552	564	314	259	197	360

11. Brian Lawrence, rhp

Born: May 14, 1976. **Ht.:** 6-0. **Wt.:** 195. **Bats:** R. **Throws:** R. **School:** Northwestern State University. **Career Transactions:** Selected by Padres in 17th round of 1998 draft; signed June 8, 1998.

Lawrence lacks size and a big-time fastball, and he was a mere 17th-round pick as a college senior in the 1998 draft. But there's no denying that he knows how to pitch. He has gone a combined 23-14 while leading Padres minor leaguers in ERA in each of the last two seasons. He shared the organization's 2000 minor league pitcher of the year award with Jacob Peavy. Lawrence has average velocity at best, but his fastball looks quicker because he effectively mixes in his slider and changeup. He throws strikes to both sides of the plate and possesses the best command in the system. His pro strikeout-walk ratio is 431-83. Lawrence thrived in eight Triple-A starts at the end of 2000, earning him the opportunity to compete for a big league rotation spot in spring training.

Year	Club (League)	Class	W	L	ERA	G	GS	CG	SV	IP	H	R	ER	BB	SO
1998	Idaho Falls (Pio)	R	3	0	2.45	4	4	2	0	22	22	7	6	5	21
	Clinton (Mid)	A	5	3	2.80	12	12	2	0	80	67	34	25	13	79
1999	Rancho Cuca. (Cal)	A	12	8	3.39	27	27	4	0	175	178	72	66	30	166
2000	Mobile (SL)	AA	7	6	2.42	21	21	0	0	127	99	40	34	28	119
	Las Vegas (PCL)	AAA	4	0	1.93	8	8	0	0	47	48	13	10	7	46
MINOR LEAGUE TOTALS			31	17	2.81	72	72	8	0	451	414	166	141	83	431

12. Nobuaki Yoshida, lhp

Born: Aug. 10, 1981. **Ht.:** 6-1. **Wt.:** 170. **Bats:** L. **Throws:** L. **Career Transactions:** Signed out of Japan by Padres, Jan. 10, 2000.

The Padres want to increase their efforts on the global market, so they hired former Orioles scouting director Gary Nickels and ex-Braves international super scout Bill Clark last offseason. In January, Nickels signed Yoshida to a bonus in the low six figures. He became the second Japanese player signed out of high school by a major league club, following Mets lefthander Juei Ushiromatsu. Japanese clubs are limited to seven draft picks per year, and many only use three or four because they have to make long-term commitments to their choices. Seibu and Yokohama told Yoshida they would draft him but ultimately passed on him. He excelled in his U.S. debut, and he won the decisive game of the Pioneer League semifinals with six shutout innings. Yoshida is a finesse pitcher with good command, but he also can reach the low 90s with his fastball and is projectable. He has good feel for his changeup and is refining a curveball and screwball. He also has learned English quickly, easing his transition. Very advanced for his age, he could reach high Class A by the end of 2001.

Year	Club (League)	Class	W	L	ERA	G	GS	CG	SV	IP	H	R	ER	BB	SO
2000	Padres (AZL)	R	0	2	2.32	7	7	0	0	31	23	11	8	7	32
	Idaho Falls (Pio)	R	1	0	3.00	4	4	0	0	18	16	8	6	3	21
MINOR LEAGUE TOTALS			1	2	2.57	11	11	0	0	49	39	19	14	10	53

13. Vince Faison, of

Born: Jan. 22, 1981. **Ht.:** 6-0. **Wt.:** 180. **Bats:** L. **Throws:** R. **School:** Toombs County HS, Lyons, Ga. **Career Transactions:** Selected by Padres in first round (20th overall) of 1999 draft; signed June 4, 1999.

One of the nation's top-rated high school defensive backs, Faison would have played football at the University of Georgia had he not signed with the Padres for $1.415 million as the first of their six first-round picks in 1999. He has been compared to Cubs center-field prospect Corey Patterson, another Georgia high school product, but while Faison has similar athleticism, he lacks Patterson's power and feel for the game. Faison was ranked the No. 1 prospect in the Arizona League in his pro debut, then struggled in his first taste of full-season ball in 2000. He does have tools, including raw speed that has allowed him to steal 58 bases in 67 attempts as a pro. He also has power potential, plus the range and arm to play center field. He'll become more of a stolen base and home run threat if he can learn the strike zone. For now, he's a free swinger who tries to pull too many pitches and gets himself out. Midwest League managers didn't think he handled adversity well, so a return trip rather than a promotion to high Class A might be best at the start of 2001.

Year	Club (League)	Class	AVG	G	AB	R	H	2B	3B	HR	RBI	BB	SO	SB
1999	Padres (AZL)	R	.309	44	178	40	55	6	6	4	28	18	45	30
	Fort Wayne (Mid)	A	.208	11	48	10	10	2	0	0	1	6	18	7
2000	Fort Wayne (Mid)	A	.219	117	457	65	100	20	2	12	39	26	159	21
MINOR LEAGUE TOTALS			.242	172	683	115	165	28	8	16	68	50	222	58

14. Kevin Eberwein, 1b/3b

Born: March 30, 1977. **Ht.:** 6-4. **Wt.:** 200. **Bats:** R. **Throws:** R. **School:** University of Nevada-Las Vegas. **Career Transactions:** Selected by Padres in fifth round of 1998 draft; signed June 4, 1998.

Eberwein is in the wrong organization. He's a competent third baseman but has no chance of playing the hot corner in an organization with Phil Nevin, Sean Burroughs and Xavier Nady. Eberwein has the bat to play at first base, where he moved in 2000 to accommodate Burroughs, but the Padres have big league starter Ryan Klesko signed through 2004. And even Eberwein's calling card, power that was rated the best in the system entering 2000, was surpassed when San Diego signed Nady. Eberwein isn't a bad athlete and probably has enough arm to try the outfield, though that also is Nady's likely destination. Eberwein drastically cut down on his strikeouts last season, though he still could draw more walks and must remember that he's more effective when he uses the whole field. He'll spend 2001 in Triple-A, where he would have been promoted last August if not for an ankle injury that ended his season and kept him out of the Arizona Fall League.

Year	Club (League)	Class	AVG	G	AB	R	H	2B	3B	HR	RBI	BB	SO	SB
1998	Clinton (Mid)	A	.296	65	247	42	73	20	3	10	38	26	66	4
1999	Rancho Cuca. (Cal)	A	.259	110	417	69	108	30	4	18	69	42	139	7
	Mobile (SL)	AA	.171	10	35	5	6	1	0	1	2	3	16	0
2000	Mobile (SL)	AA	.263	100	372	57	98	16	2	18	71	45	77	2
MINOR LEAGUE TOTALS			.266	285	1071	173	285	67	9	47	180	116	298	13

15. Kevin Nicholson, ss

Born: March 29, 1976. **Ht.:** 5-10. **Wt.:** 190. **Bats:** B. **Throws:** R. **School:** Stetson University. **Career Transactions:** Selected by Padres in first round (27th overall) of 1997 draft; signed July 15, 1997.

Nicholson became the first Canadian ever drafted in the first round in 1997, and he reached the majors three years later. He has a chance to make San Diego's Opening Day roster, perhaps as a utilityman before growing into a starting role. The question is whether he's better suited for shortstop or second base. Nicholson has the arm for short, but his hands and range are just adequate for the position. The Padres need a shortstop after moving former starter Damian Jackson to second base last year. Nicholson has good gap power for a middle infielder and runs better than his stocky build might indicate. He needs to tighten his strike zone and make better contact.

Year	Club (League)	Class	AVG	G	AB	R	H	2B	3B	HR	RBI	BB	SO	SB
1997	Padres (AZL)	R	.265	7	34	7	9	1	0	2	8	2	5	0
	Rancho Cuca. (Cal)	A	.323	17	65	7	21	5	0	1	9	4	15	2
1998	Mobile (SL)	AA	.215	132	488	64	105	27	3	5	52	47	114	9
1999	Mobile (SL)	AA	.288	127	489	84	141	38	3	13	81	46	92	16
2000	Las Vegas (PCL)	AAA	.279	91	326	48	91	26	3	6	44	35	62	4
	San Diego (NL)	MAJ	.216	37	97	7	21	6	1	1	8	4	31	1
MAJOR LEAGUE TOTALS			.216	37	97	7	21	6	1	1	8	4	31	1
MINOR LEAGUE TOTALS			.262	374	1402	210	367	97	9	27	194	134	288	31

16. Nick Trzesniak, c

Born: Nov. 19, 1980. **Ht.:** 6-0. **Wt.:** 215. **Bats:** R. **Throws:** R. **School:** Andrew HS, Tinley Park, Ill. **Career Transactions:** Selected by Padres in first round (51st overall) of 1999 draft; signed July 6, 1999.

Young catchers Ben Davis and Wiki Gonzalez combined to bat just .229-8-44 with San Diego last year. If they don't hit, the Padres will have to wait a while for reinforcements. Their only legitimate catching prospects were three teenagers who spent 2000 in Rookie ball. Trzesniak, the last of the club's six first-round picks in 1999, is the best of the crop. He offers both offense and defense. He's not a speedster by any means, but he has stolen 11 bases in 14 pro attempts. Trzesniak is a solid receiver with a strong arm. While his 28 percent success rate at gunning down basestealers last year wasn't outstanding, it was significantly better than teammate Andres Pagan's 18 percent. While Trzesniak will need to make more contact in the future, his biggest problem has been staying healthy. He had a sore arm in 1999, broke his hamate bone and required surgery in the offseason, then had back problems last year. He'll probably play at Fort Wayne this year, likely splitting time with Pagan again.

Year	Club (League)	Class	AVG	G	AB	R	H	2B	3B	HR	RBI	BB	SO	SB
1999	Padres (AZL)	R	.241	29	108	17	26	3	1	0	16	14	39	7
2000	Idaho Falls (Pio)	R	.341	36	132	32	45	6	2	7	30	23	30	4
MINOR LEAGUE TOTALS			.296	65	240	49	71	9	3	7	46	37	69	11

17. Omar Falcon, c

Born: Sept. 1, 1982. **Ht.:** 6-0. **Wt.:** 190. **Bats:** R. **Throws:** R. **School:** Southridge HS, Miami. **Career Transactions:** Selected by Padres in third round of 2000 draft; signed July 6, 2000.

Falcon added to the club's catching depth when he signed as a third-round pick last June, passing up a Louisiana State scholarship. Managers rated him the Arizona League's No. 6 prospect in his debut. He's quick behind the plate and supplements a strong arm with a short release (though he threw out just 19 percent of basestealers). Offensively, Falcon uses the entire field, has power potential and knows how to take a walk. His main needs are improving his receiving skills and making better contact. Because Nick Trzesniak and Andres Pagan probably aren't ready for high Class A, Falcon probably will begin 2001 in extended spring training before reporting to Idaho Falls or short-season Eugene in June.

Year	Club (League)	Class	AVG	G	AB	R	H	2B	3B	HR	RBI	BB	SO	SB
2000	Padres (AZL)	R	.275	40	120	23	33	9	2	4	25	22	43	1
MINOR LEAGUE TOTALS			.275	40	120	23	33	9	2	4	25	22	43	1

18. Justin Germano, rhp

Born: Aug. 6, 1982. **Ht.:** 6-3. **Wt.:** 195. **Bats:** R. **Throws:** R. **School:** Claremont (Calif.) HS. **Career Transactions:** Selected by Padres in 13th round of 2000 draft; signed June 13, 2000.

Germano is similar to Junior Herndon, a lower-round high school draftee who has moved quickly through the system despite lacking overpowering velocity. Germano's fastball can reach the low 90s, though he usually pitches at 88-90 mph. His fastball appears a lot quicker because hitters can't sit on it, having to look instead for a sharp curveball that breaks straight down. He can throw his curveball for strikes in any count, and the same is true of his fastball and changeup. Germano posted an outstanding 67-9 strikeout-walk ratio in his pro debut, though he needs to learn he'll be more effective if he's not around the plate so much because he'll be less hittable. He should open his first full season in low Class A.

Year	Club (League)	Class	W	L	ERA	G	GS	CG	SV	IP	H	R	ER	BB	SO
2000	Padres (AZL)	R	5	5	4.59	17	8	0	1	67	65	36	34	9	67
MINOR LEAGUE TOTALS			5	5	4.59	17	8	0	1	67	65	36	34	9	67

19. Kory DeHaan, of

Born: July 16, 1976. **Ht.:** 6-2. **Wt.:** 187. **Bats:** L. **Throws:** R. **School:** Morningside (Iowa) College. **Career Transactions:** Selected by Pirates in seventh round of 1997 draft; signed June 5, 1997 . . . Selected by Padres from Pirates in major league Rule 5 draft, Dec. 13, 1999.

After making him a major league Rule 5 draft pick at the 1999 Winter Meetings, the Padres stashed DeHaan on the disabled list for the first three weeks of April and then kept him on their bench for the rest of the season. While that allowed San Diego to keep him, getting a total of 158 at-bats all year didn't do much for DeHaan's development. His best tool is his speed, which makes him a stolen base threat and gives him fine range in center field. He also has an average arm and gap power. How much he'll improve depends on whether he can improve his plate discipline and make more contact. DeHaan needs to play every day in Triple-A this year, after which he'll be the club's next option in center field if Mike Darr doesn't turn out to be an acceptable replacement for Ruben Rivera.

Year	Club (League)	Class	AVG	G	AB	R	H	2B	3B	HR	RBI	BB	SO	SB
1997	Erie (NY-P)	A	.239	58	205	43	49	8	6	1	18	38	43	14
1998	Augusta (SAL)	A	.314	132	475	85	149	39	8	8	75	69	114	33
1999	Lynchburg (Car)	A	.325	78	295	55	96	19	5	7	42	36	63	32
	Altoona (EL)	AA	.268	47	190	26	51	13	2	3	24	11	46	14
2000	Rancho Cuca. (Cal)	A	.214	4	14	2	3	1	0	1	1	1	4	0
	Las Vegas (PCL)	AAA	.293	10	41	7	12	4	0	0	3	2	11	3
	San Diego (NL)	MAJ	.204	90	103	19	21	7	0	2	13	5	39	4
MAJOR LEAGUE TOTALS			.204	90	103	19	21	7	0	2	13	5	39	4
MINOR LEAGUE TOTALS			.295	329	1220	218	360	84	21	20	163	157	281	96

20. Santiago Perez, ss

Born: Dec. 30, 1975. **Ht.:** 6-2. **Wt.:** 150. **Bats:** B. **Throws:** R. **Career Transactions:** Signed out of Dominican Republic by Tigers, March 10, 1993 . . . Traded by Tigers with LHP Mike Myers and RHP Rick Greene to Brewers for RHP Bryce Florie and cash, Nov. 20, 1997 . . . Traded by Brewers with a player to be named to Padres for RHP Brandon Kolb and a player to be named, Dec. 1, 2000; Brewers sent OF Chad Green to Padres for RHP Will Cunnane to complete trade (Dec. 20, 2000).

Desperately seeking a solution at shortstop, the Padres have tried to increase their options this offseason. They signed free agent Alex Arias, picked Donaldo Mendez in the major league Rule 5 draft and traded for Perez. The 2000 Triple-A World Series MVP, Perez may have the best chance to start for San Diego among the group, though he'll also have to contend with Kevin Nicholson. Perez has the arm, hands and range teams want in a shortstop. But he also has a maddening tendency to get lackadaisical in the field, contributing heavily to his 33 errors last season, including six in 20 games with Milwaukee. He encouraged the Brewers when he batted .298 with 14 homers in 1998, but those numbers were fueled by Double-A El Paso's bandbox ballpark and he hasn't approached them since. He has the speed to steal bases, though he hinders his value by chasing too many pitches and not reaching base consistently.

Year	Club (League)	Class	AVG	G	AB	R	H	2B	3B	HR	RBI	BB	SO	SB
1993	Tigers/Cards (DSL)	R	.263	58	171	28	45	6	2	0	17	20	22	17
1994	Tigers (DSL)	R	.344	60	227	54	78	7	9	2	47	32	43	20
1995	Fayetteville (SAL)	A	.238	130	425	54	101	15	1	4	44	30	98	10
1996	Lakeland (FSL)	A	.251	122	418	33	105	18	2	1	27	16	88	6
1997	Lakeland (FSL)	A	.274	111	445	66	122	20	12	4	46	20	98	21
1998	El Paso (TL)	AA	.306	107	454	73	139	20	13	11	64	28	70	21
	Louisville (IL)	AAA	.271	36	133	18	36	4	3	3	14	6	31	6
1999	Louisville (IL)	AAA	.263	108	407	57	107	23	8	7	38	31	94	21
2000	Indianapolis (IL)	AAA	.275	106	408	74	112	26	7	5	34	44	96	31
	Milwaukee (NL)	MAJ	.173	24	52	8	9	2	0	0	2	8	9	4
MAJOR LEAGUE TOTALS			.173	24	52	8	9	2	0	0	2	8	9	4
MINOR LEAGUE TOTALS			.274	838	3088	457	845	139	57	37	331	227	640	153

21. Jeremy Owens, of

Born: Dec. 9, 1976. **Ht.:** 6-1. **Wt.:** 200. **Bats:** R. **Throws:** R. **School:** Middle Tennessee State University.
Career Transactions: Selected by Padres in eighth round of 1998 draft; signed June 5, 1998.

Owens' tools are the most impressive in the system. He's the fastest baserunner and best defensive outfielder among Padres farmhands, and he has the top outfield arm. He has stolen 151 bases and been caught just 34 times as a pro, and one scout who saw him in the California League last year said Owens is the best-running big man since Bo Jackson. Owens has power potential as well. What he doesn't have and what may keep him from reaching the majors is much hitting ability. His swing needs to be overhauled. He takes walks, but he's almost too passive at the plate and falls behind in the count too often. He'll move up to Double-A in 2001, which should be a stern challenge for him.

Year	Club (League)	Class	AVG	G	AB	R	H	2B	3B	HR	RBI	BB	SO	SB
1998	Idaho Falls (Pio)	R	.278	69	284	61	79	16	4	8	52	36	81	30
1999	Fort Wayne (Mid)	A	.281	129	513	111	144	26	12	9	66	63	153	65
	Rancho Cuca. (Cal)	A	.158	9	38	2	6	1	0	0	1	1	13	2
2000	Rancho Cuca. (Cal)	A	.256	138	570	99	146	29	10	16	63	63	183	54
MINOR LEAGUE TOTALS			.267	345	1405	273	375	72	26	33	182	163	430	151

22. Steve Watkins, rhp

Born: July 19, 1978. **Ht.:** 6-4. **Wt.:** 190. **Bats:** R. **Throws:** R. **School:** Lubbock Christian (Texas) University.
Career Transactions: Selected by Padres in 16th round of 1998 draft; signed July 28, 1998.

The Padres drafted Watkins in the 15th round out of high school in 1996 and finally signed him as a 16th-rounder two years later, after he spent time at Lubbock Christian and Texas Tech. He has averaged well over a strikeout an inning as a pro, thanks to a plus curveball. Last year opponents in the hitter-friendly California League batted just .216 against him, including a .208 mark by lefthanders. Watkins doesn't have a lot going for him besides his curve and may be nothing more than a middle reliever in the majors. His fastball is average and his changeup reaches that level intermittently. His command has been shaky as a pro, and that flaw may catch up to him this year in Double-A.

Year	Club (League)	Class	W	L	ERA	G	GS	CG	SV	IP	H	R	ER	BB	SO
1998	Idaho Falls (Pio)	R	0	1	40.50	2	1	0	0	2	10	12	9	4	0
	Padres (AZL)	R	1	0	1.31	9	3	0	0	21	15	4	3	10	20
1999	Fort Wayne (Mid)	A	0	3	8.47	4	4	0	0	17	24	17	16	9	21
	Idaho Falls (Pio)	R	5	2	4.40	12	11	0	0	61	60	39	30	25	75
2000	Rancho Cuca. (Cal)	A	7	6	3.70	27	27	0	0	151	118	75	62	90	163
MINOR LEAGUE TOTALS			13	12	4.29	54	46	0	0	252	227	147	120	138	279

23. Andres Pagan, c

Born: March 18, 1981. **Ht.:** 6-4. **Wt.:** 185. **Bats:** R. **Throws:** R. **School:** Luis Munoz Marin HS, Yauco, P.R. **Career Transactions:** Selected by Padres in 18th round of 1999 draft; signed June 10, 1999.

After Pagan batted .187 in the Arizona League, the Padres not surprisingly considered his defense well ahead of his offense. Last season, he caught the hitting fever that gripped Pioneer League champion Idaho Falls—the team batted a collective .317 to lead the minors—and raised his average 125 points. A high school hurdles champ in Puerto Rico, Pagan is an athletic backstop with strong catch-and-throw skills. Basestealers had surprising success against him last year, however, succeeding on 82 percent of their attempts. Pagan gets high marks for his ability to run a pitching staff. He still has work to do offensively, such as making more contact and drawing more walks. After sharing time behind the plate with Nick Trzesniak in 2000, he likely will do so again this year at Fort Wayne.

Year	Club (League)	Class	AVG	G	AB	R	H	2B	3B	HR	RBI	BB	SO	SB
1999	Padres (AZL)	R	.187	27	91	15	17	3	0	1	6	9	25	3
2000	Idaho Falls (Pio)	R	.312	41	154	25	48	8	0	4	24	13	41	3
MINOR LEAGUE TOTALS			.265	68	245	40	65	11	0	5	30	22	66	6

24. Omar Ortiz, rhp

Born: Sept. 11, 1977. **Ht.:** 6-1. **Wt.:** 210. **Bats:** B. **Throws:** R. **School:** University of Texas-Pan American.
Career Transactions: Selected by Padres in first round (29th overall) of 1999 draft; signed June 4, 1999.

One of San Diego's six first-round picks from 1999, Ortiz has had little success since he was promoted to Class A, totally puzzling the Padres. Ortiz can touch 95 mph with his fastball, and his slider and changeup are solid average pitches. His work ethic draws praise as well. But he has an inconsistent release point, which hampers his ability to throw strikes.

And once Ortiz falls behind in the count, he tends to just lay the ball over the heart of the plate. Lefthanders hit .343 with nine homers in 181 at-bats against him last year. He'll head back to the California League and try to get himself straightened out.

Year	Club (League)	Class	W	L	ERA	G	GS	CG	SV	IP	H	R	ER	BB	SO
1999	Idaho Falls (Pio)	R	2	1	3.41	6	5	0	0	29	25	18	11	13	24
	Fort Wayne (Mid)	A	1	2	6.75	4	4	0	0	19	17	16	14	20	9
2000	Fort Wayne (Mid)	A	2	1	4.55	6	6	0	0	30	28	21	15	18	27
	Rancho Cuca. (Cal)	A	3	9	6.36	21	21	0	0	99	111	82	70	81	97
MINOR LEAGUE TOTALS			8	13	5.61	37	36	0	0	176	181	137	110	132	157

25. Mike Colangelo, of

Born: Oct. 22, 1976. **Ht.:** 6-1. **Wt.:** 185. **Bats:** R. **Throws:** R. **School:** George Mason University. **Career Transactions:** Selected by Angels in 21st round of 1997 draft; signed Aug. 19, 1997 . . . On disabled list, March 20-Oct. 3, 2000 . . . Claimed on waivers by Diamondbacks from Angels, Oct. 5, 2000 . . . Claimed on waivers by Padres from Diamondbacks, Oct. 17, 2000.

Colangelo needed just 442 at-bats before reaching the majors in June 1999. But he hasn't played a pro game since. Colangelo, who missed half of 1998 with an ankle injury, tore ligaments in an outfield collison with Reggie Williams in his first big league game and was lost for the season. He reinjured the thumb that winter in Venezuela, then tore the labrum in his right shoulder in spring training last year, necessitating season-ending surgery. The Angels removed him from their 40-man roster in October, when he was claimed on waivers by the Diamondbacks, who lost him on waivers 12 days later to the Padres. If he's healthy, Colangelo could serve as a bat off the big league bench or possibly something more. He's an adequate left fielder who lacks the home run power teams want out of the position, but he can drive the ball to the gaps and consistently gets on base.

Year	Club (League)	Class	AVG	G	AB	R	H	2B	3B	HR	RBI	BB	SO	SB
1998	Cedar Rapids (Mid)	A	.277	22	83	13	23	8	0	4	8	12	16	5
	Lake Elsinore (Cal)	A	.379	36	145	33	55	11	3	5	21	13	24	2
1999	Erie (EL)	AA	.339	28	109	24	37	10	3	1	13	14	22	3
	Edmonton (PCL)	AAA	.362	26	105	13	38	7	1	0	9	13	18	2
	Anaheim (AL)	MAJ	.500	1	2	0	1	0	0	0	0	1	0	0
2000							Did Not Play—Injured							
MAJOR LEAGUE TOTALS			.500	1	2	0	1	0	0	0	0	1	0	0
MINOR LEAGUE TOTALS			.346	112	442	83	153	36	7	10	51	52	80	12

26. Christian Berroa, ss

Born: April 27, 1979. **Ht.:** 5-11. **Wt.:** 150. **Bats:** B. **Throws:** R. **Career Transactions:** Signed out of Dominican Republic by Padres, April 29, 1996.

The Padres spent 2000 acquiring as many shortstops as possible: Alex Arias (major league free agent), Cleatus Davidson (minor league free agent), J.J. Furmaniak (amateur draft), Donaldo Mendez (major league Rule 5 draft), Santiago Perez and Cesar Saba (trades). Before that, Berroa was unquestionably the best pure shortstop in the system, and San Diego still likes his potential. He has solid defensive tools and can make the tough plays, but he needs to be more consistent on the routine ones after making 36 errors in 129 games last year. He's aggressive offensively and defensively. He makes good contact and can steal an occasional base, though he has little power and needs more patience. Except for Furmaniak, who hasn't played above Rookie ball, none of the Padres' shortstops has distinguished himself offensively. If Berroa can do that at Double-A in 2001, he'll have a leg up on his competition.

Year	Club (League)	Class	AVG	G	AB	R	H	2B	3B	HR	RBI	BB	SO	SB
1996	Cubs/Padres (DSL)	R	.256	65	215	29	55	9	0	4	23	10	35	4
1997	Padres (DSL)	R	.352	68	273	51	96	20	4	6	27	6	31	14
1998	Padres (AZL)	R	.319	53	207	33	66	22	2	1	33	4	38	8
1999	Fort Wayne (Mid)	A	.240	119	442	49	106	12	3	4	40	14	71	25
2000	Rancho Cuca. (Cal)	A	.270	130	488	76	132	19	4	4	50	28	62	30
MINOR LEAGUE TOTALS			.280	435	1625	238	455	82	13	19	173	62	237	81

27. Oliver Perez, lhp

Born: Aug. 15, 1981. **Ht.:** 6-3. **Wt.:** 160. **Bats:** L. **Throws:** L. **Career Transactions:** Signed out of Mexico by Padres, March 4, 1999 . . . Loaned by Padres to Yucatan (Mexican), June 2-22, 2000 . . . Loaned to Yucatan, July 18-Sept. 6, 2000.

The Padres have a working agreement with the Mexican League's Yucatan Lions, and let Perez, a native Mexican, pitch there for most of 2000. He held his own against much more experienced hitters, limiting them to a .245 average and three homers in 145 at-bats. Perez has good stuff for a lefthander and is projectable. He already touches 90 mph, and he could throw harder once he adds weight to his skinny frame. He has put on 15 pounds since signing in July 1999. His curveball and changeup are average at times but need more consistency. He must learn to work down in the strike zone. Perez could open 2001 at Fort Wayne, or San Diego could be more patient and send him to its new short-season Eugene affiliate.

Year	Club (League)	Class	W	L	ERA	G	GS	CG	SV	IP	H	R	ER	BB	SO
1999	Padres (AZL)	R	1	2	5.08	15	2	0	3	28	28	20	16	16	37
2000	Yucatan (Mex)	AAA	3	2	4.36	11	6	0	1	43	39	24	21	17	37
	Idaho Falls (Pio)	R	3	1	4.07	5	5	0	0	24	24	14	11	9	27
MINOR LEAGUE TOTALS			7	5	4.50	31	13	0	4	96	91	58	48	42	101

28. Mike Thompson, rhp

Born: Nov. 6, 1980. **Ht.:** 6-4. **Wt.:** 185. **Bats:** R. **Throws:** R. **School:** Lamar (Colo.) HS. **Career Transactions:** Selected by Padres in fifth round of 1999 draft; signed June 24, 1999.

Because the Padres drafted four pitchers in the first round of the 1999 draft, Thompson received little notice. His 8-14, 5.87 record as a pro hasn't garnered much attention either, though he did lead Pioneer League champion Idaho Falls with six victories last summer. He's a product of Lamar (Colo.) High, the alma mater of the Astros' Scott Elarton. Thompson has better stuff than his statistics would indicate, as he's already capable of throwing 90-93 mph with a loose, easy arm action. He's still trying to put the rest of his game together. He's working on a slider, curveball and changeup and has been vulnerable to walks and home runs. He got a brief trial at Fort Wayne to begin 2000, and he'll head back there again this year.

Year	Club (League)	Class	W	L	ERA	G	GS	CG	SV	IP	H	R	ER	BB	SO
1999	Padres (AZL)	R	1	7	6.09	13	13	0	0	65	78	52	44	27	62
2000	Fort Wayne (Mid)	A	1	3	5.13	6	6	0	0	26	28	19	15	15	17
	Idaho Falls (Pio)	R	6	4	5.94	14	14	0	0	73	99	56	48	30	52
MINOR LEAGUE TOTALS			8	14	5.87	33	33	0	0	164	205	127	107	72	131

29. Mewelde Moore, of

Born: July 24, 1982. **Ht.:** 6-0. **Wt.:** 195. **Bats:** R. **Throws:** R. **School:** Belaire HS, Baton Rouge. **Career Transactions:** Selected by Padres in fourth round of 2000 draft; signed Sept. 5, 2000.

Moore already is well on his way to becoming a star—in college football. He averaged 89 yards rushing at Tulane last fall, finishing just four yards shy of leading all NCAA Division I-A freshmen. He was one of the best athletes available in the 2000 draft, lasting until the fourth round only because of his gridiron commitment. He signed for $250,000, taking less money so he could continue to play football. He has the tools to become an outstanding center fielder. Moore runs a 6.39-second 60-yard dash and unlike many speedsters, he has hitting ability. He should get in a couple of months with one of San Diego's short-season clubs this summer before returning to Tulane in August for football practice.

Year	Club (League)	Class	AVG	G	AB	R	H	2B	3B	HR	RBI	BB	SO	SB
2000			Did Not Play—Signed 2001 Contract											

30. J.J. Trujillo, rhp

Born: Oct. 9, 1975. **Ht.:** 6-0. **Wt.:** 180. **Bats:** R. **Throws:** R. **School:** Dallas Baptist University. **Career Transactions:** Signed by independent Johnstown (Frontier), 1999 . . . Signed by Padres, Oct. 12, 1999.

Trujillo hopes to follow in the footsteps of Brian Tollberg, who started his pro career in the independent Frontier League and climbed to San Diego last season. A second baseman/righthander at Dallas Baptist, Trujillo posted a 1.58 ERA and finished third in the Frontier League with 14 saves in 1999. He was sensational in his first year in Organized Baseball, leading minor league relievers in hits per nine innings (4.7) and saves while setting a Midwest League mark in the latter category. Interestingly, Trujillo performed so poorly in minor league spring training that he feared he would be released. A submariner, he has more velocity (83-84 mph on his sinker) and control than most pitchers who throw from that angle. His slider eats up righthanders because they can't pick it up, and they hit just .128 against him with 61 strikeouts in 149 at-bats last year. He also throws a changeup that's improving. It's almost impossible to put the ball in the air against Trujillo, who had an unfathomable 103-23 ground ball-fly ball ratio in 2000. He could skip a level this season and pitch in Double-A.

Year	Club (League)	Class	W	L	ERA	G	GS	CG	SV	IP	H	R	ER	BB	SO
1999	Johnstown (Fron)	IND	1	3	1.58	39	0	0	14	46	33	11	8	21	60
2000	Fort Wayne (Mid)	A	3	4	1.33	63	0	0	42	75	39	16	11	25	85
MINOR LEAGUE TOTALS			3	4	1.33	63	0	0	42	75	39	16	11	25	85

San Francisco
Giants

By John Manuel

Perhaps now that Pacific Bell Park is a reality, people will stop taking pity on the Giants. Last year, 3.3 million fans poured into Pac Bell, widely recognized as one of the sport's new showplaces. The National League West champions had the best record in baseball for 2000 and have a deep, young rotation back for 2001, along with closer Robb Nen and set-up man Felix Rodriguez. Second baseman Jeff Kent won the NL MVP, and Barry Bonds remains Barry Bonds. Manager Dusty Baker—retained in the offseason with a lucrative contract—has three young power righthanders in Livan Hernandez, Joe Nathan and Russ Ortiz to complement lefthander Shawn Estes.

San Francisco has at least two more high-ceiling arms on the way in righthanders Jerome Williams and Kurt Ainsworth. The farm system, which has had to accentuate mature, predominantly college players because of its structure in the past, added a Rookie-level Arizona League affiliate in 2000 and will feature a low Class A team in Hagerstown (South Atlantic) this year.

The new structure will cost more than having two California League affiliates because of travel. Yet more important, it should allow the Giants to take more chances on high-ceiling, raw athletes, such as outfielder Arturo McDowell and lefthander Chris Jones, who have had their development and confidence hurt by having to jump to the Cal League ahead of their time.

For financial reasons, the Giants lost right fielder Ellis Burks to free agency. Wisely, the organization chose not to overpay light-hitting third baseman Bill Mueller, trading him instead to the Cubs. San Francisco will turn to home-grown players Armando Rios (right field) and Pedro Feliz (third base) as replacements, and general manager Brian Sabean has proven adept at adding veteran help in midseason trades if the need arises.

With Bonds (36), Kent and first baseman J.T. Snow (both 33 on Opening Day) aging, the Giants must focus on developing a new round of players around whom to build the offense. They have three third basemen in their top 10 and catching depth in the organization, but sorely lack middle infielders (hence a new contract for shortstop Rich Aurilia) and power-hitting outfielders.

The new ballpark hasn't turned the organization into a large-revenue club yet because owner Peter McGowan's group still has to service the debt it took to build Pac Bell. One sign (other than losing Burks) the Giants need cash: An Xtreme Football League team will play games at Pac Bell this spring.

OrganizationOverview

General manager: Brian Sabean. **Farm director:** Dick Tidrow. **Scouting director:** Dick Tidrow.

2000 PERFORMANCE

Class	Team	League	W	L	Pct.	Finish*	Manager
Majors	San Francisco	National	97	65	.599	1st (16)	Dusty Baker
Triple-A	Fresno Grizzlies	Pacific Coast	57	84	.404	15th (16)	Shane Turner
Double-A	Shreveport Captains	Texas	58	81	.417	8th (8)	Bill Hayes
High A	San Jose Giants	California	53	87	.379	9th (10)	Keith Comstock
High A	#Bakersfield Blaze	California	80	60	.571	2nd (10)	Lenn Sakata
Short-season	Salem-Keizer Volcanoes	Northwest	36	40	.474	7th (8)	Fred Stanley
Rookie	AZL Giants	Arizona	22	32	.407	t-6th (9)	Lemmie Miller
OVERALL 2000 MINOR LEAGUE RECORD			306	383	.444	29th (30)	

*Finish in overall standings (No. of teams in league). #Affiliate will be in Hagerstown (South Atlantic/low A) in 2001.

ORGANIZATION LEADERS

BATTING
*AVG	Sean McGowan, San Jose/Shreveport	.330
R	Joe Jester, San Jose/Fresno	95
H	Sean McGowan, San Jose/Shreveport	173
TB	Pedro Feliz, Fresno	287
2B	Tony Torcato, San Jose/Shreveport	37
3B	**Doug Clark**, Shreveport	7
HR	Pedro Feliz, Fresno	33
RBI	Sean McGowan, San Jose/Shreveport	118
BB	Brett Casper, Bakersfield	97
SO	Brett Casper, Bakersfield	146
SB	Carlos Valderrama, Bakersfield	54

PITCHING
W	Joe Horgan, San Jose/Shreveport	14
L	Jeremy Cunningham, San Jose	14
	Jeff Verplancke, San Jose/Fresno	14
#ERA	Ben Weber, Fresno	2.42
G	Robbie Crabtree, Fresno	63
CG	Several tied at	1
SV	Jason Bullard, Bakersfield	30
IP	Joe Horgan, San Jose/Shreveport	172
BB	Chris Jones, San Jose	85
SO	**Ryan Vogelsong**, Shreveport	147

*Minimum 250 at-bats. #Minimum 75 innings.

TOP PROSPECTS OF THE DECADE

1991	Royce Clayton, ss
1992	Royce Clayton, ss
1993	Calvin Murray, of
1994	Salomon Torres, rhp
1995	J.R. Phillips, 1b
1996	Shawn Estes, lhp
1997	Joe Fontenot, rhp
1998	Jason Grilli, rhp
1999	Jason Grilli, rhp
2000	Kurt Ainsworth, rhp

TOP DRAFT PICKS OF THE DECADE

1991	Steve Whitaker, lhp
1992	Calvin Murray, of
1993	Steve Soderstrom, rhp
1994	Dante Powell, of
1995	Joe Fontenot, rhp
1996	*Matt White, rhp
1997	Jason Grilli, rhp
1998	Tony Torcato, 3b
1999	Kurt Ainsworth, rhp
2000	Boof Bonser, rhp

*Did not sign.

Clark   **Vogelsong**

BEST TOOLS

Best Hitter for Average	Tony Torcato
Best Power Hitter	Damon Minor
Fastest Baserunner	Arturo McDowell
Best Fastball	Kevin Joseph
Best Breaking Ball	Jason Farmer
Best Control	Kurt Ainsworth
Best Defensive Catcher	Yorvit Torrealba
Best Defensive Infielder	Cody Ransom
Best Infield Arm	Cody Ransom
Best Defensive Outfielder	Arturo McDowell
Best Outfield Arm	Brett Casper

2004 LINEUP

Catcher	Bobby Estalella
First Base	Tony Torcato
Second Base	Jeff Kent
Third Base	Lance Niekro
Shortstop	Rich Aurilia
Left Field	Barry Bonds
Center Field	Carlos Valderrama
Right Field	Armando Rios
No. 1 Starter	Jerome Williams
No. 2 Starter	Russ Ortiz
No. 3 Starter	Shawn Estes
No. 4 Starter	Livan Hernandez
No. 5 Starter	Kurt Ainsworth
Closer	Kevin Joseph

ALL-TIME LARGEST BONUSES

Jason Grilli, 1997	$1,875,000
Osvaldo Fernandez, 1996	1,300,000
Kurt Ainsworth, 1999	1,300,000
Boof Bonser, 2000	1,245,000
Tony Torcato, 1998	975,000

DraftAnalysis

2000 Draft

Best Pro Debut: Three players stood out in the short-season Northwest League: 3B Lance Niekro (2) hit .362-5-44 and won the batting title. RHP Jason Farmer (14), whose best pitch is his curveball, led the league with a 1.62 ERA. RHP Luke Anderson (8), who has a projectable fastball and a nasty splitter, topped the NWL with 12 saves. He also had a 1.45 ERA, 55 strikeouts in 31 innings and a .173 opponent batting average.

Best Athlete: OF Bryan Carter (42) has the speed and instincts for center and the arm for right. He's also a better hitter than the Giants originally thought. OFs Jason Pekar (30) and Mark Walker (40) offer a variety of tools, though they're both raw.

Best Hitter: Niekro's swing may be better suited for wood than aluminum. He nearly won the Cape Cod League triple crown in 1999, then added the NWL batting crown after ditching metal for good. His instincts are a tribute to his baseball bloodlines. He even has a knuckleball that would make his father Joe and uncle Phil proud.

Best Raw Power: Niekro. OF Danny Trumble (25) has big-time pop as well but isn't nearly as polished.

Fastest Runner: OF Jason Ellison (22) and Carter are above-average runners with base-stealing aptitude.

Best Defensive Player: Trey Lunsford (33) is an athletic catcher with good catch-and-throw skills and a warrior mindset.

Best Fastball: RHP **Boof Bonser** (1)

throws in the mid-90s and can blow the ball by hitters up in the strike zone but will require patience to develop. After taking Niekro in the second round, San Francisco loaded up on above-average arms in RHPs Brion Treadway (3), Kyle Gross (5) and Chad Ashlock (6) plus LHPs Ryan Hannaman (4) and Eric Threets (7).

MEL BAILEY

Bonser

Most Intriguing Background: In addition to Niekro's notable bloodlines, Gross is the son of former big league third baseman Wayne. SS Lou Colletti's (48) father Nick is an assistant GM for the Giants, while C Nick Conte's (49) dad Stan is the club's trainer. Bonser goes to the top of any list of the best names in baseball.

Closest To The Majors: Niekro has a chance to start 2001 at Double-A.

Best Late-Round Pick: The Giants are optimistic about Trumble, Lunsford and Carter.

The One Who Got Away: C Justin Knoedler (13), who has some power, is attending Miami (Ohio). He was the junior college Division II player of the year in 2000.

Assessment: Several teams thought Bonser was a reach in the first round, but Niekro may have been a steal with the 61st overall pick. As usual, the Giants targeted pitching, though they like several of their late-round position players.

1999 Draft

With two first-round choices, the Giants plucked a pair of premium starters in RHPs Kurt Ainsworth and Jerome Williams, who are also their two best prospects. 1B Sean McGowan (3) might be J.T. Snow's successor in a couple of years. **Grade: A–**

1998 Draft

San Francisco made good use of four of its five first-rounders. 3B Tony Torcato, OF Arturo McDowell and LHP Jeff Urban are among the team's top prospects. RHP Nate Bump brought Livan Hernandez in a trade. Only LHP Chris Jones hasn't worked out. RHPs Ryan Vogelsong (5) and Jake Esteves (6) round out a solid draft. **Grade: B**

1997 Draft

The Giants traded RHPs Jason Grilli (1) and Scott Linebrink (2) to get Hernandez and Doug Henry, respectively. The best players remaining are mid-level prospects, led by LHP Jeff Andra (2), RHP Kevin Joseph (6) and OF Brett Casper (8). **Grade: C**

1996 Draft

RHP Matt White (1) fled as a loophole free agent, while SS Mike Caruso (2) and LHP Ken Vining (4) were used in the White Flag trade with the White Sox. 1B Damon Minor (12) is the only player who might contribute in San Francisco. **Grade: D**

Note: Draft analysis prepared by Jim Callis. Numbers in parentheses indicate draft rounds.

. . . Williams' athletic ability and stuff draw comparisons to a young Dwight Gooden.

Jerome Williams rhp

Born: Dec. 4, 1981.
Ht.: 6-3. **Wt.:** 190.
Bats: R. **Throws:** R.
School: Waipahu HS, Honolulu.
Career Transactions: Selected by Giants in first round of 1999 draft (39th overall); signed July 10, 1999.

Before Justin Wayne went fifth overall in 2000, Williams was the highest-drafted native Hawaiian ever. While Wayne eclipsed his draft status, he doesn't eclipse Williams as a prospect. He went 39th overall the year before and remained the earliest-drafted prep player from the islands. He dominated Hawaii's high school ranks, posting a 0.30 ERA with 116 strikeouts in 65 innings as a senior. In one game, he pitched a no-hitter while hitting three home runs, and he concluded his career with 20 strikeouts in a playoff victory. California-based scout Darren Wittcke made the trip to Hawaii to scout Williams, saw him throw 95 mph with a good slider, and persuaded the Giants to pull the trigger.

Williams' athletic ability and stuff draw comparisons to a young Dwight Gooden from Giants officials. Class A California League hitters batted just .200 against Williams in his first full pro season, and he was just 18 when he pitched in the Double-A Texas League playoffs for Shreveport. He lost a 1-0 decision to Wichita but gave up just two hits, two walks and one run in seven innings. The Giants still don't know how hard he'll throw eventually. Just throwing on the side or trying to throw strikes, he throws 91 mph. When he needs it, he dials up to 94 mph and probably has another 3-4 mph to add. Combine its velocity, potential, life and his ability to throw it for strikes, and Williams' fastball is the best in the system. He was 180 pounds when drafted, and he might be 215-220 when he gets done growing. Williams also throws a solid changeup, slider and curveball. He has a smooth, sound delivery that he repeats well, and he's an excellent fielder. Despite the poker face he shows on the mound, Williams gets up for big games, which he proved in the playoffs.

The Giants don't do a good job hiding their glee over Williams' development. Sometimes his curveball gets slow and a bit too big, but it's nothing that won't improve with experience. The organization has been careful with his pitch counts, and Williams averaged less than six innings a start in 2000. As he moves up, the Giants will stretch him out and test his durability. Williams ranks among the best prospects in baseball, not just in the system. He passed Kurt Ainsworth, who would be a No. 1 prospect in several other organizations, by showing a higher ceiling in 2000. Don't look for him to pass Ainsworth on the way to the big leagues, however. The Giants would love Williams to get a full year of Double-A in 2001.

Year	Club (League)	Class	W	L	ERA	G	GS	CG	SV	IP	H	R	ER	BB	SO
1999	Salem-Keizer (NWL)	A	1	1	2.19	7	7	1	0	37	29	13	9	11	34
2000	San Jose (Cal)	A	7	6	2.94	23	19	0	0	126	89	53	41	48	115
MINOR LEAGUE TOTALS			**8**	**7**	**2.76**	**30**	**26**	**1**	**0**	**163**	**118**	**66**	**50**	**59**	**149**

2. Kurt Ainsworth, rhp

MEL BAILEY

Born: Sept. 9, 1978. **Ht.:** 6-3. **Wt.:** 185. **Bats:** R. **Throws:** R. **School:** Louisiana State University. **Career Transactions:** Selected by Giants in first round (24th overall) of 1999 draft; signed June 17, 1999.

As the 24th overall pick in the 1999 draft, Ainsworth became the first player drafted that high after major arm surgery. He missed a year in college after Tommy John surgery in 1997 and had pitched just eight innings for Louisiana State before a workhorse 1999 season that ended with first-team All-America honors. He won both of his starts for Team USA in the Olympics. Ainsworth throws a 92-94 mph fastball with good movement, and supplements it with a tight slider and good curveball. The Giants love his makeup. He pitches well under pressure and is intelligent, on and off the mound. Sometimes he can be a little too fine, and he needs to pitch more aggressively inside. He answered questions about his durability by ending a long season with a strong Olympic performance. Depth in the big league rotation has the organization hoping it can bring Ainsworth and Jerome Williams along at their own pace, with Ainsworth ticketed for Triple-A in 2001.

Year	Club (League)	Class	W	L	ERA	G	GS	CG	SV	IP	H	R	ER	BB	SO
1999	Salem-Keizer (NWL)	A	3	3	1.61	10	10	1	0	45	34	18	8	18	64
2000	Shreveport (TL)	AA	10	9	3.30	28	28	0	0	158	138	67	58	63	130
MINOR LEAGUE TOTALS			13	12	2.93	38	38	1	0	203	172	85	66	81	194

3. Tony Torcato, 3b

JOHN SPEAR

Born: Oct. 25, 1979. **Ht.:** 6-1. **Wt.:** 195. **Bats:** L. **Throws:** R. **School:** Woodland (Calif.) HS. **Career Transactions:** Selected by Giants in first round (19th overall) of 1998 draft; signed June 3, 1998.

Despite right shoulder surgery that forced him to play half of 1999 as a DH, Torcato's bat has established him as a prospect. Torcato has the best swing in the organization, one that sprays line drives to all parts of the field. California League managers walked him intentionally eight times, tops in the league. The organization is confident he will develop power as he gets stronger. He runs surprisingly well and has good instincts on the bases. His inexperience and injuries have left him flailing at the hot corner, though. He has changed his throwing stroke and rarely releases the ball from the same point twice. Staying healthy would help. He will start the year at Double-A Shreveport unless he has a big spring. His progress on defense will determine if he takes his potent bat to left field or first base.

Year	Club (League)	Class	AVG	G	AB	R	H	2B	3B	HR	RBI	BB	SO	SB
1998	Salem-Keizer (NWL)	A	.291	59	220	31	64	15	2	3	43	14	38	4
1999	Bakersfield (Cal)	A	.291	110	422	50	123	25	0	4	58	30	67	2
2000	San Jose (Cal)	A	.324	119	490	77	159	37	2	7	88	41	62	19
	Shreveport (TL)	AA	.500	2	8	1	4	0	0	0	2	0	1	0
MINOR LEAGUE TOTALS			.307	290	1140	159	350	77	4	14	191	85	168	25

4. Lance Niekro, 3b

FRANK RAGSDALE

Born: Jan. 29, 1979. **Ht.:** 6-3. **Wt.:** 210. **Bats:** R. **Throws:** R. **School:** Florida Southern College. **Career Transactions:** Selected by Giants in second round of 2000 draft; signed July 3, 2000.

The son of former big leaguer Joe and nephew of Hall of Famer Phil projected as a first-round pick after nearly winning the Cape Cod League triple crown in 1999. He even showed off the family knuckleball in an emergency relief appearance. Persistent shoulder problems, though, and a longer swing short-circuited Niekro's power last spring, so he slipped to the second round. But his short, compact swing makes him the rare hitter who hits better with wood than with aluminum. Despite a groin injury that slowed him for the first half of the season, he won the short-season Northwest League batting title. He showed the arm, hands and power to be a big league third baseman. The Giants want Niekro to get stronger and in better shape to help him avoid injuries. With his makeup and intelligence, that won't be a problem. The Giants are confident Niekro could make the jump to Double-A if needed and if Tony Torcato has the kind of spring that would put him in Fresno.

Year	Club (League)	Class	AVG	G	AB	R	H	2B	3B	HR	RBI	BB	SO	SB
2000	Salem-Keizer (NWL)	A	.362	49	196	27	71	14	4	5	44	11	25	2
MINOR LEAGUE TOTALS			.362	49	196	27	71	14	4	5	44	11	25	2

5. Ryan Vogelsong, rhp

Born: July 22, 1977. **Ht.:** 6-3. **Wt.:** 195. **Bats:** R. **Throws:** R. **School:** Kutztown (Pa.) University. **Career Transactions:** Selected by Giants in fifth round of 1998 draft; signed June 7, 1998.

Vogelsong's gangly 160-pound frame out of high school detoured him to Kutztown, an NCAA Division II program. He grew and is still growing, having added an inch and 15 pounds of muscle since being drafted. After battling tendinitis early in his career, he came back strong in 2000 and pitched well in the Arizona Fall League. He led the Texas League in strikeouts when he was promoted to San Francisco last year. The Giants like Vogelsong's stuff as much as Kurt Ainsworth's. His fastball has similar velocity (92-94 mph) and life when he pitches to both sides of the plate. He has a solid curveball, and his hard slider is effective against lefthanders. He added a changeup that has developed nicely. He lacks Ainsworth's polish, but so do most Double-A pitchers. Vogelsong gets stubborn with his curveball, which he thinks is his best pitch, while the organization prefers his slider. He will join Ainsworth at Fresno, and figures to slot behind Jerome Williams and Ainsworth in a future rotation, and has the stuff to become a reliever if the rotation gets too crowded.

Year	Club (League)	Class	W	L	ERA	G	GS	CG	SV	IP	H	R	ER	BB	SO
1998	Salem-Keizer (NWL)	A	6	1	1.77	10	10	0	0	56	37	15	11	16	66
	San Jose (Cal)	A	0	0	7.58	4	4	0	0	19	23	16	16	4	26
1999	San Jose (Cal)	A	4	4	2.45	13	13	0	0	70	37	26	19	27	86
	Shreveport (TL)	AA	0	2	7.31	6	6	0	0	28	40	25	23	15	23
2000	Shreveport (TL)	AA	6	10	4.23	27	27	1	0	155	153	82	73	69	147
	San Francisco (NL)	MAJ	0	0	0.00	4	0	0	0	6	4	0	0	2	6
MAJOR LEAGUE TOTALS			0	0	0.00	4	0	0	0	6	4	0	0	2	6
MINOR LEAGUE TOTALS			16	17	3.90	60	60	0	0	328	290	164	142	131	348

6. Sean McGowan, 1b

Born: May 15, 1977. **Ht.:** 6-6. **Wt.:** 240. **Bats:** R. **Throws:** R. **School:** Boston College. **Career Transactions:** Selected by Giants in third round of 1999 draft; signed June 7, 1999.

McGowan's big frame and athletic ability attracted the interest of football programs such as Boston College, Miami, Notre Dame, Penn State and Syracuse. He wound up at Boston College for baseball, where he led the Big East Conference in batting and home runs as a junior. He led the Giants organization in average, hits and RBIs last year. He combines the power of a man his size with a smooth, compact swing uncommon for a big power hitter. He has shown the ability to hit the ball to all fields and should hit for more power as he learns to pull the ball. McGowan has athletic ability but hasn't put in the work to be a good defensive first baseman. The Giants would like to see him be a little more selective at the plate, drawing a few more walks and turning on pitches to put his tremendous power to use. With big league veteran J.T. Snow getting older, the Giants have possible successors in McGowan and Damon Minor, or possibly Tony Torcato. McGowan, who will get a full season at Double-A in 2001, is three years younger than Minor.

Year	Club (League)	Class	AVG	G	AB	R	H	2B	3B	HR	RBI	BB	SO	SB
1999	Salem-Keizer (NWL)	A	.335	63	257	40	86	12	1	15	62	20	56	3
	San Jose (Cal)	A	.375	2	8	1	3	1	0	0	1	0	3	0
2000	San Jose (Cal)	A	.327	114	456	58	149	32	2	12	106	43	71	4
	Shreveport (TL)	AA	.348	18	69	5	24	4	0	0	12	1	8	0
MINOR LEAGUE TOTALS			.332	197	790	104	262	49	3	27	181	64	138	7

7. Damon Minor, 1b

Born: Jan. 5, 1974. **Ht.:** 6-7. **Wt.:** 230. **Bats:** L. **Throws:** L. **School:** University of Oklahoma. **Career Transactions:** Selected by Giants in 12th round of 1996 draft; signed June 6, 1996.

Minor's twin brother Ryan got more of the attention coming out of Oklahoma—where they won the 1994 College World Series as teammates of Giants righthander Russ Ortiz. But Damon has since passed his brother as a prospect thanks to his better plate discipline and ability to put his power to use. Minor has the best raw power in the organization. His confidence blossomed at Fresno in 2000, where the small park and the presence of veteran Jalal Leach helped him develop the discipline and shorter swing to make use of his power. While the Giants love Minor's power, they describe him as a stereotypical American League player. His defensive shortcomings at first base stand out in contrast to slick-fielding San Francisco incumbent J.T. Snow. Minor has little speed either. The Giants won't hesitate to use him should something happen to Snow, but Minor's chances for advancement likely would be better in another organization.

Year	Club (League)	Class	AVG	G	AB	R	H	2B	3B	HR	RBI	BB	SO	SB
1996	Bellingham (NWL)	A	.242	75	269	44	65	11	1	12	55	47	86	0
1997	Bakersfield (Cal)	A	.289	140	532	98	154	34	1	31	99	87	143	2
1998	Shreveport (TL)	AA	.239	81	289	39	69	11	1	14	52	30	51	1
	San Jose (Cal)	A	.284	48	176	26	50	10	1	7	36	28	40	0
1999	Shreveport (TL)	AA	.273	136	473	76	129	33	4	20	82	80	115	1
2000	Fresno (PCL)	AAA	.290	133	482	84	140	27	1	30	106	87	97	0
	San Francisco (NL)	MAJ	.444	10	9	3	4	0	0	3	6	2	1	0
MAJOR LEAGUE TOTALS			.444	10	9	3	4	0	0	3	6	2	1	0
MINOR LEAGUE TOTALS			.273	613	2221	367	607	126	9	114	430	359	532	4

8. Pedro Feliz, 3b

RODGER WOOD

Born: April 27, 1977. **Ht.:** 6-1. **Wt.:** 195. **Bats:** R. **Throws:** R. **Career Transactions:** Signed out of Dominican Republic by Giants, Feb. 7, 1994.

Feliz has come a long way from the skinny kid who hit .193 with no extra-base hits in the Rookie-level Arizona League in 1994. He took advantage of hitter-friendly Beiden Field to post a career year at Fresno and had a strong winter in the Dominican League. He finished fourth in the minors in home runs and was rated the best defensive third baseman in the Pacific Coast League. Feliz' power is rivaled only by Minor, who dwarfs him physically. The key to unlocking that power was plate discipline. Once he stopped putting himself in pitcher's counts, he was able to use his short swing and strong wrists to his advantage. He likely won't succeed against better pitching without improved pitch selection. He has solid tools defensively at third base, including a strong arm and good footwork. With Bill Mueller traded to the Cubs, Feliz has a chance to win the starting job in San Francisco. At worst, he'll share time with Russ Davis.

Year	Club (League)	Class	AVG	G	AB	R	H	2B	3B	HR	RBI	BB	SO	SB
1994	Giants (AZL)	R	.193	38	119	7	23	0	0	0	3	2	20	2
1995	Bellingham (NWL)	A	.274	43	113	14	31	2	1	0	16	7	33	1
1996	Burlington (Mid)	A	.265	93	321	36	85	12	2	5	36	18	65	5
1997	Bakersfield (Cal)	A	.272	135	515	59	140	25	4	14	56	23	90	5
1998	Shreveport (TL)	AA	.264	100	364	39	96	23	2	12	50	9	62	0
	Fresno (PCL)	AAA	.429	3	7	1	3	1	0	1	3	1	0	0
1999	Shreveport (TL)	AA	.253	131	491	52	124	24	6	13	77	19	90	4
2000	Fresno (PCL)	AAA	.298	128	503	85	150	34	2	33	105	30	94	1
	San Francisco (NL)	MAJ	.286	8	7	1	2	0	0	0	0	0	1	0
MAJOR LEAGUE TOTALS			.286	8	7	1	2	0	0	0	0	0	1	0
MINOR LEAGUE TOTALS			.268	671	2433	293	652	121	17	78	346	109	454	18

9. Carlos Valderrama, of

Born: Nov. 30, 1977. **Ht.:** 5-11. **Wt.:** 175. **Bats:** R. **Throws:** R. **Career Transactions:** Signed out of Venezuela by Giants, Feb. 23, 1995.

The Giants' efforts in Latin America took a huge hit with the loss of Luis Rosa, who resigned in 1997 after being accused of demanding sexual favors from Latin players in return for a chance to play for the team. Rosa signed both Pedro Feliz and Valderrama. Valderrama battled arm, back and leg injuries in 1998-99 before putting it all together with a complete, healthy season in the California League. He is the closest thing the Giants have to a five-tool prospect. When healthy and confident, he has shown good bat speed, a plus arm, the speed to be a basestealing force, and the range and savvy to play center field. Valderrama's slight build makes him injury-prone, and the Giants weren't always convinced he wanted to excel badly enough. Defensively, he has the tools to play center field, but his performance has been erratic, especially with his routes to the ball and fundamentals like hitting the cutoff man. He is the top outfield prospect in the organization but has just one solid full season under his belt. If Arturo McDowell, a superior center fielder, joins him in Double-A this year, Valderrama might move to right field.

Year	Club (League)	Class	AVG	G	AB	R	H	2B	3B	HR	RBI	BB	SO	SB
1995	Giants (DSL)	R	.228	22	57	7	13	1	0	0	4	6	10	1
1996	Giants (DSL)	R	.223	46	166	29	37	4	1	0	11	29	24	26
1997	Salem-Keizer (NWL)	A	.319	41	138	21	44	7	3	3	28	12	29	22
1998	Salem-Keizer (NWL)	A	.345	7	29	5	10	1	0	0	4	1	7	4
1999	San Jose (Cal)	A	.256	26	90	12	23	2	0	0	12	4	19	8
	Salem-Keizer (NWL)	A	.291	40	134	27	39	3	1	2	18	12	34	17
2000	Bakersfield (Cal)	A	.315	121	435	78	137	21	5	13	81	39	96	54
MINOR LEAGUE TOTALS			.289	303	1049	179	303	39	10	18	158	103	219	132

10. Jeff Urban, lhp

Born: Jan. 25, 1977. **Ht.:** 6-8. **Wt.:** 215. **Bats:** R. **Throws:** L. **School:** Ball State University. **Career Transactions:** Selected by Giants in first round (41st overall) of 1998 draft; signed July 9, 1998.

On the fast track when he signed, Urban came crashing down when he separated his pitching shoulder and tore his labrum when he fell awkwardly during a pickup basketball game in January 2000. The injury and resulting surgery kept him from pitching last year, but he returned with a strong effort in instructional league to earn a 40-man roster spot. Urban can throw four pitches for strikes, including a sneaky-fast fastball that has reached 94 mph, a cut fastball/slider that complements his tailing four-seamer, a good changeup and a developing curveball. He has excellent mechanics for his size, and they remained the same after his inactivity. Urban was 80 percent back in instructional league and will have to prove to the Giants that he has learned from his time off. Obviously, San Francisco remains intrigued by a lefthander with quality stuff. Urban will be challenged at Shreveport and could move quickly if he can shake off the rust.

Year	Club (League)	Class	W	L	ERA	G	GS	CG	SV	IP	H	R	ER	BB	SO
1998	Salem-Keizer (NWL)	A	1	2	4.98	5	3	0	0	22	21	14	12	8	22
	San Jose (Cal)	A	4	0	3.52	4	4	0	0	23	27	13	9	5	23
1999	Shreveport (TL)	AA	2	7	5.81	14	14	0	0	70	100	54	45	19	54
	San Jose (Cal)	A	8	5	3.76	15	13	0	0	81	78	41	34	18	89
2000						Did Not Play—Injured									
MINOR LEAGUE TOTALS			15	14	4.60	38	34	0	0	196	226	122	100	50	188

11. Boof Bonser, rhp

Born: Oct. 14, 1981. **Ht.:** 6-4. **Wt.:** 230. **Bats:** R. **Throws:** R. **School:** Gibbs HS, St. Petersburg, Fla. **Career Transactions:** Selected by Giants in first round (21st overall) of 2000 draft; signed July 3, 2000.

First off, he was born John Bonser, though everyone calls him Boof, a nickname his mother and friends used to toss around that just stuck with him. Considered a first-round arm with a late-round body by many scouts as a junior, Bonser dropped 30 pounds prior to his senior season in high school by sharing a personal trainer with hot 2001 draft prospect Casey Kotchman. Kotchman's father Tom, an Angels scout and minor league manager, says Bonser's weight problem was magnified to scouts by his high school and summer league uniforms, which made him look like he was in poor shape. The Giants must have seen him in better uniforms, because they liked his power arm enough to surprise many clubs by taking him with the 21st overall pick. Bonser has the power arm the Giants covet, touching 96 mph with his fastball in the Northwest League. One of the league's youngest players, he lacked command and, at times, composure. But he also showed a good curveball and solid straight changeup. With his repertoire, his role down the line could be as a closer.

Year	Club (League)	Class	W	L	ERA	G	GS	CG	SV	IP	H	R	ER	BB	SO
2000	Salem-Keizer (NWL)	A	1	4	6.00	10	9	0	0	33	21	23	22	29	41
MINOR LEAGUE TOTALS			1	4	6.00	10	9	0	0	33	21	23	22	29	41

12. Cody Ransom, ss

Born: Feb. 17, 1976. **Ht.:** 6-2. **Wt.:** 190. **Bats:** R. **Throws:** R. **School:** Grand Canyon (Ariz.) University. **Career Transactions:** Selected by Giants in ninth round of 1998 draft; signed June 4, 1998.

The organization's biggest shortcoming is its lack of impact middle-infield prospects. Ransom has the tools to be such a player, but his 2000 performance wasn't encouraging. He struck out more often than he reached base and showed little pop. He's the best the organization has to offer, though, because of his defensive tools. Ransom is one of the system's best athletes—one Giants official called him an acrobat with soft hands—and has its best infield arm, which rates a 7 on the 2-to-8 scouting scale. Ransom's offensive shortcomings undermine his defensive prowess. He has bat speed and enough strength to be dangerous, both to himself and opposing pitchers, because home runs tend to make him too power-conscious. If he made better contact, he would have the power to be an average offensive player, but his swing gets long and has plenty of holes. The organization hopes Fresno's hitter-friendly atmosphere can give Ransom the confidence to put his prodigious tools to work.

Year	Club (League)	Class	AVG	G	AB	R	H	2B	3B	HR	RBI	BB	SO	SB
1998	Salem-Keizer (NWL)	A	.233	71	236	52	55	12	7	6	27	43	56	19
1999	Bakersfield (Cal)	A	.275	99	356	69	98	12	6	11	47	54	108	15
	Shreveport (TL)	AA	.122	14	41	6	5	0	0	2	4	4	22	0
2000	Shreveport (TL)	AA	.200	130	459	58	92	21	2	7	47	40	141	9
MINOR LEAGUE TOTALS			.229	314	1092	185	250	45	15	26	125	141	327	43

13. Arturo McDowell, of

Born: Sept. 7, 1979. **Ht.:** 6-1. **Wt.:** 175. **Bats:** L. **Throws:** L. **School:** Forest Hill HS, Jackson, Miss. **Career Transactions:** Selected by Giants in first round (29th overall) of 1998 draft; signed June 24, 1998.

McDowell clearly was hurt by the Giants' previous farm system set-up, as was 1998 supplemental first-rounder Chris Jones. The organization will be able to develop such players better now with a Rookie-level Arizona League team and a low Class A team. McDowell has shown the Giants plenty of tools, as he's one of the organization's fastest players and best defenders. Some think his best tool may yet be his bat, despite his career .219 average. McDowell struggled in consecutive seasons in the California League, mainly due to his pitch selection. He swings at balls and takes strikes, club officials say, but they're pleased with his ability to draw a walk. He has shown power to the opposite field when he makes contact, and though he has the speed to control a game offensively, he has struggled with baserunning. McDowell could start 2001 at low Class A Hagerstown for a change of scenery, then move up to Shreveport if he gets out of the blocks fast.

Year	Club (League)	Class	AVG	G	AB	R	H	2B	3B	HR	RBI	BB	SO	SB
1998	Salem-Keizer (NWL)	A	.221	47	172	32	38	3	2	0	18	29	46	13
1999	Bakersfield (Cal)	A	.222	121	441	66	98	16	10	2	37	49	140	28
2000	Bakersfield (Cal)	A	.214	122	453	77	97	13	4	7	53	77	129	38
MINOR LEAGUE TOTALS			.219	290	1066	175	233	32	16	9	108	155	315	79

14. Brion Treadway, rhp

Born: April 1, 1979. **Ht.:** 6-4. **Wt.:** 215. **Bats:** R. **Throws:** R. **School:** UNC Charlotte. **Career Transactions:** Selected by Giants in third round of 2000 draft; signed June 27, 2000.

Treadway was the No. 9 prospect in the Cape Cod League in 1999 and had the best fastball in the league, topping out at 94 mph. The Giants didn't see much of that after drafting him in 2000, however. They chalk that up to Treadway's heavy college workload at UNC Charlotte, where he was the team's No. 1 starter. He had more command problems with short-season Salem-Keizer. Though his ERA was solid, he surrendered 8.7 hits and 4.5 walks per nine innings, limiting him to just over four innings a start. He had trouble keeping his sinking fastball from falling into the 85-88 mph range and from getting up in the zone. With an athletic build, solid slider and a fresher arm, Treadway figures to pitch in high Class A San Jose in 2001. The Giants think his fastball will bounce back this year. They like his upside as much as any of the power arms they procured in the 2000 draft.

Year	Club (League)	Class	W	L	ERA	G	GS	CG	SV	IP	H	R	ER	BB	SO
2000	Salem-Keizer (NWL)	A	2	3	2.31	8	8	0	0	35	35	19	9	17	29
MINOR LEAGUE TOTALS			2	3	2.31	8	8	0	0	35	35	19	9	17	29

15. Jake Esteves, rhp

Born: July 31, 1975. **Ht.:** 6-1. **Wt.:** 200. **Bats:** R. **Throws:** R. **School:** Louisiana State University. **Career Transactions:** Selected by Giants in sixth round of 1998 draft; signed June 17, 1998.

After ranking second on the organization's prospect list last year, Esteves didn't pitch at all in 2000. He came up lame in spring training with shoulder problems and doctors diagnosed a torn labrum, which necessitated major surgery. The Giants fingered an old injury that gradually worsened for the tear, which required extensive rehabilitation. The organization left him off the 40-man roster with its fingers crossed that no one would take a pitcher with two major injuries in the past. (Esteves missed the 1997 college season with personal and elbow problems.) The gamble proved successful. When Esteves returns, San Francisco plans to end his days as a starter and make him a reliever. He'll have to regain both his stuff and the confident, aggressive mentality that helps him challenge hitters with a 92-95 sinking fastball and a late-breaking slider. In the bullpen, Esteves will rely more on those pitches than on his changeup, which had developed nicely in 1999, and he may junk his curveball.

Year	Club (League)	Class	W	L	ERA	G	GS	CG	SV	IP	H	R	ER	BB	SO
1998	Salem-Keizer (NWL)	A	0	0	2.25	1	1	0	0	4	1	1	1	0	5
	Bakersfield (Cal)	A	0	2	4.29	14	6	0	1	36	43	30	17	12	24
1999	San Jose (Cal)	A	6	1	2.01	12	11	1	1	72	59	21	16	17	56
	Shreveport (TL)	AA	8	2	3.63	15	14	0	0	92	76	40	37	23	53
2000								Did Not Play—Injured							
MINOR LEAGUE TOTALS			14	5	3.15	42	32	1	2	203	179	92	71	52	138

16. Brett Casper, of

Born: Nov. 24, 1975. **Ht.:** 6-3. **Wt.:** 215. **Bats:** R. **Throws:** R. **School:** Oral Roberts University. **Career Transactions:** Selected by Giants in eighth round of 1997 draft; signed June 5, 1997.

Casper spent three years in the California League, not usually a great recipe for a prospect. Neither is hitting just .243 the third time around. But few Giants prospects have as many tools as Casper does. He has the organization's best mix of power and speed after Valderrama, though he's a completely different kind of player. Casper derives good power from his strong build and short stroke, and he has the bat speed to catch up to plus fastballs. His high strikeout numbers and low averages stem from his struggles with breaking balls. Casper isn't afraid to take a walk, though, leading the organization in that category in 2000. He has the speed to be a baserunning threat and to play center field, though he profiles as a right fielder with his solid power and arm. He'll move up to Double-A in 2001.

Year	Club (League)	Class	AVG	G	AB	R	H	2B	3B	HR	RBI	BB	SO	SB
1997	Salem-Keizer (NWL)	A	.223	61	229	31	51	14	1	7	34	31	86	17
1998	Bakersfield (Cal)	A	.194	74	237	27	46	10	3	2	18	23	75	5
	Salem-Keizer (NWL)	A	.308	7	26	2	8	1	1	0	3	2	7	0
1999	San Jose (Cal)	A	.266	121	436	71	116	22	2	16	77	56	135	20
2000	Bakersfield (Cal)	A	.243	128	436	85	106	27	3	15	70	97	146	22
MINOR LEAGUE TOTALS			**.240**	391	1364	216	327	74	10	40	202	209	449	64

17. Jeff Andra, lhp

Born: Sept. 9, 1975. **Ht.:** 6-5. **Wt.:** 210. **Bats:** L. **Throws:** L. **School:** University of Oklahoma. **Career Transactions:** Selected by Giants in third round of 1997 draft; signed June 8, 1997.

The Giants have a deep pool of promising lefthanders. Andra and Jeff Urban are the closest to the big leagues. Andra didn't pitch from July 1998 to July 1999 after shoulder woes and surgery, but he was finally healthy last year. He was inconsistent, however, giving up a .298 batting average in Double-A and getting hammered in Triple-A. The organization chalked his lack of success at Fresno to his reluctance to challenge hitters inside with his fastball. On a given night, Andra's 88-92 mph fastball is an above-average pitch, as is his slider. He needs to be more aggressive with both pitches and throw more strikes with his changeup. With his size and arm, he'll be given plenty of chances to succeed.

Year	Club (League)	Class	W	L	ERA	G	GS	CG	SV	IP	H	R	ER	BB	SO
1997	Salem-Keizer (NWL)	A	3	1	2.03	8	8	0	0	44	39	21	10	10	58
	San Jose (Cal)	A	1	4	6.98	6	6	0	0	30	36	25	23	11	29
1998	San Jose (Cal)	A	8	2	3.32	15	15	2	0	87	75	36	32	28	80
1999	San Jose (Cal)	A	4	2	4.50	13	7	0	0	50	54	28	25	19	54
2000	Shreveport (TL)	AA	6	6	3.84	17	17	0	0	91	106	51	39	35	64
	Fresno (PCL)	AAA	0	3	8.73	7	7	0	0	33	49	35	32	24	16
MINOR LEAGUE TOTALS			22	18	4.33	66	60	2	0	335	359	196	161	127	301

18. Kevin Joseph, rhp

Born: Aug. 1, 1976. **Ht.:** 6-4. **Wt.:** 200. **Bats:** R. **Throws:** R. **School:** Rice University. **Career Transactions:** Selected by Giants in sixth round of 1997 draft; signed June 7, 1997.

Joseph has the system's best raw arm. His fastball has touched 100 mph, and he throws 97-98 consistently. He also has a tight, hard slider that he throws in the mid-80s. Sounds like a top prospect, right? That's what the Giants thought when they drafted Joseph, who was primarily an infielder in college. His lack of pitching experience has stunted his development, though, as he never has gained a feel for an offspeed pitch. The Giants put him in the Double-A rotation in 2000, hoping he would pick up a changeup and get needed innings, but the plan backfired. He pitched tentatively, then went back to the bullpen and lost confidence. Despite his lack of success, the Giants decided to leave him in relief and hope he can become the organization's closer of the future. The 2001 season will be crucial for Joseph.

Year	Club (League)	Class	W	L	ERA	G	GS	CG	SV	IP	H	R	ER	BB	SO
1997	Salem-Keizer (NWL)	A	3	5	5.40	17	6	0	1	45	44	35	27	26	45
1998	Bakersfield (Cal)	A	0	4	8.14	6	6	0	0	21	35	26	19	20	17
	Salem-Keizer (NWL)	A	1	1	4.36	23	0	0	0	43	36	25	21	27	37
1999	San Jose (Cal)	A	1	2	2.35	20	0	0	2	31	17	9	8	13	30
	Shreveport (TL)	AA	0	2	1.42	7	0	0	0	13	8	4	2	5	16
2000	Shreveport (TL)	AA	3	11	5.17	27	16	0	1	103	116	60	59	48	71
MINOR LEAGUE TOTALS			8	25	4.79	100	28	0	4	255	256	159	136	139	216

19. Jeremy Luster, 1b

Born: June 10, 1977. **Ht.:** 6-4. **Wt.:** 210. **Bats:** B. **Throws:** R. **School:** DeKalb (Ga.) JC. **Career Transactions:** Selected by Giants in 44th round of 1997 draft; signed May 27, 1998.

Luster is a rare draft-and-follow in an organization that has preferred its draftees to come from four-year colleges. He helped lead DeKalb (Ga.) to the 1998 Junior College World Series before signing. Luster has good speed for a player his size, as well as solid baserunning instincts, stealing 17 bases in 19 tries last year. His power has started to develop as he gets more experience as a switch-hitter. He's a natural righthander, but the Giants like his swing from the left side better because he gets the barrel of the bat to the ball quicker and generates more pop. Luster played at first base in 2000, but he has the athletic ability to move. Giants officials have pondered moving him to third base—another crowded spot in the organization—or to the outfield, where his skills could be put to better use.

Year	Club (League)	Class	AVG	G	AB	R	H	2B	3B	HR	RBI	BB	SO	SB
1998	Salem-Keizer (NWL)	A	.304	51	181	32	55	13	3	6	48	23	30	6
1999	Bakersfield (Cal)	A	.201	52	184	26	37	4	3	0	19	22	54	9
	Salem-Keizer (NWL)	A	.219	39	146	22	32	7	1	1	14	16	48	7
2000	Bakersfield (Cal)	A	.282	137	517	86	146	35	5	14	99	77	104	17
MINOR LEAGUE TOTALS			.263	279	1028	166	270	59	12	21	180	138	236	39

20. Felix Diaz, rhp

Born: July 27, 1981. **Ht.:** 6-1. **Wt.:** 165. **Bats:** R. **Throws:** R. **Career Transactions:** Signed out of Dominican Republic by Giants, March 20, 1998.

Diaz is a testament to the Giants' revamped Dominican efforts and more player-friendly farm system. He clearly benefited from not being rushed to the Northwest League. He also was one of the organization's top pitchers in instructional league. He has one of the best arms in the system and showed an explosive fastball that reached 94 mph, a good change-up and long fingers, all of which drew the inevitable comparisons to Pedro Martinez. The Angels' Ramon Ortiz would be more appropriate. Diaz didn't throw his curveball much during the season but made strides with it in instructional league. He also throws a harder, slurvish slider. Diaz could gain more velocity on his fastball as he fills out. With their new Sally League affiliate, they won't have to push Diaz as they might have a year ago.

Year	Club (League)	Class	W	L	ERA	G	GS	CG	SV	IP	H	R	ER	BB	SO
1998	Giants (DSL)	R	0	4	7.55	14	5	0	0	39	52	44	33	26	34
1999	Giants (DSL)	R	0	0	0.75	3	3	0	0	12	6	2	1	7	19
2000	Giants (AZL)	R	3	4	4.16	11	11	0	0	63	56	35	29	16	58
	Salem-Keizer (NWL)	A	0	1	8.10	3	0	0	0	3	6	6	3	1	2
MINOR LEAGUE TOTALS			3	9	5.06	31	19	0	0	117	120	87	66	50	113

21. Giuseppe Chiaramonte, c

Born: Feb. 19, 1976. **Ht.:** 6-0. **Wt.:** 200. **Bats:** R. **Throws:** R. **School:** Fresno State University. **Career Transactions:** Selected by Giants in fifth round of 1997 draft; signed June 12, 1997.

San Francisco has plenty of solid catchers, and Chiaramonte ranks at the top of the list because of his power and Triple-A performance. He was a fan favorite at Fresno, playing in the same stadium where he was a second-team All-American for Fresno State in 1997. His brother Giachino played linebacker for the Bulldogs. Giuseppe has plenty of pop. He cut down on his strikeouts in Triple-A, and he was impressive offensively in instructional league. The reason he went to instructional league at his stage of development, though, was his defense. Chiaramonte has never looked like a Gold Glover. He's an adequate receiver and calls a decent game, but he threw out just 12 of 118 basestealers. The Giants hope offseason shoulder surgery restores arm strength. He is destined for more Triple-A time in 2001.

Year	Club (League)	Class	AVG	G	AB	R	H	2B	3B	HR	RBI	BB	SO	SB
1997	San Jose (Cal)	A	.229	64	223	29	51	11	1	12	44	25	58	0
1998	San Jose (Cal)	A	.273	129	502	87	137	33	3	22	87	47	139	5

Year	Club (League)	Class	AVG	G	AB	R	H	2B	3B	HR	RBI	BB	SO	SB
1999	Shreveport (TL)	AA	.245	114	400	54	98	20	2	19	74	40	88	4
2000	Fresno (PCL)	AAA	.255	122	443	70	113	30	6	24	79	47	81	2
MINOR LEAGUE TOTALS			.254	429	1568	240	399	94	12	77	284	159	366	11

22. Luke Anderson, rhp

Born: April 9, 1978. **Ht.:** 6-5. **Wt.:** 210. **Bats:** R. **Throws:** R. **School:** University of Nevada-Las Vegas. **Career Transactions:** Selected by Giants in 18th round of 2000 draft; signed June 11, 2000.

Anderson won four consecutive Nevada state titles at Green Valley High, where he was a teammate of Pirates outfielder Chad Hermansen. The Rockies drafted him out of high school, but he went to Nevada-Las Vegas, where he pitched infrequently as a freshman, then missed a year after having a bone spur removed from his right knee. Anderson came on with a big season in the Cape Cod League in the summer of 1999. He has the size, stuff and poise to move quickly as a closer. His fastball is fairly straight at 89-91 mph, but he has a devastating splitter. He has shown good command, especially with the splitter, which he can throw for strikes or spot out of the zone. He led the Northwest League in saves while topping short-season relievers with 16.0 strikeouts per nine innings. Opponents hit just .172 against him.

Year	Club (League)	Class	W	L	ERA	G	GS	CG	SV	IP	H	R	ER	BB	SO
2000	Salem-Keizer (NWL)	A	1	0	1.45	25	0	0	12	31	19	5	5	10	55
MINOR LEAGUE TOTALS			1	0	1.45	25	0	0	12	31	19	5	5	10	55

23. Chris Magruder, of

Born: April 26, 1977. **Ht.:** 5-11. **Wt.:** 200. **Bats:** B. **Throws:** R. **School:** University of Washington. **Career Transactions:** Selected by Giants in second round of 1998 draft; signed June 19, 1998.

Magruder does a lot of things well but nothing spectacularly. He has good pop in his bat for his size, though he'll never be a power hitter. He's at least an average runner, but he doesn't have blazing speed and hasn't become an efficient basestealer despite his added experience. If it sounds like he has plenty of limitations, he does. Magruder can play center field, but probably wouldn't be adequate in Pac Bell Park's spacious outfield. His best position would be as a corner outfielder, but he doesn't have the power to play there on an everyday basis. Magruder hits enough and has enough arm and range to become an effective fourth outfielder, but he'll have to start hitting homers to be more than that.

Year	Club (League)	Class	AVG	G	AB	R	H	2B	3B	HR	RBI	BB	SO	SB
1998	Salem-Keizer (NWL)	A	.333	47	177	43	59	8	5	3	18	37	21	14
	Bakersfield (Cal)	A	.304	22	92	21	28	7	0	1	4	13	16	3
1999	Shreveport (TL)	AA	.256	133	476	78	122	21	4	6	60	69	85	17
2000	Shreveport (TL)	AA	.282	134	496	85	140	33	3	4	39	67	75	18
MINOR LEAGUE TOTALS			.281	336	1241	227	349	69	12	14	121	186	197	52

24. Yorvit Torrealba, c

Born: July 19, 1978. **Ht.:** 5-11. **Wt.:** 180. **Bats:** R. **Throws:** R. **Career Transactions:** Signed out of Venezuela by Giants, Sept. 14, 1994.

After six seasons in the organization, Torrealba has seen plenty of other catchers come and go. He threw out 33 percent of basestealers at Shreveport and had his best offensive season last year. He never will be a power hitter because he uses an inside-out swing. The Giants like his ability as a situational hitter and hit-and-run man, but see him as a catch-and-throw defender who'll be adequate at best offensively. His presence, along with Giuseppe Chiaramonte and big leaguers Bobby Estalella and Doug Mirabelli, may move strong-armed catcher Guillermo Rodriguez to the mound. Torrealba may have to duel Chiramonte for playing time in Triple-A this season.

Year	Club (League)	Class	AVG	G	AB	R	H	2B	3B	HR	RBI	BB	SO	SB
1995	Bellingham (NWL)	A	.155	26	71	2	11	3	0	0	8	2	14	0
1996	San Jose (Cal)	A	.000	2	5	0	0	0	0	0	0	1	1	0
	Burlington (Mid)	A	.000	1	4	0	0	0	0	0	0	0	1	0
	Bellingham (NWL)	A	.267	48	150	23	40	4	0	1	10	9	27	4
1997	Bakersfield (Cal)	A	.274	119	446	52	122	15	3	4	40	31	58	4
1998	Shreveport (TL)	AA	.235	59	196	18	46	7	0	0	13	18	30	0
	San Jose (Cal)	A	.286	21	70	10	20	2	0	0	10	1	6	2
	Fresno (PCL)	AAA	.182	4	11	1	2	1	0	0	1	1	4	0
1999	Shreveport (TL)	AA	.244	65	217	25	53	10	1	4	19	9	34	0
	Fresno (PCL)	AAA	.254	17	63	9	16	2	0	2	10	4	11	0
	San Jose (Cal)	A	.315	19	73	10	23	3	0	2	14	6	15	0
2000	Shreveport (TL)	AA	.286	108	398	50	114	21	1	4	32	34	55	2
MINOR LEAGUE TOTALS			.262	489	1704	200	447	68	5	17	157	116	256	12

25. Nelson Castro, ss/2b

Born: June 4, 1976. **Ht.:** 5-10. **Wt.:** 190. **Bats:** B. **Throws:** R. **Career Transactions:** Signed out of Dominican Republic by Angels, Jan. 14, 1994 . . . Claimed on waivers by Giants from Angels, Oct. 13, 1999.

Castro was on the prospect scrap heap not long ago, waived by the Angels following the 1999 season after rising from a two-way player who pitched and played shortstop in the Rookie-level Dominican Summer League. He was slow to adjust offensively and struggled in two years in the California League. The Giants sent him back to the Cal League in 2000 before their lack of infield depth prompted his promotion to Fresno. Castro is a tools player with decent bat speed, good running speed and an excellent arm, which ranks as a 7 on the 2-to-8 scouting scale. Managers named him the Cal League's best defensive shortstop, but he could move to second base because he isn't fundamentally sound at short. His arm could help him overcome his shaky footwork and range on the other side of the bag.

Year	Club (League)	Class	AVG	G	AB	R	H	2B	3B	HR	RBI	BB	SO	SB
1994	Angels (DSL)	R	.254	59	205	44	52	6	1	1	33	38	28	15
1995	Angels (AZL)	R	.195	55	190	34	37	1	2	0	22	27	50	15
1996	Boise (NWL)	A	.000	1	1	0	0	0	0	0	0	0	0	0
	Angels (AZL)	R	.204	53	186	31	38	4	3	3	14	32	42	25
1997	Boise (NWL)	A	.294	69	293	74	86	16	1	7	37	38	53	26
1998	Lake Elsinore (Cal)	A	.234	131	470	73	110	16	7	4	41	40	101	36
1999	Lake Elsinore (Cal)	A	.250	125	444	68	111	16	12	1	50	36	75	53
2000	Bakersfield (Cal)	A	.284	53	218	38	62	14	3	5	41	20	40	27
	Fresno (PCL)	AAA	.254	67	244	27	62	7	2	5	20	14	51	10
MINOR LEAGUE TOTALS			.248	613	2251	389	558	80	31	26	258	245	440	207

Year	Club (League)	Class	W	L	ERA	G	GS	CG	SV	IP	H	R	ER	BB	SO
1994	Angels (DSL)	R	3	5	2.27	15	12	2	1	83	82	34	21	21	56
1995	Angels (DSL)	R	1	0	1.80	3	0	0	1	5	3	1	1	2	2
MINOR LEAGUE TOTALS			4	5	2.24	18	12	2	2	88	85	35	22	23	58

26. Doug Clark, of

Born: March 5, 1976. **Ht.:** 6-2. **Wt.:** 205. **Bats:** L. **Throws:** R. **School:** University of Massachusetts. **Career Transactions:** Selected by Giants in seventh round of 1998 draft; signed June 5, 1998.

Clark, a substitute teacher in Springfield, Mass., during the offseason, attended college on a football scholarship and came to baseball late. His athletic ability and breakout season in 1999 had the Giants excited. But his baseball inexperience caught up with him against better pitching in 2000. He hasn't developed the ability to turn his considerable raw power into home runs, and his plate discipline slipped in Double-A. Clark's combination of a below-average arm and poor routes to fly balls limits him to left field. On the plus side, he has good bat speed and can sting the ball to all fields with authority. His offense could get a boost at Fresno, where learning to loft the ball could lead to a 25-homer season.

Year	Club (League)	Class	AVG	G	AB	R	H	2B	3B	HR	RBI	BB	SO	SB
1998	Salem-Keizer (NWL)	A	.335	59	227	49	76	8	6	3	41	32	31	12
1999	Bakersfield (Cal)	A	.326	118	420	67	137	17	2	11	58	59	89	17
	Shreveport (TL)	AA	.220	15	50	6	11	3	0	1	6	4	9	0
2000	Shreveport (TL)	AA	.272	131	492	68	134	20	7	10	75	43	102	12
MINOR LEAGUE TOTALS			.301	323	1189	190	358	48	15	25	180	138	231	41

27. David Brous, lhp

Born: March 9, 1980. **Ht.:** 6-2. **Wt.:** 195. **Bats:** L. **Throws:** L. **School:** JC of the Redwoods (Calif.). **Career Transactions:** Selected by Giants in 18th round of 1998 draft; signed May 8, 1999 . . . Contract voided, June 4, 1999 . . . Re-signed by Giants, June 11, 1999.

The Giants signed Brous as a draft-and-follow in May 1999, then voided his contract after discovering he had elbow and shoulder problems. They re-signed him a week later after he had Tommy John surgery. He made his pro debut last July, but because he had been previously released, the Giants were forced to place him on their 40-man roster. Despite the rust and a tender arm, Brous showed what the Giants call "power equipment," touching the mid-90s with his fastball and drawing comparisons to big leaguer Alan Embree. Brous' athleticism and makeup have the organization encouraged he'll develop a breaking ball. Despite his age and inexperience, the Giants will try to wait on a lefty with such a power arm.

Year	Club (League)	Class	W	L	ERA	G	GS	CG	SV	IP	H	R	ER	BB	SO
1999					Did Not Play—Injured										
2000	San Jose (Cal)	A	1	3	4.59	9	7	0	0	33	26	17	17	23	25
MINOR LEAGUE TOTALS			1	3	4.59	9	7	0	0	33	26	17	17	23	25

28. Erick Threets, lhp

Born: Nov. 4, 1981. **Ht.:** 6-5. **Wt.:** 225. **Bats:** L. **Throws:** L. **School:** Modesto (Calif.) JC. **Career Transactions:** Selected by Giants in seventh round of 2000 draft; signed August 2, 2000.

Threets is among the hardest throwers in the system. The Giants signed him despite his commitment to Louisiana State, where he would have competed for the closer role. The Giants aren't quite sure what they have in Threets, who spent the summer pitching in the Cape Cod League. After a long season, he took instructional league off. He has a fastball that touches the mid-90s, a low-80s slider and excellent athletic ability. He may not be done growing. The Giants will see what he shows them in his first pro spring training, and he likely will start his career as a starter at Hagerstown. He has a chance to move up this list quickly.

Year	Club (League)	Class	W	L	ERA	G	GS	CG	SV	IP	H	R	ER	BB	SO
2000	Did Not Play—Signed 2001 Contract														

29. Edwards Guzman, 3b/c

Born: Sept. 11, 1976. **Ht.:** 5-10. **Wt.:** 205. **Bats:** L. **Throws:** R. **School:** Interamerican (P.R.) University. **Career Transactions:** Selected by Giants in 50th round of 1995 draft; signed Sept. 11, 1995.

Guzman overcame the odds a 50th-round draft pick faces when he reached San Francisco in 1999. He doesn't project as a starter in the big leagues, but the organization values his ability to play catcher, second base, third base and left field with aplomb. Catcher and third base are his best defensive positions, and he can make the routine plays at second. The Giants like his bat enough to think he can be a big league utilityman. But he has little power, and if he weren't a lefthanded hitter he may not have lasted this long.

Year	Club (League)	Class	AVG	G	AB	R	H	2B	3B	HR	RBI	BB	SO	SB
1996	San Jose (Cal)	A	.270	106	367	41	99	19	5	1	40	39	60	3
1997	Shreveport (TL)	AA	.284	118	380	52	108	15	4	3	42	33	57	3
1998	Fresno (PCL)	AAA	.305	102	325	50	99	17	0	9	48	24	47	1
1999	San Francisco (NL)	MAJ	.000	14	15	0	0	0	0	0	0	0	4	0
	Fresno (PCL)	AAA	.274	90	358	48	98	13	0	7	48	17	50	6
2000	Fresno (PCL)	AAA	.280	115	421	52	118	24	1	6	52	17	43	1
MAJOR LEAGUE TOTALS			.000	14	15	0	0	0	0	0	0	0	4	0
MINOR LEAGUE TOTALS			.282	531	1851	243	522	88	10	26	230	130	257	14

30. Chad Zerbe, lhp

Born: April 27, 1972. **Ht.:** 6-0. **Wt.:** 190. **Bats:** L. **Throws:** L. **School:** Hillsborough (Fla.) CC. **Career Transactions:** Selected by Dodgers in 17th round of 1991 draft; signed June 6, 1991 . . . Released by Dodgers, Dec. 10, 1996 . . . Signed by Diamondbacks, Jan. 28, 1997 . . . Released by Diamondbacks, May 20, 1997 . . . Signed by independent Sonoma County (Western), 1997 . . . Signed by Giants, Nov. 26, 1997 . . . Granted free agency, Oct. 16, 1998; re-signed by Giants, March 4, 1999 . . . Granted free agency, Oct. 15, 1999; re-signed by Giants, Oct. 22, 1999.

Zerbe's ceiling is clearly defined. He'll be no more than a situational lefthander, though he has a chance to fill that role in San Francisco this year. Drafted by the Dodgers in 1991, he has bounced around the minor leagues, including a stint in the independent Western League in 1997, where he persevered through 16-hour bus rides and $15-a-day meal money. Zerbe pitched well in his big league trial and then pitched 12 strong innings in the Arizona Fall League, showing an average fastball and good curveball that he throws for strikes.

Year	Club (League)	Class	W	L	ERA	G	GS	CG	SV	IP	H	R	ER	BB	SO
1991	Dodgers (GCL)	R	0	2	2.20	16	1	0	0	33	31	19	8	15	23
1992	Great Falls (Pio)	R	8	3	2.14	15	15	1	0	92	75	27	22	26	70
1993	Bakersfield (Cal)	A	0	10	5.91	14	12	1	0	67	83	60	44	47	41
	Vero Beach (FSL)	A	1	0	6.57	10	0	0	0	12	12	10	9	13	11
1994	Vero Beach (FSL)	A	5	5	3.39	18	18	1	0	98	88	50	37	32	68
1995	San Bernardino (Cal)	A	11	7	4.57	28	27	1	0	163	168	103	83	64	94
1996	San Antonio (TL)	AA	4	6	4.50	17	11	1	1	86	98	52	43	37	38
1997	High Desert (Cal)	A	1	6	7.43	9	8	0	0	36	61	49	30	15	26
	Sonoma Co. (West)	IND	4	5	5.42	14	13	2	0	90	117	70	54	36	52
1998	San Jose (Cal)	A	2	0	3.35	23	0	0	1	38	37	16	14	12	28
1999	Bakersfield (Cal)	A	7	7	3.64	21	21	0	0	126	124	66	51	33	81
	Shreveport (TL)	AA	1	3	1.96	7	6	0	0	41	32	13	9	10	16
2000	Shreveport (TL)	AA	2	1	2.33	9	9	0	0	39	37	11	10	9	34
	Fresno (PCL)	AAA	7	3	4.32	17	11	0	0	81	94	46	39	17	41
	San Francisco (NL)	MAJ	0	0	4.50	4	0	0	0	6	6	3	3	1	5
MAJOR LEAGUE TOTALS			0	0	4.50	4	0	0	0	6	6	3	3	1	5
MINOR LEAGUE TOTALS			49	53	3.93	204	139	5	2	913	940	522	399	330	571

Seattle
Mariners

By James Bailey

When Ken Griffey forced a trade to the Reds last winter, most predicted the Mariners would regroup in 2000. But in the end, the organization took a big step forward after parting with the man who still sits atop virtually every category in the club record book.

Alex Rodriguez managed to put his impending free agency aside and was Baseball America's Major League Player of the Year. Though the Mariners lost Rodriguez when the Rangers offered a record $252 million contract, the organization remained optimistic about the future.

For starters, the franchise is coming off just its third postseason appearance, losing to the eventual World Series champion Yankees in the American League Championship Series. And the Mariners made the first step in reconstructing the major league lineup by signing outfielder Ichiro Suzuki, the perennial batting champion in Japan's Pacific League. He joins friend and countryman Kazuhiro Sasaki, the 2000 AL rookie of the year.

Sasaki was one of several good free-agent signings that keyed the club's success last season. First baseman John Olerud, righthander Aaron Sele and lefthander Arthur Rhodes also made major contributions. The downside was the trio cost the Mariners their first three picks in the draft, but they got aggressive and spent their top choice (fourth round) on lefthander Sam Hays, who came to terms at the end of the summer for $1.2 million. The team also landed what it believed was the equivalent of a first-round pick in Korean two-way star Shin-Soo Choo.

The talent injection boosts what has gradually become a deep farm system, especially in pitching. The Mariners were so backed up with mound prospects that several pitched a level below where their talent might have dictated. The result was a .578 minor league winning percentage that was the best in baseball. Double-A New Haven and the Rookie-level Arizona League team won league championships.

While the winning was nice, the most important thing is that help is on the way to Seattle. And though the pitching stands out, the system has numerous position players to be excited about for the first time in a while. Rodriguez' departure left the team with a glaring hole, but the plethora of young pitchers should provide the currency to fill it—and then some.

Organization Overview

General manager: Pat Gillick. Farm director: Benny Looper. Scouting director: Frank Mattox.

2000 PERFORMANCE

Class	Team	League	W	L	Pct.	Finish*	Manager
Majors	Seattle	American	91	71	.562	3rd (14)	Lou Piniella
Triple-A	Tacoma Rainiers	Pacific Coast	76	67	.531	5th (16)	Dave Myers
Double-A	#New Haven Ravens	Eastern	82	60	.577	3rd (12)	Dan Rohn
High A	†Lancaster JetHawks	California	89	51	.636	1st (10)	Mark Parent
Low A	Wisconsin Timber Rattlers	Midwest	78	60	.565	3rd (14)	Gary Thurman
Short-season	Everett AquaSox	Northwest	37	39	.487	6th (8)	Terry Pollreisz
Rookie	Peoria Mariners	Arizona	39	16	.709	1st (9)	Omer Munoz
OVERALL 2000 MINOR LEAGUE RECORD			401	293	.577	1st (30)	

*Finish in overall standings (No. of teams in league). #Affiliate will be in San Antonio (Texas) in 2001. †Affiliate will be in San Bernardino (California) in 2001.

ORGANIZATION LEADERS

BATTING

*AVG	Terrmel Sledge, Lancaster/Wisconsin	.332
R	Craig Kuzmic, Lancaster	106
H	Bo Robinson, Lancaster	161
TB	Juan Silvestre, Lancaster	265
2B	Mike Neill, Tacoma	38
3B	Craig Kuzmic, Lancaster	10
HR	Juan Silvestre, Lancaster	30
RBI	Juan Silvestre, Lancaster	137
BB	Jermaine Clark, New Haven	87
	Shawn McCorkle, Wisconsin	87
SO	Juan Thomas, New Haven	128
SB	**Jamal Strong**, Everett	60

PITCHING

W	**Greg Wooten**, New Haven	17
L	Brian Fuentes, New Haven	12
#ERA	Allan Westfall, N.H./AZL Mariners	2.55
G	Three tied at	52
CG	**Greg Wooten**, New Haven	6
SV	Todd Williams, Tacoma	32
IP	**Greg Wooten**, New Haven	179
BB	Matt Thornton, Wisconsin	72
SO	Jeff Heaverlo, Lancaster/Tacoma	163

*Minimum 250 At-Bats #Minimum 75 Innings

TOP PROSPECTS OF THE DECADE

1991	Roger Salkeld, rhp
1992	Roger Salkeld, rhp
1993	Marc Newfield, of
1994	Alex Rodriguez, ss
1995	Alex Rodriguez, ss
1996	Jose Cruz Jr., of
1997	Jose Cruz Jr., of
1998	Ryan Anderson, lhp
1999	Ryan Anderson, lhp
2000	Ryan Anderson, lhp

TOP DRAFT PICKS OF THE DECADE

1991	Shawn Estes, lhp
1992	Ron Villone, lhp
1993	Alex Rodriguez, ss
1994	Jason Varitek, c
1995	Jose Cruz Jr., of
1996	Gil Meche, rhp
1997	Ryan Anderson, lhp
1998	Matt Thornton, lhp
1999	Ryan Christianson, c
2000	Sam Hays, lhp (4)

Strong   **Wooten**

ROBB STANTON

BEST TOOLS

Best Hitter for Average	Ichiro Suzuki
Best Power Hitter	Juan Silvestre
Fastest Baserunner	Jamal Strong
Best Fastball	Ryan Anderson
Best Breaking Ball	Joel Pineiro
Best Control	Greg Wooten
Best Defensive Catcher	Ryan Christianson
Best Defensive Infielder	Antonio Perez
Best Infield Arm	Antonio Perez
Best Defensive Outfielder	Sheldon Fulse
Best Outfield Arm	Miguel Richardson

PROJECTED 2004 LINEUP

Catcher	Ryan Christianson
First Base	John Olerud
Second Base	Willie Bloomquist
Third Base	Miguel Villilo
Shortstop	Antonio Perez
Left Field	Chris Snelling
Center Field	Mike Cameron
Right Field	Ichiro Suzuki
Designated Hitter	Juan Silvestre
No. 1 Starter	Ryan Anderson
No. 2 Starter	Freddy Garcia
No. 3 Starter	Aaron Sele
No. 4 Starter	Gil Meche
No. 5 Starter	Joel Pineiro
Closer	Kazuhiro Sasaki

ALL-TIME LARGEST BONUSES

Ichiro Suzuki, 2000	$5,000,000
Ryan Anderson, 1997	2,175,000
Ryan Christianson, 1999	2,100,000
Kazuhiro Sasaki, 2000	2,000,000
Shin-Soo Choo, 2000	1,335,000

DraftAnalysis

2000 Draft

Best Pro Debut: OF Jamal Strong (6) was co-MVP of the short-season Northwest League after hitting .314-1-28 with a league-best 60 steals and a 52-29 walk-strikeout ratio. LHP **Derrick Van Dusen** (5) led the Rookie-level Arizona League in victories, going 6-0, 2.63 with 58 strikeouts in 41 innings.

Best Athlete: Strong or OF Jared Jones (16), who hadn't played baseball in two years while serving as a backup quarterback at Florida State. Jones has a right-field arm and a power bat.

Best Hitter: 3B Blake Bone (11) or 2B Manny Crespo (14). Bone outhit Crespo .282 to .259 at short-season Everett.

Best Raw Power: Jones, though he'll need time to get acclimated to baseball again. He went 2-for-18 in a brief AZL stint.

Fastest Runner: The Mariners have clocked Strong in 3.88 seconds from the right side of the plate to first base, which is almost unheard of.

Best Defensive Player: Strong had tons of range in center field, though his arm has been below-average since he separated his shoulder late in the college season at Nebraska.

Best Fastball: RHP Rett Johnson (8) throws an 89-93 mph fastball and a big league slider. He's on the fast track after going 5-4, 2.07 with 88 strikeouts in 70 innings at Everett.

Most Intriguing Background: The Mariners drafted two righthanders named Chris Way, who are not related, back-to-back in the 34th and 35th rounds. LHP Sam Hays (4), the club's top draft choice, is the grandson of former big league pitcher Sid Hudson. Crespo's father Manny is a roving infield instructor with the Marlins, while SS Jason Looper (31) is the nephew of Mariners farm director Benny. Neither of the Ways nor Looper signed. In the non-relative category, LHP Ryan Ketchner (10) has overcome a hearing impairment and OF Larry Brown (22) was a quarterback at the College of the Canyons (Calif.).

Van Dusen

Closest To The Majors: Johnson.

Best Late-Round Pick: Jones. At 6-foot-4 and 235 pounds, he looks the part of the slugger. If he stops playing quarterback and sheds his football bulk, his ceiling is high. Also keep an eye on LHP Theo Heflin (27), who throws 90-93 mph.

The One Who Got Away: LHP Charlie Manning (9), who has touched 95 mph, stayed home to finish school at Tampa.

Assessment: The Mariners didn't start drafting until the fourth round, though they won't complain because they gave up their first three picks to sign John Olerud, Aaron Sele and Arthur Rhodes. Hays' signability was in question, but the Mariners got the lefty with above-average stuff for $1.2 million.

1999 Draft

The Mariners have high hopes for C Ryan Christianson (1), RHP Jeff Heaverlo (1), 2B Willie Bloomquist (3) and OF Sheldon Fulse (3). OF Terrmel Sledge (8) was sent to Montreal in a minor deal for Chris Widger. **Grade: C+**

1998 Draft

Most teams considered LHP Matt Thornton a reach in the first round, and he has done nothing to change that thinking. The only pick of value was LHP Andy VanHekken (3), and he was given to Detroit in an awful trade for Brian Hunter. **Grade: D–**

1997 Draft

Eighteen teams passed on LHP Ryan Anderson (1) before the Mariners were smart enough to grab him. RHP Joel Pineiro (12) hasn't gotten nearly as much hype, but he's also a quality pitching prospect. **Grade: A–**

1996 Draft

RHP Gil Meche (1) was a solid choice. But the pitcher who could have really helped was LHP Barry Zito (59), who didn't sign and eventually wound up with American League West rival Oakland. **Grade: C**

Note: Draft analysis prepared by Jim Callis. Numbers in parentheses indicate draft rounds.

... Anderson has the stuff to dominate, and it's only a matter of time before he joins the elite group of legitimate No. 1 starters.

Ryan
Anderson lhp

Born: July 12, 1979.
Ht.: 6-10. **Wt.:** 215.
Bats: L. **Throws:** L.
School: Divine Child HS, Dearborn, Mich.
Career Transactions: Selected by Mariners in first round (19th overall) of 1997 draft; signed Sept. 10, 1997.

When Anderson began the 2000 season by dominating the Pacific Coast League in his first few starts, the clamor began for the Mariners to call him up Interstate 5. The Mariners resisted the urge, sticking with the preseason plan of letting the Space Needle spend at least a half-season in Triple-A. They were proven correct, as the consistency Anderson has searched for since signing remained out of his grasp. His struggles may have been for the best, as pressure waned to promote the young man who has been the No. 1 prospect in the organization since signing. Anderson was shelved late in the season by shoulder tendinitis, which cost him a chance to pitch for the U.S. Olympic team. He returned to make one start at the end of the year for Tacoma and showed his mid-90s fastball was back.

When everything is clicking, Anderson works comfortably in the 94-97 mph range and mixes in a slider that should become a plus major league pitch. His changeup is an effective third pitch. He has the stuff to dominate, and many feel it's only a matter of time before he joins the elite group of legitimate No. 1 starters. Though he still walked more than a batter every two innings, his control took a step forward. He also has made tremendous strides off the field. The immaturity that dogged him earlier in his career is a footnote.

Anderson has yet to string together the season the Mariners know he's capable of. He follows Randy Johnson-like performances with back-to-back disappointing outings. That's how a pitcher with his repertoire can own a 20-26 career record. He went through three different deliveries at Double-A New Haven in 1999 and still hasn't mastered the more compact motion that will take him to the next level. When his mechanics get off he loses velocity, falls behind hitters and throws too many pitches. He needs to consistently last longer than five or six innings. After taking the winter off, Anderson will go to spring training for the first time with a legitimate shot at a major league job. Seattle's big league depth will allow the club to be patient, but many in the organization are rooting for him to push his way into the rotation.

Year	Club (League)	Class	W	L	ERA	G	GS	CG	SV	IP	H	R	ER	BB	SO
1998	Wisconsin (Mid)	A	6	5	3.23	22	22	0	0	111	86	47	40	67	152
1999	New Haven (EL)	AA	9	13	4.50	24	24	0	0	134	131	77	67	86	162
2000	Tacoma (PCL)	AAA	5	8	3.98	20	20	1	0	104	83	51	46	55	146
MINOR LEAGUE TOTALS			20	26	3.94	66	66	1	0	349	300	175	153	208	460

2. Ichiro Suzuki, of

Born: Oct. 22, 1973. **Ht.:** 6-0. **Wt.:** 160. **Bats** L. **Throws:** R. **Career Transactions:** Signed by Orix (Japan), 1992 . . . Contract purchased by Mariners from Orix, Nov. 30, 2000.

Known simply as Ichiro in his homeland, he is the seven-time defending batting champion in Japan's Pacific League. He attended spring training with the Mariners in 1999, and when the Orix Blue Wave made him available, Seattle bid $13.125 million for the right to sign him, then inked him to a three-year, $14.088 million deal with a $5 million bonus. Ichiro has been compared to Wade Boggs and Tony Gwynn as a hitter because he rarely strikes out and uses the entire field. Some scouts believe he'll contend for a batting crown right away. He runs well and has the speed and ability to play center field or either of the corners. He owns an accurate arm that plays well, even in right field. The biggest knock has been a lack of power, but he may have the ability to hit for more power at the expense of some batting average. With Mike Cameron in center, the Mariners will play Ichiro in right field. He should provide spark from the leadoff spot the team has lacked for years.

Year	Club (League)	Class	AVG	G	AB	R	H	2B	3B	HR	RBI	BB	SO	SB
1992	Orix (PL)	JAP	.253	40	95	9	24	5	0	0	5	3	11	3
1993	Orix (PL)	JAP	.188	43	64	4	12	2	0	1	3	2	7	0
1994	Orix (PL)	JAP	.385	130	546	111	210	41	5	13	54	51	53	29
1995	Orix (PL)	JAP	.342	130	524	104	179	23	4	25	80	68	52	49
1996	Orix (PL)	JAP	.356	130	542	104	193	24	4	16	84	56	57	35
1997	Orix (PL)	JAP	.345	135	536	94	185	31	4	17	91	62	36	39
1998	Orix (PL)	JAP	.358	135	506	79	181	36	3	13	71	43	35	11
1999	Orix (PL)	JAP	.343	103	411	80	141	27	2	21	68	46	35	12
2000	Orix (PL)	JAP	.387	105	395	73	153	22	1	12	73	54	36	21
MINOR LEAGUE TOTALS			.353	950	3619	658	1278	211	23	118	529	333	384	199

3. Antonio Perez, of

Born: July 26, 1981. **Ht.:** 5-11. **Wt.:** 175. **Bats:** R. **Throws:** R. **Career Transactions:** Signed out of Dominican Republic by Reds, March 21, 1998 . . . Traded by Reds with RHP Jake Meyer, OF Mike Cameron and RHP Brett Tomko to Mariners for OF Ken Griffey, Feb. 10, 2000.

When the Mariners finally pulled the trigger on the Ken Griffey deal with the Reds, Perez was viewed as a consolation prize because Gookie Dawkins and other Reds prospects couldn't be had. After leading the California League in slugging percentage in a breakout 2000 season, he looks more like the key to the deal. Perez is an exciting player who can do at least a little bit of everything. He's a strong-armed defender with good range at shortstop, and he can fly on the bases. What sets him apart is what he can do at the plate. He won't hit a lot of home runs, but he should continue to drive the ball to the gaps. At times Perez gets into a pull mode and fails to use the whole field. As with many young players, it's a matter of not concentrating consistently. He still hasn't figured out basestealing, as he was caught on 16 of his 44 attempts in 2000. Perez is still at least a year away from Seattle, but at his age there is no reason to rush him. He won't be another Alex Rodriguez, but he can be an all-star.

Year	Club (League)	Class	AVG	G	AB	R	H	2B	3B	HR	RBI	BB	SO	SB
1998	Reds (DSL)	R	.255	63	212	57	54	11	0	2	24	53	33	58
1999	Rockford (Mid)	A	.288	119	385	69	111	20	3	7	41	43	80	35
2000	Lancaster (Cal)	A	.276	98	395	90	109	36	6	17	63	58	99	28
MINOR LEAGUE TOTALS			.276	280	992	216	274	67	9	26	128	154	212	121

4. Joel Pineiro, rhp

Born: Sept. 25, 1978. **Ht.:** 6-1. **Wt.:** 180. **Bats:** R. **Throws:** R. **School:** Edison (Fla.) CC. **Career Transactions:** Selected by Mariners in 12th round of 1997 draft; signed June 7, 1997.

The Mariners were cautious with Pineiro coming into the 2000 season after he lost velocity off his fastball the previous year. He returned to Double-A and soon showed he was at full strength and ready to move on. He performed even better at Triple-A Tacoma, stringing together 19 consecutive shutout innings, and was summoned to Seattle in August. He picked up a win in his major league debut, holding the White Sox to two runs over six innings. Pineiro has good command of four pitches, with a fastball that touches above-average. His curveball has a chance to be a plus pitch, and he'll mix in a slider and changeup. He has always shown a good feel for pitching. Control, normally a strong suit, proved troublesome for him in Seattle. Perhaps it was an adjustment to working out of the bullpen, but he has to show he can throw strikes in the big leagues. Pineiro's role depends upon the makeup of the big league club. He's likely to continue breaking in as a reliever, though his future will be in the rotation. He might need more time in Triple-A.

Year	Club (League)	Class	W	L	ERA	G	GS	CG	SV	IP	H	R	ER	BB	SO
1997	Mariners (AZL)	R	1	0	0.00	1	0	0	0	3	1	0	0	0	4
	Everett (NWL)	A	4	2	5.33	18	6	0	2	49	54	33	29	18	59
1998	Wisconsin (Mid)	A	8	4	3.19	16	16	1	0	96	92	40	34	28	84
	Lancaster (Cal)	A	2	0	7.80	9	9	1	0	45	58	40	39	22	48
	Orlando (SL)	AA	1	0	5.40	1	1	0	0	5	7	4	3	2	2
1999	New Haven (EL)	AA	10	15	4.72	28	25	4	0	166	190	105	87	52	116
2000	New Haven (EL)	AA	2	1	4.13	9	9	0	0	52	42	25	24	12	43
	Tacoma (PCL)	AAA	7	1	2.80	10	9	2	0	61	53	20	19	22	41
	Seattle (AL)	MAJ	1	0	5.59	8	1	0	0	19	25	13	12	13	10
MAJOR LEAGUE TOTALS			1	0	5.59	8	1	0	0	19	25	13	12	13	10
MINOR LEAGUE TOTALS			35	23	4.43	92	75	8	2	477	497	267	235	156	397

5. Chris Snelling, of

Born: Dec. 3, 1981. **Ht.:** 5-10. **Wt.:** 165. **Bats:** L. **Throws:** L. **Career Transactions:** Signed out of Australia by Mariners, March 2, 1999.

Snelling signed as an underdeveloped 17-year-old, but he soon convinced the Mariners they had an Australian Lenny Dykstra on their hands. He was second in the Midwest League with a .342 average when he broke his hand and injured his wrist diving into an outfield wall. He wasn't at full strength when he came back at the end of the season and played on the Australian Olympic team, along with Class A Wisconsin teammate Craig Anderson. Snelling's hustle and all-out play have become his trademark. The Mariners love his attitude and knack for getting the fat part of the bat on the ball. For such an aggressive player, he knows when to be patient at the plate and has more walks than strikeouts as a pro. He runs well and is a solid defender in center field. He may learn in time that curbing his aggression might keep him healthier and in the lineup. Snelling could develop into an exciting leadoff hitter, though his bat control would be valuable anywhere in the order. He should open 2001 at high Class A San Bernardino.

Year	Club (League)	Class	AVG	G	AB	R	H	2B	3B	HR	RBI	BB	SO	SB
1999	Everett (NWL)	A	.306	69	265	46	81	15	3	10	50	33	24	8
2000	Wisconsin (Mid)	A	.305	72	259	44	79	9	5	9	56	34	34	7
MINOR LEAGUE TOTALS			.306	141	524	90	160	24	8	19	106	67	58	15

6. Jeff Heaverlo, rhp

Born: Jan. 13, 1978. **Ht.:** 6-1. **Wt.:** 215. **Bats:** R. **Throws:** R. **School:** University of Washington. **Career Transactions:** Selected by Mariners in first round (33rd overall) of 1999 draft; signed July 25, 1999.

The son of former Mariners reliever Dave, Jeff grew up in Moses Lake, Wash., and played his college ball in Seattle. In his first full pro season, he won his first three starts and struck out 24 hitters in 16 innings. It got tougher after that, but Heaverlo held his own in a hitter's league. He owns the best slider in the organization. Having grown up around the game, he knows how to pitch and mixes his breaking ball with two-seam and four-seam fastballs. His maturity allowed the Mariners to jump him to Tacoma when they needed a fill-in starter late in the season. Heaverlo's changeup is still in the developmental stages. He doesn't throw exceptionally hard and projects as a middle-of-the-rotation starter because of his velocity. Despite his gaudy record, Heaverlo was hardly dominant in the Cal League. In another organization he might move more quickly, but the Mariners are deep and he should spend most of the 2001 season at Double-A San Antonio.

Year	Club (League)	Class	W	L	ERA	G	GS	CG	SV	IP	H	R	ER	BB	SO
1999	Everett (NWL)	A	1	0	2.08	3	0	0	0	9	5	5	2	2	9
	Wisconsin (Mid)	A	1	0	2.55	3	3	1	0	18	15	6	5	7	24
2000	Lancaster (Cal)	A	14	6	4.22	27	27	0	0	156	170	84	73	52	159
	Tacoma (PCL)	AAA	0	1	4.85	2	2	0	0	13	14	7	7	6	4
MINOR LEAGUE TOTALS			16	7	4.02	35	32	1	0	195	204	102	87	67	196

7. Willie Bloomquist, 2b

Born: Nov. 27, 1977. **Ht.:** 5-11. **Wt.:** 180. **Bats:** R. **Throws:** R. **School:** Arizona State University. **Career Transactions:** Selected by Mariners in third round of 1999 draft; signed June 10, 1999.

Bloomquist spent nearly all of spring training in big league camp though he had never played above short-season ball. He led the Cal League with a .379 average when he was called to help out at Tacoma because the Mariners didn't want to disrupt Jermaine Clark in Double-A. If makeup were a tool, Bloomquist would grade out with a top-of-the-line 8 on the 2-to-8 scouting scale. He's a gamer who helps his club win by doing all the little things that don't show up in a box score. He puts the ball in play consistently and should hit for a solid average, though he'll never hit for power. He played several positions in college and could handle any assignment in a pinch, but has settled nicely at second. Bloomquist is the type of player who won't bowl you over the first time you see him, but he compensates for any shortcomings in tools with hustle and smart play. The Tigers took Clark in the major league Rule 5 draft in December, but even if he returns to the organization Bloomquist has passed him in the Mariners' long-term plans. He'll likely be in Seattle by the end of the 2001 season.

Year	Club (League)	Class	AVG	G	AB	R	H	2B	3B	HR	RBI	BB	SO	SB
1999	Everett (NWL)	A	.287	42	178	35	51	10	3	2	27	22	25	17
2000	Lancaster (Cal)	A	.379	64	256	63	97	19	6	2	51	37	27	22
	Tacoma (PCL)	AAA	.225	51	191	17	43	5	1	1	23	7	28	5
MINOR LEAGUE TOTALS			.306	157	625	115	191	34	10	5	101	66	80	44

8. Ryan Christianson, c

Born: April 21, 1981. **Ht.:** 6-2. **Wt.:** 210. **Bats:** R. **Throws:** R. **School:** Arlington HS, Riverside, Calif. **Career Transactions:** Selected by Mariners in first round (11th overall) of 1999 draft; signed July 18, 1999.

The 11th player taken in the '99 draft, Christianson made hitting look easy in his pro debut. He met reality last year in Class A Wisconsin, however, and learned what most high school catchers do: The road to the big leagues contains a few potholes. He finished the season with shoulder tendinitis, which may have bothered him more than he let on. Christianson has tremendous power to all fields but needs to learn what to do with it. When he does, he could become a solid run producer. He enjoys being in charge behind the plate and has the tools to become an above-average defender. Playing defense seems to help his offense as well. He hit .271 while catching compared to just .167 as a DH. The Mariners still haven't seen the tremendous arm strength Christianson showed off in high school, though he did regain zip in his second season. His arm now projects as average. Seattle won't let its void at catcher dictate Christianson's schedule. He'll likely move a level at a time and arrive in Seattle late in 2003.

Year	Club (League)	Class	AVG	G	AB	R	H	2B	3B	HR	RBI	BB	SO	SB
1999	Mariners (AZL)	R	.263	11	38	3	10	8	0	0	7	2	12	2
	Everett (NWL)	A	.280	30	107	19	30	7	0	8	17	14	31	3
2000	Wisconsin (Mid)	A	.249	119	418	60	104	20	0	13	59	50	98	1
MINOR LEAGUE TOTALS			.256	160	563	82	144	35	0	21	83	66	141	6

9. Rafael Soriano, rhp

Born: Dec. 19, 1979. **Ht.:** 6-1. **Wt.:** 175. **Bats:** R. **Throws:** R. **Career Transactions:** Signed out of Dominican Republic by Mariners, Aug. 30, 1996.

A converted outfielder, Soriano has come a long way in just two years on the mound. He got a late start on the 2000 season, missing the entire month of April with elbow tendinitis. He was consistently effective, never lasting less than five innings in a start and allowing more than three earned runs just twice. Soriano brings heat in the 95-96 mph range, which he complements with a hard slider and fledgling changeup. Arms like his don't come around often. He took to pitching from the start and is overpowering enough to be excused for most beginners mistakes. His slider is further along than his changeup, but both have a lot of room for improvement. Without a full arsenal and with his development time as a pitcher limited, Soriano may be better suited for a bullpen role. But there aren't many starters with his fastball and the Mariners have enough pitching, so they'll take their time with him for now. Soriano could develop into a dominant closer down the road.

Year	Club (League)	Class	AVG	G	AB	R	H	2B	3B	HR	RBI	BB	SO	SB
1997	Mariners (AZL)	R	.269	38	119	19	32	3	2	0	12	14	31	7
1998	Mariners (AZL)	R	.167	32	108	17	18	4	0	0	6	11	34	5
MINOR LEAGUE TOTALS			.220	70	227	36	50	7	2	0	18	25	65	12

Year	Club (League)	Class	W	L	ERA	G	GS	CG	SV	IP	H	R	ER	BB	SO
1999	Everett (NWL)	A	5	4	3.11	14	14	0	0	75	56	34	26	49	83
2000	Wisconsin (Mid)	A	8	4	2.87	21	21	1	0	122	97	41	39	50	90
MINOR LEAGUE TOTALS			13	8	2.97	35	35	1	0	197	153	75	65	99	173

10. Juan Silvestre, of

Born: Jan. 10, 1978. **Ht.:** 5-11. **Wt.:** 180. **Bats:** R. **Throws:** R. **Career Transactions:** Signed out of Dominican Republic by Mariners, July 4, 1994.

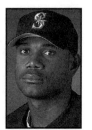

Silvestre made the Midwest League all-star team in 1999, but it wasn't quite enough to convince people. He made sure they took notice in 2000, leading the minor leagues in RBIs and earning California League MVP honors. The Mariners considered promoting him at midseason but wanted him to put two solid halves together—something he didn't do the year before. Silvestre has excellent power and already has 106 minor league home runs. The Mariners believe he'll hit for average as well. He shows a willingness to work hard on other aspects of his game, turning himself into an adequate defensive outfielder. Silvestre's bat has to be his ticket. He's a below-average runner with a below-average arm. He still strikes out a lot, but that's a common tradeoff with young power hitters. His monster numbers were inflated by Lancaster's home park, as he hit .340-20-86 at home and .265-10-51 on the road. Silvestre will report to Double-A in 2001. It will be interesting to see how he performs with expectations on him after a big season.

Year	Club (League)	Class	AVG	G	AB	R	H	2B	3B	HR	RBI	BB	SO	SB
1995	Mariners (DSL)	R	.287	59	209	38	60	4	3	11	43	23	46	0
1996	Mariners (DSL)	R	.311	64	238	51	74	9	1	19	61	28	34	1
1997	Mariners (AZL)	R	.341	34	135	32	46	11	3	7	36	15	31	4
	Tacoma (PCL)	AAA	.250	8	28	5	7	3	0	0	0	2	9	0
	Everett (NWL)	A	.315	14	54	9	17	3	1	3	9	4	19	1
1998	Wisconsin (Mid)	A	.252	106	401	44	101	20	5	15	56	22	98	7
1999	Wisconsin (Mid)	A	.288	137	534	89	154	34	4	21	107	47	124	5
2000	Lancaster (Cal)	A	.304	127	506	104	154	15	3	30	137	60	126	9
MINOR LEAGUE TOTALS			.291	549	2105	372	613	99	20	106	449	201	487	27

11. Sheldon Fulse, of

Born: Nov. 10, 1981. **Ht.:** 6-3. **Wt.:** 175. **Bats:** B. **Throws:** R. **School:** George Jenkins HS, Lakeland, Fla. **Career Transactions:** Selected by Mariners in third round of 1999 draft; signed July 12, 1999.

Fulse made his pro debut at 17, and the Mariners intended to keep him in extended spring training in 2000 until short-season Everett's season began. Those plans changed when an injury created a need at Lancaster. Fulse held his own as one of the youngest players in the California League for three weeks, then was reassigned to Wisconsin for the rest of the season. Fulse was converted from shortstop to center field upon signing in 1999. He already has taken well to the position and will develop into an above-average defender with an average arm. A switch-hitter, he doesn't offer much pop now, but the Mariners expect him to drive the ball as he fills out and end up with legitimate gap power. The key to his game, though, is his speed. He's one of the fastest runners in the organization and will steal his share of bases. Fulse should return to the California League in 2001.

Year	Club (League)	Class	AVG	G	AB	R	H	2B	3B	HR	RBI	BB	SO	SB
1999	Mariners (AZL)	R	.247	31	97	15	24	11	0	0	9	22	34	12
2000	Lancaster (Cal)	A	.274	17	62	11	17	4	3	0	7	8	18	0
	Wisconsin (Mid)	A	.255	64	216	45	55	8	0	2	22	38	58	30
MINOR LEAGUE TOTALS			.256	112	375	71	96	23	3	2	38	68	110	42

12. Cha Sueng Baek, rhp

Born: May 29, 1980. **Ht.:** 6-4. **Wt.:** 190. **Bats:** R. **Throws:** R. **Career Transactions:** Signed out of Korea by Mariners, Sept. 25, 1998.

Baek was regarded as one of the top high school prospects in Korea when the Mariners signed him for $1.3 million in 1998. His career got off to a slow start due to visa problems and a tender elbow, limiting him to eight games in his debut in 1999. Last year he was again troubled by tendinitis early in the season, but he tried to pitch through it without telling anyone he was hurt. After getting shut down and recovering, Baek saw his fastball climb back into the low 90s, and he mixed in his late-breaking slider with more regularity. He also throws a curve and changeup. He switched from a four-seam to a two-seam fastball last season, trading velocity for movement. Baek is likely to stay on the slow track through the system, both because he may need the extra development time and the organization has pitching depth.

Year	Club (League)	Class	W	L	ERA	G	GS	CG	SV	IP	H	R	ER	BB	SO
1999	Mariners (AZL)	R	3	0	3.67	8	4	0	0	27	30	13	11	6	25
2000	Wisconsin (Mid)	A	8	5	3.95	24	24	0	0	127	137	71	56	36	99
MINOR LEAGUE TOTALS			11	5	3.90	32	28	0	0	154	167	84	67	42	124

13. Miguel Villilo, 3b

Born: October 10, 1981. **Ht.:** 6-1. **Wt.:** 180. **Bats:** B. **Throws:** R. **Career Transactions:** Signed out of Dominican Republic by Mariners, July 5, 1999.

Villilo was named the No. 2 prospect in the Rookie-level Arizona League in his U.S. debut last year. A switch-hitting third baseman, he has a chance to blossom into an exciting prospect. His bat stands out as his best tool. Villilo should continue to hit for average and develop decent power as he climbs the ladder. He runs well and has one of the strongest arms among infielders in the organization. Villilo is fluid at third base and can become an above-average defender. The game comes easy for him. He should make his full-season debut at Wisconsin this season.

Year	Club (League)	Class	AVG	G	AB	R	H	2B	3B	HR	RBI	BB	SO	SB
1999	Mariners (DSL)	R	.202	30	114	22	23	7	1	3	11	12	29	3
2000	Mariners (AZL)	R	.347	44	167	30	58	14	3	3	37	23	37	2
	Tacoma (PCL)	AAA	.125	4	16	2	2	1	0	1	1	0	3	0
MINOR LEAGUE TOTALS			.279	78	297	54	83	22	4	7	49	35	69	5

14. Shin-Soo Choo, of

Born: July 30, 1982. **Ht.:** 5-11. **Wt.:** 175. **Bats:** L. **Throws:** L. **Career Transactions:** Signed out of Korea by Mariners, Aug. 14, 2000.

The Mariners took some of the money they didn't spend on early-round picks last summer and signed Choo to a $1.335 million deal, outbidding several other teams for the Korean junior team star. At the time, Mariners vice president of scouting Roger Jongewaard said Choo, who attended the same high school as Cha Sueng Baek, was the best prospect the team had ever scouted in Asia. Choo led Korea to the World Junior Championship title in 2000, earning tournament MVP honors as a two-way hero. The lefthander reaches the mid-90s off the mound and picked up the win in the gold-medal game against the United States, coming on in relief on two different occasions. That may have been his last pitching appearance, however, as the Mariners plan to keep him in center field. Though he's not especially big, Choo has tremendous power potential. He runs well and has an outstanding arm. He struggled somewhat in instructional league and has a tendency to pull that needs to be worked out. He's likely to open his career in the Rookie-level Arizona League in June.

Year	Club (League)	Class	AVG	G	AB	R	H	2B	3B	HR	RBI	BB	SO	SB
2000					Did Not Play—Signed 2001 Contract									

15. Brian Fuentes, lhp

Born: Aug. 9, 1975. **Ht.:** 6-4. **Wt.:** 220. **Bats:** L. **Throws:** L. **School:** Merced (Calif.) JC. **Career Transactions:** Selected by Mariners in 25th round of 1995 draft; signed May 26, 1996.

A draft-and-follow signing in 1996, Fuentes ranked eighth on the Mariners prospect list two years ago, but his stock slipped after a disappointing 1999 season. He was off to another rough start at New Haven last year when a change in his mechanics turned everything around. Fuentes has always thrown with a funky delivery that helped him post a lot of strikeouts because it was deceptive. But he couldn't repeat it consistently and it may have contributed to shoulder problems in '99. In the middle of 2000 the Mariners got him to drop to a low three-quarters delivery. The results were dramatic. Over his last seven starts, Fuentes went 3-2, 2.39, allowing 31 hits and 12 walks in 49 innings while striking out 61. The run began with a complete-game two-hitter in which he struck out 14 and walked none. Fuentes throws an average fastball and slider and a plus changeup. If he can stay consistent with his new delivery, he'll force his way to Seattle before long.

Year	Club (League)	Class	W	L	ERA	G	GS	CG	SV	IP	H	R	ER	BB	SO
1996	Everett (NWL)	A	0	1	4.39	13	2	0	0	27	23	14	13	13	26
1997	Wisconsin (Mid)	A	6	7	3.56	22	22	0	0	119	84	52	47	59	153
1998	Lancaster (Cal)	A	7	7	4.17	24	22	0	0	119	121	73	55	81	137
1999	New Haven (EL)	AA	3	3	4.95	15	14	0	0	60	53	36	33	46	66
2000	New Haven (EL)	AA	7	12	4.51	26	26	1	0	140	127	80	70	70	152
MINOR LEAGUE TOTALS			23	30	4.23	100	86	1	0	464	408	255	218	269	534

16. Greg Wooten, rhp

Born: March 30, 1974. **Ht.:** 6-7. **Wt.:** 210. **Bats:** R. **Throws:** R. **School:** Portland State University. **Career Transactions:** Selected by Mariners in third round of 1995 draft; signed Aug. 22, 1995.

Wooten was regarded as one of the top pitching prospects in the organization in his first few seasons, ranking in the top 10 in both 1997 and '98. But elbow trouble cost him nearly the entire 1998 season, and he didn't return to full strength from Tommy John surgery until last season. Wooten bounced back to make Baseball America's Minor League All-Star Team last year after posting more wins (17) than walks (15) and leading the Eastern League in ERA. He never did throw very hard, and since the surgery his fastball generally runs a tick below average, though it will reach average on occasion. He also throws a split-finger fastball, a slider and a changeup. Despite his outstanding 2000 campaign, Wooten has little chance of jumping to Seattle in 2001, with several pitchers in line ahead of him. He should start at Triple-A.

Year	Club (League)	Class	W	L	ERA	G	GS	CG	SV	IP	H	R	ER	BB	SO
1996	Wisconsin (Mid)	A	7	1	2.47	13	13	3	0	84	58	27	23	29	68
	Lancaster (Cal)	A	8	4	3.80	14	14	1	0	97	101	47	41	25	71
1997	Memphis (SL)	AA	11	10	4.47	26	26	0	0	155	166	91	77	59	98
1998	Lancaster (Cal)	A	2	2	7.18	6	6	0	0	31	43	26	25	12	22
1999	Lancaster (Cal)	A	10	4	4.33	17	17	3	0	114	123	62	55	30	72
2000	New Haven (EL)	AA	17	3	2.31	26	26	6	0	179	166	50	46	15	115
MINOR LEAGUE TOTALS			55	24	3.64	102	102	13	0	660	657	303	267	170	446

17. Sam Hays, lhp

Born: Oct. 7, 1981. **Ht.:** 6-4. **Wt.:** 210. **Bats:** L. **Throws:** L. **School:** Waco (Texas) HS. **Career Transactions:** Selected by Mariners in fourth round of 2000 draft; signed Aug. 23, 2000.

Hays was viewed as a difficult sign coming out of high school because of a commitment to Baylor, where eight family members had attended college. That includes his grandfather Sid Hudson, a former big league righthander. But the Mariners were in a gambling mood and spent their first pick on him. He came to terms at the end of the summer for $1.2 million. Hays has the kind of projectable pitcher's frame that scouts love, and the Mariners envision his fastball becoming above-average when he fills out. He already has shown an ability to spin his curveball effectively, and a solid changeup gives him a nice third pitch. All three could become plus pitches down the road. Hays has impressed the Mariners with the way he thinks the game.

Year	Club (League)	Class	W	L	ERA	G	GS	CG	SV	IP	H	R	ER	BB	SO
2000					Did Not Play—Signed 2001 Contract										

18. Rett Johnson, rhp

Born: July 6, 1979. **Ht.:** 6-2. **Wt.:** 220. **Bats:** L. **Throws:** R. **School:** Coastal Carolina University. **Career Transactions:** Selected by Mariners in eighth round of 2000 draft; signed June 13, 2000.

Johnson led the Big South Conference with 139 strikeouts last spring while logging 123 innings for Coastal Carolina. His velocity tailed off later in the college season, which may be one reason he was available in the eighth round. He could turn out to be a steal. The Mariners started him out in the bullpen in consideration of the number of innings he had logged. Johnson eventually moved into Everett's rotation and finished with outstanding numbers. He throws an average to above-average fastball and slider, and his changeup has become a solid third pitch for him. Johnson has a bulldog makeup on the mound and the Mariners expect him to develop into a winner wherever he goes. He should open his first full season at Wisconsin.

Year	Club (League)	Class	W	L	ERA	G	GS	CG	SV	IP	H	R	ER	BB	SO
2000	Everett (NWL)	A	5	4	2.07	17	8	0	0	70	51	26	16	21	88
MINOR LEAGUE TOTALS			5	4	2.07	17	8	0	0	70	51	26	16	21	88

19. Jason Grabowski, 3b

Born: May 24, 1976. **Ht.:** 6-3. **Wt.:** 200. **Bats:** L. **Throws:** R. **School:** University of Connecticut. **Career Transactions:** Selected by Rangers in second round of 1997 draft; signed June 12, 1997 . . . Claimed on waivers by Mariners from Rangers, Dec. 18, 2000.

Grabowski won't make up for the loss of free agent Alex Rodriguez to the Rangers, but he at least allowed Seattle to extract a small measure of revenge on Texas. When the Rangers needed to clear 40-man roster space to make room for its new signees, Grabowski was one of the victims and the Mariners claimed him on waivers. He ranked behind Ken Caminiti, Mike Lamb and Hank Blalock in Texas' long-term plans, but Grabowski might eventually become the solution to Seattle's third-base problems. He overcame a horrible start at Double-A Tulsa last year to finish with respectable season numbers. He's a disciplined hitter with line-drive power to both gaps, though his strikeouts rose in 2000 as he saw more breaking pitches than ever before. A former shortstop in college and catcher as a pro, Grabowski has defensive problems at the hot corner. His hands are good, but he has a funky throwing motion that can go haywire. He doesn't run well, though he has enough athletic ability to play any position on the field other than shortstop. He'll move up to Triple-A with the Mariners.

Year	Club (League)	Class	AVG	G	AB	R	H	2B	3B	HR	RBI	BB	SO	SB
1997	Pulaski (Appy)	R	.293	50	174	36	51	14	0	4	24	40	32	6
1998	Savannah (SAL)	A	.270	104	352	63	95	13	6	14	52	57	93	16
1999	Charlotte (FSL)	A	.313	123	434	68	136	31	6	12	87	65	66	13
	Tulsa (TL)	AA	.167	2	6	1	1	0	0	0	0	2	2	0
2000	Tulsa (TL)	AA	.274	135	493	93	135	33	5	19	90	88	106	8
MINOR LEAGUE TOTALS			.286	414	1459	261	418	91	17	49	253	252	299	43

20. Jamal Strong, of

Born: Aug. 5, 1978. **Ht.:** 5-10. **Wt.:** 180. **Bats:** R. **Throws:** R. **School:** University of Nebraska. **Career Transactions:** Selected by Mariners in sixth round of 2000 draft; signed June 10, 2000.

Strong was drafted by the Pirates out of high school in 1996 and junior college in 1997, but chose instead to stay in school. As a senior he nearly led Nebraska to the College World Series last spring. After stealing 69 bases in two seasons for the Cornhuskers, Strong swiped 60 bags in his debut at Everett, immediately grabbing the title of fastest player in the organization. Strong has been clocked at 3.88 seconds to first base—outstanding for a righthanded hitter. He did more than steal bases, though. His .314 average was third in the Northwest League and he was co-MVP of the circuit. He recognizes that he's not a power hitter and keeps the ball on the ground, draws walks and makes contact. Defensively, he uses his speed well in center field, but his arm is below-average. It will be interesting to see how the Mariners move Strong and Fulse, both of whom could lay claim to the center-field job in San Bernardino in 2001.

Year	Club (League)	Class	AVG	G	AB	R	H	2B	3B	HR	RBI	BB	SO	SB
2000	Everett (NWL)	A	.314	75	296	63	93	7	3	1	28	52	29	60
MINOR LEAGUE TOTALS			.314	75	296	63	93	7	3	1	28	52	29	60

21. Kevin Hodges, rhp

Born: June 24, 1973. **Ht.:** 6-4. **Wt.:** 200. **Bats:** R. **Throws:** R. **School:** Klein Oak HS, Spring, Texas. **Career Transactions:** Selected by Royals in eighth round of 1991 draft; signed June 17, 1991 . . . Granted free agency, Oct. 17, 1997 . . . Signed by Astros, March 31, 1998 . . . Traded by Astros to Mariners for OF Matt Mieske, June 21, 1999.

Hodges' persistence might finally pay off. He spent seven seasons in the Royals organization, never getting an opportunity above Class A, before the Astros signed him and finally gave him a glimpse of life in the high minors. Not until the Mariners picked him up in a June 1999 trade for outfielder Matt Mieske did things open up for him. Hodges enjoyed easily his best season last year and was rewarded with a call to the big leagues. He throws a good sinking fastball with average velocity and complements it with a slider. He made seven starts in the Arizona Fall League, though the Mariners see him as a contender for a middle-relief job this spring.

Year	Club (League)	Class	W	L	ERA	G	GS	CG	SV	IP	H	R	ER	BB	SO
1991	Royals (GCL)	R	1	2	4.30	9	3	0	0	23	22	14	11	11	13
1992	Royals (GCL)	R	5	3	4.71	11	9	0	0	50	60	30	26	25	24
1993	Royals (GCL)	R	7	2	2.03	12	10	0	0	71	52	25	16	25	40
	Wilmington (Car)	A	1	0	0.00	3	0	0	0	5	2	0	0	3	1
1994	Rockford (Mid)	A	9	6	3.38	24	17	2	3	114	96	53	43	35	83

1995	Wilmington (Car)	A	2	3	4.53	12	10	0	0	54	53	31	27	25	27
1996	Lansing (Mid)	A	1	2	4.66	9	9	0	0	48	47	32	25	19	23
	Wilmington (Car)	A	2	4	5.35	8	8	0	0	39	45	30	23	18	15
1997	Wilmington (Car)	A	8	11	4.48	28	20	0	1	125	150	78	62	44	63
1998	Jackson (TL)	AA	4	5	3.61	29	15	0	0	107	108	55	43	38	70
1999	Jackson (TL)	AA	1	4	2.94	8	8	0	0	49	48	22	16	16	21
	New Orleans (PCL)	AAA	1	3	7.24	5	5	0	0	27	34	23	22	11	16
	Tacoma (PCL)	AAA	3	3	3.25	14	12	0	1	83	88	31	30	27	42
2000	Tacoma (PCL)	AAA	4	3	2.76	30	11	2	3	98	87	32	30	21	73
	Seattle (AL)	MAJ	0	0	5.19	13	0	0	0	17	18	10	10	12	7
MAJOR LEAGUE TOTALS			0	0	5.19	13	0	0	0	17	18	10	10	12	7
MINOR LEAGUE TOTALS			49	51	3.77	202	137	4	8	893	892	456	374	318	511

22. Justin Kaye, rhp

Born: June 9, 1976. **Ht.:** 6-4. **Wt.:** 195. **Bats:** R. **Throws:** R. **School:** Bishop Gorman HS, Las Vegas. **Career Transactions:** Selected by Mariners in 19th round of 1995 draft; signed June 7, 1995.

Kaye has teased the Mariners with his stuff for six seasons, all but one out of the bullpen. A move to the rotation proved disastrous in 1997. He finally put everything together for a full season last year, striking out 11.7 hitters per nine innings and keeping his walks in check. He went 2-1, 6.57 in the Arizona Fall League, but his secondary numbers were solid. Kaye throws a sinking fastball and has gained command of his hard slider. The combination should be enough for him to succeed in relief. Kaye was added to the 40-man roster and likely is ticketed for Tacoma to open the season. It has taken him a while, but he should get to Seattle soon.

Year	Club (League)	Class	W	L	ERA	G	GS	CG	SV	IP	H	R	ER	BB	SO
1995	Mariners (AZL)	R	0	1	10.71	12	0	0	0	19	33	28	23	19	13
1996	Mariners (AZL)	R	1	0	3.62	20	0	0	3	32	34	23	13	19	36
1997	Wisconsin (Mid)	A	8	12	7.30	28	26	0	0	127	129	113	103	104	115
1998	Wisconsin (Mid)	A	6	2	1.71	28	0	0	9	47	25	11	9	30	79
	Lancaster (Cal)	A	1	2	6.82	16	0	0	0	30	37	24	23	13	34
1999	Lancaster (Cal)	A	3	5	5.75	53	0	0	14	61	68	42	39	40	66
2000	New Haven (EL)	AA	2	5	2.67	50	0	0	8	84	80	32	25	36	109
MINOR LEAGUE TOTALS			21	27	5.27	207	26	0	34	402	406	273	235	261	452

23. Jake Meyer, rhp

Born: Jan. 7, 1975. **Ht.:** 6-1. **Wt.:** 195. **Bats:** R. **Throws:** R. **School:** UCLA. **Career Transactions:** Selected by White Sox in seventh round of 1997 draft; signed June 8, 1997 . . . Traded by White Sox to Reds for C Brook Fordyce, March 25, 1999 . . . Traded by Reds with RHP Brett Tomko, 2B Antonio Perez and OF Mike Cameron to Mariners for OF Ken Griffey, Jr., Feb. 10, 2000.

Meyer is already in his third organization after being part of the four-player package that moved Ken Griffey to Cincinnati. Meyer has the kind of stuff that makes it easy to see why teams keep trading for him. He throws a mid-90s fastball, a slider and a splitter, and all three can be average or better. He was limited to 26 games last year by tendinitis, but made up some lost innings over the winter in Venezuela, where he closed for the Lara Cardinals. Meyer could be in the mix for a bullpen job in Seattle in 2001.

Year	Club (League)	Class	W	L	ERA	G	GS	CG	SV	IP	H	R	ER	BB	SO
1997	Bristol (Appy)	R	1	1	2.25	17	0	0	5	20	15	7	5	7	25
1998	Hickory (SAL)	A	0	6	3.21	35	0	0	11	56	58	30	20	22	47
	Winston-Salem (Car)	A	0	1	2.92	11	0	0	2	12	12	6	4	3	13
1999	Rockford (Mid)	A	3	2	2.54	33	0	0	16	46	40	16	13	18	51
	Chattanooga (SL)	AA	2	2	5.96	20	0	0	0	23	24	17	15	14	16
2000	New Haven (EL)	AA	1	0	2.29	15	0	0	2	20	17	5	5	8	20
	Mariners (AZL)	R	0	0	4.50	3	3	0	0	4	4	2	2	3	6
	Tacoma (PCL)	AAA	0	1	3.55	8	0	0	0	13	9	5	5	5	14
MINOR LEAGUE TOTALS			7	13	3.21	142	3	0	36	193	179	88	69	80	192

24. Aquilino Lopez, rhp

Born: July 30, 1980. **Ht.:** 6-3. **Wt.:** 165. **Bats:** R. **Throws:** R. **Career Transactions:** Signed out of Dominican Republic by Mariners, July 3, 1997.

Lopez led the Northwest League in strikeouts as a starter in 1999, but spent most of 2000 in the bullpen after opening the season in the rotation. His last start was a complete game, three-hit shutout. Lopez gave up runs in just five of his 34 relief outings and allowed just six hits in June and July combined. He owns a strong arm and throws a fastball, slider and

Year	Club (League)	Class	W	L	ERA	G	GS	CG	SV	IP	H	R	ER	BB	SO
1997	Mariners (DSL)	R	2	1	3.10	15	0	0	2	20	19	8	7	7	19
1998	Mariners (DSL)	R	5	1	2.19	28	0	0	3	70	53	23	17	19	100
1999	Everett (NWL)	A	7	6	3.80	15	15	1	0	88	76	44	37	30	93
2000	Wisconsin (Mid)	A	6	1	1.85	39	5	1	17	68	47	16	14	20	67
MINOR LEAGUE TOTALS			20	9	2.74	97	20	2	22	246	195	91	75	76	279

25. Derrick Van Dusen, lhp

Born: June 6, 1981. **Ht.:** 6-2. **Wt.:** 175. **Bats:** L. **Throws:** L. **School:** Riverside (Calif.) CC. **Career Transactions:** Selected by Mariners in fifth round of 2000 draft; signed June 12, 2000.

Van Dusen pitched Riverside Community College to its first California state title in May. He continued his domination in the Arizona League, forcing a midseason promotion to Everett, where he continued his torrid strikeout pace. Van Dusen already is comfortable throwing strikes and knows what to do with his stuff. His fastball and slider are both average pitches. He uses the slider effectively against both lefthanders and righthanders. His changeup is coming along nicely as well, though it's definitely his third pitch. Van Dusen has grown two inches since finishing high school and the Mariners aren't sure he's done yet. He should continue his baseball growth this season at Wisconsin. He already has shown the aptitude to move quickly, so he might not be there long.

Year	Club (League)	Class	W	L	ERA	G	GS	CG	SV	IP	H	R	ER	BB	SO
2000	Mariners (AZL)	R	6	0	2.63	10	2	0	0	41	38	14	12	6	58
	Everett (NWL)	A	1	1	3.60	4	2	0	0	15	17	13	6	5	24
MINOR LEAGUE TOTALS			7	1	2.89	14	4	0	0	56	55	27	18	11	82

26. Sam Walton, lhp

Born: Dec. 1, 1978. **Ht.:** 6-4. **Wt.:** 215. **Bats:** L. **Throws:** L. **School:** W.W. Samuell HS, Dallas. **Career Transactions:** Selected by Mariners in seventh round of 1997 draft; signed June 7, 1997.

Walton has taken slow steps since the Mariners drafted him four years ago, spending two seasons in the Rookie-level Arizona League and two seasons at short-season Everett. He has a nice frame for a pitcher and throws hard for a lefthander, which explains the fascination and the patience. In his first three seasons he walked nearly a batter per inning. Walton finally showed control last summer, but was limited to 31 innings by biceps tendinitis that cost him the last month of the season. In addition to his hard fastball, Walton throws a curve and changeup. He still has a long road ahead of him, but with the paucity of hard-throwing lefthanders in the big leagues, Seattle will be patient.

Year	Club (League)	Class	W	L	ERA	G	GS	CG	SV	IP	H	R	ER	BB	SO
1997	Mariners (AZL)	R	1	3	5.84	13	12	0	0	49	54	49	32	46	46
1998	Mariners (AZL)	R	3	6	6.44	13	11	0	0	50	55	51	36	45	52
1999	Everett (NWL)	A	3	3	4.94	14	14	0	0	62	55	39	34	60	59
2000	Everett (NWL)	A	2	0	1.44	7	6	0	0	31	27	6	5	10	39
MINOR LEAGUE TOTALS			9	12	4.99	47	43	0	0	193	191	145	107	161	196

27. Ryan Franklin, rhp

Born: March 5, 1973. **Ht.:** 6-3. **Wt.:** 165. **Bats:** R. **Throws:** R. **School:** Seminole (Okla.) JC. **Career Transactions:** Selected by Mariners in 23rd round of 1992 draft; signed May 21, 1993.

Franklin went 20-0 in two junior college seasons before signing with the Mariners as a draft-and-follow in 1993. He moved quickly his first couple of years, finishing the '94 campaign at Triple-A Calgary. He slowed down considerably after that, however, and has four Triple-A seasons under his belt with just six major league appearances, all in 1999. He also has a gold medal, having pitched for Team USA in the Sydney Olympics last September. Franklin led the tournament with three wins and didn't allow a hit or run in 8⅓ innings of relief. He doesn't throw especially hard, but what he lacks in velocity he makes up for with variety. His arsenal includes six pitches: two- and four-seam fastballs, splitter, slider, curveball and changeup. In Sydney, Franklin worked around 93 mph coming out of the bullpen, though his fastball tops out around 90 as a starter. This could be the year Franklin finally breaks through the Four-A ceiling and gets a shot as a long man in Seattle.

Year	Club (League)	Class	W	L	ERA	G	GS	CG	SV	IP	H	R	ER	BB	SO
1993	Bellingham (NWL)	A	5	3	2.92	15	14	1	0	74	72	38	24	27	55
1994	Appleton (Mid)	A	9	6	3.13	18	18	5	0	118	105	60	41	23	102

Year	Club (League)	Class	W	L	ERA	G	GS	CG	SV	IP	H	R	ER	BB	SO
	Riverside (Cal)	A	4	2	3.06	8	8	1	0	62	61	26	21	8	35
	Calgary (PCL)	AAA	0	0	7.94	1	1	0	0	9	6	6	5	1	2
1995	Port City (SL)	AA	6	10	4.32	31	20	1	0	146	153	84	70	43	102
1996	Port City (SL)	AA	6	12	4.01	28	27	2	0	182	186	99	81	37	127
1997	Memphis (SL)	AA	4	2	3.03	11	8	2	0	59	45	22	20	14	49
	Tacoma (PCL)	AAA	5	5	4.18	14	14	0	0	90	97	48	42	24	59
1998	Tacoma (PCL)	AAA	5	6	4.51	34	16	1	1	128	148	75	64	32	90
1999	Tacoma (PCL)	AAA	6	9	4.71	29	19	2	2	136	142	81	71	33	94
	Seattle (AL)	MAJ	0	0	4.76	6	0	0	0	11	10	6	6	8	6
2000	Tacoma (PCL)	AAA	11	5	3.90	31	22	4	0	164	147	85	71	35	142
MAJOR LEAGUE TOTALS			0	0	4.76	6	0	0	0	11	10	6	6	8	6
MINOR LEAGUE TOTALS			61	60	3.94	220	167	19	3	1164	1165	624	510	277	857

28. Clint Nageotte, rhp

Born: Oct. 25, 1980. **Ht.:** 6-4. **Wt.:** 190. **Bats:** R. **Throws:** R. **School:** Brooklyn (Ohio) HS. **Career Transactions:** Selected by Mariners in fifth round of 1999 draft; signed Aug. 18, 1999.

Nageotte made his pro debut last season after signing too late to play in 1999. He missed most of extended spring training for personal reasons, so the Arizona League was his first real test. He had little trouble adjusting, finishing third in ERA and fourth in strikeouts. He capped off the Mariners' title run there, striking out eight in seven innings of the championship game. His power curveball was one of the best in the league, and his fastball is a plus pitch as well. His changeup is developing but is still his third option. Nageotte's next step likely will be Wisconsin.

Year	Club (League)	Class	W	L	ERA	G	GS	CG	SV	IP	H	R	ER	BB	SO
2000	Mariners (AZL)	R	4	1	2.16	12	7	0	1	50	29	15	12	28	59
MINOR LEAGUE TOTALS			4	1	2.16	12	7	0	1	50	29	15	12	28	59

29. Josue Matos, rhp

Born: March 15, 1978. **Ht.:** 6-4. **Wt.:** 190. **Bats:** R. **Throws:** R. **School:** Miami-Dade CC South. **Career Transactions:** Selected by Mariners in 27th round of 1996 draft; signed May 24, 1997.

Matos has shown outstanding control since signing as a draft-and-follow in 1997. In 402 professional innings, he has walked just 106 batters. Since repeating the Arizona League in 1998 he has moved steadily up the ladder, succeeding without outstanding stuff. Matos is able to get by with a below-average fastball because he changes speeds well. He also throws both a slider and a curve. His arm action and delivery are quiet, befitting a player who's sneaking his way through the organization. The organization backlog of pitching could force him back to Double-A to open 2001.

Year	Club (League)	Class	W	L	ERA	G	GS	CG	SV	IP	H	R	ER	BB	SO
1997	Mariners (AZL)	R	1	0	4.17	14	1	0	1	45	48	27	21	6	50
	Everett (NWL)	A	0	0	2.08	2	0	0	0	4	5	2	1	2	6
1998	Mariners (AZL)	R	3	0	2.20	17	2	0	0	41	29	14	10	11	51
1999	Wisconsin (Mid)	A	9	9	4.63	25	22	2	0	138	143	78	71	42	136
2000	Lancaster (Cal)	A	3	3	2.64	14	14	0	0	89	78	29	26	22	93
	New Haven (EL)	AA	4	5	3.63	14	14	1	0	84	77	36	34	23	60
MINOR LEAGUE TOTALS			20	17	3.65	86	53	3	1	402	380	186	163	106	396

30. Pedro Liriano, 2b

Born: Feb. 20, 1982. **Ht.:** 5-11. **Wt.:** 175. **Bats:** R. **Throws:** R. **Career Transactions:** Signed out of Dominican Republic by Mariners, May 30, 1999.

Liriano, who ranked third in the Rookie-level Dominican Summer League with a .367 average in 1999, won a batting title in his U.S. debut. He hit an even .400 in the Arizona League, where the Mariners ran away with the league title. After finishing the season with four games in Everett, he went to Asia for a minor league exhibition tour. Liriano is an aggressive hitter who puts the ball in play and doesn't strike out much. He has a solid stroke but doesn't project as a power hitter. Instead, he'll be the scrappy guy at the top of the lineup who gets on base and causes disruptions. He's not a burner, but Liriano utilizes his speed well. Defensively, he has work to do, though he has the tools to become an adequate second baseman.

Year	Club (League)	Class	AVG	G	AB	R	H	2B	3B	HR	RBI	BB	SO	SB
1999	Mariners (DSL)	R	.367	58	199	63	73	10	3	13	47	55	26	25
2000	Mariners (AZL)	R	.400	43	170	46	68	15	2	1	30	21	11	18
	Everett (NWL)	A	.200	4	15	2	3	0	0	0	2	4	4	4
MINOR LEAGUE TOTALS			.375	105	384	111	144	25	5	14	79	80	41	47

Tampa Bay
Devil Rays

TOP 30 PROSPECTS

1. Josh Hamilton, of
2. Jason Standridge, rhp
3. Carl Crawford, of
4. Aubrey Huff, 3b
5. Jesus Colome, rhp
6. Brent Abernathy, 2b
7. Matt White, rhp
8. Bobby Seay, lhp
9. Rocco Baldelli, of
10. Travis Harper, rhp
11. Toby Hall, c
12. Jared Sandberg, 3b
13. Jace Brewer, ss
14. Jason Tyner, of
15. Travis Phelps, rhp
16. Kenny Kelly, of
17. Delvin James, rhp
18. Ramon Soler, ss
19. Jorge Cantu, ss
20. Jeff Ridgway, lhp
21. Seth McClung, rhp
22. Damian Rolls, 3b
23. Juan Salas, 3b
24. Alex Sanchez, of
25. Doug Waechter, rhp
26. Joe Kennedy, lhp
27. Ronni Seberino, lhp
28. Cecilio Garibaldi, rhp
29. Josh Pressley, 1b
30. Greg Nash, of/rhp

By Bill Ballew

Tampa Bay's marketing material last spring boasted of a "Hit Show 2000." After watching veterans such as Vinny Castilla and Greg Vaughn struggle while nearly doubling the payroll to $51.5 million, though, the primary hit experienced by the third-year franchise came in the pocketbook. The promise of a power barrage did little to excite the locals, with attendance at Tropicana Field increasing by just 14,351 to 1,549,440, second-lowest in the American League.

The result has the Devil Rays shifting gears again. General manager Chuck LaMar trimmed payroll in July by dealing Jose Canseco, Jim Mecir, Steve Trachsel and Rick White. Then he made a strong deal in January, unloading Roberto Hernandez' contract to the Royals and bringing in talented young outfielder Ben Grieve from the Athletics.

LaMar and the Devil Rays remain committed to a five-year plan that centers on building the team through scouting and player development. It's similar to the model used by the Braves, LaMar's previous employer. The hard part comes in suffering through 69-win campaigns in one of the game's best divisions. On the bright side, a thorough look reveals impressive talent is developing throughout the farm system.

Scouting director Dan Jennings' focus on raw athletes with high ceilings has stocked the farm system with a significant amount of talent, starting with outfielder Josh Hamilton, one of the game's best prospects. With additional moves expected prior to spring training, the Devil Rays could start as many as four rookies in their everyday line-up during 2001. At least one rookie will be in the rotation, and Triple-A Durham is expected to open with one of the minors' most promising pitching staffs.

The hope in Tampa Bay is that at least two or three of the first wave of young players will stick, creating a foundation when the second wave headed by Hamilton arrives in a couple of years. If all goes as planned, the Rays could field a revamped—and competitive—lineup as soon as 2004.

The downside comes in keeping the franchise afloat financially while the fans decide whether the kids are all right. The plan could wind up costing LaMar and manager Larry Rothschild their jobs, but it serves as the best route toward building long-term success in a market that has yet to prove it can support a major league team.

OrganizationOverview

General manager: Chuck LaMar. **Farm director:** Tom Foley. **Scouting director:** Dan Jennings.

2000 PERFORMANCE

Class	Team	League	W	L	Pct.	Finish*	Manager(s)
Majors	Tampa Bay	American	69	92	.429	13th (14)	Larry Rothschild
Triple-A	Durham Bulls	International	81	62	.566	4th (14)	Bill Evers
Double-A	Orlando Rays	Southern	65	71	.478	7th (10)	Mike Ramsey
High A	#St. Petersburg Devil Rays	Florida State	58	81	.417	13th (14)	Julio Garcia
Low A	Charleston RiverDogs	South Atlantic	73	66	.525	6th (14)	Charlie Montoyo
Short-season	Hudson Valley Renegades	New York-Penn	23	52	.307	14th (14)	Dave Silvestri
Rookie	Princeton Devil Rays	Appalachian	34	34	.500	6th (10)	Edwin Rodriguez
OVERALL 2000 MINOR LEAGUE RECORD			334	365	.478	24th (30)	

*Finish in overall standings (No. of teams in league). #Affiliate will be in Bakersfield (California) in 2001.

ORGANIZATION LEADERS

BATTING
*AVG	Randy Winn, Durham	.330
R	**Ozzie Timmons**, Durham	100
H	Carl Crawford, Charleston	170
TB	**Ozzie Timmons**, Durham	273
2B	Josh Pressley, Charleston	44
3B	Carl Crawford, Charleston	11
HR	**Ozzie Timmons**, Durham	29
RBI	**Ozzie Timmons**, Durham	104
BB	**Ozzie Timmons**, Durham	73
SO	Joe Pomierski, Orlando	137
SB	Carl Crawford, Charleston	55

PITCHING
W	Jim Magrane, Charleston	12
L	Delvin James, Orlando/St. Petersburg	12
	Jason Standridge, Orlando/St. Petersburg	..12
#ERA	**Jason Pruett**, Charleston/St. Petersburg	2.27
G	Lee Gardner, Durham/Orlando	57
	Jason Pruett, Charleston/St. Petersburg	..57
CG	Three tied at	4
SV	Bill Taylor, Durham	26
IP	Delvin James, Orlando/St. Petersburg	 174
BB	Matt White, Orlando/Durham	74
	Jason Standridge, Orlando/St. Petersburg	74
SO	Neal Frendling, Charleston	174

*Minimum 250 at-bats. #Minimum 75 innings.

TOP PROSPECTS OF THE DECADE

1997	Matt White, rhp
1998	Matt White, rhp
1999	Matt White, rhp
2000	Josh Hamilton, of

TOP DRAFT PICKS OF THE DECADE

1996	Paul Wilder, of
1997	Jason Standridge, rhp
1998	Josh Pressley, 1b (4)
1999	Josh Hamilton, of
2000	Rocco Baldelli, of

BEST TOOLS

Best Hitter for Average	Aubrey Huff
Best Power Hitter	Josh Hamilton
Fastest Baserunner	Carl Crawford

Timmons   **Pruett**

Best Fastball	Jesus Colome
Best Breaking Ball	Jason Standridge
Best Control	Travis Harper
Best Defensive Catcher	Toby Hall
Best Defensive Infielder	Brent Abernathy
Best Infield Arm	Juan Salas
Best Defensive Outfielder	Rocco Baldelli
Best Outfield Arm	Josh Hamilton

PROJECTED 2004 LINEUP

Catcher	Toby Hall
First Base	Aubrey Huff
Second Base	Brent Abernathy
Third Base	Jared Sandberg
Shortstop	Jace Brewer
Left Field	Carl Crawford
Center Field	Rocco Baldelli
Right Field	Josh Hamilton
Designated Hitter	Ben Grieve
No. 1 Starter	Jason Standridge
No. 2 Starter	Jesus Colome
No. 3 Starter	Matt White
No. 4 Starter	Bobby Seay
No. 5 Starter	Ryan Rupe
Closer	Delvin James

ALL-TIME LARGEST BONUSES

Matt White, 1996	$10,200,000
Rolando Arrojo, 1997	7,000,000
Josh Hamilton, 1999	3,960,000
Bobby Seay, 1996	3,000,000
Rocco Baldelli, 2000	2,250,000

DraftAnalysis

2000 Draft

Best Pro Debut: 3B Kelly Eddlemon (12) batted .293-10-42 at Rookie-level Princeton. In instructional league he played at second base, where his bat would be more valuable.

Best Athlete: OF **Rocco Baldelli** (1), only the second first-round pick ever to come out of Rhode Island, was a state sprint champion and led his high school to state titles in baseball, basketball and volleyball. RHP John Benedetti (10), believed to be the first player ever drafted out of Augustana (Ill.), can dunk despite being just 6 feet tall. He was Augustana's basketball MVP as a senior.

Best Hitter: Baldelli or 2B Mike Krga (7). Krga hit .273 at Princeton while Baldelli batted .216. The Devil Rays didn't expect a lot out of Baldelli because he didn't see top-flight pitching in high school and was recovering from a pulled oblique muscle.

Best Raw Power: Baldelli.

Fastest Runner: Baldelli runs a 6.38-second 60-yard dash. He gives Tampa Bay another outfielder with top-of-the-line speed.

Best Defensive Player: Sophomore-eligible SS Jace Brewer (5), who wrote all 30 teams before the draft to tell them he planned to return to Baylor to improve his skills. The Devil Rays gambled and changed his mind with a four-year major league contract worth $1.5 million, the first such contract ever given so low a draft pick.

Best Fastball: RHP Evan Rust, a nondrafted free agent out of St. Mary's (Calif.), can touch 95 mph. Among the draftees, the lowest-selected player signed by Tampa Bay, RHP Juan Renteria (47), can reach 94 mph.

Most Intriguing Background: SS Edgar Gonzalez (30) is the older brother of Adrian, the No. 1 overall pick by the Marlins. At 6-foot-9 and 265 pounds, LHP Hans Smith (11) is the largest player selected by any club.

Closest To The Majors: Under the terms of his contract, Brewer was promoted to Tampa Bay in September. He didn't appear in a game with a tear in his throwing shoulder.

Baldelli

Best Late-Round Pick: Back problems prevented RHP Jamie Shields (16) from pitching much as a high school senior, but Tampa Bay area scout Fred Repke monitored Shields over the summer. Once they believed he was healthy, the Devil Rays signed him. In instructional league, Shields threw 92 mph with a solid average changeup and a borderline average curveball.

The One Who Got Away: Oklahoma State OF Luke Scott (45) led the Cape Cod League with 11 homers last summer.

Assessment: The Devil Rays were deluded if they thought signing free agents Juan Guzman, Steve Trachsel and Gerald Williams would make a significant difference, and it also cost them their picks in the second through fourth rounds. They regrouped as best they could by signing Brewer and Shields.

1999 Draft

The future of the franchise is OF Josh Hamilton, the No. 1 overall pick. The Devil Rays' outfield of the future also will feature speedy Carl Crawford (2), a quarterback who had a Nebraska scholarship.

Grade: A–

1998 Draft

Tampa Bay foolishly gave away its first three picks to sign free agents. At least it found two very solid players in 3B Aubrey Huff (5) and RHP Ryan Rupe (6).

Grade: C+

1997 Draft

Tampa Bay earned a split decision with Auburn, getting RHP Jason Standridge, who would have quarterbacked the Tigers, and losing RHP Chris Bootcheck (17), a 2000 first-rounder. Another passer, OF Kenny Kelly (2), eventually left Miami football but still has a lot to prove on the diamond.

Grade: C

1996 Draft

The Rays' first-ever pick, OF Paul Wilder (1), was a reach who didn't pan out. The best choices were RHPs Delvin James (14) and Dan Wheeler (34, draft-and-follow) and 3B Jared Sandberg (16).

Grade: C

Note: Draft analysis prepared by Jim Callis. Numbers in parentheses indicate draft rounds.

... Hamilton is one of the few players with five legitimate plus tools that improve every time he takes the field.

Josh Hamilton of

Born: May 21, 1981.
Ht.: 6-4. **Wt.:** 209.
Bats: L. **Throws:** L.
School: Athens Drive HS, Raleigh, N.C.
Career Transactions: Selected by Devil Rays in first round (first overall) of 1999 draft; signed June 3, 1999.

The No. 1 overall pick in the 1999 draft and the recipient of a $3.96 million signing bonus, Hamilton built on a solid debut season with an impressive campaign at Class A Charleston. He had little difficulty adjusting to the South Atlantic League and was the league's top prospect by season's end. Hamilton shared the league's MVP award with Pirates catcher J.R. House and was voted as the best batting prospect, power prospect, outfield arm and most exciting player in a survey of Sally League managers. He was the youngest player in the Futures Game, where he went 3-for-4. The lone negative was a right knee injury he sustained after a misstep in pursuit of a fly ball. Hamilton's average dropped from the .350 range after the injury, and he missed the last month of the minor league season after having arthroscopic surgery to repair torn cartilage. He recovered in time to participate in instructional league.

Hamilton is a rare breed. He's one of the few players with five legitimate plus tools that continue to improve every time he takes the field. His power is increasing as his 19-year-old body matures. Anyone who saw his over-the-head catch, a la Willie Mays, in the 2000 SAL all-star game knows how much ground he covers in center field. His arm, which produced a mid-90s fastball while in high school, is one of the strongest among minor league outfielders. For all his tools, Hamilton's most important trait may be his baseball savvy. His knowledge of how to play the game far exceeds his experience. It's hard to find any aspect of Hamilton's game that could be deemed a weakness. He's sometimes too aggressive at the plate, resulting in 72 strikeouts against 26 walks in 2000. With less than two full seasons of professional experience, Hamilton simply needs to remain healthy and get as many at-bats as possible so he can learn to make adjustments against more talented competition.

Hamilton showed during instructional league that there's no reason to expect him to be anything less than 100 percent by spring training. He was headed for a promotion at the time of his injury, and chances are he'll bypass high Class A Bakersfield and move to Double-A Orlando to open 2001. A promotion to the big leagues could come as soon as 2002.

Year	Club (League)	Class	AVG	G	AB	R	H	2B	3B	HR	RBI	BB	SO	SB
1999	Princeton (Appy)	R	.347	56	236	49	82	20	4	10	48	13	43	17
	Hudson Valley (NY-P)	A	.194	16	72	7	14	3	0	0	7	1	14	1
2000	Charleston, SC (SAL)	A	.302	96	391	62	118	23	3	13	61	27	71	14
MINOR LEAGUE TOTALS			.306	168	699	118	214	46	7	23	116	41	128	32

2. Jason Standridge, rhp

Born: Nov. 9, 1978. **Ht.:** 6-4. **Wt.:** 205. **Bats:** R. **Throws:** R. **School:** Hewitt-Trussville HS, Trussville, Ala. **Career Transactions:** Selected by Devil Rays in first round (31st overall) of 1997 draft; signed June 6, 1997.

After not winning a game his first season and struggling during his second, the former Auburn quarterback recruit has put together two straight solid seasons. Standridge made more progress than any pitcher in the Tampa Bay organization in 2000. He got stronger as the season progressed, going 5-0, 1.80 in August before starting a playoff game in Triple-A. The Devil Rays love Standridge's character. Nicknamed "The Stallion," he's considered the hardest-working pitcher in the system. He has learned to locate his low-to mid-90s fastball down in the strike zone before retiring hitters with his hard, sharp-breaking curveball. He has matured into an all-around pitcher who has learned from his mistakes. Standridge needs to sharpen his overall command. His changeup has improved but isn't quite up to major league standards. Standridge is a strong candidate for Durham in 2001 and could move quickly to Tampa Bay if he makes the necessary progress against Triple-A hitters.

Year	Club (League)	Class	W	L	ERA	G	GS	CG	SV	IP	H	R	ER	BB	SO
1997	Devil Rays (GCL)	R	0	6	3.59	13	13	0	0	58	56	30	23	13	55
1998	Princeton (Appy)	R	4	4	7.00	12	12	0	0	63	82	61	49	28	47
1999	Charleston, SC (SAL)	A	9	1	2.02	18	18	3	0	116	80	35	26	31	84
	St. Petersburg (FSL)	A	4	4	3.91	8	8	0	0	48	49	21	21	20	26
2000	St. Petersburg (FSL)	A	2	4	3.38	10	10	1	0	56	45	28	21	31	41
	Orlando (SL)	AA	6	8	3.62	17	17	2	0	97	85	46	39	43	55
MINOR LEAGUE TOTALS			25	27	3.68	78	78	4	0	438	397	221	179	166	308

3. Carl Crawford, of

Born: Aug. 5, 1981. **Ht.:** 6-2. **Wt.:** 203. **Bats:** L. **Throws:** L. **School:** Jefferson Davis HS, Houston. **Career Transactions:** Selected by Devil Rays in second round of 1999 draft; signed June 14, 1999.

Crawford passed up football at Nebraska and basketball at UCLA. A $1.245 million bonus from the Devil Rays helped him make the decision. Despite limited experience, he has hit better than .300 and ranked among his league's top 10 prospects in each of his first two seasons. He led the South Atlantic League in hits and stolen bases in 2000. The Devil Rays rave about Crawford's ability to take instruction and put it to use. His enthusiasm is apparent, and he never seems intimidated. His best tool is his world-class speed, which helps him avoid long dry spells at the plate. He has improved his bunting ability, making his speed even more valuable. Crawford needs more at-bats to gain a better handle on the strike zone and more innings in the field to discover the nuances of playing solid defense. His arm is below-average. Crawford could bypass high Class A and open 2001 in Double-A. The Devil Rays insist he isn't on a timetable. He'll probably push Hamilton to an outfield corner when both are ready for the majors.

Year	Club (League)	Class	AVG	G	AB	R	H	2B	3B	HR	RBI	BB	SO	SB
1999	Princeton (Appy)	R	.319	60	260	62	83	14	4	0	25	13	47	17
2000	Charleston, SC (SAL)	A	.301	135	564	99	170	21	11	6	57	32	102	55
MINOR LEAGUE TOTALS			.307	195	824	161	253	35	15	6	82	45	149	72

4. Aubrey Huff, 3b

Born: Dec. 20, 1976. **Ht.:** 6-4. **Wt.:** 221. **Bats:** L. **Throws:** R. **School:** University of Miami. **Career Transactions:** Selected by Devil Rays in fifth round of 1998 draft; signed June 17, 1998.

Huff continued his rapid climb through the organization in 2000. After feeling snubbed when he didn't receive an invitation to big league camp, he was voted the Triple-A International League's best batting prospect and ranked fifth in the IL in batting average. He received an Aug. 1 promotion to the majors and held his own at the plate. Huff's calling card is his disciplined ability to swing the bat. Immensely confident at the plate, he can drive the ball to all fields with his quick swing. He isn't vulnerable against left-handers, though he shows more power against righties. Though he has shown improvement over the past two years with the glove, Huff needs to continue polishing his abilities at third base. There's talk he might be moved back to first base, his college position. The Devil Rays are satisfied that Huff is ready to compete in the major leagues. If they unload Vinny Castilla, Huff will compete in spring training for the starting job at third base.

Year	Club (League)	Class	AVG	G	AB	R	H	2B	3B	HR	RBI	BB	SO	SB
1998	Charleston, SC (SAL)	A	.321	69	265	38	85	19	1	13	54	24	40	3
1999	Orlando (SL)	AA	.301	133	491	85	148	40	3	22	78	64	77	2
2000	Durham (IL)	AAA	.316	108	408	73	129	36	3	20	76	51	72	2
	Tampa Bay (AL)	MAJ	.287	39	122	12	35	7	0	4	14	5	18	0
MAJOR LEAGUE TOTALS			.287	39	122	12	35	7	0	4	14	5	18	0
MINOR LEAGUE TOTALS			.311	310	1164	196	362	95	7	55	208	139	189	7

5. Jesus Colome, rhp

JOHN SPEAR

Born: June 2, 1980. **Ht.:** 6-2. **Wt.:** 170. **Bats:** R. **Throws:** R. **Career Transactions:** Signed out of Dominican Republic by Athletics, Sept. 29, 1996 . . . Traded by Athletics with a player to be named to Devil Rays for RHP Jim Mecir and LHP Todd Belitz, July 28, 2000.

The Devil Rays think they hit the lottery when they got Colome from Oakland. Colome posted a 3.59 ERA at one of the more favorable hitters' parks around, Double-A Midland's Christensen Stadium. The Devil Rays shut him down after he had forearm soreness near the end of the season, though he returned in time to participate in instructional league. Colome is a dominating pitcher whose fastball has been clocked as high as 100 mph. When he's in a groove, that pitch can be unhittable. He also throws a hard slider that can be particularly difficult for righthanders to hit. Colome will be a candidate for the major leagues as soon as he improves his changeup. While his velocity is impressive, Colome's fastball is relatively straight. He also tends to get sloppy with his mechanics as he tires during games. The Devil Rays see Colome moving rapidly. He should be a starter at Durham in 2001, though many scouts see him becoming a potential Mariano Rivera should he shift to the bullpen.

Year	Club (League)	Class	W	L	ERA	G	GS	CG	SV	IP	H	R	ER	BB	SO
1997	Athletics (DSL)	R	9	3	2.71	18	7	3	0	89	73	33	27	22	55
1998	Athletics (AZL)	R	2	5	3.18	12	11	0	0	56	47	27	20	16	62
1999	Modesto (Cal)	A	8	4	3.36	31	22	0	1	128	125	63	48	60	127
2000	Midland (TL)	AA	9	4	3.59	20	20	0	0	110	99	62	44	50	95
	Orlando (SL)	AA	1	2	6.75	3	3	0	0	14	18	12	11	7	9
MINOR LEAGUE TOTALS			29	18	3.38	84	63	3	1	400	362	197	150	155	348

6. Brent Abernathy, 2b

KEVIN SEIFERT

Born: Sept. 23, 1977. **Ht.:** 6-1. **Wt.:** 185. **Bats:** R. **Throws:** R. **School:** The Lovett School, Atlanta. **Career Transactions:** Selected by Blue Jays in second round of 1996 draft; signed Aug. 24, 1996 . . . Traded by Blue Jays with cash to Devil Rays for LHP Mark Guthrie and RHP Steve Trachsel, July 31, 2000.

The Blue Jays' second-round draft pick in 1996, Abernathy was the key to the trade that sent pitchers Steve Trachsel and Mark Guthrie to Toronto July 31. He spent the entire season in Triple-A before starring at the Olympics, where he batted .385 and led all players with 15 hits and six doubles in nine games. The sum of Abernathy's game is greater than the individual parts. Though his tools are modest, he has outstanding baseball instincts and does all the little things that lead to success for both himself and his team. Not flashy but always hustling, he's a true second baseman and an effective No. 2 hitter. Abernathy makes excellent contact that helps him hit for average. He's also an above-average basestealer. Scouts who don't rave about Abernathy say he lacks overall athleticism. He's steady with the leather, but his footwork at second could use improvement. He also could draw a few more walks. Abernathy will have the opportunity to win the Devil Rays' starting second-base job in spring training.

Year	Club (League)	Class	AVG	G	AB	R	H	2B	3B	HR	RBI	BB	SO	SB
1997	Hagerstown (SAL)	A	.309	99	379	69	117	27	2	1	26	30	32	22
1998	Dunedin (FSL)	A	.328	124	485	85	159	36	1	3	65	44	38	35
1999	Knoxville (SL)	AA	.291	136	577	108	168	42	1	13	62	55	47	34
2000	Syracuse (IL)	AAA	.296	92	358	47	106	21	2	4	35	26	32	14
	Durham (IL)	AAA	.264	27	91	14	24	6	0	1	15	11	11	9
MINOR LEAGUE TOTALS			.304	478	1890	323	574	132	6	22	203	166	160	114

7. Matt White, rhp

Born: Aug. 13, 1978. **Ht.:** 6-5. **Wt.:** 215. **Bats:** R. **Throws:** R. **School:** Waynesboro Area (Pa.) HS. **Career Transactions:** Selected by Giants in first round (seventh overall) of 1996 draft; granted free agency . . . Signed by Devil Rays, Nov. 25, 1996.

Inconsistency and a cracked vertebra in his back made White look like a $10.2 million bust during his first three professional seasons. That outlook changed in 2000 when he experienced his first significant success. He was among the finalists for the U.S. Olympic team but didn't make the final roster. White showed signs of learning how to pitch last season. He displayed more confidence and did a better job of mixing his pitches. He features a fastball in the mid-90s and a plus overhand power curve. White has a complex delivery and his mechanics can get untracked, which throws off his entire approach. Even when he's sound, he must work off his fastball instead of relying on his curveball when things get tough. Because his fastball has little movement, he needs to work the corners. White showed added maturity while experiencing success at both the Double-A and Triple-A levels. The Devil Rays would like to see him further establish himself at Durham in 2001.

Year	Club (League)	Class	W	L	ERA	G	GS	CG	SV	IP	H	R	ER	BB	SO
1997	Hudson Valley (NY-P)	A	4	6	4.07	15	15	0	0	84	78	44	38	29	82
1998	Charleston, SC (SAL)	A	4	3	3.82	12	12	0	0	75	72	41	32	21	59
	St. Petersburg (FSL)	A	4	8	5.55	17	17	1	0	96	107	70	59	41	64
1999	St. Petersburg (FSL)	A	9	7	5.18	21	20	2	0	113	125	75	65	33	92
2000	Orlando (SL)	AA	7	6	3.75	20	20	2	0	120	94	56	50	58	98
	Durham (IL)	AAA	3	2	2.83	6	6	0	0	35	36	14	11	16	28
MINOR LEAGUE TOTALS			31	32	4.39	91	90	5	0	523	512	300	255	198	423

8. Bobby Seay, lhp

Born: June 20, 1978. **Ht.:** 6-2. **Wt.:** 190. **Bats:** L. **Throws:** L. **School:** Sarasota (Fla.) HS. **Career Transactions:** Selected by White Sox in first round (12th overall) of 1996 draft; granted free agency . . . Signed by Devil Rays, Nov. 8, 1996.

A loophole free agent like Matt White, Seay received a $3 million bonus. For the first time in four seasons as a pro, he stayed healthy and got much-needed innings. He led Double-A Orlando with a career-high 132 innings before earning a spot in Team USA's bullpen for the Olympics. He made just one appearance, recording two key outs in the opening game against Japan without allowing a baserunner. Seay is a fierce competitor with a bulldog mentality. He throws a low-90s fastball with exceptional movement, as well as an above-average curveball. He's not afraid to challenge any hitter. A lack of maturity continues to be his greatest hurdle. He lets his mind wander on the mound, and needs a better grasp of how to use his plus stuff to his advantage. An improved change-up will help him become more effective against better competition. With a solid season in Double-A under his belt, Seay should join one of the better rotations at the Triple-A level.

Year	Club (League)	Class	W	L	ERA	G	GS	CG	SV	IP	H	R	ER	BB	SO
1997	Charleston, SC (SAL)	A	3	4	4.55	13	13	0	0	61	56	35	31	37	64
1998	Charleston, SC (SAL)	A	1	7	4.30	15	15	0	0	69	59	40	33	29	74
1999	St. Petersburg (FSL)	A	2	6	3.00	12	11	0	0	57	56	25	19	23	45
	Orlando (SL)	AA	1	2	7.94	6	6	0	0	17	22	15	15	15	16
2000	Orlando (SL)	AA	8	7	3.88	24	24	0	0	132	132	64	57	53	106
MINOR LEAGUE TOTALS			15	26	4.15	70	69	0	0	336	328	179	155	157	305

9. Rocco Baldelli, of

Born: Sept. 25, 1981. **Ht.:** 6-4. **Wt.:** 180. **Bats:** R. **Throws:** R. **School:** Bishop Hendricken HS, Warwick, R.I. **Career Transactions:** Selected by Devil Rays in first round (sixth overall) of 2000 draft; signed June 19, 2000.

A superb all-around athlete, Baldelli impressed the Devil Rays with four above-average tools, including his 6.38-second speed in the 60-yard dash. While his production wasn't exceptional in the Rookie-level Appalachian League, he showed the ability to make adjustments. Baldelli possesses all of the natural instincts to be a standout center fielder. Several Rays officials say he's the best pure center fielder they have seen. An aggressive defender with plus speed, Baldelli takes the right routes to balls and is flawless in throwing to the correct base. He showed a willingness to work hard as well as a strong desire to improve at Princeton and during instructional league. Baldelli's lone tool that isn't above-average is his arm. While he has a large frame, he needs to increase his strength. The Devil Rays think as his body matures, he'll add considerable power. He also needs to make more consistent contact. Baldelli is scheduled to play his first full season in pro ball at Charleston.

Year	Club (League)	Class	AVG	G	AB	R	H	2B	3B	HR	RBI	BB	SO	SB
2000	Princeton (Appy)	R	.216	60	232	33	50	9	2	3	25	12	56	11
MINOR LEAGUE TOTALS			.216	60	232	33	50	9	2	3	25	12	56	11

10. Travis Harper, rhp

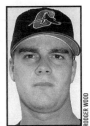

Born: May 21, 1976. **Ht.:** 6-4. **Wt.:** 193. **Bats:** R. **Throws:** R. **School:** James Madison University. **Career Transactions:** Selected by Red Sox in third round of 1997 draft; signed July 14, 1997 . . . Contract voided, Oct. 29, 1997 . . . Signed by Devil Rays, June 29, 1998.

The Red Sox voided Harper's first professional contract because he had elbow tendinitis. He has been healthy since signing with the Devil Rays and joined the big league rotation in September. He has tremendous control of a 92 mph fastball that he uses to pitch on both sides of the plate. Quiet and laid back off the field, he's an intense, intelligent and competitive pitcher who has a solid understanding of what he wants to accomplish on the mound. He showed his resiliency after getting bombed in his major league debut, improving with every outing and blanking the Blue Jays with a two-hit shutout. Harper needs to improve his curveball and changeup. Added strength would benefit him over the long haul of the season. The Devil Rays believe Harper received a good taste of the big leagues in 2000. Aided by that experience, he should earn a job in the Tampa Bay rotation this spring.

Year	Club (League)	Class	W	L	ERA	G	GS	CG	SV	IP	H	R	ER	BB	SO
1998	Hudson Valley (NY-P)	A	6	2	1.92	13	10	0	0	56	38	14	12	20	81
1999	St. Petersburg (FSL)	A	5	4	3.43	14	14	0	0	81	82	36	31	23	79
	Orlando (SL)	AA	6	3	5.38	14	14	1	0	72	73	45	43	26	68
2000	Orlando (SL)	AA	3	1	2.63	9	9	0	0	51	49	19	15	11	33
	Durham (IL)	AAA	7	4	4.24	17	17	0	0	104	98	53	49	26	48
	Tampa Bay (AL)	MAJ	1	2	4.78	6	5	1	0	32	30	17	17	15	14
MAJOR LEAGUE TOTALS			1	2	4.78	6	5	1	0	32	30	17	17	15	14
MINOR LEAGUE TOTALS			27	14	3.70	67	64	1	0	365	340	167	150	106	309

11. Toby Hall, c

Born: Oct. 21, 1975. **Ht.:** 6-3. **Wt.:** 205. **Bats:** R. **Throws:** R. **School:** University of Nevada-Las Vegas. **Career Transactions:** Selected by Devil Rays in ninth round of 1997 draft; signed June 9, 1997.

Hall established himself last year as Tampa Bay's future catcher. He learned from veteran Pat Borders and manager Bill Evers at Durham, then received a cup of coffee at the end of the season and made his first major league start Sept. 22. An intelligent player, Hall is a solid defensive catcher who has made excellent progress in his ability to call a game, though he still has more work to do. He has a plus arm from behind the plate. Hall also has an above-average bat for a minor league catcher and uses the entire field. He can turn on a pitch and has good power that should produce 20 home runs annually. Hall has made steady progress with his footwork but could be a little more nimble behind the plate. Experience should solve both minor problems. Hall should be Tampa Bay's primary receiver no later than 2002.

Year	Club (League)	Class	AVG	G	AB	R	H	2B	3B	HR	RBI	BB	SO	SB
1997	Hudson Valley (NY-P)	A	.250	55	200	25	50	3	0	1	27	13	33	0
1998	Charleston, SC (SAL)	A	.321	105	377	59	121	25	1	6	50	39	32	3
1999	Orlando (SL)	AA	.254	46	173	20	44	7	0	9	34	4	10	1
	St. Petersburg (FSL)	A	.297	56	212	24	63	13	1	4	36	17	9	0
2000	Orlando (SL)	AA	.343	68	271	37	93	14	0	9	50	17	24	3
	Durham (IL)	AAA	.304	47	184	21	56	15	0	7	35	3	19	0
	Tampa Bay (AL)	MAJ	.167	4	12	1	2	0	0	1	1	1	0	0
MAJOR LEAGUE TOTALS			.167	4	12	1	2	0	0	1	1	1	0	0
MINOR LEAGUE TOTALS			.301	377	1417	186	427	77	2	36	232	93	127	7

12. Jared Sandberg, 3b

Born: March 2, 1978. **Ht.:** 6-3. **Wt.:** 185. **Bats:** R. **Throws:** R. **School:** Capital HS, Olympia, Wash. **Career Transactions:** Selected by Devil Rays in 16th round of 1996 draft; signed July 21, 1996.

After a back injury that led to a slow first half in Double-A, Sandberg gained momentum as the 2000 season progressed. He finished in Triple-A and did well in all phases of the game against better competition. Sandberg is naturally strong and possesses above-average power to all fields. He also has a plus arm and is adept at making diving plays at the hot corner. His poise, mental approach and work ethic are exceptional. Sandberg needs to improve his judgment of the strike zone. He falls into ruts when he tries to pull outside pitches instead of hitting the ball to the opposite field. While his range is good, he needs to be more consistent on routine plays. The nephew of former all-star Ryne Sandberg is on the verge of adding another Sandberg to the major league rolls. He's expected to open 2001 in Triple-A.

Year	Club (League)	Class	AVG	G	AB	R	H	2B	3B	HR	RBI	BB	SO	SB
1996	Devil Rays (GCL)	R	.169	22	77	6	13	2	1	0	7	9	26	1
1997	St. Petersburg (FSL)	A	.333	2	3	1	1	0	0	0	2	2	2	0
	Princeton (Appy)	R	.302	67	268	61	81	15	5	17	68	42	94	12
1998	Charleston, SC (SAL)	A	.183	56	191	31	35	11	0	3	25	27	76	4
	Hudson Valley (NY-P)	A	.288	73	271	49	78	15	2	12	54	42	76	13
1999	St. Petersburg (FSL)	A	.276	136	504	73	139	24	1	22	96	51	133	8
2000	Orlando (SL)	A	.258	67	244	30	63	15	1	5	35	33	55	5
	Durham (IL)	AAA	.400	3	15	2	6	3	0	2	7	0	6	0
MINOR LEAGUE TOTALS			.264	426	1573	253	416	85	10	61	294	206	468	43

13. Jace Brewer, ss

Born: June 6, 1979. **Ht.:** 6-0. **Wt.:** 174. **Bats:** R. **Throws:** R. **School:** Baylor University. **Career Transactions:** Selected by Devil Rays in fifth round of 2000 draft; signed June 16, 2000.

A draft-eligible sophomore last spring, Brewer wrote letters to all teams saying he wanted to spend another year in college to improve his game. The Devil Rays loved his natural defensive ability and persuaded him to sign a major league contract worth $1.5 million. After a contract-mandated promotion to Tampa Bay in September, Brewer was shut down with a small tear in his throwing shoulder. He's a fluid shortstop with a plus arm, and he has above-average speed and baserunning ability. At the plate, Brewer is a line-drive hitter who realizes his power limitations. But with the days of weak-hitting shortstops gone, Brewer will need to add strength in order to drive the ball more consistently. He also must improve his knowledge of the strike zone. Brewer may require shoulder surgery, leaving his status uncertain. If he's ready at the start of 2001, he likely will head to Class A Bakersfield.

Year	Club (League)	Class	AVG	G	AB	R	H	2B	3B	HR	RBI	BB	SO	SB
2000	Charleston, SC (SAL)	A	.219	37	137	10	30	7	2	0	15	6	28	3
MINOR LEAGUE TOTALS			.219	37	137	10	30	7	2	0	15	6	28	3

14. Jason Tyner, of

Born: April 23, 1977. **Ht.:** 6-1. **Wt.:** 170. **Bats:** L. **Throws:** L. **School:** Texas A&M University. **Career Transactions:** Selected by Mets in first round (21st overall) of 1998 draft; signed July 8, 1998 . . . Traded by Mets with RHP Paul Wilson to Devil Rays for OF Bubba Trammell and RHP Rick White, July 28, 2000.

Tyner saw action in the major leagues with both New York and Tampa Bay last season. Acquired by the Devil Rays in July, Tyner was the 12th-best prospect in the International League and might have led the league in stolen bases if he had been there all season. His strengths are his outstanding speed and knowledge of how to run the bases. Tyner also puts his legs to work at the plate by hitting down on the ball and trying to keep it on the ground. He has become more patient at the plate and is willing to take a walk. His power is almost nonexistent. He hasn't homered since high school. And while he covers center field like a tarp, his arm is below-average. The Devil Rays have a logjam in the outfield, but Tyner will be among those competing for the job in center field during spring training. Even if he wins it, his hold may be short-lived, with Carl Crawford and Rocco Baldelli on the way.

Year	Club (League)	Class	AVG	G	AB	R	H	2B	3B	HR	RBI	BB	SO	SB
1998	St. Lucie (FSL)	A	.303	50	201	30	61	2	3	0	16	17	20	15
1999	Binghamton (EL)	AA	.313	129	518	91	162	19	5	0	33	62	46	49
	Norfolk (IL)	AAA	.000	3	8	0	0	0	0	0	0	0	5	0
2000	Norfolk (IL)	AAA	.321	84	327	54	105	5	2	0	28	30	32	33
	New York (NL)	MAJ	.195	13	41	3	8	2	0	0	5	1	4	1
	Tampa Bay (AL)	MAJ	.241	37	83	6	20	2	0	0	8	4	12	6
MAJOR LEAGUE TOTALS			.226	50	124	9	28	4	0	0	13	5	16	7
MINOR LEAGUE TOTALS			.311	266	1054	175	328	26	10	0	77	109	103	97

15. Travis Phelps, rhp

Born: July 25, 1977. **Ht.:** 6-2. **Wt.:** 170. **Bats:** R. **Throws:** R. **School:** Crowder (Mo.) JC. **Career Transactions:** Selected by Devil Rays in 89th round of 1996 draft; signed May 24, 1997.

An 89th-round pick in 1996 who signed as a draft-and-follow in 1997, Phelps would be the lowest-drafted player ever to reach the majors. He has a good arm with an excellent knowledge of how to pitch and has lowered his ERA for three consecutive years. His two best pitches are an above-average slider and changeup. He can be aggressive, even though he has always been considered a finesse pitcher due to his skinny frame. The Devil Rays have made several attempts to help Phelps add weight, but the results have been minimal. He needs to improve his overall strength, which would enable him to work more often off a fastball that averages 91 mph and has been clocked as high as 94. A starter throughout his career, Phelps served as a reliever in the Arizona Fall League. The Devil Rays are considering several possibilities for Phelps, which include starting in Double-A or relieving in Triple-A this season.

Year	Club (League)	Class	W	L	ERA	G	GS	CG	SV	IP	H	R	ER	BB	SO
1997	Princeton (Appy)	R	4	3	4.88	14	13	1	0	63	73	42	34	23	60
1998	Charleston, SC (SAL)	A	5	8	4.85	18	18	0	0	91	100	54	49	35	96
1999	St. Petersburg (FSL)	A	10	8	4.24	24	23	1	0	134	148	70	63	39	101
2000	Orlando (SL)	AA	7	8	3.00	21	21	2	0	108	85	44	36	46	106
	Durham (IL)	AAA	3	1	4.85	6	6	0	0	30	29	17	16	16	21
MINOR LEAGUE TOTALS			29	28	4.19	83	81	4	0	425	435	227	198	172	391

16. Kenny Kelly, of

Born: Jan. 26, 1979. **Ht.:** 6-3. **Wt.:** 180. **Bats:** R. **Throws:** R. **School:** Tampa Catholic HS. **Career Transactions:** Selected by Devil Rays in second round of 1997 draft; signed June 12, 1997.

After bypassing his role as the starting quarterback at the University of Miami in order to focus on baseball, Kelly improved as the 2000 campaign progressed. An exceptional athlete, he led Orlando in runs, stolen bases and triples. The most obvious need for Kelly is to play as much baseball as possible. While he has plus speed, he needs to use his legs by keeping the ball on the ground and dropping down bunts. Shortening his swing also would help his plate coverage. His power is minimal, so he must increase his on-base percentage. Defensively, he needs to take better routes to the ball. Other aspects of center-field play, such as throwing to the right base and hitting the cutoff man, will only come with more experience. After receiving a September callup, Kelly went to the Arizona Fall League before returning early to Florida to work individually on basic drills. He's expected to play in Triple-A this year.

Year	Club (League)	Class	AVG	G	AB	R	H	2B	3B	HR	RBI	BB	SO	SB
1997	Devil Rays (GCL)	R	.212	27	99	21	21	2	1	2	7	11	24	6
1998	Charleston, SC (SAL)	A	.280	54	218	46	61	7	5	3	17	19	52	19
1999	St. Petersburg (FSL)	A	.277	51	206	39	57	10	4	3	21	18	46	14
2000	Orlando (SL)	AA	.252	124	489	73	123	17	8	3	29	59	119	31
	Tampa Bay (AL)	MAJ	.000	2	1	0	0	0	0	0	0	0	0	0
MAJOR LEAGUE TOTALS			.000	2	1	0	0	0	0	0	0	0	0	0
MINOR LEAGUE TOTALS			.259	256	1012	179	262	36	18	11	74	107	241	70

17. Delvin James, rhp

Born: Jan. 3, 1978. **Ht.:** 6-4. **Wt.:** 222. **Bats:** R. **Throws:** R. **School:** Nacogdoches (Texas) HS. **Career Transactions:** Selected by Devil Rays in 14th round of 1996 draft; signed June 11, 1996.

A former linebacker who declined a football scholarship at Oklahoma State, James is an aggressive workhorse who has refined his ability to pitch over the past five years. He was extremely raw when he was signed out of high school, but his intelligence and strong desire to improve have made him a legitimate prospect. James' fastball reaches 95 mph on a consistent basis. In addition to a good changeup, he throws an average curveball, and the Devil Rays are considering trying to add a slider to his repertoire. While he possesses above-average command, James needs to work both sides of the plate and mix his pitches a little better. A starter for most of his career, James could be a candidate to move to the bullpen in hopes of becoming a dominating, late-inning pitcher. Regardless of his role in 2001, he's expected to continue honing his skills by returning to Double-A to open the season.

Year	Club (League)	Class	W	L	ERA	G	GS	CG	SV	IP	H	R	ER	BB	SO
1996	Devil Rays (GCL)	R	2	8	8.87	11	11	1	0	48	64	52	47	21	40
1997	Princeton (Appy)	R	4	4	4.94	20	5	0	0	58	71	57	32	24	46
1998	St. Petersburg (FSL)	A	0	0	10.80	1	0	0	0	2	2	2	2	0	0
	Charleston, SC (SAL)	A	2	0	5.40	7	0	0	0	8	12	5	5	2	8
	Hudson Valley (NY-P)	A	7	4	2.98	15	15	0	0	82	71	39	27	32	64
1999	Charleston, SC (SAL)	A	8	8	3.64	25	25	1	0	158	142	76	64	33	106
	St. Petersburg (FSL)	A	3	0	3.18	3	2	0	0	17	18	6	6	4	6
2000	St. Petersburg (FSL)	A	7	9	4.26	22	22	3	0	137	142	74	65	27	74
	Orlando (SL)	AA	1	3	2.92	6	6	1	0	37	31	15	12	7	26
MINOR LEAGUE TOTALS			34	36	4.28	110	86	6	0	547	553	326	260	150	370

18. Ramon Soler, ss

Born: July 6, 1981. **Ht.:** 6-0. **Wt.:** 160. **Bats:** B. **Throws:** R. **Career Transactions:** Signed out of Dominican Republic by Devil Rays, July 23, 1997.

Soler's season ended before it started when he separated his shoulder sliding into home plate during spring training. Surgery and rehabilitation cost him the entire year. He participated in instructional league and is expected to be at full strength for spring training. Soler is a switch-hitter with outstanding speed. He runs the 60-yard dash in 6.38 seconds and knows how to steal bases. He sprays the ball to all fields and has leadoff tools, though his hitting hasn't come around yet. He understands the importance of taking a walk, so there's hope he'll be able to hit. His hands are soft and consistent, and his range is above-average. Soler's arm is only average at shortstop, one reason he spent time at second base during instructional league. His greatest need at this point is to play everyday. Considering he has yet to put together a strong offensive campaign, Soler could begin the year back in Charleston.

Year	Club (League)	Class	AVG	G	AB	R	H	2B	3B	HR	RBI	BB	SO	SB
1998	Devil Rays (GCL)	R	.252	58	226	47	57	7	7	1	19	27	48	23
1999	Charleston, SC (SAL)	A	.237	108	389	74	92	17	2	1	28	56	93	46
2000						Did Not Play—Injured								
MINOR LEAGUE TOTALS			.242	166	615	121	149	24	9	2	47	83	141	69

19. Jorge Cantu, ss

Born: Jan. 30, 1982. **Ht.:** 6-1. **Wt.:** 169. **Bats:** R. **Throws:** R. **Career Transactions:** Signed out of Mexico by Devil Rays, July 2, 1998.

For the second straight season, Cantu was one of the youngest players in his league. Because of injuries to other players, he saw action in both the South Atlantic and Florida State leagues and displayed his maturity by batting better than .290 at both stops. Cantu is an effective line-drive hitter who is among the best in the organization at executing the hit-and-run. Scouts like the way he keeps his head on the ball, and his sporadic power will become more common as his body continues to develop. He will need to tighten his strike zone. Cantu exudes confidence on the field, and has soft hands and a slightly above-average arm. He's learning to take the right angles on grounders. His speed is below-average for a shortstop. Cantu showed he has added strength, but he must continue to do so in order to excel at higher levels. Considering how well he has handled opportunities that have come his way, Cantu is a candidate to make the jump to Double-A out of spring training.

Year	Club (League)	Class	AVG	G	AB	R	H	2B	3B	HR	RBI	BB	SO	SB
1999	Hudson Valley (NY-P)	A	.260	72	281	33	73	17	2	1	33	20	59	3
2000	Charleston, SC (SAL)	A	.301	46	186	25	56	13	2	2	24	10	39	3
	St. Petersburg (FSL)	A	.292	36	130	18	38	5	2	1	14	3	13	4
MINOR LEAGUE TOTALS			.280	154	597	76	167	35	6	4	71	33	111	10

20. Jeff Ridgway, lhp

Born: Aug. 17, 1980. **Ht.:** 6-3. **Wt.:** 195. **Bats:** L. **Throws:** L. **School:** Port Angeles (Wash.) HS. **Career Transactions:** Selected by Devil Rays in 14th round of 1999 draft; signed Sept. 7, 1999.

Ridgway made solid adjustments during his first professional season. After signing too late to play in 1999, he led Princeton in strikeouts while ranking second in starts and innings. He has a strong arm with a 90 mph fastball, a plus curveball and a solid changeup. Highstrung both on the field and off, he funnels his natural energy into aggressiveness on the mound that makes him effective when things are going well. He needs to control his emotions better while adding maturity. Once he accomplishes that, Ridgway should make rapid progress in the organization. He's targeted for the Charleston rotation in 2001.

Year	Club (League)	Class	W	L	ERA	G	GS	CG	SV	IP	H	R	ER	BB	SO
2000	Princeton (Appy)	R	3	4	2.47	12	12	0	0	55	47	24	15	30	60
MINOR LEAGUE TOTALS			3	4	2.47	12	12	0	0	55	47	24	15	30	60

21. Seth McClung, rhp

Born: Feb. 7, 1981. **Ht.:** 6-6. **Wt.:** 235. **Bats:** R. **Throws:** R. **School:** Greenbrier East HS, Lewisburg, W.Va. **Career Transactions:** Selected by Devil Rays in fifth round of 1999 draft; signed June 21, 1999.

McClung rebounded from a difficult first season to post a combined 2.41 ERA in 2000. He's an intimidating, massive, strong pitcher with a power arm. His fastball has reached 98 mph and is consistently in the mid-90s. His heater looks even better, thanks to a plus curveball that keeps hitters off balance. His changeup needs work. McClung also must mature as a pitcher, which should come with time. He was impressive last season at Hudson Valley and overcame early inconsistency at Charleston. While slated to return to the South Atlantic League, a promotion to high Class A later in 2001 is a distinct possibility.

Year	Club (League)	Class	W	L	ERA	G	GS	CG	SV	IP	H	R	ER	BB	SO
1999	Princeton (Appy)	R	2	4	7.69	13	10	0	0	46	53	47	39	48	46
2000	Hudson Valley (NY-P)	A	2	2	1.85	8	8	0	0	44	37	18	9	17	38
	Charleston, SC (SAL)	A	2	1	3.19	6	6	0	0	31	30	14	11	19	26
MINOR LEAGUE TOTALS			6	7	4.39	27	24	0	0	121	120	79	59	84	110

22. Damian Rolls, 3b

Born: Sept. 15, 1977. **Ht.:** 6-2. **Wt.:** 205. **Bats:** R. **Throws:** R. **School:** Schlagle HS, Kansas City, Kan. **Career Transactions:** Selected by Dodgers in first round (23rd overall) of 1996 draft; signed June 9, 1996 . . . Selected by Royals from Dodgers in major league Rule 5 draft, Dec. 13, 1999 . . . Purchased by Devil Rays from Royals, Dec. 13, 1999.

Rolls struggled for three years after the Dodgers drafted him in the first round and finally showed promise in the Florida State League in 1999, posting career highs across the board. But the Dodgers didn't protect him for the Rule 5 draft, so the Royals took him and sold him to the Devil Rays. He spent most of last season on the disabled list after right shoulder surgery in March, so the Devil Rays were able to keep him on the major league roster and retain his rights. Rolls is an athletic player with above-average defensive skills at third base. While he showed promise at the plate in 1999 by rebuilding his swing with his quick wrists, he doesn't have good power and struggles with his consistency because he's overly aggressive at the plate. Rolls should resume his development this year at Double-A.

Year	Club (League)	Class	AVG	G	AB	R	H	2B	3B	HR	RBI	BB	SO	SB
1996	Yakima (NWL)	A	.265	66	257	31	68	11	1	4	27	7	46	8
1997	Savannah (SAL)	A	.211	130	475	57	100	17	5	5	47	38	83	11
1998	Vero Beach (FSL)	A	.244	73	266	28	65	9	0	0	30	23	43	13
	San Antonio (TL)	AA	.219	50	160	18	35	6	0	1	9	6	28	2
1999	Vero Beach (FSL)	A	.297	127	474	68	141	26	2	9	54	36	66	24
2000	Tampa Bay (AL)	MAJ	.333	4	3	0	1	0	0	0	0	0	1	0
	Orlando (SL)	AA	.255	14	51	6	13	5	0	0	3	7	6	1
	St. Petersburg (FSL)	A	.188	5	16	2	3	2	0	0	0	2	3	1
MAJOR LEAGUE TOTALS			.333	4	3	0	1	0	0	0	0	0	1	0
MINOR LEAGUE TOTALS			.250	465	1699	210	425	76	8	19	170	119	275	60

23. Juan Salas, 3b

Born: Dec. 6, 1981. **Ht.:** 6-2. **Wt.:** 170. **Bats:** R. **Throws:** R. **Career Transactions:** Signed out of Dominican Republic by Devil Rays, July 8, 1998.

Pushed to Charleston because of injuries, Salas held his own before heading to the New York-Penn League in June. Already large, Salas is continuing to mature physically, which should enable him to hit for above-average power. He has a cannon attached to his right shoulder and good range at third base. His inexperience at the plate was apparent at times in the South Atlantic League, but he showed at Hudson Valley that he learned from his mistakes and took his game to a higher level. He still strikes out a lot because he is a free swinger. Salas had difficulty adjusting to life in the United States early in his career and displayed considerable immaturity. He has opened up to his teammates and coaches in the past year, which has coincided with his development on the field. Given his strides, Salas could move rapidly this year, beginning with a possible jump to Bakersfield after spring training.

Year	Club (League)	Class	AVG	G	AB	R	H	2B	3B	HR	RBI	BB	SO	SB
1999	Princeton (Appy)	R	.259	53	193	19	50	9	0	2	15	13	50	1
2000	Hudson Valley (NY-P)	A	.284	38	134	22	38	7	1	2	14	9	31	3
	Charleston, SC (SAL)	A	.241	60	220	25	53	11	0	1	26	3	50	6
MINOR LEAGUE TOTALS			.258	151	547	66	141	27	1	5	55	25	131	10

24. Alex Sanchez, of

Born: Aug. 26, 1976. **Ht.:** 5-10. **Wt.:** 180. **Bats:** L. **Throws:** L. **School:** Miami-Dade CC Wolfson. **Career Transactions:** Selected by Devil Rays in fifth round of 1996 draft; signed June 7, 1996.

Sanchez escaped Cuba on a raft and spent 16 months in a refugee camp, then attended junior college before getting drafted by the Devil Rays. He continued to show outstanding speed last year, leading the International League in stolen bases despite spending part of the season in Double-A. He did it thanks to his improved ability to get on base, though he still needs work. After swinging from his heels in his early days despite possessing minimal power, Sanchez has discovered that line drives, ground balls and bunts pave his road to success. He has become more mature over the past two years and is more open to instruction as he develops a better understanding of English. He needs to continue to hit on top of the ball at the plate and develop better command of the strike zone. He also can improve his routes to balls instead of relying on his legs. He faces a logjam in the Tampa Bay outfield, but has natural ability and could be a factor at the major league level as soon as this year.

Year	Club (League)	Class	AVG	G	AB	R	H	2B	3B	HR	RBI	BB	SO	SB
1996	Devil Rays (GCL)	R	.282	56	227	36	64	7	6	1	22	10	35	20
1997	Charleston, SC (SAL)	A	.289	131	537	73	155	15	6	0	34	37	72	92
1998	St. Petersburg (FSL)	A	.330	128	545	77	180	17	9	1	50	31	70	66
1999	Orlando (SL)	AA	.254	121	500	68	127	12	4	2	29	26	88	48
	Durham (IL)	AAA	.200	3	10	2	2	1	0	0	0	1	0	0
2000	Orlando (SL)	AA	.291	20	86	12	25	2	1	0	4	1	13	2
	Durham (IL)	AAA	.291	107	446	76	130	18	3	2	33	30	66	52
MINOR LEAGUE TOTALS			.291	566	2351	344	683	72	29	6	172	136	344	280

25. Doug Waechter, rhp

Born: Jan. 28, 1981. **Ht.:** 6-4. **Wt.:** 210. **Bats:** R. **Throws:** R. **School:** Northeast HS, St. Petersburg, Fla. **Career Transactions:** Selected by Devil Rays in third round of 1999 draft; signed June 27, 1999.

Waechter is a former quarterback who would have played at South Florida had he not signed. He rebounded from a horrible 1999 debut to rank sixth in the New York-Penn League in ERA last year, when he also threw the first no-hitter in the seven-year history of the Hudson Valley franchise. The owner of a low-90s fastball along with a developing curveball and changeup, he continues to battle inconsistency with all of his pitches. Waechter has a high ceiling and could develop rapidly if his mechanics are ironed out. When that happens, his control should improve as well. He should spend most of 2001 at Charleston.

Year	Club (League)	Class	W	L	ERA	G	GS	CG	SV	IP	H	R	ER	BB	SO
1999	Princeton (Appy)	R	0	5	9.77	11	7	0	0	35	46	45	38	35	38
2000	Hudson Valley (NY-P)	A	4	4	2.35	14	14	2	0	73	53	23	19	37	58
MINOR LEAGUE TOTALS			4	9	4.75	25	21	2	0	108	99	68	57	72	96

26. Joe Kennedy, lhp

Born: May 24, 1979. **Ht.:** 6-4. **Wt.:** 227. **Bats:** R. **Throws:** L. **School:** Grossmont (Calif.) JC. **Career Transactions:** Selected by Devil Rays in eighth round of 1998 draft; signed June 2, 1998.

Kennedy has had nothing but success in three years with the Devil Rays. He uses both sides of the plate and has outstanding control of a low-90s fastball. He also does a good job of mixing in a decent curveball and changeup. He has shown a willingness to use all three pitches at any time in the count. Never has his magic worked better than when he set an organization record last July with 17 strikeouts in a 16-0 victory over Capital City. Kennedy has impressive size for a lefty, but needs to improve his stamina in order to become a consistent innings-eater. While Kennedy has been penciled in to start the 2000 season at Bakersfield, a jump to Double-A wouldn't be far-fetched.

Year	Club (League)	Class	W	L	ERA	G	GS	CG	SV	IP	H	R	ER	BB	SO
1998	Princeton (Appy)	R	6	4	3.74	13	13	0	0	67	66	37	28	26	44
1999	Hudson Valley (NY-P)	A	6	5	2.65	16	16	1	0	95	78	33	28	26	101
2000	Charleston, SC (SAL)	A	11	6	3.30	22	22	3	0	136	122	59	50	29	142
MINOR LEAGUE TOTALS			23	15	3.19	51	51	4	0	299	266	129	106	81	287

27. Ronni Seberino, lhp

Born: May 27, 1979. **Ht.:** 6-1. **Wt.:** 177. **Bats:** L. **Throws:** L. **Career Transactions:** Signed out of Dominican Republic by Devil Rays, March 15, 1996.

Seberino's development has been textbook. He made the Florida State League midseason all-star team last year, moved up to Double-A and got the call to Durham when the Devil Rays needed a lefthander in Triple-A. Though he struggled with his control, Seberino showed he was comfortable on the fast track. He possesses an 89-91 mph fastball with plus life. His slider has shown steady improvement over the past two years and is on the verge of being an above-average pitch, while his changeup is average. There are times when Seberino has difficulty controlling the incredible movement of all his pitches. The Devil Rays realize he needs a stronger foundation and will start him in Double-A this spring.

Year	Club (League)	Class	W	L	ERA	G	GS	CG	SV	IP	H	R	ER	BB	SO
1996	Devil Rays (GCL)	R	4	2	3.46	18	6	0	1	52	50	22	20	15	49
1997	Princeton (Appy)	R	4	4	3.17	14	14	0	0	65	71	39	23	28	57
1998	Hudson Valley (NY-P)	A	3	2	4.15	22	5	0	0	52	47	29	24	24	61

1999	Charleston, SC (SAL)	A	6	2	2.65	50	0	0	0	75	57	29	22	38	73
2000	St. Petersburg (FSL)	A	6	0	2.75	33	1	0	4	39	30	17	12	20	33
	Orlando (SL)	AA	0	0	2.08	4	0	0	0	9	6	2	2	6	6
	Durham (IL)	AAA	1	0	2.12	12	0	0	1	17	6	9	4	14	14
MINOR LEAGUE TOTALS			24	10	3.12	153	26	0	6	309	267	147	107	145	293

28. Cecilio Garibaldi, rhp

Born: Jan. 5, 1978. **Ht.:** 6-2. **Wt.:** 214. **Bats:** R. **Throws:** R. **Career Transactions:** Signed by Mexico City Tigers (Mexican), 1997 . . . Contract purchased by Devil Rays from Mexico City, April 2, 1998.

The Devil Rays made Garibaldi a starter in 1999 to give him innings and develop his breaking ball. He missed time with injuries in 1998, and Tampa Bay hoped the extra work also would enable him to build up arm strength. Garibaldi responded by improving his fastball to a consistent 93-94 mph. He also has made steady strides with his slider, though that pitch as well as his changeup continue to need work. Garibaldi has a soft body but showed improvement with his stamina last year. While he could wind up back in the bullpen, Garibaldi is expected to pitch in Orlando's rotation this season.

Year	Club (League)	Class	W	L	ERA	G	GS	CG	SV	IP	H	R	ER	BB	SO
1997	M.C. Tigers (Mex)	AAA	1	1	6.60	18	1	0	1	30	32	22	22	22	11
1998	M.C. Tigers (Mex)	AAA	0	0	7.56	8	0	0	0	8	10	7	7	14	1
	Devil Rays (GCL)	R	1	3	5.06	22	0	0	5	27	30	16	15	9	20
1999	St. Petersburg (FSL)	A	6	6	4.36	21	15	0	0	99	109	56	48	28	52
2000	St. Petersburg (FSL)	A	5	7	3.68	25	17	2	0	110	101	59	45	36	73
MINOR LEAGUE TOTALS			13	17	4.50	94	33	2	6	274	282	160	137	109	157

29. Josh Pressley, 1b

Born: April 2, 1980. **Ht.:** 6-6. **Wt.:** 220. **Bats:** L. **Throws:** R. **School:** Westminster Academy, Fort Lauderdale. **Career Transactions:** Selected by Devil Rays in fourth round of 1998 draft; signed July 2, 1998.

Tampa Bay's first pick (fourth round) in 1998, Pressley is one of the better all-around hitters in the organization and continues to develop power as his body matures. His South Atlantic League-best 44 doubles last year show his ability to drive the ball, and the Devil Rays are trying to get him to loft the ball more to improve his home run totals. Some scouts say Pressley could follow Rafael Palmeiro as a player who added power to his solid hitting ability at higher levels, and that's often the development path for young lefthanded hitters. An all-America basketball player in high school, Pressley needs to improve his footwork around first base. He also has to work hard to remain consistent defensively, though he has shown steady improvement. Pressley could make the jump to Double-A if he has a solid spring.

Year	Club (League)	Class	AVG	G	AB	R	H	2B	3B	HR	RBI	BB	SO	SB
1998	Devil Rays (GCL)	R	.304	36	125	22	38	6	0	1	16	20	29	2
1999	Charleston, SC (SAL)	A	.243	118	437	50	106	22	0	9	64	49	80	1
2000	Charleston, SC (SAL)	A	.303	130	488	61	148	44	0	6	61	49	61	2
MINOR LEAGUE TOTALS			.278	284	1050	133	292	72	0	16	141	118	170	5

30. Greg Nash, of/rhp

Born: Feb. 16, 1982. **Ht.:** 6-5. **Wt.:** 220. **Bats:** B. **Throws:** R. **School:** St. Amant (La.) HS. **Career Transactions:** Signed as nondrafted free agent by Devil Rays, Sept. 13, 2000.

The world was introduced to the legend of Toe Nash (so nicknamed because of his size 18 shoes) when ESPN's Peter Gammons broke the story in the offseason. Devil Rays area scout Benny Latino saw him dominate as a Little Leaguer years ago in Louisiana, but didn't see him again until finding him last summer in a semipro league near Gonzales, La. Nash, who had dropped out of school, was playing baseball several nights a week on a diamond cut out of a sugar cane field. Latino arranged a workout with Devil Rays scouting director Dan Jennings at the Rookie-level Princeton affiliate's ballpark. Nash showed power from both sides of the plate, and was clocked as high as 95 mph off the mound. After receiving a $30,000 signing bonus, Nash showed he's raw but has tremendous athleticism during instructional league. His story became clouded by several criminal charges that came to light after he signed. The charges had not been resolved as spring training opened, but the Devil Rays were standing behind Nash and offering him support. The big questions are how he'll progress against more experienced players and how he'll handle the day-to-day life of a professional player. The Devil Rays had not decided whether Nash will play the outfield or pitch, but his natural talent is unmistakable.

Year	Club (League)	Class	AVG	G	AB	R	H	2B	3B	HR	RBI	BB	SO	SB
2000					Did Not Play—Signed 2001 Contract									

Texas
Rangers

By Gerry Fraley

Dissatisfaction with the player-development system figured in the Rangers' decision to hire Doug Melvin as general manager during the fall of 1994. The system has improved under Melvin, but not as much as expected.

One reason is that current ownership has created a difficult task for Melvin and the player-development group. Owner Tom Hicks wants an annual contender—as shown by his megadeal with free-agent shortstop Alex Rodriguez—and that means taking steps that work against Texas' ability to grow its own players.

The 1998 pennant-race deals in which the Rangers gave up second baseman Warren Morris and third baseman Fernando Tatis wiped out years of work. The club paid $1 million for lefthander Jeff Fassero to make seven appearances in the second half of 1999, but a year earlier let a much smaller amount prevent them from signing third-round pick Barry Zito, now a budding ace for the Athletics.

There also have been the inevitable disappointments. Texas had three of the first 32 picks in the 1996 draft and selected righthanders R.A. Dickey and Sam Marsonek, and lefthander Corey Lee. None is on the 40-man roster and only Lee has pitched in the

major leagues—for one inning.

Chuck McMichael, who resigned as scouting director in August and was replaced by national crosschecker Tim Hallgren, had four good drafts. His first two first-round choices, second baseman Jason Romano and first baseman Carlos Pena, are nearing the majors. Under McMichael, the organization looked first for strong arms and then developed pitchers. Emphasis on polished college pitchers with lower upsides brought in first-round choices who didn't produce, such as Jonathan Johnson (1995) and Dickey.

The performance of Texas' minor league affiliates is another reason for encouragement. The six farm teams had a combined .530 winning percentage in 2000, pleasing Melvin, who believes learning to win is an important part of the development process.

Of course, those trends didn't deter Hicks in the offseason. The signing of Rodriguez to a record $252 million contract was the final addition to an all-new infield. First baseman Andres Galarraga (who will see time at DH) and third baseman Ken Caminiti also arrived via free agency, while the Rangers sent pitching prospects Aaron Harang and Ryan Cullen to the Athletics for second baseman Randy Velarde.

OrganizationOverview

General manager: Doug Melvin. **Farm director:** Reid Nichols. **Scouting director:** Tim Hallgren.

2000 PERFORMANCE

Class	Team	League	W	L	Pct.	Finish*	Manager(s)
Majors	Texas	American	71	91	.438	12th (14)	Johnny Oates
Triple-A	Oklahoma RedHawks	Pacific Coast	69	74	.483	8th (16)	DeMarlo Hale
Double-A	Tulsa Drillers	Texas	64	76	.457	t-6th (8)	Bobby Jones/James Byrd
High A	Charlotte Rangers	Florida State	78	61	.561	4th (14)	James Byrd/Bob Miscik
Low A	Savannah SandGnats	South Atlantic	74	65	.532	t-4th (14)	Paul Carey
Rookie	Pulaski Rangers	Appalachian	40	28	.588	2nd (10)	Bruce Crabbe
Rookie	GCL Rangers	Gulf Coast	38	18	.679	1st (13)	Darryl Kennedy
OVERALL 2000 MINOR LEAGUE RECORD			363	322	.530	5th (30)	

*Finish in overall standings (No. of teams in league).

ORGANIZATION LEADERS

BATTING

*AVG	Travis Hafner, Charlotte	.346
R	Kevin Mench, Charlotte	118
H	Kevin Mench, Charlotte	164
TB	Kevin Mench, Charlotte	302
2B	Kevin Mench, Charlotte	39
3B	Three tied at	9
HR	Carlos Pena, Tulsa	28
RBI	Kevin Mench, Charlotte	121
BB	Carlos Pena, Tulsa	101
SO	Mike Zywica, Tulsa/Oklahoma	125
SB	**Jose Morban**, Pulaski/Savannah	33

PITCHING

W	Spike Lundberg, Tulsa	14
L	**Ryan Dittfurth**, Savannah	13
#ERA	Matt Kosderka, Savannah/Charlotte	3.35
G	Reynaldo Garcia, Savannah	49
CG	Brian Sikorski, Oklahoma	5
SV	Reynaldo Garcia, Savannah	14
IP	Colby Lewis, Charlotte	164
BB	**Ryan Dittfurth**, Savannah	99
SO	**Ryan Dittfurth**, Savannah	158

*Minimum 250 at-bats. #Minimum 75 innings.

TOP PROSPECTS OF THE DECADE

1991	Ivan Rodriguez, c
1992	Kurt Miller, rhp
1993	Benji Gil, ss
1994	Benji Gil, ss
1995	Julio Santana, rhp
1996	Andrew Vessel, of
1997	Danny Kolb, rhp
1998	Ruben Mateo, of
1999	Ruben Mateo, of
2000	Ruben Mateo, of

TOP DRAFT PICKS OF THE DECADE

1991	Benji Gil, ss
1992	Rick Helling, rhp
1993	Mike Bell, 3b
1994	Kevin Brown, c (2)
1995	Jonathan Johnson, rhp
1996	R.A. Dickey, rhp
1997	Jason Romano, 3b
1998	Carlos Pena, 1b
1999	Colby Lewis, rhp
2000	Scott Heard, c

Morban   **Dittfurth**

BEST TOOLS

Best Hitter for Average	Carlos Pena
Best Power Hitter	Kevin Mench
Fastest Baserunner	Jason Romano
Best Fastball	Colby Lewis
Best Breaking Ball	Tom Pratt
Best Control	Spike Lundberg
Best Defensive Catcher	Scott Heard
Best Defensive Infielder	Mike Young
Best Infield Arm	Mike Young
Best Defensive Outfielder	Craig Monroe
Best Outfield Arm	Craig Monroe

PROJECTED 2004 LINEUP

Catcher	Ivan Rodriguez
First Base	Carlos Pena
Second Base	Jason Romano
Third Base	Hank Blalock
Shortstop	Alex Rodriguez
Left Field	Kevin Mench
Center Field	Ruben Mateo
Right Field	Gabe Kapler
Designated Hitter	Rafael Palmeiro
No. 1 Starter	Rick Helling
No. 2 Starter	Doug Davis
No. 3 Starter	Jovanny Cedeno
No. 4 Starter	Ryan Glynn
No. 5 Starter	Joaquin Benoit
Closer	Francisco Cordero

ALL-TIME LARGEST BONUSES

Carlos Pena, 1998	$1,850,000
Scott Heard, 2000	1,475,000
Jonathan Johnson, 1995	1,100,000
Colby Lewis, 1999	862,500
Sam Marsonek, 1996	834,000

DraftAnalysis

2000 Draft

Best Pro Debut: C **Scott Heard's** bat was questioned after he hit just .292 as a high school senior, the main reason he went from the possible No. 1 overall pick to No. 24. It's an encouraging sign that he batted .345 with 16 doubles in 33 games as a pro. LHP Chris Russ (3) went 5-1, 1.88 while doing most of his pitching at Class A Savannah.

Best Athlete: A former North Carolina running back, OF Tyrell Godwin (1) was one of the draft's top athletes and agreed to a $1.2 million bonus before a physical revealed a pre-existing knee injury. The Rangers and Godwin's camp disagreed about its severity, and he chose to return to North Carolina rather than take less money. 2B Jason Bourgeois (2) and OF Laynce Nix (4) are the best among players who signed.

Best Hitter: 1B Jason Botts is a pure hitter, but he was a 46th-round draft-and-follow from 1999. From the 2000 draft it's Nix, who has a polished approach for a high school batter.

Best Raw Power: Godwin would have won, but it goes to C Brandon Pack (12).

Fastest Runner: Bourgeois runs the 60-yard dash in 6.6 seconds. Again, Godwin is faster.

Best Defensive Player: Heard is a future Gold Glove winner behind the plate, with outstanding arm strength and receiving skills.

Best Fastball: RHP Greg Runser's (5) fastball peaks at 95 mph. He was untouchable at Rookie-level Pulaski, going 3-3 with a 1.12 ERA that would have led the Appalachian League if he had enough innings to qualify.

Most Intriguing Background: Heard and Tigers RHP Matt Wheatland are the third pair of high school teammates to go in the first round of the same draft. RHP Andy Myette (17), who didn't sign, is the brother of Aaron Myette, acquired in a December trade from the White Sox for SS Royce Clayton.

Closest To The Majors: RHP Chad Hawkins (1) was the first college senior drafted. He pitched 10 innings at Savannah before being shut down with minor elbow problems. Runser could pass him.

LARRY GOREN

Best Late-Round Pick: Heard RHP Casey Berry (32), the lowest-drafted player signed, has an average fastball and an advanced feel for pitching.

The One Who Got Away: Godwin. The Rangers also missed out on RHP Virgil Vasquez (7), who has an 87-92 mph fastball but decided to go to UC Santa Barbara. RHP Nick Masset (8) had Tommy John surgery that will shelve him until March. He planned to attend St. Petersburg (Fla.) JC and if he can pass a physical, look for the Rangers to sign him as a draft-and-follow before the June draft.

Assessment: If Heard continues to hit and Texas can land a healthy Masset, Chuck McMichael's last draft as scouting director will have been productive. Losing Godwin hurt, but while his athleticism was universally admired, his baseball aptitude and desire were not.

1999 Draft

First-round RHPs Colby Lewis and David Mead are legitimate prospects. In the long run, the Rangers may get even more out of three hitters: 3B Hank Blalock (3), OF Kevin Mench (4) and 1B Jason Botts (46, draft-and-follow). **Grade: B**

1998 Draft

Texas found another impact bat in 1B Carlos Pena (1). LHP Andy Pratt (9) is a keeper, too, but the club missed out on a quality southpaw when it couldn't come to terms with Barry Zito (3), who could be the difference in the 2001 American League West race. **Grade: B**

1997 Draft

The Rangers came up with three hot-corner options in Jason Romano (1), Jason Grabowski (2) and Mike Lamb (7). Romano has moved to second base, while Grabowski was lost on waivers to Seattle in the wake of Texas' free-agent frenzy this offseason. **Grade: C**

1996 Draft

Three first-rounders, RHPs R.A. Dickey and Sam Marsonek and LHP Corey Lee, might add up to nothing. The Rangers lost 2B Warren Morris (5) to the Pirates in a one-sided deal for Esteban Loaiza. 1B Travis Hafner (31, draft-and-follow) has a shot. **Grade: C**

Note: Draft analysis prepared by Jim Callis. Numbers in parentheses indicate draft rounds.

. . . . Pena has an advanced understanding of how to play the game and can be a franchise centerpiece on and off the field.

Carlos Pena 1b

Born: May 17, 1978.
Ht.: 6-2. **Wt.:** 210.
Bats: L. **Throws:** L.
School: Northeastern University.
Career Transactions: Selected by Rangers in first round (10th overall) of 1998 draft; signed July 24, 1998.

Pena is a classic American success story. In search of a better life for his children, Pena's father brought his family to Boston from the Dominican Republic in 1992. Pena rocketed to prominence with a strong showing in the Cape Cod League during the summer of 1997, leading college baseball's top summer circuit in homers and RBIs while taking his team to the championship. He hasn't stopped hitting since. Pena batted .342-13-52 in 146 at-bats during his final season at Northeastern, after which the Rangers took him with the No. 10 overall pick in the 1998 draft. Pena has driven in 100 runs in each of his full seasons as a pro.

The Ballpark in Arlington favors lefthanded power hitters who can pull the ball. That's Pena's main asset. He smacked a combined 46 homers in his two seasons at Class A Charlotte and Double-A Tulsa. By comparison, Juan Gonzalez had 29 homers in his two seasons with those clubs (though he was three years younger). Pena is more than an all-or-nothing power hitter. He reached base in 45 consecutive games last season. He also can run, legging out 36 doubles and stealing 12 bases without being caught. Defensively, Pena is excellent at first base. He brings the intangible of outstanding character as well. He's smart and hard-working, and he has an advanced understanding of how to play the game. He can be a franchise centerpiece on and off the field. Pena sometimes gets too pull-happy and out of control with his swing. The elite power hitters can take the outside pitch to the opposite field with force, but he too often tries to yank it to right field. Pena came in with no concept of the two-strike approach to hitting the Rangers stress. He made great strides in that aspect of his game last season, cutting his strikeouts by 27 while increasing his walks by 27 over the previous season. He needs to continue that progress.

The Rangers resisted the urge to push Pena to Triple-A Oklahoma last year. They'll continue to move him pragmatically after signing free agent Andres Galarraga to a one-year deal, which should give Pena a full year at Oklahoma. He could appear in Texas late in 2001 and should be the starting first baseman in 2002.

Year	Club (League)	Class	AVG	G	AB	R	H	2B	3B	HR	RBI	BB	SO	SB
1998	Rangers (GCL)	R	.400	2	5	1	2	0	0	0	0	3	1	1
	Savannah (SAL)	A	.325	30	117	22	38	14	0	6	20	8	26	3
	Charlotte (FSL)	A	.273	7	22	1	6	1	0	0	3	2	8	0
1999	Charlotte (FSL)	A	.255	136	501	85	128	31	8	18	103	74	135	2
2000	Tulsa (TL)	AA	.299	138	529	117	158	36	2	28	105	101	108	12
MINOR LEAGUE TOTALS			.283	313	1174	226	332	82	10	52	231	188	278	18

2. Jovanny Cedeno, rhp

Born: Oct. 25, 1979. **Ht.:** 6-0. **Wt.:** 160. **Bats:** R. **Throws:** R. **Career Transactions:** Signed out of Dominican Republic by Rangers, Feb. 2, 1997.

The Rangers once worked the Dominican Republic as well as any organization, but their efforts there dropped off. The organization made a renewed push in recent years. Fernando Tatis and Ruben Mateo are the best hitters signed, while Cedeno is the most promising pitcher. Cedeno often is compared to Pedro Martinez because he's a lithe Dominican righthander with large hands that give him remarkable control of his changeup. Though Cedeno's plus fastball is his best pitch, his changeup makes him a strikeout pitcher. He finished 2000 with a seven-game winning streak during which he had 79 strikeouts in 56 innings. Cedeno needs to add strength. He had nagging injuries the last two seasons. He pitched a career-high 130 innings in 2000 but missed his final start with shoulder stiffness. Cedeno is also inconsistent with his breaking pitch. The Rangers will be careful with Cedeno, giving his body time to mature before piling innings on him. Cedeno may need at least three more full minor league seasons, which could create an option problem. He went on the 40-man roster for the first time this offseason.

Year	Club (League)	Class	W	L	ERA	G	GS	CG	SV	IP	H	R	ER	BB	SO
1997	Rangers (DSL)	R	10	2	2.56	14	14	1	0	84	70	29	24	23	73
1998	Rangers (DSL)	R	1	0	1.42	5	2	0	1	19	14	5	3	5	22
1999	Rangers (GCL)	R	3	0	0.33	6	6	1	0	27	13	3	1	4	32
	Charlotte (FSL)	A	1	0	5.40	1	1	0	0	5	7	3	3	1	5
2000	Savannah (SAL)	A	11	4	2.42	24	22	0	0	130	95	40	35	53	153
MINOR LEAGUE TOTALS			26	6	2.23	50	45	2	1	266	199	80	66	86	285

3. Jason Romano, 2b

Born: June 24, 1979. **Ht.:** 6-0. **Wt.:** 185. **Bats:** R. **Throws:** R. **School:** Hillsborough HS, Tampa. **Career Transactions:** Selected by Rangers in first round (39th overall) of 1997 draft; signed July 11, 1997.

Romano developed in the baseball hotbed of Tampa, where he attended Hillsborough High, the alma mater of Carl Everett, Dwight Gooden and Gary Sheffield. Some clubs had Romano ranked among the top 20 prospects for the 1997 draft, but he lasted until the 39th pick overall. His brother Jimmie, a catcher, signed with Texas as a 26th-round pick in 1998. Romano is a ballplayer in the best sense of the word. He's a dirt dog who loves to play and will do whatever it takes to win. Romano is a line-drive hitter with speed. He has shown pop in the past, though his slugging percentage dropped 127 points from 1999 to 2000. He can handle hitting at the top of the order, most often batting in the No. 2 spot last season. The Rangers switched Romano from third base to second after drafting him, and his defense needs work. His footwork can get tangled, and that contributed to his 24 errors in 125 games at second last season. The club has no doubt Romano will work to improve. Romano has stayed on schedule, advancing one level each season. How quickly he improves on defense will determine when he reaches the majors. The Rangers hope it's for the 2002 season.

Year	Club (League)	Class	AVG	G	AB	R	H	2B	3B	HR	RBI	BB	SO	SB
1997	Rangers (GCL)	R	.257	34	109	27	28	5	3	2	11	13	19	13
1998	Savannah (SAL)	A	.271	134	524	72	142	19	4	7	52	46	94	40
	Charlotte (FSL)	A	.208	7	24	3	5	1	0	0	1	2	2	1
1999	Charlotte (FSL)	A	.312	120	459	84	143	27	14	13	71	39	72	34
2000	Tulsa (TL)	AA	.271	131	535	87	145	35	2	8	70	56	84	25
MINOR LEAGUE TOTALS			.280	426	1651	273	463	87	23	30	205	156	271	113

4. Kevin Mench, of

Born: Jan. 7, 1978. **Ht.:** 6-0. **Wt.:** 215. **Bats:** R. **Throws:** R. **School:** University of Delaware. **Career Transactions:** Selected by Rangers in fourth round of 1999 draft; signed June 16, 1999.

As a sophomore at Delaware in 1998, Mench led NCAA Division I in homers (33) and ranked fourth in hitting (.455), but it didn't help his draft status. After a subpar junior season, he went in the fourth round. Mench hit .357 in his pro debut and was ranked the No. 1 prospect in the high Class A Florida State League in 2000. Mench has been described as a Pete Incaviglia who can play the outfield. Mench has Incaviglia's power and is a more refined hitter. He ranked among the FSL leaders in average and on-base percentage (.427) last season. Mench is muscular but runs well. He does everything with enthusiasm. Somewhat older than the competition in his first two professional seasons, Mench has been able to get away with being a pure pull hitter. He'll need to expand his swing as the level of competition increases. Because he lacks arm strength, Mench probably is limited to left field. Mench batted .354 in the Arizona Fall League, leading Grand Canyon to the league title. He'll move up to Double-A in 2001 and could push for a spot in Texas sometime during the following year.

Year	Club (League)	Class	AVG	G	AB	R	H	2B	3B	HR	RBI	BB	SO	SB
1999	Pulaski (Appy)	R	.362	65	260	63	94	22	1	16	60	28	48	12
	Savannah (SAL)	A	.304	6	23	4	7	1	1	2	8	2	4	0
2000	Charlotte (FSL)	A	.334	132	491	118	164	39	9	27	121	78	72	19
MINOR LEAGUE TOTALS			.342	203	774	185	265	62	11	45	189	108	124	31

5. Joaquin Benoit, rhp

Born: July 26, 1979. **Ht.:** 6-4. **Wt.:** 205. **Bats:** R. **Throws:** R. **Career Transactions:** Signed out of Dominican Republic by Rangers, May 20, 1996.

Former international scouting director Omar Minaya left the Rangers to become Mets assistant GM in September 1997, but his legacy endures. Minaya, who also signed Sammy Sosa, found Benoit, then a skinny righthander, in the Dominican Republic in 1996. Now 6-foot-4 and 205 pounds, Benoit looks like a pitcher. When he gets to the mound, he operates like a pitcher. He has a plus fastball and a sharp slider. He held opponents to a .237 batting average in the offense-mad Texas League last season. Getting Benoit to the mound has been the problem because he's protective of his body and worries about every twinge. His most serious injury was a strained elbow that didn't require surgery in 1998. Benoit has pitched more than 100 innings only once, and his command suffers from the erratic work. He also needs to work on his changeup to be more effective against lefthanders, who hit .308 off him in 2000. Benoit pitched well in the Arizona Fall League. He needs to put together a full and healthy season to move away from the tease category.

Year	Club (League)	Class	W	L	ERA	G	GS	CG	SV	IP	H	R	ER	BB	SO
1996	Rangers (DSL)	R	6	5	2.28	14	13	2	0	75	63	26	19	23	63
1997	Rangers (GCL)	R	3	3	2.05	10	10	1	0	44	40	14	10	11	38
1998	Savannah (SAL)	A	4	3	3.83	15	15	1	0	80	79	41	34	18	68
1999	Charlotte (FSL)	A	7	4	5.31	22	22	0	0	105	117	67	62	50	83
2000	Tulsa (TL)	AA	4	4	3.83	16	16	0	0	82	73	40	35	30	72
MINOR LEAGUE TOTALS			24	19	3.73	77	76	4	0	386	372	188	160	132	324

6. Colby Lewis, rhp

Born: Aug. 2, 1979. **Ht.:** 6-4. **Wt.:** 215. **Bats:** R. **Throws:** R. **School:** Bakersfield (Calif.) JC. **Career Transactions:** Selected by Rangers in first round (38th overall) of 1999 draft; signed June 15, 1999.

The Rangers re-emphasized power pitchers by taking Lewis with their first pick (38th overall) in 1999. Lewis had Tommy John surgery coming out of high school, but won over the Rangers with 108 strikeouts in 88 innings in his final season at Bakersfield (Calif.) Junior College. He was the top pitching prospect in the Rookie-level Appalachian League in his pro debut in 1999. Lewis throws hard. His four-seam fastball is a plus pitch and at times overpowering, reaching the mid-90s and featuring late life. He has 277 strikeouts in 228 pro innings. Lewis throws strikes more consistently than most young power pitchers. Both his curveball and slider are hard pitches, and his changeup shows promise. His elbow hasn't bothered him since his surgery. Lewis needs experience and refinement. He probably needs to settle on one breaking pitch and his changeup could use more polish. The Rangers drafted Lewis knowing he would need plenty of minor league innings. Their expectation is that he'll be ready to make a push to join the big league rotation at some point in 2003.

Year	Club (League)	Class	W	L	ERA	G	GS	CG	SV	IP	H	R	ER	BB	SO
1999	Pulaski (Appy)	R	7	3	1.95	14	11	1	0	65	46	24	14	27	84
2000	Charlotte (FSL)	A	11	10	4.07	28	27	3	0	164	169	83	74	45	153
MINOR LEAGUE TOTALS			18	13	3.47	42	38	4	0	228	215	107	88	72	237

7. Mike Young, ss/2b

Born: Oct. 19, 1976. **Ht.:** 6-0. **Wt.:** 175. **Bats:** R. **Throws:** R. **School:** UC Santa Barbara. **Career Transactions:** Selected by Blue Jays in fifth round of 1997 draft; signed June 13, 1997 . . . Traded by Blue Jays with RHP Darwin Cubillan to Rangers for RHP Esteban Loaiza July 19, 2000.

Will Young be better than Pirates second baseman Warren Morris? In a roundabout way, the Rangers essentially traded Morris for Young. Morris was the key player given up in 1998 in a deal with the Pirates for righthander Esteban Loiaza, who was dumped on Toronto last summer for Young and righthander Darwin Cubillan. The Rangers wanted Young for his athleticism. He runs well and has an excellent arm, good enough to play the outfield if necessary. The Blue Jays had Young batting cleanup at times, but the Rangers turned him into a leadoff hitter because of his quick swing. He responded, though he still needs to draw more walks to hit out of the leadoff spot long-term. Young is still learning how to use his speed on the bases. He tends to be tentative at times. Young also can be too deliberate on defense. The Blue Jays had moved him to second base, but he returned to shortstop after the trade. Settling on a position for Young was an issue—until the Rangers signed Alex Rodriguez. Young clearly won't be playing shortstop in Texas, and he's probably better suited for second base anyway. Unfortunately for him, he'll have to contend with Jason Romano.

Year	Club (League)	Class	AVG	G	AB	R	H	2B	3B	HR	RBI	BB	SO	SB
1997	St. Catharines (NY-P)	A	.308	74	276	49	85	18	3	9	48	33	59	9
1998	Hagerstown (SAL)	A	.282	140	522	86	147	33	5	16	87	55	96	16
1999	Dunedin (FSL)	A	.313	129	495	86	155	36	3	5	83	61	78	30
2000	Tennessee (SL)	AA	.275	91	345	51	95	24	5	6	47	36	72	16
	Tulsa (TL)	AA	.319	43	188	30	60	13	5	1	32	17	28	9
MINOR LEAGUE TOTALS			**.297**	**477**	**1826**	**302**	**542**	**124**	**21**	**37**	**297**	**202**	**333**	**80**

8. Aaron Myette, rhp

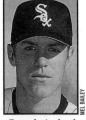

Born: Sept. 26, 1977. **Ht.:** 6-4. **Wt.:** 195. **Bats:** R. **Throws:** R. **School:** Central Arizona JC. **Career Transactions:** Selected by White Sox in first round (43rd overall) of 1997 draft; signed June 5, 1997 . . . Traded by White Sox with RHP Brian Schmack to Rangers for SS Royce Clayton, Dec. 14, 2000.

Always considered something of a loose cannon, Myette solidified his reputation by breaking his right hand against a clubhouse wall last spring. After rising quickly through the White Sox system, Myette hit the wall in an organization loaded with pitching talent. As a result, Chicago traded him and righthander Brian Schmack for shortstop Royce Clayton after the Rangers signed Alex Rodriguez. Myette was selected to represent Canada in both the inaugural 1999 Futures Game and the 2000 game. Myette has a low-90s fastball with natural sink and isn't afraid to pitch inside. Both of his breaking pitches are considered average. He also has a nice feel for pitching. The key will be whether Myette has the confidence to get ahead against big league hitters. He hurt himself with walks when he pitched for the White Sox. His changeup is nothing special, one of the reasons lefthanders teed off on him in Triple-A and the majors. If Myette had remained with the White Sox, who have the deepest farm system in baseball and particular depth in pitching, he faced another year in Triple-A. With the Rangers, who need starters, he'll get the chance to make the rotation in spring training.

Year	Club (League)	Class	W	L	ERA	G	GS	CG	SV	IP	H	R	ER	BB	SO
1997	Bristol (Appy)	R	4	3	3.61	9	8	1	0	47	39	28	19	20	50
	Hickory (SAL)	A	3	1	1.14	5	5	0	0	32	19	6	4	11	27
1998	Hickory (SAL)	A	9	4	2.47	17	17	0	0	102	84	43	28	30	103
	Winston-Salem (Car)	A	4	2	2.01	6	6	1	0	45	32	14	10	14	54
1999	Birmingham (SL)	AA	12	7	3.66	28	28	0	0	165	138	76	67	77	135
	Chicago (AL)	MAJ	0	2	6.32	4	3	0	0	16	17	11	11	14	11
2000	Birmingham (SL)	AA	2	0	3.52	3	3	0	0	15	11	7	6	8	21
	Charlotte (IL)	AAA	5	5	4.35	19	18	0	0	112	103	58	54	56	85
	Chicago (AL)	MAJ	0	0	0.00	2	0	0	0	3	0	0	0	4	1
MAJOR LEAGUE TOTALS			**0**	**2**	**5.40**	**6**	**3**	**0**	**0**	**18**	**17**	**11**	**11**	**18**	**12**
MINOR LEAGUE TOTALS			**39**	**22**	**3.27**	**87**	**85**	**2**	**0**	**517**	**426**	**232**	**188**	**216**	**475**

9. Andy Pratt, lhp

Born: Aug. 27, 1979. **Ht.:** 5-11. **Wt.:** 160. **Bats:** L. **Throws:** L. **School:** Chino Valley (Ariz.) HS. **Career Transactions:** Selected by Rangers in ninth round of 1998 draft; signed June 8, 1998.

Pratt was leading the Class A South Atlantic League in strikeouts in June 1999 when he was shut down with elbow problems that required surgery. He bounced back strong in 2000. His father Tom pitched in the Royals organization, has been a college coach and big league scout and currently is a pitching coach in the Cubs system. Like many young left-handers, Pratt relies on a changeup. Unlike many young lefthanders, he's willing to come inside with his fastball to keep hitters from sitting on it. Pratt's fastball isn't overpowering, but it's effective when he throws it in. He has good control. He's competitive and has a mound presence that reflects being around the game most of his life. Pratt's fastball and curveball are average at best. When hitters don't chase his changeup off the plate, he gets into trouble. That's what happened to him after he was promoted to Double-A. He needs to add strength to his slight body. If intelligence and guts count for anything, Pratt will do better in his return to Tulsa. He'll have to prove himself at every level.

Year	Club (League)	Class	W	L	ERA	G	GS	CG	SV	IP	H	R	ER	BB	SO
1998	Rangers (GCL)	R	4	3	3.86	12	8	0	0	56	49	25	24	14	49
1999	Savannah (SAL)	A	4	4	2.89	13	13	1	0	72	66	30	23	16	100
2000	Charlotte (FSL)	A	7	4	2.72	16	16	2	0	93	68	37	28	26	95
	Tulsa (TL)	AA	1	6	7.22	11	11	0	0	52	66	48	42	33	42
MINOR LEAGUE TOTALS			16	17	3.86	52	48	3	0	273	249	140	117	89	286

10. Hank Blalock, 3b

Born: Nov. 21, 1980. **Ht.:** 6-1. **Wt.:** 192. **Bats:** L. **Throws:** R. **School:** Rancho Bernardo HS, San Diego. **Career Transactions:** Selected by Rangers in third round of 1999 draft; signed June 4, 1999.

Blalock is a product of national power Rancho Bernardo High, coached by Sam Blalock, Hank's uncle. Hank broke into pro ball in 1999 by leading the Rookie-level Gulf Coast League in several categories, including batting average (.361), doubles (17) and RBIs (38). He easily held his own at Class A Savannah at age 19 last season. Blalock is already advanced at the plate. He has excellent bat control and good knowledge of the strike zone. In both of his pro seasons, he has walked more than he has struck out. He has power, though it's more to the gaps than over the fence. Blalock also runs well and was caught in just eight of 39 basestealing attempts last year. At times, Blalock can become too pull-conscious and lengthen his swing too much. He's OK defensively, though he's sometimes inconsistent when he lets bad at-bats affect him. Blalock will make a big jump into the pitching-oriented Florida State League this season. Another strong offensive performance would dramatically elevate his standing. The Rangers' signing of Ken Caminiti indicated dissatisfaction with Mike Lamb, so Blalock may be the organization's third baseman of the future. Putting Jason Grabowski, who hit .274-19-90 at Tulsa last year, on waivers also eliminated another obstacle.

Year	Club (League)	Class	AVG	G	AB	R	H	2B	3B	HR	RBI	BB	SO	SB
1999	Rangers (GCL)	R	.361	51	191	34	69	17	6	3	38	25	23	3
	Savannah (SAL)	A	.240	7	25	3	6	1	0	1	2	1	3	0
2000	Savannah (SAL)	A	.299	139	512	66	153	32	2	10	77	62	53	31
MINOR LEAGUE TOTALS			.313	197	728	103	228	50	8	14	117	88	79	34

11. David Mead, rhp

Born: March 21, 1981. **Ht.:** 6-5. **Wt.:** 180. **Bats:** R. **Throws:** R. **School:** Soddy-Daisy (Tenn.) HS. **Career Transactions:** Selected by Rangers in first round (47th overall) of 1999 draft; signed June 4, 1999.

Texas did a tremendous job restocking its system with its 1999 draft. Mead is the fourth player from that class on this list, and the Rangers also used sixth-rounder Aaron Harang in a trade with Oakland for second baseman Randy Velarde. Mead went 47th overall based on a projection by scout Dennis Meeks. While many teams saw Mead as a wild stringbean righthander, Meeks saw a budding power pitcher whose body and mind would mature. Mead has a legitimate plus fastball with good late movement. The Rangers believe he has enough power to succeed with average secondary pitches behind his fastball. He has averaged more than a strikeout per inning as a pro, and he also has done a pretty good job of throwing strikes. Mead's secondary pitches are far from average at this point, which is why he has yet to progress past Rookie ball. His breaking pitch has shown improvement, though his change-up is very much a work in progress. He needs to get stronger, which could add more velocity to his fastball. Minor league meal money could stand between Mead and rapid advancement. He'll get his first shot at full-season ball in 2001, most likely at Savannah. If he can't fill out his repertoire of pitches, the bullpen is an option down the road.

Year	Club (League)	Class	W	L	ERA	G	GS	CG	SV	IP	H	R	ER	BB	SO
1999	Rangers (GCL)	R	1	3	5.00	11	7	0	0	36	40	23	20	11	34
2000	Pulaski (Appy)	R	6	2	4.62	12	12	0	0	62	57	35	32	24	66
MINOR LEAGUE TOTALS			7	5	4.76	23	19	0	0	98	97	58	52	35	100

12. Travis Hafner, 1b

Born: June 3, 1977. **Ht.:** 6-3. **Wt.:** 215. **Bats:** L. **Throws:** R. **School:** Cowley County (Kan.) CC. **Career Transactions:** Selected by Rangers in 31st round of 1996 draft; signed June 2, 1997.

No one in the Rangers organization improved more last season than Hafner. Probably the strongest player in the system, he rose in Texas' judgment by dramatically changing his approach at the plate. In 1999, Hafner led the South Atlantic League in homers and RBIs but also had 151 strikeouts in 480 at-bats. He moved up to the Florida State League last season, when he began to understand the concept of hitting with two strikes and using the opposite field. Hafner again ranked among the league leaders in homers and RBIs while cutting his strikeouts nearly in half. The rap against Hafner is that he's a man without a position. He has slow feet and hands that are average at best. He simply doesn't compare to Carlos Pena at first base. Hafner is determined and fearless, traits that can make up for other deficiencies.

Year	Club (League)	Class	AVG	G	AB	R	H	2B	3B	HR	RBI	BB	SO	SB
1997	Rangers (GCL)	R	.286	55	189	38	54	14	0	5	24	24	45	7
1998	Savannah (SAL)	A	.237	123	405	62	96	15	4	16	84	68	139	7
1999	Savannah (SAL)	A	.292	134	480	94	140	30	4	28	111	67	151	5
2000	Charlotte (FSL)	A	.346	122	436	90	151	34	1	22	109	67	86	0
MINOR LEAGUE TOTALS			.292	434	1510	284	441	93	9	71	328	226	421	19

13. David Elder, rhp

Born: Sept. 23, 1975. **Ht.:** 6-0. **Wt.:** 180. **Bats:** R. **Throws:** R. **School:** Georgia Tech. **Career Transactions:** Selected by Rangers in fourth round of 1997 draft; signed June 21, 1997 . . . On disabled list, April 7-Oct. 15, 1998.

The Rangers moved Elder into the Double-A rotation last season to get him some badly needed innings. He missed the 1998 season because of Tommy John elbow surgery and worked a total of just 83 innings in his first three professional seasons. Like many recent Tommy John survivors, Elder has thrown harder since returning from the surgery, and he now can touch the mid-90s. While the added velocity is a plus, he must become more consistent with the command of his fastball. When Elder is effective with his fastball, he can dominate. When he gets overly excited and loses the strike zone, he's in trouble. He also needs to improve his slider. His future probably is in the bullpen, but he must throw more strikes to reach the majors. His height, less than the listed 6 feet, works against him.

Year	Club (League)	Class	W	L	ERA	G	GS	CG	SV	IP	H	R	ER	BB	SO
1997	Pulaski (Appy)	R	2	2	1.95	20	0	0	6	32	18	8	7	12	57
1998	Did Not Play—Injured														
1999	Charlotte (FSL)	·A	4	2	2.84	24	1	0	4	44	33	15	14	25	42
	Tulsa (TL)	AA	1	0	8.10	3	0	0	0	7	8	7	6	6	7
2000	Tulsa (TL)	AA	7	6	4.94	33	21	0	3	117	121	80	64	88	104
MINOR LEAGUE TOTALS			14	10	4.10	80	22	0	13	200	180	110	91	131	210

14. Scott Heard, c

Born: Sept. 2, 1981. **Ht.:** 6-2. **Wt.:** 190. **Bats:** L. **Throws:** R. **School:** Rancho Bernardo HS, San Diego. **Career Transactions:** Selected by Rangers in first round (25th overall) of 2000 draft; signed July 8, 2000.

Heard is a former teammate of Hank Blalock at Rancho Bernardo High, one of the nation's top high school programs. If it were a matter of defense, Heard probably could catch in the majors now. He moves well behind the plate and has a strong arm with a quick release. The only catcher better than him in the organization is Ivan Rodriguez, who's the best in the game. There is, however, the matter of offense. Heard's poor hitting in his final high school season hurt his draft status—at one point he looked like he would go to Florida as the No. 1 overall choice—though he did improve once he turned pro. Heard quickly took to the instruction of Butch Wynegar, a former major league catcher, and tore up the Gulf Coast League. The Rangers believe Heard's high school problems stemmed from trying too hard to hit home runs in hopes of impressing scouts. With Wynegar, Heard settled back into a more consistent swing and tried to hit the ball up the middle. Questions about offense will follow Heard at each level while he wows observers with his skills behind the plate.

Year	Club (League)	Class	AVG	G	AB	R	H	2B	3B	HR	RBI	BB	SO	SB
2000	Rangers (GCL)	R	.351	31	111	21	39	16	0	2	16	20	17	1
	Savannah (SAL)	A	.250	2	8	0	2	0	0	0	0	0	3	0
MINOR LEAGUE TOTALS			.345	33	119	21	41	16	0	2	16	20	20	1

15. Ryan Dittfurth, rhp

Born: Oct. 18, 1979. **Ht.:** 6-6. **Wt.:** 180. **Bats:** R. **Throws:** R. **School:** Tulsa Union HS. **Career Transactions:** Selected by Rangers in fifth round of 1998 draft; signed June 29, 1998.

Dittfurth embodies the Rangers' renewed affection for young power pitchers. He has the frame and the arm that should make him overpowering once he matures. All Dittfurth has to do is find the strike zone with the fastball. In addition to leading the South Atlantic League in walks last season, Dittfurth also threw 16 wild pitches and hit 17 batters. Righthanders need courage to step in against him. He must gain better control of his body to keep his delivery from going out of kilter. Dittfurth doesn't have a way to adjust if he can't locate his fastball. He also throws a curveball and changeup, but his fastball is what will carry him to the majors, and the Rangers hope he'll be able to control it as he gains more experience.

Year	Club (League)	Class	W	L	ERA	G	GS	CG	SV	IP	H	R	ER	BB	SO
1998	Rangers (GCL)	R	3	2	1.34	8	6	0	0	34	25	8	5	11	33
1999	Pulaski (Appy)	R	7	2	2.60	14	14	1	0	83	66	35	24	42	85
2000	Savannah (SAL)	A	8	13	4.25	29	29	2	0	159	127	83	75	99	158
MINOR LEAGUE TOTALS			18	17	3.40	51	49	3	0	275	218	126	104	152	276

16. Jose Morban, ss

Born: Dec. 2, 1979. **Ht.:** 6-1. **Wt.:** 170. **Bats:** R. **Throws:** R. **Career Transactions:** Signed out of Dominican Republic by Rangers, Dec. 15, 1996.

One of the biggest disappointments in the system last year was that Morban couldn't handle the level of competition in the South Atlantic League and had to go back to the Appalachian League. Morban is an acrobatic shortstop with good range, arm and hands. He also runs well and has pop in his bat. All of that makes his performance last year—his first full season in the United States—so frustrating to the Rangers. He didn't make contact and was erratic both on the bases and in the field. The lone positive was that he continued to draw walks, not that it helped his batting average. The Rangers will give Morban a mulligan for last season and hope his talent comes forth in 2001, when he'll get another shot at the Sally League.

Year	Club (League)	Class	AVG	G	AB	R	H	2B	3B	HR	RBI	BB	SO	SB
1997	Rangers (DSL)	R	.313	13	16	5	5	0	0	0	2	4	7	3
1998	Rangers (DSL)	R	.232	54	168	31	39	10	5	4	25	24	35	13
1999	Rangers (GCL)	R	.283	54	205	45	58	10	5	4	18	31	70	19
2000	Savannah (SAL)	A	.220	80	273	44	60	8	4	4	28	41	79	27
	Pulaski (Appy)	R	.225	30	120	21	27	3	2	3	17	12	35	6
MINOR LEAGUE TOTALS			.242	231	782	146	189	31	16	15	90	112	226	68

17. Spike Lundberg, rhp

Born: May 4, 1977. **Ht.:** 6-1. **Wt.:** 185. **Bats:** B. **Throws:** R. **School:** San Diego Mesa JC. **Career Transactions:** Selected by Rangers in 26th round of 1997 draft; signed June 5, 1997.

Give scout Jim Lentine credit for being able to project Lundberg, a junior college infielder whom Lentine envisioned as a pitcher. Lundberg made the conversion after signing. He lacks power on his fastball but gets batters out by changing speeds and throwing strikes with three pitches: a sinker, curveball and changeup. Lundberg understands his limitations and doesn't overthrow. He also doesn't try to trick hitters, preferring to let them get themselves out by beating the ball into the ground. He allowed only nine homers in Double-A last year. Though Lundberg has two consecutive 14-win seasons as a swingman, the Rangers remain somewhat skeptical. They didn't protect him on the 40-man roster during the offseason, and no one bit on him in the major league Rule 5 draft.

Year	Club (League)	Class	W	L	ERA	G	GS	CG	SV	IP	H	R	ER	BB	SO
1997	Rangers (GCL)	R	1	1	0.84	14	1	0	5	32	13	4	3	11	32
1998	Savannah (SAL)	A	6	9	5.54	50	0	0	14	88	105	69	54	27	70
1999	Charlotte (FSL)	A	14	7	2.83	30	21	4	0	156	162	63	49	44	81
2000	Tulsa (TL)	AA	14	7	3.05	40	13	0	4	151	148	61	51	54	102
MINOR LEAGUE TOTALS			35	24	3.31	134	35	4	23	427	428	197	157	136	285

18. Omar Beltre, rhp

Born: Aug. 24, 1982. **Ht.:** 6-3. **Wt.:** 192. **Bats:** R. **Throws:** R. **Career Transactions:** Signed out of Dominican Republic by Rangers, March 1, 2000.

The Rangers gave Beltre a significant bonus when they signed him out of the Dominican last February, and the early returns were promising. Despite being young and raw, he wasn't overwhelmed by coming straight to the U.S. and facing Gulf Coast League hitters. He ranked as the No. 10 prospect in the GCL. Beltre relied on a fastball-slider combination, and he throws hard enough to work high in the strike zone with a four-seam fastball. He doesn't have an advanced changeup, though he can throw strikes and set up hitters. At this point, his biggest needs are to grow stronger and gain more experience. He has a very projectable body and the Rangers believe he can be an innings-eater.

Year	Club (League)	Class	W	L	ERA	G	GS	CG	SV	IP	H	R	ER	BB	SO
2000	Rangers (GCL)	R	5	4	3.54	13	13	0	0	61	54	30	24	15	44
MINOR LEAGUE TOTALS			5	4	3.54	13	13	0	0	61	54	30	24	15	44

19. Domingo Valdez, rhp

Born: June 27, 1980. **Ht.:** 6-3. **Wt.:** 220. **Bats:** R. **School:** Moody HS, Corpus Christi, Texas. **Career Transactions:** Selected by Rangers in 16th round of 1998 draft; signed June 3, 1998.

Sensing his career had stalled, Valdez quit for a day during spring training last year. He returned contrite and determined to do something with himself. That new mindset showed on the mound. Valdez returned to the Appalachian League, where he had flopped in 1999, and dominated. He always had command of his low-90s fastball, and last season he was able to throw strikes with his curveball and changeup. He also showed improved composure on the mound, another hint that he is maturing. Valdez stuck with a conditioning program, which is important to him. He pitches best at about 220 pounds but can zoom up 260 pounds if he's not careful. Valdez is finally ready for full-season ball for the first time in his career.

Year	Club (League)	Class	W	L	ERA	G	GS	CG	SV	IP	H	R	ER	BB	SO
1998	Rangers (GCL)	R	2	2	3.09	10	5	0	0	32	24	15	11	16	27
1999	Pulaski (Appy)	R	0	0	6.75	3	3	0	0	16	20	14	12	7	14
	Rangers (GCL)	R	0	1	4.91	8	7	0	0	29	29	22	16	18	34
2000	Pulaski (Appy)	R	6	2	1.63	11	11	0	0	61	45	23	11	25	71
MINOR LEAGUE TOTALS			8	5	3.26	32	26	0	0	138	118	74	50	66	156

20. Greg Runser, rhp

Born: April 5, 1979. **Ht.:** 6-0. **Wt.:** 195. **Bats:** R. **Throws:** R. **School:** University of Houston. **Career Transactions:** Selected by Rangers in fifth round of 2000 draft; signed June 15, 2000.

In one year, Runser went from an out-of-shape junior college starter to a closer for the University of Houston, which came within one game of advancing to the 2000 College World Series. Frustrated with his bullpen, Cougars coach Rayner Noble took Runser out of the rotation and made him a closer. The switch turned Runser into a late sensation for the draft, and he went in the fifth round. A lighter and better-conditioned Runser added about 4 mph to his fastball, giving him a heater that can reach 95 mph to go with an excellent changeup that can be a strikeout pitch. His third pitch is a slider. He overmatched younger hitters in the Appalachian League and possibly could start 2001 by skipping Savannah and heading to high Class A.

Year	Club (League)	Class	W	L	ERA	G	GS	CG	SV	IP	H	R	ER	BB	SO
2000	Pulaski (Appy)	R	3	3	1.12	21	0	0	6	48	35	18	6	14	47
MINOR LEAGUE TOTALS			3	3	1.12	21	0	0	6	48	35	18	6	14	47

21. Jason Botts, 1b

Born: July 26, 1980. **Ht.:** 6-6. **Wt.:** 245. **Bats:** B. **Throws:** R. **School:** Glendale (Calif.) JC. **Career Transactions:** Selected by Rangers in 46th round of 1999 draft; signed May 15, 2000.

In many ways, Botts is the biggest sleeper in the organization. A draft-and-follow from 1999, he showed a lot more than the Rangers expected after signing last summer. They knew he could hit with power, and he did just that in the Gulf Coast League. They didn't know he could switch-hit, which Botts did when he began batting from the left side after turning pro. He knows how to lift balls and showed power from both sides of the plate. The Rangers also didn't know Botts could be so controlled at the plate. He made acceptable contact and walked nearly as much as he struck out. He fills out a uniform at 6-foot-6 and 245 pounds, but he has good footwork and can run the 60-yard dash in 6.6 seconds during workouts. Botts could come on in a hurry.

Year	Club (League)	Class	AVG	G	AB	R	H	2B	3B	HR	RBI	BB	SO	SB
2000	Rangers (GCL)	R	.319	48	163	36	52	12	0	6	34	26	29	4
MINOR LEAGUE TOTALS			.319	48	163	36	52	12	0	6	34	26	29	4

22. Alan Webb, lhp

Born: Sept. 26, 1979. **Ht.:** 5-10. **Wt.:** 165. **Bats:** L. **Throws:** L. **School:** Durango HS, Las Vegas. **Career Transactions:** Selected by Tigers in fourth round of 1997 draft; signed June 24, 1997 . . . Traded by Tigers with OF Gabe Kapler, LHP Justin Thompson, RHP Francisco Cordero, 2B Frank Catalanotto and C Bill Haselman to Rangers for OF Juan Gonzalez, C Greg Zaun and RHP Danny Patterson, Nov. 2, 1999.

Almost everyone associated with the November 1999 Juan Gonzalez trade with Detroit had a dreadful 2000 season, and Webb was no exception. He opened the season in Double-A and came undone, continuing a slump that began in 1999 with the Tigers' Double-A affiliate. That earned Webb a demotion that seemed to jar him. His commitment and maturity had been questioned, but he began throwing strikes with his changeup again in Class A and rebuilt his standing. His changeup and curveball are plus pitches, and Webb can throw strikes with a below-average fastball. But not only does his fastball lack velocity, it also doesn't move much, forcing him to pitch backward. The diminutive Webb never will have more than a narrow margin of error. He may be as good now as he ever will be, and he must pitch intelligently to advance.

Year	Club (League)	Class	W	L	ERA	G	GS	CG	SV	IP	H	R	ER	BB	SO
1997	Tigers (GCL)	R	3	1	3.74	9	8	0	0	34	27	17	14	11	46
1998	West Michigan (Mid)	A	10	7	2.93	27	27	3	0	172	110	69	56	58	202
1999	Jacksonville (SL)	AA	9	9	4.95	26	22	0	0	140	140	88	77	64	88
2000	Charlotte (FSL)	A	5	4	3.24	16	15	1	0	83	83	36	30	39	40
	Tulsa (TL)	AA	0	4	11.72	10	6	0	0	25	35	33	33	24	17
MINOR LEAGUE TOTALS			27	25	4.16	88	78	4	0	454	395	243	210	196	401

23. Kelly Dransfeldt, ss

Born: April 16, 1975. **Ht.:** 6-2. **Wt.:** 195. **Bats:** R. **Throws:** R. **School:** University of Michigan. **Career Transactions:** Selected by Rangers in fourth round of 1996 draft; signed June 9, 1996.

Dransfeldt has reached the produce-or-depart stage of his career with Texas. He's an excellent defensive shortstop, making up for a big body with good footwork and an accurate arm. He's more consistent with the glove than Royce Clayton, the Rangers' starter for the previous 2½ seasons. But Texas never used Dransfeldt for more than spot duty because he has been helpless at the plate. He has batted .239 above Class A, showing modest power and little sense of the strike zone. He can't settle on a stance and lacks bat speed. Dransfeldt obviously won't move Alex Rodriguez out of the lineup, and he'd be best served by going to a shortstop-needy organization.

Year	Club (League)	Class	AVG	G	AB	R	H	2B	3B	HR	RBI	BB	SO	SB
1996	Hudson Valley (NY-P)	A	.236	75	284	42	67	17	1	7	29	27	76	13
1997	Charlotte (FSL)	A	.227	135	466	64	106	20	7	6	58	42	115	25
1998	Charlotte (FSL)	A	.322	67	245	46	79	17	0	18	76	29	67	7
	Tulsa (TL)	AA	.252	58	226	43	57	15	4	9	36	18	79	8
1999	Oklahoma (PCL)	AAA	.237	102	359	55	85	21	2	10	44	24	108	6
	Texas (AL)	MAJ	.189	16	53	3	10	1	0	1	5	3	12	0
2000	Oklahoma (PCL)	AAA	.247	117	441	60	109	22	3	8	42	38	123	10
	Texas (AL)	MAJ	.115	16	26	2	3	2	0	0	2	1	14	0
MAJOR LEAGUE TOTALS			.165	32	79	5	13	3	0	1	7	4	26	0
MINOR LEAGUE TOTALS			.249	554	2021	310	503	112	17	58	285	178	568	69

24. Danny Kolb, rhp

Born: March 29, 1975. **Ht.:** 6-4. **Wt.:** 215. **Bats:** R. **Throws:** R. **School:** Sauk Valley (Ill.) CC. **Career Transactions:** Selected by Rangers in sixth round of 1995 draft; signed June 1, 1995.

A rough delivery caught up to Kolb last season. After pitching in pain for two seasons, he gave in and had reconstructive elbow surgery in June. The remarkable point is that despite the pain, Kolb had a 0.98 ERA for 13 relief appearances with Triple-A Oklahoma before the surgery. He had been capable of touching the upper 90s with his fastball, but has learned that he pitches more effectively at 92-94 mph. The Rangers also like his slider and go-through-a-wall makeup. The concern now is that his makeup may have pushed him too far, leaving him with a career-ending elbow injury. His command has been inconsistent as well. The Rangers hope to have Kolb back on a mound during spring training, but there are no guarantees.

Year	Club (League)	Class	W	L	ERA	G	GS	CG	SV	IP	H	R	ER	BB	SO
1995	Rangers (GCL)	R	1	7	2.21	12	11	0	0	53	38	22	13	28	46
1996	Charleston, SC (SAL)	A	8	6	2.57	20	20	4	0	126	80	50	36	60	127
	Tulsa (TL)	AA	1	0	0.77	2	2	0	0	12	5	1	1	8	7
	Charlotte (FSL)	A	2	2	4.26	6	6	0	0	38	38	18	18	14	28
1997	Charlotte (FSL)	A	4	10	4.87	24	23	3	0	133	146	91	72	62	83
	Tulsa (TL)	AA	0	2	4.76	2	2	0	0	11	7	7	6	11	6
1998	Tulsa (TL)	AA	12	11	4.82	28	28	2	0	162	187	104	87	76	83
	Oklahoma (PCL)	AAA	0	0	0.00	1	0	0	0	1	1	0	0	1	0
1999	Tulsa (TL)	AA	1	2	2.79	7	7	1	0	39	38	16	12	18	32
	Oklahoma (PCL)	AAA	5	3	5.10	11	8	0	0	60	74	35	34	27	21
	Texas (AL)	MAJ	2	1	4.65	16	0	0	0	31	33	18	16	15	15
2000	Oklahoma (PCL)	AAA	4	1	0.98	13	0	0	4	18	11	6	2	8	18
	Texas (AL)	MAJ	0	0	67.50	1	0	0	0	1	5	5	5	2	0
MAJOR LEAGUE TOTALS			2	1	5.97	17	0	0	0	32	38	23	21	17	15
MINOR LEAGUE TOTALS			38	44	3.87	126	107	10	4	653	625	350	281	313	451

25. Cody Nowlin, of

Born: Nov. 27, 1979. **Ht.:** 6-3. **Wt.:** 190. **Bats:** L. **Throws:** R. **School:** Clovis (Calif.) HS. **Career Transactions:** Selected by Rangers in second round of 1998 draft; signed June 12, 1998.

Texas took Nowlin in the second round of the 1998 draft on the basis of power potential, but after three pro seasons he has just a .396 career slugging percentage. He showed some pop in the South Atlantic League with a career-high 15 homers last year, but he also batted .244 with mediocre plate discipline. Nowlin runs well and has an above-average outfield arm, but his success will be determined by his power production. The Rangers still believe he can be a legitimate .280 hitter with power. He probably will be promoted to high Class A in 2001, which should shed considerable light on his future.

Year	Club (League)	Class	AVG	G	AB	R	H	2B	3B	HR	RBI	BB	SO	SB
1998	Rangers (GCL)	R	.272	52	202	25	55	13	2	7	34	19	42	1
1999	Savannah (SAL)	A	.181	56	204	25	37	6	1	4	26	19	58	1
	Pulaski (Appy)	R	.278	58	227	45	63	10	1	8	49	21	34	5
2000	Savannah (SAL)	A	.244	136	501	66	122	27	3	15	68	44	104	3
MINOR LEAGUE TOTALS			.244	302	1134	161	277	56	7	34	177	103	238	10

26. Chris Russ, lhp

Born: Oct. 26, 1979. **Ht.:** 6-3. **Wt.:** 190. **Bats:** L. **Throws:** L. **School:** Towson University. **Career Transactions:** Selected by Rangers in third round of 2000 draft; signed June 21, 2000.

Russ had a scintillating pro debut in 2000. He dazzled younger hitters in the Appalachian League, then pitched well against more demanding competition in the South Atlantic League. Russ is the quintessential soft-tossing lefthander. He keeps hitters confused by changing speeds and hiding the ball well. His fastball is more notable for his sink than its velocity, and he crosses hitters up by rarely throwing it in fastball counts. His curveball has developed into a solid second pitch. He's also a superb athlete who fields his position well. Russ has an intriguing ceiling, though he's not particularly polished coming from a small college program.

Year	Club (League)	Class	W	L	ERA	G	GS	CG	SV	IP	H	R	ER	BB	SO
2000	Pulaski (Appy)	R	2	0	0.83	6	2	0	0	22	14	4	2	4	26
	Savannah (SAL)	A	3	1	2.43	7	7	0	0	41	38	14	11	14	34
MINOR LEAGUE TOTALS			5	1	1.86	13	9	0	0	63	52	18	13	18	60

27. Nick Regilio, rhp

Born: Sept. 4, 1978. **Ht.:** 6-2. **Wt.:** 185. **Bats:** R. **Throws:** R. **School:** Jacksonville University. **Career Transactions:** Selected by Rangers in second round of 1999 draft; signed June 11, 1999.

Some observers believe Regilio's future is as a long reliever, but the Rangers will give him every chance to establish himself as a starter. Regilio has average stuff and never will knock the bat out of a hitter's hands. His best attribute is the late, hard sink on his fastball. He throws strikes, though almost to a fault, as he was hammered at times in 2000. In his first full season last year, Regilio was limited by occasional shoulder soreness. The Rangers don't believe the shoulder will be a long-running problem. He probably could use a return trip to Charlotte to begin 2001.

Year	Club (League)	Class	W	L	ERA	G	GS	CG	SV	IP	H	R	ER	BB	SO
1999	Pulaski (Appy)	R	4	2	1.63	11	8	1	0	50	30	12	9	16	58
2000	Charlotte (FSL)	A	4	3	4.52	20	20	0	0	86	94	54	43	29	63
MINOR LEAGUE TOTALS			8	5	3.44	31	28	1	0	136	124	66	52	45	121

28. Sixto Urena, rhp

Born: Feb. 15, 1981. **Ht.:** 6-2. **Wt.:** 198. **Bats:** R. **Throws:** R. **Career Transactions:** Signed out of Dominican Republic by Rangers, Dec. 13, 1997.

Former scouting director Chuck McMichael produced promising drafts and increased the Rangers' presence in the Dominican Republic. Urena, who has an above-average fastball, came out of the club's operation in Santiago. He pitches down in the strike zone and didn't allow a homer in his U.S. debut last season. Urena must choose between his slider and curveball because the pitches are too similar. At this point, the slider is the better pitch. He's still learning a changeup, which he'll need to progress.

Year	Club (League)	Class	W	L	ERA	G	GS	CG	SV	IP	H	R	ER	BB	SO
1998	Rangers (DSL)	R	3	0	4.50	14	0	0	1	28	29	18	14	11	23
1999	Rangers (DSL)	R	3	5	4.14	23	8	0	7	63	61	36	29	28	60
2000	Pulaski (Appy)	R	6	2	2.83	11	11	1	0	60	53	24	19	25	47
MINOR LEAGUE TOTALS			12	7	3.70	48	19	1	8	151	143	78	62	64	130

29. Jason Bourgeois, 2b

Born: Jan. 4, 1982. **Ht.:** 5-9. **Wt.:** 170. **Bats:** B. **Throws:** R. **School:** Forest Brook HS, Houston. **Career Transactions:** Selected by Rangers in second round of 2000 draft; signed June 19, 2000.

Some clubs believed the Rangers reached by taking Bourgeois in the second round of the 2000 draft. A high school shortstop, he moved immediately to second base as a pro because he has limited arm strength. Bourgeois seems to be a good fit for second base because of his range, quick feet and soft hands. He has plus speed and good instincts for the game. The Rangers hope he becomes an adequate offensive player. Bourgeois currently plays a little man's game on offense, focusing on bunts, slap hits, walks and stolen bases. He's effective in those areas, but didn't show much in terms of batting average or power in his pro debut. He'll need to get stronger to survive a full season.

Year	Club (League)	Class	AVG	G	AB	R	H	2B	3B	HR	RBI	BB	SO	SB
2000	Rangers (GCL)	R	.239	24	88	18	21	4	0	0	6	14	15	9
MINOR LEAGUE TOTALS			.239	24	88	18	21	4	0	0	6	14	15	9

30. Corey Lee, lhp

Born: Dec. 26, 1974. **Ht.:** 6-2. **Wt.:** 185. **Bats:** B. **Throws:** L. **School:** North Carolina State University. **Career Transactions:** Selected by Rangers in first round (32nd overall) of 1996 draft; signed July 10, 1996.

In 1997, Lee was the organization's pitcher of the year. Last fall, he passed through outright waivers without being claimed. Lee's decline can be blamed on a loss of control. He led the Texas League in walks in 1998 and ranked third in that category in the Pacific Coast League last season. Lee's fastball is average at best, and he loses confidence in it when it gets hit. Then he nibbles with his offspeed stuff, falls behind in the count and gets into more trouble. His curveball is his best pitch, and he also has a slider and changeup. Lee bounced back after a rough first year at Double-A. If he does the same thing in Triple-A this season, he could get another chance.

Year	Club (League)	Class	W	L	ERA	G	GS	CG	SV	IP	H	R	ER	BB	SO
1996	Hudson Valley (NY-P)	A	1	4	3.29	9	9	0	0	55	42	24	20	21	59
1997	Charlotte (FSL)	A	15	5	3.47	23	23	6	0	161	132	66	62	60	147
1998	Tulsa (TL)	AA	10	9	4.51	26	25	1	0	144	105	81	72	102	132
1999	Tulsa (TL)	AA	8	5	4.44	22	22	0	0	128	132	76	63	44	121
	Oklahoma (PCL)	AAA	3	0	2.03	4	4	0	0	27	21	6	6	8	25
	Texas (AL)	MAJ	0	1	27.00	1	0	0	0	1	2	3	3	1	0
2000	Oklahoma (PCL)	AAA	2	12	8.76	26	21	0	0	112	163	128	109	87	84
MAJOR LEAGUE TOTALS			0	1	27.00	1	0	0	0	1	2	3	3	1	0
MINOR LEAGUE TOTALS			39	35	4.78	110	104	7	0	625	595	381	332	322	568

Toronto
Blue Jays

By John Manuel

The Blue Jays had the look of a playoff team in 1999 and 2000, but a pair of third-place finishes in the American League East cost manager Jim Fregosi his job. General manager Gord Ash not only survived, but he also received a three-year contract extension when the season ended.

Ash should have more money to spend with the club's sale to Toronto-based media giant Rogers Communications. The sale has rekindled hope the organization could return to its glory days of the early 1990s. Rogers' financial stability will be an improvement over former owner Interbrew—not to mention its Canadian roots and familiarity with baseball.

"The first meeting we had with the people from Interbrew at SkyDome," one club official said, "they looked around and asked us what the R, H and E on the scoreboard meant."

Ash hired former Jays catcher and broadcaster Buck Martinez as the new manager, and he will have plenty of talent to work with at the big league level. Start with first baseman Carlos Delgado, who re-signed for four years and $68 million at the end of the season.

While the organization refused to part with some of its top-level talent, its minor league talent has thinned. Some of that happened with trades of prospects for veterans, one of the purposes of player development. Toronto dealt four members of last year's top 10: second basemen Brent Abernathy and Mike Young and righthanders Gary Glover and John Sneed. The Blue Jays re-signed Sneed after the Phillies released him.

Budget constraints the last two years prevented the organization from replacing its depth through amateur signings. Toronto is the only club that did not pay its first-round pick at least $1 million in each of the last two drafts, doing so by selecting Puerto Rican outfielders Alexis Rios and Miguel Negron.

Former scouting director Tim Wilken brought in decent talent the last two years despite the constraints, but he admits his successor, Chris Buckley, will have an easier time come June. Wilken has become vice president of baseball operations, and Buckley shouldn't have to settle for a talented but raw high school outfielder in the first round.

The organization was searching for a new farm director after Jim Lett left to become a coach with the Dodgers.

Organization**Overview**

General manager: Gord Ash. **Farm director:** Bob Nelson. **Scouting director:** Chris Buckley.

2000 PERFORMANCE

Class	Team	League	W	L	Pct.	Finish*	Manager(s)
Majors	Toronto	American	83	79	.512	7th (14)	Jim Fregosi
Triple-A	Syracuse SkyChiefs	International	74	66	.529	7th (14)	Pat Kelly/Mel Queen
Double-A	Tennessee Smokies	Southern	71	69	.507	t-3rd (10)	Rocket Wheeler
High A	Dunedin Blue Jays	Florida State	84	54	.609	1st (14)	Marty Pevey
Low A	#Hagerstown Suns	South Atlantic	63	74	.460	11th (14)	Rolando Pino
Short-season	†Queens Kings	New York-Penn	46	29	.613	3rd (14)	Eddie Rodriguez
Rookie	Medicine Hat Blue Jays	Pioneer	36	40	.474	6th (8)	Paul Elliott
OVERALL 2000 MINOR LEAGUE RECORD			373	332	.529	6th (30)	

*Finish in overall standings (No. of teams in league). #Affiliate will be in Charleston, W.Va., (South Atlantic) in 2001. †Affiliate will be in Auburn (New York-Penn) in 2001.

ORGANIZATION LEADERS

BATTING
*AVG	**Luis Lopez**, Syracuse	.328
R	Tony Peters, Dunedin	97
H	**Luis Lopez**, Syracuse	161
TB	Chad Mottola, Syracuse	286
2B	Joe Lawrence, Dunedin/Tennessee	41
3B	Brandon Jackson, Hagerstown/Dunedin	8
HR	Chad Mottola, Syracuse	33
RBI	Chad Mottola, Syracuse	102
BB	Joe Lawrence, Dunedin/Tennessee	99
SO	Tony Peters, Dunedin	164
SB	Shannon Carter, Hagerstown	33

PITCHING
W	Pasqual Coco, Tennessee	12
L	Marcos Sandoval, Hagerstown	13
#ERA	Robert Hamann, Hagerstown/Dunedin	2.52
G	Bob File, Tennessee/Syracuse	56
CG	Leo Estrella, Tennessee/Syracuse	6
SV	**Jarrod Kingrey**, Dunedin/Tennessee	30
IP	Matt McClellan, Tennessee	169
BB	Joe Casey, Dunedin	74
	Charles Kegley, Dunedin	74
SO	Pasqual Coco, Tennessee	142

*Minimum 250 at-bats. #Minimum 75 innings.

TOP PROSPECTS OF THE DECADE

1991	Mark Whiten, of
1992	Derek Bell, of
1993	Carlos Delgado, c
1994	Alex Gonzalez, ss
1995	Shawn Green, of
1996	Shannon Stewart, of
1997	Roy Halladay, rhp
1998	Roy Halladay, rhp
1999	Roy Halladay, rhp
2000	Vernon Wells, of

TOP DRAFT PICKS OF THE DECADE

1991	Shawn Green, of
1992	Shannon Stewart, of
1993	Chris Carpenter, rhp
1994	Kevin Witt, ss
1995	Roy Halladay, rhp
1996	Billy Koch, rhp
1997	Vernon Wells, of
1998	Felipe Lopez, ss
1999	Alexis Rios, 3b/of
2000	Miguel Negron, of

Lopez   **Kingrey**

BEST TOOLS

Best Hitter for Average	Vernon Wells
Best Power Hitter	Michael Snyder
Fastest Baserunner	Vernon Wells
Best Fastball	Bob File
Best Breaking Ball	Scott Porter
Best Control	Scott Cassidy
Best Defensive Catcher	Joe Lawrence
Best Defensive Infielder	Cesar Izturis
Best Infield Arm	Felipe Lopez
Best Defensive Outfielder	Vernon Wells
Best Outfield Arm	Alex Rios

PROJECTED 2004 LINEUP

Catcher	Joe Lawrence
First Base	Carlos Delgado
Second Base	Cesar Izturis
Third Base	Tony Batista
Shortstop	Felipe Lopez
Left Field	Shannon Stewart
Center Field	Vernon Wells
Right Field	Raul Mondesi
Designated Hitter	Brad Fullmer
No. 1 Starter	Chris Carpenter
No. 2 Starter	Charles Kegley
No. 3 Starter	Mike Sirotka
No. 4 Starter	Brian Cardwell
No. 5 Starter	Pascual Coco
Closer	Billy Koch

ALL-TIME LARGEST BONUSES

Felipe Lopez, 1998	$2,000,000
Vernon Wells, 1997	1,600,000
Billy Koch, 1996	1,450,000
Guillermo Quiroz, 1998	1,200,000
Miguel Negron, 2000	950,000

Draft Analysis

2000 Draft

Best Pro Debut: OF Jeremy Johnson (26) was MVP of the Rookie-level Pioneer League after batting .376-9-58. 1B/OF Ron Davenport (22) batted .345-4-46 for the same Medicine Hat club, while RHP Andy McCulloch (20) led the league with 15 saves.

Best Athlete: OF Morrin Davis (4) or OF Rich Thompson (6). Davis is stronger while Thompson is quicker.

Best Hitter: Johnson not only hit .376, but he also walked (55) nearly twice as often as he struck out (29). The Blue Jays also like the potential of 2B Dominic Rich (2).

Best Raw Power: 3B Nom Siriveaw (9) is a strong British Columbia product with a black belt in karate. Some thought 3B Aaron Sisk's (7) power wouldn't translate to wood, but he hit 13 homers at Medicine Hat.

Fastest Runner: Thompson is a flier who can run a 6.4-second 60-yard dash. Speed is OF **Miguel Negron's** (1) best tool, but it didn't warrant his first-round selection.

Best Defensive Player: Raul Tablado (4) was one of the purest shortstops in the draft. He'll need to get stronger, but he recovered from a .143 start to bat .271 in the second half in the short-season New York-Penn League.

Best Fastball: RHPs Dustin McGowan (1) and Jerrod Payne (10) both can throw 95-96 mph.

Most Intriguing Background: RHP Tracey Thorpe (11) was recruited by Central Florida to play quarterback. LHP Eric Stephenson's (15) father Earl pitched in the majors, as did SS Rich Brosseau's (16) father Frank. C Casey Martinez' (47) dad Buck once manned the same position for Toronto and is now the Jays' manager. 2B Jeremy Ridley's (19) twin brother Shayne was taken by the Orioles, and father Jim is the Blue Jays' assistant director of Canadian scouting.

Closest To The Majors: RHP Peter Bauer (2) throws in the low 90s with command of three pitches that's uncanny for a 6-foot-5 pitcher.

Best Late-Round Pick: Johnson edges out Davenport. At 6-foot-5 and 180 pounds, Stephenson is a projectable lefty with a fastball that ranges from 81-90 mph and a plus curveball.

Negron

The One Who Got Away: The Blue Jays signed 28 of their first 30 picks, and control the rights to Los Angeles Harbor JC RHP Charles Talanoa (14) and Lake City (Fla.) CC RHP Mark Perkins (18). The best player they lost is LHP Chris Neuman (29), who showed good stuff until Tommy John surgery before his senior year of high school. He's at Texas.

Assessment: The Jays haven't had the money they had in the early 1990s, so for the second straight year they spent their first pick on a Puerto Rican outfielder they could sign for less than $1 million. Following their sale to Rogers Communications, the fiscal restraints are gone. As Chris Buckley takes over as scouting director for Tim Wilken, Toronto will be much more aggressive in signing amateur talent.

1999 Draft

The Blue Jays overdrafted Alex Rios (1) so they could avoid paying a $1 million bonus. LHP Matt Ford (3) and RHPs Brian Cardwell (4), Charles Kegley (11) and Brandon Lyon (14, draft-and-follow) are all better prospects.　　　　**Grade: C–**

1998 Draft

Felipe Lopez (1) is one of the game's better shortstop prospects, though he was needlessly rushed to Double-A last year. Toronto made an astute move by drafting 3B Bob File (19), the NCAA Division II batting champ, and converting him into a closer.　　**Grade: C+**

1997 Draft

The Jays were criticized for making a signability pick in OF Vernon Wells (1), but he could be a star. The only other players of note are SS/2B Mike Young (5), who was traded to Texas, and LHP Mark Hendricksen (20), who also has spent time in the NBA.　　**Grade: C+**

1996 Draft

RHP Billy Koch (1) is Toronto's closer, and C Joe Lawrence (1) is the backstop of the future. OF Pete Tucci (1) washed out after getting dealt to San Diego. 2B Brent Abernathy (2) could start this year for Tampa Bay after a 2000 trade.　　**Grade: A**

Note: Draft analysis prepared by Jim Callis. Numbers in parentheses indicate draft rounds.

. . . Wells has the best tools in the system, and his five-tool package is among the best in the minor leagues.

Vernon Wells of

Born: Dec. 8, 1978.
Ht.: 6-1. **Wt.:** 210.
Bats: R. **Throws:** R.
School: Bowie HS, Arlington, Texas.
Career Transactions: Selected by Blue Jays in first round (fifth overall) of 1997 draft; signed June 3, 1997.

When Wells was drafted fifth overall in 1997, some chided the Blue Jays for basing their first-round choice on signability more than talent. Wells, who had agreed to a predraft deal, started his career in fine fashion in the short-season New York-Penn League and had a solid first full season in 1998 with Class A Hagerstown. But he did nothing to prepare the baseball world for 1999. Wells batted a combined .334-18-81 between Class A Dunedin, Double-A Knoxville and Triple-A Syracuse and was named the No. 1 prospect in the Florida State, Southern and International leagues—a Baseball America first. He finished with a solid month in Toronto, raising expectations for the son of the former NFL wide receiver of the same name. But he received just two big league at-bats in 2000 and struggled with the bat in Triple-A.

Wells has the best tools in the system, and his five-tool package is among the best in the minor leagues. He's a true center fielder with an accurate, above-average arm and excellent range, and he has good instincts for the position. Offensively, his speed and instincts make him an above-average basestealer, and he has plus power to all fields. Wells was caught stealing just four times, and he hit .272-12-35 with a .545 slugging percentage in his final 209 Triple-A at-bats.

Wells had never struggled before, but he was hitting .220 with four homers on July 1. Rumors abounded about his dissatisfaction with being sent back to Triple-A, and that his frustration was affecting his play. Blue Jays officials refute that contention, saying Wells took the news well. They attribute part of his poor showing to bad luck. They also agreed his struggles probably will be good for him. Wells was the player other teams asked for in deals during the season, but the Blue Jays wisely held on to their No. 1 prospect. Toronto center fielder Jose Cruz Jr. doesn't field as well as Wells, and his offensive performance shouldn't be enough to block Wells for another year. If Cruz makes it through the winter with the organization, it's up to Wells to have a big spring to force his way onto the big league club.

Year	Club (League)	Class	AVG	G	AB	R	H	2B	3B	HR	RBI	BB	SO	SB
1997	St. Catharines (NY-P)	A	.307	66	264	52	81	20	1	10	31	30	44	8
1998	Hagerstown (SAL)	A	.285	134	509	86	145	35	2	11	65	49	84	13
1999	Dunedin (FSL)	A	.343	70	265	43	91	16	2	11	43	26	34	13
	Knoxville (SL)	AA	.340	26	106	18	36	6	2	3	17	12	15	6
	Syracuse (IL)	AAA	.310	33	129	20	40	8	1	4	21	10	22	5
	Toronto (AL)	MAJ	.261	25	88	8	23	5	0	1	8	4	18	1
2000	Syracuse (IL)	AAA	.243	127	493	76	120	31	7	16	66	48	88	23
	Toronto (AL)	MAJ	.000	2	3	0	0	0	0	0	0	0	0	0
MAJOR LEAGUE TOTALS			.253	27	91	8	23	5	0	1	8	4	18	1
MINOR LEAGUE TOTALS			.290	456	1766	295	513	116	15	55	243	175	287	68

2. Felipe Lopez, ss

Born: May 12, 1980. **Ht.:** 6-1. **Wt.:** 175. **Bats:** B. **Throws:** R. **School:** Lake Brantley HS, Altamonte Springs, Fla. **Career Transactions:** Selected by Blue Jays in first round (eighth overall) of 1998 draft; signed Aug. 11, 1998.

A Puerto Rican native, Lopez moved to Florida with his father in 1990. He survived the deaths of his mother and stepmother, as well as an abusive relationship with his father, to become one of the state's top prospects. He signed too late in 1998 to make an immediate impact but has risen quickly through the system. Only Vernon Wells has better tools among Jays prospects—and Lopez has five-tool ability. He has range to spare, a plus arm and true shortstop actions. He has average power and excellent speed, though it hasn't translated into high stolen-base totals yet. Lopez jumped over high Class A in 2000, which helps explain his mediocre numbers and inability to make consistent contact. Club officials have questioned his concentration, saying he took bad at-bats to the field with him. He hasn't learned the nuances of baserunning yet. Lopez should return to Double-A in 2001. The Blue Jays wouldn't have rushed him if they didn't think it was good for him.

Year	Club (League)	Class	AVG	G	AB	R	H	2B	3B	HR	RBI	BB	SO	SB
1998	St. Catharines (NY-P)	A	.373	19	83	14	31	5	2	1	11	3	14	4
	Dunedin (FSL)	A	.385	4	13	3	5	0	1	1	1	0	3	0
1999	Hagerstown (SAL)	A	.277	134	537	87	149	27	4	14	80	61	157	21
2000	Tennessee (SL)	AA	.257	127	463	52	119	18	4	9	41	31	110	12
MINOR LEAGUE TOTALS			.277	284	1096	156	304	50	11	25	133	95	284	37

3. Cesar Izturis, ss

Born: Feb. 10, 1980. **Ht.:** 5-9. **Wt.:** 175. **Bats:** B. **Throws:** R. **Career Transactions:** Signed out of Venezuela by Blue Jays, July 3, 1996.

Izturis' brother Maicer is one of the Indians' better prospects. Cesar skipped Double-A in 2000 and was the youngest player in the International League. His build, actions and range, as well as Venezuelan descent, invite comparisons to Omar Vizquel. Managers ranked him as having the IL's best infield arm. Jays officials were pleased with the way he handled his offensive struggles, keeping his head up and remaining confident in his abilities. Izturis got the bat knocked out of his hands consistently by more experienced pitchers. He didn't help matters by chasing pitches out of the strike zone. He also needs to work on keeping the ball on the ground. Organization officials pushed Izturis hoping he would have proven more ready for the big leagues, but they are confident he could handle the jump to Toronto if need be. If not, he'll return to Syracuse.

Year	Club (League)	Class	AVG	G	AB	R	H	2B	3B	HR	RBI	BB	SO	SB
1997	St. Catharines (NY-P)	A	.190	70	231	32	44	3	0	1	11	15	27	6
1998	Hagerstown (SAL)	A	.262	130	413	56	108	13	1	1	38	20	43	20
1999	Dunedin (FSL)	A	.308	131	536	77	165	28	12	3	77	22	58	32
2000	Syracuse (IL)	AAA	.218	132	435	54	95	16	5	0	27	20	44	21
MINOR LEAGUE TOTALS			.255	463	1615	219	412	60	18	5	153	77	172	79

4. Joe Lawrence, c

Born: Feb. 13, 1977. **Ht.:** 6-2. **Wt.:** 200. **Bats:** R. **Throws:** R. **School:** Barbe HS, Lake Charles, La. **Career Transactions:** Selected by Blue Jays in first round (16th overall) of 1996 draft; signed July 1, 1996.

An all-state football player in Louisiana, Lawrence is one of three shortstops the Blue Jays have selected in the first round in the last seven drafts. Only Felipe Lopez has stayed at the position. Lawrence worked at catcher in instructional league in 1998, played third in '99 and had that season cut short by an ankle injury. He moved to catcher to stay in 2000. Lawrence took to his new duties quickly and easily, making great strides during the season in calling games and throwing out runners. He has the best plate discipline in the system and the speed to make pitchers pay for it. Rather than getting slower as a catcher, he improved his times to first base and gets down the line in 4.1 seconds. Lawrence has yet to develop more than gap power. He got tired during the last month of the 2000 season, but the club expects him to stay strong as he gets used to the grind of catching. With Darrin Fletcher signed for three more years, the Blue Jays can be patient with his successor. Lawrence could earn a spot in Triple-A with a good spring.

Year	Club (League)	Class	AVG	G	AB	R	H	2B	3B	HR	RBI	BB	SO	SB
1996	St. Catharines (NY-P)	A	.224	29	98	23	22	7	2	0	11	14	17	1
1997	Hagerstown (SAL)	A	.229	116	446	63	102	24	1	8	38	49	107	10
1998	Dunedin (FSL)	A	.308	125	454	102	140	31	6	11	44	105	88	15
1999	Knoxville (SL)	AA	.264	70	250	52	66	16	2	7	24	56	48	7
2000	Dunedin (FSL)	A	.301	101	375	69	113	32	1	13	67	69	74	21
	Tennessee (SL)	AA	.263	39	133	22	35	9	0	0	9	30	27	7
MINOR LEAGUE TOTALS			.272	480	1756	331	478	119	12	39	193	323	361	61

5. Bob File, rhp

DAVID SCHOFIELD

Born: Jan. 28, 1977. **Ht.:** 6-4. **Wt.:** 215. **Bats:** R. **Throws:** R. **School:** Philadelphia College of Textiles. **Career Transactions:** Selected by Blue Jays in 19th round of 1998 draft; signed June 11, 1998.

The Blue Jays don't hesitate to convert players with strong arms to the mound, and File is their best success story. He pitched just six innings in college, where he led NCAA Division II in batting in 1998. He hit .542-19-68 as a third baseman. File's arm strength attracted Jays scouts, and his fastball is now the best in the system. He consistently throws it 92-95 mph with good downward movement and excellent command. File's slurvy breaking ball is effective against righthanders. Despite his inexperience on the mound, he sets up hitters, holds runners well and fields the position like an extra infielder. Lefthanders see File's slurve well and batted .274 against him in 62 at-bats in 2000. Syracuse manager Mel Queen will work with File to tighten up the pitch. File also needs to throw his changeup more to fully develop it. With Billy Koch one of the game's top closers, File will break in with Toronto as a set-up man, a role he could earn with a strong performance in spring training.

Year	Club (League)	Class	W	L	ERA	G	GS	CG	SV	IP	H	R	ER	BB	SO
1998	Medicine Hat (Pio)	R	2	1	1.41	28	0	0	16	32	24	7	5	5	28
1999	Dunedin (FSL)	A	4	1	1.70	47	0	0	26	53	30	13	10	14	48
2000	Tennessee (SL)	AA	4	3	3.12	36	0	0	20	35	29	20	12	13	40
	Syracuse (IL)	AAA	2	0	0.93	20	0	0	8	19	14	2	2	2	10
MINOR LEAGUE TOTALS			12	5	1.88	131	0	0	70	139	97	42	29	34	126

6. Charles Kegley, rhp

Born: Dec. 17, 1979. **Ht.:** 6-3. **Wt.:** 205. **Bats:** R. **Throws:** R. **School:** Okaloosa-Walton (Fla.) CC. **Career Transactions:** Selected by Blue Jays in 11th round of 1999 draft; signed July 20, 1999.

The Brewers drafted Kegley out of a Florida high school in 1998 and retained his rights as a draft-and-follow when he went to junior college. They offered him $500,000 to sign, but he went back into the draft. The Blue Jays took him and signed him for $515,000. Kegley has the best arm in the system, throwing an explosive 92-97 mph fastball. Opponents batted just .240 against him and rarely got good swings even in fastball counts. He also throws a power slider. Kegley has problems controlling his fastball, though he impressed Jays officials during instructional league with his improvement toward a balance between throwing hard and throwing strikes. He needs innings and experience, which accounts for his low strikeout total. His changeup improved during the season, but it's still his third pitch. Kegley is the only Jays prospect who projects as a possible No. 1 starter on his raw stuff. He could return to Dunedin, but a good spring may vault him to Tennessee.

Year	Club (League)	Class	W	L	ERA	G	GS	CG	SV	IP	H	R	ER	BB	SO
2000	Dunedin (FSL)	A	3	9	3.88	23	23	0	0	111	96	60	48	74	66
MINOR LEAGUE TOTALS			3	9	3.88	23	23	0	0	111	96	60	48	74	66

7. Brian Cardwell, rhp

RICH ABEL

Born: Dec. 30, 1980. **Ht.:** 6-10. **Wt.:** 210. **Bats:** R. **Throws:** R. **School:** Sapulpa (Okla.) HS. **Career Transactions:** Selected by Blue Jays in fourth round of 1999 draft; signed June 8, 1999.

Cardwell passed up a basketball scholarship from Tulsa to sign with the Blue Jays. Only the White Sox' Jon Rauch stands taller among pro righthanders. New York-Penn League managers named Cardwell the No. 10 prospect in the league in 2000. He was throwing 86-89 mph in high school, but with added strength and experience his fastball now touches 93 with the good downward plane that naturally comes with being so tall. He throws it comfortably at 90-91 from a three-quarters slot, which makes him tough on righthanders. He harnessed his slider, which can be devastating at times, in instructional league. Cardwell often loses his release point and command of his fastball. He was overmatched at Class A Hagerstown but rebounded to post good strikeout numbers at short-season Queens. Only Charles Kegley has a higher ceiling than Cardwell, who projects as a No. 2 starter if he can maintain consistency. He should start the 2001 season back in low Class A with the Blue Jays' new affiliate in Charleston, W.Va.

Year	Club (League)	Class	W	L	ERA	G	GS	CG	SV	IP	H	R	ER	BB	SO
1999	Medicine Hat (Pio)	R	2	1	5.16	10	4	0	1	29	34	22	17	8	26
2000	Hagerstown (SAL)	A	0	5	9.09	11	6	0	0	31	41	38	32	21	29
	Queens (NY-P)	A	2	4	4.71	12	11	1	0	49	49	32	26	19	61
	MINOR LEAGUE TOTALS		4	10	6.08	33	21	1	1	111	124	92	75	48	116

8. Pascual Coco, rhp

Born: Sept. 8, 1977. **Ht.:** 6-1. **Wt.:** 185. **Bats:** R. **Throws:** R. **Career Transactions:** Signed out of Dominican Republic by Blue Jays, Aug. 10, 1994.

Coco signed as an outfielder, but the organization quickly recognized his arm strength (and inability to hit) and moved him to the mound. In 2000, his first year above Class A, he was added to the 40-man roster and made an emergency start in the big leagues. Coco has one of the best arms in the system. He has a fastball that touches 95 mph, though he usually throws it in the 90-92 range. His top pitch is his changeup, the best in the organization. He's quick to the plate and holds runners well.
He has added an inch and 25 pounds to his frame since signing, helping him maintain his velocity deeper into games. Coco's breaking ball for now is a sloppy slurve that's just adequate. He'll need to refine the pitch to handle righthanders more effectively. They hit .263 against him in 2000, while lefthanders batted just .212. Coco has gained experience pitching with Escogido in the Dominican League the last two winters. That will serve him well in Triple-A in 2001.

Year	Club (League)	Class	W	L	ERA	G	GS	CG	SV	IP	H	R	ER	BB	SO
1995	Blue Jays (DSL)	R	7	1	2.78	11	11	0	0	58	51	30	18	36	38
1996	Blue Jays (DSL)	R	7	2	2.99	17	16	2	0	96	77	46	32	53	92
1997	St. Catharines (NY-P)	A	1	4	4.89	10	8	0	0	46	48	32	25	16	44
1998	St. Catharines (NY-P)	A	3	7	3.20	15	15	1	0	81	62	52	29	32	84
1999	Hagerstown (SAL)	A	11	1	2.21	14	14	0	0	97	67	29	24	25	83
	Dunedin (FSL)	A	4	6	5.64	13	13	2	0	75	81	50	47	36	59
2000	Tennessee (SL)	AA	12	7	3.76	27	26	2	0	167	154	83	70	68	142
	Toronto (AL)	MAJ	0	0	9.00	1	1	0	0	4	5	4	4	5	2
	MAJOR LEAGUE TOTALS		0	0	9.00	1	1	0	0	4	5	4	4	5	2
	MINOR LEAGUE TOTALS		45	28	3.54	107	103	7	0	622	540	322	245	266	542

9. Matt Ford, lhp

Born: April 8, 1981. **Ht.:** 6-2. **Wt.:** 165. **Bats:** B. **Throws:** L. **School:** Taravella HS, Coral Springs, Fla. **Career Transactions:** Selected by Blue Jays in third round of 1999 draft; signed June 2, 1999.

Ford made a strong debut at Rookie-level Medicine Hat in 1999 and started to pull off an encore with Class A Hagerstown last year. His season ended early, though, when he developed shoulder stiffness in late July. He was back to full health in instructional league and was throwing well again. Ford's success stems from a combination of slightly above-average stuff and a competitive streak that keeps him from giving in to hitters. Ford has an 88-92 mph fastball and a curveball that ranks as one of the best in the Jays system. His changeup has the potential to be a plus pitch. His biggest need is innings, which should give much-needed polish to his changeup. He also needs to prove he can stay healthy. Shutting him down in 2000 was a precaution, whereas an injury this season would be a red flag. A healthy Ford should report to high Class A in 2001. He has a chance to move quickly, though he projects as no better than a No. 3 starter.

Year	Club (League)	Class	W	L	ERA	G	GS	CG	SV	IP	H	R	ER	BB	SO
1999	Medicine Hat (Pio)	R	4	0	2.05	13	7	0	0	48	31	11	11	23	68
2000	Hagerstown (SAL)	A	5	3	3.87	18	14	1	0	84	81	42	36	36	86
	MINOR LEAGUE TOTALS		9	3	3.20	31	21	1	0	132	112	53	47	59	154

10. Josh Phelps, c

Born: May 12, 1978. **Ht.:** 6-3. **Wt.:** 215. **Bats:** R. **Throws:** R. **School:** Lakeland HS, Rathdrum, Idaho. **Career Transactions:** Selected by Blue Jays in 10th round of 1996 draft; signed June 6, 1996.

Phelps ranks second among five catching prospects in the system, as Joe Lawrence passed him last season. The Blue Jays also have hopes for Jayson Werth, whom they traded for in December; Venezuelan Guillermo Quiroz, whom they signed for $1.2 million in 1999; and Kevin Cash, a converted corner infielder signed as a nondrafted free agent. Phelps didn't play much behind the plate in 1999 after injuring his elbow, and proved unable to handle the rigors of catching everyday and hitting tougher pitching in 2000. Never noted for his plate discipline, Phelps didn't make consistent contact at either level, though his numbers improved after he was demoted from Double-A to high Class A. While he has plenty of raw power, he may have to be brought along slowly as he learns to shorten his swing.

Year	Club (League)	Class	AVG	G	AB	R	H	2B	3B	HR	RBI	BB	SO	SB
1996	Medicine Hat (Pio)	R	.241	59	191	28	46	3	0	5	29	27	65	5
1997	Hagerstown (SAL)	A	.210	68	233	26	49	9	1	7	24	15	72	3
1998	Hagerstown (SAL)	A	.265	117	385	48	102	24	1	8	44	40	80	2
1999	Dunedin (FSL)	A	.328	110	406	72	133	27	4	20	88	28	104	6
2000	Dunedin (FSL)	A	.319	30	113	26	36	7	0	12	34	12	34	0
	Tennessee (SL)	AA	.228	56	184	23	42	9	1	9	28	15	66	1
MINOR LEAGUE TOTALS			.270	440	1512	223	408	79	7	61	247	137	421	17

11. Mark Hendricksen, lhp

Born: June 23, 1974. **Ht.:** 6-9. **Wt.:** 230. **Bats:** L. **Throws:** L. **School:** Washington State University. **Career Transactions:** Selected by Blue Jays in 20th round of 1997 draft; signed May 22, 1998.

One of the Jays' most intriguing prospects, Hendricksen isn't the typical 26-year-old just reaching Double-A. He was drafted six times before signing with the Blue Jays, who scouted him in a semipro wood-bat league in southeastern Pennsylvania. Hendricksen led Washington State's basketball team to the NCAA tournament in 1994 and was an all-Pacific-10 Conference selection in 1995 and '96. The 31st overall pick in the 1996 NBA draft, Hendricksen has averaged 3.3 points and 2.7 rebounds in 114 games for Cleveland, New Jersey, Philadelphia and Sacramento. He has played in the Continental Basketball Association and has signed three 10-day NBA contracts as an injury fill-in. His baseball career was similarly spotty until 2000. He shone in his second Double-A stint and pitched well in the Arizona Fall League. While his fastball has reached 93 mph, Hendrickson was throwing in the 85-90 mph range in the AFL with good movement and command. He employs both a slider and curveball, showing better break on the curve but better control of the slider. The organization is impressed with his changeup as well. The bottom line with Hendricksen is commitment. He will likely attempt to play in the NBA again to reach the service time required for an NBA pension, but the Blue Jays hope he will realize his ceiling is higher in baseball.

Year	Club (League)	Class	W	L	ERA	G	GS	CG	SV	IP	H	R	ER	BB	SO
1998	Dunedin (FSL)	A	4	3	2.37	16	5	0	1	49	44	16	13	26	38
1999	Knoxville (SL)	AA	2	7	6.63	12	11	0	0	56	73	46	41	21	39
2000	Dunedin (FSL)	A	2	2	5.61	12	12	1	0	51	63	34	32	29	38
	Tennessee (SL)	AA	3	1	3.63	6	6	0	0	40	32	17	16	12	29
MINOR LEAGUE TOTALS			11	13	4.68	46	34	1	1	196	212	113	102	88	144

12. Ryan Freel, 2b/of

Born: March 8, 1976. **Ht.:** 5-10. **Wt.:** 175. **Bats:** R. **Throws:** R. **School:** Tallahassee (Fla.) CC. **Career Transactions:** Selected by Blue Jays in 10th round of 1995 draft; signed June 12, 1995.

Freel improved his stock as much as any player in the system in 2000, and the organization is counting on him to contribute as a utility player in the big leagues soon. The problem is that he's clearly viewed as a utilityman at best, albeit one with offensive potential. Freel is one of the fastest players in the system—his speed rates a 6 on scouts' 2-to-8 scale—and is a good basestealer. He's a contact hitter who showed more pop after spending last offseason getting stronger, setting a career high for home runs with Triple-A Syracuse. Freel also has the patience to take a walk, making his speed even more useful. Defensively, second base and center field are his best positions. One Jays official calls him a bigger, better version of Craig Grebeck, who has carved out a 10-year big league career.

Year	Club (League)	Class	AVG	G	AB	R	H	2B	3B	HR	RBI	BB	SO	SB
1995	St. Catharines (NY-P)	A	.280	65	243	30	68	10	5	3	29	22	49	12
1996	Dunedin (FSL)	A	.255	104	381	64	97	23	3	4	41	33	76	19
1997	Knoxville (SL)	AA	.202	33	94	18	19	1	1	0	4	19	13	5
	Dunedin (FSL)	A	.282	61	181	42	51	8	2	3	17	46	28	24
1998	Knoxville (SL)	AA	.286	66	252	47	72	17	3	4	36	33	32	18
	Syracuse (IL)	AAA	.229	37	118	19	27	4	0	2	12	26	16	9
1999	Knoxville (SL)	AA	.283	11	46	9	13	5	1	1	9	8	4	4
	Syracuse (IL)	AAA	.299	20	77	15	23	3	2	1	11	8	13	10
2000	Dunedin (FSL)	A	.500	4	18	7	9	1	0	3	6	0	1	0
	Tennessee (SL)	AA	.295	12	44	11	13	3	1	0	8	8	6	2
	Syracuse (IL)	AAA	.286	80	283	62	81	14	5	10	30	35	44	30
MINOR LEAGUE TOTALS			.272	493	1737	324	473	89	23	31	203	238	282	133

13. Andy Thompson, of

Born: Oct. 8, 1975. **Ht.:** 6-3. **Wt.:** 210. **Bats:** R. **Throws:** R. **School:** Sun Prairie (Wis.) HS. **Career Transactions:** Selected by Blue Jays in 23rd round of 1994 draft; signed Sept. 4, 1994.

Thompson, the organization's No. 8 prospect entering 2000, slipped after his first full season in Triple-A. Few players in the organization have as much power, and he also has a strong right-field arm. He has been compared to Mariners slugger Jay Buhner, but only when he makes contact—and Thompson didn't do that consistently enough in 2000. He hit 31 homers in 1999, but Jays officials believe he focused on trying to hit longballs too much in 2000. When he missed a pitch, he frequently missed badly, as he was trying to jerk everything over the fence. Pitchers fed him a steady diet of breaking balls away, and he failed to adjust until the final two weeks of the season. The Jays still hope Thompson will learn to rely on his bat speed to bring out his tremendous power. He has shown the ability to draw a walk, and his power is too good to give up on.

Year	Club (League)	Class	AVG	G	AB	R	H	2B	3B	HR	RBI	BB	SO	SB
1995	Hagerstown (SAL)	A	.239	124	461	48	110	19	2	6	57	29	108	2
1996	Dunedin (FSL)	A	.282	129	425	64	120	26	5	11	50	60	108	16
1997	Knoxville (SL)	AA	.286	124	448	75	128	25	3	15	71	63	76	0
1998	Knoxville (SL)	AA	.285	125	481	74	137	33	2	14	88	54	69	8
1999	Knoxville (SL)	AA	.244	67	254	56	62	16	3	15	53	34	55	7
	Syracuse (IL)	AAA	.293	62	229	42	67	17	2	16	42	21	45	5
2000	Syracuse (IL)	AAA	.246	121	426	59	105	27	2	22	65	50	95	9
	Toronto (AL)	MAJ	.167	2	6	2	1	0	0	0	1	3	2	0
MAJOR LEAGUE TOTALS			.167	2	6	2	1	0	0	0	1	3	2	0
MINOR LEAGUE TOTALS			.268	752	2724	418	729	163	19	99	426	311	556	47

14. Jayson Werth, c

Born: May 20, 1979. **Ht.:** 6-5. **Wt.:** 190. **Bats:** R. **Throws:** R. **School:** Glenwood HS, Chatham, Ill. **Career Transactions:** Selected by Orioles in first round (22nd overall) of 1997 draft; signed June 13, 1997 . . . Traded by Orioles to Blue Jays for LHP John Bale, December 11, 2000.

In the span of three years, Werth went from the Orioles' 1997 first-round pick to commanding only a journeyman lefthander in a December trade with Baltimore. Because he's tall and rangy and has athletic tools, Werth has been compared to a young Dale Murphy, the patron saint of catching prospects. But at 21, Murphy was leading the Triple-A International League in RBIs and playing in the big leagues, while Werth was struggling mightily in Double-A. If he plays to his ceiling, Werth would be an athletic, offensive catcher. He runs well, is mobile behind the plate and has good discipline at the plate. The downside is that he's a career .266 hitter who has yet to develop power or make consistent contact. He is average defensively. His arm isn't particularly strong, and he threw out just 20 percent of basestealers last season. Werth has much improvement to make before becoming the fourth member of his family to reach the majors, joining grandfather Ducky Schofield, uncle Dick Schofield and stepfather Dennis Werth.

Year	Club (League)	Class	AVG	G	AB	R	H	2B	3B	HR	RBI	BB	SO	SB
1997	Orioles (GCL)	R	.295	32	88	16	26	6	0	1	8	22	22	7
1998	Delmarva (SAL)	A	.265	120	408	71	108	20	3	8	53	50	92	21
	Bowie (EL)	AA	.158	5	19	2	3	2	0	0	1	2	6	1
1999	Frederick (Car)	A	.305	66	236	41	72	10	1	3	30	37	37	16
	Bowie (EL)	AA	.273	35	121	18	33	5	1	1	11	17	26	7
2000	Frederick (Car)	A	.277	24	83	16	23	3	0	2	18	10	15	5
	Bowie (EL)	AA	.228	85	276	47	63	16	2	5	26	54	50	9
MINOR LEAGUE TOTALS			.266	367	1231	211	328	62	7	20	147	192	248	66

15. Dewayne Wise, of

Born: Feb. 24, 1978. **Ht.:** 6-1. **Wt.:** 175. **Bats:** L. **Throws:** L. **School:** Chapin (S.C.) HS. **Career Transactions:** Selected by Reds in fifth round of 1997 draft; signed June 5, 1997 . . . Selected by Blue Jays from Reds in major league Rule 5 draft, Dec. 13, 1999.

In the past, the Blue Jays had success with Rule 5 picks such as George Bell and Kelly Gruber. While it's hard to project that kind of career for Wise, the Jays were intrigued enough by his tools to keep him on the major league roster for the 2000 season, his first year above low Class A. He aided the cause with a toe injury that allowed him to be stashed on the disabled list for three months. When healthy, Wise is close to a five-tool player, though his power and arm are just average. He has 15-20 home run power, runs well and is a legitimate center fielder, though not on the level of Vernon Wells. The injury (and being a Rule 5 player) further limited his experience, so he's expected to start the 2001 season in Double-A. The organization will get a better read on his talent this year.

Year	Club (League)	Class	AVG	G	AB	R	H	2B	3B	HR	RBI	BB	SO	SB
1997	Billings (Pio)	R	.313	62	268	53	84	13	9	7	41	9	47	18
1998	Burlington (Mid)	A	.224	127	496	61	111	15	9	2	44	41	111	27
1999	Rockford (Mid)	A	.253	131	502	70	127	20	13	11	81	42	81	35
2000	Syracuse (IL)	AAA	.250	15	56	10	14	5	2	2	8	7	13	3
	Toronto (AL)	MAJ	.136	28	22	3	3	0	0	0	0	1	5	1
MAJOR LEAGUE TOTALS			.136	28	22	3	3	0	0	0	0	1	5	1
MINOR LEAGUE TOTALS			.254	335	1322	194	336	53	33	22	174	99	252	83

16. Brandon Lyon, rhp

Born: Aug. 10, 1979. **Ht.:** 6-1. **Wt.:** 175. **Bats:** R. **Throws:** R. **School:** Dixie (Utah) JC. **Career Transactions:** Selected by Blue Jays in 14th round of 1999 draft; signed May 31, 2000.

Lyon signed as a draft-and-follow just prior to the 2000 draft, after he overmatched hitters during the spring at Dixie Junior College, and his numbers for his first pro season raised eyebrows. Lyons has above-average command of four pitches, including an 89-91 mph fastball. He also throws a changeup, slider and curveball, and he knows how to use them well for his age and stage of development. Lyon didn't give up a walk in his final 28 innings of the season before being shut down because he was close to 200 innings for the year, including juco time. Some teams were scared off after Lyon broke his right arm in a snowboarding accident. Lyon had a pin inserted into his arm to stabilize it and has had no problems.

Year	Club (League)	Class	W	L	ERA	G	GS	CG	SV	IP	H	R	ER	BB	SO
2000	Queens (NY-P)	A	5	3	2.39	15	13	0	0	60	43	20	16	6	55
MINOR LEAGUE TOTALS			5	3	2.39	15	13	0	0	60	43	20	16	6	55

17. Alex Rios, of

Born: Feb. 18, 1981. **Ht.:** 6-5. **Wt.:** 178. **Bats:** R. **Throws:** R. **School:** San Pedro Martir HS, Guaynabo, P.R. **Career Transactions:** Selected by Blue Jays in first round (19th overall) of 1999 draft; signed June 4, 1999.

Rios and fellow Puerto Rican outfielder Miguel Negron stick out in the last two drafts as the only first-round picks who didn't sign for $1 million. Club vice president Tim Wilken, who drafted both players as scouting director, says the perceived drop in Puerto Rican talent the last 10 years is about to end. He contends talent in any area is cyclical, and that Rios and Negron are the beginning of an upward spike in Puerto Rico. Rios, long and lean, has the higher ceiling, with the potential to become a power-hitting right fielder with a plus arm. He has added almost 20 pounds since being drafted and started to drive the ball with Queens. He has good bat speed and is shortening his long swing. The Blue Jays may have to be patient with Rios, but they believe he eventually will prove worthy of a first-round pick.

Year	Club (League)	Class	AVG	G	AB	R	H	2B	3B	HR	RBI	BB	SO	SB
1999	Medicine Hat (Pio)	R	.269	67	234	35	63	7	3	0	13	17	31	8
2000	Queens (NY-P)	A	.267	50	206	22	55	9	2	1	25	11	22	5
	Hagerstown (SAL)	A	.230	22	74	5	17	3	1	0	5	2	14	2
MINOR LEAGUE TOTALS			.263	139	514	62	135	19	6	1	43	30	67	15

18. Michael Snyder, 1b

Born: Feb. 11, 1981. **Ht.:** 6-5. **Wt.:** 230. **Bats:** L. **Throws:** R. **School:** Ayala HS, Chino Hills, Calif. **Career Transactions:** Selected by Blue Jays in second round of 1999 draft; signed June 10, 1999.

Drafted with a second-round pick after Alex Rios, Snyder too has grown and added about 20 pounds. That's one reason he moved across the diamond to first base last year after he played 38 games at third for Medicine Hat. Snyder struggled with the bat in 1999 and again at the start of 2000 when he was pushed to Hagerstown, but experienced his first success at

Queens. Snyder is all about power. He has as much as anyone in the system and has (at times) the compact lefthanded swing to use it. Snyder strikes out a lot, but also has proven willing to draw a walk, a good sign in a young power hitter. As he continues to adjust to wood bats and his bigger body, Snyder should show more of his raw power.

Year	Club (League)	Class	AVG	G	AB	R	H	2B	3B	HR	RBI	BB	SO	SB
1999	Medicine Hat (Pio)	R	.209	62	196	30	41	7	0	3	19	31	47	3
2000	Queens (NY-P)	A	.278	57	227	28	63	11	3	4	34	22	49	4
	Hagerstown (SAL)	A	.182	54	165	26	30	8	1	1	13	32	48	4
MINOR LEAGUE TOTALS			.228	173	588	84	134	26	4	8	66	85	144	11

19. Chris Woodward, ss

Born: June 27, 1976. **Ht.:** 6-0. **Wt.:** 165. **Bats:** R. **Throws:** R. **School:** Mount San Antonio (Calif.) JC. **Career Transactions:** Selected by Blue Jays in 54th round of 1994 draft; signed May 17, 1995.

Woodward's ceiling isn't as high as other shortstops in the system, but he could be a useful utilityman, and the Blue Jays are encouraged by what they've seen of him in 51 big league games. He wasn't overwhelmed and showed the ability to play all three infield positions other than first base. Where Woodward really impressed the organization, though, was with the bat at Syracuse. He slugged .545 in his short time there. The Jays look at Woodward as a useful, inexpensive reserve. He'd be more effective on grass, because his modest range is more of a liability on the fast artificial surface of SkyDome.

Year	Club (League)	Class	AVG	G	AB	R	H	2B	3B	HR	RBI	BB	SO	SB
1995	Medicine Hat (Pio)	R	.232	72	241	44	56	8	0	3	21	33	41	9
1996	Hagerstown (SAL)	A	.224	123	424	41	95	24	2	1	48	43	70	11
1997	Dunedin (FSL)	A	.293	91	314	38	92	13	4	1	38	52	52	4
1998	Knoxville (SL)	AA	.245	73	253	36	62	12	0	3	27	26	47	3
	Syracuse (IL)	AAA	.200	25	85	9	17	6	0	2	6	7	20	1
1999	Syracuse (IL)	AAA	.292	75	281	46	82	20	3	1	20	38	49	4
	Toronto (AL)	MAJ	.231	14	26	1	6	1	0	0	2	2	6	0
2000	Syracuse (IL)	AAA	.322	37	143	23	46	13	2	5	25	11	30	2
	Toronto (AL)	MAJ	.183	37	104	16	19	7	0	3	14	10	28	1
MAJOR LEAGUE TOTALS			.192	51	130	17	25	8	0	3	16	12	34	1
MINOR LEAGUE TOTALS			.258	496	1741	237	450	96	11	16	185	210	309	34

20. Travis Hubbel, rhp

Born: June 27, 1979. **Ht.:** 6-1. **Wt.:** 185. **Bats:** R. **Throws:** R. **School:** Eastglen Composite HS, Edmonton. **Career Transactions:** Selected by Blue Jays in 13th round of 1997 draft; signed June 5, 1997.

The Blue Jays love athletic, projectable righties and traditionally eschew shorter pitchers. But they are trying harder to find pitchers like Brandon Lyon and Hubbel who know how to pitch. Hubbel does conform to another Jays tendency: He's a converted third baseman, like Bob File. His arm was his best tool at third, and it has translated into pure power on the mound. Hubbel's fastball rivals File's and Charles Kegley's as the system's best, ranging from 92-95 mph when his mechanics are right. Hubbel lacks command of his slurvy breaking ball and needs an offspeed pitch. He lost time last season to a flu-like virus, but with a good season in high Class A in 2001, he could move into the organization's top echelon of prospects.

Year	Club (League)	Class	AVG	G	AB	R	H	2B	3B	HR	RBI	BB	SO	SB
1997	Medicine Hat (Pio)	R	.160	42	119	10	19	3	1	0	10	10	43	1
1998	Medicine Hat (Pio)	R	.297	16	37	5	11	1	1	0	5	10	10	1
	St. Catharines (NY-P)	A	.125	10	16	1	2	1	0	0	1	3	9	0
MINOR LEAGUE TOTALS			.186	68	172	16	32	5	2	0	16	23	62	2

Year	Club (League)	Class	W	L	ERA	G	GS	CG	SV	IP	H	R	ER	BB	SO
1999	St. Catharines (NY-P)	A	0	0	1.80	5	3	0	1	20	16	5	4	7	19
2000	Hagerstown (SAL)	A	8	6	3.89	19	19	0	0	113	103	62	49	55	75
	Dunedin (FSL)	A	0	0	3.38	3	0	0	0	5	4	2	2	2	3
MINOR LEAGUE TOTALS			8	6	3.57	27	22	0	1	139	123	69	55	64	97

21. Orlando Woodards, rhp

Born: Jan. 2, 1978. **Ht.:** 6-3. **Wt.:** 205. **Bats:** R. **Throws:** R. **School:** Sacramento CC. **Career Transactions:** Selected by Blue Jays in 40th round of 1996 draft; signed May 26, 1997.

Woodards is another draft-and-follow who signed after his freshman year at Sacramento City College, where he moved from the outfield to the mound. While Woodards' pitching experience is somewhat limited, the Blue Jays thought enough of him to add him to their 40-man roster. He has electric stuff, with a 90-94 mph fastball and a power curveball that he throws in the 80-84 range. His numbers at Dunedin showed he's starting to get a feel for pitching. Because he lacks a true offspeed pitch, he'll stick to relieving, likely as a set-up man.

Year	Club (League)	Class	W	L	ERA	G	GS	CG	SV	IP	H	R	ER	BB	SO
1997	St. Catharines (NY-P)	A	2	2	5.15	21	0	0	2	37	41	23	21	24	32
1998	Medicine Hat (Pio)	R	1	3	3.58	26	1	0	3	50	48	27	20	11	58
1999	Hagerstown (SAL)	A	7	4	4.15	44	3	0	2	80	66	45	37	43	79
2000	Dunedin (FSL)	A	8	1	2.27	41	1	0	7	87	65	26	22	32	69
MINOR LEAGUE TOTALS			18	10	3.54	132	5	0	14	254	220	121	100	110	238

22. Aaron Dean, rhp

Born: April 9, 1979. **Ht.:** 6-4. **Wt.:** 180. **Bats:** R. **Throws:** R. **School:** Canada (Calif.) JC. **Career Transactions:** Selected by Blue Jays in 38th round of 1998 draft; signed May 30, 1999.

The Blue Jays have a bevy of righthanders who are close in talent, polish and ceiling. One organization official said you could pull their names out of a hat and put them in order that way. Dean is a young and somewhat polished pitcher signed as a draft-and-follow. He fits scouts' ideal for a long, lean righthander, and he is not only projectable but also has experienced success in pro ball, including a dominant debut in 1999. Dean's polish and maturity led the Blue Jays to give him an emergency start at Double-A last year. He has decent movement on his 88-92 mph fastball and should improve his velocity. His sharp, true curveball is a strikeout pitch, and his changeup has developed nicely. Dean will start at Dunedin in 2001.

Year	Club (League)	Class	W	L	ERA	G	GS	CG	SV	IP	H	R	ER	BB	SO
1999	St. Catharines (NY-P)	A	4	0	2.34	17	8	0	1	62	50	18	16	13	68
2000	Hagerstown (SAL)	A	8	3	3.28	19	19	0	0	113	99	55	41	38	89
	Dunedin (FSL)	A	1	0	6.46	3	3	0	0	15	22	15	11	7	13
	Tennessee (SL)	AA	0	1	1.50	1	1	1	0	6	5	1	1	5	4
MINOR LEAGUE TOTALS			13	4	3.17	40	31	1	1	196	176	89	69	63	174

23. Gustavo Chacin, lhp

Born: Dec. 4, 1980. **Ht.:** 5-11. **Wt.:** 170. **Bats:** L. **Throws:** L. **Career Transactions:** Signed out of Venezuela by Blue Jays, July 3, 1998.

Considering the Jays' recent struggles to develop frontline talent from Latin America, Chacin would figure to stand out in the minds of the organization's player-development staff. They jumped him to high Class A at age 20, and he responded with a decent year. The reason Chacin doesn't rank higher is that he hasn't dominated hitters since pitching in the Dominican Summer League in 1998. His fastball is average at best, and his curveball needs work. He survives by changing speeds, but he has been more hittable each time he has moved up the ladder. Toronto isn't deep in lefthanders in the majors or minors, so Chacin will continue to get opportunities to prove himself. His next will come in Double-A.

Year	Club (League)	Class	W	L	ERA	G	GS	CG	SV	IP	H	R	ER	BB	SO
1998	Blue Jays (DSL)	R	3	2	2.70	9	6	0	0	36	28	12	11	15	56
1999	Medicine Hat (Pio)	R	4	3	3.09	15	9	0	1	64	68	33	22	23	50
2000	Dunedin (FSL)	A	9	5	4.02	25	21	0	0	127	138	69	57	64	77
	Tennessee (SL)	AA	0	2	12.60	2	2	0	0	5	10	7	7	6	5
MINOR LEAGUE TOTALS			16	12	3.74	51	38	0	1	233	244	121	97	108	188

24. Scott Cassidy, rhp

Born: Oct. 3, 1975. **Ht.:** 6-3. **Wt.:** 175. **Bats:** R. **Throws:** R. **School:** LeMoyne College. **Career Transactions:** Signed as nondrafted free agent by Blue Jays, May 21, 1998.

Cassidy immediatly impressed the Blue Jays with his poise and command and as his 1998 debut drew to a close, he was going to be rewarded for his efforts with a late-season start in Syracuse, his hometown, but the game was rained out. In 2000, he almost earned the chance outright. Cassidy was a Florida State League all-star and combined with Scott Porter and reliever Chris Baker on a no-hitter in April. He earned a promotion to Double-A but struggled there. The Jays figured it was more than just the move up, and doctors soon discovered why he was always tired and losing weight—he has juvenile diabetes. Cassidy responded to treatment and regained the life on his mid-80s fastball late in the season. He throws plenty of strikes with his slider and changeup as well, but he doesn't project as a frontline starter.

Year	Club (League)	Class	W	L	ERA	G	GS	CG	SV	IP	H	R	ER	BB	SO
1998	Medicine Hat (Pio)	R	8	1	2.43	15	14	0	0	81	71	31	22	14	82
1999	Hagerstown (SAL)	A	13	7	3.27	27	27	1	0	170	151	78	62	30	178
2000	Dunedin (FSL)	A	9	3	1.33	14	13	1	0	88	53	15	13	34	89
	Tennessee (SL)	AA	2	2	5.91	8	7	0	0	42	48	30	28	15	39
MINOR LEAGUE TOTALS			32	13	2.94	64	61	2	0	382	323	154	125	93	388

25. Scott Porter, rhp

Born: March 18, 1977. **Ht.:** 6-1. **Wt.:** 195. **Bats:** R. **Throws:** R. **School:** Jacksonville University. **Career Transactions:** Selected by Blue Jays in fifth round of 1999 draft; signed June 3, 1999.

In an organization dominated by high school draftees, especially on the mound, Porter stands out. He was a closer at Jacksonville, where he led the TransAmerica Athletic Conference with 11 saves in 1999 and ranked fourth among NCAA Division I pitchers with 13.2 strikeouts per nine innings. His 2000 season was cut short by a minor shoulder injury that required arthroscopic surgery, but Porter had time to show the Blue Jays why he had such success. He combines a low-90s fastball with a hard, sharp-biting slider that's the best breaking ball in the system. He doesn't figure to be the Blue Jays' closer of the future, with Billy Koch and Bob File ahead of him. But along with Orlando Woodards, he could be another hard-throwing set-up man in the near future.

Year	Club (League)	Class	W	L	ERA	G	GS	CG	SV	IP	H	R	ER	BB	SO
1999	Medicine Hat (Pio)	R	1	3	5.49	18	0	0	8	20	23	16	12	10	29
2000	Dunedin (FSL)	A	1	2	2.67	24	0	0	4	34	20	14	10	15	41
MINOR LEAGUE TOTALS			2	5	3.67	42	0	0	12	54	43	30	22	25	70

26. Luis Lopez, 1b/3b

Born: Oct. 5, 1973. **Ht.:** 6-0. **Wt.:** 205. **Bats:** R. **Throws:** R. **School:** Coastal Carolina University. **Career Transactions:** Signed by independent Ogden (Pioneer), July 8, 1995 . . . Released by Ogden, Sept. 2, 1995 . . . Signed by Blue Jays, June 15, 1996.

Lopez would be an unlikely major leaguer, but his bat just might get him there. The Brooklyn native wasn't drafted and signed in 1995 with independent Ogden. The Blue Jays signed him in June 1996 after he finished fourth in the Pioneer League in batting, and Lopez has continued to hit. In his second full season at Syracuse, Lopez again batted better than .320, improved his home run and RBI totals, and walked more than he struck out. There's little doubt he can hit, but he lacks the power to be considered a regular, and his fielding limits him to first base or DH. One member of the organization said Lopez could be a poor man's Edgar Martinez, but even he wasn't sure if any team—let alone Toronto—would give Lopez the chance to find out.

Year	Club (League)	Class	AVG	G	AB	R	H	2B	3B	HR	RBI	BB	SO	SB
1995	Ogden (Pio)	R	.357	46	182	36	65	15	0	7	39	16	20	1
1996	St. Catharines (NY-P)	A	.285	74	260	36	74	17	2	7	40	27	31	2
1997	Hagerstown (SAL)	A	.358	136	503	96	180	47	4	11	99	60	45	5
1998	Knoxville (SL)	AA	.313	119	450	70	141	27	1	15	85	58	55	0
	Syracuse (IL)	AAA	.220	11	41	6	9	0	0	1	3	6	6	0
1999	Syracuse (IL)	AAA	.322	136	531	76	171	35	2	4	69	40	58	1
2000	Syracuse (IL)	AAA	.328	130	491	64	161	27	1	7	79	48	33	3
MINOR LEAGUE TOTALS			.326	652	2458	384	801	168	10	52	414	255	248	12

27. Jerrod Kingrey, rhp

Born: Aug. 23, 1976. **Ht.:** 6-1. **Wt.:** 205. **Bats:** R. **Throws:** R. **School:** University of Alabama. **Career Transactions:** Selected by Blue Jays in 10th round of 1998 draft; signed June 3, 1998.

Kingrey doesn't have prospect stuff, but he has the results—including a combined 30 saves last season—to be taken seriously. Kingrey was the ace reliever on Alabama's 1997 College World Series runner-up and ranked second in NCAA Division I in saves in 1998. He lasted until the 10th round because he doesn't throw hard, relying instead on a funky three-quarters delivery and a dancing changeup. Kingrey once threw his changeup 80 percent of the time, daring hitters to wait on it. He usually won those challenges, though, and has had nothing but success in pro ball. He led the South Atlantic League in games and saves in 1999. In 2000, Kingrey threw his fastball more, a mid-80s pitch with good movement and command. He keeps the ball down in the strike zone, though he'll need to refine his control at the upper levels. He'll have to keep proving himself, but he hasn't faltered thus far.

Year	Club (League)	Class	W	L	ERA	G	GS	CG	SV	IP	H	R	ER	BB	SO
1998	St. Catharines (NY-P)	A	0	0	0.48	25	0	0	16	38	21	7	2	17	58
	Hagerstown (SAL)	A	0	1	3.86	1	0	0	0	2	3	2	1	0	3
1999	Hagerstown (SAL)	A	3	2	3.10	56	0	0	27	61	49	24	21	26	69
2000	Dunedin (FSL)	A	4	2	2.97	37	0	0	23	39	33	20	13	23	35
	Tennessee (SL)	AA	2	0	2.12	16	0	0	7	17	11	6	4	15	16
MINOR LEAGUE TOTALS			9	5	2.35	135	0	0	73	157	117	59	41	81	181

28. George Perez, rhp

Born: March 20, 1979. **Ht.:** 6-4. **Wt.:** 207. **Bats:** R. **Throws:** R. **Career Transactions:** Signed out of Dominican Republic by Blue Jays, Feb. 5, 1997.

Perez entered the year with a 5.25 career ERA in 120 innings of Rookie ball and ended it on the 40-man roster despite never having played in a full-season league. His meteoric rise came as his long, lean, projectable body started producing, with dominating results in the New York-Penn League. Opponents batted just .181 against him. Perez' performance in the Dominican League in the offseason further raised his profile, prompting his protection on the roster. Perez' greatest improvement came in commanding his above-average fastball. He hasn't settled on a consistent second pitch, fiddling with both a slider and a splitter. The organization likes his considerable ceiling, so if he develops either one, he could move quickly.

Year	Club (League)	Class	W	L	ERA	G	GS	CG	SV	IP	H	R	ER	BB	SO
1997	Blue Jays (DSL)	R	1	3	3.96	20	4	0	1	48	35	24	21	29	34
1998	Blue Jays (DSL)	R	0	0	7.16	12	2	0	2	16	17	17	13	17	12
1999	Medicine Hat (Pio)	R	2	2	5.79	15	8	0	1	56	65	46	36	26	41
2000	Queens (NY-P)	A	5	1	0.78	29	0	0	12	35	21	3	3	15	35
MINOR LEAGUE TOTALS			8	6	4.24	76	14	0	16	155	138	90	73	87	122

29. Jeremy Johnson, of

Born: May 6, 1978. **Ht.:** 6-1. **Wt.:** 185. **Bats:** L. **Throws:** L. **School:** Southeast Missouri State University. **Career Transactions:** Selected by Blue Jays in 26th round of 2000 draft; signed June 14, 2000.

Johnson had a stellar college career, graduating as Southeast Missouri State's career hits leader, and the Blue Jays started him in the Pioneer League, where he was older than many of the pitchers he faced. He dominated, earning MVP honors while ranking among the top five in several offensive categories. More important, Johnson showed that he has average tools across the board to go with excellent instincts. The Blue Jays saw a loose, easy swing and solid power potential. While Johnson's speed rates a tick below-average, he gets good jumps on balls in the outfield and runs the bases intelligently. The delighted Jays now are talking about pushing him, possibly to high Class A or Double-A in 2001, depending on his spring-training performance.

Year	Club (League)	Class	AVG	G	AB	R	H	2B	3B	HR	RBI	BB	SO	SB
2000	Medicine Hat (Pio)	R	.376	67	245	66	92	24	3	9	58	55	29	5
MINOR LEAGUE TOTALS			.376	67	245	66	92	24	3	9	58	55	29	5

30. Ron Davenport, 1b/of

Born: Oct. 16, 1981. **Ht.:** 6-2. **Wt.:** 185. **Bats:** L. **Throws:** R. **School:** Leesville Road HS, Raleigh, N.C. **Career Transactions:** Selected by Blue Jays in 22nd round of 2000 draft; signed June 14, 2000.

Davenport had one of the best debut seasons by a Blue Jays 2000 draftee, rivaling Medicine Hat teammates Aaron Sisk and Jeremy Johnson, who were both drafted out of college. Most organizations figured Davenport, a product of the growing talent hotbed of North Carolina's Research Triangle area, was headed to college too. He had committed to Florida State, but the Blue Jays weren't deterred. Scout Marty Miller turned in a report encouraging the club to pursue Davenport, and Miller met with the family on a rural highway to clinch the signing. The organization loves Davenport's offensive tools, from his short lefthanded swing to his developing power, which translated into a .485 slugging percentage at Medicine Hat, impressive for his first summer with a wood bat. Davenport doesn't have a position right now. He spent most of his first pro summer at first base, though he has a good arm and decent hands, which might allow him to play third base. His lackluster footwork may result in him shifting him to a corner outfield spot.

Year	Club (League)	Class	AVG	G	AB	R	H	2B	3B	HR	RBI	BB	SO	SB
2000	Medicine Hat (Pio)	R	.345	59	229	37	79	16	2	4	46	21	28	5
MINOR LEAGUE TOTALS			.345	59	229	37	79	16	2	4	46	21	28	5

All-Time Top 100 Prospects

Baseball America assembled its first Top 100 Prospects list before the 1990 season in an effort to put all the organizational prospect rankings in perspective. The list is now one of the most popular features of the magazine when it comes out in early March. The complete list shows all the highs and lows of prospect rating, so enjoy the entire roster of 11 years of Top 100 Prospects history, from Jeff Abbott to Eddie Zosky.

A

Player, Pos.	Team	Rank/Year
Abbott, Jeff, of	White Sox	80/97, 91/96
Abbott, Kyle, lhp	Angels	84/91, 60/90
Abreu, Bob, of	Astros	38/97, 29/96, 52/95, 95/93
Acevedo, Juan, rhp	Rockies	55/95
Ainsworth, Kurt, rhp	Giants	58/00
Aldred, Scott, lhp	Tigers	98/90
Alexander, Manny, ss	Orioles	65/94, 57/93, 39/92, 59/90
Alfonzo, Edgardo, 3b	Mets	31/95, 74/94
Alomar, Sandy, c	Indians	5/90
Alou, Moises, of	Pirates	37/90
Alvarez, Gabe, ss	Padres	92/96
Alvarez, Tavo, rhp	Expos	17/93, 63/92
Alvarez, Wilson, lhp	White Sox	91/91, 26/90
Ambres, Chip, of	Marlins	80/00
Anderson, Brian, lhp	Angels	56/94
Anderson, Garret, of	Angels	93/95
Anderson, Jimmy, lhp	Pirates	88/97
Anderson, Marlon, 2b	Phillies	83/99
Anderson, Matt, rhp	Tigers	24/98
Anderson, Ryan, lhp	Mariners	9/00, 7/99, 23/98
Anderson, Wes, rhp	Marlins	43/00, 91/99
Ankiel, Rick, lhp	Cardinals	1/00, 2/99, 18/98
Ansley, Willie, of	Astros	96/91, 38/90
Anthony, Eric, of	Astros	8/90
Appier, Kevin, rhp	Royals	86/90
Ard, Johnny, rhp	Giants	77/91
	Twins	46/90
Armas, Tony, rhp	Expos	27/00, 90/99
Arocha, Rene, rhp	Cardinals	100/93
Arrojo, Rolando, rhp	Devil Rays	37/98
Austin, Jeff, rhp	Royals	55/99
Avery, Steve, lhp	Braves	1/90
Aybar, Manny, rhp	Cardinals	68/97

B

Player, Pos.	Team	Rank/Year
Baerga, Carlos, 3b	Indians	67/90
Baez, Danys, rhp	Indians	39/00
Bagwell, Jeff, 3b	Astros	32/91
Baisley, Brad, rhp	Phillies	52/00
Baldwin, James, rhp	White Sox	25/95, 8/94, 66/93
Banks, Willie, rhp	Twins	68/92, 15/91, 13/90
Barber, Brian, rhp	Cardinals	47/95, 30/94, 54/93
Barcelo, Lorenzo, rhp	White Sox	80/98
Barcelo, Marc, rhp	Twins	70/95
Barnes, Brian, lhp	Expos	57/91
Barrett, Michael, 3b/c	Expos	6/99
Battle, Howard, 3b	Blue Jays	70/92
Bautista, Danny, of	Tigers	90/94
Beamon, Trey, of	Pirates	90/96, 43/95
Becker, Rich, of	Twins	37/94, 78/93
Beckett, Josh, rhp	Marlins	19/00
Beckett, Robbie, lhp	Padres	87/94, 50/91
Belcher, Kevin, of	Rangers	82/90
Bell, Derek, of	Blue Jays	15/92, 75/90
Bell, Rob, rhp	Reds	59/00, 35/99
	Braves	68/98
Belliard, Ron, 2b	Brewers	49/99
Beltran, Carlos, of	Royals	14/99, 93/97
Beltre, Adrian, 3b	Dodgers	3/98, 30/97
Benes, Alan, rhp	Cardinals	5/96, 14/95
Benitez, Armando, rhp	Orioles	11/95, 71/94
Benson, Kris, rhp	Pirates	59/99, 7/98, 8/97
Bere, Jason, rhp	White Sox	8/93

Player, Pos.	Team	Rank/Year
Bergeron, Peter, of	Expos	61/00, 40/99
Berkman, Lance, of	Astros	37/00, 13/99, 64/98
Betemit, Wilson, ss	Braves	99/00
Blosser, Greg, of	Red Sox	72/93, 64/91
Bocachica, Hiram, ss	Expos	50/97, 73/96, 65/95
Bohanon, Brian, lhp	Rangers	45/90
Boone, Aaron, 3b	Reds	81/97
Boone, Bret, 2b	Mariners	97/93, 99/91
Booty, Josh, 3b	Marlins	100/96, 24/95
Boston, D.J., 1b	Blue Jays	66/94
Bottalico, Ricky, rhp	Phillies	68/94
Bradley, Milton, of	Expos	36/00, 86/99
Bradley, Ryan, rhp	Yankees	25/99
Brannan, Ryan, rhp	Phillies	58/98
Branyan, Russell, 3b	Indians	82/00, 29/99, 26/98, 87/97
Brogna, Rico, 1b	Tigers	87/92, 35/91, 57/90
Brown, Dee, of	Royals	11/00, 92/99, 32/98
Burke, John, rhp	Rockies	49/94
Burlingame, Dennis, rhp	Braves	50/90
Burnett, A.J., rhp	Marlins	20/00, 21/99
Burnitz, Jeromy, of	Mets	61/93, 50/92
Burrell, Pat, 1b	Phillies	2/00, 19/99
Burroughs, Sean, 3b	Padres	7/00, 82/99
Burton, Darren, of	Royals	77/92
Butler, Brent, ss	Cardinals	54/99, 69/98

C

Player, Pos.	Team	Rank/Year
Cabrera, Orlando, 2b	Expos	92/98
Cameron, Mike, of	White Sox	31/97
Carpenter, Chris, rhp	Blue Jays	28/97, 82/96, 100/95
Caruso, Mike, ss	White Sox	34/98
Casanova, Raul, c	Padres	60/95
Casey, Sean, 1b	Indians	20/98
Castellano, Pedro, 3b	Cubs	42/92
Castillo, Braulio, of	Dodgers	34/90
Castillo, Luis, 2b	Marlins	79/96
Cedeno, Andujar, ss	Astros	2/91, 55/90
Cedeno, Roger, of	Dodgers	57/96, 26/95, 38/94, 85/93
Chacon, Shawn, rhp	Rockies	67/98
Chamberlain, Wes, of	Phillies	55/91, 25/90
Chavez, Eric, 3b	Athletics	3/99, 30/98, 53/97
Checo, Robinson, rhp	Red Sox	79/98
Chen, Bruce, lhp	Braves	4/99, 27/98, 83/97
Chen, Chin-Feng, of	Dodgers	17/00
Choi, Hee Seop, 1b	Cubs	77/00
Christianson, Ryan, c	Mariners	85/00
Clark, Tony, 1b	Tigers	86/95
Clayton, Royce, ss	Giants	6/92, 23/91
Clement, Matt, rhp	Padres	10/99, 16/98
Clemente, Edgard V., of	Rockies	71/97
Cline, Pat, c	Cubs	72/97
Colbrunn, Greg, c	Expos	85/91
Coleman, Michael, of	Red Sox	51/98, 98/96
Colome, Jesus, rhp	Athletics	53/00
Colon, Bartolo, rhp	Indians	14/97, 15/96
Combs, Pat, lhp	Phillies	20/90
Conine, Jeff, 1b	Royals	45/91
Cooke, Stephen, lhp	Pirates	52/92
Coolbaugh, Scott, 3b	Rangers	94/90
Cooper, Scott, 3b	Red Sox	86/92, 68/90
Coppinger, Rocky, rhp	Orioles	19/96
Cordero, Francisco, rhp	Tigers	29/00, 41/98
Cordero, Wil, ss	Expos	6/93, 7/92, 12/91, 62/90
Cornelius, Reid, rhp	Expos	21/91, 100/90

Player, Pos.	Team	Rank/Year
Costo, Tim, 1b	Indians	17/91
Cox, Steve, 1b	Athletics	87/96
Crede, Joe, 3b	White Sox	96/00, 46/99
Cruz, Jose Jr., of	Mariners	12/97, 23/96
Cuddyer, Michael, ss/3b	Twins	18/00, 36/99
Cummings, Midre, of	Pirates	33/94, 46/93
	Twins	33/92
Cunningham, Earl, of	Cubs	87/91, 44/90
Curtice, John, lhp	Red Sox	56/99
Cust, Jack, of	D'backs	31/00

D

Player, Pos.	Team	Rank/Year
D'Amico, Jeff, rhp	Brewers	25/96, 95/94
Damon, Johnny, of	Royals	9/95, 31/94, 22/93
Darr, Mike, of	Padres	94/99
Davis, Ben, c	Padres	24/99, 49/98, 59/97, 10/96
Davis, J.J., of	Pirates	97/00
Davis, Russ, 3b	Yankees	78/95, 26/94, 60/93
Dawkins, Travis, ss	Reds	21/00
De los Santos, Valerio, lhp	Brewers	89/98, 52/97
Decker, Steve, c	Giants	52/91
Delgado, Carlos, c	Blue Jays	5/94, 4/93, 67/92
DeShields, Delino, 2b	Expos	12/90
Dickson, Lance, lhp	Cubs	23/92, 41/91
Dotel, Octavio, rhp	Mets	45/99
Dozier, D.J., of	Mets	99/92, 44/91
Dransfeldt, Kelly, ss	Rangers	65/99
Dreifort, Darren, rhp	Dodgers	11/94
Dressendorfer, Kirk, rhp	Athletics	27/91
Drew, J.D., of	Cardinals	1/99
Drew, Tim, rhp	Indians	91/00
Drews, Matt, rhp	Yankees	12/96, 79/95
Drumright, Mike, rhp	Tigers	35/97, 62/96
DuBose, Eric, lhp	Athletics	53/99
Dunn, Adam, of	Reds	56/00
Dunwoody, Todd, of	Marlins	87/98, 90/97
Durham, Ray, 2b	White Sox	28/95
Dye, Jermaine, of	Braves	30/96, 88/95

E

Player, Pos.	Team	Rank/Year
Eaton, Adam, rhp	Padres	64/00
Eischen, Joey, lhp	Expos	40/94
Elarton, Scott, rhp	Astros	28/98, 77/96, 63/95
Eldred, Cal, rhp	Brewers	85/92
Ellis, Robert, rhp	White Sox	77/94
Elvira, Narciso, lhp	Brewers	76/91, 23/90
Embree, Alan, lhp	Indians	49/93
Encarnacion, Juan, of	Tigers	15/98
Encarnacion, Mario, of	Athletics	90/00
Enochs, Chris, rhp	Athletics	100/98
Ericks, John, rhp	Cardinals	66/91, 32/90
Erstad, Darin, of	Angels	4/96
Erwin, Scott, rhp	Athletics	88/92
Escobar, Alex, of	Mets	34/00, 11/99
Escobar, Kelvim, rhp	Blue Jays	67/97
Estalella, Bobby, c	Phillies	97/97
Estes, Shawn, lhp	Giants	72/96
	Mariners	44/92
Everett, Adam, ss	Astros	76/00
Everett, Carl, of	Mets	95/95
	Marlins	52/94, 69/93
	Yankees	32/92, 88/91

F

Player, Pos.	Team	Rank/Year
Fajardo, Hector, rhp	Rangers	81/92
Farmer, Howard, rhp	Expos	69/90
Febles, Carlos, 2b	Royals	30/99
Floyd, Cliff, 1b	Expos	1/94, 3/93, 34/92
Fontenot, Joe, rhp	Marlins	66/98
	Giants	45/97, 96/96
Fordyce, Brook, c	Mets	64/93, 47/91
Frascatore, John, rhp	Cardinals	97/96
Freeman, Choo, of	Rockies	42/00, 75/99
Fryman, Travis, ss	Tigers	39/90
Fullmer, Brad, 1b	Expos	14/98, 65/97, 68/96, 67/94

G

Player, Pos.	Team	Rank/Year
Gagne, Eric, rhp	Dodgers	49/00
Garbe, B.J., of	Twins	79/00
Garces, Rich, rhp	Twins	16/91
Garcia, Carlos, 2b	Pirates	45/93, 62/91
Garcia, Freddy, rhp	Mariners	61/99
Garcia, Karim, of	D'backs	77/98
	Dodgers	20/97, 7/96, 98/95
Garciaparra, Nomar, ss	Red Sox	10/97, 36/96, 22/95
Garland, Jon, rhp	White Sox	32/00
Gates, Brent, 2b	Athletics	56/93
George, Chris, lhp	Royals	40/00
Giambi, Jeremy, of	Royals	64/99
Gibralter, Steve, of	Reds	71/96, 79/93
Gibson, Derrick, of	Rockies	81/99, 81/98, 58/97, 13/96
Gil, Benji, ss	Rangers	57/95, 23/94, 21/93, 48/92
Giles, Marcus, 2b	Braves	74/00
Glanville, Doug, of	Cubs	93/92
Glaus, Troy, 3b	Angels	36/98
Goetz, Geoff, lhp	Mets	96/98
Gohr, Greg, rhp	Tigers	94/93, 79/92
Gomes, Wayne, rhp	Phillies	96/94
Gomez, Leo, 3b	Orioles	61/91
Gonzalez, Alex, ss	Blue Jays	8/95, 4/94, 27/93, 62/92
Gonzalez, Alex, ss	Marlins	17/99, 48/98, 54/97
Gonzalez, Juan, of	Rangers	4/90
Gonzalez, Lariel, rhp	Rockies	94/98
Goodwin, Curtis, of	Orioles	68/95
Goodwin, Tom, of	Dodgers	74/91, 30/90
Gorecki, Rick, rhp	Dodgers	75/94
Granger, Jeff, lhp	Royals	74/95, 19/94
Graves, Danny, rhp	Indians	86/96
Green, Chad, of	Brewers	99/97
Green, Shawn, of	Blue Jays	6/95, 28/94, 47/93
Green, Tyler, rhp	Phillies	36/94, 31/93, 26/92
Greene, Todd, c	Angels	59/96
Greene, Tommy, rhp	Braves	80/90
Greene, Willie, 3b	Reds	24/93
	Expos	37/91
	Pirates	66/90
Greisinger, Seth, rhp	Tigers	55/97
Grieve, Ben, of	Athletics	1/98, 18/97, 37/96, 10/95
Griffin, Ty, 3b	Cubs	22/90
Grilli, Jason, rhp	Giants	44/99, 54/98
Grissom, Marquis, of	Expos	17/90
Guerrero, Vladimir, of	Expos	2/97, 9/96, 85/95
Guerrero, Wilton, 2b	Dodgers	49/97, 61/96
Guillen, Carlos, 2b/ss	Mariners	73/00, 87/99
	Astros	27/97, 74/96
Guillen, Jose, of	Pirates	24/97
Gunderson, Eric, lhp	Giants	85/90
Gutierrez, Ricky, ss	Orioles	82/91
Guzman, Cristian, ss	Twins	68/99

H

Player, Pos.	Team	Rank/Year
Halladay, Roy, rhp	Blue Jays	12/99, 38/98, 23/97
Hamelin, Bob, 1b	Royals	31/90
Hamilton, Joey, rhp	Padres	57/94, 58/93, 36/92
Hamilton, Josh, of	Devil Rays	13/00
Hammond, Chris, lhp	Reds	63/91
Hammonds, Jeffrey, of	Orioles	3/94, 19/93
Harkey, Mike, rhp	Cubs	14/90
Harris, Donald, of	Rangers	43/90
Hartzog, Cullen, rhp	Yankees	95/90
Harville, Chad, rhp	Athletics	95/99
Hawblitzel, Ryan, rhp	Cubs	73/92
Hawkins, LaTroy, rhp	Twins	70/96, 30/95, 92/94
Haynes, Jimmy, rhp	Orioles	38/96, 45/95
Helling, Rick, rhp	Rangers	45/94
Helms, Wes, 3b	Braves	86/97
Helton, Todd, 1b	Rockies	11/98, 16/97, 32/96
Henderson, Rod, rhp	Expos	88/94

Player, Pos.	Team	Rank/Year
Henson, Drew, 3b	Yankees	24/00, 100/99
Heredia, Felix, lhp	Marlins	43/97
Hermansen, Chad, 2b/of	Pirates	33/00, 37/99, 13/98, 21/97, 54/96
Hermanson, Dustin, rhp	Padres	53/96, 18/95
Hernandez, Livan, rhp	Marlins	100/97, 8/96
Hernandez, Ramon, c	Athletics	74/98
Hernandez, Roberto, rhp	White Sox	45/92
Herndon, Junior, rhp	Padres	62/99
Herrera, Jose, of	Athletics	97/95, 97/94
Hidalgo, Richard, of	Astros	19/98, 19/97, 20/96, 34/95
Hill, Glenallen, of	Blue Jays	49/90
Hill, Tyrone, lhp	Brewers	54/94, 10/93, 20/92
Hinch, A.J., c	Athletics	42/98
Hitchcock, Sterling, lhp	Yankees	84/94, 90/93
Holbert, Aaron, ss	Cardinals	96/93
Hollandsworth, Todd, of	Dodgers	44/96, 13/95, 27/94
Hollins, Damon, of	Braves	95/96, 99/95
Hollins, Jessie, rhp	Cubs	41/93
Hosey, Steve, of	Giants	83/94, 61/92, 83/91, 52/90
Houston, Tyler, c	Braves	28/91, 92/90
Howard, Tom, of	Padres	89/90
Huff, Aubrey, 3b	Devil Rays	98/00
Hundley, Todd, c	Mets	18/92, 59/91, 65/90
Hunter, Brian, of	Astros	5/95, 47/94, 87/93
Hunter, Torii, of	Twins	79/97
Hurst, Jimmy, of	White Sox	75/95
Hurst, Jon, rhp	Expos	91/92
Huskey, Butch, 3b	Mets	70/94, 92/93, 54/92
Hutchinson, Chad, rhp	Cardinals	45/00, 42/99
Hutton, Mark, rhp	Yankees	83/92

I

Player, Pos.	Team	Rank/Year
Isringhausen, Jason, rhp	Mets	37/95
Izturis, Cesar, ss	Blue Jays	67/00

J

Player, Pos.	Team	Rank/Year
Jackson, Damian, ss	Reds	62/98
Janzen, Marty, rhp	Blue Jays	40/96
Jefferson, Reggie, 1b	Indians	49/92
	Reds	78/91, 28/90
Jenkins, Geoff, of	Brewers	95/98, 78/97, 49/96
Jennings, Jason, rhp	Rockies	87/00
Jeter, Derek, ss	Yankees	6/96, 4/95, 16/94, 44/93
Jimenez, D'Angelo, ss	Yankees	89/00
Johnson, Charles, c	Marlins	7/95, 20/94
Johnson, Nick, 1b	Yankees	5/00, 18/99
Johnston, Joel, rhp	Royals	59/92
Jones, Andruw, of	Braves	1/97, 1/96, 21/95
Jones, Bobby, rhp	Mets	28/93
Jones, Chipper, ss	Braves	3/95, 2/94, 1/93, 4/92, 49/91
Jones, Jaime, of	Marlins	31/96
Jones, Kiki, rhp	Dodgers	43/91, 6/90
Jones, Todd, rhp	Astros	42/93
Jordan, Brian, of	Cardinals	66/92, 97/90
Jose, Felix, of	Athletics	54/90
Judd, Mike, rhp	Dodgers	59/98
Juden, Jeff, rhp	Astros	27/92, 48/91, 90/90

K

Player, Pos.	Team	Rank/Year
Kapler, Gabe, of	Tigers	34/99
Karros, Eric, 1b	Dodgers	94/91, 84/90
Karsay, Steve, rhp	Athletics	12/94
	Blue Jays	55/93, 38/91
Kearns, Austin, of	Reds	76/99
Kelly, Kenny, of	Devil Rays	100/00
Kelly, Mike, of	Braves	58/94, 34/93, 19/92
Kelly, Pat, 2b	Yankees	68/91
Kendall, Jason, c	Pirates	26/96
Kennedy, Adam, 2b	Cardinals	98/99
Kieschnick, Brooks, of	Cubs	47/96, 82/95, 44/94
Kile, Darryl, rhp	Astros	34/91, 11/90

Player, Pos.	Team	Rank/Year
Kim, Byung-Hyun, rhp	D'backs	81/00
Kim, Sun-Woo, rhp	Red Sox	94/00
King, Cesar, c	Rangers	31/98
Kirkreit, Daron, rhp	Indians	80/95
Klesko, Ryan, 1b/of	Braves	15/94, 26/93, 8/92, 3/91
Knoblauch, Chuck, 2b	Twins	72/91
Koch, Billy, rhp	Blue Jays	33/99, 74/97
Kolb, Dan, rhp	Rangers	61/97
Konerko, Paul, 1b/3b	Dodgers	2/98, 11/97, 42/96, 38/95
Kotsay, Mark, of	Marlins	12/98, 77/97
Kroon, Marc, rhp	Padres	69/95

L

Player, Pos.	Team	Rank/Year
Lamb, Mike, 3b	Rangers	71/00
Lane, Brian, 3b	Reds	36/90
Lankford, Ray, of	Cardinals	51/91, 19/90
Lara, Nelson, rhp	Marlins	85/98
Larkin, Andy, rhp	Marlins	56/95
LeCroy, Matthew, c	Twins	44/00
Ledee, Ricky, of	Yankees	70/99, 46/98
Lee, Carlos, 3b	White Sox	28/99, 43/98
Lee, Corey, lhp	Rangers	63/98
Lee, Derrek, 1b	Marlins	47/98, 15/97, 41/96, 81/95
Lee, Travis, 1b	D'backs	8/98, 5/97
Lewis, Darren, of	Athletics	71/90
Lewis, Mark, ss	Indians	9/91, 24/90
Lieberthal, Mike, c	Phillies	67/93
Lilly, Ted, lhp	Expos	66/99
Lofton, Kenny, of	Indians	28/92
	Astros	75/91
Lomasney, Steve, c	Red Sox	50/00
Lombard, George, of	Braves	46/00, 26/99, 93/98, 94/97
Long, Terrence, of	Mets	63/97
Looper, Braden, rhp	Marlins	23/99
	Cardinals	39/98, 32/97
Lopez, Albie, rhp	Indians	93/94
Lopez, Felipe, ss	Blue Jays	38/00, 67/99
Lopez, Javy, c	Braves	17/94, 20/93, 78/92
Lorraine, Andrew, lhp	Angels	71/95
Lowe, Derek, rhp	Mariners	63/94, 70/93
Lowell, Mike, 3b	Yankees	58/99, 71/98
Lowery, Terrell, of	Rangers	85/94, 40/92

M

Player	Pos.	Team	Rank/Year
Maeda, Katsuhiro, rhp	Yankees	85/97	
Mahomes, Pat, rhp	Twins	25/92	
Malave, Jose, of	Red Sox	94/95	
Marquis, Jason, rhp	Braves	89/99	
Marrero, Eli, c	Cardinals	33/98, 37/97	
Martinez, Angel, c	Blue Jays	77/95	
Martinez, Jose, rhp	Marlins	68/93	
Martinez, Pedro, rhp	Dodgers	62/93, 10/92	
Martinez, Tino, 1b	Mariners	18/91, 40/90	
Martinez, Willie, rhp	Indians	50/98, 47/97	
Masaoka, Onan, lhp	Dodgers	95/97	
Mateo, Ruben, of	Rangers	6/00, 9/99, 17/98	
Matthews, Gary Jr., of	Padres	73/99	
May, Derrick, of	Cubs	72/90	
McAndrew, Jamie, rhp	Dodgers	40/91	
McCarty, David, 1b/of	Twins	16/93, 22/92	
McDavid, Ray, of	Padres	55/94, 14/93, 60/92	
McDonald, Ben, rhp	Orioles	2/90	
McDonald, Darnell, of	Orioles	74/99, 21/98	
McGlinchy, Kevin, rhp	Braves	47/99, 39/97	
McNeely, Jeff, of	Red Sox	16/92, 20/91	
Meche, Gil, rhp	Mariners	78/99, 82/98	
Medina, Rafael, rhp	Marlins	72/98, 64/97	
Melian, Jackson, of	Yankees	72/00, 72/99, 98/98, 40/97	
Melo, Juan, ss	Padres	86/98, 36/97	
Meluskey, Mitch, c	Astros	43/99	
Mercedes, Luis, of	Orioles	80/92	
Mercker, Kent, lhp	Braves	47/90	
Meulens, Hensley, of	Yankees	30/91	

Milchin, Mike, lhp	Cardinals	80/91, 87/90
Miller, Kurt, rhp	Marlins	62/94
	Rangers	11/93, 14/92
	Pirates	24/91
Miller, Orlando, ss	Astros	51/95, 46/94
Miller, Wade, rhp	Astros	69/00, 80/99, 76/98
Million, Doug, lhp	Rockies	69/96, 19/95
Milton, Eric, lhp	Twins	25/98
Minor, Ryan, 3b	Orioles	35/98
Miranda, Angel, lhp	Brewers	81/91
Mitchell, Keith, of	Braves	89/92
Mondesi, Raul, of	Dodgers	51/94, 82/93, 21/92, 14/91
Moore, Kerwin, of	Royals	67/91
Moore, Marcus, rhp	Blue Jays	53/91
Morandini, Mickey, 2b	Phillies	41/90
Moreno, Orber, rhp	Royals	83/00, 57/99
Morris, Matt, rhp	Cardinals	25/97, 56/96
Morris, Warren, 2b	Pirates	84/99
Morton, Kevin, lhp	Red Sox	61/90
Mota, Guillermo, rhp	Expos	88/99
Mottola, Chad, of	Reds	48/94, 71/93
Mouton, James, 2b	Astros	72/94
Mulder, Mark, lhp	Athletics	12/00, 27/99
Munson, Eric, 1b/c	Tigers	23/00
Murray, Calvin, of	Giants	33/93
Mussina, Mike, rhp	Orioles	19/91
Myette, Aaron, rhp	White Sox	63/00, 77/99

N

Player, Pos.	Team	Rank/Year
Naehring, Tim, ss	Red Sox	46/91
Nagy, Charles, rhp	Indians	56/91, 27/90
Neill, Mike, of	Athletics	43/92
Nen, Robb, rhp	Rangers	86/91
Nevers, Tom, ss	Astros	47/92
Nevin, Phil, 3b	Astros	59/95, 24/94, 30/93
Newfield, Marc, of	Mariners	29/95, 35/94, 43/93, 17/92, 31/91
Newlin, Jim, rhp	Mariners	81/90
Newman, Alan, lhp	Twins	96/92
Nied, David, rhp	Rockies	23/93
	Braves	56/92
Nieves, Melvin, of	Padres	69/94
	Braves	39/93
Nilsson, Dave, c	Brewers	29/92
Nitkowski, C.J., lhp	Reds	87/95
Nixon, Trot, of	Red Sox	99/99, 39/96, 46/95, 13/94
Nunez, Abraham, of	Marlins	30/00
Nunez, Abraham O., ss	Pirates	65/98, 69/97
Nunez, Sergio, 2b	Royals	61/95
Nunez, Vladimir, rhp	D'backs	76/97

O

Player, Pos.	Team	Rank/Year
Ochoa, Alex, of	Mets	43/96, 35/95, 42/94, 89/93
Offerman, Jose, ss	Dodgers	4/91, 10/90
Olerud, John, 1b/lhp	Blue Jays	3/90
Opperman, Dan, rhp	Dodgers	71/91
Ordonez, Magglio, of	White Sox	56/98
Ordonez, Rey, ss	Mets	17/96, 20/95
Orie, Kevin, 3b	Cubs	42/97
Ortiz, David, 1b	Twins	84/98
Ortiz, Luis, 3b	Red Sox	86/94
Ortiz, Ramon, rhp	Angels	28/00, 75/98
Osborne, Donovan, lhp	Cardinals	35/92, 42/91
Osuna, Antonio, rhp	Dodgers	15/95
Ozuna, Pablo, ss/2b	Marlins	62/00, 8/99

P

Player, Pos.	Team	Rank/Year
Palmer, Dean, 3b	Rangers	60/91, 33/90
Park, Chan Ho, rhp	Dodgers	18/96, 41/95, 14/94
Patterson, Corey, of	Cubs	3/00, 16/99
Patterson, John, rhp	D'backs	10/00, 15/99, 45/98, 41/97
Pavano, Carl, rhp	Expos	9/98, 17/97

Payton, Jay, of	Mets	34/97, 21/96, 96/95
Peltier, Dan, of	Rangers	100/91, 74/90
Pena, Angel, c	Dodgers	41/99
Pena, Carlos, 1b	Rangers	93/99
Pena, Wily Mo, of	Yankees	88/00
Pennington, Brad, lhp	Orioles	18/93
Penny, Brad, rhp	D'backs	22/00, 5/99
Percibal, Billy, rhp	Orioles	99/96
Percival, Troy, rhp	Angels	29/93, 38/92
Perez, Eduardo, of/3b	Angels	97/92
Perez, Neifi, ss	Rockies	33/97, 63/96
Perez, Odalis, lhp	Braves	31/99
Peters, Don, rhp	Athletics	54/91
Petrick, Ben, c	Rockies	35/00, 85/99, 53/98, 62/97
Pett, Jose, rhp	Blue Jays	93/96, 75/93
Pettitte, Andy, lhp	Yankees	49/95
Phillips, J.R., 1b	Giants	73/95, 83/94
Piatt, Adam, 3b	Athletics	93/00
Piazza, Mike, c	Dodgers	38/93
Pickering, Calvin, 1b	Orioles	38/99
Pina, Michael, c	Red Sox	79/90
Pittsley, Jim, rhp	Royals	56/97, 24/96, 39/95, 82/94, 32/93
Plantier, Phil, of	Red Sox	83/90
Ponson, Sidney, rhp	Orioles	78/98, 98/97
Powell, Dante, of	Giants	92/97, 90/95
Powell, Jay, rhp	Marlins	67/96
Pozo, Arquimedez, 2b	Mariners	60/94
Presley, Kirk, rhp	Mets	59/94
Pulsipher, Bill, lhp	Mets	12/95, 21/94

R

Player, Pos.	Team	Rank/Year
Radinsky, Scott, lhp	White Sox	78/90
Ramirez, Aramis, 3b	Pirates	5/98, 26/97
Ramirez, Julio, of	Marlins	60/00, 48/99, 57/98
Ramirez, Manny, of	Indians	7/94, 13/93, 37/92
Redington, Tom, 3b	Braves	58/90
Reese, Pokey, ss	Reds	60/96, 48/95, 41/94, 48/93, 75/92
Reichert, Dan, rhp	Royals	75/00
Reid, Derek, of	Giants	95/92
Reitsma, Chris, rhp	Red Sox	88/98, 46/97
Relaford, Desi, 2b	Mariners	89/96, 92/95
Renteria, Edgar, ss	Marlins	33/96, 51/93
Restovich, Michael, of	Twins	26/00, 50/99
Reyes, Dennis, lhp	Dodgers	91/98
Rhodes, Arthur, lhp	Orioles	5/92, 6/91
Richardson, Keith, rhp	Pirates	73/90
Rigby, Brad, rhp	Athletics	91/97, 85/96
Riley, Matt, lhp	Orioles	15/00, 20/99
Ritchie, Todd, rhp	Twins	73/94, 98/92
Rivas, Luis, ss	Twins	86/00, 63/99, 55/98, 70/97
Rivera, Luis, rhp	Braves	51/00, 71/99, 44/98
Rivera, Ruben, of	Padres	40/98
	Yankees	9/97, 3/96, 2/95, 76/94
Roberts, Grant, rhp	Mets	84/00, 79/99, 29/98
Robertson, Mike, 1b	White Sox	90/92
Rodriguez, Alex, ss	Mariners	1/95, 6/94
Rodriguez, Frank, rhp	Red Sox	36/95, 39/94, 25/93, 9/92
Rodriguez, Henry, 1b/of	Dodgers	29/91
Rodriguez, Ivan, c	Rangers	7/91
Rodriguez, Nerio, c	Orioles	96/97
Rodriguez, Wilfredo, lhp	Astros	25/00
Rogers, Kevin, lhp	Giants	50/93, 89/91
Rojas, Mel, rhp	Expos	35/90
Rolen, Scott, 3b	Phillies	13/97, 27/96, 91/95
Rollins, Jimmy, ss	Phillies	95/00
Romano, Jason, 2b	Rangers	68/00
Roper, John, rhp	Reds	36/93
Roper, John, rhp	Reds	53/92
Rose, Brian, rhp	Red Sox	22/98, 44/97, 78/96
Rosselli, Joe, lhp	Giants	65/93
Ruffcorn, Scott, rhp	White Sox	23/95, 32/94, 80/93
Ruffin, Johnny, rhp	White Sox	53/94
	Reds	74/92, 58/91

Player, Pos.	Team	Rank/Year
Rusch, Glendon, lhp	Royals	89/97, 83/96

S

Player, Pos.	Team	Rank/Year
Sabathia, C.C., lhp	Indians	57/00
Sadler, Donnie, 2b	Red Sox	51/97, 28/96
Salkeld, Roger, rhp	Mariners	100/94, 3/92, 5/91, 16/90
Salmon, Tim, of	Angels	5/93, 72/92, 73/91
Sanchez, Alex, rhp	Blue Jays	51/90
Sanders, Deion, of	Yankees	53/90
Sanders, Reggie, of	Reds	11/92, 8/91
Sanford, Mo, rhp	Reds	94/92
Santana, Julio, rhp	Rangers	80/96, 44/95
Santiago, Ramon, ss	Tigers	92/00
Schmidt, Jason, rhp	Braves	11/96, 42/95
Schourek, Pete, lhp	Mets	33/91
Scott, Gary, 3b	Cubs	76/92, 39/91
Seay, Bobby, lhp	Devil Rays	82/97
Segui, David, 1b	Orioles	93/90
Sele, Aaron, rhp	Red Sox	84/93, 71/92
Serafini, Dan, lhp	Twins	76/96
Serrano, Wascar, rhp	Padres	54/00
Sexson, Richie, 1b	Indians	50/96
Shaw, Curtis, lhp	Athletics	98/94, 76/93
Sheets, Ben, rhp	Brewers	65/00
Shirley, Al, of	Mets	74/93
Shuey, Paul, rhp	Indians	67/95, 81/93
Silva, Jose, rhp	Blue Jays	33/95, 10/94
Singleton, Duane, of	Brewers	69/92
Slusarski, Joe, rhp	Athletics	64/90
Smith, Dan, lhp	Rangers	73/93, 97/91
Smith, Mark, of	Orioles	57/92
Smith, Robert, 3b	Braves	75/96
Smith, Willie, rhp	Yankees	79/91, 48/90
Snopek, Chris, 3b	White Sox	52/96
Snow, J.T., 1b	Angels	98/93
Snyder, Kyle, rhp	Royals	70/100
Soriano, Alfonso, ss	Yankees	16/00, 39/99
Sorrento, Paul, 1b	Twins	91/90
Spoljaric, Paul, lhp	Blue Jays	99/94
Springer, Russ, rhp	Angels	99/93
	Yankees	58/92, 96/90
Standridge, Jason, rhp	Devil Rays	47/00
Stanton, Mike, lhp	Braves	18/90
Staton, Dave, 1b	Padres	70/91
Stenson, Dernell, of	Red Sox	66/00, 22/99
Stewart, Shannon, of	Blue Jays	57/97, 46/96, 72/95
Strange, Pat, rhp	Mets	78/00
Stull, Everett, rhp	Expos	58/95
Suero, William, 2b	Blue Jays	92/91
Suppan, Jeff, rhp	Red Sox	60/97, 35/96, 50/95
Suzuki, Mac, rhp	Mariners	34/94

T

Player, Pos.	Team	Rank/Year
Tapani, Kevin, rhp	Twins	88/90
Tavarez, Julian, rhp	Indians	61/94
Taylor, Brien, lhp	Yankees	18/94, 2/93, 1/92
Tejada, Miguel, ss	Athletics	10/98, 6/97, 88/96
Thomas, Frank, 1b	White Sox	29/90
Thomas, Larry, lhp	White Sox	88/93
Thome, Jim, 3b	Indians	51/92, 93/91
Thompson, Justin, lhp	Tigers	79/94, 84/92
Thompson, Mark, rhp	Rockies	89/94, 77/93
Timlin, Mike, rhp	Blue Jays	69/91
Tomko, Brett, rhp	Reds	84/97
Torres, Salomon, rhp	Giants	22/94, 30/92
Trombley, Mike, rhp	Twins	53/93
Tucker, Michael, of	Royals	32/95, 25/94, 40/93

U

Player, Pos.	Team	Rank/Year
Urbina, Ugueth, rhp	Expos	48/96, 27/95

V

Player, Pos.	Team	Rank/Year
Valdes, Marc, rhp	Marlins	89/95

Valdez, Rafael, rhp	Padres	36/91, 21/90
Valentin, Jose, c	Twins	58/96
Valera, Julio, rhp	Mets	98/91, 56/90
Van Poppel, Todd, rhp	Athletics	7/93, 2/92, 1/91
Varitek, Jason, c	Mariners	51/96
Vasquez, Julian, rhp	Mets	92/92
Vaughn, Greg, of	Brewers	9/90
Vaughn, Maurice, 1b	Red Sox	10/91, 76/90
Vazquez, Javier, rhp	Expos	83/98
Ventura, Robin, 3b	White Sox	15/90
Vessel, Andrew, of	Rangers	55/96
Villone, Ron, lhp	Mariners	62/95, 91/94, 63/93
Vizcaino, Jose, 2b	Dodgers	99/90

W

Player, Pos.	Team	Rank/Year
Wade, Terrell, lhp	Braves	64/96, 54/95, 29/94
Wagner, Billy, lhp	Astros	14/96, 17/95, 78/94
Wagner, Bret, lhp	Cardinals	84/95
Walker, Larry, of	Expos	42/90
Walker, Todd, 2b/3b	Twins	7/97, 22/96, 40/95
Wallace, B.J., lhp	Expos	94/94
Wallace, Jeff, lhp	Pirates	90/98
Ward, Daryle, 1b	Astros	97/98
Wasdin, John, rhp	Athletics	84/96, 53/95
Washburn, Jarrod, lhp	Angels	73/98, 66/97
Watkins, Pat, of	Reds	83/95
Watson, Allen, lhp	Cardinals	9/93, 64/92
Watson, Ron, rhp	Angels	86/93
Weaver, Jeff, rhp	Tigers	51/99
Wedge, Eric, c	Red Sox	63/90
Wells, Kip, rhp	White Sox	14/00
Wells, Vernon, of	Blue Jays	4/00, 69/99, 52/98
Werth, Jayson, c	Orioles	48/00, 52/99
Westbrook, Jake, rhp	Rockies	75/97
Whisenant, Matt, lhp	Marlins	59/93
White, Gabe, lhp	Expos	81/94
White, Matt, rhp	Devil Rays	32/99, 6/98, 4/97
White, Rondell, of	Expos	9/94, 15/93, 12/92, 13/91
Whiten, Mark, of	Blue Jays	25/91
Wilkins, Rick, c	Cubs	70/90
Williams, Bernie, of	Yankees	11/91, 77/90
Williams, Brian, rhp	Astros	24/92
Williams, Gerald, of	Yankees	52/93
Williams, Glenn, ss	Braves	76/95, 64/94
Williamson, Antone, 3b	Brewers	81/96, 64/95
Williamson, Scott, rhp	Reds	97/99
Wilson, Dan, c	Reds	91/93, 41/92, 95/91
Wilson, Enrique, 2b	Indians	61/98, 73/97, 65/96
Wilson, Nigel, of	Marlins	80/94, 37/93
	Blue Jays	46/92
Wilson, Paul, rhp	Mets	2/96, 16/95
Wilson, Preston, of	Mets	70/98, 94/96, 43/94, 93/93
Witt, Kevin, 1b	Blue Jays	99/98
Wohlers, Mark, rhp	Braves	13/92
Wolf, Randy, lhp	Phillies	96/99
Wood, Kerry, rhp	Cubs	4/98, 3/97, 16/96
Woodson, Kerry, rhp	Mariners	65/91
Wright, Jamey, rhp	Rockies	66/96
Wright, Jaret, rhp	Indians	22/97, 34/96, 66/95
Wright, Ron, 1b	Pirates	48/97

Y

Player, Pos.	Team	Rank/Year
Yarnall, Ed, lhp	Yankees	55/00
	Mets	60/98
Young, Anthony, rhp	Mets	55/92, 26/91
Young, Dmitri, 1b	Cardinals	29/97, 50/94, 12/93, 31/92
Young, Kevin, 3b/1b	Pirates	35/93, 100/92
Yount, Andy, rhp	Red Sox	45/96

Z

Player, Pos.	Team	Rank/Year
Zancanaro, David, lhp	Athletics	65/92
Zeile, Todd, c	Cardinals	7/90
Zimmerman, Mike, rhp	Pirates	90/91
Zito, Barry, lhp	Athletics	41/00
Zosky, Eddie, ss	Blue Jays	82/92, 22/91

Minor League Top 20s

As a complement to our organizational prospect rankings, Baseball America also ranks prospects in every minor league immediately after the season. Like the organizational lists, they place more weight on potential than present performance and should not be regarded as minor league all-star teams.

The league lists do differ a little bit from the organizational lists, which are taken more from a scouting perspective. The league lists are based on conversations with league managers. It is not strictly a poll, though we do try to talk with every manager. Players were considered if they spent at least a third of the season in a league. Some players on these lists, such as Pat Burrell and Jon Garland, are not eligible for our organization prospect lists because they are no longer rookie-eligible. Such players are indicated with an asterisk (*). Players who have been traded from the organizations they are listed with are indicated with a pound (#).

Remember that managers and scouts tend to look at players differently. Managers give more weight to what a player does on the field, while scouts look at what a player might eventually do. We think both perspectives are useful, so we give you both even though they don't always jibe with each other.

TRIPLE-A

International League
1. *Jon Garland, rhp, Charlotte Knights (White Sox)
2. *Pat Burrell, of/1b, Scranton/Wilkes-Barre Red Barons (Phillies)
3. *Milton Bradley, of, Ottawa Lynx (Expos)
4. Aubrey Huff, 3b, Durham Bulls (Devil Rays)
5. Alfonso Soriano, ss/2b, Columbus Clippers (Yankees)
6. Ben Sheets, rhp, Indianapolis Indians (Brewers)
7. Vernon Wells, of, Syracuse Skychiefs (Blue Jays)
8. Reggie Taylor, of, Scranton/Wilkes-Barre Red Barons (Phillies)
9. *Tomokazu Ohka, rhp, Pawtucket Red Sox (Red Sox)
10. Brad Wilkerson, of, Ottawa Lynx (Expos)
11. *Russell Branyan, 3b/of, Buffalo Bisons (Indians)
12. #Jason Tyner, of, Norfolk Tides (Mets)
13. Jimmy Rollins, ss, Scranton/Wilkes-Barre Red Barons (Phillies)
14. Timoniel Perez, of, Norfolk Tides (Mets)
15. Randy Keisler, lhp, Columbus Clippers (Yankees)
16. Sun-Woo Kim, rhp, Pawtucket Red Sox (Red Sox)
17. Brandon Inge, c, Toledo Mud Hens (Tigers)
18. Ryan Kohlmeier, rhp, Rochester Red Wings (Orioles)
19. Grant Roberts, rhp, Norfolk Tides (Mets)
20. Cesar Izturis, ss, Syracuse Skychiefs (Blue Jays)

Pacific Coast League
1. Ryan Anderson, lhp, Tacoma Rainiers (Mariners)
2. *Barry Zito, lhp, Sacramento Rivercats (Athletics)
3. *Ramon Ortiz, rhp, Edmonton Trappers (Angels)
4. Jose Ortiz, 2b/ss, Sacramento Rivercats (Athletics)
5. Chris George, lhp, Omaha Golden Spikes (Royals)
6. *Wade Miller, rhp, New Orleans Zephyrs (Astros)
7. Carlos Zambrano, rhp, Iowa Cubs (Cubs)
8. *Ramon Castro, c, Calgary Cannons (Marlins)
9. *Ben Petrick, c, Colorado Springs Sky Sox (Rockies)
10. Matt Kinney, rhp, Salt Lake Buzz (Twins)
11. Dee Brown, of, Omaha Golden Spikes (Royals)
12. Justin Miller, rhp, Sacramento Rivercats (Athletics)
13. *J.C. Romero, lhp, Salt Lake Buzz (Twins)
14. Adam Everett, ss, New Orleans Zephyrs (Astros)
15. Luis Rivas, 2b, Salt Lake Buzz (Twins)
16. *Adam Piatt, of/3b, Sacramento Rivercats (Athletics)
17. Julio Zuleta, 1b/of, Iowa Cubs (Cubs)
18. Joel Pineiro, rhp, Tacoma Rainiers (Mariners)
19. Chad Durbin, rhp, Omaha Golden Spikes (Royals)
20. *Chad Hermansen, of, Nashville Sounds (Pirates)

DOUBLE-A

Eastern League
1. Alex Escobar, of, Binghamton Mets (Mets)
2. C.C. Sabathia, lhp, Akron Aeros (Indians)
3. Donnie Bridges, rhp, Harrisburg Senators (Expos)
4. Brad Wilkerson, of, Harrisburg Senators (Expos)
5. Brandon Duckworth, rhp, Reading Phillies (Phillies)
6. Eric Valent, of, Reading Phillies (Phillies)
7. #Drew Henson, 3b, Norwich Navigators (Yankees)
8. *Luis Matos, of, Bowie Baysox (Orioles)
9. Bobby Kielty, of, New Britain Rock Cats (Twins)
10. Michael Cuddyer, 3b, New Britain Rock Cats (Twins)
11. Danys Baez, rhp, Akron Aeros (Indians)
12. Joel Pineiro, rhp, New Haven Ravens (Mariners)
13. Luis Rivas, 2b, New Britain Rock Cats (Twins)
14. Juan Diaz, 1b, Trenton Thunder (Red Sox)
15. Doug Nickle, rhp, Reading Phillies (Phillies)
16. Pablo Ozuna, 2b, Portland Sea Dogs (Marlins)
17. Matt Kinney, rhp, New Britain Rock Cats (Twins)
18. Randy Keisler, lhp, Norwich Navigators (Yankees)
19. Cesar Crespo, of, Portland Sea Dogs (Marlins)
20. Paxton Crawford, rhp, Trenton Thunder (Red Sox)

Southern League
1. Corey Patterson, of, West Tenn Diamond Jaxx (Cubs)
2. Ben Sheets, rhp, Huntsville Stars (Brewers)
3. Jon Rauch, rhp, Birmingham Barons (White Sox)
4. Joe Crede, 3b, Birmingham Barons (White Sox)
5. Sean Burroughs, 3b, Mobile Bay Bears (Padres)
6. Felipe Lopez, ss, Tennessee Smokies (Blue Jays)
7. Matt Ginter, rhp, Birmingham Barons (White Sox)
8. *Adam Eaton, rhp, Mobile Bay Bears (Padres)
9. *Mark Buehrle, lhp, Birmingham Barons (White Sox)
10. *Juan Pierre, of, Carolina Mudcats (Rockies)
11. Carlos Zambrano, rhp, West Tenn Diamond Jaxx (Cubs)
12. Eric Munson, 1b, Jacksonville Suns (Tigers)
13. Marcus Giles, 2b, Greenville Braves (Braves)
14. Pasqual Coco, rhp, Tennessee Smokies (Blue Jays)
15. Craig House, rhp, Carolina Mudcats (Rockies)
16. Gookie Dawkins, 2b/ss, Chattanooga Lookouts (Reds)
17. Brandon Inge, c, Jacksonville Suns (Tigers)
18. Jason Marquis, rhp, Greenville Braves (Braves)
19. Brandon Larson, 3b, Chattanooga Lookouts (Reds)
20. Aaron Rowand, of, Birmingham Barons (White Sox)

Texas League

1. Roy Oswalt, rhp, Round Rock Express (Astros)
2. Carlos Pena, 1b, Tulsa Drillers (Rangers)
3. Bud Smith, lhp, Arkansas Travelers (Cardinals)
4. Alex Cintron, ss, El Paso Diablos (Diamondbacks)
5. Chris George, lhp, Wichita Wranglers (Royals)
6. Jason Hart, 1b, Midland Rockhounds (Athletics)
7. #Jesus Colome, rhp, Midland Rockhounds (Athletics)
8. Luke Prokopec, rhp, San Antonio Missions (Dodgers)
9. Kurt Ainsworth, rhp, Shreveport Captains (Giants)
10. Jack Cust, of, El Paso Diablos (Diamondbacks)
11. Keith Ginter, 2b, Round Rock Express (Astros)
12. Lyle Overbay, 1b, El Paso Diablos (Diamondbacks)
13. Wilfredo Rodriguez, lhp, Round Rock Express (Astros)
14. Jason Romano, 2b, Tulsa Drillers (Rangers)
15. Bill Ortega, of, Arkansas Travelers (Cardinals)
16. Ryan Vogelsong, rhp, Shreveport Captains (Giants)
17. Jason Grabowski, 3b, Tulsa Drillers (Rangers)
18. Aaron McNeal, 1b, Round Rock Express (Astros)
19. Luis Saturria, of, Arkansas Travelers (Cardinals)
20. Chin-Feng Chen, of, San Antonio Missions (Dodgers)

HIGH CLASS A
California League

1. Antonio Perez, ss, Lancaster Jethawks (Mariners)
2. Ryan Ludwick, of, Modesto A's (Athletics)
3. Jerome Williams, rhp, San Jose Giants (Giants)
4. Mike Bynum, lhp, Rancho Cucamonga Quakes (Padres)
5. Brad Cresse, c, High Desert Mavericks (Diamondbacks)
6. Willie Bloomquist, 2b, Lancaster Jethawks (Mariners)
7. Nick Neugebauer, rhp, Mudville Nine (Brewers)
8. Tony Torcato, 3b, San Jose Giants (Giants)
9. Jeremy Owens, of, Rancho Cucamonga Quakes (Padres)
10. Elpidio Guzman, of, Lake Elsinore Storm (Angels)
11. Gary Johnson, of, Lake Elsinore Storm (Angels)
12. #Miguel Olivo, c, Modesto Athletics (Athletics)
13. #Terrmel Sledge, of, Lancaster Jethawks (Mariners)
14. Keith Surkont, rhp, Visalia Oaks (Athletics)
15. Nelson Castro, ss, Bakersfield Blaze (Giants)
16. Sean McGowan, 1b, San Jose Giants (Giants)
17. Joe Thurston, ss, San Bernardino Stampede (Dodgers)
18. #Angel Berroa, ss, Visalia Oaks (Athletics)
19. Juan Silvestre, of, Lancaster Jethawks (Mariners)
20. Jeff Heaverlo, rhp, Lancaster Jethawks (Mariners)

Carolina League

1. C.C. Sabathia, lhp, Kinston Indians (Indians)
2. Jon Rauch, rhp, Winston-Salem Warthogs (White Sox)
3. J.J. Davis, of, Lynchburg Hillcats (Pirates)
4. Christian Parra, rhp, Myrtle Beach Pelicans (Braves)
5. Mike MacDougal, rhp, Wilmington Blue Rocks (Royals)
6. Horacio Ramirez, lhp, Myrtle Beach Pelicans (Braves)
7. Alexis Gomez, of, Wilmington Blue Rocks (Royals)
8. Billy Sylvester, rhp, Myrtle Beach Pelicans (Braves)
9. Craig House, rhp, Salem Avalanche (Rockies)
10. Dan Wright, rhp, Winston-Salem Warthogs (White Sox)
11. Tim Spooneybarger, rhp, Myrtle Beach Pelicans (Braves)
12. Jason Jennings, rhp, Salem Avalanche (Rockies)
13. Esix Snead, of, Potomac Cannons (Cardinals)
14. Juan Uribe, ss, Salem Avalanche (Rockies)
15. Matt Holliday, 3b, Salem Avalanche (Rockies)
16. Keith Reed, of, Frederick Keys (Orioles)
17. Ntema Ndungidi, of, Frederick Keys (Orioles)
18. Tim Raines Jr., of, Frederick Keys (Orioles)
19. #Mark Ellis, ss, Wilmington Blue Rocks (Royals)
20. Cristobal Correa, rhp, Potomac Cannons (Cardinals)

Florida State League

1. Kevin Mench, of, Charlotte Rangers (Rangers)
2. Juan Cruz, rhp, Daytona Cubs (Cubs)
3. Roy Oswalt, rhp, Kissimmee Cobras (Astros)
4. Brian Cole, of, St. Lucie Mets (Mets)
5. Adam Johnson, rhp, Fort Myers Miracle (Twins)
6. Pat Strange, rhp, St. Lucie Mets (Mets)
7. Hee Seop Choi, 1b, Daytona Cubs (Cubs)
8. Joe Lawrence, c, Dunedin Blue Jays (Blue Jays)
9. Tim Redding, rhp, Kissimmee Cobras (Astros)
10. Andres Torres, of, Lakeland Tigers (Tigers)
11. Ben Christensen, rhp, Daytona Cubs (Cubs)
12. Wes Anderson, rhp, Brevard County Manatees (Marlins)
13. David Kelton, 3b, Daytona Cubs (Cubs)
14. Casey Fossum, lhp, Sarasota Red Sox (Red Sox)
15. Travis Hafner, 1b, Charlotte Rangers (Rangers)
16. Alex Graman, lhp, Tampa Yankees (Yankees)
17. Michael Restovich, of, Fort Myers Miracle (Twins)
18. #Randey Dorame, lhp, Vero Beach Dodgers (Dodgers)
19. #Brian Reith, rhp, Tampa Yankees (Yankees)
20. Robert Stratton, of, St. Lucie Mets (Mets)

LOW CLASS A
Midwest League

1. Josh Beckett, rhp, Kane County Cougars (Marlins)
2. Juan Cruz, rhp, Lansing Lugnuts (Cubs)
3. Chris Snelling, of, Wisconsin Timber Rattlers (Mariners)
4. Austin Kearns, of, Dayton Dragons (Reds)
5. Albert Pujols, 3b, Peoria Chiefs (Cardinals)
6. Ramon Santiago, ss, W. Michigan Whitecaps (Tigers)
7. Jake Peavy, rhp, Fort Wayne Wizards (Padres)
8. Adam Dunn, of, Dayton Dragons (Reds)
9. Gerik Baxter, rhp, Fort Wayne Wizards (Padres)
10. Mike Nannini, rhp, Michigan Battle Cats (Astros)
11. Ben Johnson, of, Fort Wayne Wizards (Padres)
12. Dennis Tankersley, rhp, Fort Wayne Wizards (Padres)
13. Carlos Hernandez, lhp, Michigan Battle Cats (Astros)
14. Andy VanHekken, lhp, West Michigan Whitecaps (Tigers)
15. John Buck, c, Michigan Battle Cats (Astros)
16. Ryan Christianson, c, Wisconsin Timber Rattlers (Mariners)
17. Cha Baek, rhp, Wisconsin Timber Rattlers (Mariners)
18. Ryan Gripp, 3b, Lansing Lugnuts (Cubs)
19. Fernando Rodney, rhp, West Michigan Whitecaps (Tigers)
20. Rafael Soriano, rhp, Wisconsin Timber Rattlers (Mariners)

South Atlantic League

1. Josh Hamilton, of, Charleston RiverDogs (Devil Rays)
2. Chin-Hui Tsao, rhp, Asheville Tourists (Rockies)
3. J.R. House, c, Hickory Crawdads (Pirates)
4. Bobby Bradley, rhp, Hickory Crawdads (Pirates)
5. Jovonny Cedeno, rhp, Savannah Sand Gnats (Rangers)
6. Carl Crawford, of, Charleston RiverDogs (Devil Rays)
7. Brett Myers, rhp, Piedmont Boll Weevils (Phillies)
8. Brandon Phillips, ss, Cape Fear Crocs (Expos)
9. Matt Belisle, rhp, Macon Braves (Braves)
10. Keith Reed, of, Delmarva Shorebirds (Orioles)
11. Wilken Ruan, of, Cape Fear Crocs (Expos)
12. Alex Requena, of, Columbus Redstixx (Indians)
13. Jose Castillo, ss, Hickory Crawdads (Pirates)
14. Matt Butler, rhp, Macon Braves (Braves)
15. Russ Jacobson, c, Piedmont Boll Weevils (Phillies)
16. Tony Alvarez, of, Hickory Crawdads (Pirates)
17. Brad Baker, rhp, Augusta Greenjackets (Red Sox)
18. Marlon Byrd, of, Piedmont Boll Weevils (Phillies)
19. Hank Blalock, 3b, Savannah Sand Gnats (Rangers)
20. Jung Bong, lhp, Macon Braves (Braves)

SHORT-SEASON
New York/Penn League
1. Wilson Betemit, ss, Jamestown Jammers (Braves)
2. Elvis Corporan, 3b, Staten Island Yankees (Yankees)
3. Josh Girdley, lhp, Vermont Expos (Expos)
4. Chase Utley, 2b, Batavia Muckdogs (Phillies)
5. Mauricio Lara, lhp, Lowell Spinners (Red Sox)
6. Josh Wilson, ss, Utica Blue Sox (Marlins)
7. Matt Wheatland, rhp, Oneonta Tigers (Tigers)
8. Danny Borrell, lhp, Staten Island Yankees (Yankees)
9. Andy Beal, lhp, Staten Island Yankees (Yankees)
10. Brian Cardwell, rhp, Queens Kings (Blue Jays)
11. Seung Song, rhp, Lowell Spinners (Red Sox)
12. Seth McClung, rhp, Hudson Valley Renegades (Devil Rays)
13. Brett Evert, rhp, Jamestown Jammers (Braves)
14. Ryan Doumit, c, Williamsport Crosscutters (Pirates)
15. Matt Massingale, rhp, Utica Blue Sox (Marlins)
16. Chien-Ming Wang, rhp, Staten Island Yankees (Yankees)
17. David Parrish, c, Staten Island Yankees (Yankees)
18. Doug Waechter, rhp, Hudson Valley Renegades (Devil Rays)
19. Chris Basak, ss, Pittsfield Mets (Mets)
20. Dominic Rich, 2b, Queens Kings (Blue Jays)

Northwest League
1. Freddie Bynum, ss, Vancouver Canadians (Athletics)
2. Lance Niekro, 3b, Salem/Keizer Volcanoes (Giants)
3. Joe Torres, lhp, Boise Hawks (Angels)
4. Aaron Krawiec, lhp, Eugene Emeralds (Cubs)
5. Jamal Strong, of, Everett Aquasox (Mariners)
6. Ryan Jorgensen, c, Eugene Emeralds (Cubs)
7. Charlie Thames, rhp, Boise Hawks (Angels)
8. Garrett Atkins, 1b/3b, Portland Rockies (Rockies)
9. Brad Hawpe, of/1b, Portland Rockies (Rockies)
10. Wilton Chavez, rhp, Eugene Emeralds (Cubs)
11. Boof Bonser, rhp, Salem/Keizer Volcanoes (Giants)
12. Brennan King, 3b, Yakima Bears (Dodgers)
13. Todd Wellemeyer, rhp, Eugene Emeralds (Cubs)
14. Matt Roney, rhp, Portland Rockies (Rockies)
15. Chad Santos, 1b, Spokane Indians (Royals)
16. David Wolensky, rhp, Boise Hawks (Angels)
17. Sam Walton, lhp, Everett AquaSox (Mariners)
18. Nic Jackson, of, Eugene Emeralds (Cubs)
19. Mike Mallory, of, Eugene Emeralds (Cubs)
20. Tommy Murphy, ss, Boise Hawks (Angels)

ROOKIE ADVANCED
Appalachian League
1. Adam Wainwright, rhp, Danville (Braves)
2. Enrique Cruz, 3b/ss, Kingsport (Mets)
3. Corey Smith, 3b, Burlington (Indians)
4. Rocco Baldelli, of, Princeton (Devil Rays)
5. Octavio Martinez, c, Bluefield (Orioles)
6. Jimmy Barrett, rhp, Martinsville (Astros)
7. Rob Bowen, c, Elizabethton (Twins)
8. Rafael Boitel, of, Elizabethton (Twins)
9. Domingo Valdez, rhp, Pulaski (Rangers)
10. Chris Narveson, lhp, Johnson City (Cardinals)
11. Ramon German, 1b/3b, Martinsville (Astros)
12. Chad Bowen, rhp, Kingsport (Mets)
13. Cory Doyne, rhp, Martinsville (Astros)
14. Angel Pagan, of, Kingsport (Mets)
15. Bob Keppel, rhp, Kingsport (Mets)
16. David Mead, rhp, Kingsport (Mets)
17. Alejandro Machado, 2b, Danville (Braves)
18. Guillermo Reyes, 2b/ss, Bristol (White Sox)
19. Jose Morban, ss, Pulaski (Rangers)
20. Jose Reyes, ss, Kingsport (Mets)

Pioneer League
1. David Krynzel, of, Ogden Raptors (Brewers)
2. Cristian Guerrero, of, Ogden Raptors (Brewers)
3. Ricardo Rodriguez, rhp, Great Falls Dodgers (Dodgers)
4. Jason Belcher, c, Helena Brewers (Brewers)
5. Jared Abruzzo, c, Butte Copper Kings (Angels)
6. Jeremy Johnson, of, Medicine Hat Blue Jays (Blue Jays)
7. Victor Hall, of, Missoula Osprey (Diamondbacks)
8. Mark Phillips, lhp, Idaho Falls Padres (Padres)
9. Nick Trzesniak, c, Idaho Falls Padres (Padres)
10. Jose Diaz, c, Great Falls Dodgers (Dodgers)
11. Reggie Abercrombie, of, Great Falls Dodgers (Dodgers)
12. Jose Valverde, rhp, Missoula Osprey (Diamondbacks)
13. Jerry Gil, ss, Missoula Osprey (Diamondbacks)
14. Willy Aybar, 3b, Great Falls Dodgers (Dodgers)
15. Roberto Miniel, rhp, Ogden Raptors (Brewers)
16. Justin Gordon, lhp, Ogden Raptors (Brewers)
17. Luis Terrero, of, Missoula Osprey (Diamondbacks)
18. Andres Pagan, c, Idaho Falls Padres (Padres)
19. Ruddy Lugo, rhp, Ogden Raptors (Brewers)
20. Miguel Negron, of, Medicine Hat Blue Jays (Blue Jays)

ROOKIE
Arizona League
1. Luis Montanez, ss, Cubs
2. Miguel Villilo, 3b, Mariners
3. Francis Gomez, ss, Athletics
4. Jose Vasquez, 1b/of, Rockies
5. J.J. Johnson, 3b, Cubs
6. Omar Falcon, c, Padres
7. Chris Amador, 2b, White Sox
8. Beltran Perez, rhp, Diamondbacks
9. Clint Nageotte, rhp, Mariners
10. Bo Ivy, of, White Sox
11. Derrick Van Dusen, lhp, Mariners
12. Nobuaki Yoshida, lhp, Padres
13. Syketo Anderson, of, Cubs
14. Isaac Garcia, ss/2b, Athletics
15. Felix Diaz, rhp, Giants
16. Pedro Liriano, 2b, Mariners
17. Justin Germano, rhp, Padres
18. Josh Kroeger, of, Diamondbacks
19. Boomer Jones, rhp, White Sox
20. Charles Merricks, lhp, Rockies

Gulf Coast League
1. Tony Blanco, 3b, Red Sox
2. Adam Wainwright, rhp, Braves
3. Deivi Mendez, ss, Yankees
4. Justin Morneau, 1b, Twins
5. Adrian Gonzalez, 1b, Marlins
6. Yoel Hernandez, rhp, Phillies
7. Matt Wheatland, rhp, Tigers
8. Grady Sizemore, of, Expos
9. Jason Botts, 1b, Rangers
10. Omar Beltre, rhp, Rangers
11. Yhency Brazoban, of, Yankees
12. Rick Asadoorian, of, Red Sox
13. Edwin Yan, ss, Pirates
14. Denny Bautista, rhp, Marlins
15. Tripper Johnson, 3b, Orioles
16. Antron Seiber, of, Red Sox
17. Juan Francia, 2b, Tigers
18. Carlos de los Santos, rhp, Pirates
19. Jeff Randazzo, lhp, Twins
20. Miguel Cabrera, ss, Marlins

Index

Dean, Aaron (Blue Jays)	431	Freeman, Choo (Rockies)	144	Harper, Travis (Devil Rays)	399
DeHaan, Kory (Padres)	360	Frese, Nate (Cubs)	91	Harris, Willie (Orioles)	68
Delcarmen, Manny (Red Sox)	79	Fuentes, Brian (Mariners)	386	Hart, Jason (Athletics)	298
Dellaero, Jason (White Sox)	111	Fulse, Sheldon (Mariners)	385	Harts, Jeremy (Pirates)	331
DePaula, Julio (Rockies)	153			Harvey, Ken (Royals)	202
DePaula, Sean (Indians)	131	**G**		Harville, Chad (Athletics)	300
Diaz, Alejandro (Reds)	125	Galva, Claudio (Athletics)	303	Hawpe, Brad (Rockies)	149
Diaz, Aneuris (Cardinals)	348	Gamble, Jerome (Red Sox)	78	Haynes, Nathan (Angels)	20
Diaz, Felix (Giants)	374	Garbe, B.J. (Twins)	245	Hays, Sam (Mariners)	387
Diaz, Juan (Red Sox)	77	Garcia, Amaury (White Sox)	110	Heams, Shane (Tigers)	161
Diaz, Jose (Dodgers)	222	Garcia, Carlos (Dodgers)	217	Heard, Scott (Rangers)	414
Diggins, Ben (Dodgers)	213	Garcia, Jose (Brewers)	235	Heaverlo, Jeff (Mariners)	383
Dingman, Craig (Yankees)	291	Garcia, Luis (Red Sox)	80	Helms, Wes (Braves)	48
Dittfurth, Ryan (Rangers)	415	Garibaldi, Cecilio (Devil Rays)	405	Helquist, Jon (Astros)	195
Docen, Jose (Expos)	264	George, Chris (Royals)	199	Hendricksen, Mark (Blue Jays)	427
Dodson, Jeremy (Royals)	207	German, Ramon (Astros)	194	Henkel, Rob (Marlins)	176
Dorame, Randy (Rockies)	148	Germano, Justin (Padres)	359	Hensley, Matt (Angels)	27
Douglass, Sean (Orioles)	64	Gerut, Jody (Rockies)	153	Henson, Drew (Reds)	116
Doumit, Ryan (Pirates)	329	Gettis, Byron (Royals)	209	Hernandez, Adrian (Yankees)	285
Doyne, Cory (Astros)	194	Gibbons, Jay (Orioles)	63	Hernandez, Alex (Pirates)	332
Dransfeldt, Kelly (Rangers)	417	Gil, David (Reds)	124	Hernandez, Carlos (Astros)	190
Drew, Tim (Indians)	132	Gil, Jerry (Diamondbacks)	33	Hernandez, Yoel (Phillies)	316
Duckworth, Brandon (Phillies)	314	Giles, Marcus (Braves)	46	Herndon, Junior (Padres)	357
Dumatrait, Phil (Red Sox)	78	Ginter, Keith (Astros)	189	Hill, Bobby (Cubs)	90
Dunn, Adam (Reds)	116	Ginter, Matt (White Sox)	102	Hill, Koyie (Dodgers)	223
Dunn, Scott (Reds)	123	Girdley, Josh (Expos)	256	Hill, Mike (Astros)	192
Durbin, J.D. (Twins)	248	Giron, Alejandro (Phillies)	321	Hillenbrand, Shea (Red Sox)	82
Durham, Miles (Tigers)	164	Gissell, Chris (Cubs)	96	Hinske, Eric (Cubs)	91
Dushscherer, Justin (Red Sox)	82	Gload, Ross (Cubs)	95	Hochgesang, Josh (Athletics)	306
		Glover, Gary (White Sox)	108	Hodges, Kevin (Mariners)	388
E		Gobble, Jimmy (Royals)	200	Hodges, Scott (Expos)	257
Eberwein, Kevin (Padres)	358	Goetz, Geoff (Marlins)	176	Holliday, Matt (Rockies)	147
Elder, David (Rangers)	414	Gold, J.M. (Brewers)	234	Holt, Daylan (Athletics)	306
Ellis, Mark (Athletics)	303	Goldbach, Jeff (Cubs)	94	House, Craig (Rockies)	146
Encarnacion, Mario (Athletics)	298	Gomez, Alexis (Royals)	202	House, J.R. (Pirates)	325
Ennis, John (Braves)	53	Gomez, Richard (Tigers)	167	Howington, Ty (Reds)	117
Enochs, Chris (Athletics)	307	Gonzalez, Adrian (Marlins)	172	Hubbel, Travis (Blue Jays)	430
Ensberg, Morgan (Astros)	190	Gonzalez, Danny (Phillies)	320	Hudson, Luke (Rockies)	147
Ernster, Mark (Brewers)	232	Gonzalez, Dicky (Mets)	273	Huff, Aubrey (Devil Rays)	396
Escalante, Jaime (Angels)	25	Good, Andrew (Diamondbacks)	38	Huffman, Royce (Astros)	194
Escobar, Alex (Mets)	269	Good, Eric (Expos)	261	Hummel, Tim (White Sox)	107
Espinsoa, David (Reds)	117	Gordon, Justin (Brewers)	237	Hutchinson, Chad (Cardinals)	340
Espy, Nate (Phillies)	317	Grabow, John (Pirates)	328		
Esquivia, Manuel (Marlins)	180	Grabowski, Jason (Mariners)	388	**I**	
Esslinger, Cam (Rockies)	151	Graman, Alex (Yankees)	285	Infante, Omar (Tigers)	160
Esteves, Jake (Giants)	372	Gray, Josh (Angels)	24	Inge, Brandon (Tigers)	157
Estrada, Horacio (Brewers)	230	Gredvig, Doug (Orioles)	69	Ireland, Eric (Athletics)	304
Estrada, Johnny (Phillies)	318	Green, Steve (Angels)	24	Ivy, Bo (White Sox)	110
Estrella, Leo (Reds)	121	Griffiths, Jeremy (Mets)	275	Izturis, Cesar (Blue Jays)	424
Evans, Kyle (Indians)	138	Grilli, Jason (Marlins)	178	Izturis, Maicer (Indians)	133
Evans, Lee (Pirates)	335	Gripp, Ryan (Cubs)	92		
Everett, Adam (Astros)	187	Guerrero, Cristian (Brewers)	228	**J**	
Evert, Brett (Braves)	52	Guerrero, Junior (Royals)	205	Jackson, Nic (Cubs)	97
		Guerrier, Matt (White Sox)	107	Jacobsen, Bucky (Brewers)	237
F		Guzman, Edwards (Giants)	377	Jacobson, Russ (Phillies)	316
Faison, Vince (Padres)	358	Guzman, Elpidio (Angels)	20	James, Delvin (Devil Rays)	401
Falcon, Omar (Padres)	359	Guzman, Jonathan (Royals)	209	Jamison, Ryan (Astros)	190
Farnsworth, Troy (Cardinals)	348	Guzman, Juan (Orioles)	66	Jenkins, Neil (Tigers)	163
Feliz, Pedro (Giants)	370	Guzman, Wilson (Pirates)	333	Jenks, Bobby (Angels)	26
Figueroa, Juan (Orioles)	67			Jennings, Jason (Rockies)	145
File, Bob (Blue Jays)	425	**H**		Jimenez, D'Angelo (Yankees)	284
Fitzgerald, Jason (Indians)	139	Haas, Chris (Cardinals)	346	Jodie, Brett (Yankees)	291
Fogg, Josh (White Sox)	104	Hackman, Luther (Cardinals)	344	Johnson, Adam (Twins)	241
Folsom, Mark (Indians)	138	Hafner, Travis (Rangers)	414	Johnson, Ben (Padres)	356
Ford, Lew (Twins)	249	Hale, Beau (Orioles)	61	Johnson, Eric (Indians)	137
Ford, Matt (Blue Jays)	426	Hall, Toby (Devil Rays)	399	Johnson, Gary (Angels)	22
Fossum, Casey (Red Sox)	75	Hall, Victor (Diamondbacks)	39	Johnson, Jeremy (Blue Jays)	433
Foster, Kris (Dodgers)	219	Hall, Will (Brewers)	234	Johnson, Kade (Brewers)	230
Fox, Jason (Brewers)	235	Hamilton, Josh (Devil Rays)	395	Johnson, Kelly (Braves)	54
Franklin, Ryan (Mariners)	390	Hanrahan, Joel (Dodgers)	218	Johnson, Nick (Yankees)	283
Franklin, Wayne (Astros)	193	Harang, Aaron (Athletics)	306	Johnson, Rett (Mariners)	387
Freel, Ryan (Blue Jays)	427	Harper, Brandon (Marlins)	181	Johnson, Tripper (Orioles)	64

Jones, Damien (Braves)	55
Jones, Mitch (Yankees)	292
Jorgensen, Ryan (Cubs)	95
Joseph, Jake (Mets)	276
Joseph, Kevin (Giants)	373
Journell, Jim (Cardinals)	343
Judd, Mike (Dodgers)	215
Julio, Jorge (Orioles)	69

K

Kaanoi, Jason (Royals)	208
Kalinowski, Josh (Rockies)	146
Karnuth, Jason (Cardinals)	345
Kaye, Justin (Mariners)	389
Kearns, Austin (Reds)	115
Kegley, Charles (Blue Jays)	425
Keisler, Randy (Yankees)	285
Keller, Kris (Tigers)	161
Kelly, Kenny (Devil Rays)	401
Kelton, David (Cubs)	90
Kennedy, Joe (Devil Rays)	404
Keppel, Bob (Mets)	278
Kessel, Kyle (Astros)	193
Kibler, Ryan (Rockies)	152
Kielty, Bobby (Twins)	244
Kim, Sun-Woo (Red Sox)	74
King, Brennan (Dodgers)	217
Kingrey, Jerrod (Blue Jays)	432
Kinney, Matt (Twins)	243
Kirby, Scott (Brewers)	234
Knight, Brandon (Twins)	250
Knotts, Gary (Marlins)	175
Kohlmeier, Ryan (Orioles)	62
Kolb, Brandon (Brewers)	231
Kolb, Danny (Rangers)	417
Krawiec, Aaron (Cubs)	92
Kroeger, Josh (Diamondbacks)	39
Krynzel, David (Brewers)	228
Kuo, Hong-Chih (Dodgers)	214

L

Lackey, John (Angels)	18
Laird, Gerald (Athletics)	301
Lane, Jason (Astros)	193
Lara, Mauricio (Red Sox)	76
Larson, Brandon (Reds)	122
Lawrence, Brian (Padres)	357
Lawrence, Joe (Blue Jays)	424
Lee, Cliff (Expos)	262
Lee, Corey (Rangers)	419
Lee, Sang-Hoon (Red Sox)	77
Lehr, Justin (Athletics)	304
Lemon, Tim (Cardinals)	347
Levrault, Allen (Brewers)	229
Lewis, Colby (Rangers)	411
Lewis, Derrick (Braves)	51
Lidge, Brad (Astros)	189
Liefer, Jeff (White Sox)	105
Lilly, Ted (Yankees)	289
Lincoln, Justin (Rockies)	150
Linebrink, Scott (Astros)	191
Liriano, Pedro (Mariners)	391
Lockwood, Luke (Expos)	259
Lockwood, Mike (Athletics)	305
Logan, Exavier (Tigers)	161
Lohse, Kyle (Twins)	247
Lomasney, Steve (Red Sox)	75
Lombard, George (Braves)	51
Lopez, Aquilino (Mariners)	389
Lopez, Felipe (Blue Jays)	424
Lopez, Luis (Blue Jays)	432
Louisa, Lorvin Leandro (Expos)	265

Loux, Shane (Tigers)	159
Love, Brandon (Reds)	122
Ludwick, Ryan (Athletics)	298
Lugo, Felix (Expos)	261
Lugo, Ruddy (Brewers)	237
Luna, Hector (Indians)	136
Lunar, Fernando (Orioles)	69
Lundberg, Spike (Rangers)	415
Luster, Jeremy (Giants)	374
Lyon, Brandon (Blue Jays)	429

M

MacDougal, Mike (Royals)	200
Machado, Alejandro (Braves)	54
Machado, Anderson (Phillies)	313
Madson, Ryan (Phillies)	312
Magruder, Chris (Giants)	375
Maier, T.J. (Cardinals)	349
Majewski, Gary (White Sox)	105
Mallory, Mike (Cubs)	94
Malone, Corwin (White Sox)	106
Maness, Nick (Mets)	272
Maroth, Mike (Tigers)	162
Marquis, Jason (Braves)	47
Martines, Jason (Diamondbacks)	39
Martinez, David (Yankees)	288
Martinez, Octavio (Orioles)	62
Marx, Tommy (Tigers)	162
Mateo, Henry (Expos)	260
Mattes, Troy (Expos)	263
Matos, Josue (Mariners)	391
McClendon, Matt (Braves)	46
McClung, Seth (Devil Rays)	402
McDonald, Darnell (Orioles)	65
McDonald, Donzell (Yankees)	290
McDonald, John (Indians)	134
McDowell, Arturo (Giants)	372
McGowan, Sean (Giants)	369
McKinley, Josh (Expos)	263
McKnight, Tony (Astros)	186
McNeal, Aaron (Astros)	191
Mead, David (Rangers)	413
Medrano, Jesus (Marlins)	180
Melian, Jackson (Reds)	119
Mench, Kevin (Rangers)	410
Mendez, Deivi (Yankees)	286
Mendoza, Geronimo (White Sox)	109
Meyer, Jake (Mariners)	389
Miadich, Bart (Angels)	25
Michaels, Jason (Phillies)	319
Mieses, Jose (Brewers)	229
Miller, Colby (Twins)	246
Miller, Greg (Astros)	188
Miller, Jason (Twins)	248
Miller, Justin (Athletics)	299
Miller, Matt (Tigers)	163
Mills, Ryan (Twins)	247
Miner, Zach (Braves)	52
Minor, Damon (Giants)	369
Mitchell, Thomas (Expos)	261
Moeller, Chad (Twins)	249
Miniel, Roberto (Brewers)	232
Montalbano, Greg (Red Sox)	83
Montanez, Luis (Cubs)	89
Montero, Esteban (Rockies)	150
Moon, Brian (Brewers)	236
Moore, Mewelde (Padres)	363
Morban, Jose (Rangers)	415
Moreno, Jorge (Indians)	136
Moreno, Orber (Royals)	205
Morneau, Justin (Twins)	243
Morrison, Robbie (Royals)	206

Moseley, Dustin (Reds)	118
Moss, Damian (Braves)	52
Mota, Danny (Twins)	251
Mota, Tony (Dodgers)	221
Mullen, Scott (Royals)	206
Munson, Eric (Tigers)	158
Murphy, Tommy (Angels)	22
Musser, Neal (Mets)	277
Myers, Brett (Phillies)	312
Myers, Corey (Diamondbacks)	41
Myette, Aaron (Rangers)	412

N

Nady, Xavier (Padres)	356
Nageotte, Clint (Mariners)	391
Nannini, Mike (Astros)	188
Narveson, Chris (Cardinals)	345
Nash, Greg (Devil Rays)	405
Nation, Joey (Cubs)	93
Ndungidi, Ntema (Orioles)	60
Neal, Blaine (Marlins)	174
Nelson, Bubba (Braves)	50
Neugebauer, Nick (Brewers)	228
Nicholson, Kevin (Padres)	359
Nickle, Doug (Phillies)	315
Niekro, Lance (Giants)	368
Nina, Elvin (Angels)	21
Noel, Todd (Yankees)	287
Norderum, Jason (Expos)	265
Nowlin, Cody (Rangers)	418
Nunez, Abraham (Marlins)	173
Nunez, Franklin (Phillies)	321
Nunez, Jorge (Dodgers)	220
Nunez, Jose (Dodgers)	223

O

Obermueller, Wes (Royals)	208
O'Connor, Brian (Pirates)	331
Oh, Chul (Red Sox)	83
Ohman, Will (Cubs)	96
Olivo, Miguel (White Sox)	107
Olmedo, Ranier (Reds)	122
Olson, Tim (Diamondbacks)	38
O'Neal, Brandon (Angels)	26
Ortega, Bill (Cardinals)	341
Ortiz, Jose (Athletics)	297
Ortiz, Omar (Padres)	361
Osting, Jimmy (Phillies)	319
Oswalt, Roy (Astros)	185
Overbay, Lyle (Diamondbacks)	35
Owens, Jeremy (Padres)	361
Owens, Ryan (Diamondbacks)	40
Ozuna, Pablo (Marlins)	174

P

Pacheco, Enemencio (Rockies)	152
Padilla, Jorge (Phillies)	316
Padilla, Roy (Indians)	135
Pagan, Andres (Padres)	361
Pagan, Angel (Mets)	279
Paradis, Mike (Orioles)	67
Parker, Christian (Yankees)	290
Parra, Christian (Braves)	48
Parrish, David (Yankees)	293
Parrish, John (Orioles)	65
Pascucci, Valentino (Expos)	262
Patterson, Corey (Cubs)	87
Patterson, John (Diamondbacks)	32
Paul, Josh (White Sox)	108
Pearce, Josh (Cardinals)	343
Peavy, Jacob (Padres)	354
Pena, Carlos (Rangers)	409

Pena, Elvis (Rockies) 148
Pena, Juan (Athletics) 303
Pena, Juan (Red Sox) 79
Pena, Wily Mo (Yankees) 286
Penney, Mike (Brewers) 230
Peoples, Danny (Indians) 133
Peralta, Jhonny (Indians) 136
Peres, Luis (Red Sox) 80
Perez, Antonio (Mariners) 382
Perez, Beltran (Diamondbacks) 41
Perez, George (Blue Jays) 433
Perez, Josue (Phillies) 318
Perez, Oliver (Padres) 362
Perez, Santiago (Padres) 360
Perez, Timoniel (Mets) 270
Peterson, Matt (Mets) 277
Petty, Chad (Tigers) 165
Pettyjohn, Adam (Tigers) 164
Phelps, Josh (Blue Jays) 427
Phelps, Travis (Devil Rays) 400
Phillips, Brandon (Expos) 256
Phillips, Mark (Padres) 355
Philips, Paul (Royals) 207
Pierzynski, A.J. (Twins) 247
Pineda, Luis (Tigers) 167
Pineiro, Joel (Mariners) 382
Pluta, Anthony (Astros) 192
Poe, Ryan (Brewers) 236
Porter, Scott (Blue Jays) 432
Pratt, Andy (Rangers) 412
Pratt, Scott (Indians) 139
Pressley, Josh (Devil Rays) 405
Pridie, Jon (Twins) 251
Prinz, Bret (Diamondbacks) 34
Prokopec, Luke (Dodgers) 215
Pugmire, Robert (Reds) 123
Pujols, Albert (Cardinals) 340
Punto, Nick (Phillies) 321
Purvis, Rob (White Sox) 107

Q

Qualls, Chad (Astros) 192

R

Raines Jr., Tim (Orioles) 63
Ramirez, Horacio (Braves) 49
Ramirez, Julio (White Sox) 108
Ramos, Mario (Athletics) 300
Randazzo, Jeff (Twins) 245
Randolph, Jaisen (Cubs) 97
Ransom, Cody (Giants) 371
Rauch, Jon (White Sox) 101
Reames, Britt (Expos) 260
Redding, Tim (Astros) 186
Reding, Josh (Expos) 263
Redman, Prentice (Mets) 279
Redman, Tike (Pirates) 329
Reed, Keith (Orioles) 59
Regalado, Maximo (Dodgers) 223
Regilio, Nick (Rangers) 418
Reith, Brian (Reds) 120
Reitsma, Chris (Reds) 119
Repko, Jason (Dodgers) 214
Requena, Alex (Indians) 133
Restovich, Michael (Twins) 242
Reynolds, Josh (Mets) 279
Ricketts, Chad (Dodgers) 217
Ridgway, Jeff (Devil Rays) 402
Riedling, John (Reds) 118
Riggan, Jerrod (Mets) 274
Riley, Matt (Orioles) 62
Rincon, Juan (Twins) 246

Rios, Alex (Blue Jays) 429
Riske, David (Indians) 135
Rivas, Luis (Twins) 242
Rivera, Luis (Orioles) 61
Rivera, Juan (Yankees) 287
Rivera, Saul (Twins) 250
Roberts, Brian (Orioles) 63
Roberts, Grant (Mets) 271
Roberts, Mark (Marlins) 181
Rodney, Fernando (Tigers) 164
Rodriguez, Carlos (Red Sox) 81
Rodriguez, Francisco (Angels) 18
Rodriguez, Ricardo (Dodgers) 220
Rodriguez, Wilfredo (Astros) 186
Rogers, Brian (Yankees) 291
Rogers, Ed (Orioles) 60
Rolison, Nate (Marlins) 175
Rollins, Jimmy (Phillies) 311
Rolls, Damian (Devil Rays) 403
Romano, Jason (Rangers) 410
Rombley, Danny (Expos) 264
Rooi, Vince (Expos) 259
Rosamond, Mike (Astros) 195
Rosario, Carlos (Phillies) 315
Ross, Cody (Tigers) 162
Rowan, Chris (Brewers) 235
Rowand, Aaron (White Sox) 104
Ruan, Wilken (Expos) 258
Runser, Greg (Rangers) 416
Russ, Chris (Rangers) 418

S

Sabathia, C.C. (Indians) 129
Saenz, Jason (Mets) 276
Salas, Juan (Devil Rays) 403
Salazar, Oscar (Athletics) 302
Salazar, Ruben (Twins) 251
Salmon, Brad (Reds) 125
Sanches, Brian (Royals) 204
Sanchez, Alex (Devil Rays) 403
Sanchez, Duaner (Diamondbacks) 38
Sanchez, Freddy (Red Sox) 83
Sandberg, Jared (Devil Rays) 399
Sandoval, Danny (White Sox) 111
Santana, Johan (Angels) 24
Santana, Osmany (Indians) 138
Santiago, Ramon (Tigers) 158
Sardinha, Dane (Reds) 116
Saturria, Luis (Cardinals) 342
Schmitt, Billy (Cardinals) 349
Schneider, Brian (Expos) 260
Schultz, Mike (Diamondbacks) 36
Schumacher, Shawn (Cardinals) 349
Seabol, Scott (Yankees) 293
Seale, Marvin (Mets) 276
Sears, Todd (Twins) 248
Seay, Bobby (Devil Rays) 398
Seberino, Ronni (Devil Rays) 404
Seiber, Antron (Red Sox) 81
Seo, Jae Weong (Mets) 278
Serrano, Wascar (Padres) 354
Sheets, Ben (Brewers) 227
Shields, Scot (Angels) 24
Shinjo, Tsuyoshi (Mets) 273
Silva, Carlos (Phillies) 318
Silvestre, Juan (Mariners) 385
Sitzman, Jay (Phillies) 320
Sizemore, Grady (Expos) 257
Slaten, Doug (Diamondbacks) 41
Smith, Bud (Cardinals) 339
Smith, Corey (Indians) 130
Smith, Jason (Cubs) 97

Smith, Will (Marlins) 179
Smyth, Steve (Cubs) 95
Snead, Esix (Cardinals) 344
Snelling, Chris (Mariners) 383
Snow, Bert (Athletics) 301
Snyder, Kyle (Royals) 203
Snyder, Michael (Blue Jays) 429
Sobkowiak, Scott (Braves) 49
Soler, Ramon (Devil Rays) 402
Song, Seung (Red Sox) 76
Sonnier, Shawn (Royals) 203
Sorensen, Zach (Indians) 137
Soriano, Alfonso (Yankees) 284
Soriano, Rafael (Mariners) 384
Soto, Jose (Marlins) 179
Sparks, Steve (Pirates) 334
Specht, Brian (Angels) 18
Spivey, Junior (Diamondbacks) 36
Spoonybarger, Tim (Braves) 50
Spurling, Chris (Pirates) 332
Stahl, Richard (Orioles) 60
Standridge, Jason (Devil Rays) 396
Stechschulte, Gene (Cardinals) 342
Stenson, Dernell (Red Sox) 73
Stephens, John (Orioles) 68
Stiehl, Robert (Astros) 187
Stocks, Nick (Cardinals) 341
Stodolka, Mike (Royals) 202
Stokes, Jason (Marlins) 174
Strange, Pat (Mets) 270
Stratton, Robert (Mets) 275
Strong, Jamal (Mariners) 388
Stumm, Jason (White Sox) 105
Surkont, Keith (Athletics) 302
Suzuki, Ichiro (Mariners) 382
Swedlow, Sean (Indians) 138
Sylvester, Billy (Braves) 47

T

Tallet, Brian (Indians) 134
Tankersley, Dennis (Padres) 356
Taveras, Willy (Indians) 130
Taylor, Reggie (Phillies) 313
Terrero, Luis (Diamondbacks) 32
Tetz, Kris (Expos) 265
Thames, Charlie (Angels) 23
Thames, Marcus (Yankees) 293
Thomas, Brad (Twins) 244
Thomas, Evan (Phillies) 317
Thompson, Andy (Blue Jays) 428
Thompson, Derek (Indians) 137
Thompson, Mat (Red Sox) 81
Thompson, Mike (Padres) 363
Thorman, Scott (Braves) 52
Threets, Erick (Giants) 377
Thurman, Corey (Royals) 204
Thurston, Joe (Dodgers) 216
Toca, Jorge (Mets) 278
Tonis, Mike (Royals) 204
Torcato, Tony (Giants) 368
Torrealba, Yorvit (Giants) 375
Torres, Andres (Tigers) 160
Torres, Joe (Angels) 17
Torres, Luis (Expos) 262
Torres, Luis (Pirates) 329
Totten, Heath (Dodgers) 221
Towers, Josh (Orioles) 66
Traber, Billy (Mets) 272
Treadway, Brion (Giants) 372
Trujillo, J.J. (Padres) 363
Trzesniak, Nick (Padres) 359
Tsao, Chin-Hui (Rockies) 143

Tucker, T.J. (Expos)	258			Williams, Jeff (Dodgers)	221
Turnbow, Derrick (Angels)	19			Williams, Jerome (Giants)	367
Tyner, Jason (Devil Rays)	400	Waechter, Doug (Devil Rays)	404	Wilson, Craig (Pirates)	330
		Wainwright, Adam (Braves)	48	Wilson, Jack (Pirates)	327
U		Wakeland, Chris (Tigers)	166	Wilson, Josh (Marlins)	177
Ugueto, Luis (Marlins)	177	Walker, Tyler (Mets)	275	Wilson, Philip (Angels)	19
Urban, Jeff (Giants)	371	Walling, David (Yankees)	290	Winchester, Jeff (Rockies)	151
Urena, Sixto (Rangers)	419	Walrond, Les (Cardinals)	346	Wise, Matt (Angels)	21
Uribe, Juan (Rockies)	144	Walter, Scott (Royals)	208	Wise, Dewayne (Blue Jays)	429
Urrutia, Carlos (Cubs)	94	Walton, Sam (Mariners)	390	Wolensky, David (Angels)	22
Utley, Chase (Phillies)	313	Wang, Chien-Ming (Yankees)	288	Woodards, Orlando (Blue Jays)	430
Ust, Brant (Tigers)	166	Ward, Jeremy (Diamondbacks)	34	Woodward, Chris (Blue Jays)	430
		Washington, Rico (Pirates)	334	Woodyard, Mark (Tigers)	167
V		Waters, Chris (Braves)	55	Woolf, Jason (Cardinals)	347
Valderrama, Carlos (Giants)	370	Wathan, Derek (Marlins)	180	Wooten, Greg (Mariners)	387
Valdez, Domingo (Rangers)	416	Watkins, Steve (Padres)	361	Wooten, Shawn (Angels)	27
Valdez, Wilson (Expos)	264	Wayne, Justin (Expos)	257	Wright, Dan (White Sox)	103
Valent, Eric (Phillies)	314	Webb, Alan (Rangers)	417	Wright, Gavin (Astros)	190
Valverde, Jose (Diamondbacks)	35	Webb, Brandon (Diamondbacks)	40	Wright, Matt (Braves)	50
Vance, Corey (Rockies)	149	Webb, John (Cubs)	90	Wuertz, Mike (Cubs)	93
Van Dusen, Derrick (Mariners)	390	Weibl, Clint (Cardinals)	343		
VanHekken, Andy (Tigers)	160	Weichard, Paul (Pirates)	333	**Y**	
Vargas, Claudio (Marlins)	173	Wells, Vernon (Blue Jays)	423	Yan, Edwin (Pirates)	334
Vargas, Martin (Indians)	134	Werth, Jayson (Blue Jays)	428	Yarnall, Ed (Reds)	120
Vaz, Bobby (Athletics)	307	West, Brian (White Sox)	104	Yoshida, Nobuaki (Padres)	358
Vazquez, Jose (Rockies)	148	Westbrook, Jake (Indians)	132	Young, Chris (Pirates)	328
Victorino, Shane (Dodgers)	219	Weston, Aron (Pirates)	326	Young, Jason (Rockies)	145
Villareal, Oscar (Diamondbacks)	35	Wheatland, Matt (Tigers)	158	Young, Mike (Rangers)	412
Villilo, Miguel (Mariners)	386	White, Matt (Devil Rays)	398		
Vining, Ken (White Sox)	109	Whitesides, Jake (Astros)	195	**Z**	
Vizcaino, Luis (Athletics)	302	Wigginton, Ty (Mets)	276	Zambrano, Carlos (Cubs)	89
Vogelsong, Ryan (Giants)	369	Wilkerson, Brad (Expos)	256	Zerbe, Chad (Giants)	377
Voshell, Chase (Cardinals)	346	Williams, Blake (Cardinals)	341	Zuleta, Julio (Cubs)	91
Voyles, Brad (Braves)	54	Williams, David (Pirates)	333		

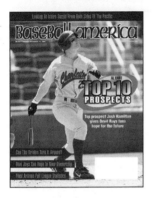